Goodnight, my servants all

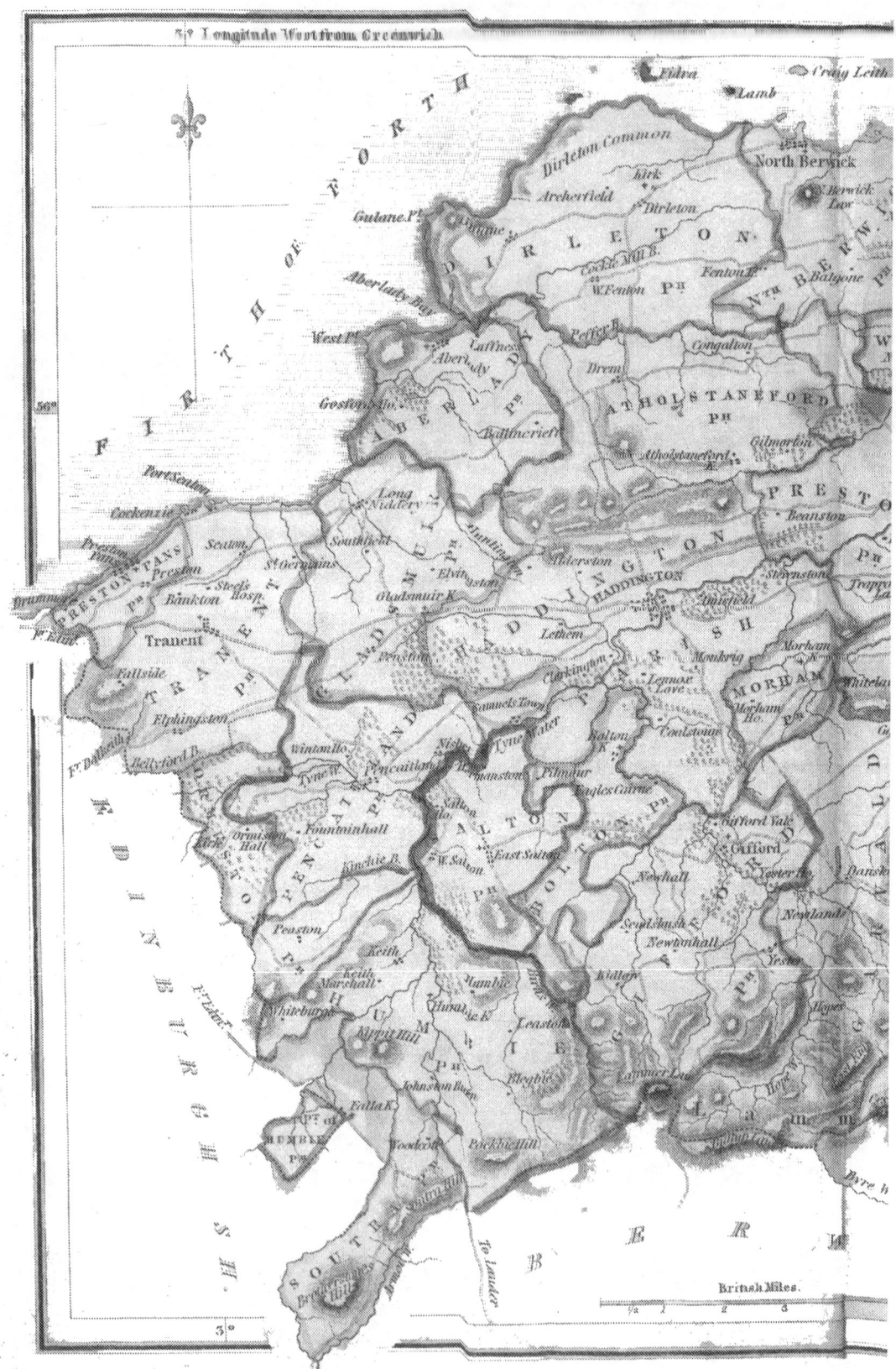

Our pleasance here is all vain glory,
This fause warld is but transitory;
The flesh is bruckle, the Fiend is slee:
      Timor mortis conturbat me.

William Dunbar

Goodnight, my servants all

The Sourcebook of East Lothian Witchcraft

David M. Robertson

The Grimsay Press

The Grimsay Press
an imprint of
Zeticula
57 St Vincent Crescent
Glasgow
G3 8NQ
Scotland

http://www.thegrimsaypress.co.uk
admin@thegrimsaypress.co.uk

Text © David M. Robertson 2008
Photographs © David M. Robertson 2008

First published in this edition 2008
ISBN-13   978-1-84530-041-8
ISBN-10   1 84530 041 6

Back cover photograph:
Witches' Knowe, near Kidlaw, East Lothian.

Tranent witchpricker (page 246) reproduced by kind permission of the National Archives of Scotland

Quotation from 'Chimes of Freedom' by Bob Dylan © 1964; renewed 1992 Special Rider Music

All rights reserved. No part of this publication may be reproduced, stored in a retrieval system, or transmitted in any form or by any means, electronic, mechanical, photocopying, recording or otherwise, without the prior permission of the publishers.

In memory of the
"countless confused, accused, misused ...."

Acknowledgements

Heartfelt thanks are due to the members of staff of the National Archives of Scotland and the National Library of Scotland, whose unfailing patience, courtesy and helpfulness do so much to ease the path of historical research.

Thanks also to my daughters, and to the staff of Longniddry Library, for guiding my faltering steps through the morass of Information Technology..

Contents

Maps of Haddingtonshire   *ii, iii*
Acknowledgements   *ix*
List of illustrations   *xiii*
Introduction   *xv*
Preface   **1**

1. The North Berwick Witches.   5
Examinations and Confessions of Geillis Duncan and Agnes Sampson.   10
Agnes Sampson.   11
The Trial of John Cunningham [Fian]   16
The Trial of Agnes Sampson.   21

2. Kirk Session Records.   65
Aberlady.   67
Athelstaneford.   69
Bara   69
Bolton.   69
Dirleton.   69
Dunbar   70
Garvald and Bara   71
Gladsmuir.   71
Haddington.   72
Humbie.   99
Innerwick.   102
Inveresk.   104
Morham.   105
North Berwick.   105
Oldhamstocks.   113
Ormiston.   113
Pencaitland.   113
Prestonkirk.   115
Prestonpans.   115
Saltoun.   120
Spott.   121
Stenton.   131
Tranent.   132
Tyninghame.   135
Whitekirk.   142
Whittinghame.   142
Yester.   144

3. Other Church Records. — 149
The Presbytery of Haddington. — 149
Presbytery of Dunbar. — 171
Presbytery of Dalkeith. — 171
The Synod of Lothian and Tweedale. — 173

4. Burgh Records. — 177
Dunbar. — 177
Haddington. — 178
Musselburgh. — 211
North Berwick. — 211

5. Trial by Commission. — 213
The Committee of Estates. — 229
Acts of the Parliament of Scotland. — 233
Privy Council. — 238

6. Justiciary Court Records — 273
The Case of Alexander Hamilton. — 347
The Stenton Witches. — 388
The Tranent Witches. — 395
Unfinished business in Tranent. — 400
A witchcraft trial in Musselburgh. — 407
Witch Pricking. — 410
Margaret Allan - a narrow escape. — 411
Agnes Williamson - another narrow escape. — 413
James Welsh. — 420
John Kincaid Questioned. — 425
Major Weir. — 425
The Peaston Witches. — 426
Porteous Roll for Haddington. — 439
Persecution in Prestonpans. — 440
Daemonologie. [1591] — 443

7 Contemporary Writers — 443
Historie and life of King James the Sext. — 446
Nicoll's Diary. 1657-59 — 446
Fountainhall's Historical Notices. — 446
The Laws and Customs of Scotland: Sir George Mackenzie of Rosehaugh. — 450
Satan's Invisible World Discovered: George Sinclair. — 453
John Bell's "Tryal of Witchcraft" — 459
The Laird of Coul's Ghost. — 460

Bibliography. — *539*
Index to People and Places — *541*

List Of Illustrations

The notorious North Berwick witch meeting was held in St Andrew's Church. All that now remains of this building is the church porch, close by the popular "Scottish Seabird Centre". 9
"Delegates" to the North Berwick meeting would have no difficulty finding their way there. "The Law" is a particularly prominent landmark. Might this have influenced the choice of venue? 9

Nether Keith (above), home of Agnes Sampson, "the Wise Wife of Keith". The mansion of Keith Marischal and the ruined church of Keith stand nearby, but the settlement of Nether Keith is long gone. 13
At Ormiston Bridge, Agnes supposedly hauled up the Devil on a rope. She was accused of using her sorcery to harm David Seton who lived nearby at Foulstruther (now "Wolfstar"). 13

The Witches' Stone. Spott. The plaque states that Marion Lillie was burnt here. In fact this is almost certainly not the case. 123
According to the records Marion, East Lothian's last recorded witch, was buried in Spott kirkyard. She could not therefore have been burnt. 123

"The Hopes". William Davidson met the Devil in 1626 while herding cattle for the lady of Blance at East Hopes. 181
Both William Davidson and the notorious warlock Alexander Hamilton seem to have been involved with others in sorcery against the lady of Woodhead, now Fountainhall 181

In 1649 witches from Penston confessed to meeting the Devil near the Three Mile House, which stood close to where Gladsmuir parish church now stands. 207
Also in 1649 Manie Hamilton, Patrick Watson, and Bess Hogg from West Fenton, were imprisoned in Dirleton Castle and subsequently executed for witchcraft. 207

An interesting record of the Tranent witch-pricker John Kincaid at work. A diagram of the pin used can be seen, with Kincaid's mark "✠K" signifying that he was illiterate. 246

Several witches from Peaston were executed in 1678, along with associates from Keith, Fala, and Crichton. 250
Gideon Penman, the minister of Crichton kirk in Midlothian, was accused of being involved with the witches executed in 1678. 250

Dunbar Tollbooth, where Catherine McTarget was imprisoned and probably also tried. 268
At Dunbar Shore (Old Harbour), observing a seaman saying goodbye to his wife, she remarked, "It will be a long goodnight!" He was lost at sea. 268

Two contrasting scenes in the Garleton hills, where Alexander Hamilton had several meertings with the Devil. 286

The Tranent witch Jean Craig was accused of bewitching cattle and horses belonging to James Smith in Little Fawside, near Fawside Castle. The cows gave blood instead of milk, the oxen ran mad, and the horses dropped dead. 373
According to Marion Logan, witches from Tranent and Prestonpans danced to the tune "Kilt thy coat Maggie and go thy ways with me" at a meeting at the Windmill on Preston Links. Cockenzie Power Station now occupies this site. 373

Several Stenton women were burned for witchcraft on the Castlehill in Edinburgh in 1659. They were interrogated in Stenton church, and Dunbar tollbooth. Church towers like this one were often used for imprisoning suspects. 394
The Register of the Privy Council records the confessions of a group of witches taken down in 1661 before the heritors and elders of Bolton church. 394

Samuelston. It was said in 1659 that there was nothing there but "whores, thieves and witches". 415
The Tyne near Samuelston. Agnes Williamson was accused of knocking James Carfrae into the water with a magic whirlwind when he was fording the river. Agnes was one of the few East Lothian witches to be acquitted. 415

St Mary's Church, Haddington served a large parish which in the 17th century included the witchcraft "hotspots" of Penston and Samuelston. Elisabeth Moodie was convicted of witchcraft in 1677 after she had been heard to exclaim "Now the turn is done! ..." 437
Isobel Eliot claimed that she left her body sitting in Pencaitland church while her spirit flew to Loanhead in the shape of a crow to visit a baby she had nursed. 437

Introduction
by Hugh V. McLachlan

Presented here is a treasury of primary material about cases of witchcraft in East Lothian. That constitutes the bulk of the book. This marvellous, vast compendium of transcribed documentation, with useful annotation and perceptive commentary, is a most welcome contribution to the study of Scottish witchcraft in the 16th and 17th centuries. It will, I am sure, be a long-lasting contribution.

One would need to have had some experience of the laborious, difficult, frustrating, eye-ball-aching task of deciphering the often tiny and indistinct unfamiliar sort of handwriting in which the documents were written to have an inkling of the vast amount of work that has gone into the writing of this book. For instance, we are nowadays used to writing and reading the letter 'h' with the loop, as handwritten going towards the top of the page. In Scotland, in centuries gone by, the letter 'h' tended to be written in an inverse way with the loop going towards the foot of the page. In the Fountain Gardens in Paisley, there is a statue to Robert Burns. It is written Bvrns. Passers-by are sometimes bemused by this. In the past, the letter 'v' stood for the letter 'u'. Hence our contemporary pronunciation of the letter 'w'. We call it a 'double u' although we write it as a 'double v'. There are many other such differences in calligraphy between the present day and the time when the documents that the author has transcribed were written. Bear in mind too that a large number of different clerks, with idiosyncratically different-looking handwriting would have been involved in writing them. The author deserves our gratitude.

Although this book is specifically written for a general readership, academic specialists will also find it to be useful and interesting. The documents are sometimes paraphrased and supplemented to make them more readable. This can be agreeable to all. Anyone who wants to be sure of the exact wording of the documents can trace them by following the meticulous references that David Robertson provides. For instance, in relation to Janet Bruce of Tranent who was tried for witchcraft in 1657 one reads: 'The papers relating to this case are in "Bundle 3" in box JC26/22. Notes on reverse side.' This is typical of the generous assistance he offers to other subsequent researchers.

Seasoned academic scholars of witchcraft will find much useful, challenging material in this book. They will, for instance, find it most refreshing to read of witches and witchcraft cases that they have never come across before. I am one such appreciative scholar. Even when one already has some familiarity with the cases that the author presents, it is fascinating to read different accounts given by different witnesses of the same case and the same alleged incidents. That the accounts are sometimes remarkably similar and sometimes subtly or blatantly different can be a source of productive reflection.

The general sort of approach that David Robertson advocates is in fact one that has an established academic pedigree. There are long names such as 'ethnomethodology' and 'phenomenology' that have been attached to it. He tries to strip away from the writing about Scottish witches layers of academic interpretation and to present the accounts of the cases as near as he can to the way in which they were presented originally. He tries to look behind the screen of what scholars have previously said about Scottish witchcraft and to see, as it were, what is actually there. It is as if he wants to try to let the accused witches tell their own stories in their own way. Hence, there is a focus in this book upon primary sources. Academics who are keen to stress the integrity of particular 'discourses', but not only they, will find this an attractive enterprise.

Of course, as the author is aware, there are difficulties. In particular, it is not always clear that accused witches actually had a story to tell, whether or not they wanted to tell it. Furthermore, it is often far from clear what one should make of the claims that accused witches were reported to have made. It is also often far from clear what one should make of the supposed reports of what accused witches were said to have done. One of the complications is that the documents in question do not seem to be the records of 'discourses' or conversations between informed and consenting adults talking freely about a mutually agreed and understood topic. They tend, rather, to suggest that those who asked the questions and those who gave the answers were, in many instances, talking at cross-purposes. Those who gave the answers did not want the questions to be addressed to them in the first place, far less to answer them. So it would often seem. Furthermore, in the past, as now, confessions are, for various reasons, frequently a weak sort of evidence despite the reliance that is put upon them. This is so even in the absence of manifest and specific physical torture, which was applied in Scotland although not, as the author indicates, in the sort of routine fashion that many people nowadays tend to suppose.

In addition to the annotated transcriptions there is, among other things, a summary of James VI and I's short treatise on witchcraft, in the form of a dialogue, called: *Daemonologie*. Notably, there is also a long, closing chapter on the analysis and interpretation of witchcraft in East Lothian. I might not agree with every single claim that David Robertson makes – for instance, I am not as sure as he seems to be that James's philosophy and theology of witchcraft was generally accepted by the legal and religious establishment in East Lothian - but I can heartily endorse the general tenor and commendable balance of his judgement. He argues that: 'We must avoid the "all or nothing" attitude, where either everything is true or everything is a farrago of ludicrous nonsense. We can accept what is probable, dismiss what is clearly impossible, but we should keep an open mind on the admittedly vast area in between'. That is an appropriate attitude with which to approach this remarkable and very fine book.

Hugh V McLachlan
Elderslie
November, 2007

Preface

This book began as an attempt to trace all the East Lothian references in *A Source Book of Scottish Witchcraft* (by Christina Larner, C. H. Lee, and Hugh McLachlan) - a fundamental starting point for studying Scottish witchcraft at a local level. The scope of my research then widened into the intention of tracing all existing references to East Lothian witchcraft in contemporary records and by contemporary writers. Ultimately I wanted to see if there was any prospect of determining what was "really" going on, in the face of the reams of conjecture, theory, and fanciful nonsense which have been written about Scottish witchcraft.

East Lothian has the reputation of having been something of a witchcraft "hotspot", but writers on the subject have tended to concentrate on the famous North Berwick trials of 1591. This is a pity, because there is much about the North Berwick affair which is not typical of the usual run of Scottish witchcraft, and concentrating on it may give a false impression of the beliefs and practices of the day. More than one famous name and erudite scholar has been led up tortuous garden paths by so doing. There is a wealth of material available in the records, which is of great interest, and which gives a much more accurate picture of witchcraft practices and beliefs in East Lothian than the more sensational North Berwick "evidence".

I have tried to gather together as many of the written records as possible dealing with or referring to witchcraft and kindred matters in East Lothian. The National Archives of Scotland are absolutely crucial for this work.

Some of the source material can be found in the printed *Register of the Privy Council*, the *Acts of the Parliaments of Scotland*, and Robert Pitcairn's *Criminal Trials in Scotland*. However, most of what is relevant consists of unpublished handwritten records stored in the National Archives. These are mainly papers from the legal processes which dealt with witchcraft suspects. Some are the "dittays" which list the crimes the accused persons were on trial for; some record the course of the trial or supporting evidence. Other papers are requests for "commissions" - special local courts to try suspects -and sometimes evidence is given to support the request. Often, however, there is no more than the bare request or the response to a request. Sometimes the result of a trial is known, sometimes not. We find some cases marked "Convict and brunt", and an occasional one marked "Clenged" [acquitted].

Some of this source material is carefully catalogued, and some of it indeed can be found in bound volumes. On the other hand, much of it consists of Justiciary Court papers stored in boxes, the contents of which are only haphazardly catalogued, if at all. The location of most of the interesting witchcraft items in the boxes is known, but in order to find out whether or not there is anything else, there is no alternative to trawling through all of the papers in all of the boxes. Fortunately, it is usually possible to recognise an irrelevant paper at a glance.

The records of the Church of Scotland covering kirk sessions, presbyteries, and synods, are also to be found in the National Archives of Scotland, and also contain much of interest - as do the Burgh Records. Very little of this material has been previously published.

There are many readily available popular books on Scottish witchcraft, some of which are quite informative. Many others - perhaps most - are of doubtful value. There is all-wise ethereal new-age "Celtic" mysticism; there is the perennial outrage against the Kirk for conducting a misogynist holocaust; there are the usual illustrations from *Newes from Scotland*, and modern pictures of withered crones with pointy hats flying around on broomsticks, which have much to do with English nursery stories and nothing whatsoever to do with genuine Scottish witchcraft practice. As for the actual cases quoted, there are the same old moth-eaten rabbits pulled out of the same battered old hats again and again.

Some interesting new research on Scottish witchcraft has been published in recent years. Unfortunately, academics tend to write for other academics, employing a style which is not likely to grab the attention or hold the interest of the ordinary reader. Thus, most of the new light shed on the subject has yet to illuminate popular perceptions of witchcraft in Scotland, and the man in the street is still stumbling among the broomsticks and black cats. What I have tried to do in *Goodnight My Servants All* is to present what seem to be the facts of East Lothian witchcraft in a way that will make the topic interesting to the general public, without arousing the complete contempt of the more keenly focused student.

Relying on original records rather than secondary sources helps the researcher to avoid the pitfalls inherent in simply repeating what other interested parties have written. Whoever said, "History may not repeat itself, but historians certainly do," made an observation particularly applicable to the study of Scottish witchcraft. Approaching original sources with an open mind also frees the interested student to a large extent from the interpretations put on the records by those with political, professional, sociological or religious axes to grind.

The original texts are written in what the clerks who wrote them would have considered to be English. However, it was an English liberally sprinkled with Scots words, phrases, and idioms. The spelling too can look decidedly odd to the modern eye. Again, what appear at first glance to be perfectly ordinary English words often had very different meanings in 17th century Scotland. Although the modern non-academic reader can happily cope with a few lines of direct quotation from 17th century documents every now and again, it is a different thing altogether to expect him to plough through several hundred pages of it. Rather than reproducing the exact words of the records, therefore, I have "translated" each piece of source material into modern English so that the reader can grasp the content without becoming frustrated by obscure vocabulary or construction. In some cases I have not only translated but summarised, so that the reader is not bogged down in repetitive or irrelevant detail. Indeed, sometimes a summary is the only way to convey the sense of a passage, on the odd occasions when parts of it may be illegible; for bad handwriting was every bit as common in the 17th century as it is today. Since 17th century "secretary hand" is quite unlike both 18th/19th century copperplate and the modern italic style of writing, when a clerk scribbles in secretary hand some of what he writes can be pretty much impossible to read. For those purists who wish to savour every word of the originals, I give reference numbers so that the sources can be traced and read without the interference of my editing.

There are various theories to explain what witches apparently got up to in 16th and 17th century Scotland. I resolved not to prejudge the issue, but to first of all read the original records, then try to come to some kind of conclusion about the true nature of witchcraft in East Lothian. Thus, most of this volume is a collection of records of what the "Authorities" of the day believed was going on, and there are only occasional asides from myself. Only towards the end of the book do I try to speculate about what was "really" going on.

Finally, as to the title: according to John Douglas the Tranent piper, "Goodnight, my servants all," was what the Devil said as he took his leave from witch meetings. It seemed to me appropriate as a title, since it conveys the idea of a more homely easy-going native Lowland Scots "devil", rather than the monster of religious myth or modern satanism. It also conveys the sense of genuine native witchcraft being a thing of the past, and lastly drops a broad hint as to the fate of most of East Lothian's witches.

D. M. Robertson.
August, 2007.

1. The North Berwick Witches.

There is no doubt that the best known East Lothian witchcraft cases are those of the so-called "North Berwick" witches of the early 1590s. Indeed, this is probably Scotland's most famous outbreak of witchcraft. The North Berwick witches have been written about so often that it is tempting to pass them by in favour of less well known but equally interesting cases. However, the "North Berwick" events were crucially important in that they did much to shape the perception of witchcraft practice as it was seen through the eyes of the law, and conceived in the minds of "the authorities" and ruling classes for the next hundred years. Also, much of what is commonly believed today about the practice of Scottish witchcraft is based on the North Berwick story. It is perhaps worth mentioning at the outset that as far as can be ascertained, none of the "North Berwick" witches actually came from North Berwick!

The best known source for the details of the North Berwick witchcraft outbreak has been in print since 1591. It is an anonymous pamphlet entitled *Newes from Scotland* - printed and published in England - which deliberately dwells on the more horrific and shocking details of the affair. Any modern newspaper or magazine article, or "popular" publication on the North Berwick witches, will have *Newes from Scotland* as its main or only source. However, the "dittays" or formal indictments of the main actors in the drama have been available in print in Robert Pitcairn's *Criminal Trials in Scotland* since 1833. Pitcairn also prints the text of *Newes from Scotland*. Most recently *Witchcraft in Early Modern Scotland* by L. Normand and Q. Roberts (Exeter 2000) reprints these dittays in full, with the text of *Newes from Scotland* and previously unpublished material dealing with the interrogation of the suspects.

The background to the story is that in the mid 1580s the young king James VI turned his mind towards marriage. Born in 1566, James had experienced a fairly traumatic childhood and youth. His Roman Catholic mother, the famous "Mary, Queen of Scots" had fled to England after a civil war, and was eventually beheaded, after many years of house arrest, on the orders of her relative Queen Elizabeth. James was given a rigorous Protestant upbringing and education, and became the pawn of competing factions of the nobility, who vied for possession of the King's person as a guarantee of power and influence. James grew up to be intelligent, scholarly, and probably homosexual. Having finally managed to assume full power in practice as well as in theory, James realised the necessity of acquiring a queen to underline his status as a monarch, and perhaps also his status as a "real man". Most importantly, he had to look to the future and provide an heir to succeed him, particularly since James himself was almost certain to succeed the ageing and childless Queen Elizabeth of England. Negotiations to marry Princess Elizabeth of Denmark fell through, and instead a marriage was arranged with her fourteen-year-old sister Anne. James and Anne were married by proxy at Kroneborg castle in Denmark on 20th August 1589, with George Keith, the Earl Marischal of Scotland, standing in for James at the ceremony. A Danish fleet set sail for Scotland to carry Anne to her royal husband, but storms and leaking ships forced the fleet to seek shelter in Norway, which was then a Danish possession. A further attempt at the end of October to sail to Scotland was again frustrated by storms, and again the fleet returned to Norway. Anne sent James a letter telling him of her decision to spend the winter in Oslo, and James decided to join her in Norway, which he reached at the end of October after another stormy voyage. On 23rd November 1589 James and Anne were married in person in Oslo. In late January 1590 they arrived in Denmark and went through yet another wedding ceremony. On 26th April the royal couple set sail for Scotland, arriving at Leith on 1st May after weathering another unpleasantly stormy passage.

It must have been well known in Scotland that the king's attempts to marry had been endangered several times by storms at sea. Perhaps this would be particularly obvious in East Lothian where James spent a fortnight in September 1589 at Seton Palace, the main residence of his good friend Robert, Lord Seton. Seton Palace had a commanding view of the Firth of Forth, and would allow James an early warning of his wife's arrival. It should also be remembered that the Earl Marischal, who had charge of all the negotiations and arrangements in Denmark, was a prominent East Lothian aristocrat with his mansion house at Keith, not far from the present-day village of Humbie.

Not long after James's return to Scotland with his new queen in May 1590 he was made aware that there had been some disturbing ongoings in East Lothian during his absence. Let us look first of all at the sequence of events as they are presented in *Newes from Scotland*, the anonymous pamphlet published in London, probably in late 1591. Although it is stated to be "published according to the Scottish copie", there is no evidence of it ever having been printed or published in Scotland. In their book *Witchcraft in Early Modern Scotland*, Normand and Roberts argue persuasively but not quite convincingly that the author of *Newes from Scotland* was James Carmichael, the minister of Haddington. The author is at least as likely to have been the 16th Century equivalent of a tabloid hack making a fast buck out of sensational "revelations".

Newes from Scotland.

Newes sets out its intention of quelling various false rumours going the rounds about the recent witchcraft outbreak, and of

declaring the damnable life of Doctor Fian a notable sorcerer who was burned in Edinburgh in Januarie last 1591, which doctor was register to the Devil that sundry times preached at North Barwick Kirke to a number of notorious witches, with the true Examinations of the said Doctor and witches as they uttered them in the presence of the Scottish King: Discovering how they pretended to bewitch and drown his Majestie in the sea, coming from Denmarke; with such other wonderful matters as the like hath not been heard at any time.

Published according to the Scottish Copie.
Printed for William Wright.

As later becomes plain, Fian was a schoolmaster, not a medical man. The Latin word "doctor" means "teacher", and was often given as a courtesy title to schoolmasters in Scotland in days gone by.

Newes goes on to explain how events originated in the household of David Seton, who is described as "Deputy Baillie in Tranent." Tranent was part of the vast estates of Robert, Lord Seton, and David Seton - no doubt a kinsman of his master - was Lord Seton's "baron baillie" in Tranent. The baron baillie was the landowner's representative in a community, deputising for him [thus the term "deputy" baillie in *Newes*], overseeing the affairs of the community as they affected his master's interests, and presiding over the baron court which administered local justice.

David Seton became aware that his maidservant Geillis Duncan was often absent from the house at night. She had also acquired a reputation as a very effective healer. Seton suspected that her healing skills might have been acquired by "unlawful means". He interrogated her, and being made none the wiser, resorted to torture [which, by the way, it was quite illegal for a local magistrate to use.]. He tried the "pilliewinkies" [thumbscrews], and screwing up a rope ever tighter around her head, all to no avail. Geillis was then searched for the "Devil's mark", which was found on her throat. At this, she immediately confessed and was imprisoned. She implicated:

"Agnes Sampson eldest witch of all dwelling in Haddington,
Agnes Thompson of Edenbrough,
George Watt's wife dwelling in Lowthiane,
Robert Grierson skipper,
Janet Blandilands,
The smith at the Brigge Hallis
with innumerable others in those parts."

Geillis also accused Euphame MacCalyean, who had supposedly killed her godfather and used sorcery against a Court of Session judge who was over-friendly with her daughter. Also accused was Barbara Napier who, it was claimed, had caused the death of the Earl of Angus, whose physician had been unable to recognise the disease that killed him. Both Napier and MacCalyean had been thought to be highly respectable women. Many others also accused by Geillis Duncan were arrested in Leith.

Agnes Sampson, the first witch named, was brought before the King and closely questioned, to no avail. She was then imprisoned arid tortured, her head being "thrawn" with a rope for an hour. All her body hair was shaved, and she was searched for the Devil's mark, which was found on her "privities". She immediately confessed, and confirmed all the others aforementioned as witches. Agnes was again brought before the King, and confessed that the previous Hallowe'en, she and the others mentioned, and about two hundred witches, had put to sea sailing in riddles and sieves and carrying flagons of wine, and sailed to North Berwick, making merry and drinking. They landed and danced a reel to the song

"Commer goe ye before,
commer goe ye,
Gif ye will not goe before,
commer let me."
[commer: woman]

As they danced Geillis Duncan went in front playing the "trump" [Jew's harp] until they came to North Berwick Kirk.

At this point in the interrogation the king sent for Geillis Duncan and had her play the tune for him. Continuing with her narrative, Agnes Sampson described how the Devil stuck his buttocks over the pulpit and made the witches kiss them as a penance for arriving late. He received oaths of good service from the company, and expressed great hatred towards the King, saying that James was "the greatest enemy he had in the world". After this the witches put to sea again and returned home.

Agnes confessed such strange and miraculous things that the king scoffed at the accused witches as "extreme liars". At this Agnes Sampson offered to prove that she was indeed telling the truth. She took James aside and told him the exact words that passed between him and the Queen on the first night of his marriage in Oslo. The king was most impressed with this demonstration of her occult powers.

She went on to confess how she had hung up a toad for three days and collected the venom that dropped from it. She had also tried to obtain an item of the King's soiled linen. She had failed in this, but said that if she had been successful she would have bewitched James to the death. He would have felt as if he were lying on sharp thorns or needles.

She and her associates had christened a cat, and tied to it the "cheefest part" of a dead man, and several joints of his body. The next night the witches again put to sea in sieves and riddles and left the cat in the sea before the town of Leith. A terrific storm arose, sinking a boat which was on its way from Burntisland to Leith, carrying jewels and gifts to be presented to the new queen on her arrival at Leith. The christened cat also caused a contrary wind to blow the King's ship away from the rest of the fleet on his way home from Denmark. Agnes stated that only James's faith had allowed him to come safely from the sea.

The arrested witches confessed that when the Devil took them as his servants he would "carnally use them" - have sexual intercourse with them. However, they got little pleasure from this, "in respect of his cold nature". (His "cold nature" has nothing to do with Satan's psychological attributes. It simply means that his penis was cold.) The Devil would also have sex with his followers from time to time after their initiation.

Fian, implicated by Geillis Duncan, was the witches' "register" or secretary, and supposedly the only man allowed to attend the Devil's "readings" (whatever they might have been). After his arrest he was invited to elaborate further, but neither coaxing, nor "thrawing" his head with a rope (as had been done to Agnes Sampson) would induce him to confess. Next, his interrogators tried him with the "bootes". The lower leg was fastened in a kind of tube, and gradually crushed by the hammering in of wedges. This is described by *Newes* as "the most severe and cruel pain in the world". Fian received three strokes of the hammer and was seemingly unable to speak. The other witches advised his interrogators to examine his tongue.

They did so and found two pins inserted up to their heads under his tongue. "Now is the charm stinted," the witches claimed.

Fian was released from the boot, brought before the King, and freely confessed as follows:

He was always present at the witches' general meetings.

He acted as clerk to all those in the Devil's service. He took their oaths and wrote down whatever the Devil instructed.

He had bewitched a gentleman near "Saltpans" [Prestonpans] where he, Fian, kept a school. This man loved a lady who had also caught Fian's fancy. For one hour out of every twenty-four this man would fall into fits of madness. He was brought before the King and fell into a fit, screeching, bending down, then capering up till his head touched the ceiling. All the men present were not sufficient to hold him. Extra help was called for and the man was bound hand and foot. After an hour the madness passed, and he came to himself believing that he had been in a sound sleep.

Having bewitched his rival, Fian attempted to "obtain his purpose" of the young lady. Her brother was a pupil in Fian's school at Prestonpans. Fian promised to teach him free from corporal punishment if he would bring him three of his sister's pubic hairs. The boy was given a piece of conjured paper to wrap them in. He apparently slept in the same bed as his sister, and when he attempted to harvest the required hairs the girl cried out and complained to her mother. The mother was herself a witch, and suspecting what the boy was up to, she thrashed him until he confessed. She then clipped three hairs from the udder of a heifer which had never been to the bull, wrapped them in the conjured paper, and had her son deliver them to Fian. He worked his magic upon them, and the heifer appeared leaping and dancing at the door of the church where he happened to be at the time,

The notorious North Berwick witch meeting was held in St Andrew's Church. All that now remains of this building is the church porch, close by the popular "Scottish Seabird Centre".

"Delegates" to the North Berwick meeting would have no difficulty finding their way there. "The Law" is a particularly prominent landmark. Might this have influenced the choice of venue?

and followed him around wherever he went, to his great embarrassment. Although Fian was a very young man, he got the reputation of being a "notable conjurer".

Fian signed his confession and was imprisoned. He renounced the Devil and all his works, and vowed to lead a Christian life in future. The next night the Devil appeared to Fian dressed all in black and carrying a white wand in his hand. He asked if Fian would continue to serve him. Meeting with a refusal, the Devil vowed Fian would be his before he died. He then broke the white wand and vanished.

The following day Fian managed to steal the prison key during the night, escaped, and fled to Prestonpans. He was recaptured, questioned again, and denied his previous confession. Needles were thrust under his finger nails, then his nails were torn off with pincers. Fian remained unmoved and refused to confess. The boots were again applied to the extent that his legs were crushed "as small as might be", while blood and marrow "spouted forth," so that his legs were rendered "unserviceable for ever". Fian still resolutely denied his previous confession, which he said he had only made for fear of torture. He was condemned to death, and duly strangled and burned on the Castle Hill of Edinburgh at the end of January 1591.

So much for the North Berwick Witches as described in the contemporary pamphlet *Newes from Scotland*. Let us now turn to the surviving records of the examination and trial of those concerned.

Recorded in the "Calendar of [English] State Papers Relating to Scotland" we find a letter of 28th November 1590 from the English ambassador Robert Bowes to Lord Burghley, the Lord Treasurer of England, which contains the following paragraph:

The King and Council is occupied with the examinations of sundry witches taken in the country and confessing both great numbers and the names of their fellows, and also strange and odious facts done by them, which upon the full trials of their causes are intended to be published. And some of good quality are like to be blotted by the dealings of the wicked sort.

[CSP, Vol X, p425].

Examinations and Confessions of Geillis Duncan and Agnes Sampson.

The first record of the interrogations can be found in the National Archives of Scotland under the reference JC26/2/13. It was recently published for the first time along with several other previously unpublished documents in Normand and Roberts' *Witchcraft in Early Modern Scotland*, where the authors refer to it as "Document 1". I have rendered thse documents in modern English

Geillis Duncan

Gillie confessed that when they were in the middle of the firth they met a woman from Copenhagen, and described this woman. The name of the place was obtained from Bessie Thomson. The Erse tailor and his wife did most of the talking to her, and they understood each other without difficulty. ["Erse" is translated here by Normand and Roberts as "Irish", but it can also mean Highland or simply Gaelic-speaking, which in the context of 16th Century Scotland is perhaps more likely.]

She swears that she did not know what the intention was in going there, but was only following the orders of "him who commanded her".

The last meeting was at North Berwick. She rode to the end of the town, put in the horse, then went to the church. There were several there dressed in "taffetas" [*i.e.* well-dressed women]. There was no conjuration or swearing of oaths, but everybody answered him [presumably the Devil] when he spoke to them. She was dancing last in the line with Greymeal, but she went in first over the kirk stile.

Greymeal was afterwards received into the Devil's service near Skugill [Scoughall].

Document JC26/2/12 in the national Archives of Scotland [Normand and Roberts "Document 2"] is a record of Agnes Sampson's confession including the intervention of the King.

Agnes Sampson.

Agnes denies healing George Newton's wife, and doesn't know whether or not she ever gave her advice.

She admits advising John Duncan's wife to take an egg steeped in vinegar for her disease. She denied knowing how the egg should be used, and later admitted it.

She denies sending any of her sons, daughters or daughters-in-law to any patient, and denies that they had any knowledge in her craft

She denies getting clothes from anyone, particularly from Edinburgh or from James Polwart's wife.

She confesses that she healed the lady of Kilbaberton with iris steeped overnight in wine; also using a prayer which she repeated for her questioners.

She confesses that she learned her skill and her prayer from her father. He told her that if her prayer stopped [*i.e.* presumably if she faltered or forgot the words while reciting the prayer] the patient would die, and if it didn't stop he would live.

She confessed that she healed the Laird of Redhall's son by rubbing *aquavitae* on him and saying her prayer.

She denies meeting John Downie coming out of Clerkington and healing him by taking him by the little finger and saying some words to him.

She admits that, using her prayer, she healed Laird Parkie's [?] girl, who was paralysed down one side. She admitted this reluctantly.

She confesses that when Robin Dickson was bewitched by grains of wheat in his doublet she told him, and advised him not to wear the doublet again unless he took out the grains of wheat. She agreed that he hadn't recovered until she told him this. She says she knows when someone is bewitched, but won't say how she knows.

She confesses that on Hallowe'en, using only her prayer, she healed the Sheriff's wife who had received "an evil blast" between the chamber and the hall.

She confesses using her prayer to heal Alison Ker in Tyninghame, who had been bewitched by Catherine Grey.

She denies knowing anything about the boat that sank between Burntisland and Leith, but she had heard sorrow expressed about it [heard "mean" made for it - *i.e.* mane: mourning].

She denies ever having been in company with Gillie Duncan and denies even knowing her.

She confesses that if her prayer stops, someone is bewitched. If it stops a second time there is no cure. [Probable reading. This part of the document is damaged.]

The next admission seems to be that someone applying for help from Agnes was told she couldn't be cured, because she didn't actually believe Agnes could help. However Agnes did eventually heal her. [Probable reading. Also damaged here.]

She denies the attestation of Mr John Kelly that... [Also damaged.]

She confesses that at Patrick Edmiston's house at Newton, when she was in the garden with his three daughters on a bright moonlit night, they saw a black dog which made them all fall down with fright.

The King intervened here because of inconsistencies and contradictions in what Agnes was saying about this incident; for example, that she said on the one hand that they had all fallen with fright and then sent for

Agnes, and on the other hand that only Lady Littledean saw the dog; then again, that they had all seen the dog come out of the well together; that she said they had killed the dog, and that the dog had escaped from them over the wall; that they had all fallen together, and that they had fallen separately. The King demanded that she tell the truth.

Agnes then continued as follows, and confessed to the King that on the day in question she had been sent for in the morning to heal the lady of the house. She told the other ladies she would tell them that night whether she would be able to heal the patient or not, and arranged to meet them in the garden after supper. Between five and six o'clock she went to the garden alone to recite her prayer, and also called on the Devil by the name of "Eloa" to come and speak to her. He appeared over the wall in the likeness of a dog. He came so close that she was afraid, telling him to come no nearer but to answer whether or not the lady would live. He replied, "Her days are gone." He asked where the Lady's daughters were, and Agnes told him they were to come to the garden. The Devil said he was going to have one of them, but Agnes forbade him and he departed howling. From then until after supper he hid in the well. When the ladies came into the garden he came out of the well and appeared to one of them, frightening her greatly. Another of the ladies was drawn running to the well, and would have been drowned if Agnes and the others had not dragged her back. The dog then disappeared howling over the wall. Agnes told the ladies that she was sorry, but she would not be able to help the patient because her prayer had "stopped". (As explained previously, Agnes assessed a patient's chances of survival by reciting a charm. If she stumbled or faltered in the recitation the patient would die. If she completed the charm without error the patient would live.)

The King asked how Agnes first came to serve the Devil. She said that after the death of her husband she was approached by the Devil in the likeness of a man, who commanded her to acknowledge him as her master and renounce Christ. She agreed because of her poverty, and because he promised that she and her children would be made rich, and that he would give her power to be avenged on her enemies. He appointed a time and a place for their next meeting, and left his mark on her. She thought at first that the mark had been caused by one of her children, who slept with her, one on each side. The wound did not heal for half a year. [This is the likely interpretation. The document is damaged here, which has also destroyed the reference to the exact location of the mark.] The second time she met the Devil he told her to call him "Eloa", which Agnes pronounced as "Hola". Agnes affirmed that when she was arrested she had vowed never to confess anything, and it was only the King's words which had now moved her to do so. She praised God that she had been brought to repentance and a sense of her sins.

After a break the interrogation resumed in the afternoon. Agnes confessed that sometimes the Devil appears like a foal, or young horse ["staig" - a more likely interpretation than Normand and Roberts' "stag"], and sometimes like a dog. However, sometimes he was like a truss of hay, or took some other form. He was always black. The Devil enabled her to fortell that Patrick Porteous would live eleven years.

She was at a meeting at Bara with Meg Steele, Kate Gray, Janet Campbell, and another now dead. They met beside the burn to the east of the church. Janet Campbell was burned after that.

Two years after that Agnes was at a meeting between Cousland and Carberry. There were three of them present, and Janet Stratton from Payston was one. She quarrelled with her master there because she got no benefit from him, and she threatened to renounce him. She didn't know what he had promised the others, for he

Nether Keith (above), home of Agnes Sampson, "the Wise Wife of Keith". The mansion of Keith Marischal and the ruined church of Keith stand nearby, but the settlement of Nether Keith is long gone.

At Ormiston Bridge (below), Agnes supposedly hauled up the Devil on a rope. She was accused of using her sorcery to harm David Seton who lived nearby at Foulstruther (now "Wolfstar").

spoke to each of them individually. She didn't stay long with him this time. He commanded them to be true servants, then left them.

She induced Grey Meal to renounce God and serve a better master. [This section is badly damaged. It probably also says that she told Grey Meal that he would never want] She gave him a drink of milk.

The Devil met her in the likeness of a man when she was going out alone to the fields between five and six in the evening. He told her to meet him the next night

She went to North Berwick on horseback escorted by a man Couper, and arrived at the churchyard in the evening. They danced in the churchyard while Gillie played the trump. John Fian led the dance; Agnes herself and a companion [Damaged here.] followed next Kate Gray was there and George Mott's wife, and Robert [Grierson ?]. Altogether there were a hundred present. Six were men and all the rest women. The women paid homage to the Devil first then the men. The men were turned round "widdershins" [anti-clockwise] nine times, and the women six times. John Fian "blew up the doors" and "blew in" the lights, which were like great black candles sticking round the pulpit. The Devil himself started up in the pulpit like a big black man. He called on everyone by name, and they answered, "Here master." When Robert Grierson was named they all ran about in turmoil, angry because it had been promised that he should be called "Robert the Comptroller".

The Devil then asked if they had kept their promise to be good servants, and asked what they had done since the last meeting. At his command they opened up three graves, two in the church and one outside. They took the joints of the fingers, toes, and noses [or perhaps knees?], and shared them out. Agnes herself got a winding sheet and two joints which she subsequently carelessly lost. The Devil ordered them to keep the joints till they were dry, then make a powder from them to work evil with. He commanded them to do all the evil they could, and before they departed they all kissed his arse. He was wearing a black gown and a black hat. Some of those present stood and some sat. John Fian was always next to the Devil at his left elbow, and Grey Meal guarded the door.

At a further session on the afternoon of the 5th of December 1590 Agnes confessed that she, the goodwife of Spilmersford, Grey Meal, Geillis Duncan, Bessie Thomson, Janet Stratton, and others, nine altogether, met at Foulstruther to discuss how to bring wrack and ruin upon David Seton.

["Foulstruther", now corrupted to "Wolfstar" from the colloquial "Foulster", is a farm overlooking the Tyne Water and the modern village of Ormiston. Foulstruther means "foul marsh" or perhaps "bird marsh", and would originally refer to the low-lying ground between the present-day farm of Wolfstar and Ormiston village. Thus the witches may have met in the marsh rather than at the farm. This may be supported by the fact that their activities centered on a bridge, presumably a bridge over Tyne Water at or near the site of the present bridge leading into Ormiston. David Seton was Lord Seton's baron baillie in Tranent, but he had a son David Seton. One of them is elsewhere termed "of Foulstruther", but it is not clear which.]

At the bridge Geillis Duncan, Bessie Thomson, and Grey Meal hauled on a rope as Agnes cried out, "Haul! Hola!" The rope was attached to something very heavy, which when pulled up turned out to be the Devil. He asked if they had all been good servants, and they asked him how they could blight David Seton. The Devil gave them some pieces of glass mixed with pieces of cord, and ordered them to scatter them on the moor. They did this. [It seems, however, that the charm affected a ploughman's possessions instead. The document is damaged here.]

Agnes confessed to have been often at sea in riddles. [*Newes from Scotland* has the witches sailing in sieves and riddles from North Berwick. The document is damaged here, but Agnes appears to be saying that they would sail to ships and foreign shores. Usually they would not stay long, but sometimes they would remain around forty-eight hours.]

The Devil foretold the storm at Michaelmas to her, and that great harm would be done at sea and on land.

John Fian wrote a letter to take to Leith for Janet Fairlie. Agnes confessed to the sinking of a ship exactly as Gillie Duncan had.

She confessed that the Devil told her that the King would have great difficulty in reaching home, and the Queen would never get there unless the King fetched her. She asked the Devil if the king would have any children. He told her that he would first have boys, then girls.

She confessed that she was in the ship called The Grace of God that perished at North Berwick. Twenty people embarked from North Berwick in a boat like a chimney [?]. Some women rowed with oars. The Devil went before them like a rick of hay. Some of them boarded the ship and some stayed in the boat. The Devil brought up wine from below deck and gave it to them, and they handed some of it over the side of the ship to those in the boat. They saw no sailors, nor did any sailors see them. When they left, the Devil remained underneath the ship. As soon as they landed an evil wind blew, and a storm arose which sank the ship. On board the ship she gave Grey Meal twenty shillings for his attentiveness in waiting on her. He also confessed this.

The Devil also told her to go to a ship where there was an "uncouth" woman whose description matches that given in Grey Meal's statement ["Uncouth" here does not have its modern meaning, but means "unknown", or perhaps more likely in this context, "foreign".]

The "Irish" [*sic* Normand and Roberts. "Highland" is perhaps more likely.] tailor and his wife played a leading part.

A Word from the English Ambassador.

In the preceding document we have for the first time in the official records a reference to the King and his difficulties in reaching home from Scandinavia However, well before this there had been indications that the royal couple's travel problems were not entirely due to natural causes. On 4th July 1590 the English Ambassador wrote to Lord Burghley, "It is advised from Denmark that the admiral there has caused five or six witches to be taken in Copenhagen upon suspicion that by their witchcraft they had stayed the Queen of Scots' voyage into Scotland, and sought to have stayed likewise the King's return." [Calendar of State Papers Vol X, p. 365.] The interrogators must have been aware of this development in Denmark, and it may well have been at least at the back of their minds throughout the interrogation sessions that something similar could have been going on in Scotland.

The Deposition of Geillis Duncan

This is JC26/2/3 in the National Archives of Scotland, and Normand and Roberts' "Document 3". There are two sections. The first is dated 5th December 1590. Geillis Duncan has been confronted with Bessie Thomson who was said by Agnes Sampson to have been at Foulstruther. Bessie has presumably given evidence against Geillis:

Geillis testifies that when they went to the ship where the foreign woman was, she and Bessie Thomson were told to stay in their boats. Robert Grierson made the boats fast to the ship's side till they came out of the ship. Agnes passed a drink of white wine through a window, but would not let her come in.

The clerk John Fian wrote a letter which Agnes Sampson brought to her to take to Leith, "to the token that" Agnes offered her a drink of wine which she refused and took a drink of ale. [Was this a sign for mutual recognition, equivalent to a password?] Agnes confesses the "token" but denies that she delivered the letter.

Gillie delivered the letter as ordered, to Janet Fairlie's house in Leith - to Janet, the two Linkups, and the two Stobies. Having delivered the letter Gillie wished to leave, but Janet Fairlie followed her to the bridge to bring her back. However Gillie "gave her on the mouth" [Hit her?], and came away. Gillie fell sick after this, and was ill for quarter of a year.

[The next part of this document is marked "Janet Campbell" in the margin, which presumably means that the interrogators had finished with Gillie and gone on to question Janet.]

Eight days after the letter Agnes Sampson, John Fian, Gellie Duncan, and Meg Din baptised a cat in the weaver's house as follows. First two of them held a finger one on each side of the chimney crook [a hook for hanging pots above the fire] with the knuckles of their fingers meeting in the crook. Then they passed the cat three times through the chain of the crook, and three times under the chimney. After that at Begie Tod's house they tied four human joints to its front feet [Beigis Tod was a Longniddry woman executed in 1608. See Pitcairn's Criminal Trials Vol 2 p.542.] Janet then took the cat to Leith. About midnight she and the four above named persons [Agnes Sampson, John Fian, Gellie Duncan, and Meg Din] went to the end of the pier, and saying, "See that there be no deceit among us" they threw the cat into the sea as far as they could and the cat swam back again.

The Trial of John Cunningham [Fian]

In December 1590 John Cunningham, alias Fian, the schoolmaster of Prestonpans, was put on trial. The record of proceedings can be found in Pitcairn's Criminal Trials Vol 1 p. 209. Pitcairn dates the trial 26th December, but as we shall see later, there may be a problem with this date.

The presiding judges were John Graham and Humphrey Blynschellis, and the prosecutor for the Crown was David McGill of Cranston Riddel. The assise [jury] consisted of:
Richard Newton in Tranent
John Hakit in Tranent
William Strathearn in Tranent
Robert Seton in Tranent
Patrick Halyeort in Tranent
Robert Trisk, merchant burgess
  of Edinburgh
James Milton in Tranent
John Donaldson, merchant there
Thomas Craig in Tranent
Robert Smith, merchant there

Johne Feane alias Cuninghame, who last lived in Preston, convicted of several items of witchcraft contained in this "dittay" [formal list of charges].

1 When he was in bed facing the wall in Thomas Trumbillis house, musing and thinking how he might get back at Thomas for not cleaning the room, the Devil appeared dressed in white and asked him, "Will you be my servant, and adore me and my servants? If so, you shall never want." The Devil promised that he would be revenged on his enemies, and persuaded him to burn Trumbill's house.

2 The second night the Devil appeared to him he marked him with a rod. He was lying feigning sickness in Thomas Trumbill's chamber when he was stricken with great ecstasies and

trances, lying for two or three hours dead, with his spirit taken and carried to many mountains, seemingly all over the world.

3 He abused his body with Margaret Spens, a widow. He promised to marry her, but the Devil persuaded him against it, because it would lose him great riches.

4 While he was lying in bed in Prestonpans, he was carried through the air to North Berwick Church. Satan commanded him to do homage with the rest of his servants. There was a candle in their midst burning blue. Satan stood as if in a pulpit preaching a sermon of dubious morality, ending with instructions to spare no effort to do evil, and to eat drink, be happy, and take things easy, for he would raise them up gloriously at the Day of Judgment.

5 He was in company with Satan at this gathering, where he saw Robert Greirsoune, Michael Clarke, Annie Sampsoune, and many others. He and all the rest kissed Satan behind, some kissing his "erse". He also bewitched William Hutsoune in Windegoul with an evil spirit.

6 Satan carried him to the sea, where they went skimming over the water in a boat. He had foreknowledge of the leak that sprang in the Queen's ship, foretold to him by Satan.

7 He raised winds when the king was sailing to Denmark. He sent a letter to Marion Linkup in Leith to meet him and the rest on the sea within five days. They were in a ship where they drank to each other, and Satan ordered them to sink the ship which they thought they did.

8 When the King was returning from Denmark he met with Satan, who promised to raise a mist and cast the King ashore in England. He took a thing like a football, which looked to Cunningham like a small parcel, and threw it in the sea, causing vapour and smoke to rise.

9 He was with Satan at North Berwick Church. Satan was in the pulpit in the form of a black man. Three graves were opened, two inside and one outside. The women dismembered the corpses with their knives in a state of ecstasy.

10 He opened locks, especially in the house of David Seytoun junior in Tranent. He opened the gate guarding the front door while the key was lying on the table. He opened the door in David Seytoun's mother's house by blowing in a woman's hand while he stood at the fireside.

11 He came from supper at Patrick Umphrais son's house in the Myls [or "at the mill"?] at night and rode to Tranent with a serving man. He made four candles appear on the horse's ears and another on the staff the man carried. This gave so much light it was like daylight. The man went back with the candles and he fell dead at the entrance to his own house.

12 He bewitched William Hutsoune by possessing him with an evil spirit for twenty-six weeks. This left him when Cunningham was arrested.

13 In the company of Annie Sampson, Robert Grierson, Kaet Gray and others, on Hallowe'en he went out in a boat beside Robert Grierson's house in the Pans. They sailed to a tryst with another witch. They boarded a ship and drank ale and wine, then caused the ship to perish with its crew.

14 He kept moles' feet in his purse, given to him by Satan. As long as he had them, he would never be short of money.

15 He was at North Berwick church at a meeting with Satan and other witches, where Satan preached. Cunningham sat at the left side of the pulpit, and when the sermon was over Satan took him by the hand, led him round anti-clockwise, and made him kiss his arse.

16 When he was chasing a cat in Tranent he was carried high above the ground at great speed, and over a wall so high he could not have touched the top of it. Satan had commanded him to catch cats at a meeting at Brumhoillis. It was to be thrown in the sea to raise winds to destroy ships and boats.

17 He claimed to be able to tell people how long they would live, and how they would die, if they gave him their date of birth. He told Marion Weddel that her son wouldn't live fifteen days, and it came to pass.

18 In a similar manner he predicted the death of the son of Alexander Bouis wife in Edinburgh.

19 He received the following commandments from Satan:

To deny all true religion.

To have faith in the Devil and adore him.

He recruited for the Devil.

He dismembered bodies, especially of unbaptised infants.

He destroyed men at sea and on land, with corn, cattle, and goods, and raised tempests and stormy weather.

20 He is a common notorious witch and enchanter.

The pamphlet *Newes from Scotland* says Cunningham was burnt in January 1591. Normand and Roberts think "late January". If this is the case, it would be unusual to have such a long delay between conviction and execution. Death sentences on witches were usually carried out within a very few days.

To complicate matters, in *Extracts from the Records of the Burgh of Edinburgh 1589 to 1603* [Ed. M. Wood and R. K. Hannay, Edinburgh, 1927] we find a record of the expenses incurred in executing Cunningham. This is dated 16th December 1590. According to Pitcairn, Cunningham was not put on trial until 26th December, so it would seem that either Pitcairn or the editors of *Extracts* have made a mistake in transcription, unless there was a 16th Century clerical error. On the other hand, perhaps 16th December was just a convenient heading for the next few weeks' expenses. Again, the treasurer might have been allowing in advance for the inevitable result of a trial the outcome of which was never in doubt. Whatever the explanation, the expense account is as follows:

The executione of Johne Feane, alias Cunninghame, witche, the 16 December.

Item, to the wricht for setting the stoupe [stake] 10s

Item, for ten laid of coiilis at Vs Vlljd the laid [coal] 64s 4d

Item, for tua turs of hedder [bundles of heather] 9s

Item, ane turs of brome [broom] 3s 6d

Item, vj tar barrellis and for careing of them to the hill 20s

Item, 2 dry barrelis 5s

Item, for towis [ropes] 3s

Item, for waiting upon the fyre 2s

Item, for carying the stoupe to the hill 8d

Item, to the lokman [hangman] and his man   6s 8d

Summa of this executioun is   5li 18s 2d

Cunningham seems to have been the first of the "North Berwick" witches to be executed. It is perhaps worth emphasising that he would not be burnt alive. Witches in Scotland were first strangled at the stake, and their corpses were then burnt to ashes.

Meanwhile, the interrogations continued.

More evidence from Geillis Duncan.

This is the second section of document JC26/2/3. It is dated 15th January, whereas the first section was dated 5th December. Normand and Roberts are of the opinion that "the deposition on 15th January also seems to be that of Gellis Duncan."

A year after the death of the Earl of Angus on Handsel Monday, about two in the afternoon Agnes came out of Lady Pogie's [?] house with Lady Pogie and Katrina Hamilton, the wife of David Nimil in Dalkeith. They went to the King's ford of Dalkeith Water [*i.e.* probably the ford where the king's highway crossed the

River Esk.] and sent Geillis Duncan up the brae to gather a broad leaved grass and to sit there till they had finished what they were going to do. She looked back and saw a black man with them whom she saw "wading out of the well" [Normand and Roberts]. She asked Agnes who he was and Agnes said, "It was not a man. It was but the waf [flapping] of my cloak."

Immediately after this they came to David Nimil's back cellar where they drove the hussie [either the housewife, or more likely, the servant girl] out of the house, and drank wine and ale, placing Geillis a short distance away from them. Agnes Sampson then addressed David Nimil's wife ... [The document is damaged here and the sense is not clear, but Agnes seems to refer to a land deal worth two hundred merks between David Nimil's wife and a landowner James Douglas. Connected with this is what may be a threat that she will never have a child to succeed to the property.]

[The next paragraph is also badly damaged and confusing. Agnes and David Nimil's wife seem to have prepared a potion of flowers and herbs, possibly to induce an abortion in someone known to David's wife. Someone called George fell in love with one of the women named in the statement to his detriment. David's wife comments to Geillis regarding some other person that his or her "well days are gone".]

Gillie Duncan states that Agnes Sampson said, "Now the king is going to fetch his wife, but I shall be here before them."

When Gillie Duncan and Agnes Sampson were confronted with Janet Fairlie, one constantly affirmed the sending of the letter, and the other that it was delivered to Janet. She constantly denies it, and also denies that the Linkups were ever in her house, or she in theirs. She also denies that when Mr Thomas Ballenden brought her from Leith, she heard the Linkups say that she was saying she was not a witch. This however is the truth.

She affirms that Janet Campbell of Carrie [?] was at the baptising of the cat and at the North Berwick gathering. She was nicknamed "Maiden". She struggled with Janet Fairly over which of them should throw the cat in the sea. She says that last Michaelmas Janet Fairlie was in North Berwick church with the Stobies and Linkups.

Evidence from Agnes Sampson.

Document JC26/2/4 in the National Archives of Scotland [Normand and Roberts "Document 4"] is the record of an interrogation of Agnes Sampson in January 1591, sometime before her actual trial on the 27th. She attempts to deny some of the accusations, but retracts the denial in one case. This might suggest the use of heavy handed methods of persuasion. *Newes from Scotland* states quite plainly that Agnes was tortured. "What this document is intent on are connections with Barbara Napier, who has not featured in previous examinations and depositions" [Normand and Roberts p. 154]. With the naming of Barbara Napier and Euphane MacCalyean the investigation is now moving to involve "gentlewomen" of much higher social standing than those exposed so far. The tentacles of the conspiracy eventually reached into the high aristocracy, and the Earl of Bothwell, the ambitious and unstable young cousin of the King was also charged, but acquitted.

[?]... January before the Master of Work John Gedde. Agnes Sampson.

Confirms raising the Devil in the form of a black dog at the death of the old Lady Edmiston.

She confesses the first appearance of the Devil.

She confesses receiving the mark.

She confesses being invited to the meeting at Bara by the Devil in visible form.

The second meeting at Carberry.

The third was about conjuring the wax image of Mr John Moscrop.

She confesses that Janet Drummond was sent to her to consult about Pumpherston.

[Janet Drummond was servant to Euphane MacCalyean, who was supposed to have been trying to impede the Laird of Pumpherston's marriage, and trying to gain his love by magic. Moscrop was Euphane's father-in-law.]

She denies Foulstruther. She denies the sending of the letter, and that she was in George Mott's house.

[Fian's letter, previously mentioned, was supposed to have been written by him in George Mott's house in Prestonpans.]

She denies sailing on the sea.

She denies the gathering at North Berwick. She confesses this again. She confesses meeting with Barbara Napier three times. The last time was in Dalkeith when their only conversation was when Barbara asked what would help Lady Angus who had an illness causing vomiting. The next time, Agnes was in Cameron, and Barbara sent her maid to say she wished to come and speak to Agnes [Or to ask Agnes to come and speak to her. The sense is not entirely clear here.], which she immediately did. Barbara's first concern was with her husband who had gone to the west country. She asked Agnes to ensure that he got home again safely and free from harm, as she feared some enemies. Agnes asked whom she feared, and Barbara replied that there was a certain "Archie" she wanted her husband protected from. Agnes promised to do her best, and promised to have "a picture of wax" [*i.e.* a wax image] ready for their next meeting, which Barbara should put under the bed of whoever she feared. She made this wax image three or four days after that, and in return was given as much linen cloth as would make a kerchief. Agnes supplied the wax herself. Agnes and Barbara had met in an old barn or some such building, sitting on a bundle of straw.

[Here, by the way, we have a good example of the dangers of placing too much faith in the interpretations of those who have little or no knowledge of Scots. Normand and Roberts say, "The meeting was in an old barn or suchlike house upon a loch stray." "Loch stray" makes no sense, and the original is of course referring to a "lock stray" - a bundle of straw.]

At their third meeting at Cameron she asked Agnes how she could get in Lady Angus's good books in order to get back some possessions of hers which Lady Angus had. Agnes asked her to lend her the ring on her finger, and that would do the trick. She would give the ring back to her within fourteen days. She recited her prayer over the ring and delivered it back again.

She confesses putting graveyard earth under Euphan MacCalyean's bed.

[On the reverse of the above document is what would appear to be part of a provisional draft of Agnes's formal dittay. Although damage causes some difficulty, the meaning is clear enough]:

You are accused that being well acquainted with Barbara [Napier] you met her at Bridgend and other places. Barbara said Archie had done her wrong and asked your advice. You replied that you would do what you could. At the next meeting Barbara brought some yellow wax in some linen cloth, which she gave you to make a wax image. You kept it for two or three days, and at the end of Craigmillar dovecot you invested the image with the Devil's power, so that as it melted away, the man whose image it was would be consumed until he was utterly destroyed. You gave it to her and she said, "Take care not to put this plan off."

Also you are accused of enchanting a ring with a stone in it for Barbara, so that she could procure the favour and friendship of Jean Lyon, Lady Angus. You gave her the ring back to use for that purpose, and for such other purposes as may later be revealed.

[Incidentally, the fact that Barbara was a resident of Edinburgh, and the mention of the Craigmillar doocot make it likely that the "Cameron" mentioned earlier is not the place of that name in Fife, as some commentators have thought, but Cameron as in "Cameron Toll", near Craigmillar on the south eastern outskirts of Edinburgh.]

The Trial of Agnes Sampson.

We come now to Agnes Sampson's actual trial, the record of which can be found in Pitcairn's *Criminal Trials* Vol 1. The trial was held on 27th January 1591 under the presiding judge Umphrey Blindschellis, before a large "assise" or jury of East Lothian men, many of whom would be personally acquainted with Agnes, and all of whom would be well aware of her reputation. They were: -

Johne Spense in Saltoune,
William Bartram in Carfra,
Edmund Bartram in Hoipis,
David Robeson in Braidwoodsyde,
William Quhyte in Coilstoun-mylne,
Robert Dicksoune in Boltoune,
William Stenhouse in Barnis,
William Peris in Hadingtoun,
Matthew Young in Hadingtoune,
James Richesone in Hadingtoune,
Alexander Young in Hadingtoune,
Robert Byris in Hadingtoune,
Robert Kyle in Hadingtoune,
William Stratherne in Tranent,
Gilbert Erdingtoune in Hadingtoune,
Richard Broune in Hadingtoune,
Robert Bagbie in Hadingtoune.

After the trial the assise removed themselves from the court. William Quhyte was chosen chancellor [foreman of the jury]. Each point of the dittay or charge sheet was discussed and voted upon. The assise then through their spokesman William Quhyte declared Agnes

1 "Fylit and convict" [guilty and convicted] of foretelling that William Markestoun, servant to Thomas Watsoune in Inveresk was "bot ane deid man" [as good as dead].

2 Guilty and convicted of saying when William Blakeis son's shirt was sent to her that his sickness was caused by an elf-shot.

3 Guilty and convicted of using witchcraft to heal John Thomsoune in Dirletoune, who remained crippled in spite of her efforts.

4 Guilty and convicted of telling Mary Nicolsoune in North Berwick that she would wager her life for hers, in spite of which she died.

5 Guilty and convicted - David Lyndesay, tinkler in Dalkeith, had lain ill for thirty weeks, and hadn't spoken for three days. Some of his friends sent a poor woman to Agnes, who told her if Lyndesay lived past Wednesday he wouldn't die. He recovered.

6 Guilty and convicted of causing John Peiry in Preston to recover when he was very ill, by using incantation and prayer.

7 Guilty of healing [?] Hallyburtoune, farmer in Incarne [?]. She said no surgeon or medicine could help him. He died as she had said.

8 Guilty of coming to Bessie Aikenhead, the wife of Thomas Vans in Haddington, and bringing her back to health with her prayer and devlish charms.

9 Guilty - She was sent for, to go to Lady Rosline who was ill. She knew by her devlish prayer that the lady wouldn't recover, so she wouldn't go.

10 Guilty and convicted of being brought to the wife of John Young, shepherd at Bairfute, last Easter when she was ill. Agnes said she would never be well living on the ground where she was. She should be transferred off the ground, and she would either die or recover. She was taken elsewhere but died shortly afterwards.

11 Guilty of having foreknowledge through witchcraft of whether diseased persons would

live or not, and knowing who had been bewitched, if she stopped once in her prayer, the sick person was bewitched, if she stopped twice he would die.

[See Item 32. This would seem to indicate that Agnes would recite her "prayer" or charm over the sick person, or while thinking of him. If she completed the recitation without hesitation or stumbling, this indicated to her that the patient would recover, if she stumbled in her recitation, the indications were as above.]

12 Guilty and convicted of knowing from the Devil and telling Patrick Porteous that he would only live another eleven years.

13 Guilty of having foreknowledge through the Devil of the storm last Michaelmas [29th September] and that there would be a great deal of damage done on land and at sea.

14 Guilty of having foreknowledge through "the spreit" that the Queen would never reach Scotland unless the King fetched her. [Pitcairn takes the "spreit" to mean the Devil.]

15 Guilty and convicted of having learned her skill and her prayer from her father. He told her that if her services were requested by a sick person, she shouldn't go if she "stopped" in reciting her prayer. If she didn't stop, she should go, and the sick person would live.

16 Guilty and convicted of telling through her devlish prayer that the wife of James Kirkaldy, burgess of Haddington, would never recover from her illness.

17 Guilty of healing by her prayers and incantations John Ker of [?] when he was lying in Alexander Fairlie's house in Langnudrie so ill that everybody expected him to die.

18 Healing John Duncan in Musselburgh by her devlish prayers.

19 Foretelling Isobel Hamilton's death, and saying nothing could help her unless the Devil was raised. Isobel's husband, being a frugal man, would not bear the expense, so Agnes refused to raise the Devil. She said that the woman was bewitched and that this had been done about six or seven years before.

20 Convicted of curing by witchcraft the gudewife of Cameron who had walked with crutches since birth. [Or possibly, after giving birth.]

21 Convicted of healing the son of the laird of Reidhallis by witchcraft when the surgeons had given up on him.

22 Guilty and convicted of curing Robert Dicksoun in Bowtoune last summer. A woman he had made pregnant, or her mother, had put some wheat or other things in his doublet. Agnes made him stop wearing the doublet.

23 Curing the wife of the sheriff of Haddington. The Witch of Mirrielawis had bewitched her one Hallowe'en with a blast of evil wind.

24 Convicted and guilty of curing Alison Ker, the wife of John Restoune, by witchcraft, incantation, and saying devlish prayers. Alison was sufering from a sickness put on her by a witch called Catherine Gray, which she'd had for three years before Agnes cured her.

25 Acquitted of curing by witchcraft the wife of Robert Caringtoune in Craprene [Traprain?] who had been bewitched by the late Johnne McGill. Agnes was said to have told Robert to go to McGill, and ask him nicely to go to his wife, if he wouldn't go willingly Robert was to get a young man to go to him, ask him who made him do it, and make him come to Robert's wife. If he refused he was to be brought against his will. McGill was brought to the woman, and twice in twenty-four hours she was mad and out of her wits.

26 Acquitted of going to Natoun church [Newton - the ruined church tower stands to the south of the Edinburgh City Bypass between Old Craighall and Sheriffhall.] at night with the witches of Carbarrie and others, digging up bodies and taking the joints from which she made an enchanted powder for witchcraft.

27 Guilty of coming to the son of Robert Bailyie in the Pannis last summer. He was seriously ill, and merely by probing his body with her hands and saying some words of charming, she cured the child.

28 Convicted of healing John Hammiltoun in Sammelstoune who was troubled with his feet. He came to her and was cured that morning.

29 Guilty and convicted of coming to the wife of James Libbertoun in Over Libbertoune and using devlish prayer for the sake of her health. When she left she said that if she didn't return shortly the woman would die. She didn't come back and the woman died within three days.

30 Guilty and convicted of healing Lady Kilbabertoune by devlish prayers, when she was seriously ill.

31 Guilty and convicted of curing the late Robert Kerse in Dalkeith when he was heavily tormented with witchcraft laid on him by a westland warlock when he was in Dumfries. She took the sickness upon herself, and kept it till morning with much groaning and obvious pain. She cast the sickness out of herself into the close so that a dog or a cat might get it, but it landed on Alexander Douglas in Dalkeyth who wasted away with it and died, while Robert Kerse was healed.

32 Convicted of foretelling by devlish prayers to the wife of Patrick Hepburn in Bangley that her sick husband would die, because her prayer had stopped. She therefore refused to come and visit him. The prayer was as follows:-

[I give this in the original language and spelling as reproduced in Pitcairn's *Criminal Trials*, because of its interest as an actual charm used by East Lothian's most famous witch. However, in line 19, Pitcairn's "cost me on the haly croce" makes little sense. Almost certainly Pitcairn has mistaken an "f" in the original document for a long "s", and it should read "coft me" [bought me]. Similarly, Pitcairn's "sellon sea" in line 25 is meaningless, and should read "fellon fea" [fae], the fellonious or cruel enemy [Satan] - all the more likely since "fae" rhymes perfectly with "slay" at the end of the next line. Several writers who ought to have known better have parroted Pitcairn's errors here, but a contemporary letter from Bowes, the English ambassador, gets it right.]

Original

I trow in Almychtie God that wrocht
baith heavin and erth and all of nocht
In his dear son Chryst Jesu,
in to that anaplie lord I trow,
wes gotten of the Haly Ghaist,
borne of the Virgin Marie,
stoppit to heaven that all weill thane
and sittis at his faderis rycht hand;
He bade us cum and there to dome
baith quick and deid as he thocht conuene,
I trow als in the Haly Ghaist,
in Haly kirk my hoip is maist,
that halyschip quhar hallowers winnis
to aske forgivenenis of my sinnis,
and syne to ryis in flesch and bane
the lyff that never mair hes gane.
Thow sayis, Lord, lovit mocht ye be
that formed and maid mankynd of me.
Thow coft me on the haly croce
and lent me body, saull and voce,
and ordanit me to heavinnis bliss
wherefore I thank the Lord of this;
And all our hallowaris lovit be,
to pray to them to pray to me,
and keep me fra that fellon fea,
and from the syn that said wald slay.
Thow Lord for thy bitter passioun in
to keip me frome syn and warldlie schame
and endless damnatioune
Grant me the joy newir will be gane
Sweit Jesus Cristus, Amene.

Translation

*I believe in Almighty God who made
both heaven and earth from nothing.
In his dear son Jesus Christ,
I believe in that only lord
who was conceived of the Holy Spirit,
born of the Virgin Mary,
He went to live in heaven so that all
    should then be well,
and sits at his father's right hand.
He ordered us to come, to judge there
both the living and the dead as he
    thought appropriate.
I also believe in the Holy Spirit;
My greatest hope is in the Holy Church,
that holy ship where priests go* [Or perhaps,
"that sanctified state where saints dwell,"]
*to ask for my sins to be forgiven,
and then to rise [from the dead] in
    flesh and bone
to the life that will never again be lost.
You say, Lord, that you must be loved,
you who formed and made mankind.
You ransomed me on the holy cross
and lent me body, soul, and voice,
and destined me for the bliss of heaven,
therefore, Lord, I thank you for this.
May all the saints be adored;
pray to them that they should pray for me
and keep me from the Cruel Enemy
and from the sin that kills the soul.
Lord, your bitter suffering keeps me
from sin, worldly shame,
and endless damnation.
Grant me the joy that will never depart,
Sweet Jesus Christ,
Amen.*

[It will be obvious that this is a vernacular rhyming "folk" version of the Apostles' Creed.]

33 Guilty and convicted: She first began to serve the Devil after the death of her husband. He appeared to her in the likeness of a man and commanded her to acknowledge him as her master. She agreed, motivated by poverty, and his promise that she and her children would be made rich, and that he would give her the power to be revenged on her enemies. He appointed a time and a place for their next meeting, when he marked her on the right knee as a sign that she had become his servant. She thought the mark was an injury given to her by one of the children lying in bed with her. The wound didn't heal for half a year.

34 Guilty and convicted: The Devil appeared to her in the likeness of a dog, from whom she sought the answers to all her questions. She dismissed him by ordering him, "Depart, by the law you live by." These words would conjure him away.

35 Guilty and convicted of sailing with certain accomplices out of North Berwick in a boat like a chimney, the Devil going ahead of them like a pile of hay, to a ship called *The Grace of God*, which she boarded. The Devil made her drink wine, and gave her other "good cheer", some of which she and her company gave to those in the boat. [Pitcairn says a "flott boit". Is this actually a "flatt boit" - *i.e.* a flat-bottomed boat?] When she was there she didn't see the sailors, nor did they see her. When they came away, the Devil, who was under the ship, raised an evil wind and caused the ship to perish. She gave twenty shillings to Gray-meill who was with her on the ship, for waiting on her.

36 Guilty by her own confession of sailing by an act of witchcraft to a ship where there was a foreign woman. The "irsch" [Gaelic-speaking, Irish, or Highland] tailor and his wife were important participants there, as was Rychard Grahame, who had done a great deal of mischief.

37 Guilty and convicted of coming to Alesoun Inglis, David Robesounis wife, who was ill. He chased her off and wouldn't allow her to use her witchcraft to heal his wife because

he knew she had a reputation as a witch. When Agnes met with David's servant she said to him that if his master had not said what he did, his wife would have been a healthy woman walking on her own feet.

38 Guilty and convicted: She was sent for to heal the old Lady Edmestoune [*i.e.* the mother of the Laird of Edmonstone, near present-day Danderhall, on the southeastern outskirts of Edinburgh.] She said to the "gentlewomen" present that she would tell them that night whether the lady would recover or not, and told them to come to the garden after supper between five and six o'clock that evening. Praying in the garden, she ordered the Devil to come and speak to her, calling him "Elva" [*sic* Pitcairn. "Eloa" is more likely. See document JC26/2/12.] He came in out of the well in the likeness of a dog, and approached so near that she was afraid, and charged him by the law he lived by to come no nearer, but to answer her question. She asked whether the Lady would live or not. He said her days were gone. Then he asked where were the gentlewomen, her daughters? And she replied that they had said they would come. He said one of them would be in danger, and that he would have one of them. Agnes said that it would not be so, and he went away howling. The dog remained in the well till after supper. When the gentlewomen came into the garden the dog appeared to them out of the well, and they were afraid. One of the ladies, the Lady Torsenze, ran to the well, forced and drawn there by the Devil, who would have drowned her if Agnes and the other ladies had not gripped her and pulled her back again. This made them all afraid. After this the dog left them with a howl. Agnes told the gentlewomen that she was sorry, but she couldn't help the lady because her prayer had stopped. After that, she and one of her sisters carried her [presumably the Lady Torsenze] unconscious to a bedroom where she lay delirious for three or four days, and was crippled for quarter of a year, until Agnes used her devlish enchantments to conjure up the spirit again. She stayed with her while she was bedridden, and when she could not stay any longer herself, she sent her son. When either was present, the lady was well enough, but when they both left her she was bedridden as before.

39 Convicted of doing some service for the gudewife of Gallowschelis, who did not pay her when Agnes asked for it Agnes said she would repent it. Within a few hours the gudewife took a mad turn, and her tongue shot out of her head and swelled like a pot [*sic* Pitcairn. Perhaps "pet" - a lump of peat - is more likely.] She sent Agnes what she had asked for and begged her to come to her. Agnes told the servant who brought the message to go home, for the gudewife was well.

40 Guilty and convicted of delivering a letter written by John Fiene, clerk, in John Mutis bakehouse in the Pannis. She is accused with the housewife of the house, Gelie Duncan, Bessie Robsoune, Jokkie Graymeill, Jonet Gaw, Erisch Marioune, the weaver's wife from Setoune, Robert Griersoune, the gudewife of Spilmourfurd Mill called Meg Begtoune, Jame Sparrow's wife called Kait Wallace.

They met there to raise a storm to stop the Queen from coming home to Scotland. They discussed whether Gelie Duncan or Bessie Thomsoune should take the letter, and decided to send Gelie Duncan. The letter was sent to Marioun Lenchop in Leith. The gist of the letter was, "Marioun Lenchop, you are to inform the rest of the sisters that they are to raise the wind today at eleven o'clock, to stop the Queen coming to Scotland." Those gathered in Prestonpans would send the same message eastwards, and meet with the others in the Prestonpans area. At their meeting they would make the storm universal across the sea.

Within eight days after the letter was delivered, Agnes Sampsoune, Jonett Campbell, Johnne Fean, Gellie Duncan, and Meg Dyn baptised a cat in the weaver's house as follows:

two of them held a finger in one side of the chimney crook, and one other held a finger in the other side, the knuckles of the fingers meeting together. Then they put the cat thrice through the links of the chain, and passed it thrice under the chimney. After that, at Begie Toddis house, they fastened four human joints to the four feet of the cat. Then Jonett took it to Leith. About midnight she and the two Linkhops and two women called Stobbeis came to the end of the pier, and saying, "See that there be no deceit among us," they threw the cat as far as they could into the sea. It swam over and came back again. Those in Prestonpans threw another cat in the sea at eleven o' clock, after which the boat perished between Leith and Kinghorn by their sorcery and enchantment. The Devil did this, and went ahead of them with a stick in his hand.

41 Guilty and convicted of making a wax image of Mr John Moscrop, father in law to Ewphane McCalyane at Ewphane's request, to destroy him. She went with the image to a hillside above a stream on the lands of Keith, and raised the "Spreit", who conjured the image to serve for a means of destroying Mr John. She delivered it to Jonett Drumond, Ewphame's servant, and told her to put it under her father in law's bed, either at the top or the bottom of the bed. She did this four years ago, before Ewphame had her last child.

42 Guilty and convicted of putting "murildis" [*sic* Pitcairn. Surely "muildis" - graveyard earth] or powder made in Natoun Kirk of human joints and body parts, under Ewphame McCalyanis bed, ten days before she gave birth.

43 Convicted of taking off the pain and sickness from Lady Hirmestoun [Herdmanston] the night before she gave birth.

44 Guilty of using a prayer and conjuration when she healed sick people, which goes as follows:-

All kindis of illis that ever may be,
in Crystis name I conjure ye.
I conjure ye baith mair and les
with all the vertewis of the mess.
And rycht sa, be the naillis sa
that naillit Jesus and na ma
And rycht sa, be the samyn blude
that reiket owre the ruithfull rud:
Furth of the flesch and of the bane,
and in the eird and in the stane
I conjure ye in Godis name.

["Sa", "na", "ma" should be pronounced as in "say".]

Translation

All kinds of ills, whatever you may be,
I conjure you in Christ's name.
Greater ills or lesser ills, I conjure you
with all the powers of the Mass.
And similarly [I conjure you] by the nails
that nailed Jesus and no-one else.
And similarly by the same blood
that steamed over the pity-inspiring cross:
In God's name I conjure you
out of the flesh and bone
into the earth and stone.

45 Guilty and convicted of charming George Diksoune's horses and cattle, after thirteen cows, bullocks, and horses had died as a result of John McGill's evildoing. No more of them died after Agnes received a stone of cheese and half a stone of butter from George's wife.

46 Guilty and convicted of charming cows and bullocks belonging to Rychard Spens, farmer at that time in Hismestoune [Surely "Hirmestoune" - Herdmanston], and James Quhyte in Gosford, by going between them in pairs in the byre, striking their backs, and repeating "Ave Maria" over and over again.

47 Guilty of being at the meeting where Meg Steel, Kate Gray, and Jonett Campbell [*sic* Normand and Roberts. Pitcairn has the obviously mistaken "Meg Stillcart, Gray, and Jonett Campbell.] were with her, and one other

person who has died since then, five people altogether. This was at the Kirk of Garvett [Garvald] to the east of Burn-syde.

48 For being at the meeting between Cousland and Carbarry where she, Agnes Straitton, and the Witch of Carbarry were present. She quarrelled with her master the Devil, saying she'd never had any benefit from him, and threatened to renounce him. However, she did not do so. He promised that nothing would go against her.

49 Guilty and convicted: She, the gudewife of Spilmourfuird, Gelis Duncan, Bessie Thomsoune, Greymeill, Agnes Stratoune, with certain others, nine altogether, met at Foulstruther and discussed how to ruin David Seytoun and his goods.

Gelis Duncan, Bessie Thomson, and Grey Meill pulled on a rope at the bridge, and Agnes cried, "Haill hola!" [This is taken to be a nautical expression meaning "Haul, haul!" However, since Agnes's name for "the Devil" was Eloa, which according to Document JC26/2/12, she pronounced "Hola", is it too fanciful to suggest that Agnes might have been chanting , "Hail Eloa!"?] The end of it was very heavy, and when they had pulled it in, the Devil came up at the end of it and asked if they had all been good servants. They asked him how they could ruin David Seytoun and his goods. He gave them clear things like pieces of glass, "brayet" [brathit - *i.e.* bound or braided] and mixed with pieces of cord, and some other things amongst them. He told them to lay a thread along the moor, and scatter the pieces of glass along the moor, so that whoever passed over them first should die suddenly. However, although they had expected him, David was late in coming that day, and the ruination landed on the goods of the ploughman, and on his daughter who ever since has been dreadfully plagued with visions and apparitions, and her body tormented by an evil spirit which has possessed her most pitifully.

Agnes was the chief participant in this. [She seems to have received either help or encouragement from James Porteous and Richard Crummy, but the reference is obscure and puzzling.] She sent Bessie Thomsoune and Anny Stratoune to Foulstruther House to ask for a handful of salt to be passed out to them from above the door. If they had got it ruination would have fallen on David Seytoune and his goods. However, because the salt was refused, the ruin fell on the ploughman's child and on his goods.

50 Guilty and convicted: As she confessed before his Majesty, the Devil in the likeness of a man met her in the fields as she went out from her own house at Keith between five and six in the evening. She was alone. The Devil commanded her to be at North Berwick church the next night. She went there on horseback escorted by her son-in-law ["guid-son" - Normand and Roberts mistake this for "godson"] John Couper, and alighted at the churchyard. A little before she came to it, about eleven o' dock at night, they were dancing in the churchyard. Gelie Duncan played the jew's harp. Johne Feane led all the rest, with his face masked [or perhaps merely "muffled up"]. Agnes and her daughter followed next Also present were: -

1 Cait Gray
2 George Mortis wife
3 Robert Griersoune
4 Cathrene Duncan
5 Bessie Wrycht
6 Issobel Gylour
7 Johnne Ramsay's wife
8 Annie Richardson
9 Jonnet Gaw
10 Nicoll Murray's wife, [?] Tailyour [or perhaps "the wife of N.M. the tailor"]
11 Christine Caringtoun alias "Lukit"
12 Masie Aitcheson
13 Marioun Patersoune
14 Alexander Quhytlaw

15 Marioun Nicolsoune
16 Marioun Bailyie
17 Jonett Nicolsoune
18 Johne Grey meill
19 Issobel Lauder
20 Archie Henillis wife
21 Duncane Buquhannane
22 Marioune Congiltoun
23 Bessie Gulene
24 Bessie Broune the smith's wife. [Bessie and the smith's wife may be two people.]
25 Thomas Burnhill [Bourhill ?] and his wife
26 Gylbert McGill
27 Johnne McGill
28 Cathrene McGill,

with the rest of their accomplices, over a hundred people, of which six were men and all the rest women. The women made homage first, then the men. The men were turned anti-clockwise nine times and the women six times. Johnne Fien then "blew up" the doors and "blew in" the lights [sic Pitcairn] which were like great black candles sticking up round the pulpit. The Devil himself started up in the pulpit like a big black man. He called everybody by name and everybody answered, "Here master". When Robert Grierson was called, they all ran hither and thither and were angry because it had been promised that he would be called "Robert the Comptroller" or "Rob the Rowar" when he was named.

The first thing the Devil asked was if they had kept all their promises and been good servants, and what had they done since the last meeting. At his command they opened up two graves in the church and two outside, and took the joints of their fingers, toes, and noses [or possibly knees - "neise"] and divided them up among themselves. The Devil commanded them to keep the joints till they were dry and to make a powder with them to do evil. He ordered them to keep his commandments, which were to do all the evil they could. Before they departed they kissed his "erse".

The Devil was wearing a gown and a hat, both black. Some of the gathering stood, and some sat. John Fiene was always the nearest to the Devil, at his left elbow. Graymeill guarded the door.

51 Guilty and convicted: When Agnes got to know Barbara Napier in Dalkeith, Camroune-brig-end, and such places, Barbara complained that a man called Archie had done her a great wrong and asked how she could be avenged on him. Agnes said she would do what she could. Agnes prepared a beautiful little image ["Pictour" in this sense should always be understood as an image, not a picture as some writers have thought] of yellow wax which she enchanted and conjured under the name of "Archie" in the east end of Craigmillar dovecot, in the Devil's name. She gave power to the image, that as it melted away in front of the fire, so should the man whose image it was pine away and be consumed until he was consumed utterly. She delivered the image to Barbara, saying, "Take good care that nothing is done to stop the plan."

52 Guilty and convicted of enchanting by her sorcery a little ring with a stone in it, for Barbara Napier. She got this so that she could influence Dame Jean Lyounn, Lady Angus, to like and favour Barbara. She sent the ring back with her daughter to Barbara within two days, to be used for that purpose.

53 She is a common and notorious witch and user of sorceries and enchantments for which she invokes the Devil, her master. She abuses poor simple people, drawing them away from their leaning towards God's mercy to believe in the support of the Devil.

Sentence

As a result of this Agnes was ordered by the judge, through the "dempster" James Scheil [the dempster was the official who read out the sentence to the court] to be taken to the Castle of Edinburgh to be bound to a stake and strangled to death, and her body afterwards to be burned to ashes. All her moveable goods to be forfeited for our Sovereign Lord's use.

Investigation of Agnes by the Church.

It is obvious from the records of Agnes Sampson's trial that she had been practising as a witch for many years. She had in fact been under investigation for some time before her arrest and interrogation around November 1590, when the details of the North Berwick gathering began to emerge.

The records of the Synod of Lothian and Tweedale [CH2 252 in the National Archives of Scotland] contain an entry for 1st April 1589 referring to Agnes: -

A complaint was given in against the Presbytery of Haddington for not calling Agnes Sampson before them. She lives in Keyth within the bounds of the Presbytery and is suspected of witchcraft. It was answered to the complaint that they could find no grounds on which to accuse her. It is ordered that they should call her before them, and inquiry should be made with a view to arresting any who have had dealings with her. To this end it is ordered that any of the brethren who can get anything proved against Any, suspected as already said of witchcraft, should give in the information within fifteen days.

[Generally speaking, the organisation of the Church was that each parish had a Kirk Session, consisting of the minister and elders; the Presbytery was a grouping of several parishes, and the Synod was a grouping of several Presbyteries.]

Several months after this first mention, an entry in the Synod minutes for 16th September 1589 reads:-

At the last meeting of Lothian Synod the Presbytery of Haddington was ordered to call before it Anny Sampson who is suspected of witchcraft, and that if anything can be proved they should proceed with her informally as far as they can. The Synod finds they have been very negligent in not calling her in, and repeats the order that she should be called before them, and that Mr Adam Lefinstoun and Mr George Ramsay should work with them to see that she is questioned.

The following year we find on 5th May 1590:

An order was given at the last Synodal Assembly in Edinburgh on 16th September that the Presbytery of Haddington call before them Anny Sampson, suspected of witchcraft, and that if anything can be proved, to proceed against her informally as far as possible. The assembly finds that some moves have been made against her, and orders them to make further efforts, and to ask his Majesty the King for a commission to apprehend her.

A very badly damaged entry in the records of the Presbytery of Haddington [CH2 185 in the National Archives of Scotland], probably from 16th September 1590, seems to record proceedings being taken against John McGill for witchcraft. Reference is made to an Elspeth Hepburn in Traprain who was sick, and advice being sought in her case from Agnes Sampson living in Keith.

On 7th October the Synod records show:-

The brethern of the Presbytery of Haddington were asked how far they had proceeded with Any Sampson and Jonet Ga, who are suspected of witchcraft. They ahiswered that they had done nothing as yet as regards Jonet Ga, but that they had already made a start with Anny Sampsone. The assembly orders that they should insist on prosecuting this case.

Thus it is plain that as early as April 1589 Agnes Sampson was being pursued by the higher courts of the church for witchcraft, months before Princess Anne of Denmark's attempts to sail to Scotland and James VI's subsequent decision to sail to Scandinavia to join her. *Newes from Scotland*'s line is that the "North Berwick" revelations began with the arrest of Geilles Duncan in the late autumn of 1590. If this is so, then it is obvious that in naming Agnes Sampson as a fellow conspirator, she was naming someone not only well known to the authorities, but already under investigation.

As to what sort of person Agnes really was, Archbishop Spottiswood in his *History of the Church of Scotland* says, "... Agnes Sampson [commonly called the Wise Wife of Keith] was most remarkable; a woman not of the base and ignorant sort of witches, but matron-like, grave and settled in her answers which were all to some purpose." The editor of the 1851 edition of Spottiswood's *History* points out that the latest of the three manuscripts of this work was written sometime between the death of James VI and the onset of the "troubles" in Scotland leading up to the Civil War - in other words probably in the decade 1625-35. However, since Spottiswood was born in 1565 he must have been at least 25 at the time of Agnes's death, so although he was writing 30-40 years later, he was describing events he would have remembered very well. The dignified and serious-minded woman he describes certainly accords well with her reported conduct during her last moments.

Agnes was executed on the Castlehill in Edinburgh on 28th January 1591. The expense account for her execution can be found in Edinburgh's records. Wood and Hannay's *Extracts* note, 'The execution of Agnes Sampson the 16 day of Januar 1590 *[sic]* quha wes burnt." Since the date of her execution is known to have been 28th January, presumably what happened on 16th January was that the expenditure was authorised [well before she had even been tried] for her confidently expected execution. Wood and Hannay point out that the items of the expense account are the same as Fian's, and that the total cost was £6-8s-10d.

It was noted at the time that "she died most penitentially for her sins and for abusing the simple people, and renounced the Devil, calling him often 'false deceiver of God's people'. She sought refuge in God's mercy, and in Jesus Christ in whom alone she was assured to be safe, like the thief who hung at his right hand." [Calender of State Papers Relating to Scotland Vol X p467].

By this time several of those mentioned in Agnes's trial had probably already been disposed of. A letter to London from the English ambassador dated 23rd February 1591 says, "Besides this Agnes Samsone, there are burnt in Haddington Gilbert Mackgill and Jhone his son, Erish Marioun, Meg Dun, and another two whose particular details would take too long to describe, one in Dalkeith and one in Dumfries. For the most part they confirmed several of the meetings Agnes was at, and many other points of her dittay, which they themselves had participated in." [Calendar of State Papers Relating to Scotland Vol X p476]. In item 25 of Agnes's dittay John McGill is described as "the late Johnne McGill", making it plain that he had already been dispatched by the date of Agnes's trial on 27th January. The others mentioned in the ambassador's letter were presumably executed in Haddington on or around the same date as McGill.

Suicide of Meg Begtoun.

Having dealt with the executions in Haddington, it may be worth pausing to consider the earliest victim of all, Meg Begtoun, the gudewife of Spilmersford Mill. She is named in Item 40 of Agnes Sampson's dittay in a list of persons accused of witchcraft, and in Item 49 as having been present at Foulstruther at the attempt to work ruination on David Seton by magic.

In Donald Robeson's confession [JC26/2/1] he claims that she was present at the witch meeting at Acheson's Haven. Janet Stratton's confession states that Meg was present in Agnes Sampson's house when Agnes prepared a magic potion containing the drippings from a roasted toad, and claims she was also present at a meeting in Prestonpans where a wax image of the King was enchanted [JC26/2/15].

Meg is also mentioned in Barbara Napier's trial as having attended the great gathering of witches at North Berwick.

However, well before the North Berwick witchcraft panic broke, Meg had already removed herself from the scene. On 12th February 1590 the Register of the Privy Seal records the gift from the King of the possessions of Meg Begtoun, spouse to Andro Cowie, to David Seyton, bailie in Tranent. Her goods had been forfeited to the Crown as a result of her "puting of violent hands on her awin person and cruellie and unnaturallie hanging herself to the deid" [RPS/LX/143.] We might guess that Meg had witnessed or experienced the initial steps taken by the Presbytery or by David Seton towards investigating local witchcraft, was all too well aware of what was brewing, and was not inclined to participate further.

The English Ambassador's View of Events.

It is worth while at this point to look more closely at the letter sent on 23rd February 1591 by Robert Bowes, the English ambassador, since he is the nearest we are likely to get to an interested but unbiased contemporary observer. This letter from Bowes to Lord Burghley includes "a note of the matters proved against the witches, whereof some are already condemned and executed." This, turned into modern English, continues as follows:-

These witches have confessed many other things, in abusing of God's name, and yielding themselves to evil spirits. Much of what they say has been said to please their interrogators [especially the King] and to win mercy, and is far more strange than true. I myself and others can bear witness to this, our involvement having been insinuated by a shameless and drunken woman. My name and position gave them enough material to ramble on about at will, and I suspect they may have been put up to it. However, their description of my personal appearance was so far out that the King and the interrogators dismissed the story, in spite of the fact that I'm informed that this rogue of a woman was convinced that soon after the King left for Denmark, the English ambassador, a little dark fat man with black hair, had been with them in a cellar and given them gold, to hang up and enchant a toad to threaten the King's life and prevent him fathering an heir.

They said many things which they recanted at their execution. John Feanne, executed in Edinburgh, at his death denied everything he had confessed, saying he had only said these things for fear of torture and to save his life. The King is going to have their interrogations printed soon after they are finished. [A footnote in "State Papers" indicates that this refers to *Newes from Scotland*, a possibility which is debateable to say the least]

At the King's request I have written to the English Border officials to arrest any witches who have escaped to England, and ask you [*i.e.* Burghley] to send a warrant to Sir John Selby and the other officials so that they can be handed over to the deputy warden of the East March of Scotland.

Enclosed with the Ambassador's letter were "Certane notes of Agnes Sampsone, her confession ..." This is interesting, because unlike the letter with which it was enclosed, it is written in Scots, and was therefore almost certainly not written by Bowes. He has presumably asked someone to provide him with a precis of the findings against Agnes, to send to London. Presumably also, this summary would be provided by someone "in the know", and might be said therefore to represent official thinking about the Sampson case at that point in time. The enclosure, rendered into modern English, is as follows:-

Some notes on Agnes Sampson's confession 27th January 1590 [*sic* Actually 1591], upon which she was convicted by an assise and burnt in Edinburgh on the 28th as a witch.

Firstly Agnes confessed that after the death of her husband the Devil appeared to her at night, when she was preoccupied with how she was going to provide for herself and her children. He told her to cheer up and not to worry about her children, and promised that if she would serve him she and her children would want for nothing. Her poverty and his promises of riches and revenge on her enemies persuaded her to take him as her master and renounce Christ. After that he gave her a painful scratch on the right thigh, just over a span above her kneecap, which continued to be painful for half a year. He arranged to meet her in a churchyard in six months' time.

Also the Devil appeared to her sometimes like a black man, sometimes like a dog, and sometimes like a truss or rick of hay, and she asked for all the answers to her questions from him.

He met with her and another two at Barro churchyard, where after general conversation with them all, he called her aside and asked if she had felt any pain since their last meeting. When she said that she had, he said it was his mark, and it would no longer be sore, which she found to be true. After she was arrested, when she was pricked with pins she felt no pricking at all.

The third meeting was just in past Garvet church at the side of the burn, on the 5th of November.

The fourth meeting was between Cousland and Carberrie on the 3rd November [*sic* Possibly rather 13th or 23rd ?] when he commanded them to be good servants to him.

The fifth meeting was at Foulestruther Mure, where they raised the Devil with a rope which she ordered them to haul up. They asked, "What shall we haul up?" and she answered, "The Devil your master," and they pulled him up and consulted him about the ruination of David Seton and his goods, after which followed a great many deaths among his livestock. The Devil gave them glittering stuff like pieces of crushed glass which he ordered them to scatter on the moor so that whatever passed over it first would perish. The ploughman's daughter has been troubled with strange and terrible apparitions of a man called John and a woman called Bessie whom she could see and hear but no-one else could. They scratch and nip her and pull her violently from the hands of those who hold her. At the beginning of this February she took yarn from the spindle she was spinning with and tied it round her neck, which would have strangled her if it had not been taken away from her neck. Also, she confessed that the Devil appeared to her in the likeness of a man and gave her word to come to a meeting at North Berwick last Michaelmas. She rode there with her son-in-law in front of her. Many people had gathered there but she knew only a few of them. The men were pushed round nine times anti-clockwise, and the women three times. The devil appeared and spoke many things to them. They paid homage to him and kissed his "ers". They opened two graves inside the church and one outside, and took some of their fingers, toes, and noses, and shared the joints among them, and kept them until they were dried and then made powder from them to do evil with.

Also she confessed that she had been out of Scotland twice by sea. She skipped away swiftly on her voyage, and sometimes stayed

48 hours, and sometimes longer, and was in ships on unknown [foreign?] coasts. She had been at sea oftener than that, namely a year past Hallowe'en. Twenty one of them sailed in a boat, and came to a ship in which they drank good ale and wine. Their master the Devil went before them on the sea and Guided them, and sank the ship they had been on. They got some of the spoil, and Agnes gave twenty shillings from her share to her servant Jhone Gordoun alias Greymeill who always attended her. Also she confessed that when a woman complained of the perversity of her father-in-law and her earnest desire to get rid of him, she made a wax image and raised a spirit at a waterside, beside a briar bush, asked him to enchant it to destroy him, and sent it to the woman to put under the foot or the head of his bed. She did the same against someone called Archie whom another person feared and wanted rid of.

Also she put enchanted powder or earth made of the dried joints of dead bodies in a cloth under the foot of some women's beds to relieve them of their labour pains. Also she confessed that she knew when someone was bewitched by the smell of their linen clothes, or the sweat in them, and by looking at them. Even if she had never seen them she would know by the words she called her "prayer" if the patient would die or live, for if she stopped in reciting it the patient would die - she would never come to visit such a person. But if she did not stop in her prayer, nothing would ail the patient. The words and verses she used were these, which she used on hundreds of people: -

I trow til Almichtie God that wroght
Both heaven and earth and all of nocht:
Into his dear sone Christ Jesu
Into that aullholie lord I trow
Was gotten of the Holie Ghost
Born of the Virgin Marie
Steppit to heaven that all went then,
And sittis at his Fathers richt hand
He bad ws come and there to dome
Baith quick and deid as he thocht quhome.
I trow als the Halie Ghaist
In halie kirk my hope is maist;
That halie ship quhair hallowaris wynnis
To ask forgivenes of my sinnis:
And syne to rise in flesh and bane
The lyfe that never mair is gane.
Thow sayis, Lord, lovit mot ye be,
That formed and maid mankind of me:
Thow coft me on the halie croce
And lent me bodie saule and voice,
And ordenit me to hevinis bliss;
Quhairfore I thank ye Lord of this,
And all your hallowaris lovit be
To pray to them to pray for me,
And keep me from the fellon fea
And from the sin that saule would slay;
Thow, Lord, for thy bitter passioun
To keep me from sin, warldlie scham
    and endless damnatioun;
Grant me the joy never will be gane
Sweit Jesus Christus, Amen.

She also used other verses which she repeated when relieving women of their labour pains, and relieving men and women, young and old, of serious diseases cast upon them by witchcraft. They were as follows:-

All kynd of evils that ever may be,
In Christis name I conjure the;
I conjure the both more and less,
With all the virtues of the mess;
And richt swa be the nailes sa,
That nailit dere Jesus and na ma
And richtsa be the samyn blude
That raikit over the ruithful rude,
Furth of the flesh and of the bane
I conjure the in Goddis name.

Also, she confessed that she charmed diseases away from innumerable animals. Her usual method was to go between every couple of them, and grip their backs and bellies, and to say "Ave Maria" over them as they stood in their stalls.

Also, she confessed that she enchanted a ring which had a stone in it, by which a woman was to gain the favour of her mistress.

Also, she raised the Devil by her evocations, to ask if a lady would live or die. He appeared to her in the likeness of a black dog before supper when she was alone. But after supper she had the lady's three daughters with her, and one of them was about to drown herself in the well out of which the dog came, and into which he went. She was barely prevented by the violent pulling and holding of her sisters and Agnes Sampson. The lady was mad for quarter of a year after this.

Generally speaking, these are the main points of her confession, and pretty much cover the rest of her particular actions. Out of the 102 articles of her indictment she confessed to 58. She died very penitently for her sins and for taking advantage of simple people. She renounced the Devil, whom she called many times "false deceiver of God's people". She had her only refuge in Christ Jesus in whom alone she was assured to be safe, like the thief who hung at his right hand.

As well as this Agnes Sampson, there have been burnt in Haddington Gilbert Mackgill and Jhone his son, Catherine Gray [no less skillful than Sampson], Jhone Gordoun alias Greymeill, Erish Marioun, Meg Dun, and another two whose particulars would take too long to describe - one in Daikeith and one in Dumfries. For the most part they confirmed several of these meetings attended by Agnes Sampson and many other points in her indictment in which they themselves had been participants.

A certain Jhone Feane alias Cunynghame confessed himself a participant with Agnes Sampson and others in several of these meetings at sea and on land, and at one meeting he wrote a letter and sent it to Leith to raise a storm there, as their meeting in the Pannes was intended to do, to stop the Queen of Scotland reaching Scotland. All of this he denied obstinately right up to his death.

There are more than forty arrested and under investigation at the moment, but we'll leave the details until we see what happens.

This summary of Agnes's activities contains some interesting new details - for example, the sniffing of underwear to determine whether a patient was bewitched or not. This does not feature in Pitcairn's printed dittay, and so presumably arose during questioning but was not included in the formal indictment. Interestingly, there is no mention whatever in the summary of Agnes being involved in a plot against the King's life. The only mention of a treasonable plot is contained almost as an afterthought in the brief paragraph relating to John Cunningham, and even then it refers only to evil intent against the Queen, not against James VI himself.

The Interrogations Continue.

Meanwhile the interrogations of the surviving suspects proceeded, although others, seeing the way the wind was blowing, attempted to put themselves beyond the reach of the law. In a letter of 3rd February 1591 the English ambassador reported, "Some of the worst sort of witches discovered here are escaped and fled into England. The King desires that they may be apprehended and delivered to him. and would send David Seaton of Tranent, gentleman - who knows them - to search them out. He has aggreed to give Seaton letters to Sir Henry Woddrington, Sir John Forster, and Sir John Selby to assist him and to arrest and keep in safety such as he shall find, that they may be delivered to Scotland or otherwise as shall please Her Majesty and her Council." [C.S.P. Vol X p457]. For those already in custody the ordeal continued.

Document JC26/2/1 in the National Archives of Scotland [Normand and Roberts "Document 5"] contains statements given by an unnamed person who is likely to be Bessie Thomson, since she was one of the participants in the ongoings at Foulstruther. The others are Donald Robeson who, since he has not appeared in previous documents, has presumably been newly drawn into the net, possibly by being named by one of the witches under interrogation. He is invariably called "Robson" by Normand and Roberts, but that is not a common Scottish surname, and since he is elsewhere called "Robeson", and "Robieson" - the usual East Lothian pronunciation of "Robertson", I suspect that was his "proper" surname. Also, he is later described as a "Highlandman" and Robertson was one of the common names of the southern Perthshire Highlands. Janet Stratton has previously come to light as another participant at Foulstruther. In JC26/2/1 we have the first mention of yet another witches' gathering, this time at Acheson's Haven [now named Morrison's Haven] near Prestonpans. The purpose of the meeting was to plot the King's death by sorcery. Two "gentlewomen", Barbara Napier and Euphane MacCalyean, are implicated in this treasonable conspiracy and we have the first mention of the involvement of the Earl of Bothwell. This document is undated but must come after the session in January 1591 where Agnes Sampson confessed a conection with Barbara Napier. In modern English JC26/2/1 is as follows:-

[Bessie Thomson ?] confesses that she got pieces of glass at Foulstruther near Ormiston Bridge from Gillie Duncan, and spread them on the ground to affect David Seton, but they affected the girl instead.

She confesses that the wax image delivered to Agnes Sampson at Acheson's Haven was wrapped in a white cloth or a piece of white paper, the length of an arm. It was passed round from hand to hand. She passed it to Gillie Duncan. Everyone said a word or two when they had it in their hands. At this meeting the Devil appeared like a heap ["quoyle"] of hay.

Donald Robeson confesses that there were more than twenty people who handled the image at the gathering at Acheson's Haven. Agnes Sampson brought it to the field. She gave it to Barbara Napier. Barbara passed it to Euphane MacCalyean. Euphane passed it to Meg Begton from Spilmersford. It was passed round eight or nine women, until at last it came to Robin Grierson, and he passed it to the Devil. As they handled the image they all said, "James the Sixth". The Devil looked like a man. Agnes said that they would get gold, silver, and food from Lord Bothwell. As well as those already mentioned, Catherine Wallace was there, Janet Stratton, and Charles Watson from Garvald who offered to give the image back to "the Thief" [presumably the Devil] again to trouble the King. Donald was once in his house. He states that there were four people wearing velvet hoods amongst them, and four or five in taffeta gowns [i.e. well-dressed people of high social standing]. There were women from Leith and Prestonpans there. He passed the image to Geillis Duncan who passed it to Janet Stratton. It was passed to him from Catherine Wallace. They met in the gloaming and conducted their business at night.

Janet Stratton confesses that there were sixty at this meeting. There were thirteen that she knew - Agnes Sampson, Barbara Napier, Euphane MacCalyean, Robert Grierson, Donald Robeson, herself, Geillis Duncan, Catherine Wallace, George Mott's wife, and Bessie Thomson. "James the Sixth" was named as they handled the image. Agnes Sampson was to have received gold, silver, and wheat.

[The two gentlewomen Barbara Napier and Euphane MacCalyean were now confronted with the other prisoners, and with Richie Graham, a warlock from the west of Scotland.]

Barbara Napier

Donald and Janet Stratton, being confronted with Barbara, testify as above that Barbara received the image from Agnes Sampson at Acheson's Haven.

Confronted with Ritchie Graham he affirms that he composed the following words, and she wrote them down: "Hominem aratum regnum valui kethi imundum prosita munda metanas dium sipilis". [Normand and Roberts comment, "This passage in what must be Latin is contracted in the MS and can be made to produce no certain sense...it seems to be something about a ploughed kingdom, and cleanliness and uncleanliness." *op. cit.* p160] They were together in the yard when this was written, with her daughter Bessie Car and a son of hers. This was a conjuration that was to be cut up and cast into the potion used in the conspiracy against the King. It was taken by Agnes Loch to Margaret [?] Sampson. He affirms that she wrote to him eighteen years ago and signed it "I Barbarie". He also affirms that she wrote him an I.O.U. for eighty pounds signed "I Bar", and that she showed him a letter sent to her from the Laird of [?], which contained a heart drawn with a dart through it.

She sent a certain John Fairlie to Fintry with a ring for Richie. She denies this, and everything else. John Fairlie was confronted with Barbara. He confesses receiving the ring about a year past Christmas, together with forty shillings in testons [a silver coin worth four shillings Scots] and a half mark piece, with an ell of linen and a pair of gloves. He was also given certain leaves. She told him to tell his master that she wanted him to heal her son who was very sick. She consistently denies all this.

Euphane MacCalyean.

She was confronted with Donald Robeson, who claims to have seen her at North Berwick church, and at the new harbour called Acheson's Haven where she had the wax image in her hands. She denies this consistently.

She was confronted with Gillie Duncan who claims to have seen her at North Berwick church.

She was also confronted with Janet Stratton who testifies that she saw her at North Berwick along with Agnes Sampson and Barbara Napier, and that she was present at the sinking of the boat where she received great riches. Janet got fifteen shillings. Donald claims that when they were at North Berwick they asked each other, "Who is that who is asking for the image?" and they all said, "It's Euphane MacCalyean." Somebody asked where they would get another king. Euphane answered, The realm will not be without a king."

We come next to document JC26/2/19 in the National Archives of Scotland [Normand and Roberts "Document 6"] which contains confessions and statements made by Geillis Duncan, Janet Stratton and Donald Robeson. As well as all the usual suspects, Napier and MacCalyean feature strongly, and the Earl of Bothwell appears as financing the whole operation. Gillie Duncan attempts to incriminate the English Ambassador. As we have seen, Bowes confirms in one of his letters that an attempt was made to implicate him by a "shameless and drunken woman".

Donald's statement is dated "the 29 of [ ]le in presence of the council". This surely is 29th April. Normand and Roberts say that the statements in JC26/2/19 must have been given before 23rd February, having seemingly jumped to the conclusion that Stratton and Robeson must have been among those stated by Bowes to have been executed in Haddington by that date [CSP Vol X p.476]. However, the witches executed in Haddington before that date are quite plainly said by Bowes to have been the two McGills, Catherine Gray, Gray Meal, Erish

Marioun, Meg Dun, and two unnamed persons - one from Dalkeith and one from Dumfries. Agnes Sampson had of course been executed on the Castle Hill in Edinburgh on 28th January, and John Fian probably also in January in the same place. As for Stratton and Robeson, not only is there no evidence for their execution by 23rd February, there is no evidence that they were executed at all, and some grounds for thinking they may have survived.

In modern English JC/26/19 reads thus:

[Gillie] Duncan confesses that she was at Acheson's Haven. There were eight or ten main participants and about thirty others there. There was Euphame MacCalyean, Barbara Napier, Agnes Sampson, John Fian, Robert Grierson, George Mott's wife, Bessie Thomson, the wife of Saltoun Mill, Gillie Duncan, Janet Stratton, Donald Robieson. Agnes Sampson proposed the business of laying a toad with "strong wash" [stale urine] in the King's way to destroy him. They named his Majesty's name in Latin.

Janet Stratton states that [some unnamed person, presumably adressing the Devil,] said, "Master, we have some business afoot, and we're keen to get on with it. We want your help." He answered, "I'll do it, but it will take a long time, because it will be thwarted." After that someone was given instructions to try to get an item of the king's linen clothing to do the job.

Gillie Duncan testifies that less than a year ago she saw Master Bowes [the English Ambassador] in Haddington riding through the street, by the cross. This was a short time before he stood sponsor at the baptism of Lord Bothwell's child. She testified that she only ever knew him in Edinburgh - she didn't see him in Barbara Napier's house, but heard him speaking in the cellar where Euphame MacCalyean, Barbara, Agnes Sampson, and John Fian were present, where the letter was read that she brought out of George Mott's house from Agnes Sampson. This was at the beginning of harvest. She delivered the letter to Barbara Napier in her own hall, where no-one else was present but Barbara's servants and children. Immediately Barbara sent her servant to tell Euphane to come to her, and she came at twilight. There were other women from Edinburgh with them, including one named Ranking who was to throw the "droppings" from the toad down in front of the King.

Janet Stratton testifies that it was the Earl of Bothwell's idea to have the image; and he was named there. She testifies that the Devil appeared first like a truss of hay.

Janet says that she neither saw nor heard John Cockburn, but Bessie Thomson agrees that she did.

Gillie Duncan again affirms that the King's life was bewitched... [the document is damaged here] by Bar[bara] N[apier] and Euphane MacCalyean. As well as that, there were Marion Ranking, someone called Nevin, Annie Sampson, and Maggie Thomson. They all met on the first floor of the house, then went down to the basement, to the cellar, and sat down to eat and drink, where they had roast fowl and sweetmeats. Agnes Sampson made Barbara give her something to eat. She [Gillie] was in the hall, but not in the cellar.

The 29th of [   ]le in presence of the council. Donald Robeson, aged over sixty, confesses that he saw Robert Grierson beside the pulpit at North Berwick church, where he found fault with the Devil because the image of the King had not been made. The Devil promised that it would be ready for the next meeting. He confesses that Grierson was in the boat, where he was "headsman". He confesses that the Devil had a black gown, and an ugly-looking skull-cap on his head. He confesses that Euphane MacCalyean made Grierson ask the Devil about the image, specifically the image of the King which was to be roasted. She shouted out so that the people nearby could hear. He testified that he only ever heard of the image on that one occasion. He confessed about the image voluntarily to begin with, without being asked about it. He confesses that John Cockburn ordered him to work to destroy David Seton's goods, and promised him fifty pounds for doing it. He ordered him to go to Agnes Sampson to ask for help. He told John Cockburn he was a witch.

[This reference to John Cockburn is intriguing. Item 49 of Agnes Sampson's dittay records a meeting near Foulstruther where an attempt was made to harm David Seton by sorcery. Donald Robeson seems to be saying here that he had put Agnes Sampson up to this on the orders of John Cockburn. Two years later, on 14th June 1593, David Seton sr in Tranent failed to obey a summons to appear before the Privy Council to answer for the "cruell slaughter" of John Cockburn of Woodhead, servant to Sir John Cockburn of Ormiston, the Justice Clerk. It would be surprising if the murder victim was not the same John Cockburn who had supposedly tried to engineer Seton's death by magic. Seton was declared "fugitive from the law and at the horn" on 29th June 1593, and his confiscated goods given to the Duke of Lennox [LPS/LXV/171]. On 25th June 1600 his possessions were gifted to Thomas Elphingstone, so presumably even at that late date David Seton remained "at the horn", and had still not answered for his crime.

Woodhead and Ormiston lie close to the house of Foulstruther which belonged either to David Seton, or to his son of the same name. It is obvious that there was bad blood between Seton and Cockburn. One might even speculate that Seton's notorious arrest and interrogation of his servant maid Gellie Duncan might have been occasioned by his getting wind of some sort of magical conspiracy instigated against him by John Cockburn. It is therefore not beyond the bounds of possibility that at least some of the roots of the North Berwick witchcraft panic may lie in a squabble or feud between David Seton and Cockburn of Woodhead, or indeed, between their respective "clan" supremos Lord Seton [later Earl of Winton], and the Lord Justice Clerk Cockburn of Ormiston, whose families had been on opposite sides of the political fence since the Reformation.

Another interesting twist to the plot is that David Seton's wife was the sister of the husband of Effie MacCalyean, an Edinburgh lady also dragged into the supposed witchcraft plot against the King, and subsequently executed [Maxwell-Stuart 2001 p. 158]. David Seton's part in all this certainly calls for further investigation.]

Returning to the interrogation of suspects recorded in document JC26/2/19: -

Following Donald Robeson's statement, there is a note in a different hand about a valuable book. This does not appear to have anything to do with the witchcraft investigations, which continue as follows.

Jannet Stratton repeated before his Majesty, the Lord Chancellor, Crawford, Morton.

She spoke of the toad dripping etc by Lord Bothwell who promised Agnes Sampson silver, gold, and food for doing it. The image was first mentioned by Robert Grierson. I was never at sea except the time the boat sank and they took me with them. As I shall answer to God Barbara Napier was there. She never heard any word of the English ambassador, whatever anybody says, whether they believe her or not. Grierson thinks that he won't be known for that kind of man; the Devil possessed him. You should hear that he could not "lease the garden and fession it about his craig" [*sic* Normand and Roberts -more likely "loose the garten and fasten it about his craig" *i.e.* "untie the garter and fasten it round his neck" - An obscure reference to strangulation? Perhaps a suicide attempt on Grierson's part?] I have no more to say, except about the wasted words as I.....

Donald said it was true what he said about the image, that Effie said, "Grierson, say it to the Devil." He denied nothing that he had said to his g....

Bessie Nisbet, servant to Martha, was sent by Euphane MacCalyean to Lady Angus to say that if any trustworthy friends were sent to Barbara to promise kindness to her she would freely confess some things well done by her and her husband that would be in her favour. Otherwise she would be ready to do her evil. The said Bessie Nisbet...

Deposition of Janet Stratton [1]

This document, JC26/2/14 in the National Archives of Scotland [Normand and Roberts "Document 7"], is concerned with Barbara Napier's relationship with Jean Lyon, wife of Archibald Earl of Angus, which features in Agnes Sampson's dittay [Item 54], and Barbara Napier's own dittay [Items 1 & 2]. Janet Stratton is claiming that the wife of the Earl of Angus is using Barbara as a go-between to arrange the Earl's murder by magic. Normand and Roberts date this document as probably January. It would seem more likely at this stage in proceedings to be April.

"The penult.of [   ]e 1591"

Janet Stratton testifies that about three years ago Agnes Sampson, Barbara Napier, and Euphane MacCalyean were at the Fiery Hills. Agnes Sampson raised the Devil and said she had something on the go about a lord. They got an image there. Agnes Sampson got it and gave it to Barbara. She gave it to Euphame who gave it back to her. It was to be roasted for quarter of a year. Every time it was roasted they were to say the word "Master" three times.

She affirms that the last wife of the Earl of Angus, Jean Lyon, sent Barbara to Agnes Sampson to do this, because of a jealousy between her husband and herself.

Deposition of Janet Stratton [2]

In Document JC26/2/15 in the National Archives of Scotland [Normand and Roberts "Document 8"], we have the finished version of Janet Stratton's testimony. The statements obtained during her interrogation have been formed into a coherent narrative setting out:-

[1] The making of a magic potion consisting of the drops from a roasting toad mixed with stale urine, which was sent to Edinburgh.

[2] A meeting at Prestonpans on Lammas Eve [31st July] 1590 where destructive magic was worked on an image of the King at the instigation of the Earl of Bothwell. This meeting, elsewhere said to have been at Acheson's Haven [now Morrison's Haven], is here said to have been at the "Fiery Hills". "Fiery" appears in other references as "Fairy", and "Hills" as "Holes". While "fairy" hills would be appropriate for a gathering of witches, the Morrison's Haven area where coal had been mined since the Middle Ages, is more likely to have had fiery holes [burning coal workings], or fiery hills [burning slag heaps].

This carefully composed precis of Janet's admissions would presumably be read out before the King and his Council, and Janet made to acknowledge it as a true statement of the facts. In modern English it goes as follows:-

At Holyroodhouse 4th may 1591 in the presence of his Majesty the King, his Grace the Duke of Lennox, the Lord Chancellor, the Clerk Secretary, the Captain Depute of Edinburgh Castle, the Laird of Carmichael, and Mr Almonsson [?] Advocate Clerk of Edinburgh.

Janet Stratton, re-examined, declares that when they came in from the sea at the time of the sinking of the boat in September 1598,

Anne Sampson told them that a gentleman had given her a job to do for which she needed to have a toad to bring ruination on a man. She said nothing else at that time, except that she had to go to Edinburgh.

Nothing else was done about this until about a month before the meeting at the Fiery Hills at Prestonpans, which was last Lammas Eve. Agnes Sampson got the toad and "dripped" it above the fire in her house, and after she had got the drippings in a brass dish she got Janet to obtain the mixture or "wash" [usually stale urine], which she brought to Agnes Sampson's house where it was mixed together, and heated on the fire while Agnes stirred it with three fingers. Those present were Agnes Sampson, Janet herself, Katie Wallace wife to James Sparrow of the Mill of Saltoun, and Meg Begtoun.

The toad dripping mixed as described was as black as pitch, and was sent to Edinburgh, to the women who were going to use it there. While mixing it Agnes Sampson called in the Enemy, saying "my Master" three times.

After that, last Lammas Eve, Agnes let Janet know she was to meet her at Kingsburn. The two of them, along with Donald and Anne Dunlop, came to the meeting at Prestonpans, where already gathered there were Barbara Napier, Effie MacCalyean, Meg Begtoun, Bessie Thomson, Gellie Duncan, Robert Grierson, George Mott's wife Margaret Acheson, and various others, as many as sixty or so. But only certain special persons stood in a ring and handled the image mentioned later.

The purpose of this meeting was to conjure or enchant a wax image which Anne Sampson brought with her, and showed to those who were with her on the way. She also showed it to all the rest of the company when she got to the Pans, and every one of them had it in their hands one after the other and spoke certain words over it. They were standing in a ring and it passed round anti-clockwise. First Anne Sampson had it in her left hand, and at the Devil's bidding passed it to Barbara Napier. Barbara Napier passed it to Effie MacCalyean. Effie passed it to Katie Wallace, and she passed it to Meg Begtoun, who passed it to Donald Robeson, who passed it to Bessie Thomson, who passed it to Gellie Duncan, who gave it to Janet Stratton. She passed it to Anne Dunlop, who passed it to Robert Grierson, who passed it to George Mott's wife Margaret Acheson. She returned it to Anne Sampson. Anne Sampson had raised the Devil and she gave the image into his hands. He was standing there in the likeness of a black priest, with black clothes like a hair [fur?] mantle.

She declares that Anne Sampson said to the Devil, "Take this image of James Stewart, prince of Scotland. And I ask you, Master Mahoun, that I may have this job done, and done to destroy him, for the sake of Lord Bothwell, and for the gold and silver that he has promised to give us, and food for me and my children."

She declares that Anne Sampson told the Devil that she had done as she was instructed about "dripping" the toad. Could the thing she had done it for not happen? He answered that he couldn't manage it.

She declares that the image was yellow, and wrapped in a cloth, and was a little less than half an ell long. [The Standard Ell of Edinburgh was 94.1318 cm/37.0598 inches]. She declares that they were home again by four o' clock in the morning, and had no further meetings until Hallowe'en at North Berwick to ask for the image back again.

Death of Robert Grierson in Custody.

A letter of 15th April 1591 from Bowes the English Ambassador recorded in the "Calendar of Scottish Papers" mentions that Robert Grierson ["Rob the Rowar", the Prestonpans seaman] had died "as is thought by the extremity of the tortures applied to him. He hath confessed little."

Examinations of Geilles Duncan, Donald Robeson, and Bessie Thomson.

This document is JC26/2/16 in the National Archives of Scotland [Normand and Roberts "Document 9"] and is dated 5th May 1591. The main purpose of these "examinations" has been to establish details of the meeting at Prestonpans and the plot to destroy James VI by means of an enchanted wax image. The King is obviously still taking a personal interest in proceedings:

Gillie Duncan, re-examined, declares that she was present at the gathering at Prestonpans, and agrees with Jenny Stratton about the number of main participants and their names. She got the image in the cloth passed into her hands, and passed it on to Jenny Stratton. She heard the king named, but not with his own name. As she remembers, he was called "Goodman" or some such word. She can't remember the words spoken by each one of them, but she remembers well that she heard Lord Bothwell spoken of. The business was done for gold and silver, and food to help Anne Sampson and her children.

Donald Robeson, re-examined, admits that he was at the gathering at Prestonpans, and came in company with Anne Sampson and Jennie Stratton. Anne Sampson told them about the image and what it was to be used for, on the way to the Pans, and announced it when she arrived there. On the road, when Anne Sampson spoke to him about the destruction of the King, he said to her, "Alas, what will become of Scotland then?" She answered, "Why should you worry? You'll want for nothing, but get enough as long as you live." As for the number of people present at the meeting and them standing in a "burgh" [*sic* Normand & Roberts. I suspect they have misread "ringe" as "burgh", not as impausible as it seems at first sight, given the peculiarities of 16th Century Secretary Hand. On the other hand, a "burgh" can be a fairy hill, which were believed to be hollow inside.] and passing the wax image from hand to hand, he agrees with Jenny Stratton and Gillie Duncan, but denies that he saw the Devil there. He says the words spoken were in Latin and he cannot now repeat them.

He declares that the business was to be done for Lord Bothwell, and Anne Sampson prepared it, and promised the "gear" [The material reward for doing it?], for gold would shortly be obtained from England, and she would give the others their share of it, and she would get food for herself and her children. Rob Grierson replied that it would be a long time before the gold came from England!

At Edinburgh in the Nether Tolbooth on Wednesday 5th May 1590 [*sic* An error for 1591.] in the presence of his Majesty the King and the members of the Council who were present the preceding day, together with Sir James Melville of Hallhill. Bessie Thomson, re-examined admits and confesses that she was present at the new harbour in Prestonpans the time there was a meeting there about the wax image. She heard the words spoken, but didn't understand them, and at the moment can't remember them. She can't tell who passed the image to her, but she well remembers that she passed it to Gillie Duncan. She admits that she was present at the lifting of the dead bodies in the church and churchyard at North Berwick. She said she can't remember if the Devil was present at the meeting at the new harbour or not, or whether she saw him. After that she said he was there in a "cloud like a [illegible] truss" [*sic* Normand & Roberts].

The Trial of Barbara Napier.

Barbara was the wife of Archibald Douglas, burgess of Edinburgh and brother to the Laird of Carschoggill. She was of a rather higher position in society than most of those involved in the North Berwick/Prestonpans ongoings.

She seems to have enlisted the services of Agnes Sampson to use magic to influence her personal and social life, and this was duly included in Agnes's dittay or charge sheet. After Agnes's trial and execution, evidence begins to appear of a second great witch meeting in East Lothian, prior to the North Berwick gathering. This was the meeting at Acheson's Haven [now Morrison's Haven], and Barbara Napier is named as having been present. Not only that, but she is now reported to have attended the North Berwick convention, although there has been no previous mention of her presence there.

Barbara of course was not from East Lothian, but since she was supposedly so involved with East Lothian events and East Lothian people, it is worth perusing her trial. It can be found in Pitcairn's *Criminal Trials*, Vol. 1, p. 244. Rendered into modern English the records read as follows:-

May 8th 1591.

Barbara Napier, wife of Archibald Douglas, burgess of Edinburgh, brother to the Laird of Carshoggill.

Accused of various charges of witchcraft contained in the indictment given in against her by Mr David McGill of Cranstoun Ryddill, advocate to our Sovereign Lord.

Pursuer, Mr David McGill, advocate to our Sovereign Lord, on his Highness' behalf.

Defence for the accused: Mr John Russell, Mr John Moscrop; William Alexander and Andro Naiper, burgesses of Edinburgh.

After hearing various allegations from the accused against the indictment, and the answers made to them, the Judge ordered Barbara to be tried by an assise for the crimes contained in the indictment.

The Assise [jury].

John Brig, master porter to his Majesty,
George Brig, master of the ale cellar,
Walter Bell, at the Mill of Dean,
Hector Clawie, burgess of the Cannongait,
James Galbraith, "averieman" to his Majesty [keeper of the royal aviary ?],
David Seytoun in Fowlstruther [!],
William Justice, merchant burgess of Edinburgh,
John Seytoun, creelman to his Majesy,
John Mowbray, merchant burgess,
David Fairlie, merchant burgess,
Patrick Sandilands, tailor, burgess of Edinburgh.
Archibald Wilkie, burgess of Cannongait,
Archibald Cuthbertson, burgess of Edinburgh,
Robert Cunninghame, burgess there,
William Harper, burgess there.

Verdict:-

The assise, by the mouth of their spokesman Robert Cunningham, found, pronounced, and declared Barbara Naiper to be guilty, culpable, and convicted of consulting with Anny Sampsoune, a witch, for help in pregnancy; consulting with Anny Sampsoune to get Dame Jean Lyoun, Lady Angus, to favour her and give her back the possessions she owed her also giving Annie a ring for this purpose, for which she sent her a linen kerchief, thus contravening the Act of Parliament in consulting her and seeking her help, she being a witch.

For consulting the same Annie Sampsoune about helping her husband Archibald Douglas when he was in the west at the military expedition to Dumfries, her husband being at that time at feud with the family of Cowhill.

For consulting with Rychie Grahame, a necromancer and abuser of the people, seeking help from him for her son, and rewarding him with three ells of bombasine [a twilled or corded fabric of silk and worsted: *Chambers Dict.*] and five quarters of brown [cloth ?]. This was in John Ramsay's house outside the West Port of Edinburgh, in contravention of the Act of Parliament concerning such things. At that same time she asked Rychie Grahame whether the king would come home or not.

For keeping company and consulting with a witch and necromancer in contravention of the Act of Parliament passed against such matters.

Barbara is acquitted of consulting Rychie about a stolen doublet belonging to her late husband George Kerr.

Consulting Annie Sampsoun about making an image of the late Archibald Earl of Angus to cause his destruction.

Being at the meeting at North Berwick.

Also acquitted of everything else in the dittay except for the counts on which she was convicted.

Thus Barbara Napier was found guilty on a handful of trivial counts of consultation, and acquitted of the most important accusations, the nature of which will shortly become apparent. Technically, even consulting a witch was a capital offence, but in practice courts almost always treated such matters more leniently. In this instance the court delayed pronouncing sentence, presumably while further advice was sought. Further advice came in no uncertain terms two days later. The King was outraged that the "wrong" verdict had been reached, and [expressed in modern English] instructed the court as follows: -

To the Justice [judge], Justice Clerk, and your deputes: We greet you well. Barbara Naper, wife of Archibald Douglas, burgess of Edinburgh, was convicted in a court of justice held in the Tollbooth of Edinburgh on the 8th of May for consulting with Annie Sampsoun, a witch etc [the verdict of the court is repeated here]. No sentence has as yet been pronounced upon her. Our will is as follows, and we order you immediately after reading this to pronounce sentence against her for these crimes, according to the laws of our realm and the acts of Parliament. She is to be taken to the Castle Hill of the burgh of Edinburgh and there bound to a stake beside the fire and strangled to death there.

Thereafter her body is to be burnt in the fire and all her moveable goods forfeited to our use because she has been convicted of the said crimes. Do this remembering that your official position and the obedience you owe make you answerable to us. This letter gives you sufficient warrant to act

Signed with our hand at Halyrudhous the tenth day of May 1591

James R [The King]

J Cancellarius [The Chancellor]

Sentence was accordingly pronounced. Barbara immediately claimed to be pregnant, and that she could not therefore be put to death until after she had given birth. Pitcairn, quoting Home of Godscroft, says, "Nobody insisting on the persute of her, she was set at libertie."

Not content with instructing the court to impose a death sentence despite the relatively trifling nature of the charges proven against Barbara, the King now directed his ire at the hapless jurors, and accused the majority of Barbara's assise of "manifest and willful error" in acquitting her. The "minority", those who had voted against aquittal, interestingly enough, included our old acquaintance David Seton in Foulstruther, and the King's creelman John Seton, who may well have been a relative of David's. The only other dissenter had been George Brig, the master of the King's ale cellar.

It is worth perusing the charges against the jurors, because they plainly set out the accusations of treason against Barbara which are missing from the records of her trial, and which detail the current state of official thinking regarding the whole East Lothian conspiracy of treason by witchcraft. The "Dittay against the assisors on Barbara Naiper's Inquest" can be found in Pitcairn Vol 1, p.244. In modern English it goes as follows:-

James, by the grace of God etc.

Barbara Napier, wife of Archibald Douglas, was accused in a Court of Justiciary held in the Tollbooth of Edinburgh on 8th May 1991 of seeking help and consultation from Rychard Grahame, a notorious known necromancer and common abuser of the people, both against the will and command of God and the Acts of Parliament of the country. Particularly, when our Sovereign Lord was at the Brig of Die, before the warning bell rang because it was feared that Earl Bothwell intended entering Edinburgh, she said to Rychard that she'd heard a woman say that the king would be harmed by a toad or a vagabond. She asked him what he thought of that and asked him to elaborate on his opinion. He consulted with the Spirit about it, and got the reply that the King would be troubled by a meeting of women, through their allowing a toad to drip; and, laughing at her, Rychard also declared that she, Effie MacCalyean, and Donald Robeson would be three of the participants. When she heard this she shook her head. This was affirmed by Rychard in her presence, and in the presence of the assise.

Also, Barbara was accused of being present at the most devlish and treasonable meeting held by her and her accomplices in the Devil's name last Lammas Eve at the new harbour called Aitcheson's Haven between Musselburgh and Prestonpans, after the King came away from Denmark. There were nine principal participants assembled, namely

Agnes Sampsone,
Jonet Straitton,
Ewfame McCalyeanne,
herself,
Johnne Fiene,
Robert Griersoun,
George Moitis wife from Preston,
Margaret Thomeson from Stirling,
Donald Robesoune.

These nine persons were thought to be those most suitable for doing the business in hand, and the Devil was with them in the shape of a black man. He therefore placed these nine nearest to himself in a group. The wife of Saltoun Mill and the rest of the less important participants, up to thirty of them, were in another group standing hardly the length of a table from the first group. Agnes Sampsoune proposed the destruction of the King, saying to the Devil, "We have a bit of business in hand, and we're keen to get on with it if we can. So help us with it." The Devil replied that he would do what he could, but it would take a long time, because it would be obstructed. He promised them a wax image, and ordered them to hang and roast a toad and let it drip. The drops from the toad were to be mixed with stale urine, an adder skin, and the thing *[sic]* from the head of a new born foal, and laid in the King's way, where his Majesty would go in or out over it, or in a passage where it could drop on the King's head or his body, in order to destroy him, so that someone else could reign in his place and the world could go to the Devil.

At this meeting the King's name was pronounced in Latin, and Agnes Sampsoun was appointed to make the image and to give it to the Devil to be enchanted. This she did, and gave it to him, and he promised to give it to Barbara and Effie McCalyean at the next meeting to be roasted. Margaret Thomson was appointed to "drip" the toad. Someone else was appointed to try to get some of the king's linen clothes to do the job with.

On 15th December last, face to face with Barbara and Effie McCalyean, Gelie Duncan swore as soon as she saw them that she saw her [Barbara?] coming to the Abbey [of Holyrood] behind her. Before she had uttered three complete sentences in her presence she affirmed that Agnes Sampson had met with her and Effie in Barbara's own house, and that Gelie Duncan and Bessie Thomson were there too. John Fiene was also there, and said to Gelie that he would go west to his father, and added that a toad had been hanging by the heels, set to drip between three oyster shells and nine stones for three nights. At that time no-one expected to have heard any such thing.

All this was manifestly made plain by the separate statements of Donald Robesoune and Jonett Strayton, who constantly upheld them, and was repeated by the King's Advocate; also the statements of Gellie Duncan and Rychard Grahame, each on his/her own behalf, when they were confronted with each other.

Barbara was similarly accused of having been physically present last Hallowe'en in 1590, at the well-attended convention held in North Berwick church, where she danced along the churchyard and Gelie Duncan played a jew's harp. John Fiene, muffled up, led the circle and Agnes Sampsoun, her daughters, and all the rest followed Barbara - up to seven score people, among whom were:-

    Effie McCalyean
    Katherene Gray
    Margaritt Aichiesoun
    Donald Robesoun
    Robert Griersoun
    Katherine Wallace
    Meg Bogtoun
    Jonett Campbell
    Jonett Logane
    Johnne Gordoun alias Gray-meill
    The porter's wife of Seton
    Jonett Straytoun
    Bessie Thomsoune
    Cathrine Duncane
    Bessie Wrycht
    Issobell Gylloun
    Johnne Ramsay's wife
    Annie Rychesoun
    Jonett Gall
    The wife of Nicol Murray the tailor
    Christian Keringtoune alias Likkit
    Marie Patersoune
    Alexander Quhitelaw
    Marioun Nicolsoun
    Issobell Lauder
    Helene Quhyte
    Margaret Thomsoune
    Marioune Schaw
    Helene Lauder
    Malie Geddie
    Duncan Buchquhannane
    Marioun Congiltoun
    Bessie Cowane
    Bessie Broun the smith's wife
    Thoman Brounhill and his wife
    Gilbert McGill
    John and Catherine McGill

with many others to the number already mentioned. At that time and place the women paid homage first and were turned round nine times anti-clockwise. Johne Fyen "blew up" the church doors and "blew in" the lights, which were like great black candles held in an old man's hand round about the pulpit. The Devil started up in the pulpit like a great black man with a black beard sticking out like a goat's beard, a high ridged nose curving down and sharp like the beak of a hawk, with a long "rumpill" [?]. He was dressed in a ragged black gown, with an ugly looking skull cap on his head, and a black book in his hand. He called on every one of them to be good servants to him, and they would have enough and never want. Robert Griersoun and Johnne Fien stood on his left hand, and Robert found great fault with the Devil, and cried out so that everyone could hear, that his Highness's image hadn't been given to them as promised. Effie McCalyan reminded Robert Griersoun to ask for the image, meaning the King's image, which was to be roasted. Robert Griersoun's words were, "Where is the thing you promised?" - meaning the wax image designed to be roasted for the king's undoing, which Agnes Sampsoune gave him. Robert cried out to get the business done. However, they did not name the King's name until the women named him, asking plainly for the King's image. But the Devil answered that they would get it at the next meeting, and because of that he'd hold the next meeting all the sooner. Robert Griersoun replied, "You promised twice and misled us!" Four honest-looking women very earnestly insisted they must have it. Barbara and Effie McCalyane got the Devil to promise them that the image of the King should be given to the two of them as soon as possible. This matter of the image of the king was the reason for that meeting, in token of which the Devil commanded Barbara and all her company to keep his commandment, which was to do all the evil they could.

Also, three corpses were dug up and dismembered, and the nails and joints shared out. The Devil commanded them to keep the joints until they dried and then to make powder from them to do evil. After that they paid homage in their own way by kissing the Devil's arse, then parted without more ado, except that Effie McCalyane, Robert Griersoune, and Barbara happened to be named there, which offended the whole company. They should not have been named with their own names. Robert Griersoun should have been called Rob the Rowar, Effie should have been called Cane, and Barbara should have been called Naip. This is true, and proven by Donald Robeson, Jonett Straittone, Gilie Duncan, and Bessie Thomson who are still alive.

All this being led in evidence at the trial, the assise nevertheless on 9th *[sic]* May 1591, out of favouritism and partiality, cleared and acquitted Barbara Naipare of, during the time his Majesty was at the Brig of Die ..... [Here all the evidence set out above is recapitulated]... None of the assise could claim to be in ignorance of all this. Neither law nor conscience could have acquitted her of it, since it had been verified by the constant assertion and deposition of some of the witnesses, who were present in court at the time as already stated, and by the production of the sworn statements of the rest of the witnesses. Therefore they obviously erred deliberately, contrary to the laws and practice of the realm, thereby committing the horrible crime of perjury.

His Majesty being sitting in judgement, they were asked by the judge whether they wished to be tried by the law and an assise for these crimes, or whether they would do as they were told. After long deliberation and consultation, they turned down the option of a trial by assise, but agreed that they would submit themselves to the King's will for committing an error in ignorance, by acquitting Barbara of the crimes and counts of the indictment given above.

Sentence.

His Majesty in public judgment in the presence of his lords of the Privy Council declared that his will was, that he understood that it was not willful error that they committed in thus acquitting her, so he therefore ordered that the aforesaid persons [*i.e.* the majority of Barbara's jury] shall every one of them be absolved from all penalties in body goods or reputation for all time to come.

Upon the declaration of the King's will, each of them asked for a written record.

An account of the above proceedings in a letter from the English ambassador Bowes dated June 8th [CSP, Vol X, p.522] makes plain how Barbara's jurors squared their volte face with their consciences. The only evidence against Barbara that they had been given was the testimony of witches, which they did not think was sufficient grounds for conviction. However, they decided that witches who have recanted are no longer actually witches, so their testimony is valid after all!

Normand and Roberts, quoting L A. Yeaman from an essay in *The Scottish Witch Hunt in Context* [Ed. Goodacre: Manchester 2001], say that Barbara was "executed with five others in Haddington in 1591". This, however, is almost certainly mistaken. P. G. Maxwell-Stuart in *Satan's Conspiracy* [East Linton: 2001, p.166] points out that the records of the burgh of Edinburgh indicate in an entry of 23rd February

1592 that Barbara had been in prison up until that date, and was now to be released on bail with her brother as her cautioner. It may be significant that 23rd February is over nine months after her trial on 8th May of the previous year. If Barbara had indeed been pregnant she would certainly have given birth by 23rd February. Whatever the truth of the matter, she was now being released rather than executed. Of course, she could have been rearrested at any time, and the sentence carried out, but there is no evidence that this ever happened. Perhaps Barbara escaped with her life in spite of the king's determination to condemn her.

The Witch of Redden.

Janet Kennedy, the Witch of Redden, was not an East Lothian woman. Redden is south of the Tweed, between Sprouston and Carham, less than half a mile from the Border. She had fled into England but had been brought back. Bowes the English Ambassador mentions her in several of his letters.

On 13th February 1591 he reminds Burghley "to give the order for Francis Dacre for warrant to Sir John Selby to send hither the Scottish witch taken in England and committed to prison in Berwick, for whom the King earnestly calleth." [CPS Vol X, p460]. On 23rd February he observes that "the King daily calls for the delivery of the Scottish witch taken in England." [ibid p.471]. On 24th March he writes, "The witch lately taken in England and committed to safe custody in Berwick is delivered into Scotland agreeable to the King's desire, wherewith the King is well pleased. This woman hath accused many others and is found to have practised sundry wicked actions by her sorceries". [ibid p.487]. Finally on 14th June, Bowes observes, "This trial of Mackallean is thought to touch Bothwell narrowly, and Kennedy the witch of Reydon, lately in England, has secretly told the king sundry matters against the Earl agreeing with Graham his chief accuser." [ibid p.530].

Although the witch of Redden was not from East Lothian, she is of interest because she had much to say about Agnes Sampson.

Document JC26/2/10 in the National Archives of Scotland [Normand & Roberts "Document 13"] is undated, but is almost certainly from June 1591. The first part describes how Janet was first recruited by an evil spirit. Rendered into modern English it then continues:-

Agnes Sampson sent word to her by her daughter, a woman named Brown, asking her to come to her. When she refused the woman threatened her in Agnes Sampson's name, and said that if she didn't come Agnes would compel the essence of her body to come to her. So it turned out, for at various times when Janet was lying in her bed at night, Agnes by her enchantments drew out her spirit and transported it to assist at their meetings. She remembers two main pieces of business done there.

The first was three or four years ago on a summer night between Midsummer and Lammas. She saw Agnes Sampson with a long slender wax image in her hand, black in colour, which had been made for the destruction of the Earl of Angus. It was put in a basin of water and made to grow weak and melt away. This took place in the fields, but she couldn't tell where because it was during the night.

[The next section of the document is damaged, making the sense unclear in places. However, the gist of it is as follows]:

The next bit of business was in the fields where Janet was shown a yellow wax image, shorter than the other. It, unlike the other image, was wrapped in a linen cloth. Agnes Sampson said this image represented King James. Great lords and ladies had shown great favour and kindliness to Agnes to have him put down by means of the image. A man stood beside Agnes, short in stature, about thirty years of age, without much hair on his face, pale and thin-faced. He wanted to take the image from Agnes, but she wouldn't hand it over until she had finished enchanting [?] it. Within a month, about Lammas, on a fair summer night with starlight, the same company met again in a little remote house on the moor, which seemed to be Agnes Sampson's house. Janet saw Agnes take the king's image out of the cloth, laid the cloth down beside the fire, and laid the image by the fire to fry it, as the custom is. However, it would not. At this, the man Janet mentioned before told Agnes to make the fire hotter, but that still did not help. Then Agnes Sampson said that what they were attempting against the King was all in vain, for nothing of their craft could get at him.

Janet affirms that the King need be afraid of nothing, for she saw from her experience on that occasion that everything the Devil could do against the King had no effect.

Not surprisingly, Janet's interrogators were not impressed by her claims that she attended the meetings in spirit only, and was not actually physically present. Document JC26/2/11 in the Archives of Scotland [Normand and Roberts "Document 14"] is another statement from Janet, headed "The wyfe of reddenis depositione". It is dated June 1591,

Janet affirms in the presence of his Majesty, Mr David [Lind]say, and Mr Robert Bruce minister, that about last Lammas, in 1590, when the image of the King was roasting in Anny Sampson's house, that Agnes said to her and the rest that there were more people involved in the business than poor folk like the present company. In particular, there were two important women whose surnames she gave as MacCalyean and Napier, but didn't name their first names. Agnes said that she and the man already mentioned, along with the two women named were the main movers, appointed to win the approval of great lords and ladies for putting the plan into action against the King.

In adition, Janet admits that she remembers that she was there "bodily" on that occasion, sent for by Annie Sampson, and that she and Meg Steel made and tended with their own hands the fire that the King's image was laid beside.

The whole aim of the above confessions would seem to be the confirmation of the involvement of the upper-class "gentlewomen" Napier and MacCalyean in the plot against the King. At the time of the Witch of Redden's interrogation, Napier was already under a suspended sentence of death, and MacCalyean's trial may actually have been in progress.

Euphane MacCalyean.

Effie MacCalyean is a puzzling figure. She was the only daughter and heiress of Thomas MacCalyean of Clifftonhall in West Lothian, an advocate and Senator of the College of Justice. Her husband was Patrick Moscrop, who seems to have taken his wife's surname MacCalyean, a fairly common practice for men who married heiresses. They had three daughters and two sons. An intriguing twist in the tale is that recent research has revealed that Effie's husband's sister, Katherine Moscrop, was the wife of David Seton, the baron baillie of Tranent whose actions supposedly first led to the uncovering of the whole "North Berwick" saga [Maxwell-Stuart: 2001 p.158] The significance of this has not yet been assessed, and there may be much more to it than meets the eye.

Because of the idiosyncracies of 16th Century Scottish handwriting, Effie's surname is often rendered "MacCalzean". Since the pronunciation was undoubtedly "Macallion", the letter "y" is more appropriate than a "z", and I shall use "y" throughout. Her first name is sometimes given as "Euphane", and sometimes as "Euphame".

Effie's marriage was obviously unhappy, and many of the accusations against her relate to the use of magic in the context of her personal and family life. She was not an East Lothian woman of course, and much of her dittay has no relevance to East Lothian. However, the accusations against her relating to the conspiracy against the King represent the final summing-up by the "authorities" of the whole "North Berwick" episode. As Normand and Roberts say [p.218] "It is in the narrative of her dittay that treason and witchcraft are most successfully combined", and [p.219], "The crimes with which MacCalzean was charged represent in miniature those that the entire group of witches is supposed to have committed against the king." Thus, since Effie played an important rote in the most famous incidence of witchcraft in East Lothian, it is worth giving her trial some attention.

She was defended by formidable lawyers, who before the trial had even begun, objected to three of the assise or jury - not surprisingly. These were David Seton, John Seton brother of David Seton in Tranent, and Joseph Douglas of Pumpherston who had given hostile evidence against both Effie and Barbara Napier. The two Setons of course, David and John, are likely to be the two Setons of the same name who were members of Barbara Napier's assise. David Seton is presumably either the Tranent baron baillie or his son, and it seems inconceivable that anyone could seriously have proposed the Setons as unbiased jurors. Effie MacCalyean's trial can be found in Pitcairn's "Criminal Trials" Vol 1, p. 247. It lasted from 9th to 11th June 1591. In modern English the preamble goes as follows:-

Accused of certain treasonable conspiracies intended to have destroyed the person of our Sovereign Lord by witchcraft, and to have deprived his Majesty of his life by those shameful and extraordinary means. Also of being art and part in the consulting and plotting with other witches of her acquaintance, and many other crimes of witchcraft committed by her, specified fully in the indictment.

Pursuer

Mr David McGill of Cranstoun Ryddell, Advocate to our Sovereign Lord.[*i.e.* Representing the Crown as prosecutor.]

Spokesmen for the defence

Mr John Moscrop, Mr David Ogilvie, Robert Kerr in Duddingstone, Henry Nisbet burgess of Edinburgh; Mr John Russell and Mr John Skene, advocates.

Mr David McGill, advocate, appeared and produced a long indictment against Euphame, and arranged for the following points to be tried by an assise.

[Pitcairn says that he gives an abreviated form of the original dittay. I shall give the items relating to East Lothian in full, in modern English, and give brief summaries of the others.]

Item 1 relates to bewitching a Michael Marjoribanks.

Item 2 relates to consulting a Gaelic-speaking woman, Catherine Campbell, on a matter concerning her children.

Item 3 is about consulting the same woman on how to kill her husband, and

Item 4 about consulting a Fife witch about how to get her husband to love her.

Item 5 accuses Effie of poisoning her husband during their first year of marriage, and in

Item 6 she is accused of bewitching him at a later date.

Item 7 accuses her of getting a witch to instruct her in witchcraft.

Item 8 says she bewitched a man and his wife for revealing that fact, and in

Item 9 she is said to have killed her nephew by witchcraft.

Item 10

Indicted that you conceived a deadly malice against Jonet Cokburne, daughter to Johnne Cokburne, maltman in Haddington, for bringing your purse, belt, mirror, and clothes down from the bedroom and laying them on the table. Your husband then lifted your purse and was going to open it, but didn't. Because of this you said to Jonet, "Well, girl, have you allowed this to happen? You shall repent it from your heart!" Catherine Carruthers, alias "Erisch Jonett" [Gaelic-speaking Janet] laid in her way enchanted graveyard earth and powder which in a short time caused a swooning to come over her heart, and such palpitations in her chest as if there had been some living thing there, gasping and panting and heaving up her body. Every time this happens she is affected for half an hour, often at night and often during the day, and has more strength at those times than when she is in normal health. You are thus accused of laying graveyard earth and powder in Jonett Cokburne's way by witchcraft and enchantment, by which she fell sick and was greatly troubled by it, as indeed she still is, by your art and witchcraft.

Item 11 accuses her of killing a Euphame Pumphray by witchcraft. Items 12-15 deal with Effie's infatuation with Joseph Douglas, Laird of Pumpherson in West Lothian. She tried to induce him to fall in love with her, gave him jewellery, then consulted "Lady Bothwell", a notorious witch living in the Canongate, about poisoning him. She sent her servant to Joseph's fiancée to persuade her not to marry him, saying that he had venereal disease, and tried to impede the marriage with charms and enchantments.

Item 16. Indicted for seeking help and consultation from Annye Sampson, known to be a notorious witch, for getting back your jewels and papers from the Laird of Pumfrastoune, sending your former nurse Jonett Drummond to Annye seven times for that purpose. One of these times she raised the Spirit, in the form of a voice, not a physical presence, which said that these things would be delivered to Jonett Drummond, the messenger sent to seek the response.

In Item 17 she is accused of killing two of the Laird of Pumpherston's children by witchcraft.

Item 18. Indicted for consulting and seeking help from Anny Sampsoune, a notorious witch, for the relief of your pains at the time of the birth of your two sons. For that purpose you got from her a stone bored through with a hole, to be laid beneath the pillow under your head. Also enchanted graveyard earth and powder in a piece of paper to be used rolled up in your hair. At the time of your labour pains your husband's shirt was to be immediately taken off him, and laid folded up under the foot of your bed. You put all this into practice as instructed by Annie, and your sickness was unnaturally cast off you at the birth of your first son, on to a dog which ran away and was never seen again. At the time of your last son's birth you did as before, and your natural and rightful pain was unnaturally cast off you on to the free-roaming cat in the house which likewise was never seen again.

Item 19. Indicted with taking part in consulting with Annie Sampsoun to destroy Mr Johnne Moscrop, your father-in-law by witchcraft about four years ago or thereabouts. You sent Jonett Drummond your servant to Annie with a wax image in a box, inside a goose wrapped in a serviette with some beef. Annie gave this image to the Devil to be enchanted. When he had enchanted it, the image was sent back to you with Jonett Drummond. Annie said it would serve to do the trick.

Item 20. Indicted for your Devlish consultation with Agnes Sampsoun, partly in person, and partly through your old agent Jonet Drummond, on how to be revenged on Mr John McGill's wife. When you and Agnes Sampsoune, a notorious witch, had decided what to do she sent you some witchcraft and enchantments through Jonett Drummond, which you threw in at Johnne McGill's window. This was a child's apron and neckcloth with something tied in it. When this was revealed by some of your servants, you made Jonett Drummond deny it when she was taxed with it. Moreover, every day and night she was troubled with terrible hallucinations and visions. At two in the afternoon she quite plainly saw a naked man standing in the middle of the floor of one of your bedrooms, with a white sheet round him. Also, Jonet Aitchesoun, your servant, was sent at twelve o'clock at night to draw a drink, and saw a naked man behind her wearing a shirt with his legs in the sleeves and the tail round his head, which terrified her. These visions must have been the result of your devlish art of witchcraft. Jonet Aitchesoun was also pestered by hedgehogs. The witchcraft already mentioned was thrown in again at Mr John McGill's window, and being found and opened out, proved to be a clay image, and an image of Elizabeth Home, Mr Johnne's wife, sewn into a shroud. An old black mutch was wrapped round this, containing five balls of different colours of wool; black, red, orange, yellow, and blue. Agnes Sampson confessed you had worked these sorceries yourself. Also Agnes Sampson confessed that Jonet Drummond brought the same old mutch to her, which she enchanted. Jonet Drummond has also confessed taking it to Agnes.

Item number 21 refers to Effie making the image of Elizabeth Home out of flour and clay, and

Item 22 concerns her killing six year old Lillias McCalyean [presumably a relative] by rubbing her face with a napkin after she had fallen.

Item 23. Indicted and accused of being present at the "conventicle" held at North Berwick church twenty days before Michaelmas [Michaelmas is 29th September] 1590, and there asking for the image of the king given by Annie Sampson to the Devil to be enchanted for the treasonable destruction of the King.

Item 24. Indicted for being at the meeting held at the new harbour called the Fayrie-hoillis last Lammas for the purpose given immediately above.

Item 25. Indicted and accused of being at a meeting held by you and other notorious witches who were your associates at the Brume-hoillis, where you and they put to sea, Robert Grierson being your admiral and chief. You passed over the sea in riddles to a ship which you boarded with your master the Devil. After you had eaten and drunk, you threw a black dog overboard, which skipped under the ship. You had the Devil your master on board, and by these means he capsized the ship. This caused the Queen to turn back due to a storm.

Item 26. Indicted for consulting with Annie Sampson, Robert Griersoune and various other witches for the treasonable delay of the Queen's homecoming by storm and wind; for raising a storm either to accomplish that or to drown Her Majesty and her company, by conjuring cats and throwing them into the sea at Leith and at the back of Robert Grierson's house.

Item 27. Indicted for being art and part in the destruction of a boat between Leith and Kinghorn, and of sixty people on board, by meeting with witches and by your and their witchcraft - as is notoriously known.

Item 28. Indicted for a common witch.

Effie's assise found her guilty on the following counts:-

Item 2 - Consulting with Catherine Campbell for help with her children.

Item 9 - Killing her nephew by witchcraft.

Item 13- Consulting with a notorious witch to poison Joseph Douglas, the Laird of Pumpherston.

Item 16 - Consulting Agnes Sampson about getting jewels and papers back from the Laird of Pumpherston.

Item 18- Getting help from Agnes Sampson to ease her labour pains through magic, and transferring the pains on to a dog and cat.

Item 19 - Consulting with Agnes Sampson about using a wax image to destroy her father in law John Moscrop.

Item 21 - Making an image of flour and clay to bewitch Elizabeth Home.

Item 23 - Being present at the meeting in North Berwick church.

Item 24 - Being present at the meeting at Acheson's Haven.

Item 28 - Being a common witch.

She was acquitted of all the other charges. Being proved to be a "common witch" was enough to ensure the death penalty. However, her crimes were obviously felt to be so dreadful that exemplary punishment was required. Effie was sentenced to be burned alive, one of the very few times that this cruel and inhuman sentence was ever handed down in Scotland after the passing of the Witchcraft Act of 1563. Indeed, this, as far as I am aware, is the *only* official record of such a sentence being passed. Effie was duly burned on the Castle Hill of Edinburgh on 24th June 1591. Pitcairn comments, "She does not seem to have repented her crimes, but rather seems to have gloried in what she attempted." However, Pitcairn is probably basing this statement solely on Effie's refusal to confess, rather than on any hard evidence of her glorying in her supposed crimes.

Since death sentences were normally carried out almost immediately, it seems rather odd that Effie was sentenced on 11th June, but not executed until 24th June. A week after her trial, on 19th June, Bowes the English Ambassador wrote, "On Tuesday last judgment was given that Effam Mackallean should be burnt alive. The execution is stayed because she alleges herself to be with child, and still denies all matters in her indictments, though some appear very evident against her." Perhaps Bowes is confusing Effie with Barbara Napier here, who certainly did claim pregnancy, or perhaps he is just quoting an official line spun by the authorities to account for the delay. The real reason for delaying the execution is probably that Effie had been found guilty and condemned to death while persistently refusing to confess to any of the accusations - a most unusual situation, since the confession was normally the crucial part of the evidence against a witch. The King personally ordered that the execution should be delayed so that further pressure could be brought to bear on Effie to extract a confession. This is made plain in the final paragraph of a communication from James IV to Secretary Maitland [C.S.P. Vol X, p.508] which at first sight is striking in its callousness. The attributed date of this letter is "April", but this must certainly be wrong since it has patently obviously been written after Barbara Napier's trial, and since it also alludes to the "dome" or sentence passed on MacCalyean, it must therefore date from after 11th June. In modern English it reads as follows:

Put the medical men on oath to find out if Barbara Napier is pregnant or not. Take no delaying answer. If you find that she's not pregnant, to the fire with her immediately, and have her publicly disembowelled. Let Effie Makkaillen see the stake for two or three days, and then delay matters suddenly in the hope of getting a confession. If that does the trick let me know. If not, dispatch her next week, but not according to the harshness of the sentence. As for the rest of the less important witches, "off at the nail with them", but make sure Ritchie Graham doesn't lack his usual allowance, until I take further steps with him.

Thus, Ritchie Graham is being kept alive meantime [he was finally executed at the end of February 1592], Barbara Napier is to be examined by doctors to prove the truth of her pregnancy claim, and Effie MacCalyean is to be put under psychological pressure to confess. If there is no confession, she is to be executed, but not according to the "rigour of the dome". This, surely, can only mean that the King does not after all want her to be burnt alive.

In a letter dated 25th June [C.S.P. Vol X, p.537] Bowes the English Ambassador writes, This afternoon Effam Mackalzon was executed by fire and died very obstinately without confessing any crime." The phrase "executed by fire" certainly suggests that Effie was indeed burned alive, but it was common practice throughout the history of Scottish witchcraft to refer to the "burning" of witches rather than to the strangling which actually dispatched them. All the known written references to Effie being burnt alive are based on the sentence rather than the actual execution, and as far as I am aware, there is no eyewitness account of the burning. If she had indeed been burnt alive, surely more notice would have been taken of this horrific and unusual event, and someone somewhere would have left an account of it. On the contrary however, the historian Calderwood in his "history of the Kirk of Scotland" says quite plainly, "She was wirried [*i.e.* strangled] and burnt to ashes upon the 25th of June." [Calderwood: ed. Wodrow Society 1849, p.128] Calderwood was writing in 1627 about events which occurred when he was around 16 years of age, and almost certainly a student at Edinburgh University. Is it plausible that he could have forgotten that Effie had been burnt alive?

Let us hope, therefore that the King's instructions to avoid the full "rigour of the dome" were obeyed, and that Scotland's best-known [and possibly only] instance of the judicially sanctioned burning to death of a living witch, post-1563, is in fact a myth.

The treasurer's accounts in the Burgh Records of Edinburgh [Wood and Hannay p.643] have an interesting reference to "The execution of Euphane McCalyeane quhilk wes upoun the XV day of Junij 1591 - Payit for the carying of the maist part of the coilis with the rest of the fire appointit for Barbarie Naper into ane house in John Edyearis cloiss and for carying out of the samyn quhen Euphame McCalyeane was execute - 16s." In other words the materials prepared to burn Barbara Napier in the second week of May were not used for their original purpose. Instead, they were kept in store until 25th June and used to burn Euphane MacCalyean. Wood and Hannay comment that the other items in the execution expenses are the same as Fian's, previously quoted, and the total cost of the execution was £11-7s. Here too there is a discrepancy in the date given for the execution. Wood and Hannay quote "15th June", but the English ambassador's letter of 25th June clearly says that her execution was "this afternoon". Perhaps as I have suggested before in similar cases, the treasurer authorised the expenses well in advance, or perhaps the clerk slipped up and wrote "XV Junij instead of "XXV Junij"

The following year the King magnanimously returned much of Effie's forfeited estate to her family, saying he did not wish her children to suffer. However, he kept Clifftonhall and gifted it to one of his favourites, Sir James Sandilands.

Returning briefly to questions of execution: although it is almost universally believed that witches in Scotland were routinely "burnt at the stake", in fact, as has previously been emphasised, they were dispatched by strangulation. Dead bodies were burnt, not living witches. However, there is one oft-quoted description from 1608 of witches being burnt alive in Brechin. The original can be found in the Register of the Privy Council, Vol 14, p.605, and comes from manuscript notes kept by the Earl of Haddington of items of interest arising during Privy Council meetings, many of which [including the witch-burning reference in question] do not appear in the official minutes of the Privy Council.

"The Erle of Mar declarit to the Counsell, that sum wemen wes tane in Breichin as Witches; and being put to ane Assyse, and convict albeit they perseveirit in their denyal to the end, yet thay were brunt quick in sic a crewell maner that sum of them deit in despair, renuncand and blasphemand, and utheris half brunt, brak out of the fyre, and wes cast quick in it agane, quill thay were brunt to the deid."

Obviously this incident was considered considered important enough by the Earl of Mar to raise in the Privy Council, presumably because he found it not only shocking but unusual - perhaps even unprecedented. However, it was not considered important enough by the Council even to be minuted, far less acted upon. Why should such a flagrant breach of the law have been ignored? There may of course have been many politically expedient reasons. Another reason may have been that the Earl of Mar was reporting only hearsay. There is no other evidence for the incident, and the story could quite plausibly be wildly exaggerated or even unfounded. It could also of course be true, but the mere fact of its being raised by an Earl in a Privy Council meeting does not make it so; far less does it make it typify the fate of Scottish witches, although it has often been used so to do.

With the evidence for the Brechin burnings hanging from a rather "shoogly nail", and room for serious doubt about Effie MacCalyean being consigned as a living sacrifice to the flames, and no other cases of live burning in the official records, it would seem that Scotland's reputation for witch-burning barbarity may not be wholly deserved.

Depositions of Janet Stratton and Donald Robeson to a Notary Public.

On 19th June 1591 statements were taken by Alexander Cook, notary public, from Janet Stratton, imprisoned at Seton, and Donald Robeson, who was in the custody of David Seton, baron baillie of Tranent. This is an obvious attempt to gather evidence favourable to the Earl of Bothwell, who had been imprisoned in Edinburgh Castle since 16th April under suspicion of plotting with witches against the King. These statements are contained in document JC26/2/11 in the National Archives of Scotland [Normand and Roberts "Document 15"].

At Seton and Tranent respectively, the nineteenth of June 1591.

Which day, in presence of myself, the notary public, and the witnesses whose names are written below, appeared the right noble and potent lord, Robert Lord Seton. He proceeded into the presence of Janet Stratton, at that time imprisoned in the dungeon at Seton for the crime of sorcery allegedly committed by her, and earnestly asked her to tell him everything she knew about the Earl of Bothwell, and if she understood him to have consulted with witches or practised witchcraft himself, and particularly if he had ever dealt with her or anyone else in such matters. She answered the noble lord as follows, "As I shall answer to God, I never knew Earl Bothwell to be anything but a noble man." To her knowledge, he never had any kind of dealings with her or anyone else to harm anyone. She never saw him face to face, nor did she know him apart from any other man, except that she had heard it said that he was a noble man. This I testify to be the truth. Signed with my hand, the foresaid day year and place, in the presence of the noble lord Robert Lord Seton, Thomas Seton of Northrig, and George Seton his son.

This same deposition was given in the presence of David Seton in Tranent the same day, by Donald [   ], Highland man, who also was detained captive for sorcery.

Alexander Cook notarius ad premissa requisitus.

Bothwell escaped from Edinburgh Castle two days later, and was not finally put on trial for witchcraft until August 1593.

Effie MacCalyean's family attempt to clear her name.

On 4th July 1591 Donald Robeson, still imprisoned in Tranent, was visited by David Ogilvy, Effie MacCalyean's son-in-law, who had been one of her prolocutors [spokesmen for the defence] at her trial, and a statement was taken from Donald before two notaries public. Similarly, a statement was taken at Seton the same day from Janet Stratton. Both now claim to have known absolutely nothing about the whole "North Berwick" saga. It is certainly quite possible that all their previous revelations may have been fed to them by "the Authorities" accompanied by torture or the threat of torture. On the other hand, tucked away in Seton and Tranent, they could be threatened or ill-treated at will by Lord Seton and his baron baillie, and it is perfectly possible that their sudden change of tack could have been "suggested" to them.

Janet Stratton's statement to David Ogilvy at Seton is JC26/2/8 in the National Archives of Scotland [Normand and Roberts "Document 17"]. In modern English it reads as follows:-

At the palace of Seton, 4th July 1591 in the 20th year of the reign of our sovereign lord the king.

This day in the presence of ourselves, notaries public, and the witnesses named below, an honourable man David Ogilvy, lawful son of Lord Ogilvy, personally visited Janet Stratton in prison at Lord Seton's palace and required her to tell what she knew of the late Euphane MacCalyean, wife of Patrick MacCalyean, concerning any kind of witchcraft. She made a particular and general declaration of her knowledge of this. That declaration was as follows:

Firstly Janet Stratton was asked by Mr David when and where she knew the late Euphame MacCalyean, wife of Patrick MacCalyean. Janet declared that as she should answer to God she never knew Euphame MacCalyean until she met her in the presence of the King.

Mr David further inquired of Janet if she had been at the great convention of witches at North Berwick church, and if she knew Euphame there; or if she saw Euphame at Acheson's Haven, Broomhills, or any other place or time where they asked for an image of the King. She answered declaring that as she should answer to God she was never in these places, or at any convention, or at any place where there was any witchcraft. She never saw the late Euphame there, never knew her to make any use of any kind of witchcraft, and knew nothing of the image of the King. She also declared that whatever she had said about Euphame was out of fear for her life, and fear of torture, and by compulsion. She declared that whatever she had said before about Euphame concerning witchcraft was false and invented, as she should answer to God. At the same time Janet declared that she had unconditionaly denied before Euphame's death absolutely everything she had said about her concerning witchcraft

After this formal request and statement made by these persons as specified above, Mr David asked us, the notaries public, for a written record. This was done at the gate of Lord Seton's prison house on the wall of his Lordship's palace where Janet was at that time, about three o'clock in the afternoon before these witnesses.

Sir John Seton of Barnes, knight, Mr Walter Ogilvy,

Steven Bannatyne, schoolmaster to Lord Seton's children,

Mr John Pap, servant to John Seton,

Patrick [   ], servant to Patrick MacCalyean.

Signed:

Robert Gardner, notary public,

Stephen Bannatyne, notary public.

A similar statement had been taken from Donald Robeson at nine o'clock in the morning. It is JC26/2/23 in the National Archives of Scotland [Normand and Roberts "Document 16"]. In substance it is word for word the same as Janet's, and is in the same handwriting. The differences are that Donald is "in the house and keeping of David Seton, elder, in Tranent". The formal record was made "in the dwelling house of the said David Seton elder, on the east side of the town of Tranent", and the witnesses were:

David Seton elder [*i.e.* senior],
George Weddell,
Alexander Bell,
John Adamson, collier,
Ninian Weir,
Robert Gardiner, notary public,
Steven Bannatyne, ditto .

These efforts by her relatives to clear Euphane MacCalyean's name may not have been entirely altruistic. Effie was not only a convicted witch but a convicted traitor, and her entire estate was thus forfeit to the Crown. Her family may be engaged here in an attempt to salvage their inheritance.

Did Stratton and Robeson survive?

Interestingly enough, in 1595 a Fala woman was tried and acquitted of murder by magic. [Pitcairn Vol 1 pt2, p397-9]. She was accused of having enlisted the help of a "notorious witch" Janet Straton, then resident in Lauderdale. It would be an odd coincidence to have two notorious witches of the same name, so it looks rather as if Lord Seton may have eventually released Janet, perhaps as a reward for saying the right thing at the right time. As Peter Maxwell-Stuart says, "If this were so, it would be a remarkable indication that not everyone concerned in the treason plot was executed, not even someone who had played a major part in its magical operations." [Maxwell-Stuart 2001: p.196]. The same of course could be said of Barbara Napier's apparent escape from the stake.

If Janet Stratton survived, perhaps Donald Robeson also was allowed to live, but as far as I am aware his fate is unknown. If David Seton did release him, perhaps as a "Highland man", he would see his safest course of action in quietly disappearing back to the Gaidhealtachd.

Geilles Duncan changes her tune.

One of the last victims of the East Lothian magical treason plot was Gellie Duncan, with whose arrest, according to *Newes from Scotland*, the whole business began.

Document JC26/2/20 in the National Archives of Scotland [Normand and Roberts "Document 18"] is a record of statements given by Geilles Duncan and Bessie Thomson immediately before their execution on the Castle Hill of Edinburgh on 4th December 1591. This appears to be a further attempt to clear the names of Barbara Napier and Euphane MacCalyean. In modern English it reads as follows:-

At Edinburgh, 4th December 1591, in the 25th year of the reign of our Sovereign Lord. This day, in the presence of ourselves, notaries public, and the witnesses whose names are written below, appeared Patrick MacCalyean, Mr David Ogilvy his son-in-law, and Archibald Douglas, brother to Robert Douglas of Carschogil. They then went to where Geillis Duncan and Bessie Thomson were standing waiting to be executed on the Castle Hill of Edinburgh for certain crimes of witchcraft.

There, after they had been untied, they were asked by John Cairns, reader in Edinburgh, to acknowledge and confess their sins in the presence of the people gathered there, and to speak the truth. When they had cried out their confession before God and in presence of the people for the relief of their souls and consciences, they were asked with heartfelt urgency by Patrick, Mr David, and Archibald if they had ever known the late Euphame

MacCalyean and Barbara Napier to be witches or ever to have used any sorcery or witchcraft at any time or in any place in this kingdom, particularly in North Berwick church or Broomhill against any person or persons, and particularly against the most noble person of his Majesty the King. To this it was answered and declared first by Geilles Duncan, that as far as she was concerned, as she should answer on her soul and conscience before God, she never knew Barbara or Euphane to be witches or use any sort of sorcery or witchcraft in any of these places or anywhere else, against the King or any other person or persons. Neither did she know of any vice or crime committed by either of them at any time in the past. When she was asked why she had previously made such slanderous allegations, she answered that she was forced and persuaded to do so by the two David Setons in Tranent, and by others, and that it was all just lies, for which she craved God's forgiveness.

In the same way, Bessie Thomson, when asked by the same people about her knowledge in the matter, answered and made a declaration the same as that made by Geillis. Whereupon Patrick MacCalyean, Mr David Ogilvy, and Archibald Douglas asked for one or more written records from ourselves the undersigned notaries public. This was done about three o'clock in the afternoon on the date and at the place already given before the following witnesses:

James Nicholl and Thomas Fisher, baillies of the burgh of Edinburgh,

John Cairns and James Henryson, gravediggers there,

William Shaw, master of work to the King,

John Clerk, Robert Forrester, Alexander Henryson, Mingis Baker, servants to the burgh,

John Leirmont, messenger there,

George Bisset, scribe,

and many others.

Signed: Adam Schaw, notary public. James Justice, notary public.

It is surely significant that Geillis Duncan and Bessie Thomson apparently made no attempt to deny their own sins, but vehemently insisted that MacCalyean and Napier had not been involved, and that the accusations against them were "all just lies". Standing minutes from death, with the fuel for the fire which was to consume their corpses waiting ready before their eyes, would they have lied about this? It looks very much as if Geillis and Bessie considered themselves guilty at least to some extent, but believed Barbara Napier and Euphane MacCalyean had been deliberately framed.

The Earl of Bothwell.

It would not be fitting to leave the North Berwick conspiracy without a word or two about the Earl of Bothwell, whose trial and acquittal in August 1593 on charges of witchcraft was the final postscript to the whole sorry business.

Francis Stuart, Earl of Bothwell, was of royal blood on his father's side. His father, Lord John Stuart, was the illegitimate son of James V, King of Scots, and Katherine Carmichael. On his mother's side his connections with East Lothian were long and widespread. His mother was Lady Jean Hepburn, the sister of James Hepburn, 4th Earl of Bothwell who was third husband of Mary, Queen of Scots. They were descended from the ancient East Lothian family of Hepburn of Hailes. In 1480 the head of that family had been created Lord Hailes. Soon afterwards Crichton in Midlothian was added to the family's possessions, and also the Earldom of Bothwell near Glasgow. In 1491 the 1st Earl of Bothwell was given the Lordship of Liddesdale with the use of the royal castle of Hermitage. By the time the 4th Earl married Queen Mary the Hepburns had amassed further estates in Kirkcudbright, Dumfries, North Berwick, Lanark, Selkirk, and Berwickshire, and had become one of the most powerful families in Scotland.

Francis, son of Lord John Stuart and Jean Hepburn, was born in 1563, and lost his father at the age of 13. Francis's uncle, James Hepburn, 4th Earl of Bothwell, had abandoned his wife Queen Mary at the confrontation of Carberry Hill in 1567, fled to Orkney and on to Norway, and was eventually imprisoned in Denmark. He was presumed dead in 1576, and young Francis was formally recognised as 5th Earl of Bothwell by his even younger cousin James VI. As well as his uncle's title and lands, Francis inherited the offices of Sheriff of Edinburgh, Haddington, and Berwickshire, and High Admiral of Scotland. At a very early age he married Margaret Douglas, daughter of the Earl of Angus.

Thus on his mother's side Francis, Earl of Bothwell, was descended from the Hepburns of Hailes, and related to an extensive tribe of lesser Hepburn lairds and tenants in East Lothian. On his father's side he was descended from the Royal House of Stewart [albeit on the wrong side of the blanket], and was cousin to the King.

Francis seems to have been the very epitome of the handsome dashing young blade, displaying all the attributes most highly regarded in a young nobleman. By contrast his younger cousin James was scholarly, timid, and unimpressive in appearance. Possibly Francis nurtured resentment that James was king, and he, possessing all the qualifications except an ancestral marriage certificate, was not. He was certainly a fiercely ambitious young man, and headstrong to the point of instability. It may be significant that his mother's brother, Queen Mary's Bothwell, died in prison hopelessly insane.

The highlights of Francis's various escapades may be briefly summarised as follows. In April 1589 there was an unsuccessful rising of Catholic earls in the north against the King. Bothwell, although a Protestant, led a parallel rebellion in the Borders. In May Bothwell was declared a traitor. Sentence was suspended, but he had to make public repentance for his misdeeds, in St Giles church in Edinburgh in November of the same year. With all seemingly forgiven, Bothwell was appointed a prominent member of the regency council which ran Scotland while James VI was in Scandinavia attending to his marriage. In September 1590 he was appointed Lord Lieutenant of the Border.

In November and December 1590 the King was much taken up with investigating the newly discovered witchcraft plot against him. The interrogations and executions continued into 1591, with Bothwell now being named as the instigator of the whole conspiracy. In the middle of April Bothwell was brought before the King and Council and charged with consulting Agnes Sampson and the warlock Richard Graham with treasonable intent.

In a letter dated 15th April 1591 [CSP Vol X, p.501] the English ambassador Robert Bowes describes how Ritchie Graham claimed that an Italian necromancer had prophesied to Bothwell that he would achieve great things but would eventually lose his life at the King's hands. Since much of the prophecy had come true, Bothwell was now anxious to avoid his predicted fate - thus the enchantment of a wax image of the King and other magical activities. Gelly Duncan and other witches had at first confirmed Bothwell's involvement but later denied it. [Bowes also mentions here that both Ritchie Graham and Gelly Duncan had accused him of involvement, but since at one of the crucial times someone completely different had been England's ambassador, the accusations were dismissed.] Ritchie Graham is now described by Bowes as "the pryncipall of the witches heere", and it would seem that he is the main source of the accusations against Bothwell, and not the East Lothian witches or the two Edinburgh "gentlewomen".

In a letter of 17th April [ibid p.508] Bowes says that both Bothwell and Graham have been brought before the King, and Ritchie Graham had persisted in his allegations.

Bothwell was imprisoned in Edinburgh Castle, and the King attempted to convene a meeting of Bothwell's peers to put him on trial. However, so many sent their excuses that the plan had to be abandoned. In the early hours of the morning of 21st June Bothwell escaped from the Castle. He was proclaimed traitor and outlaw and active preparations began for hunting him down. Still at large at the end of December, Bothwell made an unsuccessful attempt to raid Holyroodhouse and seize the King. In June 1592 Parliament formally ratified the forfeiture of Bothwell's lands and possessions. At the end of the same month he made another unsuccessful attempt to capture the King, this time from Falkland Palace in Fife.

In the early hours of the morning of 24th July 1593 Bothwell succeeded in entering Holyroodhouse and confronted the King who was in his nightgown "with his breeks in his hand". Bothwell and his allies engineered a coup which allowed him to dominate the King and virtually govern the country for several weeks. Bothwell now felt himself strong enough to face down his own trial for witchcraft by an assise of lords and barons. He was acquitted unanimously.

With Bothwell's trial we come to the culmination of the whole "North Berwick" saga. He, after all, was suspected of being the main mover, and in the case for the prosecution we should find a record of events in their final official version. Frustratingly, as Pitcairn says, "Another unfortunate hiatus in the records of the High Court of Justiciary takes place at this period; the Books of Adjournal from October 1591 to May 18th 1596 having been lost."

However, although the official records of the trial have disappeared, the "Calendar of Border Papers" [Vol 1, p.486] contains a letter from Carey to Burghley dated 12th August 1593 giving what would appear to be a reliable account of proceedings. Rendered in modern English [and summarised in places] it goes as follows:-

I have delayed writing so that I could report on the Earl of Bothwell's trial which began last Friday, the tenth of August at one o' clock in the afternoon, and continued until ten at night. He was acquitted by his peers of the acts of witchcraft he was accused of. I am here giving Your Lordship an account of this, word for word as I received it from Scotland, along with the names of the noblemen on the jury.

Bothwell's indictment was read in court. David McGill the King's Advocate delivered certain depositions by Richard Greyme which had formed the basis of the indictment. The substance of the depositions was as follows:

Bothwell used his servant Renian [*recte* Ninian] Chirnside to arrange more than thirty meetings between Bothwell and Greyme.

The main points alleged by Greyme were that Bothwell said to him that he had been told in Italy that the King would favour him well, but that all the same he would lose the King's friendship and that his life would be in danger from the King. He had asked Greyme's help to prevent this. Greyme says he consulted with other witches and they decided to send Bothwell a poison made of adder skins, toad skins, and the "hipomanes" from the forehead of a young foal. [*Hippomanes*: an ancient philtre obtained from a mare or foal. Greek hippo: horse and manes: madness. - Chambers Dictionary] This was to be mixed together and left where the King would come so that it would drop on his head. It would be a poison of such strength that it would immediately prove fatal.

Also, a wax image was to be made mixed with other things which would degenerate and melt away in time, causing the King to waste away as it did.

Also, he should be enchanted to remain in Denmark and not return to Scotland.

Bothwell's lawyers were John Russell, John

Preston, and Thomas Craig. They said Greyme's depositions were contradictory. What he said in one interrogation he denied in another. They argued that Greyme could not be both witness and accuser, since he was a man excommunicated from the church and professing witchcraft. He should be accounted an "infidel", and therefore had no legal right to accuse anyone, far less a peer of the realm.

Bothwell's speech.

A friend had asked him to let Greyme, an excommunicated person, live within his bounds to save him trouble. This friend and Greyme asked Bothwell to try and get the king's protection for him. Bothwell agreed, but did nothing. When the Earl of Angus was ill his wife asked Bothwell to send Greyme to her husband, and he got his servant Chirnside to take Greyme to Angus. Bothwell had been present when Greyme arrived. Soon after this Bothwell met Greyme by chance in Kelso.

A long time after that Angus was again ill, and his wife again asked Bothwell to send Greyme, and again he sent him along with Chirnside. Once again he was present when Greyme arrived and talked with him. Angus died.

Bothwell met Greyme again at the Chancellor [Maitland]'s house. As they were out riding Greyme showed him and the Chancellor a stick with nicks in it wrapped about with long human hair, and said it was an enchanted stick. Bothwell paid little attention to this.

Bothwell affirmed that these were the only times he ever saw Greyme, although Greyme's depositions and the indictment claimed that Chirnside brought Greyme to John Provan's house in Edinburgh, and that Bothwell met him at a shepherd's house within two miles of his own house at Crichton - all of which was untrue.

The King's Advocate then brought up the confessions of several other witches, Greyme's confederates, who were burned at Edinburgh, such as Agnes Sampson, Effam Mackenell [i.e. MacCalycan], Barbara Naper, another two who were burned, and another two who were set free. Although they had often been questioned, they always said that they knew nothing of Bothwell, except that he was a noble man. Nor had they had any conference with him as Greyme alleged. Also, Greyme had never accused Bothwell until he got a warrant from the Council saying that if he told simply and truly what he knew, his life would be preserved; he would live in Stirling Castle where he need fear no-one's ill-will, and he would receive a good allowance. After this, all his depositions had mentioned Bothwell.

Bothwell's counsel then made the point that Greyme had been offered his life if he spoke the truth. In taking away his life they had therefore proved his accusations to be untrue.

Several honest men from Edinburgh claimed Greyme had said to them that he would either have to accuse the Earl of Bothwell or else undergo torture such as no-one could endure. His own brother claimed that Greyme had said to him many times that he was forced to accuse Bothwell for fear of maiming with the boots and other tortures.

Bothwell then made another speech to the court, saying that the King had been set against him firstly by the Chancellor [who had plotted the death of the King's father, had a hand in his mother's death, and had been involved in all sorts of conspiracies]; also by Sir John Carmichael who was in the pay of the Queen of England, and opposed to Bothwell because Bothwell had meted out justice to the English "Officers of the Borders", and Carmichael was afraid he'd lose the Queen of England's favour; also by Sir George Hume because Bothwell had killed his brother.

The jury consisted of
The Earl of Atholl
The Earl of Montrose
Lord Leviston

Lord Seton
The Laird of Bas
The Laird of Cawdewell
Laird Blowhen [Blairquhan?]
Laird Roslen
Lord Furbos
Lord Sinclair
The Master of Gray
Laird Combulton [Congalton?]
Laird Hermaston
Laird Colston
Laird Markeston
Laird Redhaule.

They found the Earl not guilty of the charges.

Bothwell had in fact been acquitted unanimously. Thus, not only do the revelations of the treason by witchcraft conspiracy end in something of an anticlimax, but the verdict must cast doubt on at least some of what had gone before.

Although Bothwell's acquittal was undoubtedly a triumph for himself and his friends and allies, the King was able to consolidate his own support over the ensuing months, and eventually gain the upper hand. Bothwell once again aligned himself with the rebel Catholic Lords in the north. When they had been worn down and banished, Bothwell had no remaining allies or supporters, and was also forced into exile in April 1595, and finally deprived of his estates. He died in Florence in 1624.

Accounts by two contemporaries.

The historian David Calderwood has already been mentioned in connection with Euphane MacCalyean. His family was from Dalkeith where he was born in 1575. He attended Edinburgh University and is likely to have been a student there while the witchcraft trials were going on. [Students went to university at a much earlier age then than nowadays.] He became minister of Crailing, and suffered imprisonment then exile for his religious beliefs. The first manuscript of his "History of the Kirk of Scotland" dates from before 1627. Around 1641 he was appointed minister of Pencaitland and died in 1650. He deals with the "North Berwick" affair in some detail. The following quotations are from "The history of the Kirk of Scotland", Vol. V. [Wodrow Society, Edinburgh, 1849]. Spelling has been modernised.

In the months of November and December [1591], many witches were taken: Richard Graham, John Sibbet alias Cunninghame, Annie Sampson midwife, Jonet Duncan in Edinburgh, Ewfame Makcalzeane daughter to umquhile Mr Thomas Makalzean, Barbara Naper spouse to Archibald Douglas of Pargill, Jonet Drummond a Highland wife, Katherine Wallace. They conspired the overthrow of the Queen's fleet at their return out of Demark by raising of storms upon the seas. Sundry of the witches confessed they had sundry times company with the Devil at the kirk of North Berwick where he appeared to them in the likeness of a man with a red cap and a rump at his tail, and made a harangue in manner of a sermon to them; his text, "Many go to the market but all buy not." He found fault with sundry that they had not done their part in ill. These that had been busy in their craft, he said were his beloved and promised they should want nothing they needed. Playing to them on a trump he said, "Cummer, go ye before; cummer go ye!" and so they danced. When they had done, he caused everyone to the number of three score, kiss his buttocks. Johne Gordoun, alias called Graymeale, stood behind the door to eschew, yet it behoved him also to kiss at last. John Feane, schoolmaster of Saltpreston confessed he was clerk to their assemblies, yet at his execution he confessed only he had abused the people that way, and had committed adultery with two and thirty women, but denied witchcraft. Of Richard

Grahame, Ewphame Makcalzean, and Barbara Naper, we will hear more hereafter. [Calderwood, Vol. V, p. 115]

Upon Saturday the 8th of May, Barbara Naper, sister to Willian Naper of Wright's Houses, was convicted by an assise for art part and consulting with witches. The next Tuesday she was condemned to be wirried till she was dead, and thereafter to be burnt. When the stake was set in the Castle Hill, with barrels, coals, heather, and powder, and the people were looking for a present execution, her friends alleged she was with child, wherupon the execution was delayed till that alledgance was tried. In the mean time, those that were upon her assise were summoned to underlie the law upon Monday the seventh of June for willful error in "cleanging" [acquitting] her in treason agaihist the King's person. The jurymen came in the King's will. Upon Monday the 9th of June, Euphame Makcalzean was accused of witchcraft and practice to take away the King's life. The procurators pleaded so subtly for her that the assise could not be resolved before the 13th of June. She was wirried and burnt to ashes upon the 25th of June. She took it on her conscience that she was innocent of all the crimes laid to her charge. [Calderwood: Vol V, p.128]

Some other witches were also wirried and burnt about this time, as Donald the Man, the gleyed Highland witch etc. Barbara Naper was convicted only of consulting with Richard Graham and Agnes Sampson. That she connsulted for the death of the King or the Earl of Angus she denied. In respect of the Act of Parliament against naked consultations was not put in execution it was thought hard to execute her. [ibid P. 129]

[Calderwood would seem to be saying that Barbara was not executed because the law prescribing death for simple consultation was never put into practice.]

John Spottiswood was born in 1565, and would thus be well able to remember the witchcraft trials of the early 1590s. He became minister of Calder, and then around 1603 was appointed Archbishop of Glasgow. His "history of the Church of Scotland" was published in 1655. His third and final manuscript copy is thought to date from some time between 1625 and the commencement of the religious troubles in the late 1630s. His earlier manuscripts must obviously predate the final version. Spottiswood's "history" was reprinted in 1851 in Edinburgh with a biographical sketch and notes by the Right Rev. M. Russell. In Volume One, page 411, Spottiswood writes as follows:-

Most of this winter [1590-91] was spent in the discovery and examination of witches and sorcerers. Amongst these, Agnes Samson [commonly called the wise wife of Keith] was most remarkable; a woman not of the base and ignorant sort of witches, but matron like grave and settled in her answers which were all to some purpose. In her examination she declared that she had a familiar spirit who upon her call did appear in a visible form and resolve her of any doubtful matter, especially concerning the life or death of persons lying sick. And being asked what words she used when she called the spirit, she said her word was, "Holla, master," and that he had learned her to do so. She further confessed that the Earl Bothwell had moved her to inquire what should become of the King, how long he should reign, and what should happen after his death; and that the spirit having undertaken to make away the King, after he had failed in performing and was challenged by her, confessed it was not in his power, speaking words she understood not, but as she did take them the words were, "Il est homme de Dieu." Richard Graham, another notorious sorcerer, being apprehended at the same time made the like confession of Bothwell, which was the cause of his committing in April following, [*i.e.*

the reason for Bothwell being put on trial the following April.]

The entire "North Berwick" saga is a complicated and confusing story. It may be worth while therefore to finish this section with a brief summary of the progression of events.

In November 1590 Geillis Duncan is arrested in Tranent, and confesses witchcraft. Many others are subsequently implicated, including Agnes Sampson "the Wise Wife of Keith" who had already been investigated for witchcraft, and John Cunningham nicknamed "Fian", the young schoolmaster of Prestonpans. King James VI takes a personal interest in the interrogation of the suspects. A tale unfolds of a large convention of witches at North Berwick where the Devil was present, and of plots to raise winds by magic to delay or prevent the King's return from Scandinavia after his wedding.

Cunningham and Sampson are executed in January 1591 and attention becomes focused on two "gentlewomen", Barbara Napier and Euphane MacCalyean, and on a plot hatched at North Berwick and Acheson's Haven to kill the King by roasting a wax image, and through a magic concoction containing drips from a roasting toad. MacCalyean is sentenced to be burned alive for her crimes, which she denies to the end. [She may have been executed more humanely, however, and Napier may have escaped punishment altogether.]

As the tale unfolds increasing emphasis is placed on the involvement of the King's cousin, Francis, Earl of Bothwell, who is supposed to have initiated and financed the plot against the King. He finally stands trial in 1593, but is acquitted.

Large numbers of other supposed witches are arrested and investigated in connection with the affair. As well as Cunningham, Sampson, Napier, and MacCalyean, eight others are burned in Haddington in February 1591, Robert Grierson from Prestonpans dies in custody, and Geillis Duncan and Bessie Thomson are burned in Edinburgh in December of the same year. Magical plots against numerous other people are uncovered; ships had been sunk, and many people had been made to fall sick or die. A great many attempts to cure sickness by charming come to light, and much in the way of divination, raising of spirits, and meetings with the Devil. Some of these activities date back many years into the 1580s or even earlier.

We shall return to the "North Berwick" witches in the final chapter, in an attempt to decide if it is possible four centuries after the events to come to any sort of conclusion about "What was really going on?"

2. Kirk Session Records.

Church business in each parish was run by a committee, the Kirk Session, consisting of the minister and elders. The elders were chosen from amongst those parishioners deemed to be solid respectable citizens of blameless life. Session meetings were chaired by the minister in his capacity as "moderator", but he by no means always had his own way.

The Kirk Session was not just a management committee, however. It was also an ecclesiastical court with powers to impose sanctions. The Session was empowered to deal with cases of fornication, slander, drunkenness, profanity, Sabbath-breaking, and minor offences against public order such as "scolding", "flyting", and less serious assaults. Sessions were also required to deal with "charming" - attempts to cure or ward off sickness and disease by performing superstitious rituals or actions. Punishments ranged from a mild private rebuke before the Session, through various degrees of public humiliation before the congregation, to the ultimate horror of excommunication. Fines were also levied on occasion. It was more prudent, for example, to fine an aristocratic fornicator than to attempt to force him into public repentance before the congregation. Any ordinary person wishing to move from one parish to take up residence in another was supposed to obtain and produce a "testificate", a certificate of good behaviour. Thus, anyone failing to satisfy church discipline would find escape very difficult, and excommunicates were virtually non-persons who in theory had no right to live anywhere.

It is a commonly held notion that witches in Scotland were usually harmless old women convicted by kangaroo courts consisting of the local minister and his elders, who consigned their victims to the flames with relish and without hesitation. The reality was in fact rather different.

Kirk Sessions were absolutely *not* empowered to try cases of witchcraft, which like murder, treason, and other serious crimes, was far beyond the competence of a mere church court. Admittedly, there was sometimes a very fine line between charming and witchcraft, but since witchcraft involved *malefice* [deliberately evil actions or intentions] and making a formal commitment to serve the Devil, it was usually apparent what amounted to witchcraft and what was only charming.

Where witchcraft arises in the course of Kirk Session business is when someone complains to the Session that he or she has been called "Witch", or has been publicly [but informally] accused of practising witchcraft. These are cases of slander, which the Session is competent to deal with. Also, sometimes when cases of "charming" come before the Session it will be found that matters are more serious than was at first believed, and that actual witchcraft seems likely. If this is the case, the matter is then referred out of the Church's hands to the "Civil Magistrate". Similarly, if when investigating a complaint of slander it is found that the description "Witch" is indeed well-founded, the case is passed to the Civil Magistrate.

In the case of Royal Burghs like Haddington, North Berwick, and Dunbar, or "regalities" like Musselburgh, the civil magistrates are the Baillies appointed by the town council. Everywhere else the civil magistrate is the local landowner, who more often than not delegated such duties to his representative and depute, the Baron-baillie. The civil magistrate could order the detention of the witchcraft suspect to allow "examination" to take place, and it was common for the minister to be involved in working with the suspect in an attempt to "bring her to a confession". Some confusion may have arisen here in modern minds, because in the idiom of the day, interrogation is often referred to as "trying" the suspect; but this of course is not what is meant by a "trial" or "trying" in 21st Century English. It is commonly assumed nowadays that suspects were subjected to torture as a matter of course to force confessions, but in fact throughout the 17th Century torture in witchcraft cases could not be used without the express permission of the Privy Council. Indeed, many witchcraft "dittays" take pains to make it clear that confessions were "freely given". It is more than likely however that ill-treatment of suspects was common, amounting to torture to all intents and purposes in many cases, particularly when a "pricker" was called in to search for the Devil's mark. Burgh tolbooths and baronial "pits" were hardly likely to be luxuriously appointed. Elsewhere, barns, church towers, and cellars were utilised as temporary prisons. Heating and hygiene were probably not the first priority in any of these places, and feeding is likely to have been more basic than bountiful. Sleep deprivation seems to have been often used to persuade suspects to confess, but perhaps not as often as is assumed. Certainly, relays of trustworthy people, often church elders, were frequently used to guard suspects day and night, but it must not be taken for granted that "wauking" or "waking" the suspected witch necessarily meant keeping her awake. The word is cognate with the Dutch "waken" and the German "wachten", and simply means "to watch". After all, none of the places of imprisonment mentioned, even burgh tolbooths, were reliably secure places. We should perhaps remember that the old song "The Waukin o' the Fauld" refers merely to guarding the sheepfold, not keeping the sheep awake! Only when a confession had been obtained, or enough incriminating evidence gathered, could the prisoner on remand stand trial. He or she could be tried by the High Court of Justiciary in Edinburgh, or when the High Court went out on circuit. Alternatively, a commission could be sought from the Privy Council, or less frequently from Parliament, to hold a court locally to try the suspect. In all cases the verdict was decided by an "assise" or jury, and the accused was entitled to "prolocutors", or spokesmen for the defence, who might or might not be lawyers, and were indeed on occasion eminent legal luminaries.

Witches could *not* be tried and convicted by baron courts, burgh courts, sheriff courts, or church courts. Attempts to do any such thing would be illegal, and those involved would themselves be answerable to the law. It is of course not beyond the bounds of possibility that witches were sometimes processed by illegal courts, but I have found no record of this happening in East Lothian. Similarly, spontaneous lynchings may have occurred from time to time, but as far as I am aware there is no record of any such thing in East Lothian. Thus in the minutes of the Kirk Sessions of East Lothian we will emphatically *not* find records of ministers and elders trying and sentencing witches, but we will find witchcraft rearing its head in cases of slander and charming; we will find ministers being asked to assist with interrogations; elders being recruited to guard suspects; and appeals for information and evidence being made from the pulpit.

The records of each Kirk Session meeting were written up by the Session Clerk, who was often the parish schoolmaster, but if not, was at least someone literate and reasonably intelligent. Human nature being what it is, some clerks took more pleasure in their duties than others, and so some records are much fuller and vastly more interesting than others. Since there are virtually no records surviving from the 16th Century, and since witchcraft cases had more or less petered out by 1700, the Kirk Session minutes considered here are, with very few exceptions, records from the 17th Century. Not surprisingly, the survival of 17th Century East Lothian session books is far from complete. For some parishes a great deal of material is still extant, for others little has survived, and for some there is nothing. However, there is more than enough available to enable us to form a vivid impression of how ordinary folk in the 17th Century regarded witchcraft, and how the kirk dealt with the problems it generated. The revelations are sometimes surprising.

I shall deal with each of the parishes of East Lothian in turn, in alphabetical order. The session clerks wrote in what they no doubt considered to be English. It is, however, an English full of Scots words and idioms. In addition, many words and phrases which appear familiar may in fact have had very different meanings in the 17th Century. Spelling and punctuation, although they followed the rules and conventions of the day, can often appear bizarre to the modern eye. I shall therefore give the quotations from the Kirk Session minutes in modern English, and summarise some of the repetitious and less interesting material. Those who wish to read the entries in the original idiom can find them all in the National Archives of Scotland.

Aberlady.

The Aberlady Kirk Session Minutes are designated CH2/4 in the National Archives of Scotland. Records survive for 1632 - 45 and 1697 -1712.

1632

2nd February: ffrancis Elphingstone appeared this day...[damage here]... He and his wife have been resident in our parish for three years and have not obtained a testimonial. The Session ordered him to bring a testimonial from Tranent, from which parish he last came, his wife being suspected of witchcraft, and orders him to appear on the Sabbath day.

9th February: ffrancis Elphingstone appeared and produced the testimonial from Tranent for him and his wife, signed by John Hastings, clerk to the session there. Robert Dowglas is ordered to appear between now and Easter for slandering his [*i.e.* Elphingstone's] wife of witchcraft, as soon as he is able to travel, he being infirm of body due to illness.

30th March: On this day, being called, Robert Dowglas appeared. The said Robert most vilely broadcast slander about Elspeth Meik, accusing her of witchcraft, and said that she had taken his health from him. Because of this, he in his ignorance and because of the seriousness of his disease, forsook his Creator and knelt down before her and asked his health from her three times in God's name, if she had the power to restore his health in her hands, thus abusing the sacred name of the Lord. The Session thus orders him to be called before the congregation on the Sabbath day to give a sign of repentance for his offence, firstly for slandering Elspeth of witchcraft, and secondly for forsaking his God and going to the Devil to seek his health. He is therefore to kneel before Elspeth Meik and ask forgiveness for the offence caused to her, and that he should be reconciled to her and her husband.

1638

19th August: This day, appeared George Gulan for blaspheming by calling Patrick Chrystisone's children "witch's gets" [*i.e.* brats, bastards], which George admitted and confessed... [Becomes illegible here.]

1640

6th September: This day a paper was given in by Marioun Taillyur in Gosford complaining about David Baxter there who is supposed to have called her a witch. The Session therefore orders her to hand over a dollar in pledge that she will produce her accusation [to the Session], or find security in some other way. Alexander Rae became "cautioner" [guarantor]. David is ordered to appear next Sunday, and the evidence is to be produced for examination.

13th September: This day Marion Taillyor was called and appeared complaining about David Baxter. David also appeared for calling Marioun a witch. She then produced her proof, namely James Blaikie, gardener, and William Johnstoun, carter. Being sworn and admitted, they confirmed that David called her a witch. Being convicted, the Session orders him to appear next Sunday in the presence of the whole congregation, and there to acknowledge the offence done to Marioun Taillyour, and to beg her forgiveness for that scandal.

Undated, but obviously shortly after the above: On this day the Session orders Marione Taillyeor to appear before it by next Sunday to submit to authority for her wicked and unchristian words in our church, in not forgiving David Baxter who called her "witch", when David had done everything the Session had ordered him to do.

27th September [some parts illegible]: Marioun appeared... she said in great fury in a devlish temper, in the presence of the whole congregation, "Lord, let never God forgive him!" with many other wicked words... She is to appear in the presence of the whole parish next Sunday, and publicly acknowledge her offence.

4th October [parts illegible]: Marione appeared... She acknowledged her offence and begged God's and the people's forgiveness, and forgave David.

1644

1st September: On this day a bill of complaint was given in by John Frissell, complaining about Johne Waldie. This Johne was going to Edinburgh on Friday to the market there with George Vert and John Ewane before daylight, and said in his own house in front of several reliable witnesses that he saw and heard Catherein Arnot, John Frissell's wife, with others on the Bogle Hill and that she must therefore be a witch. John Frissell is therefore ordered to present his proofs at the next meeting, under the penalty [of forfeiting] one dollar which he has found as security. If he does not present his proofs his dollar is to be confiscated, and disposed of as the Session pleases.

8th September: This day John Frissell was called, but did not appear to prove his bill of complaint against Johne Waldie. His dollar is therefore confiscated.

1706

17th February: Henry Donaldson, miller in Reedhouse, complains about Katherine Allan, the wife of Alexander Reed in Reedhouse, slandering him by calling him a warlock. Moreover, Katherine said to Henry, "Rascal, where are you going? Home to that witch your wife?" Again, when Henry was coming out of the cherry orchard of Reedhouse, Katherine met him and said, "Mansworn knave! Ye said that ye should have amends of me at the Session, but I defy you and Mr Glass [the minister] both to cause me compear before the Session. Kiss ye Mr Glass his arse, and let him scratch your elbow!"

17th March [in the course of investigating the above]: Margaret Provan heard Katherine Allan say, "Hold your tongue you warlock dog. Go home to the witch your wife!", but he avoided her. Mary Bouston heard her call Henry and his wife "warlock and wizard or witch" in her house about four months and three weeks ago.

Athelstaneford.

There are no 17th Century Kirk Session minutes for Athelstaneford.

Bara

See Garvald, below.

Bolton.

Bolton is designated CH2/37 in the National Archives of Scotland. The index lists Kirk Session minutes for 1640 - 83, and for 1683 - 1745. However, the first is in fact merely an account book, and the second contains no witchcraft references.

Dirleton.

Dirleton is designated CH2/1157 in the National Archives of Scotland. Kirk Session minutes remain for 1655-68.

1657

March 10th: Elspeth Darge complained against Jean Nicolsonne and Marion Hendersonne. She complains against Jean for slandering her as a witch, saying her mother was a witch, her grandmother a witch, and she was one. She complains about Marion for the selfsame slanders, and also because she said the witch and the witch's get were "holding a court on her mother", meaning of the [illegible deletion]. These persons are ordered to be summoned to the next meeting.

[Presumably this means that the witch and her brat were meeting together to judge and punish Marion's mother through witchcraft.]

15th March. [The first part of this entry is badly damaged.]: ... for saying that the Devil was Marie Crek's father ... she was reluctant to confess these words voluntarily, but ... her confessions, and so the Session summons her to the next meeting ... saying the Devil's father's sister I have, and ... spoke so, but confessed that she said God ... had a father's sister.

Jean Nicolsonne appeared, and when she was questioned whether she spoke these reproachful and slanderous words about Elspeth Dargue, she denied that she said Elspeth Dargue's grandmother was a witch and her mother a witch, and that all the world would not free her from being a witch.

Elspeth Dargue appeared, and the moderator [*i.e.* the minister] told her that Jean Nicolsoune had denied all that she alleged in her complaint, and asked if she had any witnesses to lead against Jean. She answered that she had these witnesses - Alex [ ], John Nicolsonne Jean's brother, and John Nicolsoune his son, who are all ordered to appear the next day.

Marion Hendersoune appeared, and was asked if she called Elspeth Dargue a witch and her grandmother a witch, and if she said the witch and the witch's get were holding a court on her mother. She denied the words of the complaint, but confessed this much, that she said it was the way of witches to pray [illegible] prayers and to pray for curses against a woman and her children.

Elspeth Darge appeared and being asked if she had any witnesses to uphold her complaint against Marioun Hendersoune she named the following witnesses - Alexander [ ], John Duncan, and Alexander Dune, who are all to be summoned to the next meeting.

Marioun Henderson appeared again, and being asked if she called Margaret Kemp "fairy lady, runt that the Devil rode upon," she denied it altogether.

March 17th

Jean Nicolsonne appeared, and again denied what was laid to her charge, whereupon the witnesses were called in, firstly the John Nicolsons, elder and younger. When Jean was asked if she had any objections to either of these witnesses, one being her brother and the other her brother's son, she said they bore ill-will against her. The session did not sustain this objection. Jean was removed and the moderator asked the John Nicolsons younger and elder to testify on oath what they heard Jean Nicolsonne say about Elspeth Dark, as far as they knew and could remember. Having taken the oath, they promised to do this.

[The next section is badly damaged.] John Nicolson was removed, and his father being sworn ... he had no hatred at all against his sister ... he heard his sister say that Elspeth ... suffer herself to be ripped ... of the mother and ... Johnne Nicolson younger ... Nicolson call Elspeth ... that she doubted not ... herself and hoped for ... appeared ...

Marion was removed and the witnesses were all sworn to tell what was required of them as far as they knew or remembered.

John Duncan was called first, and after the rest were removed, testified on oath that he heard Marioun Hendersone call Elspeth Darg a witch and...[damaged]... witch's get who held a court on her mother.

Alexander Dune testified on oath that he never heard Marion Henderson say that Elizabeth Darg was a witch, and that the witch and the witch's get held a court upon her mother, but only heard Elspeth Darg say that Marion Henderson had called her a witch.

John Duncan was called again to say what he knew about Margaret Kemp's complaint, and testified that to his certain knowledge he heard Marion Henderson call Margaret Kemp "fairy lady, runt that the Devil rode upon".

Alex Dune being called testified that he heard ...the same of Margaret Kemp.

The Session, after removing the witnesses, and reading over and considering their statements, finds that Jean Nicolsonne has slandered Elspeth Darge as a witch, and that Marion Henderson, partly by her own confession and partly by the evidence of one of the witnesses, has slandered Elspeth Darge as a witch. The Session also finds that Marion called Margaret Kemp "fairy lady, runt that the Devil rode on", and unanimously judge that Jean and Marion should be publicly rebuked before the congregation.

Jean Nicolson and Marion Henderson were called in and it was made known to them that by the statements of the witnesses and by Marion's own confession they were both proven guilty of slandering Elspeth Darg with the name of a witch, and especially that Marion was found guilty of calling Margaret Kemp "fairy lady, runt that the Devil rode upon", and that the Session ordered them to make public confession of that before the congregation.

[They were both accordingly publicly rebuked on 29th March.]

1658

March 28th: [Jean Brown is being investigated for verbally abusing her mother.]... Bessie Knox complained about Jean for calling her "witch", and saying that she conceived a bastard child with her husband. Jean was called in and questioned ... She denied that she called Bessie Knox a witch, but she admitted that she said, "God forgive Bessie Knox, for her husband was never well after she threw muck after him." She heard her husband say this before his death. [It is not clear whether the victim is actually Bessie's husband, or perhaps Jean's.]

Dunbar

Dunbar is designated CH2/647 in the National Archives of Scotland. The only surviving kirk session minutes from the 17th Century cover the years 1659-1662. I could find only one reference to witchcraft.

Sunday 25th August 1661: The minister reported that he was at Spot last Monday, and heard George Boyd confronted with a confessing warlock there. Alison Sheall was also confronted. A record of thse accusations was produced today for the clerk. The Session appoints a letter to be written to the Earl of Glencairne to have Alison Sheal apprehended, since she lives within the bounds of Belton; [illegible] to the Earl of Tuedale, with a copy of the record of her confrontation in each letter.

Garvald and Bara

The parishes of Garvald and Bara were united in 1702, although both churches were used until Bara fell into disrepair around 1743 (Martine, 1999, p.69). The fact that kirk session minutes for Bara continue after 1702 suggests that although they were sharing a minister, both parishes continued to have their own kirk sessions, at least for a time.

The parish of Garvald and Bara is designated CH2/167 in the National Archives of Scotland. There are no surviving 17th century minutes from Garvald. Bara minutes covering 1694-1709 seem to contain no witchcraft references.

Gladsmuir.

Gladsmuir did not exist as a parish until 1692, when it was formed from large portions of Haddington and Tranent, and a smaller piece of Aberlady. Penston and Samuelston seem to have been hotbeds of witchcraft in the 16th Century, but were part of Haddington parish at the time. Gladsmuir is designated CH2/169 in the National Archives of Scotland. The first volume of Kirk Session minutes covers the period 1692 -1711.

1693

April 9th: William Dick was called. He appeared and denied that he called Margaret Broun a witch. He is referred to the next session day.

April 30th: William Dick was called and appeared. He still denies. Mr Alexander Gray and John Carmichell are appointed to discuss the matter with him between now and the next session day.

May 14th: Mr Alexander Gray and John Carmichell report that William Dick still denies.

June 18th: William Dick is appointed to be summoned to the next session day.

June 25th: William Dick was called and did not appear. He is referred to the Civil Magistrate.

1695

May 12th: A complaint was given in by Agnes Corser, wife of David Wadell, about William Baillie's wife Grissel Hamilton, who called Agnes Corser a witch. The witnesses are Isobel Frank, Margaret Thomson, and Janet Raff. Grissel Hamilton and the witnesses are to be summoned to the next session day.

May 24th: Grissel Hamilton was called and appeared, and denies Agnes Corser's complaint. Witnesses were called. Isobell Franck appeared, having been sworn, and purged of malice and partiality. She is aged fifty and married. She testifies negatively, and declares that she cannot write.

Janet Raff, 58 years old and married: being sworn, purged of malice and partiality, she testifies negatively and declares that she cannot write.

Margaret Thomson, aged 50: being sworn, purged of malice and partiality, testifies negatively and declares that she cannot write.

Considering the complaint, and the statements of the witnesses, the Session finds the complaint not proven.

September 15th: A complaint was given in by George Reid about Robert Hunter, that Robert had called the complainer a warlock. The witnesses are John Greive and Georg Scugall. The officers [*i.e.* elders] are appointed to summon Robert Hunter and his witnesses to the next session day.

September 19th: Robert Hunter was called. He appeared and confessed. His censure is referred to the next session day.

October 13th: Robert Hunter was called and appeared. He repents and professes grief for slandering George Reid. He is appointed to pay thirty shillings Scots to the poor box and was rebuked.

1698

April 24th: Elspeth Wate in Penston complains about John Mitchell, coalhewer there, and his servant Jean Dickson for slandering her and calling her a witch. She claims to have witnesses. John Mitchell and his servant are to be summoned to the next session day, and the witnesses Barbara Alan, Janet Mure, and Bessie Hogard.

May 1st: John Mitchell was called, appeared, and being questioned about the slander, denies it. The witnesses were called and appeared. Robert Masson, about 24 years old, married, was sworn and purged, and testified that he did not hear John Mitchell call Elspeth Wate a witch. Janet Murrey, aged 40 ... did not hear. Barbara Allan, aged 26, ... did not hear. Bessie Hogard, 23 ... did not hear. [The witnesses all declare that they cannot write.] The Session finds the complaint not proven, and rebukes Elspeth for lying about John Mitchell.

Jean Simson was called, appeared, and denied that she called Elspeth Wate a witch. Janet Murrey testified affirmatively that she heard Jean Simson call Elspeth Wate a "maiden witch". Bessie Hoggard testified that she did not hear her call her a witch. Barbara Alan asked Bessie Hoggard, "Who is the maiden witch?" and she said that it was Elspeth Wate. She heard Jean Simson say, "Faith, it's true." The Session finds the case not proven, and she is rebuked for that also.

1699

September 10th: This day a bill of complaint was given in by Mary Goold, in which she alleges that Jenet fforest slandered her, calling her a witch. She says George Sinclair and his wife Margaret Johnson can prove it. Both parties and the witnesses are to be summoned to the next session day, September 17th.

September 17th: Margaret Goold, having complained about Jenet fforest calling her a witch, was asked if she still stood to her complaint, and answered yes. Jennet fforest was called, appeared, and was asked what was the reason for calling her a witch. She answered that she had no reason but that she had lost her temper. The Session delays deciding on her censure till the next meeting.

September 24th: Jenet fforest was called, and appeared. The Session appoints that her censure should be that she should come in before the congregation the next Sabbath Day, acknowledge her offence upon her knees, and be rebuked for it.

October 1st: Jenet fforest appeared before the congregation and was rebuked and absolved.

Haddington.

Haddington is designated CH2/799 in the National Archives of Scotland. Kirk Session minutes survive for 1629 - 31, 1640 - 56, 1656 - 65, 1665 - 85, and 1685 -1703, and contain many references to witchcraft, some of them in Penston and Samuelston, both of which became part of Gladsmuir parish in 1692.

1641

February 23rd: Margaret Wait appeared and confessed she called Agnes Broune "witch". Her reason was a common report she had heard about her in the countryside. Another reason was the advice she gave her when her child was ill. She told her to put a piece of raw meat under his head and he would recover, and told her to cut a piece of rowan tree between the two Beltanes [apparent reading], at the back of the furthest down [..illegible..] and put it above the lintel of the door, and it would protect him against witches and witchcraft. A third reason was that she had been blamed and accused previously by some others who were burnt for the same sin. She denied that she called her daughter a witch, but claimed that George Eidington's son said to her that the woman and daughter had blown out Jean Straquhan's husband's eye. Agnes Broune confessed that she had laid down the raw meat and cut the rowan wood as [advised] previously.

The Session orders them both to appear at the next meeting, and all the elders were urged to try to find out what they could to shed light on the business before then.

March 16th: Margaret Wait appeared and declared as before that she called Agnes Broune a witch, but that she cannot prove it, except by the reasons already mentioned. She declared that Agnes Broune gave her the advice two years ago when the child was ill.

Agnes Broune appeared and confirmed that when Margaret Wait asked her what would prevent her child falling into a fever again, she told her to put a piece or two of raw beef under the child's head.

Since they can get no further information the Session referred them to the magistrates to be locked up and to fine each of them forty shillings for the benefit of the poor. They give no advice as to what should be done next.

1642

January 17th: Margaret Bryson appeared, after Margaret Denholme complained that she had called her a witch's get and common whore. She admitted this with what appeared to be great penitence, and most humbly upon her knees craved Margaret Denholme's forgiveness for the sin, promising never to do it again to her or anyone else, under the penalty of standing in the jougs. [An iron collar with a chain usually attached to the wall near a church door, or to a mercat cross.]

1647

June 20th: Eupham Johnston gave in a letter of complaint against Helinn Burnmoore for calling her a witch. Helein appeared and denied it. Thomas Lindores appeared, was admitted as a witness, sworn in, and testified that he heard Heleine Burnmoore call Effie a witch and a witch's get. James Meikie [?], witness, was admitted and sworn, and testified as above. The Session, finding the complaint clearly proven, rebuked Helline for her fault, and urged her not to do anything like it ever again, and to crave Effie's pardon for it. Fined £1 - 7s - 6d.

1648

August 22nd: [Note in the margin, "Issabell Smith for charming."] Issabell Smith in Newmilnes appeared and confessed and declared, concerning the man "turning" his child, that Agnis Andersone took the child and put him twice round an oak tree, but was afraid the third time. She also declared that she told her to take the child between two barn doors and turn him three times heels over head, and that would cure him.

Agnes appeared and confessed that she took the child and put her twice round a tree in the presence of the child's mother, but denied that she uttered any words, and said that she had heard tell that to turn the child heels over head three times between two barn doors would cure the child.

1649

March 13th: [The Session was obviously worried about the implications of the above case, and had referred it to the higher church court, the Presbytery of Haddington.]

Issabel Smith in Newmilne appeared, referred back by the Presbytery to the Session for consulting with Agnis Anderson for charming her child, which she admitted. She was ordered to make her public repentance for this next Sunday in sackcloth, which she promised to do.

March 18th: Agnis Anderson appeared, and for charming Isabell Smith's child was ordered to make her public repentance "this day eight days" [*i.e.* a week today, "today" being included in the reckoning] in sackcloth, which she promised to do.

Issabell Smith made her satisfaction today [*i.e.* satisfied church discipline - appeared before the congregation in sackcloth as ordered].

June 3rd: Margaret Vaitch gave in a letter of complaint against various people for calling her a witch. She and they were summoned to appear the next Lord's Day.

June 12th: Patrick Young, weaver, appeared and testified that last Fastings-even [Shrove Tuesday] a horse pulling a cart broke its neck on his stair, and broke a step of the stair. He had the horse removed to the other side of the street, and the flesh had hardly been eaten off it when Margaret Vaitch set up the bones at her door. Margaret confessed that she took the bones and boiled them, and took the grease for rubbing her arm that was subject to the gout. She still has some of the grease. She stated also that she could not think of anyone who had told her to do it, and that John Simsone's servant broke the bones for her. The boy was ordered to be summoned.

James Lyll appeared, and declared that Margaret Vaitch came to him and offered to give him ten pounds she had put by, if he would go with her to Mr Robert Broune's and help her to make out a bill [of complaint] against those who called her a witch. Margaret confessed that this was true.

Alexander Robertson declared that he boiled four of the horse's legs whole to get the horse-flesh off, which had been standing at Margaret Vaitch's door forty-eight hours after the horse died. Margaret admitted that three of the legs were at her door, but there was no flesh on them apart from the joints.

James Kirkwood, Francis Cockburne, William Anderson, and Elspeth Dobbie are ordered to be summoned to declare what they know about Margaret Vaitch.

June 19th: ffrancis Cockburne appeared and declared that after Margaret Vaitch was knocked over by his cow, the cow gave no milk for twenty weeks after that, till she had calved. Before that she had been as good a milk cow as was required.

Elizabeth Dobbie appeared and declared that about thirty years ago when she was living on the laird of Adirstone's land [Alderston?] she had a milk cow. Margaret Vaitch lived beside her and had another milk cow which stood beside hers in the byre. One night she milked her cow which gave her a quart of milk, and while she was milking the cow Margaret came into her house [*sic*], and after that the cow never gave any more milk, just blood. She declared that there was no malice or quarrel between them before that. After that, when they both lived in Garmiltoune two of her calves died.

[Note in margin] James Kirkwood appeared and declared he knew nothing about Margaret Vaitch.

Christine Kirkwood appeared, since she had heard from others a report that she called Margaret Vaitch a witch when she came to her house.

George Young and his wife Thomas [*sic*] Macall, and David Couper are ordered to be summoned to declare what they know about Margaret.

June 24th: David Couper appeared and declared that Robert Watherstone, who was a shepherd at Garmiltoune at one time, and still lives in Garmiltoune, told him that when he was living in Garmiltoune he had two heavily pregnant cows. He saw Margaret Vaitch come out of his byre, and after that the cows never gave birth, but dwindled away. When he told her off, she answered telling him to keep it quiet till her husband came home. "For," said she, "ane ill word waxes wyd." [Bad news spreads quickly]. Margaret denied all this. The Session ordered the clerk to write a letter to the minister of Tynninghame to get Robert to appear next Sunday.

James Thomsone, smith in Rottinraw, is ordered to be summoned to be questioned on Tuesday on what he knows about Margaret Vaitch.

June 26th: George Young and his wife appeared, and denied that they ever called Margaret Veatch a witch. They never knew her until five weeks ago, except that her daughter Margaret Murray said to them when they were considering flitting out of their house, that if they did not flit they would repent it.

July 1st: Robert Watherston in Tynninghame appeared and declared that when he and John Murray were both living under the laird of Aderstone, early one Sunday morning before the sun had risen he saw Margaret Vaitch come out of his byre with a coat round her head. Robert had two heavily pregnant cows in this byre, one of which was "faire seedit" [?], and after that the calves vanished and were never seen.

Margaret confessed that she looked in at the door, and that she had a stick in her hand to call the sheep and goats out of his yard, and that it was reported that she was measuring the walls with an ell-measure.

James Thomson in Rottinraw testified that the dog ran in and out over his wife, and fell down sick in front of his cow. He took the dog out from in front of the cow and laid it down on the ground where it died soon afterwards. It lay for a year after that, untouched by any beast. The cow never gave any milk after that but only red blood, and his wife got better every day from then on. [She had presumably been ill.]

Robert Smith in Caldro is ordered to appear next Tuesday.

July 3rd: Thomas Sinclar in Hadingtone appeared, and declared that when he was locked up in the Tolbooth of Hadingtone because of James Riddel, at the time when Patrick Young was collector of the exise duties, Patrick locked up Grissell Andersone from Painstone for her exise money. When she came into the Tolbooth, and the doors were locked behind her, she cursed Patrick upon her knees, and uttered these words - she hoped in God that before long he and his family would present an "evil sight".

July 15th: Robert Spence appeared as a witness and was admitted and sworn. He testified that he heard William Sandie say that the witches in Haddington would never confess as long as the baillies [*i.e.* magistrates of the burgh] drank sack [Spanish white wine] and sugar with them. When he was asked who was drinking with them he replied, "John Aytone and John McCaill." William Smith, witness, admitted and sworn, testified likewise. John McCaill [*sic*] witness, admitted and sworn, testified likewise. [Obviously some confusion here.] Robert Forrest, witness, admitted and sworn, testified that he doesn't recall the details, but in general terms he had said the magistrates gave them too much leeway.

The Session defers censure until they consult with the Presbytery. William Smith was ordered to appear in a week's time to hear the Presbytery's decision.

July 22nd: Mr William Trent [the minister] reported that the Presbytery had advised that William Sandie should do public penance in sackcloth on two Sabbath days for slandering and reviling the magistrates. William was called, appeared, and was ordered to do penance the next Sabbath Day in sackcloth. He was also fined £2-15-0.

August 19th: Reminder - Get all the parish churches in the Presbytery to make intimation about Helleine Gyllour, witch, who has fled from Painstone.

August 28th: Agnes Murray in Painstone appeared, and declared that about four years ago, when she was living there with Grissell

Anderson, she and Grissell were coming from Hermiston Mill, and the Devil came all the way with them, to the end of Painstone village. He left them there with [a noise like] a great rumbling of carts and horses. Another time, about half a year after that, about the middle of the day, she saw the Devil and Grissell Anderson lying in bed together, and when they got out of bed, the Devil flew out at the side of the house where they were. She also testified that last Sunday Grissell came to her bedside with a candle in her hand, in the house of her master Alexander Broune.

September 16th: John ffairbairn testified that after his child was eight days old, the child had a piece of his lip missing, and subsequently died because of it. When this was done there was nobody in the house but his wife and Elspeth Dobbie. John ffairbairne's wife testified that the child had a sore lip, but she didn't know whether Elspeth Dobbie had done it when she was giving the child hot food. It healed up afterwards, but the child died.

Christiane Douglas appeared and declared that after she had her last child, Elspeth Dobbie came into her house one particular night, and when Janet Martein was breast-feeding the baby Elspeth came in, and touching her breast, she said she had no milk. The child never sucked again till he died. Also, she testified that Elspeth took the child and looked at him, and took the cross-cloth [?] off his head and put it in her pocket. She took a long pin out of his clothes and put an eyeless needle in instead of the pin. When Christine Douglas was asked if she had ever done Elspeth any wrong, she replied that she can't remember any wrong done by her to Elspeth ; only that she said to her before she gave birth that people said she was a witch and had the mark on her shoulder.

John Thomsone testified that when he was in James Broune the candlemaker's house, James was making candles, and he saw that the tallow was very white. Elspeth Dobbie came in quarter of an hour later, and went out shortly afterwards. As soon as she went out the tallow became bloody, and the candles he was dipping were all red.

Elspeth Dobbie, and James Broune and his wife are ordered to be summoned.

September 23rd: James Broune appeared and declared that Elspeth Dobbie came into his house when he was making candles. The tallow was boiling very white, and he made some small candles with it, then went outside. As soon as he had gone out the tallow turned red, and all the candles that he dipped were all like red blood.

Janet Gray his wife testified as above.

Elspeth Dobbie appeared and confessed that she took the child's cross-cloth out of Alexander Edgar's house by mistake, and that she did not know whether she handled Christiane Dowglas's breast or not.

Patrick Goodaill is ordered to be summoned again.

September 30th: Christiane Dowglass appeared in the presence of Elspeth Dobbie, and still affirmed that Elspeth took a pin out of the child's clothes, and put in an eyeless needle in its place. Elspeth denied this but admitted that she did lay her hand on Cristiane Dowglas's breast. Also, Cristiane declared that Elspeth "wand" the child [*i.e.* swaddled it - bound it tightly with strips of cloth to prevent over-exertion, as was the usual custom] without her or her husband's permission, and that she did this herself, on her own, and nobody else was with her. Elspeth said that she swaddled the baby at Cristiane's direction, and that a stranger woman from Aberdouer was with her when the child was swaddled.

Elspeth was questioned about the death of her son, who died suddenly twenty years ago or thereabouts, and if she had been in any way an accessory to his death. She declared as follows - that he had put the ewes in the sheepfold early in the morning, then she told him to go and "mand a calf's chivill" [?]. She came home later with the milk, and found him lying with his hands on his face. Finding him breathing weakly, she went to the door and called in one of the neighbours. Wine was brought out to him from Clerkington, and the lairds of Clerkington and Blackbarronie, came to see him, and said he had died of a "pleurrasie of blood".

October 7th: The Session unanimously thought it advisable to have Elspeth Dobbie searched to find out whether or not she has the witch's mark, and therefore recommended her to the magistrate to be locked up.

October 9th: Patrick and James Kellie appeared, Elspeth Dobbie's sons, and since John Kinkaide who is the usual searcher for the witch's mark is in England and won't return for another twenty days, they asked that their mother might come out on bail till John Kinkaid gets back. The Session advised the baillies that if they could find sufficient "caution" [bail-money], that is a thousand pounds officially recorded in the town court-books, then she could be set free, as soon as her cautioner guarantees that she will return to the Tolbooth whenever she is required to do so.

October 14th: William Tait and Jonet Seatone appeared. Jonet complained about him for calling her a witch, which he admitted. However, she denied that she called William and his wife and son a nest of thieves. He could not prove this allegation, and so William was rebuked for his sin and ordered not to do it again or he would be punished, and Janet was urged to live more peaceably with her neighbours.

November 20th: Alexander Rae appeared, after a complaint by Issabell Heamone [?], for calling her a witch, which he admitted. He also promised to give in a letter of complaint against Issobell.

December 20th: Bessie Watherstone and Margaret Scuggill appeared, in connection with the statement from William Stillie, who being present, and after being sworn in, testified that he heard Bessie Watherstone say to Margaret Scuggill that there were three sievewrights' wives in Samilstone, and that one of them was a witch, and that she feared that Margaret was that woman. Also, he stated that Margaret said nothing else except, "If I am a witch, may witches eat the meat from you." Bessie was sharply rebuked, and ordered to make public satisfaction [*i.e.* repent in church before the congregation] for it next Sunday. Fined £1-10-0.

It is recommended that the elders of Samilstone should try to find out if Margaret Scuggil is a charmer or not.

William Achesone in Painston appeared in connection with his letter complaining about John Stoddirt there for alleging that Isabell Alexander is guilty of the sin of witchcraft, and saying that he would pledge his head on it. As proof he produced James Winlae and John Herring as witnesses. After being sworn in, both of them stated that they heard John Stoddirt say these words. John Stoddirt said in his defence that when Agnis Hunter was in prison she accused Isabell of being at meetings with the Devil, and that she said this in the presence of Richard Broune, Thomas Winton, Thomas Fouler, James Winla, Alexander Baillie called Little Alexander, and James Baillie his brother. John was ordered to appear the next session day, and those persons were ordered to be summoned.

1650

February 24th: William Johnstone and James Fortone, James Caldwell and William Lamb, James Wilkie and George Cathkit, and Thomas Antcaill [?] were ordered to keep the keys of the prison door where the witches are locked up, for this week.

February 29th: Bessie Watherstone appeared, affirming to Margaret Scuggall's face that she was a charmer. To verify it she produced George

Shorswood, William Lorimoure, and George Simsone. William Lorimoore and George Shorswood, being sworn and admitted, testified that they heard Bessie Watherstone say that Margaret Scuggill was a charmer and that she would prove it, but that they know nothing else about it.

George Simson and his son John agree with the last statement but never knew her to charm anyone

George Simsone's wife, and Paul Hamiltone and his wife are ordered to be summoned for next Sunday.

As regards the action of slander pursued by Issabell Alexander, Thomas Fouler appeared as a witness, was admitted and sworn, and testified that he heard Jean Hunter say when she was in prison that Issabell Alexander was at several meetings with the Devil and the rest of them, and that Barbara Purdie said the same - however, they had both gone back on their statements against Issabell.

James Baillie testified that he heard his mother Jean Hunter say the same thing, but never knew her to go back on it, and that Andrew Douglas and John Weire also heard her make the same statement. Andrew and the rest of them were ordered to be summoned for next Sunday.

March 3rd: William Bene, John Bene, John Cowdane, George Lairmoth, Peter Cunninghame, John Simson weaver, and Alexander Robisone senior were appointed to keep the keys of the Tolbooth for the following week.

Alexander Baillie appeared as a witness, and was admitted and sworn in the action of slander pursued by Issabell Alexander against John Stoddirt. He stated that he heard his mother Jean Hunter say that Issabell Alexander was at a meeting with her and others between the Thrie Myll Hous and the Lough Hall [?] but never heard her go back on it. [Other entries make it clear that the Three Mile House was near the present Gladsmuir Church.]

Andrew Douglas, witness, admitted and sworn, stated that when Jean Hunter and Barbara Purdie were in prison, and he was watching them, he heard them both say that Issabell Alexander was at several meetings with the Devil in their company.

Thomas Rentone, witness, admitted and sworn, stated that he heard Jean Hunter say when he was watching her, that Issabell Alexander was with her at the back of John Hamilton's yard with the Devil, but heard nothing about Barbara Purdie.

James Winlaw, witness, admitted and sworn, stated thet when he was watching Jean Hunter and Barbara Purdie, he heard both of them say that Issabell Alexander was at that meeting with the Devil at the end of John Hamilton's yard, and at another to the east, in the moor.

Richard Broune, witness, admitted and sworn testified exactly the same as James Winlae.

Having heard the statements of the above witnesses, clearly testifying that Issabell Alexander was reported to be a witch, and that she was at several meetings with the Devil, the Session therefore ordered their clerk to write to the laird of Lamington to "keep the said Issabell close", [*i.e.* keep her locked up, or possibly keep a close watch on her. The laird of Lamington in Lanarkshire owned land in the Penston and Hoprig area of what later became Gladsmuir parish.]

March 5th: The Session has thought fit that seven men shall be chosen out of the Session each week to keep the keys of the places where the witches are locked up - four men to watch them at night, and two during the day - going round the town in turn, honest men to either do it themselves, or use their servants or others for whom they will be answerable.

Paul Hamilton, witness in the case of slander between Margaret Scuggall and Bessie

Wathirstone, agreed with the testimony of William Lorimoure, George Simsone, and the other witnesses.

Janet Maisson, witness, admitted and sworn in the case of slander between Margaret Scuggill and Bessie Watherston, agreed with the testimony of Paul Hamiltone and Richard Lorimour and the others.

March 10th: Jonet Allene appeared in correction with her letter complaining that Bessie Adamsone called her a witch and a bitch. Bessie denied these words, and as proof John Wightman, being sworn, stated that he did not hear Bessie Adamsone call Janet witch or bitch.

John Hamiltone, witness, admitted and sworn, testified that he heard Bessie Adamsone call Jonet Allene bitch and heard her say that she might have been burnt.

John Murray, witness, admitted and sworn, testified that he heard her call Jonet Alane [illegible] whore, but not witch.

James Achesone, witness, admitted and sworn, stated that he heard nothing, but he has heard it said that Bessie's husband Alexander Baillie was over-familiar with Jonet Allane.

John Moore, witness, admitted and sworn, stated that he had not heard any slander.

John Wood, witness, admitted and sworn, stated that he heard no scandalous words.

Bessie Adamson confessed that she called Issabell [sic] Allane whore but never witch, and that she had great justification for calling her a whore, because until he died she was always following her husband Alexander Baillie around. Also Jonet Allane confessed that she called Bessie Adamson whore. The Session found both of them guilty of "flyting" and ordered each of them to acknowledge the wrong done to the other, which they did in the presence of the Session. Both were ordered not to do it again, or they would receive double censure and further punishment. Each of them was fined twenty shillings.

March 28th: The case of Marjorie Aytone against Thomas Crafoord came before the Presbytery yesterday. It was remitted by them to our Session, accompanied by by some of the members of the Presbytery to examine her witnesses for proving her bill.

The Provost, Patrick Young and John Aytone baillies, John McCaill, James Hay, Helleine Cockburn, John Dyit [?], and William Lauder, all burgesses of Hadingtone, were present as witnesses. They were admitted and sworn and all of them were removed till they were called, and testified individually as follows: -

John Cockburn, provost, testified that he heard Thomas Craford say to the baillie Patrick Young that he would stand to every thing that he had said before Mr Robert Ker and John Sleich, but knew nothing else about the business.

Patrick Young testified that when he was in his house on 13th March, Thomas Craford, in the presence of the Provost and baillie John Aytone, and various other honest men, was asked by John Aytone whether what he had said against Marjorie Aytone was true or not that she had tried to get certain persons to influence him in his investigation of her. Thomas refused to tell John Aytone, but said, "I have told all that business already to Mr Robert Ker and John Sleich," and that he would stand by it. After that Patrick took him aside to a window, and he declared to him that John Dyit and William Lawder came to him, asking him to come to Marjorie Aytone and search her for the mark, and promised in her name to give him a thousand merks for his trouble. Being asked by Patrick if it was to conceal the mark or not, he answered, "I warrant you that it was so," [You bet!] and that there was a round-faced woman came to him for the same purpose. When he was going away he said to the whole company, "I have told Patrick Young everything, and he will tell you and John Aytone everything."

John Aytone declared that he had heard nothing, except that Thomas Crafoord said in

Patrick Young's that he would abide by what he had said to Mr Robert Ker and John Sleich. He offered to tell them what it was, but he [John Aytone] refused to listen.

James Hay declared that he heard nothing at all.

John McCaill declares that he heard Thomas Crafoord say that Marjorie Aytone sent some people to him offering him a thousand merks to search her in private. Being asked if this was to conceal the mark if she had it, he answered, "I warrant you." Thomas said this publicly in the presence of everyone in the house and room belonging to Patrick Young.

William Lawder testified negatively to the bill.

March 31st: Margaret Scuggill appeared and was ordered to appear the next day and confess that she could charm, as was proven by witnesses, and to crave God's forgiveness for it, or else proceedings would be taken against her with a view to excommunication.

April 2nd: In the case of Bessie Kennedie against Thomas Broune and William Kyle, she produced William Poerk [?] in Dalgownie [?] to prove her bill, and promised to produce William Allane the next day. William Poerk [?], admitted and sworn testified that he heard Robert Broune say there was a woman within the bounds of the place, and as long as she was there they would get no good from the mill [Probable reading. Text says "jois of the milne"]. James Broune his son said to Bessie Kennedie that she was that same woman. William Kyle said that Bessie had the same marks as his mother who was burned as a witch. She was ordered to appear a week today, and to bring her money [?], witnesses, and bill.

April 14th: William Lawder appeared and was asked on his solemn oath whether he had spoken to Thomas Craford asking him to go and search Marjorie Aytone privately in her own house. He answered that Mr John Drummond and Michael Melvine were coming to ask the minister and magistrates if she might be searched in her own house. He said, "Go back to your house. You have nothing to do with it," and he never spoke to him about it until a few days before they were arrested. He never spoke to him about that business either before or after that. [It is difficult to make out here who is speaking to or about whom.]

John Dyit appeared, and was asked on his oath if he offered Thomas Crafoord anything in Marjorie Aytone's name to come and search her privately in her own house, or if he had any offer in connection with it made to him by anyone else. He said no.

Jonet Maine appeared, and was asked on her solemn oath if she had offered anything to Thomas Crafoord in Marjorie Aytone's name to search her privately in her own house. She said no, but confessed that Marjorie asked her to go to James Haye's house and ask his wife Helleine Cockburne to come to her house before she was arrested. She denied that she ever said anything to Thomas Crafoord, but there were men drinking in her house, and she does not know if he was there.

April 16th: James Hay's wife Helleine Cockburne appeared, and being sworn, testified that William Lawder came to her house and asked Thomas Crafoord to come to Marjorie Aytone's house and search her privately. Thomas answered, "Supposing you offered me a thousand merks, I wouldn't do it, unless the minister and magistrates asked me to." Jonet Maine came to her house to take her to Marjorie Aytone. Seeing Thomas Crafoord, she asked if that was the man that searched the witches, and if he and William Lawder had agreed that he would be rewarded for his trouble. Marjorie Aytone had said to her, Thomas Crafoord comes about your house. If he would come and search me privately in my own house he'd get ten dollars for his pains." Thomas Crafoord and Jonet Maine went out to her stair in private, but what they said, and what passed between them, she does not know. She is ordered to appear next Thursday.

Jonet Main and James Hay are to be summoned for next Thursday.

April 18th: William Lawder appeared and declared that he did not ask Thomas Crafoord to come to Marjorie Aytone's house and search her privately, "nor noe other person bot in general." [Meaning obscure - perhaps he means that there was a general feeling that Marjorie should be searched privately, but no-one actually made such a request.]

Helleine Cockburne claimed that in her hearing William Lauder asked Thomas Crafoord to come and search Marjorie Aytone privately in her own house.

James Hay was sworn as before, and testified as on 28th March, but added that he heard his wife say that Marjorie Aytone had promised her ten dollars... [Several words deleted here.] ...arrange with Thomas Crafoord to come and search her in her own house privately.

Jonet Main testified that when she came to James Haye's house for his wife to come to Marjorie Aytone, James Hay refused to let her go. She also testified that she drank with Thomas Crafoord, but still claimed that she never spoke to him.

It is decided to find out if Thomas Crafoord is at Tranent.

April 28th: Margaret Scuggall was recommended to the magistrates.

May 2nd: Isoble Aytone produced Issobell Maccail and Marion Wilson as witnesses that Helleine Cockburn called her a witch, which Helleine denied. An objection was made to Issobell [Maccail] for alleged malice. She was sworn and purged of partiality, and testified that she heard Helleine Cockburn say, casting up to her some of her relatives, "Witches like you were to blame for it." However, she heard nothing of what is alleged in the bill of complaint.

Marion Wilson was admitted and sworn as a witness, and testified similarly to Issabell McCaill.

It is ordered that Mr James Fleming should be spoken to, to make Issabell appear on Sunday night and declare what she heard in this business between Issabell Aytone and Helleine Cockburne.

5th May: Issabel Saidler appeared and was admitted and sworn as a witness in the case of slander pursued by Issabell Aytone against Helleine Cockburne. She declared that she heard Helleine Cockburne say to Issabell Aytone in her own house when she was talking about some of her forebears, "Devilry was to blame for that," and she would have thought that she [Issabell Aytone] should have been suspected to be a witch, rather than her sister Marjorie. And if she was a witch, she was not a wise witch; for she had her son-in-law's purse, and thought she could come with the money from it to her son-in-law's house to buy cloth with it.

The bill is not proven, but words of slander are. The Session finds that Helleine Cockburne spoke these words in anger, having been provoked by Issabell Aytone, who came to her house and abused her. The Session rebuked her sharply for it. She acknowledged her rashness and was ordered not to do it again.

The sentence against Issabell Aytone is postponed until a week today, and both parties are ordered to be summoned.

[Four men are appointed "captors" for the forthcoming week.]

May 12th: Issabell Aytone appeared and was ordered to make satisfaction [*i.e.* apologise] to Helleine Cockburne, which she did, and craved God's and her pardon. She was ordered to pay ten pounds.

Issabell Wightman in Painstone is ordered to be summoned for slandering Catherine Anderson, and Marjorie Romanes for calling Catherine Thomson "king of witches". [The continuation of this case makes no more mention of witches or witchcraft.]

June 25th: Syrie [?] Ayton was admitted and sworn as a witness, and declared she heard James Lyll say that the witch in Tranent had told him the those who had done him wrong "were near his doors" [*i.e.* lived near him]. Others had told her that the bung of his vat was between John Sleiche's and John Graye's, but she denied that she heard James Lyll name any names.

July 7th: Thomas Renton and John Sinclair appeared, John being complained about by Thomas for saying that there was more being spoken about against John's wife concerning witchcraft, than was spoken about his. John was sharply rebuked for slandering Thomas Renton's wife, was ordered to satisfy [church discipline] publicly in sackcloth, and was fined £2-0-0.

Robert Smith testified that about fifteen years ago he had some barley being threshed in Marioun Hastie's barn. The threshers had gone home "to ease them" [*i.e.* to have a rest, or possibly to ease their bowels]. He stayed in the barn, and Marioun Hastie came to him and said that she was keen that he should get his barley threshed so that she could get hers in. He looked towards the shell of the old kiln and he saw something like a mist or a whirlwind rise out of it, about the height of a human body. He was very much afraid when he saw it because his mother had been burnt as a witch before that.

[There is a break in the records here until 9th March 1651, almost certainly caused by Cromwell's invasion, his resounding victory at Dunbar, and his subsequent military occupation of Scotland. It is usually supposed that under Cromwell's "Commonwealth" government, witchcraft executions became very rare, and that many imprisoned witchcraft suspects were released. The Commonwealth was abolished and the Monarchy restored in 1660.]

1651

November 20th: Margaret Sivis in Nungate is ordered to be summoned for consulting with the dumb boy in Peastone.... [Damaged].

December 30th: Robert Carmichaell and Robert Howlatsone's wife appeared. Robert [Carmichaell] claimed that three years ago the said Jonet Fergusone [*i.e.* Howlatsone's wife] came into his house with a live mouse. She rubbed it between her hands then let it fall to the ground. When Robert and his wife reproved her for it, Jonet called his wife a drunken jade and also said to her, "It would be good if you swelled as big as a barrel." Both of them were ordered to appear the next session day to prove their bills.

1652

January 8th Janet Fergusone and her husband Robert Howlatsone appeared, both of them complaining about Robert Carmichaell for calling her a witch and saying that she had caused the death of his former wife. Robert Carmichaell also appeared, denying the allegation. To prove it Jonet and her husband produced James Whylae and his wife. Both of them were sworn and testified individually that they heard him call her a witch but they deny the rest.

July 4th: Janet Steine testified that she heard Ewphane [   ] say that if there was a devil out of hell, Helleine Baillie was one.

Catherine Wightman declares that she knows nothing.

Hellein Loch testified that she heard Effie Broune say that they should search Helleine Baillie, and if she didn't have the mark she would pay for investigating her.

Margaret Sinclair declares that Helleine Baillie goes up and down like a mad lion, calling everybody "witch", and striving to blood them above the breath. ["Blooding above the breath" involved drawing blood from a suspected witch above the nostrils - usually from the brow. This was supposed to counteract the effects of her witchcraft.]

Janet Stein denied that she heard anything.

Heleine Loch declares she heard nothing.

The Session finds both parties guilty of "flyting" and rebuked them for their scandalous carriage. Helleine Baillie was fined £1 -19 - 0 and both of them were ordered to be here a week today to confess their fault before the Session.

July 17th: Effie Broune humbled herself before the Session, and craved pardon from God and Helleine Baillie for her unchristian behaviour.

September 5th: Alexander Baillie was admitted and sworn as a witness in the action of slander pursued by John Sincler's wife in Painstone against William Sandersone's wife there.

He testified that he heard William's wife call John Sinclar's wife a witch, and that his neighbours also heard it.

James Taes was admitted and sworn as a witness, and declares that he heard William Sandersone's wife call John Sinclar's wife a witch.

These persons, "scolders", were ordered to appear the next session day.

September 12th: William Weire was admitted and sworn as a witness and declared that he heard John Sinclar's wife Issabell Crafourd, and his daughter Margaret Sinclar call William Sanderson and his wife Bessie Watherstone "evil-favoured witches", and that they had been put out of Samilstone for witchcraft.

George Bartrome was admitted and sworn as a witness, and declared he heard John Sinclar call Williame Sandersone "knave" and "evil-faced knave", and that he was known for a knave in the place he came from.

September 19th: Margaret Wood was admitted and sworn as a witness and testified negatively to the bill, but said that Isabell Craford called Bessie Watherstone "hairy-mouthed blaide".

Janet Fisher was admitted and sworn, and testified negatively, and that she had heard nothing at all.

George Smith was admitted and sworn as a witness and declared he heard nothing.

Thomas Rentone was admitted and sworn as a witness and declared he heard nothing except that Margaret Sinclar called Bessie Watherstone a "heavy-browed thief."

James Young was admitted and sworn as a witness and declared he heard John Sinclar say that William Sanderson was a banished thief, banished out of the place he had come from, and that he heard Bessie Watherstone call Issobell Craford, John Sinclair's wife, an exposed witch.

October 17th: Adam Hamilton against Jonet Carkettil. None of the others appeared.

Heleine Cockburne was admitted and sworn as a witness, and testified that she heard Jonet Carkettil witch's get. [*sic* Presumably Janet had called Adam Hamilton a witch's get.]

Thomas Simsone, witness, declared he heard a great noise, but heard no articulate voices.

John Thin, being sworn, declared he heard a great din, but heard no articulate voice.

[Jonet confesses on 19th October and promises not to do it again.]

1653

January 4th: Hendrie Hoggart was sworn and declared that he heard Helline Dickson call Helleine Baillie a marked witch.

Jonet Fisher declared the same.

John Cowane declared he heard a mutual quarrel but didn't hear "witch" mentioned.

March 13th: Janet Seatone gave in her bill of complaint against Marione Forrest for calling her "odious witch". [Marion confesses and is rebuked.]

May 1st: Mark Carraill appeared in connection with his bill complaining about

Bessie Littell for calling him a witch's get. Bessie also appeared and confessed she did, but denied that she called him anything else. The rest of the allegations in the bill have still to be proved. Bessie Littel is required to prepare her bill in time for the next session day.

May 8th: James Greive was admitted and sworn as a witness, and testified that Bessie Littell did call Mark Carraill a witch's get, but he heard none of the other things contained in the bill.

John Darumpill was admitted and sworn as a witness and testified that Bessie Littell called Mark Carraill a witch's get, and told him to go and fetch his mother out of the Sandes. [This was a particularly cruel jibe. The "Sands" was the spot by the river Tyne where witches were executed and where their ashes were presumably left to be scattered by the wind.]

Bessie Ridpeth was admitted and sworn as a witness, and testified that Bessie Littel called Mark Carrail a witch's get, but denied the rest of the bill.

Bessie Littell gave in her bill of complaint against Mark Carraill for calling her a "landlouper blaide" [good-for-nothing vagabond], and saying that an Englishman was supposed to have given her gold for lying with her.

[Mark denies calling her "landlouper", but admits saying the Englishman paid her money for sex.] Both rebuked and fined £1-0-0.

July 10th: Elspeth Wood appeared, accused of sorcery, and for getting her son to steal the tether from George Forrest's cow, which after that gave no milk, but only blood, until the tether was given back again. After the tether was given back she gave milk as before. Elspeth was questioned but denied it. George Forrest was ordered to have his witnesses here the next day.

[It is rather surprising that the Session should presume to try a case of "sorcery" rather than mere "charming", or slander involving accusatons of sorcery. There is no further mention of this case, so perhaps it was dropped or referred to the civil magistrates, as would have been more appropriate in the first place.]

1654

January 29th: Issabell Donaldson appeared in connection with her bill complaining about Bessie Rankine for calling her a witch. Bessie appeared and denied it. However, Issabell Gibson and William Gibson were admitted and sworn as witnesses, and by their testimony Bessie was convicted of calling her a witch, and apologised to her for saying so. She was also sharply rebuked and promised not to do the like again, under the penalty of being severely punished.

May 14th: A bill of complaint was given in by Jonet Dicksone against Marione Wightman for calling her a witch. Marione denied this allegation. To prove the complaint Alexander Broune and James Baillie were admitted and sworn as witnesses and both declared that Marione called Jonet Dicksone a witch; and said that if anybody called her a witch, she would stop their mouths with a boll of meal. [A boll was a large capacity measure comprising around 211.6 litres.] She was fined £2-6-6.

Marione was ordered to give in her bill of complaint about Jonet Dickson a week today. [On May 21st Marion testified that Jonet called her a "collier jade's wife and bitch". The Session decides it is a case of "mutual flyting" and orders them to live more peaceably. Both parties were from Penston.]

November 28th: A bill of complaint was given in by George Helliday against John Sinclar for calling him a "condemned devil", his wife a witch, and his children witch's gets. John appeared and confessed everything in the bill, but denied calling George a condemned devil. The Session found John guilty of slander and rebuked him sharply. John craved God's pardon for the offence caused to George and his wife and children, and promised not to do anything of the sort again. He was fined £2-0-0.

1655

February 13th: A bill of complaint was given in by Agnes Williamson against Anna Pilmoore for calling her a witch and alleging that she had her child's heart boiling in her pot, and that a woman had come to her and told her to wash a vessel [?] at midnight with green flax and throw it in front of her neighbour's door. Anna denied this.

William Carraill was admitted and sworn as a witness and testified that he heard Anna Pilmoore say that her child's heart was boiling in Agnis Williamson's pot, but denied the rest of the bill.

Since Anna Pilmoore is out of her mind ["distracted"] the Session thinks it expedient to resolve the quarrel between her and her neighbours, and Mr William Trent [the minister] undertook to go to Samilstone to reconcile them if possible. [Agnes Williamson actually stood trial for witchcraft six years later, and presumably already had a reputation as a witch.]

February 18th: A bill of complaint was given in by Alisone Wilson against John Ewart and his wife for calling her "bitch-faced canting witch, and witch's get". They denied this accusation and James Ridpeth and George Jaksone were produced as witnesses, and being admitted and sworn, testified as follows: -

James Ridpeth testified that John Ewart's wife called Alisone Wilson witch and witch's get, but heard nothing else.

George Jaksone denies that he heard George Ewart and his wife say anything against Alisone Wilsone. Alison is ordered to summon the rest of her witnesses, and John Ewart and his wife were also summoned to appear the next day.

February 25th: Mariane Hendersone appeared and was admitted and sworn as a witness. She declared that she heard John Ewart and his wife call Alison Wilson witch and witch's get.

Isabell Watson appeared and was admitted and sworn as a witness. She declared that John Ewart called Alison Wilsone "bitch-faced canting witch", and his wife called her witch and witch's get.

James Tait appeared and was admitted and sworn as a witness, and testified as above.

The Session found the bill proven and ordered John and his wife to acknowledge their fault and to apologise to her for it., which they did in the presence of the Session, and promised never to do the like again under the penalty of making public satisfaction. They were fined £2-0-0 by the magistrate.

April 15th: Jeane Watherstone appeared in correction with a bill given in against her by John Ogilvie, for wishing that nothing would prosper with him, and cursing him. Jean denied the points made in the bill, but to prove it he produced as witnesses Robert Dickson, Robert Hucheson, and Jonet Vaitch. After being admitted and sworn, they testifies as follows: -

Robert Dicksone testified that he did not hear Jeane Watherstone utter any words such as were in the bill, but she said to John Ogilvie's wife that she had a fair face but a foul heart.

Robert Huchesone testified as above, and also that Jeane said that John Ogilvie had taken her land from her, and that she wished a curse upon it.

Jonet Vaitch declared that she heard her curse John Ogilvie, but could not remember the words.

John Ogilvie asked to have his bill back so that he could make corrections to it. This was granted, and his witnesses were appointed to be summoned.

April 25th: Mr William Trent, Patrick Young, James Smith, James Cockburne, and David Wilsone met according to a previous decision of the Session, for the purpose of reconciling the quarrel between John Ogilbie and Jeane Watherstone. Having informed themselves sufficiently of the quarrel and its causes, they found that Jeane Watherstone had not only uttered words of blasphemy to the great contempt of God and scandal of the gospel, but had also most injuriously slandered both John Ogilbie and his wife, causing them great unhappiness. This was acknowledged by Jean Watherstone, and so the above-named persons ordered her to confess her fault to John Ogilby and his wife, and also to promise to behave more sensibly in future. Jean accordingly did so, and promised to live more peaceably with them. In the case of her offending in the same way again, she promises to give public satisfaction before the congregation, quite apart from any other punishment inflicted on her at the Session's pleasure.

May 6th: Patrick Learmonth and Agnis Balfoure appeared. Patrick claimed that Agnis had called him a "Mutter" [a term of abuse or contempt; origin obscure - *Dict. O. S. T.*] and a witch's get, and that she called his father the Devil's servant. She denied this allegation, and claimed that Patrick was full of drink and had intended beating her. The Session found there was provocation from both sides, and that it constituted mutual scolding between them. They were rebuked and ordered to live more peaceably in future, under the penalty of making public satisfaction.

May 27th: [John Scot and Alison Murray in Penston. She calls him a whoremonger and adulterer, he calls her a witch and a witch's get. John proves his bill. She acknowledges her fault and is fined £2 - 0 - 0. He is told to live "christianly and soberly" in future.]

1656

July 20th: Marie Robisone and Heleine Richesone appeared. Marie confessed she called Heleine a witch. Heleine denied calling Marie anything. By the testimony of John Maisson Sr. and John Broune in Painston the Session found that they are mutual "flyters", and referred them to be punished by the magistrate, who fined each of them one merk. August 24th: A bill of complaint was given in by David Meikie, John Johnstone, William Stillie, and William Bookie in Samilstone against James Bartilman and his wife Beigis Sandersone, and against James Paterson and his wife Agnis Williamson for calling them thieves, and claiming that they had stolen meal out of their sacks. All were summoned to be present the next session day with their witnesses.

August 31st: Margaret Rid and Christiane Watherston appeared who by their own confession were convicted of calling each other witch and "loune" [a sexualy immoral woman]... [They were sharply rebuked, referred to the magistrates, and each fined one merk.]

[Witnesses were led in the Samuelston case. This of course has nothing to do with witchcraft, but it is of interest because it involves Agnes Wiliamson who was later to stand trial in the High Court of Justiciary for witchcraft. It also throws some light on the fraught state of affairs in Samuelston. The complainers in this case are millers. It was alleged they had been stealing meal from their customers' sacks, and it was claimed that William Stillie had "stolen himself rich in Hermistone Milne". The Session found Beigis Sanderson had slandered Stillie. All were rebuked and ordered to live more peaceably. Beigis had to apologise to William Stillie.]

1657

July 12th: Agnis Cudbertsone was admitted and sworn as a witness in the matter of the scandal between Helein Waker and her husband. She testified that she heard Helein say that her husband James Stewart was in the house with Agnis Williamsone with the door closed, and that he was lying with Agnis Williamsone as he did with her.

Margaret Hendrie appeared and was admitted and sworn as a witness, and testified that James Stewart came to Agnis Williamsone's house, and sent for a pint of ale. They drank it all, and sent a drink from it to his wife Helein Waker, and closed the door while a little boy waited [?]. She heard Helein say that her husband James Stewart was lying with Agnis as he did with her.

August 23rd: Helen Waker appeared declaring that her husband James Stewart was lying in the bed with Margaret Williamson ... [On August 30th Margaret Williamson denied the accusation and claimed James only brought her a pint of ale. On September 6th Margaret again denied "carnal dealing" and was referred to the magistrates to be locked up. On September 23rd the ministers - Haddington Parish Church had two - were asked to go to the Tolbooth to speak to Margaret regarding alleged adultery, which was then considered a serious crime.

Again, this has nothing to do with witchcraft, but it gives some idea of how the Williamsons were regarded by at least some of the inhabitants of Samuelston. Margaret is presumably Agnes's sister, since a daughter would have Agnes's husband's surname Paterson.]

1659

May 15th: A bill of complaint was given in by Jonet McNab against Margaret Smith for saying that evil things were spoken about her, and she hoped to God that more would be said about her before long. Margaret was present and was questioned on the matters raised in the bill. She confessed, and when asked what the evil things were that were said about Jonet, she declared that Alexander Young in Saltone is supposed to have said that some of them had taken his bonnet off his head, and that the people in Samilstone are "evil spoken". Margaret Argyll told her about it in Drem, in front of Jonet Carfra from Samilstone. Margaret and Jonet Carfra are ordered to be summoned. Margaret was summoned to appear a week from today.

May 22nd: Margaret Argyll appeared, confessing that she said to Margaret Smith that Jeane Kirkwood told her that Jonet McNab was a witch. Jean, Margaret, and Margaret Smith were therefore summoned to appear the next session day.

May 29th: Margaret Argyll and Margaret Smith were summoned to appear next session day. Jean Kirkwood is to be summoned for the second time.

June 5th: Jean Kirkwood appeared, denying that she called Jonet McNab a witch as Margaret Argyll alleged.

Marg*ret also* appeared, affirming to Jeane Kirkwood's face that she called Jonet McNab a witch, and said it to her and others when they were sitting on a corn-rig between Saltone and Samilstone. She is referred to the magistrate to be locked up until she declares who else was with them when Jean told her about Jonet McNab being a witch. Jeane and Margaret Smith were warned to appear when they are summoned again.

Memorandum:- to write to Mr Thomas Kirkaldie to make his parishioner Adam Brotherstones appear. He is accused of slandering John Blak's wife, and saying that there was nothing in Samilstone but whores, thieves, and witches.

June 12th: Margaret Smith appeared, again reported for calling Jonet McNab's mother a witch, and her father a "dubskelper" [vagabond, fly-by-night]. When questioned whether she said these things or not she denied it. To prove it Jonet produced Andrew Lorimoore and John Hastie, who being admitted and sworn, testified as follows: -

John Haistie declares that Margaret Smith said that Jonet McNab's mother was a witch and that her father was a dubskelper, and that she was deemed to be a witch herself.

Andrew Lorimoore testified as above.

The Session finds by the declarations of the witnesses that Margaret was guilty of calling Jonet McNab and her mother witches. Since Margaret did not seem to be conscious of the wrong done to Margaret, she is referred to the magistrates to be locked up until she acknowledges the wrong done to Jonet McNab. She is also ordered to be set publicly at the market cross for one Friday night with a paper on her face, to deter other people from airing similar groundless scandals about Jonet McNab and others.

Margaret Argyll appeared, still claiming that Jeane Kirkwood said to her that Jonet McNab was a witch. However, since she was unable to prove it, the Session declared that she was guilty of the calumny, and referred her to the laird of Hermiston on whose land she lives to have her put in the [illegible] prison of Samilstone, and also to make her find surety to appear before the Session again, and to answer for the crime of witchcraft for which she is to be challenged whenever she is summoned again. She is fined £0 - 6 - 8 for her absence from the investigation.

Adam Brotherstones appeared, denying that he said that the whole village of Samilstone were whores, thieves, and witches. As proof he named Isabell Mill, Walter Hunter's daughter in Nisbet, and Nicoll Stillie in Samilstone as witnesses. They were ordered to be summoned to appear a week from today, and Adam was summoned to appear the same day.

June 19th: The baillies reported that Margaret Smith could not be set at the cross last market day because she was so late in coming to the town. However, she is recommended still to the magistrates to be set at the cross next market day.

June 26th: The baillie reported that according to order Margaret Smith was set at the cross last Friday for slandering Jonet McNab.

Catherine ffoster is to be summoned, accused by Mr George Hepburne of saying that he was supposed to have called her a witch.

July 3rd: Catherine Foster appeared, declaring that Jeane Greinla in Gimmersmilnes said to her that Mr George Hepburne had called her a witch. Jeane is ordered to be summoned to the next session day.

July 10th: Adam Brotherstones appeared, still denying that he had said that in Samilstone they were all whores, thieves, and witches. As proof John Blak cited Isabell Mill, Adam Hunter's daughter in Nisbet, and Nicol Stillie in Samilstone, and Adam was asked if he had any objections why they should not give evidence against him.

Isabell Mill, being solemnly sworn, testified that John Blak's wife threatened to strike Adam, and that he invited her to hit him with her own staff. John's wife said that by God's bread she would make the highest blood in his body the lowest, and Adam answered that he defied all the whores, thieves, and witches in Samilstone. He is ordered to appear the next session day.

July 17th: Office bearers chosen: -
Samilstone

Elders
Wm Lorimore
John Blak

Deacons
Jas Johnstone
Rid [Ritchard] Sharpe

Painstone

Elders
John Sheill
John Bower
Adam Mason
Pat Hog
John Allane

Deacons
John Hog
Wm Patersone

[It is obvious from this that the embarrassing "whores, thieves, and witches" altercation about Samuelston involves the wife of the church elder John Black. Some of the other names appear in other cases from the fraught communities of Penston and Samuelston.]

July 19th: Jeane Greinla appeared, declaring that David Smith told her that George Cassils said in his house that Mr George Hepburne had said that Catherine Foster was a witch. George is ordered to be summoned.

July 24th: George Cassils was called, but did not appear. He is referred to George Bainne, baillie in Nungate, to make him appear.

Nicol Stillie appeared, and was admitted and sworn as a witness to testify in the process between John Blak's wife and Adam Brotherstones. He declared that Adam Brotherstones told John Blak's wife to "ride out of the way, for he wanted none of her company. There was no grace in the toun she came from but whores, thieves, and witches."

July 1st: George Cassils appeared, denying that he said Mr George Hepburne had called Catharine Foster a witch, but declared that he heard John Turnbull say that Mr George had said Catherein was a witch.

August 14th: Adam Hunter's daughter appeared as a witness led by John Blak and his wife against Adam Brotherstone. Having been sworn he testified that three times John Blak's wife threatened to strike Adam, and Adam said to her that he defied all the whores, thieves, and witches in Samilstone to strike him. This business is remitted to John Blak for further evidence, and he is ordered to be summoned for that effect.

August 21st: Isabel Rid, John Vaitch's wife appeared, denying that she called James Drew and his wife thief and witch's get, but confessed that she said that James Drew's mother-in-law was a witch. Isobell was removed [from the room] and John Neilson and John Thomson, elders for that district, declared that both John and his wife had called James Drew and his wife all the words alleged in the bill. John and his wife were called in again, and convinced of the wrong done to these persons. They were sharply rebuked and ordered never to fall into that kind of fault again, under the penalty of a public punishment and a double fine. They were remitted to the magistrate who fined them £4-0-0.

As far as the quarrel between John Blak's wife and Adam Brotherstones is concerned, the Session finds that the evidence of the witnesses shows that Adam Brotherstones' words reflect very badly on the whole village of Samilstone. He is ordered to appear the next session day to give particulars about such persons as he knows to be whores, thieves, and witches in Samilstone.

August 28th: Adam Brotherstones appeared and was sharply rebuked for reviling the whole village of Samilstone, and was ordered not to do the like again, under the penalty of public punishment.

September 4th: James Drew appeared, complaining that John Vaitch's wife came to his door at twelve o'clock at night, calling his wife a witch's get. She is summoned to appear a week today. John Vaitch is also summoned to appear next session day for harbouring ["resetting"] vagabond beggars. [Vaitch was rebuked at the next session day, but his wife was ill and was summoned to the next meeting.]

1660

February 7th: Concerning the complaint given in by Jonet Spavine against Alison Murray for calling her a witch and common whore,

Alison appeared and denied the points of the bill. As proof Jonet Spavine produced William Inglis and Thomas Lason. Being questioned individually they testified as follows: -

William Inglis solemnly swore that Alison Murray called Jonet a witch, and said she would prove she was one. He denied that she called her a common whore.

Thomas Lasone was purged by his oath of malice or envy against Alison, and his testimony agreed in everything with the above.

Alison Murray appeared, and was ordered to satisfy Jonet Spavine by craving her pardon for the wrong done to her. She refused to do it, alleging openly that Jonet and another four with her came into her house at midnight. There was no-one else in the house but her husband and children, and the doors were closed. They took hold of her arm and nipped it. She also affirmed that she [illegible] in her ear, and did not speak openly about it [?]. She also declared that Jonet lent money to a man in Painstoune and that he never prospered after that. The Session therefore remitted her [Alison] to the magistrate to be locked up until she finds surety to appear next session day and give full satisfaction as ordered.

February 14th: Alison Murray appeared, still insisting that Jonet Spavine came into her house at cockcrow when the doors were shut, and took her by the arm. Also, that Bessie Edmistone who was burnt as a witch had testified against Jonet Spavine. The Session appoints Mr Robert Ker and John Bower to try to find out if there is any truth in this business, and to report next session day. [Rober Ker is the minister. John Bower is a Penston elder.] Both parties are therefore summoned to appear the next session day.

February 26th: Mr Robert Ker reported that he had examined three witnesses in Painstone in connection with the business between Alison Murrey and Jonet Spavine. He finds by the testimony of the witnesses that Alison Murrey had called Jonet a witch "in face of court" [Before the baron court perhaps?], and persistently calls her so on a daily basis. Alison is referred to the magistrates to be locked up until she acknowledges her fault.

March 19th: Alison Murrey appeared, insisting confidently that at nightime when the doors were locked, Jonet Spavine came [and stood] above her bed where she was lying. She undertook to prove her to be a witch a month from today, or else give satisfaction as a slanderer.

April 8th: Considering that the Laird of Lamington had asked the Session to suspend further proceedings against Alison Murrey and Jonet Spavine until he had investigated the business, the session appointed John Shiell, elder in Painstone, to convey any information on the Laird of Lamington's progress in the business, in writing from the clerk of the court of Painstone, by the 29th of April.

April 29th: Alisone Murrey and Jonet Spavine are ordered to be summoned.

May 6th: Alison Murrey and Jonet Spavine appeared. Both of them were ordered to appear whenever they shall be cited, and James Edmistone the clerk of Lamington's court was also summoned to appear a week today to declare what has been done in the business between these two persons.

May 13th: James Edmistone appeared, and declared that three witnesses have been examined in the business between Jonet Spavine and Alison Murrey. He promised to give in the account of the proceedings of the Laird of Lamington's court when the other witnesses have been examined.

June 10th: James Edmistone gave in several written statements from witnesses taken before the court of Painstone against Janet Spavine and Alison Murrey. The statements were not clear enough, and therefore the besiness was continued. James Edmistone was requested to have the rest of the witnesses examined, and their statements brought before the Session.

[While the baron court in Penston attempted to get to grips with the bitter accusations of witchcraft there, Samuelston also seems to have been in its usual state of ferment. An entry of 5th August summons several boys for making the Samuelston schoolmaster "ride the stang" at the instigation of his wife whom he had locked out of their house two nights running. "Riding the stang" entailed being paraded through the community astride a pole or beam, the rougher the better, with much bouncing up and down - a painful business.]

August 5th: A bill of complaint was given in by Dame Margaret Preston against Patrik Thomsone for calling her a witch, and a debauched witch, and saying that he would see her burnt as a witch. Patrik appeared and admitted that the lady had called him a knave, and a beggar knave, and also said that she hoped he would lose his job. Provoked by her scandalous words, he said to her that he hoped he would see her burnt like a witch. The business is continued till a week today, and the witnesses are ordered to be summoned to declare what they heard between the lady and Patrik Thomson.

[Patrik has also been the subject of a complaint from Patrik Brown for calling him whoremaster, adulterer, etc.]

August 12th: George Broune was admitted and sworn in the action of slander between the Lady Beirford and Patrik Thomson... [She called him knave, and he hoped to see her burnt like a witch. Oner witnesses are led. The Session finds that Lady Bearford's bill is "materially proven". Since Patrik alleges provocation, he is instructed to give in his bill of complaint in writing.]

James Edmiston is ordered to be summoned to give an account of what has been done in the business between the parties in Painston.

August 19th: [John Hepburn appears on behalf of Patrick Broune and the dowager Lady Bearford who want to have back their bills against Patrick Thomson, in order to complain to the Presbytery. The Session refuses. Thomson gives in his written complaint against Lady Bearford for calling him a knave. The whole business becomes very complicated, but there is no more of substance about witchcfaft.]

September 2nd: Margaret Walker appeared, who was being harboured by James Carram. She confesses that she was married in Winton. Before she was married she was a servant to George Renton in Pencaitland, and her name is not Margaret Walker but Christian Summer.

Robert Dewar who was burnt for witchcraft in Wintone accused her of being a witch, but at his death he went back on what he had said. She was ordered to appear a fortnight today, and the minister was requested to speak to Mr Alexander Vernor to get him to seek out the statements and report on them.

The case of the women in Painstone is continued.

September 9th: Reminder - Christian Summer in the Abbey.

September 16th: Christian Summer was called but did not appear. She is ordered to be summoned again.

September 30th: James Sives has reported that Christian Summer has fled. James was requested to inform the Session if she returns.

1661

March 24th: A report was received of Young, servant to Alexander Burnet, speaking secretly with Agnis Williamson and Christian Deans, imprisoned for the sin of witchcraft and sorcery. She is to be summoned to the next session day.

March 31st: Catharine Young appeared, confessing that she came to Agnes Williamson when she was in prison, nobody knowing about it. However she alleged that she was looking for her half year's wages. She spoke to Christiane Deanes, but only said that Agnis Williamson would not confess. At this, Christiane went back on everything she had said, and denied the sin of witchcraft. Cathreine was sharply rebuked, and ordered to make public satisfaction the following Lord's Day in presence of the whole congregation.

Elspeth Tailloure has been imprisoned for sorcery and witchcraft.

April 21st: Marie Taes is ordered to be summoned, having been reported for calling Alexander Robison's wife a witch.

April 30th: John Haistie appeared, complaining that Marie Taes and Rachell Coudin had slandered Alexander Robison's wife, and his own wife, by calling them witches. The Session therefore ordered him to give in his bill on Sunday. Since these persons were present they were summoned to appear the next session day, and told that it was expected that they would live peaceably.

May 5th: John Haistie withdrew his complaint.

A bill of complaint was given in by John Speires's wife against James Lindsay for calling her a witch and a charmer. He is to be summoned to the next session day.

George Broune, baillie in the Nungate, was asked to take Bessie Kennedie, accused of witchcraft, to Samilstone to be confronted with her accuser Heleine Deanes.

May 12th: Concerning the complaint given in by John Speirs's wife against James Lindsay, he appeared and admitted calling her a witch. He was sharply rebuked and ordered not to do the like again, and ordered to make public acknowledgement of his rashness the next Lord's Day.

A bill of complaint was given in by James Lindsay against John Speirs's wife for calling him a warlock. When she appeared she denied that she called him a warlock, but only said if she were a witch, he was a warlock. She was sharply rebuked and ordered not to do the like again, under the penalty of making public satisfaction.

David Wilson complained that Jean Thomsone was naming him as a warlock along with various other honest people in the town. Jean appeared, and being asked who were the people she named as witches, she declared that William Allan in Newmilns told her that David Wilson, Marion Lindsay, Marion Livington, Jeane Steine, and Jean Sinclar were named as witches, and that a woman in Tranent had accused them. She said Robert Dason and his wife could prove it.

Baillie Forrest declared that in his presence she named David Wilson, Marion Lindsay, and Jeane Steine as witches, and that she claimed that David Wilson could be nothing else but a witch, because the Devil had carried him to Makmirrie.

Robert Dason and his wife appeared, declaring on oath that they never heard William Allane say any such words as Jeane Thomsone alleged.

The Session found that Jean had raised a filthy slander against David Wilson and the rest of the aforenamed persons. Her punishment was deferred to the next session day, at which she was ordered to appear.

May 19th: The Session orders James Lindsay, in spite of his plea, to make public acknowledgment in the presence of the congregation of the wrong done by him to John Speirs's wife.

James Lindsay undertook to prove that when John Speirs's wife was in labour, she laid her pains on her husband. She set up a needle in the frame of the bed, and when he took it down on her instructions, she was eased of her pains.

Jean Thomsone appeared. For the scandalous words uttered by her against David Wilsone and other honest persons, she was ordered to stand at the church door in sackcloth the next Lord's Day, and then appear thus dressed before the congregation and make public acknowledgment of her rash and scandalous words. The magistrates were asked to make her stand at the market cross on Friday with a paper on her breast showing the reason for her standing in such a public place.

May 26th: This day Jean Thomsone appeared publicly in sackcloth, and in front of the congregation confessed her rash and ill-advised calumniation and slandering of David Wilson, Marion Lindsay, Marione Livingtoune, and several other honest people under the name of witches. She humbly craved God's pardon and promised never to do the like again.

June 2nd: James Lindsay appeared and gave in a request expressing grief and sorrow for slandering John Speirs's wife, and humbly entreating the Session to cancel their sentence against him of making a public acknowledgment. The Session dispensed with the public satisfaction, and ordered him to acknowledge his fault in the presence of the Session, and to crave pardon for the offence done to John Speirs's wife. This he did, and promised never to do the like to her or any other person.

June 16th: Heleine Nicolsone in Samilstone is ordered to be summoned, accused of calling her husband a warlock. [Again, the actual word used here is "warla", which was presumably the usual East Lothian pronunciation.]

June 23rd: Helein Nicolsone, wife of William Bartilman, apeared confessing that she had prayed God to forgive those who had brought her to Samilstone amongst warlocks and witches. However, she denied that she called her husband a warlock. Thomas Crumbie appeared, declaring upon oath that in her drunkenness Helleine called her husband a warlock. Thomas Spotiswood also declared exactly as above. The Session by the witnesses' declarations finds Helleine guilty both of the sin of drunkenness and of slandering her husband by calling him a warlock. Therefore they sharply rebuked Helleine and ordered her never to do the like again under the penalty of making public satisfaction as well as any other punishment to be inflicted on her at the Session's pleasure.

July 28th: The Session requested the baillies to lock up Helleine Buckon, since she had confessed to the magistrates her pact with the Devil, and that she had renounced her baptism.

September 8th: A bill of complaint was given in by Thomas Strayn against Robert Lindsay for calling him a "warla carill" [warlock fellow], and claiming that he turned round three times anti-clockwise with a sheep round his head. Robert appeared and denied the allegation. Both parties were summoned to appear next session day, and the witnesses are also to be summoned.

September 15th: Robert Lindsay appeared and objected to Peter Carkettil and John Wilsone being led as witnesses against him by Thomas Strayne, because he claimed they were ill-disposed towards him. The Session found the objection irrelevant, and admitted them to tell what they knew of the matter between the persons involved, as long as they purged themselves of partiality.

John Wilson appeared, and was admitted and sworn as a witness, and testified in agreement with everything in the bill

James Patersone appeared, and was admitted and sworn as a witness, and testified in agreement with everything alleged in the bill.

Finding the bill proven, the Session recommended Robert to be civilly punished by the magistrates, but postponed his ecclesiastical punishment until a week today. He was therefore summoned to appear that day.

September 29th: Robert Lindsay appeared, confessing with sorrow his abusing of Thomas Strong *[sic]*. He was sharply rebuked, and ordered not to do the like again under the penalty of making public satisfaction, and was referred to the magistrates.

October 13th: Thomas Strong appeared and expressed his agreement with the Session's decision on Robert Lindsay's satisfaction of church discipline for wronging his good name. Robert appeared and confessed the wrong done by him to Thomas Strong in wronging his good name. He craved God and Thomas's pardon humbly upon his knees, and promised never to fall into the same fault again, under the penalty of making public satisfaction before the congregation, as well as any other punishment to be inflicted on him by the magistrates and the Session.

A bill of complaint was given in by William Stillie and his wife against George Hutson for calling him a "thief knave", and his wife a witch. They are ordered to appear a week today, and George is ordered to be summoned.

October 20th: George Hutsone appeared confessing with sorrow his slandering of William Stillie and his wife, and craved their pardon, promising not to do the like again, under the penalty of making public satisfaction. Fined £1 - 0 - 0 by the magistrate.

December 22nd: Concerning James Welsh, imprisoned in the tolbooth for the horrible sin of witchcraft: the Session resolved today to send him to Edinburgh to be imprisoned there until he is put on trial. The charges for his upkeep during his imprisonment there will be paid by the Session, not exeeding two shillings a day.

1662

January 14th: The Session orders James Welsh imprisoned in the tolbooth of Haddington for witchcraft, to be taken to Edinburgh and kept at the Session's expense for one month, at a cost of four pounds over and above the man's wages for taking him there.

To James Dounie £2 - 0 - 0

For keeping James Welsh in the tolbooth for 74 days at two shillings a day £7 - 8 - 0

For keeping him in the tolbooth of Edinburgh for one month £4 - 0 - 0

Given to the man who took him to Edinburgh £1 - 0 - 0

For a night's quarters on the way £0 - 8 - 0

1663

March 10th: A bill of complaint was given in by Isabell Deanes, wife of William Carrail in Samilstone, against Jonet Baigbie, wife of George Cauldcleuch there, for calling her a "wizet-faced beast" [wizet: shrivelled, wizened], and saying that she should have been burnt, and that she hoped to see her burnt. Jonet appeared and denied the allegation, and referred to the witnesses, John Bartilman, Beigis Sandersone, and John Vaitch, who being admitted and sworn testified as follows:-

John Vaitch testified that Jonet Baigbie called Isabell Deanes a shrivelled beast, and also said she might have been burnt.

John Bartilman denies the allegation contained in the bill, and declared that Jonet Baigbie said she would do her an evil turn.

Beigis Sanderson testifies negatively to everything in the bill.

Jonet Baigbie and Isabell Deans were therefore summoned to appear a week today, and William Carrail to fetch the rest of his witnesses.

March 15th: Martin Shanks and Christiane Bartilman were led as witnesses in the action of Isabell Deanes against Jonet Baigbie. They were sworn, and testified as follows:-

Christian Bartilman testified negatively to the bill.

Martin Shanks agreed with everything in the bill.

The Session found by the statements of the witnesses that Jonet Begbie has wronged Isabell Deanes in her good name, and postponed their sentence until a week today because Jonet Baigbie alleged that Isabell had wronged her good name as well, and that she would give in her bill of complaint that day. Both parties were therefore summoned to appear the next session day.

May 22nd: [The above case is continued. Isabell had wished the Devil to be in Jonet's belly; and said she deserved to be put in the jougs, and that she should drink less and pay her debts. It all becomes very complex and involved, but there are no further references to witchcraft.]

June 14th: A bill of complaint was given in by Helleine Romannos against William Bichit for calling her a witch. William is ordered to be summoned to the next session day. John Rae, elder in that district, says he heard William Bichet call Hellein a witch.

June 21st: A bill of complaint was given in by William Bichit against Helleine Romannos for calling him a devil and a common thief, and saying that both he and his father should have been hanged. Both parties were summoned to appear the next session day and to bring their witnesses with them.

July 5th: Concerning the bill of complaint given in by William Bichet against Helleine Romannus, Helleine appeared, denying the allegation contained in the bill. William offered to prove it through John Summervaile and John Martine. John Summervaile appeared and was sworn as a witness, and testified that Heleine Rommannos said to William that he lay in the Devil's arms, that he and his father were thieves, and that he himself would either be hanged or burnt. Both parties were summoned to appear the next session day, and to bring in with them the rest of the witnesses.

July 19th: John Martine appeared, and was admitted and sworn as a witness in the action of slander between William Bichet and Helein Rommanos. He testified negatively to the bill given in by William against Heleine. The Session finds that William Bichit has not proved the bill given in by him against Helleine Rommannos, and declared that he had forfeited the forty shillings given by him when he produced the bill, because he had not proved it against her, and ordered that the [illegible] should keep the money and be accountable to the Session for it. As for the injury done to Helleine which she has sufficiently proved, they ordered William to ask her forgiveness, which he did, and promised not to do the like again, under the penalty of making public satisfaction. He was fined £4 - 0 - 0 by the magistrate.

September 20th: A bill of complaint was given in by Helleine Romanes against William Bichit for calling her a confronted wrtch, for saying that he would [illegible] her to the thieves' hole [*i.e.* prison cell] and to the fire, and for calling her children witch's gets. William is ordered to be summoned to appear the next session day.

October 6th: William Bichit appeared, denying all the allegations contained in Hellein Rommanos' bill against him for slandering her good name. As proof Heleine produced John Martine and Isabell Grahame who being admitted and sworn, testified as follows:-

Isabel! Grahame testified in agreement with everything in the bill.

John Martine testified in agreement with the bill.

Margaret Hume was admitted and sworn as a witness and testified in agreement with the bill.

The Session found the bill proven, and ordered William to appear before the congregation next Sunday, and to acknowledge the wrong done by him to Hellein in the presence of the congregation. Fined £4 - 0 - 0 by the magistrate.

November 3rd: A bill of complaint was given in by Jonet Landels against Jonet [*sic*] Gray for calling her a witch, and saying that she had caused her brother's death. Christiane appeared and confessed that she called her a witch, but denied the rest of the bill. She is ordered to appear the next session day.

November 17th: Jonet Landels and Christiane Graye's business is postponed until the next day.

[It continues until 15th December. "Whoore", "theife", and "lowne" are bandied about, but there is no more mention of witchcraft.]

1664

March 6th: A bill of complaint was given in by Jonet Todrig against James Shorswood for bidding the Devil thrash the soul out of her, for calling her an arrant witch, and for hoping to see her burnt.

James appeared, confessing that he called Janet an arrant witch, but denied the rest of the allegations.

A bill of complaint was given in by James Shorswood against Jonet Todrig for calling him a thief, and for saying in a threatening manner that she had "seen her own time of him", and before long she would see more. Jonet denied this, and therefore both parties were summoned to appear next session day, and to bring their witnesses with them.

March 13th: William Yorkstane and William Middlemast were led as witnesses against Jonet Todrig, and being admitted and sworn, testified that James called her a witch, but denied the rest of the details.

Adam Brotherstone was admitted and sworn as a witness, and testifies as above.

James Nisbet was admitted and sworn as a witness, and testifies that Jonet Todrig called James Shorswood a "thief-like limmer" and "beggarly rascal", but denied the rest of the allegations.

James Wilkie was admitted and sworn as a witness, and testifies that Jonet Todrig called James Shorswood a thief and a beggarly debauched rascal.

William Middlemost testifies in agreement with James Nisbet and James Wilkie.

The Session found both parties guilty of mutual flyting, and ordered both of them to crave each other's pardon, and since James Shorswood was most in the wrong they ordered him to acknowledge the wrong done to Jonet Todrig's good name in the presence of the congregation next Sunday.

April 24th: A bill of complaint was given in by Margaret Clerk against David Baird for calling her a common whore and thief, and for saying he hoped to see her burnt on the top of Lammerlaw.

David appeared confessing everything in the bill. David also gave in a bill of complaint against Margaret for calling him witch's get, and for saying that his wife was a witch and he was a thief.

Margaret appeared confessing that she had called David a witch's get, but denied that she called his wife a witch. However she offered to prove that she was a thief. Both parties were therefore summoned to appear the next session day and to bring their witnesses with them.

May 9th: John Menzies and William Steinstone appeared as witnesses led by David Baird against Margaret Clerk. After being admitted and sworn they testified in agreement with everything in David's bill.

May 15th: Having considered the process between David Baird and Margaret Clerk, the Session found both of them guilty of mutual flyting, and since Margaret Clerk is unwell at present and unable to travel, their censure was delayed until she has recovered. David was ordered to live peaceably with Margaret and his other neighbours until then. June 12th: David Baird and Margaret Clerk appeared, and confessed with grief their sorrow for their mutual scolding and flyting with scandalous and injurious words. They were sharply rebuked and ordered to live peaceably with each other in future, under the penalty of making public satisfaction. David was fined £4-0-0.

1665

September 24th: A bill of complaint was given in by Alison Wilson against Issoble

Downie for calling Alison a warlock's get. Issoble denied these words. Witnesses were called and sworn to declare the truth as in the sight of God. Patrick Wood testified that Issoble called Alison warlock's get. William Black testified that Issoble said to Alison, "You are all devils together." The parties were called in and Issoble was told that the case was proved by witnesses. Issoble, being very old, began weeping bitterly, saying if she spoke any such words it was in the heat of the moment, and she could only apologise for it. The Session, feeling compassion for the old woman, made her kneel down and ask God's mercy for offending. She was not to offend Alison in future by speaking any such words. She accordingly promised to fulfill these obligations.

1666

January 16th: A bill of complaint was given in by Bessie Romanoes against Margaret Dicksone, who had abused the complainer and her son, calling him in a very public place a witch's get whose mother was an exposed witch. The complainer having proved the bill by witnesses, and the Session finding that Margaret is a stranger, rambling through the countryside without any "testificate", the Session refers Margaret to the baillies to use their civil power to deal with her as they thought fit.

January 28th: A bill of complaint was given in by Besie Romanoes against Margaret Dicksone, who in a very public place called the complainer's son a witch's get, and the complainer an exposed and adulterous witch. When enquiries were made, the baillie reported that the civil magistrate had Dicksone put out of the town by the hangman, banished as a "worigat" [vagrant] and vagabond.

[From here until 1677 the kirk session minutes become progressively more concentrated on financial matters, with only brief references to fornicators and occasional cases of Sabbath-breaking and "scolding". There is, as far as I can make out, no further mention of witchcraft. However, the handwriting is very poor, and it is possible that I might have missed something.]

1677

October 28th: A bill of complaint was given in by Greissell Seatoun, that George Yeamane had abused her good name most outrageously in the hearing of many, by calling her a witch. George appeared., [illegible] ...and members of the Session and others proved the bill in his presence. George claimed he spoke in the heat of the moment and was not in his right mind. [The handwriting here is atrocious, and the sense also appears somewhat garbled. The gist seems to be that George is to satisfy church discipline publicly. Some of his friends ask for the punishment to be delayed until they can speak to Greissel Seatoun. The Session agrees, but appoints Baillie Lamb and George Cockburn to go along with them.]

November 18th: [Again, much of this is illegible. Greissel has been consulted and does not wish George to suffer public censure. He is apparently related to kinsfolk of hers. Several of the elders are to meet to decide what to do.]

December 2nd: [A new clerk takes over] This day George Yeaman again appeared and was sharply rebuked on his knees. He acknowledged his great fault in slandering Grissell Seatoun. He promised ammendment and never to do the like again, under the penalty of the highest censure the church can inflict on him. He was referred to the baillies to be locked up until he pays whatever fine they decide to impose upon him.

1678

June 9th: [William Hunter and John Aitchison. One called the other a knave. He in turn called the other's mother a witch. They were reconciled and fined.]

July 21st: A bill of complaint was given in against Margaret Manderston for calling Margaret Cathie and Margaret Young witches. The witnesses were John Somervail, Grissel Broun, Margaret Grein, and Isobell Smith. John Somervail and some of the other witnesses declared upon oath that they had heard Margaret Manderson say, "God forbid that it's all true, what they're saying; for your wife will weep as sadly as I do for the connection she has to Margaret Young her half sister." However, the Session finding the business unclear, made Margaret Manderson and Margaret Grein humble themselves and agree to be severely punished if they said anything to the prejudice of the complainers.

1683

February 18th: A complaint was given in by John Bartilman against Margaret Jackson who had called him a witch's get, and uttered several insulting expressions against him. Margaret Jackson appeared, acknowledged the bill, and claimed she had been just as much injured by him, which the complainer's witness Anna Lamb freely admits. Because of this the Session thought fit to refer it to two or three of their members to deal with privately, since the injury had been mutual.

1685

May 10th: A bill was given in by Patrick Hunter and his wife against Margaret Douglas, who called his wife behind her back, and not in her presence, a whore, a thief, and a witch. Margaret Douglas appeared and denied the bill, except that she had called ... [The text is garbled here. The clerk seems to have missed a line. Both parties are to bring their witnesses to the next meeting.]

June 14th: Patrick Hunter and Margaret Douglas appeared in connection with the bill given in by him claiming she abused his wife. She had no objection to his witnesses Marion Carbreath and Margaret Ruscastle, who proved the bill. Therefore the session thought fit that she should humble herself before the Session and acknowledge her fault, which she refused to do, and was therefore sent to prison by the magistrate.

1691

September 20th: A complaint was given in by Margaret Macnab against William Maine and Agnes Shannoch his wife for calling her an exposed witch and devil. The witnesses were called and declared as follows: -

George Deane and Patrick Learmouth were called separately, and declared that they never heard William Maine or his wife slander Margaret in any way. The Session therefore ordered her to bring the rest of the witnesses the next session day.

October 11th: Bessie Baptie appeared as a witness and declared on oath that she heard William Maine's wife call Margaret McNab a witch.

Agnes Aytkine appeared and declared the same on oath.

William Maine and his wife are ordered to be summoned to the next session day.

[Nothing further seems to have been done, however.]

1694

April 29th: A complaint was given in by Barbara Gladstaines against Katharine Mylne and Agnes Mylne for calling her witch and whore. The parties appeared with the witnesses and were examined as follows: -

Katharine Mylne declared that she said that Barbara harboured thieves, but did not call her whore or witch. Agnes Mylne also denied the accusation. John Wood was called as a witness and declared that he heard Katharine Mylne call Barbara Gladstaines what was alleged.

May 13th: Barbara Gladstanes and the rest were called but did not appear. They are ordered to be summoned to the next meeting.

[No more seems to have come of this.]

1697

July 8th: This day appeared Helen Wyte, accused of witchcraft by the deceased Alexander Brocky on his death bed. Being questioned, she declared that the cause of that report was that one day she was seeking an alms [*i.e.* a free handout] of seed corn from Alexander. He called her an old ridden witch, and she answered that his own mother had bewitched his wife. That was all she knew, except that she said witches would be the death of him.

James Smith was called as a witness, and being questioned, he declared that he heard Helen Whyte say that Alexander Brockie was sowing the corn but would not see it cut down. He denies that he saw her turn round three times anti-clockwise.

Margaret Thomson was also called as a witness, and being questioned, she declared that when Helen Whyte came to seek seed from Alexander he refused to give her any because she had been there twice before. She denies that he gave her any evil words, but heard her say that witches would be the death of him, and that he would not see the corn cut down. She denies that she saw her run round anti-clockwise, but that she heard her say again that "if he were hanged, he should not see the corn cut down", and said that since then she had taken blood from above Helen's brows.

Helen was asked how she came to know that Alexander Brockie's mother had bewitched his wife. She answered that it was just what everybody said. Being asked what she said about the cutting down of the corn, she replied that he said that he would remember her, and she said, "May God remember me, but you and I may never see the corn cut down."

Margaret Thomson declared that Helen had threatened her and said that if she lived seven years she would make her repent it.

The minister asked the opinion of the Session whether the evidence along with her own confession gave sufficient grounds for imprisonment, and it was decided in the affirmative. [Earlier in the 17th Century Helen would have been referred to the magistrates to be imprisoned while further evidence was sought. This would usually have resulted in an application to the Privy Couneil for a commission to put the suspect on trial, or a transfer to Edinburgh to be tried by the High Court of Justiciary. At this late date it is unlikely that matters would proceed so far. There is no record of a commission being sought. By the late 1690s witchcraft trials were few and far between in the High Court, and in any case were usually "deserted" by the prosecution. The High Court records have no mention of a case involving a Helen Whyte.

Humbie.

Humbie is designated CH2/389 in the National Archives of Scotland. It was formed from the two pre-Reformation parishes of Humbie and Keith. The famous "North Berwick" witch Agnes Sampson lived at Nether Keith. Humbie Kirk Session minutes survive for the period 1643 - 77.

1646

September 6th: Margaret Mackenzie appeared and complained that Jonet Bald called her witch, thief, and landlouper. Jonet Bald is ordered to be summoned to the next session day with the witnesses who heard it.

September 13th: Jonet Bald appeared, and being questioned declared that Margaret MacKenzie called her witch and thief. The witnesses John Clegorne and James Miller appeared and testified that both of them were guilty of using abusive words to each other. Therefore both of them were found guilty, and each of them was ordered to pay 20 shillings next session day, or else be put in the jougs for their flyting.

The same day it was ordered that whoever complains about his neighbour to the Kirk Session must give in his complaint in writing and deposit 30 shillings before he is heard. If the complaint is proved the money will be given back. If not, it will be kept for the use of the Kirk Session.

1649

September 16th: It was reported to the Session that Agnes Gourley was lying under a scandal of charming cattle so that their milk gave no cream. The Session ordered her to be summoned to the next meeting.

September 23rd: Agnes Gourley was questioned about charming the cattle, and testified as follows: -

About three years ago Anna Sympsone, who was then servant to Robert Hepburne of Keith, was dissatisfied with the milk of their cows because it gave no cream. Agnes said, "Can you not throw some of it into the drain? They say, God save us, that there are those under the earth who have as much need of it as those above ground." She also confesses that she went and watched the cows being milked, but she doesn't remember whether she milked them herself or not. However, she confesses that she threw the milk into the drain herself, and said, "God save us, there may be those under the earth that have as much need of it as those above ground." [The milk was presumably thrown into the drain as an offering to the fairies, who were often supposed to live underground.]

She also admits that she put salt and wheat bread into the cows' ears. She was asked where she got the wheat bread, and how long it was between the time she threw the milk in the drain, and putting the salt and bread in the cows' ears. She replied that it was the same day or the day after, and Anna Sympson and Rachell Forrester were there at the time. When she was asked who taught her, she said she heard it from a "going man" [*i.e.* a vagabond, itinerant]. The Session, after considering her statement, referred her to the Presbytery.

December 9th: The minister reported that the Presbytery had ordered that Agnes Gourley was to make public repentance in sackcloth for charming cattle.

December 16th: This day Agnes Gourley gave public evidence of her repentance in sackcloth for charming cattle.

1659

May 1st: William Fleck gave in a bill of complaint against James Moore for slandering his good name by saying that he could tell if he liked what was wrong with the mill at Over Keith the day it ground bran like blood. James was ordered to be summoned. May 8th: James Moore appeared. When questioned whether he had slandered William Fleck, he denied that he had originated the story. William Forsyth had said it to him, and so he was the source of the slander. William Forsyth was ordered to be summoned. May 15th: William Forsyth appeared, and denied that he said any such thing about William Fleck to James Moore. All he said when they were speaking about the mill grinding the corn like blood was that if anybody knew who had caused it, it would be a good thing to say so. He affirmed all this in the presence of James Moore.

James Moore was asked if he could prove if William Forsyth or anybody else had previously said this about William Fleck. He said no, and so since James Moore had admitted speaking these words, and couldn't prove that anyone had previously said any such thing, the Session judges that he has slandered William Fleck, and orders him to be publicly rebuked for it.

1661

June 9th: Intimation was made concerning George Miltone and Alison Berrie, fugitives from a charge of witchcraft in the parish of Haddington, and Bessie Dickson, fugitive from a charge of witchcraft in the parish of Bothans [Yester]. Anyone knowing where they are should declare it.

1664

April 17th: Elizabeth Kemp and Jenet Fereis have been reported for charming, and taking off a heavy sickness from a young woman in Costertone in the parish of Crichton. They were ordered to be summoned to the next session day.

April 24th: The two persons named above appeared, and because the scandal was in the parish of Crichton, they were referred to the kirk session there to be investigated and censured.

The witnesses and parties concerned were all within that parish, and the minister of Crichton was informed of it by the minister of this parish.

1669

April 11th: The Session was informed that some corn and clothes had been stolen from James Hog in Overkeith, and that James went to a certain Seal, an Englishman living in Newbottle to ask him who had stolen the things out of his house. Seal directed him to a man in the Cannongate who would inform him who the thief was, and wrote a letter for that purpose. James Hog sent his servant to David Ewart, the man in Edinburgh, who gave him a paper containing a description of the man who had stolen the goods from his house. They were both ordered to be summoned to the next session day.

April 25th: James Hog appeared, and confessed he went to Seal in Newbottle and asked him who had stolen the things out of his house. He answered that he had promised the Presbytery of Dalkeith not to meddle with anything in that line, but he would direct him to a man in Edinburgh who would tell him who had stolen the missing articles. James said he did not go himself, but sent his servant John Wood with the letter from Seal and also some money. David Ewart sent him back a paper giving a description of the person who had stolen these things.

James Wood was called and confessed that he went to Edinburgh and delivered the letter to David Ewart and gave him some money. He promised to tell him who had stolen the corn and clothes. The paper was produced to the Session and read. In it David Ewart claimed that by astrology he knew that the person who was the thief lived to the south [of James Hog's house presumably], that he had sandy coloured hair, blue watery eyes, a big brow, and a scar on his head where no hair grew. He was an old soldier or a smith.

James Hog and Johne Wood were sharply rebuked for their sin, going to consult somebody they supposed to be a magician or wizard. Their sin was explained to them and they were urged to mourn for it. However, as to what their censure should be, the Session thought fit to refer that to the Presbytery.

It was decided that the paper received from David Ewart should be sent to the ministers of the Canongate, and that they should be informed of how David Ewart was abusing the people, so that they could take some course of action to restrain him and censure him.

May 16th: The minister reported that the Presbytery had ordered that James Hog and Johne Wood should be publicly rebuked for consulting with David Ewart, supposing him to be a magician, and that they should acknowledge their sorrow for their heinous sin before the congregation.

May 30th: James Hog and John Wood acknowledged their sorrow for their heinous sin of consulting David Ewart, a supposed sorcerer, about their stolen goods.

Innerwick.

Innerwick is designated CH2/1463 in the National Archives of Scotland. CH2/1463/1 contains minutes and accounts for 1648 - 49, and 1654 - 58. CH2/1463/2 contains transcript minutes and accounts from 1608 to 1695.

1612

June 20th: Patrick Neilson appeared, summoned for slandering Janet Lytster, the wife of John Chanslere. He affirms that what he said was no slander, but that it was all true. He declares that he will maintain it till his death that he bought a cow from John Chansler on Martinmas Day 1611. After he had brought the cow home, Janet Lytster, John Chansler's wife was very angry that the cow had been sold, and after that the cow would not allow Patrick Neilson's wife Catherine Grey to milk her for the two or three days that she was kept. After Patrick's wife took off the milk, she began sweating continuously, and soaked two shirts every twenty-four hours until the cow was burnt, and after that the sweating decreased somewhat. But she had no appetite for her food, and had a "raw" sweat, although not so much as before.

He declares that between Martinmas and Yule, on a day which had formerly been styled a fast, he saw Janet Lytster at night standing over him in the bed above his wife. She tried to tear the child that was in her arms away from his wife. He saw a fire burning in the hearth beside the chimney, and standing on the floor with Janet Lytster was Agnes Smyth, Christian Grinton, and Janet Hendrie. When he saw them he cried, "Lord be in this house!" With that Janet Lytster gave a leap upon the floor, and they all went away in an instant.

Catrein Gray, Patrick Neilson's wife, confirms all the above points to be true. She also heard one of them say, "Take the bairn, for she loves the bairn best," and Christian Grinton replied, "God forbid, for she loves it better than all her possessions." She wakened her husband and said, "Woeful man, what are they doing? Are they tearing at your child?" Janet Lytster looked her in the face as [illegible], and she [Catherine Grey] said, "Lord, how many women are here?"

Patrick also testifies that about the beginning of last March, when Christian Grinton was coming out of Skateraw, and Patrick was going down there, he said to her, "Christian, what's this you have done, coming to my house under silence of night with Agnes Smith, Janet Lytster, and Janet Hendry? Trying to take away my child, and torturing my wife so that she sweats continually?" She replied that whatever ailed him, she had done him no harm by word or deed, and she would come up and bring his wife something. He declares that she came up and gave him two fish, and two to his wife. After she had got the fish and eaten them she stopped sweating, and began to eat, whereas before she could eat nothing. Thus she got over her serious illness.

Catrine Grey declares concerning this, that Christian gave her a piece of rowan before she gave her the fish, and instructed her always to keep it in her purse. She also gave Catherine another piece of rowan which she kept in her chest. This was on St Helen's Day. Catrine affirms this to be true.

These two, Patrick Neilson and his wife Catrine Grey declared these things before the Session of Innerwick Kirk, the day and place foresaid, and promise to abide by their statements to the end.

Because of the gravity of the matter, the Session postpones discussion of this to the next session day.

[There sems to be no further reference to this case, but the Register of the Privy Council records the granting of a commission in 1613 to put Janet Lytster and others on trial for witchcraft.]

1614

John Walker appeared and was ordered to pay 13s 3d, and to satisfy church discipline as an absentee. [Having failed to appear when summoned.] He was also ordered to be here in a week's time in connection with his slandering of Kathrane Fleck by calling her a witch.

1654

April 23rd: Margaret Fender and Janet Muffet appeared and acknowledged their scolding. Janet Muffet complained against Margaret, alleging that she prayed for an accident like the one which befell John Denholm's cow. She named Alexander and Janet James as witnesses, and admitted that she had called her a witch.

Christian Denholm in Thurston complained about Marion Denholm there for calling her a witch, and named Thomas Brown and John Lawrie as witnesses. They were appointed to be summoned to the next session day.

April 30th: Alexander James appeared as a witness. Margaret Fender was called and asked if she had any objections to him as a witness. She declared that she had none, after which he was heard. He declared that as far as he could remember, he never heard Margaret Fender say any such thing as was alleged by Janet Muffet - that she cursed John Denholm's cow so that she would give nothing but blood to her calf.

Janet Muffet appeared, and named Alexander James, and Thomas Gray and his wife as witnesses who had heard Margaret Fender call her a witch just as much as she had called Margaret one.

Alexander James was called, appeared, and declared he heard both of them call each other witches. Thomas Gray and his wife are appointed to be summoned a fortnight today.

Marion Denholm in Thurston appeared and confessed that she called Christian Denholm a witch. She claimed that Christian said she had borne a "gait" [bastard] by her husband, and so would soon get a "gait" from her. However, she produced no witnesses, and Christian Denholm denied it. [The sense of this is difficult to unravel. It seems to be an accusation of adultery.]

The Session orders both of them to be publicly rebuked for scolding. Marion is to stand at the church door in white sheets a fortnight today, and then come in before the pulpit and ask Christian Denam's pardon for calling her a witch.

May 14th: Thomas Gray and his wife appeared, and both testified that they did not hear Margaret call Janet Moffat a witch. The Session orders Janet Moffat to stand at the church door in white sheets for calling Margaret Fender a witch. After that both of them are to come in before the pulpit and declare their repentance for their scolding and calumniating. May 21st: The scolders and calumniators who were ordered at the last meeting to make satisfaction did not appear today, and are recorded as "obstinat" [i.e. defying church discipline]. George Watt and John Denholm are appointed to speak to and deal with the obstinate persons in Overthornton, and William Denholm in Triplaw to speak to those in Thurston. [Probable reading. The original wording is confusing here.]

May 28th: George Watt declared that Janet Moffat was still obstinate. The Session refers her to the Presbytery.

June 4th: The Session was informed that Marion Denholm was still obstinate, and therefore refers her to the Presbytery.

June 18th: The minister reported the Presbytery's advice on the obstinate persons referred to them. If those concerned made a request to that effect to the Session, the white sheets should be dispensed with. Since these persons were in the churchyard, they were allowed in. They made an earnest supplication to the Session to be spared the white sheets, which was granted. They therefore undertook to satisfy church discipline the next session day.

1659

July 17th: A request was presented from William Cowan in Wallacemill, asking to be admitted to the Lord's Supper [*i.e.* Communion] when it is celebrated. The Session's answer is that since he was investigated some time ago by the Presbytery under suspicion of witchcraft, and had never yet shown a certificate that he had been cleared, they judged that he should bring one first.

1661

May 19th: William Pettiloe was reported for the scandal of using a charm. He went to five different houses in Eastbarns; the Laird's, John Brown's, Mr Robert Bryson's, John Dickson's [*Sic*; only four mentioned] to ask for "meet loomes" [measuring vessels for loose solids or liquids - *Dict.O.S.T.*] and old shoes for God's sake. He was confident that if he got them he would recover his health. Being present, he was called and confessed that not long ago as he was coming out of Dunbar he met a woman in Dryburn who advised him to do it. He denied that he had done it, and said he didn't know the woman. She was a poor itinerant and a stranger to him. The elders are appointed to make further inquiries about the deed, as the report about it is quite definite. He is to be present next session day.

June 9th: William Pettiloe was called but did not appear. The elders reported that he has fled. The Session recommends all possible inquiries to be made for him, since his flight increases the suspicion of his guilt.

October 14th: Public intimation was made that if any person had anything to say against William Cowan concerning witchcraft, for which he is now in prison, they should declare it at the convenient time and place. This was called three times at each door of the church to all and sundry, so that they could come to the Session with their declarations, but no-one appeared.

Inveresk.

Inveresk is designated CH2/531 in the National Archives of Scotland. Seventeenth century kirk session minutes survive for the period 1651 -1677. Inveresk parish contained the ancient burgh of Musselburgh and the adjacent fishing community of Fisherrow. Other sources show that witchcraft was certainly not unknown, and local tradition says that Musselburgh's witches were burned at the Bogle Hole, off Campie Road. Perhaps surprisingly, references to witchcraft in the kirk session minutes are few and far between.

Until recent local government reforms, Musselburgh was of course part of Midlothian, not East Lothian.

1651

December 14th: James Wickedshaw [?] complained that Gelles Finlason called him a witch's get, a thief, and a traitor hog. The bill was proved, and she was ordered to make her repentance the next Sabbath Day.

1653

July 12th: Robert Paistoun and his wife confessed that they went to a dumb man to ask about the stealing of their cloth. He said that he had been advised to go there. Archibald Hislop said to him, "Go to him if you like, and take the man with you that they say took it, and confront them with each other." Robert Paistoun is referred to the Presbytery.

Helinor Stevenson confessed that she went to the dumb man about her money that was missing.

August 16th: John Ker made his public repentance for the base scandal of attempting to "turn the key" to find money which had been stolen from a certain woman.

1659

April 5th: Marion Wilson appeared, servant to Thomas Mitchell, summoned before the Session for saying she saw the Devil sitting with Agnes Anderson ... [Unfortunately the rest of this is partly illegible, and the sense unclear.] ... and is now referred to the Justices of the Peace.

1661

June 4th: The Session has decided that whoever verbally abuses anyone who has had his mother or a relative burnt for the sin of witchcraft, will be liable to the censure of the church as well as being liable to a civil penalty from the magistrates. [This was intimated from the pulpit on June 9th.]

July 4th: John Whytfurd appeared and confessed that he fell in fornication with Helen Conker who is now in the Tolbooth for witchcraft. He is ordered to satisfy the penalty and make his repentance for committing such a sin.

July 7th: John Whytfurd made his repentance for fornication committed with Helen Concker.

August 18th: Marion Baker appeared, and was questioned as to how she was cured of the disease she had five or six years ago. [Several lines are left blank here.]   It was decided to have a further interrogation.

November 5th: The Session and the Baillies request the minister to make an announcement from the pulpit about Janet Stoddart who was imprisoned on suspicion of witchcraft. If anyone has anything worth considering to charge her with, they should come within ten or twelve days; otherwise she would be freed, since she was a great expense to the magistrates.

December 8th: The minister intimated from the pulpit that nobody should give shelter to Helen Brechenrig or Euphame Adare, who have fled from the parish of Dirleton after being accused and condemned for witchcraft.

Morham.

No 17th Century kirk session minutes have survived from Morham.

North Berwick.

North Berwick's kirk session minutes are designated CH2/285 in the National Archives of Scotland. Seventeenth Century minutes survive as follows:-

CH2/285/1 Transcribed extracts 1608 -1720
CH2/285/4   Minutes 1661-1684
CH2 7285/5 Minutes 1694-1721

Obviously any references from before 1661 only exist in transcription, and the originals have been lost. Some, but not all, witchcraft references after that appear both in the original minutes and as transcribed extracts.

1611

January 13th: Bessie Mansoun appeared, summoned for using rituals of charming to heal her child of whooping-cough. In particular, she put the child nine times into the hopper of a mill as it was grinding, and secondly, she gave the child a drink from a horn she had sent for with that intention. She admitted everything she was accused of, saying she had taken that course of action because she had heard from many people that both rituals were good for getting rid of whooping-cough. She did it with the intention of getting good health for her infant, after receiving sound advice. When she was asked who gave her the information about putting the child in the hopper, she couldn't remember, but she particularly remembers that when her servant woman was in Dirletoun, William Nielsoun [?], a weaver there, and his wife told her about it. She did it after that because they had said that if she performed that ritual it would heal the child.

When she was asked who had told her about the horn, she replied that when Jhone Hodge, a weaver now living in North Berwick, was in her house she asked him what was good for whooping-cough, and he said that he had heard that it would cure any child with that illness if it was given nine drinks out of the horn of a living ox. There was just such a horn in the house of his father-in-law Jhone Cluk [?] in Fysher Raw. The ox had broken its horn by chance, and it was still living at Saltcotts. After hearing this she sent for the horn, repaired it, and made the child drink out of it as she had been told.

She was asked if drinking out of the horn had cured her child, and she said that because the child was young and couldn't drink out of it, it did no good. Bessie then claimed that Jhone Hodge had told her that this horn had been used in this way for eight weeks among the children there.

Jhone Hodge appeared, and being asked about all this he admitted it, except the ritual of the nine drinks, which he denied. He was asked who had told him about the properties of such a horn, and he said he had heard it from people in whose company he had been, but could not now remember who. When he was asked where this horn was now, he replied that it was in his house. He was ordered to bring it to the Session. He went and brought it and laid it down before them. The clerk was ordered to keep it, and the parties concerned were dismissed until further notice.

January 22nd: Bessie Mansoun appeared. Questioned about the ritual of the hopper, she answered as she had done previously, and when asked who had told her about the horn being used in Saltcotts, she could not remember if it was Jhone Hodge or his boy. As far as the name Saltcotts is concerned, she didn't know whether it was Saltcotts or Estfeild. A name like that of course made a difference.

Thomas Buikless appeared about the horn. He confessed that he fetched the horn from Fysherraw for Jhone Clerk's wife, who was told to take care of it and send it back again. A letter is ordered to be sent to Musselburgh about this.

March 3rd: Bessie Mansoun appeared, confessing humbly upon her knees her offence in using charming for her child as described, and craving God's forgiveness for it. She was ordered to pay 20 shillings to the poor, which she consented to willingly.

June 16th: James Cook's wife Bentie [?] Miller appeared in connection with the scandal raised against Bessie Thomsoun, wife of Adame Harlaw in Weitscha, alleging that she is a witch. Bentie Miller declared that one of Bessie's sons had struck her painfully with a nail. She had kept the nail, and Bessie said it would be the dearest nail that had ever been taken in Weitscha. This was on the Saturday. The next Tuesday there fell on her [Bentie Miller] such a dizziness of heat in her heart which afflicted her for ten weeks until she came to Bessie and asked for her health for God's sake. At that Bessie answered that she had no more witchcraft than that cat. She took the cat by the ear and threw it past her. Bentie claims that within two days she recovered, and was improving daily. She had been told that the cat died shortly afterwards. Bessie, however, claimed that the cat was still alive, which she offered to prove to her neighbours.

Alison Fenton appeared, alleging that because she had cut corn in a "balk" which then belonged to Bessie she was angry with her. [A "balk" was usually a strip of uncultivated ground dividing one person's "rigs" or cultivation strips from his neighbour's. It would not be unusual for broadcast seed from an adjacent rig to fall and grow on the balk.] Bessie said she would cut as much of Alison's corn. A minute after that Alison fell down sick on the rig where she was cutting, and dreamed at night that Bessie was struggling and quarrelling with her. She was continually ill at ease until a bullock of hers died, and after that she recovered.

Nans Alexander appeared and affirmed that when her cow was giving birth, and the calf half born and half unborn, Bessie came in and asked for fire. She pushed towards the fireplace to take fire. Nans claims that her cow let go her milk. With great difficulty she stopped Bessie taking fire from her, and forcibly put her out. She saw there was fire in the smiddy and the smith's house, which were nearer Bessie's house than she was. Bessie, however, alleges that after the first refusal she willingly left the house and went her way.

Alison Howison appeared alleging that after a minor quarrel between her and Bessie, Bessie held her in sickness for a whole year together, having promised her a bad turn. Bessie had fetched fire out of her house in the morning when Alison was going to milk her cow. The cow had always given sufficient milk before, but immediately after this it would give no milk, and as yet still gives none. Bessie claims that the cow gave milk after the following Martinmas. It was alleged that Bessie had given shelter to Redcap's wife in [illegible] and given her a plateful of meal. She denied this but admitted giving her the meal. However, she had never done this since Redcap was burnt, which was at least seven years ago. If it could be proved otherwise, she was content that all the other allegations should be held to be true.

1654

April 10th: The minister reported that it was necesary for the Session to do something about those accused of witchcraft, and therefore the Session decided that all of those persons should be brought to the next session day so that they could be referred to the Justices of the Peace.

April 12th: The names were given in of those who have been accused of witchcraft, and who are to be referred to the justices when they sit. Considering that there have been many instances discovered in the county of the abominable sin of witchcraft; and considering that John Nicolsone's wife Elspeth Carter in this parish had confessed herself guilty of that sin in the year of God 1650, and that her confession had been attested by the Presbytery; also that William Wheit, John Guild, and Marie Lauder in this parish were arrested and imprisoned at that time on information given by dying and confessing witches, although they did not themselves confess; also that several other persons - Agnes Yeaman, Elspeth Pattersone, Margaret Mill, and Alison Hill - were accused by one or more confessing witches, although they were not apprehended; the Session thought it their duty to lay this before the honourable Justices of Peace within the County, so that they can take whatever course of action they judge to be in keeping with the supposition of the foresaid persons' guilt. John Bennet is delegated to attend to the first letter from the honourable Justices of Peace, and to communicate with them. The Laird of Sydserf Robert Aitcheson is asked to assist him in making his representations. July 19th: 49 shillings given for bread and drink for Marioun Patterson, and 30 shillings lent by her son-in-law for her upkeep in prison.

1661

August 25th: [This is dated 1654 in the "extracts", but it is in fact 1661 in the original minutes.] Andrew Stuart appointed to speak to the "tutors" [*i.e.* the guardians of a minor] of the Marquis of Douglas about Marion Paterson in the Mains of Tantallon who confessed to witchcraft.

November 17th: A bill of complaint was read which had been given in by Anna Home against Janet Macklurge for calling her a common whore and a witch's get. They are to appear next session day. [Janet was called twice and did not appear because of illness. She finally appeared on 15th December and "confessed sorrow on her knees"]

1663

May 15th: A bill of complaint was given in by James Blackie against Elspeth Curr for calling his wife a witch. They are to be summoned to the next session day.

May 17th: [The minutes mistakenly say March.] Elspeth Curr was called and appeared. Challenged about the complaint, she admitted it, but said he called her a squint-eyed bitch. He denies this. They are summoned to the next session day.

May 24th: Elspeth Curr was called and appeared. Challenged again about the complaint, she admitted it and professed grief for it. She was appointed to appear and testify to this before the congregation next Lord's Day. She was also warned that if she did not live more peaceably she would be put out of the parish.

A complaint was given in by Adam Gilles and his wife Christian Watsone against John Kummine and his wife Margaret Hannin for calling them witches. John was called and appeared, and being challenged about this, declared that Christian called his wife a common whore first, and then she called her a witch. Being asked what grounds she had for this, he answered that they had no grounds, only that they were doing some things which people disliked, such as tying grains of wheat with the same number of grains of salt to their cow's horn. Andrew Blair, Samuel Yeul, William Leslie, and Margaret Hercus can verify this. Adam was again called in and challenged for doing this. He replied that there was no witchcraft in so doing. Livestock was vulnerable to harm, and they would do all they could for their preservation. When asked who had taught him to do this, he said that when his cow had not been well for eight or ten days, a certain Thomas Bookles had told him to do it. Adam's wife was called and challenged on this particular, and replied that it was true they had tied grains of wheat with salt to the cow's horn. Adam didn't know what more he could do. He'd only used nine grains of wheat with the same amount of salt. The Session couldn't make them out to be witches for doing that! They are appointed to appear next session day with the witnesses. John Hog is to enquire where Thomas Bookles is living so that he can also be summoned.

November 1st: Adam Gilles was called and appeared with the witnesses. Asked if he had any objections why these witnesses might not be admitted to testify in the business, he said he had none. They were then charged upon oath to declare what they knew of the matter. Margaret Hercus testified that when she and Andrew Blair were in the cattle fold they saw a piece of cloth tied round the cow's horn. She untied it, and there were eleven grains of wheat with the salt. Then she put it back again. Asked if she knew the cow was sick, she said that she didn't know. The rest testified similarly, and said that the cloth had been tied to the cow's horn for fourteen days.

John Hog reported that Thomas Bookles had no settled residence, but at present was in the parish of Dumbar. A letter was therefore appointed to be written to the minister there, to cause Thomas to appear before the Session at their next meeting.

November 8th: John Hoge reported that when he was out, Thomas Bookles had by chance come to his house, and his wife had asked him about the matter. He said that when Adam said his cow was not well, he told him that wheat and salt would do her good, but he didn't tell him to apply them. She asked him to come to the Session to tell them this, but he said he would not. Walter Smart is therefore appointed to take some others with him next Wednesday to hear what Thomas has to say about the matter.

November 22nd: Walter Smart reported that he had spoken to Thomas Bookles before several honest men. He declared that Adam Gilles had been bemoaning the fact that his cow was so sick that he feared she was "forespoken" [bewitched]. He said rowan tree was a good thing to keep both on man and beast. The matter is referred to the Presbytery for advice. December 20th: The minister reported that it was the Presbytery's advice that John Kummin's wife should be publicly censured for making allegations against Adam Gilles and his wife which she cannot prove. Adam Gilles should be publicly censured for practising that which gave just offence to his neighbours, and Adam's wife for calling John's wife a common whore. They are all appointed to appear when John Kummine's wife has been delivered of her child.

1664

March 20th: Adam Gilles and his wife, and John Kummin and his wife are appointed to appear before the next meeting of the Session.

March 28th: Adam Gilles and his wife appeared with John Kummin and his wife. John and his wife professed grief for alleging against their neighbours that which they could not prove, as did Adam and his wife for offending them by using scandalous customs. They promised to beware of doing this sort of thing again, as the Presbytery commanded. They were all appointed to testify to this next Lord's Day.

April 3rd: The foresaid persons appeared before the congregation, confessed as aforesaid, and promised to live more peaceably in future.

1668

June 21st: A bill of complaint was given in by Issobell Anderson against Catharin Wilson for calling her a blackened and exposed witch. Catharen was called and admitted this, but said Issobell had first struck her in the face. They were appointed to appear next session day.

June 28th: Issobell Anderson was called and appeared, and was asked if she could prove Catharene Wilsone was a thief. She answered that everybody knew that she stole corn with her father, and that William Mitchell caught her stealing the Chambers' whins. When Catharen Wilson was asked if she could prove that Issobell Anderson was a witch, she replied that she could not, but several people had called her so. The Session considered that they had both wronged each other, and appoints them both to admit this before the Session, or before the congregation next Lord's Day if they can't agree. They are referred to the magistrates of the burgh for further censure.

That same day a bill of complaint was given in by George Hendersone against Jeane Hoge for calling him a "runnagate beggar dog", and in the streets called his wife a "witch carlene" and himself a "runagate warlow carle". Jeane was called and denied this, and said that George called her a common whore and thief, and said that she had not thriven and would not thrive. She said to him that if she was not going to thrive, then he must be a warlock. They are appointed to appear next session day with the witnesses.

July 5th: George Henderson's case was deferred because of Jeane's illness. July 12th: Jeane Hoge was called and appeared. Being challenged as above, she continued in her denial, alleging that George called her as above. He denied this. Robert Thomsone and his wife were called as witnesses. Asked if they had any objections against these persons testifying, they said they had none. Robert testified on oath that Jeane called George "runagate beggar carle", and George called her "false toun, theife, and whoore".

Helene Darlene appeared and declared as above. The Session considered that they had both dishonoured God and wronged each other's good name, and orders them to confess their faults before the Session on their knees, and to take each other by the hand, which they did. They were referred to the civil magistrate for a "pecunial mulct" [fine].

July 19th: Issobell Anderson appeared before the Session with Catharene Wilsone. They testified their repentance on their knees for wronging each other's good name, and in token of friendship took one another by the hand, and promised to beware of similar behaviour in future.

1669

May 2nd: The minister reported that Bessie Clarke claims that William Weit had bewitched her child, and that Lady Beill had told her that the child would not recover till she could get blood from him above the breath. Thus, she suddenly attacked him and bled him several times about the nose with a needle, then fell down on her knees three separate times and asked her child's life from him. She is to be at the Session next session day.

May 9th: Bessie Clarke was called and appeared. She acknowledged as above, and professed to be truly sorry. Since the case is difficult and out of the ordinary, the Session refers it to the presbytery for advice.

May 16th: The minister reported that the Presbytery had appointed Bessie Clarke to appear before them so that they could be clearer in their minds before giving judgement and advice. Bessie has been summoned to appear before the Presbytery at Hadingtoun on Thursday twenty days from now. In the meantime, the Session appoints Robert Sandilands to acquaint Lady Beill with the calumny laid to her charge by Bessie, and to report her answer to the Session [Note that although the Session does not shirk its duty to investigate Lady Biel's role in the affair, it does so with rather more circumspection than it would have shown to someone of more lowly status!]

July 18th: Bessie Clark refused to obey the Presbytery's orders, and was referred to the civil magistrate. She promised him that she would satisfy church discipline the next session day. July 29th: Bessie Clarke had agreed to answer church discipline during divine service. She was summoned, but since she did not confess her sin she was appointed to appear again before the Session in sackcloth, and then appear next day before the congregation. October 30th: Bessie Clarke was called and appeared. She was asked if she was any more aware of her grievous sin in seeking her child's life from the Devil. She answered that ever since she had been begging mercy from God for it, and would do so as long as she lived. After sending her out, the Session decided that she should testify her repentance for the sin before them on her knees. Being called in again, she did as she was told, and was referred to the civil magistrate. The minister is to declare this from the pulpit next Sunday. November 11th: The minister declared from the pulpit that Bessie Clark had satisfied the discipline of the church for the foresaid sin, and was absolved from the scandal.

1672

March 17th: A bill of complaint was given in by Adam Gilles against John Cargill and his wife for calling his daughter a witch's get, and saying that her father had turned many [illegible] and laid her father twenty weeks in his bed with sickness. They are to attend the next session day with the witnesses.

March 24th: Adam Gilles's wife was called and appeared. She declared she said nothing at all to Margaret Leslie, but Margaret's daughter had called her a scourged thief. Margaret Leslie appeared and said that Adam's daughter had called her a thief's get, and hit her on the head with a staff. Adam's daughter was called and denied this.

Adam Gilles and John Cargill were asked if they had any objection to John Sandie and Bessie Nielsone [as witnesses] and they said they had none. John Sandie then testified upon oath that John Cargill had a calf which was in the habit of butting people. The calf was butting at Adam's wife who was lying under it, and when her daughter came to chase it away Margaret Leslie came and hit her, and called her a witch's get. Adam's daughter said that Margaret had been scourged round Tantallon. Bessie Nielsone was also called, and declared that she came and helped up the woman who had been lying under the calf, but knew no more about it. She was appointed to appear again at the next meeting with the rest of the witnesses.

March 31st: John Cargill and Adam Gilles were called and appeared with their witnesses. Adam and his daughter were asked if they had any objections to Thomas Macklennen, Marion Littel, and Margaret Scougal as witnesses. They replied that they had none. Thomas Macklennen declared that he heard them miscalling each other, but neither heard nor saw anything more. Margaret Scougal declared that John's calf used to butt the children in the place. Margaret Leslie struck Adam's daughter first, then Adam's daughter did the same to her, and they miscalled each other. Issobell [sic] Littel declared as above. The civil magistrates, therefore, with the advice of the Session, appointed John Cargill to pay 40 shillings Scots, and to kill his calf. His wife Margaret professed repentance on her knees for calling her neighbour that which she could not prove. Adam's daughter did the same. Being reconciled, they were informed that if they fell out again they would pay double and satisfy church discipline publicly. They agreed to this and were dismissed.

June 2nd: Adam Gilles was called, appeared, and was challenged for not living at peace with his neighbours. He said he was not at home when his wife and daughter fell out with John Sandie and his wife Helen ffoster, but if they were at fault at all it was because Sandie and his wife had called his children witch's gets, which they could not put up with. Helen ffoster was called and confessed that she had said this. Asked what evidence she had for saying it, she said that when she was a servant in Robert Scougal's house, Adam's wife Christian Watson often came on the Sabbath Day asking for yeast, and afterwards neither the yeast nor the ale was any good.

John Sandie was called, appeared, and being similarly questioned he sajd that a long time ago, late at night in harvest time, Christian Watsone came to him and said, There's a pea-drying kiln on fire. Will you go to it?" His wife had taken him by the shoulders and pushed him into the house and said he was not to go, for he would get the same as the people in Prestoun who went to see a pea-drying kiln. He said that Christian, Adam's wife, came and took a piece of turf off the house [Roofs were often covered with turf.] and his wife was never well after that. He would never deny that he called them what he did. The Session gives then a week from today to prove it, and to find surety under the penalty of £10 from each of them that they would not fall out again with Adam and his wife and children. Also that they should attend when the Session summoned them.

June [No date given in the minutes.]: John Sandie and his wife Helen ffoster were called and appeared. Asked what further proof they had of the above allegations, John said there was nobody present that time but himself, and said that he was truly sorry for the allegation. His wife said the same. The Session appoints John to acknowledge his fault before them, which he did. Because his wife was the guilty party, and the one who had started off the whole business, she is to testify her repentance for slandering her neighbour, before the congregation next Sunday. They were ordered to pay ten pounds if they fall out with them [Adam and Christian] again, or anyone else. Adam and his wife and children were ordered to pay the same if they did likewise.

[Adam Gilles was complained against on 6th April 1673 for calling a weaver a thief on a Sunday, and asking if his patches had stolen thread in them. Adam admitted this, and repented on his knees. George Youl, one of the elders, stood surety that Adam would "never do the lyke in all time coming."]

1676

June 18th: George Anderson appeared, complaining about Robert Johnston and his wife. Robert had come to his house alleging that George's servant woman had struck his dog. He hit her and knocked her over, and said to George that if he didn't dismiss her he would do him an evil turn. He also called George's wife a white-faced bitch. ["White-faced": the word used in the minutes is "bleaken", meaning bleached or blanched. It could in fact refer to her clothes, hair, or complexion; and rather than "white-faced", might mean washed-out, pallid, peelly-wally, etc.]

Robert Johnston appeared. He denied striking her, but did knock her over. When asked if he said he would do George an evil turn if he did not dismiss her, he denied it, but said he would give his life to be revenged on her. He was asked, what if it could be proved that he had said so, and he replied that it would not be.

Robert's wife appeared and denied that she had miscalled George's wife, but said George's wife had given ten ill words for every one of hers, and had called her a witch.

Margaret Bennet appeared and said Jean called her a witch's get and a white-faced bitch, in front of Robert Smart and Adam Gillis and his daughter. They are appointed to appear next session day. When Margaret was asked if she had called Jean a witch she denied it. She was appointed to appear again next session day with the witnesses.

June 25th: Robert Johnston and his wife were called and appeared. They were asked if they had anything against Adam Gilles, Robert Smart, and Margaret Wait being admitted to testify in the case. They answered they had nothing. Adam Gilles was asked if he heard Robert say that if George Anderson would not dismiss his woman [servant], he would do him an evil turn. He declared that he heard him say that if he would not give him satisfaction, he would take it! He was asked if he heard Jean Reid going through the loan cursing and miscalling Margaret Bennet. He answered that she called her a squint-eyed kestrel and such like. ["Stainchel" can mean an iron bar or a kestrel. "Kestrel" is perhaps more likely here, suggesting that she is hawk-faced.] Asked if he heard Margaret Bennet call her a witch, he replied that he did not. Robert Smart declared that Robert Johnston said if he did not get satisfaction he would be "full of George's flesh", and his wife said she would be full of Margaret Bennet's flesh. Going through the loan she called Margaret a white-faced bitch and cursed frequently. Margaret Weit appeared and declared as above.

The Session appoints Jean Reid to apear before the congregation next Sunday to testify her repentance for slandering and cursing her neighbour. She is to pay 13s 4d, or stand an hour in the jougs. Robert was referred to the magistrate.

July 2nd: Robert Johnston professed true repentance for turning his mind to wrong his neighbours. He humbled himself before the Session, and promised to beware of doing the like in future, and handed over thirteen shillings and fourpence for the use of the poor. His wife was appointed to appear next session day.

1677

September 10th: A "testament" was signed for Margaret Shireffe and her children who were going to London to the King to be helped for "the creualls", otherwise called the "king's evil". [The king's evil was the skin disease scrofula, which it was believed could be cured by the touch of the King. Charles II regularly "touched for the king's evil". It is interesting to consider that attempts by anyone else to cure a disease by touch would have been treated as charming or witchcraft, and therefore sinful, illegal, and punishable. Margaret's "testament" is a sort of travel-pass certifying her good character and intent.]

1678

18th August: Adam Gilles was called, and appeared complaining about Robert Johnston.

Adam's daughter had driven away Robert's pigs from their feed with a stick, and Robert called Adam Gilles a warlock dog, and told him to come out or he would burn his house down on him. Robert Johnston appeared and admitted this. He was appointed to appear next session day to prove it [*i.e.* to prove the epithet "warlock"].

24th August: Robert Johnston was called and appeared. He confessed that he was very sorry for what he said to Adam Gilles, and that he could not prove it. He agreed that if he should fall out again with him or anyone else, he should be imprisoned until he could pay ten pounds, and he should then be banished from the parish.

[In September Adam Gilles was summoned for making ropes from pea-straw on the Sabbath, and had to repent before the congregation on 6th October.]

1679

June 1st: Walter Smart reported that Robert Johnston and his wife, and Adam Gilles and his wife had fallen out again. Robert Johnston appeared and declared that he wasn't there when they fell out, and didn't know what had happened. Adam Gilles appeared and declared that Robert and his wife miscalled him and his daughter.

Considering that they had fallen out so often, and been processed by the Session so frequently, the Session referred them to the Sheriff and put them out of the parish.

Oldhamstocks.

Oldhamstocks is designated CH2/288 in the National Archives of Scotland. Kirk Session minutes survive for the period 1642-1707. The records are copious and legible, but although there are the usual droves of fornicators and adulterers, as far as I could see there was not a single reference to witchcraft or charming.

Ormiston.

Ormiston is designated CH2/292 in the National Archives of Scotland. Seventeenth Century Kirk Session minutes survive as follows: -

CH2/292/1   -   Minutes 1648-49
CH2/292/2   -   Minutes 1683-89
CH2/292/3   -   Minutes 1690-1703.

There appear to be no references to witchcraft or charming. In June 1649 Margaret Gait denied blasphemy, saying that she had only remarked, "Over holy was hanged." She had said to her neighbour who had reproved her that the neighbour was not one of the "holy women of Longniddry". Who the holy women of Longniddry were, and why they were hanged, is a mystery.

Pencaitland.

Pencaitland is designated CH2/296 in the National Archives of Scotland. Kirk Session minutes [CH2/296/1] are extant for the period 1633-1703 with gaps from 1659 to 1662, and 1674 to 1684.

1651

October 5th: Agnes Burnet to be summoned before the Session for putting a nail in a dead corpse after it was... [Final word illegible, but probably means "dressed in its winding sheet or shroud]

November 18th: The session meeting was chaired by Mr James Calderwood, minister at Humbie. Enquiries were made whether there was any new scandal. Agnes Burnet was summoned, appeared, and confessed that she got a "kist" nail [This could be a chest nail or a coffin nail - probably the latter.] from her sister and put it between the winding sheet and the corpse. She said this was to stop her spirit coming back again. She denied that she brought the nail for this on purpose, but that it was a nail from the coffin. [Probable reading. The original is confusing.] She confessed she had heard about doing this from Bessie Crail in Saltoun.

November 20th: Alexander Gray in Templehall gave in a bill of complaint that he was being falsely accused of witchcraft, whereupon Jenet Paterson was ordered to be summoned to the next session day.

November 27th: Jenet Patersone appeared, and denied that she called Alexander Gray a witch. The business was then deferred until the witnesses could be heard - John Coalston, Thomas Fowles, and William Uttersyde.

December 18th: The witnesses in Alexander Gray's case appeared. But since the parties themselves were absent the case was postponed till the next session day, and the witnesses appointed to be present then.

1654

February 26th: Alexander Gray appeared and gave in a bill of complaint against Jonet Patersone for calling him a witch. She denied it. Alexander promised to prove it with two witnesses who had heard her say it, namely William Uttersyde and John Coalston. They are ordered to be summoned to the next session day.

March 19th: John Coalstone and William Uttersyde appeared as witnesses against Jonet Pattersone. They testified that they heard her say that Alexander Gray was to blame for her child's death. She admitted this and promised to satisfy church discipline.

July 18th: Elspeth Plaine appeared and gave in a bill of complaint against Thomas Gilchrist for calling her a witch, a thief, and a "lowne" before two witnesses, Willian Long and George Gibsone, who were ordered to be summoned to the next session day.

July 23rd: Thomas Gilchrist and Elspeth Plaine appeared. The witnesses supported Elspeth Plaine's bill of complaint. Thomas Gilchrist was ordered to satisfy church discipline.

1663

January 11th: Marion Painstone and Jennet Mill are ordered to be summoned for going to a dumb woman to enquire for something that was missing. Also John Biggins for the same fault.

January 18th: Marioun Painstone and Jennet Mill were called and appeared. They acknowleged their fault and were sharply rebuked, and earnestly admonished to beware of this sort of thing in future. Likewise John Biggin, who was dealt with accordingly.

1688

April 29th: The minister reported that Agnes Bartleman had told him that John Watsone had given her herbs to destroy the child she had conceived. Robert Hay declared that he had got these herbs from the gardener of Walliford.

1694

May 20th: John Gray gave in a bill of complaint against Margaret Sinclare and her daughter Margaret Conquer for calling him a witch's get, wishing that his soul was boiling in Hell's cauldron, and saying that his soul had been in hell long before now. She also called him a drunken "slate" [a dirty, slovenly, or nasty person - *Concise Scots Dict.*] and much more, as witnessed by William Bell, Wiliam fford, and Alexander Smyth.

June 3rd: Margaret Sinclare was summoned and appeared today.

June 17th: Margaret Sinclare was rebuked today for her slanderous speeches against John Gray.

1698

May 15th: Marion Carfrae was summoned and appeared. She declared that some of David Allan's servants came in to see the dumb woman. Agnes Harper was summoned and appeared, and confessed that she was guilty. She declared that Jean Williamson and Janet Hog were there, and that Adam Laing, James Clerk, and Robert Rid were also there. Agnes Hay was summoned and appeared, and declared that Jean Robertson and Isabell Turner were there, and that they each gave the dumb woman money. Janet Hog and Jean Robertson gave her a plack [four pence Scots], and Agnes Wedderburn gave her a plack.

Prestonkirk.

The parish of Prestonkirk was often known as "Prestonhaugh" in the 17th Century. The parish has East Linton as its main settlement, and should not of course be confused with Prestonpans. Prestonkirk's kirk session minutes are designated CH2/306 in the National Archives of Scotland. CH2/306/1 contains "Minutes and collections 1691-97 and 1692-1733". CH2/306/2 contains "Minutes and collections 1692-1724". There appear to be no references to witchcraft or charming.

Prestonpans.

Prestonpans is designated CH2/307 in the National Archives of Scotland. Seventeenth Century kirk session records survive as follows
CH2/307/6 Accounts and discipline 1671-77
CH2/307/22 Discipline 1690-97
CH2/307/23 Discipline 1697-1702
CH2/307/28 a] Extracts from records 1637-42
b] Notabilia interspersed throughout Records of Discipline in Prestonpans

Obviously CH2/307/28 will contain extracts from original minutes which are now lost. These include: -

1606

December 25th: It is decided that Robert Hamilton, baillie, Mr Wm Hamilton, John Cubie [?], George Ker, George Hamilton are to go in to Edinburgh to speak to the Council, to purchase a commission for the arrest of Isobel Griersone, and that the commission should invest the Sheriff of Haddington, David Seyton, Robert Hamilton, baillie, Mr Alexander [?] Hamilton, David Hamilton, Alexander Cranston, George Hamilton, George Ker, and John Cubie with power as judges.

[Isobel Grierson from Prestonpans was tried by the High Court of Justiciary for witchcraft in 1607. Might she have been related to Robert Grierson from Prestonpans, one of the "North Berwick" witches? She was sentenced to be strangled and burnt on the Castle Hill of Edinburgh, which makes the next extract a bit of a puzzle.]

1609

Isobel Grierson is to be imprisoned in the steeple until she pays 40 shillings for slandering Elspet Christie.

[CH2/307/6 contains no reference to witchcraft. However, there is much of interest in CH2/307/22 and 23.]

1691

4th May: [I have summarised this lengthy and verbose entry. The clerk is addicted to ponderous polysyllables and complex sentence structure.] Elspet Russel appeared at the instance of Barbara Ramsay who gave in a bill last session day against her. The witnesses were Rebecca Whinton, Helen Hog, Isabel Brown, Rebecca Kerr, and Barbara Glass, and all of them declared unanimously that Elspeth Russel called Barbara Ramsay a devil, and said that she deserved to go the same way Agnes Kelly went who was burnt as a witch. She called Barbara's son an imp of the Devil, who had come out of the loins of the Devil. The bill was judged sufficiently proved, and Barbara was asked what punishment would satisfy her. She said she would consult with her husband when he came home.

1692

February 24th: Alexander Hamilton in Newhaven [i.e, probably Morrison's Haven] gave in a bill of complaint to the Session against Robert Taylor, the Laird of Prestongrange's overseer, for calling him and his wife the Devil's servants. As proof Thomas Vint, William Muir, Robert Wilsone, and Malcolm Robison were named as witnesses. They and Robert Taylor were ordered to be summoned to the next session day.

March 9th: [Summarised] Robert Taylor appeared and admitted his fault, that he had rashly and inadvisedly slandered Hamilton and his wife. He was heartily sorry, and received a grave admonition.

June 1st: Agnes Cuthbertson in the Grange appeared, complaining about Agnes Locke, also in the Grange, for alleging not only that she and her husband James Summervaill had stolen some money from her, but had also slandered Agnes's good name. It was also claimed that persuaded by Doctor Makie's advice, Agnes Lock had gone to Edinburgh and consulted James Cathcart, an astrologer, about the money that had been taken from her. She had also consulted Robert Alane, a servant man in Seatoun, about it. Also Robert Irvine, overseer to the Laird of Prestongrange, had written some figures and had them put in water to enquire after the money. Doctor Makie and Robert Irvine were ordered to be summoned to the next session day. The complainer Agnes Cuthbertson and the defender Agnes Lock are to wait upon the Session accordingly.

June 22nd: Agnes Cuthbertson and Agnes Lock appeared, but the case was postponed until the next session day. [The session clerk's post then fell vacant and there is no further mention of this case.]

1693

July 20th: Janet Cousing appeared, complaining about Janet Reid for slandering her and calling her a witch. Janet Cousing was appointed to draw up her case for next Sunday, with the witnesses to prove it, and produced forty shillings to be forfeited if the case should fail.

July 23rd: [Summarised] Janet Reid was called but did not appear. She was appointed to be summoned to the next meeting. In the meantime she was referred to the civil magistrate to be punished for her defiance, and to be compelled to appear. Two witnesses appeared, but their evidence was deferred until the next session day.

December 3rd: Janet Reid appeared, following several citations to answer Janet Cousing's case against her, which up until now has been delayed by the defender's alleged sickness.

Janet Reid was sharply rebuked for her long absence, and was afterwards asked by the minister if she could prove Janet Cousing was a witch. She replied that she had often called Janet Cousing a witch, but could not prove she was one. At this the minister and Session ordered both parties to be removed, and declared the bill sufficiently proved by Janet Reid's own confession. Janet Cousing was therefore ordered to uplift her 40 shillings surety, and it was unanimously decided that Janet Reid should stand before the whole congregation next Lord's Day and acknowledge her sin and fault in slandering and taking away her neighbour Janet Cousing's good name by calling her a witch, which she could not prove. As regards Janet Reid's allegation that Janet Cousing had also slandered her, they appointed her to draw up her bill against Janet Cousing with witnesses to prove it for the next session day, with forty shillings Scots as surety in case of failure.

10th December: Jennet Reid appeared as appointed before the congregation, standing opposite the pulpit, for slandering her neighbour Jennet Cousing by calling her a witch. When she was called upon by the minister, Mr James Hay, she justified herself instead of confessing and acknowledging her sin and fault. She was therefore not absolved of the scandal, but referred to the civil magistrate to be suitably punished for mocking God and the congregation.

1695

January 6th: Janet Reid appeared, convicted on page 91 [of the minute book] for slandering her neighbour, and for mocking God and the congregation by excusing and justifying herself instead of confessing and acknowledging her sin and fault, as she was appointed to do on the same page 91 of this book. All of this she acknowledged and confessed, referring herself to the Session's pleasure in the matter, and wholly submitting to the sentence and punishment. After she had been sent out, and the Session had considered and discussed the whole complex business, it was decided by majority of votes, that Janet Reid should be sharply rebuked, and should acknowledge her sin before the Session by falling down upon her knees and humbling herself before God and the Session. When called on, she willingly acquiesced, and falling down on her knees and acknowledging her great sin before the minister and Session, she was absolved of the scandal, and dismissed with an exhortation to live more circumspectly in future.

1696

January 22nd: William Cuthbertson, skipper, gave in a bill against Helen Purves, wife of James Drummond, sheriff officer. He complained that she abused him and called him witch's get. He named James Chalmers, William Broun, and William Davidson as witnesses to prove it, and deposited 40 shillings surety in case of failure, according to act of Session. All parties were appointed to be summoned to appear at the next meeting.

January 29th: Today, Wednesday, the beadle summoned as ordered Helen Purves who was reported by William Cuthbertson, skipper. When called by the beadle she did not appear, sending the excuse that she was not able to come so far. The case was therefore delayed until the next meeting. In the meantime the Session nominated Alexander Blunthorn, Robert Jamieson, and James Chalmers to investigate the truth of her indisposition. February 12th: Summoned as ordered, and called thrice by the beadle, Helen Purves did not appear. Alexander Blunthorn, Robert Jamieson, and James Chalmers reported that she was perfectly able to appear, being in ordinary health. She was therefore again summoned to the next meeting.

February 26th: Summoned for the third and last time, and thrice called by the beadle, Hellen Purves did not appear. She was therefore unanimously referred to the civil magistrate to be suitably punished for defiance and contempt of church discipline, and to be compelled to appear.

1697

August 3rd: A charge brought by Helen Hoge and Agnes Bizet her daughter, both living in Prestonpans, against Margaret Auchterlony, daughter to James Gardner in Prestonpans, for slandering Helen Hoge's good name by calling Helen a witch, and Agnes a witch's get. As proof, the following witnesses were led - John Grege, Robert Dawson, and James Smout, all salters. Forty shillings was deposited until the charge should be proved, as required by act of Session. The Session appoints all parties to be summoned to the next session day; pursuer, defender, and witnesses.

August 4th: Today, Wednesday the fourth of August 1697, was summoned Margaret Ouchterlony reported to the last meeting on Tuesday the 3rd of this month of August 1697 for slandering Helen Hoge and Agnes Bizet her daughter, both of whom also appeared. Margaret denied that she called Helen either witch or warlock, but had asked her why she called her [Margaret's] brother a dog. Helen said that her brandy, which had been seized by the customs officers ["waiters"], was drunk at Margaret's brother's funeral feast ["dergie"]. She named Anna Johnston, Isabell Watson, and Isabell Low as witnesses who could prove this. John Grege and James Smout, salters, were summoned and called as witnesses to prove Helen Hoge's case. John Grege gave his oath, and James Smout was objected to and discarded as "not worthy of the King's unlaw." [i.e. a worthless and destitute person]. However, only one witness could prove nothing.

August 4th: Anna Johnston, Isabell Watson, and Isabell Low appeared as witnesses in Margaret Ouchterlony's defence. When they had all been solemnly sworn before the minister and Session they testified unanimously that Helen Hoge said that her brandy had been drunk at the funeral feast of John Ouchterlony, whom she called "the dog". The Session unanimously concluded that the bill was proven.

Christopher Knolls, indweller in Prestonpans, gave in a charge to the minister and Session against Helen Hoge, widow there, as follows:-

"Helen Hoge, widow in Prestonpans, came to my house on the 5th of July 1697, while my son-in-law John Ouchterlony was alive, and ran to the bedroom where John was lying, and could not be stopped although my wife told her that her son was breathing heavily and sleeping, and could not be disturbed. She looked into the bed and said, 'Young man, you have been raving as my daughter-in-law did; for she said there was a witch in the house who had bewitched her. But jo, jo, [i.e. my dear] there was no witch there.'

My wife Janet Gardner took her out of the bedroom, and took her as far as the foot of the stair. Helen Hoge, kneeling down and holding Robert Ouchterlony by the hand, said to her, 'God's curse come on him, [John] and let him never come out of the bed, but let him pine like a head-hair until he declares my innocence.' She would have gone into the bedroom again, but Janet Gardner closed the door and would not allow it She also said that she hoped to see him in hell, with other horrid imprecations and curses, and said that she would be revenged on Janet Gardner and her daughter Margaret Ouchterlony.

The following Wednesday, July 7th, the minister had sent two elders to hear what John Ouchterlony had to say against Helen Hoge. It was written down by John Hepburn and Samuel Forrest in the presence of William Cuthbertson, skipper. [There is no mention of this in the July Kirk Session minutes.] After the elders and the skipper had gone away, Hellen prayed that John might never leave this world, and that he might pine like a hair of her head till he asked her pardon. She said that she trusted to see him in hell, with many other unchristian and horrid expressions. About six hours before John died, about the dead time of the night, John cried out, 'Mother, mother, there's Helen Hoge!' Janet Gardner [his mother] answered, 'No, my bird. God be present here, you cause my hair to creep!' He replied, 'Oh mother, I see her!' But we saw nothing but a cat, and after it had been thrown out of the window, a woman's head appeared looking in through the glass, which was seen by everyone sitting there. The witnesses for proving this are Alexander Seton, collector [of customs dues]; James Smith, clerk; James Robertson; Henry Linn; James Bell; Robert Ouchterlony; Thomas Eison; Elspeth Sands; Helen Tomson[?]; Marion Waddel; Eupham Steill; Agnes Burton."

The Session appointed everyone to be summoned to their next meeting. Christopher deposited forty shillings until the case is proved.

[Oddly enough there is no further mention of this case. Nor is there any evidence from other sources that Helen Hogg was ever put on trial for witchcraft.]

1699

April 10th: A most opprobrious letter of complaint was given in by Helen Bizet against Alexander Drummond, salter, which she offered to prove with witnesses. She deposited two pounds in the hands of the clerk. Alexander Drummond appeared before the Session and affirmed that he did nothing to provoke Helen Bizet, but only said that it was very good salt her salters were putting in the girnel [store-house]. She told him, "Begone filthy slave and villain." He denied the part of the complaint where it was alleged that he said she had got her gear [possessions and wealth] from the Devil, and that the Devil would get her and it both.

Helen Bizet produced witnesses to prove her case. Mrs Hog appearing as a witness declared that Alexander Drummond called Helen Bizet a witch's get, and said that he would knock her head to pieces, and that she had got her gear from the Devil.

Andrew Pirie was led as a witness and said that Alexander Drummond came into his house and took up a place, and would not go away. Helen Bizet grew angry at this and said, "How can you be so impertinent as to come into my company, when you say that my father died with a plate full of bubbles at his head." Alexander Drummond replied calling her a witch's granddaughter. [The significance of the plate full of bubbles is not immediately obvious. Perhaps Helen's father died coughing up blood, and it was suspected that witchcraft was the cause.] Ana Johnstone corroborated what Mrs Hog had witnessed.

Alexander Drummond was appointed by the Session to produce his witnesses to prove the truth of what he had said. Otherwise the Session would look upon him as guilty and Mrs Cuthbertson's complaint as proven. [Mrs Cuthbertson is presumably Helen Bizet.] This was to be done for the next meeting.

April 18th: The minister, Thomas Vint, and John Robertson were commissioned by the Session to report Alexander Drummond's behaviour to the Laird of Preston Grange. Since he has also failed to produce his witnesses today, as ordered by the Session, they defer the inflicting of any censure or punishment until a magistrate can be present. April 26th: Those who were delegated to report Alexander Drummond's behaviour towards Mrs Cuthbertson to the Laird of Prestongrange are also authorised to speak to him with reference to James Drummond and his wife's defiance of and disobedience to church discipline, for their slighting of church ordinances, and for reviling and abusing their neighbour.

May 10th: Being the principle member of the group appointed by the Session to speak to Preston Grange about the Alexander Drummond business, and about James Drummond and his wife, the minister reported that he had applied to Preston Grange, who had promised to take action against these persons for their abuses.

Saltoun.

The minutes of Saltoun Kirk Session are designated CH2/322 in the National Archives of Scotland. Seventeenth Century records survive as follows:-
CH2/322/1 - Minutes and accounts 1635-46.
CH2/322/2 - Minutes and accounts 1663-95.
CH2/322/3 - Minutes and accounts 1695-1715

1642

December 11th: John Howdone and Christen Paterson his wife, residing in Overkeyth, satisfied church discipline as ordered by the Presbytery, and confessed their fault in linens [*i.e.* wearing linen robes or sheets]. He had sought his health thrice for God's sake from a woman that his wife brought to him. They craved God's pardon for this. A sermon was preached which was applied to the purpose.

1643

April 23rd: Jeals Murray and Effie Rae in Saltonhall appeared and complained about Agnes Paterson there, who is distracted in her wits. She invents dreams and fantasies, and goes around saying that she sees many people in the night, particularly Jeals and Effie, tormenting and vexing her. They offer to prove this with the following witnesses: Agnes Mairsone, Jock Finlason, Christen Chooshead[?], and Barbarie Headone, All parties are ordered to be present next session day.

April 30th: Agnes Paterson appeared, and was asked about what she had been saying. She denied that she named Jeals Murray and Effie Rae, but they did appear to her to vex her more than the rest did.

All of the foresaid witnesses appeared, and testified unanimously that Agnes had said in their hearing that she saw many people in her dreams, particularly Jeils and Effie.

Considering that the rumour has been spread abroad, giving those concerned a bad reputation and resulting in slanderous stories about Jeals and Effie, and considering the woman revealing her dreams is distracted in her wits, the Session orders Agnes to give an open and public confession of her fault before the congregation next Sabbath. [This she did on 7th May.]

May 7th: Thomas Finlasone was accused of charming, but his accusers failed to prove their case.

1646

October 9th: Agnes Renton appeared. She was convicted by witnesses of calling Bessie Elgear "rigwoodie witch", and was ordered to make a public confession of the scandal next Sunday, and to pay forty shillings.

October 25th: Agnes Renton gave a public confession of her fault, and craved God's mercy for it.

1673

February 2nd: James Patersone, Jean Forest, and Christiane Bouars appeared. James Paterson and Jean Forrest confessed they had wronged Christiane Bouars in that Jean had called her a witch, and that both she and her husband James had struck Christiane's daughter. However, they had been provoked. Christiane confessed that she and her daughter had given them ill words because they accused her daughter of stealing some salt from them. The Session found that Christiane and her daughter had been wronged.

Christiane asked for herself, and on behalf of her daughter who was sick, that since they were reconciled to James and his wife Jean, the matter should not be heard in public. The Session decided that they should all be rebuked for their unchristian contention and strife, and that James and his wife Jean should confess their fault on their knees before them, and promise to live more peaceably. This was duly done.

1678

October 6th: The minister reported that a certain Alison Montgumbrie had complained about James Bouar, weaver in Morvindean[?] for calling her a witch and saying she had taken away his health. Alison earnestly desired that she might be cleared before the Session. They are both appointed to be summoned to the next meeting.

October 3rd [*sic* - actually October 13th]: Alison Montgumbrie appeared and renewed her complaint against James Bouar. He also appeared and denied that he had ever called her a witch, but confessed that he had uttered some rash words for which he was sorry, and craved her pardon, promising never to say such things again. The woman was satisfied with this, and in token of their reconciliation took James by the hand.

Spott.

The Kirk Session records of Spott are designated CH2/333 in the National Archives of Scotland. Relevant minutes survive as follows:-

CH2/333/1 1662-1683;
CH2/333/2 1683-1703;
CH2/333/3 1704-1727;
CH2/333/9 Transcribed minutes for 11th May 1665 and 27th January 1689

1663

June 21st: Patrick Muir complained against George Liddaill for calling him a witch. George Liddaill is appointed to be summoned. Also Johne Thomson and John Forrester, witnesses in the case.

July 5th: John Forrester appeared and declared that George Liddaill called Patrick Muir a witch. The Session finds that George Liddaill has slandered Patrick Muir as claimed. George Liddail is appointed to make public satisfaction of church discipline before the congregation for the slander.

July 20th: Today George Liddail made satisfaction for his slandering of Patrick Muir, and he was appointed.... [Entry apparently unfinished.]

There are no further references to witchcraft in the 17th Century records of Spott Kirk Session. This is in direct contradiction to statements made in the Old Statistical Account, in the article on the parish of Spott written by the minister Mr Broune. He notes that the Kirk Session Minutes are extant from 1662, and says that the following items are extracted from them:-

a] That in 1698, "the Session, after a long examination of witnesses refers the case of Marion Lillie for imprecations and witchcraft to the presbytery, who refer her for trial to the civil magistrate. - Said Marion Lillie generally called the Rigwoody Witch."

b] "October 1705. Many witches burnt at the top of Spott Loan."

There is no better illustration than this of the old adage, "History may not repeat itself, but historians certainly do." These references from the Old Statistical Account have been quoted time and time again, not only in local histories, but in several works on witchcraft in general. Taken together with the existence of a "Witch's Stone" at the roadside to the west of Spott, the impression is sometimes given that Spott was some sort of centre of witchcraft in East Lothian. However, if we go back to the contemporary records instead of putting blind faith in the Old Statistical Account, we find that all is not as we have been led to believe.

The Spott Kirk Session minutes for this period are exceptionally legible, written in a clear neat hand, and there is *no reference whatever* in 1705 to "many witches burnt at the top of Spott Loan". Nor as far as I can see after careful perusal is there any such reference in that volume of the minutes [1704-1727], nor in the preceding one [1683-1703]. It is not unknown for parish clerks to make an occasional brief note of important events, in the registers of baptisms, marriages, and burials, but there is no such note in the Spott registers concerning witch burning. The church accounts for the period are also extant, and neither is there any mention there of the burning of witches.

Thus, wherever the writer of the Statistical Account of Spott got the idea that many witches were burnt at the top of Spott Loan in 1705, it was not from the parish records. In any case, 1705 is very late for witch burnings, which had all but petered out by then, although the supposed last Scottish witch burning - at Dornoch [for which, incidentally, there is no written evidence] - was not until a couple of decades later. Might Mr Broune perhaps have seen some reference in a record from 1605, not 1705, now lost? Whatever the explanation for the statement in the Old Statistical Account, it must be emphasised again that there is no evidence whatsoever for witch burnings in the surviving records of Spott parish.

As regards Marion Lillie, contrary to the reference in the Statistical Account, there is no mention of her, nor of witchcraft, in the Spott Kirk Session minutes for 1698. She does appear a few years later, however, and was indeed referred to the civil magistrate. The statement that she was known as the "Rigwoodie Witch" should be taken with a pinch of salt. "Rigwoodie witch" is an epithet rather than a nickname [c.f. the entry for Saltoun, 9th October 1646; also Burns' reference in Tam o' Shanter to "rigwoodie hags"]. Describing someone colloquially as a "rigwoodie witch" simply means a "thoroughgoing" or "out-and-out" witch. The likely original derivation arises from primitive rope being twisted from withies, and "rig" meaning to risk or dare."Rigwoodie" therefore would originally mean someone in constant danger of the rope. The lengthy saga of Marion Lillie appears as follows in the Spott Kirk Session minutes. I have, as always, rendered it in modern English.

1702

November 15th: The minister told the Session that Robert Kemp, weaver in Spott, and Marion Lillie his mother had been at him complaining about Janet Logan for slandering Marion Lillie. He had appointed them to come and table their complaint before the Session. Therefore the Session thought fit to instruct their officer to call them in. Being called, Marion Lillie appeared with her son Robert Kemp. The minister asked them if they had anything to say to the Session, and Marion Lillie answered that Janet Logan her neighbour had slandered her name, speaking evil things of her. Her son, to whom these things were said, could confirm this. The minister enquired of Robert Kemp what Janet Logan had said about his mother. He answered that last Tuesday morning as he was passing Janet Logan's door he heard William Young, her son, roaring and making a noise. At this he went in to see him, and as soon as he entered the house Janet Logan said that heart hatred was "slockened" [satisfied] now. Robert Kemp said, "What do you mean by that, Janet? Who are you blaming for your son?" Janet Logan answered, "I am blaming your mother, for she has been doing the Devil's work on me and mine since Lammas." He undertook to prove this by John Guilly and Jean Lochland who were present, and whom he asked to bear witness to the matter at the time.

Also, Marion Lillie said that on the following day, the eleventh of this month, Janet Logan came in to Marion Lillie in her own house when there was nobody with her, and threatened her, saying she would tear her all to pieces if anything killed her son. She therefore asked that the Session would require Janet Logan to prove what she had said, or suitably punish her according to the laws of the church governing such cases.

The Witches' Stone. Spott. (Above.) The plaque states that Marion Lillie was burnt here. In fact this is almost certainly not the case.

According to the records Marion, East Lothian's last recorded witch, was buried in Spott kirkyard (below). She could not therefore have been burnt.

After they had been removed from the meeting, the Session, considering the grossness of the scandal, appointed their officer to summon Janet Logan to appear before the Session next Lord's Day, and also John Guilly and Jean Lochland to bear witness in this matter if needed.

November 22nd: The Session asked their officer if he had summoned Janet Logan and the others to the meeting, and he answered that he had, and that they were all present. Janet Logan was called and appeared, and was asked if she said, "Heart hatred is satisfied," when Robert Kemp came into her house a week past Thursday. She confessed she did say so. She was asked if she said, "I am blaming your mother, for she has done the Devil's work on me and mine since Lammas," when Robert Kemp asked her whom she blamed for her son. She answered that she did not say, "I am blaming your mother for my bairn," but Robert Kemp asked her what she meant by saying that heart hatred was satisfied now, and she replied that she meant that his mother had been doing the Devil's work on her and her family since Lammas. She was asked if she went into Marion Lillie's house the following day saying that she would tear Marion Lillie all to pieces if anything killed her child, and she confessed that she did go in and say so, and that ever since the child had been better.

She was asked to leave, and the Session saw no need to examine witnesses, since Janet had admitted the most important points of the case. There was no time to stay any longer, and further consideration of this affair was postponed until the next meeting.

December 3rd: The minister and elders having met for prayer, they took into consideration the business of Janet Logan and Marion Lillie. After some deliberation they decided that they would have to question Janet Logan about the reasons why Marion Lillie had done the Devil's work on her and her family for some time. They therefore appoint their officer to summon her to the Session next Lord's Day.

December 6th: The Session asked their officer if he had summoned Janet Logan to the meeting and he answered that he had. Janet Logan was called and appeared in the presence of Marion Lillie and her son Robert Kemp. Janet Logan was asked what reasons she had for saying that Marion Lillie had done the Devil's work on her and her family since Lammas, and she answered that she had grounds for saying it. She had done it now, and about three years ago. She explained, "My son William Young had no master at the time, and offered to apprentice himself to Marion Lillie's son Robert Kemp. Marion was present, and when she heard this she said, 'We will have no apprentices!' After this William Young came into my house, took a book, and was reading it when Marion Lillie came into our house asking for fire. As she passed William Young she said, 'Are you reading, Will?' and he said, 'Yes.' Shortly afterwards my son became blind and dumb, and never got any better [Probable meaning. The original is obscure here.]. She wronged my son then, and he was not right for a month after it.

Not only that, but Marion Lillie has had the name of working in the Devil's service for many years, and I am not the only person to say so, for others have said worse. Her daughter-in-law Barbara Caulder called her a witch to her face several years ago. Also, James Baillie called her a rigwoodie witch and blooded her in the face on the main street ['high towngate'] and it was well enough known that she had wronged other peoples' livestock. William Colme had blamed her for the loss of his beasts about ten years ago. She had threatened that she would make him repent it because he wouldn't allow her to keep a tethered ewe. Within a few days he had two mares that ran mad till they died ['ramaged to dead']. And there was still more to be said, and would be said, against her. That Wednesday when I went into her house, three of us couldn't hold my son in his bed. And when I was speaking to her she said, 'Do you think I have wronged your son?' and I said, 'You wronged him before; why may you not have wronged him now?' I admit that I said that if anything ailed my child I would tear her to pieces, and I no sooner came into my house after that than he began to settle and has been better ever since. These things are all true, as is well known in the community."

Being asked why she said that Marion Lillie had been doing the Devil's work on her only since Lammas, she answered, "It was because she was coveting my house and my piece of land, and trying to take it over my head. She told lies about me, and was malicious and envious of me."

After all this, Robert Kemp asked that the Session would require Janet Logan to prove these things against his mother, for he was sure she would not be able to do it. Having no further time, the Session delays consideration of it until the next session day.

December 13th: The minister told the Session that Janet Logan came to him last night and asked if she could tell the Session the rest of what she had to say against Marion Lillie. If the Session wished, they could get their officer to call her in and hear her. The Session agreed, their officer called her in, and Janet Logan appeared. She was asked what else she had to say against Marion Lillie, and she answered that she had this to say, "Some years ago Catharine Deans, who now lives in Bouden, was in this village seeing her friends [or relatives], since she was pregnant with her first child. Marion Lillie came to her and gripped her belly. Soon after this Catharin Deans was siezed by pain and was never free of it until six weeks after that she gave birth to a dead child. All that time she thought she still felt pain as a result of Marion Lillie's grip. Ever since she has not been right or as she should be. Catharine Deans had told this to several honest women in the village."

Not only that, but Janet Logan also said, "About a year past Martinmas, Marion Lillie's son Robert Kemp came into my house, took out a tether, and hanged his mad dog over my little house [?], on a beam above my cow's fodder, which I think was very unseemly, since there were trees round the walls [or perhaps ditches] that he could have hanged his dog from. And I can say this, that ever since then I have got neither milk nor butter from my cow as I used to.

Also, one day last harvest, Marion Lillie laid down a pair of stockings in the main road in front of my door, and they lay there all day. Neither the poor folk nor the reapers passing by had power to lift them, and I wouldn't allow any of my family to meddle with them because I feared they had not been put there for any good purpose. Towards evening John Whyt came by and called to me to take in my stockings, and threw them in at my door. I told him they were not my stockings, and I took the tongs and threw them out again. When John Whyt asked Robert Kemp if they were his stockings he said no, and although Marion Lillie was sometimes at home that day, she didn't acknowledge that they were hers until at night when everybody was going home. Then she came out and lifted them, and said, 'These are my Robbie's stockings which Margaret Logan made for him.' I think this was a strange thing, that she should have laid them down there and let them lie all day until night time."

Judging that there may be difficulties in this affair, the Session thinks it best if the minister asks advice from the brethren of the Presbytery as to what the Session should do next, and then reports back.

December 20th: The minister reported to the Session that the opinion of the brethren regarding this affair was that if those concerned insist on going on with it, then Janet Logan will have to prove what she claims against Marion Lillie. The Session leaves it to the minister to speak to them. If he finds that they insist on proceeding, he is to summon them to the next session day.

December 27th: The minister said that Marion Lillie demanded that Janet Logan should be made to prove what she alleged against her. Therefore he had summoned them both to the Session. Being called, they both appeared, and Marion asked that the Session should make Janet Logan prove these things against her, or else punish her as a slanderer. When Janet Logan was asked how she would prove tha various things she had alleged against Marion Lillie, she replied, "By several people; namely James Young in Little Belton, William Colme in Spott village, James Baillie there, Margaret Wightman there, John Whyt there, and Barbara Caulder there." She wished the Session to have them summoned as witnesses, and have their statements taken regarding what they know about these things.

Also, Janet Logan alleged that within these past few days Marion Lillie had prayed that the heavy curse of God might come upon her; that is upon Janet Logan, and all those who spoke to her. Some of the witnesses could testify to this.

The next meeting about this affair is to be a week on Wednesday. The officer is appointed to summon all the foresaid persons who live within the parish to appear before the Session that day to bear witness in this affair. Janet Logan and Marion Lillie are also to be present at that time.

1703

January 6th: The Session asked their officer if he had summoned all the witnesses as he had been asked. He answered that he had and that they were all in attendance. Janet Logan and Marion Lillie were both called and both appeared. Marion Lillie was asked if some weeks ago she had wished the curse of God to come upon Janet Logan and all who spoke to her or took her part. She confessed that she did say so, in an outburst of rage. Then the Session went on to call the witnesses. Marion Lillie and her son were present and objected to none of the following witnesses:-

William Colme in Spott was called and appeared; aged about forty and married. He was solemnly sworn and purged of malice and partiality. Asked if at any time about ten years ago Marion Lillie had threatened him that she would "make him repent it", he declared that Marion Lillie said in the "Barlae Court" [a local court for regulating grazings, boundaries etc.] when he was present, that it would be a costly course of action for some of them, and they would rue it before the year was out. This was because they would not let her keep a ewe tethered on the green. Asked if any harm came of it, he replied, "A few weeks after that my father-in-law and I went to Pressmenen Wood to buy timber, and someone came to us to fetch us home as my mare was dying. She had been in her usual health when I went away, feeding in the Well Myrs with the rest of the beasts, and before night time she ran mad till she died, leaving a young foal behind her. Robert Burnet had a mare still in milk, and I got her to give the foal milk. I gave her a handful of fodder in the evening to make her take with the foal, for she was tethered in the barnyard. In the morning when I went out, she was sitting on her rump like a dog and couldn't stir. She was at the far side of the hemp, and there was no sign of what way she had gone through the hemp. Then I went away to John Houme in the Barns [?]. He came to see the beast, took out a penknife and pricked her - beginning at the fore parts and going back. After he had passed her heart he said all the power had gone from her hindquarters, and suppose I had five hundred merks to spend on her, I needn't bother, for she would do no good. He enquired if I was envied by anyone, and said that either seven or nine of my beasts of one kind or another would go that way before it was at an end. After that the hen went out at the back door of the barn, with a number of young birds with her. Seven of them fell over, and they all swelled up and died, and yet there was nothing wrong with any of the rest."

Asked if anything passed between him and Marion Lillie after that, he said, "All that passed between Marion Lillie and me was, one time after that as I was walking past Marion Lillie she asked how I was doing, and I answered, "None the better of your evil prayers. For if your evil prayers have any power, they have landed on me." And I also prayed that the Lord would keep me from any harm.

He was also asked if he knew anything about Janet Logan or her son William Young blaming Marion Lillie for his trouble about three years ago. He declared that he heard Janet Logan say more than a year ago that her son said it would be more fitting for him to take blood from Marion Lillie, than anyone to take blood from him, and that he wanted to go and take blood from her. He also declares that he has heard Marion Lillie called a witch, or deemed as such by the opinion of the neighbourhood.

[Signed] William Colme.

Jean Lochard in Spott was called and appeared; a widow aged about fifty-five. Being solemnly sworn and purged of malice and partiality, she declared that Catharine Deans, now living in the parish of Bouden, said to her that Marion Lillie came to her as she was passing through the village of Spott, and asked her how she was doing. She laid her hand on her belly and gripped it. Catharine was soon afterwards seized with pain, after she had gore about half a mile, and her husband had to take her off the horse, as she seemed about to faint. She was never well until she brought forth the child, which died shortly after. It was her first child. She also declares that she has heard Marion Lillie deemed a witch by the opinion of the neighbourhood. In addition, she declares that she has heard Janet Logan say that she could not get butter or milk from her cow as she used to, since Robert Kemp hanged his mad dog over her cow's fodder. However, she knows no more about it.

She was asked if she heard Marion Lillie curse Janet Logan, and declared that she heard Marion Lillie bid the curse of God come upon Janet Logan and everyone who listened to her or took her part; and that Marion said, "Near-hand tales will not serve out. They must fetch far-off ones." [*i.e.*" Recent stories won't do. They've got to bring up stories from long ago." or perhaps "Local stories won't do. They've got to fetch them from further off."] Asked if she knows about William Young getting better when Janet Logan threatened Marion Lillie, she declared that she did not see him that day, but she heard others say that he was [illegible] that morning before she went to the market, and when she came home at night they told her he was better, and has been ever since. She declares that she cannot write, but allows the clerk to sign for her.

[Signed] Andrew Whyt.

Margaret Wightman was called and appeared, a widow aged about fifty-six. She was solemnly sworn, purged of malice and partiality, and testified that she heard Catharine Deanes say that Marion Lillie came to her as she was passing through Spott village, and gripped her belly - the witness was also present. She had not gone far when she fell sick and her husband was forced to take her off the horse. She still felt the pain of Marion's grip till she brought forth her child, which was her first. She also declares that she has heard Marion Lillie deemed to be a witch by the opinion of the neighbourhood. She declares that she cannot write, but allows the clerk to sign for her.

[Signed] Andrew Whyt.

James Baillie was called and appeared, aged about thirty or more and unmarried. Being solemnly sworn and purged of malice and partiality, he was asked if he had heard Marion Lillie deemed to be a witch. He declares that is the word that is going through the countryside, and that he had heard it before he came to this village.

[Signed] James Baillie.

John Guilly was called and appeared, aged about fifty, married. Being solemnly sworn and purged of malice and partiality, he was asked what he knew about William Young getting better when Janet Logan went in to Marion Lillie. He testifies that he heard the story in the village that he was no better in the morning, and better before night time. He was also asked if he heard that Marion Lillie was believed to be a witch. He said that he had heard it going through the countryside. He declares that he cannot write, but allows the clerk to sign for him.

[Signed] Andrew Whyt.

Janet Grieve was called and appeared, aged about 19 and unmarried. Being purged of malice and partiality she declares that on Martinmas day in the morning she heard Janet Whyt asking Elisabeth Young how her brother Will was. She answered that he was no better. However, at night, after she came home, she went in and saw him better, and speaking quite sensibly. Janet Whyt was there, and Isabell Muir, and Janet McCall. Janet Logan said she had been in at Marion Lillie that day, and her son got belter immediately. She declares this is the truth, as in the sight of God. She cannot write.

Barbara Caulder was called and appeared, and said that she never called Marion Lillie a witch.

Janet Muet was called and appeared, aged about fifty and married. Being solemnly sworn and purged of malice and partiality, she was asked if she had heard Marion Lillie deemed to be a witch. She answered that she had. She was asked what she knows about William Young getting better when Janet Logan went in to Marion Lillie. She says that she did not see him in the morning, but when she came home at night she heard people saying he was better. She declares that she cannot write, but allows the clerk to sign for her.

[Signed] Andrew Whyt.

John Whyt was called and appeared, aged about thirty-one and married. Being solemnly sworn and purged of malice and partiality, he was asked if he had heard that Marion Lillie was believed to be a witch. He testifies that he has heard it. He was asked if he knew anything about William Young getting better after Janet Logan went in to Marion Lillie. He testifies that he was ill in the morning and better at night last Martinmas Day, and that this is the truth.

[Signed] John Whyt.

Janet Whyt was called and appeared, aged about eighteen and unmarried. Being purged of malice and partiality, she declares that last Martinmas, when she went out with their cow in the morning, she asked Elisabeth Young how her brother Will was, and she said he was no better. At night when she came home from the fair she went in to see him, and saw he was better. Janet Logan said that she had been in at Marion Lillie, and that he had been better ever since. She had heard Marion Lillie blamed as a witch. She declares this is the truth in the sight of God.

[Signed] Janet Whyt.

January 1703 [Date not given]: The Session met to consider the Marion Lillie affair. After mature deliberation, the Session finds that by her witnesses Janet Logan has proved several things that she alleged Marion Lillie to be guilty of, particularly that she had threatened William Colm and others in the "berlie court". Following that, harm came upon William Colme's beasts, and he blamed her for it.

Secondly, Catharine Deanes said that she was taken with pain in her belly after Marion Lillie had laid her hand upon it and gripped it, and she was never free of pain until she gave birth to her child.

Thirdly, Marion Lillie has been reputed to be a witch in the opinion of the countryside for a long time.

Fourthly, Marion Lillie uttered bitter imprecations against Janet Logan and others, as is proved by her own confession, and the testimony of others.

Fifthly, Janet Logan has given some reason to presume that Marion Lillie had wronged her son both before and recently.

Considering the difficulty of the affair, the Session judges it more suitable to refer it to the Presbytery for their opinion and advice. Since Janet Logan has proved such things against Marion Lillie, should she now be censured as a slanderer? And what should the Session do next about Marion Lillie?

January 31st: The minister reported to the Session that he had referred the case of Janet Logan and Marion Lillie to the Presbytery. Having considered the matter, the Presbytery were of the opinion that since Janet Logan had proved such things against Marion Lillie, she was not to be censured as a slanderer because of what she had said about her. The Presbytery also gave it as their opinion that Marion Lillie was to be rebuked before the congregation for her cursing and brtter imprecations against Janet Logan and others. An account should be given to the congregation of the things proved against Marion Lillie, and she should be referred to the civil magistrate for further "tryall" in these matters. [It should be noted that "tryall" here almost certainly means "investigation" rather than "trial" in the modern sense.]

February 4th: The Session appoints their officer to summon Marion Lillie to appear before them a week on Sunday, so that they can question her further about the things that were proved against her, and to see how she regards her cursing and swearing before she appears before the congregation.

February 14th: Marion Lillie was called and appeared. She was questioned on whether she knew anything about witchcraft or a compact with the Devil. She was seriously exhorted to give glory to God by confessing it, but she obstinately denied that she knew anything of these things. She was also rebuked for her sin of cursing and swearing, and exhorted to humble herself and mourn for it before God. She was told that the Session had appointed her to appear before the congregation to be publicly reproved when called for.

The Session was informed that Marion Lillie seems to have done the same kind of harm to a woman in this parish about a year ago, as she is recorded in the process to have done to Catharine Deans. The Session desires the minister to speak to Janet Haliburton, the woman to whom she is said to have done it, to see what truth there is in it, and to report back.

February 21st: The minister reported to the Session that he had spoken to Janet Haleburton, who told him that just over a year ago Marion Lillie came into her house when she was baking. Janet told her to sit down and gave her a piece of bread. When she had eaten some of it she rose from her seat, came to her, and stretched her hand over the "backboard" [baking board ?]. She laid her hand on Janet's belly and gripped it, and said, "What, woman? Are you not growing big yet?" or something like that, and she went back to her seat and sat down again. At this, Janet Haleburton was seized with fear, and about two or three days after that she miscarried, having met with no stress or any other thing that she thought could have caused it. However, she would not take upon herself to say that Marion Lillie's touching her had caused it. The Session desires the minister to send for Marion Lillie to come to his own house and have further discussion with her about the things alleged against her, particularly this business with Janet Halleburton, and to try to bring her to a confession of these things. George Turnbull and James Manderson, two of the elders, are to be present with him.

March 7th: The minister reported that he and two of the elders had spoken to Marion Lillie and dealt with her as effectually as they could to bring her to a confession of her guilt in the matters she was charged with. As far as the business with Janet Haleburton is concerned, she did not deny it altogether, but said that if she had laid her hand upon her belly, it was not with the intention of doing her any harm. When they spoke to her about her cursing and imprecations against Janet Logan, she tried rather to vindicate herself than to show regret for it. Thus, she does not seem to have the sense of her sin that she ought to have. The Session thinks it fit that she should be spoken to again before she appears in public.

April 4th: The minister reported that he had spoken to Marion Lillie again, and he found that her attitude had improved, and she acknowledged her sin in cursing and uttering imprecations. Considering the circumstances of the whole affair, the Session thinks fit not to delay any longer, and appoints their officer to summon Marion Lillie to appear before the congregation next Lord's Day to be rebuked for her cursing and imprecations against Janet Logan and others.

April 18th: The minister reported to the Session that according to their instructions Marion Lillie had appeared before the congregation last Lord's Day, and was rebuked for her sin as appointed. According to the advice given to him by the Presbytery, he had given an account to the congregation of the things proved against her, so that they might beware of her. He said that the church had done all that was required of it as regards persons alleged to be guilty of witchcraft, and therefore she was to be left to the civil magistrate for further investigation.

A routine Presbyterial visitation in October 1705 "commended the Minister and sessions accuracie in discipline, they having had some difficult processes before them." There is no mention of witchcraft in the report of the visitation, and most certainly no reference in 1705 to "many witches being burnt at Spott Loan"; and as already emphasised, neither is there any such statement in that volume of the minutes, as far as I can see, nor in the preceding volume.

"The Witch's Stone" lies to the west of Spott village, at the roadside. This is generally believed to mark the place of execution of a witch or witches. According to Martine's "Reminiscences and Notices of the Parishes of the County of Haddington", the last witch burnt in the south of Scotland was supposed to have died here. However, this may be nothing more than an assumption based on the old chestnut of "many witches burnt at Spott Loan in 1705", which Martine also quotes.

On occasion it has been assumed that the Witch's Stone marks the place of Marion Lillie's execution. For example, in "The Deil's Ain" [Roy J. M. Pugh: Balerno 2001] the author remarks of Marion Lillie on p. 157, "She is remembered today only by the Witch's Stone enclosed by railings outside the village, thought to mark the place of her execution." And on p. 158, "Although the records are incomplete, it is certain that Marion was strangled and burnt at the stake." Alas for the "certainty" of jumping to conclusions, the Spott register of burials records in 1705, "Febry 11th Deceased Marion Lillie in Spott & was interred at this kirk." The record of parish expenses for the period 30th January 1705 to April 23rd 1705 records, To bell and Mortcloath to Marion Lillie 02-10-00."

A condemned witch is most unlikely to have been buried in consecrated ground, far less with the usual accompaniments of bell and mortcloth. Indeed, an executed witch could not possibly have been buried at all, since the sentence specifically required that the body should be burnt to ashes! Thus, whoever was burnt at the Witch's Stone, it could not have been Marion Lillie, who must have died a natural death on 11th February 1705.

Marion's case had been passed to the civil magistrate almost two years before her death, and since thare is no record either of a trial in the High Court of Justiciary, nor of an application to the Privy Council for a commission to try her locally, it seems likely that the local civil magistrate decided not to pursue the case; possibly because the evidence for what was "proved" to the Kirk Session's satisfaction would not have been deemed sufficient for a civil court. The stresses involved in all this may of course have contributed to Marion's death, but on the other hand, she was presumably already elderly and may well have been in poor health. At the beginning of the 18th Century death was everyone's constant shadow.

Anyway, whatever the cause of Marion's sad demise, I must repeat and emphasise that in spite of all that has been written elsewhere, there is no evidence whatsoever that witches were burnt at Spott in 1705, and every reason to believe it to be at least rather unlikely. Also, there is written evidence to show that Marion Lillie died a natural death in February 1705, and was buried in the churchyard with the usual ceremonial trappings of the kirk's bell and mortcloth.

Stenton.

Stenton is designated CH2/335 in the National Archives of Scotland. The only 17th Century records surviving are contained in CH2/335/1 which runs from 1690 to 1724.

1700

November 24th: Robert Manderson appeared and gave in a complaint against Jane Brock in Stentoun, mentioning that some time ago Jane had said in Lochhouses that Robert or his wife had given Isoble Lylle a drink to hinder her conception.

[Robert had complained in September that a former servant of his was saying he was guilty of adultery with his current servant Isoble Lylle.]

After considering this complaint the Session appoints their officer to summon Jane Brock to appear before them a week today.

December 1st: The officer reported what he had done, and Jane Brock was called and appeared. When the charge was read to her she denied it as it was written, but admitted that she had said in Lochhouses that there was a "bad report" going the rounds, that Isoble had a drink to stop her conceiving. However, she denied that Robert and his wife were the instigators. Questioned further about her authority, she blamed Helen Whyt, whereupon the Session appointed their officer to summon Helen to appear before them next Sabbath.

December 8th: [In summary:- Helen Whyt was summoned and asked if she had said anything to Janet Brock about Isoble Lylle getting a drink to hinder conception. She said she'd heard it from Alison Anderson, a former servant of Robert Manderson's. On December 10th Alison denied this, but said that a little before Martinmas 1699, when she and Janet Morton were both in service with the Manderson family, they were walking together and Janet asked Alison if she had ever seen any misbehaviour between Robert Manderson and Isoble. She said no, if anything like that was happening, since Isoble was young she would conceive and become pregnant. To which the said Janet Morton gave no answer for some time, but a little after that said she had heard before she came out of the west country that a woman might get a drink to hinder conception. Alison had subsequently relayed this statement to Helen Brock. On December 17th Janet Morton denied having any such conversation.

The Session sought advice from the Presbytery, who subsequently advised them that the scandal was "groundless".]

Tranent.

Tranent is designated CH2/357 in the National Archives of Scotland. CH2/357/1 contains unbound minutes covering the period 1651 -1657. CH2/357/2 and CH2/357/3 are both in fact bound together into one volume and cover the periods 1670-1680 and 1684-1686 respectively.

1652

July 27th: Jonet Krige[?] was ordered to stand before the congregation on the following Sabbath in sackcloth for calling John Clunie a witch's get. It was also decided that if she should trouble John Clunie or his wife again that she would have to pay ten pounds Scots.

1670

June 21st: Robert Wilson appeared before the Session and complained that Helen Cowan called his wife a witch, and said that she would maintain it. Hellen also appeared and was questioned about this. She denied it, but Robert offered to prove that she had called his wife a witch by the evidence of Andrew Sinclair, James Weir, John Stevenson, and William Man. They are to be summoned to the next Session meeting, immediatelly after the last communion service.

July 5th: Robert Wilson and his wife appeared, and Helen Cowan. They were reconciled to one another, and promised the Session that, God willing, such things should never again be heard between them. They were dismissed after a rebuke.

1671

January 10th: Jean Young appeared and confessed "scolding" with Jannet Berrie on the Sabbath Day. Jannet Berrie also appeared and confessed doing so, but says she was provoked by Jean Young calling her mother a witch in front of John Manners jr., and Margaret and Barbara Fyffe. They are to be summoned to the next session day.

January 17th: John Manners jr. appeared, and Margaret and Barbara Fyffe, witnesses in Jean Young and Jannet Berne's process. They declared that Jean and Janet are both guilty, for Jean offered to throw stones at Jannet, and Jannet immediately struck Jean. Jean and Jannet were appointed to be summoned to the next meeting of the Session.

January 24th: The Session examined the scandalous behaviour of Jean Young and Jannet Berrie in Seton on the Lord's Day on their way to church. They were both found guilty of gross Sabbath breaking and continued malice against each other. The Session therefore refers them to the magistrate to be punished for their riot, earnestly recommending that the punishment should be exemplary, to prevent them and others behaving so badly in future. It is also decided that next Lord's Day it should be publicly announced from the pulpit that they are both publicly suspended from the Lord's Supper and other church benefits until they show evidence of better behaviour, and more of the spirit of the Gospel in living in love and peace with one another as becomes those who profess the name of Christ. The elders of the village of Seton are advised to keep an eye on their behaviour, and report to the Session if either of these persons give them reason to do so.

1673

April 13th: Margaret Crooks gave in a letter to the Session complaining that Agnes Martin called her a witch, witnessed by Robert Mackendly, Alexander Strathearn and John Samson. All of them are ordered to be summoned to the next session meeting with Agnes Martin.

April 20th: Agnes Martin appeared and denied that she called Margaret Crookes a witch. Robert Mackendly, Alexander Strathearn, and John Sampson appeared. Agnes declared that she had no objection to them as witnesses, and they were sworn to declare what they knew about Agnes Martin calling Margaret Crooks a witch. John Simson declares that he heard Agnes calling Margaret a sharp-nosed witch. Robert Mackendlay and Alexander Strathem declared the same. The Session finding the case proven orders Agnes to stand in the branks at the kirk porch from the second to the third bell, then to come in before the congregation to humbly confess her fault and crave pardon, and after that to be publicly rebuked the following Sabbath.

May 13th: The Session was informed that Agnes Martin has not yet satisfied church discipline as ordered for slandering Margaret Crooks. She is ordered to be summoned to satisfy next Lord's Day, or be punished for defiance. [She duly satisfied the following Sunday.]

1678

April 16th: William Rammage, weaver in Tranent, appeared and gave in a letter to the Session complaining that John Nicolson, weaver there, called his wife a witch in the presence of Mr George Turnbull and Adam Porteous. John Nicolson was called and appeared, and denied calling William Rammadge's wife a witch. Mr George Turnbull and Adam Porteous appeared, summoned as witnesses in the matter, and the minister laid before each of them the nature of the oath, and the danger of perjury. John Nicolson was asked if he had any objection to either of them being received as witnesses, and he answered no. At this the minister took their oath, and they declared as follows:- Mr George Turnbull declared that he did not remember hearing John Nicolson calling William Rammadge's wife a witch. Adam Porteous declared the same.

The case was not proven, but since it was found that John Nicolson is an "ill-tongued man", he was called before the Session and very sharply rebuked. He promised that if ever he should be brought before the Session again for that sort of thing, he would submit to any censure the Session should impose, submit to be punished as the magistrate should think fit, and pay twenty pounds Scots.

October 15th: Alexander Hunter appeared and gave in a letter to the Session complaining that James Hislop had called his wife Marion Scot a confronted witch and a reported devil, in the presence of John Muir, Lilias Marr, and William Allan. James Hislop appeared, and denied calling Marion Scot either a confronted witch or a reported devil. John Muir, Lilias Marr, and William Wilson appeared as witnesses in the case, and after James Hislop had declared he had no objection to them appearing as witnesses, they were sworn, and unanimously declared that they heard James Hieslop call Marion Scot a reported devil, but not a confronted witch. Since James Hieslop was found guilty by the declaration of the witnesses of slandering Marion Scot, after the minister had exhorted him to live in peace and unity with his neighbours, he ordered him to go to Alexander Hunter and his wife and daughter, and acknowledge his offence in the presence of John Henderson and ffrancis Seton. It is recommended to the magistrate that he should impose a fine [a "pecuniale mulct"] upon him, and that if he does not pay, he should be imprisoned until he appears in public.

December 24th: Elizabeth fford and her daughter Elizabeth Scot appeared and gave in a letter complaining that George Russell's wife Isabell Murray called Elizabeth's daughter "witch's breed", and Elizabeth a witch; that she hoped to see her led to the Muir-brow and burnt, and that she would "cast coals to her" [*i.e.* dig coal to be used to burn her body]. This was said in the presence of Elizabeth Martin and Elizabeth Armstrang.

Elizabeth Murray appeared, and confessed that in a temper she called Elizabeth Scot "witch's breed", but denied saying that she hoped to see her led to the Muir-brow to be burnt, and that she would dig coal for her.

Elizabeth Martin and Elizabeth Armstrang appeared as witnesses in this matter. The minister asked Isobell Murray if she had any objection to them being received as witnesses against her. She answered no, and after being sworn they testified unanimously that they heard Isobell Murray call Elizabeth fford a witch, and that she hoped to see her led to the Muir-brow to be burnt. However, they did not hear her say she would dig coal for her.

Isobell Murray also gave in a complaint against Elizabeth fford that Elizabeth said in Alexander Hog's house that she was "great with the soldiers" [*i.e.* over-friendly with them]. She also complained against Elizabeth's daughter Elizabeth Scot that she said that the only thing that angered her about it was that Mr John was not brought to her. Elizabeth fford appeared, and denied that she said that Isabell Murray was great with the soldiers. She had been telling the company what she had just heard a drunk soldier say in the street about Isabell and the soldiers. Elizabeth Scot appeared and confessed that when Isabell Murray abused her mother, she turned round and said, "If you don't hold your tongue I'll bring Mes John [*i.e.* the minister] to you."

Isabell Murray and Elizabeth Scot were rebuked for their rashness in slandering one another, and were exhorted to more Christian behaviour in future, and to live in peace and friendship with each other. Forgiving one another, they bound themselves to pay ten pounds Scots and be liable to public censure if they were found transgressing in this way again.

1679

May 20th: Alexander Clunie gave in a complaint against Thomas Dick complaining that Thomas called him a "witch's nephew" last Wednesday, and told him to go up to the Muir Brow and bring down his lucky's clothes. ["Luckie" was a familiar term for an elderly woman, often meaning "granny", but obviously here an elderly aunt. The Muir Brow may refer to Tranent Muir which lay to the east of the town, and which may have been the regular local place of execution. On the other hand Cowan's aunt may have been one of the witches burnt at Peaston Muir the previous year. It sounds as if the victim's clothes had been left lying at the place of execution. Who, after all, would want the clothes of a condemned and executed witch?] Also, Thomas had called his wife a crow-faced lean-faced bitch in front of Margaret Thomson, Margaret Dalziel, and William Bell.

Thomas Dick appeared and denied the charge. Margaret Thomson, Margaret Dalziel, and William Bell appeared as witnesses in the matter. Thomas Dick was asked if he had any objection to these persons being received as witnesses against him, and he answered no. They were all solemnly sworn and testified as follows:-

Margaret Thomson, being sworn, declared that she heard Thomas Dick call Alexander Clunie an ill-hued dog and a witch's nephew, and told him to go up to the Muir Brow and fetch down his lucky's clothes. Also, he called his wife crow-faced. Margaret Dalziel and William Bell declared the same.

Since the charge is proved, Thomas Dick is ordered to appear in the place where he committed the scandal. In the presence of William Watson, Robert Gilmur, and Thomas Waugh, elders, and those who heard him, he is to kneel down before Alexander Clunie and humbly confess his fault. He is also to be referred to the magistrate to be suitably fined.

When Thomas Dick was called in and exhorted to more circumspect and Christian behaviour, he appeared very impudent and obstinate, and so was delayed to the next Session meeting.

July 1st: Thomas Dick was summoned and did not appear. He is ordered to be summoned a second time.

July 8th: Thomas Dick did not appear, and is to be summoned a third time.

July 15th: Thomas Dick has been lawfully summoned three times. The last time he was summoned personally to today's meeting, and has not appeared. The Session finds that not only has Thomas been defiant in refusing to obey the sentence the Session imposed on him for slandering an elder, Alexander Clunie, but has also refused to appear before the Session to give an account of his disobedience. Therefore they think fit that the civil magistrate should be asked to make him appear. Otherwise, he will be referred to the Presbytery to be proceeded against with a view to excommunication.

August 31st: Margaret Colstoun appeared, and complained against Agnes ffairnie, wife of John Rae in Cockenzie. Agnes called her a witch in the presence of John Lanson[?] and Alaster Morison, and said she would prove she was one. Agnes ffairnie and the witnesses are to be summoned to the next Session meeting.

November 11th: Agnes ffairnie appeared with her husband John Rae. Having been convinced that they had slandered Margarit Colstoun, Agnes acknowledged her fault and was humbled upon her knees and fined forty shillings Scots. Both she and her husband promised that if ever they were found slandering or scolding with any other person or persons in the future, they would be liable to pay ten pounds, and if unable to pay they would flit and remove themselves out of the parish. The Session recommends to the magistrate that he should see that this is done.

Tyninghame.

Tyninghame has not existed as a separate parish since 1761 when it was united with Whitekirk. Tyninghame's kirk session minutes are designated CH2/359 in the archives of Scotland. The surviving minutes from the 17th Century are unusually extensive. CH2/359/1 covers the period 1615-1650, and CH2/359/2 covers 1650-1694.

1615

May 14th: [This entry is damaged.] Jonet Shortus, servant to Alexander Knoxe ... appeared ... ... Janet Shortus, wife of Patrick Benn ... a slanderer of Janet Shortus, sevant to Mr Alexander ... sacrament[?], appeared but were not called, and they are both ordered to be ... for the second time next session day.

William Gaitgude, the slanderer of Jonet Utterston, was called upon and appeared. Accused of calling Jonet Utterston a witch, he confessed it, but at the same time alleged that Jonet called him a thief.

Jonet Utterston was called and appeared, and accused of calling William Gaitgude a thief. Eventually she confessed. Both parties were sent out, then called in individually. After a serious rebuke, the Session ordered William to make public satisfaction the following Sunday before the congregation, and to pay one merk. After a serious rebuke, Jonet was ordered to do the same.

If Jonet is ever here again, if the quarrel was started by her, or if she has made any reply to whoever started it, it is ordered that she is not to be heard, and will pay double. If a quarrel is initiated against her she is to hold her peace and come and complain to the minister. [This seems the most likely meaning of this paragraph. The original is rather obscure and convoluted.]

1631

November 20th: John Ewart complained about Alison Foullar, wife of George Ra. [I had thought at first that this name was "Fa" - there were Faas/Falls in Dunbar - but came to the conclusion that on balance the name was probably "Ra", *i.e.* Rae.] In David Nicolson's house Alisone spoke some words about Alexander Jaksone's death. [Jaksone had recently been drowned crossing the "creek" - the Tyne estuary - on his way to Dunbar.] These words were partly slanderous against Alexander Jakson, who has now departed this life, and partly prophetical against him [John Ewart]. She said that he would die the same death and go the same way that Alexander Jakson did. This was because they found her husband with peas during the night and complained about him to the civil magistrate. He was asked if he could prove this with reliable witnesses. He answered that he could, and named Andrew Strong, Patrick Basinden, Margaret Hunter, Adam Skugall, and Manis Clerk. He was ordered to come to the next session day and bring his witnesses with him.

November 27th: John Ewart and Robert Ewart his father, being present, were called in. He was asked if his witnesses were present. He answered that some of them were. James Bucan affirmed that he had summoned some of them - Andrew Strong, Patrick Bassenden, and Margaret Hunter.

Andrew Strong appeared and was asked what he heard Alison Foullar say in David Nicolsone's house. He said that after some conversation between David Nicolson's wife and her, Alison Foullar said to Margaret Huntar, "Fye, Alexander Jakson's neighbour will go the same way that Alexander Jaksone did." Patrick Bassinden was called in and also asked what he heard Alison Foullar say. He answered that she said, "It may be that he makes so ane end." [*i.e.* dies like that]. Margaret Huntar and the others were called but did not appear. They are ordered to be summoned to the next session day.

December 4th: Margaret Huntar was called and appeared, and was asked what she heard Alison Fouler say about the late Alexander Jakson and John Ewart. She replied that Alison was at variance with the late Alexander Jaksone because of the peas, as is written above. Alison said, "It is well done to have good company, and it's well done for parents to tell their children to do well." Margaret Huntar would say no more and was rebuked for it. She is kept in mind until she is summoned again.

Robert Ewart also affirmed that Alison Foullar said to his wife, "if I burn before noon for what I've said, Margaret Huntar will burn after noon." Adam Scugail and Manis Clerk were called but did not appear. They are ordered to be summoned to the next session day. December 8th: On Wednesday 21st December George Ewart, son to Robert Ewart, was buried.

Manis Clerk was called, and asked what he heard Alison ffouller say about the late Alexander Jakson and John Ewart to Margaret Huntar. He replied that he heard her say nothing but, "God send everyone a good end," and, "It would be well done if parents told their children to keep good company." It was answered to this that he was saying otherwise in peoples' houses, where he had said that Alison said that Robert Ewart's son John Ewart, his neighbour, would go the same way. Manis Clerk denied this.

Adam Skugill was called and appeared, and was asked what he heard Alison Fowllar say. He answered that he was not paying attention, and did not heed what she said, for he was at the fireside with company, and she was in the parlour with Margaret Huntar. He was rebuked, and he and Mainis were ordered to appear again next session day. The rest of the witnesses are to be present with Andrew Strong.

1632

January 1st: All the witnesses in the case between John Ewart and Alisone Foular were called and appeared, and were confronted with Andrew Strong. They testified as above. This is referred to the Presbytery for advice.

January 22nd: The minister informed the Session that the advice of the Presbytery concerning the case of Alisone Foullar and John Ewart was that if Robert Ewart and his son could prove that Alison ffouler had said what they alleged, it would be better for them to persist, and call their witnesses before the Presbytery to be questioned again there. They should find surety that if he or his son fail to prove the matter, they should make amends to her accordingly. If they thought they could not prove the words Alisone ffoular is accused of, it would be more fitting that they should be brought to an agreement with her, and she with them. Robert Ewart appeared, and complained about Jeane Ra, Alison ffowler's daughter. The minister explained to the Session that Robert Ewart came to him and asked that she might be summoned to the Session today. Because they were dealing with this business anyway, he had got the clerk to summon her.

This Jeane Ra was called and appeared. Robert Ewart claimed that she spoke ill and despiteful words in the mill against his son George Ewart, who has now departed this life. When somebody said in the mill that George Ewart was dead, she said the Devil had judged[?] him. William Martein the miller heard her say it, and he is present. William Martein was asked by the minister to say whether she had spoken these words or not. He said he heard no such thing, but there were other harsh words between them. Margaret Ewart spoke more harshly to Jean Ra than she did to her. This is deferred for further investigation.

Jean Ra was accused of saying to Robert Ewart's wife that if her mother was burnt before noon, Margaret Hunter would be burnt after noon. She replied that it was true that she had spoken these words. What she meant was that her mother had said nothing but what Margaret Hunter had said, and yet they were not challenging her. If they thought Margaret had only said what was tolerable, then her mother was no more a witch than Margaret Huntar.

January 29th: The minister explained to the elders that concerning the Alison ffoular business, he had told Robert Ewart and his son of the Presbytery's advice as set out above, and asked him whether he was going to proceed or not. Robert Ewart and his son said they would not be able to prove what she said, except by a minor [*i.e.* except by the evidence of a child ?], since she denied it. Therefore the minister had asked Robert Ewart and his son John Ewart to come to today's session meeting, and had also summoned Alison Foular and Jean Ray her daughter to appear, so that this business between them could be brought to a conclusion either by proceeding further or by agreement.

Robert and John Ewart were called in and asked if they wished to proceed with the matter concerning words between them and Alison ffowler. They answered that since they could not get her words proved as they had thought, they were willingly content to do whatever the Session ordered. Alison Fowlar was also called in, and appeared. She was asked what she had to say against John Ewart or Robert Ewart. She answered that she had nothing to say against them; only that the late Alexander Jaksone had been very much against her husband and her when he was alive, and that John Ewart had enthusiastically supported the late Alexander Jaksone in his severity against her husband and her. However, she had now forgotten all their quarrels and forgave John. John Ewart answered that he supported Alexander Jakson against her and her husband George Ra only in those matters for which he had just cause, which everyone knew.

The minister urged them to speak and love as became neighbours and Christians, and in the end both parties, in presence of the Session, took each other by the hand and promised to agree in future as became Christians, God willing. Alison asked Robert and John Ewart to forgive her if she had said anything hasty against him or his son. They forgave her, and took her by the hand, as she did to them. Asked if they had anything to say against Jean Ra, they said they had nothing against her, and nothing to accuse her of. They were therefore dismissed.

1633

December 3rd: Jeremie ffergison and Jonet Utterstone are to be summoned to the next session day for using foxglove leaves on a child of Marion Laing's, which is now dead. December 22nd: Jeremie ffergisone appeared. When he was accused by the minister he answered that he fetched the foxglove leaves at the request of the child's mother. Jonet Utterstone was called and appeared, and affirmed that although it was true that the foxglove leaves were used in her house, she had not given her consent to it

Since the child's mother Marion Laing is half mad with sorrow, and acting as a wet-nurse to William Mirst's[?] child, her appearance was postponed for a time. Jeremie Fergison and Jonet Utterston are ordered to appear again a fortnight from today. It was thought fit that the minister should seek advice from the Presbytery next Thursday. The minister also asked the elders to try to ask the child's mother Marion Laing who had given her the counsel or advice to use the foxglove leaves.

1634

January 5th: The minister reported the Presbytery's advice regarding the parties who used the foxglove leaves. Those at fault are to make public satisfaction, and such practices are to be publicly forbidden under the penalty of the most severe censure.

Jeremie Fergiston was called in to hear this, confessed, and was ordered to satisfy publicly next Sabbath. Jonet Utterston was called, appeared, and accused. Since it was found that she had not given her consent, she was dismissed.

The minister reported that he had spoken, along with some of the elders, to Marion Laing the mother of the dead child. The explanation she gave was that the child had lain sick for a long time, and never seemed likely to either die or live. Alexander Peter's woman servant, who saw the child, told her to use foxglove leaves, and the child would either "end or mend". The woman was half mad with grief that she had done anything to offend the minister and elders, and since the child was nearly dead before the foxglove leaves were used, she was called in before the Session where the minister explained her error to her before the Session, and ordered her never to make use of such practices again. Since she showed signs of repentance, she was dismissed.

The same day Bitriche [*i.e.* Beatrice] Milton in Belpotis complained that Alexander Cugilton in Belpotis had slandered her, claiming that she was the cause of his daughter's illness. She also said he claimed that she was the cause of his cow aborting her calf. Alexander Cugilton was lawfully summoned, called, appeared, and was accused of this. He denied it, and declared that he had killed a pig, and his wife - as she usually did - sent Bitrich Milton a piece of it with some pudding the same day. When his daughter came back from Bitrich's house with the meat, his other daughter became very ill. Near evening, the cow came home and aborted her calf, and after that his daughter became well. There were crows crying around the house, and in the morning the cow came in heat again. After that he sold the cow to a butcher.

When Alexander was asked why he blamed his neighbour Bitrich Miltoun for these things, he answered confidently, saying that he never said - nor would he say - that Bitrich Miltun was the cause of it. Bitrich was present, and when called brought in George Shenkis in Kirklandhill to prove that Alexander Cugiltoun had slandered her. When George was questioned he affirmed that Alexander Cugiltun did not slander her or give her the blame, but only told her about the cow's sickness and how she had come into heat the next morning. The Session asked Bitrich if she had any more witnesses against Alexander Cugiltun, and she said she had none. The Session therefore thought it would be better to seek the Presbytery's advice about it.

January 12th: The minister reported to the Session the Presbytery's advice about Alexander Cugiltun and Bitrich Milton in Belpotts. Since Alexander Cugilton could prove nothing against her, and since she could not prove that he had slandered her, it was thought that since they were neighbours and had been good friends to each other in the past, they should be brought to an agreement. If there is any [illegible] in the matter, it is left to God until his majesty sheds further light on it.

[Alexander Cugilton's wife Helen Crystison was reconciled with Bitrich Milton on 19th April.]

April 6th: [Agnes Kirkland, Christen Nisbet, and Janet Neilson had been quarrelling.] George Wood says, " Agnes Kirkland, in a great passion, prayed ill against Janet Neilson and her husband, and wished that his 'gear' would never prosper... [illegible]". James Anderson was called, appeared, and declared that Agnes Kirkland said she hoped that no gear would thrive that twenty pounds came among, and spoke many other despiteful words. [The meaning is obscure here. Is the £20 the cause of the quarrel, or is it the value of the "gear"?] William Ra testified similarly. Agnes Kirkland was called, appeared, and was accused of these spiteful words. She confessed that she had spoken such things in anger. However, she did not say it should never thrive, but wished it so. Christen Nysbett had provoked her first by calling her a witch, and she answered that she was in the company of one, or worse. [This is continued to the next meeting where they all appear and say that they are reconciled. The minister rebukes them, and says they deserve to be punished.]

1644

July 7th: According to the orders of the Presbytery, intimation was made today that if anyone had any accusation to make against the people suspected of witchcraft who are imprisoned in Dumbar, they should give in their accusations tomorrow - Monday. If they are ill and it is not convenient to come to Dumbar that day, their accusations or whatever they have to say against them should be given to the minister before witnesses.

July 11th: Intimation was made again, that if anybody had anything to give in against the four persons suspected of witchcraft, they should come to Dumbar again next Monday, the fifteenth of this month. The parties suspected and imprisoned are John Steill, Catherin Reck, Cirsten Forster in Thorntonloch, and Cirsten Jaimesone in Dumbar.

October 20th: Public intimation was made to the people about the sickness among livestock called "rowting evill". [The Dictionary of the Older Scots Tongue quotes the definition, "a strange and sudden disease wherewith an ox could never lie down, but rowted [bellowed] continuously till he died."] No-one is to to try to cure this by making a grave and burying or interring a live beast in it, under the penalty of taking upon themselves the crime of charming and witchcraft. Since this was done recently in Whittinghame parish and some others, intimation is being made about it in all the parishes of this presbytery, by order of the Presbytery, so that in future no-one can claim ignorance. Anyone using this practice will be judged guilty of charming and witchcraft as previously stated.

1649

August 12th: Public intimation was made this day that if any person or persons within this parish had anything against Alexander Wilson and his wife, or against Jennit Niclsone[?] in Hailis, or Catharin Bee, who are all arrested on suspicion of witchcraft, they should tell it to the Session, the Presbytery, or [illegible]. If anybody knows anything against anyone in this parish or within the presbytery or elsewhere concerning witchcraft, they should similarly report it to the Session or the Presbytery. If it is found afterwards that they knew or had heard of anything and did not report it, they should be censured according to the law, and the orders dealing with such cases.

The minister earnestly desired the elders to say if they knew of anyone suspected of witchcraft in this parish. They said they knew of nobody.

September 2nd: Again, everyone was formally asked individually if he knew anybody suspected of witchcraft. They answered that they knew of nobody.

September 17th: Jonet Nicolson was executed and burnt at Hailes for witchcraft.

October 14th: It was publicly intimated from the pulpit about Agnes Angus who is suspected of witchcraft, that anybody in this parish having anything to say against her is summoned to appear at Stainton.

November 4th: The minister asked the elders individually if they knew of anybody suspected of witchcraft within this congregation, since witchcraft was so common. They answered that they knew of nobody, but promised to inquire diligently.

November 25th: [This entry is damaged.] ... minister asked the elders individually if they knew of anybody... ... of witchcraft. They answered that they knew of nobody, but... ...the minister and all the elders thought it necessary that public... ...about it should be made from the pulpit, that if anybody knew of any persons suspected of witchcraft they should report them...

Public intimation was made from the pulpit that if anyone knew of any person or persons suspected of witchcraft, they should report them to the Session or the minister... ...public intimation, earnestly exhorted the people of his parish to make thorough enquiries about it.

Public intimation was made from the pulpit about a certain Helen Hunter, fugitive from [Er?]ingtowne, suspected of witchcraft.

Public intimation was made from the pulpit about Patrick Yorstone and Cristen Yorstoun in Whrttinghame. If anybody in this parish either knew or had any dealing with both or either of them, they should report it to the Kirk Session.

[Between November 1649 and April 1650 the handwriting is very poor, the ink is badly faded, and the pages are damaged - all of which causes some problems in interpretation.]

1650

January 6th: [damaged] ...to enquire if there was anybody suspected of witchcraft. Some of our people were confronted with some witches in Prestonkirk today... ...minister asked the elders if they knew of anybody suspected of witch... ...and told them they were to search dilligently [illegible] in this parish... ...accused by the witches of Prestonkirk [illegible].

January 27th: It was reported that the man who searches the witchcraft suspects had not yet come to Prestonkirk to search those that are accused and suspected here. The baillie of the parish promised to make it known when he comes to Prestonkirk, and will make him come here to us.

February 3rd: It is reported that the searchers of witches from Tranent have not yet returned from the south. In the meantime Agnes Kirkland and David Steward should be apprehended.

George Shortus promised to tell his son Robert Shortus in Tranent to get one of the searchers in Tranent to come east to here when they come back from the south.

[Damaged] ...on Thursday the seventh of February 1650 Agnes Kirkland and David Stewart, both in this parish, were imprisoned... ...being accused... ...witches in Prestonkirk.

...and on Wednesday I went to Dumbar beach where ten witches were executed... [damaged].

February 10th: The Session sent down orders about the watch ... ...who have been arrested for witchcraft, one appointed each night.. ... the parish to be taken up, and so to watch overnight, and two... ...daytime, time about in order. This was done accordingly.

February 17th: The Session appoints the watch to be punctually kept. This was done... February 29th: [damaged] ...Robert and James Kirkwood in Skugall, and John Cowie in Auldham... ... desired to send up their folks to watch by [illegible], promised to do this, but wished that if anybody in their area was arrested... ...witchcraft, that Lord Hadington would watch as it see[?] them... ...they agreed to this willingly.

It is appointed as before, that those whose turn it is to watch... ...an elder should watch with them there, time about, as was done before... ...promised to continue.

The searcher from Tranent came on the twentieth of February and found the ... ...that were suspected of witchcraft, and [illegible] and shortly...

March 5th: [damaged] The people given up by Agnes Kirkwood and David Stewart, both in this parish and in Prestonkirk parish... ...with again, finished with this, and found...

March 24th: [damaged] The Session orders the watch on the witches to be kept better...
...promised to do.

March 31st: [damaged] Because the [illegible] about the witches was not... ...it was decided to attend to the watch... ...of them still... ...it was hard to get people to watch all day... ...observed all night, and therefore... ...thanked God and commended the elders for their good... ...holding hand and watching the witches in their [illegible]... ...as they were desired and employed.

April 7th: [damaged] The minister informed the elders that concerning David Stewart and Agnes Kirkwood, that the commission to put them to an assise was now... ...brought east, and had come into our hands. Some of those appointed... ...and put in the commission met yesterday, and appointed all... ...to be done and is meeting together next Tuesday to be [illegible]... ...send them to an assise. The watch was therefore appointed to be well... ...these two night two nights to come, and all the elders and [illegible]...on Tuesday, to which they agreed.

...of the great [illegible], refers the matter of the [illegible] the next... ...Having been appointed to do so by the Session, James Kirkland reported that the Laird of... ...was happy that a "justicierie" should be... ...his bounds of... ...and Aldhame, with the advice of James Kirkwood... ...not... ..[illegible] day of April 1650, a Tuesday, David Steward and Agnes Kirkwood were executed.

...and being officers at the court, since George Shortus... ...that belonged to Agnes Kirkwood.

George Shortus was promised twelve pounds out of Agnes Kirkwood's [illegible]...and gear... the box likewise, if there are any ...[several illegible words].

[It is a great pity that these entries from 1649 and 1650 are so fragmented. They were made during one of the great "witchcraft panics" and a complete version would have been valuable. It is interesting that although the Presbytery requires the minister to persistently quiz the elders about whether there are any witchcraft suspects in the parish, and to announce from the pulpit that parishioners should report any such people, no suspects are to be found until two Tyninghame people are named by confessing witches in a neighbouring parish. The entries also mention obtaining the services of "searchers" [witch-prickers] from Tranent, and detail the arrangements for "watching" the suspects. Arrangements for holding the court are also noted, and the fact that local men appointed as court officials are to be recompensed from the confiscated estates of the executed witches. It looks as if the parish poor-box also benefited.]

1661

July 21st: "Given for candle to watch the witch" - £0 - 11 - 0. [This was during another "witchcraft panic", but no other information is given, and there is no further mention of witchcraft or charming in the 17th Century Tyninghame records.]

Whitekirk.

Whitekirk Kirk Session minutes are designated CH2/371 in the National Archives of Scotland. CH2/371/1 contains minutes for the period 1691 to 1717, but no 17th Century references to witchcraft as far as I could see.

Whittinghame.

Whittinghame Kirk Session minutes are designated CH2/327 in the National Archives of Scotland. CH2/327/1 contains minutes from 1674 to 1690, and CH2/327/2 contains minutes from 1694 to 1702.

1677

October 21st: William Knocks, one of the assistants here, reported that Robert Yourstoun and George Smyth are still at variance because Patrick Yourstoun had vilely upbraided and calumniated both George Smyth and his wife, calling them witches and thieves. They are to be summoned to appear here at the next Session meeting. William Knocks is appointed to tell them to bring in their witnesses to the meeting, if they have any. [There is no further mention of witches in this case. The argument centres on Robert calling George and his wife thieves. They are finally reconciled on 16th December.]

1680

April 2nd: Thomas Moor gave in a letter of complaint against William Comb, saying that William detracted from his good name by calling him "warlock's get", and saying that he had "stolen himself rich". Patrick Douglas and John Henderson, assistants here, witnessed this, and George Wood in Pople. [Whittinghame seems to refer to its elders as "assistants".] Both parties are to be summoned to the next meeting, with their witnesses. [There is no further mention of this case, however.]

1681

May 8th: William Johnstoun gave in a bill of complaint against John Kincaid, specifying that John had calumniated his good name by calling him "warlock carle". Both parties and the witnesses are ordered to be summoned to appear at the next meeting. Our minister is to write to the minister of Garvit kirk, since one of the witnesses is a parishioner of Garvit, to get him to appear here at the next Session meeting.

May 29th: John Kincaid was called for calumniating William Johnstoun as specified above. He appeared, and was sharply rebuked by the minister for detracting from William's good name. He acknowledged that he was heartily sorry for doing it. The minister exhorted him to walk more circumspectly with his neighbours in future, and he promised to do so. John is ordered to appear publicly before the congregation a week today, to give satisfaction for the offence. [He duly appeared on 4th June.]

1685

January 18th: John Calder in Grayhaughs gave in a bill of complaint against Jean Finlison in Yarrow, specifying that Jean had maliciously detracted from his good name as follows: -

Firstly by saying that he had said that he would "staint thair ground" [*i.e.* stunt or wither the ground; destroy its fertility]. Secondly by saying that he had taken away all the strength and fruitfulness of the ground, for within two or three days after he had said that he would "staint" the ground, it happened that two of their cows died. At this, Jean inferred in the hearing of William Woolans in Whittinghame, and James Craw and James Knowes in Yarrow, that John was a warlock, and had actually taken away all the strength of the ground. Both parties are to be summoned to appear with their witnesses at the next meeting.

February 22nd: Jean Finlison was called, and appeared. She was sharply rebuked for calumniating John Calder as stated above. She denied that she said anything injurious to his good name. The minister questioned her on the points of the complaint, that is, whether or not John was a warlock, and if he had taken away the substance of the ground. She replied that she had only said John would "staint" the ground badly if he brought all the beasts on to it that he intended. The minister immediately had all the witnesses called. They were individually questioned and sworn about the points of the complaint. Each of them declared that they heard Jean say nothing but that the ground would be sufficiently "stainted" if John if John brought the lambs to it that he said he would bring. The Session thought that the witnesses statements did not prove the complaint, and asked the minister to make some overtures in the matter. The minister then called John in, and told him that he was very sorry that he and Jean should have given such great offence to God and his people. He exhorted them to be more vigilant over their hearts in future. He also told John that his complaint was null unless he could find new witnesses for the next meeting. However, John was unwilling to proceed any further, and said he would try hard to be reconciled with Jean. The minister therefore ordered some of the assistants of the Session to meet John and the woman at Patrick Douglas's house, to work at reconciling them, and to report the outcome at the next meeting.

March 22nd: William Knox, Robert Dixon, Adam Skin/in, and John Henderson reported that they had met with John Calder and Jean Finlison with a view to reconciling them, and had reconciled them.

June 21st: Jean Finlison, having been summoned, was called, appeared, and acknowledged her fault in expressing some rash and inconsiderate words against one of her neighbours. Being sharply rebuked for her offence, she gave great evidence of her repentence, and promised to live soberly and in a Christian manner in future.

1686

May 9th: The minister reported that a complaint had been made by James Whytlaw and Alison Shanks against Christian Arther, and so he had ordered Christian Arther to be summoned to today's Session meeting. She had knelt down publicly and cursed, calling James Whytlaw "thief of thieves", and Alison Shanks an old devil or witch. Christian was called but did not appear. She is ordered to be summoned for the second time to the next Session meeting.

May 16th: Christian Arther was called, appeared, and confessed that in her anger she had uttered the word "thief or similar slanderous things" against James Whytlaw, calling him a thief, and against Alison Shanks, calling her an old witch or devil. She declared that she was heartily sorry for offending God and her neighbours. The minister sharply rebuked her, and explained to her the heinousness of her sin. She was ordered by the Session to appear publicly the next Lords Day before the congregation to acknowledge her offence, and to beg mercy from God and forgiveness from her neighbours. The Session delayed modifying her fine until they saw how she behaved at her public satisfaction of church discipline. Appointing some of their number to go with the minister to see her reconciled with James Whytlaw and Alison Shanks, was also delayed until the next meeting.

May 30th: Christian Arther again appeared before the Session, and after many pious and godly exhortations from the minister regarding reconciliation with her neighbours, she declared that she was very willing to beg pardon of her neighbours whom she had offended. To that end the Session appointed John Henderson and James Skirvin, with the minister, to see them reconciled between now and the next Sessiom meeting, and to report back.

Also, since the Session was satisfied with Christian's behaviour during her public repentance, she was ordered to pay into the Poors' Box two "rex dollars", one for slandering James Whytlaw, and the other for slandering Alison Shanks, to be paid between now and next Lammas term. Christian also desired a "testificate" that she had given satisfaction. Therefore the Session appointed an extract of the process to be written for her by the Clerk.

July 4th: John Henderson and James Skirvine reported that they had met in order to reconcile Christian Arther with James Whytlaw and Alison Shanks, since Christian had declared before the Session as is written above, that she was very willing to crave pardon of her neighbours whom she had offended, and be reconciled with them. However, James Whytlaw and Alison Shanks showed their unwillingness to be reconciled with Christian by absenting themselves, although Christian had turned up. The minister therefore informed the Session that he would deprive James and Alison of the benefits of the church until they had come to an agreement with Christian, since she was very willing to agree with them, as God's holy word allows.

[The above lengthy and admittedly not terribly exciting case is included in full as a prime example of how calling someone "witch" did *not* normally set the hounds of the Kirk Session snapping at that person's heels, but instead was much more likely to rebound with serious and humiliating consequences upon the slanderer. It is also a good example of the kirk's tenacity in sorting out such matters; and furthermore, shows that even the offended parties could feel the weight of the Kirk's displeasure if they did not accept the slanderer's appology with good grace.]

Yester.

The modern centre of this parish is the village of Gifford, which did not exist in the 17th Century. The old church and village of Yester, often known as "Bothans", were situated near the present mansion house of Yester. Yester Kirk Session minutes are designated CH2/377 in the National Archives of Scotland. CH2/377/1 runs from 1613 to 1643. CH2/377/2 runs from 1643 to 1707. The minutes therefore cover almost all of the 17th Century.

1628

June 29th: It was ordered that John Halliday should satisfy church discipline for consulting Patrick Chrystisoun about stolen goods.

July 13th: John Halliday is ordered to satisfy for consulting Patrick Chrystisone.

July 23rd: John Halliday satisfied in linen clothes for consulting Patrick Chrystison.

1629

March 18th: Today Andro Mathieson in Yeaster satisfied church discipline for charming. It is ordered that if ever again Andro Mathieson should be found charming or meddling in any way with charmers and witches, that he shall be delivered into the hands of the civil judge to be punished according to the laws of the land as an obstinate person persevering in the Devil's art.

March 22nd: Today David Diksone made his satisfaction for charming. It is ordered that if David Dikson is ever again found charming or meddling in any way with charmers and witches, then he shall be delivered into the hands of the civil judge to be punished according to the laws of the land.

It is ordered that John Wheatlie jr. should be summoned again for slandering Jonet Begbie as a witch.

March 29th: John Wheatlie jr. satisfied in linen clothes for slandering Jonet Begbie as a witch.

1632

April 8th: It is ordered that Meg Hunter [illegible] and Patrick Harlaw's wife should be summoned for slandering Johne Merkhouss.

Meg Barker in Yeaster appeared, accused of slandering her neighbours. Regarding Agnes Scott, she confessed that six years ago she gave Agnes Scot six shillings to charm her daughter. She had asked for it back again since then, but never got it.

April 28th: Meg Hunter in Yeaster and Patrick Harlaw's wife satisfied publicly for slanderously accusing John Merkhous of witchcraft.

1646

July 12th: Thomas Carfrae appeared, having been summoned previously, and declared that he put a live toad round a ewe's neck, because of sickness among them, but did not use any words. He also declared that he was told about this by Jeane Deanes, a parishioner of Bolton. He is referred to the Presbytery for investigation.

1650

March 17th: Intimation was made concerning fugitive witches who have fled from the parish of Carriden - Janet Kennedie, Agnes Penny, Isobeil Simpson, Elspeth Thomesone, and Andrew Anderson.

July 2nd: Some reports of malefice [*i.e.* evil-doing through witchcraft] were given in against Margaret Turner... [This entry has been cut off at the foot of the page.]

July 7th: Margaret T[urner?], midwife in Newtoun appeared, having been summoned to answer the declarations pf certain persons given with reference to an accusation in our hands of malifice committed by her. She denied it. Because of the inconvenience of apprehending her and investigating the matter, and the troubles that would result from it she was asked to find surety that she would answer when called for. She could not find anyone to stand surety, and so the business is postponed until a more opportune time.

1651

October 24th: It is reported that John Watherstoune in Yester consulted the parents of the dumb boy about some stolen money. He is ordered to be summoned to the next Sesson day.

November 2nd: John Watherstoune appeared, summoned for consulting the parents of the dumb boy in Paistoun, and for abusing his own parents. He confessed consulting but denied the other scandal. He was sent out, and after considering his fault and his ignorance, the Session ordered him to make a public acknowledgement of consulting, next Sabbath. It was also ordered that if he was found guilty of this sort of offence again, he would be liable to church censure and to whatever sum of money the Session should think fit to fine him. The other scandal is to be investigated.

November 16th: John Watherstone in Yester made public acknowledgement of consulting the parents of the dumb boy about his lost money.

December 23rd: Issobell Breddin complained against Bessie Heriot that Bessie had called her a witch. The first two witnesses called as proof did not appear. The case is therefore postponed.

[Somehow associated with the above case in a way that is not entirely clear - to me anyway - is a case of adultery between Bessie Heriot and Walter McKinnel. Also somehow connected is the strange business of drawing blood from Bessie and baking it, which follows.]

1652

February 28th: Margaret Sked appeared, and testified that the blood which was drawn from Bessie Heriot was baked, and that she ate three bits of it, not knowing what it was. It was bitter and salty, and she got it from Janet Kemp when she was baking, and gave the rest of it to Christian Watherstone and Margaret Wood.

April 25th: Margaret Sked and Janet Kemp appeared, who had previously been questioned about the scandal of the baked blood. Questioned individually, they declared that Margaret Wood brought down the blood and kneaded it, and Janet Kemp put it on the girdle. There was no other blood in the house at the time, and it was the last time Bessie Heriot's blood was drawn. They both declared that Margaret Wood told them to deny it and say it was lamb's blood.

May 16th: Margaret Wood appeared after being summoned. She denied baking the blood and that the other two, Janet Kemp and Margaret Sked were present. However, they affirmed their declarators in her face. Since this is a civil matter, as advised by the presbytery, she is referred to the civil magistrate, and Alexander Ogilvie is to speak to lady Newhall about her punishment.

[An entry of 30th May notes that Bessie Heriot and Walter McKinnel have fled the parish.]

[There is a gap in the minutes from 1654 to 1663.]

1667

March 6th: William Home appered and complained that Agnes McCrie had scolded and reproached him, calling him "dyvore dog" [dyvore: a debtor, bankrupt – Dict. OST]. Agnes appeared, complaining that William had struck her and called her a witch and a witch's get. She was asked if she had verbally abused William and called him a "dyvore dog". She admitted that there were abusive words between them, and that she called him a "dyvore". William was called and questioned about his complaint. He confessed that he gave her a blow with a spade shaft and called her a witch's get.

It seemed to the Session that neither of them have any sense of their sinful ill-temper and the injury they have done to one another, and so the business is delayed until a week today, when they are both appointed to appear.

March 13th: William Home was called and appeared, and was asked what sense he had of the injury done to his neighbour. He said that if he had fallen short in calling Agnes a witch's get, he was sure that her husband John Brown was a witch's get since his mother had been burnt as a witch. John Brown appeared and complained that William had reproached him as stated above. This business is delayed while the Session give it further consideration. The parties concerned are to be heard a fortnight today.

[Date missing]: William Home was called but did not appear. The Session appoints him to be summoned to appear a fortnight today. [Unfortunately, there seems to be no further mention of this matter.]

1671

June 25th: It was reported that Robert Whit in Carselwood Hall had gone to a wizard to consult him about some cloth which had been stolen from him. The Session appoints him to be summoned to appear a week from today.

July 2nd: Robert Whit was called, appeared, and confessed that he was at a man in the Cannongat and consulted him about his lost cloth. He had been told that if he went looking for it, he would find it, and that it was a woman who had stolen it. The Session appoints that Robert should speak to the minister this week, and appear here a week today.

July 9th: Robert Whit was called and appeared. The Session found him obstinate, and unwilling to satisfy church discipline for the offence he has given. He is referred to the Presbytery, and is summoned to appear before them next Thursday.

July 16th: Robert White appeared and confessed his sin. The Session appoints him to appear before the congregation next Lord's Day to acknowledge his sin in consulting with a wizard to find his stolen cloth.

1672

July 14th: It was reported that Jean Pearson had gone to consult that person in the Cannongat who claims to have skill in finding thieves, about the loss of some curtains belonging to the Countess of Tweeddall about which she had been challenged. The Session appoints her to be summoned to appear a week today.

July 21st: Jean Pearson was called and did not appear. The Session appoints her to be summoned to appear a fortnight today.

August 4th: Jean Pearson was called and did not appear. The Session appoints her to be summoned for the third time, to appear a fortnight today.

August 18th: Jean Pearson appeared and declared her sorrow for her sin of consulting as stated above. She is ordered to acknowledge her sin before the congregation, and to be publicly rebuked.

September 8th: The minister reported that the Presbytery had eased the severity of Jean Pearson's sentence after she had applied to them to that effect, and she is now to be rebuked before the Session.

1673

June 15th: The Session appoints David Blake to be summoned to appear before them a fortnight today to answer for consulting a person in Edinburgh who claims skill in discovering stolen goods, about some clothes stolen at Yester a few months ago.

June 29th: David Blaik was called, appeared, and confessed his sin. He was rebuked, and promised amendment.

We shall return in the final chapter to the question of what light the Kirk Session Minutes can shed on witchcraft and attitudes to it in 17th Century East Lothian. In the meantime, suffice it to say that if there is one thing that should be blindingly obvious, it is that calling someone "witch" was a dangerous game. It is commonly believed that in 17th Century Scotland all you had to do was point the finger at some poor innocent old soul and call her "witch", and a fanatical Calvinist kirk session, red in tooth and claw, would hustle her off to a cruel and horrible death. As even the most cursory reading of the surviving East Lothian kirk session minutes makes clear, calling someone a witch almost always ended with the accuser or name-caller being processed as a slanderer, and having to repent and apologise, sometimes in the most humiliating circumstances. Curiously, this even happens in cases where the victim of the "slander" clearly has a reputation as a witch. What is also striking is the thoroughness and tenacity with which kirk sessions would investigate such slander cases, and the effort often put into bringing about reconciliations.

Seventeenth Century kirk sessions may have had many faults, but it would appear that consigning innocents to the flames was not usually one of them.

3. Other Church Records

Parishes were gathered together into Presbyteries. Ministers and elders from each parish met regularly to discuss business and make administrative decisions. The Presbytery was also a church court superior to the kirk sessions, to which the sessions could refer their difficult cases. The Presbytery made regular visits of inspection to the parishes, and entered the reports of these "trials" in their records.

Presbyteries were in turn similarly overseen by "Synods", which were in theory overseen by the General Assembly of the Church of Scotland. There were however lengthy periods of Episcopacy in the 17th Century when the Presbyterian system in the lower echelons of administration operated in tandem with a "top management" of bishops and archbishops, and the General Assembly was not allowed to meet.

The Presbytery of Haddington.

The records of the Presbytery of Haddington are designated CH2/185 in the National Archives of Scotland, and begin in 1587. Interestingly, these early leaves are bound in what appear to be sheets of parchment cut from a book of Catholic church music. The first few pages are very badly damaged, to the extent that reading them is more an exercise in conjecture and guesswork that transcription and interpretation. Records are extant as follows:

1587-96	CH2/185/1
1596-1608	CH2/185/2
1612-27	CH2/185/3
1627-39	CH2/185/4
1640-48	CH2/185/5
1648-61	CH2/185/6
1686-86	CH2/185/7
1698-98	CH2/185/8 and 9
1698-1715	CH2/185/10

I shall render the entries in modern English and occasionally summarise where it seems justified. The Presbytery records of course help to fill out the Kirk Session records, since they include items which must have featured in kirk session minute books which are now lost.

1588

June 12th: Johne Makgil, suspected of witchcraft.

[This occurs as part of the report on a Presbyterial Visitation to Garvald. It seems that the life of James Reid the minister has been threatened, perhaps by witchcraft. The entry continues:-] ...... in Hadington which he had made his principal place of residence, and accused a certain John Makgill in Garvatt who is suspected of witchcraft.

1589

August 27th: [Contained in a report of a visitation of Gullane.] ...reported that Bessie Gray, a witch, had fled from the [illegible] and is in their parish.

1590

September 15th: [This page is particularly badly damaged. It refers to John McGill as "an idle beggar menacing the simple people", and seems to say that he has no difficulty making a living since people are so afraid of him. However, this does not seem to have been the case in Traprain.] ... except that in the settlement of Traprene where Esspet Hepburne was lying sick. Advice was sought from Agnes Sampsoun in Keith. She said... [What she appears to have advised was that McGill should not be allowed to pass by, but should be apprehended and taken into the sick woman's house. As soon as she saw him she would be delivered from her complaint.] ... found to be true in all circumstances... ... John Macgill is to appear eight days from now.

September 30th: [John] Macgill appeared and was asked if it was true that he did not go to church. [Probable reading. There is damage here.] ... he promised to amend. He was asked how long he had been a beggar, and he admitted that it had been sixteen years. When asked what the reason was, since he appeared to be a physically able man, he alleged that he had been ill with kidney stones ["the gravell"] for fourteen years. He was asked when he had been in Traprene, and he replied that he had only been in Traprene twice since the marriage of Robert Hepburn's bastard daughter. The last time, Robert's daughter had been lying sick, and her husband and Patrick Hepburn, son of the said Robert Hepburne of Over Haillis, said to him, "John, you thief, you've taken my sister's health away from her." In the meantime Keringtoun came in behind him and felled him with a fork, and kept striking him till the fork broke. Then they carried him violently to where the woman lay sick. On entering the house he said, "God be here." [Probable reading.] After this they gave him some food and drink, but being weary with travelling and with the blows... [Damaged.]

[It would seem that Agnes Sampson diagnosed that the sick woman at Traprain had been bewitched by McGill, and that the cure was to confront him with his victim. He, like Agnes Sampson, was caught up in the "North Berwick" investigations, and executed early in 1591.]

1595

June 25th: Marion Congilton, the wife of Jhone Storie in Hadington, has been accused of being a witch, and is to be put to an assise next Tuesday The Presbytery therefore orders that this should be intimated in all the churches within the bounds of the Presbytery, to see if anyone has any complaint to make about her.

1597

November 23rd: It was reported to the brethren that Helen Porteous, the wife of Hary Broun in over Keyt, and Mr Robert Broun their son, had consulted with Janet Steill in Over Keyt, who is suspected of witchcraft, and with the dumb boy, about Helen's husband's health and other matters. It was decided that both of these persons should be ordered to appear in fifteen days time to answer the accusation.

December 7th: A summons was given to Helen Porteous, wife of Hary Broun in Over Keyt, and Mr Robert Broun their son, to appear today for the reasons contained in the communication sent to them. The summons was duly delivered, executed, and endorsed in the usual way. Both of these persons appeared and were accused of consultation with Jonet Steill in Overkeyt who is suspected of witchcraft, and with the dumb boy who is reputed to be a diviner and soothsayer, and possessed by an evil spirit. The consultation concerned the health of Hary Broun - Helene's husband and father of Mr Robert. Helene answered that it was true that her husband was seriously ill, so Janet Steill was sent for and did most of the nursing of her husband while he was ill. She washed him several times in south-running water after sunset, and Helen was aware of this. However, this was not done on her orders, but on her husband's orders. As far as the dumb boy is concerned, she admitted that she sent her son for him, and enquired about some missing articles, but said nothing about her husband.

Mr Robert answered that on his mother's orders he went in search of the dumb boy and brought him to her. However, he knew nothing about Jonet Steill.

After some discussion of these matters with the brethren, they both confessed that they had offended God and scandalised his church by seeking help from [illegible], indeed from the Devil in their desperation. They submitted themselves to the discipline of the church. After discussion, the Presbytery decided on further investigation. As regards their satisfying church discipline for the scandal, the opportunity should be taken to investigate the matter further and question Jonet Steill in Overkeyt. In the meantime they were ordered to hear the Word [i.e. attend church] diligently, and be ready to appear again when requested to do so.

1598

February 1st: It was decided that Jonet Steill in Overkeyt, who is suspected of witchcraft, should be summoned to appear at the next meeting to be charged with magical practices concerning the health of Harie Broun in Overkeyt.

February 8th: Jonet Steill in Overkeyt was summoned to appear before the Presbytery today, for the reasons set down in the communication duly delivered, executed, and endorsed according to order. Jonet was called, appeared, and was questioned about her dealings with Hary Broun, and confessed as follows:

That she was born in the Stow of Weddell, in a place called Praintatoun, where she lived till she was eleven years old. From there she came to the Raschaw, where she stayed eight years, and from there she came to Howdaine in Lauderdaill. She stayed there three years and then went to the Bourhouss, where she stayed for a year, then stayed for another year in Nather Howdene. From there she went to Overkeyt, where she has been for the past seventeen years.

About thirteen years ago, when she was seriously ill with swollen hands and feet, there came a poor man who said he used to go about with the Jews. He washed her in south-running water, and healed her of her illness at the time of the great plague ["greit pest"].

Since Harie Broun was seriously ill, his wife Helen Porteous came to her. After she had looked after him for eight days, she told him how south-running water had healed her. After that, with the consent of Henry and his wife, she went three different nights to a well called the Well of Saynt An, after sunset, and brought back water. The first night she met Robert Roger's wife, the next night Katherane Smyt, and nobody the third night. Every night she washed Hary in the following way; first she saved the water [or possibly, "sained" it - i.e. blessed it], then after putting it in a tub she mixed it with water-cress ["welcarse"], and said the Creed and the Lord's Prayer in Latin as the man had taught her. Then Harie stood up in the tub, and she and his maidservant Bessie Spens washed him. And when they had finished they threw the water out.

The Presbytery continues this for further investigation, and ordered her to appear when next required, which she promised to do.

[There seems to be no further record of this case.]

1623

January 22nd: Evidence relevant to James Dik's witchcraft case was produced from Hadinton kirk session. It was presented to the brethren, and the session's dilligence was approved.

1628

November 12th: Mr Archibald Davidson [minister of Saltoun], reported on his going to Dalkeith on the Presbytery's orders to question the witch Margaret Muirhead, detained in the tollbooth of Dalkeith, about the case of William Davidson alias Hadtheraike. He has progressed against William to the extent that he has been imprisoned in Hadington with accusations against him which may be enough to convict him.

[This nickname is almost illegible in the original. It seems to be "Hadtheraike". "Hatteraik" was a notorious warlock who is named in Sinclair's "Satan's Invisible World Discovered" as Sandy Sinclair or Hunter. Since Davidson and Sandy Sinclair/Hunter were contemporaries, the author of "Satan's Invisible World" may have confused them - perhaps even deliberately, since that author's own name was Sinclair. The trials of both William Davidson and Sandy Sinclair/Hunter are contained in the Haddington burgh records. Several writers have unquestioningly followed Sinclair's lead in naming "Hatteraike" as Sandy Hunter. In fact it seems more likely from the evidence of the Presbytery minutes that "Hatteraike" was William Davidson.]

1629

August 20th: James Balfour appeared, having been complained against by the Presbytery of Dalkeith. [This entry is very difficult to decipher. The gist seems to be that James is suspected of witchcraft. He claims that the "Goodman of Emmet" has deposited surety for him and he should be released. However, it seems the "Goodman" doesn't know him. James is apparently "content to confess his fault" - whatever it might have been - before the Presbytery of Dalkeith or elsewhere.]

1630

January 20th: Patrick Broun, baillie of Haddington, presented to the brethren a commission from His Majesty's Secret Council to examine the women who were accused by Alexander Hamilton [another notorious warlock] of the crime of witchcraft. So that they can proceed with this business more conveniently, the brethren have ordered them to be summoned to each Presbytery day to be questioned.

January 27th: Two of the women accused by Alexander Hamilton of being guilty of witchcraft had been ordered to be present, but did not appear. Because the brethren of the Presbytery did not have all the statements against them ready, they were appointed to be summoned to the next Presbytery day, so that they can hear the commission read to them which was sent to the ministers of the Presbytery, and so that the brethren can then proceed to a formal investigation.

February 3rd: According to the decision made at the last meeting, the women suspected of witchcraft and accused by Alexander Hamilton, whose names are contained in the commission sent to the Presbytery, appeared before the brethren of the Presbytery, with the exception of Margaret Alexander who has lately departed from this life, and Agnes Lauder who is seriously ill. The commission for the investigation was read. Two of them, Katharein Lauder and Bessie Duncan, are ordered to be present next Presbytery day.

February 11th: Bessie Duncan and Katharen Lauder appeared, and various important and serious accusations were made besides those made by Alexander Hamilton.

April 7th: A commission was brought and presented to the Presbytery from the Lords of Council for the imprisoning and further investigation of the women named by the warlock Alexander Hamilton as being guilty of witchcraft. Proceedings are to be reported to the Lords by the 20th of April. Therefore, all the brethren in whose parishes there is anyone who can bear witness against these women, are ordered to make public intimation next Sabbath Day from the pulpit that the witnesses should be present in the tollbooth of Hadington the following Monday.

June 23rd: The brethren are ordered to be present in Hadington on the 2nd of July to attend the commissioners who are to try by an assise the four women imprisoned in the tollbooth of Hadington - Alison Carrick, Katharen Kirktoun, Bessie Duncan, Kathren Hunter. The brethren are ordered to intimate next Sabbath that any of their parishioners who have any accusation against any of these persons, should be present in the tollbooth on the day of their trial.

1639

August 7th: Bessie Hogge appeared, the wife of Hew Walker in West Fenton. She was examined on oath, and questioned in particular on whether her sister Isabell Hogge had told her to ask Helen Carfrae, servant to David Cowan, for ashes from under the chimney of David Cowan's house. This had been between the time of his wife's delivery, and her being laid up in bed. She affirmed that she had indeed said that her sister had asked her to do so, but when she said this she was lying about her sister. Helen Carfrae was also examined on oath, and questioned in particular on whether Bessie Hogge had said to her that her sister Isobel Hogge had asked her to get the ashes at the time and from the place mentioned above.

As regards the process pursued by William Smith against the two Hogges, the brethren decided that they could do nothing but give a copy of the statements of the persons examined by them. This was accordingly done, and sent with William Smith to Mr John Dalyell.

1641

March 10th: The minister of Haddington sought the advice of the brethren about two women in Hadinton who had quarrelled with each other. One called the other a witch, and said she would prove it by what was commonly said in the district, and by some advice which had been given to her. Taking the matter into consideration, the brethren found that there is no point in the allegations substantial enough to warrant detaining the woman in prison as a witch. However, neither is the other party to be held to be a slanderer, since there is some likelihood that there may be grounds for calling her a witch. The brethren therefore think it best that the magistrates of Hadinton should cause them both to find surety to live peaceably in future, and that they should be punished for their public quarrel. In addition, both of them shall answer to Hadinton kirk session if it can be proved in future that either the one has consulted, or that the other has used any kind of charming.

October 12th: John Howden in Over Keith is ordered to be summoned fourteen days from today for craving his health from Isabell Wood. Also Isabell for pronouncing some words by way of a charm, as a result of which John is said to have recovered from his sickness and infirmity. His sister Jonet Howden is said to have fallen sick at the uttering of some words by Isabell.

October 26th: John Howden in [blank] appeared. When he was asked about his illness he declared that when he was at variance with Isabell Wood, she had taken him by the arms when he was in the fields. Shortly after that he lost the power of his arms. Then about two years after that he took a pain in his heels which continued a long time, and a [blank] told his wife to go to Isabell Wood and ask his health from her thrice for God's sake. He did this, leaning on his staff, but not kneeling, and after that he grew better little by little. Immediately after that Isabell came to John's sister Janet Howden and said, "Let God never allow your brother to prosper or thrive!" Shortly after that Jonet became sick, and is now bedridden.

Isabell Wood appeared, and confessed that John Howden came to her and asked his health from her. She had knelt down and said, "Goodman, if ever I did you any harm more than an unborn child could do, may the Lord make me like a crow to fly about the world, and may the same happen to you if it be otherwise." She had said to Janet Howden, "May God's forgiveness light on your brother. How can anything thrive that he has?"

All parties - the man and his wife, the woman that instructed his wife, and Isabell Wood - are ordered to be summoned to the next meeting by Mr John Cockburne, but not before the Sabbath preceding the day of [illegible].

November 16th: Jhone Howdane appeared, consulter with a supposed witch, and stood by everything in his last statement. His censure is postponed until his wife can come. The Presbytery orders that he and his wife should appear a week from today.

Issobel Wood, the supposed witch, also appeared, a parishioner of Humbie, and denied everything. In order to investigate Issabell further, the Presbytery desires the minister of the parish to make public intimation from the pulpit to see if anyone can be found to shed further light on the matter, so that the Presbytery can proceed with it more methodically. The Presbytery also desires Mr Richard Broun, minister at Salton, Mr Jhone Logan, minister at ffallaw, and Mr Hewie [?] Cockburne, minister at Chengenkirk [Channelkirk in Lauderdale], neighbouring ministers, to join with the minister of Humbie for the same purpose.

Mr Jhone Cockburne reported Janet Gourlaw, a parishioner of Humbie, for consulting with a witch. The Presbytery orders her to be summoned a week from today.

[Obviously the situation in Humbie was causing the Presbytery some disquiet. Following the above entry comes a report from the Laird of Humbie suggesting that a helper should be appointed to assist the minister of Humbie. This person should be a qualified minister so that he can "use discipline among the people".]

November 23rd: Jhone Howdone and his wife appeared. She was asked whether or not she advised her husband to seek his health from the supposed witch. She confessed that she did, and also confessed that he obeyed. Both of them humbled themselves before the Presbytery, acknowledging their sin with sorrow. They were ordered to satisfy church discipline in linens in three separate churches - Humbie, Fallay, and Pencaitland, a day in each. Also, the ministers in each of these churches are to preach about Janet Gourlaw, because of her confession before the kirk session of Humbie. The Presbytery refers her to that kirk session to receive her instructions.

Mr David Calderwood produced a referral from Pencaitland kirk session, regarding James Mill's accusing Margaret Dicksone of witchcraft. Further investigation of their parishioners is referred back to their own session. Mr Robert Broun, reader in [Haddington?] is ordered to summon Jhone Sinclare, a parishioner there, to Pencaitland session to shed further light on the matter.

1643

February 8th: John Clarke appeared, from Bankreiff in the parish of Aberlady, and confessed that he had gone to Johne Lyndsay to ask him who had stolen his balls of thread. He also declared that he had given him 40 shillings for his pains. He then confessed that he drank with him in the blacksmith's house at Dirletowne, and met with him in Cocklemill in the presence of a certain Gawen Guyler. The Presbytery orders him to satisfy church discipline in his parish church of Aberlady, and also in Dirletown, two separate Sabbaths in linens.

John Lyndsay is to be summoned a week from today.

February 15th: John Lyndsay in Dirletown was called and did not appear. He is ordered to be summoned for the second time.

April 12th: John Lindsay appeared, the suspected abuser of the people. He denied that he was guilty of abusing anyone, and denied it when he was asked whether he had received money from Jhone Clerke for telling him who had stolen his ball of thread. Jhone Clerke was also called, and when he was confronted with Johne Lindsay, swore that he had given him forty shillings and stood by all his previous statements.

The Presbytery orders John to be investigated further in this wickedness. To this end, intimation is to be made publicly in Dirleton and Aberlady from the pulpit, to see if anyone can be found who can give an example of Jhone Linsaye's abusing someone. If so, it is to be diligently reported to the Presbytery. The Presbytery also orders Jhone Linsay, and he binds himself at their orders, never to make use of his former methods to abuse anyone. If anyone can be found who when questioned reveals abuse committed by him, it will add to the seriousness of his conviction.

[Perhaps "deceiver" and "deception" would convey the sense of the above extract better than the original terms "abuser" and "abuse".]

April 19th: Mr David Calderwood produced and read the notes from Pencaitland kirk session which contain statements of alleged witchcraft, the wording of which is as follows: -

"James Mill's Complaint

I, James Mill, complain against Margaret Dickson in Nisbet. About two years ago when I was sick she offered to free me from my sickness if I would go through a hank of yarn. This was on a Sunday, before noon, at the time of preaching. Last harvest time I reproved her daughter for pulling my wheat. 'Yes,' she said, 'he's so angry about the pulling of two or three ears of wheat! It won't be long until he loses a better quantity of goods!' ["block": a quantity of goods - Concise Scots Dictionary]. William Baxter witnessed this, and John Thomsone heard her say she would see me stabbed in a gutter and my children come to a bad end. After this I found my livestock seized with a kind of trembling disease, and some of them died. Since she said what she did, I have a suspicion that she is the one who has done me the wrong she spoke about."

James refers the investigation of this to us, and gave his oath that his statement was true.

Witnesses' Statements

John Thomson declares that Margaret Dickson said every grain of wheat would bring down a pound, and she hoped to God that James Mill would be stabbed in a gutter as his grandfather was, and that the Lord might not let anything thrive that he does.

William Baxter declares that Margaret Dickson said that James Mill would lose a better quantity of goods before Christmas Day, and various other evil words, and she said to Willliam himself that she hoped to see him go an ill road, and hoped to see him carried in a barrow by Martinmas Day. She denies this.

John Sharp declares that Margaret came to his house, and when she saw his daughter sleeping she said that she also had a daughter and had got her cured. She said to Jhone, 'If this has been done by evil spirits, this is what you should do. Take a peck of meal, take nothing out of it, and bake it. Take 12 [?] eggs, and take the contents out of them, lay the bread and the eggshells in front of the fire, and put your daughter behind the fire. Then about midnight go round the house nine times, and when you come in again say, 'Rise up elf, and go back where you should go in the Devil's name, and give me my daughter again.' If the child is to recover, the bread and eggs will be away, and if not, the shells and bread will still be there.' She told him to keep quiet about it. Margaret Dickson confesses that it was an old woman who said these things to her. She admits the whole story, except that she said thrice round the house in the evening at ten o'clock, and Jhone said nine times.

Isobell Jhonstone declares that Margaret Dickson washed her child's shirt, and the child, twice in south-running water, and put the shirt back on the child. After the second time the child began to sweat, and Margaret said she would need to be washed thrice. However, Isobell would not allow Margaret to wash her again, for the child gasped and sweated and burned for thirteen weeks after that. Because the child was so emaciated, Margaret told Isobell to put on a good fire and throw the child into it, for the child was not hers, she was a hundred years old. When Isobell blessed the child, Margaret said she had blessed her as well, and that was what had made her last so long. Isobell also said that ten days after that Margaret came to her and told her to deny it all. She said she wouldn't deny it. Margaret said that in that case it would be the worse for her, and asked Isobell to forgive her if she had done her child any wrong.

Margaret Dickson said that Isobell had asked her a quarter of a year previously to come to her. Six or seven times in an hour she came to her and offered her sixpence to fetch a pint of burn water to wash her child. She also said that James Mill had been saying that if one devil laid on the sickness, another devil took it off."

The Presbytery orders all parties to be summoned to appear a week from today.

April 25th: Margaret Dickson appeared, suspected of witchcraft. Being asked about James Mill's complaint, she confesses she came in to see him, but denies that she told him to go through a hank of green yarn. She told him to use it by winding it round the affected part, as somebody else had told her. In response to John Thomson's statement, she confessed that she said his father was always a good brawler ["payker" - a thumper], as could be seen since he was stabbed in a gutter.

William Baxter was called, appeared, and was accepted by Margaret as a witness of good reputation. When William was questioned, he testified as he did at Pencaitland. When she was confronted with the first part of the statement, she admitted it, but with one addition - that she "hoped in God" that every grain etc. To the latter part she admitted as above.

Lastly, when she was confronted with James Mill, when he affirmed his previous statements and complaint against her, she said no more than she had declared previously in reply to all the particulars.

Jhone Sharp was called, and testified as at Pencaitland, but said he did not remember well whether it was nine times or three times she told him to go round the house.

Margaret Dicksone answered just as she had done at Pencaitland, as is contained in the records, and said she was told to practise the cure mentioned there on a child of her own. When asked if she did it, she denied it. Asked why she did not do it, she answered that God would not let her. She was asked why she told someone else to do it, since she did not think it was right, and she replied that she only told him about it, but didn't tell him to do it However, he declared that she told him to do it.

Isobell Johnstone appeared and testified as at Pencaitland. Margaret Dickson confessed to most of what Isobell Johnstoun had testified, but said that she told her to throw the child in the fire in loose soil. She also admitted that she received a sixpence from Isobell. The Presbytery orders that a copy should be made of the whole process and sent on. [Presumably to the civil magistrate, or to the Privy Council.]

October 25th: Mr John Courtney is requested to copy the case of the witch in Pencaitland parish, and produce it a week from today.

November 1st: Mr John Courtney brought the copy of the case of the witch in Pencaitland, and delivered it to Mr David Calderwood.

[In 1649 the Privy Council records show a Margaret Dickson in Penston confessing to witchcraft, and a commission being sought to put her on trial. Since she speaks of meeting the Devil in the Nisbet area around five years previously, this may well be the same woman. If so, it makes it very unlikely that the revelations before the Presbytery in 1643 had been taken any further.]

1644

February 28th: Andro Kerr, charmer in Castleton, was summoned by Mr Henrie, appeared before the Presbytery, and confessed that he had practised charming for the past twelve years. He was therefore ordered to be present the next Presbytery day, and the brethren also ordered Patrick Lyll of the Heuch to be summoned before them, whose ox Andro had charmed and cured. The record of Andrew's previous investigation by the session of North Berwick was duly read to the clerk, the content of which is written below: -

"The session had cause to summon the persons later specified to appear before them, in order to investigate a frequently repeated report of a cow in Castleton out of whose belly a flame of fire is supposed to have issued.

First appeared Andro Ker, the owner of the cow, who declared that the cow was greatly swollen and dead. They made a little cut in her belly, and first a blast of wind came out. At the next cut came a flame like the flame of brimstone, which he knocked down with his hand. It had risen about an ell [94.1 cm], and he felt the heat of it. In his opinion, if he hadn't held it down it would have set fire to the house.

Next, Alexander Gaylour appeared, and declared that after the hide was taken off, he made a nick in the cow's belly, and a puff of wind came out. Then he made another nick, and a flame came out, blue and red, which was knocked down by Andro.

Thirdly, William Sandie testified similarly, that a flame came out a [illegible] high which was first blue and red, and flashed three or four times, and if it had not been held down it would have set fire to the house.

Fourthly, Robert Darling also declared that he saw a flash of blue and red fire. Andro Ker's wife said it would save her a better gift. [Probably meaning that this occurrence had prevented something worse.]

Fifthly, John Mitchell declared that the flame was like a blaze of gunpowder, and made them all afraid.

The same day, Andro Ker appeared in connection with the scandalous report alleging him to be a charmer. Being asked in regard to this if he had practised any such thing, he replied that one Sunday morning he came to Patrick Lyll's house in Heuch, having been asked to come, and bled an ox of his [Patrick's] by cutting its ear. The ox was diseased. Asked if he used any words of charming, he answered yes. When asked what the words were, he answered as follows:-

'Three things are tain fra thee; the heart, the hand, and the eye maist;

There is nane can remeid thee bot the father, the sonne, and the haly ghaist.'

Asked from whom he had learned these words, he answered from his mother Isobell Waitt, who taught him to charm bewitched animals in this way, and had died eight years ago. Asked how long he had used that form of charming, he said for the past twelve years, for those who asked him.

The said kirk session [*i.e.* North Berwick], 25th February 1644.

For further investigation of this scandal, Patrick Lyle in Heuch was summoned, appeared, and when asked if Andro Ker had cured his ox, he answered yes. When asked why he had employed Andro, he said that his ox was diseased, and when he described the disease to Johne Chrystisone in Weitschot, he told him the ox was bewitched and that Andro Ker in Castletowne would charm him. At this, he sent a boy on horseback for Andro, who didn't come right away, but came soon afterwards on a Sunday morning when Patrick was in bed. He told Andro about the ox, and Andro went to the byre and made use of some cure or other before Patrick came out to him. Whether he cut the ox's ear or not, he doesn't know, but it was cut, and before ten o'clock the ox recovered and was better each day after that. Before Andro performed the cure, for five days and nights previously the ox had done nothing but sometimes lie, and sometimes rise and stretch itself."

March 13th: Patrick Lyle in Heuch, within the parish of North Berwick, appeared before the Presbytery. Asked about Andro Ker charming his ox, he replied that he did, and confirmed the truth of the process drawn up by the clerk of Northberwick.

Also, when Andro appeared today, the moderator asked him whether, as a popular report among the people has it, he had ever heard anyone say these words of cursing to him, The fire of hell be in your cow's belly." He declared that he had never heard any such words said to him. Asked whether he had repeated the words of the charm [*i.e.* Three things are tain fra thee... etc.] to his own cow or not, he said that he had, but to no avail. The Presbytery requests the moderator to summon Andro before his own kirk session to find out any further particulars about his charming, and to report back. The Presbytery orders the neighbouring ministers, or one of their number, to use their elders to search for any information about this charming in any parish or congregation near at hand or far off.

June 26th: Andro Ker, the charmer previously mentioned, is ordered to satisfy church discipline in sackcloth, and if anything more can be found out about him, the Presbytery recommends the session of Northberwick to try diligently to do so.

July 3rd: Mr Home reports that Andro Ker is to enter to his public satisfaction next Sabbath.

July 17th: Andro Ker has entered to his public satisfaction.

1646

May 27th: George Beir [?], who professes skill in curing "cruells" [scrofula, a form of lymphatic tuberculosis, also known as "the king's evil"], is ordered to appear next Presbytery day.

June 24th: George Beir was called and did not appear. He is ordered to be summoned for the second time.

July 2nd: George Beir in Haddington appeared. When questioned about his skill in curing "the King's seekness", he replied that he didn't learn it from anyone, but he was a seventh son. The late Mr James Knox, minister at Kelso, understanding that he was a seventh son, told him when he came to a patient to lay his hand on the sore part and say, "I touch thee; Lord cure thee" three times. He had never tried to cure anyone before Mr James had told him to. But ever since he has employed the cure when he had occasion to do so. He applies nothing to the patient but clean cloths, and ties two black silk threads round the patient's neck. Amongst others, he used this cure with Farquhar Anderson's daughter, Richard Chaplain's son, somebody in Samuelstoun, James Westoun's daughter in Tranent, Marioun Skedd's daughter in Humbie, James Black's daughter in Cinglekirk, a servant of the Laird of Tofts in Lambe Burn in Eccles parish, and [blank] Stobart's daughter in Hermistoun Mill. Several had benefited from his cure, and several had not. He himself had had the disease, and cured himself. The brethren order him to desist from using the cure until he is summoned before them again, which he promised to do.

July 2nd: It is ordered that the brethren of Dunbar Presbytery should be consulted in the matter of curing scrofula.

August 5th: The Presbytery of Dumbar's advice regarding George Beir's curing of scrofula is that the Commission [?] should be consulted. It was resolved to follow this advice. Thomas Carfra and Jeane Deanes appeared separately before the Presbytery, and confessed that they tied a toad round the neck of one of their sheep to cure the "kreakshaw" [stiff or feeble legs due to disease of joints - Scot. Nat Dict.]. This was a cure used by Andrew Yooll, a neighbour. The Presbytery orders Andrew Yool to be summoned before them fourteen days from today, and the others to appear the same day.

August 19th: Mr John Courtney is ordered to summon Androw Yool to the next Presbytery day.

September 23rd: George Bair is ordered to be summoned again, fourteen days from today.

October 14th: George Beire appeared and promised that if ever he was found practising the curing of scrofula again, he would satisfy church discipline as a charmer. Andrew Yooll did not appear. It is ordered that he should be given a summons in writing.

October 21st: Andrew Yool was called and appeared. The moderator sharply rebuked him for taking so long to appear. He was asked if he was in the habit of curing his sheep by tying a live toad round one of their necks, and from whom he had learned it. He replied that he had done so, and had learned it from George Brown of Dernidykes. Asked if it actually cured them, he answered that he thought it did them good.

Asked if he said any words or made use of any ritual when he tied the toad round he sheep's neck, he replied that he made use of no ritual and spoke no words. The Presbytery orders him never to use this cure in future, under the penalty of being censured as a charmer, to which he agreed. He is ordered to appear whenever he should be summoned in future, which he also promised to do. It is ordered that the minister in whose congregation George Brown lives should be acquainted with this case so that he can be questioned and processed for it.

1647

June 2nd: Mr John Magkie reported on Helen Bull, a midwife in Dirletoune parish, for being in the habit of laying a piece of bread in the bosom of children brought to be baptised [*i.e.* putting a piece of bread in the clothing covering their chests]. The Presbytery orders her to be summoned to Hadintone in a week's time.

June 9th: Helen Bull's absence today is excused because Mr John Mackgie reports that she is detained out of necessity with some women in labour. She is to be summoned to the next Presbytery day.

June 16th: Helen Bull was called but did not appear. She is ordered to be summoned to the next Presbytery day and informed that if she fails to appear the Presbytery will proceed against her.

June 23rd: Helen Bull in Dirletoune was summoned and appeared. She declares that she laid bread in the bosoms of children when they were baptised because it was an old custom which she had always seen followed. She was severely rebuked and ordered never to practise any such thing again, otherwise she would be censured as a charmer.

Hearing that this was common practice, the brethren exhorted everyone to enquire about it diligently. Particularly, the Presbytery appoints

Mr John Mackgie to forbid it publicly from the pulpit, since it has been practised in his parish more than elsewhere.

1648

Mr Robert Ker informed the Presbytery that a certain Agnes Anderson being processed before his session [Haddington], has confessed that she advised Isobell Smith in Newmilnes to take her child between two barn doors and turn it three times heels over head. Alternatively she could turn it three times round a post of oak, uttering the words that she would teach her. That would cure her child of nausea ["maw turning"], which was what the child was suffering from. Mr Robert also informed the Presbytery that Isobell Smith confessed that she did as Agnes Anderson advised her, and turned her child twice round an oak tree, but was afraid to do it a third time. From then on her child began to recover.

Mr Robert also informed the Presbytery that Janet Symie, Agnes Andersone's daughter, had advised Janet Cosser, when it looked as if her marriage to James Watsone would not come off, to go in to James in the morning and look three times into his face, and three times at the ground. He would then either marry her, or never do well.

All this was put into writing by the session clerk, and referred by the session to the Presbytery for judgment. The Presbytery finds Agnes Andersone and Janet Symie her daughter guilty of charming, and Isobell Smith and Janet Cosser guilty of consulting or relying upon a charmer. The punishment of these persons will be decided next Presbytery day, before which time the clerk is requested to search the register with regard to the censure of charmers, particularly as practised in Northberwick, and report back.

1649

January 3rd: The clerk, Mr Andro Makghie reported that he had found in the Presbytery records, a certain Andro Ker in Castletoun, convicted of charming sick oxen. When he confessed this, he was ordered to satisfy church discipline in sackcloth on three separate Sabbaths. The Presbytery orders Agnes Anderson and Janet Symie her daughter, now found guilty of charming, to satisfy in the same way before the congregation of Haddinton.

March 28th: Mr Robert Balcanquhall reports that a certain Jean Craig in Tranent has been arrested and imprisoned under a warrant from the Lord Chancellor for the scandal of witchcraft. He requestd the Presbytery to nominate some brethren to assist him in dealing with her, so that she can be brought to a confession. The Presbytery directs Mr John Oswald and Archibald Douglas to agree to assist him with this.

April 12th: Mr Robert Balcanquhall showed a copy of the statements and formal accusations of witchcraft concerning Jean Craig in Tranent. After this was read the Presbytery's advice was to ask the Council, or whoever it concerns, for a commission to try her and judge her according to law. [Jean was sentenced by the Justiciary Court to be executed at the Muir Brow, Tranent, on 1st May 1649.]

18th April: The brethren of Dumbar Presbytery reported Johne Lindsey in Dirleton for deluding George Craig in Markle, by making him believe that he could tell him within forty-eight hours the whereabouts of the Laird of Markle's money, which George is accused of stealing. John Duncan in Dirleton witnessed this. John Lindsay and John Duncan are ordered to appear the next Presbytery day. Mr John Dalyel is to cause George Craig to appear next Presbytery day.

25th April: George Craig in Markle was called, appeared, and being interrogated declares that he went to John Lindsay in Dirletoun and consulted with him concerning the whereabouts of the money that William Whyte alleged George had stolen and taken away. He said he would give John Lindsay everything he had if he would tell him where it was. John had answered that he didn't do that sort of thing, but if he could help him he would send him word within forty-eight hours. However, he never did send word.

Mr Robert Balcanquhall wished some of the brethren to be nominated to be present at Tranent next Friday when the assise on Jeane Craig's witchcraft case is due to sit.

May 16th: John Lindsay was called, appeared, and confessed that John Duncan told him that the Laird of Markle had some money missing, and that Markle's servant George Craig had come to him to ask who had the money and where it was. John Lindsay had answered, "Don't let him come to me, for I will break his face!" John Duncan replied, "Why not do it? We can trust him as much as we trust ourselves." George Craig had come with John Duncan, and George Craig's wife and daughter had been to him before that. Yet John Lindsay denies that he ever promised to send him word within forty-eight hours, or that he ever made arty sort of contract with him.

John Duncan was called, appeared and was questioned. He declares that he thinks George Craig came to John Lindsay before his wife and daughter. There were two or three days between George coming, and his wife and daughter coming. Craig was the first to break off the dealing between himself and John Lindsay. John Lindsay had asked where Craig lived, what did he want with him, and had he anything missing. He asked how old his daughter was, and alleged that she had the money.

John Lindsay was called in again, and declared that after thinking about it, he remembers that George Craig came to him first. Confronted with John Duncan, John Duncan affirmed in his face the truth of his above-written statements, and also affirmed that John Lindsay had said, "If I can do any good for you, I shall send you word in two or three days." John Lindsay still denies that he said this. He is therefore summoned to appear in fourteen days time.

Mr James Carmichael is ordered to request Mr John Dalziell to summon George Craig and his wife and daughter to appear the same day.

May 23rd: George Craig was called and appeared. His wife Janet Whittle was called and appeared. Their daughter was called but did not appear. When questioned, Jannet declared that she went to John Duncan in Dirletoun to get him to take her to John Lyndsay, because she had heard that John Lyndsay could give her good advice. John Lyndsay had said to the girl, 'Tell the truth if you've got it," and she had been in tears. John had told her to pray to God. George Craig declares that he went down to Dirletoune before his wife. The Presbytery postponed proceeding further in this business until John Lyndsay could be present. It was ordered that he should be summoned to the next Presbytery day.

June 6th: The Presbytery took the matter of John Lindsay into consideration. He was called and appeared. It was decided that it was clear that

1. George Craig and his wife and daughter had come to John Lyndsay to consult him about the stolen money.

2. John had promised them an answer within 48 hours.

The Presbytery refers the consumers to the Presbytery of Dumbar, within whose bounds they reside. Since John Lyndsay has been dealt with before regarding this sort of thing, Mr Andrew Mackgie is appointed to search the register to see what was done about him then, and to report next Presbytery day. Lyndsay is therefore summoned to appear then.

June 13th: John Lindsay was called but did

not appear. He is ordered to be summoned to the next Presbytery day. The records are to be searched concerning him.

June 20th: John Lindsay's case postponed until a week today.

Patrick Watson, Marione Miek, and Bessie Hodge in the parish of Dirletone, imprisoned for being guilty of the crime of witchcraft, have given statements and confessions accepted by the Presbytery to be sufficient grounds for seeking a commission for trying and judging them according to law.

Also, the confessions of Isabel [blank] and Margaret Dicksone in Penstone were similarly accepted by the Presbytery.

July 2nd: The statements of [long blank], imprisoned in Hadinton for being guilty of the crime of witchcraft were accepted as sufficient grounds for seeking a commission for trying and judging these persons according to law.

The statements of [blank] in Dirltoune were similarly accepted.

Mr John Mackenzie is requested to confer with the witchcraft suspects in North Berwick.

July 9th: The statements of Sybella Wyllie and Elizabeth Hamiltoune, prisoners in North Berwick for the crime of witchcraft, were accepted as sufficient grounds for seeking a commission for trying and judging these persons according to law.

The statements of Margaret Hamiltoun, Margaret Tulleis, Marjorie Forrester, prisoners in the said burgh [*i.e.* North Berwick] for the same crime, were read and considered. The Presbytery finds the contents give sufficient grounds for seeking a commission, but because they have not been subscribed by a minister or a magistrate the Presbytery cannot attest them. Mr Andro Mackgie is ordered to question them again. If in his hearing, or in the hearing of any magistrate or elder, they make the same statements as are contained in the paper presented, then Mr Andro is warranted to attest these statements in the Presbytery's name. This is to be done because the magistrates wish to get a commission for them all at once.

Statements from Helen Fairlie, Barbara Purdie, and Helen Lawsone, prisoners in Haddintoune for the crime of witchcraft, were read, considered, and accepted as sufficient grounds for seeking a commission for trying and judging these persons according to law.

July 18th: Mr Andro Mcgie reported that he had interrogated the witches in North Berwick upon the same particulars that were presented to the last Presbytery meeting. They confessed them in his hearing and in the hearing of one of the baillies who was with him. He therefore attested the declarations in the Presbytery's name as he had been authorised to do.

A letter was received from the baillies of North Berwick desiring some ministers to be present at the execution of their witches next Friday. The Presbytery appoints Mr Robert Ker and Mr John Magie to be present.

Mr Robert Ker and John Mackgie were commissioned to question some of the witches about certain persons they had mentioned before who, it is alleged, had been suggested to them.

July 25th: Johne Lyndsay is referred to the next meeting when all the brethren can be present.

Mr Robert Ker brought the statements from the witches he had questioned, as he had been appointed to do. They were ordered to be recorded, because some of the people they concerned wished to have copies of them. They read as follows:-

"July 20th 1649, in the presence of Mr Robert Ker, minister at Hadintoune; John Hepburne of Craige; John Levintoune, baillie in North Berwick; and Archibald Stewart, chamberlain to William Dick of Breade[?]. Margaret Hamiltoune was questioned about the meeting at Fortonmoore she had previously mentioned in her statement of [date left blank].

She declares that as far as the house they went to is concerned, where they ate, she does not know the owner of it. She said only that he was an old man she never saw before or since. As she shall answer to God she doesn't know him, and doesn't know his name. What she said in her previous statement about his name was only suggested by some of those who were present at the interrogation.

Signed: Robert Ker
Robert Hepburne, elder
John Levintoun, elder
Archibald Stewart, elder

" I hereby declare that being commanded by the Presbytery of Hadintoune to question the foresaid persons, I questioned them as previously described, and also asked them if they now remembered if they saw at that time whether he person they mentioned in their statements had any mark on his face [or perhaps 'outstanding facial characteristic']. Did he have both his eyes, or did he have any noticeable defect in his face? Both of those questioned declared that they did not notice any such thing.

Signed: Robert Ker"

August 1st: [Presumed date. No date actually given in the original.] Hearing that Catherine Whitley[?], wife of Mr Johne Cockburne, was under grave suspicion of witchcraft, the Presbytery earnestly recommends that the magistrate for the district should investigate the business.

Statements were read from Marion Goodfellow in Dirletone; Margaret Robertsone, Margaret Bartilman, Janet Burg, Margaret Patersone, and Jean Hunter in Hadintoune; George Ker, James Reid, Adam Moffat, Margaret Brotherstone, Jean Ker, Agnes Wilsone in Humbie; Agnes Broune in Saltone and [long blank] in Pencaitland - all imprisoned as guilty of the crime of witchcraft. The statements were considered and accepted by the Presbytery as sufficient grounds for seeking a commission for trying and judging these persons according to law.

August 8th: John Lindsay was called but could not appear. He is referred to the next Presbytery day, and ordered to be summoned.

Statements were read from Richard Umpherstone, Christina Leitch, Euphaim Wallace, Janet Smith, Margaret Fortune, and Helen Umpherstone in Aberladie, prisoners for the crime of witchcraft. The statements were attested as sufficient grounds for trying and judging these persons according to law.

[Marginal note: "Deposition of a witch"]
The statement of Janet Thomsone in [blank] was attested.

August 15th: Concerning John Lindsay - Mr John Mackgie and Mr Andro Mackgie have searched the register and can find no evidence of anything against him.

Statements were attested from James Paterson, Bessie Johnstone, Adam Johnston, Margaret Murray, Marion Laurie, and Janet Carncorse, imprisoned in Humby as guilty of the crime of witchcraft.

Francis Capie appeared, and gave in a plea on behalf of his wife Margaret Richardson, that since she has been imprisoned for a long time under suspicion of witchcraft, somebody should be sent to interview her, and that she should be quickly brought to trial. The Presbytery appoints Mr John Oswald and Andro Makgie to question her between now and the next Presbytery day.

August 22nd: Concerning the witches in Pencatlane - because the Presbytery is unclear about their statements, and because the magistrates think it is too long a delay to wait until the next meeting to seek a commission, Mr Robert Ker and William Trent are warranted to attest their statements in the Presbytery's name if they find them confessing "pactione" [*i.e.* a pact with the Devil to serve him].

September 14th: The confessions of Agnes Johnstone, Janet Cockbarne, Marione Hay, Christiane Forrest, and James [blank], all imprisoned in Pencaitland for the crime of witchcraft, were read, considered, and attested by the Presbytery.

Francis Capie presented the statements made by Margaret Richesone his wife. Some others involved in the same case also presented supplications. The Presbytery has John Kincaid's testimony that these persons have the mark. Mr John Mackgie is appointed to investigate these persons before the kirk session and report back, so that their statements can be sent to the Council afterwards.

September 26th: Mr John Mackgie reports that he questioned the persons in Tranent suspected of witchcraft. Margaret Richesone's statements were ordered to be sent in to the council, which was done.

October 4th: Elisabeth Wilsone and Janet Lyddell, fugitives from Pencatland, and John Foster from Humbie, who have all been processed for witchcraft, are to have their names publicly intimated in all the congregations within our bounds, so that if they are here amongst us they may be apprehended.

October 19th: Mr James ffleming is appointed to.go to Tranent next Tuesday.

Agnes Angus, who was being processed for witchcraft, is a fugitive from Stentoune. Her name is ordered to be intimated in all our congregations.

October 24th: Mr John Mackgie reports concerning John Lyndsay that there is a process against him before he session at Dirletowne, which is the same sort of thing that the Presbytery are processing him for - that is, giving advice about finding stolen money; with the help of the Devil, it is suspected. The Presbytery postpones his censure until they see what is proved in this latest scandal.

Margaret Brounfield appeared, reported as having consulted a witch in Salton about taking away her brother's life. She declares that she told Janet Whitley in Breadwoodsyd that she had been at Salton begging for meal. She said Janet asked her how all their friends [or possibly "relations"] were. She told her they were all well, but her brother was ill and she wished, if it was the Lord's will, that he was out of the world so that she might get an inheritance from her father. However, she denies altogether that she consulted with a witch. She is ordered to be here next Presbytery day, and Mr John Courtney is appointed to have Janet Whitly summoned in this parish, and also Marion Kirkwood, to throw some light on Margaret Brounfield's case.

[There is a theory that witchcraft panics tend to coincide with periods of political and/or natural crisis and disaster. It is therefore perhaps significant that October 24th also contains a reference to "apprehension of great dearth and famine by reason of the unseasonableness of the weather."]

October 31st: Margaret Brownfield appeared. She still denies that she consulted a witch for taking away her brother's life. She was further questioned about whether, when she came to Janet Whitlae's house, she was on horseback or on foot, whether she was barefoot or not, and where Janet Whitlaw was when she came to her house. She answered that when she arrived, Janet was standing in her own doorway. Margaret was on horseback and had on her stockings and shoes.

Janet Whitlaw appeared, and testified that Margaret Brownfield came into her house. She had not seen her for about seven years until then. Margaret said, "My brother is sick. I wouldn't mind being rid of him so that I could go home, for I've had an unhappy life." Janett asked her, "You want to get rid of your brother? It would always be there to punish you. I've a good mind to tell Mr Andro!" Margaret replied, "I only said it to see what you would say." Janett also declares that she did not tell Mr Andro. [Presumably the minister.] She says that when Margaret came to her house she was not at the door, but in the house.

Marioun Kirkwood appeared and testified that Janet Whitlaw told her that Margaret Brownfield wanted to have her brother dead, and that Brownfield had been at Saltoune looking for a woman to devour him. Marioun Kirkwood and Janett Whitlaw were confronted with each other. Before Margaret Kirkwood said anything in her presence, Janett said that she could not say whether she told Marion Kirkwood that Margaret Brounfield told her she had been at Saltoun looking for a woman to devour her brother. Margaret Brounfield and Margaret Whitlaw are ordered to appear next Presbytery day.

Mr John Courtney reports that a certain William Measlit[?] in Colstoune was given a message from Margaret Brownfield to tell Janett Whitlaw to deny anything that she'd said about her to Mr John Courtney. Mr Archibald Douglas is appointed to question Measlit.

November 28th: John Lyndsay was called but did not appear. Mr Johne Maghie is ordered to summon him to the next Presbytery day.

The statements of Isobell Boyd, Agnes Broun, and Jennet Wilsone in Hadington; and of Jennet Bard and Margaret Fodringhame, all confessing witches, were attested by the Presbytery.

December 5th: John Lindsay is to be questioned by John and Andro Maghie. A letter was received from the clerk of the Synod, requesting that intimation should be made in all the churches of the Presbytery by order of the Synod, regarding Isobell Hunter, a fugitive witch from the parish of Ormiston.

December 26th: [In the margin, "Deposition of a witch."] The statements of Catherine Whitley are attested by the Presbytery.

1650

January 5th: John Lyndsay was called but did not appear. George Gyler was called and appeared, and was recommended to the civil magistrate on presumption of his guilt in consulting with John Lindsay.

January 16th: Petitions were presented from Margerie Aytone, Marion Eastie, Margaret Dunkanlaw, and Isobel Rammanous, imprisoned for the crime of witchcraft. They request the Presbytery to take up their case with the magistrates of Haddington with a view to releasing them from prison on bail. Request denied.

George Gylar, after being referred to the civil magistrate on presumption of guilt, declared that he had lost a purse with sixteen pounds Scots in it at the time of the herring fishing [the "drove", more usually "drave"] last harvest. After that, he met with John Lindsay from Dirleton on the shore at North Berwick. They went from there to Robert Pringle's house in North Berwick, where they drank a pint of ale. While they were drinking he asked John Lindsay if he knew who had his purse, and asked him to tell him who had it, and he would reward him. John Linsey asked, "Who was nearest you?" He replied that the first person he saw was Mr James Atchison. John answered, That man has your purse." George Gyler declared this in the presence of John Sligh, baillie, and Robert and William Smith, merchants and burgesses of Hadington. George Gyler was called before the Presbytery and testified to it. Moreover, he added that when he asked John Lindsey to tell him who had his purse, John said he would look and see, and come back within two hours and give him an answer. Two hours later John came to him and gave him the answer.

February 6th: The brethren reported that they had made intimation concerning Isobell Hunter in their individual churches.

February 20th: John Lindsay was called and did not appear. He is excused because of his old age and sickness.

George Gyler was called, appeared, and was ordered to be present when he is informed that John Linsey is to appear.

The statement of Margaret Bishop, imprisoned for witchcraft, is attested by the Presbytery.

March 6th: A petition was presented by Michael Melvin from Margerie Aytone who is imprisoned for witchcraft, desiring the Presbytery to confer with the magistrates of Haddington with a view to liberating her from prison because of serious illness. After mature deliberation, the Presbytery thinks it inconvenient to grant the petition.

Petitions were also received from Marion Hastie and Margaret Duncanlaw, imprisoned for the crime of witchcraft, desiring the Presbytery to negotiate with the magistrates of Haddington for their release. The Presbytery answers as before, and thought that they should see the magistrates about giving them a more frugal diet. ["A more spare dyet" probably means less to eat, but it might just possibly mean "a less complicated and therefore speedier court process".]

A letter was received from Patrick Dicksone, clerk to the Synod, enclosing a list of names of fugitive witches and adulterers from the parish of Carrein in the presbytery of Lithgow. It is requested that their names should be intimated in all the churches of the Presbytery by order of the Synod. The Presbytery ordered sixteen copies to be made, and the brethren are to make intimation next Sabbath.

Margaret Skuggal is ordered to be summoned to the next Presbytery day, as she has been under the scandal of charming.

March 13th: The brethren reported that they had intimated the names of the fugitive witches and adulterers from the parish of Carein, and the declaration of the Church was also read.

Margaret Skuggal appeared, and is referred back to Haddington session to investigate matters in connection with her charming.

March 27th: John Lindsay was called, appeared, and was asked if George Gyler came to him and asked him to go to George Pringell's house in North Berwick to speak to him about his missing purse. John Lindsay answered that he spoke to George Gyler and went to Robert Pringell's house with him, but without any such intention. George Gyler never asked him directly who had his purse. George Gyler was called, appeared, and stood by his previous statement, and testified to the truth of it in John Linsay's presence. The Presbytery finds that George Gyler is a consulter, and therefore orders him to stand three days at the church door in sackcloth, and to go afterwards to the place of repentance to satisfy church discipline both for consulting and for slandering Mr James Atchison. Mr John Maghie and Mr Andrew Maghie are appointed to work with John Linsay to bring him to a confession.

Thomas Crawfurd was called and appeared. The Presbytery read the bill of complaint given in against him by Margerie Aytoun. Thomas denied the accusation. The Presbytery took this bill into consideration, arid decided that he could not be censured as a slanderer since Margerie Aytoun was already imprisoned for the crime of witchcraft, and was therefore "infamous" [i.e. devoid of reputation, and therefore not a reliable witness]. It was decided that they should see the magistrates of Hadington about binding Margerie Ayton to prove the bill under penalty of a sum of money. When this is done the ministers of Haddington, Mr John Maghie and Mr James Fleming are to interview the witnesses against Thomas Crawford.

April 10th: Jennet Couts, a confessing witch, declared judicially before the commissioners of her trial that she had been moved and enticed to accuse innocent people of witchcraft, principally by George Kathie. Within three days of her first confession, he made a bargain with her that she should accuse many people so that he would get the job of searching them for the witch's mark, and therefore profit from it. He would try to get her life prolonged for long enough. The commissioners ordered this to be copied and registered by me.

Signed: Andrew Watson, clerk.

This is an accurate copy, revised and prepared before the Presbytery by me, Mr Thomas Abernathie, at command of the Presbytery.

The Presbytery orders George Cathie to be summoned to the next Presbytery day.

April 17th: George Cathie was called and did not appear. Mr William Trent, who is to go to Tranent on Tuesday, was appointed to see the civil magistrate there to make Cathie appear before the Presbytery.

April 24th: The Presbytery attested the statements made by Marion Johnston who is imprisoned for witchcraft.

The case of Robert Bishop, imprisoned for witchcraft in Aberladie, is referred by the Presbytery to the Synod for advice.

May 1st: The Presbytery attested the statements made by James Vetch, a confessing witch in Pankaitland.

A supplication was received from Isobell Ramanoe who is imprisoned for the crime of witchcraft. Since she has been fifteen weeks in prison she asks the Presbytery to take up her case with the magistrates of Hadington with a view to setting her at liberty on payment of sufficient bail. The Presbytery thinks she could be set at liberty because of the reasons in her bill:-

1. The shortage of space in the prison.
2. The woman who named her was inconsistent in her evidence.
3. No witch mark was found on her.

Supplications were also received from Margerie Ayton, Marion Hastie, Margaret Duncanlaw, and [blank], asking the Presbytery to take up their cases with the magistrates of Haddinton with a view to setting them at liberty on payment of sufficient bail. The Presbytery decided that their case is different from that of Isobel Ramanous, and refers it to the Synod.

George Cathie was sent to the Presbytery from Tranent kirk session. He was called, and asked whether he knew Janet Cootes. He answered that he had spoken to her, and searched her for the mark. He was asked whether he had spoken to her after he found the mark, and he answered that he had often spoken to her after he found the mark on her. He was asked if he wanted her to accuse many people so that he would get employment. He replied that he never wanted any such thing. The Presbytery requests John Smith, elder in Tranent, now present at the Presbytery meeting, to see the baron baillie about either having George Cathie arrested, or to make him find surety to appear at Musselburgh on Tuesday before the Presbytery of Peebles. [There is no clue here to explain why Peebles Presbytery wanted to interview Cathie.]

The Presbytery attested the statements made by Marion Baptie, a confessing witch in North Berwick.

May 15th: The Presbytery ordered that they should convey to the magistrates of Hadinton the Synod's advice that the women imprisoned for witchcraft should be treated rather more harshly, and treated as others have been in the same circumstances. Mr James Oswell[?] and Mr John Maghie are appointed to speak to them to that effect.

May 29th: The brethren who were appointed to speak to the magistrates of Hadingtoune reported that they had spoken to them, and the magistrates resolved on the Synod's advice to treat them [*i.e.* the imprisoned witches] more harshly. [This is not so pointlessly cruel as it appears. There had been allegations over the preceding months of baillies drinking in the tollbooth with witchcraft suspects, and of attempts by one or some of them to bribe the witch-pricker. See the Haddington Kirk Session minutes.]

The Presbytery attested the statements of Margaret Veich, Thomas Sandersone, Elizabeth Holieday, Alexander Bell, and Agnes Bouglosse, confessing witches in Pencaitland, and of Janet Ballenie in Salton.

The Presbytery attested the statements of Alison Blackburne, Alison Johnstoune, Barbara Park, Mariom Bryson, Christian Burnet, Margaret Park, Elspeth Martine, Jeane Parke, Helen Guild, and Elspeth Falconer, confessing witches in North Berwick.

June 19th: The Presbytery attested the statements of Thomas Andersone, Bessie Andersone, Archibald Skugail, Agnes Stevenstone, William Hunter, Margaret Broun, Katharine Ferguson, all confessing witches in Pencaitland.

The Presbytery attested the statements of Janet Haistie, Jean Shanks, Bessie Adamsone, and Isobell Alexander, all confessing witches in Haddington.

June 26th: The Presbytery orders that intimation should be made in all its parishes, that if anyone has anything to say against Marjorie Aytoune, Marion Hastie, and Margaret Duncanlaw, they should come and report it. These women are imprisoned for witchcraft, but have not confessed.

July 4th: Statements were attested from Isobell Dickson in Pencaitland, who has confessed witchcraft.

A supplication was received from William Whyte and his wife, who have both been imprisoned for witchcraft. They desire the Presbytery to take up their case with the magistrates of North Berwick so that they can be set at liberty. The Presbytery has been informed that they have too much liberty in prison, and they request that the magistrates see to this. Until this has been remedied the Presbytery can give no advice about liberating them.

The Presbytery attested the statements of George Johnstoune, Bessie Gordoun, Robert Thomsone, Elspeth Cunninghame, Jean Crawford, Barbara [illegible], and Elspeth Oarther[?], who have all confessed witchcraft.

July 8th: The Presbytery attested the statements of Jilly Murray, who has confessed to witchcraft.

July 17th: The Presbytery attested the statements of Agnes Gray and Margaret Williamson in North Berwick, who have confessed to witchcraft.

[The Presbytery did not meet after 17th July 1650 until 13th August 1651 "In respect of the present troubles and violence of warres". Oliver Cromwell had invaded Scotland, smashed the Scottish army at Dunbar on 3rd September 1650, and subsequently incorporated Scotland into union with England under the "Commonwealth". Most witchcraft scholars claim that witchcraft prosecutions declined dramatically under the Commonwealth, and the Presbytery minutes would certainly support this view. It is also believed that those witches still in prison were freed by the English army of occupation. Many of the astounding numbers of witches whose cases were attested by the Presbytery for trial during the "panic" of 1649-50, may therefore have escaped with their lives after all.]

1651

August 13th: The Presbytery were informed that several persons within their bounds had gone to a dumb boy in the parish of Ormestoune to consult with him about things they had lost. The Presbytery ordered a letter to be sent to Mr John Sinclair, the minister there, asking him to find out who from within Haddington

Presbytery had consulted the dumb boy, and to acquaint them with their names. [Ormiston was in the Presbytery of Dalkeith.]

August 27th: Certain persons, namely John Clerk, Robert Mitchell, David Cold, and Isobell Lindesay, were summoned by the session of Salt Preston for consulting with a dumb woman about some things that had been stolen from them. They were called, appeared, and acknowledged their sin, and seemed to be sorry for it. They were rebuked by the Presbytery and remitted to their session to make public satisfaction before the congregation.

September 10th: An answer was received from Mr John Sinclair, minister at Ormistoun, to the Presbytery's letter. He explained that he had made James Cockburne, the father of Robert Cockburne, a dumb boy, appear before the session and tell who the people were from Hadington Presbytery who had tried to consult with his son about stolen articles or suchlike. He declared that William Cockburne in the parish of Bathans came and consulted with the boy, causing him to give some sign indicating what had become of his money. After that, William and his brother James came again and wanted the boy to signify what had become of it. He also said that William had brought a letter from William Home, requesting James Cockburn to come east with his son to try for the lost money. Also that a certain Watherstone from Yester came and asked him to signify what had become of some money he had lost. Also, John Blaik in Kirkland and Margaret Gives in Nungate came to consult him about the same thing. The Presbytery therefore ordered that the brethren in whose congregations these people were, should investigate them and make them satisfy church discipline in public if it was proved they had actually done it.

1652

February 18th: George Davie appeared, accused of consulting with John Lonesay. He acknowledged that he had consulted John about some money which had been stolen from him. He had accused Alisone Fergusone of being the thief because that was what John Lindesay had suggested. The Presbytery referred him to North Berwick session to make public satisfaction. Because John Lindesay is very infirm, a very old man unable either to walk or ride, the Presbytery appoints Mr John Maghie and Dr Turuett to go to him and look into what part he played in this.

July 19th: Mr Archibald Douglas, minister at Saltoun, reported Marion Hunter in his congregation to the Presbytery for consulting John Lindsay of Dirletoune about recovering a web of cloth that had been stolen from her. Since the woman was present the Presbytery decided to call her in. She was called, appeared, and was asked whether or not she went to John Lindsay. She answered that she did go, and was sorry for it. Secondly, she was asked what passed between John Lindsay and her. She declared that when she spoke to him he was in his bed, and his wife was present. He got up, and walked up and down the house, and asked if she suspected anyone. She replied that she suspected no-one, but people had said that hawkers had come that way. He asked their names which she told him. He said that he could not tell her that day, but would tell her another day. She drank with him, paid for the drink with a shilling, and gave him the rest of it. After that he told her that a man in Ormestoun, John Mark, had the web. She accused John Mark and he denied having the web. Then she and John Mark went to John Lindsay, who denied everything that he had said to her. The Presbytery withdrew to consider the business seriously, and postponed proceeding any further until the next Presbytery day. The woman Marion Hunter is ordered to appear before the Presbytery when told to do so by her minister.

August 18th: The Presbytery took the business with Marion Hunter into consideration, and referred it to the session of Dirleton for further examination. Marion Hunter was ordered to appear before that session when requested to do so, so that she could be confronted with John Lindsay to prove what she testified against him last day. The session was instructed to be diligent in the matter and to report back.

1654

August 2nd: Mr John Makghie reported that according to the Presbytery's orders, John Lindsay had been dealt with privately by Mr John and some of his elders. He had signed a confession acknowledging his great guilt in advising various people from time to time about stolen goods by that kind of divination called "the turning of the key", in frequently prevaricating when he was called before the Presbytery about it, and in various other aggravations of his sin. The confession signed by him had been read before the congregation of Dirletown and he had publicly acknowledged it and professed his unfeigned sorrow for all the trouble he had caused the Presbytery. The confession was then inserted in the session book of Dirletoun. The Presbytery is satisfied with this, and appoints the brethren to intimate his repentance to their individual congregations, so that this great public scandal may be removed, and so that the people may be warned not to go to him any more, nor to any other, for finding stolen goods by such a sinful and blasphemous means.

1663

December 24th: Adam Gilles and his wife, parishioners in North Berwick, were accused of witchcraft by John Cumming and his wife, also parishioners there, because they had tied eleven grains of wheat and a little salt round their cow's horn. This was referred by North Berwick session to the Presbytery for advice. The brethren discussed this case, and since no words had been used as far as they knew, they judged the deed to have been done out of gross ignorance and superstition ["vane observance"], and so is not sufficient evidence to prove them to be witches. However, because of the offence given on both sides by verbal abuse, and because it would set a bad precedent if it went unpunished, the Presbytery advised the minister of North Berwick to rebuke all the aforementioned persons publicly before the pulpit. [See the North Berwick kirk session minutes.]

1668

December 31st: Henrie Davidson appeared, referred from the kirk session at Saltpreston, and confessed that he had consulted for the recovery of some stolen goods with a certain David Howat who lives on the south side of the Cannogate a little above the cross. This David Howat told him that his servant woman was the thief. The Presbytery orders him to stand before the congregation at Salt Preston in sackcloth, and appoints Mr James Calderwood and Mr Patrick Cook to speak to the ministers of the Abby about David Howat.

1669

June 10th: Bessie Clerk appeared, referred from the session of Northberwick, and confessed that the night after she had a disagreement with William Whyt, who lives in Northberwick, her child fell dangerously ill. Next day she went to this William and blooded him with a pin, then went down on her knees and asked her child's health from him. The Presbytery orders her to appear in sackcloth before the congregation of Northberwick and make public confession of her sin.

[William had been imprisoned for witchcraft during the 1649-50 "panic", and had apparently survived unscathed, with his reputation for witchcraft undiminished. See Haddington Presbytery minutes 4th July 1650. How many others similarly survived?]

1672

September 5th: Mr Laurence Charteris reported that the kirk session of Yester had appointed [blank] to be publicly rebuked before the congregation for consulting [blank] in Edinburgh in order to solve a theft which she was being blamed for. She earnestly desires the Presbytery to mitigate the censure. The Presbytery was informed that she was a stranger, and did not know that the crime was liable to punishment She had been greatly provoked and tempted to take the course she did. The minister was therefore advised to take her confession and acknowledgment before the session, and to rebuke her there for her fault.

1679

January 16th: Elspet Paterson lately vented a wicked and scandalous expression at the burning of some witches. What she said was, "The Devil receive their souls!" Being summoned to the Presbytery, she appeared and confessed that she was in a rage because the witches had slandered her and taken away her good name, but whether she had uttered those exact words she did not know. Elspet was appointed to make public satisfaction before the congregation of Haddinton.

February 13th. Elspet Paterson has given satisfaction according to the orders of the Presbtytery.

1684

January 3rd: Mr James Cockburn reported on two women, namely Helen Mayten[?] and Barbara Haddo[?]. They have been referred from their session to the Presbytery, and summoned for "scolding". One had called the other a witch. They were called but did not appear. He is to summon them for a second time, to the next meeting. [Note in margin: "Helen Mayston and Barbara Claddo in Pencatland"]

March 29th: Pencaitland session's case was again postponed because Mr Cockburn is sick in Edinburgh.

Presbytery of Dunbar.

The Presbytery of Dunbar is designated CH2/99 in the National Archives of Scotland. Seventeenth Century Presbytery Records survive as follows:-

CH2/99/1   1652-57
CH2/99/2   1657-84
CH2/99/3   1694-1704

Surprisingly, as far as I can see, there is only a single reference to witchcraft in the 17th Century presbytery records.

"Last day of May 1652

Appoints a reference to be made to the Synod anent advice concerning witches. What should be done by ministers concerning them?"

Presbytery of Dalkeith.

The Presbytery of Dalkeith in Midlothian included the parish of Inveresk [Musselburgh], which is now part of East Lothian. Oddly enough, Ormiston parish was also under the jurisdiction of Dalkeith Presbytery, although as far as I am aware, Ormiston has always been considered part of East Lothian. Apart from inhabitants of these two parishes, there are occasional mentions of residents of other East Lothian Parishes. Dalkeith Presbytery is designated CH2/424 in the national Archives of Scotland. Records for the relevant period are

CH2/242/1   1582-1630
CH2 7242/2 1630-39
CH2/242/3   1639-52
CH2/242/4   1652-62
CH2/242/5   1673-88
CH2/242/6   1692-94
CH2/242/7   1694-1700

1594

June 27th: [This is part of the case of a woman in Catcune, near present-day Gorebridge, who is suspected of witchcraft.]   Johne Lyddell appeared, who used to live in Maldsly. He testified against Jennet Brus in Catcune that Agnes Samson the witch lay in bed with her. She denied this. He also affirmed that a little girl lay in bed with her and Agnes Samson in [illegible] and the girl was frightened out of her wits. This she also denied.

1641

February 4th: Mr Oliver Colt presented to the brethren the statements and free confessions of Christian Drupes[?] and Katherin Wod, regarding their practising of sorcery and witchcraft. He wished to have the opinion of the brethren. They were publicly read and carefully considered by the brethren, and they unanimously thought them sufficient and convincing grounds for investigation by the civil magistrate. The moderator and the clerk are ordered to sign their names to them. [Oliver Colt was the minister of Inveresk.]

February 11th: Mr Oliver Colt reported that he had applied for a commission to put the foresaid women to the trial of an assise.

1642:

March 31st: Mr Oliver Colt asked the advice of the brethren about some women accused of witchcraft. Should they be allowed to take Communion ? It was thought convenient to suspend them this year until further investigation is made.

1647

July 22nd: [The ministers are asked to condemn from the pulpit the superstitious custom of people washing their horses on Lammas Day.]

1649

August 2nd: Mr Johne Sinclair reported there were eight persons in his parish [Ormiston], who had confessed various items of witchcraft. He desired the assistance of some of the brethren for further investigation. The brethren appointed Mr Jhone Logan, Oliver Colt, Adam Penman, and Gideon Penman to meet with our brother at Ormeston on Monday at ten o' clock for that effect. If they found sufficient grounds for seeking a commission for further investigation, they should sign the confessions and report back to the next Presbytery day.

[John Sinclair was minister of Ormiston. His brother George Sinclair, scientist, engineer, and professor at Glasgow University, was the author of "Satan's Invisible World Discovered", a collection of "true" tales of witchcraft and the supernatural.

Gideon Penman was deposed from his charge of Crichton in 1678 for adultery, and was then imprisoned on a charge of witchcraft. He was subsequently freed on bail.]

August 9th: The brethren appointed to assist at Ormiston reported that they went and assisted our brother Mr John Sinclair in investigating some alleged witches, and that the Lord so blessed their labours that eleven persons in that parish had given an ample confession of witchcraft, which they signed. The report was approved.

Having heard and considered the confessions of Margaret Pringle and Patrick Anderson in the parish of Ormiston, the brethren judged them sufficient grounds for seeking a commission for further investigation. They were signed by the moderator and the clerk in the name of the Presbytery. [Many other confessions were coming in from the Midlothian parishes at this time.]

October 15th: The moderator and clerk attested the witchcraft confessions of Jonnet Paton, Margaret Oliver, and Phemie[?] Steil in the parish of Ormiston, and of Robert [blank] and Christian Steil in Borthwick, as sufficient grounds to seek a commission to investigate them further.

November 6th: [This is the note of a decision made by the "Provincial Assembly" - i.e. the Synod - of Lothian and Tweedale held in Edinburgh on 6th November.] The Assembly requests Lord Lothian to speak to the Committee of Estates, with a view to their Lordships ordering their clerks to issue commissions free of charge for the trial aid burning of witches.

November 15th: The statements of Bridget Flesher in Haddington [and another woman in Cockpen and three in Dalkeith] were read and considered, and were attested by the moderator and the clerk.

1650

June 20th: Mr James Robertson and Mr Gideon Penman were appointed to investigate the witches in Ormestoun.

1697

May 31st: Mr Richard Howison reported Agnes Broun as suspected of witchcraft, and gave account of some evidence against her noted by the session of Musselburgh, and asked the Presbytery's advice about it. The Presbytery appointed Messrs Cummine and Traill to consult with the Commission about the matter. [The significance of the"Commission" is not clear.]

The Synod of Lothian and Tweedale.

This is the administrative layer between the presbyteries and the General Assembly - when it was allowed to meet. The Synod's records are designated CH2/252 in the National Archives of Scotland. Minutes for the relevant period survive as follows:-

CH2/252/1 1589-96
CH2/252/2 1640-48 [transcribed]
CH2/252/3 1655-59
CH2/252/4 1659-61
CH2/252/5 1687-90
CH2/252/6 1691-97
CH2/252/7 1698-1710

There is nothing in the 17th Century minutes relating to witchcraft in East Lothian. However, there are several interesting entries from the late 16th Century, which show the Presbytery of Haddington to have been strangely reluctant to take action against Agnes Sampson, one of the major figures in the "North Berwick" affair. As always, I have "translated" the entries into modern English.

1589

April 1st: A complaint was considered against the Presbytery of Hadingtoun for not calling Any Sampsone before them, since she is a resident of Keyth within the bounds of that presbytery, and is suspected of witchcraft. The first answer to this complaint was that they can find no evidence to accuse her of witchcraft. It is ordered that they call her before them, and after investigation, if it can be arranged, they should deal with her. For furthering this business, it is ordered that all of the brethren who can get anything proved against this Any, who is suspected as previously mentioned, should give it in within fifteen days after today.

September 16th: According to the orders of the last Synodial Assembly of Lowthian, the Presbytery of Hadingtone was ordered to call before it Anny Sampsoun, who is suspected of witchcraft; and after investigation, if it can be arranged, they should deal with her as far as they can "ex officio" [*i.e.* informally]. The Assembly finds them greatly negligent in not calling her in, and orders that according to the said decision they call her before them, and that Mr Adam Lefinstown and Mr George Ramsay work with them to this effect so that she may be investigated.

1590

May 5th: According to the decision of the last Synodial Assembly which met at Edinburgh on the 16th of September last, the Presbytery of Hadington were ordered to call before them

Anny Sampsoun, who is suspected of witchcraft. If an investigation could be arranged they were to proceed against her informally as far as they could go. The Assembly finding that some action had been taken against her, orders them to apply further diligence, and also to seek a commission from His Majesty the King for her arrest.

October 7th: During the assessment of the Presbytery of Hadingtoun they were asked how far they had proceeded with Any Sampson and Jonet Ga who are suspected of the art of witchcraft. They answered that as far as Jonet Ga was concerned they had done nothing, but they had begun with Anny Sampsone and got going with her. The Assembly has ordered that they insist on prosecuting this case.

1591

April 6th: A request is ordered to be sent in to the King and Council, to deal with the persons suspected of witchcraft who were formerly in the tollbooth of Hadington and are now relinquished, ready to stand trial at law.

September 5th: A question was put by the brethren of the Presbytery of Hadingtoun, asking for the Assembly's decision on [illegible], because there are certain persons in Tranent parish who are rumoured to be involved in, and are accused of, witchcraft. Since they have neither been condemned nor acquitted of it, an answer is desired from the Assembly resolving whether or not such persons should be received at the table of the Lord [*i.e.* should be allowed to take Communion]. The Assembly's answer is that they should not be received.

1594

April 3rd: Assessment of the Presbytery of Dunbar.

It is ordered that by the advice of the Presbytery of Haddington, the Presbytery of Dumbar should deal with Jonet Lyndsay in Lyntoun who is suspected of witchcraft. October 1st: The last assembly ordered the Presbytery of Dumbar, with the advice of the Presbytery of Hadingtoun, to deal with Jonet Lyndsay in Lintoun, who is suspected of witchcraft. When they were asked what they had done about this matter Mr Robert Hepburne reported that after her arrest no-one accused her, and so the magistrate set her free on bail. If anyone has anything to accuse her of, the magistrate will apprehend her. After considering this report, the Assembly orders all the brethren of Dumbar Presbytery to try to find whatever information they can get against her, and after receiving information, to proceed against her in line with previous instructions.

October 7th: According to order of the last assembly, the Presbytery of Hadingtoun was ordered to give up accusations against Jonet Lyndsay in Lintoun who is suspected of witchcraft, and on receiving this confirmation the Presbytery of Dumbar were to proceed according to the decisions taken at the last assembly. These presbyteries were asked how far they had proceeded against this Jonet. Since the Assembly understands that no proceedings have been taken against her, they instruct the Presbytery of Dumbar to make serious efforts to seek further accusations against Jonet. For this purpose the Presbytery of Hadingtoun is ordered to seek out for Dumbar Presbytery all the information they can find, if it is required.

[Reading the records of the Synod and Presbyteries, we could hardly draw the conclusion that the Church was permanently obsessed with witchcraft. The exception of course was during the witchcraft panic of 1649-50, when the behaviour of Haddington Presbytery was nothing short of shameful, rubber-stamping the acusations against droves of witchcraft suspects with seemingly minimal discussion. So many indeed were sent for trial, that it might be interesting to compare East Lothian delations for witchcraft with the rest of Lowland Scotland to see how far the panic of 1649-50 in other areas matched the East Lothian holocaust.

The Synod's insistence on browbeating Haddington Presbytery into pursuing Agnes Sampson might stand as a significant piece of evidence on behalf of the "top-down" theory of witchcraft persecution; that is, that it was used as a form of social control by the country's "elite". However, we shall return to themes arising from the records of the Church's higher courts in the final chapter.]

4. Burgh Records.

Burgh courts were not qualified to try witchcraft cases, which could only be tried by the High Court of Justiciary, or by courts set up under commissions from the Privy Council, or occasionally from Parliament. Just prior to Cromwell's invasion of Scotland the ruling power was the "Committee of Estates", which also issued commissions to try witchcraft cases.

However, although burgh courts could not legally put witches on trial, the burgh magistrates could and did imprison and interrogate witchcraft suspects. Also, a commission to try witches might be given to the provost and baillies of a burgh, so that to all intents and purposes the burgh court then became a special court empowered to try a specific witchcraft case before an "assise" or jury.

It is obvious from church records that baron courts also questioned witchcraft suspects, and no doubt these sessions would be minuted. Unfortunately, I could find no East Lothian baron court records in the National Archives of Scotland. This is not to say there are none there of course. There might well be interesting material lurking in "Gifts and Deposits" from families or individuals whose East Lothian connections are not immediately obvious. It is perhaps worth stressing yet again that baron courts were absolutely not entitled to try witchcraft cases. Recent colourful "reconvening" of the Prestongrange baron court to pardon witches supposedly condemned by that court in Prestonpans, is good entertainment but bad history.

Dunbar.

Surviving records in the National Archives of Scotland are:- B18/13/1   1671 – 1687. B18/13/2 1687- 1715

Although it does not directly concern witchcraft, it is perhaps worth mentioning an entry in the burgh minutes for 23rd January 1678. Witches were executed by the professional hangman of the nearest burgh. In East Lothian this official was usually termed the "lokman", which has caused some confusion in some quarters, leading those who ought to have known better to make nonsensical statements like, "The town hangman was often the locksmith." In fact, a "lock" was a small quantity, such as a handful, and the euphemism "lokman" came into use because one of the hangman's perquisites was a handful from each sack of grain on market days, as is made clear by the entry for 23rd January 1678, when Dunbar burgh council was "considering the taking and exacting of ane loke corne be the lokman out of everie sack or pack upon the marcat days."

The only references to witchcraft in the Dunbar burgh records concern Catherine Mactarget. A very full account of her case will be found in the Privy Council records. She must have been one of the last, perhaps the last, in East Lothian to stand trial for witchcraft. She was found guilty, but there seems to be no record of her ultimate fate.

In this chapter, as previously, I shall give all the extracts quoted in modern English.

1683

February 26th: Act against Katherein Mactarget. Reliable information was received that Katherein Mctarget - wife of William Broun, burgess of this burgh - had been summoned before the Court of Justiciary to undergo the law for the sin of witchcraft. She was counted as guilty and declared fugitive for non-appearance. The magistrates and council therefore order John Laidlaw the executioner to put Katharein out of the burgh and its bounds.

1688

May 7th: The Clerk reported from Edinburgh that he had been to Edinburgh, and the King's Advocate had caused a request to be drawn up to the Privy Council for a commission for the trial of Catherine Macktargatt, which he obtained. The commission was issued by the Council on May 3rd. The charges incurred amount to £118-0-0.

Mr Patrick Brown is delegated to ride and deliver the letter at the town's expense to the gentlemen commissioned to try Catherine Macktargatt.

June 22nd: Act concerning Katharein Mactarget.

Baillie George Purves produced an order dated 19th June from the Privy Council, directed to the Sheriff or his deputes, for transporting the person of Catharin Mactarget to Edinburgh. Mr Patrick Brown is delegated to take this order and ride with it to the Sheriff or his deputes, and to see that they accept it.

Haddington.

GD1/413 in the National Archives of Scotland contains the research notes of Dr J. G. Wallace James, a former provost of Haddington. Dr Wallace James transcribed Haddington's court and council records, which of course makes the modern researcher's task much easier. Dr Wallace James's handwriting is not always of the highest standard, but it is incomparably more legible than 17th century "secretary hand". The Wallace James papers contain:

GD1/413/1   Haddington Burgh Court and Council records 1530-1602

GD1/413/2   Haddington Burgh Court and Council records 1602-1624

GD1/413/23   Haddington Burgh Records and court books "1637-1690" *[sic]*

[This also contains transcriptions of Dunbar records.]

There are no references to witchcraft in GD1/413/1. An interesting entry dated 2nd July 1619 in GD1/413/2 tells how Haddington recruited a new "lokman". He was William Elliot, a native of Hawick who had been condemned to death for stealing ten sheep from Letham. The Haddington magistrates got permission from the Privy Council to offer him the post of executioner. Since the alternative was death, Elliot accepted, and "...obliged himself to exercise the office of 'lokman' as it is called, in executing and putting to death whichever persons shall be convicted of murder, slaughter, theft, witchcraft, or such like, and condemned to die by the magistrates or sheriff of this burgh; also in scourging, marking, and inflicting other punishments on such others as shall be convicted and condemned." Elliot's job was for life, and he was forbidden to leave the burgh on pain of death.

There are no references to witchcraft in GD1/413/2. However, GD1/413/23 contains a great deal of interesting material. It consists of notebooks and loose papers, and supposedly deals with the period 1637 -1690. In fact it contains transcripts of cases going back to 1628. Some of these are invaluable, since because they were tried locally under commission, there is no central record of them. I have arranged the extracts in sequence, and put them into modern English.

1628

November 10th: In the presence of Mr James Cockburne, provost; and Patrick Broun and John Cockburn, baillies of the burgh of Haddington, appeared personally Robert Learmouth, merchant burgess there, and enacted and obliged himself, his heirs, and executors, that John Sinclar of Hirdmanestoun; Sir Johne Sinclair his son; Patrick Abernethie of Netterstaill, Baillie of the Barony of Saltoun; and Mr George Butler of Blans, will follow up and prosecute William Davidson who has been reported to them and arrested by them as a witch. This shall be done between now and the last day of November. To that effect, between now and that date they shall purchase a commission from the Lords of His Highness' Secret Council [*i.e.* the Privy Council] directed to the said John and to Sir Johne Sinclair, Mr George Butler, and Patrick Abernethie, or any two of them, appointing them commissioners or sheriffs in that district to try and execute him. In the meantime, during his imprisonment in the burgh tollbooth they shall sustain and provide for William Davidson with food and drink, and provide two men at night and one man during the day throughout the period to attend and watch William in prison. The expense is to be charged to John and Sir John Sinclair, Mr George, and Patrick, under the penalty of 90 [?] merks of the money of the realm.

Johne, Sir Johne, Mr George, and Patrick appeared personally, and renouncing their jurisdiction, submitted themselves to the jurisdiction of the Burgh of Haddington for this particular case only. They enacted themselves individually and together with their heirs and successors to relieve Robert Learmouth and his heirs etc, and keep them free of liability arising from his guarantee of surety, and any damage or loss they may incur.

November 15th: William Black, burgess, appeared before Patrick Broun, James Bartrem, and John Cockburne, baillies, and enacted himself as surety that John Home, bailie of the Barony of Keith; Richard Skirving, feuar of Plewlandhill; and Mr John Cockburne, minister at Keith, will prosecute Elizabeth Duncan in Blacksheillis for witchcraft, and also for the expenses of her imprisonment in the Tollbooth.

December 11th: Mr James Cockburne of Wester Monkrig, Provost; Patrick Broun, James Bartrim, Johne Cockburne, baillies.

In the presence of the above judges, Thomas Waderstoun in Samelstoun appeared for judgment, accused by the witch William Davidson of being guilty of the same crime of witchcraft. Renouncing his own jurisdiction [*i.e.* that of his local laird], he submitted himself to the jurisdiction of the Provost and Baillies of the Burgh for this particular case only, and obliged himself to appear and enter into confinement in the Tollbooth of the Burgh at whatever time it pleases the above judges to require him to do so. He is to submit to whatever criminal process they or any others shell charge him with or pursue against him in connection with the above crime. If he shall fail to appear when required, he is in that case content that he shall be held and declared to be guilty of the crime and punished accordingly.

December 16th: The case of William Davidson, Saltoun.

Commission of the Lords of His Majesty's Secret Council to John Sinclair of Herdmanston, Patrick Abernethy of Netterdaill, Mr George Butler of Blans, and Mr James Cockburn of Wester Monkrig for the trial of William Davidson, witch.

16th December 1628 – John Wilkie, procurator fiscal, produced the following indictment of the most odious, abominable, and devilish crimes of witchcraft, soothsaying, enchantment, invocation of devils, consulting with the dead and familiar evil spirits [This is a stock "catch-all" formula, which does not necessarily mean that the accused has actually done all of these.], to the great dishonour of the true and everlasting God, whom he has renounced and forsaken. He has renounced his baptism and turned himself over body and soul to the service and obedience of the Devil, the common enemy to the salvation of mankind, against the express law of God, and in high contempt of the loveable laws of this realm.

In token of this, when he heard that he had been named as a witch by a certain Meg Muirhead - recently tried, convicted, and put to death for the same crimes - he feared he would be apprehended, and fled from Saltoune where he was residing. He was followed and searched for by Johne Sinclair of Hirdmistoun, Sir Johne Sinclair his son Mr George Butter of Blans, Patrick Abernethye of Netterdaill, and Mr Archibald Levingstoun the minister of Saltoun.

He was arrested and imprisoned for a time in the mansion house of Hirdmestoun, and transported from there to the burgh of Haddington, and put in secure confinement in the Tollbooth. During that time he confessed as follows:-

That he has been a charmer of men, women, and beasts for the past thirty two years, and that he was taught and instructed in charming at the age of thirty two by a certain Bessie Gray. At that time he came to Lauthian and entered into service with Marion Lauder, then Lady of Blans. Since then he has remained in Lothiane, doing and practising various kinds of witchcraft, and often having intimate meetings and communications with the Devil. During that time he has never attended church on Sundays, because his master the Devil forbade him, saying that he was holy enough already. From the Saturday night till the Monday morning each week he was with the Devil, and was never to be seen, as those with whom he was in service have testified. He met with the Devil at night in the byre at Blans, as he confessed, in the likeness of a tall black man. The Devil took him in his arms saying, "Rise up Willie, in the Devil's name. You are very heavy." He then left him. Next William met him at Nelans Burne. Thirdly, he met him on Nisbet Common, where he appeared to him first in the shape of a great black dog entangling itself among his feet. Walking further on, it was transformed into the shape of a man. They were interrupted by some servants from Nesbitt nearby, and so they parted company at that time, and the Devil arranged to meet him at Hirdmiston Myln in fourteen days' time. At the appointed time William met him at the mill of Hirdmestoun about midnight, where he renounced God his creator, and renounced his baptism and became the Devil's servant. In return for his service the Devil said he should want for nothing, and he would have liked to take him away with him. When William was lying in the cow byre at Hirdmestoun about midnight, the Devil came to him and said to him, "What are you doing here? Should you not have been serving me according to your promise, since you have no master but me?" After a long conversation, the Devil gripped and laid his hand on all the cattle in the byre. Gripping the bull, he said to William, "I must have this bull." When William asked what he would do with him, he replied that he would have both William and the bull. He said no harm would befall the rest of the beasts, and immediately leaped on the bull and rode him up and down the byre. That bull fell sick, wasted away, and died shortly afterwards. Not long after that, the Devil met William and said to him, "I won't have this bull. Neither you nor he are fit for the work I have to do with you." When William was looking after the cattle from Blans in the East Hoipes in the summer of 1626, the Devil appeared to him again, first in

"The Hopes". William Davidson met the Devil in 1626 while herding cattle for the lady of Blance at East Hopes.

Both William Davidson and the notorious warlock Alexander Hamilton seem to have been involved with others in sorcery against the lady of Woodhead, now Fountainhall (above). Sir John Lauder of Fountainhall, an eminent 17th century judge, mentions several East Lothian witchcraft cases in his "Historical Notices".

the form of a black dog, and next in the form of a man. They had a long conversation with each other beside a cairn. Also, last Beltane [*i.e.* early May] in Salton Wood he met Bessie Mak from Saltoun, Sara Keith from Wintoun, Alexander Hamiltoun the vagabond, Alizon Tailyour from Pencaitland, and Thomas Walderstoun from Nesbitt, all guilty of similar crimes of sorcery and witchcraft.

At these meetings with the Devil, William out of malice consulted with him, and questioned him about how he could lay on and take off sickness from men, women, and animals, and undo or destroy them at the request of others who came to him for that purpose, or out of his own personal ill-will against those who had offended him in some small measure. All the above accusations William openly confessed in the presence of the said judges and jurymen.

As proof of William's devilish mind, ill-will, and desires: Andro Wilkiesone in Blaikbie was seriously troubled with a lengthy wasting disease. Agnis Wilsone his wife was informed of William's skill and claims, and came to him asking him to cure her husband. He came and saw him and claimed that he was blasted by an evil spirit. Just after that he treated him with his charms, and with a drink made from foxglove leaves. After this Andro became so hungry and eager for food that, marvellous as it seems, for many days after that he ate and drank more than six men would have done. By his abominable art, without pity or compassion, this sickness taken off Andro was laid by William upon his nephew William Wilkiesone, who had never offended or wronged him, so that he died as a result. William confessed that he had performed the cure, but denied that he had done any wrong to William Wilkiesone. Also, Janet Howiesone, the wife of James Young, the Laird of Hirdmestoun's carter, being bewitched and seriously ill, came to William and asked her health from him for God's sake. He immediately cured her by his unlawful medicines, and took her sickness on himself. It stayed with him for the space of two hours or thereabouts. He claimed that the sickness had been laid on her by Sara Keith in Wintoun, an expert in that craft. William confessed all this openly. Also, William was indicted and accused that when Agnes Sinclair, the wife of William Swanstoun in Ovir Saltoun was heavily tormented with intolerable pain in her whole body, William Swanstoun came to him and asked him to heal her. He came and saw her, and said she was bewitched, and could not be cured simply by charming, but salt or musk should be applied to her. Then William went and fetched foxglove leaves from Saltoun, which he mixed with fresh butter and made a salve from it, which he applied to her arm, even though her whole body was sore. She was cured immediately. This pain and sickness he laid by his witchcraft on William Finlasone in Saltoun, who sent for William Davidson to cure him. When he came he admitted he had done him wrong, and asked his forgiveness. William Finlason died shortly afterwards of this sickness. William Davidson confessed the cure, but denied laying on the sickness.

Agnes Stanehous, the daughter of George Stanehous in Saltoun was blasted - as William called it - in her arms, and had lost the power of them. She came to him asking him to remedy it. He cured this with south-running water which he got George's son David Stanehous to fetch from a south-running well. He directed him to leave either a rag or else two pins at the well. On the way he was not to speak to anyone nor answer them, otherwise the charm would not be effective. He washed Agnes's body with the water, and her arms recovered their usual strength. William confessed this.

Similarly, when Robert Spens in Ovir Saltoun had been blasted and lost the power of his whole body, his wife Marioun Smith went to [blank], a witch in Home for a remedy for his disease. She gave Marioun an enchanted shirt to put on Robert, and directed Marioun to William Davidsone to get him to wash Robert with south-running water. After washing him the water should be thrown away in some out-of-the-way place where nobody ever went. After William had done this, it fell out that shortly after that Marioun contracted a deadly sickness because of him. She sent for him to come and cure her, which he did with a drink of foxglove leaves. After that she felt an extraordinarily acute pain in her finger which he cured by applying the [blank] of a cow, taken from her own byre. He could not have done this in any other way but with the assistance and working of the Devil his master, which William confessed.

Also, when [blank], a grandchild of Isobell Wilson in Abbay was sick, at Isobell's request William sent a drink to give to the child with the intention of killing it. Being curious, after William left the house, Isobell tasted the drink and died within a few hours. Thus he is guilty of poisoning her and therefore liable to the law for manslaughter. William denies this.

Also, he cured John Hill in Hirdmistoun of a serious illness by his charms, and by laying a salted hake and a piece of raw flesh under his head. He confessed this.

Also, William was accused that when James Halyday in Wester Pencaitland was blasted and his body was severely wasted away, Henry Wilsone in Saltoun got William to come to James Halyday in his house where he was lying sick. As soon as William came into the house James became so mad and furious that he could not be held by those who were with him, but struck out at everyone near him and continually cursed and blasphemed. When William approached him and gripped him by the arms he immediately became sensible and quiet. Then William took a salted hake and a piece of raw flesh and laid them under James's head, and immediately he was freed from his sickness. William confessed to this.

Also, William conceived a deadly hatred and malice for no reason against Euphame Cathie, the daughter of Johne Cathie in Samelstoun. Looking for an opportunity to put his malice into action against her, he came to her father's house and bewitched her, so that when she came to her door after him, she fell and not only lost the power of one side, but contracted a serious illness. After she had been troubled and weakened by it for a long time, her parents sent for William and asked him to come and help her. When he came, he sat down in the corner of the long bench near the fire ["lang sadle"] where Euphame was lying. He gripped her by the arm and said she had been blasted by an evil spirit - which of course he well knew since he himself was the cause of it - and said he would not take her in hand because he liked neither the father, the mother, nor the daughter. As he was leaving the house he said she would not shake it off, so that instead of helping her he made her illness worse. Until she died she could lot rest until she had been laid in the corner of the long bench where he had sat. Just as he had said, she never recovered, but died of the sickness laid on her by him. William denied this.

Also he cured with his charms a cow belonging to Andro Hunter in Kirklandis of Bolton.

He also cured a farm worker to George Lies in Howden, and he took the disease upon himself. William confessed to this.

Also, he cured [blank] the wife of Hairie Lister in Saltoun of a serious illness with south-running water in the same way as he had cured others. He also confessed to this.

Chancellor [*i.e.* foreman of the jury]: Thomas Elder in Ovir Saltoun. The same day, the whole assise [jury] by the mouth of Thomas Elder the foreman of the jury unanimously finds William Davidsone culpable and guilty of all the points of his indictment by his own confession, except for the two points concerning the alleged wrongs done to Issobell Wilson and Euphame Cathie. He denied them and they could not be proved or confirmed. Therefore William is found guilty of all the points of the indictment except for these two points, of which he is acquitted. It was therefore ordained by the judges and pronounced as sentence by the mouth of William Sinclair, dempster [the official whose job it was to pronounce sentence], that William Davidson should be taken this day, his hands bound behind his back, and brought by the hangman ["lokman"] of the burgh to the Sandis, the usual place of execution. First he is to be strangled and hanged at a wooden post, and after that his body is to be burnt to ashes.

"Desuper acta" [The above was done.]

December 20th 1628: Robert Learmonth, burgess, appeared to give surely for Johne Sinclair of Hirdmanston; Sir John Sinclair, feuar of Hirdmanston; Mr George Butler of Blans; and Patrick Abernathie of Netterdaill, that they will prosecute Bessie Mak in Salton as a witch. He also stands surety for the expenses of her imprisonment.

December 26th: David Kyll, baker, burgess, appeared to give surety that he will purchase a commission to try as a witch Alexander Sinclair who is in prison and alleges himself to be a vagabond. He also gives surety for the expenses of his imprisonment.

December 31st: Andro Hepburne, burgess, appeared before Patrick Brown, baillie, and gave surety that George Cockburne of Ormistoun would prosecute Sara Keith in Wintoun as a witch, and gave surety for her expenses while imprisoned in the Tollbooth.

1629

17th February 1629: The trial of Sara Keith and Besse Mak.

Commission from the Lords of His Majesty's Secret Council to Sir Robert Hepburn, knight, of Alderston, Sheriff Principal; Patrick Abernethy of Netterdaill; Mr James Cockburn of Wester Monkrig, Provost; Patrick Brown and John Cockburn, Baillies, 17th February 1629 for trial of Sara Keith and Besse Mak, witches.

John Wilkie, notary, procurator fiscal, produces the following indictment against them:-

Firstly, Sara confessed that her first entry into the sin and her pact with the Devil was when wrong and injury had been done to her by the late George Harlaw in Garvald Kirk [i.e. he settlement in which the parish church of Garvald was situated], and out of a desire to e avenged on him. Her father the late [blank] Keith, had died in a house belonging to George Harlaw around twenty-four years ago. George had dealt with a large amount of money belonging to him, amounting as Sara alleged to a peck of silver and gold. He would give her none of it, although it all belonged to her.

Shortly after this, when she was among the broom at Litill Newton, greatly grieved and angered at this wrong, she burst out with these desperate words, "May either God or the Devil grant me revenge on this man!" Immediately the Devil appeared to her in the shape of a handsome boy and asked her what had caused her to be so sad. She told him about her recent misfortune, and knowing him to be the Devil, desired to be revenged on this George. He promised her sufficient amends if she would become his servant and renounce her God and her baptism. She then consented to renounce her God and her baptism, and to be his servant. For these renunciations the Devil promised that George would possess as little before he died as she did then, with the result that although at that time he was wealthy and rich, he became so poor that he had to beg for his food before he died. Sara openly confessed these promises in court as she had done before, craving pardon and forgiveness at the hands of almighty God.

Also, she confessed that about a year after

she was married, now being nineteen years old and living at that time in Adinstoun, she was weeding her flax in her garden about eleven o' clock in the morning, when the Devil appeared to her in the likeness of a man. There, with her own consent, he had the use of her body. He then gave her a name, calling her "Mistress Keith", and marked her on the joint [?] of her right arm by gripping her, which she said she found very painful. Then he asked her for a gift, and she offered him her only son, who was then about half a year old. The Devil expressed himself very pleased with this, and came to her house in Adniston within nine or ten weeks to take away the child she had promised him. The child was lying in the cradle, and the Devil took him out of the window with a whirlwind, and in the place of the child in the cradle left a long lean deformed creature which shouted and cried continually for three days till it died. Sara made ample confession of this indictment or accusation with great penitence.

Also, Sara was accused, and she confessed, that last Beltane she and Besse Mak, who was also in court with her for the same crimes, and the vagabond Alexander Hamilton, went to Saltoun on purpose to meet the Devil. It was Alexander Hamilton who persuaded her to go with them. However, since she and Besse were outside the wood, and the rest in the wood, they did not see the Devil that time. After that, last Michaelmas, Sara and Besse went to meet the Devil at Dryden Dein where he appeared to them riding on a fine spirited horse. The reason for the meeting was to find out what would become of them, since there was such an intensive search being made for witches, who were being arrested, tried, and punished. When they asked what would become of them, he answered that he had to take such care of his servants "beneath Tyne Water" that he could not take as much care of Sara and Besse as he would like. However, he ordered them to always deny everything, and nothing would [blank] them.

Sara declared that Besse Mak, there in court with her, became very earnest with the Devil, hanging on to his horse's bridle, repeatedly begging him to save her from the approaching danger. The Devil said to her, "Besse, you are very frightened. Don't be so frightened. You shall have feet to flee, but the rest will not have feet to flee."

Sara affirmed that Besse was an expert in the devilish art of sorcery and witchcraft, and more familiar with the Devil and more acceptable to him than she herself was. She confessed this again and swore in Besse's face that this was the truth.

Sara was also accused that she confessed that about [blank] years ago a certain Bessie Makgil found her and Besse Mak at the house of Gilbert Bathcatt, a shepherd at Trabroun. They all went to the Thrie Mile House [at present-day Gladsmuir village], and met with the Devil there in the likeness of a fine gentleman. She also confessed this again.

She also confessed that she and Alexander Hamiltoun and various other beggars were begging at the gate of Wodeheid. Amongst them was Alison Hunter, a lunatic person, and this Alison got an old shirt from the late Lady Wodeheid, which the Lady sent out to the gate to be given to Alisone. Alexander Hamilton wanted the Lady to give part of the shirt to him. She refused, and reproved him for going begging when he and and his wife were two strong able people. Being offended by this, he said to Sara that the next time he came back she would have [blank]. He meant that he intended to do the late Lady Wodeheid some great harm. She declared that Alexander bewitched the Lady by laying a serious illnes on her, of which she died. Shortly after her death Sara met Alexander Hamiltoun at the birch valley of Wodeheid, and she reproached him for causing the death of such a good lady. He answered, "I have done so giff he can helpit." [The sense of this is unclear. Perhaps some words have been omitted.] She confessed this again.

You [*i.e.* Sara] also confessed that Besse came to you, sent by the late William Davidson, a witch, asking you to meet them at the end of Pencaitland village immediately after Lady Wodeheid's death. When you met William he told you to come with him because he had a job to do with you. From there you went to Wodeheid, and around twilight William and Besse ordered you to fetch a tub full of water for them from the "syke" [a stream in a hollow, or in boggy ground] at Wodehead. You brought this to the Birch Valley, and after that they made you bring it into the mansion house of Wodeheid. When it was set down William and Besse carried it over to the bedroom where Lady Wodeheid's body was lying, and washed her with it. Sara also confessed this again. [The mansion house of Fountainhall was formerly known as Woodhead.]

You are accused of curing Agnes Litster, the daughter of Henrie Litster in Saltoun of a long-standing wasting disease by your charms and by washing her with south-running water. No-one had expected anything but that she would die. Sara also confessed this.

You are also accused of curing William and James Stanehous, the sons of George Stanehous in Saltoun with your devilish art of sorcery and charms. You cured them of a blindness in their eyes by annointing them with south-running water, and with some small [blank], so that a short time after that they received their sight. Sara denied this.

You are also accused of bewitching Jonet Thomsome, the wife of James Young, carter to the Laird of Hirdmistoun, by laying a serious illness on her. She denied this.

Besse Mak

Likewise, you Besse Mak, are accused and indicted for the crimes of sorcery, soothsaying, enchantments, invocation of devils, consulting with the Devil, and practising various kinds of witchcraft.

Firstly, you and the late William Davidson, Alexander Hamilton the vagabond, Alison Tailzeour in Pencaitland, Thomas Wadderstoun who then lived in Nisbet, and Sara Keith there beside you in court, all met together at Saltoun Wood last Beltane, as was declared and confessed by William at various times before his death, and then by Sara. Besse denied this.

You, Bessie Makgil, and Sara Keith met with the Devil at the Thrie Mile House. He appeared to you in the likeness of a fine gentleman.

Also, last Michaelmas you and Sara and your above-named associates went to Dryden Dene and met with the Devil there to learn what was to become of you. He answered you and Sara as previously mentioned. You were very earnest and insistent with him, continually hanging on his horse's bridal, fearing a miserable and shameful death, and demanded an answer from him about your final end. Being a liar and deceiver of mankind from the beginning, he answered you with ambiguous and evasive words, saying that you would have feet to flee. The deception was proved by the fact that when you were accused by William, and arrested and brought to this prison as being guilty of these crimes, he affirmed this to your face when you were confronted with him. When you most obstinately denied everything, you were freed until further notice, and you enacted yourself to enter into confinement again to answer for your crimes when you were required to do so.

When you were blamed for these sins a second time by Sara you were arrested again and imprisoned in the Tollbooth. She swore these things against you, and also declared that you were more amenable and familiar with the Devil than she was.

Also, around Martinmas 1627[?] when you were coming out of Scheilfield to Brigis Hauch along a hollow track, you met with the Devil who struggled with you and hurt your nose. You came to Brigishauch bleeding, and [blank] the man of the house asked you how you came to be bleeding, with an injured nose. You replied that you had been frightened by the Devil.

Also, as proof of your guilt, when you heard of Sara's arrest and feared for your own, your daughter-in-law Christian Schorswood passed through Saltoun village where you lived and you called her. When she came to you, you said to her that she need not go by your house, for there was as much meal there as would do you as long as you lived. In fact there was very little meal or bread in the house, and you knew Sara Keith would denounce you as a witch.

Similarly, you came to Samuelston to the house of George Schoriswoode, the brother of your daughter-in-law, and said to him when you met him, "Yon Sara Keith in the Tollbooth will denounce me as a witch." You said that if you were arrested and accused, and if you were found guilty, you would put the blame on nobody else but yourself.

You are also accused that when Helene Bathcat, the wife of the late Cuthbert Hendersone in Saltoun, was very sick and confined to bed, he came to you out of consideration for her health and asked you to come for God's sake and cure her. When you came to her, instead of curing her, out of the malice of your heart which you had conceived against her, you caused her to die. Shortly afterwards, continuing your malice against Cuthbert himself, when he had married another wife you bewitched him and laid a serious illness on him. His second wife came to you on his instructions to ask for his health. You came and dispatched him in the same way [as his first wife]. The late William Davidson avowed this to your face.

You are also accused of causing a certain Janet Johnstoun in Thrieburnfurde by your enchantments to hang herself in despair from a beam in her house. Knowing all about it, you came in without fear and saw her hanging there, and the Devil in the likeness of a black dog on the beam the woman was hanging from. When you came out of the house you gave no sign of pity or sorrow, but seemed rather to be rejoicing, and asked a poor woman named Kathren Hiltoun to go into the house to see Janet hanging there. When she went and looked, and saw the Devil above her as described, she immediately lost the sight of one eye and never regained it again. This was done by you, by unlawful means.

You are also accused of being art and part in the death of Lady Wodeheid, and doing various things as described in Sara Keith's indictment.

Also, you were a near neighbour of Peter Douglas, weaver in Saltoun, and you wanted some money from Peter's wife. One night you lit a great smoking fire in your house which sent so much smoke through the dividing wall between your house and theirs, that it fouled their house to the extent that they could neither work nor stay in it. After he had complained to you several times about this, and asked you to throw back part of the fire so that there wouldn't be so much smoke, you refused. Since Peter was greatly incensed by this, in a rage he took an earthenware vessel of water, went into your house, and doused your fire with it. Being offended, you said that you would make him repent it. You laid a serious illness on Janet Broun his wife, from which she pined and wasted away for a long time. Because you were able to take the sickness off as you had laid it on, Peter carried her to your own house, since she was not able to go herself. Falling on his knees, he begged her health from you thrice for God's sake. You put aside your former malice against her and her husband, and declared that it was only a decline in health and she would recover from it shortly. After that you went away from Saltoun, begging through the countryside for eight days. When you returned, you brought a piece of raw meat with you, and gave it to Janet, telling her to roast it and eat it, and she would be cured right away. She took the piece of raw meat from you and laid it down beside her, but was afraid to eat it. Suspecting harm from you rather than good, she did not eat it until Thomas Smyth in Saltoun came in to visit her and advised her to roast it and eat it saying, "Whatever happens, you can be no worse than you are, and fire purifies everything." She roasted it and ate it, and was immediately cured of her illness.

You are also accused of claiming to be able to bring about marriage through your enchantments, and to induce men and women to love others, even those they had formerly disliked. You came to Helen Palmer, the wife of James Young in Saltoun, and offered to procure a marriage for her son George Young in return for some acknowledgment of your pains. She told you to go and discuss it with George himself, saying that she did not want to choose his wife for him. You tackled George about it, and wanted him to follow your advice regarding marriage, saying you would get him an honest marriage to an honest woman, namely Adame Arnot's sister in Fala Myln. He replied that he would take other people's advice about his marriage, and would have none of yours. You were offended at this, and went away speaking some words heard and known only to yourself. The same day, within a few hours, George went to his father's barn to thresh, and you laid such a severe pain on his back that he was unable to stand. This continued till he was forced to take to his bed. He faded and wasted away for a long time, and eventually died. When he was lying sick, perhaps repenting of your cruel deed, you came to visit him to cure him; or perhaps out of malice to finish him off and dispatch him, which is more likely. You wanted to go into the room where he was lying to see him, but when he heard of this, the young man would not allow them to let you near him. Being refused entry, you sat down on the floor in the hall, and leant your head against a chest, gazing at the door for a long time. Then you got up and went to the door muttering and talking to yourself. Shortly after this George died of his sickness. Several times before his departure, George affirmed that you had bewitched him, and he left his death to your charge. He also wished to live long enough to see you burnt.

Also, Marioun Allane in Saltoun had three or four ells of linen doth which she had kept to be her winding sheet. Being poor and destitute she came to you and offered to give it to you as a pledge in return for some money. You took a fancy to the cloth and offered to buy it, and to give her corn or meal for it, but would not have it in pawn. When she refused to sell it you said to her, "You will leave it to those who will give you less thanks for it." The same night - a Wednesday - she fell ill with an extremely painful sickness and died on the following Monday. This sickness was laid on her by you, which was declared by Marioun herself throughout the period of her illness. As further confirmation of this, you said to Elizabeth Fortun, the wife of Marioun's son Richard Cowane, just after Marioun's death, that if she had forgiven you she would still have been alive.

You are also accused of bewitching James Robesone in Wintoun, and laying a sickness on him at the request of Sara Keith, but sparing his life and possessions because he was a crony of her son's. She wanted revenge on James for killing her husband. He lay sick from the beginning to the end of harvest, until Sara went to William Davidson and asked him to take the sickness off him. This he did, and she gave him a peck of wheat for it.

The same day, the whole jury ["assise"], by the mouth of Thomas Elder their jury foreman ["chancellor"], finds them guilty on all counts except the last two. Therefore it was ordained by the judges, and pronounced as sentence by the mouth of the dempster William Sinclair, that Sara Keith and Besse Mak should be taken this day by the hangman of Hadington to the ordinary place of execution, with their hands bound behind their backs, to be first strangled to death, and their bodies thereafter to be burnt to ashes.

3rd April 1629: The trial of Alexander Sinclair alias Hunter.

Special commission of justiciary to Sir Robert Hepburne, knight, of Aldistone, Sheriff Principal; and to George Hepburn, feuar of Alderston, Sheriff Depute; Mr James Cockburn of Wester Monkrig, Provost; Patrick Brown, James Bartrem, and John Cockburne, baillies of Haddington; for the trial of Alexander Sinclair alias Hunter, witch, 3rd April 1629.

Alexander Sinclair alias Hunter, vagabond, appeared in court accused on a capital charge for the most odious, unnatural, and devilish crimes of sorcery, soothsaying, enchantment, invocation of devils, consulting with the dead and familiar evil spirits, and practising various kinds of witchcraft, to the great dishonour of the true and everlasting God, as is specified at length in his indictment. Being asked if he had anyone to speak for him, or wished anyone to do so, he answered there was none but God in heaven. Therefore the above-named judges put him to the knowledge of an assise. [*i.e.* put him on trial before a jury].

John Wilkie, notary, as procurator fiscal produced the following indictment:-Alexander Huntar, you are accused and indicted for the most odious, abominable, and devilish crimes of sorcery, soothsaying, enchantment, invocation of devils, consulting with the dead and familiar evil spirits, and practising various kinds of witchcraft to the great dishonour of God, whom you have forsaken. You have renounced your baptism and rendered yourself body and soul to the service and obedience of the Devil, the common enemy to the salvation of mankind, against the express law of God, and in high contempt of the loveable laws of the realm. This was declared to be true by the late William Davidson, a witch, recently condemned and put to death for similar devilish crimes. Amongst his other confessions he declared you guilty of the same crimes.

For example, this William confessed and declared that Susanna Sinclair, the elder Lady Samuelstoun, had conceived an unnatural hatred and malice against her brother John Sinclair of Hirdmestoun. She resolved to undo and ruin his house and estate by whatever unlawful means she could. William confessed that she consulted with him how she could manage this, and promised him a reward. He refused to get involved, so then she consulted with you and Patrick Lermonth to the same effect. You agreed to this, and at her request - or so he believed - you laid some devilry and witchcraft around the mansion house of Hirdmestoun, which he declared had still not been purged away.

This Susanna Sinclair was no better inclined towards her late husband. She had a mind to dispatch him with your help, and sent for you. She brought you into the bedroom where he was lying sick. You put on one of his shirts and went away with it, and by your sorcery and witchcraft he died shortly afterwards.

You frequented the house of the late Bessie Littil, a witch also lately burned for these crimes, and used to stay there a month or more at a time. In the presence of Tranent kirk session she affirmed and declared that you were a notorious witch, even though she had no particular quarrel or ill-will against you, as you know. She first came to know this when you were in Panistoun and sent a girl to her for some money. She refused and said she had none. Then you sent the girl to her again, who told her that she had a five-merk piece in a cloth in her chest, which she thought nobody knew about but herself.

This same Bessie declared that you had a bee

in a tin box which you fed every day with three drops of your own blood, and you went once a year to Norhame in England and got a new bee in place of the old one, and there you renewed your wicked and desperate pact with the Devil.

Also, when John Heres, an inhabitant of the burgh of Hadingtoun, was seriously ill with a lengthy wasting disease, you came to his house shortly before his death. You called yourself Seaton, for this was your usual habit, to change your name and surname as it suited you. Claiming to be a skilled physician, you offered to cure him, and for that effect asked for one of his shirts, promising to return with it within eight days to cure him. He refused to allow you to do this, and declared you were a witch, and only able to do it by means of charms and witchcraft. After that his wife Elizabeth Seaton offered you bread and drink, but you refused this and demanded money. She said she had none, arid you replied that she had both money and gold, for she had on her a double pistolet [a foreign gold coin] and a gold five-merk piece. Not only that, but you told her that her husband had gold that she did not know about. He had four double angels [an English coin bearing the figure of the archangel Michael] lying in a napkin under his head. This was true. You also said that he would not live long and that he would be dead within a week, and in fact he died about the end of the week. Elizabeth declared this and swore to your face that it was true, in the presence of the baillies of this burgh.

You are also accused of coming to the house of Adame Nycolsone in Langnudre sixteen years or so ago, and demanded food from Issobel Turnbul his wife. Seeing you were a beggar, she offered you half of a grey loaf ["grey" bread was coarse rye bread, sometimes also of oats – Dict. OST.] You refused to take it, and demanded white bread. This she refused to give you, declaring that what she offered was quite sufficient for you, since, after all, her reapers working hard in the harvest field got nothing but grey bread. You were offended at this refusal, and immediately bewitched her so that when you went out at the door she fell down dead on the floor. Being made aware of this sudden accident, her neighbours in Langnudrie came in to help her, but were not able to. They went after you and brought you back again to her house. When you came in you called for whisky which you said was in her cupboard, and having tasted a little, she recovered. This sickness, which you took off as described, you laid on a greyhound walking by on the floor, which instantly fell down dead. And an ox yoked to her plough died at the same moment. About a year after that, you came back again to her house, and as soon as you came in you said to her, "Lord! Are you still living?" She replied that she did not have you to thank for it. After that you said that she had five evils laid on her, and you were amazed that she was protected from them. You foretold that she would go far away, as far as Ireland, and that she would return again. After that she did go to Ireland, and lived there for a long time, and then came back again. Issobell affirmed all this to your face when she was confronted with you, and she is here at this moment to swear to the same things again.

Foreman of the jury: Thomas Bane in Langnidrie.

The same day, the jury, by the mouth of their foreman Thomas Bane, finds Alexander Huntar alias Sinclair guilty of the foresaid abominable and devilish crimes of sorcery, soothsaying, enchantment, invocation of devils, consulting with the dead and familiar evil spirits, and practising various kinds of witchcraft, taking into consideration the statement given by the late William Davidson above mentioned. This statement was produced in court, signed by the provost and baillies of Haddington and Mr Robert Balcanquell, minister of Tranent. He is found guilty of

Putting on the late Laird of Samuelston's shirt and bewitching him as described in the foresaid statement and confession.

Also, of the charges regarding... [The page is damaged here.]... a gold five-merk piece sent for by him from the late ... Little, and concerning the bee which he fed in a tin box ... as described in the statement and confession of William ... Bessie Little was produced, signed by the said minister... various other persons in Tranent kirk session.

Also... Alexander of the charge concerning... made by him to cure the late John Hares, and of ... devilish knowledge of the four double angels under his head in a napkin, and of the other gold in Elizabeth's purse, considering that there is sufficient verification from the baillies who heard Elizabeth swear to it to Alexander's face.

Also, of bewitching Issobell Turnbull, and foretelling to her that she would go to Ireland, as given in her statement. Being personally present, sworn, and questioned by the judges, she affirmed this to be true.

Therefore the judges ordained, and it was pronounced as sentence by the mouth of William Sinclair, dempster, that Alexander Sinclair shall be taken, his hands bound behind his back, and conveyed by William Allat, hangman of Hadingtoun, to the ordinary place of execution, strangled to death at a post, and his body thereafter to be burnt to ashes.

Desuper acta.

July 6th 1629: Andro Hay, burgess, obliges himself on behalf of Lord John Hay of Yester that he will prosecute John Carfrae in Yester, his wife Alison Borthwick, and his brother Thomas Carfrae in Yester Mylne, who are allegedly guilty of witchcraft; and that he will sustain them while imprisoned in the Tolbooth.

July 7th 1629: Burgh Court. In presence of James Bartram and James Cockburne, baillies. Andro Hepburne appeared as surety that [blank] Cockburne of Ormestoun should prosecute the vagabond Alexander Hamilton to the death for the detestable sin of witchcraft, and that he will bear the expenses of his imprisonment. [See the Justiciary Court records for Hamilton's trial.]

August 20th 1629: Trial of John Carfrae *et al.*

Court of Justiciary held on 20th August 1629 by Sir Robert Hepburn of Alderstoun, knight, Sheriff Principal; George Hepburn fuar of Alderstoun, his depute; Mr James Cockburn, provost of Haddington; Mr George Butler of Blans; under special commission sent to them on August 1st 1629, for the trial of John Carfrae, his wife Alison Borthwick, and Thomas Carfra his brother for witchcraft etc.

Mr John Wilkie, notary, appears for the accused.

John Cranston of Skedsbush appeared, brother to the late Marioun Cranston; also, William Hay the lawful son of Marioun Cranston and the late James Hay; and also James Barnes, procurator fiscal to our Sovereign Lord for his Highness' interest. They produced the underwritten indictment accusing John and Thomas Carfrae and Alison Borthwick on a capital charge as follows: -

John and Thomas Carfrae and Alison Borthwick, you are accused and indicted of the most odious, abominable, and devilish crimes of sorcery, soothsaying, enchantment, invocation of devils, consulting with the dead and familiar evil spirits, practising various kinds of witchcraft, and consulting with other witches how to undo and wrong your neighbours in their bodies, goods, and gear, and bereaving them of their lives, to the great dishonour of the true and ever-living God, whom you all three have forsaken. You have renounced your baptisms and rendered yourselves body and soul to the service and obedience of Satan, the common enemy o the salvation of mankind, against the express law of God, and in high contempt of the loveable laws of this realm, particularly as written below.

Firstly, this is verified by the fact that after you had been imprisoned in this Tolbooth, you John and Thomas Carfrae were confronted with the witch Alexander Hamilton, who at that time was in the same prison. He affirmed frankly, and swore to your faces, and still stands by it, that you were notorious witches and had several meetings with the Devil. You were with him and various others of that persuasion at the following times and places: about two years ago you met with the Devil at Coldingham Law; next you met him at Pencraik Hill, where John renewed the contract and pact he had previously made with him. On your knees, in a most submissive manner he made you swear - and you gave your oath in the presence of your associates who were there - that you would be a true servant to him. He then promised to be a good and true master to you. the third meeting was at Monkrig Hill; and you, Thomas, and Alexander Hamiltton had intimate meetings with the Devil in William Dennam's house in the burgh of Haddington. The Devil appeared there to dine with you, and you had for your dinner ale, bread, and a piece of boiled mutton.

At these various meetings you consulted with the Devil and questioned him how you could lay on and take off sickness from men, women, and animals; how you could undo and ruin them in their goods and resources, and bereave them of their lives - all that with little or no provocation, which you cannot deny.

As evidence of this, you all dispatched and murdered the late Marion Cranston, wife of the late James Hay, baillie of the Lordship of Yester, where you were living. This you did with the counsel, advice, and assistance of the Devil your master, and of his servant the late Margaret Hamilton lately condemned and burnt at Dalkeith for similar crimes of witchcraft and sorcery. To put it into effect, the three of you went to this Margaret Hamilton and consulted with her about how you might take Marion's life. She agreed to your wishes and promised to carry them out. To achieve this more easily, she asked that she might have the opportunity to have a drink with Marion. Shortly after that you found that there would be the opportunity to drink with her at a marriage in the village of Yester. Knowing that Margaret would be there, you told Margaret Hamilton about it, and arranged to meet her there. The day of the marriage, you went with her to the house where the wedding was being held, and sat down to drink. When Marion passed, you invited her to drink with you and Margaret. By that means she laid a heavy and grievous sickness on her, of which she died not long afterwards. All this was clearly stated and confessed to be true by Margaret Hamilton several times before she was put on trial. Not only that, but Alison Borthwick revealed and confessed it to your mother Cristiane Walderstoun. She in turn told the late Bessie Carfra, the sister of John and Thomas. Burdened with this, on her death-bed Bessie made an open declaration and confession of it, and you cannot deny it.

Also, the three of you are accused that persevering with your malice, and not content with your murder, you made up your minds to cut off and murder the late James Hay by the same unlawful means, for no other reason except that as baillie of the Lordship of Yester he brought you to justice and punished you for your faults and riotous behaviour committed there. For that effect you contacted Margaret again, and she arranged to meet you in Haddington on a Saturday, which you did. After she had seen James Hay on the street, Margaret bewitched him by rubbing a piece of enchanted gold on the palm of her hand, which caused James to contract a serious illness the next morning, of which he died within twenty days. During his illness James constantly imagined that you were at his back, and he left his death upon you [*i.e.* blamed them for his approaching death].

Margaret Hamilton also confessed to have thus committed this murder at your desire and instigation. When you were confronted with her she swore to it and to the other murder in your faces. For carrying out the murders each of you gave her two pecks of rye. Bessie Carfra also claimed this to be true on her death-bed, which you cannot deny.

Also, you, Thomas, are accused of the most cruel and unnatural murdering and dispatching of your wife Janet Hay by the same devilish means, with the help of Margaret Hamilton. This is evidenced by the fact that your sister Bessie Carfra who lived with you was sent by you to Margaret Hamilton with a "penwark" [?] mutch of your wife's. She was to say this to Margaret, "I would be pleased to be rid of my wife, for she is not at all pleasant or attractive, and I can't love her." Bessie went to her and came back with the answer that you were to go and see her yourself. So shortly after that you went, and received from her certain instructions which you were to put into practice against your wife. By those means you murdered and made away with her.

In the same way you sought to dispatch your mother-in-law Issobell Scot in Park, in the hope of getting the wealth you thought she had, and which would have come to you at her death. However, you could not manage to achieve this because you could not get any of her clothes to take to Margaret Hamilton. Also, since during your late wife's lifetime you had conceived a child in adultery with a certain Magdalen Heriot, you consulted with the same Margaret Hamilton about bewitching Magdalen and the child. She undertook to do it, but failed. All this was affirmed to your face by Bessie Carfrae on her death-bed, which you cannot deny.

Also, you, John, are accused of sending your servant John Brown between Martinmas and last Christmas to borrow a horse from your neighbour Edward Part to carry some corn. He refused and you were offended, and so by your devilish art you bewitched three of his horses, and laid strange and unfamiliar diseases on them. Two of them died within forty eight hours of the refusal. Their eyes were hanging out of their heads by the strings. This you cannot deny.

Also you, John and Alison, are accused and indicted that around May 1628, John Quhitlie, the beadle of the Kirk of Bothans complained about you to the birleymen because your cattle had been eating and destroying his corn [The beadle was a church officer who performed duties such as bell-ringing, grave-digging, Bible-carrying, etc. The birley court was a local court for adjudicating in boundary disputes, grazings, straying of livestock, and other agricultural matters.] You were fined and your cattle impounded, and afterwards Alison said to John Quhitlie's wife with great spitefulness, "Those who weep after noon will weep as sorely as those who weep before noon." Within about ten days, when John Quhitlie was driving his cart over the end of one of your furrows, John Carfrae said to him, "Your mare is strong enough to drive over my plough-land." And with that, by your art of witchcraft, the rim of his cart-wheel broke, and his mare contracted a serious sickness which lasted around ten days, and then she died. A poor vagabond woman, perhaps guilty of the same profession as yourselves, came by and declared that the sickness had been laid on the beast, and that it would not recover. She told John Quhitlie not to kill it. This you cannot deny.

Also, you, John, are accused of bewitching and ruining the goods and corn of John Broun in Yester, a very painstaking and hard-working man. The evidence for this is that you were offended with him, and threatened him, declaring that if it wasn't for the fact that it would shame you in the eyes of the world, you wouldn't leave one of his sacks dry, although you'd never lay a hand on him [*i.e.* presumably Carfrae meant Broun's sacks of grain to rot]. This you accordingly did to him, for ever since then, in spite of his great efforts and industry, his goods have decayed and he has sustained great losses, all brought about by you. This you cannot deny.

Also, you, Alison Borthwick, are indicted and accused of the most detestable unnatural and inhumane murder and putting down of your own child, a twin which was being fostered in Fala village. The evidence is that you asked Bessie Carfra, who was then living with you and your husband John Carfra, to go with you to the village of Fala, ostensibly to visit your child, and keeping your devilish intention to yourself till you got there. Having arrived, you went to Margaret Hamilton and said to her that you had a lot of children and were afflicted by them, and you asked her to get rid of this child for you. She told you to come back, and gave you another time to come back to her, telling you to bring a winding sheet for the child. You and Bessie went to the house where the child was. The child showed no signs of dying. Then you went and brought Margaret Hamilton to the house where the child was. Immediately, by your art of witchcraft, the child died. Bessie also affirmed and confessed this to your face on her deathbed. The day that you were all confronted with Bessie, when you were returning to your house and passing by Castle Wood, you were constantly advising the other two to stand by your denial of these charges, saying, "Keep your tongues quiet for me, and I'll keep mine quiet. They'll never make me confess, whatever they do." James Wilsone from Newtonhall was nearby in the wood and heard you say it, and is here ready to affirm and swear to it, and you cannot deny it.

Also, you, Alison, are accused that having conceived a deadly hatred and malice against George Carfra your brother-in-law for no reason, you consulted with the same Margaret Hamilton how to wrong him in his goods and possessions. She told you that if you could get blood from him, he would fail and decay in his goods. Accordingly, you fell out with him, and you grappled with each other. You got his thumb in your mouth and bit it badly, and made it bleed, so that ever since then his wealth has declined in spite of his dilligent labour and industry. Bessie Carfra also declared this to be true before her death, and you cannot deny it.

You, Alison, are also accused that when you and your husband John fell out with Patrick Walderstoun in Yester, you impounded two of his oxen. When they were standing in your courtyard you busied yourself to bewitch them, so that the next morning the better of the two oxen suddenly fell down. It was at the point of death, and would have died if you had not been interrupted in the middle of your charm. While you were busy doing it, James Hunter, Patrick's servant, came to take the oxen away. He saw your lips moving and heard some words, so he gave a cough. When you heard it and saw him, you crouched down and disappeared in at your door. Not only that, but in the same way you killed one of Patrick's cows by laying a great sickness on it. When it was dead and opened up, it was found to be without blood, as if the meat had been chicken. This you cannot deny.

Taking these counts into consideration, all three of you, both by the laws of God and the laws and acts of Parliament of this realm, deserve the punishment of death as is recommended by the testimonies of Scripture and Acts of Parliament, particularly the 20th chapter of Leviticus, the 6th verse: "The saule that turneth efter sic as have familiar speiritis and efter wizards to go a hooring efter thame, I will even set my face against that saule and will cut him off from amongst this people." It also says in the 18th chapter of Deuteronomy, in the 10th, 11th, and 12th verses, "Thair sall not be fund amongst yow any one that maketh his sone or dochter to pas throw the fyre or that useth divinatioun, or ane observer of tymes, or ane inchanter, or a wiche, or a charmer, or a consulter with familiar sperittis, or a wizard or a necromancer; for all that do these things ar ane abhominatioun unto the Lord. And becaus of these abhominatiouns, the Lord thy God doth dryve them out before the [*i.e.* thee]." Also, in the 9th Parliament of Queen Mary it is expressly forbidden for any person to seek help from or consult with any witches, sorcerers, or necromancers, under pain of death. These Scriptures and Acts of parliament each and every one of you has contravened, and so you ought to be punished accordingly.

Foreman of the jury: John Yule in Braidwodsyde.

The same day the whole jury unanimously by the mouth of their foreman Johne Youle in Braidwodsyde finds John and Thomas Carfra guilty of being notorious witches and warlocks and of having meetings and consultations with the Devil as specified in the second charge of the indictment based on the statements and confessions of the witch Alexander Hamilton, which were produced duly subscribed by reputable persons who had heard these things declared and confessed. Also, John and Thomas Carfra and Alison Borthwick are found guilty of the third charge of the indictment concerning their consulting the late witch Margaret Hamilton and murdering and dispatching Marion Cranston as detailed in the statements and confessions of their sister Bessie Carfra, produced and subscribed by reputable witnesses, and verified in court by two of these witnesses who were on the jury - Robert Smyth and John Wadderston in Newtoun. This was also supported by the statement of the late Margaret Hamiltoun, produced in judgment against her at her trial, copied from the court records of Dalkeith, and produced in this court.

Also, these three persons are found guilty of murdering and dispatching James Hay, and of all of the fourth charge of the indictment concerning this. Again, this is supported by the statements and confessions of the witch Margaret Hamiltoun, and Bessie Carfra their sister, and by the verifacation of the same two witnesses on the jury.

Thomas Carfra is acquitted of the alleged murder of his wife, the late Janet Hay, and of Issobell Scot in Park, his mother-in-law. William Makie, one of the jurors affirmed that he was present at Margaret Hamilton's trial, and heard her deny the alleged murders of Jonet and Issobell.

Johne Carfra and Alisone Borthwick are acquitted of the sixth, seventh, and eighth charges of the indictment, concerning the bewitching of John Quhitlie's cart and horse, and the bewitching of John Brown in Yester's goods and corn. None of these points were proved, and John Brown himself said they were innocent of the last of the three charges.

Alison is found guilty of the murdering and putting down of her own child, the twin fostered in Fala village, and of all the particulars contained in the ninth charge of the indictment, based on the declarations of Margrit Hamiltoun and Bessie Carfra, and the supporting evidence of the aforementioned two jurors.

Alison is acquitted of the tenth and eleventh charges of the indictment concerning the bewitching of the goods and gear of George Carfra and Patrick Wakterstoun, because nothing was proved.

Lastly, Johne, Thomas, and Alisone are found guilty of breaking and contravening the laws, Scriptures, and Acts of Parliament as detailed in the last charge of the indictment, in that they were found to have consulted with the witch Margret Hamiltoun as set out in the declarations made by her and Bessie Carfra.

Therefore the judges ordained, and it was pronounced as sentence by the mouth of the dempster William Sinclair, that Thomas and Johne Carfra, and Alisone Borthwick, shall be taken this day, their hands bound behind their backs, and conveyed by the hangman of Hadingtoun to the Sandis, as the place appointed for execution. There they are first to be strangled to death on a gallows, or individual stumps or trees ["tries" can also mean "posts"], and immediately thereafter their bodies are to be burnt to ashes.

[The idea of having witnesses for the prosecution serving on the jury would seem rather unfair nowadays!]

1630

July 17th 1630: Patrick Brown, baillie.

According to a warrant granted to them, the moderator and brethren of the Presbytery of Haddington imprisoned Janet Alexander, the wife of Alexander Finlasone in Hagstoun, in the Tollbooth. However, they are now setting her free until she can be more conveniently tried, on condition that she appears again, after eight days' warning, under the penalty of 500 merks[?], for which George Thomson, fisherman and resident in Haddington becomes surety.

1631

June 15th 1631: Mr James Cokburn of Wester Monkrig, Provost.

George Blackburn, burgess, appeared. Mr Robert Balcanquell, moderator, and Mr Archibald Levinston and the other brethren of the Presbytery have obtained a commission from the Bishop of St Andrews to "try" Christina Patisone, wife of George Carmichal in Hirdmanston, who is charged with witchcraft. George stands surety for the expenses of her imprisonment in the Tollbooth.

[Perhaps this commission was for an initial interrogation rather than a "trial" in the modern legal sense. It seems rather strange that a bishop could give permission for a "trial", unless he was doing so on behalf of Parliament or the Privy Council.]

August 9th 1631: Trial of Christiane Patersone.

Court of Justiciary held under special commission by Mr James Cockburne of Wester Monkrig, Provost; Patrick Brown, James Bartrem, and John Cockburne, baillies; for the trial of Christiane Patersone, witch.

This day Christiane Paterson, wife of George Carmichael in Hirdmestown, was put on trial accused of the detestable crime of witchcraft. Asked if she had anyone to speak for her, she declared that she had no-one but God. The judges therefore referred her to be tried before a jury ["put her to the knowledge of an assise"]. John Wilkie, procurator fiscal, asked for a written record of this. The names of the jurors were called in her presence, and she was asked if she had any objections against any of them serving on her jury. She answered that she would not decline or appeal against any of them. The jury was sworn and admitted.

The same day the procurator fiscal Johne Wilkie produced Christiane Patersone's indictment, accusing her of the capital charge of being guilty of the abominable crime of witchcraft, consulting with the Devil and various witches, and of practising various acts of witchcraft, of which she has been found guilty and convicted.

The same day the jury unanimously by the mouth of their foreman Alexander Wyllie, finds Christiane guilty of the crime of witchcraft, laying on a heavy sickness and diseases, and committing murders, as follows:-

Firstly she is found guilty of laying a serious illness by the art of witchcraft, upon Janet Forrester, the wife of George Baillie in Templefield. Ther was no other reason for this than the fact that Janet had sent Margaret Muirhead, a notorious witch who was burnt for witchcraft, to her to find out from her whether her husband George would live or not, since he was mortally ill at the time. Janet took [blank] with her. George and Janet swore in the presence of the judges that it was true she had taken the sickness off him. [This seems a little confused. Presumably Christiane had taken the sickness off George and laid it on his wife Janet. It is unclear whether Margaret Muirhead played a part in this, or was just a messenger.]

Also, by similar enchantments and by her devilish art, Christiane laid a pitiful and frenzied madness on Katherin Allan, her servant at that time, which lasted for several days. This was because she would not lie in bed with Margarit Muirheid the witch, who was lodging in Cristiane's house. Cristian also took the madness off again.

She is also guilty of the cruel murder by the same devilish means of the late Elizabeth Caldcleuth, wife of Archibald Masone in Samuelstoun, and of Bessie Masone their daughter, and of Margaret Litster, Archibald's wife. This was verified and sworn against her by Archibald in the presence of the judges. [Presumably Elizabeth was a first wife and Margaret a second wife.]

She is also guilty of the similar cruel murder of the late John Keith in Hirdmestoun, by laying on him by her enchantments and sorcery a deadly wasting disease from which he died. This was because James and her son-in-law James Carmichael fell out with each other, and she was offended with James Keith. On his deathbed this James blamed her for his death, and this was proved and verified in the presence of the judges by George Symsone in [blank] and Gavin Mitchell in Wodeheid.

She is also guilty of bewitching Elizabeth Andersone, the wife of James Mackae in [blank], three years ago, by laying a serious illness on her, which is still with her, and of causing death, decay, and wasting away of their goods and livestock. This was also sworn to and verified by Elizabeth Andersone, who was present.

She is also found guilty of bewitching the corn and possessions of James Wadie in Saltoun. By doing so she has utterly ruined and undone him. This was because she reaped for him for several days last harvest in 1630, and when he sent her wages home to her house she thought it too little for her work. James Wadie testified and declared this to the kirk session of Saltoun, and most of the jurors knew it to be true.

The judges, in accordance with their commission and in obedience to its terms, postpone pronouncing sentence against Cristiane until the lords [of the Privy Council] are acquainted with the process of her conviction, so that after consideration, they may give their opinion on pronouncing sentence.

October 5th 1631

In obedience to a commission from the Lords of His Highness' Secret Council, directed to them on 24th July, the foresaid judges postponed sentence on Cristiane Patersone, the wife of George Carmichael in Hirdmistoun, for the abominable crime of witchcraft, until the Lords had been acquainted with the process of her conviction, so that they could give their opinion on sentencing her. Christiane Patersone was again brought before the court, and in accordance with a warrant and Act of Council issued at Perth 21st September last, directed to the judges and signed by Mr Gilbert Primrois, clerk to the Council, it is publicly announced and read out, decreed, and ordained, and also pronounced as sentence by the mouth of the dempster William Sinclair, that Cristiane should now be taken to the ordinary place of execution called the Sandis of the Burgh of Hadington, and first strangled at a stake there, and her body thereafter to be burnt to ashes.

1635

January 6th 1635

Special commission of justiciary to the Provost and Baillies of Haddington, against Anna Tait alias Hownome, the wife of William Johnstoun, miller in Haddington, for witchcraft, the murder of her first husband John Cathcart, and the murder of her daughter.

James Cockburne, Provost; Robert Leremouth, John Cockburne, and John Sleich, baillies. 6th January 1635. This day Anna Tait, alias Hownome, the wife of William Johnston, miller of the burgh of Haddington, accused, arrested, and imprisoned in the tollbooth of this burgh, appeared in court held within the "bos window" [a bay window, or concave window] of the Tollbooth, accused on a capital charge of the most odious abominable and devilish crimes of sorcery, soothsaying, enchantment, invocation of devils, consulting with the dead and familiar evil spirits, and practising various other kinds of witchcraft to the great dishonour of the true and ever-loving God as is contained at length in her indictment. She was asked if there was any person to speak for her, and she answered, "None but God in heaven." Therefore the judges put her on trial before a jury.

The same day Jak Wilkie, notary, appeared personally in judgement as procurator fiscal for our Sovereign Lord His Highness' interest, and accused Anna Tait alias Howname of the abominable and devilish crimes, and produced his indictment as follows:-

Anna Tait alias Howname, you are accused and indicted of the most odious, abominable, and devilish crimes of sorcery, soothsaying, enchanting, invocation of devils, consulting with the dead and familiar evil spirits, and practising various other kinds of witchcraft; and consulting with various witches to undo and ruin your neighbours in their bodies, goods, and gear, and depriving them of their lives to the great dishonour of the true and everlasting God your creator, whom you have most wickedly forsaken. You have renounced your baptism and your covenant made with Him, and rendered yourself in soul and body to the service of the Devil. You have made a devilish covenant with him, the common and deadly enemy of man's salvation, against the express law of God, and in high contempt of it and of the laws of this kingdom.

As evidence of this, for a long time your conscience has been so troubled by your devilish practices, and you have been in such fear of the shame if these should come to light and be revealed, that you have several times attempted to kill yourself, sometimes by hanging yourself with your kerchief, sometimes by other unlawful means, and recently after you came into this tollbooth by putting a knife in your own throat, which you would have cut if you had not been prevented. Since your hands were bound and your feet made fast in the stocks, and there was no other way to accomplish your devilish designs, you knocked your head against the wall and the stocks, attempting to kill yourself, which you would never have done nor attempted if it were not for fear of a more shameful death for your abominable and devilish practices, which you have also confessed since you arrived in prison, and which you cannot deny.

Further, you are indicted and accused of being many times in company with and in the society of the Devil, who, as you confessed, sometimes appeared to you in the likeness of a wind, and sometimes as a black man as follows:-

1. He often appeared to you in the likeness of a man, and in particular recently on Monday 8th December last, when you went to your own bed in this town, and there he had sexual intercourse ["carnal copulatione"] with you.

2. Also, he appeared to you in the likeness of a wind, particularly on Thursday 11th of December last, when coming to you in the likeness of a wind as described, he took you by the hair of the head and dragged you along, and nipped your left cheek. The mark is still there and you cannot deny it.

3. You have also confessed that you attempted to meet him at Alderslie[?] within a short space of time, and that he said you would not die until he had first met with you, which you cannot deny.

Also, you are indicted and accused of the cruel, detestable, unnatural, ungodly, and inhuman murder and putting down of your first husband, the late John Coltheard, cattle drover, to whom you were married in Ford Kirk in England about twenty eight years ago. You had committed fornication with William Johnstoun your present husband long before your marriage to John Coltheard, and as a result contracted such lust and intimacy with him, that not only could you not refrain from his company during your marriage to John, but committed adultery with him, for which you deserve death, both by the laws of God and this realm. To enjoy him more freely, you nurtured an abominable malice and hatred against your lawful husband John, and resolved to dispatch him by any possible means. To that effect you consulted with the Devil how you could most conveniently carry it out. He advised and counselled you to make a drink of foxglove leaves and some other devilish ingredients best known to you and him who concocted it, and gave it to John. You maliciously took this devilish counsel and advice, made up the drink, and gave it to your husband. Within three hours of drinking it he died from the same devilish and venomous drink. You did this for no other reason or provocation from your husband, but that he was old, and was an impediment to your enjoyment of your present husband who then lived in Mynram [Mindrum?] near to where you and your late husband lived, which you have already confessed and cannot deny.

You are also indicted and accused of the cruel, abominable, ungodly and unnatural murder and putting down of your daughter Elizabeth Johnston, conceived by you and William Johnstoun in your adulterous marriage, and also of an infant in her womb. Suspecting Elizabeth was pregnant - only you know to whom, and you will not reveal the truth of the matter - and apparently reluctant to let it be known to whom the child belonged, you both sought out all possible ways to kill and murder the child in her belly. This was so that it might not come to light who the father was or how it was conceived, whether in adultery or incest or some other unlawful way. You consulted with several of your confederates about it, and got various pieces of secret advice. Following this advice you administered potions to your daughter, but when none of them worked, and you could think of nothing else, you went to your old master the Devil and consulted him for advice on how it could be done. Being as cruel and maliciously inclined as yourself, he advised you to buy a mutchkin [quarter of a Scots pint, *i.e.* 0.43 litres] of white wine, mix some of it with salt, give it to your daughter, and that would do the trick. You willingly obeyed this cruel and devilish advice, fetched the wine, mixed it with salt, and gave it to your daughter to drink. As a result, she presently began to swell and shortly afterwards both she and the child died. As evidence, you have confessed that the Devil gave you enough money in real genuine turners [Money from the Devil often turned to leaves or stones. A "turner" was a coin worth 2 pence Scots.] to buy the mutchkin of wine and the [salt?]. It is dread of the consequences of all your devilish and abominable actions which has most troubled you, and been the main cause of your desire to murder yourself. By consulting and plotting with the Devil and his other servants, and administering your poisons and devilish drinks, and by the cruel and unnatural murders of your husband, your daughter, and her infant, you are guilty both by the law of God, and the laws of this realm, and ought to die the death. James Nelson in Quhittinghame: foreman of the jury.

The same day the whole jury by the mouth of their foreman James Nelson unanimously finds Agnes Tait alias Hownome guilty of the abominable, cruel, unnatural, and devilish crimes of sorcery, soothsaying, enchantment, invocation of devils, consulting with the dead and familiar evil spirits, and practising of various kinds of witchcraft. [As has perhaps become apparent from previous cases, this is a stock catch-all rigmarole which does not necessarily mean that the accused had actually done all of these things.] She is also guilty of consulting and advising with the Devil and his servants in connection with the murder of her first husband John Coltheard; also of the murder of her eldest daughter Elizabeth Johnston with the child in her womb; also of keeping company with the Devil on the 8th and 12th of December last, when he appeared to her first as a black man, and secondly as a wind. She is also guilty of attempting to kill herself in prison, first by by hanging herself with her kerchief, and secondly by trying to cut her own throat. She is found guilty on the basis of her own confession, having confessed to the whole indictment against her, except for the general clause [*i.e.* the rigmarole including soothsaying, enchantment, consulting with the dead, etc.], of which she was also found guilty, although she denies most of it.

Therefore the judges declared, and it was pronounced as sentence by the mouth of the dempster William Sinclair, That Agnes Tait should be taken, her hands bound behind her back, conveyed by William Allot hangman of Haddington to the ordinary place of execution, strangled to death at a post, and her body thereafter burnt to ashes.

1649

June 23rd 1649: Trial of John Dickson *et al.*

Court of justiciary held 23rd June 1649 by James Broun of Coalstoun, Provost of Haddingtoun; Patrick Young and John Aytoun, baillies; for the trial of John Dicksone, Marion Richieson, Agnes Hunter, Margaret Dickson, and Isobell Murray, witches.

Indictment.

John Dicksone, you are accused and indicted of the most odious, abominable, and devilish crime of witchcraft, and practising various kinds of witchcraft, to the great dishonour of God, whom you have forsaken. You have renounced your baptism and rendered yourself body and soul to the service of the Devil, common enemy to the salvation of mankind, against the express law of God, and in contempt of the loveable laws of this realm. The particulars are as follows:-

Firstly, last barley sowing time you were asked by Margaret Dickson, who is also the Devil's servant, to come and see a man. However, she would not say who it was until you came out to see him. Then she told you it was Lucifer. He desired you to become his servant, and this request you granted. He asked you to renounce Christ and your baptism, which you did. Then he gave you a mark by laying his hand on your left shoulder. In company with you and the Devil that time were Agnes Hunter, Grisell Andersone, and Margaret Dicksone. When the Devil gave you the mark, he called you "Grot Bage" [a bag for holding groats or hulled grain], which you cannot deny.

You had a second meeting with the Devil and the forementioned persons, and met in Glaiddismoor, where the Devil appeared to you and to them in the likeness of a man, and was with you for about an hour. The Devil and the others did nothing that time but dance, and Margarit Dicksone sang. The Devil went away like a [blank] foal. This you cannot deny.

Also, you, Johne Dicksone are accused of meeting the Devil another time at a well on the north side of Painstoune. With you and those already mentioned was the Devil, who appeared in the likeness of a black man, and asked what service you had done. This you cannot deny.

You, Marione Richesone, are accused and indicted of the most abominable and devilish crime of witchcraft., sorcery, and others as written above, and of meeting the Devil. The first time was at the Kirk Hill in company with Agnes Hunter. The Devil appeared to you in the likeness of a black man. He took hold of you and wrestled with you, and wanted to have sex ["carnal copolatione"] with you, which you refused that time. After that he went away in the likeness of a black shaggy foal. It was then that you realised that he was the Devil. You asked Agnes Hunter, "Who was that man?" and she said he was a gentleman. This you cannot deny.

You are also accused and indicted that when one of your children was ill, you came to Agnes Hunter. She told you to go to a well below the Boges, to bring a pint of the water, and she would wash the child who was badly bewitched. She told you to see that you were there before the sun rose. Accordingly, you followed her advice and directions, and went to the well. When you had filled your bucket with water from it and were coming away, the Devil met you and said, "What now, my dove? Where did you get the water?" You said, There at the well." Then the Devil struggled with you and kissed you, and told you the water wouldn't be much use to you. This you cannot deny.

You are also accused of meeting the Devil in Margaret Hunter's house, where he was in the shape of a man sitting with Agnes in her bedroom. You had come to the house for a pint of ale. The Devil had sex with you on the lid of a chest in Agnes Hunter's bedroom, and promised you that you would never lack enough in the way of worldly possessions. After that he called you "Miraklis". Another time you saw the Devil at the end of Alexander Mallire's[?] garden, in the likeness of a man in drab coloured clothes. With you were John Dickson senior, Grissell Andersone, and Issobell Murray, and they were all dancing round the Devil while he stood in the midst of them. This you cannot deny.

You, Agnes Hunter, are accused of the most odious and devilish crimes of witchcraft etc. specified above. Firstly, about ten years ago you were coming from Ormestoune and saw the Devil in the likeness of a gentleman, and suspected that he was the Devil. However, he did not approach you, and did not try to touch you that time, but went away in front of you in the likeness of a greyhound. The second time the Devil appeared to you at the foot of your own garden about five years after that in the likeness of a man in green clothes, and desired you to become his servant. You asked what service you could do, for you were not able to go out of doors. The Devil replied that you would never need to get out except when Marioun Richesoun got out. You promised to become his servant, and he asked you to renounce your baptism and Jesus Christ, which you old. The Devil had sex with you and he was "cauld of natour" [*i.e.* his penis was cold]. He laid his hand on your shoulder at the time and gave you his mark. This you cannot deny.

You also met him a third time, about half a year after that, in your own garden. He appeared to you in the likeness of a black man, and asked you to meet Marioun Richesone and several others in Langniddrie, in Thomas Dicksone's house. You asked him what reward he would give you, and what good you would get from him. He answered that you would get something when you came to the meeting with the rest. He had sex with you that time, and you found his penis cold.

Also you are accused of meeting the Devil at Langniddrie, as arranged. With you were Marioune Richesone, Marioune Adisone, Marjorie Russel, Margaret Ritchesone, Meg Staige, and another long-backed woman. You all met in Thomas Dicksone's house, but Thomas did not know you were there. Food and drink were provided for you, and you all ate and drank. You had a quart of wine and stayed about an hour and a half. The Devil promised to give you your reward at Easter. You had a fifth meeting with the Devil in the same house on Shrove Tuesday ["Faster-night Even"] with the same company. You all had supper together and arranged another meeting for Easter, where you were to get your reward. The Devil arranged for you to part company with them; he would come to Panistoune and enter you, Agnes, in the company he had there. At Easter the Devil met you as arranged at Panistoune where Grissell Andersone and Johne Dicksone were in company with you. You were just in the act of meeting when Marioun Richeson came by and said, "God speed!" whereupon the Devil vanished away and you all parted company. This you cannot deny.

Margaret Dicksone, you are accused of the same abominable and devilish crimes of witchcraft etc as written above. The occasion of your coming into the Devil's snare was the trouble caused by your daughter's illness. Thinking she had recovered a little, you asked her to go out to the harvest field. She refused, whereupon you struck her and said, "Since you are a burden to me, may either God or the Devil part me and you." That same night about midnight the Devil appeared to you at the side of your bed. He lay down a while with you, and asked you to become his servant. Although unwilling at first, you were persuaded by his plausible conversation, and you became his servant. He had sex with you and ordered you to forsake your God and take yourself to him. This you did, saying you would do as he wished, become his servant, and renounce your baptism. All this was about five years ago. The Devil also gave you a name, calling you "Marrit", and gave you a nip under the right arm, where there has been a mark ever since. He arranged to meet you half a year after that at Nisbet Dame Heid, and promised to give you some kind of reward. He kept this appointment, appearing to you in the likeness of a gentleman in green clothes, about twelve o' clock at noon, and had sex with you again. This you cannot deny.

You are also accused of having a third meeting with the Devil at the "balk heid" of Nisbet. [A "balk" was an unploughed strip of land often used as a boundary, so this may signify "at the top edge of the lands of Nisbet"]. There you saw Agnes Broune lying between two rigs [cultivation strips]. She got up and came over to you, and as you were meeting, the Devil appeared and came in between you. He went to Agnes and embraced her in his arms. When you saw that, you left them, and shortly after that you met the Devil at the lime kiln at the west side of the More Shote, where he wanted to lie with you. When you refused, he struck you and flew at you like a wild animal, which caused you to became very sick. You never saw him after that until you were at Panestoune, where he fell upon you in the night, and forced down your head until you cried out, thinking he was about to rape you. Then Johne Dicksone came to you and told you not to go near the place where you saw the Devil. John Dicksone, Johne Weir, Isobel Murray, Agnes Hunter, and Grissell Andersen all met together, but you did not do much, for you were scattered by Marion Richeson coming by and bidding you "God speed!" [The last two sentences are somewhat unclear. This is the best sense I can make of them.] This you cannot deny.

You are also accused of being at another meeting with the Devil in Gladismoore with Johne Dicksone, John Weir, and his wife Marioun Richesone, and that the Devil lay with Marioun Richesone that time. This you cannot deny.

You are also accused of meeting the Devil in Agnes Broun's house in Nesbit. While you were sitting with Agnes, the Devil came in, and said he didn't know which of you to turn to. Agnes answered, "Whichever of us you like," whereupon he turned to Agnes. She winked at you, and told you to go out. While you were going out the Devil pulled you back again and joined your hands with Agnes, and told you both to be good servants to him, and you would not lack your wages when you liked to ask for them. You and Agnes promised to do so. This you cannot deny.

You are also accused that Issobell Johnstoune, having a sick child in Nesbit, came to you and asked you to get some south-running water to

Several people from Penston (above) were executed for witchcraft in 1649.

One of the Penston witches described what appeared to be a lighthearted flirtation between the Devil and Agnes Broun in Agnes's house at Nisbet, below.

wash the child in. She said some people had been advising her to do this, and asked you if it would do any good. You told her to try it, and the next time you met the Devil you asked his advice about it. He told you to fetch the water and give it to the child's mother. He directed you not to use the water yourself. The mother of the child should apply it, and you were only to fetch it. This you cannot deny.

Isobell Murray, you are accused and indicted of the most odious and devilish crimes of witchcraft abovewritten, and of being a servant to the Devil since last Easter. You were lying in your bed when "the spirit" took you out of your bed. You walked around the garden. The Devil was in the likeness of a great black dog, and he nipped you on the left shoulder, which you found very painful. After that you returned home in the likeness of a cat. As soon as you got back to your own house you returned to your own likeness. This first time was on a Monday, and the following Tuesday you came to Johne Hamiltoune's garden in Painistoune, and met Johne Dicksoune, Heilling Andersone, and Maggie Hoge. This was about two o'clock in the morning. Marion Richesoune came by and said, "God be with you," and the Devil broke her arm and fled. Before the Devil and the rest of you danced, you knelt down at the top of the garden, renounced your baptism, and became the Devil's servant. He made you throw a stone over your left shoulder, and he called you Lisbie". He lay with you like a rough [*i.e.* probably "hairy"] man, all black. This you cannot deny.

Foreman of the jury: John Forrest

The same day the whole jury unanimously by the mouth of John Forrest their foreman found guilty John Dicksone, Marioune Richisone, Agnes Hunter, Margarit Dicksone, and Isobell Murray as notorious witches and warlocks, and of their individual indictments, and of being consulters with the Devil as specified in the individual indictments and accusations based on their own confessions. Therefore the judges ordained, and it was proclaimed as sentence by the mouth of the dempster Thomas Broune, that Johne Dicksone, Marioune Ritchesone, Agnes Hunter, Margarit Dicksone, and Isobell Murray shall be taken this day, their hands bound behind their backs, and conveyed by the hangman of Haddingtoune to the Sandis. There about three o'dock in the afternoon they are to be strangled to death, and their bodies thereafter burnt to ashes.

July 24th 1649: The case of Helen Fairlie *et al.*

Court of justiciary held by Patrick Inglis of Elvingston; Patrick Hepburn of Wester Monkrige; Alexander Cockburn; John Cockburne, Provost; and John Aytoun, baillie of Haddington; for the trial of Helen Fairlie, Barbara Purdie, Helen Lawsone, and John Weir, witches.

Heillein Fairlie, you are accused of the most odious, abominable, and devilish crime of witchcraft, enchantment, invocation of devils, and practising of various kinds of witchcraft, to the great dishonour of God whom you have forsaken. You have renounced your baptism and rendered yourself body and soul to the Devil, common enemy to the salvation of mankind, against the express law of God and in contempt of the loveable laws of this realm. The particulars are as follows:

Firstly, you conceived a deadly hatred, malice, and ill-will against James Wilsone in Langnudrie after your mother was burnt for the same crime that you are now accused of. You were in your father's house in Langnuderie when the Devil came in to you in the likeness of a man. He promised that if you would forsake your saviour Christ, and become his servant, he would grant you revenge on James Wilsone. This you did. Then he had sex with you, and told you to give James a piece of bread and a drink, and then you would get sufficient revenge on him. You did as the Devil wished, and as soon as James had got the bread and the drink, he went mad and then died. This you cannot deny.

Secondly, you had another meeting with the Devil in the company of Marjory Adamsone in [blank], Margaret Simsone in [blank], and several others. You had a feast in Thomas Dicksone's, and the Devil was with you. This you cannot deny.

Thirdly, you had another meeting with the Devil in Haprig in your own house about the end of last harvest. The Devil had sex with you, and demanded to know why you had stayed away from him so long. This you cannot deny.

Fourthly, you were with the Devil and Heillein Gylour, Margaret Patersone, and various others at a meeting in Butterdain. There the Devil had sex with you and all the rest. This you cannot deny.

Fifthly, you had another meeting with the Devil between the Thrie Myll Hous and Lochhall. The aforementioned persons were with you. You danced and the Devil played for you. This you cannot deny.

Sixthly, you had another meeting with the Devil where you and Marjorie Adamsone, Margaret Simsone, Margaret Russel, Isobele Baine and several others went with the Devil to Jeanot Carfra's house. She was in bed and you all went to her bedside. Marjorie Adamsone wanted to take Jeanot's child from her out of the bed, but she could not get it. You made Jeanot become insane, and then left her. This you cannot deny.

Seventhly, you, Heillein Gyloure, Marjorie Nesbit and various others had a meeting with the Devil in Butterdaine. The Devil played to you, and you and he all danced. This was at the end of harvest in the gloaming of the evening. This you cannot deny.

Barbara Purdie, you are accused and indicted of the same most odious and devilish crime of witchcraft and others above mentioned. Also, of going to meet the Devil at the foot of the gardens at the south boundary wall of Painstoun. With him was Issobel Murray who had brought you from your own house, John Dicksone, John Weir, and Margaret Dickson. The Devil was in the likeness of a gentleman. He came to you, took you by the shoulder, and asked you to forsake your saviour Christ, and become his servant. You, like the rest, would always have a sufficiency of wealth and possessions ["eneuch of geir"]. You then knelt down and forsook Christ, and promised to serve the Devil. He had sex with you and you thought his penis cold and thin. This was about a year ago, and you cannot deny it.

Secondly, you were at another meeting with the Devil at the top end of the gardens on the north side. In your company were John Weir, Johne Dickson, Grissell Andersone, Heilleine Lawsone, and Issobell Murray. Marioun Richesone passed you, coming back from the well, and wished you "God speed." At that you all went away, and the Devil went down the rig [cultivation strip] opposite James Baize's garden. This you cannot deny.

Thirdly, you had a meeting with the Devil at Pannistoune Heuch where the above named persons were with you. This you cannot deny.

Heillein Lawsone, you are accused and indicted of the foresaid abominable crime of witchcraft, and others as written above. Also, that Issobell Murray came to your house and asked you to come to Richard Broune's garden to have a word with someone. When you got there you saw a black man, who came to you and asked you to be his servant. You promised to do what service you could, and at his desire you knelt down, renounced your baptism, and became his servant. Then he lay with you. This meeting was last Whit Sunday, and you cannot deny it.

Secondly, you had a meeting with the Devil at the top end of John Hamilton's garden, about thirty days after the first one. He was in the likeness of a man, and the same people were in your company. The Devil asked you how you were and what you had done since the last meeting. This you cannot deny.

John Weir, you are accused and indicted of the same abominable and devilish crimes of witchcraft, and others mentioned above. Also, last Easter, you were with the Devil in Richard Broune's garden in Pannistoune. After daylight had faded, when you were lying in your bed, you were brought out by Grissell Anderson and your own wife. Your wife asked you to engage with the Devil who was there in the likeness of a gentleman, and to enter into the same trade and service that she herself was in. You consented to this, knelt down and renounced God and Jesus Christ, believed in the Devil and became his servant. At the same time the Devil gave you a nip on your [blank] bone, which was very painful for a long time after that. At your desire, the Devil promised you money. Heillen Lawsone was in company with you and the others mentioned. This you cannot deny.

Secondly, you had a meeting with the Devil last barley-sowing time at the bottom end of the stackyard[?]. In your company were John Dicksone, Isobel Murray, Margarit Dicksone, and Barbara Purdie, who were all dancing. Isobel Murray yourwife was singing to you and dancing, holding you by the hand. When the Devil embraced and kissed the women, he only shook hands with you. After staying about half an hour he said he would meet them after the next meeting was intimated. Then he bade, "Be with you", and went away heading northwards. This you cannot deny.

Thirdly you had a meeting with the Devil after your wife had told you about it, in John Hamilton's garden in Panistoun, in the evening twilight, at about the end of barley-sowing time. You, the Devil, Grissil Andersone, Johne Dicksone, Margaret Dicksone, and Issobell Murray arrived, but when the rest of the company were coming the meeting was prevented and you were scattered by someone coming by at the time. This you cannot deny.

Taking into consideration these charges, you, Heillein Fairlie, Barbara Purdie, Heillein Lawsone, and John Weir, all four of you, deserve the punishment of death according to the laws of God, and also according to the laws and acts of the Parliament of this realm. This is verified and proven by the following testimonies of Scripture and Acts of Parliament, in particular as is said in the twentieth chapter of Leviticus, verse six, "And the soule that turneth after sutch as have familear speirits and visards to goe a hooring after them I will even sett my face against that soule and will cut him of from amongst the people." It is further said in the eighteenth chapter of Deuteronomy in verses ten, eleven, and twelve, "Thair sall not be found amongst yow that makis his sone or his daughter to pas through the fyre or that useth divination or ane observer of tymes, or ane enchanter or a witch or a charmer or a consulter with familiar spirits or a visard or a necromancer for all that & this thingis ar ane abhominatione unto the Lord and becaus of these abhominations the Lord thy God doth drive them out before thee." Also, in the ninth parliament of Queen Mary it is expressly forbidden for any person to seek help or response, counsel or advice, from any witch, sorcerer, or necromancer, under pain of death. These Scriptures and Acts of Parliament require every one of you to be punished accordingly.

Foreman of the jury: John Sharpe.

The same day the whole jury, by the mouth of their foreman John Sharp, finds Heillein Fairlie, Barbara Purdie, Heillein Lawsone, and John Weir guilty of being notorious witches, and John Weir a warlock; also of the various charges and accusations and points of witchcraft given in against them. Each and every one of them is found guilty in accordance with their own confessions.

Thereafter the judges ordained, and it was pronounced as sentence by the mouth of the

In 1649 witches from Penston confessed to meeting the Devil near the Three Mile House, which stood close to where Gladsmuir parish church now stands.

Also in 1649 Manie Hamilton, Patrick Watson, and Bess Hogg from West Fenton (below), were imprisoned in Dirleton Castle and subsequently executed for witchcraft.

dempster Thomas Broun, that Heillen Fairlie, Barbara Purdie, Heillein Lawsone, and John Weir should be taken this day, their hands bound behind their backs, conveyed by the hangman of Haddinton to the Sandis, and there between three and four o'clock to be strangled to death and their bodies burnt to ashes.

Desuper acta.

August 17th 1649: The trial of Agnes Broun, Margaret Robisone, Margarit Bartilman, Jeannie Hunter, Hellein Gylloure, Jeannot Burgane, Margarit Patersone, and Marjorie Nisbet.

Court of justiciary held under special commission by Patrick Inglis of Elvingstone; Mr John Butler of Blance; John Cockburne, Provost; and John Aytone and John Sleich, baillies of Haddington; for the trial of Agnes Broun, Margaret Robisone, Margaret Bartillman, Jeannie Hunter, Hellein Gyllour, Jeannot Burgone, Margaret Patersone, and Marjorie Nisbet for witchcraft, 17th August 1649. John Wilkie, procurator fiscal.

Margaret Robesone, you are accused of the most odious and devilish crimes of witchcraft, and practising various kinds of witchcraft to the great dishonour of God whom you have forsaken. You have renounced your baptism and rendered yourself body and soul to the Devil, the common enemy to the salvation of mankind, against the express laws of God and the loveable laws of the realm. In particular, you had a meeting with the Devil last Easter when you were going looking for seed about four or five o' clock in the morning. He took you by the shoulder and asked you to kneel down and renounce your baptism, which you did. He threw a cloak over your shoulder [So says Wallace Brown, but a "clod" is more likely than a "cloak". See Margaret Bartillman.] and gave you the name "Margaret Bealls" [bealls = festers].

Also, twenty or thirty years ago when you were living in James Fleming's barn, you were pulled up and down the house [sic] by the hair of the head by some invisible creature which also went to your mother's bed and said, "Old woman, you must shift."

Mr George Hepburn and John Trotter were sworn in court, and testified that she had said no more; that she had thought God would save the weak, but saw no evidence of it now.

Agnes Bown, you are accused and indicted of the most odious crime of witchcraft, and that you have been the Devil's servant for the past six years. When you were living in Nisbet, and Meg Dickson was also living there, she came to your house one Sunday night with a pint of ale under her apron. The Devil was with her, and you both drank with the Devil, who had the appearance of a man wearing black clothes. You went out with him to the top end of Nisbet where he made you kneel down and renounce God and your baptism. He lay with you and gave you the name "Meg". Also, you had a second meeting with the Devil at the top end of a rig of corn. Meg Dicksone was with you, who has already been burnt, and a certain Meg Brown who was then living in Nesbit, and who has since then died in Elvingstone.

Margaret Bartillman, you are accused of the same crime of witchcraft. About last Christmas you met with the Devil at the side of a wall to the east of Panistone. Issabell Murray and John Weir were in your company. The Devil ordered you to renounce God, Jesus Christ, and your baptism, and become his servant. This you did by kneeling down and casting a clod of earth over your left shoulder, and he called you "Margaret Shortill". After that he lay with you, and you thought his penis was cold, like a lump of cold iron. He promised to give you worldly possessions, and told you to serve him, keep his commandments, and use every opportunity to draw others into his service. He arranged to meet them again in six weeks' time, and went away in the likeness of a dog.

You had a second meeting with the Devil at the appointed time, beside Painstone about twelve o' clock at night. The same people were present, and all you did was dance. You had a third meeting with the Devil about twelve days after that, and he asked what service you had done. You said, "None," and he said you were a bad servant.

Jeannet Burgane, you are accused of the same sin of witchcraft. The first meeting you had with the Devil was in Patrick Hog's garden. You had been asked to come there by Heillein Gyllour to have a word with a gentleman. When you arrived you saw the Devil in the likeness of a gentleman dressed in black, and he was rough and hairy. You asked Heillein who the gentleman was, and she said he was "a gentleman". Then the Devil came to you and kissed you, and asked you to become his servant. You wanted a gift from him, and he promised to give you one. He made you kneel down, renounce your baptism and your interest in Jesus Christ, and become his servant. This you did. The Devil had sex with you, and you thought his penis cold. In company with you were Heillin Fairlie, Jeane Hunter, Margarit Patersone, and Marjorie Nisbet. They all danced, and then the Devil bade, "Be with you," and vanished away.

Secondly, you, Heillin Gyllour, Heillin Fairlie, and Marjorie Nisbet had another meeting about two years ago between Martinmas and Chrstmas. First you met at Heillin Gylloure's door, then at Heillin's request you all went down to Patrick Cowdan's house. The Devil unlocked the door and you all went in. The Devil took three of Patrick's oxen and tied their tails together where they lay. Then the Devil and the rest of you took hold of the tails of the oxen and drew them backwards. Then you let the tails go, and went away in the flesh as you had come. [The interrogator would seem to be making sure here that Jeannot was actually physically present, and not merely present in spirit.] Immediately after you, Jennot, had lain down in your bed, Patrick sent someone to get your husband Johne Storie to come and bleed two of his oxen. The third died the next night.

Thirdly, you had a meeting with the Devil and Heillein Gylloure, Heillein Fairlie, Marjorie Nisbet, Jean Hunter, and Margarit Patersone, to the east of the Thrie Myll Hous about last Christmas. The Devil was in the likeness of a man. He had sex with you there, and after that you sent Margarit Nisbet to the Thrie Myll Hous for a quart of ale. The Devil and all the rest of you drank and danced for about half an hour. When you arrived there the Devil had embraced you and said you were very welcome, and then he made you kneel down and renounce your baptism and your share in Jesus Christ, and become his servant, all of which you did. [This is rather odd. Jeannot is supposed to have done this already!] He called you "Jeanis" and then he had sex with you, and you thought his penis cold. After that you all danced for about an hour there, then went down to the middle of the "balk" [unploughed boundary strip]. Heillein Gyllour went to her own house and brought back a quart of ale for you, and the Devil and the rest of you drank for about half an hour. Then the Devil bade, "Be with you all," and went away.

Margaret Patersone, you are accused and indicted of the same crime of witchcraft. Your first meeting with the Devil was last Christmas when Heillein Gyllour came to your house and asked you to come with her and speak to a gentleman. You went with her up to the east of the Thrie Myll Hous, and the Devil was there in the likeness of a black man. With you were Heillein Fairlie, Jeanie Hunter, Jennot Burgone, and Marjorie Nesbit. The Devil came to you, took you round the neck, kissed you, and asked you to become his servant. This you promised to do, and then he made you kneel down, renounce your baptism and your interest in Jesus Christ, and become his servant. All of this you did, and he called you "Magdaline". You and the rest danced for about an hour, and Marjorie Nisbet sang. Then the Devil bade, "Be with you," and you all went away home.

Secondly, you had another meeting with the Devil and the above-mentioned persons beside Patrick Hog's garden. There you got Heillein Gyllour to ask leave from the Devil for you to go home because your children were crying. Then you went away home and left the three of them.

Thirdly, you and the above-named persons had a meeting with the Devil in John Bailzie's garden. They said to the Devil that they were afraid that they would all be burnt. He said that he didn't think that they would all be arrested. Then they all danced. When you were coming away, the Devil took hold of you and both of you fell over the wall. He had sex with you, but you thought his penis was as cold as a clod of earth. He bade everyone, "Be with you," and you went your way home.

Jeannie Hunter, you are accused and indicted for the same abominable sin and crime of witchcraft, and for entering into the Devil's service around Shrove Tuesday last. Your sister Agnes Hunter came in when you were lying in your bed and took you out to the back of the gardens. The Devil was there in the likeness of a man with grey coloured clothes. Your sister Agnes told him she had brought someone with her who would be pleased to be his servant. He came to you and embraced and kissed you. However, he got nothing else done at that time, because someone came by and bade you "God speed", and so everyone went away. That time Grissel Anderson, John Weir, Issabell Murray, and Heillin Gyllour were in your company.

You had a second meeting with the Devil between the Thrie Myll House and the Loch Hall. In company with you were Heillein Gyllour, Heillein Fairlie, Marjorie Nisbet, Jonet Burgone, and Margaret Patersone. Then the Devil bade, "Be with you all." He went away, and you and Heillein Gyllour went home.

Thirdly, you and the Devil and the above-named persons had a third meeting in Patrick Hog's garden, where you danced for about an hour. Then the Devil bade, "Be with you all," and he went away in the likeness of a black man. This was about a fortnight after the previous meeting.

Marjorie Nisbet, you are accused of being in the Devil's sevice. The first time was on Shrove Tuesday at the back of Patrick Hog's garden. With you were Jeane Hunter, Jennot Burgone, Margaret Patersone, and Heillein Gylloure. You saw a black man who spoke to you and asked you to become his servant. You consented, and promised to become his servant. He asked you to leave the service of God and Christ, and forsake God and your baptism. This you did by kneeling down and throwing a stone over your left shoulder. After that he gave you a nip on the back of your left shoulder, and gave you the name "Mugilie"[?]. You had a second meeting within fourteen days near the Thrie Mile Hous about nine o' clock at night. The Devil looked like a man, but his face was unpleasant. He was black haired and had black teeth. The same people were present at this second meeting. Then the Devil had sex with you, and you thought him cold. Heillein Gyloure sent for a quart of ale out of the Thrie Myll Hous, and the Devil and everyone else drank. When he went away he bade, "Be with you," and vanished away. You had a third meeting with the Devil and the same people, and some others whom you did not know as they were masked women. They danced, and someone you did not know sang. The woman who sang was masked.

Foreman of the jury: John Quhyt.

The same day the whole jury by the mouth of their foreman Johne Quyte, found Margaret Robertson, Margaret Bartillman, Agnes Broune,

Jannet Burgane, Margaret Paterson, Jeane Hunter, and Marjorie Nisbit guilty of being notorious witches, and guilty of various charges and accusations given in against them. Each and every one of them is also guilty by virtue of their own confessions.

Thereafter, the judges ordained, and it was pronounced as sentence by the mouth of the dempster Thomas Broune, that Margaret Robertson, Margaret Bartilman, Agnes Broune, Jonnet Burgane, Margarit Patersone, Jeane Hunter, and Marjorie Nisbet, should be taken that day, their hands bound behind their backs, and conveyed by the hangman of Haddington to the Sands of that burgh. There this day, between now and four o' clock, they are to be strangled to death and their bodies thereafter burnt to ashes.

1689

[Haddington Court Book 1683-1701: B30/10/17. This entry does not seem to be included among the Wallace James transcriptions.]

June 14th 1689: This day in the presence of Alexander Smyth, one of the baillies of the burgh, and Mr James fforman, minister of the same burgh, appeared Robert Byres, tailor burgess of Haddington. According to his own confession, he was found guilty of inhumanly and unchristianly slandering the good name of John Lamb, merchant burgess of the same burgh, by calling him witch's get and witch's grandson. Being now conscious of his misbehaviour, and having craved God's and John Lamb's pardon, Robert Byres legally binds and obliges himself to behave discreetly and civilly towards John Lamb, and not to slander and calumniate him, nor utter any such words against John Lamb or any of his predecessors. This under the penalty of a hundred pounds Scots over and above any corporal and personal punishment given at the judges' pleasure.

Signed: Robert Byres.

Musselburgh.

The only 17th Century burgh records for Musselburgh in the National Archives of Scotland are contained in a minute book spanning the period 1679-1714 [B56/3/1]. As far as I could see, there is no mention of witchcraft in it. The Musselburgh court books in the National Archives do not begin until 1718.

North Berwick.

The National Archives of Scotland contain a North Berwick court book covering the period 1638-1720, designated B56/6/1. Council minutes do not begin until 1727. There seems to be only one relevant entry in the court book.

1649

October 15th 1649: The court of the burgh of North Berwick held in the Tollbooth by the honourable John Levington and George Baillie, baillies of the said burgh, on 15th October 1649. Court affirmed.

James Achesoun, now resident here, appeared before the baillies this day in the action pursued against George Gyler, pedlar, burgess of North Berwick.

George had claimed that he lost a purse in Tynninghame Links at the time of the last herring fishing ["drave"] this year. As he alleged in presence of the baillies, it contained £129 Scots in money. He also said in the presence of reliable witnesses that it had cost him ten shillings sterling for John Lindsay to tell him that Mr James Acheson had his purse. Mr James cited as witnesses to these allegations Robert Seyton in Fenton, David Cowan, John Lawder [illegible], John Craig, and Thomas Kemp, of whom appeared Robert Sytoun. Having given his oath, he declared that he heard George Gyler say that it had cost him six [illegible, but probably "pounds Scots"] to Johne Lindsay, who told him Mr James had the purse that he had lost. David Cowan appeared, but would not give his oath. He declared that George Gyler said the man who took his purse was... [several illegible words here]... and John Hume's within the burgh. Because this action was a case of slander [a "scandal"] and belonged to the ecclesiastical jurisdiction, and since the witnesses lived outwith the baillies' jurisdiction, the case was referred to the kirk session.

[Haddington Presbytery was greatly concerned about John Lindsay's activities. See "Other Church Records"]

5. Trial by Commission.

We have already seen some trials by commission which survived among the Haddington burgh records. Trial by commission was the usual way of dealing with witches. They could also be tried by the High Court of Justiciary, and since Edinburgh was not at an inconvenient distance, several witches from East Lothian did stand trial there. It was more usual, however, to seek a "commission" from Government to try witches locally. Normally the government body which granted such commissions was the Privy Council. During the chaotic Civil War years of 1649/50, however, the Scottish Parliament and its Committee of Estates also granted large numbers of witchcraft commissions. Parliament also granted a few immediately after the Restoration of 1660.

The idea of a commission was that a group of dignitaries from the area concerned, usually local lairds, and usually including local magistrates in the case of burghs, were empowered by Government to set up a court to try a specific case, and to appoint the various officials required - procurator fiscal, dempster, clerk, messengers, etc. They also had to summon witnesses and draw up a "dittay" or indictment on the basis of witnesses' statements and the confession, if any, of the accused. The commissioners were also required to summon a pool of jurors from which an "assise" or jury could be chosen, usually numbering fifteen. Sometimes all the commissioners would preside over the court, but often a "quorum" of perhaps three or five was stipulated, which would suffice.

No doubt meticulous records of these trials would be made, but the vast majority of them seem to have been lost. What survives in the records of the Privy Council is usually nothing more than a note of the granting of a commission. Sometimes, however, supporting evidence has been sent to the Council and kept, and there is much interesting material of that kind. There are also a few "supplications" over, for example, wrongful imprisonment. By the time of the trial of Catherine McTarget in 1688, a more sceptical Privy Council was keeping a very close eye on a trial which it seems to have been rather uneasy with, and we have a lengthy and detailed account of proceedings from beginning to end.

The Privy Council was in theory a meeting of the selected advisors of the monarch, although for much of the 17th Century the job of the Privy Council was not so much advising the monarch as running the country. "The primary duty of the Lords of Council was the preservation of domestic peace, and the devising and enforcing of other regulations leading to an efficient internal police administration. The Lords of the Council also, however, administered justice by pronouncing on litigation." [RPC 1st Ser. Vol i, P. xi]. The Privy Council appointed after the Restoration by Charles II contained 29 members, mostly aristocrats, but also included two archbishops, the Lord Provost of Edinburgh, the President of the Court of Session, and the Lord Advocate. Thus, in the case of witchcraft trials, this august gathering of the great and good, to whom power was delegated by the King, in turn delegated power to groups of responsible and trustworthy people to administer justice locally.

Charles I offended many in Scotland by his attempts to make the Church of Scotland more like that of England. Those who opposed him, the "Covenanters", eventually became the ruling power in the land, and exercised control over the Privy Council and Parliament. The Committee of Estates originated as a committee for regulating parliamentary business, but from 1643 to 1651 it sat continuously when Parliament was not in session to ensure the unbroken influence of Parliament in Scotland's affairs. Since the Covenanters were above all a religious party, it is not surprising that both Parliament and Privy Council between 1638 and 1649 were very much influenced by the General Assembly of the Church of Scotland. Also, since the Covenanters were predominantly Presbyterian fundamentalists, striving to establish their own particular vision of the Godly Society, it is not surprising that at the height of their power in 1649 there was a flood of commissions granted against witches.

Parliament and the Privy Council did not exist from August 1651 until the Restoration. After the execution of Charles I in 1649 the Covenanters proclaimed his son King Charles II, thus offending the English leader Cromwell, who invaded and occupied Scotland, forcing it into union with England. Cromwell's republican "Commonwealth" government lasted until 1660 when the monarchy was restored.

The Privy Council records were published as the "Register of the Privy Council" in Edinburgh in 1877, edited by John Hill Burton Ll D, Historiographer Royal for Scotland. As in previous chapters, I have rendered the extracts in modern English. The editor of the RPC summarised many of the original records to some extent, and updated the language in places. Some entries in the published RPC are obviously a combination of summarised passages and large chunks of the originals. What is given here therefore is a modernised version of what has already been processed by the editor of the RPC. Readers unwilling to trust my interpretations should have no difficulty finding a set of the published Registers of the Privy Council to compare them with, and real enthusiasts can always consult the original documents in the National Archives of Scotland.

The records of the Committee of Estates are as yet unpublished. The original papers are designated PA11/8 and PA11/9 in the National Archives of Scotland.

The "Acts of the Parliament of Scotland" were published in Edinburgh in 12 volumes between 1814 and 1875, edited by T. Thomson and C. Innes.

Register of the Privy Council.

1609

July 18th 1609: Complaint by George Earl of Dumbar, treasurer, and Sir Thomas Hammiltoun of Bynnie, advocate for His Majesty's interest:-

On the 6th of this month Jonet Drysdaill, servant to James Newtoun in Creichtoun, known as "Sir James", appeared before the Presbytery of Dalkeith suspected of witchcraft, sorcery, and the subsequent murder of a certain Andro Mitchelsoun, the son of Jonrme Mitchelsoune of Currie. She was questioned by the Presbytery in the presence of Sir William Hairt of Prestoun, His Majesty's representitive, and the baillies of the regality of Musselburgh. By their advice it was thought expedient to commit Jonet to prison to await trial. Thus she was committed to prison in the tollbooth of Mussilburgh. The baillies of Mussilburgh were ordered to transport her to the tollbooth and keep her there until she could stand trial in Edinburgh. For that purpose she was therefore handed over to their officer James

Wilsoun, but while he was on the way with her, George Newtoun, legal messenger; the already mentioned Sir James Newtoun; his nephew Mr James Heislip in Creichton; and Mark Briswell from Creichton; took her from Wilsoun by force and carried her off to the village of Creichton where she has been detained ever since.

Not only that, but the following day George Newtoun came from Mussilburgh to Creichton on purpose to assault William Penman, the minister at Creichtoun. Finding him at his own house with the masons at work there, he addressed him in a threatening manner, declaring that the minister had accused him before the judge and Sir James Richardson the baillie, as guilty of deforcing the Mussilburgh baillies' officer, and rescuing Jonet. When the minister confirmed the truth of this Newtoun laid his hand on his sword, and said that if he got him out of his house he would knock out his brains. Hearing of this, Sir James Richardson had instructed the baillies of the burgh of Musselburgh to imprison Newtoun. However, when commanded to go into confinement Newtoun refused to do so, declaring that he would acknowledge no orders except from the Lyon Herald.

The defendants were ordered, except for Boiswell, to present Jonet Drysdaill before the Privy Council and to answer for their insolence. Both parties appeared, and the defendants promised to produce Jonet before the Council. The Lords of Council ordered the defendants to be imprisoned in the tollbooth of Mussilburgh, and Jonet in the tollbooth of Edinburgh. [RPC 1st Ser, Vol vii, P322.]

July 20th 1609: Thomas Gourlay in Dalkeith and William Clerk there stand surety for 500 merks that Jonet Drysdaill in Creichtoun will answer before the Council when required, for the charge against her of witchcraft and the murder of Andro Mitchelson in Currie. [RPC 1st Ser, Vol vii, P701.]

July 20th 1609: Complaint by Gelis Johnstoun, widow of Johnne Duncane in Mussulburgh: -Some malicious persons, her enemies, reported her to the Presbytery of Dalkeith as a person suspected of witchcraft. The Presbytery therefore summoned her before them, and have subjected her to their proceedings against her for the past seven weeks, although the truth of the matter is that the complainer is an honest woman who has lived in the town of Mussilburgh for the past thirty years with a blameless reputation. She has never been suspected or rumoured to have had anything to do with such devilish and detestable doings. She has presented herself before the Presbytery every time they have called upon her to attend their interrogations, or whatever procedures they were pleased to use against her. The crime of Witchcraft is one of the Pleas of the Crown which are to be tried by His Majesty's Chief Justice and his deputes. The Presbytery has no jurisdiction over witchcraft, and can have no warrant or authority to adjudicate in or determine such cases. Nevertheless, they continually pester the complainer with citations and summonses to appear before them, on purpose it would seem, to call her reputation into question and to foully slander her with this detestable crime, of which she is completely innocent. If they had any evidence of her guilt in this crime, they should have given the information to the lord of the regality where she lives, and before whom the complainer has found surety that she will answer the charge whenever she is called upon to do so. Ether that, or they should have given the information to His Majesty's Justice General and his deputes, agreeing to submit it as evidence for her prosecution. They should not have proceeded with her themselves in such a preposterous way, which cannot produce any sort of decision or sentence. The ministers of the Presbytery therefore ought to be forbidden to proceed in any way against the complainer in the above matter.

Mr Andro Blackhall, minister at Inveresk, Mr Patrick Turnour, minister at Borthuik, Mr William Penman, minister at Creichtoun, Nathaniel Harlaw, minister at Ormestoun. Mr Alexander Ambrois, minister at Newbottle, Mr Johnne Nymbill, minister at Cranston, Mr George Ramsay, minister at Laswaid;

all ministers of the Presbytery of Dalkeith, had been called upon to answer the complaint. Now, the pursuer being represented by her son William Duncan, and the defendants also being present, the Lords forbid these ministers to take any form of procedure against the pursuer. They remit her to be tried either by the Justice General, or by the lord of the Regality of Dunfermling. [The Earl of Dunfermline was Musselburgh's feudal superior.] This is. however, without prejudice to the right of the Presbytery to use all means for the discovery of her dealings, and to give the information to the Judge Ordinary. [RPC 1st Ser, Vol vii, P. 322]

[This case is important, because here an over-zealous presbytery is reminded by the Government that presbyteries are only allowed to question and gather information in witchcraft cases. They are not allowed to prosecute the suspect, as they seem to have had ambitions to do in this case.]

1612

October 9th 1612: Christian Grintoun living in [Domicile left blank. Larner's "Sourcebook" says Dunbar, but there is no mention of that in the RFC.]   is reported suspect of witchcraft, sorcery, and various other devilish practices. A commisson of justiciary is given to commit her to secure confinement, where she is to remain at her own expense until justice is administered. [RPC, 1st Ser, Vol ix, P. 471]

December 2nd 1612: The Lords of Council are reliably informed that Jonet Henry, wife of Robert Wood in Scaitraw; Jonet Litster, wife of Johnne Chanceter in Innerweik; Katherine Vertie, wife of George Wallace in Corhous; Agnes Smyth, widow of the late Hew Hammyltoun in Skaitraw; and [blank], wife of Alexander Burghie in Dumbar, are suspected of being guilty of the devilish crime of witchcraft, and of many other strange practices dishonourable to God and hurtful to our Sovereign Lord's good subjects. A commission is therefore granted to Sir [blank] Hammyltoun of Innerweik; Sir James Douglas of Spott, knight; [blank] Home of Pinkertoun; Jasper Home of Lawfield; and to the provost and baillies of Dunbar; or any two of them; to send for and apprehend these suspects, to imprison and question them regarding that crime, and on such suspicious circumstances and evidence as might lead to clearing up the crime. Also to confront them with others who have been arrested for the same crime. The results are to be reported to the Council. [RPC, 1st Ser, Vol ix, P. 490]

December 22nd 1612: Robert Allane, fisherman, living in Dumbar, and his wife Katherine Hammiltoun are imprisoned in the tollbooth of Dumbar, suspected of being guilty of the devilish and detestable crime of witchcraft. Clear evidence was given against them by some persons who were recently put to death in the same burgh. Commission under the Signet, signed by the Chancellor, Johnne Prestoun, R. Cockburne, and Alexander Hay, is therefore given for trial of the accused to Sir Alexander Hammiltoun of Innerweik, knight; Sir James Douglas of Spot, knight; and the provost and baillies of Dumbar. [RPC 1st Ser, Vol ix, P. 522]

1613

March 2nd 1613: Commission given to Sir George Home of Wedderburn, knight; Sir Patrick Hepburn of Waughtoun, knight; Sir Alexander Hammyltoun of Innerweik, knight; Sir William Seytoun of Kyllismure, knight; Sir

Patrick Home of Aytoun, knight; Sir James Dowglas of Spott, knight; William Arnot of Colbrandispeth; or any four of them; and the provost and baillies of Dunbar; for the trial of Jean Litster, wife of John Chancellor, gardener in Innerweik; Catherine Vertue, wife of George Wallace in Corhouse; and Euphame Young in Cockburnes Peth, suspected of witchcraft, sorcery, and other devilish practices, as stated in the report of the previous commission appointed to examine the evidence against them. [RPC 1st Ser, Vol x, P. 4]

April 7th 1613: Commission given to Sir James Home of Coldenknowis, Sir George Home of Wedderburne, Sir Patrick Home of Aytoun, Sir Patrick Hepburn of Kyllismure, Sir James Douglas of Spott, and the provost and baillies of Dunbar, or any four of them as long as two of the above-named barons are included, to apprehend and try Alesoun Denis, widow of the late William Patersone in [blank], Alesoun Angus in Dunbar, Jonet Harlaw in Innerweik village, and Jonet Henry in Scaitraw, who are suspected of witchcraft, sorcery, enchantment, and other devilish practices. [RPC 1st Ser, Vol x, P. 28]

1622

June 6th 1622: Commission under the Signet to Richard Adinstoun of that Ilk, and Robert Seaton elder in Tranent, to hold courts as judges to try Jonet Maglene, wife of William Naismith, gardener at Seaton, and Helen Mure in Tranent, who have been apprehended as suspected witches and dealers in sorcery, charms, etc. Signed: Mar, St Androis, Mortoun, Melros, Lauderdaill, and Carnegy. [RPC 1st Ser, Vol xii, P. 734]

1624

February 24th 1624: Commission to Sir Alexander Hammilton of Innerweik, knight; Sir Archibald Douglas of Quhittinghame, knight; Sir James Baillie of Lochend; Mr Patrick Hepburne of Smeytoun; George Home of Freirlandis; William Sydserff of Ruchlaw; James Hopper of Bourhouses; and the baillies of the burgh of Dunbar; or any two of them along with the baillies, to apprehend Margaret Mewros and Jonet Acheson, living in Pinkerton, who have long been suspected of witchcraft. They are to keep them in secure custody and question them regarding the statements already made by Margaret and others. They are then to report to the Council in writing. [RPC 1st Ser, Vol xii, P. 443]

March 30th 1624: Commission to Alexander Hammilton of Innerweik, knight; Sir James Baillie of Lochend; Patrick Hepburne of Smetone; George Home of Freirland; William Sydserff of Ruchlaw; James Hopper of Bourhousis; and the baillies of the burgh of Dunbar; or any two of them along with the baillies, to hold courts as judges to try Margaret Mewros and Jonnet Acheson, living in Pinkertoun, for witchcraft, which they have freely confessed after being arrested and questioned. [RPC 1st Ser, Vol xiii, P. 485]

1628

July 3rd 1628: Commission to Sir John Hamilton of Preston and Samuel Johnston of Elphinstone to hold courts as judges to try Margaret Young, Agnes Rankin, Janet Reid and her daughter Margaret Ridpeth, all in Prestonpans, who have long been suspected of witchcraft. [RPC 2nd Ser, Vol ii, P. 353]

July 15th 1628: Commission to the lairds of Preston and Elphinstone to try Bessie Riddell, Agnes Dempster, Agnes Liddell, Margaret Oliver, and Barbara Mathie, living in Prestounpannes, who have long been suspected of witchcraft, and whose statements have been shown to the Council. [RPC 2nd Ser, Vol ii, P. 379]

August 8th 1628: Commission to Sir John Hamilton of Preston and Sir Samuel Johnstoun of Elphinstone to try Janet Strauchane, wife of Walter Finlaysoun; Beatrix Cuthbertsoun; Janet Darling, wife of David Thomsoun; and Janet Boyd, all living in Prestounpannis. They were suspected of witchcraft, and on being questioned confessed to renouncing Christ and their baptism, serving the Devil, and various other points of devilry and witchcraft. [RPC 2nd Ser, Vol ii, P. 439]

September 27th 1628: Commission to Robert Seaton elder in Tranent; Archibald Turnbull, baillie there; Alexander Turnbull, baillie in Langnidre; and Archibald Wedell, baillie in Seaton; or any two of them, against Elspitt Hislop, wife of James Fairlie in Langniddrie; and Isobell Miller, wife of George Lumisden, shoemaker in Langniddrie, for witchcraft. [RPC 2nd Ser, Vol 11, P 439]

[Elspitt's daughter Helen was burnt for witchcraft in 1649. See "Burgh Records"]

November 11th 1628: Complaint by Margaret Jo in Mussilburgh: -

Eleven or twelve weeks ago she was arrested by the baillies of Mussilburgh, and imprisoned in the tollbooth, accused of being a witch. Although she insisted most earnestly that she should be put on trial, she has been refused. She is willing to find surety that she will appear before a judge for trial whenever lawfully required to do so. Orders were given to John Calderwood, William Scot, Walter Smart, and William Duncan, baillies of Mussilburgh, to attend and bring the complainer with them. The pursuer [i.e. Margaret] was represented by Alexander Walker, tailor, burgess of Edinburgh. John Calderwood and William Duncan appeared for themselves and on behalf of the rest of the baillies. The Lords order the defendants to put the pursuer on trial before a jury within fifteen days, and failing that to set her free. [RPC 2nd Ser, Vol ii, P 487]

November 11 1628: Commission of Justiciary under the Signet to George, Earl of Winton and his baillies, within whose bounds the crimes of witchcraft, sorcery, and using charms have become very frequent. The perpetrators of these crimes have become emboldened by the fact that there is no-one authorised with the power to question and expose them. Since this crime is most offensive to God, and cannot be allowed in a Christian and well-governed state, the Earl is empowered to search within his bounds for such offenders, who are his own removable tenants, to imprison and interrogate them, and to report their statements to the Council so that further proceedings can be taken. [RPC 2nd Ser, Vol ii, P482]

[This would seem to indicate that witch-hunting was not exclusively a Presbyterian obsession. The Earl of Winton, whose lands included Tranent, Seton, Cockenzie, and Longniddry, was a Catholic. Of course, the Earl may have been pressurised into seeking the commission, or thought it expedient to do so.]

November 8th 1628: [sic - actually some date between 11th and 20th Nov.] Complaint by Margaret Jo in Mussilburgh: -

On the tenth of this month it pleased their Lordships to order the baillies of Musselburgh to try her on a charge of witchcraft within fifteen days or release her. In so doing their Lordships dealt with her most fairly and justly after her her long imprisonment of twelve weeks. However, the baillies of Mussilburgh still continue in their malice against her. She is still kept fettered in irons. They refuse to allow her relatives and friends access to her, or to allow them to give her any comfort in her time of trouble. She has been informed that they intend to take her out for trial without allowing her as much as an hour's notice, and without allowing her to read her indictment so that she can prepare her defence as she is legally entitled to do. In so doing they will deprive the complainer of the usual benefit which the law of God and nature allows to persons in such cases for the defence of their lives. The baillies of Mussilburgh who intend to be her judges in this matter are the complainer's professed and avowed enemies. In a position of authority over her, or over her life, their motives would be very suspect Their judgment and experience is too limited to investigate and judge such obscure crimes, or to discuss the objections and defences which will be raised in this matter. The complainer's life is in extreme peril, and in danger of being taken from her without a lawful trial or a legal investigation beforehand.

Instructions were given to William Duncan and John Calderwood, baillies of Mussilburgh, to appear to hear themselves ordered to free Margaret from the irons and stocks in which she has been miserably detained for the past twelve weeks. Also, to address the other complaints, they are to bear witness to the appointment of Mr Laurence McGill and Mr David Prymrois to vet the judges who are to sit in judgment on the complainer, or such other advocates as the Lords of Council are pleased to appoint. The complainer was represented by Alexander Walter, tailor in Edinburgh, and the defendants were personally present. All parties were heard, and the Lords ordered the defendants to produce to them their indictment against the complainer next Thursday, the 20th of this month, so that it can be passed on to her advocate for his inspection. If any other accusations are brought up against her before the day appointed for her trial, which is to be the 25th of this month, they are to be given to her in good time for the preparation of her defence. Also, her trial is to be continued to the 26th if her advocates require it. Her friends are to have access to her in the presence of the minister and one of the baillies. Meanwhile, she is to be kept where she is till the day of her trial. [RPC 2nd Ser, Vol ii, P. 487]

[Unfortunately, the result of the trial is not known.]

December 4th 1628: Commission to Robert Seaton elder in Tranent; Archibald Turnbull, baillie there; Archibald Weddell, baillie in Seaton; or any two of them, to try Bessie Littil and Margaret Bain, both living in Langnuddre, who have long been suspected of witchcraft. [RPC 2nd Ser, Vol ii, P.51]

[Bessie was found guilty and burned. She is mentioned in the trial of Alexander Sinclair alias Hunter. See "Burgh Records".]

December 4th 1628: Commission to John Sinclair of Hirdmestoun; John Sinclair of Hirdmestoun his son; Patrick Abernethie, Baillie of Saltoun; Mr George Butler in Blance; and the provost and baillies of Haddington; against William Davidson, lately living in Saltoun, for witchcraft. [RPC 2nd Ser, Vol ii, P. 517]

[William was a notorious warlock, and was tried and burned in Haddington on 16th December. See "Burgh Records".]

December 9th 1628: Commission to George Cockburne of Ormiston to seek, search for, and apprehend Alesoun Tailyeour in Pencatland, Sara Keith in Wintoun, and the vagabond Alexander Hamilton, who are suspected and reputed to be guilty of the crime of witchcraft. Also to detain them in secure confinement until permission is given for their trial and punishment. [RPC 2nd Ser, Vol ii, P. 518]

[See "Burgh Records" for the trial of Sara Keith. See "Justiciary Court Records" for the trial of Hamilton, another notorious warlock.]

December 19th 1628: Commission to the provost and baillies of Dumbar, Douglas of Kilspindie, Mr John Hepburne of Gilmertoun, John Arnot in Colberspeath, and George Hoome of Furde, or any one of them, to search for, apprehend, and imprison Margaret Baxter from Dumbar and Marion Bathcat from Eistbarns, who have long been suspected of witchcraft. Thereafter any three of them are empowered to hold courts to try the suspects. [RPC 2nd Ser, Vol ii, P. 540]

1629

January 13th 1629: Warrant to the Bishop of Dumblane and others to examine Isobel Young, prisoner in the tollbooth of Edinburgh for witchcraft, and to report her statements to the Lords of Council. [RPC 2nd Ser, Vd iii, P 4]

[Isobel was from East Barns. See "Justiciary Court Records" for her trial.] January 20th 1629: Commission to the provost and baillies of Hadintoun, Sir Robert Hepburn of Aulderstoun, and Patrick Abernethie of Netterdene, or any two of them - of whom the provost and baillies should provide one - to to try Sara Keyth, wife of [blank] in Wyntoun, and Bessie Make in Saltoun, long suspected of witchcraft. [RPC 2nd Ser, Vol iii, P16 - See "Burgh Records" for their trial.]

March 24th 1629: Commission under the Signet to the Sheriff of Haddington and his depute, and the provost and baillies of Hadintoun, or any three of them - the Sheriff or his depute being one - to hold courts to try the vagabond Alexander Hunter who has long been suspected of witchcraft. [RPC 2nd Ser, Vol iii, P110] [See "Burgh Records" for his trial.]

June 9th 1629: Complaint by Janet Hardie, wife of Robert Clerk, skipper in Fischerraw, and Janet Barclay, widow there: -

Last March the baillies of Mussilburgh came to the complainers' house in Fischerraw, apprehended them, and put them in the tollbooth, where they are still keeping them in the stocks and in irons, alleging that they are guilty of witchcraft. They have offered themselves for trial, and to find surety to appear for trial, but the baillies have refused. William Duncan and John Calderwood were ordered to appear and produce the complainers. Janet Hardie was represented by her husband, and Jonet Barclay by Robert Clerk her son, and the defendants also appeared. The Lords remit the case to the Lord of the Regality of Dunfermline and his baillies.[RPC 2nd Ser, Vol iii, P162]

July 16th 1629: This day Alexander Hamilton was brought before the Council by the Laird of Aytoun, having been arrested in England by a warrant from His Majesty, and sent to Scotland. The Lords order Hamilton to be committed to prison in the tollbooth of Hadinton, to remain there until arrangements are made to deliver him to the provost and baillies to be dealt with as described above. A warrant for this was authorised by the Council. [RPC 2nd Ser, Vol iii, P 222]

[See "Justiciary Court Records" for Hamilton's trial.]

August 1st 1629: Commission to the Sheriff of Haddington and his deputes, the Provost of Haddington, Mr George Butler of Blance, George Hepburne of Alderstoun - the Sheriff or his depute being one - to try John Carfra in [blank], Alison Borthwick his wife, and Thomas Carfra his brother. They are accused of consulting Margaret Hamilton and Bessie Carfra, persons burnt for the crime of witchcraft, with a view to murdering the late James Hay and Marion Cranston, whose deaths immediately followed the consultation. They are also accused of other charges of witchcraft and other devilish practices. [RPC 2nd Ser, Vol iii, P. 269] [See "Burgh Records" for their trial.]

August 15th 1629: Alexander Hamilton the warlock, who is now a prisoner in the tollbooth of Edinburgh, has named as persons guilty of witchcraft [Catherine Kirktoun, Alison Carrick, Bessie Hepburne, and Margaret Mitchell in Haddington; Bessie Duncane in Walkerland; Katherine Lawder in Stobstane; Bessie Lawder in Nunland; [blank] Sinclare in Burnehead; and Margaret Alexander in Pickiltillane. They have been brought to Edinburgh and confronted with Alexander Hamilton in the presence of the provost and baillies of Edinburgh, and he upheld all his statements against them.

They now need to be questioned more closely, and so a commission is granted to the Sheriff of Haddington and his deputes, and the provost and baillies of Haddington, to find and arrest the above-named persons, and bring them to the tollbooth of Edinburgh to be again confronted with Alexander Hamilton, and to be questioned and examined by His Majesty's Advocate and Justice Depute. [RPC 2nd Ser, Vol iii, P. 261]

August 21st 1629: Commission to Sir John Hamilton of Preston, and Robert Hamilton and John Hall, baillies of Preston, to try Beigis Wallace in Preston and Margaret Matheson in Prestounpannis, long suspected of witchcraft. [RPC 2nd Ser, Vol iii, P 271]

[Beigis Wallace's daughter Jean Craig was burned in Tranent for witchcraft twenty years later in 1649.]

September 5th 1629: Commission to His Majesty's Advocate, the Justice Depute, or whichever one of them is in town, or to the provost and baillies of Edinburgh, to examine the warlock Alexander Hamilton. [RPC 2nd Ser, Vol iii, P. 290]

November 6th 1629: Commission to Sir John Hamilton of Preston, and Robert Hamilton and John Hall, baillies of Preston, for the trial for witchcraft of Marion Porteous, daughter of the late James Porteous, alias Playfair. [RPC 2nd Ser, Vol iii, P. 340]

November 12th 1629: The Lords of the Privy Council hereby give warrant and commission to the Bishop of Dumblane, His Majesty's Advocate, and the Justice Depute, or any two of them, to examine Johne Hoge and Margaret Nicolsone regarding their guilt of the crime of witchcraft, with power to confront them with others who can give best evidence, and after questioning them to commit them to prison, or otherwise to allow them to return home upon surety that they will answer before His Majesty's Council when lawfully required to do so. [RPC 2nd Ser, Vol iii, P. 345]

November 26th 1629: The Lords of the Privy Council free John Hog and Margaret Nicolsone his wife from their restraint and confinement within the burgh of Edinburgh, and grant them liberty to go home to attend to their lawful affairs, provided that they find surety to be recorded in the Books of Adjournal, that they will appear before the Justice to undergo legal proceedings for the alleged crime of witchcraft, each under the penalty of a thousand merks. [RPC 2nd Ser, Vol iii, P. 358]

[John Hog from Markle and his wife had been denounced by the warlock Alexander Hamilton. See "Justiciary Court Records" for the results of their investigation. There is no reason to think they ever had to stand trial.]

December 3rd 1629: Bessie Hepburne, Katharine Kirktoun, Aleson Carrick, and Margaret Mitchell in Hadintoun; Bessie Duncane in Walkerland; Katharine Lauder in Stobstane; Bessie Lawder in Nunland; Agnes Sinclare in Burneheid; and Margaret Alexander in Pickletillane, have been reported as being guilty of the detestable and odious crime of witchcraft by Alexander Hamiltoun the warlock, who is a prisoner in the tollbooth of Edinburgh. They have been confronted with him as a result of various statements made by him against them, which he has constantly stood by. However, it will be very expensive for the aforenamed persons to be questioned and examined in this burgh, and impossible for some of them because of their lack of means. Also, it may cause hardship for such persons as are led as witnesses against them. Therefore, so that the guilt of these people in the crime of witchcraft may be more easily and clearly brought to light, the Lords of the Privy Council hereby give and grant full power, warrant, and commission, and express instructions to the moderator and bretheren of the Presbytery of Hadintoun where these people live, to call each of these persons before them at whatever times may be convenient. They are to question them and examine them on the statements made by Alexander Hamilton against them, and also on any other points raised against them by any of His Majesty's subjects.

Authority is given to confront them with others, and to lead witnesses against them. The statements taken down against these forementioned persons are to be reported to the Lords of His Majesty's Privy Council. [RPC 2nd Ser, Vol iii, P. 361]   [There seems to be no record of this in the Presbytery minutes.]

1630

February 2nd 1630: There have been some foul and most scandalous reports spread by the warlock, the late Alexander Hamilton, against Dame Helene Arnot, Lady Manderston, that she used devilish practices against her husband... [RPC 2nd Ser, Vol iii, P. 443]

[On being questioned Hamilton withdrew his original statement, and ratified the withdrawal at the time of his execution, saying he knew nothing about the matter except what he had been told by John Neill from Tweedmouth. In "The Scottish Witch-hunt in Context" Louise Yeoman says that Lady Manderston's husband had been involved in tracking down Hamilton and Neill, and had almost certainly pressurised Hamilton into making false statements against his wife. She began divorce proceedings against him later in the year.] [Goodare ed.: Manchester 2002: p.112-3]

April 21st 1630: Commission to George Forrester of Corstorphine for the trial of Patrick Murray in Clerkington for witchcraft.   [RPC 2nd Ser, Vol iii, p. 535]

April 21st 1630: The Lords extend the commission granted to the Presbytery of Hadintoun concerning the questioning and examination of witches until the next Council day. Statements are to be sent to the Bishop of St Andrews.   [RPC 2nd Ser, Vol iii, P. 535]

May 26th 1630: John Neill, prisoner in the tollbooth of Edinburgh for witchcraft, has said certain things against [blank] Home, Lady Samwelstoun, which closely concern her reputation, especially his reference to her consultations about the death and destruction of her last husband by witchcraft. To clarify this it is necessary that she should be confronted with this John with regard to the reports made by him against her. The Lords of the Privy Council order letters to be sent to Lady Samwelstoun requiring her to appear personally before them on 10th June, so that she can be confronted with John regarding the statements he made against her. [RPC 2nd Ser, Vol iii, P. 541]

June 10th 1630: John Neill, prisoner in the tollbooth of Edinburgh for witchcraft, has made certain statements against [blank] Home, Lady Samwelstoun, for consulting about the death and destruction of her last husband by witchcraft. It is necessary for making the truth clear that she should be confronted with this John Neill. Instructions in this matter having been given to her, she appeared, and the Lords ordered her to remain within the burgh of Edinburgh until they give her permission to leave. This under the penalty of 1000 merks, for which she pledged herself.

Adam, Bishop of Dumblane; Sir Archibald Acheson, Secretary; Sir John Hamilton, Clerk Register; Sir Thomas Hope of Craighall, His Majesty's Advocate; and Sir John Scot, Director of Chancery, are appointed as commissioners to examine Lady Samwelstoun and confront her with John Neill.   [RPC 2nd Ser, Vol iii, P. 563]

June 15th 1630: Today [blank] Home, Lady Samwelstoun enacted and obliged herself under the penalty of a thousand merks, to remain within the burgh of Edinburgh, and not to leave it until given permission by the Council. [RPC 2nd Ser, Vol iii, P. 565]

[Janet Home, Lady Samuelston, was the cousin of George Home of Manderston who had pressured Alexander Hamilton into denouncing Home's wife Lady Manderston. Manderston had grave financial problems, and seems to have swindled his cousin Lady Samuelston out of a substantial amount of money. John Neill is the same John Neill from Tweedmouth who was inolved in the Alexander Hamilton case. It looks as if Manderston may have been trying to get rid of his cousin as well as his wife. She was exonerated by the investigating commission. [Goodare Ed: Manchester 2002: P. 113-4]]

July 1 st 1630: A letter is to be written to Lady Bass requiring her to deliver her servant Johnne Smith to Sir Johnne Hoome of North Berwick, to be brought in by him to His Majesty's Council to be questioned under suspicion of the crime of witchcraft. [RPC 2nd Ser, Vol iii, P. 587]

1631

September 21 st 1631: Petition by the provost and baillies of Hadintoun: -Commission had been granted to them By the Privy Council to try Cristian Paterson, wife of George Carmichael in Hirmestoun on a charge of witchcraft. On 9th August she was convicted of

1. Laying a serious illness on Jannet Forrester, the wife of George Baillie of Templefield.

2. Laying madness and frenzy on her servant Catherine Allan.

3. Cruelly murdering by witchcraft the late Elizabeth Caldcleuch, wife of Archibald Maisson in Samwelstoun, and his daughter Bessie Maisson.

4. Cruelly murdering James Knight in Hirdmistoun by witchcraft.

5. Laying a serious illness on Elizabeth Anderson by witchcraft.

6. Causing the death, decline, and decay of their livestock and goods.

7. Ruining and undoing James Wade in Saltoun by witchcraft.

The provost and baillies now wish to know what they should do next. The Lords of the Privy Council order them to pass sentence of death on Christian Paterson for the crime of witchcraft, and to see to her execution. [RPC 2nd Ser, Vol iv, P. 334]

[See "Burgh Records" for Christian's trial. The commissioners had apparently been forbidden to pass sentence until the Council had been acquainted with the result of the trial.]

1632

February 23rd 1632: James Balfore in Corsehous claims to have the skill to find out who is guilty of the crime of witchcraft, by spotting the Devil's mark on some part of their bodies, and by thrusting pins into it. On the basis of this expertise he goes around the countryside abusing simple and ignorant people for his private gain and advantage. He was ordered to appear to be questioned regarding his skills and how he acquired them. The first time was when Robert Balcanquall, the minister of Tranent, ordered him to search a gardener's wife in Tranent for the mark. He found it on her arm and she acknowledged he was right. By that, and similar marks on others, he came to know about the mark and how to find it. He has been employed to search for and find the mark, and has exposed several people publicly in the church and in the tollbooth.

The Lords decide that his knowledge is only conjectural, and has been used most unlawfully within God's church. He is not to exercise this art and trade again, otherwise he will answer for it at his peril. [RPC 2nd Ser, Vol iv, P. 487]

1649

[The Privy Council extracts for 1649 are from the "Miscellaneous Documents" in the records of the Privy Council. These are not minutes of meetings or decisions of the Council, but evidence submitted by those who have been given commissions for investigating witchcraft suspects, and who are now seeking commissions to put the suspects on trial.]

June 7th 1649: In presence of Mr Johne Makghie, minister of Dirltoun; Alexander Levingtoun of Saltcottis; James Borthwick, chamberlain; William Ferguson; George Temple; Walter Marshall; and William Daliel, notary: -

Agnes Clarkson appeared, a widow from Diriltoun, now prisoner in the Castle of Diriltoun. She confessed that about eighteen weeks ago the Piper's Mother from Longniddry who was recently burnt as a witch, came to her house in Diriltoun and stayed with her all night She got up in the middle of the night, and with fearful curses and execrations tried to persuade Agnes to become the Devil's servant. She refused to consent to it at the time, but afterwards she saw what seemed to be a black wind and mist filling the house, which made her very much afraid. In the morning as she left the house, the Piper's Mother continued trying to entice her, and when Agnes still refused she said, "I'll make you regret it!"

She also confessed that at "the dead time of the day" [late at night?] the Devil came in, in the likeness of a black dusky-coloured dog which went up and down the house and seized Agnes by her clothes. It then took the shape of a black man and had sex with her. She found his penis cold. He also spoke to her and asked her to become his servant, saying she would want for nothing. He asked her to renounce God, Christ, and her baptism. She says she did all of this, and asked us, "How shall I get mercy now?" She was asked how she renounced Christ and her baptism - whether she had expressed it in actual words. She said no, but she had done it in effect by having sex with him, and that he had not failed in his intentions. He also gave her a mark at the time, on the back of the left arm below her elbow. She also confessed that he changed her name, and called her "Nan Clark", or "Nan Clatt". He said that he would meet her again, and then left the house as he had come in.

Also, about fourteen days ago the Devil and several others with him had a meeting on the green at Diriltoun in front of James Nicolson's house in the twilight. Hearing a tremendous noise, she came out and they all danced there. The Devil appeared amongst them in the likeness of a black man with a staff in his hand, with which he knocked them on the head. She did not know any of them except Patrik Watson in West Fentoun, his wife Manie Haliburtoun, and Besse Hogge.

The rest of them all went away with him down below the wall, with black hoods, and danced with the Devil. [RPC says "black heids". The Concise Scots Dictionary suggests "heid" as an alternative spelling for "huid" - a hood. "Hoods" would seem more sensible than "heads".] Agnes came home to her house, and she thinks Patrik, Manie, and Besse went home to Fentoun.

Also, Agnes testifies that eight days ago, when the Chamberlain told her in Marion Temple's house that he would have her investigated for witchcraft, she went over to West Fentoun, met with Besse Hogge and Manie Halyburton, and told them at the end of Patrik Watson's house that the Chamberlain had threatened to investigate her. She said that as soon as she was arrested she would have Patrik, Manie, and Besse arrested as well, and when she said this they slapped their thighs and mocked her.

After this statement had been made, Patrik, Manie, and Besse were sent for and confronted with Agnes individually. She boldly upheld her statement to their faces, in the presence of the previously named persons.

Signed: J. Makghie, Minister at Dirilton.
Alexander Levingtone.

At Hadintoun June 13th 1649: The Presbytery having read and considered the statement and confession of Agnes Clarksone, finds them sufficient grounds for requesting a commission to hold a court to try her.

Signed A. Makghie, clerk. [RPC 2nd Ser, Vol viii, P.189]

June 8th 1649: At Painstone. Today Agnes Hunter in Painstone, suspected of witchcraft, was questioned by Mr Robert Ker, minister at Haddington, before Thomas Foullis, John Eastone, and John Baillie. She testified as follows: -

1. Firstly, when she was coming from Ormestone about ten years ago she saw the Devil in the likeness of a gentleman, and suspected him to be the Devil. He approached her, but did not speak or try to touch her. He went away in front of her in the likeness of a large greyhound.

2. The second time the Devil appeared to her was about five years later at the bottom of her own garden. He was in the likeness of a man in green clothes, and wanted her to become his servant. She asked what she could do for him since she wasn't able to go out of doors, and he replied, "You'll never need to come out except when Marion Richesone comes." She promised to become his servant, and at that he asked her to renounce her baptism and Jesus Christ, which she did, and for which she is now greatly grieved. She cannot at the moment remember whether he had sex with her at that time or not, but remembers clearly that he lay with her after that occasion.

3. She met with him for the third time about half a year later in her own garden. He appeared in the likeness of a black man, and asked her to meet Marioun Richesone and several others in Langnuddrie in Thomas Dicksone's house. She asked him what benefit she would get from him and he answered that she would get something when she came to the meeting with the rest. He had sex with her this time, and she found him cold - not like a man.

4. She met him for the fourth time at Langniddrie, as previously arranged. With her were Marion Richeson, Marjorie Adamsone, Margarit Russell, Margarit Richesone, Margarit Staig, and another big tall woman whom she does not know. They met in Thomas Dicksone's house, although he did not know that they were there. Food and drink had been provided for them, which they ate and drank. They had a quart of wine and stayed about an hour and a half. The Devil promised to give them their rewards at Easter.

5. The fifth time that she met him was in the same house on the Shrove Tuesday after that, in the same company previously mentioned. They had supper together and arranged another meeting at Easter, when the Devil promised he would give them their rewards. He arranged to divide their company, and said he would come to Painstone and enroll Agnes in the company which he had there in Painstone.

6. He met with her at Easter as arranged. Johnne Dicksone, Grissell Andersone, and Margaret Dicksone were with her. Just when they were gathering together Marion Richesone came and said, "God speed," and at that the Devil vanished and they all parted company. [RPC 2nd Ser, Vol viii, P 202]

June 8th 1649: At Painstone. Today Margaret Dicksone testified as follows in the presence of Mr Robert Ker, minister of Hadintone, Thomas Foullis, John Eastone, and John Baillie: -

She came into the Devil's snare because of the serious difficulties she was in over her daughter's illness. She had spent everything she had on healing and curing her, and being in great poverty, she expected her daughter who was now a little better to go out and gather in the harvest field. She refused, and so Margaret struck her and said, "Since you're such a burden to me, I wish that either God or the Devil would part me and you!" The same night, about midnight, the Devil appeared to her, came into her bed, and lay with her for a while, and asked her to become his servant. At first she was unwilling to do this, but he kept talking and persuaded her in the end. He had sex with her, and asked her to forsake God and ally herself with him. This she did, and said she would obey him and become his servant. She renounced her baptism, and he promised her that she would never want for anything. This was about five years ago. She declares that he gave her the name "Marret", and gave her a nip under the right arm, where there has been a mark ever since. He arranged to meet her half a year later at Nisbet Dein Heid, and promised her a reward of some kind.

The second time he met her was at Nisbet Dein Heid as arranged. He was in the likeness of a gentleman in green clothes. It was twelve o' clock in the middle of the day, and he had sex with her. She asked for the reward he had promised her, and he replied, "You'll get it when the rest get theirs."

The third time she met the Devil was above the bank at the road down to Nisbot ["the gait bank heid of Nisbot"]. She saw Agnes Broun lying between two "rigs" [cultivation strips]. Agnes got up and came over, and just as they were meeting the Devil appeared between them in the road. He went to Agnes and embraced her in his arms. Seeing him acting in this way towards Agnes, Margaret left them, and what else they did she does not know. Shortly after this, Margaret met the Devil at the lime kiln on the west side of the Moor Shot [*i.e. a* piece of cultivated land on or near a moor]. He wanted to have sex with her but she refused. At that he struck her and attacked her like an animal. She became very ill because of it, and never saw him again after that until she was here in Painstone, where he fell upon her in the night and forced her head down until she cried out, thinking she was going to be raped by him. [Or perhaps "smothered"; "opprest", the word in the original text, could mean either.] After this Johnne Dicksone came to her and asked her to come out. She saw the Devil together with Johnne Dicksone and John Weir, Issobell Murray, Agnes Hunter, and Grissel Andersone. They did not do much since they were hindered by Marion Richesone coming and wishing them, "God speed."

About half a year ago she was at a meeting in Gladsmoor [*i.e.* The moor of that name. There was no village of Gladsmuir in those days.]. The Devil was there with Johnne Dicksone, John Weir and his wife, and Marion Richesone, and they danced for an hour. The Devil had sex that time with Marion Richeson, but not with anyone else.

She also met with the Devil in Agnes Broun's house in Nisbet. When she was sitting with Agnes the Devil came in, and said he didn't know which of them to turn to. Agnes answered, "Whichever of us you like." At that he turned to Agnes who winked at Margaret and told her to go out. While she was going out, the Devil pulled her back again, joined Margaret and Agnes's hands together, and told them to be good servants to him, and they would not lack their wages when they liked to ask for them. This they promised to do.

Issobell Johnstone in Nisbet had a sick child and came to Margaret and asked for some south-running water to wash the child in. She told Margaret that some people had been advising her to do this, and she asked Margaret if it would do any good. Margaret told her to try it, and the next time she met the Devil she asked his advice about it. He told her to fetch the water and give it to the child's mother. He instructed her not to use the water on the child herself, but that only the mother should apply the water. All Margaret should do was fetch it. [RPC 2nd Ser, Vol viii, P.190]

June 9th 1649: At Haddington. Today, having been imprisoned after an allegation that she was a witch, Issobell Murray, wife of John Weir, meal-maker in Painstone, appeared in the presence of Mr William Trent, minister; John Cokburne, provost; and Patrick Young, baillie of the burgh of Hadingtone. She confessed that she has been a servant of the Devil since last Easter. When she was lying in bed "the Spirit" took her out of bed and she walked about in the garden. He was in the likeness of a great black dog. He nipped her on the left shoulder, which she found very painful. After this she returned home in the likeness of a cat, and resumed her own shape as soon as she returned to her own house. This first time was on a Monday. The following Tuesday she came to Johnne Hamiltone's garden in Painstone and there met with Johne Dicksone, Agnes Hunter, Grissell Andersone, Barbara Purdie, Margaret Dicksone, Helen Lausone, and Margaret Hog, about two o' clock in the morning. Marion Richesone came by and said, "God be with you." The Devil broke her arm and fled, and they had no conversation with him. Before they danced she knelt down at the top of the garden and renounced her baptism. He made her throw a stone over her shoulder, and he called her "Lisbie". He had sex with her in the likeness of a rough [*i.e.* hairy?] man, all black.

[The editor of the RPC says that the following reference to Grissell Anderson has been deleted in the original. Grissell's husband is given as "Alexander Baillie, elder in Painston". However, the comma may well be an insertion by the editor. The husband is perhaps more likely to be "Alexander Baillie elder", *i.e.* senior.]

Grissell Anderson, wife of Alexander Baillie elder in Painston, having also been accused of being a witch and imprisoned, appeared in the presence of the above-named judges... [RPC 2nd Ser, Vol viii, P. 192]

June 12th 1649: At Hadington. Today, in the presence of Mr William Trent, minister; John Aytone and Patrick Young, baillies of Hadingtone; George Cockburn, treasurer; James Borthuick and Patrick Dausone; appeared Issobell Murray, who accused Margaret Bartilman, wife of [blank] Forrester, saying that she was at two different meetings with her and her neighbours at which the Devil was present. The first meeting was at the loch called Painstone Loch. Johne Dicksone, Marione Richesone, Grissell Andersone, Margaret Hog, and Agnes Hunter from Painstone were there, and Barbara Purdie. The Devil took Margaret Bartilman aside and spoke to her. She doesn't know whether he had sex with her. This was about the first week of last Easter, and the meeting was about an hour after midnight. She declared that Grissell Andersone told her that night to meet her, saying they would get their pay at the meeting.

The second time that they met with the foresaid persons and Margaret Bartilman was within a week after last Easter. The meeting was arranged, and they called him "Sir". The meeting was at a place called Butter Dam [*Sic* RPC. - More likely "Butter Dein"] at ten o' clock at night. The Devil danced among them holding Grissell Andersone's hand. Margaret Dicksone sang that time. When he went away that time he only said, "Be with you." She didn't see him have sex with any of them.

She said that she would stand to the confession that she previously made on 9th June in the presence of the Provost and Mr George Gray, the clerk to the burgh of Hadingtone. [RPC 2nd Ser, Vol viii, P.193]

June 20th 1649: At Hadintoun. This day the above statements and confessions of Agnes Hunter, Margaret Dicksone, and Isobell Murray were found to be sufficient grounds for seeking a commission for trying and examining them according to law. [RPC 2nd Ser, Vol viii, P.193] [No time was lost. A commission was granted by Parliament next day on June 21st - see later in this chapter - and they were tried and executed along with Marion Richeson and John Dickson on 23rd June! Several others named in the confessions were also executed at the Sands in Haddington over the next few months. See "Burgh Records".]

June [blank] 1649: In the presence of Johnne [blank], baillie of Dirletoun; James Levingtoun there; John Stalker in Lairhill there; James Speir, Richard Ferguson, William Hansey, and William Daliell. Manie Halliburton appeared, a prisoner in the castle of Dirleton, suspected of the crime of witchcraft, reported as guilty by Agnes Clarkson who was recently executed for the same crime, and also by Manie's husband Patrik Watson who was also executed for it. She confessed that about eighteen years ago her daughter was ill. She first sent for Patrik Chrystisone in Aberledie to come and cure her daughter. He refused to come, so she went for him herself. However, he refused to cure her. Within [blank] days the Devil came to her house in the likeness of a man, calling himself a physician and saying that he had some good ointments and animal-fat oil ["oylespeck"] with which he would cure her daughter. She agreed to take some of his ointments, which he gave her, and she gave him two English shillings. He went away and promised to come back within eight days, which accordingly he did. Before he went away the first time, she gave him milk and bread, and when Patrik Watson came in he sent for a pint of ale. However, the second time he came he stayed all night, and early in the morning after Patrik had gone out, in came the Devil when she was still in bed, lay down with her, and had sex with her. His penis was cold. He asked her to renounce Christ and her baptism and become his servant, which he did. She says her daughter was to blame for all her woe, and wishes she had never been born.

This statement was reaffirmed in all particulars by Manie in the same place on Sunday 1st July before Alexander Levingtoun of Saltcottis; James [blank]; John Stalker; William Daliell, notary; and Mr John McGhie, minister at Dirleton.

Signed: J Makghie.

Witnesses: Alexander Levingtoun, James Borthuike, James Lauder, John Stalker, W. Daliel, Walter Marechall.

July 2nd at Hadintoun. Today, having read and considered the statements and confession of Manie Haliburton, the Presbytery finds them sufficient grounds for seeking a commission to try her and judge her according to law.

Signed: J. Stirling, clerk.

[RPC 2nd Ser, Vol viii, P194]

Undated. [But obviously around the time of the previous extracts.]: At Dirleton, in the presence of Alexander Levintone of Saltcottis; James Borthuik, chamberlain of Dirilton; John Stalker, baillie there; James Foirman in Drem; Mr James Acheson in Northberuik; and William Daliell, notary. Patrik Watson in West Fenton and Manie Hailyburton his wife, with a reputation for witchcraft, and long suspected of it, hearing that I, the undersigned John Kincaid was in the village of Dirleton, and had some skill and dexterity in searching for the Devil's mark on the bodies of persons suspected to be witches, of their own free will and under no compulsion they asked me, John Kincaid, to examine them as I did with others. When I had finished, I had found the Devil's mark on Patrik Watson, a little below his left shoulder blade, and on the left side of Meinie Halliburton's neck, a little above her left shoulder. They had no feeling in these marks, nor did any blood come from them after I had tested them in the same way as I had always done with others. This I testify to be true, on my reputation and conscience, in confirmation of which I have signed this with my hand, the foresaid day and place, before the above-named witnesses.

Signed: IK

Witnesses: Alexander Livingtone, W. Dalliel, Ja Borthuik, John Stalker, James Terman, Mr J. Acheson.

[RPC 2nd Ser, Vol viii, P.195]

[Kincaid was from Tranent. His method was to run long pins into the suspected witch-marks.

Lack of feeling and lack of blood supposedly confirmed their diabolic origin. Eventually, suspecting fraud, the Privy Council had him arrested in 1662 and made him promise not to exercise his profession again. See also "Justiciary Records"]

July 13th 1649: At Hadingtoun. Today, in the presence of Mr Ker, minister at Hadingtoun; George Patersoun, clerk of Hadingtoun; John Pow, John Dicksoun, and Richard Whyt, burgesses: Margaret Vaith [Vaitch?], a prisoner in the tollbooth of Haddington for the crime of witchcraft, declared and confessed that the first time that she met with the Devil was at the "seneins" before last Easter. [To "sain" means to bless or carry out some ritual or ceremony with the intention of blessing. What the "sainings" might be in the context of the Presbyterian church is not immediately obvious unless this was a term for the high jinks of Fastern's E'en/Shrove Tuesday.] He appeared to her in the likeness of a gentleman and wanted to have sex with her. She refused, and he said that the next time they met they would not part on such terms. The Devil arranged to meet her in fourteen days' time in the same place. Secondly, she declared and confessed that she had a second meeting with the Devil as arranged, at the same place where they had first met. This time the Devil had sex with her, and she thought his penis was cold. She renounced her baptism, went down on her knees, and became his servant.

We hereby attest this to be true, and sign as follows: G. Paterson. Ro Ker.
[RPC 2nd Ser, Vol viii, P. 198]

July 16th 1649: At Hadingtoun. Today in the presence of Mr Robert Ker and ... [Blank. Presumably damage in the original document.] ... at Haddington Margaret Vaith acknowledged her above-written statement to be true, and confessed further that she had a third meeting with the Devil at the Byrilaw, and that she saw a certain Margaret Robertsone from Hadingtoun a short distance from her, gathering sticks. The Devil approached her and stayed with her about half an hour, but she does not know what they did or said. He came back to her again, and after that he went away.

Signed: Ro. Ker , The Laird of Smaitoun, John Aiton, baillie of Hadingtoun, Patrick Young, baillie there, The Laird of Beinstoun, Patrick Hepburne of Munkrig
[RPC 2nd Ser, Vol viii, P198]

July 18th 1649: The Presbytery having read and considered the enclosed statements from Margaret Vaitch in Hadingtoune, find them sufficient grounds for seeking a commission for trying and judging her according to law.

Signed: R. Stirling, clerk. [RPC 2nd Ser, Vol viii, P.198]

[As previously mentioned, the Privy Council did not meet during the Commonwealth period when the monarchy was abolished and Oliver Cromwell ruled as Lord Protector.]

The Committee of Estates.

For much of 1649 the Committee of Estates was effectively running the country, and in that year it granted a substantial number of commissions for witchcraft trials. The Registers and Minutes of the Committee of Estates are designated PA 11/8 and PA11/9 in the National Archives of Scotland.

1649

April 20th 1649: The Committee of Estates gives power and commission to His Majesty's Justice Depute to go to Tranent to examine and try Jeane Craig there, against whom several allegations of the crime of witchcraft have been given in; also to administer and do justice upon her according to the laws of the kingdom and the usual practice in such cases. [PA11/8, p. 49]

[See "Justiciary Court Records" for the well-documented case of Jean Craig.]

May 22nd 1649: [Marginal note - "Commission for burning Agnes Affleck and others"] A Commission given to Mr James Ramsay, baron baillie of Tranent; the Laird of Elphingston; John Seaton of St Germains; Robert Seaton of Fentountoure; Thomas Turner of Skaitbush; John Adniston of that Ilk; or any three of them, Mr James Ramsay being one: to try and burn Agnes Affleck, Catherine Craig, Margaret Strachan, and Margaret Gibsone, all in Tranent ,and Margaret Allane in Longniddry. They have confessed several points of witchcraft which have been attested by the hands of the minister and several elders of Tranent, and studied anew by the Presbytery which found them sufficient for seeking a commission [illegible] in the usual way. [PA11/8, p.90]

[The original text says "revised" by the Presbytery, but the sense in the 17th century was almost certainly "looked at again" rather than the modern meaning of "revised", which implies making changes. A "Commission for Burning" certainly does not sound as if the defendants had much chance of being found not guilty!]

August 16th 1649: [Marginal note, "Commission for burning Patrik Andersone and Margaret Pringle."] Patrik Andersone and Margaret Pringle in Paiston have confessed several points of the abominable crime of witchcraft, and the statements have been attested by the minister and several elders within the parish of [blank], studied anew by the Presbytery and found by them sufficient for seeking a commission to put these prisoners on trial according to law, and shown to the Committee of Estates. Therefore it is necessary for justice to be administered on these persons in accordance with the laws of the kingdom. The Committee of Estates therefore authorises James Skirving of Plewlandhill, Alexander Borthwick of Johnstonburn, Richard Skirving in Over Keith, John Carins in Ormestoun, Robert Cairnes younger in Pencaitland, and John Blair in Paiston, or any three of them, with full power and commission to meet at [blank] on the [blank] day of [blank], or any other day or days they shall appoint. They are empowered to call before them Patrik Andersone and Margarit Pringle, cause them to be accused of witchcraft, have indictments given in for it against them, and put them on trial before a jury. If they are found guilty and culpable of the crime of witchcraft they are empowered to convict and condemn them, pronounce the sentence of death against them, cause them to be strangled and their bodies thereafter burnt to death [sic]. To this effect power is given to the commissioners or their quorum to hold one or more courts of justice and continue them as long as need be; to appoint clerks, procurator fiscals, officers, dempsters, and whichever other members of court are required, for all of whom the commissioners will be answerable; also to administer oaths, and to summon and instruct a sufficient number of jurors of least suspect reputation to sit on Patrik and Margaret's jury, each under the penalty of forty pounds Scots for non-appearance. Generally speaking, they are firmly and stably to do all and sundry things which might be lawfully done, or have been done in the past, by any other judge or judges delegated in similar cases. [PA11/8 p.114]

August 16th 1649: Commission for burning Janet Cairnecroce and others. Commission is given to James Skirving of Plewlandhill, Patrik Abernethie of Neitherdein, Alexander Borthwick in Johnstonburne, Richard Skirving in Nether Keith, William Skirving in Ewingstoun, John Blair in Paistoun, and James Borthwick in Whytburgh, or any three of them, to administer justice upon Janet Carnecroce in Lystoun, Janet Patersoun, Bessie Johnston, Andrew Johnston, Margaret Murray, and Marioun Laurie, all in the parish of Humbie. They have confessed several points of witchcraft. These have been sufficiently studied anew by the Presbytery, who found them sufficient for putting these persons on trial according to law. This commission is given in the usual form, with the same provisions as the preceding commission. [PA11/8 P. 115]

[August/early September] 1649: Commission against James Dalgliesh and others. Commission is given to Robert Sinclare, brother of the Laird of Hermiestoun; Patrick Abernethie [blank]; John Pringle in Milnetoun and James Allan there; or to any three of them; to administer justice according to the laws of the kingdom upon James Dalgliesh, Geilles Wood, Rachael Horseburgh, and Marion Broun in Wester Pencaitland; Elizabeth Wilsone in [blank], and Marion Broune in Woodhall; all in the parish of Pencaitland, and all confessing witches. Their statements have been studied by the Presbytery of Hadingtoun etc. Commission passed in the usual form.[PA11/8 P. 134]

September 7th 1649: At Edinburgh. Commission for administering justice on Isobel Keith and others. Commission given to James Skirving of Plewlandhill, Alexander Borthwick in Johnstouneburne, Richard Skirving in Over Keith, John Blair in Paistoun, Robert Cairns jr in Pencaitland, William Skirving in Ewingstoun, James Borthwick in Whyteburgh, and James Johnstoun in West Byres, or any three of them, to administer justice according to the laws of this kingdom on Isobell Keith in Keithmarshall, John Forrester in Laistoun, Elspet Douglas, wife of Thomas Hunter[?], and Rachael Forrester in [blank], who are confessing witches. Their statements have been studied by the Presbytery of Haddingtoun and found sufficient for putting these persons on trial before a jury. The commission passed in the usual form and signed. [PA11/8 P.143]

September 7th 1649: Commission for administering justice on Janet Nicolsone. Commission given to Mr John Hepburne of Smetoun, James Hepburne of Beinstoun, William Whyte of Markill, James Millar of Gourlabank, John Butler in Benstoun Milne, and George Johnstoun in Morhame, or any three of them, to administer justice according to the laws of this kingdom on Janet Nicolson in Nether Hailes, a confessing witch. Her statement is attested by the minister of Preston and several others in that parish, and studied anew by the Presbytery of Haddingtoun who found it sufficient for putting her on trial before a jury. Signed etc. PA 11/8 P. 143]

September 14th 1649: Commission against Jonet Speid. Another commission to Robert Calderwood, James Brown, and Robert Strachan, baillies of Mussilburgh; and William Scot, a former baillie there; or to any three of them; to administer justice on Jonet Speid in the parish of [blank] within the Presbytery of Dalkeith. Her deposition has been studied by that presbytery, and the commission is passed in the usual form.[PA11/8 P. 163]

September 27th 1649: Commission Given to Robert Sinclair, brother of the Laird of Hermeston; Patrick Abernethie of Ettirdaill; John Pringle of Saltwell[?]; James Allan in Wintoun; and Robert Games sr, "portioner" [i.e. joint owner of land] of Pencaitland; or any three of them; to administer justice according to the laws of the kingdom upon Agnes Johnstoun, Janet Cockburne, Marjorie Hog, Margaret Temple, Margaret Hamilton, Christian Forrest, Agnes Cairnes, and Agnes Gourlay, all in the parish of Pencaitland, who have confessed several points of witchcraft attested by the minister and several elders of that parish, and studied anew by the Presbytery of Haddington. The commission is passed in the usual form, and signed in the usual way. [PA11/8 P. 169]

October 24th 1649: Commission against Margaret Barbour and others, which was omitted on 11th October. Margaret Barber, widow in Woolmet; and Jonet Thomsone, wife of William Ratchiman[?] in Edmistoun, have confessed and acknowledged several points of the fearful and abominable crime of witchcraft. Their statements have been attested under the hand of the minister and several of the elders where they live, and studied anew by the Presbytery of Dalkeith on 11th October. The committee of Estates therefore hereby authorise with full power and commission Robert [blank], now elder in Inveresk; Thomas Forman there; Thomas Smith there; William Scot in Mussilburgh, and William Duncane there; or any three of them to meet and convene in the usual way.

[PA11/8 P. 179]

[These women are not of course from East Lothian, but they are included because they are to be tried by a commission of worthies from Musselburgh.]

October 24th 1649: Commission against Agnes Gray, wife of Robert Cockburne in Ormestoun; Janet Sympson, servant to Jonet Hunter there; Marioun Halyburton; Jonet Paton, wife of Andrew Thomson in Paiston; Margaret Oliver there; and John Steil. They have confessed witchcraft. Their statements were attested by the minister and some of the eiders of the parish where they live, and studied anew by the Presbytery of Dalkeith. Commission given to James Skirvin of Plewlandhill; Alexander Borthwick in Johnstoun Burn; Ritchard Skirvine in Overketh; Robert Cairns jr in Pencaitland; Johne Cairnes in Ormestoun ;John Blair in Paistoun; James Johnstoun in Westbyres; or any three of them. This commission passed in the usual form, and signed as before. [PA11/8, P. 179]

October 26th 1649: Commission to Patrick Inglis of Elvingstoun; Sir John Sinclair of Harmistoun; John Hepburne of Allerstoun; John Cockburne, Provost of Haddingtoun; and John Sleich, baillie of Haddington; or any three of them to be a quorum; for administering justice upon Marion Dobie, midwife and confessing witch. Her statement was attested under the hand of the minister of Hadintoun, and studied anew by the Presbytery. With the same clause as in the previous commission. *[sic]*. They are to report back between now and the tenth of December. [PA11/8, p.181]

November 9th 1649: Commission to Mr James Sydserff of Ruchlaw, Mr Alexander Hay of Baro, James Millar of Gourlabank, George Wood in Newmilne, John Johnstoun in Papill, and Patrick Whytlaw of that ilk, or any three of them, to administer justice upon Marion Honeyman, Beatris Dolsoun[?], and Elspit Skuggall in the parish of Whittinghame, confessing witches. Their statements have been studied anew by the Presbytery of Dumbar. The commission is passed in the usual way, with a clause appended providing for investigation of the goods and possessions belonging to Beatris Dolsoun and Elspet Skouggall ,and the reporting of the result to the Exchequer by the tenth of December. [PA11/8, P. 189]

November 20th 1649: Commission against Agnes Anderson, wife of John Adie in Wolmet, a confessing witch, to Robert Vernor sr, portioner of Inveresk; Thomas Forman there; Thomas Smith there; and William Scot, Robert Strachan, and James Brown, baillies of Mussleburgh; or a quorum of any three of them. The statements have been attested by the minister and others in the parish of Newton, and studied anew by the Presbytery of Dalkeith. A clause added to report to the Exchequer between now and 20th December. [PA11/8, p.196]

[Again, these are not East Lothian witches, but they are to be tried in Musselburgh. They may well have already been imprisoned in the tollbooth there.]

December 4th 1649: At Edinburgh. Commission against Janet Baird and Margaret Fothringhame. Commission administering justice upon Jonet Baird and Margaret ffothringhame in Keith Marshall, confessing witches. Their statements have been attested under the hand of the minister and some of the elders of that parish, and studied anew by the Presbytery of Hadington. Commission given to Patrick Abernethie of Netherton, James Skirving of Plewlandhill, Alexander Borthwick in Johnstoun Burne, Ritchard Skirving in Nerkeith, William Skirveing in Elphingstoun, Jhone Blair in Paystoun, and James Borthwick in Whitburgh, or any three of them, with a clause to report to the Exchequer between now and 20thDecember. Signed as previously with the L Borthwick. [*i.e.* Signatories include Laird Borthwick? Or perhaps signed in his presence?] [PA11/9, p.5]

December 6th 1649: Commission for administering justice upon Catherine Veitch. Commission to Patrick Abernethie of Netherdeane, James Skirving of Plewlandhill, Alexander Borthwick in Johnstonburn, Richard Skirving in Overkeith, William Skirving in Ewingston, John Blaie in Paiston, and James Borthwick in Whyteburgh, or any three of them, to administer justice according to the laws of the kingdom upon Catherine Veitch in Keith Marshall, a confessing witch. Attested by the minister and some of the people of Keithmarshall, and studied anew by the Presbytery of Haddington, with a clause for the taking [illegible] all of her goods and reporting to the Exchequer between now and the 25th of this month.

Subscribed as the previous commission except Sir James Stewart. The commission in the same form as the preceding.[PA11/9, p. 5]

Acts of the Parliament of Scotland.

As previously mentioned, commissions were also granted by Parliament. This was particularly common in 1649, perhaps because the Privy Council was being swamped with applications during the witchcraft panic of that year. The Scottish parliament was abolished by Cromwell and did not meet again until after the restoration of the monarchy in 1660. The restored parliament also granted a handful of commissions in 1661. The "Acts of the Parliament of Scotland" were published in Edinburgh in twelve volumes between 1814 and 1875, edited by T. Thomson and C. Innes.

June 21st 1649: Commission for burning Agnes Hunter and others. The Estates of Parliament now convened has considered the statements of Agnes Hunter, Margaret Dickson, and Issobell Murray from Painstone, taken by the ministers and magistrates of Haddington and several of the elders there. In these statements they confess and acknowledge several items of the crime of witchcraft. The Presbytery of Haddinton has perused the statements and found them sufficient for seeking a commission according to law. Since the Estates of Parliament desire to clear the land of wickedness, and desire those who are guilty of the crime of witchcraft to suffer the death their faults deserve, the Estates of Parliament therefore hereby give full power warrant and commission to the Laird of Lamington; Patrick Inglis of Elvingston; John Cockburne, Provost of Hadington; John Aitun and Patrick Young, baillies of Hadington; to the effect underwritten, hereby authorising them, or a quorum of any two or three of them, to sit at [blank] on the [blank] day of [blank], or any other day they decide upon; to call before them Agnes Hunter, Margaret Dickson, and Issobell Murray for the crime of witchcraft; to cause them to be accused of it, and to have indictments given in against them; to swear in, question and receive witnesses; to lead and make use of all kinds of relevant evidence; and to put these persons on trial before a jury. If they are found guilty of the crime of witchcraft the commissioners are empowered to convict and condemn them, pronounce sentence of death against them, and to have them strangled and their bodies burned to death. To that effect they are to hold courts of justice, one or more, and continue them as long as need be. They are to create clerks, procurator fiscals, serjeants, dempsters, and other necessary members of court. They are to be answerable for them, and take their oaths to perform their duties faithfully. They are to summon a sufficient number of persons of least suspect reputation to sit upon the jury, each under the penalty of a hundred merks Scots for non-attendance. They are also, generally speaking, to do anything else deemed appropriate for the arrangements, that other delegated judges have done, may do, or might have done at any time in the past in similar cases. [APS, Vol 6 part 2, Appendix "Parliamentary Proceedings", p. 732-3]

[See earlier in this chapter for the suspects' confessions in the records of the Privy Council. The three suspects along with two others were tried and executed in Haddington only two days later on June 23rd. See "Burgh Records"]

June 21st 1649: This day commission was granted by Parliament to certain persons for doing justice upon three witches whose statements, signed by some of the Presbytery of Hadingtoun, were read in the hearing of Parliament and found to be grounds for granting a commission. [APS, Vol 6 part 2, p. 240] [This is the record of the "Act" passed as a result of the decision recorded in the previous extract.]

July 5th 1649: This day the Estates of Parliament grants commission to certain persons for administering justice upon some persons guilty of the crime of witchcraft in Aberdour, Inverkeithing, Haymouth, and Dirltoun.

[APS, Vol 6 part 2, p. 463]

July 19th 1649: This day the Estates of Parliament find unanimously that the sin of witchcraft is daily increasing in this land. Therefore they have given and granted full power and commission for trying and executing certain persons guilty of the crime of witchcraft according to their statements signed by the ministers and elders in the parishes of Northberwick, Borroustounes, Quenisferie, and Haddington. [APS, Vol 6 part 2, p. 490]

July 26th 1649: This day the Estates of Parliament grant commission for the execution of certain persons guilty of the crime of witchcraft according to the statements signed by the ministers and elders in the parishes of Humbie and Keith Marschell.

[APS Vol 6 part 2, p. 463]

July 30th 1649: This day the Estates of Parliament grant commission for the execution of certain persons guilty of the crime of witchcraft according to their statements signed by the minister and elders of Tranent.

[APS Vol 6 part 2, p. 506]

August 2nd 1649: This day the Estates of Parliament grant commission for the execution of certain persons guilty of the crime of witchcraft in the parishes of Haddington and Dirltoun according to their statements signed by the ministers and elders of these parishes. [APS, Vol 6 part 2, p. 518]

August 7th 1649: The Committee of War of the various districts is to investigate whether any torture has been used against any person suspected or guilty of the crime of witchcraft, and to report back to Parliament or the Committee of Estates before they are executed. [APS, Vol 6 part 2, p. 538]

[Parliament is unlikely to have issued this instruction unless it suspected that torture was taking place at least to some extent. It also suggests an uneasiness with the numbers of confessions leading inevitably to trial and immediate execution.]

August 7th 1649: This day the Estates of Parliament grant commission for trying and executing certain persons guilty of the crime of witchcraft according to their statements signed by the ministers and elders of the parishes of Aberdour, Innerkeithing, and Ormestoun. [APS, Vol 6 part 2, p. 538]

[As previously stated, Parliament was abolished by Cromwell and did not meet again until 1660. On 3rd April 1660 Parliament considered a petition from the Earl of Haddington seeking a commission to deal with confessing witches and other suspects living in Samuelston, part of his property. A section of this petition saying that witchcraft had greatly increased because "the laws are now silent on the subject" has been much quoted as evidence that witches had been tolerated during the English occupation, and that by extension, English attitudes to witchcraft were therefore more enlightened. In fact witches continued to be tried and executed in Scotland under the Commonwealth - see "Justiciary Court Records" - although admittedly not at the exceptional rate of the "panic" of 1649. However, judging by the surge in witchcraft trials in 1661 there seems to have been a genuine feeling that the Justices of the Peace appointed by the "Usurpers" had not been rigorous enough in these matters.]

April 3rd 1661: To His Grace the right honourable His Majesty's Commissioner, and the Lords and others of the Parliament appointed for the Articles. The humble petition of John Earl of Hadintoun:-

After several "malefices" were committed on and around my lands of Samuelstoune, several persons suspected of the abominable sin of witchcraft were apprehended and searched. Witch marks were found on them in the usual way, and several of them have made confessions, named various others in the district, and acknowledged making a pact with the Devil. Their names are Elspeth Tailyeour in Samuelstoune, Margaret Bartilman, Marioun Quheit, and Jonet Carfrae - they have already confessed. The others they have named as participants with them in the same crime are Christiane Deanes and Agnes Williamson. They have been named by the others, the marks have been found on them, and they have also been apprehended. Others who have also been named are Helene Deanes, George Milnetowne, Patrik Cathie, Anna Pilmure, Elizabeth Sinclair, Margaret Baptie, Jonet Maissone, Margaret Argyill, and Elspeth Crawford. They have been named in previous confessions, but have not yet been apprehended and searched.

It is true to say that because of the frequency of this sin in the area, all my tenants there threaten to leave my ground unless justice is done on these persons. Because the laws are now silent, this sin daily becomes more frequent.

Two others have also been arrested for theft in the district, and I have kept them in prison in the tollbooth of Hadingtoun at my own expense for the past ten weeks. Another two have been arrested for a robbery they committed within my bounds on the lands of Byres twenty weeks ago, and are in the tollbooth of Edinburgh at my expense.

May it please your Lordships to give commission to Alexander Cockburne in Lethame; James Cockburne in Clerkingtoun; Mr John Butler of Kirkland; Thomas Halyburton of Inchcairne, the Provost of Hadingtoun; and Patrik Young, baillie of Hadingtoun; or any three of them; or any others your honours think suitable; to put the foresaid witches thieves and robbers on trial for execution, with the lawful evidence to be used against them according to the laws of the land, so that my ground and the countryside may be freed from these abominable sins. Alternatively, Your Lordships might order that they should be brought to Edinburgh to be tried there as Your Lordships might appoint, so that I may be freed from the trouble and expense they are causing. I humbly crave Your Lordships' answer.

Edinburgh 3rd April 1661: The Lord Commissioner and the Lords of the Articles, having heard the petition, answer as follows: -

It is their opinion that the Estates of Parliament grant commission to Sir John Sinclare of Harmestoun; Mr Alexander Hay of

Baro; James Cockburne in Clerkingtoun; Mr John Butler of Kirkland; Thomas Haliburton of Inchcairn; [blank] Seatain, Provost of Hadingtoun; and Patrick Young, baillie there; or any five of them; for trying sentencing and putting to death such persons as they shall find guilty of witchcraft by confession. Also for investigating the rest and reporting to Parliament or the Privy Council.

Signed: Glencairne. [APS Vol 7, Appendix, P. 31]

May 3rd 1661: Heleen Gibesone and Christian Blaikie have confessed the abominable crime of witchcraft in entering into a pact with the Devil, renouncing their baptism, and many other ways, as shown in their statements signed under the hands of Mr Patrick Cook, minister; William Robertoun, baillie; Johne Hamiltoune, baillie; and Johne Clerk, Robert Drumond, and Hector Wood, elders of the parish of Salt Preston. It is necessary that the kingdom should be purged of such vile sin, and justice administered upon the offenders. Therefore the King's Majesty with the advice and consent of the Estates of Parliament gives full power and commission to Robert Cockburne of Butterdeane; John Hamilton of ffalsyde; John McMorran in Prestoun; George Hepburn of Adiestoun; Niniane Hendersone and Ninian Rid in Prestoun; William Robertsoun and Johne Hamiltoun, baillies there; Mr Andrew Rutherford, schoolmaster in the Pans; Mr James Oswald there; Thomas Home and Alexander Hendersone, baillies there; or any five of them; to meet at such times and places as they should think fit, fix and hold courts there, call cases, fine absentees, and uplift fines and financial penalties. They are empowered to create clerks, servants, dempsters, and all necessary officers and members of court, and put them on trial before a jury. If they are found guilty the commissioners are to cause justice to be administered and executed upon them. They are also to do all other things with regard to carrying out this commission according to the laws and customs of the kingdom.

Since Margaret Butler, Margaret Auchinmoutie, and Margaret Hall are suspected and reported as guilty of witchcraft, power is given to these commissioners or their quorum to secure them and such others as have been or may be reported as guilty, and to question them and use all fair means to investigate them and bring them to a confession of their sins. They are to report back as soon as possible concerning their proceedings and investigations to Parliament, or to His Majesty in the case of their not sitting.

[APS Vol 7, p. 192]

May 3rd 1661: Commission is similarly given to Patrick Broun of Colstoun; Mr Alexander Hay of Baro; Mr Johne Butler of Kirkland; Mr Johne Dougall of Nunland; Mr Richard Cairns of Pilmore; Patrick Young and Alexander Swintoun, former baillies of Haddington; David Kyle, baillie there; or any five of them; against Jonet Maisson and Margaret Barclay whose statements have been attested by Mr Robert Ker, minister at Hadingtoun. Also, for securing and investigating Elizabeth Crafford, Agnes Cuthbertsone, Jonet Home, Cristine Waderstoun, Jonet Wilsone, Catherine Coupland, and Issobell Ker.

[APS Vol 7, p. 192]

May 3rd 1661: Commission similarly given against Robert Crafford in ffisherraw, Helen Cass there, and Bessie Doughty there, to Sir William Murray of Newtoun; Sir James Richardson of Smeitoun; Robert Dobie of Staniehill; Mr John Prestoun; Major John Bigar; William Rig of Carberrie; John Jossie of Westpans; Thomas Smyth, Robert Ramage, and the baillies of Mussillburgh; or any five of them, with the baillies making up two of their number. The statements are attested by Mr Oliver Colt, minister, and Robert Strachan and Robert Douglas, baillies of Mussilburgh.

[APS Vol 7 p. 197]

May 9th 1661: Commission to George Seaton of Barnes; Patrick Broun of Colstoun younger; ffrancis Hepburne of Beinston; Mr George Butler of Kirkland; Mr Johne Dougal of Nunland; Thomas Halyburtoun of Egliscarno; Mr Ritchard Cairnes of Pilmore; Patrick Young, baillie in Haddingtoun; Alexander Borthwick in Johnstounburne; Archibald Eliot in Drem; or any five of them; for judging Nicoll and Issobell Steille, Elspeth Baillie, Issobell Ritchardsone, Elspeth Lasone, and Issobell Cairnes, reported as guilty of the abominable sin of witchcraft, and apprehended.

This commission is the same as the one recorded on the third of this month. [APS Vol 7, p. 199]

May 22nd 1661: Commission for judging Bessie ffouler, widow in ffisherraw; Agnes Patersone; Kathrine Cruikshank, wife of [blank]; and Jonet Douglas, wife of Thomas Patersone. They have been reported as guilty of witchcraft as shown intheir statements signed under the hands of Mr Oliver Colt, minister, and Robert Strachan and Robert Douglas, baillies of Mussilburgh. To Sir William Murray of Newtoun, Sir James Ritchardsone of Smeitoun, Robert Dobie of Stainehill, Mr Johne Prestoun, Major Johne Bigger, Wiliam Rig of Carberrie, Johne Jossie of Westpans, Thoman Smyth, Robert Ramage, and the Baillies of Mussillburgh; or any five of them, the baillies being two etc. The form of the commission is registered on 3rd May. [APS Vol 7, p. 233]

May 22nd 1661: Similar commission against Jonet Gray, wife of Johne Glorrat[?], and Agnes Aird, wife of David Bald in Prestoun. Their confessions are signed under the hands of the commissioners appointed by Parliament for arresting those accused in the parish of Salt Preston etc. To Robert Cockburne of Butterdeane; Johne Hamiltoun of ffawside; Johne McMorrane in Prestoun; George Hepburne of Adistoun; Ninian Hendersone in Prestoun; Ninian Red there; William Robertsone, baillie in Saltprestoun; John Hamilton, baillie in Prestoun; Mr Andrew Rutherfoord, schoolmaster in the Pans; Thomas Home and Alexander Hendersone, baillies there; James Jollie there; or any five of them etc. [APS Vol 7, p. 233]

May 28th 1661: Commission for judging Elizabeth Crafford, widow in Samuelstoun; Katherine Coupland, wife of Thomas Johnstoun; Christine Watherstoun, wife of James Home in Samuelstoun; Jonnet Wilsone, wife of James Bichel in Templefield; and Margaret Bannatyne in Samuelstoun, all reported as guilty of the abominable crime of witchcraft. Their statements signed under the hands of Mr Robert Ker, Mr Johne Butler, Mr Patrick Skougall, and Mr Richard Cairns, ministers. To Dr George Hepburne; Mr Alexander Hay of Baro; Mr Johne Dougall of Nunland; Mr Johne Butler of Kirkland; Mr Richard Cairnes of Pilmoir, Thomas Haliburton of Inchcarny; Alexander Halyburtoun of Johnstounburne; Patrick Young and Alexander Swintoun, former baillies of Haddingtoun; or a quorum of any three of them. [APS Vol 7, p. 234]

June 7th 1661: Commission to Sir Robert Hepburne of Keith Marshall, Patrick Broun younger of Colstoun, Alexander Cockburne in Letham, Mr Alexander Hay of Baro, Thomas Halyburton of Egliscarno, Mr John Butler of Kirkland, Doctor [blank] Hepburne of Monkrig, or any four of them, for trying and judging Anna Kemp in Beltoun [*sic* for Bolton], Issobel Smith there, Margaret Ker there, and Issobell Smyth in Pilmore, who have been reported as guilty of the abominable crime of witchcraft.

[APS Vol 7, p. 247]

June 7th 1661: Commission to George Levingstoun of Saltcoats; William ffergusone, baillie of Dirletoun; [blank] Couper of ffentounbarnes; and Adam Maxwell of Hiefield; for trying and judging Bessie Knox in

Westfenton and Issobell Johnston in Gullane, reported as guilty of the abominable crime of witchcraft. The commission requires a quorum of any three of the aforemamed commissioners. [APS Vol 7, p. 274]

June 7th 1661: Commission to Mr John Dougall of Nunland; Mr John Butler of Kirkland; Mr Ritchard Cairnes of Pilmore; Patrick Hepburne, former baillie of Haddington; Francis Hepburn of Beinstoun; Thomas Halyburton of Egliscarne; and Alexander Borthwick of [blank]; for judging Jonnet Wast, Issobell Cathie, Issobell Thomson, Cristine Blak, Jonnet Kemp, and James Welsh, all in Samuelstone, and Barbara Scott in Rottenraw, who have been reported as guilty of witchcraft etc. Any three of the commissioners make a quorum.

[APS Vol 7, p. 248]

[James Welsh was eventually dismissed as a time-waster. See "Justiciary Court Records".]

June 13th 1661: Commission to George Home of ffuird; Patrick Hepburne of Smeitoun; ffrancis Hepburne of Beinstoun; ffrancis Kinloch of Gilmertoun; James Miller of Gourlaybank; Patrick Butler of Harpardane; David Congiltoun in Overhaills; Alexander Wood in Stentoun; or any three of them; for judging Jonet Hog, who is guilty of the abominable crime of witchcraft. Her statements have been attested under the hands of the minister and elders of the kirk session of Prestonhaugh etc. The foresaid commissioners are empowered to secure any other accused persons. [APS Vol 7, P. 269]

June 13th 1661: Commission to Mr Alexander Hay of Baro; Thomas Halyburton of Eliscamie; Doctor Hepburne of Nunrig; Mr Johne Butler of Kirkland; Mr Johne Dougall of Nunland; James Hay in Cairnehaugh; Patrick Young and [blank] Swintoun, baillies of Haddingtoun; or any three of them; for judging Marion Ingrahame living in Newtoun, Euphame Bartieman in Woodfoote of Newhall, and Cristine Umpherstoun, who are guilty of the abominable crime of witchcraft. Their statements have been attested under the hands of the minister and kirk session of Bathans etc. They are empowered to secure Margaret Allane, wife of Thomas Corser, who is reported as suspect, and also any others etc. [APS Vol 7, p. 288]

Privy Council.

Parliament seems to have issued no further commissions for the trial of witches in East Lothian after 17th June 1661. Thereafter, the practice of issuing witchcraft commissions was taken up again by the newly restored Privy Council. Also, documents relating to several of those named in commissions issued by Parliament can be found among the "Miscellaneous Papers" in the Register of the Privy Council.

May 28th 1661: The confession and statement of Bessie Todrig taken down verbatim before several witnesses, and without searching her.

Bessie Todrig declared that about last Martinmas, when she was in her own house, the Devil came to her like a man in brown clothes. His cloak was a different colour from his clothes. He stood up beside the end of her bed and laid his hand on her shoulder. Then he laid it on her head, struck down on her shoulder again, and said she was his own. He asked her to become his servant and she said yes. He asked her to renounce her baptism, which she did, and gave herself soul and body to him. She laid one hand on her head and the other on her feet, and gave soul and body to him. He told her to be a good servant to him and come when she was called.

She said she was at a meeting on Sammelstoun Haugh, and was summoned by what seemed to be a sound or a cry. This was on the 24th of April last, the same day that three or four witches were burnt. It was the second time she had been at a meeting. She saw Elspeth Baillie, Elizabeth Lawson, And Issobell Richardson there. She confesses she has been at several meetings since then.

This was taken from her own mouth without any violence or compulsion being used against her, before these witnesses: Andro Yull in Braidwoodsyd; George Patrick and John Baylies in Boltoun [*sic* for George, Patrick, and John Baigbies - *i.e.* George Baigbie, Patrick Baigbie, and John Baigbie]. [RPC 3rd Ser, Vol 1, p. 647]

May 29th 1661: Bessie Dawsone's confession, taken from her own mouth. Bessie Dawson declared that a year ago, when she was going to Hadingtoun, Bessie Todrig asked her to take a dozen eggs with her and bring her back twelve pence worth of tobacco.

She did this, and got two herring from her. She left them with the things she had brought from Haddingtoun, went to the mill, and got a handful of meal from Kirkland's servant. At night, when she was lying in her bed, she was stung by a cleg on the shoulder. A day or two after that she went to Kirkland and Elizabeth Lawson gave her a handful of meal. After that she couldn't see or hear very well for a long time, until in harvest she went to Kirkland Burne to gather barley. Elizabeth Lawson was there, and the Devil appeared like a man in black-coloured clothes. She gave herself to him and consented to be his servant. She renounced God and her baptism, and gave herself to him laying one hand on her head and the other on her feet, and then he called her Katharein. [Bessie appears to be suggesting that the misfortune with the cleg and her eye and ear troubles were the result of accepting food from Bessie Todrig and Elizabeth Lawson.]

She was at a meeting beside Pilmore with the Devil, Elizabeth Lawson, Issobell Smyth in Pilmore, Margaret Bower, Katharein Cowpland, Margaret Bannyntyne, and a big woman with a red coat [or perhaps petticoat] and a green apron. After that Elizabeth asked her to come to her house to get a pound of "tow" [flax or hemp fibre for spinning], and a peck of barley. She saw Issobell Smyth there, and got the tow. However, then she was asked to come back again before the men working in the barn finished, which she did, and Elizabeth and Issobell were together.

Since then, she was at a meeting at the Back Burne beside the calf enclosure. Elizabeth Lawson was there, and Issobell Smyth, Christian Umpherstoun the wife of Gilbert Lamb the tailor, Margaret Ker, Anna Kempe, and Issobell Smyth. They went to Bagbie Mure where there were a lot of people. There was a small white [pale ?] woman among them whom she did not know. They went towards the West Field. She was summoned to the meeting by Margaret Ker.

Further, she declared that she was at a meeting in Over Boltoun More. Margaret Allan, Thomas Cosser's wife was there. Also Gilbert Lamb's wife, Anna Kempe, and Margaret Ker.

This confession was made without violence or compulsion in the presence of Patrick, John, and George Bacbie.

[RPC 3rd Ser, Vol 1, p. 647]

29th May 1661: Statement and confession of Jonet Baigbie.

Janet Baigbie declared that about half a year ago or thereabouts, Bessie Todrig came to her window at night and called to her to come out. However, she did not come out that night. Bessie came to the window again another night and called to her, but she didn't answer. She came a third night and called to her. This time she came out to her. She was standing beside the sticks at her door, and the Devil was with her like a man in black clothes. He took her by the hand. His hand was cold, and he laid it on her shoulder and asked if she would be his servant. She consented and he then asked her to renounce God and her baptism. This she did, laying one hand on her head and the other on her feet, and gave soul and body to him. He called her "Magie".

She declares that she was at a meeting at the Backburne and Baigbie Mure, where she saw Bessie Todrig, Bessie Dasoun, Anna Kempe,

Margaret Ker, Issobell Smyth, Jeane Deans in Godspeid[?], Margaret Maislet from Maristoun, Marion Wood from Ewingston, and several others whom she did not know. The Devil was with them in the likeness of a man. He took them by the hand and they danced. She was summoned to that meeting by Bessie Todrig.

Taken before these witnesses: George, Patrik, and John Baigbie in Bolton, and Richard Mathie there. [RPC 3rd Ser, Vol 1, p. 648]

30th May 1661: Confession of Margaret Ker, taken from her own mouth. Margaret Ker declared that about a half or a quarter of a year ago, after she was in bed a dog came to her house and pulled off her bedclothes. She got up, put on her clothes, and went up the cattle track from her house to the west side of Boltoun More. On the way there, the Devil who had first appeared like a dog as described, appeared as a man and then asked her to be his servant. She promised to do so. Then he kissed her and asked her to renounce God and her baptism, which she did, laying one of her hands on her head and the other on her feet, and gave soul and body to him. He called her Elizabeth, and had sex with her after throwing her down to he ground. She suspected something was wrong when she found his penis cold; and when he kissed her his breath was unpleasant. He then asked her to be a good servant.

He came to her house again, and she was taken to a meeting in Sammilstoun Hauche, summoned by Jeane Deanes. There she saw Helen Deanes, Issobell Cathie, Jonet Wast, Jonet Kempe, Issobell Smyth. Ana Kemp, Bessie Todrig, Bessie Dawson, and Jonet Baigbie. Satan was there with them. They danced there; he spoke to them, and to her, and told her again to be a good servant.

Also, she declared that she was at a meeting beside Pilmore, summoned by Elspeth Baillie. She saw many people there, but knew none of them, except Elspeth Baillie, Issobel Richardson, and Margaret Maislet. Elspeth summoned her to another meeting, but she didn't go.

Also, she was at a meeting, first at the Back Burn of Boltoun, and from there went to Baigbie Mure. She saw many people there with the Devil amongst them. She knew none of them except Elspeth Baillie, Isobell Richardson, Margaret Maislet, Bessie Todrig, Bessie Dawson, and Janet Baigbie. She was summoned to that meeting by the Devil, and she summoned Anna Kemp and Issobell Smyth.

This was taken down from her own mouth, without using any manner of violence or compulsion, before these witnesses: George Baigbie and James Gottray in Over Boltoun; John Cantlie, servant to the Earl of Lauderdale; and Thomas Makcoull.

[RPC 3rd Ser, Vol 1, p. 648]

31st May 1661: At Bolton. The same day Mr Robert Ker and Mr William Trent, ministers of Hadingtoun; Mr John Butler of Kirkland and Thomas Halyburtoun of Egliscarnie, heritors and elders of trie parish of Bolton; with other elders of Boltoun Kirk Session, had brought before them Bessie Todrig, Bessie Dawsoun, Jonet Baigbie, and Margaret Ker, referred to above. After exhortations had been made to these persons, their confessions were read to them, and being taken aside individually, they confessed their guilt and adhered to ther confessions, without any violence or compulsion being used on them, or any one of them. This we hereby attest. Signed on the day and at the place foresaid: Robert Ker, Mr William Trent, Mr J. Butler, Thomas Halyburton

Bolton, 2nd June. This day the above statements were read to the persons named in them. They confessed them to be true and adhered to them.

Signed: Jas. Provane, Mr R. Cairnes

[RPC 3rd Ser, Vol 1, p. 648]

31st May 1661: Issobell Smyth declares that she came to be the Devil's servant because of

Margaret Ker and Anna Kemp, last oat-sowing time. The first to speak to her was Margaret Ker. When they were together she asked her to join them, and she would want for nothing. At the Backburne she saw a black man with green clothes. He made her welcome and asked her to be his servant. She undertook to be his servant, and he said that she would not lack enough of the necessities of life. He told her to renounce her baptism and renounce Christ, and be his. He told her to lay one hand on her head and the other on her feet and give herself to him, which she did. Asked about having sex, she said she did what the others did.

She was at a second meeting on Baigbie Mure. Margaret and Anna were there, and Bessie Todrig, Bessie Dawson, and Jonet Baigbie.

This was taken down from her own mouth before Mr Robert Ker, minister at Haddingtoune; Mr William Trent, minister there; Mr Johne Butler of Kirkland; and Thomas Haliburton of Egliscarno.

Signed: Robert Ker   Mr Wm. Trent   Mr J. Butler   Tho. Halyburton   Boltoun 2nd June 1661.

The abovewritten statement was read to Issobell. She confessed it to be true, and added that the Devil had sex with her, that his penis was cold, and that he gave her the new name "Magie".

Signed: Jos. Provane   Mr R. Cairnes
[RCP 3rd Ser, Vol 1, p. 649]

June 2nd 1661: Issobell Smyth in Pilmore declares that about eight years ago when she was living in Blause [sic for Blanse], and Elizabeth Lawson was also living there, Elizabeth asked her to come to her house to see a gentleman. When she came in he welcomed her, kissed her, and asked her to renounce her baptism and give soul and body to him. This she did by laying one hand on her head and the other on her head [sic]. She gave soul and body to him. His penis was cold, and she suspected then that she had gone wrong. In company with the Devil, besides herself and Elizabeth Lawson, were Margaret Bewar[?] and Katherein Cowpland. She also had a second meeting with him, Elizabeth Lawson and Catherein Cowpland in the "great yaird" at Blanse. [Most likely a "big garden", but possibly a stackyard or courtyard.]

Also, she was at a third meeting at the Backburne, where the Devil put his hand round her neck. Elizabeth Lawson said she would be a good servant. Bessie Todrig was there, and Bessie Dawson, Jonet Baigbie, Margaret Ker, Anna Kemp, and Issobell Smyth from Over Boltoun. They danced there, and had a piper, but she did not see who he was.

Also, she was at a meeting at the Cadger Well with the previously mentioned persons and many others, who went towards Saltoun with candles. [Surmised meaning. The last sentence does not make sense in the RPC]

Taken down from her own mouth in the presence of Mr Joseph Proven, minister at Morhame, who preached at Boltoun today; and in presence of the eiders of the kirk session of Boltoun, 2nd June 1661.

Signed: Jos. Provane, Tho. Halyburton, Mr R. Cairnes   [RPC 3rd Ser, Vol 1, p. 649]

June 2nd 1661: Anna Kempe declared that she was enticed to go to the Backburne by Margaret Ker. There she first saw a greyhound, and after that there was a man clad in black clothes, who made her welcome, took her by the hand, kissed her, and asked her to renounce her God and her baptism. This she did, laying one hand on her head and the other on her feet, and gave soul and body to him. Then he had sex with her and his penis was cold. He gave her a new name - "Janet".

Taken from her own mouth in the kirk session 2nd June 1661 in the presence of Mr Joseph Provan, minister at Morhame, and the elders of the parish of Boltoun undersigned. Signed: Jos. Provane   Tho. Halyburtone   Mr J. Butler   Mr J. Cairns

[RPC 3rd Ser, Vol 1, p.649]

"Undated c. 1649" [So says the RPC 2nd Ser, Vol viii, p. 198. However, many of those named feature in commissions and confessions dated 1661. Also, the signatories of this document were signatories to others in 1661. One of them signs himself "William Seatoun, Provost of Hadingtoun". The provost of Haddington in 1649 was John Cockburn, as can be seen from the commissions issued in that year. I would place this extract somewhere in the summer of 1661.]

Accused this day in my... [Blank. Presumably damage to the original document.] ...George Hutson, Issobell Hutson, Marion Hutson, Euphame Halyburton, Marion Wood in Ewingstoun, Begis Bathcat in Baigbie, Jean Deans in Braidwoodsyde, and Agnes Murray. The commission empowers the commissioners to question and examine them, and report back.

Agnes Williamson, Helen Deanes and Anna Pilmore have confessed and are named in the old commission. ["Nicoll Stillie, Issobell Stillie" - deleted] confesses; Elspeth Baillie and Issobell Richardson in Pilmore and Elisabeth Lawson in Kirkland have confessed. Georg Milton and Christian Blek have been accused and arrested. Patrik Meikkie, Helen Reid, Jonet West, Issobell Cathie, Jonet Kemp, and Susana Bannyntyne have been accused and are to be apprehended, having signed an undertaking to present themselves. Adam Harlaw, John Home, Margaret Blek, Helen Scharp, Issobell Cairnes and others have been accused and are to be arrested.

Memorandum for Thomas Crumbie: Let My Lord know that the judges named in the old commission were angry that it did not empower them to summon a jury with a penalty for non-attendance. In the past, when naming the persons to be judges and setting their quorum, previous commissions used to say, "With power to them to hold courts and appoint officials, such as clerk etc, and to summon and convene such persons as are known to be honest and beyond suspicion to sit upon the jury, under the penalty of sixty or fifty pounds for non-attendance."

Signed: George Seton of Barnes; Patrik Broun of Colstoun younger; Francis Hepburn of Beinston; Mr John Butler of Kirkland; Thomas Hallieburton of Edgcarnie; Alexander Borthwick of Johnstounburn; Patrik Yong, baillie of Hadinton; Mr John Dougall; [Doctor Hepburne -deleted]; Archibald Elot in Daurein[?]; Mr Alexander Hay of Baro; Mr [blank] Abercrombie; Sir James Sinclare of Harmistoun; William Seaton, provost of Hadingtoun.

[RPC 2nd Ser, Vol viii, p.204]

[This may have followed on from the Earl of Haddington's request for a commission to clear his lands of witches, since some names appear in both documents. It sounds as if the initial request was granted, but because the procedure had been out of use for a decade, the commission was not as tightly worded as in the "good old days" before the Commonwealth.]

July 25th 1661: Issobell Johnstoune from Guillan in the parish of Dirltoune has confessed herself guilty of witchcraft in that she has entered into a pact with the Devil and renounced her baptism; also in other ways as shown in her statements signed by several of the heritors and other honest men. Since it is necessary that the kingdom should be purged of such vile sin, and justice administered on the offender, the Lords of His Majesty's Privy Council give full power and warrant to George Livingtoune of Saltcoatts; George Hoome of Foord; William Fergussone, baillie of Dirletoune; [blank] Cowper of Fentounbarnes; and Adam Maxwell of Hiefield, to meet at such times and places as they think most convenient; to fix and hold courts, fine absentees and uplift the fines; to create clerks, serjeants, dempsters, and all other necessary members of court; and to call before these courts Issobell Johnstoune and put her on trial before a jury. If she is found

guilty they are empowered to cause justice to be administered and carried out against her according to the laws of the kingdom, and to do everything else necessary for the fulfilling of this commission according to the law and custom of the kingdom. The commissioners are empowered to arrest such others as are or shall be reported as guilty, to question them, and make use of all fair means for their interrogation and bringing them to a confession of their sins. The commissioners are to report as soon as possible on these investigations and proceedings to His Majesty's Privy Council.
[RPC 3rd Ser, Vol 1, p.11]

July 23rd 1661: Considering the commission presented by the heritors of Spott for a commission to proceed against Margaret Nisbitt, who is imprisoned on suspicion of witchcraft, it is ordered that Mr Andro Wood, the minister at Spott, should make further investigations and send in a report. [RPC 3rd Ser, Vol 1, p. 12]

July 25th 1661: [Summarised] Petitions from the heritors and others in the parishes of Mussilburgh, Dalkeith, Newbotle, Neatone, and Duddingstone, that there are a great many persons in prison who have confessed witchcraft or are accused of it. The Council appoints Mr Alexander Colvill of Blair, Mr George McKenze, and Mr Johne Cunnyngham as judges, or any two of them, to meet at Mussilburgh next Monday, and hold courts for the trial of those belonging to the parishes of Mussilburgh, Neatoune, and Duddingstone. [RPC 3rd Ser, Vol 1, P. 11]

[George Mackenzie was an eminent legal luminary who wrote later in life about his experiences in Musselburgh, which had influenced him to become sceptical about the truth of most witchcraft confessions - see "Other Sources". Considering this scepticism, it is perhaps ironic that his tomb in Greyfriars Churchyard in Edinburgh should now feature in "Ghost Tours" as a source of recurring psychic phenomena.]

August 2nd 1661: Mr John Henderson, macer [one who delivered legal messages and proclamations], is ordered to summon John Ramsey, an ordinary pricker of witches, to the next Council meeting to answer for pricking Margret Taitt, who died immediately afterwards.
[RPC 3rd Ser, Vol 1, p. 123]

[John Ramsay was from Ormiston – See Justiciary Court Records JC26/27 item 18. It may be that this incident influenced the Council's decision the following year to lock up John Kincaid, the notorious Tranent witch pricker.]

September 6th 1661: It is ordered that a commission be directed to Sir Robert Douglas of Blakestoun, Archibald Douglas of Spott, Mr Cornelius Inglis of Eistbarnes, Hendry Hopper of Burnouses, Robert Douglas in West Barnes, Robert Lauder in Belheaven, Mr John Darleith in Dumbar, or any five of them, as judges in that area for putting to legal trial Margret Moffat, Margarit Elleot, George Watson, James Johnstoun, Elspeth Yester, and Margaret Nisbitt, all living in the parish of Spott. They have confessed the abominable sin of witchcraft in that they entered into a pact with the Devil, renounced their baptism, and also in other ways as their statements show. For that effect the commissioners are empowered to meet at such times and places as they shall think most suitable to fix and hold courts there, to call cases, create clerks, and do everything else required to carry out the commission.

Signed: The Chancellor, Rothes, Roxburgh, Weymes, Hoom, Callander, Register, Advocate, Provost of Edinburgh. [Lords and officials of the Privy Council.] [RPC, 3rd Ser, Vol 1, p.33]

September 6th 1661: Commission granted to Sir William Murray of Neaton; Mr George Prestoun; George Hepburne of Aldinstoun; Major John Biggar; Mr Mongo Murray of Carlaverock; Robert Strauchan, baillie of Mussilburgh; Alexander Borthwick of Johnstounburne; John Huntar in Cousland; or any five of them; as judges in that area to legally try Jean Huntar, Jean Getgood, Jean Knox, Margaret Hawie, Bessie Turnbull, Katherin Johnstoun, and John Harlaw, all living in the parish of Ormestoun, [and others in Newton parish, Midlothian] who have either confessed the abominable sin of witchcraft in entering into a pact with the Devil, renouncing their baptism, or in other ways; or are at least imprisoned as being accused and suspected of that horrid sin. This is shown by the statements of several of them, and by a supplication from others of them asking to be either tried or set at liberty. Therefore the commissioners are empowered to meet at such times and places as they shall think most expedient.

Signed: Glencairn, Hoom, Roxburgh, Tweedale, Callander, Duffus, Register, Advocate, Alexander Bruce. [RPC 3rd Ser, Vol 1, p. 34]

November 7th 1661: A petition has been presented by the Earl of Haddintoune showing that a certain Agnes Williamson was imprisoned after being denounced for witchcraft. Ever since she has lain in prison for the past eight months at the expense of the same lord, causing great trouble to his tenants, without being put on trial. He asks therefore either that a commission might be granted to put her to a legal trial, or else that she should be set at liberty, so that the supplicant and his tenants may be put to no further expense or trouble with her in future, as shown in the petition.

The Lords of Council ordain that this Agnes Williamson should be tried and proceeded against by the Justice Depute as soon as possible according to the laws of this kingdom. For that effect the Earl of Haddingtoun is appointed to have her sent to the magistrates of the burgh of Edinburgh, who are to have her taken and put in secure confinement in the tollbooth, and to present her to the Justice deputes for trial, for which this order shall be sufficient warrant.
[RPC 3rd Ser, Vol 1, p. 78]
[Agnes was tried by the High Court of Justiciary, with an unusual outcome. See "Justiciary Court Records"]

1662

January 9th 1662: It is recommended to the Lord President of the Council that he should have John Kincaid apprehended. He takes upon himself on his own authority, without warrant or order, to prick and investigate persons suspected to be guilty of the abominable crime of witchcraft. He should be imprisoned until he finds surety to appear before the Council to answer for this. [RPC 3rd Ser, Vol 1, p. 132]

January 9th 1662: The Justice deputes are appointed to consider the confessions and witnesses' statements given in against several persons suspected of witchcraft within the parishes of Rind, Pennicook, Falkland, Innerwick, Innerleithen, and Queensferrie. They are to report in writing to the Council whether there is sufficient reason to grant commissions for trying and judging these persons or not.
[RFC 3rd Ser, Vol 1, p. 132]

January 16th 1662: Commission granted to Archbald Douglas of Spott; Mr Cornelius Inglis of Eistbarnes; Hary Hopp of Bourhouses; Mr John Darleith in Dumbar, Robert Lauder, portioner of Westbarnes; Robert Douglas there; Richard Cook, chamberlain to the Lord Cranborn; Lodovick Cant of Farstoun[?]; or any five of them; for trying and judging William Cowan living in the parish of Innerweick who has acknowledged the crime of witchcraft by entering into a pact with the Devil, and in other ways.

Signed: Glencarn, Cancelarius, Rothes, Mortoun, Cathnes, Southesk, Halcartoun, J. Lockhart, A. Bruce, Robert Murray. [RPC 3rd Ser, Vol 1, p. 143]

March 31st 1662: Information has been received that great abuses have been committed by John Kincaid who takes upon himself the pricking and investigating of witches, through which in all probability many innocent people have suffered. It is ordered that he be imprisoned in the tollbooth of Edinburgh until further measures are taken and investigations made.

[RPC 3rd Ser, Vol 1, p.187] ["Suffered" here probably means not that these innocent people had suffered the pain of pricking, but that they had suffered the death penalty for witchcraft.]

May 19th 1662: Supplication from John Kincaid from Tranent as follows: - He is imprisoned in the tollbooth of Edinburgh for the alleged pricking of witchcraft suspects without warrant. He has now become so physically infirm and ill that if he is not quickly set at liberty his life will be in great danger. He craves warrant for his liberation on payment of surety that he will return when requested to do so, and that he will not practise that sort of thing in future without a special warrant from the Council.

Before giving an answer, the Lords recommend that the Justice Depute should investigate his conduct in this business of pricking, and report back.

[RPC 3rd Ser, Vol 1, p. 210]

June 12th 1662: Supplication from John Kincaid from Tranent as follows:- He has been a prisoner in the tollbooth of Edinburgh for the past nine weeks for the alleged pricking without warrant of persons suspected of witchcraft. He was referred to the Justice general and his deputes for investigation, and they are ready to give in their report. The petitioner has now become so physically infirm and ill, that being an old man, if he is not quickly put at liberty his life will be in danger. He asks that the report should be considered, and that he should be liberated on payment of surety to enter prison when required to do so, and to stop the practice of pricking in future without a special warrant. Having seen the report, the Lords give permission to the magistrates of Edinburgh to free the petitioner from imprisonment on the above charge, on guarantee of sufficient surety, recorded in the Council books or Books of Adjournal, not to prick or torture any person suspected of witchcraft in future without a warrant from the Council or from His Majesty's Justice deputes. He will be answerable for this at his utmost peril. He is to appear when required, under pain of £1000 Scots. [RPC 3rd Ser, Vol 1, p. 226]

June 13th 1662: Registration by [blank] of a bond of caution by John Somervale, skinner, burgess of Edinburgh, for John Kincaid from Tranent, that he will desist from pricking or torturing any person suspected of witchcraft without having a warrant from the Council or justice Depute. Also that he will appear to answer any charges laid against him under the penalty of £1000 Scots. John Kincaid is therefore set at liberty from the tollbooth of Edinburgh by their Lordships' act of 10th June, and obliges himself to relieve his "cautioner" [i.e. the man who put up the money], and to register the conditions of the bond.

The bond is written by Hew Stevensone, servant to James Wright, solicitor ["writer"], and dated at Edinburgh 13th June 1662.

Witnesses to John Somervale's signature: Hew Stevensone. Alexander Ramsay, servant to Sir Peter Wedderburn of Gosford.

Witnesses to John Kincaid's signature: Robert Griersoun and James Johnstoun in Edinburgh. [RPC 3rd Ser, Vol 1, P. 226]

[The text of this bond of caution can also be found on RPC 3rd Ser, Vol 1, P. 657.]

August 8th 1662: Supplication by John Forrester in Tranent.

Mr Robert Hodge of Gladsmoor and the deceased Mr Andrew Marchbanks were appointed justices of the peace by the "usurpers" [i.e. the English army of occupation during the Commonwealth period]. They commanded John Forrest to take on the office of constable in Tranent, under penalty of £100 sterling. As

An interesting record of the Tranent witch-pricker John Kincaid at work. A diagram of the pin used can be seen, with Kincaid's mark "IK" signifying that he was illiterate.

he could not pay this sum, he was forced to obey and gave them his bond. He was entrusted with the goods and effects of certain persons accused of witchcraft, and disposed of them by order of these justices.

He is being troubled every day by certain persons before various judges because this Mr Robert Hodge will not come to terms with him or return his bond to him. It is requested that he be ordered to do so, and the Lords ordain accordingly. Mr Robert is to give a report of this to the Council for their consideration. In the meantime the Lords forbid any further proceedings against the supplicant.

[RPC 3rd Ser, Vol 1, p.252]

[The Justiciary Court records contain the trial of Jonet Bruce in Tranent in 1657 before Hodge and Marchbanks, but the phrase "certain persons" implies that there were others. It is usually believed that there were very few witchcraft trials under the Commonwealth, but this may be a misapprehension. For example, the box of Justiciary Court processes JC26/25 contains papers referring to 42 witches in seven Ayrshire parishes in 1658. It is not impossible that other witchcraft trials were being conducted by local justices of the peace throughout the Commonwealth period. Far from proving that trials were not taking place under enlightened English rule, lack of written evidence may simply indicate that records were not normally being held centrally.]

1677

May 2nd 1677: Commission to the provost and baillies of Haddington, Patrick Broun of Colstoun, Sir Robert Hepburne of Keith, and Mr John Preston, to try Elizabeth Moody, widow of John Moor, living in Haddington, who has been arrested and imprisoned in the tollbooth of the burgh on suspicion of witchcraft by entering into a pact with the Devil, renouncing her baptism, and in other ways.

If she is found guilty after making a voluntary confession, without any sort of torture or "direct means" [*i.e.* physical violence] being used against her to bring her to a confession, or if acts of evil intent or other charges can be legally proven, "etc etc..." [*sic* RPC. Presumably empowerment to set up courts, and to try and execute the suspect is to be understood.] [RPC 3rd Ser, Vol v, p. 161]

August 10th 1677: Supplication by Marion Phin living in Haddington.

She is 80 years of age and was slanderously accused by a wretched woman who was executed at Haddington for witchcraft and said that the petitioner was as guilty as she was. At this, the magistrates of the burgh, without any further proof or investigation, put her in the tollbooth where she has been for the past three months in a most deplorable condition because of her great age and because of her sorrow for her good name. She is a person who lived always with a good reputation, never stained with the least disgrace, far less with the abominable crime of witchcraft. Being of such well-known integrity, it is hard that she should suffer because of such lying accusers who may, and often do, cause the best of God's servants to blunder.

Since the petitioner is happy to find sufficient surety to answer when called, she craves her liberation.

Considering the petition along with a report from the Laird of Colstoune about the petitioner and others apprehended and imprisoned for the same crime, the Lords renew the commission previously granted to the same persons for questioning the petitioner and the others, and for trying and judging them. [RPC 3rd Ser, Vol v, p. 231]

1678

May 2nd 1678: The Lords of the Privy Council are informed that Agnes Kelly, widow of [blank] Brown in Prestoune Panns, and her servant Marjorie Anderson, have been arrested and imprisoned in the tollbooth of Prestoune Panns under suspicion of being guilty of witchcraft by entering into a pact with the Devil, renouncing their baptism, and committing several acts of evil intent.

Sir Alexander Moriesone of Prestongrange; Patrick Broune of Colstoune, sheriff depute of Haddington; and [blank] Seatoun of St Germans; or any two of them; are authorised to call a jury and witnesses and put the suspects on trial. If they are found guilty after making a voluntary confession, without any sort of torture or "indirect means" [persuasion?] being used to bring them to a confession, or if acts of evil intent are proved, the commissioners are to cause justice to be administered to them according to the laws of the kingdom. [RPC 3rd Ser, Vol v, p. 449] [Why "indirect means" in this case, and "direct means" on 2/5/77 ?]

August 15th 1678: The Lords considered a petition by Katherine Liddell, widow of Thomas Keddy in Salt Preston. She has always been known as a person of entirely good fame and integrity, and yet has been imprisoned by John Rutherfoord, baillie in Prestounpanns, on suspicion of witchcraft, and suffered torture at the hands of a certain [blank] Cowan from Tranent. She craves liberty and the punishment of the perpetrators of these cruelties. The Lords order John Rutherford to set her free immediately, as she has found surety of 500 merks, recorded in the books of the Privy Council, to appear and answer the charge when required. They order John Rutherford and [blank] Cowan to be summoned to appear before them to answer for imprisoning and torturing the prisoner. [RPC 3rd Ser, Vol v, p. 501]

September 13th 1678: Complaint by His Majesty's Advocate, and by Katherine Liddell, widow of Thomas Keddy in Saltprestoun.

Although the imprisoning and torturing of His Majesty's good subjects, and branding their good name with the epithet of witch are crimes severely punishable; and although Katherine has hitherto been known as a person of known integrity and unblemished fame, and in no way suspected of any diabolical practices or engagements; yet John Rutherfoord, baillie of Prestounpanns has with groundless malice slandered her good name and Christian reputation by calling her a witch and a servant of the Devil. Along with William Atchesone, "officer" [the equivalent of a constable] in Prestonpanns; David Seaton, drummer there; David Cowie and John Stevinsone, salters there; James Robertsone, sailor there; James Anderson who lives there, and others, on 9th July last he violently seized her and imprisoned her in the tollbooth of Prestounpanns. There these persons by night and day most cruelly and barbarously tormented and tortured the complainer by pricking her with pins in several parts of her body to the great effusion of her blood. As a result the skin is raised and her body highly swollen, and her life is in danger. Also, they kept her from sleep several nights and days with the intention of extorting any confession they pleased from her, if they possibly could, since she was in such a desperate and forlorn condition.

The complainer continued under this cruel and unchristian treatment for the space of six weeks, until after application to His Majesty's Privy Council, she was ordered to be liberated.

Having been summoned, all parties appeared personally, and the Lords discharged the pursuer Katherine Liddell from her imprisonment. They declare that from such evidence as has so far appeared, she ought not to be troubled or vexed for witchcraft. They forbid John Rutherfoord, one of the defendants, to seize or torture any person for witchcraft without warrant from one of the Council or Commissioners of Justiciary. Because of the practice of others in a similar station in life with the same lower-class misapprehensions, and similar responsibilities, they dismiss him without punishment. They order David Cowan the pricker, another of the defendants, to be taken as a prisoner to the tollbooth of Edinburgh until the next meeting of the Council, and until it has considered what further punishment they shall inflict on him for presuming to torture or prick any person without warrant from the Council, the Commissioners of Justiciary, or those who have a commission from them. [RPC 3rd Ser, Vol vi, p.13]

[Although it would be rash to draw too many conclusions from a single RPC extract, this hints strongly that it had previously been common practice for baron baillies in the area to imprison suspects without warning, ill treat them, deprive them of sleep and prick them for the witch mark without necessarily making reference to any higher authority. The Privy Council is signalling in no uncertain terms that these days are now gone. Cowan was made to promise not to prick again. See below, 27th February 1679.]

September 13th 1678: Warrant for carrying out the sentence of death against the witches Isobel Eliot, Marion Veitch, Margret Dods, and Helen Laying, prisoners found guilty by a jury of the crime of witchcraft. They are sentenced by us, the Lords Commissioners of Justiciary, to be taken to Paistoun Muir next Friday, the 20th of the month, between two and four o' clock in the afternoon. There they are to be strangled at the stake till they be dead, and thereafter their bodies are to be burnt to ashes. Sir Robert Hepburne of Keith and Sir John Pringle of Woodhead are commanded to see that the sentence is duly carried out.

[RPC 3rd Ser, Vol vi, P. 627]

September 20th 1678: Certification of the burning of four witches in Peastoun Moore.

We the undersigned - William Baylie of Lamingtoun; Adame Cockburne of Ormestoun; William Cunynghame of Eterkine younger; David Hepburne of Randerstoun[?]; Mr Robert and Mr George Cockburne, uncles to the Laird of Ormestoun; William Borthwick of Johnstounburne; John Belshes of that Ilk; Mr John Sinclar, minister at Ormestoun; Mr James Calderwood, minister at Humbie; Mr Robert Spottswood, minister at Crightoun; Mr James Cockburne, minister at Pencaitland; Mr George Moodie, minister at Fala; and Mr James Griersone, reader at Ormestoun - hereby testify and declare to the honourable Lords of His Majesy's Justiciary that according to and in obedience to the sentence of death pronounced upon the thirteenth day of September ordering Issobell Elliot, Maryon Vaitch, Margarett Dodds, and Hellene Lainge, found guilty of the crime of witchcraft, to be taken to Peaston Moore this Friday 20th September between two and four o' clock in the afternoon, and there to be strangled at a stake till they be dead and their bodies thereafter to be burned to ashes.

We the undersigned testify that we were all present, saw, and were eyewitnesses to the due execution of the foresaid sentence of death upon the bodies of the four witches above-named, at the time, day, and place above mentioned. This conformed to the foresaid sentence of death in all particulars.

In witness of this, and of the truth of these particulars, we, the forenamed persons have signed this with our hands at Peaston Moore, 20th September 1678.

[Their signatures follow.]
[RPC 3rd Ser, Vol vi, P. 672]

[Several others from East Lothian were involved in this case, and were executed in Edinburgh. There were also many others involved from neighbouring Midlothian parishes, including the disgraced former minister of Crichton, Gideon Penman. See "Justiciary Court Records".]

Undated 1678: Account of the expenses incurred over the witches [*i.e.* the witches

Several witches from Peaston were executed in 16785 along with associates from Keith, Fala, and Crichton.
Gideon Penman, the minister of Crichton kirk in Midlothian (below), was accused of being involved with the witches executed in 1678.

executed at Peaston. These expenses seem to have been borne by the local laird.].

1. In the first week of July David Chalmer went to Edinburgh with the confessions and a letter requesting a commission to try them locally. Expenses including payments to the clerks of the Council: £18-13-4
2. The Council refused a commission. The Laird went to Edinburgh himself and delivered a second letter requesting a commission. He gave the clerk to the Council two rex dollars, which is… 8 - 14 - 0
3. To George Rae, Mr Thomas Hay's employee, for writing several commissions. He was given two dollars as the number of witches increased. 5 - 16 - 0
4. To the Council's legal messengers when letters were presented on two separate occasions:- 2 - 18 - 0
5. Dues for the indictment of 13 witches: 85 - 12 - 0
6. To the Laird's servant Archbald Buntein: a dollar - 2 - 18 - 0
7. To the clerk to the Criminal Court when the witches' confessions were first presented: a dollar - 2 - 18 - 0
8. To the clerk for reading the confessions to the court twice: five dollars – 14 - 10 - 0
9. Hire of horses for bringing the witches in 1 - 6 - 8
10. A messenger on horseback to hurry through the night to stop them coming after all, since their coming would be of no use: 1 - 0 - 0
11. Fees to the legal messengers of the Criminal Court for seeing the assessors in Edinburgh about getting warrants from the Lord Advocate to indict the witches: 8 - 14 - 0
12. To one of the legal messengers for coming out on the 24th of August to charge the witches and inform several members of the court who live in the country: 5 - 16 - 0
13. For his horse hire: 1 - 12 - 0
14. Paid to David Chalmer for getting the indictments drawn up etc.: 26 - 2 - 0
15. "Sentence money" due to the legal messengers of the *Criminal Court for the four witches comdemned and the nine declared fugitives - 5 dollars - 14 - 10 - 0*
16. *To John Anderson, the clerk's employee, for his efforts in this process:* 11 - 12 - 0
17. *To the "keepers of the house" [Is this the house where the trial was held, or is it perhaps where the witches were imprisoned?]: 4 merks -* 2 - 13 - 4
18. *Clerk Marline claimed two merks were due to him for each indictment, as well as the sentence money. Beaten down and settled for less.* 95 - 9 - 4

Total 310-9-4

i.e. The cost to the Laird has been £23 -17 - 7 for each of the 13 witches indicted.

Account of the expenses incurred in burning the four witches.

£

Item: To the dempster £2.

To the hangman 13s 4d; 6s more paid to him to give back their plaids.

To the "officers" [constables or guards] £1: 5 - 19 - 4

Item: For 8 cart loads of coal at 14 shillings per cart: 5 - 12 - 6

Item: For wood and nails for the gallows and scaffold: 2 - 5 - 6

Item: For four tar barrels 2 - 9 - 4

Item: To the wright [joiner] and his men for building the gallows and scaffold: 1 - 10 - 0

Item: For the hangman's wages, and expenses incurred at Haddington on two separate occasions before he came out.

Also for sending him back with a merk to buy ropes. In all - 2 - 7 - 4

TOTAL 38 - 3 - 0

Divide £38 - 3s into four parts.

Each fourth part will be £9 -10- 9. [RPC 3rd Ser, Vol vi, p.628]

[The sums of money are of course in pounds Scots, which were worth a twelfth of pounds sterling. All the same, the costs were substantial, and seem to have been borne by the laird. He may have been compensated to an extent by the forfeited moveable possessions of the witches, but these are not likely to have amounted to much. In her book "Enemies of God" Christina Larner cites instances of relatives of witches being billed for the execution expenses.

There is something strangely modern about the implied typical local government cock-up, where the hangman appears to have arrived expecting ropes to be provided, and the organisers seem to have presumed that he would bring them. He then has to be sent back to Haddington to buy this vital equipment. Spare a thought for the miserable wretches kept waiting by this delay.]

1679

27th February 1679.

Bond by David Cowan, drummer in Tranent, with William Cowan who lives there providing surety. Having been imprisoned in the tollbooth of Edinburgh for pricking witches without a legal warrant, he guarantees in future not to follow this line of work without a licence from the Council. He will appear before them when required under a penalty of 500 merks. Clauses of relief and registration apply. This bond was written in Edinburgh by George Rae, employee of Hugh Stevensone, solicitor in Edinburgh, and dated at Edinburgh 27th February 1679.

Witnesses to the signature of the "cautioner": Patrick Vause[?], master of the Tollbooth. George Rae, writer of the bond.

Witnesses to Cowan's signature: John Gray, solicitor in Edinburgh, and Alexander Bell, solicitor in Kircalde. [RPC 3rd Ser, Vol vi, p. 645]

1688

[The following case of Catherine McTarget is, as far as I can see, the last mention in the records of the Privy Council of witchcraft in East Lothian. Neither do there seem to have been any Justiciary Court cases involving East Lothian witches after this trial. Catherine McTarget's process is therefore almost certainly the last East Lothian witchcraft trial. Although it is extremely lengthy, it is interesting in that it gives a very clear picture of what ordinary people at the end of the 17th century believed witches got up to. Catherine's name is probably a version of the surname now rendered as Mactaggart, so Catherine must at least have had Highland ancestry, and may well have been a Highlander herself.]

May 10th 1688: Commissioners of Justice for summoning a jury and witnesses against Catherine McTarget and her judicial confession.

Sitting of the commissioners for the trial of Catherein Mactargett, suspected to be guilty of the crime of witchcraft:
Sir John Sinclair of Lochend
James Mure of Burehousses
Sir William Baird of Newbyth
Mr Robert Lauder, one of the clerks
 of exchequer
Robert Hamilton
James Forrest, former baillie of Dumbar
Archibald Murray of Spott
William Kirkwood and James Smith,
 merchants
Mr George Purves
George Rutherford
George Sinclair
Present baillies of the burgh.

Mr George Sinclair was chosen to be chairman.

William Kirkwood, town clerk of Dumbar, chosen to be clerk for the legal process and trial.

Mr Patrick Broun, solicitor, to be public prosecutor.

Robert Innes and Alexander Crombie chosen to be officers of court [*i.e.* to keep order, carry messages, perform general duties etc.].

After the prisoner Katharein Mactargatt had been exhorted by the minister Mr Thomas Wood, he came in to the commissioners and reported to them that she had confessed to him that she is a witch. She was then brought in before the commissioners, and there made a formal confession that she is a witch. The commissioners appointed and fixed May 30th at eight o'clock in the morning to be the meeting to which the accused is to be summoned with a jury and witnesses, and have signed a warrant to that effect. The commissioners recommend the minister Mr Thomas Wood to exhort the accused further, and to take one or two of them along with him, as well as the clerk, to see if she can be brought to a further confession of her guilt, and the times and circumstances concerned.

Signed: Mr George Purves, chairman [and the other commissioners]. [RPC 3rd Ser, Vol xiii, P.234]

May 10th 1688: Warrant sent by the above named commissioners to their court officers Alexander Crombie and Robert Innes communicating the Privy Council's commission of 3rd May to the foresaid persons, or any three of them, to act as judges and to call Catherin McTarget, prisoner in the tollbooth of Dunbar to appear on 30th May at the request of Mr Patrick Brown, solicitor, public prosecutor for His Majesty's interest. Also to summon

George Miller, portioner of West Barnes,
James Nisbet in Cockburnspath,
William Dun in Cockburnspath Tower,
David Simpsone in Thursetun,
William Craig in Innerweik,
William Murray in Crawhill,
Henry Neilsone in Innerweik,
James Smith in Eastbarnes,
James Crambie there,
Johne Brysone there,
Archibald Cuthbertson in Brunt,
Alexander Kirkwood in Pinkertoun,
William Kirkwood there,
Thomas Wightman in Broxburne,
William Lausone there,
Andrew Robisone in Wester Broomhouise,
Francis Dudgeon in Hallhill,
William Home in Cocklaw,
George Broune in Standarts,
Gideon Broune in Chesterhall,
John Dausone in Beltoun,
Thomas Hog and Alexander Crombie in North Belton,
Thomas Logan in Stentoun,
William Logan in Pleasants,
Patrick Douglas in Whittinghame,
Patrick Temple in Lintoun,
Robert Constable there,
William Shirriff in Tynyngham,
Thomas Yewart there,
John Sked, Alexander Young, Robert Wands, and Robert Sked in Belhaven,
William Cockburn, wright
William Cockburn, cooper burgesses of Dumbar.
Nicol Kellie, wright
David Robison

They are to appear on 30th May to attend Catherine's trial as jurors.

Certain witnesses are also to be summoned....

[blank].

The jurors are summoned under penalty of 100 merks for non-attendance.

Dated at Dunbar 10th May 1688.

[RPC 3rd Ser, Vol xiii, p. 235]

May 14th and 15th 1688: "Note of execution" [*i.e.* that he has carried out his instructions] by Alexander Crombie, sheriff officer in Dunbar, of the above-mentioned warrant summoning George Miller etc etc to appear in court under the penalty of 100 merks.

Witnesses to the serving of the order:

David Ker, baker, burgess of Dunbar.

Robert Innes, one of the ordinary officers of the burgh.

[RPC 3rd Ser, Vol xiii, p. 242]

May 14th and 15th 1688: Note of execution by Robert Innes, one of the officers of Dunbar. He has served the warrant on 14th May against Catherine McTarget, wife of William Brown in Dunbar. She was personally informed in the tollbooth of Dunbar. A warrant also against Robert Home, postmaster at Cockburnspeth.

The following people have been personally informed and summoned to appear under penalty of 100 merks, except John Home and Arthur Simpsone:

Margaret Vertue, John Home's wife,

John Ker, their servant,

Helen Patterson, a former servant of theirs,

James Simpson, mason, and Thomas Lamb, hawker, in Cockburnespeth,

John Hog, mason in Dunglas,

George Lyall in Saltpanhall,

Isobel Restoun, wife of George Milne in Eastbarnes,

Janet Chisholme, widow of Thomas Ross, blacksmith there,

Margaret Ross, daughter of the late Thomas Ross,

George Wallace, baker, burgess of Dunbar,

Alexander Affleck elder, burgess there,

James Forrester in Spott and Catherine Forrester his wife,

Patrick Fergussone, mason, burgess of Dunbar,

Marion Bairnesfather, widow of John Fergusone, mason there,

Richard Merstone, seaman there,

Sarah Atchesone, widow of John Laurie there,

John Smith, indweller there,

Janet Symontoun, wife of John Affleck, shoemaker there,

Thomas Thomasone in Westbank and Mary Johnstoun his wife,

Arthur Simpsone in Easter Broomhous and Janet Hamiltone his wife,

William Bryson, slater, burgess of Dumbar, and Lucress Smith his wife,

Agnes Colm, wife of George Kemp, cooper, burgess there,

Margaret Jacksone their servant,

Maurice Fergusone, mason, burgess there,

Jean Boig, servant to Mr Patrick Broun,

Christian Dumbar, servant to Patrick Mathie, burgess there,

George Shirrif in Knous and Christian Orme his wife,

Patrick Shirreff there and Helen Pringle his wife,

Patrick Wood, maltman, burgess of Dumbar,

Andrew Stevinsone in Newtonlies,

Margaret Aitken in Drem,

James Congiltone, burgess of Dumbar, and Helen Milne his wife,

George Walker, wheelwright, burgess there, and Jean Johnstoun his wife,

George Restone and Patrick Kellie, ordinary officers of the burgh,

James Lauder and Catherine Sandilands his wife,

William Smail, resident there,

Witnesses to the serving of the warrant: Alexander Crombie, sheriff officer; David Ker, baker, burgess of Dumbar.

[RPC 3rd Ser, Vol xiii, p. 343]

[A total of 48 witnesses. John Home and Arthur Simpsone were presumably not at home when the messenger arrived.]

May 30th 1688: Indictment: Mr Patrick Broun, procurator fiscal, against Catherin Mactargett for witchcraft.

Catherin McTarget, wife of William Broun,

weaver in Dumbar, now prisoner in the tollbooth of Dumbar, you are indicted and accused that although the law of God and the laws of this and all other well governed nations - particularly Act 73 of the 9th Parliament of Queen Mary - forbid under pain of death and confiscation of their moveable possessions all persons to use any kind of witchcraft, sorcery, or necromancy, or to claim to have any such skill or knowledge of it, thereby abusing the people; in spite of this, it is true that having shaken off all fear of God and respect for the laws of the nation, you took up the trade of begging. There was no necessity for this, as you and your husband had a perfectly adequate income. While begging you have made use of such odd and strange words, gestures, and practices, that the people where you went begging became convinced you were a witch. You had that public reputation for a long time, and never complained to any magistrate that people were calling you a witch. On the contrary, in a way you gloried in it, and terrified the people to such an extent that you became insolent and imperious in your begging. When you got alms from the people, which they could hardly spare, you were not satisfied and used to demand more. Out of fear and terror people felt forced to satisfy you. If anyone refused, you used to threaten and predict damage to them for refusing, which many times accordingly came to pass. You came to the point where if you were displeased in any way you threatened damage and hurt, which would accordingly came to pass. In this way you have deluded the people by making them superstitious and distrustful of Almighty God, and afraid of the Devil and of yourself, to the extent that whenever they saw you they used to bless themselves. Your usual words on these occasions were that they never prayed so much before they saw you, and they'd never pray so much till they saw you again.

As proof that you are guilty of this black art of witchcraft and sorcery, and thereby committing acts of evil intent, using charms, terrifying and abusing the people as described, contrary to Act of Parliament, it is true that

1. You, Catherin McTarget were in the house of Thomas Ross, blacksmith in Estbarnes, in one or other of the months of the year 1685. Thomas's daughter was making oatmeal porridge, and when you asked if the porridge was for you, she answered as a joke, "I hope you choke on it then." You replied that some of her relatives would choke before long. Accordingly, that young woman's father choked on a piece of beef that same night in the house of the wright Patrick Lougan, and died.

2. Also, in one or other of the months of July or August 1672 your husband William Brown was engaged in selling a young cow to James Reid, a butcher in Dumbar. You came to the foot of the stair of the house where they were, and shouted up to your husband in a great rage, and said that if James Reid bought your cow he would never draw blood from her. Accordingly, although he was a very fit man at the time, and in perfect health, he fell ill within a day or two and died

3. Also, on [blank] 1677, you were on the shore at Dumbar when John Fergusson was getting coal. You stole a piece of coal out of his cart, and he quite rightly struck you. At that, you said that this would be dear coal to him, and he would never strike again. Although he was a healthy young man he went home, immediately fell ill, and never came out again till he died.

4. Also, in one or other of the months of the year 1683 you got alms from James Forester's wife in Spott, and asked for some milk as well. She refused, and you went away very angry. The next time their cow was milked, to everyone's astonishment she gave only blood. This went on for two or three days, and then the cow died.

5. Also, not only were you in the habit of making explicit threats as described, and not only did damage and destruction immediatelly

follow, but also if anybody had offended you they immediatelly fell ill with extraordinary diseases and died. In one or other of the months of the year 1674, you came to Andrew Stevensone in Bourhousses where he was out sowing oats. You said you wanted a boll of his oats, and he replied that what you deserved was more like a boll of coals to burn you with. Immediately, you went to his house and got a drink of water. A day or two later his wife was at the mill where you met her, and after some conversation between the two of you she came home and "ramished to death". [Rammish: to rush about in a frenzied state - SND . Livestock often died in this way as a result of witchcraft. I suppose the modern equivalent is "going berserk".]

6. Also, you practised charming and other magical acts. In particular on [blank] October 1676 you came to the house of John Lawrie in Dunbar on a Sunday morning, and threw down a tether made of horsehair, something usually done by witches. After that you looked into where John Laurie was sleeping, and he awoke. He looked up and saw you, and immediately fell ill with a most unnatural disease, and never closed his eyes till he died the following Thursday.

7. Also, on 1st January 1682, Handsel Monday, you came to Ruchlaus Close in Dumbar to Patrick Fergussone the mason, where he was watching some people playing at quoits. You offered him cheese and bread. When he refused you pressed him to take it. He took it and tasted a little and gave it back to you. You let it fall on the ground, and immediately his wife [blank] Richesone took ill, lost all her senses, and died within ten or twelve days. [Handsel Monday was the first Monday after New Year, and was kept as a holiday. A "handsel" is a good luck gift to mark something new, in this case the New Year. The bread and cheese here was presumably meant as a New Year gift.]

8. Also, in one or other of the months of the year 1684 you came to George Colme's house in Spott seeking alms. There were two girls in the house who were frightened when they saw you and prayed to God to bless them. You said they had not prayed so much till they saw your pleasant face, and you told the Evil Spirit to take note of them. You put your hand down by your side, dipped your fingers in the water pail, put your finger on the sole of your foot, and went on your way. Shortly after this, three of George Colme's cows and two of his bullocks died.

9. Also, in one or other of the months of the year 1685, you were in the street in Dumbar where you saw George Fergusone, the son of Maurice Ferguson the mason, a child about four years old. He was playing, and throwing his bonnet around. You picked up the bonnet and put it on his head with the crown downwards by way of a charm. The child went home to his father and told him what you had done, and said his head was hurting. He cried pitifully for three or four days till he died.

10. Also, at Michaelmas 1687 you came to Patrick Mathie's house in Dumbar, sat down, asked for some milk, and repeated the words of this charm three times, "If I break my nose, I spoil my face, and when I spoil my face I break my fortune." The following Sunday, you came to the same house with a piece of unshrunk coarse woolen cloth ["rau pledden"], and offered it in pawn for some money. Patrick Mathie had allowed you to have the milk, and his daughter Issobell Mathie was very angry that you should have been given any milk, and that you should come to the house with cloth on such a day [*i.e.* the Sabbath]. Ever since, Issobell has been in a melancholy and troubled frame of mind, and continues thus at the present time, although before she was a person of perfect judgment and discretion.

11. Also, on the [blank] of June or July 1677, on a Sunday about three or four o'clock in the morning, you brought a bullock through the street in Dumbar. You left it outside a byre

belonging to the slater William Brysone when he lived at Crauswindhead. It was left standing in the same position as his cow was standing inside the byre. You picked up some dung from the midden, held it to the beast's mouth, and uttered some words and charms. Immediately William Brysone's cow began to decline in health, and never thrived afterwards.

12. Also, in one or other of the months of 1678, at ten o' clock at night when it was dark, you came west through the High Street of this burgh riding on a white-faced calf, with one of your legs on each side of it. [*i.e.* she was riding like a man, and not "sidesaddle" as a woman would usually have done]. When you were asked where you had been at such a time and in such a posture, you answered that you had been in the "east country", and had found the bullock at the kirk style. It was Margaret Liddel's and you were going to take it home. [Presumably Catherine had been in the countryside to the south-east of Dunbar. Due east would have been in the sea!]

13. Also, in one or other of the months of 1677 you came to the Knous to George Shirreff's house where they were making porridge, and asked for alms. His wife offered you the pan to lick, and you asked for some milk or ale for it. Some of the family gave you some of a weak unfermented malt mixture which was boiling on the fire, and you said it would be good ale if it had salt. George Shireff's wife Cristian Orme was angry with you for saying it, and said, "You witch thief, who would put salt in ale?" You said that there was better drink in the house. Cristian said there was some, but it had not fermented yet. You replied that they would get enough fermentation shortly, and went away out of the house. When some of the family went into the room where there was a barrel with a mixture in it which had never had yeast added, they saw it foaming up in such a fearful manner that it touched the beams of the ceiling. They got vessels to catch it, and were greatly astonished since no-one had ever put any yeast in it. [Since the word "barme" can mean yeast, the fermenting mixture, the foam produced, or indeed the process of fermentation, this passage is easy enough to understand in the original, but difficult to translate literally into modern English. This is a loose interpretation.]

14. Also, in one or other of the months of 1682, you came seeking alms at James Lauder's house in Dumbar, and got a handful of meal from his wife. After that you asked for a drink of fermenting ale ["barme" again], which she refused to give you. You stood still and would not go away without it, and in the end she was forced to give you some. You had no sooner gone away from the house than his wife took such a violent pain in her hand that she was like to go mad. A stranger, Doctor McKullo, who happened to be in the house, drew blood from her, but since it made her no better he said some evil person was affecting her. After that you came back to James's house and said the woman would never be well till either she or her child died. She had a young child at the breast, who fell ill and died within a month. She herself recovered and grew better every day after that. This caused such terror and fear in that family that they could never see you after that without their flesh trembling.

15. Also, in either November or December 1685 you were trying to buy a sheep's head from the wife of William McKie, butcher in Dumbar. However, George Walker's wife Jean Johnsone bought it, and gave more for it than you were offering. You said it would do her family no good. So it turned out. When it was boiling Jean Johnsone became extremely sick and was tortured with such pain for three or four days that when you heard people saying that you had bewitched her, you came to her house and got her to provide the entrails of a sheep. You gave her five onions, and told her to take three of them and boil them with the entrails, then take

some of the broth and that would cure her. This she accordingly did, and as soon as she tasted the broth she was well. This is clearly a laying on and taking off of sickness.

16. Also, in one or other of the months of 1675 John Affleck's wife Janet Symontone asked you for a peck of barley, for which you abused her, and she called you an incarnate devil. You immediately took off your head-cloths and threw them at her. She had some satisfactorily good malt steeping beside her from which she had been brewing good ale, but after the quarrel neither she nor anyone else in the town could make a drop of good ale from that malt.

17. Also, in one or other of the months of the year 1658, when you and the late John Milne had quarrelled, you threatened that he would never thrive, which accordingly followed. Although he was then a sober man of substantial means, his possessions vanished away until he came to a state of extreme poverty. He had a horse which accidentally came into your vegetable garden and trampled some of your plants. When you were driving the horse out you said it would never go home till it broke its neck. This accordingly fell out, for the same night the horse fell over the cliffs and broke its neck. [RPC says that Catherine was "calling the horse out", but it is perhaps more likely, given Catherine's temperament, that the writer of the original meant that she was "ca'ing the horse out" - driving it out.]

18. Also, in 1671 James Congiltone owed you some plants, which you came looking for a month before they were due. You would not go away from his house, but sat all night "over in the stair" [on the stair opposite James's house?], with your hair hanging over your eyes, and he was so terrified and afraid that he paid you. However, he never thrived after that, and could not even get meal for his children, although he had been doing well before then.

19. Also, you used to lay on and take off sickness, which is the height of witchcraft. In particular, on [blank] 1678, when you were at the post-house at Cockburnspeth, you asked for a drink from Hellen Paterson who was a servant in the house. She refused, and you went away uttering some words. A little while after you had gone, although she had been in perfect health, Hellen fell down dead. She remained a considerable time as if she were dead, and was then violently delirious ["in ane high and mighty distemper"]. The family, and the strangers who were in the house were convinced that the woman had taken such a strange and sudden sickness because of some of your devilish arts, and they sent a manservant of the postmaster's to look for you and bring you back, saying that you could take the sickness off again. Accordingly, when the man brought you back, you gave the woman a drink, and she immediately recovered her perfect health without the application of any other art or effort.

20. Also, in one or other of the months of 1673 you were lodging in Patrick Shirreff's house in the Knoues, with two bundles of onions. Helen Pringle his wife was reluctant to buy any of the onions. When she took her childbirth pains you were put out of your lodgings. You came over to Christian Orme, George Shirreff's wife, who was then lying sick at the point of death, and said to her, "Cheer up, for what was intended for you will land on another. Within four days you'll be as well as ever you were." It so fell out that four days after that she was so fully recovered that she not only got up from her bed, but went and visited her neighbours, which was wondered at by everyone who had known the condition she was in. Her neighbour Hellen Pringle came to be tormented with extreme pain, and remained so for a quarter of a year. Everyone in the countryside around was convinced that Helen Pringle had been wronged by your sorcery.

21. Also, on the [blank] of August 1687: Patrick Wood, maltman in Dunbar, has two

daughters, one eleven years old, and one seven. When they were going out at the end of the town near your house, you frightened them by some strange position you were lying in on the road. You got up and chased them. They immediately came home anid fell sick. The younger daughter became speechless, and the elder told her father how you were lying on the main road, then shot out your head and your feet, and got up and chased them. The next day you came to Patrick's house asking for milk. Patrick happened to come in, and drew his knife on you, saying he would be the death of you if you did not make his child speak again. At this you immediately collapsed at his feet, and his wife took him away from you. You got up and hurried home, and immediately the girl spoke again. They both recovered from that moment on.

22. Further evidence that you are guilty of that black art is that you can know of and indicate damage and danger to come. On the [blank] of March 1684 William Henderson, a sailor from Dunbar, was going to sea, and his wife Jean Murray was escorting him to the shore. When they were taking their leave of each other you repeated these words twice over, " It will be a long goodnight." It turned out that William was lost in a shipwreck within a few days.

23. There is further proof that you are guilty of the black art, and have the marks of it. On the [blank] of August 1683 you were at Dunbar shore where there were many strangers at the fishing. A dumb man came to you and put a great long pin into your shoulder. At that time you never said a word about feeling any pain, and when he took it out and held it up before several people you called him a dumb devil, and moved away from him.

24. Also, in one or other of the months of 1684 you came to a house in the West Links where you heard a young calf lowing. You asked what was wrong with the calf that it was roaring. Thomas Thomson's wife answered, "God save us all, it needs its dinner." "Hout," you said, "it was calved at an ebb sea. It will roar till it dies." Accordingly, it bawled continually in an extraordinary manner for three or four days, and died.

25. Also, on 2nd January last, on Handsel Monday, you came to the house of Thomas Whyte, cooper in Dumbar, asking for alms, which his wife gave you. You knew his brother John Whyte was in the house and had sent for a pint of ale. After going away you came back to the door again and asked for a drink of the ale. John Whyte replied that he would rather see you hanged and burnt before you got any of it. He called you a witch, and you said that you wished that there would be a hanged man about his house before long. And so it was that last March George Lumsdean from the Cove, John Whyte's next door neighbour, hanged himself and was carried close by his door.

26. Also, on 10th May this year, when you were in the tollbooth of Dumbar before the commissioners appointed by the Lords of the Privy Council for investigating you as highly suspect of witchcraft, you publicly acknowledged that you were a witch.

27. Also, on the 19th of this May, Mr Thomas Wood the minister of Dumbar was visiting you in prison, and asked if you were a witch. You answered that you were. He asked you how long ago you became one; twenty years? You answered, "No, not so long." He then asked you how you entered the service of the Devil. You answered that a Highland woman called Margaret McClain taught you. He asked, "How did she teach you? Did you renounce your baptism?" You answered that you did what she told you. He asked again, "Did she tell you to renounce your baptism?" You answered, "Yes." Then he said to you, "Did you do it then?" You answered that you did. The he said, "Will you abide by this confession?" You answered, "I will, for God knows everything."

Because of all this, and your usual devilish cursing against those who refused your unreasonable demands - for some of which you were committed to prison - it is obvious that you are guilty of the crimes of witchcraft, sorcery, necromancy, superstition and abusing the people, using spells and charms, laying on and taking off sickness, and committing malefices. You are art and part and a perpetrator of all these, and if this is found to be so by a jury, you ought to be punished by the penalty of death and confiscation of your moveabe possessions, to deter others by terror and example from committing the same crimes in future.

Signed: William Kirkwood

[RPC 3rd Ser, Vol xiii, P. 245ff]

May 30th 1688: Court of Justiciary held in the Tollbooth of Dumbar by Sir John Sinclair of Lochend, Sir William Baird of Newbyth, Mr Robert Lauder, one of the Clerks of Exchequer, James Mure of Bourhouse, James Forrest, former baillie, William Kirkwood and James Smith, merchants, Mr George Purves and George Sinclair, two of the baillies of Dumbar, on 30th May 1688, as empowered by our commission. Court lawfully constituted and cases called.

Catherine McTargett "entered in pannall" [*i.e.* appeared as the accused]. Mr Patrick Broun, solicitor in Dumbar and procurator fiscal for His Majesty's interest, produced along with the indictment a commission granted by our sovereign lord, His Majesty the King and the Lords of the Privy Council, which constitutes

Sir John Sinclair of Lochend,
Archibald Murray of Spott,
Sir William Baird of Newbyth,
Sir John Hall of Dunglass,
Robert Hamilton of Pressmennan,
Mr Robert Lauder, one of the
Clerks of Exchequer,
John Mure of Bourhousses,
James Forrest, former baillie,
William Kirkwood and
James Smith, merchants,
and the present baillies of Dumbar,

or any three of them as judges in the area for the trial of the accused, signed at Edinburgh on 3rd May. He also produced an act of the Committee of the Lords of Privy Council, of the same date as the commission, ordering that before sentencing the accused, the commissioners should return the verdict of the jury, and the whole process against the accused, to the Clerks of the Privy Council so that the commissioners can be given further direction in the matter. He also produced an act of the commissioners dated 10th May electing and constituting Mr George Purves, one of the present baillies of Dumbar, chairman of the commissioners in these proceedings, and nominating and electing William Kirkwood, clerk of Dumbar, as clerk to the process; Mr Patrick Broun as procurator fiscal; and Alexander Crombie and Robert Innes as court officers. These all appeared, accepted their responsibilities, and were sworn in etc. Also, today was appointed to be the meeting for trying the accused. He also produced an authorisation signed by the commissioners on 10th May directing the officers to summon the accused, the jurors, and the witnesses. These orders were duly carried out and certified.

On this day the indictment and grounds for prosecution were read, and the accused was asked if she had any objections to the relevance of the indictment, or anything to say against it. She acknowledged in open court the confession she made to the minister Mr Thomas Wood on 19th May - the last point of the indictment - that she is a witch and was acquainted with a Margaret McLane who instructed her. She admits that she said she had renounced her baptism, but says that in fact she did not do so. Mr Partick Broun, procurator fiscal, ordered a written record to be made.

Andrew Robisone in Wester Broomhous; Francis Dudgeon in Halhill; and Thomas

Brysone, slater in Dumbar; are fined a hundred merks each by the commissioners for defying the court. Having been lawfully summoned, and personally informed of the time they should attend as jurors in the process against the accused, they have been called several times but have not appeared.

The commissioners now reinstate these persons [*i.e.* Robisone, Dudgeon, and Brysone], since they appeared before the decision to fine them had been intimated. [This is a loose translation of a fairly dense passage.]

Having considered the indictment and the individual charges contained in it, the commissioners find all the charges taken together to be relevant. Not only that, but several individual articles separately and in themselves are sufficiently relevant to infer the contravention of the Act of Parliament, and to infer the crimes mentioned. The indictment is therefore referred to the procurator fiscal to prove, and for the consideration of the jury.

Signed: Mr G. Purves, chairman.

The accused was questioned in the presence of the commissioners on several points of the indictment. Regarding the seventh article, she confessed that the reason she gave Patrick Fergusone bread and cheese was because she alleged he had a grudge against her. Regarding the eighth article, she confessed that she dipped her hand in George Colme's water bucket and put her hand to the sole of her foot to take out some gorse spines. Regarding the ninth article, she admits that she laid George Fergusson's bonnet on his head with the crown downwards, but "cannot help it" [*i.e.* There's nothing she can do about that now. Possibly she also intends the meaning, "So what!"]. She confesses using the expressions in the tenth article. In the thirteenth she confesses the business of the salt and the fermentation, but says she was only joking. In the fifteenth article she says she prescribed syboe heads and sheeps' innards to Jean Johnstoun to make broth that would cure her. She also admitted in the presence of the commissioners and the jury the confession she made to the minister Mr Thomas Wood on 19th May, as stated in Article 27; also her judicial confession before the commissioners on 10th May contained in Article 26.

Signed: Mr G. Purves, chairman.

Mr Patrick Broun, procurator fiscal, brings forward these confessions in support of the witnesses' statements which are to be produced. He brought forward several reputable witnesses to prove the indictment, who took the oath, were purged of malice and partiality, were solemnly sworn, and were questioned individually in court in the presence of the accused and the jurors named below. Being asked, the accused raised no objections to the witnesses and jurors, who were all called before her. The commissioners fined Margaret Vertie, wife of John Hume, postmaster at Cockburnspath, and Marie Johnstoun, wife of Thomas Thomsone in West Links, the sum of a hundred merks each for defiance, since they had been lawfully summoned to bear witness and had not appeared.

Signed: Mr G. Purves, chairman.

Out of forty five, the commissioners elected and chose the following jurors:

George Miller, portioner of Westbarnes,
William Craig in Innerweik,
William Murray in Crahill,
James Smith in Eastbarnes,
Alexander Kirkwood in Pinkerton,
Thomas Wightman in Broxburne,
William Lausone there,
Alexander Crambie and Thomas Hog in Belton,
James Crombie and John Brysone in Eastbarnes,
Robert Sked in Belhaven,
William Cockburne and Nicill Kellie, wrights, and William Cockburne, cooper; burgesses of Dumbar.

[A total of 15 jurors.]

All of these were lawfully summoned and solemnly sworn. The commissioners referred the indictment to the jury for consideration. After mature and serious deliberation over the indictment and all the evidence produced, the jurors were removed from court. Entering again, they returned the following verdict, sealed. It was opened and read to thecourt.

Dumbar 3rd May 1688. The above-mentioned persons sitting as a jury unanimously chose James Crombie as foreman of the jury ["chancellor of the said inqueist"]. By the judicial confessions of the accused and the witnesses' statements produced, they found that the accused, Catherein Mactarget, is guilty of the crimes of witchcraft, sorcery, and superstition as indicted.

Signed: James Crumbie.

The commissioners have ordered this verdict, with a record of the whole process to be returned to the Clerks of the Council for the purpose previously specified.

Signed: Mr G. Purves, chairman. [RPC 3rd Ser, Vol xiii, p. 251 ff]

[The following is a record of the witnesses' statements which has also presumably been sent to the Privy Council with the indictment and the account of the proceedings of the trial.]

Dumbar 30th May 1688: Witnesses led at the instance of Mr Patrick Broune, procurator fiscal, against Catherein Mactargett, charged with witchcraft as set out in the indictment. They were all sworn, and testified before the jurors as follows: -Issobell Restoun, wife of George Milne in Eastbarnes:

Purged of partiality and malice, aged 36 years, solemnly sworn, she testifed that about three years ago, in oat-sowing time, she was at Thomas Ross's house where his daughter was making porridge. Catherein Mactargett came to the house and got alms from Thomas Ross's wife. After that she asked for porridge, and Margaret Ross replied that she would rather see her choke on it. The accused answered that some of her family would choke before long. It turned out that the same night the woman's father Thomas Ross choked on a piece of beef in the house of Patrick Logan the wright in East Barnes. She declares that she cannot write, and that this is the truth as she shall answer to God.

Signed: Mr G. Purves.

Janet Ross, servant to Alexander Home in Westbarnes:

Daughter of the above-mentioned Thomas Ross. Aged 24 years. Being purged, sworn, and questioned as above, declares in accordance with the above-written statement in everything. She declares that she cannot write, and that this is the truth as she shall answer to God.

Signed: Mr G. Purves.

George Walker, baker, burgess of Dumbar:

Aged 47, purged, sworn, and questioned, he testifies that in July or August 1672, the accused's husband William Broun was in his [George's] house selling a young cow to James Reed, butcher in Dumbar. The accused arrived in a great rage and shouted up that if James Reid bought her cow he would never draw blood from her. Accordingly, although he was a fit man and in perfect health at the time, he took ill the next day and died within three or four days. This is the truth as he shall answer to God.

Signed: George Wallace Mr G. Purves.

Alexander Affleck, butcher, burgess of Dumbar:

Aged 66; purged, sworn, and questioned, testifies in agreement with George Wallace's statements in all points. This is the truth as he shall answer to God. He declares that he cannot write.

Signed: Mr G. Purves.

Richard Merstoun, seaman in Dumbar:

Aged about 60; sworn, purged, and questioned, testifies that about eleven years ago he was at Dumbar shore and saw John

Fergusone take a piece of coal from the accused which she had taken out of his cart. He heard the accused say that they would be dear coals to him, and that he would not strike so much in future. He knows that John Fergusone came home to his house and took ill. He never came out again till he died, and he sweated to death. This is the truth as he shall answer to God, and he cannot write.

Signed: Mr G. Purves.

Mareon Bairnsfather, widow of the late John Fergusone:

Aged 60; sworn, purged, and questioned, testifies that eleven years ago her husband was getting coal at the shore, and Catherein Mactargett, the accused, took some coal out of his cart. She heard her husband say when he came from the shore, that when he struck her for stealing the coal, the accused said to him that these would be dear coals to him, and that he "should never stryk als much". [This might mean either that he ought not to be so ready to strike, or that he would never strike so much in future.] He came home immediately, and took a languishing sickness and never came out again till he died. This is the truth as she shall answer to God, and she cannot write.

Signed: Mr G. Purves.

Patrick Fergusone, mason, burgess of Dumbar:

Aged 46, married; sworn, purged, and questioned, testifies in complete agreement with the above testimony of Mareon Bairnsfather. Also, regarding Article 7 of the indictment, she declares that on the [blank] of January 1682, on Handsel Monday, the accused came to where the witness was at Ruchlawes Closse and offered him cheese and bread which he refused. She pressed it upon him and he took and tasted a little and gave it back to her again. She let it fall to the ground, and within a few days his wife Margaret Ritchesone lost all her senses, and was buried on the 13th of the same month. This is the truth as he shall answer to God.

Signed: Patt. Fergusone Mr G. Purves.

James Forrester, farmer in Spott:

Aged 39; sworn, purged, and questioned. Testifies that about five or six years ago the accused came to his house seeking alms, which his wife gave her. After that the accused asked for milk and was very determined to have it. However, he heard his wife say to her, "You'll get no milk here!" and the accused went away not very pleased. The next time his cow was milked she gave nothing but blood instead of milk. This continued for three or four days until she died. This is the truth as he shall answer to God.

Signed: James Forster Mr G. Purves.

Catherein Forrester, wife to the above James Forrester:

Aged 36; sworn, purged, and questioned. Testifies in complete agreement with the above testimony of her husband James Forrester. This is the truth as she shall answer to God. She further declares that the cow never ate again after the accused went away. She cannot write.

Signed: Mr G. Purves.

Andrew Stevinsone, servant to George Kirkwood, farmer in Newtonlies: Aged 61; sworn, purged, and questioned. Declares that that in the year 1674 when he was sowing oats on the land of Bourhousses, the accused came to him asking for a boll of the oats. He answered that he would rather give her a boll of coals to burn her with. The accused immediately went into his house to get a drink of water. Within the next two days the accused met with his wife, and his wife came home and fell ill with a very strange sickness and died raving mad ["ramished to death"]. The witness remembers now that he had struck the accused in the kitchen at Bourhousses because she would not get up and go away. This is the truth as he shall answer to God. He cannot write.

Signed: Mr G. Purves.

Sara Atchesone, widow of the late John Laury in Dumbar

Aged 53; solemnly sworn, purged, and questioned. Testifies that in 1678 her husband was lying in bed on a Sunday morning. She saw the accused come to her house and look in at her husband. She had a hair tether in her hand, and she laid it down and looked in at the witness's husband where he was lying quietly. He looked up and never closed his eyes again till he died the following Thursday. She saw a great many crows, more than forty, flying round her house and the houses of her neighbours in the close. Her husband took such a fearful "distemper" [fever?] that she had to get some others to hold him in the bed. For three years after that the accused would never look her in the face, but ran away from her. This is the truth as she shall answer to God. She cannot write.

Signed: Mr G. Purves.

John Smith, living in Dumbar:

Aged 40, married; solemnly sworn, purged, and questioned. Testified that at the time of the events described above he was living in the close beside the late John Laurie, and he saw the accused coming out of Laurie's house on a Sunday morning with a hair tether in her hand. He saw a great number of crows round the house, and was astonished at the noise of these crows. He was immediately called on to tie up John Laurie who had fallen into an extraordinary "distemper". When he went in he saw John Laurie snapping and biting at anything near him. He stared up and said, "There she is! There she is!" This is the truth as he shall answer to God. He cannot write.

Signed: Mr G. Purves.

Agnes Colme, wife of George Kemp, cooper, burgess of Dumbar:

Aged 20; sworn, purged, and questioned. Testifies that about three years ago when she was in her father's house in Spot, the accused came there seeking alms. The witness and Margaret Jacksone were there. They were frightened when they saw her, and prayed to God to bless them. The accused said that they wouldn't pray so much until they saw her pleasant face, and told the Evil Spirit to take notice of them. She put her fingers down by her side and dipped them in the water bucket, and put her fingers on the sole of her foot, staring at the witness all the time. Then she went away, and shortly after that three cows and four bullocks died belonging to her father George Colme.

Signed: Agnes Colme   Mr G. Purves.

Margaret Jaksone, servant to George Kemp, cooper, burgess of Dumbar: Aged 20; solemnly sworn, purged, and questioned. Testifies that she was in George Colme's house in Spot at the time of the above events, and knows and heard of everything exactly as is written in Agnes Colme's testimony. This is the truth as she shall answer to God. She cannot write.

Signed: Mr G. Purves.

Maurice Fergusone, mason, burgess of Dumbar:

Aged 40; sworn, purged, and questioned. Testifies that as described in Article 9, the accused laid the bonnet on his son George Fergusone's head with the crown of the bonnet downwards. The boy came home and told his father what the accused had done, and cried that his head was all hurting. He cried most piteously for three or four days and died. This is the truth as he shall answer to God, and he cannot write.

Signed: Mr G. Purves.

Jean Boig, servant to Mr Patrick Broun, solicitor:

Aged 24; sworn, purged, and questioned on Article 10 of the indictment. Declares that at the time mentioned the accused came to Patrick Mathie's house where the witness was a servant, and asked for some milk. She repeated these words three times. "If I break my nose I spoil my face, and when I spoil my face I break my fortune." After that she came to the house on a Sunday and offered Issobell Mathie some unshrunk coarse woolen cloth in pawn for money. Issobell was very angry with her for coming to the house to ask for milk or to pawn cloth, and sent her away. Since then Issobell has lain greatly troubled in mind, as explained at length in Article 10. This is the truth as she shall answer to God. She cannot write.

Signed: Mr G. Purves.

Christian Dumbar, also servant to Patrick Mathie:

Aged 24; sworn, purged, and questioned on Article 10. Testifies as above, except as to the offer of the unshrunk woolen cloth. She was not present, but when she came in she was told about it. This is the truth as she shall answer to God. She cannot write.

Signed: Mr G. Purves.

Lucress Smith, wife of William Brysone, slater, burgess of Dumbar.

Aged 30; sworn, purged, and questioned. Testifies according to Article 12 of the indictment. This is the truth as she shall answer to God. She cannot write.

Signed: Mr G. Purves.

William Brysone, slater.

Aged 48; sworn, purged, and questioned. Testifies according to Article 11 of the indictment about bringing the beast through the street.

Signed: W. Brysone   Mr G. Purves.

George Shirreff, farmer in Knowis: Aged 50; sworn, purged, and questioned. Says he knows nothing except by hearsay. This is the truth as he shall answer to God.   Signed: George Shirreff   Mr G. Purves.

Christian Orm, wife of the above George Shirreff:

Aged 48; sworn, purged, and questioned on Articles 13 and 20 of the indictment. Declares that the accused came to her house seeking alms, which she got. She also got the pan with porridge to lick. The accused asked for a drink, and got something to drink from the witness. The accused said that the witness had better drink in the house. She replied that this was so, but it needed yeast. The accused said that she would get yeast enough before long, and went away. When the witness went into the room where the brew was, the foam was rising up and gushing out in such a fearful manner that she shouted to some servants to see to the fermentation, and got buckets and caught it, although there was never any yeast put into it, which frightened them all. [As previously mentioned, this is tricky to put into modern English, since "barme" can mean yeast, or the fermenting brew, or the resulting foam.] She also declares that as stated in Article 20, the accused came to her unexpectedly when she was extremely ill, and said that what was intended for her would land on another. Helen Pringle was newly brought to bed, and was tortured in the way described in Article 20. This is the truth as she shall answer to God, and she cannot write. [*Sic* Her signature follows.]

Signed: Christian Orm

Mr G. Purves.

Patrick Shirreff, farmer in Knowes:

Aged 50; sworn, purged, and questioned. Declares concerning Article 20 that he knows nothing except by hearsay, and this is the truth as he shall answer to God.

Signed: Patrick Shirreff

Mr G. Purves.

Hellen Pringle, wife to the above Patrick Shirreff:

Aged 48; sworn, purged, and questioned on Article 20. At the time mentioned in the Article, the accused came to her and offered to sell her onions which her neighbour Christian Orm had refused. The witness took them, and the accused said Christian Orm would have further trouble. Immediately afterwards Christian's husband George Shirreff took ill and lay so for a long time. This is the truth as she shall answer to God. She further testified that at the same time or thereabouts, the accused came seeking lodgings and the witness let her into the "pease barn" where she slept amongst the pea-chaff. The chaff was given to some of the horses and their two best horses died within a fortnight. The servants were angry about the accused getting lodgings. She cannot write.

Signed: Mr G. Purves.

Margaret Aitken, widow of the late William Denholme in Knowes:

Aged 60; sworn, purged, and questioned on Article 13. Declares that the accused came to the Knowes where the witness was a servant, and got some porridge with some weak ale on it in the pan. The accused said it was tasteless and needed salt. The mistress of the house said, "How does ale need salt?" The accused said there was better ale in the house. The mistress said there was, but it needed yeast. The accused said she would get yeast enough before long, and went away. Shortly after that, the mistress went into the room where there was a barrel with a brew that had never got yeast in it. Seeing the foam rise up to the ceiling, she shouted to the servants to come in and see what was happening. The witness went in with the rest and saw it, and this is the truth as she shall answer to God. She further declares that she remembers that there was just about a gallon of fermenting ale burst out of the barrel.

Questioned on Article 20, she declares that she knows Helen Pringle fell sick the fourth day after she was brought to childbed. She was in great pain and remained so for half a year. This was the fourth day after the accused met Christian Orm, so the one recovered and the other fell sick, as the accused said would happen. It was the opinion of the whole surrounding countryside that Helen Pringle was wronged by the accused's witchcraft. This is the truth as she shall answer to God. She cannot write.

Signed: Mr G. Purves.

James Lauder, burgess of Dumbar:

Aged 48, married; sworn, purged, and questioned on Article 14, he testifies that in the year mentioned the accused came to his house asking for alms, and got a handful of meal. She asked insistently for yeast [or perhaps fermenting ale], and although she was refused several times, in the end they were forced to give her it. The witness's wife had no sooner given her the yeast than she took such a violent pain in her arm that it almost drove her mad. A Doctor Maccullo was in the house, and drew blood from her, but she was no better, and he said some evil person had acted against her. She had a young child at the breast, which took ill and died. His wife then immediately recovered. This is the truth as he shall answer to God.

Signed: J. Lauder Mr G. Purves.

Katherine Sandilands, wife of James Lauder, burgess of Dumbar:

Aged 46; solemnly sworn, purged and questioned. Testifies exactly in accordance with the preceding testimony from James Lauder. She also says that the accused came back to the house and the witness said, "Away with you!" The accused answered, "God help you, you will never be well until either you or your child die." Thus it was that the child died within a few days and the witness recovered. This is the truth as she shall answer to God. She cannot write.

Signed: Mr G. Purves.

John Home, postmaster in Cockburnespath:

Present in court, aged 48, married; sworn, purged, and questioned. Testifies concerning Article 19 that the accused came to his house in the year mentioned and asked for alms from his servant Helen Patersone, which she got. She asked for something else and the girl refused. The accused went away, and Helen Paterson, who had been healthy enough, fell unconscious and was carried to her bed in a great fever. When he heard how it had come about he sent a servant man to look for the accused and bring her back. When she arrived, she said the girl would be well enough if she had a drink, and the accused had a drink made up and gave it to her with her own hand. Immediately Helen Paterson got up and got on with her work as usual, without any other trick or cure. This is the truth as he shall answer to God.

Signed: Jo. Hoome   Mr G. Purves.

Helen Purves, referred to above:

Aged 28, married; sworn, purged, and questioned on Article 19. Testifies that in the year mentioned she was in perfect health when the accused came to the Post House where she was then in service. She asked for a drink from the witness, which she refused. The accused went away muttering some words, and immediately the witness fell senseless as if she were dead. She was carried out of the cellar to her bed, and lay delirious until the accused was brought back, which was for about three or four hours. She was brought in to the witness, and got a drink made up of ale with an egg, and gave it to her out of her own hand at the witness's bedside. When she had tasted a little of it she soon recovered. This is the truth as she shall answer to God. She cannot write.

Signed: Mr G. Purves.

John Ker, servant to John Home, postmaster at Cockburnspath:

Aged 38; purged and questioned on Article 19. Testifies that he was a servant in the house at that time, and was sent away by his master to search for the accused and bring her back. He found her at Birnieknowes and brought her back. When he came back with the accused, Helen Paterson the servant woman was lying in bed delirious, with several people holding her. He heard the accused say to Helen Pattersone that she had not been well "sained" that day. [To "sain" means to bless, or protect oneself from harm or evil by a ritual sign, act, or prayer.] This is the truth as he shall answer to God.

Signed: John Ker   Mr G. Purves.

James Simpsone, mason in Cockburnespeth: Aged 54, married; sworn, purged, and questioned. Testifies concerning Article 19 that he was in the Post House at the time, and saw the accused brought back, and Hellen Patersone lying in bed with some women holding her down. He heard the accused give directions to heat her a drink and boil her an egg, and the poor thing would be well again. The witness went away, and he heard that the girl got up and got better. This is the truth as he shall answer to God.

Signed: James Simsone   Mr G. Purves.

John Hog, mason in Dunglas:

Aged 50, married; sworn, purged, and questioned on Article 19. Testifies that at the time mentioned he was at the Post House. He knew the accused was at the Post House, and that after she went away Hellen Patersone the servant woman became delirious as mentioned. He saw the women holding her in the bed. He knows that when the accused was brought back the girl recovered, but does not know what the accused prescribed - only that everyone there was frightened, thinking that the accused was the cause of it. This is the truth as he shall answer to God.

Signed: John Hoge   Mr G. Purves.

George Lyle, farmer in Saltpanhall:

Aged 48, married; sworn, purged, and questioned on Article 19. Declares that at the time mentioned he was at the Post House and saw the accused there seeking alms, which she got. After that she asked Hellen Pattersone for a drink, which she refused her. The accused went away, and he heard her say Hellen Patterson would rue it. Then the girl fell into a fever, both dumb and senseless, and was carried to her bed where she lay in that state until the accused was brought back. He knows that Hellen Patersone got up and grew better after the accused was brought back. This is the truth as he shall answer to God. He cannot write.

Signed: Mr G. Purves.

Thomas Lamb. Hawker in Cockburnspath: Aged 38, married; sworn, purged, and

Dunbar Tollbooth (left), where Catherine McTarget was imprisoned and probably also tried.

At Dunbar Shore (Old Harbour, below), observing a seaman saying goodbye to his wife, she remarked, "It will be a long goodnight!" He was lost at sea.

questioned on Article 19. Testifies that he was in the Post House at the tme mentioned, and saw the servant women lying in a great delirium, and several women holding her in the bed. He knows that the accused was brought back, and he saw the girl get the drink. Afterwards he heard the girl say that she was better after the accused came back and gave her the drink, and she worked as usual. This is the truth as she shall answer to God.

Signed: Thomas Lamb Mr G. Purves.

Jean Johnstoune, wife of George Walker, wheelwright, burgess of Dumbar: Aged 28; sworn, purged, and questioned on Article 15. Testifies in agreement with it in everything. This is the truth as she shall answer to God. She declares that she cannot write.

Signed: Mr G. Purves.

George Walker, above-named:

Aged 56; sworn, purged, and questioned on Article 15. Agrees with the content of it in everything. This is the truth as he shall answer to God.

Signed: George Walker. Mr G. Purves.

Patrick Wood, maltman, burgess of Dumbar:

Aged 50; purged and questioned on Article 21. Testifies in agreement with it in everything. This is the truth as he shall answer to God. He cannot write.

Signed: Mr G. Purves.

Rachal Darra, wife of Patrick Wood:

Aged 44; sworn, purged and questioned on Article 25. Testifies in agreement with it in everything. This is the truth as she shall answer to God. She cannot write.

Signed: Mr G. Purves.

Jonet Symontoun, wife of John Affleck, shoemaker, burgess of the burgh: Aged 65; solemnly sworn, purged, and questioned on Article 16 of the indictment. Testifies in agreement with its content in everything. This is the truth as she shall answer to God. She cannot write.

Signed: Mr G. Purves.

Hellen Milne, wife of James Congiltoun, burgess of Dumbar:

Aged 40; sworn, purged, and questioned on Article 17 of the indictment. Testifies in agreement with its content in everything. This is the truth as she shall answer to God. She cannot write.

Signed: Mr G. Purves.

James Congiltoun above mentioned:

Aged 50; sworn, purged, and questioned on Article 18. Testifies in agreement with it in everything. This is the truth as he shall answer to God. He cannot write.

Signed: Mr G. Purves.

William Smeall, living in Dumbar:

Aged 27, married; sworn, purged, and questioned on Article 22 of the indictment. Declares that at the time mentioned he saw a woman with a coarse woolen coat standing on the shore. He heard her say the following words twice over - this was when the seaman William Henderson was going to sea and taking leave of his wife - "You may take leave of each other, for it will be a long goodnight." It was rather dark, and he is not sure if it was the accused, but he thinks it was her because William Henderson's wife could never look at her after her husband was lost at sea on that voyage. This is the truth as he shall answer to God. He cannot write.

Signed: Mr G. Purves.

Alexander Affleck, butcher, burgess of Dumbar:

Aged 66, married; sworn, purged, and questioned on Article 23. Testifies in agreement with its content in everything. This is the truth as he shall answer to God. He cannot write.

Signed: Mr G. Purves.

Thomas Thomason in West Links:

Aged about 40, married; sworn, purged, and questioned on Article 24 of the indictment. Testifies in agreement with its content in everything. This is the truth as he shall answer to God. He cannot write.

Signed Mr G. Purves.

Thomas Whyte, cooper in Dumbar, and John Whyte in Cove, his brother: Aged about 30, both married; both sworn, purged, and questioned on Article 25 of the indictment. They both testify to the truth of this article as it is in the indictment. This is the truth as they shall answer to God. They declare that they cannot write.

Signed: Mr G. Purves.

As for Article 26, the procurator fiscal Mr Patrick Broun produces the statement written below, signed by the chairman and commissioners who were present on 10th May, containing the judicial confession of the accused as recorded.

Signed: Mr G. Purves.

George Cairnes, living in Dumbar: Aged 53, married; sworn, purged, and questioned on article 27 of the indictment. Testifies that on 19th May when the accused was in prison, the minister Mr Thomas Wood went to visit her, and asked if she was a witch. She answered that she is one. Then he heard the minister ask how long it was since she became one - twenty years? The accused answered, "No, not so long." Then the witness heard him ask how long it was since she entered into the service of the Devil. She answered that a Highland woman called Margaret McClain taught her. Then he asked how did she teach her? Did she renounce her baptism? The accused answered that she did what she was told to do. Then he asked again if she told her to renounce her baptism. The accused answered, "Yes." Then the witness heard the minister say to the accused, "Did you do so, then?" The accused answered that she did. Then he asked if she would abide by that confession. She answered that she would, for God knew everything. This he declares to be true as he shall answer to God. He further declares that this confession was made in the presence of James Smith, one of the commissioners.

Signed: George Cairns   Mr G. Purves.

Alexander Carnes, church officer in Dumbar:

Aged 36; sworn, purged, and questioned. Declares concerning Article 27 that he was present in the tollbooth with the minister and the accused, and heard the above confession word for word as written above. The accused was on her knees when she confessed. This is the truth as he shall answer to God.

Signed: Alexander Carns   Mr G. Purves

John Inglis, burgess of Dumbar:

Aged about 60, married; sworn, purged, and questioned. Declares as above in everything. This is the truth as he shall answer to God. He cannot write.

Signed Mr G. Purves.

George Restone, one of the public officers of the burgh:

Aged 64, married; sworn, purged, and questioned. Declares as above in everything. This is the truth as he shall answer to God. He cannot write.

Signed Mr G. Purves.

Patrick Kellie, burgess of Dumbar:

Aged about 48; sworn, purged, and questioned. Declares as above in everything. This is the truth as he shall answer to God.

Signed P. Kellie   Mr G. Purves.

[3rd Ser, Vol xii, P. 251 ff]

[In his "Historical Notices" the judge Lord Fountainhall remarks that after being found guilty by the commissioners in Dunbar, Catherine McTarget was subsequently called twice before the Privy Council, since they were sceptical about her guilt. Apparently the jury found her guilty by a majority of only two votes. However, on 12th July she was finally returned to Dunbar "to be burnt there if her judges pleased". Her confession seems to have been the deciding factor. I have been unable to find any record of Catherine's execution, although the Dunbar records mention her being sent to Edinburgh to be interviewed by the Privy Council. It would be nice to think that the commissioners decided to spare her life after all, but given that she was such a long-standing nuisance, it is perhaps unlikely.]

6. Justiciary Court Records

As previously stated, there were two ways of putting witches on trial. The commonest method was trial by commission, but witches could also be tried by the High Court of Justiciary. It is generally believed that suspects had a marginally better chance of acquittal in the High Court, which was of course conducted by professionals instead of the local bigwigs involved in trial by commission. Suspects were also entitled to a "proloquitor" to speak in their defence. He could be a layman, but was often a qualified advocate. Incidentally, some writers have surmised that suspects were not allowed this benefit in courts set up by commission. However, in some of the Haddington trials the accused was specifically asked if she had anyone to speak for her. The reply was always in the negative, but the fact that the question was asked at all would suggest that defence "proloquitors" were not actually forbidden. [See "Burgh Records".]

There are three main sources of Justiciary Court material in the National Archives of Scotland. Firstly, there are the JC26 boxes of court processes. These contain preparatory work for the case, including confessions, statements taken from the suspect, statements from witnesses, lawyers' letters and casenotes, and the formal "dittay" or indictment which presented the case for the prosecution. There are sometimes also what appear to be notes jotted down during the course of the trial, and occasionally a note of how the individual members of the jury voted on each charge in the indictment. The documents range from thick wads of carefully written records to tiny scraps of paper bearing a few illegibly scrawled words. The contents of the JC26 boxes are uncatalogued, although Larner's *Sourcebook of Scottish Witchcraft* lists the numbers of the boxes where witchcraft material is known to be stored. In the boxes, most of the witchcraft processes are clearly labelled "WITCHCRAFT". It has always been suspected that there was other witchcraft material lurking unnoticed in the boxes, and unfortunately there is no other way to find it but to search laboriously through each box. As far as East Lothian is concerned, however, there is not much that is not already known about.

The second source of witchcraft material is the High Court Minute Books [JC6], where the clerk of the court would write up a sort of diary of each day's events.

Finally, there are the Books of Adjournal [JC2], where an account of each trial and its result was entered as an official record. Witchcraft trials which have appeared in print in various publications have usually been taken from the Books of Adjournal.

Thus, in theory, each witchcraft trial should have its documentation collected in a JC26 box, should have been minuted in the High Court Minute Books, and should have finally been entered in its "finished" version in the Books of Adjournal. It will come as no surprise to learn that this ideal state of affairs is not always the case.

Where a published version of the trial exists, I have used it. Sometimes there is a dittay in a JC26 box which is more or less the same as what appears in the Minute Books and the Books of Adjournal. Clearly in such cases there is little point in regurgitating all three, and usually I will use the source to which Larner's

"Sourcebook" first directed me. If I quote more than one version of a trial it will be because there are interesting or significant differences. Obviously there can be material gathered in the preparation of a case which does not appear in the final version of the trial, and I quote a substantial amount of this. The JC26 boxes also contain evidence gathered for cases which never came to trial, and which therefore do not appear in the High Court Minute Books or Books of Adjournal.

Sometimes I summarise repetitious passages. Sometimes, admittedly, I summarise because I have quite simply found the source documents impossible to read [not too often, fortunately]. As in previous chapters, I have "translated" the original text into modern English. Those unhappy with this can follow up my references and read the original documents for themselves.

Most of the documentation for the "North Berwick" trials can be found among the Justiciary Court Records. Having already dealt with these, however, I do not propose to go over the same ground again. The first East Lothian case to come to trial after North Berwick for which records still remain would seem to have been in 1602. It can be found in Robert Pitcairn's *Criminal Trials in Scotland 1488 - 1624*, published in Edinburgh in 1833. Pitcairn's material is taken from the Books of Adjournal. His transcriptions are usually held to be trustworthy, but there are occasional lapses. I have already mentioned, for example, his mistaking of long "s" for "f" in Agnes Sampson's prayer.

1602

July 21st 1602: James Reid, formerly servant to George Anderson in Mussilburgh. Reported, accused, and prosecuted. Indicted for the following crimes: -

For being a common sorcerer, charmer, and abuser of God's people by purporting to be able to heal all kinds of sickness. This skill he learned from his master the Devil in Bynnie Craigs and Corstorphin Craigs, where he met him and consulted him in order to learn it. The Devil gave him three pennies on one occasion, and a piece of lard out of his bag another time. He appeared to James on many occasions, sometimes in the likeness of a man, sometimes in the likeness of a horse. James has consulted with him on many different occasions since his first meeting with him about thirteen years ago. The Devil instructed him to take south-running water to heal these diseases.

He cured Sara Borthuik by his sorcery and devilry when she was grievously troubled and diseased, by bringing south-running water from the well at Schyreff Braes, and scattering a certain quantity of salt and wheat round her bed. She was healed by this cure.

Being particularly persuaded by Jonet Crystie, daughter of John Crystie at Crystiesounis Mylne, and by his mother [blank], he consulted with the Devil to destroy David Libbertoun, baker, burgess of Edinburgh, and also his wife, their corn, and their goods. The Devil made him take a piece of raw meat, on which he made nine nicks, and enchanted it. He delivered this to Jonet, and got her to lay part of it under the mill door, and the rest under the stable door to destroy his horse and cattle. He also enchanted nine stones for him, which James scattered on David Libberton's land to destroy his corn.

Also, James, and Jonet Crystie and her mother, made a wax image which the Devil enchanted. The image was turned at a fire in Johnne Crystiesone's house to destroy David Libbertone himself. [As in the case of the North Berwick witches, "pictour", the word used here, should be understood as an image rather than a "picture".]

He cured Johnne Crystie, who was suffering from a swelling, by putting three silk laces in a devilish manner round his waist, which he wore for ten weeks. Then they went away from him, but he did not know how. [It is not quite clear here whether it was the laces or the swellings which went away.]

Verdict: By the mouth of their foreman John Howie, the jury unanimously found, pronounced, and declared James Reid to be found culpable and convicted of all the crimes specified above.

Sentence: To be taken to the Castel Hill of Edinburgh and there to be strangled at a stake, and his body to be burned to ashes. Since he is convicted of these crimes, all his moveable goods are to be forfeited and collected for His Highness's use.

[Pitcairn, Vol 2, P. 421]

1607

March 10th 1607: Issobel Griersoune, wife of John Bull, workman in the Pannis.

Mr William Hairt, Justice depute.

Witchcraft, sorcery, incantation etc.

Indicted and accused of the crimes recorded below: -

Having conceived a cruel hatred and malice against Adam Clark in Prestounpannis, for the past year and a half she has continually used all kinds of devilish and ungodly means to be revenged on him. Particularly, in the month of November in the year of God 1606, between eleven and twelve o' clock at night, Adam was lying in bed with his wife, and his servant woman was lying in another bed. Then Isobel, in the likeness of her own cat, and accompanied by a great number of other cats, entered the house in a devilish manner and made a great and fearful noise and commotion. Adam, lying in bed with his wife, and his servants who were in the house at the time were seized with such a great fear that they were almost going mad.

Then the Devil in the likeness of a black man appeared in the house in a fearful manner, came up to the servant woman who was standing on the floor, and hauled her up and down the house by the hair, after he had snatched the kerchief off her head and thrown it in the fire. The poor woman became so seriously ill after this that she lay bedridden for six weeks with her life in great danger, and still has not regained perfect health. All this is well known.

Also, Isobel was accused of conceiving a deadly feud, rancour, and evil will against the late William Burnet in Prestoun-pannis, husband of the widow Margaret Myller. She devised all sorts of devilish and ungodly means to bereave him of his natural life. To achieve this, as a manifest sorcerer and witch, in January 1600 she laid a fearful and unfamiliar sickness on him by throwing a piece of raw meat in at his door. For half a year after that the Devil appeared in the house every night in the shape of a naked infant. He appeared in front of the fire with an enchanted image in his hand.

After that the Devil appeared in Isobel's likeness in William's house, in front of the fire and in various other parts of the house, and in a most discourteous and filthy manner she urinated ["pischit"] on Margaret Myller, and in various parts of the house. In the end William named Isobell by her name, and she immediately vanished. After this, William Burnet continually wasted and pined away with the previously mentioned strange sickness. For three years no cure could be found, and at length about September 1605 he departed this life in great anguish and pain. Thus, he was most devilishly bewitched by her as described, and she is art and part in this the late William's sickness and death.

Also she is accused of casting a serious illness on Robert Peden in the Pannis by devilish means in the month of October 1593. He remained sick for a year and eighteen weeks, swooning and fainting away, and although he tried all the usual ways of recovering his health, he grew worse every day. At length he remembered that he owed Issobell nine shillings and four pence from before he had fallen ill. He had refused to pay her the money until she brought back some plates of his she had kept. After addressing several blasphemous words to William, she said he would repent it, and said he would not have all his clothes at the same time. [*sic* Pitcairn, who I think is confusing "plaittis" and "claithis", and has misread one for the other.] He went to her immediately, repaid the money, and asked her thrice for his health for God's sake, saying, "If you have done me any wrong or injury, repair it, and restore my health to me." After that, Robert Peddane recovered his health within twenty four hours.

Also, she was accused that having lost her cat half a year before, about last January, as she was passing Robert Peddane's window she pulled out his cat. At that time there was good new ale fermenting and brewing in the vats. Several honest neighbours had been drinking it, but by her devilish incantation and sorcery, from that time onwards this batch of ale turned in such a way that it became rotten and black, thick like the dirt of the gutter, and with a filthy and pestilent smell. Nobody could drink it or bear the smell of it.

Also, she is accused and indicted that having conceived a deadly ill-will, hatred, and malice against Robert Peddane's wife Margaret Donaldsone, around Hallowe'en in 1605 she came in her devilish manner under silence and cloud of night to Robert Peddane's house. She entered in some devilish and unknown way. Inside the house Margaret Donaldsoune was lying in bed with her husband, sleeping soundly. Isobel then pulled Margaret out of bed by the shoulder, and flung her violently to the floor. As a result, Margaret's spirits failed her and she remained unconscious for a long time. Afterwards, when she came to herself, she fell into a fearful and unfamiliar sickness, so the once in every twenty four hours her head and breast were so seriously troubled that for the space of an hour she was mad, and did not know what she was doing. This went on with great force for five or six days. After six days Isobel heard that she was being blamed for this wicked and devilish turn of events, and so she asked the neighbours to arrange for her and Margaret to drink together. When this was done she recovered her health again, and continued in perfect health for eight or ten days. After that, hearing her name slandered, and hearing herself called a witch who could lay on and take off sickness, she came to Margaret's house, roused again by rage and envy. She addressed many devilish and horrible words to her, saying, "May the faggots of hell land on you!" and "May you boil in hell's cauldron!" With these and similar devilish expressions she went away, and after that the previously mentioned fearful sickness overtook Margaret again. For nine weeks altogether she was affected in a most fearful manner for an hour every twenty four hours, until a poor woman came to Margaret's door to ask for food. When she saw Margaret visited by this fearful sickness she declared that she was bewitched and had all the symptoms of it. After that the sickness ended, and did not come back to her until the beginning of last December when Isabel came by her door with a creel on her back and said, "Away, you thief! I'll have your heart for spreading tales about me so falsely!" Immediately after that the sickness came upon her again, and she was most heavily vexed and troubled with it until the 25th of January last when Isobel and Margaret were confronted with each other, and questioned in the presence of the Lord Justice regarding the devilish crimes described above.

Also, she is indicted as a common sorcerer, a witch, and abuser of the people by laying on and taking off sickness and diseases, using all sorts of devilish and ungodly means to earn her living, and using charms and other devilish practices.

Pursuers: Adam Clark, blacksmith in the Pannis; Margaret Myller, widow of the late

Williame Burnet; Robert Pedane, and his wife Margaret Robiesone.

Spokesmen for the accused: Robert Hammiltoune; John Bull in the Pannis.

Verdict: By the mouth of their foreman David Seton, baillie in Tranent, the jury found, pronounced, and declared Issobell Griersoune to be guilty, culpable, and convicted of all and sundry of the points contained in the indictment, and of the particular crimes described there.

Sentence: The Justice Depute, by the mouth of the dempster James Hendersoun, ordered Issobell to be taken to the Castell-hill of Edinburgh, to be strangled to death there at a stake, and her body to be burnt to ashes as convicted of the crimes described. All her moveable goods are to be forfeited and collected for our Sovereign Lord's use, since she is convicted of these crimes.

[Pitcairn, Vol 2, P. 523]

[Might Isobel Grierson have been related to the Robert Grierson from Prestonpans who features strongly in the "North Berwick" ongoings of 1590-91?]

1608

May 27th 1608: Beigis Tod in Lang-Nydrie.

Mr William Hairt, Justice Depute.

Reported, accused, and prosecuted at the instance of Mr Robert Foulis, Advocate Substitute to our Sovereign Lord's Advocate, of the following crimes of sorcery: -

In the month of August 1594, she, accompanied by her sister the late Cristiane Tod, John Graymeill, Margaret Dwne, and Ersch Marian, met with their accomplices, all witches and abusers of the people, at Dien-fute of Lang Nydrie. There the Devil appeared to them and reproved Beigis Tod very sharply for being so late. She replied, "Sir, I couldn't get here any sooner." Immediately after this they all went to Beigis's house in Lang Nydrie, where after they had drunk together for a while, they took a cat in their devilish manner and drew it nine times through the hook above Beigis's fire, and then came as quickly as they could to Seaton-thorne, to the north of the gate. There the Devil called for Cristiane Tod, and went to Robert Smart's house. Then he brought her out, and as she was coming with him she became very frightened, and said to him, "Sir, what are you going to do with me?" He replied, "Don't be afraid. You're going back to your sister Beigis and the rest of the company who are waiting for you at the thorn tree."

Then they all went together with the Devil to the iron gate of Seatoun where they took a cat again, and drew it nine times through the iron gate. Immediately after this they came to the barn [*sic* Pitcairn. Perhaps more likely "burn".] in front of George Feudar's door, where they christened the cat and called her Margaret. Then they all came back again to the Deane-fute where they had first met, and cast the cat to the Devil.

For these devilish practices Cristian Tod, John Gray-meill, Ersche Marioun, Margaret Dwne were convicted and burnt; and Beigis Tod is art and part of the crime of sorcery and witchcraft described above, as was well known.

[These events could not in fact have happened in 1594. In a letter dated 23rd February 1591, Bowles, the English ambassador, names most of Beigis Tod's associates as already having been executed. - Calendar of State Papers, Vol X, P. 476 ff.]

Also, Beigis Tod fell out with the late Alexander Fairlie in Lang Nydrie. In the month of June 1591, to be revenged on him and his children, she cast a heavy and unfamiliar sickness on his son Alexander Fairlie by her sorcery and witchcraft. He fainted away with severe sweating and burning at the heart. This illness lasted for two months, so that no-one thought he would live. Every night Beigis appeared to him in her own likeness, and he called upon her continually for help. During the day she appeared to him in the shape of a dog, which almost put him out of his wits. Because of this, his father Alexander went to Beigis Tod, and after he was reconciled to her, beseeched her most earnestly to come and cure the sickness. She refused to come, but at the earnest request of Archibald Galloway, she came to the house accompanied by her two sons. As soon as young Alexander saw her, he became better and better from that time on, and recovered from the illness. She thus committed manifest devilry and witchcraft by laying on and taking off sickness as described.

Also, she was accused by the Advocate, and by the dyer Robert Woid, of casting a similar uncanny sickness on Robert last November by her sorcery and witchcraft.

Verdict: By the mouth of David Seatoun, baillie in Tranent, the jury unanimously found Beigis guilty of the first two points of the indictment. By a majority, they found, pronounced, and declared her to be innocent and aquitted of the sorcery and witchcraft used by her against Robert Woid in laying the sickness on him as described in the indictment.

Sentence: For the two crimes of which she is convicted the judge ordered her to be taken to the Castell-hill of Edinburgh, and there to be strangled at a stake and her body burnt to ashes. All her goods are to be forfeited.

[Pitcairn, Vol 2, p. 542]

[As well as the material recorded in Pitcairn, envelope JC40/3 in the National Archives of Scotland contains a paper marked "Beigis Tod wiche hir dittay". The first charge of this version of the indictment, dealing with the meeting at Longniddry Dean, the ceremonies with the cats, and the mention of the burning of Christian Tod, John Graymeill, and Ersch Marion, is almost word for word the same as Pitcairn. A marginal note in JC40/3 says "Fylit all in ane voce of this poynt", although another note seems to indicate that there was no actual evidence - presumably because the others involved had been executed long before. As for the second charge, this also carries the marginal note "Fylit of this poynt all in ane voce". It is also almost word for word the same as Pitcairn, up until the point where Beigis is persuaded to visit the sick boy Alexander Fairlie, and ends slightly differently.]

... At this request she came with him to his house accompanied by her two sons. As soon as she had spoken to him and given him certain instructions on how to treat himself, the sickness left him, and by her devilish practices he recovered his health.

[The next charge, relating to John Fairlie, is deleted by pen strokes, and a marginal note reads "past fra", indicating that this charge has been dropped. It reads as follows: -]

Also, immediately after this, out of [illegible] and ill-will against Alexander Fairlie and his children, by your witchcraft and enchantments you laid a similar serious illness on John Fairlie, a young infant, who lay wasting away for ten days after that in great agony and pain. The child died of this sickness, and therefore you by your enchantment and sorcery are art and part of the murder of this child.

Also, a quarrel arose between James Bain her son, and Robert Woid, a dyer, because Robert had caused legal officers in Edinburgh to arrest him and put him in the Tolbooth for a debt owed by him to Robert. To be revenged on Robert, in November of last year, when he came to the village of Langnydrie to visit his sister, by her devilish practices Beigis cast a grievous disease and sickness upon him. For a period of four hours every day, and sometimes at night, he fell down in a trance, having his heart torn from him so that all his senses left him. He was also as cold as iron the whole time, then a great sweat would come upon him with such tremendous heat that it was as if he had been in a hot furnace. This terrible sickness seized him every day and continued with him for [blank] weeks until fourteen days before last Easter. He got no relief from it until the time that through the great efforts of his brother in law James Markill, he got Beigis's son James Baine to come into the town of Edinburgh where Robert Woid was lying, and they were reconciled. After that he began to recover from his illness. Also, several times since then Beigis has asked James Adnistoun in Langnydrie to effect a reconciliation between herself and this Robert, so that he would not accuse her of this crime or pursue her for it. [Marginal notes show that this charge was sworn to by the "pursuer" - presumably Robert Woid - but that the jury acquitted Beigis of it by a majority.]

As evidence of this, on the Tuesday after Easter, understanding that Robert Woid had gone to Seaton to report you to My Lady, you came to Nicoll Cuike's door and said, "Alas and woe is me. Robert Woid has gone to Seaton to accuse me, and you'll be rid of me now. God grant that the earth would open and swallow me before I am made a public spectacle and a shame to my children." As further evidence, you sent Issobell Couk to James Wilson in Langnudrye to earnestly plead with him to leave off pursuing you for witchcraft.

[The following sentence looks like an insertion, possibly a memo.] To ask why he threw salt in the fermenting brew before he brought it in to make your ale.

[The next sentence begins as a marginal note, but eventually crosses the page. Its meaning is not altogether clear but the following makes most sense..] Every time you brewed your ale, along with certain charms and incantations you always threw salt in the tub and other vessels and [illegible] in which you bring in your brew to ferment. [Another marginal note indicates that Beigis was acquitted of the accusations recorded in this paragraph.]

Also, in 1603, a quarrel arose between your daughter and Davie Fairlie's wife in Langnidre about a comb that went missing. Your daughter Beatrix went over and asked Davie Fairlie's wife for it. She replied that she didn't have it, and what's more, had never seen it. As this turned into an argument, your daughter said to her that it would be the dearest comb she had ever seen, and she would repent it from her heart. Since then her ale would never ferment, and David will take on his conscience that he is 500 merks worse off because of her.

[Marginal note: Acquitted.]

Also, David Fairlie's maidservant's brother in law happened to be in Beatrix Tod's house. He sent for the maid because Beatrix's ale was finished, and told her to go and fetch a pint from William Patterson's, and bring it to Beatrix's house. It was twenty days after that before David's maid had any other errand to William's house, but then his housekeeper sent her to get some yeast to start off a new brew. Their answer to this was, "Sorrow on you, for we've never had ale nor yeast since you took that pint to Beatrix Tod's house." Taking offence, the woman came east to Beatrix Tod's and reproved her, saying, "What's this you've done to William Paterson's folk? They say they've never managed to *get ale* nor yeast since I brought that pint of ale to you and my brother in law. I ask you for God's sake to give them their luck back again, if it's the case that you've done them wrong." Beatrix answered,"If there's any evil, blame them for it!"

[Marginal note: Acquitted.]

Also, a disagreement fell out between your daughter and David Fairlie's wife in Langnydrie in the month of [damage] 1602, about a missing comb of yours. You directed your daughter to go to David Fairlie's house to look for it, and she and David Fairlie's wife quarrelled in [illegible]. Then your daughter shouted loudly at her that it would be the dearest comb she ever saw, and she would repent it from her heart. [Some of the following sentence is deleted. Probably the whole sentence is meant to be taken out.] Since that time, by your enchantments and devilish devices, David has never got any good out of his brewing. Neither he nor his wife could ever get any good from the stuff. Since then, David's wife could never get any good from her brewing but [Deleted: "gave up brewing ale"] their ale stopped fermenting. They could get no fermentation in it, to their great loss, namely 500 merks. [Apart from the date, this seems identical to the item before last. A marginal note reads "Acquitted".]

Also, for casting enchantment on William Patersone's ale ...

[The document ends here. It is odd that Beigis was acquitted of all the most recent charges, but condemned to death for her earlier activities, for which there were no surviving witnesses, and which are wrongly dated in her indictment. Presumably the evidence for her guilt was contained in the confessions of other participants. Since these persons had been tried and found guilty, the truth of their confessions would be deemed to have been proved, thereby providing "trustworthy" evidence against Beigis Tod. Unfortunately there seems to be no surviving record of these prosecutions. Interestingly, however, the records of Agnes Sampson's trial mention a cat being prepared "in Begie Tod's house", before being thrown in the sea at Leith to raise a storm. Beigis must have been lucky to escape the North Berwick roundups.]

1629

Issobell Young

[A transcription of Issobell Young's trial appears in "Justiciary Cases 1624 - 1650", Vol. 1, published by the Stair Society, Edinburgh 1953, edited by Stair A. Gillon. It has been taken from the record in the Books of Adjournal. It gives a blow by blow account of what happened in court, but only gives summaries of most of the charges in the indictment. However, box JC26/9 of Justiciary Court processes in the National Archives of Scotland contains a bundle of fifteen items relating to Issobell Young. Item 1, which contains Item 2, is Issobell's "dittay" or indictment. Item 3 is the record of her trial, and appears to be identical to the record published by the Stair Society. The other items comprise witnesses' statements, memos, and other papers relevant to the case. This is one of the most extensively documented East Lothian witchcraft cases, and it is worth giving in full because of the light it sheds not only on withcraft beliefs, but also on rural life at the time.]

[On reverse] Issobell Young's indictment: 4th February 1629. Witchcraft etc. At Edinburgh 22nd April 1629. Received by me from John Bannatyne - the statements taken before the Presbytery of Dumbar in April 1624 concerning Issobell Young, Margret Baxter, and Marion Bathcat. Also the evidence given against Margaret Melrois and Jonet Achiesone, who were convicted of witchcraft before the Laird of Innerwick, the Laird of Smetoun, Sir James Bailyie, James Bailyie, and the baillies of Dumbar, Commissioners, on 9th April 1624; all of which were produced as evidence in this process.

[Item 1, Page 1 ff]

Issobell Young, wife of George Smyth, portioner of Eist Barnes.

1. You are indicted and accused because not only by the divine law of Almighty God, but also by the laws of this kingdom - particularly the 73rd Act of the 9th Parliament of our Sovereign Lord's grandmother Queen Marie of worthy and reputable memory, held by Her Majesty and the Estates of this kingdom on 4th June 1563 - it is expressly enacted and ordained that no person or persons of whatever estate, degree, or condition should thereafter make use of any manner of

witchcraft, sorcery, or necromancy, or claim to have any such skill or knowledge of it in order to abuse the people. Neither shall any person seek any help, response, or consultation from any such users or abusers of witchcraft, sorcery, or necromancy under the pain of death, which will be executed against both the user and the person who seeks the response or consultation. This is ratified by the said Act of Parliament and approved by all subsequent parliaments.

In spite of this, it is true that you, Issobell Young, in the year 1620 [20 deleted] came about Martinmas time to the mill called Brandsmyln, then tenanted by the miller George Sandie. For many years you had been having hulled corn ground there, and you earnestly requested George Sandie to grind a load of ears of corn and dirt for you. He refused to grind it because there were a great many poor folk waiting at the mill to have some bags of corn ground there to relieve their destitution. You violently flung the ears of corn over his shoulder into the hopper, and out of great spitefulness barged against George and the hopper in so doing, so that he, along with the burden of corn which was in his arms ready to be thrown into the hopper, and the hopper itself, all collapsed on the bedding of the millstones, and broke the mill with ten or eleven of the cogs. Then in great rage and fury you burst out with outrageous threats, and swore to God you would make him regret it, and that the mill would lie idle when he least expected it and would be most needed. Accordingly, when the mill had been sufficiently repaired, and there was sufficient water to drive it, nevertheless by your devilry and witchcraft laid on the mill, it would neither go nor grind anything for eleven days. After that, little by little, it returned to its usual state. Through this witchcraft and devilry which you laid on the mill, all its customers forsook it, the volume of grain processed there vanished away, and the mill became completely unprofitable to George.

Also, about a year after that, you brought some bran and other grain to the mill. After it had been ground you were asked to pay the usual duty, along with the mill's usual fee in grain. You not only refused, but offered to pay the duty using a peck measure of your own, which you brought to the mill, and which you were in the habit of using to measure out your fee. It was a third less than the right measure, and you would use it and no other. George Sandie refused to use it, and retained a quantity of your grain for the payment of duty. You then went home in great anger, taking with you a load of your meal. The water [*i.e.* the Brox Burn] was in spate and so high that a big horse of George's was hardly able to cross it, and could not pass through with a load, without the sack on its back becoming wet both at the mouth and the other end. You had in the meantime left two of your servant women in the mill to stay there till all the rest was ground. During the night these servants sent for a quart of ale and gave Alexander Symson, who was then employed at the mill, as much meal as would pay for the quart of ale. The night was extremely stormy and tempestuous with wind and rain, and all these servants were baking some bannocks in the fire, when you yourself came into the mill. To the great surprise of everybody in the mill you were clean and dry, with no rain on your clothes. You went to the fire and took out the bannocks, went to the recess in the wall and took out the meal that had been given in payment for the ale, and then went away back again. You crossed over the water to your own house without a horse or any other help except your devilish and unlawful means of extraordinary transportation.

After that, both by direct and indirect unlawful means, you worked against George Sandie, not only by devilry against him personally, but by moving his master the Laird of Broxmouth to break his agreement and put him out of the mill. Thus, by your devilry and witchcraft he was reduced to great poverty and necessity. All his wealth vanished away and he was left in debt to the extent of over 3000 merks.

Fourteen years later, by your devilry and witchcraft practised against him, George Sandie was brought to the point where he had nothing left but a coble with which he went to sea at the time of the herring "drave". Because you still continued in your wicked and devilish disposition towards him, he was so heavily crossed by the devilish sorcery and witchcraft you practised against him, that in spite of his hard work and diligence, he could not get as much as the tail of a herring in his boat, while all the other boats accompanying him in the fleet were getting full loads of herring. All the herring then fled eastwards, and he was then forced to fish for mackerel. While he was so doing, the shoal of herring came past his boat, playing above the water, and the gulls diving at them and taking them up in abundance. George and his crew then rowed back to land as fast as they could, got their nets, and shot them - as they thought - in the middle of the shoal of herring. When they hauled the nets they scarcely got a score of herring in them, although all the boats in the sea which came a long time after George, all got full loads. By the devilry and witchcraft you used against him George was prevented from getting his herring, and was completely disappointed. When he came to land he was greatly pitied by his neighbours, and a Highlandman then came to him and told George that you, Issobell Young, had done him all that damage and hurt. He said that George should come to you and ask for his herring three times in God's name. So because of the great poverty and misery to which he had been reduced by your devilish machinations, he took the Highlandman's advice and came to you at Eist Barnes, and asked you three times for God's sake to give him back his fish, and the other commodities you had taken from him. At that, you leaped at him, took him by the wrists, and said, "Do you think I'm a witch, man?" He said, "God knows," and left you. Then George put to sea in his boat, and he got more herring that night than all the rest of the fleet. When he sold that load of herring he got £200, to the great admiration of the people of Dumbar. Thus, by the devilry and witchcraft you practised against George Sandie when he was miller at the mill mentioned, and by taking his herring at sea as described after he had requested it three times for God's sake, you have declared yourself to be an obvious and manifest sorcerer and witch.

[A marginal note indicates that the jury acquitted Issobell of this charge by a majority.]

2. You are also indicted and accused because nine years ago Thomas Kers in Dumbar was asked by William Lowrie, a legal messenger, to go with him to Eist Barnes to witness a summons being given to you and your husband George Smyt at the instance of Patrick Sinclare, to give your [illegible] in an action he was pursuing against you. When William Lowrie came to your house at Eist Barnes, neither he nor any of the witnesses would risk going in to deliver the copy of the summons, except Thomas Kers. Without fear, he came forward to the door, and after declaring his errand he put the copy of the summons in the lock of the door. You immediately came out to the door, and first in great wrath and fury gave him a cuff on the side of the head that made him stagger. He was just a young boy, a scholar no more than eighteen years of age. [Eighteen seems rather old for a "scholar" in those days, but that's what the Roman figures seem to say.] Then you threatened Thomas with execrations and curses, saying that you would make him repent coming there.

That same day he went to Hadingtoun with William Lowrie, went home, and lay down in his bed seemingly healthy and sound. However, next morning, by the sorcery and witchcraft you practised against him, his right hand - the hand that put the copy into the lock of your door, a "pipe lock" - became powerless and dead, so that with grievous and intolerable pain it swelled and drew his wrist bone together. [It is not clear what is meant by "drawing together" his wrist bone.] He continued in this painful condition for a month, and then the pain moved down his side to his thigh and leg. This extremely agonising pain settled above and below his knee, and drew his leg up so tight and close to his body that nothing was able to hold it out straight, and anything it was tied up with broke apart. He remained in extreme pain for a long time until Lady Heidrik saw it. She claimed to have some knowledge of surgery, and declared that he was bewitched. She said there was no remedy for Thomas except to have his leg cut off, even though George Adamsone in Dumbar and the best doctors in the area had worked to try to help and cure him. His leg is still in this pitiful state, drawn up to his body. He has thus been made a cripple by the witchcraft and sorcery practised on him by you, in accordance with your threat that you would make him regret coming to your house on such an errand for the rest of his days. This you cannot deny.

3. You are also indicted and accused of having conceived a cruel and deadly hatred and ill-will against the late William Meslett in Eist Barnes, and his wife Margaret Ogill. This was because you and George Smyt your husband had a piece of land belonging to George Home of Mekill Pinkertoun pledged to you until he could redeem it for 400 merks. William Meslet lent that sum to George Home, and he used it to redeem the land from you. You then conceived this deadly hatred against William Meslett and his wife, and you vowed and threatened to do him an evil turn for it, saying that he would never again have so much money to lay out on land. William and his wife at that time were well to the fore in worldly goods. Not only that, but in your devilish spite you cried out that for all their wealth, they would be forced to sell and forfeit what they had before they ever bought any more. In accordance with this fearful threat, to bring the malice you bore against him to its desired conclusion by sorcery and witchcraft practised against him, you first bought from the late William Meslett a chalder of wheat. This was not because you needed it, but to get it in order to effect your devilish practices on him. When you came to get it, and you first came in to William's barn to load the wheat, you at once in your devilish manner pulled the kerchief off your head. This was the instruction given to you by Sathan your master. You then turned yourself three times round about anti-clockwise, as you and the sorcerers and witches you associated with were in the habit of doing as a way of saluting your master the Devil at your meetings with him. He told you to do the same to anyone you wished any harm to, either in their own person or in their goods. This taking off your kerchief was done three separate times in the barn before you got the wheat. As a result, and by other devilish practices used by you against William, sixteen of his best oxen and eight of his horses and mares dropped dead very suddenly shortly afterwards.

However, William Meslet accepted all this with resignation from the Lord's hands. He never suspected that you were the cause of his ruin until when he was sowing his barley seed, and Jonet Lyndsay, a witch who was then living in Lyntoun Brig, married to a saddler, came to William when he was sowing his barley seed and told him that all his wrongs and losses were the result of the devilish practices you had used against him and his possessions. Also, when you got the chalder of wheat out of William's barn, William had two pet sheep standing at the door. They were chased by two of his greyhounds, and came running through the grain. You were annoyed about this, and threatened with a curse that they would break their necks. In accordance with this threat, by your witchcraft and sorcery one of these sheep broke its neck another day, and died immediately.

[Marginal note: "Convicted by a majority."]

4. You are also indicted because you are not only a wicked practitioner and user of witchcraft yourself, but consult with other witches on a daily basis, and shelter them in your house: for example, Cristiane Grintoun, Margaret Melrois, Janet Atchieson, and others of that devilish sect. It is true that this Cristiane Grintoun was seen by your husband George Smyt coming out of a hole in the slates of his house, at first in the likeness of a cat, and then turning and growing progressively into her own likeness and shape. After seeing this he came to you and told you about it, and was very angry with you for entertaining and sheltering such devilish people. You made this answer to him, "Husband, I'm sorry you saw that sight, for it will be the worse for you after it."

The next morning George was ploughing, and in accordance with what you foretold, he fell down dead in the field. When you were told of this by Barbara Kelly you ran as fast as you could to William Meslett's house and took away a chair with the intention of practising some evil against him. You didn't take a chair from your own house or from any of your neighbours' houses. You ran with this chair to the field where your husband was lying dead, put him in the chair, and brought him home in it through William Meslett's barn doors. You went no other way, although there was a wide public road nearby, on which horses and carts come and go. Having done your turn [*i.e.* worked your magic] with the chair, you sent it back to William Meslett's house. By the sorcery and witchcraft you practised against William and his wife, after the chair came back neither their livestock nor other worldly goods belonging to them would thrive, but everything went backwards with them, in accordance with your previous execrable and devilish threats.

[Marginal note: Convicted by a majority.]

5. You are also indicted and accused because after your husband had been struck down by the sickness as described, having seen Cristiane Grintoun appearing out of a hole in your roof as mentioned, and after you had brought him home in William Meslet's chair through the barn as described; in order to relieve your husband of that serious illness and to cure him of it more quickly, you used sorcery and witchcraft with the help of the witch Cristiane Grintoun, whom you sent for. Within four days the sickness was taken off him, and put in the threshold of the barn door, so that whoever first came that way would take the sickness.

Shortly afterwards your husband's brother's son William Smyt was coming from ploughing, and came in at the door first. He no sooner came over the threshold of the door, than by the devilry and witchcraft practised by you and laid at the entrance to the barn, as he constantly affirmed, the sickness overtook him. He said that as he came in at the barn door, where Johnne Fergusson was about to get a boll of wheat, he saw the measuring tub ["the firlot"] running around the floor, bubbling up in the middle like a cauldron. Thus, since he was the first person to come into the barn after you and Cristiane Grintoun had been in there making your plans and practising devilry to relieve George Smyt of his serious illness, the sickness was taken off George and laid on his nephew William. After this, George recovered daily, and William Smyt was driven insane. In the delirium of his sickness he came running at you, and took you by the throat, shouting that you had tormented him by your sorcery and witchcraft. He drew a sword and struck at you. You dodged the blow and he hit the lintel or arch of the chimney, where the mark can still be seen.

Thus by your sorcery and witchcraft, the

sickness was taken off your husband and laid on his nephew William Smyt, as is notoriously well known, and you cannot deny it. Also, William Smyt swore afterwards that if he got the opportunity he would pursue you by law to the death for bewitching him.

[Marginal note: Convicted unanimously.]

6. You are indicted and accused because one Lammas Day about [blank] years ago, a quarrel broke out between Thomas Smyt your son and Thomas Symsone, the son of William Symsone in Eistbarnes and his wife Issobell Frude. They were both schoolboys at the time. William Symsone was told about it, and came out and parted the two boys. In his anger he threatened them for fighting and wrestling with each other. When this threatening from William came to your ears from Thomas Feinla, John Brysone's servant, you were highly offended that he should have menaced your son. In revenge you came to William Symsone's house pretending that you wanted to buy some pigs. As soon as you came in, you sat down in the doorway, and in your devilish manner, in accordance with your usual greeting towards those to whom you bore any malice, you uncovered your head by taking off your kerchief. When those in the house told you they had no pigs there, you went away without wishing them goodnight. However you came back again to the house the following Sunday, passing through the courtyard in the shape of a hare, into which you had transformed yourself by your devilry and witchcraft. Immediately afterwards William's daughter Margaret Symsone contracted a sudden serious sickness through the sorcery and witchcraft you practised against her, because she had nipped your son's leg when he was wrestling with her brother Thomas Symsone. She died of this sickness. And so, by your sorcery and witchcraft Margaret Symsone's life was taken from her in a most piteous manner, to the great grief of her parents and the others who knew her. By transforming yourself into the likeness of a hare you have shown yourself to be a manifest witch and sorcerer, which you cannot deny.

[Marginal note: Convicted by a majority.]

7. Isobell Frude, wife of the above-mentioned William Symsone, portioner of Eistbarnes, was ordered to appear before the Presbytery to tell what she knew about you, particularly about the bewitching of her children, and the other wicked deeds people were accusing you of. Realising she had returned from the Presbytery, you laid a heavy and serious disease on her by your sorcery and witchcraft. Her face broke out into a great heat and inflamation, like an eruption of the skin. This caused her continuous pain, and to get relief from it she went to Edinburgh and other parts of the country to get help by ordinary lawful means. She got no better, but when she got home and the complaint broke out again on her face, you met this Issobell one day and verbally abused her horribly and outrageously. You alleged that after she had made her statement before the Presbytery of Dumbar, she confirmed what she told them with this attestation, "If this statement is not true, may God make it appear on my forehead!" After Issobell had come home, grievously pained with this disease by the sorcery and witchcraft you had practised against her, you came to her and in great malice burst out with these words, "I thank my God I have got the upper hand over you. For you confirmed your statement to the Presbytery with a prayer that God would show it on your forehead if what you had said was not true, and this is just what has happened to you!"

However, Issobell made no such attestation before the Presbytery, but only attested that what she said was true in itself. Nevertheless, since Issobell Fruid had tried all lawful means for a cure, and had got none, and the disease continued to pain her greatly, she was advised by some people that the disease had been laid on her by witchcraft - by none other but you,

Two contrasting scenes in the Garleton hills, where Alexander Hamilton had several meetings with the Devil.

Issobell Young. She was advised to address herself to you, and to beg her health from you three times for God's sake. This she did, coming to you and asking her health from you three times in succession for God's cause. After she had done this, she convalesced day by day, and recovered from the painful disease. Thus it is most evident that this disease was laid on Issobell Fruid by the witchcraft and sorcery practised on her by you, and that she was cured of it in the manner described.

[Marginal note: Convicted by a majority.]

9. You are also indicted and accused of having conceived a deadly hatred against Thomas Home in Eistbarnes, the husband of Cristiane Lumisden, because he had bought John Purves's land, which you'd had your eye on. Knowing that he had gone to Dumbar to get the papers drawn up, you laid a heavy and greivous sickness on him by your sorcery and witchcraft as he was coming home. He continued to be affected by this sickness for fifteen days, pining away, and continually sweating and fainting. At the end of fifteen days he died as a result of your sorcery and witchcraft. Ever since then you have always been in the habit of bragging and boasting that nobody could thrive or get on if they meddled with anything you had an eye on or a desire for, as the results of doing so were apparent with Issobell Fruid, William Meslet, Thomas Home, and others.

[Marginal note: Convicted by a majority.]

10. You are indicted and accused of being at various meetings and gatherings with the Devil in the company of Margaret Melrois and Jonet Achesone who lived in Pincartoun and were both notorious witches, burnt for witchcraft. In particular, you and they were at a meeting with your master the Devil at the Doun Hill of Spott, at the place called Maiddeyis Loupe. You and the other two had a conversation there about the death and destruction of George Clerksone. Since you were at this meeting in the capacity of a leading figure, your opinion was sought as to what should be done with him. You replied that you had christened him with cold water, and that he was therefore your godson. All the same, you said, "Let him go the way he is going." Margaret Melrois and Jonet Achesone affirmed that this was the truth in your presence, and in the presence of His Majesty's Commissioners in the tollbooth of Dumbar, both before and after their conviction, and at the hour of their death when they were bound to the stake.

[Marginal note: convicted]

11. You are also indicted and accused of having conceived a deadly hatred and ill-will 34 years ago against Patrik Brysone, the father of John Brysone in Eistbarnes, for cutting your pig's tether. You abused him most maliciously for this, and in a great rage flung the cut tether in at the door of his house. After doing this, by your sorcery and witchcraft you laid a grievously painful disease on him whereby he lost the power of one of his sides, which became dead and without feeling. He never recovered from this as long as he lived. A woman called Dame Bet, who was supposed to be a "wise wife" and to have skill in curing various diseases, was asked how this could have happened to him. She said Patrik Brysone swore that it was through sorcery and witchcraft laid on by you between the dovecot and the knoll where the pig's tether was cut.

[Marginal note: Acquitted.]

12. You are indicted and accused because Marion Wolf in Eistbarnes took a serious illness and tried everything in order to be cured. In the end she went to a witch named Catherine Gray, with whom you were in the habit of consulting and keeping company, and who was burnt for witchcraft in Haddington. [Catherine was one of the North Berwick witches. See Chapter 1.] She had tried to find Catherine Gray several times, and at length found that you were keeping her in a little back outbuilding

[or possibly "bakehouse"]. When Marion Wolf discovered this, she came to the outbuilding and found Catherine Gray inside with you. When Catherine saw Marion, she said she was there consulting and seeking help for her, if any could be had, and that she had been discussing it with you. You and the witch Catherine Gray were together in secret in that outbuilding with no-one else with you. Therefore, through your familiarity and keeping company with this witch, and consulting and advising with each other for curing Marion Wolf, and releasing her from the disease she was troubled with by sorcery and witchcraft, you have declared yourself to be a witch and a consulter with witches for curing sickness and disease by sorcery, witchcraft, and other unlawful and godless methods.

[Marginal note: Acquitted.]

13. You are also indicted and accused of conceiving a grievous hatred and ill-will against Elizabeth Brysone, the wife of William Kellie in Wast Barnes, the daughter of the above-mentioned deceased Patrik Brysone, and also against her husband William Kellie himself. This was because they claimed that Patrik Brysone was bewitched by you 34 years ago for cutting your pig's tether. About eighteen years ago William Kellie came to your house to discuss some business of his with your husband George Smyt, in the company of George Purves his son in law, and Archibald Ogill from West Barns. In your usual manner, as you had been directed by your master the Devil to greet those to whom you bore ill-will, or desired to inflict harm upon, as soon as William came in at your door, as you stood there on the floor you uncovered your head, and took off your kerchief and all your headgear as a sign that some fearful accident would befall him, either in his person or in his possessions. There was some conversation between him and you, and you described his wife to him in a scornful taunting manner, saying she had become a wealthy woman with abundant possessions, and also affirming that before too long you would have more of your own. Then when William had finished his business with your husband and was coming away, it is true to say the you took off your kerchief to him twice more, showing your bare head. By the sorcery and witchcraft practised against this William Kellie, and discussed caused and devised by you and the witches and sorcerers who were your accomplices, his house and the grain in his barn and barnyard, 84 bolls of corn or more, was completely burnt, to his utter ruin hurt and prejudice. This was the result of your witchcraft and sorcery, and the fearful and devilish greeting and salutation you gave him, as described above.

Also, a year after that, William Kellie was coming through Eist Barnes accompanied by his brother in law John Faa, going to look for a chimney breast. They met you on the way, and you took off your headgear to William in your usual manner, and asked him where he was going. He was unwilling to speak to you because of the evil reputation you had for sorcery and witchcraft, so he passed you by, and as he went away you said, "Adew upon you." [*i.e.* "adieu" - goodbye.] Then, in your sight, and and by the sorcery following upon the devilish form of greeting you had given him, William and his horse crashed to the ground, and William himself was knocked unconscious. At that, his brother in law John Faa cried out, "Fye brother, this unhappy woman has bewitched you!" However, you came up to him, clapped him on the shoulder, and said, "I'll let him off this time." He then got up, jumped on to his horse, came home, and immediately went to bed. By the sorcery and witchcraft you laid upon him, he remained in bed seriously ill for thirteen weeks after that. That same night the horse he had been riding dropped dead, as a result of your sorcery and witchcraft.

[Marginal note: Convicted by a majority.]

14. You are indicted and accused of having conceived a deadly hatred and ill-will against George Umphrastoun in Innerweik, and his wife Jonet Hodge, because George had taken the job of shepherd on the Links over the head of your brother Thomas Young who had previously held the post. In revenge for this, and in order to practise your sorcery on them, you came to George Umphrastoun's house [blank] ago, and asked to buy three pounds of butter from his wife. Because she refused to sell you any, saying she had none, out of the malice of your heart you said to Jonet Hodge, "You're lying. I know you have just churned three pounds of butter, so let me have it, for I will not go without it!" When Jonet Hodge heard you say that, she did not know how much butter had been taken put of the churn, since she had not weighed it. She brought you the butter, and when she weighed it, she found there was exactly three pounds of butter, no more nor less. So you went away with it.

After that time, by the sorcery and witchcraft laid by you on George Umphrastoun and his wife, so long as they remained there [*i.e.* in Innerwick], which was three years altogether, Jonet Hodge could never get as much as an ounce of butter out of her churn, although she would have sometimes eight and sometimes twelve pints of cream in the churn, as good as any in the countryside round about. Neither did they or their livestock thrive. Through the sorcery and witchcraft you laid on them, everything went backwards with them as long as they lived in that place, until they moved away. [Marginal note: Acquitted.]

15. Also, you are indicted and accused of having conceived a deadly rancorous and malicious feud against the late Thomas Home in Eistbarnes and his wife Lilias Knowis, [illegible] six years ago. This was because you and your husband George Smith had your eye on a piece of land you fancied in the Eist Barnes, which then belonged to William Woid. You offered eighteen hundred merks for its disposal and transfer to you. However, the piece of land was disposed of and sold to Thomas Home and Lilias for the sum of two thousand merks - 200 merks more than you had offered. Because Thomas and his wife bought this land over your head, ever since then you did everything in your power by all manner of devilry sorcery and witchcraft, to utterly ruin the late Thomas Home, and bring him to beggary in his lifetime. You have done the same to his widow Lilias Knowis since he died. To bring this about, twenty two years ago in a single year, by the sorcery and witchcraft you practised against them, you made twenty seven of his horses, cattle, and their followers [*i.e.* foals and calves] suddenly drop dead. You also inflicted a heavy and grievous sickness on Thomas himself, of which he died in the end. During the time when you inflicted this serious illness on him he was so unmercifully tortured and tormented with pains throughout his body, and with continual sweating, that he was advised for his relief to retire from his own house in Eistbarnes and to come to Prestounpans. Finding no relief there, and his sickness still getting worse, he wasted away with it like a skeleton [an "anatomie"]. In the end he died from the sorcery and witchcraft you inflicted on him. Before he died he steadfastly affirmed in the presence of his brother, Mr John Ker, minister of Prestoun Pans, and Mr David Home of Godscroft, that he had been wronged by you, and that all the trouble he had received was by your sorcery and witchcraft, for buying the previously-mentioned piece of land over the heads of you and your husband.

[Marginal note: Acquitted.]

16. You are also indicted and accused because you were not satisfied with causing the destruction by the godless means of sorcery and witchcraft, of Thomas Home, his possessions, livestock, and other worldly goods as described. After his death you continued with your malice

and inveterate hatred against his wife Lillias Knowis and the worldly estate allotted to her for the maintainance of her and her children. By your sorcery and witchcraft, and by the actions of witches and devils directed and incited by you, you burned down and destroyed Lillias's steading and her adjacent house in the middle[?] of the night, about Michaelmas, immediately after Thomas Home's death. There were also four houses burnt belonging to William Watt, together with various other houses nearby, belonging to neighbours. These fires were started at your direction, planning, and instigation. The woman you incited and directed to do this was lodged secretly, kept and fed by you in your house for twenty days before the burning of these houses, and afterwards was liberally rewarded by you for doing that wicked deed before being sent away. She has since confessed that this is true to several people who heard her declare it. The fire was thus raised by you, and the houses burned and destroyed by you; or at least, this was done on your particular orders, at your direction and instigation, as described above.

[Marginal note: Acquitted]

17: You are indicted and accused of still continuing in your malice against Lillias Knowis, so that six years ago you came into her house, and swore and raged at her in the most outrageous manner, alleging that her husband had struck a pig of yours in the courtyard. Lillias was greatly frightened and terrified at this, and replied calmly and modestly, saying that if it was true she would give you such compensation as would satisfy you, to redress your loss. Seeming to be well pleased with that, you sat down on a stool in the house, and after some conversation took her daughter on your knee, a baby a year and a half old. You said to Lillias that she was a fine-looking child, and you'd have to get your grandson - your daughter's child - to marry her. After staying a short time in the house you then went away. After you came away, by your sorcery and witchcraft, the child contracted a strange and fearful disease, being drawn all together with pain. She continued like that for about a year and a half. This sickness and disease was laid upon the child by your sorcery and witchcraft, which you cannot deny. [Lillias has obviously remarried after the death of Thomas Home.]

[Marginal note: Acquitted.]

18. You are indicted because by the sorcery and witchcraft practised by you against the late Thomas Home and his wife Lillias Knowis, all the pigeons in their dovecot in Eistbarnes were driven out of it, and none have lived in it for the past sixteen years, although previously it had been the richest dovecot in all the countryside.

[Marginal note: Acquitted.]

19. You are also indicted and accused of having conceived a deadly malice and ill-will against Johne Brysone in Eist Barnes because he had affirmed that you had bewitched his father Patrik Brysone for cutting your pig's tether. About five years ago by your sorcery and witchcraft you entered Johne Brysone's stable under silence and cloud of night, about four o' clock in the morning. His servant David Nisbet was sleeping in the stable at the time. He saw a bright light on the far side of the horse and mare standing in the stable, shining round about them, and by this light he made out you and a man riding on the mare. At this, David Nisbet rose out of his bed, drew his sword, and came forward to the horse meaning to strike at you. Immediately the light went out. He went to the horse and the mare to find out what sort of state they were in, and found them dripping with sweat from the ears to the tail, as if they had been over their heads in a river. The next morning by your sorcery and witchcraft the mare aborted her foal, and the horse wasted away and died. All this was done by your sorcery and witchcraft as described.

[Marginal note: Convicted by a majority.]

20. You are indicted and accused because

sixteen years ago Cuthbert Symson, shopkeeper [or perhaps "chapman" - a pedlar] in Eist Barnes, sold you [illegible] webs of linen cloth for £44. After you had paid for them and received them from him, you returned and asked him to take back one of the pieces of cloth - about twelve ells in length - which you said was full of tufts and was thus not as good as the rest. You wanted him to give you another better piece of cloth for it. Because Cuthbert refused to do this, you burst out in great anger, cursing and threatening him, saying that twelve months from that day he would dearly repent it. The next morning you came to Cuthbert again. You greeted him in your devilish manner by taking the kerchief off your head, according to your usual practice with those towards whom you were ill-disposed. You requested him as before to take back the piece of cloth and give you a better one for it, saying that if he did not, he would repent it before long. Because of his refusal that second time, by the sorcery and witchcraft practised by you on Cuthbert for his ruin and overthrow, and in accordance with the fearful threats you uttered against him, his horse suddenly dropped dead not long afterwards. From being well off in terms of worldly goods, and worth a hundred pounds, it all vanished away through your sorcery and witchcraft, and nothing since then has ever thriven or prospered with him.

[Marginal note: Acquitted.]

21. [A diagonal line has been drawn across the first eleven lines of Article 21, and a marginal note reads "Passes from this article." In other words, this charge has been dropped from the indictment.]

You are indicted and accused because six years ago Alieson Patersone in the Myreside was dangerously ill with a serious ilness. You came to visit her to cure her, and knowing no better method to cure her than taking the disease off her and making it land on someone else by your sorcery and witchcraft, you laid some enchanted yarn and other materials on the threshold of the door to the house. Thus whatever living creature - beast or human being - was the first to come in or out would catch the disease, thereby relieving your patient Alieson of it. James Liddel, a shoemaker from Spote, Wiliam Liddell's brother, had come to James Hopper[?] to negotiate with him for some land which he wished to cultivate. Hearing that Aliesone Patersone was at death's door with no hope of survival, he came to Aliesoun's house to visit her. Since you, Issobell Young were present with her, when James first came in you took him by the hand and bade him welcome, although he did not know you at all. By doing this, and by the devilry and witchcraft you laid at the door, since James Liddell was the first person to come in, he suddenly took a grievous sickness and disease, and was not able to stay any longer. As he went away, he said that his "deid evil" had come upon him [*i.e.* the illness or evil which would cause his death]. He died of this grievous sickness within a week, and Alieson Patterson convalesced and recovered. Thus, by the sorcery and witchcraft practised by you as described above, the disease was laid on the man and taken off the woman. This is notoriously well known, and you cannot deny it.

22. You are indicted and accused of making a habit of resorting to sorcerers and witches, and keeping company with them - namely with the late Katherine Gray and Jonet Lyndsey who were both burnt at Haddington for witchcraft. Also with Crystiane Gryntoun, Margaret Melrois, and Jonet Aitchiesoun, all three burnt at Dumbar for sorcery and witchcraft. You were told, and expressly commanded by your master the Devil, that before you practised any cure for helping or relieving any of your beasts, or any livestock belonging either to yourself, your children, or any other relatives, for a successful outcome and a more certain effect, you must on all such occasions dig a deep hole or pit in

the ground. Then as a sacrifice to your master the Devil, you should throw into it a live ox, a live cat, and a certain amount of salt. If possible, this hole or pit should be dug towards the north, between two lords' lands, or if not, in any inconspicuous place. Accordingly, for the past forty years, when any disease occurred among the livestock belonging either to yourself or your children, to recover their health you have always been in the habit of taking a live ox and burying it alive in a deep hole or pit in the ground. Then you would throw in a live cat and a great quantity of salt as a sacrifice to your master the Devil as previously described. Then you would close up the deep hole and cover it with a board[?] with earth on it. After that the rest of the livestock was driven over it to relieve their sickness or disease. You first practised this cure with a deep pit made beside the dovecot of your house at your own back gate. The second time was at the north side of the Lady Well, between the lands of Pinkertoun and the King's Lands at the side of the [illegible: possibly "mercat"] road. The third time was in the yard belonging to Casper Home, which he rented from your son the late William Smith, at the back door of the barn there. In doing all this you have declared yourself to be a manifest sorcerer and a notorious witch.

[Marginal note: acquitted.]

23. You are indicted and accused because five years ago Andro Meirton, who then lived in Eist Barnes but now lives in Prestoun, owed you a certain sum of money. On the Sunday before Martinmas you came to his house and asked for the repayment of this debt. He refused to make immediate payment of the sum of money to you, and answered in sober terms that it was not yet Martinmas - which was the day of payment - but by the grace of God you would be satisfied at the term. At this, in great rage and fury you burst out with the most execrable and hellish blasphemy, saying to Andro, "If you trust too much in that God, he'll beguile you. Pay me now, since I have come for it, or else you will repent it all your days!" Not satisfied with that disgraceful threat uttered against him on that occasion, shortly afterwards you met Andro Mairtoun's wife, who had been newly delivered of a child. She was on her way to church to be "kirkit" [*i.e.* A mother's first appearance in church after giving birth - an event invested with spiritual and superstitious significance.], and to give thanks to God for his merciful deliverance, when you burst out with the most outrageous words against Andro and his wife, saying that neither she nor her husband would stay two years together in that community, nor would they have the wherewithal to feed or clothe themselves. In accordance with this execrable and devilish threat uttered by you against Andro and his wife as described, and by the sorcery and witchcraft practised by you against them, all their horses and cattle suddenly dropped dead, and all their worldly goods and gear vanished away from them. At that time they were reasonably well off, and well to the fore. However, in less than a year, by the sorcery and witchcraft you practised against them, their livestock, goods, and resources, Andro and his wife were compelled to leave, in accordance with the devilish threat quoted above.

[Marginal note: Acquitted of the losses inflicted on Andro Mortoun.]

24. Finally, you Issobell Young, are indicted and accused that you are, and have been for the past forty years, a manifest witch and sorcerer, and a keeper of company with various witches and sorcerers at various trysts and meetings with your master the Devil; especially with Margarit Melrois, Jonet Achiesone, and other notorious witches. When you and they met with the Devil, the death and destruction of George Clerkson was plotted and planned out amongst you. You also renounced your baptism and engaged yourself in the service of Sathan, the enemy of

man's salvation. You received from him power, expressed by threatening, cursing, and taking off your kerchief, to inflict by sorcery and witchcraft various strange and fearful diseases on the men women and children to whom you uttered these threats and curses. These were also inflicted on their beasts and livestock for their ruin and destruction. Then he gave you his mark under your right breast. You put these devilish practices into execution by your witchcraft and sorcery against various of our Sovereign Lord's good subjects living in Eist Lothian and other parts of the countryside round about, for their utter overthrow and destruction. This is notoriously well known, and you cannot deny it.

[The folded sheet containing charges 23 and 24 is marked "JC26/9/2", and is inserted inside the back page of JC26/9/1. Item 3 in Box JC26/9 appears to be the same as the transcription of Issobell's trial taken from the Books of Adjournal, which can be found published by the Stair Society in "Justiciary Cases 1624 -1650" edited by Stair A. Gillon, Edinburgh 1953. This repeats much of the material in items 1 and 2, but it is interesting because it gives the arguments between the prosecution and the defence. My "translation" of Gillon's transcription now follows.]

February 4th 1629   Issobell Young
Colville and Robertoun, Justice Deputes.

Accused: Issobell Young, wife of George Smyth, portioner of Eist Barnes.

Pursuers: Sir Thomas Hope of Craighall, baronet, Advocate to our Sovereign Lord for His Highness's interest. Mr George Fleschear, Advocate Substitute to His Majesty's Advocate.

Spokesmen for the defence: Johnne Smyth, James Smyth, and Thomas Smyth, sons of the accused. Mr David Primrois and Mr Laurence McGill, advocates.

The Lord Advocate produced the indictment with the official letters and the list of jurors, and began proceedings.

1. [Proceedings begin with a stock preamble stating that witchcraft is forbidden by Scripture and by the laws of the land]... In spite of this, it is true that Issobell Young became ill-disposed towards George Sandie, the miller at Brandis Mylne, around Martinmas 1600. She laid her sorcery and witchcraft on the mill and made it incapable of grinding anything for eleven days altogether, thus making the mill unprofitable for him. Also, about quarter of a year after that she came to the mill to grind some husked oats and other grain. George asked for his dues for grinding it and she refused, so he kept back some of her stuff as payment. In revenge for this, by devilry and witchcraft practised against him, she caused all aspects of his business to go back until he was reduced to great poverty and necessity.

On a foul and stormy night of wind and rain, when the mill horse was scarcely able to cross the water between her house and the mill, Isobel was noticed to have come back from her house through the water, where there was no bridge of stone or wood. She had conveyed herself over without a horse, and without any other help but from the Devil.

Finally, by Issobell's sorcery and witchcraft, George Sandie was reduced to extreme poverty and utter ruin, as already mentioned. He had no other means of trading or making a living but a fishing boat which he used to fish during the herring "drave". Continuing in her constant hatred and malevolence, when he had gone to sea to catch herring at the time of the "drave", she practised her witchcraft and devilry against him with the result that all the boats from the town of Dunbar received full loads, but he was frustrated and disappointed, as is set down at greater length in the first article of the indictment.

This first article with its three charges was absolutely denied by the accused.

After the first article of the indictment had been read, and denied by the accused, the spokesman for the accused, Mr David Primrois, declared in an introductory statement that since witchcraft is condemned by the Word of God as altogether diabolical in itself, those who practise it and receive the name of witches and sorcerers are always odious and detestable, and should be condemned and detested by all good Christians as not worthy to live. "Witch" is defined as one who strives to attain unlawful ends by diabolical and unlawful means. The crime which the accused is alleged to have committed in the first article against George Sandie, even if it were true, does not fall under that definition of witchcraft, nor is it covered by the act of parliament on which the indictment is based. This was set out by the spokesman for the defence as an introductory statement.

It is alleged that the first article of the indictment is in no way relevant, because the alleged prediction was a threat made against George Sandie that the mill would not work. The ensuing stopping of the mill for eleven days is in no way relevant, because the indictment itself says that George fell into the hopper, and the hopper and the cogs of the mill were broken. It is quite common and usual that with a mill which had been broken and newly mended, there might have been an interval of ten or twelve days before it could resume its normal work. If her prediction had any real force, it is likely that its power would have lasted more than eleven days, and yet it is nowhere mentioned that the accused took away her impediment to the running of the mill, although the mill eventually resumed its normal work."

Also, as to her going through the water when it was in spate, that point is in no way relevant, because it is claimed that she had the miller's horse, and that the top and bottom of the sack were wet. Surely if she had crossed by unlawful means she would have kept her own meal dry? And as for her coming back to the mill dry, although it was a stormy night; it is not alleged that she came through the water. It is presumed that she crossed on a wooden bridge. And although the night was stormy, she might have come between showers when it was fair, or she might have had a plaid or cloak around her and taken it off at the mill door, and thus come in dry.

Then, as regards her speaking to Home, the Laird of Broxmouth, about dismissing the miller George Sandie from his service as claimed in the indictment, that cannot infer witchcraft, because it is the usual practice of enemies to go to the masters of servants against whom they bear ill-will. Probably Broxmouth would not keep him as his employee because he was a debauched character. As for George Sandie's financial resources, it is probable that he was never worth £20 Scots!

As for the loss of George Sandie's herring, this cannot infer any instance of witchcraft, because there are no actions alleged, no, not as much as menacing expressions spoken by the accused to George, by which she could have engineered his bad luck. This could be put down to his lack of skill, lack of hired help, or not enough nets, as it is acknowledged that he was a poor man, and was known to have a very lewd lifestyle. We have a good example of this in Livy, where a certain Furneus had achieved great worldly possessions, but was accused of having obtained them by sorcery. To prove his innocence, he paraded his servants, horses, oxen, and so on before the judges, saying, "These are what make my land fertile, and myself prosperous." Similarly, George Sandie's poverty came from himself, as a result of his laziness and lack of equipment to further his trade. Lastly, as to the Lowland man *[sic]* and the instructions given by him to George Sandie to recover his health, and his sending of him to the accused for that purpose, this is in no way relevant, because it is not claimed that the accused ever had any conversation with the Lowland man. When George asked the accused to give him back his hearing [*sic* The editor has mistaken "herring" for "hearing".] in God's name as is claimed, there is no suggestion that she made any promise or prediction regarding his future success. On the contrary, it is recorded that she had him up for slander, for which he had to make satisfaction in church. Even if she could have helped him, she would probably never have done so, since he deserved nothing else from her but what could be expected from an irritated and angry woman. If this point of the indictment were true, it could actually be seen in her favour, as obeying the Gospel precept to do good to her enemy - remembering of course that the allegation of the crime contained in the indictment is completely untrue, and in no way admitted by the accused. Therefore this first article of the indictment should certainly not be submitted for consideration by a jury.

My Lord Advocate replies to this that these allegations should be rejected, because the indictment shows that the deeds contained in the indictment were done by the accused through ill-will which preceded threats, after which losses imediately followed. There was no obvious or apparent cause for the harm, except the devilish sorcery and incantations of the accused. Also, since it is stated that all the deeds recorded were done by means of her sorcery, the indictment is without question relevant in law. This is sustained every day by the procedures and laws of the realm, as was recently decided in the case of Margarit Wallace.

The accused answers that in spite of this reply, the defence made against the first article of the indictment is still relevant, and repeats it. Not only that, but the Lord Advocate's reply is as irrelevant as the indictment, since it does not explain by what examples of sorcery and witchcraft she brought about the effects of her threatening words and the ensuing bad luck. The example given is his bad luck in fishing for herring. It is not claimed that he had no success in fishing. [*i.e.* Presumably this is suggesting that Sandie might have had better luck with other kinds of fish.]

My Lord Advocate replies that the only connection that is necessary is in terms of "from whom and to whom". As for making witchcraft the means of connection, denying it would be a defence for the accused.

To this it is answered that the connection is absolutely necessary. In terms of "from whom and to whom", the relationship must be connected by some means - that is, the devilish practices which are not described.

2. The second article of the indictment was read, which states that she conceived ill-will against Thomas Kers for being in company with the court messenger William Lawrie, and summoning her at her house, and putting a copy of the summons in the lock of her door. She threatened him that he would regret coming there and doing that, Accordingly, first his right hand, and then his right leg "drew up", and he became a cripple by her sorcery and witchcraft.

It is alleged by the accused concerning the second article, that as far as wronging Thomas Kers is concerned, may it please the judge to be informed that William Lawrie will declare that he never knew Thomas Kers, and that he was a cripple before the time mentioned. As to the business of putting the copy in the keyhole, it can be proved by a witness present in court that the doors in George Smyth's house have been the same doors unaltered for twenty years, and there never was a "pipe lock" or any other lock, nor a hole, or any trace of one in the door, but only bars inside. As for threatening him, this has no connection with the ensuing misfortune, because it is not stated that she threatened either his hand or his leg, but only uttered some angry words, which might be thought normal for women cited by messengers. She denies knowing this Thomas Kerse, or ever having seen him.

The Advocate replies that this should be rejected in respect of the indictment, and that the lock is of minor importance.

[What the Lord Advocate means by rejecting arguments "in respect of the indictment" is that he is saying that because something is stated in the indictment, it must be relevant because of that very fact. On the face of it, this would seem to be manifestly unjust, but it must be remembered here that the lawyers are arguing about the "relevance" of the articles of the indictment. The Lord Advocate is not necessarily saying that something must be true because it is in the indictment. He means rather that if something is considered to be important enough to be in the indictment, it must be "relevant" enough to be considered by the jury.]

3. The third article of the indictment was read, dealing with the misfortune, damage, and losses sustained by William Meslet and his wife Margaret Ogill through the sorcery of the accused. There was also the business of her taking off her kerchief and then going round thrice anticlockwise at the time of these misfortunes. There was also the sudden death of their livestock which followed the accused threatening and menacing them for outbidding her and her husband in buying a piece of land. They had the intention of giving two hundred merks more than the accused and her husband, as is described in the indictment, and as was declared by the witch Jonet Lyndsay.

The accused and her spokesmen allege that the third article contains a tedious history of William Meslet's misfortune, with the death of a number of horses and bullocks suddenly occurring, and caused by the accused. It can never be verified that twenty years ago he had so many cattle or horses either living or dead. As for the menacing words described, they are only ordinary blasts of anger which people are in the habit of letting out when they are dispossessed of their possessions. The falsity of the story is shown by the fact that it is well-known and obvious, and will be proved in court, that at the time when the land was redeemed by George Home, two hundred merks of the money was lent by the accused and her husband to this William Meslet. For this, William paid money back annually to the accused for five years after the redemption. As for Isobel supposedly taking off her kerchief and running round anticlockwise in the barn, this is not relevant, because it is quite possible that her kerchief might have been blown off going in at a windy barn door, and in order to save it from landing on the ground she might have turned round twice or thrice to catch it. If this sort of behaviour was designed to cause the death of cattle, it is more likely that she would have done it at the door of the stable or the byre, than at the barn door. As for Jonet Lyndsay's declaration, she is stated by the indictment to have been a witch, and so no trust should be put in her declaration, since she must be presumed to be a liar like her master the Devil. As for the two pet sheep it is alleged were bewitched by the accused so that they broke their necks, it is unlikely that her words could have caused misfortune to one and not to the other, since they were both innocent beasts. As for the decay of William Meslet's estate, allegedly brought about by the accused's sorcery, our response is that this should be ascribed to the secret judgment of God, for it is well known that he took upon himself to be father to a child begotten in adultery by his own father. As for the slander given out by William Meslet's wife Margaret Ogill, the truth is that Thomas Lowrie the schoolmaster in Eist Barnes was given board and lodging by the accused and her husband in their household. The accused suspected that Margaret Ogill was up to no good in visiting him. When she told William Meslet this he became so jealous and watchful that he caught them in the act. Thomas Lowrie was banished from the community for this, and Margaret Ogill could not think of a more malicious way of taking revenge than making up this slander. Because of this, it is not relevant.

My Lord Advocate answers that these allegations should be rejected because of what the indictment says.

4. The fourth article of the indictment was read, about sheltering the witch Cristiane Grintoun in her house, and that she was seen by the accused's husband George Smith, coming out of a hole in the roof in the likeness of a cat, and then changing herself into her own shape. There is also the prediction made by the accused to her husband about him seeing this, that things would not go well with him, and that in accordance with this prediction George Smith fell down dead at his plough, and was brought home by the accused in William Meslet's chair.

It is alleged against the fourth article of the indictment, that as for sheltering Christiane Grintoun, Margaret Melrois, and Jonet Acheson in her house - not granting it to be true - if neighbours frequent each others' houses, this cannot impute witchcraft, and it is not stated that she knew they were witches. As for the accused's husband George Smith seeing Christiane Grintoun appearing in the likeness of a cat and changing herself back to her own shape again, it is not stated that anybody saw that change, or the change back. As for her husband being brought back in William Meslet's chair, and carrying him through the barn, that is not relevant, because he fell ill at William Meslet's back door, or in his barnyard, and that chair was handiest. Through the barn door was the most convenient and discreet way to go. As for William Meslett's estate going back because of it, we repeat the answer of the accused to that claim.

The prosecutor answers that the allegations should be rejected because of what the indictment says.

5. The fifth article was read, about the sickness that was taken off George Smyth by sorcery, and put upon William Smyth his brother's son, when he came to the barn door and saw the "firlot" [a tub for measuring meal or grain] running about with the contents bubbling up onto the floor. He then confronted the accused with a sword with the intention of striking her for bewitching him.

It is alleged by the accused that the fifth article about taking the sickness off George Smyth and laying it on his nephew William Smyth is both improbable and impossible. It can be proved that two years intervened between these illnesses. Also, the indictment contains absolute nonsense in claiming that an illness can be laid beneath a barn door, because an illness cannot be anywhere but in a living creature. This is just like a fable related in Ariosto.

The prosecutor answers that the indictment is still relevant in spite of this allegation, and should be considered by the jury.

Also, as to the alleged sight of the firlot with wheat in it going about as claimed, it is obvious that the disturbance was in the subject, that is to say, in the brain of the person who saw the sight, for he was mad. As for pursuing her with a sword, and the lintel of the door bearing the mark of the stroke, there is no such mark on the lintel, as will be proved. As regards health or curing, the accused can prove that William Smith was cured by John Purves the surgeon, lived for eleven years after that, and had children.

The prosecutor answers that the allegation should be rejected as above, because of what the indictment says.

6. The sixth article records that William Symsone's daughter Margaret Symsone was visited by a serious illness laid on her by the

sorcery of the accused. The accused alleges that the sixth article is not relevant. No action performed or words spoken are recorded in this article, only that Margaret fell ill and died of her illness. As for the accused taking off her kerchief as described in the article, a greeting of that kind is contrary to what is said in the third article, which claims that she usually took off her kerchief by going round anticlockwise three times. Here however, she is said to have sat down on the threshold of the door and taken off her kerchief. As for the part of the indictment about the ridiculous transformation of herself into a hare, it has not been properly established which persons saw the woman change into the hare, or the hare change back into the woman. Therefore the hare still remains a hare, and the woman still remains a woman, and the indictment is not relevant.

The Advocate answers that the allegation should be rejected because of what the indictment says.

7. The seventh article concerns the disease inflicted upon Issobell Frude's foot [*Sic* "Fute" and "face" can look very similar in 17th Century secretary hand and the editor is mistaken here. The indictment definitely concerns Issobell Frude's face.] by the accused's witchcraft, and the cure after she had asked for her health for God's sake as described in the seventh article. As to what is said in the seventh article about the breaking out of Issobell Frude's face, there is nothing recorded indicating that this was caused by the accused. As for coming to the accused and seeking her health from her, that can only be taken as an indication of the continuation and further progress of Issobell's malice, in an attempt to slander the accused as a layer-on and taker-off of sickness. Neither is it recorded that when she asked for her health, the accused promised to give it to her. To highlight the lies and deceit contained in this article, it can be proved by Thomas Bois[?] the blacksmith in Eist Barnes, that the breaking out of her face followed from her intemperate drinking of the dregs of an old ale barrel in Thomas's house, and by drinking after that a great quantity of raw unfermented wort. She is known to be a drunken wretch, and it is no wonder that the effects of it broke out in her face. It is also known that she was cured by John Chisholm, Lord Heries' gardener.

The Advocate answers that this allegation should be rejected because of what the indictment says.

8 & 9. The eighth and ninth articles concern the malice borne to Thomas Home for buying John Purves's land over the head of the accused, and also the sickness she laid on him because of it, from which he died. It is alleged against this article that it is in no way relevant, because nothing is recorded that the accused either did or said to cause Thomas Home's sickness or death. As for the empty bragging words inserted in the article, that people who meddled with anything she had a liking for never throve, they are not witchcraft, or examples of it. If they were spoken - which is not admitted - they are only the bragging of an angry woman. Also, it can be proved that this point of the indictment is false, because Thomas Symsone bought the land at that time, and not Cristiane Lummisden's husband Thomas Home. What caused his death was a tremendous drinking bout he had in Nicoll Kellie's house in Dumbar with five other cronies - Nicoll Kellie, William Cullane, Andro Ros, John Lermouth, and others, who drank all day and a good part of the night, until midnight. He himself slept outside for the rest of that winter night in the open hearth of a kiln, without warmth or covering, and died with the rest of his associates because of it.

10. The tenth article states that the accused was at a meeting with the Devil, in company with the witches Margaret Melrose and Jonet Achiesone, who were burnt for witchcraft at

Dumbar. This was at the Doune Hill at Spote, concerning the death of George Clerksone in Dumbar. The tenth article is based on a statement from Margaret Melrois and Janet Achiesone, and is not relevant because they were witches and persons of ill repute. Their confessions served well to destroy them, but cannot now be used in this court to have the accused counted among their detestable fellowship, since both they and their master the Devil are all liars, and the law regarding persons of ill repute will not allow trust to be put in their statements.

The Prosecutor answers to this that the allegation should be rejected because of what it says in the indictment, based on the statement of Margaret Melrois and Jonet Achiesone, who were convicted of witchcraft. They died penitent, and gave this confession. The law and practice of this kingdom is that persons with a bad reputation arising from conviction for a crime are always received in atrocious circumstances such as these as strong evidence for the case in question. Just such circumstances, along with a bad reputation in the community are alleged against the accused. Such statements are always admissible in order to secure a conviction. This has always been the practice in the past, and is warranted by a Statute of Session in the year 1591 as used against Euphane McCalyeane in her trial of the same year. [This summary is the gist of a very difficult passage. Evidence from convicted criminals was usually disallowed, but had been permitted in the case of Euphane McCalyeane, thus setting a precedent for witchcraft cases.]

The accused replies to this that her objection is relevant in spite of the answer, because no matter whether persons of ill repute are classified thus by law or by their deeds, they cannot be trusted or produced before a judge. Statements from accomplices are only supporting evidence and presumptions, and cannot be accepted unless they are supported by other very convincing evidence. Bodene in the second chapter of his fifth book declares that three things are necessary for clear proof: the fact being well-known, along with sincere voluntary and unextorted confession, and the statements of witnesses without reproach. Judges cannot inflict the punishment of death on the basis of presumptions, but only other corporal punishment or fines.

The Prosecutor answers that it is certainly not relevant to cite Bodene, because in the passage quoted he is dealing with criminal acts with permanent effect, such as murder, not with criminal acts of transient effect, as is the nature of witchcraft.

11. The eleventh article states that she conceived a deadly hatred against the late Patrik Bryson for cutting her pig's tether, and inflicted a serious illness on him by which he lost the power of one side.

The accused alleges that the eleventh article about cutting Patrik Bryson's tether [sic] is frivolous and inept, since no action or menacing words of hers are mentioned. It is well known that Patrick Brysone recovered, and sixteen years after that died in the accused's arms as a sign of full reconciliation.

It is answered that the allegation should be rejected because of what the indictment says.

12. The twelfth article concerns her consultation with the witch Katharine Gray for curing Marioun Wolf by sorcery of an illness with which she was visited in the manner described. It is alleged by the accused that this twelfth article about the alleged consultation with the witch Katharine Gray as described in the indictment is not relevant, since it does not indicate any words or deeds either done or spoken at that consultation for relieving or curing Marioun Wolf from Eist Barnes of her disease. It is answered to this that it should be rejected because of what is said in article twelve.

13. The thirteenth article of the indictment was read, concerning the burning of William Kellie's corn by witchcraft out of ill-will conceived against him by the accused, for blaming her for bewitching his father in law, the late Patrik Bryson. Also for inflicting a serious illness on this William by sorcery and witchcraft as described in the indictment.

It is alleged against this thirteenth article that it is a mere childish tale of harm supposedly done to William Kellie resulting from a grudge dating back 34 years. Nothing of what she either did or said is recorded. As for his fall from horseback caused by her sorcery, which is mentioned in the thirteenth article, it can be proved that the fall was the result of a great drinking session which got the better of him. What caused it was that as he was coming in at John Brysone's door, he was felled by hitting his forehead on the lintel of the door. The accused was in Dumbar at the time, two miles away from William Kellie. After his fall he was picked up by John Bryson's daughter, not by the accused.

It is answered to this by the prosecutor that the allegation should be rejected, since the indictment says that the fire was raised and the sickness inflicted on William Kellie by the witchcraft and sorcery of the accused.

It is alleged further by the accused that as to the burning of the corn, that is a manifest calumny and untruth. It is well known that this happened because of the laziness and negligence of William Kellie's own wife, who had a lighted candle under her own bed. This is known to all the people in the district.

The prosecutor answers as above.

14. The fourteenth article concerns the bewitching of the dairy produce of George Umferstoun and his wife Janet Hodge, so that they could get no butter from their churn. This was for taking the job of shepherd of the Links over the head of her brother Thomas Young. Everything went back for George and his wife by the sorcery of the accused, and all they had in this world vanished away from them.

The accused alleges that this fourteenth article about George Umpherstoun is not at all relevant, because this George Umpherston was the accused's own employee on the Links, and the livestock was hers as well. She had discharged Thomas Young from her service as a ne'er-do-well, and hired George Umpherstoun in his place, and so could never have used sorcery on him or his wife Jonet Hodge to cause their butter to do badly or fail. Even if the dairy produce had been Jonet Hodge's own, the article is not relevant because many accidents can happen during the churning of butter, as Bodene alleges in his third book, concerning a servant in Vallois.

It is answered that this ought to be rejected, since the indictment shows this to be "actus continuus" as affirmed by Bodene.

15. The fifteenth article concerns the sickness of Lilias Knowis' husband Thomas Home. This was inflicted upom him by the sorcery of the accused, which was also practised upon their goods and means of earning a living, and caused the death of 27 of their horses, oxen, and other livestock, as described in the fifteenth article.

It is alleged by the accused about this article concerning Thomas's illness, that it is well known and can be proved in court by his own son that he died of dropsy in Preston Panes. In any case, the article is not relevant since it does not record that the accused did or said anything to cause his death. The indictment is manifestly untrue when it says that this Thomas Home got a continual right for himself and his wife Lilias Knowis to rent William Woid's land. Lilias was his third wife, and he acquired the right in the time of his second wife Marioun Craw, who died long before. The indictment affirms that before his death, in the presence of his brother Mr Alexander Home, the minister of the Pannis Mr John Ker, and Mr David Home of Godscroft, Thomas Home declared and affirmed to them that the accused was the cause of his death. Although this was affirmed and the affirmation was verified, it is not relevant in itself, since it does not legally infer or prove witchcraft just because a dying man blames his death on someone to whom he bears ill will.

It is answered that this should be rejected because it is part of the indictment.

16. The sixteenth article concerns the burning of the houses and steading belonging to Lilias Knowis, the widow of Thomas Home, by the sorcery of the accused and other witches. Also her hounding out as described in the sixteenth article.

The accused alleges against the sixteenth article that this has nothing to do with witchcraft. It is negligence, and that is not what is alleged. In any case, it is in no way relevant, since it does not name the man or woman who did it. And if it was relevant - which it is not - it can be proved that the fire happened because of Lilias Knowis' own negligence in handling her lint beside the fire.

It is answered that this allegation should be rejected because of what the indictment says. This article is connected with the previous one, as resulting from the menacing and threatening of the accused.

17 & 18. The seventeenth article concerns the sickness laid upon Lilias Knowis' child, and her subsequent death caused by the sorcery and witchcraft of the accused, as described in the seventeenth article of the indictment. Also, Thomas Home's dovecot failed to thrive, and the pigeons flew away from it, as described in the eighteenth article. This was also caused by the sorcery and witchcraft of the accused.

It is alleged by the accused and her spokespersons, that as far as the sickness laid upon Lilias Knowis' daughter is concerned, nothing is shown to have been done to the child except an indication of neighbourly kindness, when the accused took the child upon her knee and stroked her head. And the child is not dead, but recovered from the sickness and is still alive. As to the dovecot not thriving, and the pigeons flying away, as contained in article eighteen, that is in no way relevant, because it is common for pigeons to leave for various reasons, such as cats or other animals.

It is answered that this should be rejected because of what the indictment says.

19. The nineteenth article describes the apparition of the accused in John Brysone's stable at night, riding on the horse and mare which were there, and seen by the servant David Nisbet. He drew his sword and the accused vanished. The horse died and the mare aborted her foal as a result of the accused's sorcery and witchcraft.

It is alleged concerning the apparition of the accused in John Brysone's stable, that there is no evidence for this. It is obviously mere fiction, and might have been a dream or fancy of the drunken fellow mentioned named Nisbet. As for drawing a sword, it is confidently affirmed that he never had a sword, and so could not draw one! As for the mare casting her foal, that could have been caused by the fellow not looking after the mare, or some other accident, and not by sorcery.

20. The twentieth article concerns the ill will and hatred borne by the accused towards the shopkeeper [or possibly "pedlar"] Cuthbert Symson for not changing a web of cloth out of four webs which he sold her. The web was not big enough. By her sorcery she caused him to fail to thrive, and his worldly goods to diminish, reducing him to poverty although he had previously been worth £100. She also caused the death of his horse by devilish means. It dropped dead that same night.

It is alleged against article 20, that as regards Cuthbert Symsone failing to thrive, or being worth £100, this is in no way relevant since it does not specify any act, word, or deed connected with it. It is well known that she never used to buy cloth from shopkeepers [or "pedlars"], but sold many webs to them and others. In particular she never bought any from this Cuthbert Symsone. It is a ridiculous conclusion to say that his horse died and that the accused was the cause, or that he became poor after being worth £100. A hundred pounds are soon spent by a lazy and debauched man, as this person is known to be, and in any case he was never worth £20!

It is answered to this by the prosecutor that the allegation should be rejected, because the indictment shows that threats preceded and damage followed.

The accused replies that his answer should be rejected, because of what has just been said, and repeats again the answer made to the Lord Advocate's previous reply.

21. Article 21 concerns curing Alisone Patersone in Myreside of a serious illness by witchcraft, using enchanted yarn. The sickness was taken off her and laid on the shoemaker in Spott, James Liddle, when he was the first to walk through the door where this enchanted yarn was laid. Through this, she recovered and he died.

It is alleged that this article is a manufactured slander, because it cannot be proved that the accused has ever been in Alisone Patersone's house for the past nine years. She never knew any such man as James Liddell, nor where he lived, nor what he did for a living. And whereas it is stated that this was done six years ago, it can be proved that this Alisone died nine years ago.

22. Article 22 says that for the past forty years, for curing her livestock or her children's livestock, she has been in the habit of taking a living ox, with a cat and a great quantity of salt, and burying the ox and the cat alive with the salt in a deep hole in the ground as a sacrifice to the Devil, so that the rest of the livestock should be freed from sickness or disease. Doing this is obvious sorcery and witchcraft.

Concerning this 22nd article of the indictment, the burial of the ox with the cat in a deep pit is in no way relevant. It does not state where it was done, in whose presence, or with whose help - for the accused could not bury a live ox with a live cat on her own. As for the salt, no-one ever heard or read of witches using salt, for it is a symbol of eternity, and therefore loathed by witches, who delight in all sorts of filthy and unsavoury things, as Bodyn alleges. The truth behind the claims of this article is that William Smyth and John Smyth his brother, both sons of the accused, had livestock diseased of the "routting evil" [a disease which caused cattle to run about bellowing till they died]. They intended to go to the Laird of Lie to borrow his curing stone, but they were advised by their servant James Nisbet that they had no need to undertake such a journey, for he had seen livestock cured by taking a living sick ox, digging a deep pit, and burying it there. Then the rest of the oxen and livestock should be driven over the place. John and William did this once or twice, but were none the better of it, so they went to the Laird of Ley's house and asked for a loan of the curing stone. The Lady refused, but gave them a quantity of water in flagons, in which the stone had been dipped. This was given to their livestock to drink, and in their opinion it healed them of the sickness. It can be proved by the minister, and other witnesses present, that they were challenged by the kirk of Dumbar for trying this charm, and they were ordered to satisfy church discipline publicly for this scandalous action, to deter others from doing it. The accused was never challenged for it. As for the way the cure was carried out, it has been the common practice of the best farmers in the kingdom, and they were never suspected or accused of witchcraft.

23. The 23rd article of the indictment was read, concerning the fearful threats uttered by the accused against Andro Mertoun, who then

lived in Eist Barnes, but now lives in Prestoun, for not promptly paying her a sum of money he owed. She said that he and his wife would not stay in the community two years before they would have nowhere to live, and neither food nor clothing. Accordingly, by the sorcery practised against this Andro and his wife by the accused, all their horses and cattle suddenly dropped dead. Andro had said to her that with God's grace he would pay her back the money before the day it was due. She replied with most blasphemous words that if he trusted too much in God, God would beguile him, thus committing the most hellish and horrible blasphemy.

The accused alleges that the decay of Andro Morton's estate described in article 23 is no less slanderous than all the preceding articles. He was never in debt to the accused or her husband for any sum of money at any time for any reason whatsoever. The article is not relevant since it does not mention the cause of the debt. As for the blasphemy alleged to have been uttered by the accused, it would have been most abominable if it had been said - not admitting that it was - but it cannot infer any point of witchcraft, and can only be punished by His Majesty's High Commission. As for the decaying of Andro's estate, it is well known, obvious, and can be proved that he had neither a livelihood nor any estate, and was a spendthrift vagabond fellow given to drunkenness and womanising, which are the main causes of poverty and misery, as is well known. If he had possessed any estate, he would have used it up by his riotous spending and his life of vice, and made an end of it.

It is answered that the allegation should be rejected because of what the indictment says about the menacing and threatening words uttered first, and the losses following on caused by her sorcery.

24. The 24th and final article of the indictment was read, declaring that for the past forty years the accused has been an undoubted witch and sorcerer, and a consulter and keeper of company with the Devil and various witches, particularly Margaret Melrois, Jonet Achesone, and other witches who were their associates. They kept company to practise sorcery on various decent people to destroy them and their goods. She also renounced her baptism, and applied herself to the service of Sathan, receiving a mark from him under the left breast, as described in this article.

It is alleged that what this article has to say about the alleged mark is in no sense relevant, since it is not recorded that she was ever searched for the mark, nor that it was found to be the Devil's mark. On the contrary, it is well known that it was an ulcer, an infection in her breast normal in women, something which many other honest women were subject to in the parish where she lives, and cured by Alexander Foirtoun. As for the alleged renouncing of her baptism, this is not relevant, since there is no mention of anyone who heard her renounce her baptism. Thus, this article, like all the rest, has been framed most maliciously and unjustly, and is completely false and untrue.

It is answered to this by the prosecutors that the allegation ought to be rejected because of what the indictment says, which is all very relevant. As for the truth of the article, proving that is for the jury to decide.

The accused and her spokesmen deny all of the articles of the indictment as inherently absolutely false and untrue, and they ask for a written record to that effect. My Lord Advocate asks for a written record to the contrary.

The judge postpones making an interim decision on the preceding allegations and the answers made to them, until tomorrow. He orders the accused to be taken back to prison, and the members of the jury to be informed, each under the penalty of 500 merks for non-attendance.

February 5th 1629: The interim decision of the judge is that the first two points of the first article of the indictment, dealing with the mill called Brandis Mylne and the witchcraft laid on it are found relevant, and also the transportation of the accused by devilish means; also the 18th article concerning the bewitching of the dovecot. These should all be taken and considered together. The third point of the first article is also found relevant in itself, about the fishing and George Sandie's herring being taken from him by sorcery and witchcraft. Similarly the 2nd, 3rd, 4th, 5th, 6th, 7th, 8th, 9th, 10th, 12th, 13th, and 15th articles of the indictment are each relevant in themselves. Also the 14th article taken with the 18th article and the first two points of the first article, are all jointly relevant. The 16th article is also found relevant when taken together with the 15th, and the 17th, 19th, and 20th articles are relevant in themselves, along with the 21st, 22nd, 23rd, and 24th articles. Each and every one is relevant in itself in spite of the allegations made to the contrary. All the articles of the indictment mentioned, taken together or separately as indicated, are to submitted for consideration by the jury. My Lord Advocate asked for a written record of the judge's interim decision.

The Jury
Robert Mure in Poppilhall [Foreman],
John Arnote in Pethhead,
Johm Home in Pinkertoun,
John Gullane in Eist Barnes,
John Hog of Drylawis,
William Dicksone in Beil,
James Nicolsone in Quhytekirk,
James Lermonth in Lyntoun,
Robert Aliesoun there,
Thomas Dawsone in Brokisburne,
David Nisbet in Dumbar,
John Aliesone in Lyntoun,
Johnne Quhyte there,
George Woid in Newmylne,
Adam Lermonthe in Frude.

My Lord Advocate had a written record made of the swearing in of the jury. To clarify the guilt of the accused of the crimes contained in the indictment, the first witness produced was George Sandie, who was the victim of the sorcery and witchcraft in the 1st article. Having been sworn, he declared on oath that the first article was true, and the crimes described in it. My Lord Advocate had this recorded.

Next was produced Thomas Kerr, to whom the injury described in the 2nd article was done. Having been sworn, he declared on his solemn oath that the whole article was true.

Margaret Ogill was also produced. Having been sworn, she declared that the point in the indictment concerning her was true. The 5th article was also true, regarding the accused taking the illness off her husband George Smyth, and laying it on William Smith as described in the indictment.

Issobell Frude was produced and sworn. She declared on oath that the 5th article was true, as was reported to her by William Smyth who went mad with the sickness laid upon him. She also declared on her solemn oath that the 6th, 7th, and 8th articles of the indictment are true as they are set down.

Cristane Lummisden was produced, and being sworn on the 9th article she declared it to be true as she should answer to God.

To prove the 10th article the statements of Margaret Melrois and Jonet Achiesoun were used and produced. These were made before the Presbytery, and show her to have been in company with them at a meeting they had with the Devil. The accused was there as a "special commander" [a person in authority?], as specified in the statements. The statements made before the Commissioners were also produced, which say the same thing.

It is alleged by the accused and her spokespersons that the testimony to prove the 10th article, signed by Mr Patrik Hamiltoun [clerk to the Presbytery of Dunbar], should not be admitted because it has no legal standing, being only a collection of accusations given in against Margaret Melrois and Jonet Achiesoun, and presented to the Council for purchasing a commission. No faith can be put in them, especially as they have been extracted by the minister Mr Patrik Hamilton who is appearing against the accused as someone who contributed accusations to the indictment. The second point is that the main accusation in the process against these two persons should not be admitted to prove the 10th article of Isobel's indictment. The article says that Margaret Melrois and Jonet Achiesone said both before and after their conviction, and at the time of their death, that the accused was one of their company and associates. Their trial does not record that they declared or admitted their confessions either at the time of their conviction or afterwards, but only before their conviction. Thus the article is in no way proven, since the character and credibility of witnesses count for more than their testimony. Besides, this evidence was not given on oath.

My Lord Advocate answers to this that the statement recorded in the Presbytery's extract has legal standing, although not in civil law [*i.e.* Its legal standing is in church law]. Thus it can be trusted. The second statement has legal standing in a civil court since it was made before His Majesty's judges by sworn commissioners whose oaths had been taken. There is no need to prove this part of the indictment by using statements from living persons, since it has been found relevant because of the statements from Margaret Melrois and Jonet Achiesoun, who gave evidence first before the Presbytery, and afterwards before the King's commissioners. It is alleged that the indictment says that their statement was made before and after their conviction, and at the hour of their death, which is supposedly not proven. It has been said that their confession and confrontation with the accused was able to prove a change. However, the contrary can only be true, since reference has been made to a sworn statement from Mr Patrik Hamilton that there was a change, but he has denied this on oath. [This is the best I can make of the last couple of sentences. The original seems rather confused.] In any case it is perfectly well known to the whole court that these two witches died without any change to their confession, and we are happy to produce sufficient witnesses - that is to say, the baillies of Dumbar, and others who heard them die with the same confession.

George Anderson, a baillie of Dumbar appeared, and after being sworn testified that he was present at the death of Margaret Melrois and Janet Achieson. However, whether they stood by the confessions made before their conviction or not, he doesn't know, since he was not near them when they were put to death, but stood further away as a spectator, and thus knows nothing about it.

George Purves, town clerk of Dumbar appeared, and after being sworn testified that he was present at their execution and heard what they said. Also, when they were confronted with the accused he heard the declarations about Isobel which were set down in their statements. When they were at the stake with the fire built round about them, they never varied from their previous confessions and affirmations, and both died as penitent persons.

Mr James Home, minister [of Dunbar] appeared. He was also sworn, asked to declare the truth of these matters, and testified in complete agreement with George Purves.

Thomas Corsbie, currently a baillie of Dumbar, appeared. Being sworn, he declares that he knows nothing.

My Lord Advocate asked for a written record of the declarations of Mr James Home and George Purves.

The accused answers that her previous allegation is still relevant in spite of the

Prosecutor's reply to it, in spite of the two Acts of Presbytery produced, and in spite of the legally ratified witnesses' statements produced. This article is in no sense proven, because it was created to suit the witnesses' statements. The Acts of Presbytery only record the assertions and declarations of two condemned witches, which cannot be received in law, since they were disreputable and devilish persons. Their testimonies cannot be admitted or received, because they were notoriously known to be of ill repute. It cannot be proved that they died penitent, although they may have seemed to be so. Such wretched people as they were, weary of the world's hardships, and brought to a state of great misery by their imprisonment, are often enough willing to die, and those eager for death are not to be trusted.

In order to prove the 11th article, My Lord Advocate produced John Bryesoun. Being sworn, he agreed that the tether was thrown in by the accused, and after that the sickness and disease took hold of Patrik Brysone, which he never recovered from - at least, not as far as his hand was concerned. As regards the Wife of Norham, he heard his brother report the truth of the matter just as is recorded in the indictment. He further declared that the accused has had an evil reputation for witchcraft for the past forty years. Being sworn and questioned about the 12th article, he knows no more than that it was reported to be true.

George Wat in Eist Barnes was produced and sworn in connection with the 12th article, but declares that he knows nothing about it. Questioned about the life and conduct of the accused, he testifies that she has been reputed to have been a witch for the past thirty six years, but he knows nothing specific about her.

George Purves, Andrew Ogill, and William Kellie are produced in order to prove the 13th article. William Kellie was present, was sworn, and testified that the 13th article was true as recorded in the indictment. George Purves and Andrew Ogill cannot be received as witnesses, because George Purves is the son in law of William Kellie who made the accusation, and Andrew Ogil is the brother of Margaret Ogil who did likewise. The notoriety of the 14th article was referred to the jury.

As for the 15th article, Lilias Knowis, Jasper Home, and Jeane Alexander were produced to prove it. Being sworn, Lilias Knowis declares that she saw the accused take off her kerchief, and she has had a reputation in the district as a witch for the past twenty six years. As for the rest of the indictment, concerning the sickness laid on her husband, the burning of her houses, and the sickness laid on her children, her conscience would not allow her to say that these losses, injuries, and evil turns of events, were caused by the sorcery and witchcraft of the accused. However, she had been told that the accused was the cause of it.

Jasper Home was sworn, and declares that he knows nothing about Issobell Young being a sorcerer or a witch, except for the 18th article of the indictment, about the pigeons flying away from the dovecot. However, he will not say that this happened as a result of her witchcraft.

Jean Alexander was sworn, and declares that she knows nothing about the burning of the houses in the 16th article - just what was said by one woman whose name she does not know, and who she never saw before or since.

To prove the 19th article concerning John Brysone's horse and mare, and the vision seen at night in his stable by David Nisbet's servant, David Nisbet's statement was produced signed by the ministers of the Presbytery of Duns.

As for the 20th article about Cuthbert Symsone and the injuries done to him as described, Cuthbert was put on oath to prove the truth of the article. Being present, Cuthbert was sworn and declared that the part of the indictment concerning Issobell taking off her kerchief was true. Also, for the past twenty years the accused has had a bad reputation as a witch among all the country people. As for the losses sustained by him as described in the indictment, this is true, but she was not the cause of them. He accepts them from God for his sins.

As for the 21st article concerning taking off the sickness from Aliesone Patersone and laying it on James Liddell, the prosecution abandons it, and desires that it should be deleted.

For proving the 22nd article concerning the burial of the live ox, and the circumstances of it, Issobell's own statement about it was used. Also, Aliesone Lummisden in Eist Barnes is produced, who was a witness to it. This Aliesone Lummisden appeared, was sworn, and declared that she saw a live cat in the accused's apron, together with some salt, but does not know what was done with it. Asked what she knows of the accused, and what her reputation in the countryside was, she declares that as far as she is concerned she was her servant for several years, and saw her as nothing but a virtuous, careful, and honest woman, although the gossip of the countryside said otherwise against her, amongst those who did not like her.

For the information of the jury concerning the truth of the 23rd article, regarding Andro Mertoun and the threats made against him by the accused, and the losses and harm which followed, Andrew Moirtoun is produced to swear to the truth of the article. Andro Mertoun, formerly of Eist Barnes, but now in Prestoun, was sworn and testified that it was true about the threats uttered by the accused against him, and about the loss which followed, but says that he will not take it upon his soul that Issobell Young was the cause of the death of his livestock, or any other harm sustained by him.

To prove the final article, the statements are repeated from witnesses who declare that for the past forty years she has been reputed and held to be a notorious witch, who resorted to and kept company with witches. Also, the declaration was submitted from Alexander Foirtoun taken before the Presbytery of Dunce and signed by Lenard Houstoun, clerk to the Presbytery.

To verify her custom of taking off her kerchief at the times when she intended to do harm, and to prove that she kept company with Margaret Melrois and Jonet Achiesone, the statements of Margaret Melrois and Jonet Achiesone are produced, along with the statements of Margarit Baxter and Marioun Bathcat made before the Presbytery of Dumbar on the 22nd and 24th April 1624, extracted from the Presbytery's books by Mr Patrik Hammiltoun their clerk, and ratified by My Lord Archbishop of Sanct Androis.

It is answered by the accused that Alexander Foirtoun's written statement in no way proves the last article of the indictment. It can be given no credence, since he never appeared in court, nor was he ever sworn before a judge. The law in all known judicial systems is that no trust is put in the testimony of deceased persons, but only to the supporting testimony of ministers who have been sworn to it by their soul and conscience. The same answer is repeated regarding the Act of Presbytery for verifying the 19th article. As for the statements of a number of witnesses who were questioned in the criminal process against the witches Melrois and Achiesone, these cannot be used again here in this court unless witnesses are produced in person, sworn, and made to testify in the presence of the accused, as those who swore to the indictment did. Since they have not been produced in this court to testify to the truth about the guilt of the accused in the crimes she is charged with, their statements cannot be relied on to convict her. If written evidence of this kind was produced in court in any civil case, unless it was only a matter of £5, no judge would respect it, and far less can the honest men of a jury receive or admit these unsubstantiated statements in such an important case as this, which threatens to take away an honest woman's life for accusations made by her malicious enemies.

Because of the evidence produced by him to the jury to prove the various articles of the indictment against the accused, My Lord Advocate claims that the jury will be guilty of willful error if they acquit.

The members of the jury having been chosen, sworn, and admitted, they once again heard Issobell Young accused in their presence and hearing of all the crimes contained in her indictment, all of which she denied were true. After the evidence was produced as proof by His Majesty's Advocate, and objections were made by the accused and her spokespersons against this evidence, a written record was requested by both sides and granted.

The jurors adjourned from court to the Council House, where they elected Robert Mure in Poppilhall as foreman by a majority. They then discussed and voted upon all the points of the indictment. After long and mature consideration of it and the supporting evidence, they returned again to the court where by the report and declaration of the foreman, they found pronounced and declared as follows: -

By a majority the found pronounced and declared Issobell Young to be guilty, culpable, and convicted of the sorcery and witchcraft practised by her upon Thomas Kerse in Eist Barnes, as described in the 2nd article of her indictment, and of the sorcery and witchcraft practised against William Meslet's horses, oxen, and other livestock, as described in the 3rd article.

Also, of keeping in her company Cristiane Grintoun, a notorious witch who was seen by Issobell's husband coming out of a hole in the roof of his house in the likeness of a cat, and afterwards changing back into her own likeness. Also of the fearful prediction uttered by the accused to her husband, and the accident and the sickness which befell him afterwards, as described in the 4th article of the indictment.

Also for being art and part in taking the sickness off her husband and laying it on his brother [sic] William Smith as described in the 5th article of her indictment.

Also, of inflicting a serious illness on Margarit Symsone, the daughter of William Symsone in Eist Barnes, followed by her death caused by the sorcery and witchcraft of the accused as described in the 6th article of the indictment.

Also, of the sickness and disease inflicted upon Issobell Frude by her sorcery and witchcraft, and the cure received by Issobell Frude from Issobell Young as described in the 7th and 8th articles of the indictment.

Also, of the sickness and disease laid on the late Thomas Home in Eist Barnes, husband of Cristiane Lummisden, and his death which followed as a result of her sorcery and witchcraft, as described in the 9th article of the indictment.

Also, the members of the jury unanimously find her guilty of the meeting she attended with the Devil, Margaret Melrois, and Jonet Achieson, at the Doune Hill of Spot at the place called Madeis Loup, where they planned and accomplished the death of George Clerksone as described in the 10th article of her indictment.

Also, by a majority, the jury finds and declares Issobell to be guilty and convicted of laying the sickness on William Kellie in Wast Barnes, the death of his horses, and the burning of his corn by sorcery and witchcraft as described in the 13th article of her indictment.

Also, of the bewitching of John Brysone's horse and mare, and transporting herself into his stable at night by sorcery and witchcraft, as described in the 19th article of the indictment.

The jury unanimously found Issobell to be guilty, culpable, and convicted of common sorcery, of witchcraft, and of using and practising it for the past forty years as described in the

24th and final article of her indictment. She is found clear, innocent, and acquitted of all the remaining crimes contained in her indictment and its various articles.

A written record was then made by His Majesty's Advocate of the above-written crimes of which Issobell was convicted.

By the mouth of John McAirtour, dempster of court, the judge decreed and ordained her to be taken to the Castel Hill of Edinburgh, and there to be strangled at a stake until she is dead, and thereafter her body to be burnt to ashes. All her moveable goods are to be forfeited and confiscated for our Sovereign Lord's use, since she has been convicted and found guilty of the above crimes. This was pronounced as sentence.

[Issobell was thus convicted of 12 of the 24 accusations in her indictment. She was convicted unanimously on only two, one being the important catch-all article 24 which accused her of having been "an undoubted witch and sorcerer for the past forty years". Thus in spite of her lawyer's skillful defence and sensible arguments, her local reputation sealed her fate with the jury, who if not from her immediate neighbourhood, mostly lived not far off. On the other hand, many of the jurors would also be familiar with the characters of the witnesses and accusers. They would know well, for example, who was a "spendthrift vagabond fellow", and who was a decent hard-working chap whose failure to thrive was indeed puzzling. Local knowledge must surely have been a factor in Issobell's acquittal on half the charges in the indictment. Unfortunately, it only needed a conviction on one of the articles to send her to her death.

This case is discussed by Hugo Arnot in his "Celebrated Criminal Trials" published in Edinburgh in 1785. He observes, "The celebrated Sir Thomas Hope who was counsel for the prosecution replied that these defences ought to be repelled and no proof allowed of them because contrary to the libel; that is to say, in other words, that what was urged by the prisoner in her defences contradicted what was charged by the public prosecutor in his indictment……This most incredibly absurd and iniquitous doctrine of repelling defences because contrary to the libel was till the present century a received maxim of criminal jurisprudence in Scotland."

To be fair to the prosecutor in Issobell's case, however, as I remarked earlier, I feel that he is not actually saying that the arguments of the defence must be wrong because the indictment contradicted them. He was meaning rather that because an accusation was thought important enough to be put in the indictment, it must be held relevant for the jury's consideration in spite of the defence's arguments.]

Witnesses' statements and other evidence in the Issobell Young case.

[As previously stated, box JC26/9 contains not only Isobell Young's dittay and the record of the court proceedings, but several other items connected with the case, which now follow.]

JC26/9/4

At Edinburgh 15th January 1629, in the presence of My Lord Bishop of Dumblane and Alexander Colvile of Blair, Justice Depute.

Issobell Young was solemnly sworn on her knees and asked how it came about that for the past forty years she has been spoken of and held to be a witch. She declares that she never was slandered with such a crime until she was in Bryanes [Brands?] Mylne. When she got some grain there she broke a firlot measure because it was too small and not sufficient measure. Because of this, George Sandie the miller slandered her most dishonestly after that, out of malice.

She was asked if at any time she was in the habit of taking the kerchief off her head when she wished or threatened harm to anyone. Was this a ritual given to her so that her threats would take effect? She declares as she shall answer to God that she never took the kerchief off her head at any such time, or with any such intent. She took it off when she was going to bed, as other honest women do.

She was asked if she had a live ox buried, or buried a live ox, at any time. She declares that she never buried any ox. However, when her livestock had the "routting evil", Johne Brysonne and his wife cried out that their livestock would infect the whole community if one of the beasts infected by the disease were not buried alive. She declares that she gave no orders to bury it, but her servants proposed burying one of her oxen in the barnyard. When she heard of this, she forbade them to do it there in case it infected the stacks [Or perhaps merely "dirtied" the stacks]. Instead, it should be taken to some other place beyond her bounds. She says that this ox was then taken and buried in the corner of her barnyard, and that the rest of the beasts were then driven over the place where it was buried to free them of the disease of the "routting evil". After that, none of her cattle died.

The Lords ordered her to show the mark on her breast. She loosened and lowered her clothing, and showed it, under her left breast. She says that she received it three years ago, through a pain and "humour" that fell out of her breast, which lasted a quarter of a year. It was cured by Alexander Fairbairn in Dunce, who got twelve pounds from her for curing it, and half a boll of wheat.

[The human body was believed to contain a balance of "humours" or fluids which each governed various traits, inclinations, or states of mind. An imbalance would cause illness. A "humour" breaking from the body might refer to pus from an infection. Issobell's mark, therefore, was probably the healed scar from a boil or ulcer.]

She says she believes it was four or five years since it was cured. When he cured it, he made her swallow a handful of small stones, and drink two quarts of a drink made with bark.

She was asked about the time when Johnne Fall and William Kellie were going to look for a chimney breast after William Kellie's house was burnt down. When they came past, was she not standing at her own door? She declares that she was not in her house, nor at her door at the time, but was in Dumbar church, and did not see William Kellie as had been affirmed during the interrogations.

She was asked if Marion Wolfe was sick at any time, or if she knows Marion Wolf. Also, whether she asked a certain Katharene Gray to cure her of her sickness. She denies ever asking anyone to help or cure Marioun Wolf. She says she knows Marion Wolf, and knew her both when she was healthy and when she was ill, but never spoke to Katharene Gray or anyone else about curing her.

JC26/9/5

Statements and accusations given by the parties named below against Isobell Younge, the wife of George Smyth in Eist Barnes, before the Presbytery of Dumbar when she was suspected of witchcraft, on 22nd April 1624, and on 29th April the same year.

Margaret Melrois and Jonet Acheson: Margrat Melrois and Jonet Acheson, living in Pincartoune in the parish of Dumbar, were accused before the Presbytery and confessed that they had learned the devilish art of incantation and witchcraft from the Devil, and that they had many different meetings with him, including one last August in 1623. This was on a windy Tuesday which blew away many boats, and shook a great deal of green barley. They had a meeting at the Dounhill of Spott, at a place called Maiday's Lowpe, about the death of George Clerkeson. Isobell Young was there amongst the rest at this meeting as a "special commander"... [several illegible words here] "...with cold water. He is my godson. Let him go the way he is going." Before they declared this before the Presbytery, they declared it in [illegible], and swore to it in the tollboth of Dumbar before His Majesty's commissioners, before they were put on trial. They also affirmed it at their deaths, where they were very penitent.

William Meslet [Marginal note - "Dead. To prove the third and fourth articles".]: On the 23rd of April William Meslit in Eist Barnes appeared and stated that he had lent the sum of 400 merks in money of this realm to George, the son of Meiklepinkerton, to free a croft of land which George Smyth in Eistbarnes and Isobell Yong his wife had as a pledge. Because of this Isobell Yong was angry with William Meslet and his wife Margrat Ogill, and vowed that she would do them an evil turn. And further, that he would never again have so much money to lay out on land. At that time they were very rich. Also, Isobell Yong declared that for all their wealth, before they bought any more they would sell the things they had. All this came to pass as follows through her devilish malice, by God's permission. William Meslet sold half a chalder of wheat to Isobell Yong, which she did not need to buy from him - as if she could not have got it from others. It was just to accomplish her devilish malice over the redeeming of George Home's land. When she came in to William Meslet's barn to get the wheat, she took off her headgear and turned round anticlockwise three separate times. Margaret Melrois in Pincartoun declared before His Majesty's commissioners in the tollboth of Dumbar, and also before the brethren of the Presbytery of Dumbar, that this touching the head and lifting headgear and kerchiefs was a significant example of witchcraft which had been given to them by the Devil. They lifted it to hurt those … [damage] ...to whom it was lifted either in their bodies or in their possessions. This was when they first greeted the Devil, every time they did so they used to take off their kerchiefs and salute their master. This was the reason he gave them this power. She lifted her headgear in this manner on three separate occasions, as William declared before the Presbytery of Dumbar and His Majesty's commissioners in the tollboth of Dumbar. He stated that through this devilish incantation, through her behaviour, he lost sixteen oxen and six or eight horses and mares which all died, although they had been very fat and active and nobody could see any thing wrong with them. Then the witch Jonet Lyndsay, who was living at the time in Lynton Brigges married to a fiddler, and who was afterwards burnt in Hadingtoun, told William Meslet while he was sowing his barley seed that he was being wronged by his neighbour Issobell Yong. She was the cause of the loss of all his livestock. This loss was all within the space of half a year after she had taken off her kerchief, and the beginning of it was immediately after she had bared her head.

He also declares that he had two pet sheep and two greyhounds. The pet sheep ran through the corn which Isobel Yong was receiving, and the greyhounds followed them, spilling the corn. Isobel Yong was angry at this and prayed to her god that they might break their necks. In accordance with her devilish request and desire, it followed that the next day one of them broke its neck.

He also declared that he was informed by a certain William Smythe, the nephew of George Smythe mentioned above, that George Smith senior was on the Dowcat Know and saw a woman called Cristian Grinton come out of his house through a hole in the slates. She was a witch, and George Smythe was angry with his wife Isobel Yong over it. She said to him, "I'm sorry you saw that, for it will be the worse for you." The next day when he was at the plough he fell down dead. When Isobell Yong was told by Barbara Bellne that her husband had fallen down dead at the plough, she would neither take a chair out of her own house nor borrow one out of anyone else's house. Instead, because of her promise and her usual malice, planning to destroy him, she came to William Meslett's and took his chair although there were many houses between his house and their house. She brought her husband in through Wilyam Meslett's barn doors in Wilyam Meslett's own chair, although there was a road nearby to allow carts and wagons to go to and fro. When they had done, they turned with the chair and sent it back to William Meslett's. After that time, by her devilish malice, nothing throve with him and everything went continually backwards.

Also, he was informed for certain that George Smythe's sickness was laid on his brother's son William Smyth. William Smyth told him so himself - that he was the first to go in at the door after the sickness was taken off his uncle George Smyth, and laid upon him. Isobell Frud's statement will explain this more clearly. After that time George Smyth grew continually better, but William Smyth grew worse, howled for his mother in a mad rage, and was never well the [illegible] time of his life. William also declares that the witch Cristian Grinton took him by the hand when he was watching her in the tollboth of Dumbar, and said to him, "Willem ... [half a line of damage here] ...neighbour Isobell Yong, for she is the cause of all the misery you've sustained in your loss of livestock."

Margaret Ogil [Marginal note - To prove the 4th and 9th articles."]

The same day appeared Margaret Ogill, the wife of Williame Meslet in Eistbarnes. She declared that when Isobell Younge from Eistbarnes was in Auldhamstoks at the baptism of a child of Hary Andersen's, somebody called her "Lady Young". She answered, "No, call me Lady Home, for my purse has got some of Home's land, and it will get more yet." When the wife of George Home of Mikell Pinkertoun heard of this, she came and borrowed the sum of four hundred merks from Wilyam Meslet and his wife Margrat Ogil, and redeemed the Hawch of Laide out of the hands of George Smythe and Isobell Young. Isobell Yong was exceedingly angry about this, and said to Wilyam Meslet and Margrat Ogill that when he put his plough to the land at Martinmas he would never redeem land again, but would sell what he had. Through her devilish malice and witchcraft this came to pass. Wilyam and Margrat were exceedingly wealthy at that time, but from then on they never did well and everything went backwards with them, by Issobell Young's devilish malice. Isobell Yonge also said, "Margrat Ogil would like to carry coals in the lap of her gown to burn me, but before I'm burnt she shall have few gowns or other things." This also came to pass by her devilish malice.

Secondly, Margaret declares that when Isobell was receiving half a chalder of wheat from her, she took off her headgear three separate times, and turned round anticlockwise three times saying, "What do you think of this crop-headed [or bald] old woman?" Margrat Ogil saw this once, and her people in the barn saw the other two times before she came into the barn. Isobell Young said to them and to Margrat Ogil that it was just a habit of behaviour that she had. However, as previously stated, Margrat Mellrois affirmed that it was a command from the Devil to do evil to people or their possessions.

Thirdly, she declares that one of her pet sheep that Issobell had cursed, hoping in her god that it would break its neck, that same night had its neck broken by her devilish execrations, and died shortly after that. Also, within four days of Isobell lifting her headgear in the barn, their oxen and horses began to die, and before half a year had passed, Margrat Ogil and her husband had sixteen oxen and eight horses dead, although they had all seemed healthy and in good condition.

Fourthly, she declares that her husband went to Dunbar about Lammas to sell some wheat. Isobel Yong and Bessie Downandson from Cockbrandspethe were going on the same errand. He said he had promised some wheat to Agnes Acheson in Dunbar, but Isobel said, "I'll buy it." He replied that if his wife would sell some, Isobel could get it from her, but what he had with him was promised to someone else. Isobel went to Margrat Ogill and said, "Go and get me the [six?] bolls of wheat which I have bought from your husband." She answered, "I'll sell nothing, and give you nothing until he comes home." At this, knowing her master's mind, Isobell Young said in her devilish malice to two women who were carding, "Go and lay out the cloths and thresh this wheat, for I promise her she will never have so much to sell again at this time of year." And so it happened, in accordance with her prediction.

Fifthly, she declares that William Smyth, George Smyth senior's brother's son, was the first man to come into George Smyth's after the sickness had been taken off him. He took the sickness, became very weak, and was never free of it till his death. He told her this himself.

Jhon Thomson [Marginal note - "Dead".]

Jhon Thomson in Aistbarnes appeared. He testifies that he saw Isobell Yong take off her kerchief in Wilyam Meslet's barn, and turn herself round about anticlockwise three separate times. Marian and Alison Broun were also present. He also heard Isobel Yong cursing the pet sheep, wishing it would break its neck, which came to pass that night by her devilish incantation. He saw George Smyth's people bring George Smyth through Wiliam Meslet's barn, when they could have gone by the road, where any cart could have gone through. He says that William Meslet never did well after that. He also says that he heard that Christian Grinton being seen by George Smyth coming out through a hole in the slates of his house was the cause of his illness, and this illness was taken off him and laid on his brother's son William Smyth.

Jhon Bryson

Jhon Bryson in Eistbarnes appeared, and declared that about 34 years ago his father Patrick Bryson cut a pig's tether of Isobell Yong's. In a great rage, and with many malicious words, she railed at his father Patrick Bryson in a threatening manner, and flung the cut tether through the door into his house. Jhon both heard and saw this. Immediately he took a serious disorder in his leg and arm on one side, and was cruelly tormented with it. Hendrie Bryson, Jhone's brother, therefore went to the Wife of Noram, known as Dame Bett, who was said to be a wise woman, to see if he could get any help for his father. When she had [illegible] she left him for a short time, then came back and asked him if his father was at variance with any of his neighbours. He said no, for they never suspected Isobell Yong. She said, "Yes, but he is at variance with somebody. He has cut a pig's tether belonging to one of his neighbours, who has given him the disease between a dovecot and a knoll." This is just where he was first affected by the disorder, and it was there the tether was cut, just as she said. She also said that he would die of it between then and such-and-such a night, or else he would waste away. In any case he would never regain the power of that side of his body as long as he lived, and this certainly also came to pass.

He also declares that he knew Isobell Yong resorted to and consulted with witches, and she sheltered one who had done wrong to Alexander Home's mother in Thurston Mill. She was called Agnes Craw. There was also a witch called Cathren Gray who was burnt in Hadington, and who stayed with Isobell Yong for a long time before her execution. To illustrate the truth of this, for example, Marion Wolf in Eistbarnes had spoken about her ill health to Cathren Gray.

She subsequently went looking for Cathren Gray, and knowing she was staying with Isobell Yong, she came upon Katren Gray and Isobell Yong sitting in a little outbuilding in George Smyth's steading. The witch Katren Gray said to Marion Wolf, "I'm here consulting and seeking health for you, if any help can be had. That's why I'm speaking to this woman." Marion Wolf said to Katren Gray, "God reward you!"

He also declares that he heard a servant boy called George Gourly who was living with Isobell Yong, say that Isobell Yong had an ox which spoke while he was driving it to the field. It cried out three times, "Oh God! Oh God! Oh God!" The boy said he would die from this, and because he spoke about it, he was threatened to the extent that he had to leave the district and go away. Also, another servant of Isobell Young's, Jhon Millar, heard this same ox speak and say, "What's wrong with me that the rest were fed and I wasn't ?" [Probable meaning. The wording of the original is obscure here.] Hearing this, Isobell Yong called Jhon Millar and paid him his wages, saying, "If you mention this again, you'll die where there will be no-one to help you." After speaking of it again he subsequently fell ill, continually wasting away, until when he was going to North Berwick to the mill, he lay down in the fields and died miserably with no-one to help him. This came to pass in accordance with her prediction, out of her devilish malice. George Watt [Marginal note: To be produced in court to prove the 4th and 5th articles.]

The same day George Watt in Eist Barnes appeared, and declared that he can bear witness to the statements of Wilyam Meslet and his wife Margrat Ogil, and Jhon Brysone, because those who made the statements, and other people who were present, confirmed them to him -for example Marion Broun and her sister, when Isobel Young took off her headgear, looked to the far end of the barn, and said, "There won't be so much corn here next year, or ever again in his lifetime." He also declares that he heard Hendry Bryson confirm the same things declared by Jhon Bryson about his father's illness. He went to Norram to see about this, and declared that if his father lived beyond a certain date, as he understood it, he wouldn't die of the disease, but he would never recover from the loss of power in his leg and arm, or ever live fully independently. Also George Gourly was worried that he would die, because the ox spoke that morning when they were setting off to the fallow ground, crying out, "Oh God!" He also heard Jone Millar swear that he heard the ox speak, saying, "What have you got against me more than the rest ?" Also how Issobell Yong threatened the man with the words previously quoted, that he would die a miserable death, which came to pass within a short period of time. William Kellie

William Kellie in Wastbarnes appeared, and declared that he came to the Eist Barnes with his son in law George Purves, and Archibald Ogill from Wast Barnes. They had some business to conduct with George Smyth. Isobell Young had a particular grudge against William Kellie's wife, because of her father Patrik Bryson cutting her pig's tether. She had bewitched him for this. Her ill will was extended to William Kellie because of his wife, and so when they were going into the house, she lifted her headgear according to her usual custom, as they came in at the door. She does this to harm either people or their possessions. Also, when she was eating, she roundly condemned William's wife's thrift. However, she declared that before long she would save more of her ground. [The implications of this prediction are unclear.] Within five days her whole house and all her corn was burnt. The corn in the barnyard was also burnt - a hundred and sixty bolls or more.

After that, William Kellie was going through the Eistbarnes with his father in law, the mason Jhon Faa, when Issobel Yong met them, lifted her headgear, and asked, "Where are you going?" Standing in the road she said, "Goodbye then." ["Adew upon you".] Then both the horse and William fell to the ground senseless, and Jhone Faa said, "This woman has bewitched him!" He got up and went away home on horseback. When he got home he went to bed and lay sick for thirty weeks, not daring to move. The horse died immediately afterwards, however. All this happened when she lifted her kerchief, through her malicious and devilish disposition and her witchcraft.

George Umphraston [Marginal note: "Dead."]

George Umphraston from Innerwick village appeared. He declares that he and his wife took on the job of looking after the sheep on the Links. Isobel Yong's brother Thomas Yong had previously done this job, and so Isobel was angry with George Umphraston and his wife Jonet Hoge over this, and kept a deadly malice in her heart against them. Thus, on one occasion Jonet Hog had churned about three pounds of butter, and Isobell Yong came down wanting to buy some butter from her. She replied, "I have none." Using her devilish knowledge, Isobell answered, "I know you've just churned three pounds of butter, and I must have it." When Jonat Hog heard this she was frightened, so she brought out the butter and sold it to her. When it was weighed it came to three pounds, neither more nor less. After that, for the three years they lived there, Jonet Hoge never got as much as an ounce of butter, although she would sometimes have eight pints of cream, and sometimes twelve, as good as any in the land. She never got butter, but if any did appear it was filthy and stinking. Furthermore, from the time they came there neither they nor their livestock did well. They acknowledge that this was the result of Isabel's devilish malice. When George Umphraston was seriously ill before his death he swore to this before Mr Patrick Hamilton. He also declared this when he was still on his feet, before John Bryson in Eist Barnes.

Isobell Frude [Marginal note: "Witness in the matter of Cristen Grynton, George Smyt, and his nephew William Smyt."]

Isobell Frude from Eistbarnes appeared, the wife of Wilyam Sympson. She declares that William Smythe, George Smythe's nephew, said to her that one morning in barley seed time George Smyth was standing on the road, and he saw Crystion Grinton come out at a hole in the slates, wriggling like a cat. Then she gradually increased in size until she came to her own likeness. He heard George say to his wife Isobell Yong, "What made you lock Crystian Grynton in? You …[illegible] …her coming out." When he went to plough he fell down dead on the Wakraft. [I can only surmise that "Wakraft" is a proper noun, the name of a piece of ground, perhaps "well-croft" or "wall-croft".] They had a chair taken out of Willyam Meslet's, and he was carried through between Wilyam Meslett's barn doors, although there was a convenient road. The result was as declared by Margaret Ogill. Then four days after that the witch Crystan Grinton was sent for. She came and took the sickness off George Smyth, and when William Smith came in from ploughing, he was the first to come into the house, and the sickness was laid on him. When he came into the barn where Jhon Ferguson was, to get a boll of wheat, he saw the firlot measure full of wheat running about and bubbling up in the middle like a cauldron. He was the first person in the barn after Crystion Grinton and Isobell Young came out of it, and then he fell sick while George Smythe recovered day by day. The sickness drove him almost mad, and he came and took her by the throat and vowed to have her life. He left a mark on the lintel of the chimney breast, and vowed that if he got the opportunity he would pursue her to the death for bewitching him.

Secondly, Isobell Frude declares that a quarrel

broke out on a Lammas day between her son Thomas Sympson and Isobell Yong's son George Smyth. They were both schoolboys, and Isobell Frude's daughter Margaret Sympson, seeing who her brother was wrestling with, came and told off Thomas [sic] Smyth for it. Isobell Yong was very angry about this, having been informed of it by Thomas Fender[?], John Bryson's servant. She came to Willyam Sympson's house on the pretence of buying vegetables, sat down in the doorway, and took off her headgear as her usual custom was. The following Sunday a great quarrel broke out between Isobell Yonge's sons and William Sympson for the same reason. That same Sunday in the evening, as witnessed by Willyam Sympson's illigitimate daughter Jonat Sympson who called to Isobel Frude to come and see it, a hare came through Willyam Sympson's courtyard. It moved no faster than a man [Surmised meaning. The text seems garbled here.]. However, Isobell Frude's daughter Margrat Sympson had nipped Isobell Young's son's leg, and fearing Isobell Young's malice, and fearing that this was Isobell Young in the shape of a hare, she would not allow her mother to go any further. After that the child fell ill, and wasted away until she died, through the devilish malice and incantation of Isobel Young.

Thirdly, she declares that about April 1624, after she had come back from the Presbytery where she was giving evidence against Isobell Yong, a serious skin complaint broke out in her face like a "hive" [A general term for rashes and skin complaints.]. She went to Edinburghe, Jedburghe, and to Doctor Arnot with this, and could get no lasting remedy; for after she had been at home for two or three days and saw Isobell Yong, the disease always broke out again and her face became worse, which is evidence of Isobell's devilish intent against her. When she came home and the cures were not working, Isobell Yong said, "I thank my god I've got the upper hand of you, for you said in Dunbar before the Presbytery that if your statement wasn't true, may God [illegible] in my forehead. So," said Isobell Young, "now it has happened." All this was false, however, for no such thing was spoken before the Presbytery, it was Isobell Yong who caused it all through her devilish malice, with God's permission... [Some illegible words here,]... Isobell Yong was the cause of her disease, for she had been at some of the most skillful physicians in Scotland and could get no means of relief, until she came and asked Isobell Young for her health three times for God's sake. From that time she improved continually. A third reason why it appears to have proceeded from her malice was that she said to Isobel Purves who bore a child to her son Thomas Smyth, "Will you take it on your conscience to name my son as the father of the child, as you have done with many others? [Probable meaning. The wording is rather obscure here.] In any case, I can have the Purves land whenever I like. And as for Sympson's land, I should have had it rather than him, and it's my wish that anyone who has an eye on it will never thrive." And truth to tell, her son William Smith got the Purves land, and Wilyam Sympson and his wife, whose land she had her eye on, never throve. The same could be said about Wilyam Meslet and Margaret Ogil and their possessions, for they had their eye on the land which her daughter Isobell Smyth got after that Christian Lumsden

Christian Lumsden from Eist Barnes appeared, and declared that her late husband was coming from Dumbar about midnight, having been supplied with a horse for the road by George Rutherforde. About midnight a great shower of rain came on. He came to the schoolhouse and sheltered with his back to it and saw a great number of candles burning in George Smyth's hall. Her late husband Thomas How[?] came to an agreement for Purves's land, which Isobell Younge had an interest in. He went to Dumbar and Markal about the securities

[Probable meaning. Some of this is illegible.], and after he came home, presently he fell ill. Nevertheless, he walked to Dumbar to church, and when he got home was very weak. They said a drink made with honey would do him good, so Christan went to Isobell Younge and bought a mutchkin of honey. She said, "Oh, has your husband been at Dumbar?", surprised that he had gone because she knew about the sickness she had laid on him. After he had got the drink he became steadily worse. He died fifty days after he signed the papers for Jhon Purves's land, and during that time Isobell or Marion Cathcart never left him. This Marion is now in Dumbar tollbooth charged with witchcraft. Isobell had been interested in this land for William Smythe her second son, and she got it for him later. All this happened as a result of her devilish malice in accordance with what she had said to Isobell Frude, that nobody would thrive who took what they [*i.e.* Isobell Young and her family] had a mind to. It was also evident in Isobell Yong's malice towards Crystian; for after the death of her husband she came to Inerweik to Silvester Craig's house to deliver the papers which had been drawn up in Dumbar. On the way home she got a slight scrape on her forehead, and after that lay from around Martinmas to oat-seed time. When she got up, the first time she went out at the gate, the lintel of the gate broke and fell her own length away from her. No doubt this was done so that Isobell could take her life as well as that of her husband, and have more peaceable possession of the land.

[Document JC26/9/5 is cut off here. The tops of the tall letters from the next line are visible, indicating that there has been more.]

JC26/9/6

[This seems to be a note of the Prosecution's tactics in their case against Issobell.]

Instructions for proving each of the articles in the indictment against Issobell Young.

1. As regards the first article, the prosecution will use George Sandie's oath and declaration to prove it before the court.

2. As for the second, Thomas Kers's oath and declaration will be used.

3. As for the third article, we will use the oath and declaration of Margaret Ogile, the widow of William Meslet. The following witnesses are to be sworn and are to give evidence - Give the witnesses' names.

Also the statements made by the late William Meslet on 23rd April 1622 before the Presbytery of Dumbar. Also Margaret Melrois's statements about taking off her kerchief, and the statements of James Fairlie made before Mr John Weymes the minister at Duns.

4. The fourth article: this is about Cristiane Grintoun coming out of the roof of the house in the likeness of a cat, and then in her own likeness, seen by your husband. Also about the sickness which befell your husband according to your prediction; all the other circumstances contained in this article; and also taking the sickness off him as mentioned in Article 5, and laying it on his nephew William Smyt. We will use the statement of William Meslet and his wife Margaret Ogle, along with the statement of the late John Thomesone in Eist Barnes which was taken before the Presbytery - Also the statement of George Wat in Eist Barnes. Also Issobell Frude's statement.

6. We will use Issobell Frude's statement for the sixth article, about the quarrel between the two schoolboys William Smyt and Thomas Symson, and your anger against the boy's father William Symsone for threatening your son Thomas Smyt. Also your coming through the courtyard in the likeness of a hare, and the sickness and death of his daughter Margaret Symson which followed.

7. The seventh article concemes the disease laid upon Issobell Frude's face, and the cure

8. Contained in the eighth article. The statement of Issobell Prude will be used.

9. The ninth article concerns the fatal illness laid on Thomas Home, Cristiane Lumisden's husband. Cristiane Lumisden's deposition will be used.

10. The tenth article concerns her being in company with Margaret Melrois, Jonet Achesone, and the Devil, and contributing to George Clerkstone's death. We will use the attestations of the Presbytery, the judges and the jury. Her son William Smyt was one of the jury, and he signed with the rest.

11. As for the eleventh article about the disease laid on Patrik Brysone for cutting the pig's tether, the statement of his son John Bryson will be used.

12. For the twelfth article, about Marion Wolf's sickness and cure, John Bryson's statement will be used. Also, the statement made by George Wat before the Presbytery.

13. The thirteenth article concerns the burning of William Kellie's house and corn, the subsequent death of his horses, and the sickness laid on William himself. William Kellie's own statement will be used, together with the declaration by John Faa and George Purves made in court. Archibald Ogill in West Barnes is also to be a witness.

14. As for the fourteenth article, concerning the ruin of George Umphrastone, and the devastation inflicted on him and his wife Jonet Hodge, George Umphrastone's statement made before the Presbytery will be used.

15. The fifteenth article concerns the hurt and loss inflicted on Thomas Home and his wife

16. Lilias Knollis. This also features in the sixteenth article about the burning of Lilias Knollis' house and corn.

17. & 18. There is also the sickness laid on Lilias's child, contained in article seventeen. The statement given by Lilias Knollis will be used for all of this, and also for the eighteenth article about the doves flying away. Jasper Home will be used as a witness to inform the jury of this under oath. He will declare it in court in the presence of the judge and jury. The statements and declaration of Jeane Alexander in [illegible] will also be used and sworn to judicially before the judge and jury.

19. The nineteenth article concerns the harm done to John Bryson's horse and mare, and the visions or light seen by David Nisbet, his servant at the time, who was sleeping in the stable. We will use the statement made by David Nisbet in the presence of Mr John Weymes, minister at Duns, and others.

20. As for the twentieth article about Cuthbert Symson's horse, and the harm done to him, his own declaration on this article under oath will be used in court in the presence of the judge and jury.

21. The twenty first article concerns the curing of Alesone Patersone in Myreside, and the curing of her serious illness and laying it on James Liddell, the shoemaker in Spot. The statement made by William Liddel will be used, and sworn to in court in the presence of the judge and jury.

22. As for the twenty second article about burying the live ox, the following notes will be used. [Conjectured meaning. This paragraph is very difficult to read and seems to be written in a different hand.]

23. As for the twenty third article about Andro Mertoun and the harm done to him and his wife, we will use the statement made by him in the presence of the Laird of Preston and his baillie on 27th January last.

24. As for the last article about the Devil's mark, we will use the statement taken from Alexander Foirtoun before the Presbytery of Duns on 27th January 1629.

JC26/9/7

[This document seems to be a list of witnesses numbered 1-17, with brief comments on each. Much of it is illegible and the notes are fragmentary and difficult to interpret. They could have been jotted down as memos for either the defence or the prosecution. There is probably little to be learned from pondering over them.]

JC26/9/8

[This is Andrew Mertoun's statement referred to in document JC26/9/6, article 23.]

On January 27th in the presence of the Laird of Preston and his baillie, Andro Mairtoun declared on oath that Ysball Young in Eistbarnes came into his house on a Sunday before Martinmas fourteen or fifteen years ago and asked for some money he was owing her. It was to be paid at Martinmas, but he had no guarantor for the money. [Probable meaning. The sense is obscure here.] Andro replied that by the grace of Almighty God he would pay her the money at Martinmas as agreed. Ysball Young answered, "If you trust too much in God, he'll beguile you!" When Andro's wife was going to church, having just had a baby, she said to Andro's wife that neither he nor she would stay in the community as long as a year, and they would have neither food nor decent clothing. After that, everything that Andro had vanished away. All his horses and cattle died, and he left the community before a year had passed. He declares this on oath that all these things are true, and much more that he will express to her face.

This was written before the Laird of Prestoun by James Purves, the son of George Purves in Dumbar, and before his baillie John Hall.

Signed: Prestoun   John Hall

JC26/9/9

[This lengthy statement by Lilias Knollis gives a fascinating insight into the 17th century mindset. Interestingly, it also mentions the notorious warlock Alexander Hamilton.]

I, Lilias Knollis, declare and testify that for many years past, and in the lifetime of my husband, I have been oppressed by the malicious and devilish enchantments and sorcery of Issobell Young, as I am well aware, and which may be seen from the following particulars, and for the following reasons: -

Firstly, about twenty years ago, my husband the late Thomas Hume was known as a good Christian man by all his neighbours, both in his knowledge and in his conscience. About twenty years ago he had an extraordinary number of deaths among his livestock, to the extent of 27 horses, oxen, cows, and bullocks in a single year. He himself falling sick of what was to be a fatal illness, we left the Barnes and went to live in the Pannes.

About five weeks before he died, between Christmas and Candlemas, we were lying in bed abut ten or eleven o' clock at night. It seemed that I ...[illegible] ...when a strange vision appeared to me that greatly frightened me. I thought I was in Eistbarnes in the house where my husband and I lived. I was about to clean a pan to cook some food for my husband, and it seemed to me that I came to the door of our house. I looked up opposite me and I saw George Smyth and his wife Issobell Young walking on the roof of my husband's dovecot, on a very narrow ledge made for the pigeons. It seemed to me that I shouted to my husband about this in great consternation, and told him to come and see. However, when he came out he said he could see nothing. He stepped up to the wall of the dovecot to urinate. Then it seemed to me that Issobell Young reached her hand down to catch hold of the night-cap on his head, She pulled it up, but she couldn't get it off. At this I cried out in terror in the dream, lying beside him, "John, John, pray to God! Pray to God that the Devil doesn't get possession of our souls in the way that he has got possession of our goods and bodies!" He was lying awake, and when I cried out he wakened me and asked me what had made me call out, and had I been frightened? I replied, "My heart,

I have been greatly frightened, and God is not in heaven if something does not follow upon my dream." Being an understanding man and a good Christian, he realised it was just a stupid fantasy, wouldn't listen to me, and was grieved at my ignorant words. However, I insisted again, "John, God is not in heaven if I don't hear more of this dream!" He was quite annoyed at me about this, but he spent much of the rest of the night reasoning and praying with me.

In the morning, his own eldest son, Caspar Hume, who is still alive, came riding from the Eist Barnes. As he came in, his father asked how all the neighbours were, and what news there was from the east. He answered that there was no news, but early in the morning, about ten or eleven hours before he had mounted up [or possibly "earlier that night, about ten or eleven o' clock, before he mounted up..."], all the pigeons in his father's dovecot, and there were a great many of them, came out, and sat crowded on the roof of the dovecote. He and John Wood his father's farm manager were sitting at their supper, and suddenly all the pigeons took off from the roof of the dovecot, making such a noise in their flight that they thought their neighbour's steading had collapsed. They went out to see if this was the case, and seeing that the pigeons were away, surmised that it had been the noise of their flight. Then Caspar took a candle and went into the dovecot, taking two men with him. They searched all the holes as closely as they could to see if a cat or some other animal had got in and frightened the pigeons, but found nothing, indeed, no animal could have got in there. Then he took his horse and rode to see his father.

As he told us this story I cried out in bed, lying beside my husband, "There's the explanation of my dream!" After explaining this, in a great passion my husband pulled off his nightcap and spoke to God from the heart, saying, "Lord, I have been a long time between hope and despair, and now I see I am like Job. You have allowed the Devil to lay hands on my goods and my body, but Lord, you shall have my soul and he shall have no power over it! Now I am persuaded that Issobell Young is a witch!" Then he related again a story which he had often told me before, that George Smyth and Issobell Young had offered eighteen hundred merks for a strip of land in Eistbarnes. However, he gave two thousand merks, and bought it - the same land as provided for myself and my children. Ever since then, he knew they had a secret resentment against him and his family, and now he realised that she had wronged him by devilry and witchcraft.

After that, my husband sent for his brother Mr Alexander Hume who was then schoolmaster in the Pannes, and after he had given him all the details they sent for the minister Mr Jhon Ker, and Mr David Hum of Godscroft, who was then living in Prestoun. After they had conferred together for a long time over how strange and fearful the details were, they asked my husband if there was any man or woman he suspected of having wronged him by witchcraft. When they heard the story of George Smyth and Issobell Young's anger against my husband because we had bought the land, they thought that he must have been wronged by them for that reason. Therefore it is clear that Issobell Young is a witch, and she cannot deny it. As for the pigeons in the dovecot, everybody knows that it is true that they did not come back for twenty days, and even then only a few of them, and they have been scarce ever since. Since then, from one year to the next there have only been a dozen pairs of doves to be had in it, whereas before they were always plentiful.

Next, less than a year after this, after God had taken my husband to his rest, about Michaelmas time a sudden fire broke out in my steading at the Eistbarnes, which I thought very strange, for even yet I cannot think how it can have happened. It burned four buildings to the south of the steading, belonging to the late William Watt. On the north side it leaped over a little thatched house where a woman was lying in childbed, and burned the farmhouse belonging to Gibye Maselate[?]. As the whole district knows, and still remembers, it burned so fiercely with a great wind, that it was a wonder that all the corn which had been newly put into the barnyards was safe, although the fire came so close that it was reported to have broken out four times in Jhon Brysson's yard. I thought this was strange, but I did not imagine that Issobell Young had any hand in it. In fact, I didn't think she had anything to do with it, but about twelve or thirteen years after that, Jean Alexander had a daughter living with me. Jean is still alive, and lived at that time in the Hordweill, and is now living there again. She came to my house to see her daughter, and since two witches were to be tried by jury in Dunbar the next day, I said to her, "Jean, have you come to see the witches burnt?" "No, by my faith, mistress," she replied, "I've come to see your maidservant, my daughter. Are there no witches in this community?" I answered her, laughing, "No Jean. Not one!" And at this she said, "Well, I'll tell you a strange tale I heard from a little old woman in my house about twelve or thirteen years ago. William Douglasse's cattle fell sick, and my husband and I took two of them. They gave blood instead of milk, and I often wept over this. A little old woman saw me weeping and asked what was wrong. I replied that it was something she could help me with. What do you want, daughter?' she said. I've done good to many a one, and never evil to anybody, except to one, God forgive me, and woe is me for it!' When asked who that was, she replied, 'A gentlewoman who was a neighbour living in the Eistbarnes, daughter. Have you not heard of a fire there?' I said, yes, I had heard there was a fire, but did not know whom it had harmed. The little old woman said, 'Daughter, I am tired. I have come from Auldhamstocks Mill where the lady of the house refused to give me a piece of bacon, although I knew she had it. She wouldn't have done that when I arranged her marriage for her. If I was in the Eist Barnes I would lack neither bacon nor rye bread. There are two people there who bought steadings and lands...' [Lillias Knollis interpolates here.] - Now it's true that along with Issobell Young's husband George Smyth my husband bought two cottages and a strip of land. In compensation my husband gave a strip of ground in Eistbarnes which had formerly been worked by George Smyth, which my son works now, and the strip which my husband then used, which George Smyth's son John now works.

"The little old woman went on, 'One of them may well regret this bargain. Issobell Young fed me for twenty days in the house, unknown to anyone, and though she's as great a witch as any in Scotland, and could have done it herself, she got me to set fire to the lady's house. Not only that, but whatever the lady does as long as she lives, nothing will go well for her.' [Lilias Knollis again comments.] - This I have found to be only too true, to my great sorrow. In fact everything I take in hand continually goes back or does poorly, although the whole district knows that I have striven, and do strive to get on, with as much effort as anyone in the area. That, and similar things, have all been the result of her devilish practices against me by witchcraft, and she cannot deny it.

When I heard Jean Alexander relate this story, I said to her, "Jean, we who have heard that tale are too few!" She replied that she would tell it in front of anybody, and did in fact tell it over again before William Simson and George Wat. William Simson said,"... [illegible] ...witness to it, as I think she would still testify to it in front of anybody as she promised." [It is not actually clear whether it is William or Lilias making this suggestion.]

Thirdly, about five years ago Issobell Young came into my house in my husband's absence. [Lilias has obviously remarried after the death of Thomas Home.] She alleged that my husband had struck a pig of hers in the courtyard. To tell the truth I was afraid of her, because I knew she had done me so much harm, and I avoided her. So I was unhappy about her coming there, and spoke to her soothingly, hoping to get rid of her with calmer words. She seemed to be pleased, and sat down beside me, and lifted my child, a little girl about eighteen months old, on to her knee. She said she would get her grandson, her daughter's son, to marry her. Then after a while she went away. Within a very short time the child took a fearful kind of disease. Whenever she [illegible] to her foot she crept [illegible], and was as if she had been choked. She was like this for nearly a year. I tried all the usual ways to find out what was wrong with her, and to get help for her, but was wasting my time until finally an English vagabond woman heard of her disease when she was in East Barns - I don't know from whom - and sent George Watt to me, and Isobell Ford another time, offering to cure her. I feared this would be unlawful, and refused to let her use her cure, or allow her to see the child. Then, however, she sent word by them just to keep the child's urine so that she could see it. When this had been done, she asked permission to go into a room on her own to examine it. After she had been alone for about half an hour, partly because I was fed-up waiting, and partly because I was afraid her skill was not lawful, I came to her, and found her apparently crouching down looking at the urine. I asked her what she thought of it, and she answered that my child had been wronged by my neighbour Issobell Young, and was bewitched. She offered to cure her, and when I refused she demanded payment for what she had done. When I said I would not pay her anything, because she had done nothing, she said she had done the child good, and after that the child improved steadily. Issobell Young did this by her devilish witchcraft, and cannot deny it, for that Englishwoman said she recognised the Devil's mark on her breast. Fourthly, about three or four years ago, a certain Alexander Hamilton came to the East Barnes, known by the whole countryside to be a venomous warlock, and lived there for a week in a house belonging to one of Issobell Young's sons. One day this Alexander Hamilton was speaking to Thomas Murray in East Barnes, when a horse of my husband's came by, looking unwell. "Whose is the horse?" he asked. Thomas Murray. He answered, "It belongs to John Douglas and Lilias Knolls." At this, the warlock remarked, "God help them, poor folk! They have been wronged by their neighbours. They can do what they will, but nothing will go well with them." And it is true that the horse died shortly after that, as many had done with us before. If Thomas Murray is properly questioned, he will tell you about this, and much more. Before God, I am sure she is a witch. She has done these things and much more against me and my husband by witchcraft.

JC26/9/10

Questions to be put to Issobell Young.

[I would guess that these questions were part of the pre-trial information gathering process, and would be put to Issobell during an interrogation after her arrest, or perhaps at a previous appearance before the Presbytery, rather than questions to be asked at her trial.]

1. How did she come to get the horrible reputation of a witch over forty years ago, which has increased steadily ever since?

2. What has caused everyone without exception who knows her to be afraid of her, and be loath to have business or social dealings with her? How is it that everyone who has anything to do with her either receives harm or is tainted with the same reputation?

3. How is it that if anyone ever fell out with her or any of her family, particularly if she threatened them, or took the kerchief off her head, that some mischief quickly befell them afterwards; for example, leprosy to Issobell Fruid, the loss of a leg to Thomas Kers, etc.?

4. How was it that when such accidents could not be cured by any ordinary means, if those who had been harmed sought their health from her thrice for God's sake, they quickly recovered?

5. Why did she associate with witches, for example over forty years ago with Katharen Gray and Jonet Lindsay who were both burnt in Haddington; Christian Grintoun, Margaret Melrois, and Jonet Achiesone, all burnt in Dumbar, and many more?

6. How is it that so many witches have testified against her? The Witch of Norime, for example more than thirty years ago said that she had bewitched Patrick Brysone in East Barns and caused his death. The Ladie Herdrid[?] said that she bewitched Thomas Kers in Dumbar, and Heiland May said that she bewitched George Sandie there. Another witch said that Isobell used sorcery to make her burn Lilias Knowllis' houses in Eistbarnes. An Englishwoman said that she bewitched a child of Lilias Knollis'. And Alexander Hamilton said that she bewitched Lilias Knollis' livestock, and that Lilias would never thrive as long as Issobell Young lived. Margaret Melrois and Jonet Achiesone already mentioned, swore that Isobell was with them consulting with that Thief, the Devil, about the death of George Keresone.

7. What was the reason for her custom of taking off her kerchief to those she was angry with, especially since Margaret Melrois and Jonet Achiesone claimed it was the rite whereby the Devil gave power to her to bewitch people?

8. Why did she use sorcery and witchcraft to cure her beasts, and her children's livestock, when they were diseased? She buried live oxen, live cats, and salt together, which is without doubt a sacrifice to the Devil.

9. What about the mark on her breast, which Margaret Melrois and Jonet Acheson declared was the Devil's mark?

10. What makes her without spiritual perception in all this, so that she does not humbly apply to God to be free from such a fearful reproach, from which only God can liberate her?

11. What can be the sin which has drawn this reproach upon her? It must surely be some gross impiety and wickedness against God. It is the usual course of God's justice to punish men and women with public scandal for the sins with which they offend him by practising in private, especially idolatry, witchcraft, etc.

12. If she is innocent of this crime, what has caused her to avoid being questioned about it? It is the only thing able to clear her, yet she uses all direct and indirect means through her children and others to hinder this and keep her from it. And now she contradicts those who know most about her, and those who complain about her.

[The last three questions are hinting that Isobel may have something to hide because she has not complained to her kirk session that she is being slandered as a witch. Certainly, it would appear that most people who did this were in fact vindicated - see the chapter on "Church Records".]

JC26/9/11
[This is an order to summon jurors to try Isobel. It is the Privy Council's response to Item 14, which is a request from Isobel to either be put on trial or released from prison.]

Charles, by the grace of God king of Great Britane, ffrance, and Ireland; Defender of the Faith: Greetings to our committees, messengers, and our sheriffs specially constituted in that part of the kingdom.

It has been explained to us by a trusted and

intimate advisor, Sir Thomas Hoip of Craighall, baronet, Advocate for the King's interest, that Issobell Young, wife of George Smyt, portioner of Eist Barnes, has been recently accused of various charges of sorcery and witchcraft practised by her against several of our good subjects. She has therefore been committed to prison in our tollbooth of Edinburgh to remain there until she can be tried before our judges and their deputies, and found either guilty or innocent of these crimes.

Therefore the lords of the Privy Council have appointed 4th February for our judges to put her to a lawful trial for these crimes she is accused of. Those persons of least suspect reputation who best know the truth about Issobell Young's guilt, who live within or round about the bounds of the sheriffdom where she lived, and where her sorcery and witchcraft was put into practice, have been several times ordered to come to our burgh of Edinburgh, and to attend when called to serve on a jury to try Issobel for the crimes specified above.

However, they will not appear for that purpose unless they are commanded and compelled to do so. It is therefore our will, and we charge you, that you lawfully summon and order these persons of least suspect reputation, who best know the truth about Issobell Young's guilt in these crimes of sorcery and witchcraft contained in her indictment, should appear before our judge or his deputes, not exceeding the number of forty-five persons. Their names are to be on a list, and they are all to be resident in our sheriffdom of Eist Lothian or round about. They are to appear on 4th February to serve on Issobell's jury, each person under the penalty of a hundred merks according to the law, or you will answer to us for it. In order to do this, we grant you conjointly and separately our full power by this document, which you are to duly endorse and give back to the bearer. Given under our seal at Edinburgh, 28th January 1629, the fourth year of our reign. [Stamped with the royal seal.]

28th January 1629   John Bannatyne.

JC26/9/12

[Items 12 and 13 are evidence against Issobell given in Berwickshire before the Presbytery of Duns.]

At Duns, 27th January 1629.

This day Alexander Fortoune appeared in Duns parish church before the moderator and the brethren. He was asked what he had to do with curing Issobell Young in the Eastbarnes. He declared that he was at the mansion house of Innerweik, attending the elder Laird of Innerweik, who had broken his leg, with a view to curing him. Issobell came to him with her husband. Her belly was greatly swollen, and she asked him to try to cure her, for which she promised to pay him. He came to her house and made a potion of oil, vinegar, onions, and mallows, and gave it to her to drink. He also made a waterproof cloth with wax and resin, and applied it to her belly. He went away, and when he came back after fourteen days, he asked her if the potion he had given her had done any good. She replied that she was much the better of it. Also, Alexander declared that Issobell Young heard that he had cured John Fender[?] of an ulcer on his chest, which he had contracted when he had fever. She therefore asked him to cure a little wound, a hole about the size of a large pea, which she had under one of her breasts. As he was attending to this he asked her if she felt any pain. She answered, "Not at all," whereas John Fender fainted when he treated him. He said that he applied ointment three times to the wound. He said the ointment was made up of "kemp leaves, bawort roots, curldodies, waybraid leaves, and butter". ["Kemps" are the flower spikes of ribwort plantain, "curldodies" are ribwort plantain, and "waybraid" is plantain. I have been unable to trace "bawort".] However, the wound was never one whit the better, but remained unhealed. Alexander said to her that the common report was that this was the Devil's mark and that it would never heal. She answered that that was what some people said who were evilly disposed towards her. Several people there said she could cure herself as well as any doctor, and she was only doing this to make the word go round that she wasn't able to do it. For his pains he got nothing more from her or her husband than five pounds Scots, and half a boll of wheat which he promised to pay her for. When he went back to her about a quarter of a year after that he asked her how she was. She answered, "I'm very well now, and well recovered."

Leonard Houston, clerk to the Presbytery of Duns.

JC26/9/13

At Dunse 6th January 1629, before the undersigned persons, David Nisbet, servant to John Nisbet in Putonmilne[?], declared what he knew about Issobell Young in East Barnes, the wife of George Smyth there. When he was living with Johne Brysone in East Barns about five years ago, he was sleeping in a stable, and woke from his sleep about midnight. He saw a bright light beyond a horse and mare that he usually worked with. It seemed to him that a man and a woman were riding on the mare. He then got up from his bed, and took a drawn sword in his hand with the intention of striking at them as soon as there was any moonlight, in case he had been deceived in what he saw, and it was only an illusion. However, there was no moonlight, and so he went back. A certain George Mortoun who was schoolmaster in Eastbarnes at the time, cried to him, "David, what's the matter with you?" He answered, "Let God never allow to any good fellow what has happened to me!" Asked if he knew the persons who were riding on the mare, he replied that as far as he could judge, it was Issobell Young. He went to the horse and mare in the dark and felt them, and they were dripping with sweat from the ears to the tail.

The mare aborted her foal that same night, and the horse wasted away and died. Marion Broune also gave a statement. She is the wife of James Fairlie in Dunse. When she was servant to William Macelat in Eastbarnes, Issobell came into William's barn where they were threshing wheat. She saw Issobell take her mutch off her head. While she was bending to lift a measure of wheat, the others in the barn saw Issobell run round three times anticlockwise. She also declares that on one particular day Issobell's husband George Smyth was suddenly taken ill working at his own plough. The alarm was raised, and Issobell Young came into William Macelet's house, took out his chair, carried it to the field where her husband was, and put him in it. She would not bring him directly home, but brought him through William Macelet's courtyard.

Mr Johnne [illegible], minister at Dunse.
Leonard Houston, minister at Preston.
Thomas Lyn, baillie.

JC26/9/14

[If the documents were numbered in chronological order, JC26/9/14 should in fact come before Item 11. Item 14 is an appeal from Issobell to be either freed from her imprisonment in Edinburgh, or put on trial. Item 11 is the Privy Council's response.]

My Lords of the Privy Council,

I, your humble servant Issobell Young, wife of George Smith in East Barnes, respectfully inform you that in order to clear myself of the foul imputation of crimes of witchcraft of which I was accused, I found surety to appear before His Majesty's justice when called, within fifteen days, to undergo legal process for that crime, under penalty of 500 merks.

I found caution to put my case to [the magistrates of] this burgh on the 15th of this month, and to prepare for my trial, which Your

Lordships appointed to be on the 20th of the month. In obedience to this, I came to this burgh on the 13th, and expected that my trial would be on the 20th. However, those bearing malice against me got me into secure confinement in the tollbooth of Edinburgh, where my life is endangered because of the unseasonable time of year. I am now over eighty years of age, and heavily afflicted with complaints and illnesses. They have taken nothing further to do with the business, and never intended to. Their intention is to keep me continually in custody, holding me under suspicion on hearsay for the crime mentioned.

I therefore beseech Your Lordships either to appoint a definite date for my trial, and to give orders to those whom it may concern to give me an accurate copy of the indictment, so that I can familiarise myself with it, and have the time and leisure to prepare a just and lawful defence. Otherwise I request that your Lordships will command the provost and baillies of Edinburgh to set me free and allow me to go where I please, on condition that I find surety to appear before His Majesty's justice at fifteen days' notice, to undergo the law for the crime specified, under such penalties as Your Lordships please.

I await Your Lordships' answer.

[On reverse]

At Halyrood House 20th January 1629.

The Lords appoint a date fifteen days from tomorrow for the trial of the supplicant. Her indictment is ordered to be produced in Council eight days from today, so that it can be delivered to you.

Signed: Menteith

[And near the foot of the page]

J. Prymrois.

JC26/9/15

[Item 15 is a list of those summoned for jury service. Many of the names are decorated with cryptic symbols and numbers. Names marked "p" seem to be those chosen to serve on the jury of fifteen. It is not obvious what "p" stands for, unless it simply means "picked".]

Robert Mure in Poppilhall	p
John Harriot in Pethhead	p
Thomas Forest of [illegible]	
John Home in Pincarton	p
William Grey in [illegible]	p
John Gullan in Est Barnes	p
John Hog of Drylawes	p
William Dicksone in Beill	p
John Kirkwood in West Barns	p
George Wod in Newmyln	p
James Nicelsone in Quhytkirk	p
James Kirkwod in West Barnes	p
Patrick Arnot in Lynton	
James Lermont there	p
John Aliesone there	p
Robert Aliesone there	p
John Whyte there	p
William Lermont in Furde	
Adame Lermont, Edinburgh	
John Dun in Helden [?]	
Archibald Stobe in Dunglas	
Patrick Tait in Colbrandspeth	
Richard Guidfellow in Crawhill	
George Sendert[?] in Westhall	
James Pettigrew in Burnehead	
Silvester Craig in Innerweik	
William Charles in Trapren	
David Patersone in Pethheid	
John Craig there	
James Manderston in Haitsyd	
Robert Manderston there	
James Hoppringell in Spot Myln	
Robert Sked in Belhevin	
Robert Lauder there	
John Manderston there	
Thomas Denholm there	
Thomas Dasone in Broxburne	
John Nisbet in Hawhill	
[illegible] Young there	
David Nisbet in Dumbar	

Richard Sandie there
Alexander Nisbet there
Robert Quhyte there
John Kellie, merchant
Alexander Affleck there
William Home, baker.

All the above persons lawfully summoned by William Lowrie.

[On reverse] On the 30th and 31st of January, and the 1st and 4th of February 1629, I, William Lowrie, summoned all of the persons contained in the list on the other side, and informed them in person that they were to appear on 4th February to participate in the trial of Issobel Yong for the crimes contained in the indictment. I informed all those on the list. [Probable meaning. The last sentence is obscure in the text.] This I did before these witnesses:

Robert Andersone in Dumbar, James Foirtoun there.

And as further testimony, signed with my signature:

William Lowrie, messenger.

[As a final footnote to Issobell Young's case, it might be worth observing for the benefit of those who imagine that witchcraft suspects in Scotland were invariably bundled off to a cruel death at the drop of a hat, that cruel as it undoubtedly was to strangle an old woman at the stake, Issobell had survived to the - for those days - unusually ripe old age of over eighty, having enjoyed a fearsome reputation as a witch for over forty years. She must indeed have already had this reputation at the time of the "North Berwick" roundup, had been investigated by the Presbytery at least once before her criminal trial, had been denounced by other witches, and yet survived unscathed until 1629.]

John Hog and his Wife.

[John Hog and his wife Margaret Nicolson, living in Markle near East Linton, were denounced by the notorious warlock Alexander Hamilton. A lengthy investigation followed, but they were eventually freed on condition that they would present themselves to be tried for witchcraft if required to do so. Since there is no record of any such trial in the Books of Adjournal, it can be safely presumed that the charges were dropped. It is difficult to see why, since many other suspects were condemned and executed on evidence no more persuasive than was gathered in this case. John and Margaret's smartest move was without doubt their refusal to confess, since confession almost inevitably led to conviction. It is often assumed that witchcraft suspects in Scotland were tortured or at least ill-treated as a matter of course. John and Margaret's refusal to confess would suggest that this was not always the case.

Apart from Hamilton's initial denunciation, the investigations concentrate on John Hog's unexpected recovery when he was lying at death's door, on a mysterious black man seen in Hog's house by an overnight guest, and on a mad horse which arrived in Markle after its owners prayed that it might indicate who had bewitched it.

None of this material has been previously published, possibly simply because it is not recorded in the Books of Adjournal. It may be, however, that some of the allegations were rather strong meat for douce Victorian researchers.

The relevant records are contained in the Justiciary Court Processes in the National Archives of Scotland, in box JC26/9. The bundle is tabled as containing 17 items, but some of them appear to be missing. As previously, I have "translated" the text into modern English.]

JC26/9/1

Edinburgh 24th November 1629, in the presence of My Lord of Dumblane, My Lord Advocate, and Mr Alexander Colme, Justice Depute. List of names to be sent for:

- [A scribbled list of names follows, which is extremely difficult to make out, and often completely illegible. It seems to include most of those whose interrogations are recorded in subsequent items.]

JC26/9/2

My Lords, ask William Learmuith, smith in Merkill, whether or not when he was in his bed one night, two cats came in, set upon and killed two of his cats, and were dragging them away when William stood up and took a piece of wood in his hand to strike them. The cats spoke to him and said, "Where are you going, my good man?" He replied, "Wherever I like. Get out!" This was alleged to have been an example of conferring with the Devil, and was cast up at him when he was arrested.

JC26/9/3

I, Patrick Karkettle, your Lordships' humble servant, most humbly address your Lordships as follows: - By the cruelty, witchcraft and devilry of John Hog in Markill and his wife, within the past nine years they were the sole cause of the death of the former farmer of Markill my father's brother, and of his wife who was my mother's sister. They were very suddenly bereft of their lives by them within a short space of time, along with two or three of their young children who were similarly cruelly and suddenly cut off by their malice. John Broun of Colstoun, my mother's brother, was with them at the time, and was also very suddenly bereft of his life. After that, my father... [illegible]...

On one occasion my father discovered John Hog's son in the meadow, and struck him. John openly vowed that either directly or indirectly, he would have amends of my father for it. He kept that vow very well, for after that nothing went forward or prospered with my father, until his life was suddenly cut off. All these people were cruelly bereft of their lives within less than a year. The whole countryside was aware of it and can bear witness to it. Also, my Lords, I am able to prove that John Hog is not ashamed to say that whoever angers him or his wife or children, he will destroy and overthrow them, both in their bodies and possessions. This cruel false devilry and witchcraft should neither be suffered nor tolerated. I humbly beseech you for a just response.

JC26/9/4

May it please your Lordships, Johne Bell knows a woman in the community of Merkill called Marioun Fruid, who knows more about the doings of Johne Hog and his wife than twenty others. Your Lordships may like to ask Johne Bell whether or not Johne Hog grew well immediately after Ewphame Johnston's child died. Also, ask John Bell if he or his father were told to bring in a lamb to bake for the funeral meal, and before they ever brought the lamb in, they were told not to bother because Johne Hog had recovered. Ask John Bell also if he heard of a supper that was prepared after the people in the house had all gone to bed, and who it was who ate it. This was reported by Thomas Hog's wife Isobell Thomson who is John Hog's own daughter in law, and who was in the house with them at the time. Also, there was a village blacksmith in Merkill, William Leirmuith, who is said to know a lot about them. Your Lordships might also like to ask Sandie Gray whether or not it is true that Johne Hog was away from home, it was very late in the evening, and the household had become anxious about him. His wife took a pan and some water, went into the stable, and said she could soon tell if he would come home that night or not. Ask him also if he saw her put each of the horse's four feet into the water in the pan, then come in and say that her husband would arrive home soon, healthy and unharmed. By the time she had finished speaking it had turned out just as she had said. Alexander Gray says all the lords of Scotland could not remedy his falsehoods, whatever he says.

[On this same piece of paper there is a scribbled list of names, dated 2nd November 1629. Some are illegible, but the list includes Thomas Low, Issobel Thomson his wife, Richard Hog, Bessie [illegible] to Issobell Hogis, Marioun [illegible] living in Markil, William Leirmouth in Sigis[?]: John Bell and his wife Issobell Neilson.]

JC26/9/5

My Lords,

You may like to ask Thomas Quhyt whether or not when his brother Robert Quhyt was sleeping in John Hog's house, he saw a great grim black man come in at the north end of the room where he was lying, after he had been sleeping. This grim-looking man went to a chest, and there was a clinking noise as if he was counting money. Robert shouted to John Hog that here was a thief in the house, and to watch out for the money he had received the previous day. John Hog came with a light in his hand and said, "Don't be afraid, there is no thief here. As for the money I got yesterday, it's lying under me between two matresses. Take a drink out of the barrel and go back to bed." Robert refused to do this, but took his clothes in his arms and ran as fast as he could to Thomas's house in a terrible state of fear, and told his brother Thomas all this, as is written above.

[On the reverse side of Item 5 are some scribbled notes dated 18th November 1629. Most of this is completely illegible. However, there is a memo to inquire about someone's public reputation, and to inquire if anyone saw the mad horse go to John Hog's house. There is also something about James Sandis wife, and a note that Part Neilson in Markill told John Keir that the servant women in John Hog's house were complaining about great activity at right in John Hog's stable.]

JC26/9/6

Sir Thomas Hope of Craighall, baronet, His Majesty's Advocate.

Mr James Robiesoun, Justice Depute.

Edward Edgar[?], burgess of Edinburgh.

At Edinburgh, 7th November 1629, in the presence of My Lord Bishop of Dumblane, and Mr William Strutheris, one of the ministers of Edinburgh.

Alexander Hamiltoun was solemnly sworn upon his knees to declare the truth. He testifies that at the end of harvest five years ago he was in John Hog's house in Markill, where he was in the habit of staying. Margaret or Jonet Nicolsoun, John's wife, took him into the parlour or inner part of the house, gave him a choppin of ale to drink, and asked him if he was one of "the Society". He was unwilling to reveal himself as one of their number, but after serious enquiry he told her he was one of them. Nicolson then asked him if he would be at a meeting with her and the rest of the Society within the next week, where the Devil would be present He gave in, and promised to attend the meeting. Accordingly, within a week, he came to Johnne Hog's house in Markill before evening, and after he had taken some refreshment at the fire ... [damage] ...house, where he stayed till about eleven o' clock at night. At this time, between eleven and twelve, he and Nicolson and her husband John Hog all went out together. Going out at the door, John Hog came up to him and said, "My wife has been telling me that you're one of our number. Please keep it secret so that nobody knows about it but God and ourselves." This he promised to do.

After making this promise, Hamilton, along with John Hog and his wife, went behind Markill House into a hollow between two hills to the south of Markill House. Sathan was walking there in the shape of a grim black man. They all went up to him, and Nicolson greeted him first, saying, "Good evening Master," and kneeling down before him, as Hamilton and John Hog also did. Then Nicolson said to the Devil, "I've been told to seek a gift from you." He answered, "Ask what you will, and it will be granted." So she asked for power from the Devil to harm James Sandie the miller of Lyntoun Brige in his goods and gear. The Devil answered, "Go on with what you plan to do. It shall be done just as you wish. Work on to harm him as you please, and it shall come to pass." She thanked him and kissed his hand. Hamilton declares he and John Hoge were beside them and in their presence when the Devil granted her request, and said that within a year George[?] Sandie lost six horses and fell seriously ill himself. He says that before they parted the Devil appointed another meeting with him in a month's time, on the south side of Markill in a hollow beside a little bridge. Then the Devil commanded them to be his true sevants, and at that he vanished. Hamilton returned to the house with John Hog and his wife, and he went to the building facing the door where he was accustomed to sleep, and lay down to rest. He declares that as they were coming home they swore to each other with execrable curses that they would keep all their doings secret.

He also declares that a month after that, according to the Devil's appointment, Hamilton came to John Hog's house before evening and stayed till eleven o'clock at night, at which time he got up along with John Hog and his wife, and went to the appointed place on the north side of Markill, in the hollow between Markill and the bridge. There they saw the Devil waiting for them in the likeness of a black man. with a hat on his head. When she approached him he took Nicolson aside the length of a house, where they had sex while Hamilton and John Hoge turned their backs to her and the Devil. He declares that he rode her as if she had been a beast during that filthy act. After that, Hamilton, the Devil, and John Hog and his wife, all returned to John Hog's house. Candles were lit, the table cleared, and mutton, beef, and bread set down.

The Devil sat down at the head of the table with John Hog's wife next to him. Next to her sat John Hog himself, and Hamilton sat next to John Hog. They all ate and drank and made merry together until a little before cock-crow, at which time the Devil vanished away.

He declares that before the Devil left, since there was a fiddler in the house, the Devil took to the floor, and took John Hog and his wife by the hand. John Hog took Hamilton by the hand, and they all danced across the floor. Then the Devil vanished from their sight. After that, Hamilton went to his bed in the outhouse where he was in the habit of sleeping, and stayed until eight o'clock in the morning.

Before he went away, he got certain fermenting brews from John Hog's wife, which he sipped, and then went away. Since that time he has never come back to the house nor been in their company. He declares that every word of this statement is true as he shall answer to the great God of Heaven for his salvation or damnation on the Great Day.

At Edinburgh, 7th November 1629.

In presence of my Lord Dumblane; my Lord Advocate; Edward Ethie[?], baillie of Edinburgh; Mr William [damage] Struthers, minister; Mr James Rotsone, judge.

John Hog and Margaret Nicolson his wife were confronted with Alexander Hamelton, and solemnly sworn on their knees to declare the truth. When he was asked about it before, John Hog denied it, but now confesses that he has seen this Alexander Hamelton in the hall of his house, but never in his chamber. He declares that he cannot remember how long ago it is since he saw Alexander in his house, whether it was a year ago, two years ago, more than that, or less than that. As for the rest of the statements made by Alexander against John Hog and his wife as written above, John Hog and his wife Margaret Nicolson upon their knees and on their great oath solemnly given, deny every word of these statements and declare them altogether false and untrue. Alexander was again sworn in their presence, and confirmed his previous statement to be true on his great oath. Margaret was twice or thrice sworn on her knees to declare truthfully if she had ever seen Alexander Hamilton at any time in her house. By her great oath, she declares that to her knowledge she never recognised him in her house apart from any other man.

Signed: B. of Dunblane, witness.
Thomas Hope
James Robertsoune
Edward Edgar, baillie.

At Edinburgh, 14th November 1629. In presence of my Lord of Dumblane; my Lord Advocate; and Mr Alexander Colmbe, Justice Depute.

John Hog in Markill, being solemnly sworn, declares he knows Euphame Yorstone. About last Easter he was coming between Markill and Lyntoun, and on the way met Euphame coming from Houstoun with a load of straw on her back. She and Hog came back to Markill together, and on the way he said to Euphame, "It would do you a good turn if I had sex with you." To which she replied, "You have a wife of your own, and I have a husband. You can get that frisky notion out of your head!" He denies that he threatened her, or promised to do Euphame a bad turn for refusing what he desired. He also denies that he ever mentioned any such thing to Euphame before or since, but only on that occasion.

He was asked when he last became ill and was confined to bed. He said it was abut the beginning of May, when the beans were being sown. He was asked how long he was ill before the Communion Sunday at his parish church of Prestoun Hauche. He declares that he was ill for a month before that, and on the Communion day he was bedridden, otherwise he would have gone to church and taken Communion there with the rest of the parish. He was asked how soon he recovered from his illness after Communion Sunday. He declares that as far as he can remember it was about twenty days after the Communion. He was asked if he knew that Euphame Yorstoun had a young child which died suddenly. He admits that he knew that she had a baby girl about half a year old, who died when he was bedridden. The morning after the child's death he heard that she went to bed with her mother in good health, and was dead before daybreak. He was asked who told him about the child's death in the morning, and he declares on his great oath that he cannot remember, but he heard that Euphame Yorstoun blamed Helen Lermonth, his mother's sister, for bewitching the child. He declares that he was told about this business of Helen Lermont bewitching the child by Helen Lermouthe's daughter after Helene's death. He was asked how soon after the child's death he was told by Helene Lermonth's daughter about the rumour that her mother was blamed for bewitching the child. He says it was eight or ten days after the child's death. He declares on his conscience that as far as he knows, this rumour was not going about at any time before Helene Lermonth's death. He was asked when Helen Lermonth died. Did she die before or after the Communion? He declares that he cannot really tell, but as far as he remembers it was after the Communion day. His mother's sister died before the child died. As far as he can remember the child died about fourteen days after his mother's sister. When asked if he was at the burial of his mother's sister, he declared that he was lying bedridden, and could not rise from his sickbed at the time of her burial. Asked how long he lay bedridden, he declares that he lay in bed for a month. After that he stayed indoors for six weeks walking up and down the house.

He was asked if he had heard that his own wife was rumoured to have bewitched the child.

He declares on his solemn oath that he never heard such a rumour about her while he was ill. However, when he came out of the house around the end of harvest there was some quarrelling between Euphame Yorston and other women in the place. He heard then that Euphame had blamed his wife for bewitching her daughter. He says that it was after harvest when he heard this gossip, because Euphame reaped right through harvest for him, and if she had said it before that time neither he nor his wife would have kept her in service.

He declares that as far as he remembers, he lay bedridden for fourteen days after Helene Lermonthe's death and was never out of his bed all that time. The sickness he was suffering from began to abate some eight days or so after Whitsunday. When asked how soon he got out of bed after the death of Yorstoun's daughter, he says he cannot remember, but knows he was bedridden at the time. He declares that it was certain that the child went to bed healthy and was found dead in the morning. He was asked if there was any quarrelling or argument between his mother's sister and her daughter in Markle, and Euphame Yorston and har husband or anyone else. Or was there any grudge between them? He declares he knows of nothing. However, after Helen's death her two daughters had struck and beaten Euphame Yorston for slandering his mother's sister. He never heard anyone say before his mother's sister's death that she was a witch.

He was asked if there was ever any grudge between him and James Sandie. He says there was none, but now and then his wife and James Sandie would argue about the "moutter" of the mill [*i.e.* the fee for milling, usually paid in grain]. He certainly knows about the death of four or five horses of James Sandie's, four or five years ago. They all died suddenly together. They ran wild till they died, in a kind of madness. One of them came to Merkill, to several houses in the place, and came by his house too, as was reported. It also came to John Charles's house. He was asked who was blamed for this harm done to James Sandie, and he declared that James Sandie blamed Margaret Dudgeon, George Raeburne's wife, for bewitching his horses. This Margaret Dudgeon and George Raeburn were [illegible] before James Sande. James Sandie had taken the mill over their heads about a year before the business with the horses. He testifies that George Raeburn and his wife were not living in Markill, but five miles away in [illegible] Mills, belonging to Lord Haddington or Lord Reidhouse. He never heard that Margaret Dudgeon was rumoured to be a witch. Both she and her husband are still living. He declares that as far as he knows his own wife was never said to have harmed James Sandie by witchcraft until Alexander Hamilton accused her of it.

He was asked if he ever saw Alexander Hamilton in his house before he saw him testify in Edinburgh. He says he had seen him in his house with other beggars, and has given him food and lodging, but he never saw him in his private rooms.

He was asked if his wife Margaret Nicolsoune told him about the mad horse coming to his house. He declares on his solemn oath that neither she nor anyone else told him about this, or whether it came by Prestoun. If this is not so, he is content to lose his life.

John Hog's wife Margaret Nicolsone was sworn solemnly upon her knees to declare the truth, and asked how long she had known Alexander Hameltoun. She declares that she did not know him apart from anyone else. She declares after looking at him that as far as she can remember, she never saw him in her house.

She was asked if she ever saw any of the mad horses belonging to James Sandie in the village of Merkill. She declares that she never saw any, but she heard that there was a mad horse in the place which came to John Charles's house, and that it ran between the wall and the "post" of the house. However, neither she nor her husband, nor any of the household went to see this mad horse, since it had put the whole place in a state of fear. She says that she heard of no upset, because the horse was away out of George Charles's house long before she heard about it. If it can be proved that she saw the horse, or heard of the upset while it was in the village of Merkill, she is content to be counted as a false and dishonest woman.

She was asked if she met James Sandie the morning after his mad horse was in Markill, or within the next two days. She denies it. She was asked if at any time she said to James Sandie that she was never so frightened in her life as she was with the mad horse. She denies this also.

The afternoon of 14th November 1629, in the presence of the previously mentioned commissioners: Margaret Nicolson was asked if she would abide by the statement she made in the forenoon.

When it was read to her she said she would abide by it. She was asked particularly if she would abide by that part of her statement where she said she knew nothing of the alarm and amazement in Markill over the mad horse when it was there, and that nobody told her about it. She stood by this part of her statement.

James Hog, the son of John Hog in Markill, was solemnly sworn on his knees. He declared that he was in Markill the day the mad horse came there. He saw the mad horse in his own garden, and drove it out with a fork, but did not follow it any further. He does not remember if he met his mother and father that day, because he lives by himself, separately from his mother and father.

He was asked where he was the night Effie Yorstoun's child died. He declares that during the night of the day before the Communion, he came to attend his father with a number of the neighbours. He stayed in his father's house till past midnight because it was thought that his father would not live, and he was continually expecting his last breath. He does not know how many of his brothers were there that night, but it is certain that there were seven or eight of them at least. Amongst them was John Keir, a neighbour in Markle. He was asked if he saw Euphame Yorstoun with her baby in her arms, come into his father's house that night. He declares that he did not, but has heard that she came. He declares that about midnight Adame Cuming, Euphame Yorstoun's husband, came into his father's house, lit a candle, and said that his child had taken a strange disease, and looked as if she would soon die. At this, the witness with some of the neighbours, particularly John Keir, went into the house where the child was dying. He saw the child's mother wringing her hands over her child, and saw the child struggling in great extremity. He knows that the child died shortly after that, and that as far as he knows she had lain down healthy and well.

He was asked what state his father was in after the death of the child. Was he better or worse? He says that they saw no change in his father. In his opinion his father remained in the same state the following Monday and Tuesday. The minister came to see him on the Tuesday, but he doesn't know whether he had been sent for or not. He declares that his father was no better all that week, but at the beginning of the next week Helene Leirmonth died, and when he was told about it he expressed some regret, and wished that he could get out of bed for the burial. This was the first sign they saw of the change in him. He was asked when Helene Lermonth left his father's house. He answered that she left on the Monday or Tuesday after the death of Euphame Yorstoune's child. He was asked if Helene Lermonth was in his father's house on the Sunday night when the child died, and he says that as far as he remembers she was there. He did not hear Euphame Yorstoun blame Helene Lermouth for the death of her child for four days afterwards. On the contrary, he says Euphame came to his house three days after the child's death and said that it would be fitting for her to ride at horses' tails, for she had ridden on her own child. [The sense of this is not quite clear, and the handwriting is particularly poor in this part of the text. Euphame may be saying that she deserved to be dragged to the place of execution as she had overlain her baby and caused its death.] However, he says that the rumours started within the next two days that Euphame Yorston was blaming Helene Lermonth for the death of her child.

He was asked who his father had in his household the time George[?] Sandie's mad horse came to Markill. He says that as far as he remembers, he had four of his sons with him - Robert, John, Thomas, and William Hog were in his service, and others whose names he cannot remember. He was asked what servants were with his father at the time of his last illness, and he declares that he had two of his sons, Thomas and William, and other servants namely Alexander Nicolsone, John Allane, Thomas Quhyte, a servant woman Jonet Davie who is still in his service, and an old blind body named Will Hog.

William Hog, the son of John Hog in Markill, solemnly sworn on his knees to declare the truth, was asked if he was with his father the day the mad horse came to Markill, or if he saw it. He says he was in his father's house, but did not see the mad horse, and doesn't know if his father or mother saw it.

Asked about Euphame Yorstoune's baby, he declares as his brother James Hog did. He went into the house with his brother to see the child. He insists that John Lermonth came to his father's house that night, and moreover that his father began to improve after that within two or three days at most He says that when Helein Lermonth died, which was about twenty or twenty-four days after the child died, his father was walking up and down the house with a stick; and all the week following the Communion Sunday, as far as he can remember, his father got up once a day and was led through the house. However, he thinks that he certainly did not begin to get out of bed that week until the Tuesday.

Johnne Hog, the son of John Hog in Markill, solemnly sworn on his knees, declares that he was in his father's household at the time the mad horse came to Markill. He did not see the horse that died, and admits that his father was in Markill either at the leading in of the corn, or at its assessment for the teinds [a church tax to support the minister's stipend]. Asked about his father's last illness he says that he was sent for the night before the Communion Sunday to come and see his father die. He came from his house at East Craig to his father's house at Markill, a distance of about a mile, and stayed there till ten o'clock on Sunday. He got back to his own house at East Craig about twelve o'clock. Immediately after dinner he came back to see his father and stayed until night time. Then he came home to East Craig again. Between twelve and one that night he was sent for again to come and see his father, who was poised between life and death. When he came, his father could scarcely speak. All night both of his sons were waiting in the house for the end to come. The witness remained there till four o'clock on the Monday afternoon, and then came back to his own house. He remembers perfectly that when he left, his father seemed a little easier, but was speaking little better than he did before. He says he was not sent for again to see his father poised between life and death.

He declares that at midnight on the Sunday when he was sent for to see his father die, just after he arrived, Adam Coming, Euphame Yorstoun's husband, came into his father's house to light a candle, and he heard him say his child was not well. The witness went in and saw the child, which appeared to him to be a healthy and lively child. At that time it was quiet and not struggling, and died before sunrise. He says that Helein Lermonth was with his father that night, but does not know when she left.

Robert Hog, the son of John Hog senior in Markill, solemnly sworn on his knees, declares that he lives in Markill. He does not remember seeing the mad horse in Markill when it came there. Asked about his father's illness and if he was wrth him, he says he was with his father at the time of his illness, in particular on Communion Sunday at night when a number of his brothers, relatives, and neighbours were in the house waiting for his father's last breath. He declares that he heard the fuss about Euphame Yorstoun's sick baby girl, but didn't go into her house that night to see the child. Heleine Lermonth was in his father's house.

Signed: Lord Bishop of Dunblane, witness. Thomas Hope.
[illegible].
JC26/9/7
[On the outside cover in a modern hand: "Alex Hamiltoun 1629 Witchcraft ex JC26/9"]
[On the outside cover in a 17th Century hand: "Alexr Hameltoun his depositions wt Jon Hog Margaret Nicolsoun his spouse yr depositiones examinat in Nor. 1629"]

At Edinburgh 18th November 1629, in the presence of My Lord of Dumblane; Mr Alexander Colme, justice depute; Mr William Struethers, one of the ministers of Edinburgh.

Margaret Carrail, the wife of William Harlaw in Markill, sworn on her knees and questioned in particular on the following points: -

Firstly, she was asked what was the reputation, and what was said in the countryside about John Hog senior in Markill and his wife Margaret Nicolson. Had they ever been talked about in connection with witchcraft or seeking the advice of witches? She testifies that she never heard of any report or gossip about witchcraft concerning them from anyone before they came to Edinburgh.

Also, she was asked if she had heard that John Hog began to convalesce from his serious illness at the time when Euphame Yorstone's child died. How soon was it after that? She says that she heard Euphame Yorstoune and her husband Adam Coming say that immediately after the death and burial of the child, John Hog began to recover from his serious illness. She says that as far as she can remember she heard this said by nobody else but the child's parents.

Also, she was asked if she had heard whether or not James Sandie's mad horse came into John Hog's house after it came from Lyntoun. She says she heard that the mad horse came first of all to Andro Keir's house, and then to John Charles's house, but never heard that it came to John Hog's house. This she swears on her solemn oath.

She was asked if she ever heard her late husband Richard Small blame anyone for the death of fourteen of his horses, oxen, and cows, which suddenly dropped dead eight years ago. She says that she heard her husband say, "I don't like Margaret Nicolson's ominous looks, for great harm has been done to us. However, I won't say that John Hog or his wife are the cause of it." The witness had replied to her late husband, "God forgive you, my dear, if you suspect either John Hog or his wife for that business."

William Harlow, living in Markill, solemnly sworn on his knees, says he never heard any talk about John Hoge or his wife before they came to Edinburgh, that they were said to be witches or had doings with witches. Asked about the mad horse previously mentioned, his statement agrees with that of his wife. He was asked if he could remember how soon John Hog recovered from his illness after the death of Euphame Yorstoune's child. He says he was not in Markill at that time, but he understands that it was about a month after the child's death before he was fully recovered from his serious illness, or came out of his house.

Niniane Dudgeoin from Beinstoun, married, aged about 39, was sworn and asked if he had ever heard any talk or stories repeated about John Hoge or his wife being witches. He declares that he never heard any such tales about them until after Alexander Hamilton the warlock was arrested and questioned in Hadingtoun. He was asked about James Sandie's mad horse. Did he ever see it, or did it come to John Hog's house in Markill after it had broken out of its stable in Lyntoun? He says that he never heard that it came to John Hog's house. He was asked about Euphame Yorstoun's baby, and he declares that as for the sickness being taken off John Hoge and put onto the child so that she died of it, he never heard of this until within the past twenty days. Since then it has become the talk of everybody in the surrounding countryside, but he knows nothing more about it.

William Bennet from Merkill, married. aged 60, was sworn upon his knees and asked how long he has lived in Markill. He says for the past eleven years, and that he is the public swineherd for the community. He says that he never heard it rumoured or talked about by anyone that John Hoge or his wife were witches. Asked about the mad horse belonging to James Sandie, he says that since he was on the spot he got hold of the mad horse in the village and poinded it, and brought it to Andro Keir's house in Markil. However, the horse broke out of the house and came to John Charles's house. It came in furiously between the post and the wall of the house. It was brought out of John Charles's house with great difficulty. He says that this horse was never in John Hog's house as far as he knows. He was asked about Euphame Yorstoune's child, and if the sickness was laid on her and taken off John Hog. He says that as he shall answer to God, that he knows nothing about it.

Thomas Quhyte from Markill servant to Andro Quyte now living in Markill, aged 40, was sworn and asked if he ever heard John Hoge or his wife slandered for witchcraft He testifies that he never heard of any such slander before the arrest of Alexander Hamiltoun. He says that his father was a weaver to trade, and occupied a husbandland, half of which was in the community of Markill, which he paid for with his own goods. [The text is rather obscure here.] He died in Markil thirty years ago or so.

JC26/9/10x and 11 [Items 8 and 9 appear to be missing.]

[Written on the outside: " [damage]... Jon Hog and Margaret Nicolsoune his spouse in Markill confronted wt Alexr Hamiltoun [illegible] Nor 1629."]

Edinburgh, 16th November 1629, in the presence of My Lord Bishop of Dumblane; the Lord Advocate; and Mr Alexander Colme, Justice depute.

John Keir in Markill, solemnly sworn on his knees, says he was in John Hog's house on the morning of the Communion Sunday visiting him, since he was critically ill and not likely to live. He was also in the house at night, the same night that Euphame Yorstoun's child died. He was present when her husband Adam Coming came into John Hog's house to light a candle about twelve o'clock at night. He said that his child had taken a sudden attack and was likely to die. At this, a great number of those who were in the house went to Adam Coming's house to see the child, and stayed there about three quarters of an hour. After that they came back to John Hog's house. From what they said, the witness gathered that the child was badly affected and not likely to live, so he went in to see her. He saw the child flailing with her hands, and struggling furiously to breath. He stayed until he saw the child die about half an hour after he came in. The night before, he had seen the child in her mother's arms as healthy as any child could be. When asked who was blamed for the child's death, he said the rumour went through the village that the child's mother was saying that her baby had filled John Hog's grave. [The last few lines are damaged in the text, but the sense is almost certainly as above.]

Also, he declares that he never heard Heleine Lermonth blamed for the child's death; except that Heleine Lermonth's daughters assaulted Euphame Yorstoun at Lyntoun, but he has no idea why.

Also, he was asked if he knew anything about John Hog and his wife. He says he knows nothing else, except that he admits that Margaret Craill and her husband William Harlaw in Markill blamed them for some harm or loss caused by mischief-making with their possessions and work. Also, Pait Neilsone in Markill told him that the servant women in John Hog's house were muttering that there had been strange noises in his stable lately.

Euphame Yorstoun, wife of Adam Coming in Markill, solemnly sworn on her knees to reveal the truth, testifies that John Hog met her between Lyntoun and Merkill and wanted to have sex with her, which she refused. This was about last July. After that, about last Easter, she came to his house on some errand, and he pressed her to have sex with him. He put his hand round her throat, and because she refused, said to her, "Shame on those who refuse such a thing. I'll work at doing them a bad turn if I can." [Probable meaning. The text is obscure.]

Concerning her child, she declares that the baby was fit and healthy on the Sunday night. The whole community knew she was a robust and lively child. About nine o'clock at night she went to John Hog's house with her child in her arms to get some yeast, and as soon as she came in, met Margaret Nicolsone and asked her for the yeast. Margaret took the child by the hand and gripped it saying, "My burd, my burd." [A term of endearment.] After that, Euphame went back immediately to her own house, and laid the child down in the bed beside her. The child slept quietly in her bosom until about twelve or one, then wakened with a great cry or screech. From that time she struggled valiantly until about three o'clock in the morning, and then died. She declares that John Hog fell ill on the Tuesday or Wednesday before the Communion Sunday, for she remembers perfectly that he was in the church the Sunday before that, and that he went to Dunbar on the Tuesday to arrange a marriage between his younger son William and Issobell Sibbet in Auldhamstockis. When he came home on the Tuesday or Wednesday he fell ill. She also declares that on the Communion Sunday after that his sons were at the morning service, and came out of the church to see their father die, since none of them expected him to live. However, on the Monday, after the death of her child, she heard Robert Hepburne in Lynton say that he believed with God's grace John Hog would live and surprise them all. She declares that she never suspected John Hog or his wife for the death of her child, and still doesn't. But it was openly said in the community, and in the whole parish, that her child had filled John Hog's grave.

She says that she never blamed Helene Lermonth for bewitching her child. However, when she was told that John Hog's mother's sister Helen Lermonth had died, she said, "If she had greater skill and cleverness than me, it might be that Helen took the sickness off John Hog and laid it on my child." She declares on her solemn oath that she never said any such thing to James Hog's wife, that her child had been smothered. It was just that James Hog's wife said that she had given her child the cold by keeping her up too late at night. Euphame had replied to her, "How could she have caught a cold on a summer night like that, with her clothes on?" If she had caught cold by any oversight of hers she prayed God to forgive her. She knows Catherine Lermonth's daughter assaulted her with [damage] in Lyntoun, and drew blood from her head.

She was asked if she knew anything else about John Hog and his wife, and she declared that if William Harlaw and Margaret Carrail were called, they could give further information.

Adame Cumming, tailor in Markill, Euphame Yorstoun's husband, being sworn, testifies in agreement with his wife regarding the details of the child's death. The child had not been harmed by himself or his wife when she was was lying between them. The child wakened between twelve and one with a cry, and was screaming. He felt her, and found that she was cold below the waist, and hot above it. [These last few sentences are damaged but the meaning is clear.] The child struggled furiously after that, till she died. He takes it on his conscience that the child died a strange kind of death, and if children can be bewitched, then his daughter was bewitched. However, he could not take it on his conscience to say by whom.

As for John Hog pestering his wife to have sex with him, his wife told him about it, and also told him about the last time, when, because she refused him, he said he would do her a bad turn for refusing him what he wanted.

John Hog senior in Markill... [illegible] ...and sworn, says that regarding his illness before the Communion Sunday, he cannot remember. Asked if he would stand by his previous statement that he was confined to bed at the time of the death of his mother's sister Helene Lermonth, and not coming to the [illegible], he says he is not sure about that. He was confronted with Euphame Yorston. She affirmed in his face that the Wednesday after her child's death he was sitting in a chair at his door, to which he had been carried from his bed. He replied that he cannot remember. Euphame also declared in his presence that the same day that she was assaulted in Lyntoun by Heleine Lermonth's daughter, when she came home John Hog was sitting outside his own house at the gable end. This was twenty days after her child's burial. Asked about this, John says he cannot really remember.

Margaret Nicolsone, John Hog's wife, questioned again today and sworn on her knees to declare the truth, says she was not at the last Communion in Prestoun, before last Whitsunday. On the last Communion Sunday her husband was at the point of death, and her sons and neighbours were sent for that Sunday to see him die. This had happened once or twice before, but whether they were sent for on the Monday [illegible] she does not remember. Asked how soon after that her husband was carried out of his bed to the door on a chair or stool to sit there, she says that as far as she can remember he was in bed for three weeks after Communion Sunday, before he was brought to the door. She says that before the Communion Sunday she had bread baked for her husband's burial. It was baked in John Friskin's bakehouse in Lyntoun. The wheat was carried to Lyntoun on the miller's horse, and after it had been ground it was taken from the mill to the bakehouse and baked into bread. She declares that as far as she can remember there was half a boll, or ten pecks. There was nothing baked after that for her husband; only the bread for the burial.

She was asked if she knew about the day that was [illegible] for Adam Coming and Euphame Yorstone's child. She admits that Adam Coming came to her house about midnight to light a candle, and said that his child had taken a fit and seemd likely to die. Most of the people in the house went out to see the child, but she didn't go out herself. She says the child died suddenly that night. She was asked if Euphame Yorstoun came to her house with her child in her arms that night to ask for yeast. She answered that she cannot remember whether she came or not, but she is certain that she took neither Euphame nor the child by the hand that night. She also declares that Euphame did not come to the witness herself to ask for yeast, nor did she come and say the words alleged when she was looking for yeast [illegible] because her son Thomas's wife Issobell Thomson was in charge of selling the yeast and ale. Alter being confronted with Euphame Yorston, she admitted after several denials that she saw Ewphame come into her house that Sunday night. She also remembers that the child was in Euphamne's arms when she came in. Asked if she handled the child or not, she says she cannot remember, but it could be that she did.

When Euphame was sworn and confronted with Margaret, she consistently stood by her previous statement, and the manner of her child's death as described in that statement. After this Margaret Nicolson was asked if she would stand by her previous statement about bringing her husband to the door to sit on a chair three weeks after he fell ill. She said that she could not say with certainty how long it was before he was brought to the door. She was asked if her husband was brought to the door from his bed within three days of contracting his last illness. She swears on her solemn oath that she cannot remember if it was three days or three weeks. When she was confronted with Euphame Yorston on this point, Euphame stood by the part of her statement where she said John Hog was sitting at his door in a chair on the Wednesday after her child's death and burial.

James Sandie, miller at Lyntone Mill, was sworn solemnly on his knees and asked if there was ever any quarrel between himself and John Hog and his wife. He declares that there was no quarrel, except about receiving his fee, which they would settle the next day. Asked about the interference with his horses, he declares that four years ago at harvest time he had four horses which all went mad one after another within six weeks. The last horse to go mad, he put in a stable healthy and well in the evening. At about [illegible] at night it ran wild. His servant heard it, and came and told the witness. He got up, came to the stable, took the horse out of the stable, and put it in to lie in another outbuilding. Before daylight the next day, the horse had jumped out of that building at the eaves. The witness and his wife fervently prayed God that the mad horse would run to the place where the hurt had come from. When he got up in the morning he went to the outbuilding and saw the horse was gone. He had no idea where it had gone, but heard later that it had gone to Markill, and had been impounded there by the impounding officer, taken to John Charles's house, and kept there as an impounded horse. John Charles came into his own stable, not knowing the horse was there, and found the horse stuck between the post and the wall. He brought in a number of the neighbours to pull the horse out. When they got it out he put it at the side of the road. After that the horse went wandering through the village of Markill to the houses of various honest men, and among the rest, the story goes that it went to John Hog's house.

The witness declares that his wife said to him that the next day or the day after, she met John Hog's wife, who told her that the horse came in through her door and frightened her, and that she was never so frightened in her life as at the sight of that mad horse.

Margaret Nicolson was again asked about the mad horse. Did she ever see it, or did it come into her house after coming out of John Charles's stable? Did she say to James Sandie's wife Margaret Hamilton at any time that she was never so frightened in her life as she was when she saw the mad horse come in at her door? She denies altogether that she ever saw the horse, or said any such words to Margaret Hamilton, as far as she can remember.

After this, John Keir was questioned about whether he had seen the mad horse come to Markill. He declares that he never saw the horse, but had heard it said that this horse came to Markill, and came first of all to his brother Adam Keir's house. After that it went to John Charles's where it lay between the post and the wall of his house. After it had been put out of Charles's house the story was that it had gone to John Hog's house.

Signed: Thomas Hope,   Lord Bishop of Dunblane,   J. Colville.

JC26/9/12

[This appears to start in the middle of a paragraph, so there was presumably at least one preceding page which is now missing.]

... before that time all the witness's plough oxen and horses died. After the deaths of those beasts John Hog senior in Markill came to the witness's father and asked him if he would let John Hog have the tenancy of a husbandland and a half, since the wrtness's father's oxen had been lost. John Hog promised to give him back two rigs of land on which he could lay his dung, and also the possession of the house during his lifetime, which would suit him better

The witness's father refused John Hog's offer. Then it fell out that his father was dispossessed of the land by Richard Flemyng and Mr George Butler, who at the time were employed by the Countess of Cassleis, the liferenter of the lands. This was brought about by John Hog. After this, Richard Flemyng and Mr George Butler had the witness's father's corn threshed and used it to pay Lady Cassillis her dues. After that John Hog asked the witness's mother Jonet Neilsone to go up to Lethington to confer with the Countess of Cassills, and while she was away John Hog took the roof off the house. Thus, when the witness's mother returned she was forced to take herself to a little cottage nearby, provided for her by John Hog.

The witness further declares that he has a brother Robert Quhyte at present living in the Half Land Barne, opposite Tantallon, under Lord Angus. He told the witness that about St Androis Day 1625 three years ago, he was sleeping in a bedroom in John Hog's house in Markill. After he had been sleeping for a time, Robert saw a big black man in the moonlight between himself and the bedroom window. He came in at the window, and it seemed to Robert that he was counting or clinking money on the lid of a chest. At this Robert got out of bed terrified, drew his sword, and struck at the black man. In his fear, he shouted to John Hog and woke him up saying, "There's a thief in the room stealing your money!" At this, John Hog got up and came through to the room with a lighted candle. He said to Robert, "Go back to bed. My money is between two matresses which I sleep on myself in this room." However, Robert refused to lie down. He lifted all his clothes in his arms, and came out to the witness's house after midnight, and told him this story. Then he went to bed in the witness's house where he stayed until morning.

He was asked about the mad horse coming to John Hog's house. Also about John Hog's sickness being taken off and laid on Euphame Yorston's child. He says he knows nothing about either of these events.

John Charles in Markill, married, aged fifty, was sworn on his knees and asked if he had ever heard John Hog or his wife slandered for witchcraft or doing harm to their neighbours. He declares on his solemn oath that he never heard any such tales before Alexander Hamilton the warlock was arrested. He was asked about the death of Adam Coming's child, and the business of taking the sickness off John Hog and laying it on the child. Who had he heard this story from? He declares that he never heard anybody say this except Euphame Yorston the child's mother. Asked about the mad horse, and if it had come to John Hog's house, he says he saw the mad horse in his own house. It ran between the post and the wall of his house. He heard that people were saying that after that it ran in at John Hog's door. However, he says that he did not see it in John Hog's house himself. He also declares that he remembers that a certain Jonet Lyndsy from Lynton was burnt in Hadintoun for witchcraft.

Adam Keir in Markill, married, aged thirty, was sworn and asked if he had heard any talk about John Hog or his wife being involved in witchcraft. He declares that he never heard any such stories about them before the arrest of Alexander Hamilton. Asked about the mad horse and if he saw it in John Hog's house, he said he was leading-in and stacking corn at the time, and heard that the horse had come to his house, then to John Charles's house, and after that ran to the Yellowstanes. However, he does not know if it went to John Hog's. He never heard that. He was asked if he knew about, or had heard reports about John Hog's illness being taken off him and put on Euphame Yorston's child. He testifies on his solemn oath that he knows nothing about it.

Patrick Neilsone, married, aged about 34, was sworn on his knees and asked if he had ever heard gossip about John Hog or his wife being involved in sorcery or witchcraft before Alexander Hamilton was arrested. He said he never heard it talked about before then. He also testifies that he knows nothing about the sickness taken off John Hog and laid on Euphame Yorstone's child. He knows nothing about the mad horse or if it came to John Hog's house or not. He was asked if he ever heard any of John Hog's female servants say that they heard a great din or rumbling in John Hog's stable among the horses' feet, and if he had told John Keir about it. He declares he never heard any such story from the women, nor dd he tell any such story to Johne Keir.

Issobell Lermonth, servant to Adame Keir in Markill, was sworn on her knees and asked if she had been in service with John Hog and his son James. She says she was a servant to both of them, and before last Whitsun was a servant to John Hog senior. She was asked if she ever heard any rumour or scandal going around, about John Hog or his wife being involved in witchcraft. She declares that she never heard any such stories before the middle of last harvest when Hamiltoun was arrested. She was in their service and saw no sign of witchcraft in any of them, either by night or by day. She declares that she never heard anybody but Euphame Yorstoun say that the sickness was taken off John Hog and put on her child. She says she knows nothing about the mad horse, because that was long before she came to Markill in service.

Alexander Nicolsone, servant to John Hog senior, aged about twenty one or twenty two, was sworn on his knees and asked if he ever heard any scandalous tales repeated by anyone about John Hog or his wife. He says he never heard anything like that - only since John Hog came to Edinburgh. He was asked if he knew whether John Hog's recent illness was taken off him and laid on Euphame Yorstone's child. He knows nothing about it, nor about the mad horse belonging to James Sandie. He never saw nor heard anything about it before his master's recent coming to Edinburgh.

Richard Allane, servant to John Hog, was sworn, and agrees with Alexander Nicolson in everything, except that he heard Euphame Yorstone say that the sickness was taken off John Hog and put on her child. He says it was ten days after the child's death before John Hog recovered from his illness.

Jonet Davie, aged 22, born in Bairfute, and now servant to John Hog, was sworn and asked if there had been scandal at any time about John Hog and his wife being involved in witchcraft. She says she never saw anything to hold against them, and never heard any such tales from anyone before he came to Edinburgh last harvest. She knows nothing about this sickness laid on Euphame Yorstone's child, nor of any other scandalous report about her master or mistress, either by night or by day.

Signed: Lord Bishop of Dunblane,
[illegible],   Mr A. Colme.

JC26/9/13

At Edinburgh 21st November, in the presence of My Lord of Dumblane; the Lord Advocate; and Mr Alexander Colme, Justice Depute.

Margaret Hamilton, the wife of James Sandie, miller at Lyntoun Mill, was sworn and asked about the death of her horses which went mad. She testifies in agreement with her husband. As for the last of the four horses, which jumped out at the side of the house, she says she prayed to the Lord to bring about a miracle to make the horse run to the house of the person who was the author of the harm done to them. When he heard her, her husband did the same, both of them upon their knees.

Also, she declares that her husband got up and took the last mad horse out of the stable about eleven o' clock at night, and put it in the barn. About dawn - this was around the beginning of harvest - the witness and her husband heard a great rumbling as if the barn was falling down. They could hear this because the house where they were sleeping was joined to the barn. They were frightened to get up, but in the morning they and all their neighbours saw the mad horse in their own garden, and saw the part of the barn through which the horse had come was knocked down much more than as if a big dog had come out of it. [The word in the text seems to be "dog", but the last sentence admittedly does not sound very sensible.] Then they and the neighbours saw the horse run round four or five times anticlockwise, and then run to Markill. However, she does not know to which house in Markill the horse went. Nor did she know until John Hog's wife Margaret Nicolsone came to the mill. This was the first time she had been there since the death of the mad horse. It was the same harvest-time, but she cannot tell how soon or how many days afterwards. Without any prompting from the witness, Margaret Nicolson said to her, "I was never so frightened in my life as when your mad horse frightened me." The witness replied, "Jesu Marie, how did he frighten you?" Margaret answered, "I was kneading dough in my own house, and the mad horse came in at my door where there was a tub full of water. The mad horse put his two forefeet in the tub of water." And she said that for her life she dared not drive it out, but went to the barn to the children, and got some of them to come and drive the horse out. However, the witness declares that she was told by a little girl in John Hog's household, the daughter of John Mason the tailor in Markill, that their son Thomas Hog had taken the horse out.

Margaret Nicolsone was this day sworn again on her solemn oath, and asked if she ever saw James Sandie's mad horse in or near her house in Markill. She swears on her solemn oath that she never saw it in or outside her house. She consistently denies that she saw it. Asked on her solemn oath if she ever said to James Sandie's wife that she had never been so frightened as she was at the mad horse, she said that she never said so as far as she knows or can remember. She was urged to give a straight answer, did she say so or not? At length she declared on her solemn oath that she said no such thing to her or to anyone else.

After this, Margaret Nicolsoun and Margaret Hamiltoun were confronted with each other upon their knees. Margaret Hamiltoun affirmed by her solemn oath in Margaret Nicolsone's face that her previous statement was true. Margaret Nicolson also denied by her solemn oath that Margaret Hamilton's assertion and affirmation was true, and swore that she never said any such words to Margaret Hamiltoun about the mad horse coming to the house, nor did she ever see it in the house, nor was she frightened by it.

Robert Quhyte in Hafflandbarne, under the Earl of Angus, aged 34, was sworn, and testifies that the night his brother Thomas Quhyte was married three years ago last November, he was sleeping in John Hog's house. He went to bed at nine o'dock at night, and slept till about two or three in the morning. He then woke up, spontaneously, and not wakened by anyone else. When he awoke, between himself and the light from the north window, he saw a grim broad black man. He saw him move up and down the little parlour at the north end of the bedroom where the witness was lying. He heard a tinkling as if there were coins in his hand going into open chests, and sometimes as if he had been counting out dollars. [This sentence is difficult to decipher in the text.] The witness suspected that this was some thief who had come to steal John Hog's money. He put out his hand, and lifted his sword which was lying on the table by his bed. He drew the sword out of the scabbard in his bed, and then jumped out of bed and lashed out at the walls with his drawn sword. The man he had seen went between him and the light, and obscured it so that he could see nothing. Before that he could see him perfectly between himself and the light from the window, as there was a full moon shining. Then the witness began to be greatly frightened, and trembled with terror, and then he cried out.

JC26/9/14

Edinburgh, 18th November 1629. In the presence of the Lord Advocate, My Lord Dumblane, and Mr Alexander Colme.

John Hog senior was sworn and questioned. He was asked if he ever knew a certain Jonet Lyndsay who lived in Lyntoun and was burnt for witchcraft in Hadingtoun. He declares that he knew her, and he may have given her some seed corn at some time. He was asked if he had known John Maison before he died. He says that he knew him, and that he got the land he had possessed. He was asked if he knew that Jonet Lyndsay had confessed before her death that she had done harm to John Maison by bewitching his two sons and one of his horses. They had all died within the space of an hour. He says he never heard of this, but if it is true it will be shown in the Haddington records.

He was asked if he knows Robert Quhyte, Andrew's son. He say he knows him and that he stayed in his house three years ago, and about eleven o'clock at night he came through the house to the witness in a fury or fit of madness saying, "Get up John, for there are thieves in the house!" At this, John and his servants came through with lighted candles and found nothing. He told Robert to go back to bed. He says that if there was anything that frightened him, it was the shepherd's cat that came in at the window with a piece of chain round her neck. [The text says that the cat had a "pair of suiellis" round her neck. This could indicate a swivel with an iron ring, and "sweels" can also be large flat baskets. However, it is clear from the text that the cat had been chained up but had broken away. What remained round its neck therefore was obviously part of the means of restraint, and so it would seem sensible to translate it as "a piece of chain".] The shepherd's name is Pait Bell. He was asked when the shepherd told him that it was his cat with the chain round her neck that had gone in at the window. He says it wasn't the shepherd who told him, but his family who missed the cat at home and came to Markill to look for her. He was asked which of the shepherd's family told him this, and he replied that they went through the whole village saying so, but he can't remember who told him. He says Pait Bell's wife is called Issobell Wilsone, and his son is called John Bell, and that as far as he knows it was they who came looking for the cat. He was asked if the disturbance made by Robert Quhyte caused his wife to get up and come through to the room. He says he cannot remember, but his sons Thomas and William were in the house at the time. After that, he was questioned further about Robert Quhyte, and said that as far as he could remember Robert Quhyte came through with a short sword in his hand.

Margaret Nicolsone, John Hog's wife, was sworn, and testifies that she has seen the late Jonet Lyndsay, and that she had come to her house more than twenty times looking for food. It is possible that she might have stayed a night in her house. She was asked if she ever knew that Jonet was believed to use witchcraft. She declares that she never heard that until she was arrested, accused, and executed for witchcraft. She says that she knew the late John Mason, but never heard that Jonet Lyndsay confessed at her death that she had done wrong to John Masone or to his children or livestock.

She says she knows Robert Quhyte, and that he was in her house the night that his brother was married, sleeping in an inner room. About eleven or twelve he got up in great excitement saying there was a thief in the house and that all the money for the wedding was stolen. At this, her husband and the servant got up, lit candles, and came through to the room, and found nothing. She was asked if she knew the cause of the rumbling noise, and said that the next day or a couple of days after that the shepherd's wife missed her cat and came to Markill looking for her. She found her in the witness's house with a chain round her neck. She had broken away from the shepherd's house, where she was kept with the chain round her neck to keep her from wandering. She was asked whether she had found the cat in her house before the shepherd's wife came. She says they found the cat with the chain in an upright barrel containing hansel bread. [Presumably bread given to the Hogs as a good luck gift, or bread which they intended giving as such. Perhaps something to do with Quhyte's brother's wedding?] This barrel was left in the bedroom. She didn't know it was the shepherd's cat until the shepherd's wife came for it. This was about Martinmas three years ago. She was asked if the barrel where the cat was found had a cover. She says it has a cover, but it could have been left off. She cannot remember whether she herself or one of the servants found the cat. She declares that as soon as they found the cat they told Thomas Quhyte, Robert's brother - who was their next door neighbour - that they had found the cat which had caused the disturbance. She was asked whether after that disturbance Robert Quhyte went back to bed or not. She says he was told twenty times to go to bed, but can't tell if he did or not, or if he left the house or not.

John Hog was asked whether Robert Quhyte went back to bed or not after the disturbance.

He says he does not remember. He was asked if the cat was found in his house. He says that he cannot tell. If the shepherd who lost his cat hadn't told him about it he would never have known. He was asked if the cat was found in a barrel of bread in the room. He says that he doesn't remember, or whether his wife or one of the servants told him about it. Then Margaret Nicolsone and John Hog were confronted with one another, and John remembered that Margaret had told him about it.

Signed: Lord Bishop of Dumblane, witness.

Thomas Hope.

J. Colme.

JC26/9/15

[The first part of this is obviously missing.]

... with a loud noise upon John Hog, saying, "Come through! A thief has broken into your house and is stealing your money!" John Hog answered from his bed, "What ails you, Robert? I'm not so foolish as to have my money lying around loose." To which the witness replied, "Where is it then?" John answered that it was between two matresses. After that John Hog got up out of his bed in the hall and came with a lighted candle into the bedroom where the witness was lying. The witness said to John that he had seen a black man or thief in the house. Then John and the witness went and searched the whole house, and the beds and barrels there. They searched above and below the beds, and in three barrels, one of which contained feathers, the second contained herring, and the third contained nothing as far as he could remember. After that John told the witness to go back to bed, for they had found nothing in the house. However, he refused to go to bed, but lifted his clothes with his cloak in his arms, and went out of the house to his brother's house where he stayed until morning. In the morning he went back early to John Hog's where he remained all day, drinking and making merry all night. When he came in in the morning Margaret Nicolsone said to him, "Jesus, Robert, what made you so frightened?" He replied that he had good reason, since he had seen a [illegible] thief in the house stealing their money. She answered that there was nothing in the house unless it was Pait Bell's cat with a chain and a swivel round her neck." However, he says that he saw no cat in their house all that day as long as he was in the house. He swears on his solemn oath that he was not under the influence of drink on the night of the wedding before he saw the thief or black man as stated above.

John Bell, son of the shepherd Patrick Bell, was sworn on his knees and asked if he knew about John Hog's illness. He declares that he knew about it and that he was at death's door. He was asked how quickly he recovered. He says he knows nothing about that, except that he grew better and better within three days after Yorstone's child died. He also says that John Hog's son John went to the witness's father who is a shepherd for a lamb to be baked for his father's burial. He knows that his father brought the lamb, but when he came with it they didn't take it, and it was sent back again. He cannot tell when it was sent back again, but says it was about the Communion Sunday. However, whether it was before or after that he cannot remember.

Concerning his father's cat, he admits that his mother tied the cat with a chain and swivel. It got away, and was away for eight days. It came back home of its own accord after eight days, but the swivel was delivered to them by Margaret Nicolsone before the cat came home.

Alexander Gray in Markill, being sworn, declares that within the last twelve months he heard that James Sandie's mad horse had come to Markill. He says he was a servant to John Hog ten years ago, only for half a year, and left his service after that. He says that in that time he never saw nor heard of any wrong, or any other fearful things done either by John Hog or his wife. Asked about the particular question addressed to him, he solemnly swears that he knows nothing about it.

John Hog senior was confronted with Robert Quhyt and asked if he and Robert Quhyte had searched the three barrels, the night of the disturbance in his house about the thief or black man Robert saw in the house. Robert Quhyte claimed that they did, but John Hog constantly denied that either he or Robert Quhyte searched any barrels in his house that night. He says Robert Quhyte was drunk that night.

Robert Quhyte affirms the contrary. He was sober and in no way drunk at the time, nor when he had gone to bed earlier that night.

Margaret Nicolson solemnly swears that the cat was not found in any of her barrels that night, nor before sunrise the following day. She was confronted with Robert Quhyte who declares that in the morning, when he came in about sunrise he met her in her own house, and she said that he'd had no need to be afraid, for it was Pait Bell's cat. If there had been any noise to frighten him it had been Pait Bell's cat.

Signed: Lord Bishop of Dumblane, witness; Thomas Hope; A. Colmbe.

JC26/9/16

At Edinburgh, 23rd November 1629, in the presence of My Lord of Dumblane; the Lord Advocate; and Mr Alexander Colmbe, Justice Depute.

Marion Fruid, widow, living in Markill, was solemnly sworn to declare the truth about John Hog and his wife, and testifies that she knows nothing.

Thomas Hog, was solemnly sworn and asked if he carried his father in a chair to the door, or helped to carry him, on the Tuesday, Wednesday, Thursday, or Friday, after the death of Euphame Yorstone's child. He declares that he does not remember which day it was, but he thinks it was towards the end of the week that he was brought to the door. He says that as far as he can remember his wife was in the house. He was asked if he saw James Sandie's mad horse the day that it came from Lynton to Markill, or if he brought it out of his father's house. He swears on his solemn oath that he neither saw the mad horse that day, nor brought it out of his mother's house.

He was asked if he was in his father's house the night that Robert Quhyte saw the black man. He says that he was in the house that night, but swears on his solemn oath that he did not get up out of bed that night, but heard about it in the morning. What gave him the fright was the shepherd's cat which was found the next day in the house with a pair of iron rings. He says that he saw the cat in his father's house the next day before twelve o' clock, with the iron rings round its neck. The shepherd's wife came and got the cat, but he can't remember what day she got it back from his mother. He was asked if his mother told him that she had found the cat in a barrel in her house. He denies this, and swears on his solemn oath that his mother never told him this.

Issobell Thompsone, wife of Thomas Hog, was sworn, and declares that she cannot tell if Euphame Yorstoune or her child or her husband Adam Coming came into her father's *[sic]* house at night, the Sunday of the Communion, when the child died. She gave neither drink nor yeast to Euphame. She says she heard of the child's death about three o' clock in the morning. She also testifies on her solemn oath that she never saw the mad horse in her father in law's house, or in the village of Markill, the day that it came from Lyntoun. Nor did she see it in any other part of the district, or even heard about it until within the past ten days.

William Lermonth, from Markill, married, aged 50, was solemnly sworn on his knees and asked if he was in Markill the night that Euphame Yorstone's child died. He says he saw the child in good health on Sunday night before she died. He says that he was in John Hog's house that night, sitting up with him, and saw Adam Coming come in to light candles. Asked whether the mad horse came to John Hog's house the day it came to Markill, he says that he heard the horse came to Markill, and was in John Charles's house, then came out and ran through Markill, but doesn't know if it came to John Hog's house or not that day. He was asked if he had heard John Hog or his wife talked about in connection with witchcraft or any other wicked doings. He swore on his solemn oath that he never heard any evil rumours about either of them until after the arrest of Hamilton the warlock.

He swears solemnly that last Michaelmas, when he was in bed with is wife about twelve o' clock at night, a number of cats came into his house, fell upon his own three cats, and killed two of them. He and his wife were wakened up by the great screeching and crying they were making. He got up with a stick in his hand to put the cats out. He solemnly swears that when he got up he heard a cat speak and say to him, "What's all the hurry?" to which he answered,"Never mind my hurry. Get out!" At this they all ran out at the hen-hole under the door and took one of the dead cats with them. They left the other dead cat behind with a hundred holes in her. He testifies that his wife Elspeth Broun heard the cat speak as well. He says nobody could have spoken but the cats, for there was no-one else in the house but himself and his wife, and a boy of nine lying sleeping at the end of the house.

Signed: Lord Bishop of Dunblane, witness. Thomas Hope.   A. Colmbe.

Item 17

Robert Hog, son of John Hog, was questioned and solemnly sworn on his knees. He declares that he knows that the cat with the iron rings was in his father's house, and that this cat with the iron rings came into his own house and gave him a bad fright during the night. However, he never saw it because he had just put out the fire and was going to bed. When he heard the cat he took a stick and chased her. He searched the house for her but couldn't see her because it was dark. He thinks the cat went out at the upper window where she had come in. This he declares to be true on his solemn oath.

Signed: Dunblane, witness.
Thomas Hope.   A. Colmbe.

25th November 1629

Elspeth Brown, wife of William Lermonth, was sworn upon her knees and asked about the cats that came into her house about Michaelmas at night, when she and her husband were lying in bed and were wakened by the noise of the cats as described in her husband's statement, and how one of the cats spoke to him as is recorded there. She swears on her solemn oath that her husband's statement is true. Her declaration agrees with his in everything.

Signed: Dunblane, witness.   Thomas Hope. A. Colmbe.

[John Hog and Margaret Nicolson were freed on 26th November 1629 by order of the Privy Council, on condition that they found surety to appear for trial if required - see the chapter on "Trial by Commission". There is no record of them ever being put on trial.]

1630

The Case of Alexander Hamilton.

[Hamilton was a native of Prestonpans and worked as a coal miner there in his youth. Later he worked as a miner in Northumberland, and seems to have been pressed into military service. Latterly he lived a roving life as a beggar. He was arrested as a result of the efforts of George Home of Manderston, who seems to have interfered illegally in the taking of statements from Hamilton. Louise Yeoman, in "Hunting the rich witch in Scotland", contained in *The Scottish Witch-hunt in Context*, ed. Julian Goodare, Manchester 2002, shows that there is compelling evidence to indicate that Manderston was using Hamilton and others to blacken the characters of Manderston's wife Helen Arnot, and his cousin Lady Samuelston, with charges of witchcraft. Hamilton was undoubtedly an unsavoury character who probably did dabble in witchcraft and charming, but was also almost certainly a dupe forced into perjury by the unscrupulous "gentleman" George Home.

A transcription of Hamilton's trial as recorded in the Books of Adjournal was printed in *Justiciary Cases 1624 - 1650* Vol 1, ed. Stair A. Gillon, published by the Stair Society, Edinburgh 1953. Here, as with other records, I have rendered Gillon's transcription in modern English.]

22nd January 1630

Judges: Colville and Robertoun.

Alexander Hamilton, warlock.

Accused of various charges of sorcery, witchcraft, and consultation with the Devil regarding the destruction of various persons by sorcery and witchcraft as specified in his indictment and in statements made by him.

Prosecutors: Mr Robert Burnet and Mr John Oliphant, substitutes to Sir Thomas Hope, His Majesty's Advocate.

The prosecutors produced the indictment and the list of jurors. After reading the indictment the judge asked Alexander Hamiltoun if the statements made by him in the presence of the Lords Commissioners, and sworn by him to be true, were in fact true, and if he would abide by them, or wished to withdraw anything. He was now requested to declare the truth in court, and must not lie about any person, as he should answer before the judgment seat of Christ where he would shortly appear. In answer to this by his great and solemn oath, down upon his knees, Hamilton ratified and approved all he previous statements made by him since his arrest, in every particular, excepting only the charge made by him against Lady Manderstoun, which he declared is completely untrue. On his knees before God, he craved God's mercy for it, and declared that this story against her was information reported to him by John Neill in Tueidmouth, as is recorded in the last statement he made in Edinburgh.

After the indictment had been read, and he had been accused of the various charges contained in it, Hamilton confessed that the indictment and all the charges contained in it were true. At this, the prosecuting advocates asked for a written record.

[A list of the jurors follows in the original text, which Gillon does not give, indicating merely that the jury consisted of "15 Edinburgh burgesses".]

The jury was received, sworn, and admitted, after Alexander Hammiltoun had been indicted of the various and particular crimes mentioned, namely:

The divine law of Almighty God set down in his sacred word against all witches, sorcerers, users and practitioners of sorcery and witchcraft, appoints the deserved punishment of death to be inflicted on all such persons who are guilty and culpable of such things. Also in the Acts of Parliament and civil laws of this kingdom made in the days of our Sovereign Lord's most noble ancestors, namely in the ninth parliament held by His Majesty's dearest grandmother of worthy and famous memory, it is expressly provided, prescribed, and ordained that no manner of person or persons of whatever degree, estate, or condition should presume to take in hand at any subsequent time the practice or use of any manner of witchcraft, sorcery, or necromancy. Nor should they advertise themselves as having any such skill, craft, or knowledge with which to abuse His Majesty's good people. The punishment for this is death, as indicated in the said laws and Acts of Parliament.

In spite of this, it is true that, shaking off all fear of the almighty and omnipotent God, all reverence and regard for his divine laws and commands set down in his sacred word, and all regard for the laws and Acts of Parliament of this kingdom, Alexander Hammilton in a most fearful manner applied himself to the service of Satan, the enemy of his salvation.

About Michaelmas 1624 he entered into a pact and covenant with the Devil on Hugston Hills while coming from the Nunland [now Huntington] to the burgh of Haddingtoun. About midday the Devil appeared to Alexander there in the likeness of a black man dressed all in black, without a cloak, and with a wand in his hand. After some conversation, Alexander promised to be his servant, on condition that the Devil would not allow him to lack food, clothing, or money. Alexander asked him for money. The Devil refused this at that time, but arranged for Alexander to meet him a few days after that on Gairnetoun Hills at night, between twelve and one o'clock. There Alexander was to renew his covenant and promise, and the Devil would then give him money.

So, shortly after this, Alexander went to Garnetoun Hills as arranged, and he met with his master the Devil, who appeared to Alexander riding on a black horse. He asked Alexander how he was and whether he wanted to remain in his service or not. Alexander replied that he was happy to do so.

Then the Devil in a most fearful manner made Alexander renounce his baptism and promise once again to become his bondsman. After this he gave Alexander four shillings sterling in English money. Alexander was carrying a stick in his hand, and after the pact had been made and agreed between them, the Devil then commanded Alexander to take the baton whenever he wished to consult him, strike it three times on the ground, and to command him with the words, "Rise up, Foul Thief!" When Alexander struck the ground three times with his baton as directed, the Devil would appear to him, sometimes in the likeness of a crow, sometimes in the shape of a cat, and at other times in the shape of a dog. In this way Alexander would receive answers from him. Before the Devil left him, Alexander was in the habit of making payment to him either with a cat, a loaf, a dog, or any other such beast as he came by.

Alexander kept the baton until he was arrested at Killene Mure three miles from Newcastell. When he arrived in Newcastell he was drinking in a house by the wayside, and he threw the baton in the fire. When he threw it in the fire, it gave a loud crack. When the onlookers expressed surprise Alexander said to them, "Don't be afraid. It's nothing but the knots in the fir-wood making the noise."

Shortly after this, Alexander met certain other accomplices and associates at a tryst with the Devil in the hills to the west of Dunse Castle. There, every one of them asked leave from the Devil to do harm to any person against whom they bore any ill-will or malice. Alexander bore a grudge against Mr James Cockburn, the provost of Haddington, because of an injury done to him by Mr James. Alexander was commanded by his master the Devil to pull three ears of corn out of every one of Mr James's stacks which were standing in his barnyard Then he was to take them to Gairneton Hills and burn them. In obedience to this command, Alexander drew the three ears of corn out of the stacks and burned them in Gairnetone Hills. At the time when they were burnt, the provost of Haddington had a kiln full of corn which was drying. By Alexander's devilish sorcery, and with the assistance of his master the Devil, ail this corn was completely burnt up.

Thomas Home in Clerkingtoun was bewitched with a fearful sickness laid on him by a beggar woman who is now dead. She laid an enchanted thread in front of his door. The witchcraft was directed against his father James Home because he had previously struck her. Alexander Hammiltoun came to Thomas Home's house, and when he saw he was infected whith this sickness, he told him he was bewitched arid promised to cure him. In order to do this, Alexander went shortly afterwards to Clerkingtoun Burne beside the Rottonraw, with a cat under his arm. With his stick he raised his master Sathan, who appeared to him in the likeness of a crow, and informed him by what means he could cure Thomas of his illness. He was to take oil of animal fat, camomile, and heart-fat, mix them together, dip a woollen cloth in it, and rub Thomas with it. When he got this answer from the Devil, Alexander cast the cat to him, and he vanished away with it. Thomas was cured of his disease by Alexander's sorcery, applying the cure to him as was instructed.

Also, Alexander Hamiltoun conceived a deadly hatred against the late Elizabeth Lausone, the younger Lady Ormestoun, besause when he was at her gate asking for alms she chased him off, saying, "Away, you custroun carl [base fellow]! You'll get nothing here!" To get his revenge Alexander then went to Saltoun Wood accompanied by two women mentioned in his statements. There he raised the Devil, who appeared to him and his associates in the likeness of a man dressed in grey. Alexander and his associates explained why they had come, and asked him to tell them how they could be revenged on Lady Ormestoun. The Devil then gave Alexander a ball of blue thread, with instructions to lay the thread in front of the gate leading to her house. He guaranteed that by doing this they would get their intended revenge on her. According to this devilish direction, the blue thread was laid down by Alexander and his associates in front of Lady Ormestoun's gate at Wodheid. Within a short time after that, by the sorcery and witchcraft practised against the lady as described, she and her eldest daughter suddenly fell ill and were both bereft of their natural lives.

Also, he is accused of having conceived a deadly malice against George Broun of Colstoun because he banished Alexander from his land as an idle beggar and vagabond. In revenge for this Alexander raised his master the Devil at a place called the Monkrig, above the Stob Stane, There he asked the Devil for power to do harm to the Laird of Colstoun, either in his person or in his possessions. However, the Devil answered that he could not do so, because he had already granted the gift of harming the Laird of Colstoun to Wilsone's wife in Stobstane.

Also, he is accused of being in company with Agnes Thomesoun from the Pannes, the wife of John Woid there, at a meeting with the Devil on the Links of Prestoun, where plans were laid and approved by the Devil for the destruction of the possessions and ships of various people.

He is also accused of being in company with the late Katherine Oswald and Katharine Gilmoir from Nidrie at a tryst and meeting they had at the top end of the Broken Causway at Nydrie, near the hollow of the Deane on the way to Edmistoun. The Devil appeared to them there in the likeness of a black man dressed in black clothes, and spoke to the two women for half an hour. He then took them up the side of the hollow of the Dean, where he stayed with them for quarter of an hour, leaving Alexander behind with orders to stay there till the Devil and the women returned. When they came back again he arranged for a new tryst for them to meet together in fourteen days' time on Cauldcoit Mure. Alexander did not keep the appointment, and for breaking the tryst he was most vigorously beaten by the Devil with a baton at a subsequent meeting on the Garnetone Hillis.

All of the above individual charges, and several other meetings Alexander and his associates had with the Devil, were plainly confessed by Alexander to be true, as his statements show. For these heinous crimes and for the damnable life led by Alexander in his devilish service to Sathan for many years, he has incurred the punishment of death as a person not worthy to live among Christian people.

Verdict: Guilty. [This is presumably the editor's summary of a passage in the original text describing the withdrawal of the jury and the presentation of the verdict.]

Therefore, by the mouth of the dempster of court, Andro McCairtour, the judge sentenced

Alexander Hammiltoun to be taken to the Castell Hill of the burgh of Edinburgh, there to be strangled at a stake until he is dead, his body thereafter to be burnt and consumed to ashes, and all moveable goods he may have to be confiscated and forfeited to His Majesty's use. This was pronounced and given out as the sentence of the court.

[Editor's note: "He was dead by 2nd February 1630, and described on 5th July 1631 as lately burnt for witchcraft. RCP iii, P.443; iv, 265."]

The same day the warlock Alexander Hammiltoun was presented in court by the magistrates of Edinburgh, and brought out of their prison where he has been held since August 1629. He was accused and prosecuted by Mr Robert Burnet and Mr Johnne Oliphant, advocates substitute to Sir Thomas Hope of Craighall, baronet, advocate to our Sovereign Lord for His Highness' interest. He was charged with various crimes of sorcery, witchcraft, and consultation with the Devil for the destruction and depriving of their lives of various persons specified in the indictment, and in the statements made by him at Dunce, Haddingtoun, and Edinburgh. The statements made by him were produced, and remained in court before the admission and election of those summoned to serve as jurors, and also after the jurors had been elected. [The exact sense of the preceding sentence is difficult to pin down.] In court, in presence of the judge and jury, solemnly sworn and on his knees, Alexander Hammiltoun ratified the truth of his previous statements in all their contents, except for the details he gave against Lady Manderstoun, which he affirmed were completely untrue, and for which he craved God's mercy. He declared that the details about Lady Manderstoun had been given to him by John Neill from Tueidmouth, as he said in the last statement he gave in Edinburgh. Humbled and prostrate upon his knees, by his solemn oath he declared that he is absolutely certain that all the foresaid statements made by him, with the exception mentioned, were made and taken down without being suggested, given, or ordered by any other person whatsoever.

He swears particularly that Sir George Home of Manderstoun never said a word to him except to encourage him to make a true confession and declare the truth. Also, that his servant Andro Fraser who brought Alexander from Beruik to Dunce, said nothing else to him in Beruik or on the way to Dunce, except to tell the truth about what he knew. Fraser said, "Alexander, if you do so my master will be good to you, for he is a compassionate man." At this, Sir George Home of Manderstone ratified and approved in court before the judge and jury all the statements he had made in court against John Hog in Markle and his wife, as they had been taken down and sworn to him in the presence of the lords and judges who interrogated him. He declared on his solemn oath that he was never induced or persuaded by anyone to make any statement either for or against John Hog and his wife. He has declared the truth about them according to what he knows for certain. At this, Andro Quhyte who was present asked for a written record.

[It is not absolutely clear whether Manderston here is ratifying statements made by Hamilton about John Hog, or statements made by himself, but it would seem sensible to take it that he was ratifying his own statements. Since Manderston was apparently engaged in blackening the characters of his wife and Lady Samuelston for his own financial gain - see Yeoman in Goodare ed. 2002 - we might assume that accusations made by him against John Hog might well have had similar motives. However, what his connection with John Hog might be is not immediately obvious, since none of the Justiciary Court papers dealing with Hog's case make any mention of Manderston. Nor does Hog seem to have been summoned for trial, in spite of Manderston's ratification of whatever he had said against him.]

Justiciary Court papers relating to Alexander Hamilton.

[Box JC26/9 in the National Archives of Scotland contains a bundle of papers relating to the case of Alexander Hamilton. Much of the material deals with the activities of Hamilton and his supposed associates outwith East Lothian. I shall therefore summarise those parts of it.]

Item 1.

[This is dated 14th March at Eyemouth in Berwickshire, and records the confessions of Christian Wilsone, Jonet Williamsone, Barbara Sluit[?], and Margaret Loche before the minister of Eyemouth and several local lairds including Home of Manderston. There were meetings in Eyemouth with the Devil and other witches, some of whom had already been burnt or had made their escape. None of the confessions make any mention of Alexander Hamilton.

However, Item 1 subsequently records a statement made by Hamilton in Haddington on 15th July 1629. He claims that Alisone Colme in Duns had asked the Devil for power to take the life of the Sheriff Clerk in Duns, James Douglas. In another statement he declares that he and the women in Duns had consulted with the Devil to kill Margaret Cockburn and John Weymis's wife and her brother. He confessed to being at several meetings with the Devil and other witches. Among the witnesses to these statements was Sir George Home of Manderston.

A third statement is dated at Haddington, 22nd July 1629, and was made in the presence of the ministers of the Presbytery of Haddington. Hamilton swears to the truth of his previous statements, and claims that a certain John Smyt was the Devil's "heid man" in the various Berwickshire ongoings.

All this was again ratified by Hamilton at his trial on 22nd January 1630.]

Item 2.

Copy of the statement made at Dunce 14th July 1629.

Alexander Hamiltoun, vagabond, fled to England under suspicion of witchcraft. When Sir George Home of Manderston was informed that this Alexander had bewitched Lady Woodheid's daughter he obtained a warrant under His Majesty's hand to the justices of England and Ireland to apprehend Alexander. After his arrest Sir George procured another warrant under His Majesty's hand referring him to the Privy Council in Scotland. He brought Alexander to the tollbooth of Dunse on 13th July 1629, and on 14th July 1629 Alexander declared as follows, freely and of his own accord, in the presence of we, the undersigned:-

Firstly, being aware of his sins, he asked God's mercy, and declared he was a witch and had been in the Devil's service for the past five years. The Devil first appeared to him at the hills of Hukstoun near Hadintoun, in the likeness of a gentleman riding on a black horse, dressed in black, who asked if he would be his manservant. Thinking this was some gentleman, and being in great need, Alexander agreed to be his servant. He made him deny his baptism and the cross of Christ. He wanted him to receive the mark, but Alexander declares that he refused to have it. He declares that he met him several times after that in several places around in Hadintoun, and that the Devil promised he would never lack resources.

[The next four paragraphs refer to various ongoings in and around Duns, including a meeting where the Devil had sex with all the women present. His example was then followed by John Smyth who "gott upon the women abovenamed and usit them all behind, and raid them lyk beastes" - Hamilton seems to have had a fixation for this: see the case of John Hog and his wife. There were plots against the lives of various people, and the witches raised a flood to drown James Mowat and his wife, but failed.

After that Hamilton declares that Sir George Home of Manderston is in danger from witchcraft practised by John Neill from Berwick at the instigation of Manderston's wife Helen Arnot. She had consulted with Neill and the Devil several times and made payments to Neill in grain and money. This paragraph goes on, "Particularly Dame Helen Arnot met with the Devil about twelve o'clock at night about two years ago on the south side of Coldingham Law, where he and John Neill, all the Dunse people already named, and some from around Hadingtoun were all present. Dame Helen asked the Devil that night to take Sir George Home's life. She had a man's hand taken up from a grave, and at the Devil's direction put it in a corner of Sir George Home's garden in Berwick where he used to go every day. If he had been the first to see it he would have died, but somebody else saw it before him so God preserved him from their intentions."

In the final paragraph Hamilton declares that John Neill is a notorious witch, and that if they are not prevented Neill and Dame Helen will take Manderston's life and property. Hamilton adds that three years before, Neill and Dame Helen had put a foal into Manderston's stable in Berwick. If he had been the first to see it there he would have died.

The copy of these statements was made on 30th October 1629 by James Rucheid in the presence of the Lord Advocate.]

Item 3

At Edinburgh, 8th August 1629, in the presence of Mr Alexander Colmbe of Blair, Justice Depute; Archibald Tod and Alexander Harlot, baillies of Edinburgh.

Alexander Hamilton, about 60 years old, was sworn upon his knees and asked when he first saw Sir George Home of Manderston. He says it was fourteen days before he left the prison in Newcastell. There was no further conversation with Nm except that Sir George asked Hamilton if he recognised him. The witness answered that he had heard his name, but never knew him before then. He asked for some money but Sir George answered that he would get no money from him. He says he was committed to prison in Newcastell by Lord Bamburgh, who asked him at the time if he had been at Humbie or Ormestoun. He denied that he had.

He was asked to tell the truth about the first time he met and had conversation with the Devil. He says the first time was about five years ago, as far as he remembers, and it was at harvest time. He was coming out of Nunland near Hadingtoun, and going up Hugstoun Hills above Hadingtoun on the way to Gairnetoun. Going up the hill between twelve and one o'clock he met with a gentleman all in black, without a cloak, who had a wand in his hand. [Or perhaps more prosaically, a "stick" in his hand.] He was ill-favoured in the face, without the company of either human being or beast, and without a horse. He asked Hamilton to come and be his servant, and he would never want. He agreed on condition that he should want for neither money nor food. The Devil then "passed away in an obscure manner", and as he went, asked Hamilton to meet him at Gairnetone Hillis on the following Tuesday, eight days after that, between eleven and twelve o'clock at night. He declares that in accordance with the agreement between them, he came to the appointed place, where he encountered Sathan mounted on a black horse. The night before he kept this appointment he slept in a cottar's house in the Geigging[?] Hillis. The next day, on the Tuesday, he asked lodgings for God's sake at Pepper Craig, and stayed there till about midnight. When he left he was - as far as he can tell - carried to the Gairnetoun Hills he knows not how.

He declares that the first time he met the Devil at the place mentioned, the Devil asked him now he liked being his servant. Hamilton answered that he was content to serve him. The Devil then gave him four shillings sterling, which Hamilton accepted. Then they parted, and Hamilton came back to Peppercraig, he knows not how, and stayed in bed in Peppercraig until eight o'clock in the morning. There was no other meeting or further conversation between them.

A month after that Hamilton was going to Lyntoun Brigis during the day between eleven and twelve, and met with the Devil on Penkraik Hillis in the shape of a black man riding on a black horse. The Devil asked him, "How are you doing now?" and Hamilton answered, "Very well," and at this the Devil rode away from him.

[The next four paragraphs relate how Hamilton was sleeping in an outhouse in Duns when he was wakened by a spirit in the shape of a foal which carried him to a witches' meeting with the Devil at Coldingham Law. He names several people from Duns who were present. After the meeting they all came back to supper in Bessie Sleiche's house in Duns, which was followed by dancing. The Devil appointed them to meet again in the hills to the west of Duns in a fortnight's time.]

Item 4

[This seems to be a continuation of the statements made in the previous document.]

He declares that fourteen days after that all of the six persons already named, along with Hamilton, met as arranged in the hills to the west of Duns Castle. Each one of them asked permission from the Devil to do evil to those persons against whom they bore a grudge or ill-will. Hamilton wished to do evil to the provost of Haddingtoun, Mr James Cockburne. The Devil ordered Hamilton to go to the Provost's barnyards and draw three ears of corn out of his stacks, and then burn them on the Gairnetoun Hillis. Hamilton accordingly did this in the company of James Darling from Hadingtoun, Elspeth Bartie[?] who is now dead, and Catherine Crystell, the wife of a certain [blank] Denholme, all from Hadintoun. He declares that these three, Darling, Bartie, and Cristell, were at the meetings with the Devil in the places previously mentioned. He declares that immediately after he burned the ears of corn at the place mentioned, the Provost had his kiln full of drying corn all burnt up by Hamilton's devilish intervention as described.

After that he met the Devil a second time on Hugstoun Hillis. The Devil was dressed in brown clothes. He cannot remember whether it was in the daytime or at night. He asked power to do evil to Archibald Broun in Hugstoun. The Devil refused because he had already granted that power to three others - Archibald Sharp's wife, a woman in Pikkiltillim, and the third was Amy Sinclair in Bourne Heid. This was to take the goodness ["phisson" - strength, pith, or essence of something] from his corn and goods.

He was asked how he could manage to meet with the Devil so easily when he wanted something from him. He said that when he first agreed with the Devil to be his servant, Hamilton had a baton of fir-wood in his hand. The Devil told him to take the baton and strike the ground with it three times, saying, "Rise, Foul Thief!" It was according to these instructions that he used to raise the Devil whenever he pleased. The Devil would sometimes appear to him in the likeness of a crow, other times like a cat, and at other times in the shape of a dog. When he went away, Hamilton would strike the Devil on the head with the baton, saying, "Go away to hell, Thief!" He declares that he kept the baton till he came to Killene Mure, three miles from Newcastell. On his way to prison in Newcastell they drank in a house there, and Hamilton burned the baton in the fire. When he threw it in the fire the baton gave a loud crack. When those present marvelled at this, Hamilton said to them that it was nothing but the knots in the fir-wood cracking.

He was asked if he had the power of charming. He says he learned it from the Devil. Thome Sanders's wife brought him to Thomas Home in Clarkingtoun Mylne, who had been bewitched by the laying of a blue thread in front of the door where people came out. This was meant for his father James Home. He says that it is usual with all these enchantments, that whoever comes over the thread first, catches the disease. He says this thread was laid there by a vagabond woman who had been struck by James Home when she was begging. She swore to make James Home regret that blow. This woman had died since then. After Hamilton looked at Thomas Home and told him he was bewitched, he said he would come back later and apply something to Thomas to cure him. Hamilton then took the opportunity to raise the Devil and consult him about curing Thomas Home. To do this, he came at night to Clerkingtoun Burne beside the Rottenraw with a cat which he had killed with a stone. He raised Sathan with his baton by striking it three times on the ground under his foot, saying three times, "Arise Foul Thief, in the Devil's name!" The Devil then rose "half out" [of the ground?] in the likeness of a crow, and Hamilton asked him what he should do to cure Thomas Home and put him out of his pain. The Devil's response was to tell Hamilton to buy a quantity of animal-fat oil ["ulie spek"], camomile oil, and heart-fat; mix it all together, and then rub the patient with it. Then when that was done to take a warm cloth and rub him with it, then throw the cloth into a stream so that it would not harm anyone after that. So according to these instructions, Hamilton came to James Home and got five or six shillings sterling from him, then went to Edinburgh and bought the ingredients mentioned, which he mixed and made up, and rubbed over Thomas Home and cured him, without using any words. Then he rubbed him with the warm cloth, which he threw in the mill dam or Clerkington Burn, and it was carried away by the stream.

When he raised the Devil that time, a man called George Harlaw - a tenant of the Laird of Clerkington - and Thomas Sanderson's wife were present along with him, and when he laid the Devil that time he cast down the dead cat. Similarly at other times he was in the habit of casting down a loaf to him. When the Devil arose as a foal, he would cast him a dog. When he rose in the likeness of a cat he gave him nothing, and laid him with his baton as already mentioned.

He declares that after that, Agnes Allain in Saltoun, accompanied by Bessie Sinclare and a woman from Fala whose name he cannot remember called on Hamilton when he was at James [illegible]'s house in Saltoun, and told him that it was necessary for either him or her to kill the young Lady Ormestoun and her daughter. If Hamilton would undertake this he would get a half peck of wheat and a peck of barley. He undertook to do this, and got the barley and wheat, which he sold. After that they all met together at Saltoun Wood with the Devil who appeared to to them in the likeness of a man dressed in grey. He stood in their midst, and the three of them stood round about him more than six ells distant from each other. Then the Devil gave to each of them their particular instructions. Hamilton was to take a ball of blue thread, and lay a piece of thread - part of the ball given to him by the Devil - in front of the gate of Humbie. The women were to speak certain words when the thread was being laid down, but Hamilton did not know what they were, because the Devil whispered them in their ears. Thus, about twelve or one o' clock at night, accompanied by the women, Hamilton came to the gate of Humbie where Lady Ormestoun and her daughter were living at the time. They laid the blue thread in front of the gate, and then they all came away together.

He declares that a short time after that Lady Ormestoun and her daughter died. The reason that he was so willing to assist Agnes Allane in this wicked business was because half a year previously he was asking for some food at the gate of Ormestoun. The young lady was at the gate and said, "Away, you layabout ["custroun carl"; a base fellow], you'll get nothing here!" That is why he put the devilry into practce.

He declares that he went away to Sweden with Captain Diksone, where he remained for two years, and did not come back until a year past St James's Day.

Signed: J. Lolluller[?]. J. Flocker, baillie. Alexander Heryott, baillie.

Item 5.

At Edinburgh, 8th August; in the afternoon, in the presence of My Lord Justice Depute; Alexander Herote, baillie of Edinburgh; Alexander Tod, baillie.

In the afternoon Alexander Hameltoun was re-examined. He was solemnly sworn on his knees to declare the truth and not to conceal it, nor to lie, nor to give false statements against himself or any other person.

He declares that about Martinmas about five years ago Aliesone Carrik; Bessie Hepburne in Haddington; the wife of Andro Banes the "officer" [*i.e.* constable] in Haddington, whose name he cannot remember; Margaret Blak in Samelston; Christiane Bartilman the falconer's wife there; And Andro Allane's wife, whose name he doesn't know, were all in company with Hamilton at a meeting they had with the Devil on the Gairnetounhillis, Andro Allan's wife asked for power from the Devil to do evil to the blacksmith in Samilstoun whose name is Veitche. This was granted, and he pined away till he died through the wicked designs she practised on him. [Hamilton goes on to talk about John Neill from Tweedmouth, and how he had put a dead man's hand in Sir George Home's garden, and a dead foal in his stable. Hamilton claims not to know why this was done. He describes meeting Neill several times coming from Coldingham Law with supplies of food on his back, and says that eventually Neill told him that he had got this from Home's wife. Hamilton is pressed to say whether he ever met Lady Home, and says that her daughter once gave him a handful of beans in Lady Home's presence, and another time gave him a piece of bread, also in Lady Home's presence. He swears he knows nothing more either about John Neill or Lady Home.]

He declares that he had a grudge against the Laird of Colstoun because he banished Hamilton from his land. Hamilton went to a place near the Stob Stane, called Monkrig, where he met the Devil and asked him for power to do evil to Colstoun. The Devil replied that he could not do that because he had already given power to the goodwife of the Stobbestane, [illegible] Wilsone's wife, to do that. However, what she did to Colstoun, Hamilton does not know. [Hamilton then denies ever meeting the Devil or other witches in Berwick. He is then asked if he ever had any dealings concerning witchcraft with Cathareine Wilsone in Duns. He replies that he has received food from her when begging, but has had no conversation with her. However, he thinks he saw her at several witches' meetings. Hamilton says the Devil appeared to him several times when he was in England, and repeats that at their second meeting he renounced his baptism and agreed to serve him. He now craves God's mercy for this, and renounces the Devil.]

Item 6.

Statement of Alexander Hamilton, 30th October 1629.

Hamilton did not turn up at that time, and so because he had not kept the appointment, at the next meeting with him in Gairnetoun Hillis the Devil struck him most violently with a baton. Signed: Thomas Hope. J. Cochrane, baillie. Wm. Reid, baillie. Edward Edgar, baillie.

Item 7.

Edinburgh, 30th October. In the presence of Sir Thomas Hope of Craighall, knight baronet, His Majesty's Advocate; James Cochrane, William Reid, and Edward Edger, baillies of Edinburgh.

Alexander Hameltoun, being sworn, declared that he was born in Salt Preston under Lord Newbottall, and is now sixty years old. He remained in Preston working as a coal miner there and on other gentlemen's lands round about, until around the time of the death of the minister John Davidson 25 years ago or so. During that time he had no meetings with the Devil, but he did keep company with some of the Devil's servants, for example Elspit Crystie and Agnes Thomesone. He long suspected that they were witches, but was not certain until he met them afterwards in the Devil's company.

When he left Preston he and his wife headed towards the Eastern Borders of England and Scotland, at Tweedside, and he left his wife Alesone Edington in Hinklie[?]: which is on Lord Gray's land on the south side of Tweed. Hamilton went on alone to the coal pits of Schoirswoid and worked there for three or four years. Then he worked in the coal pits at Duddo and other places in England, until he was taken by Captain Diksone at the end of Twedismouth bridge, and sent away to the wars. This was about three years ago.

Marginal note: There for twelve years or so. Then when they left the coal pits in England he came and lived in Tweedmouth and remained there. However, because of his poverty he was wandering in Louthiane and Merss for seven years.

He declares that about the beginning of the last two years of these seven years, about 1624 he thinks, at Michaelmas, he was coming out of Nunlands to Hadintoun between eleven and twelve o'clock during the day...

[Hamilton then repeats his story of meeting a man on horseback dressed in black on the hills at Ugston, who recruits him to his service and appoints to meet him in the Garneton Hills a fortnight later. He also solemnly swears to the truth of statements made by him on 8th August. He admits that he was interrogated in private in Duns on 13th July by the sheriff clerk James Mowat. A copy of his statements to Mowat is read, and Hamilton is questioned on each paragraph, particularly about witch meetings in Duns, and about Sir George Home's wife Lady Manderston. He now vehemently denies the truth of what he had previously said about her. He denies that he said Lady Manderston attended witch meetings, consulted with the Devil about killing her husband, or had a dead man's hand put in her husband's garden, or a dead foal put in his stable. Hamilton swears as he shall answer to God that he said no such things, but only declared that he had heard them said by John Neill. He admits that the statements he made to James Mowat in Duns were read out to him, but now claims that he was not paying attention to what was read. He emphasises again that he never claimed to have seen Lady Manderston with the Devil, but only repeated what John Neill had said.]

Asked if he knows any other witches who were familiar with the Devil or had meetings with him, apart from those already mentioned in his previous statements, he declares that Agnes Thomesone in the Pannis, the wife of John Woid, and Elspeth Crystie in Preston met with the Devil when Hamilton was present, in the Links of Preston the year before he went to Sweden. This meeting had been arranged beforehand by the Devil, and Hamilton was told about it by Elspeth Crystie when he was lodging in her house.

Finally, Hamilton claims that two women from Niddrie, along with himself, had a tryst with the Devil at the head of the "Broken Caisay of Nydrie". The Devil appeared as a black man, took the women away for quarter of an hour, then returned to arrange the next meeting on Cauldcot Moor in a fortnight's time. Item 7 appears to break off in the middle of a sentence.]

Item 8.

At Edinburgh 25th November 1629. In the presence of My Lord of Dumblane, the Lord Advocate, and Mr Alexander Colme, Justice Depute.

[Hamilton relates how after his arrest Sir George Home brought him to Berwick and locked him up. A servant of Home's came to him and urged him to say what his master told him to say, for his master was merciful and would help him. Home himself first accused Hamilton of putting a dead man's hand in his garden, then said a woman in Eyemouth told him that someone in Berwick had done it to harm him on his wife's orders. Hamilton continued to deny that he had anything to do with this, so Home had him put in irons. On the way to Duns, Home's servant again tried to persuade him to say what his master wanted him to say. If he did so, his master would be good to him and be a father to his children. Hamilton then promised to do all that was required of him.

He claimed further that Home and James Mowat visited him in the tollbooth in Duns, where Home repeated the promise that his servant had made to Hamilton. The following day he was questioned by Mowat, and admits that he told him "certain things" as he had been asked to do. However, if he said anything about Lady Manderston it was only what he had heard from John Neill.

When Hamilton was brought to Haddington, Sir George Home urged him to stand by the statements he had made in Duns, and repeated his promise to be good to him and to be a father to his children. Home then gave him a shilling, and gave him another three shillings during his imprisonment in Haddington.]

Also, he was asked while solemnly sworn upon his knees if his previous statements about John Hog and his wife were true. He declares on his solemn oath that he abides by his previous statements about being in their company at two meetings with the Devil at the times specified in his statements. This, as he shall answer to God upon the dreadful day of Judgment, upon his salvation or damnation.

Signed: Lord Bishop of Dunblane, witness. Sir Thomas Hope.   A. Colmbe.

At Edinburgh, 8th January 1630, in presence of the Lord Advocate, the Lord Justice Clerk, and Lord Scottistarvet.

After the preceding statements made by him on 25th November were read to him, Alexander Hameltoun was questioned again and sworn. He ratifies and approves every part of these statements as set down.

Signed: [illegible]

Sir Thomas Hope.   Scotistarvit.

At Edinburgh 14th January 1630, in presence of Lord Scottistarvit and Mr Alexander Colme, Justice Depute.

Alexander Hameltoun was sworn in the presence of the examining lords. His statements made on 25th November 1629 were read to him. By his solemn oath given upon his knees, Alexander ratifies these statements in every particular as they are set down, except for the following details. He said that Sir George Home said to him, "Alexander, remember my servant Andro spoke to you? If you keep your promise I'll do you good and be a father to your children." Alexander Hameltoun now denies that Sir George Home said these words to him. When he came to the tollbooth he only said to Hamilton, "Are you there Sandie?" Sir George said this to Hamilton in Duns tollbooth on the Monday evening and did not speak to him again that night.

Item 9.

[On reverse side: "Alexr Hamiltoun 16th Decr 1629   Anent Agnes Allane in Saltoun."]

At Edinburgh 16th December 1629 in the presence of the Lord Advocate and the Lord Justice Depute.

Alexander Hamiltoun was solemnly sworn on his knees in the presence of those above-mentioned. Two women were shown to him; Agnes Allane from Saltoun, and Agnes [blank]. Being solemnly sworn, he was asked if he knew them. He declares that he thinks he has seen [blank] before, but cannot remember if he has seen Agnes Allane before. He was made to come close and have a good look at them. When asked if either of them was Agnes Allane from Saltoun, after again being solemnly sworn on his knees, he said that [blank] was not Agnes Allane because Agnes Allane was not so tall. Asked if the other woman was Agnes Allane, he declares that she is not Agnes Allane, because Agnes Allane had a mark on her cheek which he did not see on this woman. He was asked if he would know Agnes Allane if she were present. He says that he would hardly know her, because he had only ever seen her twice - once in daylight when he got a half peck of wheat and a peck of barley from her in her own house in Saltoun, and the other time was at night, about twelve o' clock.

He was asked how he dared to take upon himself to bear witness against Agnes Allan since he would not know her if she were present. He answered that he could well testify against her, because he saw her at a meeting with the Devil on a bridge between Salton and the Woidheid, and they heard her called by her name, Agnes Allane. He was asked about the mark he claims she had on her face. He says it was reddish in colour under her eyes and near her nose, but cannot tell whether it was on her right or her left cheek.

After that both women were called in separately and presented to Hamilton. He was urged to look and see if the mark was on either of their faces, or if either of them had some small mark on their cheek. Alexander constantly affirmed that without doubt neither of the two was Agnes Allane. He was asked what punishment he would be happy to suffer if one of these two was Agnes Allane. He answered that he was content to be quartered alive, and that all the statements he had made against her should be counted as false, if any of these two women were Agnes Allane. He was asked again if he would know Agnes Allane if she were presented to him. He answered that he believed he would know her. Asked how old Agnes Allane was, he declared that she is middle-aged, about forty or so.

Agnes Allane from Saltoun, solemnly sworn on her knees, denied that she ever saw Alexander Hamiltoun before this time. If it can be proved that she ever saw him in any place whatsoever, apart from in this building, she is content that everything he has said about her should be thought true.

Alexander Hamiltoun was called in again. The truth was declared to him, and he was informed by his interrogators that Agnes Allan, presented to him again, is the very woman in question. He was told to look closely at her face, and then Alexander on his solemn oath declared as he should answer to God that he could not say whether or not it was she who had called him into her house in the middle of the day before eleven o' clock - there is no-one else of that name in Saltoun. The house was almost at the upper end of the village of Saltoun, a little above James Cinquerrour's, on the other side of the road. She had asked Hamilton if he would go with her on a visit, and she would give him half a peck of wheat and a peck of barley. The next day he came to her and she explained that the outing was to the Woidheid to harm the lady there. When he agreed to go with her she gave him the peck of barley and the half peck of wheat. Three or four days later he went with Agnes Allane and Bessie Duncan from Walkerland near Boltoun, to the bridge [or possibly "bog" - "brig" and "boig" can look very similar in secretary hand] between Saltoun and the Woidheid, and met the Devil there. At this meeting Agnes asked the Devil for the gift of the ability to do harm to the younger Lady Ormestoun. This was granted, and the harm followed as related in his previous statements.

Agnes was then confronted with Alexander on the matter of the above statement. On her solemn oath she denied it altogether. She says she never knew him before today when she was confronted with him in this place. Then she was asked if she ever saw any man resembling him in her house. She answered that it was possible, but as she shall answer to God she cannot tell him from any other man who has been in her house.

[On the reverse side of this document, in a different hand, are the notes given below.]

Edinburgh 27th January 1630.

Received by me, Patrick Broune, baillie of Hadingtoun. Statements made by Alexander Hamiltoun, warlock, on 4th December 1629 in the presence of My Lord Bishop of Dunblane and Mr Alexander Colme, Justice Depute; together with the statements of Bessie Duncan, Bessie Lauder, Alesone Carrile, Margaret Mitchell, Katharine Kirktoun, and Agnes Sinclar, who were questioned on the same day, and confronted with Alexander Hamiltoun in the presence of the above interrogators. These statements received by me will be delivered back again to John Balnetyne, depute clerk in the Office of Justiciary, whenever they are asked for.

Signed: Patrick Broune, baillie.

Also received by me from John Bannatyne; Alexander Hamiltoune's statements, together with the statements made by Besie Lauder, Bessie Duncane, Kathrine Creichtoun, Alisoune Carrile, Margaret Mitchell, Katharene Lauder, and Bessie Hepburne, on the basis of which they were confronted with Alexander Hamiltoun. These were made on 23rd September 1629, in the presence of David Alkenheid, provost, and Archibald Tod and Alexander Fernie, baillies of Edinburgh. These statements are required back again when asked for. Received by me, John Thomesone, burgess of Hadingtoun, in the absence of the baillie. They will be delivered back again as instructed above.

Signed: J. Thompson, with my hand.

Item 10.

At Edinburgh 19th January 1630. In the presence of Mr Alexander Colme, Justice Depute. [Hamilton is quizzed about various people in Duns. He declares that he was questioned there by James Mowat, and had never seen him before then. John Smith and Catherine Wilson had plotted with Satan against Mowat for some reason unknown to Hamilton. He repeats the story of a meeting in Bessie Sleich's house, and is ordered to describe John Smith's appearance and Catherine Wilson's domestic circumstances. He mentions again that he has been away to the wars in Sweden for the past two years.]

Item 11.

[This fragment is obviously part of the record of the interrogation of an unnamed woman, perhaps Agnes Allan from Saltoun.]

Also, she was asked if she had ever seen Bessie Duncan in Walkerland. She solemnly swears that she has never seen her and does not know her.

Item 12.

After reading everything in this paper, the Officers of Arms to our Sovereign Lord are to go and summon a jury of honest and steadfast persons to appear before His Majesty's Justice or his deputies in the tollbooth of Edinburgh on 22nd January at the time appointed for the trial. They are to serve on the jury in the trial of the warlock Alexander Hamiltoun, who is accused of various meetings with the Devil and of practising various examples of sorcery and witchcraft for the destruction of several people and their livestock and goods, as specified at length in his indictment. Each person is to be summoned under the penalty of a hundred merks for non-attendance. This document serves as sufficient warrant for you.

Signed with our hands at Edinburgh, 21st January 1630:Thomas Hope. A. Colme.

[A list follows of 34 merchants and tradesmen, all presumably from Edinburgh, except one from "Bruntylland". Fifteen are marked "qt", four are marked "ab", and fifteen have no marks against their names. Those marked "qt" are recorded in Item 14 as those who actually served on the jury.

A note records that they were all personally summoned, before witnesses, on 21st and 22nd January 1630. Another note records the appointment of George Wast as court "officer" and his subsequent swearing in.]

Item 13.

The King's Court of Justiciary held in the tollbooth of Edinburgh 22nd January 1630 by the discreet, honourable, and great man Alexander Colme of Blair, Justice Depute. Court Affirmed.

This day Alexander Hamilton, warlock, was presented for trial by the magistrates of Edinburgh, and brought from their prison where he had been detained since August 1629. He was accused and prosecuted by Mr Robert Burnet and Mr John Oliphant, advocates substitute to Sir Thomas Hoip of Craighall, knight baronet, advocate to our Sovereign Lord for His Highness's interest. He was accused of various charges of sorcery, witchcraft, and consulting with the Devil for destroying various persons and depriving them of ther lives as specified in his indictment and in the statements made by him at Dunce, Hadingtoun, and Edinburgh - these statements were recorded and produced as part of the court process.

Before the election and admission of the jury, and also after the jurors had been elected and admitted, Alexander Hamilton, faced with judgment, in the presence of the judge and jury, on his solemn oath and on his knees, ratified and confirmed the truth of all the statements he had previously made in every article and clause, except what he had declared against Lady Manderstoun. This he affirmed to be altogether untrue. He craves God's mercy for this, and declares that the information about Lady Manderstoun was reported to him by John Neill from Tweidmouth, as recorded in his last statement made at Edinburgh.

Extract from the Book of Adjournal made by Sir George Elphinstons of Blythswood, Justice Clerk.

Witnessed and signed: John Bannatyne.

Item 14.

[On the reverse side: "22nd January 1630. Alexander Hameltoun warlok his dittay and conviction."]

[Hamilton's indictment is given in Item 14 almost word for word as published by the Stair Society. The record then continues in a different hand as given below.]

Court held 22nd January 1630 by Mr Alexander Colme.

Alexander Hamilton, accused of certain crimes of sorcery contained in the preceding indictment.

Prosecutors: Mr Robert Burnet, Mr John Oliphant; substitutes to His Majesty's Advocate.

My Lord Justice asked the accused if he would abide by his previous statements as they are recorded, sworn by him, and signed by the Lords Commissioners who questioned him. He ratifies and approves them in every particular except that part declared by him against Lady Manderstoun, which is altogether untrue. He craves God's mercy for it on his knees, and says the information was reported to him by John Neill from Tweidmouth, as his last statement made at Edinburgh records.

The accused confesses all the charges of the indictment to be true. The advocates asked for a written record of this.

The Jury;

John Couper, Robert Burne, Robert Wilsone, Mungo Hunter, James Steill, Hew Wallace, Thomas Ireland, William Mayne, John Fegusson, Patrick Smeitoun, Robert Reid, John Ritchie, Thomas Armestrang, Barnard Shaw, David Reyming.

He declares as he shall answer to God that all the statements made by him, either in Dunce, Hadingtoun, Edinburgh, or elsewhere, were declared by him without the information being suggested, and without being ordered by any other person. He solemnly swears it to be what he saw and heard, and has declared of his own accord, without being induced to do so by anyone, except what he heard from John Neill.

He also ratifies the statements made by him against John Hog and his wife in Merkill as they are set down. He has not been induced or persuaded to make any statement for or against them, as he shall answer to the great God. Andro Quhyte then asked for a written record of this.

Andro Fraser spoke to him in at the [illegible], saying, "Sandie, speak the truth. Don't lie about anyone, and my master will do you good, for he is a compassionate man."

He says Sir George never said a word to him, except to tell him to make a true confession and tell the truth.

[The next paragraph is identical to Item 13. He exonerates Lady Manderston, then continues as given below.]

Also, humbled and prostrate upon his knees as described, he declared that all these statements made by him were made and recorded from his own certain knowledge without being suggested to him, or the information supplied to him or requested from him at the command of any person whatsoever. All this is declared, with the previously mentioned exceptions, particularly that Sir George Home of Manderston never said anything to him, but only to come to a true confession and declaration of the truth. Also that Home's servant Andro Fraser who brought Hamilton from Beruick to Dunce said nothing either in Beruick or on the way to Dunce, except to tell him to tell the truth about what he knew, saying, "Alexander, if you do so my master will do you good, for he is a compassionate man."

At this, Sir George Home, who was himself present, asked for a written record, asking that these points might be recorded and remain in the record, and a copy made for him.

[It might be thought that there is something fishy about the great emphasis placed on having Hamilton swear that Home of Manderston had not put words in his mouth. It smacks a little of protesting too much.

The women denounced by Hamilton were referred to the Presbytery of Haddington for further questioning - see "Trial by Commission". However there seems to be no record of this ever actually happening, and there is certainly no record of any of them ever standing trial for witchcraft. As previously mentioned, neither were any charges brought against John Hog and his wife from Markle. This would suggest that the authorities basically regarded Hamilton's statements as a pack of lies. Unfortunately for him, however, they seem to have found it expedient to believe what he testified against himself!]

1649

The case of Jean Craig in Tranent.

[The case of Jean Craig, as recorded in the Books of Adjournal Vol JC2/8, was published by the Stair Society in *Selected Justiciary Cases 1624 - 1650*, Vol iii, Ed. J. Irvine Smith, Edinburgh 1974. As with previous cases, I have put the original text into modern English.]

Tranent, 27th April 1649. Judges: Colvill and Robertoun.

Jean Craig in Tranent. Convicted and burnt for witchcraft and murder.

Accused: Jean Craig, wife of William Steill, coalminer in Tranent.

Accused of contravening the Acts of Parliament made against committing sorcery and witchcraft, particularly the 73rd Act of the 9th Parliament of Queen Mary 1563, forbidding any person or persons from using any manner of witchcraft, sorcery, or necromancy, or to advertise themselves as having any such skill or knowledge in order to abuse the people. Forbidding them also from seeking any help, response, or consultation from any such practicioners or abusers under pain of death, as is contained at length in the said Act. In cotravention of this Act of Parliament, for many years Jean Craig employed sorcery and witchcraft, by the advice and counsel of her lord and master the Devil, with whom she was familiar at all times. She kept trysts and meetings with him and with her mother Beigis Wallace.

Twenty two years ago her sister in law Agnis Steill was pregnant and near to giving birth. Jean earnestly begged Agnes for the gift of the child she was expecting. After Agnes Steill had given birth to the child, in order to destroy it by her sorcery and witchcraft, Jean rubbed and stroked it with three enchanted stones which she got from her mother Beigis Wallace. As a result of being rubbed with these three enchanted stones the child afterwards died by Jean's sorcery and witchcraft, and was thus cruelly murdered and slain by Jean's sorcery and witchcraft.

2. Accused of laying a fearful sickness on Beatrix Sandilandis, wife of John Parkie in Tranent, by her sorcery and witchcraft. This was laid on Beatrix about twelve years ago, and caused her to become mad and bereft of her natural wits. As a result of this madness laid upon Beatrix by Jeane's sorcery and witchcraft, she was bereft of her natural life.

3. She is accused that because she had a deadly hatred against James Smyth in Little Fawsyd, she came early in the morning to his byre in Littlefawsyd, and walked through the byre where his oxen and cows were. By the sorcery and witchcraft laid by her on the cows and oxen, she took away the milk from the cows so that they gave nothing but blood after that instead of milk. His oxen immediately ran mad, and the herd boy who looked after them, who had also been in the byre and had seen her there, died by her sorcery and witchcraft, or at least was never seen again.

4. Also, early one morning shortly after that, continuing in the malice she had previously borne against James Smyth, she met an employee of his, leading out six of James's horses. She greeted him with these wicked words, "What the Devil are you doing, man, up so early in the morning?" Crossing his path, Jean laid her sorcery and witchcraft on three of his horses so that presently they dropped dead. The other three horses and the manservant himself died shortly afterwards as a result of her sorcery and witchcraft laid upon them.

5. Finally, she is accused of being a common sorcerer and witch, of keeping trysts and meetings with other witches, including Beigis Wallace her mother, a notorious witch; also Margaret Mathiesone and Jonet Reid, both witches convicted and burnt for witchcraft at Preston Panes. She is accused of seeking advice from the Devil on how to be avenged on various people by witchcraft - particularly Beatrix Sandilands, making her go mad as described. She is accused of becoming the Devil's servant and of receiving his mark. He appeared to her in several different shapes. The first time was in Penstoun in the Laird's kitchen in the form of a cat. Another time the Devil appeared in her own house in the likeness of a man, where he had sex with her, and made her renounce her baptism and become his servant. This was all confessed by her to be true, today the 27th of April, in the presence of the minister of Tranent,

and various reliable witnesses specified at length in her indictment and the various charges contained in it quoted above.

Prosecutor: George Ramsay, son of the late Mr Symone Ramsay of Quhythill, substitute to Mr Thomas Nicolsone, His Majesty's Advocate for His Highness's interest, as appointed in the letter sealed with his hand dated 26th April 1649.

After reading the indictment with ite various charges, the judge found it relevant, and referred the proving of the facts and deeds in it to a jury composed of the following lawfully summoned persons:

    Archibald Purves in Tranent
    James Allane in Wintoun
    Peter Wylie there
    Robert Heriot in Langnidrie
    John Craig there
    James Carfra in Wintoun
    Ritchard Trumble there
    Patrik Spence in Prestoun Panes
    James Congletoun in Langnidrie
    John Reid there
    Ritchard Waddell in Seatoun
    James Affleck there
    Adame Waddell there
    Hectour Wood there
    Robert Qilmour there

These members of the jury found, pronounced, and declared Jean Craig to be guilty, culpable, and convicted of all the various crimes of sorcery and witchcraft specified and contained in her indictment. For this reason, by the mouth of Mark Broustene the dempster of court, the judge decreed and ordained that Jean Craig should be taken next Tuesday, the first day of May 1649, to her place of execution, that is, the Murebrow. There she is first to be strangled at a stake until she is dead, and her body thereafter is to be burned to ashes. All moveable goods belonging to her are to be forfeited and collected for the use of our Sovereign Lord since she has been convicted of the crimes specified. This was pronounced as sentence. [The Stair Society's editor J. Irvine Smith has summarised the part dealing with the jury's deliberations and the sentencing of the accused as it appears in the Books of Adjournal.]

[Jean Craig's supposed activities and the investigations into them can be found in much greater detail among the *Justiciary Court Processes* in the National Archives of Scotland. Box JC26/13 contains a bundle comprising 12 items dealing with Jean's case.

Item 1 seems to be a draft indictment, it is much longer and more detailed than the list of charges recorded in the Books of Adjournal and printed by the Stair Society. Thus, Item 1 may be a draft indictment subsequently abandoned in favour of something more concise and believable, or it may be that Item 1 was indeed the indictment read at the trial, and that it was subsequently summarised for the records.

Item 1 begins with a typical lengthy preamble detailing the secular and divine laws which Jean has broken. Such introductions are all pretty much par for the course, and I have therefore omitted it here.]

Item 1.

1. ... Jean Craig has for many years past, by sorcery and witchcraft, and with the advice and counsel of her lord and master the Devil, laid on and taken off various horrible diseases and sicknesses from many of our Sovereign Lord's good people and subjects, and also their livestock and goods. Namely, [blank] years ago or thereabouts you conceived a devilish hatred and malice against the late James Wilson, the husband of Helen Cowane who is now married to John Naper in [blank]. Also against the late James Bradie in Elphinstoun, and against the late Johne Crawfurd in Tranent; also against the late William Ekfurd there. After consulting with your master the Devil, by your sorcery and witchcraft you laid on James Wilsone, James

Bradie, John Craufurd and the late William Eckfurd, various fearful sicknesses and diseases from which they all died, and were thus in fact murdered by the sorcery and witchcraft you laid on them. This is well known to their neighbours and all the people in the district where you were living, which you cannot deny.

2. You are accused of continual devilish consultation with your mother Beigis Wallace, a notorious witch who was burnt for witchcraft in Prestoun Pannis about 22 years ago. In particular, in connection with your constant involvement with your mother Beigis Wallace, you solicited and begged night and day for the gift of a baby boy which your sister [sic] Agnes Steill was then carrying, and about to give birth to. Your intention was that as soon as this child came into the world, you would offer him to your lord and master the Devil. Beigis confessed this to be true shortly before she was burnt at Prestounpannes. Thus, after your sister in law Agnes Steill had been delivered of this child, in order to destroy him by your sorcery and witchcraft you rubbed and stroked him with three little enchanted stones all over his joints and various parts of his body. You had obtained these stones from your mother Beigis Wallace. After you had rubbed and stroked the child over and over at various times with the three devilish enchanted stones you got from your mother, the child wasted and pined away by your sorcery and witchcraft day by day till he died. Thus the child was cruelly slain and murdered by your sorcery and witchcraft, which is notoriously well known. All the time after Agnes Steill had given birth to the child, you continually frequented the house, and declared to Agnes that you knew the child was not hers, but your lord's. By this you meant your master the Devil. You said nothing would benefit him but foxglove leaves and south-running water. You promised to get these and apply them to him, but never did so.

3. After the bewitching and death of this child caused by your sorcery and witchcraft as described, your sister in law Agnes Steill gave birth to six children. Bearing a secret grudge and malice against her, by your sorcery and witchcraft you caused her milk to vanish away altogether from her breasts, so that she never had any milk to nourish any of them. Finally, still continuing in your cruel hatred and malice against Agnes Steill, her husband, and children; by the sorcery and witchcraft you practised against them, you made various fearful sights appear on several nights in their house. Namely, you caused great numbers of ugly beasts like pups to appear. As a result of these ugly beasts running every night around a "knocking stane" [a hollowed-out stone in which meal was pounded] which was standing in their house, Agnes Steill's husband and son contracted fearful sicknesses and diseases, which were laid upon them by your sorcery and witchcraft. As a result they wasted and pined away in great anguish and pain, and in the end died. Thus they were both murdered and slain by your sorcery and witchcraft, which you cannot deny.

4. You, Jeane Craig, are also accused of having conceived a deadly hatred and ill-will against John Parkie in Tranent, and his wife Beatrix Sandilandis. In the month of [blank] in the year 1637[?] or thereabouts, you came to their house, and after some devilish things had been said by you against Beatrix Sandilandis, by your malicious devilish sorcery and witchcraft, you blew on her face with great violence. By the devilish blast blowing on her face, and by the horrible and devilish words you uttered against her, Beatrix immediately became mad and bereft of her wits, so that four or five strong men were not able to hold her. This was done by your devilry and witchcraft which you laid on her. Shortly after that, still persevering in your devilish malice, you came to John Parkie's house under silence of night, with some devilish

enchanted animal like a cat on your staff. You stayed in the house all night, and went to the fire and roasted this ugly enchanted beast. Then by the sorcery and witchcraft you practised in John Parkie's house, you caused a great number of ugly cats, or rather devils in their likeness, to come dancing and leaping in about John Parkie's fire. At this, to rid himself of that horrible and fearful sight, John picked up a rope to chase them away. All the cats in the house then went out at a hole near the chimney. When they went away out through the hole, the last one turned and cried out with a clearly heard voice and words, "Hey! What's wrong with Beatie now?" All this time Beatie Sandilandis, on whom you Jean Craig had blown in your devilish manner, was lying bound hand and foot because of the devilish madness you had laid on her as described. Also, by the devilry and witchcraft you practised in John Parkie's house, you threw down and scattered all over the house, several ugly lumps of red raw flesh with horrible red blood. To everybody who looked at it, it seemed that everything was swimming in flesh and blood. You were never satisfied until you had bereft Beatrix Sandilands of her natural life by your sorcery and witchcraft. She was tormented with continual fevers and horrible pain wherever she went. Yes, in the end by your sorcery and witchcraft you bereft her of her life in the very coal pit itself. This is notoriously well known to the whole parish of Tranent, and to the country people round about.

5. You conceived a deady malice and evil intent against the late John Craufurd in Tranent, who was most fearfully bewitched and bereft of his life by your sorcery and witchcraft as previously described. At the hour of his death he affirmed in the presence of several reliable witnesses, including Mr Robert Balcanquill the minister, that this was true, and blamed you for being the sole cause of his death. You also continued your ill will against his brother Thomas Crawford because of some argument and disagreement between him and your husband William Steill. In revenge you laid a serious illness on Thomas Crauford's son by your sorcery and witchcraft, so that he lost all power in both legs, and he has been unable to walk ever since.

6. You, Jean Craig, are also accused of conceiving a deadly hatred and malice against James Cowan, a miner in Tranent, because of some angry words that passed between this James Cowan and your husband William Steill about a year before that. You took revenge for this by your sorcery and witchcraft, under the orders and with the advice of Agnes Affleck, one of your fellow students of devilry, this Nans Affleck says that one night James Cowan was so vexed and troubled in various parts of his body, especially his face, that the blood sprang out of it in great abundance. Every night since then, by the sorcery and witchcraft you laid on him, he is so bereft of his natural wits that he has lost the power and ability to control himself. By your sorcery and incantation he is weak in mind, and compelled whether he likes it or not to tear and rend himself, particularly in the face, until he draws blood in great quantities. Also, by your devilish sorcery and witchcraft this James Cowan is terrified every night by your appearing at his fireside, at his bedside, and in his bed. When he should be sleeping he is hurled out of bed, and pulled and tumbled up and down the floor by wicked spirits which come running out from under his bed in great numbers like ugly black dogs. Because of these and other fearful apparitions James Cowan can often be seen crawling under beds and hiding in holes here and there. Sometimes he will climb on the bed-heads and hide himself between the ceiling and the joists and beams of his house. This is well known and has been seen by his neighbours. Finally, since you were put in prison you have continued in your malicious hatred and evil intent towards James Cowan. By the

sorcery and witchcraft practised by you, and by others who were your associates on your orders, when James Cowan's son John was working in the coal pit he broke his leg there. This was done by your devilish witchcraft. Afterwards he was carried home to the house of his father James Cowan. Some relatives of John Cowan's came to visit you in prison, got into various topics of conversation with you, and finally mentioned the injury received by John Cowan who broke his leg in the coal pit. You immediately asked him what way John Cowane was carried home to his father's house. You were told that after he broke his leg he was carried home and carried through Patrick Craig's house to his father's house. On hearing this account of how he was brought home, you said to this Patrick Craig who was one of those who had come to visit you in prison, "He was taken through your house?"

"Yes indeed Jean," said Patrick, "the youth was carried through my house."

"That's a pity," you replied.

"Why's that, Jean?" said Patrick.

"That's for me to know," you answered him. "I'd rather he'd been carried through Catherine Smith's house." [This is a summary and personal interpretation of a rather difficult passage in the original text.] This conversation will be proved and verified by Patrick Craig, James Craufurd, and William Johnstoun.

In all this you have revealed yourself quite happy with the fearful witchcraft practised by you against James Cowan and his son John Cowane. You are an obvious sorcerer and witch, familiar with the Devil, and acted for their destruction as the Devil's student and servant

7. You, Jean Craig, are also accused of having conceived a deady hatred and ill will against James Smith in Littil Fawsyde. Several years ago, you did all you could by your sorcery and witchcraft to destroy him, his cattle, and his goods, and bring him to extreme poverty. Namely, in the month of [blank] in the year [blank], seeing this James Smith's cows and oxen standing in his byre, you combed the hair of your head, and by doing this, after you had walked through the oxen and cows, by your sorcery and witchcraft you took all the milk from all the cows, so that when they were milked nothing but blood came from them instead of milk. Immediately after this, all the oxen ran mad, and the boy that kept them and looked after the oxen and cows, and had seen you in the byre that morning, shortly afterwards he dropped dead by your sorcery and witchcraft. So by your sorcery, witchcraft, and particular actions, you were art and part in his death, and in the bewitching of the oxen and cows as described.

Also shortly after that you met a servant man of James Smith's in Littel Fawsyde early in the morning He was leading six horses belonging to his master. You greeted him with these wicked words, "What the devil are you doing up so early in the morning, man?" By your devilish sorcery and witchcraft you cursed the man with the horses so that shortly afterwards three of the horses dropped dead and never ate grass again. The man himself and the other three horses also died not long after by your sorcery and witchcraft. You were the particular cause of this man's death and destruction by the devilish and unlawful means of your sorcery and witchcraft.

Finally you are indicted and accused as a common witch and sorcerer, associating and keeping familiar company with your lord and master the devil, and with several witches who were his servants, especially your mother Beigis Wallace and other notorious witches. For her devilry and witchcraft Beigis Wallace was tried, convicted, and burnt for witchcraft at Prestonpans. Before her death she declared that you were the sole cause and instrument of the death of Nans Steill your sister in law's child, as previously described. You have excercised this devilish trade of sorcery for the past twelve years, and for that reason you ought to be punished with death, in accordance with the laws of Almighty God, and the Acts of Parliament of this kingdom, as an example to strike terror into others.

Item 3.

[This is a letter to the minister of Tranent from the baron baillie of Penston, who was the brother of the laird, Baillie of Lamington. It is addressed on the reverse side, "For the right reverant in ye Lord Mr Rot Mackanquell minister of god's word at Tranent."]

Right Reverend Sir,

I got a letter from Tranent from some of your people there, asking me to let you know about the behaviour of William Steill's wife Jean Craige. To tell the truth, she had a very bad reputation, for she kept company with witches, for example Margrat Mathiesone and Janet Reid who were both burnt at Prestoune. Jean Craige kept company with Margrat Mathieson for a long time till I put her away out of Penstoun. One incident I remember involving Jean Craig concerned a poor man, one of our coal miners, and as far as I remember his wife was called Beatrix Sandilands, a Tranent woman. She and Jean fell out at our coal pit in Penstoune. She alleged that Jean Craig blew in her face, and in fact the woman went mad, so that four or five of us could scarcely hold her. The women told me that Jean Craig had blown in her face. They all said she had shouted some words at her, which as far as I remember were that she would see a black sight of her. When I was told that, I sent for her, and at first she refused to come. I sent for her again, and ordered her husband to bring her, which he did. I discussed the matter with her, and she certainly did not deny the words that the poor woman accused her of speaking. I made her get down on her knees and ask for the poor woman's forgiveness. I told her that if the woman continued [in ill health] any longer I would question her further. In fact after that the woman became fairly well and recovered, so that was the end of that business. When my brother arrived I told him about it, and he gave orders to evict them, which I did. Most of the laird's tenants knew all this was true. Thomas Rentoune, and Alexander Baillie and his son of the same name know this to be true, and I am informed that John Parkie himself is still living, and will declare that it is true. I have no further information at present.

Wishing you and yours all health and happiness, I remain

Your affectionate friend

[Illegible] Baillie.

John Dicksone in Penstone knows this to be true, for the victims lived in a house belonging to him.

[The statements and confession which follow also appear in Item 3, written on the page facing the preceding letter.]

At Tranent 31st March 1649.

Alexander Baillie senior in Penstone testified and bore witness that he knew the aforementioned Beatrix Sandilands, and having recovered a little she finally died, but how and in what circumstances he did not know.

The same day Johne Diksone in Penstoune testified as Alexander Baillie did.

The same day Alexander Baillie junior declared that at the very time that the poor woman Beatrix Sandilands became mad, she said quite clearly to him that Jean Craig blew in her face. This he declared upon his salvation and damnation.

Also the same day James Winla in Penstoun declared that he heard the woman say many a time that Jean Craig had blown in her face, and that he heard Jean Craig say that one of these days she would see a black sight of Beatrix Sandilands. Also that he heard after that… [This statement is broken off here.]

On the morning of April 2nd before the minister of Tranent and the baron baillie Mr

James Painson[?], Jean Craig confessed that she was acquainted with Margaret Mathesone and Janet Rid ... [illegible]. She also confessed that she fell out with Beatrix Sandilands, and that she asked Beatrix Sandilands' forgiveness for the ill she had done her.

[The next paragraph is in a miniscule cramped hand, much of which I found illegible.]

Confession

Jean Craige confessed herself to be a witch and asked God's pardon for the sin of witchcraft. She was asked how she came to be the Devil's servant, and says...[illegible]... to her in Penstoun and enticed her ...[illegible]. Asked how the Devil appeared to her she answered, "In the likeness of a cat." ... [illegible]...from the Devil and what he gave her, she answered that with a piece of coal or anything, and saying these words, "A black sight upon that face." When she said these words to Beatrix Sandilands she went mad. She also confessed the words spoken to James Smith, servant in Little Fawside, and that the Devil had...[illegible]... with her many times.

Item 4.

Thomas Crauford etc. in Tranent.

[In more ordinary times this would have been an application to the Privy Council for a commission to try the suspect. However, in the fraught political conditions of 1649 the Privy Council was not sitting, so the request was directed to the Committee of Estates to allow the High Court of Justiciary to sit in Tranent.]

To the lords and other members of the Committee of Estates.

Your lordships' servants Thomas Crawford, John Parkie, John Naper, James Cowan in Tranent, and James Smith in Little Fawside humbly inform you that we and several others in the area have been seriously wronged by Jean Craig, a notorious witch who has been accused and questioned before the Presbytery of Haddington on many grave and execrable charges of witchcraft. Our case will be supported by the accusations produced before the Presbytery, and will be made clear by further investigation.

Since there is at present no quorum of the Privy Council, we humbly request that your lordships would be pleased to recommend and grant commission to His Majesty's Justice Deputes to go to the place where these crimes and acts of evil intent were commited, and with the assistance of such gentlemen in the area as they think fit, to investigate these charges and administer justice upon the accused, and inflict upon her such suitable punishment as she shall deserve.

20th April 1649.

[Then in a different hand:]

The Committee of Estates duly give warrant to His Majesty's Justice Deputes to go to the place and administer justice as requested.

[Signed with two illegible signatures.]

Item 5.

This is from Mr Thomas Nicollson, Advocate to our Sovereign Lord, to inform everyone that Jean Craig, wife of William Steill in Tranent, has been accused of several charges of sorcery and witchcraft committed by her against various people, subjects of His Majesty, specified in her indictment. She has been charged and will be tried and prosecuted before His Majesty's Justice Deputes in the tollbooth of Tranent next Friday, 27th April. George Ramsay is therefore created and constituted my depute in that district, with full power committed and granted to him on my express instructions to appear in this court of justice to deputise for me, His Majesty's Advocate, on the day and at the place appointed. He is to prosecute Jean Craig on my behalf and in my name for the crimes specified in her indictment, and to do everything necessary for her trial and her prosecution for the foresaid crimes. I shall back up his actions as if I had been present myself; in confirmation of which I have signed this with my hand at Edinburgh 26th April 1649 before these witnesses:

James Chalmers [illegible] of the witnesses, and my employee James Douglas.

Signed: Thomas Nicolson.

J. Chaimers, witness.

Ja. Douglas, witness.

Item 6.

[This is a list of accusations against Jean, with supporting evidence and a so-called "confession", sent to the Presbytery of Haddington to be certified as sufficient grounds for seeking a prosecution.]

Accusations against Jean Craig, wife of William Steel in Tranent.

Firstly Jean Craig is accused by John Naper and his wife Heline Couane of causing the death of James Wilson, Heline's first husband. Also, the death of James Braidie in Elphingston, John Crafoord in Tranent and William Eskfoord there.

2. Jean Craig is accused by her own sister in law Agnes Steill of never allowing her mother Beigis Wallace respite from continually asking her and begging her night and day for the gift of a child which at that time was in Agnes's belly and as yet unborn. This was so that Jean Craig might give it to her lord as soon as it came into the world. Beigis confessed this to be true a little before she was burnt at Prestonpans.

3. Jean Craig is accused by Agnes Steill that after the child was born she touched and rubbed all the joints and parts of his body with three little stones which she had obtained from her mother Beigis. After this touching and rubbing the child wasted and pined away day by day till he died.

4. Agnes Steill on her solemn oath and with tears declared that one time Jean Craig had told her that she knew well the child was not hers, but her lord's. Nothing would help him but foxglove leaves and south-running water. She promised to get these, but did not. Also, after Agnes bore the child, she had not a drop of milk for him.

5. On several nights Agnes and her husband had a great number of black ugly beasts like little pups going round the knocking-stone that stood in her house. After these terrible sights, her husband and son were terrified, and both of them pined away and finally died after a long and lingering sickness.

6. Jean Craig is accused by John Parkie of many instances of witchcraft. Firstly of blowing in his wife's face, and uttering some devilish words so that she became so mad that four or five strong men were not able to hold her.

7. Jeane is accused of entering John Parkie's house at night, and putting on her staff some ugly thing like a cat, which she roasted at the poor man's fire all that night.

8. Jeane is accused of making a number of cats skip and trip round about John Parkie's fireside. At this horrible sight he found himself taking up a stick to make himself chase them away. As the cats went out at a hole near the chimney, the last turned his head round and cried, "Aye, what's wrong with Beatie now?" Meantime the poor man's wife Beattie Sandilands, on whose face Jeane Craig had blown, was lying bound hand and foot because of her madness.

9. Jean Craig is accused of laying ugly lumps of red raw flesh everywhere in John Parkie's house, and sprinkling so much blood on the ground and all the floors there, that to everybody who saw it, the house seemed to be swimming with flesh and blood.

10. The devilish malice of Jean Craig never left this poor man John Parkie until by her devilries she had killed his wife Beatrix Sandilands in the very coal pit itself, without either mark or wound, as many people in Tranent parish can testify.

11. Jean Craig is accused by Tomas Crawfoord of killing his brother John Crawfoord, who at

his last hour blamed his death on Jean Craige, Mr Robert Balcanquell being the only witness. Also, when this Thomas fell out one day with William Steal her husband, all power to stand or walk was then taken away from his son's legs, and ever since then he has had no strength or power in them.

12. Jeane Craig is accused by James Cowan, that one night after exchanging some words with her husband, he suddenly began bleeding. Since then, every night whether he likes it or not, like someone unable to control himself, he is forced to tear and rend himself till he bleeds, particularly in his face.

13. Jeane Craig is also accused by James Cowan of appearing in his house, in his bed, at his fireside; and indeed when he should be resting he is tumbled and dragged up and down the floor. She is also accused of causing numbers of evil spirits like ugly black dogs to run out from under his bed and run about his house. At these and similar fearful sights James Cowan is often seen to crawl in under beds, hide in holes here and there, and sometimes climb up on bed-heads, as neighbours who have seen it can testify.

14. Jean Craig is accused by James Cowan of saying certain things since she was imprisoned. James Cowan has a son named John Cowan who recently broke his leg in the coal pit. He was carried home to his father's house through Patrick Craig's. When Jean Craig heard this she demended of Patrick when he came to visit her, "What, man? The youth John Cowan was carried home? What way?" Patrick said, "Indeed, Jean, he was carried through my house." "I'm sorry to hear that," she said. "Why is that, Jean?" he asked. "That's for me to know," she replied. "I'd rather he had come through Catherine Smith's!" Patrick Craig, James Crawfoord, and William Johnson can testify to this.

15. Jean Craig is accused by Jeams Smith in Little Fasyde of having been seen one morning in his byre amongst his cows and oxen combing her hair. After that his cows gave blood instead of milk, and the oxen went mad. The boy who looked after them, who had seen her, died shortly after that.

16. Very early in the morning, Jean Craig met with a servant of James Smith's, and greeted him with these words, "What the Devil are you doing up so early in the morning?" Jean crossed the road the man was on with the last three horses. They never cropped grass again, but died, and so did the man not long after that. The three horses in front also died a few days later.

Statements.

Saturday 31st March 1649 in the tollbooth of Tranent, before the minister, the elders, and many honest men of the town, Alexander Baillie junior from Penstoun appeared. He was solemnly sworn, and bore witness that Beatie Sandilands said to him that she was driven mad at the exact time that Jean Craig had blown in her face.

James Winlay in Penstoun on his solemn oath also declared that he had heard Beatie say many times that Jean Craig had blown on her face. He also said that he had heard Jean Craig herself say that she would see a "black sight" on Beatie Sandilands within a week, which happened accordingly.

Libra Smithsone[?], a former servant woman to James Smith, declared on oath that she knew that her master's cows had given nothing but blood instead of milk, his oxen had gone mad, and his horses had dropped dead. His two manservants who looked after them were never well from the morning they saw her till they died.

10th April: Jean Cockburn, the Laird of Butterdane's sister, testifies and declares that Jean Craig came one day through her house in Prestoun [Penstoun?], took her by the wrists muttering some words, and she became so mad and disturbed that for many days after that she was not herself, and is not herself even to this day, as is well known to her neighbours, and as is witnessed by her brother and signed by herself.

Jean Craig's confession, taken 31st March 1649.

Firstly, she confessed before the ministers of Tranent and Pans, and before Mr James Ramsay the baron baillie, the elders, and many other honest men of the town, that she had known Margaret Mathesone and Jonet Rid who were both burnt as notorious witches. This is confirmed by a letter from the Laird of Lamintoun's brother, and Mr Balcanquell. She confessed that Beattie Sandilands in Penston had angered her one day, for which she had angered Beattie worse. On the orders of the Laird of Lamintone's brother she had fallen on her knees and asked Beatie's forgiveness for the wrong she had done her, and after that the woman had got a bit better. She admitted that when she lived beside him she knew James Smith had cows that gave blood, oxen that went mad, and horses that dropped dead, and that the man who looked after them was in ill health. However, she was not to blame for that.

At Hadington, April 11th 1649.

Having heard the above accusations, depositions, and confessions today, the bretheren of Hadintoun [Presbytery] think it necessary for the parties pursuing the prosecution to apply to His Majesty's Privy Council, or whoever is responsible, for a commission to sit and try the case against Jean Craig and pass judgment according to law.

Signed: J. Makghie, clerk.

Item 7a

[This seems to be a brief scribbled note of the jury's verdict on each point of the indictment.]

1. Assise clenges her of the first, 3d, and fylles of... [illegible].
2. Fylled
4. fyled
6 clenges of ye 6t art.
7. fyllis
8. fyllrt
10. fyllit

[In other words, Jean had been found guilty of the 2nd, 4th, 7th, 8th, and 10th charges of the indictment..]

Item 7b.

[This is a small piece of paper containing what appear to be closely written scribbled comments on the case. I found it almost completely illegible.]

Item 8.

[This contains brief scribbled notes on the verdict reached on each point of the indictment. It is very difficult to read.]

Item 10.

[Similar almost illegible notes on the 9th point of dittay.]

Item 13.

[Items 9, 10, and 11 appear to be missing. Item 13 is written in a very clear italic hand. It is almost word for word the same as Item 6, detailing the charges, the witnesses' statements, Jean's "confession", and the Presbytery's endorsment.]

[All the preceding items from Box JC26/13 dealing with Jean Craig are tied together in a bundle. However, there is a separate envelope labeled "Ex JC26/13 Bundle B 2 docs. These have been extracted from Bundle B for conservation."]

Document 1. is bady damaged but has been restored. The handwriting is poor. It is a list of Jean Craig's jurors, followed by notes of witnesses' statements.]

Document 1.   The Jury.
And. Hunter[?] in Tranent
Peter Wylie there
John Craig there
Ritchard Tinble[?] there
James Congltoun in Longnidrie

The Tranent witch Jean Craig was accused of bewitching cattle and horses belonging to James Smith in Little Fawside, near Fawside Castle (above). The cows gave blood instead of milk, the oxen ran mad, and the horses dropped dead.

According to Marion Logan, witches from Tranent and Prestonpans danced to the tune "Kilt thy coat Maggie and go thy ways with me" at a meeting at the Windmill on Preston Links. Cockenzie Power Station now occupies this site.

Ritchard Wadell in Seaton
Adame Wadell in Seatoun
James Alane in Wintoun
James Carfra in Wintoun
Patrick Spence in Prestounpans
John Read there
[damage] Fleck there
[damage] Wood there
The Accusers.

Thomas Crawfoord in Tranent. Sworn on Part 2 of Article 5.

Helena Cowane [deleted]

John [illegible] her husband.

Agnes Steill was sworn on the indictment and the malefice done to her husband and son. Also on Article 3... [illegible]...also the articles.

John Parkie swears Article 4 is true, concerning the malifice done to his wife.

Witnesses:

James Winla, living under the Laird of Lamington, was sworn, and declares he saw raw flesh in the house. Declares that he heard the accused promise that a black sight would come upon Beatrix Sandilands within a week. This accordingly happened, but he connot tell if the accused... [damage].

Alexander Bailzie, senior, living in Penstoun under the Laird of Lamingtoun. He was sworn and declares he saw Betie Sandilans go mad. But he does not know who caused her to go mad, or how she came by her madness.

John Dicksone, living in Penstoun under the Laird of Lamingtoun. He was sworn, and declares that Betie Sandilandis went mad, but does not know how she came by it. However, Betie Sandilands blames the accused for her madness.

Jeane Smith, living in Penstoun. She was sworn and declares that she knows nothing about the bewitching of Agnes Steill's child. She says she only saw her come... [The rest of this paragraph is so badly damaged as to be almost incomprehesible. However, the witness seems to be saying that she could not swear that Jean Craig was the cause of the child's death.]

Janet Smith in Litle Fawsyde: [This is damaged in places and illegible in others.] Declares that Jean Craig by her witchcraft ... the oxen went mad and the cows gave blood after that instead of milk. She declares that she spoke to the boy, saying ... the boy was never seen again, and could never be found, although he was born in the Pans ... went away from the witness to the Pannes by ... bed and thinks the boy was killed by her witchcraft.

Libra [illegible - Smithsone?], widow in Tranent. She was sworn, and declares that she milked the cattle that gave blood that day. The oxen were [illegible] for their sickness, and the horses died when they were coming from the plough that night The herd boy ran away and was never seen again. That boy never throve again, but begged and died ...[illegible]

James Cowane in Tranent was sworn and declares... [illegible]

Cristiane Mertoune was sworn and declares ... [illegible] ... three or four nights after her husband that the ... [damage]... she saw Jean Craig sit behind... [damage]... the bed.

Jeane Cokburne was swom, and declares that she was not well before Jean Craig gripped [illegible] by the arms, and that shortly after that, within three days, she found herself worse, and was so for a long time after. However, she could not say that it was through her sorcery and witchcraft.

Document 2.

[This document is in clear and legible handwriting, but is very badly damaged.] The statement... declared before the minister... elders in the parish... James Baillie declared that Jeane Craig fell on...

James Bailie declared that Jeane Craig fell ... Beatrix Sandilandis on the coal-hill at Painestoun ... that Jean Craig blew in her face and... this Beatrix went mad. And when she blew ... words, "A black sight be upon that face!"...

1652

Dittay Roll

[Some of the JC26 boxes in the National Archives of Scotland contain "dittay rolls". These are lists of persons charged with serious crimes in the various sheriffdoms during the year in question. These seem only to have survived sporadically, and those which do survive do not always contain references to witchcraft and related matters. The Haddington dittay roll for 1652 in box JC26/14 contains the items given below.]

James Mitchell in Bolton: You are indicted and accused of the crime of adultery, and as a common and notorious charmer and vagabond. You have no master or means of making a living, and you go up and down the country with a bad reputation deluding many of the people with your devilish art of charming and sorcery, for which crime you were condemned and accused before the Presbytery of Dunbar. [This entry is marked "Abs", presumably indicating that Mitchell was summoned but did not appear for trial, or fled before he could be summoned.]

Beatrix Nisbet, wife of George Broune in Stentoune. Absent. You are indicted and accused of the abominable crime of witchcraft, which you committed in the manner and at the times contained in your statements, which are in the custody of Mr Robert Davidsone, minister at Stentoune. For these crimes you were condemned to die by a jury, and a commission was purchased for that purpose. However, because of the distractions of the times, and the troubles in the country when the English army invaded, you were dismissed out of the prison where you had been locked up.

Witnesses:

Robert Lauder in Belhevine;

Mr Robert Davidsone,
    minister at Stentoune.

Elizabeth Cunninghame in Northberwick	Present
Robert Thomson there	Absent
Elspet Carter there	Present
Bessie Gordone there	Absent
Barbara Morgone there	Absent
Jeane Park there	Absent
Agnes Gray there	Absent

Each and every one of you is indicted and accused of the abominable crime of witchcraft and sorcery committed by you for several years past. You have forsaken God and taken on the service of the Devil. You have renounced your baptisms and the holy sacrament, and done many other malefices and deeds contrary to the law of God and man. These are specified at length in your individual statements, which are in safe keeping ready for production. Each and every one of you has confessed to the crime of witchcraft.

Witnesses: William Dalyell, notary in Northberwick; Mr James Atcheson, schoolmaster there; Andro Dick there.

John Wilson in Dunglass

[Also in box JC26/14 is the case of John Wilson in Dunglass.]

June 1st 1652, at Dunglass.

Today, in the presence of Mr William Symsone, resident in Dunglass; Alexander Lermott, chamberlain there; William Peeres, schoolmaster; and James Riddoch, notary public; John Wilson appeared, having returned after escaping from Dunglass about two years ago. He had been arrested by lawful authority on grave suspicion of witchcraft, and was named by varies confessing wtches who were then put to death for the same sin. Having free access to go out and in without any molestation, John Wilsone freely of his own accord confessed as follows: -

1. Firstly, that his first meeting with Satan was after that business of the ball of yarn which Margaret Geddes stole from Margaret Home, wife of the proprietor of Dunglas Mill. A court was set up to try this Margaret Geddes for stealing the yarn. Because she had the yarn, but was not living with a craftsman, she was accused by Margaret Home. James Wilson had a twist of the yarn, and taking it into consideration, the Judges decided to choose some [illegible] workers to investigate it. After further consideration the court was dismissed, and when John Wilson was returning to his own house at night, he met Agnes Henderson and her two daughters Margret and Helene Geddes in the hollow of Bilsdene. They had the ball of yarn and the Devil was with them. He told Johne to keep the bit of wool he had, and not show it. If he would do that, he would always have enough work and money.

2. His next meeting with the Devil was in Bilsdene. Robert Chisholme was there, Stephen Hewat and his wife Helen Litster, Jeane Mearnes, Agnes Henderson, and her two daughters. At that time he renounced his baptism, got a new name from the Devil - Alexander - and had "carnal copulation" with the Devil.

[This is most unusual. This is the only reference in East Lothian witchcraft to a man having sex with the Devil.]

3. His next meeting was at the "rutch-house"[?] of Dunglase, where he helped to eat a goose with Robert Chisholme, Stephen Howat and his wife Helene Litster, Margaret Herrone, Jeane Mearnes, Elspet Haistie, and Margaret Clift. James Cotthird brought him drink, but he could not testify to where it came from.

4. His next meeting was at Bilsdene again, in company with those already named. Margaret Henrie asked the Devil for revenge on her master Sir John Ruthven, which the Devil granted her. He gave her an image of his body made from wax, and told her to torment his body as she pleased.

[The word used for "image" in the text is "portrait". This of course is similar to the "pictour" of wax handled by the witches at Acheson's Haven, which has often been wrongly interpreted as a "picture" in the modern sense. We should think rather of a "portrayal" or "depiction" of the victim's body, which for convenience's sake would almost certainly be an image.]

5. [illegible]

6. [illegible]

7. He confessed to a meeting at the Lillie Law, and another at the Foulisch Strype, beyond Thraitonley with all those already named, together with David Hog and his wife.

Item 2.

At Dunglas the first [or perhaps fifth] of June 1652.

In the presence of Mr William Sympsone; Alexander Heriot, chamberlain to the Lady Dunglasse; William Peires there; and James Riddoch, notary public. John Wilsone, having returned to Dunglas after his escape two years or so ago... [This continues word for word as in Item 1, but continues after paragraph 7 as follows: -]

At Dunglas, 9th July 1652, in presence of the judges constituted for that effect by a commission granted by the Commission Appointed for Administration of Justice to the People in Scotland for investigating and examining persons guilty of the abominable sin of witchcraft, we the undersigned declare on our solemn oath that John Wilsone confessed to all the forementioned matters. Witnessed with our hands, the day, month, and place foresaid.

Mr William Symsone, witness.

William Peires, witness.

Johne Quarioir, witness.

We the undersigned, having power to examine persons guilty of the abominable sin of witchcraft, by authority of the Commissioners Appointed for Administration of Justice to the

People in Scotland, summoned Johne Wilsone before us. On being examined, he freely of his own accord confessed in our presence all these matters, which we hereby testify to be true. Signed with our hands, the day place, and year of God foresaid.

James Nicolsone
Thomas Reidpeth
James Tait,

Item 3.

July 19th 1652. The confession of John Wilsone before the Commission for Administration of Justice in Criminal Cases.

John Wilson says that the Devil has appeared to him several times, sometimes in the shape of a man, sometimes of a woman. Jonn Wilson had money owed to him by several of his neighbours, which he could not get from them. Because of this he asked the Devil to give him something so that he could be revenged on them. The Devil gave him several silver coins which he was to stick in the walls of their houses. This he did, and within a short time after this their goods and cattle wasted away. He also says that he has made several agreements and had sex with the Devil. He has renounced his baptism and had a new name given to him by the Devil, which was ["Alexander" deleted] Saunders.

John Wilson, his mark. [a squiggle]

Item 4.

[Item 4 is a list of names of people denounced by Wilson, and people against whom acts of evil intent - "malefices" - were perpetrated. See Item 6.]

Item 5.

On December 10th 1652, I John Reidpeth, messenger, lawfully summoned Robert Chisholm in Cruiknowis, Jeane Mearnes there, Stein Hewit in Painkertoun and Heilen Litster his wife, Margarit Geddies in Auldhamstoks, David Hog in Thomtonloch, and Issobell Airther his wife. They were informed personally, and a copy of the summons was delivered to them ordering them to appear before the Commissioners in the criminal case arranged for 17th December, for the reasons contained in the summons. I did this before these witnesses: - James Herit, J. Ridpeth

Deliver this proof of execution to Patrick Young, sheriff depute, or Patrick Broune, procurator fiscal, to be sent to Edinburgh between now and Friday.

Item 6.

[This is a list identical to that contained in Item 4, but with brief comments added]

Persons named by Wilsone and his accomplices.

Agnes Henrysoune   dead
Margaret and Helen Geddes, her daughters
Robert Chesome
Stephen Hewit
Hellen Litster his wife
Jeane Mearnis
Elizabeth Haistie   burnt
Margaret Clift   burnt
James Couthard   dead
Margaret Henrie   burnt
David Hog and his wife.

Persons against whom malefices were done:-

Issobell Hamiltone, daughter to Sir Alexander Hamilton of Innerweik
Elizabeth Glen, widow of the minister of Innerweik

Item 7.

To the honourable Commissioners for Administration of Justice to the People in Scotland. The petition of William Ruthven of Dunglas in the shire of East Lothian. Some years ago several witches and warlocks were arrested and executed for devilish actions and detestable practices of witchcraft, which are all too common in this country. Amongst the rest, a fellow called Johne Wilson was arrested as being guilty of that crime. He escaped from prison, and after wandering up and down the country for a long time, he has now returned to Dunglas, and willingly confessed to various acts of evil intent, He has also accused various others of this vile crime of witchcraft, as his attached statement will show. His detestable acts call for justice to be administered on him and the rest of his companions, lest the land should be polluted by suffering such vile persons to live in it. Your honourable petitioner therefore humbly desires that according to the practices formerly observed in such cases, your honours may be pleased to commission Sir James Nicolsone of Colbrandspeth; Mr Cornelius Inglis of East Barnes; Mr Thomas Reidpeth of Foulordleyes; Thomas Sympsone of Dryburghfurd; Mr John Sandielands, portioner of Eastbarnes; and James Tait in Colbrandspeth; or any two or more of them, as your honours think fit, to be judges for trying and sentencing this John Wilson and his associates according to the law of Scotland, and according to equity and conscience, so that if he and they deserve it, they can be put to death. These judges or their quorum should have power to hold courts for that purpose, to choose clerks and all other members of court, and to do everything relevant, just as others similarly commissioned have done in the past

[The commission is being sought from Cromwell's occupying forces. There is of course no Privy Council, but the Laird of Dunglass obviously hopes that the occupying administration can be persuaded to grant the same sort of powers to a local commission as the Privy Council would have formerly done. Unfortunately, there is no indication of what Wilson's ultimate fate was. It has usually been assumed that witches were treated more leniently during the English Occupation/Commonwealth period. Indeed, Wilson may have returned to Dunglas with the intention of facing his old charges of witchcraft, banking on them being dismissed. However, that was not always what happened, as the next case shows.]

1657

Janet Bruce in Tranent

[The papers relating to this case are in "Bundle 3" in box JC26/22 in the National Archives of Scotland.]

[Notes on reverse side.]

Statements made against Janet Bruce in Tranent 1657.

Case not called 7th Jul 1657.

4th August 1657. To a jury for proving the articles of her indictment

Sentence delayed. To be pronounced against her on 5th October 1657.

Tranent 22nd June 1657.

Today in the presence of Mr Andrew Marjoribanks and Mr Robert Hodge, two of His Highness's [*i.e.* Oliver Cromwell's] justices of the peace in the county of East Lothian, appeared the persons named below. They were solemnly sworn in the presence of the said judges, and questioned on what they knew of the behaviour of Janett Bruce, who is now in prison in Tranent, under suspicion of witchcraft and charming. The witnesses testified as follows:

The statement of James Melvill, salter in Preston Pans, and others.

James, 30 years of age, married, was sworn, and testifies as follows: that about a year ago he had occasion to come into Elspeth Baptie's house in Preston Pans where he found Jonet and Elspeth drinking. Jonet had a little black dog which made to bite the witness. In his anger he threatened to throw the dog in the fire. At this, after she had muttered several words privately to herself, Jonet Bruce spoke out loud, and declared that she would do him a bad turn before long. It so happened that the same right the salt pan he was working in was blown over by the wind, and all the contents belonging to the witness were completely spoiled and thus made valueless to him. He valued the contents at the sum of £30. [This paragraph is marked in the margin "pluralitie clainges", that is, the jury has acquitted the accused by a majority.]

He also declares that the same day he heard the widow Kathren Kniblo in Preston Pans say in public before witnesses that when she had asked Jonet Bruce how she had learned all these cures, Jonet replied that if she would become her servant, in seven years she would make her as expert as herself. [This paragraph is marked "All clainges" - acquitted unanimously.]

Signed: Robert Hodge. A. Marjoribanks.

Johne ffine. Absent. Aged about 25, married. Being solemnly sworn, he declares as follows: his wife had been lame and confined to bed for a quarter of a year or longer before "fastingeven" [Shrove Tuesday] 1656. John's mother in law Marion Fa had heard that Jonet Bruce could cure many strange diseases. She was sent for, and accordingly came to John's house, and after some discussion undertook to cure John's wife. John agreed to give her £14 Scots for her pains. After that, Jonet came in secret to John's wife and asked her to give her a gift, otherwise she could not cure her. When she was asked what she wanted as a gift she replied, "You must give me a child." At this John's wife replied that she hoped in God's mercy that the Lord had given her no children to give to her. Then Jonet asked her to give her her [illegible] shirt, with her "beginet"[?] and the clothes she was wearing beneath it. Accordingly, she gave these to Jonet. Then Jonet invited Johne to take supper with her. He arrived a little before supper was ready. She sent her daughter for a mutchkin of wine, and when he and Jonet were alone she expressed the same desire to him that he would give her a child, and if he did, she would cure his wife. He replied that he hoped in God that He had not given him children to be given to the Devil. After he had taken a drink he left, and would take no supper with her, and his wife is still in the same condition as she was in the beginning. [This paragraph is marked "plurality ffylles" - guilty by a majority verdict]

Signed: Johne Finie.

Margaret Strathearen's accusation against Jonett Bruce.

Firstly, in the year 1649, Jonett was away in the south as was her custom. She was a tenant of Margaret and her late husband's, and a man came wanting to rent Jonett's house, since she had been away so long. Margaret observed that all the goods in the house would not be enough to pay her rent. The next night Jonett came home and began to quarrel with Margaret, because she as her landlady had defamed her behind her back to a certain Alexander Strathearn. That same night, in the middle of the night, after Margaret had been greatly troubled in her bed, she saw Jonett standing on the floor in front of her bed, with her hand in her side [Her hand in a side pocket, perhaps?]. She was troubled with this four rights in succession, but there were no other appearances. Then a brood-sow of Margaret's which had newly given birth, began refusing any kind of food, and Margaret was troubled no more. However, the sow deteriorated day by day, and at length Margaret asked Jonet to take a look at her sow. She replied that she knew nothing about her sow's disease, but went to see it. When she saw the sow, she said that it had received a wrong done to it, which had not been meant for the sow, but for another. Margaret replied that she was glad it had turned out that way, and laughed. Jonett said, "Are you laughing? This sow was worth £20." Then she took the sow between the doors, barred them front and back, told Margaret to close the entry gate on her and the sow, and called to her to heat a mutchkin of ate. Then she went up the stair to her own house to fetch a little powder, and stayed there for quarter of an hour. She forbade Margaret to open the doors until she came back.

When she did come back she told Margaret that the sow would die. Margaret said that she had expected as much. [Probable meaning, the text is obscure here.] So it turned out, eight days after it had gone off its food.

At the term-time following that, Jonett came to pay her rent to Margaret and her late husband. When she had done so, she asked her landlord if he had anything else to say to her, and he told her no, but he had rented her house to someone else. She went away then, without saying any more at that time. However, early next morning, before four o'dock, she came back and began to ask Margaret if her landlord had [illegible] her the night before or not Margaret said no, but her house had been let. At this Jonett swore, "By the head of you, that will make it the dearest house that was ever built in Tranent!" Margaret replied, "I trust that you have no power." Then she swore again with curses that she would make him shit his breeches for it. This is in fact what happened, and it continued with him till he died, after wasting away for a year and a half.

Margaret was taken and solemnly sworn on the above-written particulars before Mr Andrew Marjoribanks and Mr R. Hodge, two of His Highness's justices of the peace, and declared that they were true.

Alexander Johnstoun, salter, about 30 years of age, married, was solemnly sworn, and testified as follows: -

About two years past May he had a child who had lost all power of movement below the loins. He had spent a great amount on doctors, but the child was no better. Elspeth Baptie sent for him and his wife and offered to get a woman who would cure the child completely. So the witness and his wife came to Elspeth's house, and she sent for Jonet Bruce. When she arrived, she undertook to cure the child and get him to stand within five days. Later, she came to Alexander's child, laid a waterproof cloth on him, and rubbed him with oils. He got better every day, and for this cure Jonet got about twenty or thirty shillings sterling from his wife. He knows no more about the matter.

Signed: A. Marjoribanks. Robert Hodges.

Agnis Bardie, wife of the above Alexander, was also solemnly sworn, and testifies as above. Signed: A. Marjoribanks. Robert Hodges.

Barbara Smyth, widow of the late Robert Seaton, portioner of Tranent, was also solemnly sworn, and testifies as follows: -

About five years ago she and her husband were living in Tranent, and were about to move. They sold Jonet Bruce and her son John Thomson the fruit from their garden for the sum of £46, half to be paid when the bargain was made, and the other half when the fruit was shaken down. The witness and her husband received a dollar in acknowledgement of the striking of the bargain. After the fruit was shaken down, she and her husband asked several times for the money, and since it seemed unlikely that they would get any of it, at length Robert went to John Thomsone's house to speak seriously in person to him about it. He could not find him that night, so after that he had him arrested. Thomson was bailed by Jacob Nicolsone who stood surety for him. About four or five days after that the witness and her husband were in bed about twelve o'clock at night. A fire was burning in front of them in the room, and the doors were shut. Suddenly, when she was asleep, the witness's husband was seized and his nightshirt pulled over his head. The witness wakened and saw her husband naked and lashing out with his arms to defend himself. She asked her husband what was wrong with him, and he told her that Jonet Bruce and another two with her had set upon him to murder him in his own bed. He had seen Jonet in the clothes she usually wore going towards the fire from his bed, but he did not recognise either of the other two. The next day her husband went to Jonet's house to be revenged on her, but he was stopped by neighbours, and came back without touching her.

Signed: A. Marjoribanks. R. Hodges.

Robert Seaton, son of the above Robert, was also solemnly sworn, and testifies as above; that is, that he heard his father relate all of the above particulars.

Signed: Robert Setoun.

James Johnstoun, widower, about 60 years of age, was also solemnly sworn, and has nothing to say about her.

William Brysson, aged about 30, married, was solemnly sworn and declares that about six years ago he was ill, and Jonet Bruce smeared him with oils.

Alexander Wilsone was also solemnly sworn and testifies as above.

Patrick Kemp was also solemnly sworn, and testifies as above.

Robert Sandelands, about 40 years of age, married, was also solemnly sworn and testifies that about five years ago Jonet was a tenant of his. He had heard evil rumours about her, and wanting to get rid of her, he terminated her lease. She challenged him about it in his own house, and after they had exchanged some words, she went to the door, sat down at the threshold and urinated ["scailed her watter"]. When the witness objected she promised him an evil turn of events. In particular, she would make him hang himself behind his own bed. Shortly after that one of his children lost the power of his legs, and has not yet recovered it.

Signed: A. Marjoribanks. R. Hodges.

Bessie Ronold, wife of Thomas Bell, was solemnly sworn and declares that about four years ago she had a child who was not well. At Thomas Wedle's suggestion she went to Jonet, who undertook to cure the child. She came to the witness's house for that purpose. Jonet took the child on her knee, but the witness was not present and does not know what she did to the child. However, Thomas Weddle's wife was present, and declares that she took a piece of red velvet trimming and measured the length of the child wth it. The child recovered. The witness refused to give Jonet anything to drink, since Jonet wouldn't pay for it when she was requested to do so. Jonet declared that she had done her a good turn, and that a good turn could never be paid for. She added these words, "Whoever has the child, I have the measurement of it."

Signed: A. Marjoribanks. R. Hodges.

James Brotherstanes, aged about forty, was also solemnly sworn, and testifies that last Sunday night, the 21st of this month, when he was guarding Jonet Bruce in the house belonging to Patrick Ersken in Tranent, about twelve o'clock at night, a rat came to the candle and took it out of the candle-holder. It carried it away to the thatch of the house before he could reach the rat, even though he was within his own length of it when it seized the candle. Soon the whole house was on fire, both on the one side and on the other, and the fire could not be put out until the whole house was destroyed.

Signed: James Brotherstones.

[Would a rat carry off a burning candle? Or has James concocted a story to cover up some negligence or carelessness on his part?]

Elspet Nisbet, about forty years of age, married to William Clerk, coal miner in Tranent, was also solemnly sworn, and testifies that last Sunday night when Patrick Erskene's house was fire, she was watching the fire, and she saw a black horse rise up on the top of the house [The "boss" of the house. The precise meaning is not clear.] at the back of the chimney. It first stood with its face to the east, then turned its face to the north. The fire was burring to each side of it, and it beat upon the roof ["boss" again] of the house with its fore-feet until the fire destroyed it, and both roof and horse went down together.

Signed: Robert Hodges.

[There is not necessarily anything

supernatural about this. Animals often shared the same building with their owners until long after the 17th Century. This might well have been a real horse making its way up through the house to escape the flames.]

Margaret ffrank, servant to John Clerk, aged about eighteen, being also solemnly sworn, testifies as above.

Tranent 29th June, 1657.

Also, Marion Hammiltoun appeared, the wife of William Heriot from Huckstoun in Lauderdaille [i.e Oxton]. She was also solemnly sworn in the presence of Sir John Johnston of Elphingstoun and Mr Robert Hodge, two of His Highness's justices of the peace. She was questioned, and declares that a year ago Jonet Bruce came to her house. She declared that she could cure any disease, and the witness asked her if she would cure her of a cyst she was troubled with. Jonet replied that as God should judge her on the Great Day, she would make her as perfect as the day she was born. She got three dollars from the witness and then went her way. Then one of her neighbours told her that Jonett was a witch, and so the witness, and another man with her, went after her to get the money back. They overtook her at Ginglekirk, a mile from her house, and struggled with her to get the money back, but failed. They took her plaid from her in John Dewer's house in Ginglekirk, and found there were some things tied up in a corner of the plaid. When it was opened, it was found that it was the flesh and bones of dead children. There was an arm and thigh - it was not clear whose. This she declares on oath to be true.

Signed: J. Johnston. R. Hodges.

Kathren Kniblo in Prestounpannis, a widow, was also solemnly sworn and testifies that Jonet undertook to cure a sick child of Alexander Johnstoun's. The witness came to Alexander Johnstoun's house in Prestoun Pans when Jonet was there. She asked her what disease the child had, and how she knew. They were both alone, and so Jonet said that if she would become her servant for seven years, she would make her as expert as herself, as if she were as old as she was. She declares on oath that this is true, and that she knows no more about it.

Signed: J. Johnston.

Margraret Liddle, wife of James Brotherstones, aged about fifty, was solemnly sworn and testifies that on the Sunday night, between twelve and one, when her husband had delivered Jonet Bruce into her keeping at the time of the fire, the witness was standing at the top of the stair at her own door. Jonet was inside the house, and suddenly a raven came over the house that was on fire, to the witness's door, so near to the witness's face that it seemed to want to go into the house. The witness cried out, and Jonet heard her and asked what was the matter. The witness answered that a raven had come at her. Jonett replied, "You might well enough have gone with him."

Signed: J. Johnston. R. Hodges.

Issobele Smyth, being solemnly sworn, declares that she saw the raven come over the house where the fire was, towards Margaret Lidle's door.

Signed: J. Johnston. R. Hodges.

Elspeth Wedle, being solemnly sworn, declares that she saw this raven fly over the house as described.

Signed: J. Johnston. R. Hodges.

Tranent 27th[?] June 1657.

Today, according to the orders of His Highness's justices of the peace in the western division of Eist Lowthiane, John Kincaid, witch investigator, searched and examined the body of Jonett Bruce, now imprisoned in the prison-house of Tranent. He found four marks, into which he inserted a pin of this length: -

[59 mm]

This he did in four separate places in her body

without drawing blood, before the following witnesses: -

James Anislie, son of Mr Cornelius Anislie in Prestoun.

Archibald Purvis and David Howison, elders in the parish of Tranent.

Alexander Mudy and James Cowan, constables there.

Walter Scot, clerk to the justices of the said division, and writer of this record.

[Their signatures follow.]

Also, John Kincaid declares that the four marks are of diabolical origin, and he will declare this upon oath, in confirmation of which he signs with his mark of two letters, at Tranent 30th June 1657, before these witnesses: William Forester in Tranent, Robert Borthwick, and the above-named Walter Scot.

Signed: IK

[The witnesses' signatures follow.]

[This is an interesting and rare insight into the activities of the notorious Tranent witch-pricker John Kincaid. Bundle 3 also contains a deposition subscribed by John Kincaid certifying that he found the Devil's mark on Agnes Robert in Linlithgow. He was therefore obviously continuing to ply his trade under Commonwealth rule.]

[Janet Bruce's indictment can be found in the High Court Minute Book JC6/5. It is entered under 7th July 1657, and presumably the case was scheduled for that day. It seems to have been postponed, however, because it is marked "Not callit". The indictment corresponds closely to the witnesses' statements, but there are some extra details.]

Witchcraft: Jonet Bruce in Tranent, prisoner in the Tollbooth of Edinburgh. Prosecutor: The Solicitor General.

7th July 1657.   Not called.

You are indicted and accused that whereas the laws of Almighty God and Acts of Parliament of this nation make committing the crimes of sorcery and witchcraft punishable by death, it is nevertheless true that you Jonet Bruce have shaken off all fear of God, reverence for his divine law, and the acts of parliament of this nation, and for the past sixteen years have taken yourself to the service of Sathan, the enemy of man's salvation. You have entered into a pact and covenant with him, renounced your baptism, received his mark, and with his devilish assistance you have by your sorcery and witchcraft committed many acts of evil intent, laid on and taken off various sicknesses and diseases from many of His Highness's good people in this country, and have caused the deaths of many of them. You have also laid on and taken off various sicknesses and diseases from their livestock and goods.

[This preamble is presumably considered as the first article of the indictment, since the next paragraph is numbered "2".

2. Witness: James Melvill, salter in Prestonpans. Firstly, twelve months ago you conceived a devilish malice, hatred, and envy against James Melvill, salter in Prestonpans, because he threatened to throw a dog of yours in the fire because it seemed likely to bite him as he was coming from Elspeth Baptie's house in Prestonpans where you and Elspeth were drinking by the fireside. After muttering some words to yourself, you spoke out and said to James in a threatening manner that you would do him a bad turn. This followed accordingly, for the same night the salt pan he was working in was overturned by your sorcery and witchcraft, and by an evil blast of wind sent by you. Everything James had in it, to the value of £30 Scots, was spoiled in the fall and made useless and unprofitable to him.

3. Witness: Katherene Kniblo in Prestonpanes. The same day as that wrong you did to

James Melvill, he heard Katharene Kniblo, a widow in Prestonpans, declare openly before witnesses that she had asked you how you learned all those cures you practised, and you replied that if she would become your servant for seven years you would make her as expert as yourself.

4. Johnne Phinnie. You are also indicted and accused that a quarter of a year before Shrove Tuesday 1656, [blank], the wife of John Phinnie, who was lame and bedridden, heard that you could cure many strange diseases. John's mother in law Marione Falle sent for you. Accordingly, you came to John's house, and after some discussion between you, you agreed to cure John's wife for £14 Scots. After that, you came to John's wife in private and asked her for a gift. She asked you what gift you wanted and you replied that she must give you a child. She answered that she hoped in God's mercy that the Lord had not given her children to give to you. You then suggested threateningly that she might give you the shift she wore as a bride, along with her "begnet", and the cloth she wore under it. These she accordingly handed over to you. After that you invited John Phinnie to supper. He came a little before supper was ready, and you sent your daughter for a mutchkin of wine. When you and John were alone together in your house, you expressed again your desire that he should give you a child, and you would cure his wife. He replied that he hoped in God that He had not given him any child to be given to the Devil. After taking a drink, he went away and would not take any of your supper. His wife, therefore, is still in the same condition as before. All of these unlawful requests you made as described for effecting the cure - asking for a child and for his wife's clothes - were nothing but devilry and witchcraft, which is notoriously well known, and you cannot deny it.

5. Margaret Stratherne [witness]. You are also indicted and accused that about Whitsunday 1649 when you paid your rent to your landlord [blank] and his wife Margaret Stratherne, after paying, you asked your landlord if he had anything else to say to you. He answered that he had no more to say, just that he had let your house to someone else. At that, you went your way without saying a word, but early next morning, before four o'clock, you came back and asked Margaret if her husband, your landlord, had renewed your lease the night before or not. She said no, the house was let. You then swore a great oath by the bread of God that you would make it the dearest house that was ever built in Tranent. Margaret replied that she trusted in God that you had no power. Then you swore most dreadfully that you would make her husband shit his breeches for it. This is just what happened, for by your sorcery and withcraft he continued in great pain for a year and a half with violent diarrhoea until he departed this life. You, by your sorcery, witchcraft, and devilish curses, were the sole cause of this cruel murder.

6. Witnesses to the 6th Article: Alexander Johnstone, salter in Prestonpans, and Elspeth Bardie, Alexander's wife. You are indicted and accused that about two years ago last May, Alexander Johnston, a salter in Prestonpans, had a child who was paralysed below the loins, on whom he had spent a lot of money on doctors to bring him back to health. However, he was no better. He came to you in Elspet Baptie's house in Tranent, and you undertook to cure the child and to make him stand within five days. So according to your promise, you came to Alexander Johnstone's house, and after you had laid a waterproof cloth on the child, and rubbed him with oil, by your sorcery and witchcraft he was able to stand within five days, and grew better day by day after that. You got about twenty or thirty shillings sterling from Alexander's wife for this cure, which was all done by your sorcery and witchcraft.

7. Witnesses to the 7th Article: Barbara

Smyth, widow of the late Robert Robertson [*sic*] in Tranent; Robert Seatonn junior there. You are indicted and accused that about five years ago, you conceived a deadly hatred against Barbara Smith, widow of the late Robert Seitoun, portioner of Tranent, because Robert Seatonne pressed you and your son John Thomsone for payment and threatened you with imprisonment for the sum of £46 owed to him by you for the fruit from his garden, which he had sold to you for that sum. Immediately after that, by your devilry and witchcraft you came to Robert Seatoune's house at night about twelve o'clock, with another two witches or devils like yourself. Although his doors were shut, by your devilry and witchcraft you entered his house. He and his wife were both sleeping in their bed before the hall, and a fire was burning in front of them. With your two devilish associates you suddenly seized him in his bed, and pulled his nightshirt over his head. At this, his wife Barbara Smith woke up, and saw her husband lying naked beside her, fighting with his arms to defend himself, and asking what was happening to him. She told him that you, Jonet Bruce, and the other two devils had set upon him to murder him in his own bed. He saw you in the same clothes you were in the habit of wearing, going away from his bed towards the fire, but as for the other two, he knew neither of them. The next day he was going to your house to be revenged on you, but he was dissuaded by his neighbours. All this was done by your sorcery and witchcraft, in revenge against Robert Setoun, because he was seeking what rightfully belonged to him. This article is ratified by Robert Setoune junior, the son of the above Robert Setoune.

8. Witnesses to the 8th Article: William Brysone, Alexander Wilsone, Patrik Kemp, and Robert Niddrie. You are indicted and accused that about six years ago when William Brysone was ill, you came to him, looked him over, and smeared his body with oils. Shortly afterwards, he recovered as a result of your sorcery and witchcraft.

9. Wrtness to the 9th Article: Robert Sandelands in Tranent. You were a tenant of Robert Sandelands in Tranent. Because of the bad reputation you were given as a witch, he let the house you had been renting from him to someone else. You then conceived a devilish hatred against Robert, and challenged him in his own house with letting your house over your head. Then you went to the door and sat down at the threshhold and urinated. When Robert protested to you over this you replied that you would do him an evil turn. In particular, you said that you would make him hang himself behind his own bed. By your malicious threats and your sorcery and witchcraft, shortly after that one of Robert's children lost the power of both of his legs, and still has not recovered.

10. Witness to the Article 10: Bessie Ronald. Bessie Ronald, the wife of Thomas Bell in [blank], had a sick child and sent for you. You undertook to cure him, and for that purpose you came to Bessie's house, and took the child on your knee in the presence of Thomas Wedle's wife. You had a length of broad velvet trimming in your hand, and using your sorcery and witchcraft, you measured the length of the child with it. After that the child grew better day by day. You got some free drink from Bessie Ronald after that, but when you wanted more drink from her she refused to give you any more without payment. You then said that you had done her a good turn, and that a good turn could never be paid for. Then you added these words, "All the same, if you have the child, I have its measurements."

11. Witness to the 11th Article: James Brotherstanes in Tranent. On the 21st of June last, on a Sunday night, James Brotherstaines in Tranent had you in his keeping within the dwelling house belonging to Patrick Erskeine. About twelve o'clock at night, by your sorcery

and witchcraft, a rat came to the candle burning in front of you, took it out of the candle-holder, and carried it away to the thatch of the house before James could reach it, even though James was within his own length of the rat when it got hold of the candle. Soon the whole house caught fire, both on the one side and on the other. The fire could not be put out until the house was completely destroyed. All this was done by your sorcery and witchcraft.

12. Witnesses to the 12th Article: Elspeth Nysbet; Margaret Frank, servant of William Frank. Also, the same night that the house caught fire, Elspeth Neisbeit was watching the fire as the house was burning, and she saw a black horse rise up on the roof of the house at the back of the chimney. It stood first of all facing east, then turned to face north. The fire was burning on each side of the horse, and it beat on the roof of the house with its forefoot until the fire consumed the roof, in the end both fell down together. All this was done by your sorcery and witchcraft.

13. Witnesses to the 13th Article: Marion Hamilton, wife of William Heriot in Huckston. About a year ago you came to Marion Hamiltonne, the wife of Willism Heriot in Huckstoune in Lauderdaille. You claimed to her that you had the skill to cure any disease, so Marion asked you to cure her of "ane wind" [This appeared as "wene" in the previous statement - *i.e.* a cyst] she was troubled with. You said to her that as God should judge you at the Great Day, you would make her as perfectly healthy as the day she was born. You received three dollars from Marione, and went your way. But then one of her neighbours told her that you were a witch, so with another man with her, she followed you to get her money back. She overtook you at Ginglekirk a mile from her house, and struggled with you to recover her money. She did not manage this, but took your plaid from you in John Deware's house at Ginglekirk. Rolled up in the corner of the plaid she found the flesh and bones of dead children, that is, a thigh and arm, not yet putrified.

14. Witnesses to the 14th Article: Margaret Liddell, Issobell Smyth, Elspeth Wedle. The night the house caught fire James Brotherstaines delivered you into the keeping of his wife Margaret Liddell in his house. He himself was busy trying to put out the fire. As Margaret was standing at the top of the stair, in front of her door, while you were in the house, suddenly a raven came flying over the house that was on fire. It flew to Margaret's door, close to her face, as if it meant to go into the house. At this Margaret cried out, and when you, Janet, heard her, you asked what was the matter. She answered that a raven had come at her. You replied, "You might have gone with him well enough."

[As previously mentioned, Jonet's trial was postponed. Nineteen pages further on in the High Court Minute Book, the above indictment is repeated. The articles of the indictment are numbered differently however, since this time the preamble has not been considered as an "article". The overturning of James Melvill's saltpan therefore becomes Article 1, whereas it was previously designated as Article 2, and all the other articles follow suit, numbered one less than in the previous indictment. A brief note beside each article records the decision of the jury. These show Jonet was acquitted of all charges except the 3rd and 12th - 4th and 13th in the indictment quoted above . Article 7 - numbered 8 in the first indictment - seems to have been struck out. Thus she was found guilty of asking for a child from John Phinnie's wife, and being in possession of a child's severed limbs in Channelkirk. The Minute Book then continues as given below.]

Pleads not guilty to all. To a jury trial 4th August 1657. Mosely and Goodear.

4th August 1657: By the mouth of Andro

Gray the jury by a majority finds the accused, Jonet Bruce, guilty of witchcraft in the 3rd article of her indictment, of asking for a child from James Phinnie and his wife to cure James's wife, and of saying that she could not cure her without a gift. She was acquitted by a majority of votes of the remaining articles of her indictment.

Signed: Andro Gray.

Jonet Bruce's sentence delayed to the first Tuesday of October 1657.

[This verdict does not square with the scribbled notes beside the original indictment, which indicate that as well as trying to obtain the gift of a child from her sister in law, the jury also found her guilty by a majority of having a child's thigh and arm tied up in her plaid at Channelkirk.]

8th October 1657: The commission sentenced Jonet Bruce, found guilty of witchraft by a jury, to be taken on Wednesday 14th of this month to the Castell Hill between two and four in the afternoon, to be strangled at a stake there until she is dead, her body thereafter to be burnt to ashes, and her possessions forfeited.

[Janet's case is a good example of how the odds were stacked against witchcraft suspects. The nonsense about diabolical ravens, rats, and horses has all been dismissed, run-of-the-mill cures, curses, and charming have been overlooked, but Janet must still die because she has been found guilty of a single charge - or perhaps two - out of the thirteen in her indictment.]

1658

[The High Court Minute Book JC6/5 which contains Jonet Bruce's case, runs from 6th November 1655 to 5th July 1659, and contains several other East Lothian cases. We also find the notorious East Lothian witch-pricker John Kincaid at work in Midlothian in the case of Kathrine Casse from Dalkeith on 2nd February 1658, where he appears on oath before the justices of the peace as "witness to the mark, John Kinkaid, pricker.]

Margaret Anderson

February 2nd 1658 Witchcraft

Margaret Anderson, prisoner. Pursuer: Advocate general.

Witnesses

Mr Robert Ker, minister of Hadington.

Mr William Trent, minister there.

Richard Schaipland, baillie there.

Mr James Gray, session clerk there.

Mr Georg Hepburne, schoolmaster there.

David Wilson, burgess there.

Patrick Broun, burgess there.

You are indicted and accused because by the divine law of Almighty God and Acts of Parliament of this nation those who commit sorcery, witchcraft, charming, and soothsaying, or those who seek help, response, or consultation with any such persons are punishable by death. Also by the same laws, those who commit the crime of adultery are likewise punishable by death. Nevertheless it is true that contrary to these laws and Acts of Parliament, you, Margaret Anderson, having shaken off all fear of God and reverance or regard for the laws of the nation, have upon the 1st, 2nd, 3rd, and remaining days of the months of January, February, March, April, May, June, July, August, September, October, November, and December 1645 and 1646, or at least on one or other of these days and years, polluted your body and had carnal copulation with John McKie, a married man. You and he were at the time in service in the household of the Laird of Bass. Also in 1650, in one or other of the days and months of that year, you fell into the sin of adultery with a certain Johne Kerd, a married man, when you were both in service with Sir John McKenzie of Tarbat. Also, at the time of your employment with Sir John McKenzie, you fell into the sin of fornication with a certain James Innes. You were disappointed of your intention of marrying him, but some Gypsies came to the Laird of Tarbat's gate at that time, and one of them claimed to have skill in charming. You took her into the great hall and consulted her, asking her to tell you whether this James would marry you or not. She asked you to give her a shilling and your linen apron, and bring her three straws from your bed. When you asked her what she was going to do with these things she answered that she would put them under the head of his bed. She then asked you to turn your back on her. This you did, but when you turned round again you could not see the apron or the other things you gave her, although you made a thorough search for them, and although there had been nobody in the room but yourself.

Also, James had shaved his head at that time, but by your consulting with this charmer, and by the sorcery and charming you used against him, his hair never grew on his head again.

Lastly, on the [blank] day of the year [blank], when you were in James Moniepenny's house in the Chanonry of Ross and possessed by vile and unclean thoughts, you entered into a covenant and pact with the Devil by renouncing your baptism, becoming his servant, and having sex with him.

All the above-written crimes you have confessed to be true by your signed statements.

[Marginal note]

Margaret said she made a confession. She says she was out of her mind. She stands by her confession of adultery. Mr Robert Ker declares that as far as he is aware, she was in her right mind when she confessed. Mr William Trent says the same. Baillie Chapland[?] says that as far as he could tell she was not out of her mind.

[Footnote]

Margaret Anderson alleges she was ill when she made this confession. She now denies she ever saw Sathan, or that she is a witch. She confesses the two adulteries and one fornication.

2nd February 1658: The jury by the mouth of their foreman found the accused Margaret Anderson guilty by a majority of votes of making a pact with the Devil as described in the confession which was ratified by the witnesses as being a true confession made by her, and that she was not out of her mind when she made it. The jury unanimously found her guilty of the adultery and fornication mentioned in the indictment confessed by her. The Commissioners judged Margaret Anderson and John Ross to be guilty of making a pact with the Devil, and of the various adulteries mentioned in the indictments. They are to be taken to the Castel Hill of Edinburgh and strangled at the stake until they are dead, their bodies to be thereafter burnt to ashes, and their possessions confiscated.

1659

The Stenton Witches.

[Box JC26/26 of Justiciary court Processes in the National Archives of Scotland contains the following records in "Bundle 2".]

Item 11.

Part of the process of the Quarter Sessions at Dumbar held by His Highness's Justices of the Peace, 8th February 1659.

February 7th 1659, at Stentoune.

This day was appointed for confronting the persons named by Bessie Lacost with her. They were all individually brought before her one by one as follows:-

Jonet Wood was brought before her. Bessie Lacost was asked if she had anything to say against Jonet Wood, and she made the following statement. Jonet was at several meetings with the Devil at the Gallowhop, the Home, and

Sande's Hill. She asked the Devil to get revenge on John Crumbe for the money he owed her, and for not marrying her. The Devil answered that he could not manage to do it, because John's house was protected by effective prayer. They went to Mr Robert Davidson's courtyard and finished off a whole barrel of his ale, and Jonet got the last drink of it. They were at Ruchlaw and got some wine there, and she was among them. She was a witch before Bessie knew her. Jonet denies all this.

Marrion Angus was brought before Bessie Lacost, who was asked if she had anything to say against Marrione. She declared that she was as guilty as she herself was. She was at meetings with her at the Gallowhope, Home, and Sandie's Hill. She asked the Devil for revenge on Mr[?] Abbot for a bag of peas that Jonett Yooll stole out of his house, which she brought back again. The Devil said that she would get revenge, but she never got it until two years before he died, when she got a grip on him as he was eating his porridge one morning, and took the power from his tongue and one side.

[Box JC26/26 also contains a bundle labelled "Witchcraft including Items 1, 2, and 3 from a 'bundle Z' ". This contains a document "Ex JC26/26 Bundle 2 Item 3", which would appear to follow on from Item 2 given above. This bundle also contains several items from cases outwith East Lothian, and "Ex JC26/26 Bundle 2, Item 4", which I give after Item 3 below.]

Item 3.

The abovementioned court was adjourned until 21st February in order to proceed further with the interrogation of the witches who were accused and confronted as described above. On that day Captain Thomas Simnell and Captain Robert Home of Whytloch[?] met in the tollbooth of Dumbar, the court was constituted, and proceeded as follows under the chairmanship of Captain Robert Home.

First to be dealt with were the accusations, declarations, and statements in connection with Bessie Lacost's judicial confession and confrontation.

Marion Angus was again called in and questioned about the declarations and accusations of witchcraft. She confessed that about two years ago or so she was asked by the witches Bessie Lacost and Alliesoune Fermer to go wth them. She confessed that she went with them to a place in Stentoune parish called the Horn, where she met several people, the Devil being amongst them. He told her to renounce her baptism, which she did in these words, "I take my baptism from Christ and give it to you."

Secondly, she confessed that she was at another meeting at the Gallowhope about a month after that. The Devil was there. He lay with her and had sex with her. His body was hard and cold. Jonett Wood, Aliesoune Fermer, Hellin Heriott, Jean Sydserffe, and Bessie Lacost were there. She repents of this pact with the Devil from her heart, and for the sin of witchcraft she confessed she says she deserves and desires to die.

Hellin Heriott was questioned, having been denounced as another suspected witch, and against whom many acts of evil intent are alleged and affirmed by Bessie Lacost and others. She confessed that about eight years ago in Bessie Lacost's house in Stentoune, the Devil appeared to her in grey clothes, with a grey cap on his head, when she and Bessie Lacost were sitting by the fire. He asked her if she would be his servant, and she said she would.

She confessed that the reason she had come was to seek revenge from the Devil on an Englishman, a sutler, who was quartered in her house. [A sutler was a person who sold liquor or provisions to soldiers in a camp or garrison.] When she promised to be his servant, he promised he would whip the Englishman out of the village. She renounced her baptism to the Devil in Bessie's house. When she renounced her baptism, the Devil called her Bessie, and that is what she was called at every meeting after that. The Englishman was called Keiver.

About half a year after that, she and Allissoun Fermer, Jean Sydserffe, Marrioun Angus, Jonett Wood, and Bessie Lacost had a meeting at night in the Gallow Hope. They had a piece of meat like beef there, and after they had all eaten some of it, the Devil - who had a bonnet on his head - took Bessie Lacost by the hand. They others took each other by the hand and danced in a ring around the Broad Stonn on the Gallowhope, and sang to each other. They stayed there for an hour, then the Devil told them to treat him and each other honestly, and bade them goodnight.

About three quarters of a year after that they all met at Sandie's Hill, where they sang and danced for a while, then returned home. Bessie Lacost was in charge there.

After that, they were with the Devil in the courtyard at Ruchlaw at night. He called himself Simone. Wine was brought out of the house that time. Aleissonne Fermer got it for them, and they drank it in the courtyard.

Alleissonne Fermer, another witch, was questioned on the previous statements. She confessed that she is guilty of witchcraft by making a pact with the Devil, and that she ...[illegible]. The first time she met the Devil was in her own garden. He was dressed in grey clothes and he asked her if she would be his servant. She answered that she would not. He asked why she would not be his servant when others were, and promised to give her revenge on anyone who wronged her. So she consented to be his servant, and then he put his hand on her head, and another on the sole of her foot, and she said, "Now I renounce my baptism to thee. I renounce my baptism from Christ and give it to thee." He called her by the name Jonett on that occasion, and she was always called Jonett after that. She confessed that the Devil put his hand on her right shoulder, which left it very painful. This did not go away until the Devil came back again and laid his hand on it, and she was freed from the pain.

Bessie Lacost invited them to the Gallowhope to a meeting with the Devil. He met her along with Heline Heriott, Jonet Wood, Marion Angus, Jean Sydserff, Bessie Lacost, and she thinks William Richesone was there. The Devil had sex with her there. She would tell Jonet Wood to her face that she had sought revenge on George Crumble from the Devil. She cannot remember clearly how long she has been the Devil's servant She also confessed that at the meeting in the Gallowhope she fell when they were dancing in a ring and hurt her knee slightly, and the Devil took her by the hand. She got the ale when they were in Mr Robert Dayidson's courtyard, and helped to drink wine at Ruchlaw. For all this she says she neither desires nor deserves to live.

Jean Sydserff, another witch, was questioned and confessed that the Devil came to her bedside and asked her to be his servant and renounce her baptism. At first she refused, but he insisted, and he persuaded her. She confessed that she renounced her baptism to him, and he called her by the name of Jonett.

All the previously named persons, and a man she did not know, met in Mr Robert's courtyard in the evening. They had ale to drink, and it was Aleisome Fermer who got it. After Bessie Lacost was arrested, she and those previously named, and a man she thinks was William Richesoune, met at the end of William Mandersonne's barn in Stentoun. There was a man in grey clothes with a round bonnet on his head, and he ordered them to deny that they were witches. He would vouch for them, and give them anything they wanted to ask for. They met in the courtyard at Ruchlaw at night and drank some ale. Aleisonne Fermer got it and brought it to them.

Having considered the interrogations and the confessions of evildoing through witchcraft by the above named Bessie Lacost, Aleison Fermer, Jeane Sydserffe, Marionne Angus, and Helline Heriot, the evil acts of renouncing their baptism, sex with the Devil, and the other practices, are found to be capital crimes. These five persons are ordered to be escorted to the tollbooth of Edinburgh by William Mandersonne and Robert Wat, the constables of Stentoune, assisted by Patrick Nisbet, Hew Hay, and Rayntoun Pringalle. There they are to be tried on Tuesday 1st March before the judges for criminal cases.

This evidence is ordered to be copied and registered by our clerk of court, and sent on to the clerk of the Criminal Court for the reasons already given, along with the indictments, and complete records of proceedings. Given under our hands in court on the foresaid date. Robert Hume.   Thomas Simnel.

[From the High Court Minute Book JC6/5.] March 1st 1659:

Bessie Lacost , Mareon Angus, Jean Sydserff, Alesoun Fermer, Helen Herriot - Stentoun witches

Pursuer: The Advocate General for the interest of the Commonwealth.

[A standard indictment follows in which the suspects are accused of meeting and having sex with the Devil, renouncing their baptisms, committing malefices, laying on and taking off sicknesses, and causing deaths as described in ttieir "confessions made before His Highness's justices of the peace for the shire of East Lothian". No details are included. However, there is a lengthy note written at the left hand side of the page, which is given below.]

All confessed that they are witches. Bessie Lacost confessed that the Devil lay with her and got a promise from her to be his servant. They had sex in the Gallowhope a couple of years ago.

Marion Angus confessed that she was a witch, that she renounced her baptism and became his servant. She says the Devil lay with her. This was a year ago.

Jeane Sydserfe says she only saw the Devil once. She renounced her baptism to him and promised to be his servant. He did not have sex with her. He gave her the name Jonet, although her name is Jean.

Aleson Fermer declares she only saw the Devil once, at last Martinmas. All four of them were with him. This was "in the land" [in the countryside?]. She renounced her baptism and he called her Jonet. He had sex with her.

Helene Heriot says she renounced her baptism, and met them with the Devil. These four were with her every time. They danced when they met. He gave her the new name of Bessie. It was malice towards an Englishman brought her to the Devil.

March 1st 1659: The jury unanimously find the accused Bessie Lacost, Marion Angus, Helen Heriot, Alison Fermour, and Jean Sydserf guilty of the sin of witchcraft mentioned in their indictment, because it was judicially confessed by all of them.

Since Bessie Lacost Marion Angus, Helen Heriot, Alison Fermour, and Jean Sydserf have confessed judicially and been found guilty by a jury of the sin of witchcraft as described in their indictment, the Commissioners sentence them to be taken to the Castell Hill of Edinburgh on 9th March between two and four o' clock in the afternoon. All of them are to be strangled at a stake until they are dead, their bodies burnt to ashes, and all their goods to be forfeited.

[The interrogation and trial of Bessie Lacost and her co-accused seems to have prompted further investigations, presumably because the suspects Janet Man and Helen Cumming had been implicated by one or more of the first batch of Stenton Witches. The documents dealing with this are in the previously mentioned Box

JC26/26 of Justiciary Court Processes in the National Archives of Scotland, Bundle 2.]

Item 4.

March 11th 1659, at Stentoun.

After being denounced, and arrested by order of the justices of the peace, Jonnett Man was seriously exhorted to make a frank confession. She then absolutely freely and of her own accord declared as follows:-

She began about two and a half years ago when she came to Alesounne Farmer's one day - one of the witches who was recently burnt. She was begging for alms, and Christ was not in her mind. Aleisonne said to her, "Why are you going about like this, Jonet? Can you not find a better way of getting assistance?" She replied that she had grown old and weak and couldn't work for herself. Aleisoun said, "You can get it more easily than that." Then Aleisonne took her into the west room of her house, where the Devil was siting like a man in grey coloured clothes, and a hat on his head like a gentleman.

Right away, the Devil wanted to have sex with her. She had no power to refuse him, so Aleison slipped out and the Devil had sex with her. She thought his penis was cold and he had a sour smell of earth.

He asked her to renounce her baptism. She renounced Christ, and all she had received from Christ, and became the Devil's servant. He called her Bessie and touched her right hand and arm, which left a pain in her arm above the elbow. She promised to be ready to do whatever service he called her to, then the Devil kissed her and went away.

Another time Alleisome Fermer came and told her to come with her. She went to Gallowhop, where they were all dancing and whooping it up ["making goravage"]. The Devil and Bessie Lacost led the ring. She saw about eleven people there altogether. There was Bessie Lacost, Janet Wood, Aleisonne Fermer, Jean Sydserff, Marion Angus, Hellene Heriot, herself, and Helline Cumine, and another three she cannot remember. It was about eleven o'clock at night. The Devil whistled, and they all danced. The Devil took his leave of them courteously, and said they were all his good and joyful servants. Every one of them answered, "My Lord, I am thy servant."

Sometimes she was absent from the meetings, and the Devil was very angry and frowned on her. She could not find it in her heart to repent, for the Devil was locked in her heart, until on one occasion after the minister had prayed she thought her heart was lifted up a little. Now she thanks God that she has found it in her heart to confess the sin of witchcraft. She confessed that she was guilty of many other sins. She had not been to communion for twenty years, and had got no benefit from the church. She had lived in sin for nine years with Alexander Cathil and had three children to him, for which she had never yet repented.

At Stentoun, 14th March 1659.

Helline Cumine was exhorted to declare frankly whether she was guilty of witchcraft or not, and freely declared as follows: -

She is guilty of witchcraft. The first time she ever saw the Devil was at Carfrae Burn where the Devil was riding a horse and came plunging into the water. She was frightened, and cried, "Lord save me!" At that, the Devil ducked down and she saw no more of him then.

The next time she saw him was when he came to her bed and lay on top of her. She turned to the other side of the bed and he went away. Another time Aleison Fermer came to her at night and told her to get up and come away with her. She got up and went to the Gallowhope, but Aleisone Fermer went so fast that she couldn't keep up with her. She decided to go back, but the Devil came to her and cried, "Wait Janet!" He came and threw her down, made her renounce her baptism, and called her Janet. She saw a great number of women there

- about forty, she thought. However, there was a mist between her and them, and she couldn't recognise them. Similarly, she saw a great number of men in another place, but there was a thick mist between her and them too.

At the Court of Justice held by His Highness's Justices of the Peace at Stentoune, 2nd April 1659.

This day, the previously named Janett Man and Helline were produced in Stentoune church before the court. They were indicted for witchcraft, joining with the Devil, and other acts. They were judicially examined before the court in the presence of Captain Thomas Simnell and Archibald Sydserff of Howdine whose signatures are appended. They ratify their confessions and testify as previously recorded.

Tho. Simnell.
Arch. Sydserf.

Court held during the continuation of the Quarter Sessions in the tollbooth of Dumbar, 7th April 1659, by the undersigned justices of the peace.

Having seen, read, and considered the indictments, declarations, examinations, re-examinations, and confessions recorded above against Janet Man and Helline Cuminge, we find malevolent witchcraft sufficiently proved by their own judicial confessions of meetings and get-togethers with the Devil, renouncing their baptisms, having sex with him, and other actions. They therefore declare Janett Man and Helline burning to be found guilty of witchcraft. They are to be taken by the constables of Stentoun and escorted in secure custody to His Highness's prison in Edinburgh. They are to remain there to receive their sentence from the criminal court according to law, on the first Tuesday in May. A warrant for this is ordered, and directed to the keeper of His Highness's Tollbooth of Edinburgh.

Signed on the foresaid day:
Tho. Simnel.   Rot. [illegible].

[On the reverse of this document JC26/26, Bundle 2, Item 4 is the note given below.]

Indictment, charges, evidence, interrogations, and confessions against the witches Janett Man and Helline Cuminge, taken down before the Justices of His Highness's Peace for the East Division of the shire of East Lothian. 1659.

For Mr William Scharpe, or Mr Alexander Hawthorne, clerks to the Criminal Court - either of them, or their deputes.

Signed: J. Lesse.

Item 5

[This is a small loose sheet of paper which properly belongs not with the papers concerning Janet Man and Helen Cumming, but with the case of Bessie Lacost and her associates.] You, Bessie Lacost, Marion Angus, Jean Sydserffe, Aleisone Fermer, and Helline Herriott, are hereby indicted in the name of His Highness Richard, Lord Protector of the Commonwealth of England, Scotland, and Ireland, for joining with and making pacts with the Devil, renouncing your baptism, taking it from Christ and givng it to the Devil, for having sex with the Devil, and in general for living remaining and acting in his service for several years past. These are capital crimes punishable by death according to the laws of this nation.

[Finally, there is a slip of paper marked "Ex JC26/26 Part 2".]

You Jonnett Man and Helline Cumming are hereby indicted in the name of His Highness Richard, Lord Protector of the Commonwealth of England, Scotland, and Ireland, for joining with and making pacts with the Devil, renouncing your baptism, taking it from Christ and giving it to the Devil, for having sex with the Devil, and in general for living remaining and acting in his service for several years past. These are capital crimes punishable by death according to the laws of this nation.

[The record of the trial of Janet Man and Helen Cumming can be found in the High

Several Stenton women were burned for witchcraft on the Castlehill in Edinburgh in 1659. They were interrogated in Stenton church (left), and Dunbar tollbooth. Church towers like this one were often used for imprisoning suspects.

The Register of the Privy Council records the confessions of a group of witches taken down in 1661 before the heritors and elders of Bolton church (below).

Court Minute Book JC6/5, which is given below.]

May 3rd 1659

The case of Janet Man and Helen Cuming, both in Stentoun parish.

To read their confessions.

To call their minister and the constables of Stentoun.

Witnesses: Mr Richard Tweddall, minister, Robert Wat, constable.

[The case begins with a standard preamble citing divine and secular law, and accusing the suspects of making a covenant with the Devil, renouncing their baptism, receiving marks, sex with the Devil, etc. etc. It continues as given below.]

... The confessions made to His Highness's justices of the peace for East Lothian follow: - Namely, you, Janet Man, entered the Devil's service two years ago, and kept an appointment with him in the house of Alesoun Fermour, a witch who was recently burnt. The Devil had sex with you there, and you renounced your baptism, Christ, and all you had received from Christ, and became the Devil's servant. You took the new name of "Bessy", and he touched your right hand and arm, leaving a pain there. You promised to be ready to do all the service the Devil should ask you to do. Then the Devil kissed you and went away. You had a meeting with the Devil another time at the Gallowhope with Aleson Fermor, Bessy Lacost, Helene Cummine, and others, where the Devil whistled and you all danced. When the Devil went away he said you were all his good and joyful servants. You answered, "My Lord, I am thy servant."

[Marginal note.] Jonet Man confessed everything.

And you, Helen Cummine, have confessed yourself guilty of the sin of wfthchcraft. The first time you ever saw the Devil was at Carfraeburne, where the Devil was riding on a horse. The next time was beside your own bed. Another time, Aleson Fermor came to you at night and told you to get up and come away. At that, you came to the Gallowhope where the Devil met you. You renounced your baptism and took the new name of Janet from the Devil.

[Marginal note.] The minister was sworn and testifies that she confessed many times with tears, both to him and to the justices of the peace. All the items contained in her confession and at her interrogation are expressed in her own words. He knows nothing about her being insane. Robert Wat declares that he heard her confess that she renounced her baptism and took a new name.

The Tranent Witches.

[This case is also taken from the High Court Minute Book JC6/5, where it in fact appears recorded before the case of the two Stenton women heard the same day.]

Edinburgh 3rd May [1659]: Judges Mosley and Goodeir.

Christian Cranstoun, widow in Tranent.

Janet Thomson there; wife of William Spence, shoemaker.

Elspeth Fouler, widow there. [Deleted, and marked "dead".]

Barbara Cochrane, widow there.

John Dowglas, living in Tranent.

Janet Crooks, servant to John Achinteck in Prestonpans.

Mareon Lyn, widow, and midwife in Salt Prestonpans.

Helen Simberd, widow there.

Helen Wilson, widow there.

Mareon Guild, wife of Michel Fukcart, shoemaker in Tranent.

Pursuer: The Lord Advocate for the interest of the Commonwealth.

Witnesses:

Archibald Purves,
    living in Tranent parish - present

James Cowan there - present

John Forrester there
James Scot.
John Kincaid
John Hepburn.

[These last three are entered in a different hand, but presumably are also present in court. Once again we see the notorious witch pricker Kincaid.]

[The indictment begins with a standard preamble, and then goes on to set out charges based on the individual confessions of the accused made before "His Highness's Justices of the Peace for East Lothian".]

1. You, Christian Cranstone, for the past fourteen years have used sorcery and witchcraft to cure diseases. Among these cures you used foxglove leaves, and applied them to Robert, the son of George Seutie in the Myles, and to the sons of Adam Johnstone and Patrik Cowane in Tranent. They had asked you to do this for God's sake. When you went to Humbie Wood to look for these leaves, you used to say these words, "These I seek for God's cause." And when you brought them back to the patient you used to say, "This I give for God's sake, and may God give a blessing to it." You also made use of south-running water for curing Patrick Cowan's son, and asked for a mutch [a kind of bonnet] belonging to the child from his mother. You got this and left it beside the well. All the way to the well you said, "I seek it for God's cause," and on the way back you would not say anything until you came to the patient. You did all this by your witchcraft, charming, and sorcery. Also, the Devil's mark was found under your right armpit and leg.

[Marginal note in a different hand.] Confessed that she did these things, but denied witchcraft or that she renounced her baptism. She cured two or three people. Does not know that she has any marks. All the witnesses testify to the "carnal copulation" with the Devil. She denies having sex. Says he lay above her. Kincaid declares he found the mark. James Cowan testifies that he saw it. Says she saw John Thomson [illegible].

2. Also, you, Janet Thomsoune had a meeting with the Devil about two years ago at the dean or Heugh of Tranent, at the place called the Stone Well, where the Devil had sex with you. You received his marks, renounced your baptism, and danced in company with the Devil and several other witches. Also, within the past nine weeks you attended another witches' meeting in the Bray Grein between Tranent and Seatoun about twelve o' clock at night.

[Marginal note] Jonet Thomsone denies everything. She never saw the Devil. Says any confession she made was for fear of torture and putting the gown on her. Mr Robert Hodge declares that her confession was voluntary. John Kincaid declares that she confessed this before the minister in the church. He testifies that she has the marks, and the witnesses declare they saw them. James Scot, Cowane, and the others testify that the confession was voluntary. The accused says she was threatened.

3. And you, Elspeth Fowlar; the Devil appeared to you last harvest in your own house in Tranent, and promised that you would lack none of the necessities of life if you would become his servant. At that you became the Devil's servant, renounced your baptism, and received your own name back from the Devil. Immediately after that the Devil had sex with you in the middle of the floor. Also, within the past six weeks or so you were at another meeting with the Devil and other witches in the Bray Grein between Seatoune and Tranent at night for about two hours. You all danced, and the Devil kissed you when he left, and said, "Be with you." He had sex with you and all the rest.

[Marginal note]: "Dead".

4. Also, you, Barbara Cochrane; the Devil's mark was found on the back of your neck towards your left shoulder. You thereupon

acknowledged that you were a witch, and that the first time you met with the Devil was at the late Meg Maitland's festivities. You saw the Devil there, and he kissed you and had sex with you. You were at another meeting with the Devil at the above-mentioned Bray Grein, with other witches. There were twelve of you. You did not know them as they were masked.

[Marginal note.] Admits that the Devil kissed her, but did not have sex with her. She confessed two twilight meetings with the Devil. She was taken [illegible]. When this and her statements were read over, she confessed it was all true, except having sex with him. The witnesses testify that she confessed everything voluntarily. She confessed that she was at the Bragrein.

5. Also you, Johne Douglase; the Devil appeared to you in your own house last winter about ten o' clock at night, asking if you would be piper to his servants, and he would pay your wages. You promised to do this. The Devil said you would want for nothing and gave you his mark by nipping your neck. A fortnight later you were in the Hewghe or dean of Tranent in company with the Devil and several witches, where they all danced. The Devil kissed them all and told you to play well. Also, last March you were at the Braygrein between Seatoun and Tranent, playing your pipes to the Devil and the other witches, where they all danced. The Devil was in the likeness of a big black man. He kissed them all, and when he left he said, "Goodnight my servants all." The tune that they danced to was "Hulie, the bed will fall" [Be careful, the bed will collapse]. You have two Devil's marks, one on the roof of your mouth, and the other on the outside of your left leg.

[Marginal note.] John Douglas confessed to everything in the indictment. He says there were five with him at the meeting - Christian Cranston, Janet Crooks, Barbra Cochrane, and another two. The Devil gave him [illegible] pipe and took it back from him again. The Devil gave him nothing although he had promised. Confessed the marks. Says he was very much afraid to confess to begin with. They threatened they would put him in the [illegible] and stocks. The witnesses testify that no threats were made.

6. You, Janet Crooks, had a meeting with the Devil about twenty four years ago, in Elphingstoune Garden in the company of a certain Anna Nesmith. There at the Devil's request you renounced your baptism, and became his servant. Since then you have had several meetings at that place with the Devil, and he has had sex with you. You also met the Devil at Gillohaslip between Tranent and the More House, where the Devil took you by the finger and said to you, "Will you serve me?" Then he vanished away. Since last Christmas the Devil appeared to you in your own house where he had sex with you.

[Marginal note.] Denies everything. Says only that she has the marks. James Cowane and the rest of the witnesses testify that she confessed everything voluntarily without torture.

7. Also, you, Marion Logane, a notorious witch, have had many meetings and trysts with the Devil. The first was about ten years ago when the Devil appeared to you at Janet Balfoure's well in Tranent. Shortly afer that, when you were contracting yourself to a certain Elspeth Baptie, your servant girl Jean Craige who was afterwards burnt as a witch, said to you that if you would stay still she would get a gentleman to pay you your wages. Immediately the Devil appeared to you and told you not to worry about your wages, for he would pay them. It seemed to you that he put a coin in your hand, saying it was your hiring penny. Then he had sex with you. Shortly after that the Devil appeared to you like a black dog, beside William Steille's midden, threw dirty water in your face, and called you "Tapok" in the name of Belljebub. ["Tapok" probably has the same meaning as

"taupie" - a scatterbrained young woman.] Also, within the past three years you and your servant girl Margaret Auchemitie had another meeting with the Devil in her garden at Salt Prestoune, where the Devil had sex with both of you, and called your servant "The Brave Dancer". After that, the Devil appeared to you alone at Alexander Lambe's saltpan, and asked if you would continue as his servant. When you said no, he said he would make you be his servant. Also, three months ago you were at the windmill in the Links between Cokeny and Prestoune Pannes with several other witches, where you danced a spring called "Kilt the coat Maggie, and go thy ways with me". [Marginal note.] Marione Logan says it is all very true, and the Devil had sex with her at Archibald Mitchell's garden. The midwife Marione Lyne was at the last meeting at Preston, and many others. Also Helen Simeard and Helen Mesone.

8. You, Marion Lynne, had a meeting with the Devil and several other witches at the windmill at the east end of the Panes. You became the Devil's servant and renounced your baptism. The Devil kissed you and danced with you. Six weeks ago the Devil came to the back door of your house accompanied by three women. However, he was scared away when some men came out of John Nemoe's house.

[Marginal note.] Marion Lyne confessed that the indictment was true. Says she only met the Devil once, and that was nineteen weeks[?] ago. Logane confessed this.

9. You, Helen Simbeard, became the Devil's servant about a year and a half ago, renounced your baptism, and received the Devil's mark on your shoulder where he kissed you. [It is not quite clear whether this means that the Devil left the mark by kissing her on the shoulder, or whether it means that he kissed her at that particular meeting.] You were also at two other meetings with the Devil, one at the Old Kirk at Lammas time, and the other at the windmill. Arrangements were made to meet for merrymaking which did not come off. Also, you have another two marks from the Devil, one over your heart, and the other a little above your left armpit.

[Marginal note.] Helen Simbard denies everything. The witness Robert Donalson and the rest testify that they heard her confess voluntarily. James Scot, James Cowan, and John Hepburne say the same. She admitted that she has the marks, but does not know how she got them. Marione Lynne and Marione Logan say she was at meetings with them.

10. You Helen Wilsone, have had several meetings. You first kept company with the Devil about three years ago in your own house where he had sex with you. The next was at the windmill at the Pannes, where the Devil appeared to you like a big black man. He laid his hand on your shoulder, and you heard a noise like the sound of a jews' harp. ["ane trumpe". This could conceivably also mean a trumpet.]

[Marginal note.] Helen Wilsone confessed this. Says Agnes Thomsone first took her to the meetings, that she renounced her baptism, and that the Devil nipped her shoulder. Helene Simbard was with her; also Lyne and Logane. The Devil kissed her ["but did not have sex with her" deleted]. The Devil had sex with her two years ago at night. She was sleeping, and he was very heavy on her.

11. You, Marione Guild, had a meeting with the Devil and certain other witches about three months ago at the Bray Grein between Seatoune and Tranent, where you engaged yourself in the Devil's service. The next day the Devil appeared to you when you were coming between the Blake Gutter and Olivestob. He was in the likeness of a black man. He gripped you by the left shoulder and gave you his mark. A little after that he came to you again and arranged to meet you at the Blake Gutter, and promised to give you a gift. You did not keep

that appointment, but had another meeting with the Devil at Braygrein.

[Marginal note.] Says she never saw the Devil except at Olivestob, and that she was never at the Braegrein. She denies that she ever engaged in the Devil's service.

Everything written above was confessed by each and every one of you in the presence of the Commissioners for His Highness's Peace.

Edinburgh 3rd May 1659.

[Fifteen Edinburgh merchants and tradesmen are listed in the High Court Minute Book as members of a jury which seems not only to have tried the Tranent suspects, but also the two women from Stenton. There may have been two separate trials, but it reads as if both sets of suspects were tried together.]

The jury by the mouth of their foreman unanimously find the accused Marion Guild innocent and not guilty of the crime of witchcraft mentioned in her indictment, and by a majority find the accused Janet Thomson and Helen Cuming innocent and not guilty of the crimes of witchcraft mentioned in their indictments.

Signed: George Cairncross, foreman of the jury.

May 4th 1659.

The Commissioners sentence Marione Logane, Marione Lyne, Jonet Man, Cristiane Cranstoun, Barbara Cochrane, John Douglass, Jonet Crooks, Helene Simbeard, and Helene Wilsone, having been found guilty of the crimes of witchcraft contained in their indictments, to be strangled at stakes, their bodies burnt to ashes, and their goods to be confiscated. This is to be done at the times and places indicated: -

Marione Logane, Barbara Cochrane, John Dowglass, Jonet Crooks, Helene Simbeard, and Helene Wilsoune are to be taken back to Tranent to be strangled and burnt there on 5th May at the head [*i.e.* the upper end] of Tranent.

Marione Lyne and Cristiane Cranstoune are to be strangled and burnt at the same place on the 14th of this month.

Janet Man is to be taken to the Castellhill of Edinburgh on Wednesday 11th of this month between two and four o' clock in the afternoon to be strangled there and her body to be burnt afterwards.

A Stenton Acquittal

May 4th 1659. Edinburgh. Judges Mosley and Goodear.

Helen Cuming appeared, accused and prosecuted at the instance of Mr Robert Hodges, Solicitor General. Forasmuch as by divine law ... [A standard preamble follows.] ... namely she confessed she was guilty of the sin of witchcraft, and that the first time she saw the Devil it was at Carfraeburn, where the Devil was riding on a horse. The next time was beside her own bed, and another time Aleson Fermor came to her and told her to get up and come away. She then came to the Gallowhauch *[sic]* where the Devil met her. She renounced her baptism and took the new name of Janet from him in the way specified in her indictment. Helen denied the truth of this indictment. The court then referred her to a trial by jury composed of the persons in the attached list.

Gavin Williamson, bookbinder in Edinburgh etc etc

The jury having been chosen sworn and admitted, and the statements of various witnesses received read out and examined, the jury retired from court. They elected George Cairncroce their foreman, and discussed and voted upon the charges of the indictment. Having considered these maturely and well, along with the witnesses' evidence, they entered again into court, where by the mouth of their foreman, by a majority verdict they found the accused Helen Cumming innocent and not guilty of the crime of witchcraft mentioned in her indictment At this, Helen asked for a written record from the court. This was extracted by me, Mr Alexander Hamilton, clerk to the Criminal Court.

Signed: Alexander Hamilton.

[Similar entries in the High Court Minute Book record the acquittals of Janet Thomson, wife of William Spence, shoemaker in Tranent; and Mareon Guild, wife of Micheall Fuchcart in Tranent.]

1660

Unfinished business in Tranent.

[These papers are from Box JC26/26 of Justiciary Court Processes in the National Archives of Scotland. The bundle is marked "JC26/26/5/1 - 5 Tranent Witches". They record proceedings taken against the two Tranent women acquitted of witchcraft the previous year. The new Restoration regime may have been dissatisfied with the verdict reached under the Commonwealth authorities, or it may be that the two women had never actually been released after their acquittal, and the new regime is wondering whether their release is justifiable or not.]

At Tranent, 25th November 1660.

This day the kirk session met, and the minister read a letter to the elders which had been sent to him by the right honourable Earl of Cassilis, Lord Justice General, to be communicated to the session. He is asked to make all possible inquiries in order to obtain information for His Lordship regarding the guilt of Jonet Thomson and Marion Yool, who are in the tollbooth of Edinburgh. To do this, he is to gather information from the kirk session, their neighbours in the parish, or any others who know most about their guilt and their complicity in the crime of witchcraft. An answer is to be returned by next week.

In obedience to His Lordship's request, the minister asked the elders what they knew in particular about Janet Thomson and Marion Yool concerning their involvement in the crime of witchcraft which they are suspected and accused of. They answered that at present they could remember nothing except what was contained in their papers, that is, the confessions which were in the hands of Walter Scot, one of the elders present, who had been depute clerk to the justice of the peace at the time.

Walter Scot was asked to produce these papers and show them to the session next Tuesday, which he promised to do. The rest of the elders, especially Richard Turnbul, Archibald Purves, and Jacob Nicolson, in whose districts the suspects lived, were asked to search their own memories, and to inquire in the suspects' guilt and involvement in this crime from the neighbours living beside them. They are to report back on Friday night.

At Tranent 27th November 1660.

Walter Scot showed the session two papers. One contained the confession of Marion Yool, attested and signed by the minister and the elders Richard Turnbull and Walter Scot. The other contained the confession of Janet Thomson attested and signed by Mr John Sinclair, minister at Ormeston, Ninian Reid who lives in Preston, and Mr James Cowan in Tranent.

The minister announced that a search had been made for further information on the suspects, but he had heard nothing more than what is contained in the papers, except that when he asked several of the neighbours if they knew of any malefice done by them, or if they made use of charms or superstitious practices, they answered that they knew of no such thing.

He also declared that as far as Jonet Thomson is concerned, when the marks were found on her it was thought strange that they were in such sensitive places, on each side under her ears. She confessed very freely to him what is in the record of her confession, until it came to the part where it says, "Devour her, devour her." After that she never confessed anything else in his hearing. Marion Yool also confessed very freely in his hearing the things contained in the record of her confession.

Particular inquiry was made of the elders, especially Robert[?]Turnbull in whose district Marion Yool lived. He replied that he had heard nothing more than is contained in the record of her confession.

Archibald Purves and Jacob Nicolson, in whose district Jonet Thomson lived, reported that after making inquiries, they heard nothing more than is contained in he record of her confession, except that when she and Janet Thomson [sic] and Marion Yoole were brought in to the tollbooth of Edinburgh, a certain Patrick Creighton visited them and said to them that if they would consistently deny everything he would stake his life for them. After that they could never be brought to confess. One time when Janet Thomson's husband William Spens came to visit her, she said to him, "My heart, you needn't worry, for a man came in and said that if we denied everything he would stake his life for us." Also, the elder Archibald Purves reported that he had been informed that some time after she confessed, Janet Thomson said to her husband William Spens when he came to visit her, "My heart, I don't know how this has happened to me. I want you to share my clothes among my sisters." William Spens was called in and questioned on these particulars. He answered that it was true that this was what Janet said to him when he came to visit her.

The rest of the elders were asked individually if they knew anything more than the information already given about the guilt of these two persons Marion Yoole and Jonet Thomson. They answered that they knew nothing more about them. However, they remembered that others had been denounced and imprisoned, and some of them had been released on bail, as can be found in the records of the justices of the peace who sat at Tranent. Some had been released without bail, and some were denounced who were not imprisoned.

Taking all these points into consideration, the session orders a copy of the minutes of the meeting to be made and given to the minister, together with the two papers signed by Walter Scot, who was depute clerk at the time. The minister is requested to present these to the Lord Justice General.

Copied from the records of the church of Tranent by me, Mr Adam Kilgour, clerk to the session.

Signed: A. Kilgour.

[This is an unusually neat and legible document. The spelling is good, and the punctuation remarkably so.]

[The rest of the papers in this bundle are in fact records of the evidence taken down in the process leading up to the trials of the previous year which resulted in the execution of several of the accused, and the acquittal of Janet Thomson and Marion Yool/Guild. These documents are probably the confessions mentioned as being in the possession of Walter Scot, which have been sent on to the Lord Justice General as described.

It is most unlikely that the two women would be retried on the charges of which they had been acquitted, so the Restoration authorities were probably checking to see if there was any evidence to justify trying them on new charges of witchcraft. There seems to be no record of the ultimate fate of Janet and Marion, but since no new evidence was forthcoming, it seems likely that the authorities would have little option but to release them. The fact that there is no record of another trial would seem to support this happy conclusion.]

Item 3. [The numbering of the items in "Bundle 5" seems rather confused. However, I give them as I got them.]

Tranent 24th April 1659.

Marion Guild, wife of Michele Focker,

shoemaker in Tranent, a witchcraft suspect named by Elspeth ffouler, a confessing witch. She denied that she had been involved with Elspeth in the crime of witchcraft. However, Espeth Fouller still insisted and maintained that Mareon was a witch and that she had seen her at a meeting at the Brae Greane between Tranent and Seatoun where the Devil was in their company, and that they danced, and that she ... [A whole line is illegible here.] ... Therefore Mareoun was searched for the Devil's marks by the common searcher, who found a mark beneath her left armpit with a "dug" or teat of insensible flesh. This was done before Mr Thomas Kirkadye, minister at Tranent, David Huiesoune, James Scot, and Walter Scot, elders in the parish, and witnesses to the finding of this insensible mark.

Mareone was once again questioned in tile presence of the minister; Ritchard Trumble in Tranent, elder; and Mr Alexander Dunbar[?], clerk of the peace. She confessed that eleven weeks ago or so she was at a meeting with certain witches at the Brae Green between Tranent and Seatoun with Elspeth Fouller, Christiane Cranstoune, Jonett Watsone, Jonnet Cruiks, Jonnett Thomsone, and Barbara Cochrane. Jonnet Watson played to them on two stones[?]... [Several illegible words.]... This was the first meeting she was at with them. She confessed it was there she engaged in the Devil's service. The day after this meeting the Devil appeared to Mareon when she was coming by the stone between the Black Gutter and [illegible]. He was in the likeness of a black man. He looked at her and gripped her by the left shoulder where the mark is. She said, "Where... [illegible] ... at me?" and he went away. Shortly after that he came to her again, and arranged to meet her the next day at the Black Gutter. He promised to give him a gift if she would meet him there. He was dressed all in black with a side-cloak. She did not turn up for that meeting, but she was at a later meeting with the persons already mentioned at the Brae Greane. However, she did not see the Devil there.

Signed:

Thomas Kirkaldie, witness.

R. Turnbull, witness.

Walter Scott, witness.

"Ex JC26/26   Bundle 5 Item 1."

[On the reverse side.] Tranent Witches. Mr Robert Hodges of Wester Gladsmuir and Mr Andrew Marjoribanks in Salt Preston, Justices of His Highness's Peace for the County of East Lothian, hereby certify and declare to the commissioners for criminal confessions sitting at Edinburgh that the enclosed confession was taken from and acknowledged by Marion Guild on the day and at the place indicated.

Witnessed by our hands at Tranent, 27th April 1659.

A. Marjoribanks.   Robert Hodges.

Tranent, 27th April 1659. Present: Mr Andrew Marjoribanks and Mr Robert Hodges of Wester Gladsmuir, Justices of His Highness's Peace for the County of East Lothian.

You, Christian Cranstoun, widow in Tranent, are hereby indicted in the name of His Highness for the horrid and damnable sin of witchcraft committed by you, and of which you are guilty, contrary to God's law and the statutes of this nation.

Christian Cranstoun appeared and confessed that about fourteen years ago she used to cure diseases. She learned this from a certain Joke Cranston in Humbie wood, and Issobel Hepburn, a vagrant woman. Among the various cures she used, she used to make use of foxglove leaves. She applied them to Patrik, the son of George Hendrie in the Myllis, and to the sons of Adam Johnstoun and Patrick Cowan in Tranent. These persons had asked the cures from her beforehand for God's sake. When she went to Humbie Wood to get the leaves, she would say these words, "These I seek for God's comfort[?]." When she brought them back to the patient she used to say, "This I give for God's sake. God give a blessing to it."

She also confessed that she made use of springs and running water for curing Patrick Cowan's son in Tranent. She asked the child's mother for a "mutch" [a kind of close-fitting bonnet] belonging to the child. She got it and left it beside the well. She sought the cure for God's comfort[?] all the way to the well, muttering it in her mind. As she was returning she would say nothing, although many people tried to speak to her. When she came in to the patient she said, "God be here," when she first came in.

She also confessed that about two years ago the Devil appeared to her for the first time in the Heugh or dean on the west side of Tranent, in green clothes. He had sex with her, and as she was going away he appeared bigger and bigger, and uglier. This sight frightened her, and afterwards she was ill for eight weeks.

She confessed that a quarter of a year after that, the Devil came to her in her own house during the night, about midnight, when the doors and windows were shut, and laid his face against her brow. She found it cold like lead. He laid the rest of his body on her body above the bedclothes. The doors and windows were also shut when he went away, saying, "Be with you."

She confessed that another time she was in the Heugh or dean of Tranent, gathering snails in the morning about sunrise, and she saw that ugly thief the Devil dressed in green, in the company of Jonet Crooks, Jonet Nalsone, Catherine Gray, and John Douglas, who all live in Tranent. She declares that Janet Crooks, and a certain [illegible] Millen in Tranent used foxglove leaves to cure diseases as she herself did.

She freely acknowledged this to be true in the presence of the Justices of the Peace. Witnessed by James Cowan, Jeams Scot, and John Forrester in Tranent.

As a result of this confession she was searched for the Devil's mark. When she was examined by John Kincaid the common searcher, he found the Devil's mark under her right armpit, into which a great long pin was put; also another mark on her leg. Both were insensible and there was no blood at all.

Extract made by me,
Alexander Dick, clerk of the peace.
James Couane, witness.
James Scott, witness.
J. Forrester, witness.

Mr Robert Hodges of Wester Gladsmuir and Mr Andrew Majoribanks in Saltpreston, Justices of His Highness's Peace for the County of East Lothian certify and declare to the Criminal Council sitting in Edinburgh that the enclosed confession was taken and acknowledged in our presence by Christian Cranstoun, on the day and at the place indicated. Witness our hands at Tranent, 27th April 1659.

Robert Hodges.   A. Marjoribanks.

"ExJC26/26/5 Item 2."

Mr Robert Hodges of Wester Gladsmore and Mr Andrew Marjoribanks in Saltpreston, Justices of His Highness's Peace for the County of East Lothian, humbly certify and declare to the commissioners for criminal confessions sitting at Edinburgh, that the enclosed confession was taken and acknowledged in our presence by Elspeth Fuller on the day and at the place mentioned. Witness our hand at Tranent, 27th April 1659.

R. Hodges.   A. Marjoribanks.

You, Elspeth Fowler, living in Tranent, are hereby indicted in the name of His Highness for the horrid and damnable crime of witchcraft committed by you, and of which you are guilty, contrary to the command of God's laws and the statutes of this nation.

Elspeth Fuller appeared and confessed herself to be a witch. She said the Devil appeared to her last harvest in the likeness of a great big black man. This was in her own house during the day about twelve o'clock. She was standing between her [illegible] bench and her bed. He asked her what she wanted, and she answered that she was poor and had no means of support. The Devil replied that if she would become his servant she would want for nothing. She therefore became his servant and renounced her baptism; and the Devil called her Elspeth Fuller, her own name. Immediately after this he had sex with her in the middle of the floor.

She also confessed that within the past five or six weeks, she was at a meeting with her master the Devil at the Bra Green between Seaton and Tranent. This was at night, for about two hours. She was accompanied by Barbara Cochran, widow in Tranent; Margaret Robertson, wife of the weaver John Nicolson in Tranent; and Marion Lowrie, wife of John Clerk jr, butcher in Tranent. They all danced with their master the Devil, and he kissed each of them. When he went away he said, "Be with you."

She declared also that Christiane Cranston, Catherine Gray, Janet Watson, Jonet Crook, and John Douglas, who all live in Tranent, were allied with her in the Devil's service.

She confessed all this to be true in the presence of the above-mentioned justices of the peace; Mr Alexander Dick, clerk of the peace in Tranent; James Couane there; and John Forrester, constable in Tranent.

New extract made by me, Alexander Dick, clerk of the peace.

Archibald Purves, witness
James Scot, witness
James Couane, witness
J. Forrester, witness

Tranent, 27th April 1659.
Elspeth Fouler appeared in the presence of the forementioned justice of the peace, and was further questioned about how she came to be involved in the crime of witchcraft, and the extent of her guilt, which she had previously admitted. She declared that Marion Gray, the wife of Thomas Logan, coal miner in Tranent; Jean Lauson[?], widow there; Marion Guild, the wife of Michael Fockart, shoemaker there; Elspeth Potts[?], wife of John Faicer[?], weaver in Tranent; and Jonet Thomson, the wife of William Spens, shoemaker there, were all present at a meeting at the Bragreen. The Devil was like a big black man, and they all danced there. The Devil kissed them all, and had sex with her and the rest. When he went away he said, "Be with you all."

She also confessed this freely in the presence of the justice of the peace, witnessed by James Scott, John Forrester, and James Cowin in Tranent.

Extract made by me Alexander Dick, clerk of the peace.

J. Forrester, witness.
James Scot, witness.
James Cowane, witness.

[The text of "Ex JC26/26/5 Item 2." is written on a long folded sheet. The note below is given on the reverse side.]

Elspeth Fouller mentioned in this record died this morning in prison of diarrhoea ["ane flux"]. As witness my hand 28th April 1659, before these witnesses - Robert Hendrie and John Forester, constables for the parish of Tranent. Alexander Dick, clerk of the peace. J. Forrester, witness. Robert Hendry, witness.

[Janet Thomson is the subject of the first item on the next page. Since this is identical to "Item 5", it is omitted here and given later.]

You Barbara Cochrane, widow in Tranent... [A standard indictment follows.] Barbara Cochrane appeared, accused as described, and was confronted with Elspeth ffowler who affirmed to her face that she had been present with herself, the Devil, and the rest of the previously named persons at the Bragrein between Tranent and Seatone, on the occasion previously described. However, Barbara denied this. She said that she would be happy to admit that she was the Devil's servant, if any mark was found on her, apart from the normal marks women have. She was then searched and examined by John Kincaid, the public examiner of witches. He found the Devil's marks on two separate places on her body, on the back of her neck towards her left shoulder. He put a great long pin into each of them, which she did not feel. Immediately after that Barbara cried out in the presence of the justices of the peace, "Foul thief, you have deceived me now! You have deceived me now!" She admitted she was a witch, and that the first time she met the Devil was at the "feasts" of the late Meg Maitland, who was burnt as a witch. She saw the Devil there wearing green clothes. He kissed her, and the others who were there with her, and had sex with her. In company with her and the Devil were Meg Maitland; Issobell Home[?], widow in Tranent; the late Hellen ffleck; the late Cristian Harper; and Elspeth Colville, the wife of Adam Purves, baker at the West Port of Edinburgh. She was with the Devil at the Bragrein. He was dressed in green. There were many others there, twelve of them; people of a higher social class, dressed in black. She did not recognise them as they were all masked.

She declared all this to be true before these witnesses: John Forrester, constable in Tranent; James Scot, Archibald Purves, and James Cowin there.

Extract copied by me, Alexander Dick, clerk to the peace.

J. Forrester, witness.

James Cowane, witness.

Archibald Purves, witness.

James Scott, witness.

[On the reverse side of this page is the usual declaration by Hodges and Marjoribanks endorsing the confession. If the above account of events is in fact an accurate record, it would seem to be a remarkable confirmation of the reality of witch-marks. It sounds as if Barbara believed herself to be under the Devil's protection, and was horrified to find that he had let her down. On the other hand, perhaps the outburst of "foul thief!" was not meant for the Devil, but addressed to Kincaid, whose tricks of the trade had enabled him to stick pins in her without her feeling them.]

Tranent 27th[?] April 1659.

You John Douglas, living in Tranent... [A standard indictment follows.] This day John Douglas appeared in the presence of the previously named justices of the peace, and confessed that the Devil first appeared to him in his own house about ten o' clock at night, and said to him, "John, will you be a piper to my servants? I shall pay you your wages." John promised to do so, and the Devil said that he should not want. The Devil was dressed in green, and something nipped John's neck.

He also confessed and declared that about a fortnight after that he was in the Heuch or dean of Tranent with the Devil, who was in the likeness of a big black man. John played the pipes there. In company with him and his master the Devil were the previously named Barbara Cochran, widow in Tranent; Cathren Gray there; Elspeth Fuller, widow there; and Jonet Crooks, widow there. They all danced. The Devil kissed them all, and told him to play again and he would not want.

He also confessed that about twenty days ago, or a month or thereabouts, he was at the Bragreen between Seaton and Tranent, playing his pipes to the Devil. Barbara Cochrane, Elspeth Fowler, Catherine Gray, Cristiane Cranstoun, and Janet Crooks. They all danced there, and the Devil kissed them all. He was like a big black man. When he went away he said, "Goodnight my servants all." The tune they danced to was

"Hulli the bed will fall" ["Be careful, the bed will collapse" - no prizes for guessing the activity inferred.] He freely confessed the truth of all this before the justices of the peace and John Forrester, constable in Tranent; James Scot, tailor there; and James Cowane; witnesses to the confession. John was searched and two marks were found on him, one in the roof of his mouth, and another in the outside of his left leg, both of which were insensible.

Extract copied by me Alexander Dick, clerk of the peace.

James Scott, witness.

Archbald Purves, witness.

James Couane, witness.

J. Forrester, witness.

[Endorsed on the reverse side by Hodges and Marjoribanks.]

You, Jonet Crooks, widow in Tranent... [A standard indictment follows.] The same day Jonet Crooks appeared, and declared that the Devil first came to her in the garden of Elphingstoun, in green clothes. Anna Nasmith first introduced her to the Devil. She said to her, "Jonet, I'll get you a good master." The Devil appeared to her in the garden in green clothes, and made her renounce her baptism and become his servant. This was about twenty four years ago. She was at several meetings at that place, and the Devil had sex with her. There were several other people at these meetings. They were masked and she knew none of them.

She also declares that she met the Devil at Gilwhaslip between Tranent and the Crosshouse, where he took her by the finger and said, "Will you serve me?" and then vanished. Since around Christmas time the Devil has appeared to her in her own house, where he lay with her and had sex with her.

She freely acknowledges all this to be true, in the presence of the justices of the peace; John Forrester, constable in Tranent; James Cowane there; and James Scott.

Extract copied by me Alexander Dick, clerk to the peace. James Couane, witness. Archibald Purves, witness. James Scot, witness. J. Forrester, witness. [Endorsed on the reverse side by Hodges and Marjoribanks.]

"ExJC26/26/5" Item 5. Tranent 27th April 1659.

Today, Jonet Thomson, wife of William Spence, shoemaker in Tranent, a suspected witch on whom the Devil's marks were found by John Kincaid the public searcher, was questioned about her guilt in the sin of witchcraft. She confessed that she was a frequent curser and blasphemer, and in particular she often cursed her husband and children. What was frequently in her mouth was that the Devil would take either her or them away. She acknowledges that this, with her many previous sins, was the first factor in the Lord's deserting her and turning her over to the power of Sathan.

Also about two years ago she was taken out of her own house by a witch, Jonet Dowglas, to the dean or Heuch of Tranent, and at a place called the Shirrie Well the Devil appeared to her for the first time in the likeness of a black cow. He then changed his shape into the form of a man clad in green clothes. Jonet Douglas was sitting beside him, and said to the Devil, "Devour her, devour her!" Then the Devil, in the form of a man as described, threw her over [illegible] to the well and had sex with her. After that he put his hands round her neck where the marks are. She supposes that she got these marks from him, although she was not aware of them. He called her by name, and asked her to renounce her baptism and become his servant. She had no power to refuse, and immediately became his servant. Immediately after that several witches, ten or eleven of them, came up to her in the dean or Heuch. She did not recognise them as their faces were covered, and it was at night. They all danced there, she along with them. When they parted, the Devil said, "Be with you."

She also confessed that she was at another meeting with certain other witches at the Bra Green between Tranent and Seaton, about twelve o'clock at night, within the past eight weeks or so. In company with her were Marion Guild, who took her to the meeting, Jonet Balfour, Jonet Nealson, Margaret Robertson, Elspeth Robertsone, Jonet Crooks, Jonet Bartelman, Cristian Cranstoun, Elspeth Fouler, Barbare Cochran, Jonet Douglas, and John Douglas. They all danced and made merry, and John played to them.

She confessed this to be true before J. Sinclar, witness to the [illegible] of this confession. B. Reid, witness. James Birnie[?], witness.

[On the reverse side of this page is the note given below.]

Jonet Thomson, the person named in the text, appeared and completely denied all of the confession. Asked why, she said that she thought it would save her from burning. She then immediately admitted again that it was true.

[As we have seen, Janet Thomson and Marion Yool/Guild were acquitted of witchcraft in 1659, and now in 1660 the evidence was being reviewed. As previously observed, however, there is no evidence that they were ever retried.

John Forrester, the Tranent constable mentioned, was entrusted with the duty of disposing of the forfeited possessions of the Tranent witches. See the previous chapter "Trial by Commission", 8th August 1662.]

1661

A witchcraft trial in Musselburgh.

[This trial is recorded in the Books of Adjournal JC2/10, P. 4. The suspects seem to have lived not only outside the actual burgh of Musselburgh, but outwith the parish of Inveresk, so they could not be called East Lothian residents, either in terms of ancient or modern boundaries. However, they apparently resided within the jurisdiction of the Regality of Musselburgh, and so were imprisoned in Musselburgh and tried there by a jury composed mostly of Musselburgh people. Because of this I have included the case, albeit mostly in summary form.]

July 29th 1661.

Mr John Prestoune, bailie of the Regality of Mussilburgh appeared for the Earl of Lauderdaill, and wished to be allowed to sit with the Justice Depute in the trial of the following persons, all living within the regality. The request was granted. [The Earl of Lauderdale was Musselburgh's feudal superior.]

The accused: David Johnstoune.

Agnes Loch, wife of Patrick Robertson in Sunniesyd.

Margaret Rammage.

Jonet Lyle in Edmistoune.

Jonet Dale, wife of George Bell, coal miner.

Indicted and accused of the crimes of sorcery and witchcraft specified in the indictment. Prosecutor: Mr Robert Douglas, for His Majesty's Advocate.

After the reading of their individual indictments in court, all of the accused named above confess and acknowledge them to be true. The prosecutor asked for a written record.

The jury:

Adam Greinlaw, burgess of Mussilbrugh.

Patrick Carfra, burgess there.

David Alexander in ffischerraw.

Walter Clerk in Mussilbrugh.

John Hill in Edmistoune.

William Thomesone,
 burgess of Mussilbrugh,

Wm. Leslie, burgess there.

Thomas Baillie in Edmistoune.

David Ros, burgess of Mussilbrugh.

Patrick Cass[?] in Sunysyd.

Robert Robiesone in Brunstoun Milne.

Thomas Hog in Mussilbrugh.

John Meikle in Brigend.
Oliver Calderwood in Mussilbrugh.
Wm. Ramage, shoemaker there.

The jury was lawfully sworn, and no objections were made against them. The Prosecutor then asked for a written record of this. He declared that the jury would be guilty of willful error if they acquitted the accused of the crimes contained in their indictments.

David Johnstoune;
Agnes Loch, wife of Patrick Robertson in Suniesyd;
Margaret Rammage;
Jonet Lyle in Edmistoune; and
Jonet Dale, wife of George Bell, cottier;

accused and pursued by Robert Dalgleish, substitute to Sir John Fletcher, His Majesty's Advocate for His Highness's Interest, for the crimes of sorcery and witchcraft contained in their indictments…

[Since none of the "crimes" were committed in East Lothian, I have summarised the indictments as follows. David Johnstoun was accused of entering the Devil's service eleven years previously. He met the Devil at the Burrowmuir, received the Devil's mark on his leg and the new name of William. The Devil was in the shape of a big grim-looking man dressed in black. David met the Devil again at Wolmet Bank with several other people, and again at the Grein Lawes.

Agnes Loch entered the Devil's service twelve months previously when she was returning from Dalkeith. The Devil met her at the Sheriffhall Burn as a man dressed in green. He promised her money, and marked her on the shoulder and upper thigh. She agreed to serve him, and at a subsequent meeting in the same place, she had sex with him and renounced her baptism. She attended several meetings with other people during the following year.

The previous winter, between Christmas and Shrove Tuesday, Margaret Rammage met the Devil in Elspet Haliburtone's house in the likeness of a black man. He marked her on the shoulder. Five weeks later she entered into the Devil's service and renounced her baptism at the Sheriffhall Burn, and she later had another meeting in the same place with the Devil and other notorious witches.

Jonet Lyle, widow in Edmistoun, entered the Devil's service a year previously. She met the Devil as she was going round the back of Edmistoun House. The Devil asked her to be his housekeeper because his wife was dead. He gave her what she thought was a silver coin, but she found afterwards that it was just a stone. Three months later she met the Devil at Wolmet Bank where she renounced her baptism and agreed to become the Devil's servant various other notorious witches were present.

Jonet Dale, wife of George Bell, coal miner, first met the Devil fourteen years previously in the company of two other women, the Devil laid his hand on her shoulder. Not long after that she attended another meeting on Sheriffhall Muir with various others. She renounced her baptism and entered the Devil's service, taking the name Jonet Cleirkeyes. She was at another meeting at Wolmet Bank with other notorious witches fifteen weeks before her trial. The accused were all found guilty and sentenced to be taken to the "ordinary place of execution of the brugh of Mussilbrugh" between two and four o'clock in the afternoon of 30th July, which was the following day. They were to be strangled at the stake and burned. Their moveable goods were to be forfeited to the King's use. At this, the baillie of the Regality of Musselburgh protested that the sentence must not prejudice the Earl of Lauderdale's right to the forfeited goods, as feudal superior of the Regality.]

[By tradition, the place where Musselburgh's witches were executed was at the "Bogle Hole", off Campie Road.]

[Box JC26/27 contains a bundle of Justiciary

Court papers labelled "Musselburgh Witches". This is supposed to contain eleven items. However, a note explains that some items have been misplaced, and some ought to be elsewhere. In any case, as far as I can see. very little of the material actually relates to Musselburgh people, and much of it concerns Janet Cock from Dalkeith.

Item 4, part of Item 6, and Item 7 concern David Johnston, one of the accused in the case summarised from the Books of Adjournal. He is described as living in Musselburgh.]

Item 4.

11th July 1661: In the presence of Walter Gewine[?], John Strachan, John Carfrae, John Bennet and James Ogilvie, David Johnstone confessed that about thirteen years ago he was going to Edinburgh with a load of coal. Near the Barowmure the Devil appeared to him in the likeness of a man in black clothes. The Devil asked David where he was going. He replied that he was a poor man going to the town with a load of coal. The Devil told him that if he served him he would never want. He agreed, and a year after that, at about ten or eleven at night at Wollmet Bank he met the Devil in the company of William King, Elspet Helebourtone, Janet Dells, and Walter Couane, The Devil gave him a mark on the leg and made him renounce his baptism, which he forgot *[sic]*. David also said that just before Janet Deall's daughter was married they had a meeting at the Grain Law with the people mentioned, where they had dancing and piping.

John Graham, witness. John Bennet, witness.

At Musselburgh 17th July 1661: Today in the presence of Mr George Rhine, James Hodge, James [illegible], and James Byres, David Johnston ratified his previous statement.

M. Phin, witness. James Hodge, witness. James [illegible]. James Byers, witness.

Item 6.

[This document is written in dreadful handwriting, with many deletions and insertions. Only part of it relates to David Johnston, and the others mentioned are not Musselburgh people.]

Musselburgh tollbooth 26th July 1661, in the presence of Alexander Colville.

David Johnstoun, portioner in Musselburgh appeared, when questioned he confessed that the Devil appeared to him at the Borrowmore eleven years ago, and he entered his service there. The Devil promised him more, but never gave him anything. He renounced his baptism and was called William, and then the Devil gave him a mark on the leg. Another time, he was at a meeting with the Devil at the Wolmet Bank. Margaret Dailies, William King, and Walter Cowane who is now dead, were present. His third meeting with the Devil was at the Grienlawis, where the people previously named were present. He declares that he has not been to communion since he entered the Devil's service, nor has he often been to church since that time. [Probable meaning. This sentence is difficult to decipher.]

[The statements and confessions of several others follow, then there is another passage relating to David Johnston.]

["He confesses that he did not know..." deleted] the Devil the first time when he appeared as a big grim-looking man in black clothes... [illegible]... Within two days of doing so he was sorry that he had renounced his baptism. The Devil promised him money when he did it. When he was asked how he knew it was the Devil when he first met him, he answered it was because the Devil wanted to hire him, but had nothing for him to do but to follow him around ["walk at his foot"]. When he was asked how he knew him at the second meeting, he said he was angry[?] with him because he had told him to renounce his baptism.

Item 7.

Musselburgh 28th July 1661: David Johnston appeared and was asked if he was guilty of the sin of witchcraft. He says that he [illegible] little of it. He says that he knows no more about witchcraft than a child in its mother's womb. When he was arrested he was put in a garment of horsehair ["ane hair cloath"] which made him confess that he had been with Janet Dailies and others at the Borrowmure. He only confessed that he renounced his baptism because he was forced to say it. He would not go back on what he said in front of the minister. Questioned again, he declares that he will not deny what he has already confessed, whether it is true or not.

After that he declared that it is about eleven years since Sathan beguiled him. When he was going to Edinburgh with coal Sathan said to him at the Borrowmuir, "Poor man, do you lack money? I'll give it to you." He says that Sathan asked him if he would be his man, and he promised to be his servant. Sathan gave him a name, calling him William. He met him three times; once at the Borrowmuir, once at the Wolmet Bank, and another time at the Greenlaw. In these places he danced in company with Janet Dailies and the rest. He says that the Devil was black, and at the Wolmet Bank looked to him like a man. He said that all the above-written confessions were true.

He declares that he made his first pact with him at the Borrowmuire. He said to him, "Poor man, where are you going?" He answered, "Sir, I am following a poor beast with coal." The Devil asked if he lacked money. If he did, he would give it to him. If he would be his servant he would have nothing to do but go up and down with him. This he undertook to do.

He says that when he appeared to him, Sathan looked terrifying. He knew it was the Devil because he was black. He confesses that he was tricked by the Devil into everything described above. He says Jonet Dailies, William King, Elspeth Halyburton, and [blank], were at the first meeting with the Devil at the Borrowmoor. He says that the Devil gave him the mark on his leg at the Wolmet Bank wih his hand. He put a finger to his leg. He always had black clothes when he saw him, and a black cloak with a hat on his head.

He declares that all of the confession written above is the truth.

[As previously noted, Johnston and his co-accused were sentenced to be strangled and burnt in Musselburgh on 30th July 1661. His claims of ill-treatment are significant. Perhaps if he had clung more tenaciously to them, and consistently refuted his confession, he might have escaped with his life.]

Witch Pricking.

[Box JC26/27 contains a bundle labelled "Dalkeith Witches", in which there are several descriptions of the Tranent witch pricker John Kincaid at work. There is also mention of a John Ramsay from Ormiston engaged in the same business - see also "Trial by Commission", 2nd August 1661 for an unfortunate mistake of Ramsay's.]

Excerpt from JC26/27 Item 10.

At Dalkeith 11th July 1661: John Kinkade, the public examiner of such persons had been sent for, and came for that effect today to examine Elspeth Graham. Before Johne went about his business the "balif" William Scot charged him on his solemn oath that in carrying out his duties he should do nothing and declare nothing but what was the truth. In carrying out his duties he found a mark on her right side, and another below her left breast. He pricked these marks and put a pin into each one of them, right up to the head, then pulled them out, without tiie appearance of any blood. This was done in the presence of William Scott, "ballife" [i.e. probably the local landowner's baron baillie]; Alexander Dicksone, church elder; James Hog,

John Sheill, and Thomas Harvie. [Elspeth confessed the following day.]

Excerpt fron Item 16.

At Dalkeith 11th July 1661: Today John Kinkade from Tranent, the public examiner of those who are guilty of the sin of witchcraft, had occasion to be in the place to examine some other witches. Although she had not been accused, Kathrine Hunter wished to be examined because of her uneasy conscience. The baron baillie William Scot charged John on his solemn oath to carry out his duties honestly and faithfully, and do nothing but what was the truth. In going about his business he found a mark on her left shoulder, and another below her left armpit, which he declared to be the Devil's marks. He pricked them, and left both the pins sticking in the marks without any sensation or feeling on her part until she had put on her shirt again, after which she pulled them out with her own hand. All this was done in the presence of William Scott, baron baillie; John Stevin, Alexander Dicksone, and Thomas Hog. [Katherine confessed the next day.]

Excerpt from Item 18.

Evidence of Issobel Fergusson's guilt in the sin of witchcraft...

Then Issobell asked that a man should be sent for, to search for the mark, and accordingly John Ramsay from Ormeston came on the 5th of July and found two marks on her. So that same night, without any appearance of torture being used on her, she made the following confession...

Excerpt from Item 22.

[A letter has been sent to the minister of Newton informing him that Janet Paiston has been named by two confessing witches. She is arrested, taken to Newton, and confronted with her accusers.]

At this the minister and the baron baillie sent for John Kincade in Tranent, the public pricker and examiner of such persons. He came for that purpose, and was charged on his solemn oath to go about his duties faithfully, and to declare and do nothing in that connection but what was true. He found two marks on her which he declared to be the Devil's marks. They did indeed appear to be so, for she had no sensation or feeling when they were pricked, nor could she tell in what part of her body the pins were. After that, having been exhorted several times by the minister to repent and confess her sins; at length, out of the remorse of her conscience, Jennet Paistoune on this same day in June, earnestly asked for the minister; and out of the sense of her sins, without any kind of compulsion in the least, either then or beforehand, she declared... [She gave a detailed confession, and named Janet Cock as a witch. Janet Cock was subsequently confronted with Jennet Paistoun, leading to the events described in the excerpt given below.]

At Dalkeith 18th June 1661: ... After that, John Kinkade the public pricker was sent for to examine this person. He was deeply sworn on his solemn oath, went about his duties, and swore that he would do nothing in that connection but what was true. He found two marks on her, one on her throat, and one on her left arm. He pricked them without any feeling or sensation on her part, or the least appearance of blood. The holes stayed open and unclosed, as if the pins had been put in white paper.

Witness John Kincaid with the other undersigned witnesses... [She sent for the minister the following day and confessed.]

Margaret Allan - a narrow escape.

[This case is also to be found in Box JC26/27. It consists of one paper, tied, and marked "Margaret Allane, her dittay, desertit 14 Nov 1661". She is from the parish of "Bathanes", now known as Yester. In other words, Margaret was from the Gifford area. The indictment begins with a typical preamble, and continues as given below.]

... Namely, about fourteen years ago Dina Kemp asked you to go with her to ["Hadingtoun" deleted] Hodindean. When you got there you encountered the Devil in the likeness of a man in black clothes and a bonnet on his head, along with other notorious witches, all dancing together. He came out from among them, gave you a kiss, took you by the hand, and asked you to be his servant, promising that you would never want. You agreed to this. You also renounced your baptism by putting one hand on the crown of your head, and the other on the sole of your foot, and giving to him everything between. You received a new name from him, Jenni, [or possibly "Jeani"], and also received his marks on different parts of your body, one on your shoulder, and another on your thigh. At this meeting, you also saw Bessie Davidson, Bessie Dicksone, Dina Kemp, Elizabeth Smyth, Margaret Ker, and other notorious witches.

Also, in the year 1660, a servant woman sleeping with you at Newhall was seized about midnight with such a strange and terrible fit of trembling by your sorcery and witchcraft that she thought she was about to die of it. At this time you were lying as if dead, and however she tried, you could not be wakened. Immediately after she wakened the trembling and the pain ceased, and the woman seemed healthy enough. It therefore seems evident that this pain and trembling was laid upon her by your sorcery and witchcraft. This servant woman was to be brought to Edinburgh as a witness against you, but she has again been seized by that same trembling and sweating, and she is in such a state, fainting and crying with pain, that nobody expects her to live. Therefore it seems obvious that you have laid on this pain and sickness by your sorcery and witchcraft.

Also, in the year 1659, by your sorcery and witchcraft you caused the death of four horses ploughing for James Bannatyn of Newhall, because there was a legal case between James Hog of [blank], who looked after these horses, and your son. You went in among the horses saying certain words to yourself. Soon, one of the horses went mad and ran up and down the fields for two or three hours, then lost all power in its body, and was carried home and died within the space of [blank] hours. The other three horses also died of the same disease within half a year. All this was done by your sorcery and witchcraft.

Also, in 1650 you contracted a hatred against William Tate in Woodhead because he had poinded your husband's goods for debt. At that you threatened to do him an evil turn, and shortly after that, by your sorcery and witchcraft, William's horses and oxen were dying every day. Ever since, this has happened with calf, foal, or any young animal [probable reading], so that over the past eleven years his entire livestock and goods have been destroyed, and he himself has been ruined by your sorcery and witchcraft.

Also, in the year 1659 you conceived a malice and hatred against Gilbert Lamb. You threatened to cast him out of his house, and the same night as you made the threat he contracted a strange and grievous sickness, trembling and sweating, so that he almost lost his life.

In the same year of 1659 you contracted a hatred and malice against Thomas Hoge because he had taken some land which had been in the possession of your husband. By your sorcery and witchcraft Thomas went insane.

In the year 1660, when the Laird of Newhall was away from home, one of the sevants in the house saw a black man go into the room where you were. As he walked up and down the room his feet were like those of an ox, and made a great din. During this time there was such a cacophany of voices in the house that nobody dared to come in.

Also in the year 1660, any time you were offended by James Barmatyne of Newhall or his servants, immediately afterwards he or some of them would fall into an extraordinary sweating and trembling by your sorcery and witchcraft, and at such times you were always found lying as if you were dead.

Also, in the year 1658, Margaret Sinclar, Lady Newhall, fell out with you several times, and immediately afterwards took sudden fits of trembling and sweating, and at length died of it, blaming you for her death.

For many years you have been held and reputed to be a rank notorious witch, and you have been reported for it to the kirk session of Bathenes, as can be seen in their records. You have therefore contravened the laws and acts of parliament made against sorcery and witchcraft, and if this is found proven by a jury you ought to be punished with death as an example to terrify others who commit similar crimes in future.

[The bundle marked "Mussellburgh Witches" in JC26/27 contains the following paper, designated "Item 3".]

14th November: Margaret Allan, accused of the crime of witchcraft as recorded in her indictment.

This day, Margaret Allan was brought out of the tollbooth to be tried for the crime of sorcery and witchcraft recorded in her indictment, and declared herself willing and ready to undergo a trial for it. Because James Bannatyne of Newhall abandoned the prosecution of Margaret for these crimes, the judge with the consent of both of them cancels the trial and orders Margaret to be freed, on condition that she enacts herself in the Books of Adjournal to be of good behaviour for all time to come, and never to come to or enter the lands of Newhall in future, under pain of death..

In obedience to this order she is confirmed to be judicially bound for all time to come to be of good behaviour, and never to enter the bounds of Newhall, under pain of death.

[It is probably significant that the indictment does not mention any confession or diabolic pact. Perhaps the Laird of Newhall was advised that his case was likely to fail in the absence of a confession, since the various charges of malefice would be very difficult to prove. It is also probably fortunate for Margaret that the pricker Kincaid does not seem to have been called in.]

1662

Agnes Williamson – another narrow escape.

[Agnes Williamson was from Samuelston, a community which the Haddington kirk session minutes indicate had a formidable reputation for witchcraft. Agnes is also mentioned in the Haddington records, and seems to have been known as a witch before she came to trial. It was the activities of Agnes and others in Samuelston which prompted the Earl of Haddington's famous appeal to the Privy Council to clarify the law and grant a commission for clearing his lands of witches [See "Trial by Commission"]. The following text is from the Books of Adjournal JC2/10, P. 60, dated 17th[?] January 1662.]

Agnes Williamsone in Samuelstoune, prisoner in the tollbooth of Edinburgh.

[After a standard preamble, her indictment proceeds as follows.]

1. ... namely on Shrove Tuesday three years ago George Culdcleuch in Samuelstoune had bought a horse from John Hepburne, and brought it home to his house. You, Agnes Williamsone and your husband James Paterson, and John Bartilman and his wife Christian Deans, came to his house, and after calling for ale, insisted on drinking with him and having a look at his horse. You were invited to see the horse yoked some fourteen days or so after that [probable reading], and when George was drinking with your husband the same night, he heard your voice and the din of many people around his house. He heard you cry out aloud, "Aha! Aha!"

The next morning he went to see his horse, and found that by your sorcery and witchcraft the horse would neither eat nor stir. When he brought some neighbours in to see it, they found its mouth bloody. A piece the size of a golf ball had been cut out of his lip, and two pieces of flesh, round like tobacco pipes, were through his teeth. Immediately after this the horse died. All this evil was caused by your sorcery and witchcraft. The same night George Grundisone, a workman of George Culdcleuch's, thought he saw a woman at his stable, and advised him to chain his stable door.

2. Also, at Candlemas 165[blank] George Cauldcleuch had ten bolls of oats made into meal, and brought a load home from the mill. When he went back for the rest, you, Agnes Williamson sent to his wife asking for a "fourth part" [*i.e.* a "forpit" or quarter of a peck] of the meal. This he sent you, but by your sorcery and witchcraft you took all the substance and strength from the rest of the meal, so that he never got any good of it, and has never had enough money since to have any meal made from his oats.

3. James Carfra, mason in Samuelstoune was drinking with some neighbours in Robert Gourdie's house in Samuelstoune last Shrove Tuesday. On his way home to Pilmore where he was living at the time, he was taking off his stockings and shoes at the ford to wade the water [*i.e.* the Tyne], when you, Agnes Williamson, raised a sudden blast of whirlwind which carried him headlong back to the East Mill and over the dam. With God's help he gripped the kiln-spout in his arms, and used it to climb out. Then as he was struggling to climb the bank, you gripped him by the heel to pull him down, and he turned and struck at you with his mason's rule. With you were Margaret Bannatyne, Elizabeth Baylie, and others who were burnt for witchcraft. He heard you say at the time, "Shall we make away with him? He was never good to his mother."

The next morning James went to your house and called you a witch, and demanded to know from your husband where you were the day before. Whereupon you said to your husband, "Get the bottle out of the cupboard and stop this glowering fellow's mouth!" You husband took him in and they drank together. [Probable meaning. The last few sentences are illegible in parts.]

4. Also, you conceived a hatred against the maltman Thomas Crombie, and threatened him that he would lose another five hundred merks over and above what he had lost at Whyttinghame Fair. Accordingly, it fell out that about four days later, when he was brewing a container of malt belonging to [illegible], by your sorcery and witchcraft the outside of the kiln was set on fire at the part nearest the fire, by a sudden blast or whirlwind. Several penitent and confessing witches said you had caused the fire, and had invited them to be present when it was done.

5. Also, you Agnes Williamson asked for the loan of ten pounds from Thomas Steell in Samuelston. When he refused, you threatened and menaced him that he would repent it before long. Accordingly, next morning, a fire broke out in his house, the cause of which could not be found. Several condemned and confessing witches declared that you were the cause of this, and that you had invited them to assist you in doing it.

6. About seven years ago you were pregnant. Near the time of your delivery when you had your pains, you invited your neighbours in. When you were brought to bed, by your sorcery and witchcraft the child was taken away ["substracted"]. Some clothes were given to your husband to bury in its place. It is evident that you used devilry, witchcraft, and sorcery in taking away the child.

7. Johne Veatch in Samuelstoune was in bed with his wife and child when he wakened from his sleep and saw you and another woman

Samuelston. It was said in 1659 that there was nothing there but "whores, thieves and witches".

The Tyne near Samuelston. Agnes Williamson was accused of knocking James Carfrae into the water with a magic whirlwind when he was fording the river. Agnes was one of the few East Lothian witches to be acquitted.

sitting by the fire which was burning there. He got up, meaning to beat you with his sword, but you made your escape from the house, and the next morning by your sorcery and witchcraft the child was dead in the bed.

8. Also, on several occasions you confessed you were a witch and that this came about because of a quarrel between you and your husband about a sack. He went away with some meal, and it was then you got involved with the Devil. You renounced your baptism, he gave you the new name of Maisie Luckifoot, and gave you his mark upon your shoulder. Also you have been held and reputed to be a notorious witch, have been accused and confronted by several penitent and confessing witches, and have had several meetings and trysts with them. Through this you have contravened the laws and acts of parliament against sorcery and witchcraft. If this is proved you deserve to be punished with death as an example to terrify others so that they will not do the same in the future.

[JC2/10 goes on to record the legal arguments over the various articles of the indictment. The indictment and legal wrangling is repeated almost word for word in JC2/11 in the Books of Adjournal, but rather more legibly. I have taken the following part of the process from JC2/11.]

Prosecutor: Mr Andro Birnie, substitute to the Lord Advocate. Spokesman for the Defence: Mr Nathaniel Fyffe, advocate.

After the indictment was read the accused denied altogether that it was true. The prosecutor declared that he was abandoning the seventh article of the indictment, but insisted on pursuing all the remaining articles. His Majesty's Justice Deputes then ordered the accused to set out her defences against the indictment, and whether its relevance justified its being tried by a jury.

It is alleged by the spokesman for the accused, Mr Nathaniel ffyfe, that the first article is not relevant because the horse might have been killed, or died, without the use of witchcraft or colaboration with the Devil. For example, the horse might have been diseased, or there might have been an externally caused accident. So this first claimed incidence of malefice is not an article of indictment against the accused.

The prosecutor Mr Andro Birnie answers to this defence opposed to the statement in which the crime of witchcraft is relevantly described; that there was a horse which was struck down and killed by an extraordinary disease which could not have occurred as the result of any ordinary cause, since the horse had been abruptly and suddenly affected, and a piece the size of a golf ball taken out of its upper lip. in addition there was evidence of practices which were customarily used by witches in their enchantments and spells – in this case, raw flesh wrapped round the horse's teeth. That the accused was the cause of this is a relevant accusation, because under cover of night, with others unknown, she was heard to utter strange and unusual expressions, with a resulting effect on the horse.

Mr Nathaniel ffyfe replies to this that the defence put forward is still relevant in spite of that answer, because, firstly, however extraordinary the disease was that killed the horse, it was not outwith the bounds of a natural disease. As far as the raw flesh is concerned, and the accused being there, all these things could have happened without making any agreement with the Devil. Thus the defence remains relevant, notwithstanding.

It is alleged by Mr Nathaniel ffyfe that the second article of the indictment is not justified in inferring witchcraft, because the giving of substance and quality to things created for the sustenance of man comes from a higher power than the Devil and his accomplices. Therefore this cannot be taken away by an inferior power. Even if it could, the article is not relevant unless it can describe the particular act of sorcery and witchcraft by which this was done.

Mr Andro Birnie answered in explanation of the indictment, that although all being and substance proceeds from the First Being of all things, there is no doubt that it is known from everyday experience that the Devil may be permitted to take the spirit and substance from created things to make them unprofitable. Just as these are the productions of natural causes, so contrary causes may result in quality and substance being taken away. These causes are well known to the Devil. As for the accused, the particulars of this act of sorcery are described; that is, that she got a parcel of the same foodstuff, which is the normal course of action taken by witches.

Mr Nathaniel ffyfe replies that the defence for the accused is still relevant in spite of these answers. As for borrowing meal from the person mentioned, and the removal of quality and substance from the rest of the corn and meal; even if it were granted that such an act could only be done by diabolical power, unless it is proved that it was done by the accused by virtue of an express agreement with the Devil, it is not relevant to infer witchcraft.

It is further alleged by Mr Nathaniel fife that the third article of the indictment is not relevant unless it can be proved that the accused raised a whirlwind by virtue of an agreement with the Devil, to attack this person while he was returning home. Unless that can be proved, the evil act described cannot infer the crime of witchcraft.

Mr Birnie answers that there is no need for an express agreement. Doing something using enchantment and sorcery is enough to indicate witchcraft, and this deed is relevantly described.

Mr N. ffife replies to this, that unless those deeds are individually described and expressly proven - for example, a pact with the Devil - the articles cannot be relevant. It is further alleged by Mr Nathaniel ffife on behalf of the accused, that the rest of the articles of the indictment are in no way able to infer the crime of witchcraft, because some of them consist of [illegible]. That is a weak argument in law. At best it is a ground for interrogating, but in no way for condemning. As for the alleged confession from the accused, this was illegal, and the result of torture. In the first place, the tortures used were not legitimately used. Thus, although the accused confessed, she may retract the confession, which in fact she does. As for the accusations from other confessing and penitent witches condemned to death, these can never infer that she committed a crime. The sentence passed on witches declares them to be unreliable, and therefore not worthy of attention. Secondly, as for the lifestyle of the accused, her reputation can never be a reason to condemn her, but only something which might lead to questions on particulars.

Mr Andro Birnie answers for the prosecution that the testimony of dying and penitent witches, along with fame and reputation, are important indications of guilt. Any person who has despaired of her life, especially if she is penitent, is the fittest person in the world to bear witness. This is sufficient proof in cases of witchcraft, which is one of the "reserved crimes", and special standards of proof apply. Although it is alleged that the threat, and the the effect which followed - in this case fire - is not sufficient proof, it is answered that witchcraft is a deed of darkness done by hidden means. The person involved is the only cause, and the serious consequences are not a normal accustomed result, but something extraordinary - in this case the malt kiln catching fire in the part furthest away from the fire, while the part nearest the fire was unaffected. There is also the accused's judicial confession taken before a Commission of Parliament which had power to put her on trial.

Mr Nathaniel ffyfe contradicts with his previous reply, and alleges that unless her confession be made before the jury, it can have no significance.

The Justice depute finds the third, fourth, and fifth articles relevant, linking with them her reputation and the accusations mentioned. The other articles are not found justified as relevant in themselves, but only relevant when considered with the other articles specified above.

[The judge has ruled relevant:

Article 3 - James Carfrae's falling in the Tyne.

Article 4 - The burning of Thomas Crombie's malt kiln.

Article 5 - The mysterious fire in Thomas Steill's house.

What the judge appears to be saying is that if Agnes can be proved to have been the direct cause of the events described in Articles 3, 4, and 5, then her guilt can be assumed in the other articles of the dittay.]

The Jury.
William Steinson, sievewright;
Alexander Guthrie;
Robert Wilson, baker;
George Charteris, merchant;
Oliver Dumbar, stabler;
David Wightman, pewterman;
William Weir, merchant in Edinburgh;
John Cralo[?], merchant there;
George Glover, sievewright there;
George Young, dyer there;
Cuthbert Carridine;
Andrew Grinlay, baker;
William Cochran, tailor;
William McCulloch,
    brewer in the Canongate;
William Crawford in St Ninian's Law.

The jury was lawfully sworn and no objections were made.

The prosecutor produced the following witnesses to prove the indictment:

Article 1. George Caldcleuch, aged about 50, was sworn, purged himself of malice, and testifies according to the indictment in every thing. Also that he heard Sussanna Bannatyne say that the accused and Christian Deans caused the death of his horse, and that a certain [blank] Cairns had confessed this.

Patrick Baptie, aged 33, married, was sworn and testifies that he was the first to discover this business concerning George Cauldcleuch's horse. He saw the horse's lip, but he knows of no complicity that the accused had in this. He testifies that she is reputed to be a witch. She was accused by thirteen penitent witches, who confessed that she had undone most of Samuelston, and they were drawn in by the ale in her house. He declares that she confessed to renouncing her baptism before she was put in the stocks.

William Lorimer, aged 23, unmarried, was sworn and purged himself of malice, and testifies that he heard the accused at George Cauldcleuch's stable door. He heard her voice and knew it was her. She cried out, "Aha! Aha!" He heard Christian Deans's voice with her. He also declares that he told George that he had heard her voice, and that the horse died within twenty four hours after that.

Article 2. George Caldcleuch was again questioned on the 2nd article of the indictment, and he testified in agreement with everything in it. However, he testifies all the same that he ate bread made from that meal, and was satisfied with it. He says it was just that the meal was used up faster than it usually was.

Article 3. James Carfrae, aged 25, married, purged himself of malice, and after being sworn testified that he knows the accused, and that he was going to wade over the water when a rush of wind knocked him over and threw him into the water. He caught hold of the kiln-spout. Coming up the bank, he recognised the accused by her voice, but didn't see her face. He declares she said, "Away with him! He was never good to his mother!" There were other women with her, and he sruck at them, but did not hear them cry out. The next morning the accused was ill. He came to see her next morning and challenged her as it says in the indictment. He said he wanted to look at her shoulder. Also, after she made her confession she told him that she had confessed. She was believed and reputed to be a witch. She was named by Margaret Baptie, Elspet Taylor, and several others.

John Veach, aged 36, married, was sworn and declared that James Carfrae came to his house to sharpen his mason's chisels. After that, they went to the accused's house and called for ale. He gave her a drink and called her a witch. She said to her husband, "Take the measures and fill them up." James Carfra looked as if he had been frightened. James also told him how the accused had blown him back. She has always been reputed to be a witch, and he heard that she had been named by Elspeth Taylor and Marion Whyte.

Article 4. Thomas Crumbie, aged 44, married, was sworn, purged himself of malice, and testifies that he did not hear the accused utter the threats in the indictment, but Jean Paiston had told him that she had said it. He testifies that the kiln did not catch fire, but the strong winds blowing at the time might have done it[?]. Also, he heard Sussanna Bannatyne say the accused had invited her to set fire to the kiln. The accused is reputed to be a witch and was accused by many people. She confessed to him and William Carrail that she was a witch before she was put in the stocks.

James Forrest, aged 30, married, was sworn, and purged himself of malice. He testifies that he heard Susanna Bannatyne say that the accused told her and others to set fire to the kiln. The kiln gave a crack, but it did not catch fire. Both Agnes and her mother were reputed to be witches, and he heard that she had confessed that she was a witch before she was put in the stocks.

Article 5. Thomas Steill, aged 30, married, was sworn and purged himself of all malice.

He declares that the accused's servant came to him to borrow ten pounds, but declares that the accused did not threaten him. After that his house caught fire, and Susanna Bannatyne declared before the judges and ministers that Agnes had set fire to the house. She is reputed to be a witch, and was named by Elspeth Taylor and others who saw her at meetings. She was free when she made her confession, but had been in the stocks before that, for her restraint, not to torture her.

Article 8. [*Sic* Presumably no witnesses were questioned on Articles 6 and 7.] William Carraill, aged [blank], was sworn and declares that what she confessed accords with what is in her indictment. She had been in the stocks before her confession.

The chosen jurors were sworn and admitted after the indictment of the accused and the questioning of the witnesses. They left the court and proceeded to the jury room, where by a majority they elected William Weir as foreman of the jury. They debated and voted on all the points of the indictment, and after adequate discussion of it they came back into court where unanimously, except for one, they declared through their foreman that they found pronounced and declared Agnes Williamson innocent and not guilty of the 3rd, 4th, and 5th articles of the indictment, but guilty of having the reputation mentioned, and of having been accused as mentioned [*i.e.* named by confessing witches]. Since these points and the other articles of the indictment are not relevant in themselves, they are referred to the judges for consideration. At this, the accused and her spokesman Mr Nathaniel Fyfe asked for a written record.

[Since the judges had already ruled that all the accusations were irrelevant unless Articles 3, 4, and 5, could be proved, they would have little option but to dismiss the charges. In fact JC2/11 is marked "Witchcraft clenged" - *i.e.* acquitted of witchcraft. Agnes Williamson would therefore almost certainly be freed. She had of course the advantages of a good lawyer, a trial in Edinburgh, and a jury of Edinburgh tradesmen and merchants. She also had the good sense to repudiate her confession.]

[Box JC26/28 of Justiciary Court Processes contains a bundle of papers dealing with Agnes Williamson's case.]

a] "Agnes Williamson her dittay". This is her indictment as given in the Books of Adjournal. It is covered with scribbles and doodles.

b] "Agnes Williamson clenged January 27 1662." [This is identical to JC2/11, and ends with the same verdict - "referred to the justices' consideration". Brief notes at the end appear to be memos relating to other cases.]

c] Memorandum to draw up an indictment against Agnes Williamson and others, 6th instant[?] 1662. [This is a short note relating how Agnes confessed before her arrest that after she had quarreled with her husband, the Devil came to her, had sex with her, marked her, and gave her a new name. It ends as given below.]

Also, on 20th May 1661 Agnes confessed in the presence of the judges comissioned by Parliament. She confessed sex, name, and mark as mentioned. To conclude, she is held and reputed to be a witch, confronted and blamed by repentant witches at their death.

d] Almost identical to JC2/10.

e] Witnesses' statements similar to those given during the trial.

James Welsh.

[James Welsh seems to have been a vagrant boy or youth caught up in a witchcraft investigation, who gave his captors the benefit of his vivid imagination. In doing so he implicated large numbers of other people. He was imprisoned for a year and a day with a view to questioning him further, but there is no evidence that this was ever done, and he does not seem to have stood trial for witchcraft. He would therefore presumably be freed at the end of his spell in the "Correction House". The bundle of papers relating to James Welsh can be found among the Justiciary Court Processes in Box JC26/28.]

Item 1

April 3rd 1662: Petition - James Welsh, alleged wizard, prisoner.

To His Majesty's Justices of the Peace: the humble petition of James Welsh, prisoner.

On February 16th, 1662, the petitioner was sent from Haddington to the tollboth of Edinburgh to be tried before Your Lordships as an alleged wizard, as explained in a letter to the Lord Provost of Edinburgh from Robert Ker, one of the magistrates of Hadingtone, and that he was a ghost [sic]. Ker said that he would come in himself to speak to Your Lordships regarding the trial of the petitioner. However, neither he nor anyone else seems likely to insist on this. Neither has he given the petitioner anything but £3 - 8s Scots since he came here, although he had promised.

Therefore I beseech Your Lordships to make Robert Ker proceed against the petitioner, and also to pay for his past and future upkeep during his imprisonment. Otherwise let the prisoner be liberated, after enacting himself to appear when called upon, on pain of death. Hoping for Your Lordships' answer.

[In another hand at the foot of the page: The Justice Depute ordains the petitioner James Welsh..." Breaks off here.]

Item 2.

James Welsh for witchcraft. Letter from Mr Robert Ker.

[This must be the letter mentioned in Welsh's petition, Item 1. In a different hand from the text of the letter is the note, "Condemned to be kept in the Correction House for a year and a day, 17th April 1662."]

To his much loved friend Mr Alexander Hamiltoun.

Sir,

According to my promise [illegible] of the boy's statements [illegible] not doing it. [This is probably an apology for not sending in the evidence against James Welsh.] However, he made statements very freely, without any compulsion that I ever knew of, not only before me and my colleagues, but before several other ministers of the Presbytery; also, before the gentlemen who were commissioned by Parliament to sit and judge him and others at Samilstoun. These statements were attested by them and sent on to Parliament. A commission was then obtained for putting him on trial. This was postponed at the time because of his age, and particularly because he had named several other people, but had not been confronted with them. The judges therefore postponed trying him according to their commission until another day. Once it had been delayed, it was put off again until a decision about his age could be obtained from the judges, since they had some scruples about putting a minor on trial.

Since I thought there was little likelihood of getting the judges out to these parts, I arranged with the magistrates to send him on to Edinburgh, where the judges might have the opportunity to speak with him at their leisure. Spotswood, who was clerk for all his statements, can tell you that he said many other things about various other people, but since there was no magistrate or minister present, these were not put down on paper. He is a very cunning rogue, and what he is presently denying, he was brought to confess after being laboured with. I have no doubt that if he was dealt with wisely, before the judges themselves if they have the opportunity, or any of the ministers, if they took the trouble to discuss matters with him and press him on the details in the paper, I am confident that he could be brought to confirm them. It seems very likely that he is guilty. Managing this business will certainly take some more time and effort. For the present, you... [illegible].

Thus, I earnestly entreated the judge to think of some way of keepng him for a while. He promised to speak to the Provost about taking him into their Correction House. He has been there for some time now, maintained by our Kirk Session from our poor box. Since the Session is not meeting now, he cannot have any allowance that way. The magistrates think themselves greatly inconvenienced in this, because he was a poor begging boy, accidentally arrested in their parish, if they cannot find some way of maintaining him, it would seem that he must either perish or be dismissed, which would be a pity. Some arrangement should be made, at least until he can be brought before a commision. I meant to acquaint the Justice Depute with these things, but I know he is very busy, so I have contented myself with informing you. I hope you can represent matters to them soon.

I am your most respectful friend and servant,

Ro: Ker.   Hadintoun, 7th February 1662.

Item 3.

Statement and confession of James Welsh. [Some of this is vey difficult to read.]

Before he was accused or arrested for witchcraft, James Welsh declared that when he was coming home from Herdmiston Mill one night about five years ago, he saw many women and men on Nisbet Hauche. Among them he recognised Marion Houm, who brought Agnes Williamson, Christian Deans, George Shoreswood and his wife [illegible], Patrick Cathie and his wife Jonet West, and John Carfrae. Marion had intended to have his life, but Agnes Williamson said, "Let him alone. He will be my son in law." Christian Deans said, "Let him go. He won't speak about me, for I've given him many a handful of meal." He confessed this several times before being arrested, and as a result was confronted with Agnes Williamson and Christian Deans before Christian's death.

James Welsh was denounced as being guilty of witchcraft by Jonet Wood, and was then arrested and searched for the mark. He was found to have several marks. It was after this accusation and searching, and not in his previous statement, that he acknowledged his own guilt.

He said that the Christmas after he had been frightened, his mother was in his grandmother's house. He was at home all alone, and had gone out in the evening to the end of the barn to ease himself. A bonnie lass appeared to him, and wanted him to have sex with her, but he refused. Then, a short distance from there, a man appeared to him who tempted him to become his servant, and asked him what he did. James replied, "I beg for food, as other poor things do." The man then asked him to become his servant, and said that he would have enough and never want if he did his bidding. So he promised to be his servant. During all this time he could not say, "God have mercy on me." [It is not clear whether this sentence is referring to James's interrogation, or to his period of service with the Devil.] Then he [illegible] the next night beside John [illegible]'s house, and the Devil, looking like a gentleman, as already mentioned, appeared before him at the appointed time. Then he asked him to be his servant as described... [illegible]... and his baptism. James agreed to do this, and laying one hand on his head and the other on the sole of his foot, he gave himself soul and body to him. The Devil then called him James Scot and gave him the mark which he has between his thigh and his body. This was sore forty eight hours [or possibly "this was sore for eight hours"] after that, till he met with the Devil again. The first time he gave him two silver coins which he later found to be two peices of slate. He threw them in the pool at the West Mill at Samuelstoun.

He testified that the Devil appeared to him in black [illegible] clothes, and declared that the first meeting he went to after his recruitment, his mother was to one side of him and his grandmother behind him. At that meeting he saw Marion Broun who saw him and said, "James, are you now one of our own?" At that meeting he saw John Home the miller in Samuelstoun, Martin Black's wife, Patrick Meikle and his wife Helen Herd, Janet Robeson, Robert Scot and his wife Jeane Aikwood, [illegible] Thomson, Marion Broun already mentioned, Meikle her husband, George Schoreswood and his wife Anna Pilmore, Elspet Tailer, Margarit Paterson, Janet Kempe, Nicol Bailie and Christian Clarke his wife, Susanna Bannatyne's daughter Isobell Stillie, Patrick Cathie, James Wast and his wife Issobell Cathie, their daughter [illegible], Agnes Spans, John Bartleman and his wife Christian Deans, Beigis Sanderson, and Agnes Williamson, all from Samuelston. Also Archibald [illegible] from Blans and his wife [blank], [illegible] Smith and Alexander Hunter from Saltoun, James Finlason in Over Saltoun and his wife, An Finlason's husband [blank], Agnes Baptie in Spinnelfoord, Marion Stevinson and [blank] Dobson's mother from Nisbet. [This long list is entirely without punctuation in the original text, making it difficult in places to determine just who is "spouse" to whom. I may therefore have mismatched some of the couples.]

He declared that he was at a meeting at Tranent Moore Croce where the Devil and John Kincaid were sitting side by side, and everyone passed by them. He wanted to go over to where they were sitting, but was prevented. He has been at several other meetings, and at all the meetings Patrick Cathie played to them on his pipes.

He declared that he was at a meeting at the West Port of Edinburgh, and went there as if they had been going to a market. They were in a house where they had food and wine brought out from Edinburgh. The company he was in drank from dishes *[sic]*. However, the Devil was not in the company James was in, but in another company there at that time. He thought that the man who brought them the food and drink was someone who lived about Musselburgh or Fisherraw.

He declared that he was at several meetings at Gladismore, Mr Robert Hodges Kirk, the Lauch, Robswalls, the Round Knowe, Layeshope, Samelstoun village, and Bailhauches. Patrick Cathie was always there playing his pipes to them.

He declared that he was at a meeting in Saltoun Wood on the Back Hill there, and went from the wood to Blans dovecot. That night was the 22nd or 29th of May past, a Wednesday. There was no dancing, but they followed their master who rode on a horse with a gentlewoman behind him - they were always at the front. He saw the following people: Archibald [illegible] and his wife; Alexander Hunter whom he recognised and went along with, and they went home together; [blank] Mirrilies; Thomas Finlason and his wife and daughter in law, who nearly broke her neck coming over Saltoun Wood Dyke; George Lacost in Saltoun and [illegible] his wife, [blank] Pepper and his wife who lived about Saltounmylne. Many people came in later to that meeting, and others he did not know.

He declared he was at a meeting to the west of Wester Saltoun. Before that time he was never present when any evil was done. At that meeting Agnes Williamson and Issobell [illegible] "cut a horse lip of Patrick Baillie's". [It is not clear whether James means that they cut the horse's lip off at the meeting, or whether they cut up a lip at the meeting, which had been previously sliced from a horse.] Elspeth Tailyour helped them. This was on a Wednesday at night.

He declared that fourteen days past Sunday there was a meeting at the Threiplaw. The Devil was there, and he recognised Agnes Williamson and David Schakes[?]. David told Agnes that he had made two parcels [illegible] and laid them at Patrick Baylie's door. He recognised Robert Bartleman's wife Helen Nicolson at that meeting.

He declared that one night they were going to cut the [illegible] mare belonging to Patrick Baylie. He sat in the [illegible] to prevent them. The perpetrators of this were Margaret Blak and Issobell Thomson. After going out to Samelstoun Holme they struck James with staves like whip handles while the rest were passing by. He saw the aforementioned Issobell Thomson, Margaret Black, and Agnes Williamson.

He declared that at a meeting at Thrieplaw they planned to knock down the mill at Painstoun, but that night there was a man in the mill, and they could not manage it. The women from Painstoun went nearest to the mill. He saw and recognised Old John Sinclair's wife. [The next few lines seem very garbled, with several illegible words. There is a reference to someone getting a chopin of ale from someone else, but I can make no sense of the rest.]

He declared that he has been at several meetings, for example one at the West Kill of Haddingtoun on 5th September 1659. At these meetings he saw Nicol Maen and his wife Marion Raeburn, Alexander Athin's wife Jonet [illegible], Helen Dickson, Edward Dikson, William Martin, Janet Wilson, Walter Dykis, Bessie [illegible], Violet Nymmo, Barbra Cungiltoun, Richard Gulit's wife Jonet Todrig, Marioun Lindsay, Jonet Blythe etc [sic].

He declared that he lived as a servant to the minister's wife at Stentoun, for about seven or eight or nine weeks. During that time he was at three meetings, one at the draw well, one at the end well, and a third above Newbane[?]. George Lacost, then miller at Newmylne, was present at these meetings, and George Binnie who was then servant to the minister's wife. Also, Marion Cumming and various other people.

He named several people who had been at meetings with the Devil where he had been present: Thomas Hay in Wintoun's wife, John Lyll in Boigis, John Russell in Nisbet, and others. He also declared that on Saturday 3rd September, before the great flood, there was a meeting at the Back Burn of Boltoun[?]. Bessie Lamb, Agnes Williamson, and Jonet Symson were there, having taken some sheaves of peas from Samuelston Hauch belonging to Patrick Baylie, which they burned there and gathered up the peas. John [illegible] and his wife, Patrick Meikkle and his wife Sussana Bannatyne, and Isobel Thomson came to them and wanted some of the peas. Jonet Symson said she had children at home, and asked for some to to give to them. She wished that the owner of the peas might get no more good or profit from them, which is what happened, because all the peas on the Haugh were taken away by the water. There were several others there that he didn't know. Also, around the Christmas after that, they had a meeting with the intention of burning the malt kiln and barn, but they could not manage to do it. [Much of this paragraph is difficult to make out, but this seems a sensible interpretation. I am not quite sure about the "Back Burn of Boltoun". I initially read "Boltoun" as "Colkiny" - not so impossible as it sounds, considering the vagaries of Secretary Hand - but considering the geographical location of the associated events, Bolton seems more likely.]

He declared that at a meeting in Gladismuire, Matthew [illegible] and Jeanne Crose his wife were there with twenty people in their company.

He also declared that two years ago or more he was at Eistbarnes and Broksburne, and lodged in the house of [blank], the mother of the miller of Broksburne. He was at a meeting there, and at this meeting with the Devil, he recognised [blank], the miller's mother, Jean Martin from Dumbar, and John Tosh from Eistbarnes.

He declared that in barley-seed time two years ago he and his mother went to the coast to get seed barley. They lodged with Issobel Johnstone in Gullane. They went to a meeting on Gullane Links at that time. His mother and he were lying down, and a little boy lay down beside him. When they all met he saw Issobel Johnston and [blank] Craik, who lived a little to the west of Issobel Johnston, in at an entry. They took a fine mare of Johne Nicolson's and rode on it from Gullane Links to Dumbar. [Blank] rode in front. When they came back to the rest, the mare fell to her knees and they carried her home. She died immediately afterwards of a [illegible], running herself against the walls.

He declared that he was at several meetings in the countryside when he was begging for food, and recognised at meetings with the Devil, Margaret Fokkart, Euphan Neilson, Marion Wood, and Margaret Acheson. There were six meetings at that time. There was [illegible] Dikson, a farm labourer's wife. He doesn't know where she lives, but suspects it is about Garvald Mill; also Johnne Foster.

He named the following persons whom he knew to have been at several meetings: John Manners in Tranent, Margaret Focker, Jonet Lowrie the baker's wife, and Archibald Manners's wife ... [I can make no sense of the rest of this sentence. It seems to be a comment made by someone, and an answer given by Manners's wife.]

He also named the following persons whom he knew to have been at several meetings: Janet Lidell, Bessie Thomson, Marion Black, Alexander Bell and his wife, all from Pencaitland; Thomas Baylie and his wife, whom they called "Lady Falconer", and George [illegible] from Winton. At all the meetings Jonet Liddell is always on the Devil's right hand.

He has also been at several meetings with the Devil in and around Athelstaneford, where he saw and recognised [illegible] Lamb the wife of George Walker, [blank] the wife of the pauper George Sandie, Robert Caphie senior and his wife [blank] Logie, [blank] Goodfellow the wife of Robert Baptie junior, Anna Hunter the wife of John Nicolson in Medles[?], and others.

[This case is remarkable for the droves of people denounced by James, which may indicate that he was continually being pressed for names, and obliged by naming anyone who came into his head. It is a good example of how large numbers of people could be sucked into witchcraft investigations. Fortunately, although the authorities in Haddington seem to have taken James seriously, those in Edinburgh must have been more sceptical. The case is also therefore a good example of how being denounced did not always mean automatic trial and execution.

All the same, there is a niggling matter-of-fact plausibility about some of James's statements.]

John Kincaid Questioned.

[The Register of the Privy Council records how suspicion began to fall on the notorious Tranent witch-pricker John Kincaid. He was brought in for interrogation, and eventually released after promising never to practise his profession again. The following little gem comes from Box JC26/36 of Justiciary Court Records, and casts interesting light on Kincaid's methods. It also speaks volumes about the "personal freshness" of some witchcraft suspects!]

Edinburgh, 4th April 1662.

This day in the presence of His Majesty's Justice Depute, John Kincaid the pricker was interrogated, and was asked how he came to learn how to examine witches. He declares that he acquired the knowledge only by sight, and by doing what other witches have often told him to do. He was asked why when examining them he will not let them go over the threshhold, and why he uses rituals such as placing them an ell from the wall. He decares that he does it only because witches have so informed him, and told him to do it He declares that he pricked anyone he was asked to by any gentlemen or ministers. He says witches have directed him to take them into a house backwards and keep them away from the wall, and from water. He says anyone who has seen him prick could do it after that. The first place he searches is their hands and arms. He consistently denies that he ever said to witches that he knew they were witches because they were with the Devil on such-and-such a day at such-and-such a place, but says that he has told them they were witches because they had an unpleasant smell. Witches have told him that when the Devil leaves them after they have had sex, they had an unpleasant smell. They said this was because the Devil put on and inhabited a dead corpse.

Signed: John Cunigham

[There is a certain logic in the suggestion that if the Devil, a spiritual being, wished to have sexual intercourse with a woman, he would have to clothe himself in human flesh, and what better choice than a body no longer needed by its departed soul. This is the only overt example of this gruesome belief that I have come across in the field of East Lothian witchcraft, although it would explain why the Devil's "nature" was always cold, and why he frequently had an earthy smell. Kincaid claims to have been getting advice from witches on how to proceed against their own kind, which seems odd. Were they just stringing him along and laughing at him behind his back?]

1670

Major Weir.

["Major" Thomas Weir and his sister Jean are famous in the annals of Edinburgh's "true" horror stories. Weir was a well respected pillar of the community who suddenly confessed to bestiality, and incest with his sister. They were popularly supposed to be deeply involved in witchcraft.

However, it was their sexual adventures they were executed for, not witchcraft. The records of their case can be found in the Books of Adjournal JC2/13, where we find this statement on p.11 from an East Lothian witness.]

Mr John Sinclair, minister at Ormiston, aged about 50, married, was sworn and declares that yesterday Major Weir sent for him. He went to the tollbooth to see him, and asked why he had sent for him. The Major told him that he was going to tell him what was on his conscience, and make a free confession. The Major accordingly confessed to him that he was guilty of incest, adultery, and bestiality, and asked the witness to pray for him as a person guilty of these grievous crimes. He also declared that after the Major was brought down from the tollbooth, the witness asked to retire with him to the little room in front of the council chamber. He confessed again that his sister had been taken out of bed from him several times. The witness asked him if he had seen the Devil. He answered that any feeling he ever had of him was in the dark. This is the truth, as he shall answer to God.

Signed: John Sinclair.

[There is no mention of why Weir should have sent for Sinclair to unburden himself. Sinclair's brother later published a book on witchcraft which is generally understood to rely heavily on the Rev John's experiences.]

1678

The Peaston Witches.

[The Register of the Privy Council records the expenses incurred for the execution of four witches at Peaston in 1678. These were quoted in the previous chapter Trial by Commission". These women were victims of a witchcraft panic centred on neighbouring areas of Midlothian, and involving the disgraced minister of Crichton, Gideon Penman, who seems to have escaped with his life. The burnings at Peaston are the last authenticated executions for witchcraft in East Lothian, although it is not unlikely that Catherine McTarget from Dunbar suffered the same fate ten years later. The papers connected with the Peaston witches can be found in Box JC26/49 of Justiciary Court Records.]

For the Lords of His Majesty's Justiciary.

Verdict of the jury against Douglas and other witches 13th September 1678. Burnt Edinburgh 15th September 1678.

By the mouth of their foreman James Paterson, the jury unanimously find the accused Margaret Dowglas in Crightoun; Margaret Low; Margrett Smell; Issobell Elliot; Mareon Vetch, the wife of George Thomson in Keith, Helen Laying in Peston; Margaret Dods; Isobell Schankes in Crightoun, and Helen Forester there; all guilty of the crime of witchcraft, since they have all confessed paction with the Devil and renouncing their baptism.

Signed: James Paterson, foreman of the jury.

[Apart from the above note, the rest of the material in Box JC26/49 relevant to this case is in a bundle marked "Isobel Elliot, Marion Veitch and others Ex JC26/49. 6 items."]

Item 1. [On the reverse side.] Testificate of the burning of four witches in Peastone More 20th September 1678"

We the undersigned
William Baylie of Lammingtoun;
Adame Cockburne of Ormestoun;
William Cunninghame
    of Enterkine younger;
David Hepburne of Ronderstoun[?];
Mr Robert and George Cockburne,
[illegible] to the Laird of Ormestoun;
William Borthwick of Johnstounburne;
John Belshes of that ilk;
Mr John Sinclar, minister at Ormestoun;
Mr James Calderwood,
    minister at Humby;
Mr Robert Spotswood,
    minister at Crightoun;

Mr James Cockburne, minister at Pencatland; Mr George Moode, minister at Fala; and Mr James Griersone, reader at Ormestoun, hereby testify and declare to the honourable Lords of His Majesty's Justiciary as follows:

Conforming to and in obedience to their sentence of death pronounced on 12th September, ordering Issobell Elliot, Marion Vaitch, Margaret Dodds, and Hellen Lainge, found guilty by a jury of the crime of witchcraft, to be taken to Peastoun Moore this Friday 20th September between two and four o'clock in the afternoon, to be strangled to death at a stake, and their bodies thereafter burned to ashes, we the undersigned testify that we were all present. We saw and were witnesses to the sentence of death being put to due execution on the bodies of the four witches above named. This was at the time day and place mentioned above, and conforming to the sentence in every particular. In confirmation of the truth of this, we the forementioned persons sign with our hands at Peastoun More, 20th September 1678.

[Their signatures follow.]

[Attached to the "testificate" is the claim given below.]

To the Lord Justice General, and the other Lords of His Majesty's Justiciary: The humble supplication of Sir Robert Hepburne of Keith and John Pringall of Woodhead.

Issobell Elliot, Marion Vaitch, Margarett Dodds, and Hellen Lainge were found guilty by a jury of the crime of witchcraft. By Your Lordships' sentence dated 13th September 1678 they were ordered to be taken to Peastoun Moore on Friday 20th September between two and four o'clock in the afternoon to be strangled to death at a stake, and thereafter their bodies to be burnt to ashes. Your lordships also commanded us, Your Lordships' supplicants, to be answerable for putting the sentence to due execution. Your Lordships' clerk Mr Robert Martein took our bond for the sum of ten thousand merks that we would see the sentence carried out. We caused this sentence to be executed on these witches at the place day and hour abovementioned, as testified by the attached certificate signed by a nimber of barons, gentlemen, ministers, and others who were there as witnesses.

We therefore humbly beseech Your Lordships to order your clerk Mr Robert Martein to cancel and return our bond, as we have punctually observed and obeyed Your Lordships' orders. We await Your Lordships' answer.

Edinburgh 9th December 1678: The Lords grant the desire of this bill, and order the petitioners' bond to be delivered up.

Edinburgh 2nd January 1679: The bond received by me.

Robert Hepburne.

Item 2. Margaret Russell.

At Pestoun, 29th June 1678: There follows the free and voluntary confession of Margreat Russel in Peastoun, given without any torture or threatening. She made this confession in the presence of Sir Robert Hepburne of Keith; Mr Jone Sinclar, minister at Ormestoun; John Ker in the Windymains; David Chalmer in Keith; William Cockburne, schoolmaster there, and writer of the confession; James Lyddell in Pestoun; George Haliday there; James Carentoune there; and John Adamsone, schoolmaster there.

Margreat Russell confesses firstly that about four and a half years ago, she and Marion Campbel were coming home from Seatoun to Wintoun when a grim black man appeared to them. He kissed Marion Campbell. She told Margreat it was the Devil. At the Devil's request Margreat then renounced her baptism. When she did this he made her put one hand on the crown of her head and the other on the sole of her foot. This happened during the day, in the afternoon. She denies that the Devil ever had sex with her. She also denies that she ever had any other meeting with the Devil, except at the time and place mentioned where he made her renounce her baptism. She denies that the Devil gave her any new name when she renounced her baptism. She denies that she ever did any wrong to man woman or beast. She denies that she knows any other person to be guilty of witchcraft apart from Marion Campbell.

[The signatures of the witnesses named above follow.]

Margaret Dodds.

At Pestoun 1st July 1678: There follows the free and voluntary comfession of Margret Dodds in Pestoun, given without any torture or threatening. Margaret Dodds confesses that about three years ago the Devil appeared to her in her own house in Pestoun at night when she was in her bed. At the Devil's request she renounced her baptism, and he made her put one of her hands over the crown of her head, and her other hand to her knee, because she was not able to put it on the sole of her foot, and she gave over to the Devil everything that was between her two hands. She declares that the next time the Devil appeared to her was at the Rowting Stair above Olestop, when she was going to the Panns with her creel on her back with eggs in it. The Devil had sex with her there. His penis was cold and he had no breath. [Here we seem to have corroboration of Kincaid's claim that the Devil put on the flesh of a cadaver for his sexual adventures.] She declares that after that she was at a meeting at the Murraisburne. However, she did not see the Devil there. Hellen Laing, Sarah Cranstoun[?] and her servant Margaret Banontine, Marion Veitch, Margaret Russell, and Margaret Cowan[?] from Falla were all present at this meeting. They had a piper and they ail danced. However, she was not able to dance. She denies that she ever had any other meetings or dealings with the Devil, or that she ever did any harm to man, woman, beast, or goods. This statement was taken in the presence of Sir Robert Hepburne of Keith; James Yule in Keith; William Symson there; William Cockburn, schoolmaster there, writer of the statement; Alexander Ramsay in Pestoun; James Lyddell there; and John Adamsone, schoolmaster there.

[The witnesses' signatures follow.]

Item 2.

At Peastoun and Templehall 1st July 1678: This day in the presence of Sir Robert Hepburne of Keith; John Pringal of Woodheid; Mr James Calderwood, minister at Humbie; Mr John McMath, minister at Leswad; Mr James Cockburne, minister at Pencaitland; and Mr George Moddy, minister at ffala, the statements of the following witches were read: -

Marion Cambell, her statement of 19th June last,

Issobell Elliot, her statement of 27th June last,

Hellien Lainge and Margaret Russell, their statements of 29th June last,

Margaret Doddes, her statement taken today.

These were all read to the five confessing witches named, in the presence of the above ministers and gentlemen. These five women all adhered to and acknowledged their previous statements and declared them to be true. Mr James Calderwood and Mr George Moody were not present at Temple Hall when Issobel's statement was read to her, but were present at the four in Peastoun. The forenamed gentlemen and ministers testify to the truth of the record of proceedings with their signatures, day, year, and place as mentioned.

[The witnesses' signatures follow.]

At Keith 1st July 1678: This day Marion Veitch in Keith, a confessing witch, was again called into the presence of Sir Robert Hepburne of Keith; Mr James Calderwood, minister of the parish; and Mr George Muddy, minister at

Fala. Marion's previous statements, dated 21st and 27th June last, were read over to her, and she adhered to all the points of her previous confessions and declared then to be true; to which this testifies, signed by the above-named persons, day year and place as mentioned.

[Their signatures follow.]

Item 3.

Confession: Agnes Dalgleish in Keith. Mariyon Vaitch.

At Keith 20th July 1678: This day Marion Veitch in Keith and Elspeth Knox there, two confessing witches, declared without being asked to do so by anybody, that Margreat Cowper, the wife of James Moffat in Keith; Agnes Dalglish, wife of Thomas Thomson in Keith; and Jennet Wilson, wife of James Dewar in the Birks, were all three at several meetings with the Devil where the above named witnesses were present. This was at the Waird Hauch and the Reid Ford, all within the past two years. Elspeth Knox also declared that the hen wife in Woodheid, who is married to a weaver there, was also at all three of the meetings. When Margaret Cowper and Agnes Dalglish were confronted with Marion Veitch and Elspeth Knox, they constantly upheld the truth of all this to their faces, and the other two accused women forcefully denied it. This was done day year and place foresaid, in the presence of Sir Robert Hepburne of Keith; Alexander Ramsay in Pestoun; and James Yule, William Sheill, and William Cockburn the writer of this record, all living in Keith, Their singatures follow as witnesses to this.

[Their signatures follow as indicated.]

Agnes Dalglish's confession.

Agnes Dalglish, accused above as described, was questioned again in the presence of Sir Robert Hepburne of Keith; Mr John Sinclair, minister at Ormestoun; Mr James Calderwood, minister at Humbie; Mr James Cockburne, minister at Pencaitland; and the others whose signatures appear below. Freely and voluntarily, without subjection to any threatening or torture, she confessed that before last Whitsunday she was in Sara Cranstoun's house in Keith, when a black man appeared to her in black clothes. This was during the day, about two o'clock in the afternoon. There was nobody else there but Sara. The Devil first kissed Agnes. His mouth was as cold as lead, and he had no breath. He then had sex with her, and he was monstrously heavy and exceedingly cold. At the Devil's request she renounced her baptism, the Devil made her put one of her hands on the crown of her head and the other hand on the sole of her foot, and at the Devil's command she gave over to him all that was between her two hands. The Devil gave her a new name, Eppie. She declares that right at the beginning Sara Cranstoun took her hand and put her hand in the Devil's hand. His hand was cdd like lead. She declares that after this, Sara Cranstoun roused her out of her bed at midnight, and took her over to Sara's front door where the Devil was waiting. On that occasion the Devil neither did anything nor spoke to Agnes, except to ask her how she was doing. She also confesses that since the times mentioned, she was taken to two meetings at the Cowburne and the Mains Park Burne. She thought there were about a hundred people at these two meetings, but she did not know any of them, except Sara Cranstoun who was masked, Grissel Waker, and David Yorstoun's mother, who is now a fugitive. She says they all danced for about an hour, but denies that she saw the Devil at these meetings. Marion Veitch, a confessing witch, testifies that she saw Grissel Walker at these two meetings with David Yorstoun's mother. This confession is attested and signed by the above-named and undersigned persons, day year and place mentioned. [Their signatures follow.]

Item 4.

The statements of Margaret Russell in Peastoun, Margaret Dods there, Elspett Knox, Jennet Burtoun, and Marion Veitch.

At Keith, 9th July 1678: There follows the third statement from Marion Veitch in Keith, which she confessed freely in the presence of Sir Robert Hepburne of Keith; John Pringel of Woodhead; Mr James Calderwood, minister at Humby; and Mr James Cockburne, minister at Pencaitland. Marion Veitch declares that Agnes Thomsone and Elspeth Wood, both from Over Keith, Barbara Howden in Saltoun Mylnehill, and Elspeth Knox the wife of Andro Smyth in Netherkeith, were all four of them at several meetings with the Devil where Marion was present. These were at Keith Bridge, the Crosshill, and the Waird Hauch. She saw the four women at these meetings. Marion Veitch stands by her two previous confessions dated 21st and 22nd June. Her confession is signed by the two gentlemen and ministers above-named as witnesses to its truth, day year and place mentioned.

[Their signatures follow.]

Elspeth Knox

At Keith, 9th July 1678. After Marion Veitch had accused Elspeth Knox, this Elspeth Knox was called for and questioned by the two gentlemen and ministers, and the other undersigned persons. Immediately Elspeth Knox freely and voluntarily confessed that about two years ago she was coming home fron Ormestoun to Keith. Night came down, and Elspeth lay down to sleep at Keithbank Folds. Marion Veitch, "in bodily likeness", wakened her, got her up, and brought the Devil to her. She set him down beside Elspeth. He did nothing to her on that occasion. Jennet Burtoun, Sara Cranstoun's servant was also present there. She left her with the Devil along with Marion Veitch. About eight weeks after that, Elspeth had a meeting with the Devil in the Waird Hauch. The Devil had sex with her there. He was as heavy as a horse and his penis was cold. At the Devil's request she renounced her baptism. He made her put one of her hands over the crown of her head, and her other hand under the sole of her foot, and she gave over to the Devil all that was between her hands. The Devil gave her a new name and called her Lady Know. At this last meeting Marion Veitch was present, and Jennet Burtoun, Margreit Anderson from Ormestoun, Jennet Hunter who was then living in Ormestoun, and Jennet Maitland from Hielie.

Jennet Burtoun.

The following is the free and voluntary confession of Jennet Burtoun, servant to Sara Cranstoun in Keith, given by her, day year and place foresaid, in the presence of the gentlemen and ministers named above, and the other undersigned witnesses. Jennet Burtoun declares that about two years ago she was in her bed, when her mistress Sara Cranstoun got her up out of bed and told her that she must come and speak to a gentleman. She brought her to the hall where Jennet saw a grim black man, who took her in his arms and kissed her, but did nothing more that night. The next night when she was going to bed the Devil came again, brought her to the fireplace in the hall, and had sex with her there. He told her that she must be his servant when he called for her, and she promised she would. About fourteen days after that, her mistress Sara Cranstoun took her to the ford already mentioned, to a meeting with the Devil. She made her renounce her baptism, and put one hand over the crown of her head and the other under the sole of her foot. She delivered over to the Devil all that was between her hands. The Devil gave her a new name, calling her Sara's Drudge. At this meeting Sara Cranstoun was present, and

Marion Veitch, Marion Campbell, Helen Laing, Katherin Haliday, Margreit Russell, Margreit Banantyne, Isobell Elleat, Margreat Dodds the wife of Walter Spence in Pestoun, the mother of William Allan in Pestoun, and Jennet Maitland from Hielie.

[The witnesses' signatures follow.]

Also, Jennet Burtoun confesses that she was at some other meetings with the Devil at Ormestoun Wood, the Lint Hauch, and the Waird Hauch. She did not know any of the people at these meetings except those already mentioned. She declares that about five or six weeks ago Sara Cranstoun burst and rode to death a horse belonging to her own eldest[?] son John Anderson. She took the horse out to meetings. She declares that Marion Veitch took her own grandchild Marion Thomsone, a child a year old, and gifted her to the Devil in her father William Thomesone's house in Templehall. This was in the presence of Jennet and all the others she has named. The child died within eight days after that

The two gentlemen and ministers above-named testify and subscribe to the truth of the confessions of these two persons, Elspeth Knox and Jennet Burtoun. Also signing are David Chalmers, James Yule, Malcome Grive, and William Shiell, all from Keith; John Fowler at Humbiemylne; Richard Dalglish at Woodhead; and William Cockburne, schoolmaster at Keith, the writer of this record.

[Their signatures follow.]

Item 5.

The statement of Marion Campbell, a confessing witch, at Pestoun 19th June 1678.

Marion Campbell. The following is the statement and confession of Marion Campbell, the wife of William Laing in Pestoun, freely and voluntarily confessed without any torture or threatening whatsoever after being denounced and arresetd on suspicion of witchcraft.

Firstly, Marion confesses that about four and a half years ago, she and Margreat Russell, who is now married to Thomas Attkine in Pestoun, were coming from Seatoun to Wintoun when a man in green clothes appeared to them. He kissed Marion, and he had no breath. He said to her that she was his servant. After he had stayed with them for half an hour he vanished. When she asked Margreat Russel who he was, she answered that she would find out later.

A few days later she had a meeting in Ormestoun Wood with the Devil at night, along with Margaret Russel; Margreat Dods from Pestoun; William Laing's widow Helen Laing from Pestoun, and Isobell Elliot who was then her servant, and now lives in Templehall; Kathrin Haliday, the wife of William Hare the cooper; Margreat Bannantyne, the wife of John Goudy in Pestoun; Sara Cranstoun, widow of the late George Andersone in Keith; and Marion Veitch, the wife of George Thomesone in Keith. There were also many others who Marion did not know. The Devil had sex with her there, and his penis was cold.

About eight days after that, Marion and all the other women mentioned had another meeting with the Devil at Cousland Dean where the Devil again had sex with her. She also confesses that he made her renounce her baptism, and become his servant by laying one of her hands on the crown of her head, and the other hand on the sole of her foot, and giving to the Devil everything that was between her two hands. The Devil gave her a new name, calling her Tousce[?].

After that, Marion and all the women named above, with many others she did not know, had another meeting with the Devil at the Cow Bume, where they all danced, as they did at the previous meeting. She also declares that they ail had another meeting with the Devil a while after that near Wintoun, where they all danced. The Devil had sex with her there again. She also confesses that she had several other meetings with the Devil. Many of the women named were at all these meetings, except Sara Cranstoun. Marion could be certain only that she was at three of the meetings, as far as she could tell.

She declares that when she and the others went to and returned from these meetings, they were sometimes in the shape of crows, and sometimes in the shape of magpies. Sometimes they were in their own shape, wearing their own clothes. She absolutely denies that she ever did any harm to either man woman or beast, but confesses that when some people fell out with her she intended to do them harm, but could never have managed it She declares that the Devil gave them all new names. He called Margaret Russel "His Own Post Horse". He called Margreat Dods "Drodlin", and he called Margreat Balentine "Lout Shoulders" [*i.e.* stooped shoulders]. He called Cathren Haliday "Dancewell", but she cannot remember the names he gave to the rest.

Margreat Russell, Margreat Dods, Kathrine Halyday, Margreat Balantine, and Helen Laing were all confronted with Marion Campbell. She affirmed all this to their faces, but they all obstinately denied it.

This statement was taken in the presence of Sir Robert Hepburne of Keith; Mr Johne Sinclar, minister at Ormestoun; Mr James Calderwood, minister at Humby; and the other undersigned persons. [Their signatures follow.]

Marion Veitch.

At Keith 21st June 1678: The following is the free and voluntary confession and declaration of Marion Veitch, wife of George Thomesone in Keith, concerning her guilt in the sin of witchcraft. She made this confession without any compulsion or threatening, in the presence of Sir Robert Hepburne of Keith; Mr James Calderwood, minister of the parish; Thomas Kamaway, one of the gentlemen of His Majesty's Lifeguards; David Chalmer, James Yule, and John Spavine, servants to Sir Robert; William Shiel, gardener in Keith; and William Cockburne, schoolmaster there and writer of this record.

Firstly, Marion Veitch confessed that she entered into the Devil's service about the end of 1650 or the beginning of 1651. About that time the Devil appeared to her at the Rid Ford. She had been brought there by the late Barbry Veitch. The Devil had sex with her, and made her renounce her baptism. The Devil gave her a new name and called her "Broadback". He made her put one of her hands on the crown of her head, and the other at the sole of her foot, and deliver up to the Devil all that was between her two hands. This she did, and the Devil required her to serve him by destroying her neighbours, and to blaspheme God's name. However, God did not permit her to do these things. She declares that the next meeting she had with the Devil was in Ormestoun Wood, where there were many people present, and they all danced with the Devil. Helen Laing and Margreat Dods were at that meeting. She declares that she has been at many meetings with the Devil over the past twenty seven years, and remembers clearly that Helen Laing and Margreat Dods were present at many of them; also Kathrine Haliday, Marion Campbell, Margreat Russell, Margreat Balantine, all from Pestoun; and Isobell Elliot who then lived in Pestoun but now lives in Templehall. She knows that Sara Cranstoun was certainly present at two of the meetings, one at the Cowburne and the other at Ormestoun Wood. She confesses that after her first meeting the Devil had sex with her several times. She declares that she was present when Helen Laing's husband William Laing died. She says that Helen Laing, along with Isobell Elliot who was then her servant, killed her own husband William Laing on his death bed, and pulled out his heart. One of them sat on one side of him and the other by the side of the bed. Marion was present but invisible when the two women committed this horrid act of murder.

This is attested as the true statement of Marion Veitch, and is signed by the persons named above who were witnesses to the confession, day year and place above-mentioned.

[Their signatures follow.]

At Keith, 27th June 1678: Marion Veitch freely and voluntarily confessed in the presence of those signing below that she was present at, and an accessory to, the death of William Laing in Peastoun. Also present and an accessory was Helen Laing his own wife, and Isobell Elliot who was then her servant. Also Marion Campbell and certain other witches. She further confesses that she, along with Marion Campbell and Isobell Elliot, also killed a young daughter of William Thomsone's at Templehall. The Devil tempted her and the rest to commit these two wicked acts. She declares that Sara Cranstoun's servant Jennet Burtoun carried Sara's mantle to the meetings where Sara was present. These were two or three meetings, at Ormestoun Wood, the Wairdhaugh, and the Cowburne.

Signed: Da. Chalmer, Ja. Yule, Malcolm Grieve, Ro. Hepburne, W. Cockburne, John Spevin, William Simpsone, Ja. Calderwood.

Isobell Elliot.

At Peastoun 27th June 1678: The following is the free and voluntary confession given by Issobell Elliot in Templehall without any threatening or torture. She was accused of witchcraft by Marion Campbell in Peastoun and Marion Veitch in Keith. This confession is made by Issobell Elliot in the presence of Sir Robert Hepburne of Keith; John Pringall of Woodhead; Mr James Calderwood, minister at Humby; Mr James Cockburne, minister at Pencaitland; and the other witnesses signing below.

Firstly, Issobell confesses that about two years ago, when she was servant to Hellene Laing in Paistoun, one Sunday morning Hellen kept her at home from the church, saying that a friend was coming to the house. Issobell stayed at home, and was carrying in water from the well when she found Hellen Laing and Marion Campbell with the Devil sitting between them. The two women went into the parlour, and the Devil came and kissed her, and suggested having sex with her. She refused, because she was pregnant at the time, and the Devil said he would leave her alone until she had been delivered of her child. At his request she renounced her baptism. The Devil baptised her on her face with a wave of his hand, like a sprinkling of dew, and called her Jean. After she was "kirked" [*i.e.* after she had attended church for the first time after the birth of her child] the Devil had sex with her. Since that first time she had several meetings with the Devil and had sex with him several times. She thought the Devil had the weight of four men when he lay with her, and he was very cold. At several of these meetings with the Devil the following people were present: Sara Cranstoun, Jonet Bruntoun her servant, Maryon Vaitch in Keith, Marion Campbell, Kathrin Halyday, Margaret Dods, Margaret Balenden... [damage]...Laing, and Margaret Russel, all from Peastoun; Jonet Hunter who was in Ormestoun until recently; and Margreat Andersone, widow of James Vaitch in Ormestoun. She also testifies that Bessie Bell and Margarett Little in Laiswaid Loanhead are witches, and killed a child of Mr John McMath's, the minister of Leswaid, when the child had been put out to nurse at Caringtoun. They also killed a daughter of John Whyt's, a coal miner there. She denies that she had any hand in the death of William Lainge who was then her master, and whatever part his wife Hellen Laing or any other person played in his death, she does not know. She confesses that she and many other witches were present at the contriving of the death of the child who was the daughter of Kathrin Halyday and her husband William Hair. Kathrine Halyday the child's mother, Hellen Laing, Sara Cranstoun, Margaret Russel, and Margaret Balenden were all present.

Signed:... [damage]... James Liddell, J. Calderwood, R. Hepburne, J. Pringall

Hellen Laing.

At Peastoun, 29th June 1678. The following is the free and voluntary confession of Hellen Laing in Pestoun, made without any torture or threatening. This confession was given in presence of Sir Robert Hepburne of Keith; Mr Johne Sinclar, minister at Ormestoun; Mr John Ker in the Windymaines; David Chalmer in Keith; William Cockburne, schoolmaster there, and writer of this record; James Liddell in Pestoun; George Haliday there; James Cairintoune there; and John Adamsone, schoolmaster there.

Firstly, Hellen Laing declares that about seven years ago the Devil appeared to her in her own garden in Pestoun in the shape of a black man. She does not remember what he did or said to her on that occasion. About a year after that the Devil appeared to her at the Ward Burn in the shape of a black man as before, in black clothes, and at his request she renounced her baptism. She declares that there were several women present, but she knew none of them except Marion Campbell and Margreat Dods. After that, she had another meeting with the Devil at the Black Sauch. There were several women there but she knew none of them except Marion Campbell and Margreat Dods already mentioned. She cannot remember having any other meetings with the Devil, and denies that the Devil ever had sex with her. She denies that she ever saw any other person at meetings with the Devil except for the two women already named, and denies that she did any wrong to her husband William Laing, or to any other person. She denies knowing that any other person did wrong to man woman or beast, and denies that the Devil gave her any new name when she renounced her baptism. She was confronted with the three confessing witches, Marion Campbell, Marion Veitch, and Isobell Elliot, who affirmed to Hellen Laing's face everything contained in their statements against her. She denied everything, and confessed nothing of her dealings with the Devil, except the particulars noted above which were admitted by her.

Item 6.

List of jurors for the trial of Marion Veitch and other witches, 7th September 1678. [This is presumably a pool from which a jury of fifteen would be chosen. "P" stands for "present", and "D" indicates absence, probably standing for "delinquent".]

   Patrick Banklie[?] in Samulston
P Robert Selkirk, merchant
      in Edinburgh
P Robert Pringle in Templehall
P James Selkirk, merchant
      in Edinburgh
P John Hempseid in Murrays
P Thomas Gray, merchant
      in Edinburgh Netherbow
P John Henson[?] in Ormestoun
P Thomas Fisher elder, tailor
      in Edinburgh
P Robert ffouler in Overkeith
P James Symson, merchant
      in Edinburgh
P George Robertson in Wintoun
P Robert Hogg there
P James Edmonstoun,
      merchant in Edinburgh
P James Paterson, skinner there
P John Adam, merchant there
P Alexander Laying, white
      iron man [*i.e.* tinsmith]
P William Pollock elder, baker there

P John McGill, merchant
P George Menteith, merchant there
P James Dixon, merchant there
P Richard Lothian,
    merchant in Edinburgh
P Mr Alexander Paterson, merchant there
P John Selkirk, merchant there
P William Lawson, merchant there
P James Warrock, merchant in Edinburgh
P Robert Hamilton elder in the Bow
P Henry Barclay, baker there
D Willliam Johnstoun elder, skinner there
D Hugh Blain, merchant there
P Robert Broun, stationer there
P John Broun, merchant at
    Baxter's Close head
P Alexander Hume, His Majesty's tailor
P Alexander Wilson,
    hammerman in Cannogate
P William Burne, baker there
P Johne Howesone, brewer in Potterawe
P David Howieson,
    merchant in Edinburgh
D John McLurge, merchant there
P James Ardbuckes elder, merchant there
D William Brown, skinner there
P John Paterson, shoemaker ther
P James Tait, merchant there.

[The trial records of the Peaston/Crichton witches can be found in the Books of Adjournal JC2/15. The evidence produced closely follows the statements contained in the Justiciary Court Processes box JC26/49. In the case of Isobel Elliot from Templehall, however, the following additional information is given on JC2/15 page 19.]

She was at many meetings, particularly at Crighton. Many others were present and there was a flaming fire. The Devil gave them a kind of sacrament, preached to them, and blasphemed God. She declares that she was present at the poisoning of William Thomson's child, who was poisoned by Marion Veach the child's grandmother. She declares that she and Marion Veatch were in the shape of bumble bees when the child was poisoned, and that Marion Veatch carried the poison in her claws, wings, and mouth. She declares that she left her body in Pencaitland Kirk, and went in the shape of a crow to Lesswade Loanhead to see a child she had nursed for William Ramsay there. She declares that she cannot write.

[The following is extracted from the Books of Adjournal JC2/15, page 17.]

13th September 1678.

Marion Campbell, wife of William Logan in Paiston; Grisell Walker, wife of Alexander Couper in Keith; Margaret Dalgleish, wife of Thomas Thomson there; Margaret Anderson, widow of the late Thomas Waugh in Ormestoun; James Campbell in Wintoun; Margaret Russell in Paistoun; Elizabeth Wood in Overkeith; Elspeth Knox in Keith; and Agnes Thomson in Overkeith, were called several times to appear here in court before the Lords Commissioners of Justiciary to submit themselves to the law for the crime of witchcraft committed by them. Having been lawfully summoned to that effect at the time of day ordained, none of them appeared. The Lords therefore sentenced each one of them to be outlawed as fugitives from His Majesty's laws, and ordered them to be put to the horn, with all their moveable goods and gear to be forfeited and confiscated to our Sovereign Lord's use; which sentence was formally pronounced.

[Being "put to the horn" simply means to be outlawed. There seems to be no record of any of these people ever coming to trial, so it looks as if they saved their lives by fleeing from justice. Perhaps the safest and most easily reached refuge might be Northumberland. At that late date in the 17th Century it is rather unlikely that the English authorities would look sympathetically on extradition requests for witchcraft.

The Books of Adjournal also record the fining of a juror who failed to turn up for the trial of the Peaston witches.]

13th September 1678.

Alexander Hume, His Majesty's tailor, was called several times to appear in court here today to serve on the jury of Issobell Elot and other witches. He was lawfully summoned for that effect at the time of day ordained, and did not appear. The Lords Commissioners of Justiciary therefore, by the mouth of the court officer Gilbert Mair, judged Alexander Hume to in breach of the law, and fined him a hundred merks in accordance with the relevant Act of Parliament; which sentence was formally pronounced.

[Several Midlothian people were caught up in the same witchcraft panic as the witches from the Peaston/Keith/Ormiston area, and some of what they had to say has relevance to East Lothian. The Books Of Adjournal JC2/15, page 20, record the trial of Bessie Gourlie, midwife in Fala, and Agnes Somervall and Margaret Sonus, also from Fala. They made the usual pact with the Deil, putting one hand on the head and the other on the sole of the foot, and giving him everything in between. They attended various meetings at the Cowe Burne, at Keith Bridge, behind the "toun" of Nether Keith, and at the Ward Burn. The record is accompanied by the blunt marginal note "Convict and brunt".]

4th November 1678. The statements of Bessie Gourlie, one of the confessing witches from Fala, which she gave voluntarily without any violence being offered or done to her, before the following witnesses: George Mudie, minister at ffala; John Crightoun, precentor there; Thomas Rae and Thomas Findleyson, elders there; John Findleyson there; Andrew Wallace, weaver there; David Borthwick, elder there.

Bessie Gourlie in ffala, denounced by Isobell Eliot in Templehall for several acts of evil intent, and also by Agnes Somervaill, a confessing witch in ffala, confessed that Sara Cranstoun in Nether Keith led her into becoming the Devil's servant. She met with her on one particular occasion when Sara promised to give Bessie her daughter, Laird Skirvin's lady, to be with her in childbirth if she would do her bidding. She took her to the back of the garden to meet a gentleman, and there she saw the Devil. Sara promised her that she would never want if she would be a servant to that gentleman. She promised that she would. After that, Sara took the Devil into her house, and Bessie said, "Who is that gentleman?" She replied, "He is a gentleman who has come from my daughter at Ladyside." Bessie said to him, "Well sir, how is the goodman, and the mistress and the child?" The Devil said, "They are all well." Sara promised to give Bessie a cheese, but never gave her it.

She also declared that she met with the Devil at the Cowe Burne, and another time at Keith Bridge. Also, Sara Cranstoun, Marion Veatch, and Sara's female servant came to ffala after sunset. Bessie went out, and Sara was at the end of her barn. She beckoned Bessie with her finger, so Bessie went to her, and Sara said, "Go in with me." Bessie refused, but she said, "You must go." And so Bessie went with her up to the Whithouse to meet the Devil. He appeared to me [sic], and at his request I renounced my baptism. He laid one of my hands on the crown of my head and the other on the sole of my foot, and I delivered up all between the two, soul and body, to the Devil's service. The Devil promised her [sic] that she would be well-loved among women. She says it was through greed for employment that she engaged in the Devil's sevice.

She also declares that the last meeting she was at was twenty days after Whitsunday this year, at the back of Nether Keith village. Sara Cranstoun was present, Marion Veitch, and many others she did not know. Sara Cranstoun had a mask on her face, and a cloak wrapped

St Mary's Church, Haddington (above) served a large parish which in the 17th century included the witchcraft "hotspots" of Penston and Samuelston. Elisabeth Moodie was convicted of witchcraft in 1677 after she had been heard to exclaim "Now the turn is done!" in church at the very moment when her mistress hanged herself at home.

Isobel Eliot claimed that she left her body sitting in Pencaitland church (left) while her spirit flew to Loanhead in the shape of a crow to visit a baby she had nursed.

round her. Sara said, "The witches will be arrested now, but I won't confess. I've been in his service for a long time, but now I'm going to give it up." She also declares that about twenty days before that, she was at a meeting with the Devil at the Ward Burn. She went to the meeting after sunset when her husband and family were in bed, and came back at midnight, but did not go to bed that night. Sara had told her when the meeting was to be a few days before.

This true confession is attested by the forenamed witnesses at Fala, 17th September 1678.

[Their signatures follow.]

Edinburgh, 4th November 1678.

Bessie Gourlie was brought into the presence of the Lords Commissioners of Justiciary, and questioned on the confession quoted. She declares this confession to be true, and voluntarily given by her, and she abides by the truth of it. She declares that she cannot write.

Signed: Thomas Wallace, Robert Norvie[?,] David Balfour, J. Falconer.

[The Books of Adjournal also record statements from Bessie Gourlie's co-accused Agnes Somervaill and Margaret Sonnes. They contain no clear East Lothian references however.]

6th November 1678: [The sentence passed on Gourlie, Somervaill, and Sonnes.] ... to be taken to the Gallowlie between Leith and Edinburgh between two and four o'clock in the afternoon, and then to be strangled at a stake until they are dead, and thereafter to have their bodies burnt to ashes, and all their moveable goods and gear to be forfeited and confiscated to His Majesty's use; which was pronounced for doom.

[A petition from two East Lothian lairds, recorded in the Books of Adjournal JC2/15 draws a final line under this outbreak of witchcraft.]

3rd December 1678: A petition was presented by Sir Robert Hepburne of Keith and John Pringle of Woodhead relating how the Lords of Justiciary had ordered them to see the sentence of death put to execution against the witches Isobell Elliot, Marion Veatch, Margaret Dods, and Helen Laing, on the moor of Paistoun, 20th September last. They were required to give surety to that effect under the penalty of 10 000 merks, which they accordingly did. The sentence of death was carried out against these four witches at the place day and hour mentioned in their sentence, as a certificate testified, signed by a number of barons, gentlemen, and other eyewitnesses. This certificate was shown to the Lords of Justiciary. It is therefore requested that the Lords would order the clerk to cancel the petitioners' bond.

The Lords Justice General, Justice Clerk, and Commissioners of Justiciary grant the request, and order the petitioners' bond to be delivered up.

[It might be thought puzzling that there is no record of the much-mentioned Sara Cranstoun being questioned, never mind being "convict and brunt". She may of course have been dead, but on the other hand she may have escaped arrest because her station in life protected her. She was, after all, a woman who kept servants and whose daughter was married to a laird. Indeed, the eminent legal figure Sir John Lauder of Fountainhall wrote of this case that the suspects were "ready to fylle by their deletion sundry gentlewomen and others of faschion, but the justices discharged them." The judges purported to believe that claims that such people had taken part in witches' meetings could only have sprung from malice, madness, or diabolicaly-inspired imaginings. See the next chapter - "Contemporary Writers".]

There are no further records of witchcraft in East Lothian in the Books of Adjournal or the High Court Minutes. As previously remarked, the executions on Peaston Moor are the last authenticated witch-burnings in East Lothian. Although Catherine McTarget from Dunbar was found guilty of witchcraft in 1688, there seems to be no record of sentence being passed, and no record of an execution - see "Trial by Commission".

1678

Porteous Roll for Haddington.

[In theory these lists of criminal cases should have been made each year. Few of them seem to have survived however. This one is from Box JC26/51 of Justiciary Court Processes. It is interesting in that it records an attempt to process Catherine McTarget from Dunbar ten years before she was finally put on trial. It also indicates how at least one baron baillie treated witchcraft suspects. The fact that he felt able to behave in that way tempts one to believe that such behaviour had been common practice in such cases.]

Fugitives.

James Hunter in Lumhnay Mains. [Wamphray? Luffness?]

Janet [blank], servant to William Hunter in Sandersdale. [Saundersdean?]

Katharin McTargaret in Dunbar.

Witnesses: The ministers, elders, and neighbours of the parishes and places where they live, who had given in their names and were cited as witnesses against them. They are indicted and accused of the crime of witchcraft, sorcery, and necromancy; renouncing our blessed saviour and their baptisms; giving themselves over soul and body to the Devil; and destroying the persons and goods of His Majesty's good subjects by their sorcery and witchcraft.

Case defeated.

John Rutherford, baillie in Prestounpannes; William Aitcheson, officer there; William Cuthbertson there.

Witnesses:

Gilbert Glover in Prestounpannes;
David Simpson, salter there;
John Thomson, skipper there;
James fforest, apothecary in Tranent;
George Whytt, maltman in Prestoun;
John Robertson, glover in the Caldtoun, and his daughter [blank] Robertson;
John Whytt, merchant in Prestoun;
George Keddie, merchant there.

They are indicted and accused of torturing, tormenting, and wrongfully imprisoning Elspeth Chousley in Prestounpannes in the month of May 1678, and for coming to her house in the month of June last about eleven o' clock at night, and surrounding it with cocked pistols and drawn swords, committing "hamesuken" with the intention of taking her life, which they would undoubtedly have done had they not been scared off by people who came to her rescue.

William Aitchieson and William Cuthbertson are also indicted and accused of beating, pricking, and drawing blood from Andrew Williamson, mason in Edinburgh, to the great hazard of his life on [blank] September 1678, and for railing against the Lords of His Majesty's most honourable Privy Council, cursing them, and saying, "God damn such sitting sheriffs, especially the lord Chancellor and Lord Advocate." John Rutherford and the others named above are perpetrators and art and part of these crimes.

Fugitive: Christian Lockhed in Prestonpanns. Case defeated:

Elspeth Chouslie there.

Fugitive: Margaret Wightman in Hadingtoun.

Witnesses: the minister and magistrates of the place where they live, and those who heard the penitent and dying witches confess against them.

They are indicted and accused of the crimes of witchcraft, sorcery, necromancy, renouncing our blessed saviour and their baptisms, giving themselves up soul and body to the Devil, receiving his marks, and destroying the persons and goods of many of His Majesty's subjects by their sorcery and witchcraft.

1679

Persecution in Prestonpans.

[The following "memorandum" is contained in Box JC26/50 of Justiciary Court Processes. If I have read the date 1679 correctly this would indicate a further attempt by Elspeth Chouslie to prosecute the baron baillie after his apparent acquittal in 1678. However, it may be that the memorandum is connected not to a new case, but to the one mentioned in the 1678 Porteous Roll.]

Memorandum for Elspeth Chouslie.

To raise letters against John Rutherford, baillie in Prestounpans; Andrew Anderson there; William Ritchison in Prestoungrange; James ffinich there; David Cowan, pricker; and Christian Lockart in Prestounpans, making mention that although the crimes of hamesucken [assault of a person in his own home], robbery, wrongful imprisonment, and torture of His Majesty's subjects are designated serious crimes by the laws and Acts of Parliament of this country, and severely punishable:

Nevertheless, it is true that these persons conceived a deadly hatred and malice against Elspeth, and came to her dwelling-house on the [blank] day of June or July 1677, and by force and violence broke down her doors with sledgehammers and other instruments of force. They stole and carried away her furniture such as chimneys *[sic]*, tables etc, and broke up her other possessions, rendering them useless.

When dealing with the witches Agnes Kellie, Marjorie Anderson, and Christian Lockart, they tortured them and persuaded them to denounce Elspeth as a witch. After condemnation, they indicated Elspeth's innocence at the stake, and declared that everything they had said against her was false. Having made this conscientious denial, they craved pardon from God and from her for this calumny, in the presence of the baillie and the ministers. However, the malice of these people was such that after the death of the witches, they arrested her and put her in prison, keeping her there in great pain and torture for sixteen days and nights.

They brought a pricker in, and stripped off her clothes in a most disgraceful and shameful manner, and would not let her out of prison until she bought her freedom by giving them £23 6s 8d, and paying over 300 merks due with a bond to "enter her person" [*i.e.* turn up for trial when required]. Not satisfied with that, they came back to Elspeth's house in June or July 1678 with twelve soldiers who were then camped at that place. With drawn swords they beseiged and assaulted Elspeth in a most fearful manner at twelve o'clock at night, broke down her doors, broke her glass windows, and would undoubtedly have killed both her and her [husband? servant?] if they had not been prevented by some soldiers who were then quartered in Elspeth's house.

After that, this baillie J. Rutherford came to her dwelling-house on 16th June 1679 at about eleven o'clock at night with a sword and pistol. He threatened her with violence and would have killed her if some people had not taken her away when the baillie was drunk.

Witnesses: John Thomson in Prestounpans; Gilbert Glover there; David Coul, salter there; Ninian ffin, salter there; David Sampson, salter there.

[See Trial by Commission" for a similar case in Prestonpans involving Rutherford and the pricker Cowan.]

I was unable to find any subsequent papers in the JC26 boxes relating to witchcraft in

East Lothian. Taken together with the other Justiciary Court records, and the evidence provided by the Register of the Privy Council, this, as I have already observed, would appear to indicate that the last East Lothian witchcraft executions were at Peaston in 1678, with the possibility of another in Dunbar in 1688.

7 Contemporary Writers

Apart from the official records of witchcraft in East Lothian, a few published works have come down to us from writers who took notice of the activities of witches in the county, and were alive at the time of the events they describe. Some indeed were directly involved.

None were more directly involved than James VI, King of Scots. His *Daemonologie* was "probably published in the autumn of 1597", [Larner 2000; p. 204], and is the result of his wide reading on the subject, and his personal experience of interrogating the "North Berwick" witches. Normand and Roberts [Exeter 2000] are of the opinion that it was actually written in 1591, when the events of the North Berwick witchcraft panic must have been well to the fore in James's mind. *Daemonologie*, however, is not a narrative of actual events or particular cases. It is a dissertation on the theory and practice of witchcraft, which for the next hundred years was to provide a handy reference book for investigating authorities, enabling them to formulate their ideas of what constituted witchcraft and sorcery, and what sort of behaviour they could expect to hear described by witchcraft suspects. This was not always the same as the behaviour attributed to witches by popular belief, but we will tackle the subject of what witches "really" got up to, in the next and final chapter.

The relevance of *Daemonologie* to East Lothian, therefore, lies in the fact that anyone in the county arrested on suspicion of witchcraft was likely to find herself being interrogated by men who were bearing in mind the main points of James VI's treatise, and who were likely to have been keen to work towards eliciting a confession of behaviour compatible with James's ideas.

What I offer below is a summary of James's *Daemonologie*. Anyone wishing to read the original dissertation will find the most recently published text in *Witchcraft in Early Modern Scotland*, ed. Lawrence Normand and Gareth Roberts [Exeter 2000].

Daemonologie. [1591]

The reason James gives for writing his Demonology is that several recent writers had been sceptical about witchcraft, and James wishes to put forward proofs of its reality. His treatise is divided into three sections or "books".

Book 1 takes the form of a dialogue between Philomathes and Epistemon. It is stated that whereas witches are merely the servants of the Devil, necromancers have the power to command him. The basic powers the Devil gives to his servants include charms using words, herbs, or stones; clever deceitful tricks; and such superstitious rituals and practices as tying rowan twigs to livestock, curing tapeworms, staunching bleeding, healing lameness in horses, and "turning the riddle" - divination used in the detection of theft and recovery of lost property, involving a pair of shears stuck into a riddle and held by two persons. The Devil's servants can also cause impotence in men by tying knots in a cord.

James condemns using astrology to predict future events, and goes on to discuss the conjuring up of spirits. Two things are necessary for this - holy water, and the gift to the Devil of some living thing. However, in such rituals the Devil only pretends to be commanded by the practitioner. James goes on to discuss the use of magic circles and diagrams, and dismisses them as a waste of time.

Discussing the contract made by the Devil with his servants, James states that the Devil will appear to the "base sort" as an animal or merely a voice, and will answer questions on curing diseases, or on particular problems. With more advanced practitioners, tire Devil will enter into a human corpse, and give answers on questions of current affairs and such more complex and important topics. The Devil may serve other adepts as an attendant page, or perhaps as a spirit in a ring. The contract itself will be written in blood, or perhaps after it has been agreed the Devil will touch his pupil's body and leave a mark. This is always the case with witches, but not always with magicians and necromancers.

Book 2 deals specifically with sorcery and witchcraft, as opposed to the more elevated sciences of magic and necromancy. James points out that not all witches are "pale, lean, melancholy, solitary", but are often "rich, worldly-wise, fat, and corpulent". In other words, we can't tell a witch merely by looking at her. Most witches are addicted to the pleasures of the flesh, good company, and merriment. Witches are reluctant to confess without torture; in fact this unwillingness to confess is to be taken as a sign of their guilt.

When cultivating a potential servant the Devil will prepare the way by cunningly encouraging her in her state of mind, for example by increasing her despair and desperation. When the time is ripe he will reveal himself, perhaps when the victim is walking alone in the fields, lying in bed deep in thought, but always when the victim is alone. In the shape of a man, or as a voice, he will ask the victim to tell her troubles, promise a remedy if she will follow his advice, and will set a date for another meeting. At the second meeting he will persuade the victim to commit herself to his service. He will then reveal his true identity, make his servant renounce God and her baptism, and will mark her body "in some secret place". This mark will remain painful and unhealed until the next meeting, and will thereafter be permanently without feeling. The mark is a symbol of the Devil's power to both hurt and heal his servant.

Having dealt with how witches are recruited, James goes on to discuss what they actually do. He states that witches meet together to worship Satan. There he instructs them on how to work mischief, and he demands from each of them an account of what "horrible and detestable" things they have done since the last meeting. Sometimes these meetings take place in churches, where according to some witches' confessions, the Devil has on occasion occupied the pulpit. The witches express the worship of the Devil by kissing his backside.

Witches not only travel to meetings by the normal means of walking, riding, or sailing, but are sometimes carried by spirits through the air, or sometimes travel in the shape of some animal. They can enter buildings when doors and windows are closed. Sometimes they can travel to meetings in spirit form while their bodies lie in a trance. James thinks, however, that these are mere illusions.

At their meetings witches propose their intentions to the Devil - such as how to obtain riches or revenge, and he will tell them how to do it; perhaps, for example, by preparing powders made from corpses and other ingredients.

Witches are more likely to be women than men, because women are morally weaker than men, and it's easier for the Devil to trap them in his snares. He may teach them how to make images of wax or clay, or give them charm-stones or powders to enable them to lay on or take off diseases. Witches' main activities include causing men and women to love or hate each other, taking sickness off one person and laying it on another, bewitching and taking life by roasting images, raising storms at sea or on land, driving others insane, causing people to be frightened or troubled by spirits, or houses to be haunted by them, and causing people to be possessed by spirits. All this is permitted by God in order to punish the wicked, to make the godly more alert, and to try the faith of the best - as was done to Job in the Bible. It is not permissible to use a witch to undo the harm done by another witch. The only lawful remedy is prayer to God, or amendment of the victim's [presumably sinful] life.

Witches must be diligently pursued, and punished by death. A negligent magistrate may be vulnerable to witches, but one who is diligent in questioning and punishing them will be safe. Once witches have been justly arrested and detained by a lawful magistrate, they have no power. The Devil may appear to them in prison to give them vain hope or to drive them to suicide, but God does not permit him to trouble penitent witches who have confessed.

How is it that witches can experience the Devil as being solid to their sense of touch? After all, as a spirit, his body is formed out of air. Perhaps he feels solid because he is inhabiting a dead body, or perhaps because he deludes the witches' sense of touch as well as their sense of sight. This would not be difficult, because all our senses can be "oftentimes deluded", for example during illness. James finishes this section by declaring that during the time of Catholicism the Devil walked much more frequently among men, and ghosts and spirits were much more common because of the gross ignorance which then prevailed.

In Book 3 of his *Daemonologie* James discusses spirits which have sexual intercourse with human beings - "incubi" which have sex with women, and "succubi" which have sex with men. He suggests that the Devil may steal the sperm from a dead body and have sex with a woman when he is in spirit form, and nothing distinct will be seen or felt, in other cases he may borrow and inhabit a dead body and have apparently natural intercourse with a woman. However, the woman will feel his sperm as unnaturally cold, because it had come from a corpse. James dismisses stories of monsters being born from such escapades as old wives' tales.

After touching on the belief in fairies as a complete illusion, rife in the days of Catholicism, James goes on to deal with the detection and punishment of witches. Two helpful indications of a witch's guilt are firstly the finding of the Devil's mark and proving it to be without feeling; and secondly, a witch will float in water, because since she has shaken off the sacred water of baptism, water will not allow her to sink. Also, until she repents, a witch will not shed tears, even when threatened and tortured. Witches must always be punished with death, and there should be no exceptions made. Fire is often used, but the actual method is not important, and whatever is the custom of the country is acceptable.

Normand and Roberts comment that we can gather from James's preface to *Daemonologie* that he was familiar with a wide range of 16th Century works on witchcraft and demonology, and that "many of the points James makes are the often-iterated commonplaces of most demonical writings" [Normand and Roberts 2000, p.331]. They also note that some of *Daemonologie*'s contents are very close to the contents of the North Berwick dittays, and they emphasise that the Bible is one of James's main authorities. It is his "first court of appeal in an argument" [Normand and Roberts 2000, p. 329].

Before passing on from James VI's wise words on witchcraft, we might remind ourselves of the events which had stimulated his interest by looking at a passage from *Historie and Life* of *James the Sext*. The author of the *Historie* is unknown, and it was published by the Bannatyne Club in 1825. The editors believe that "it was written within the period within which it treats". I have rendered the passage in modern English. It can be found on page 242 of the Bannatyne Club's text: -

Historie and life of King James the Sext.

"With his great ability to deceive Christian people, Satan assembled some of his supporters, some of them men, and others women, in the church of Northberwick at midnight on the last day of October. Several of them were put to death, for example Johne Cunynghame alias Johne Fean, schoolmaster at Tranent; Agnes Sampsone, a midwife, otherwise called "The Wise Wife of Keith"; and various others.

The purpose of the assembly was to raise storms at sea to prevent Queen Anne from arriving safely in Scotland. Among the various admissions in her confession, this Agnes Sampsone admitted that Francis, Earl of Bothuel consulted her several times about his own affairs and worldly success. A certain Richert Grayame, a sorcerer, also confessed the same thing. After the King's return, therefore, Bothuel was summoned to appear before the Privy Council. He obeyed, and was immediately imprisoned in Edinburgh Castle for further investigation. The King, under the influence of Chancellor Maitland, suspected that Bothuell harboured evil intentions towards him, and remained convinced of it for several years after that."

Nicoll's Diary. 1657-59

[Another text issued by the Bannatyne Club is the diary of John Nicoll, which was published in Edinburgh in 1836. John Nicoll was a native of Glasgow, long resident in Edinburgh as a Writer to the Signet and notary public. As with other texts, I have put Nicoll's diary entries into modern English.

On 14th October 1657 there was a woman burnt on the Castlehill of Edinburgh for witchcraft. She was an inhabitant of Tranent or thereabouts.

[This was Jonet Bruce.]

9th March [1659], a Wednesday. There were five women, witches, burnt on the Castlehill for witchcraft. They all confessed making a covenant with Satan. Some of them renounced their baptisms, and all of them confessed often dancing with the Devil. All five of them were brought from Dunbar.

[These were the Stenton Witches - Bessie Lacost, Marion Angus, Helen Heriot, Alison Fermour, and Jean Sydserf.]

[May 1659]. At this time great numbers of witches were arrested and burnt. They all confessed having sex, renouncing their baptism, taking new names from Satan, and receiving marks in their flesh. Nine of them were condemned and executed in May 1659, all of them in the parish of Tranent.

[Marion Logan, Barbara Cochrane, John Douglas, Janet Crooks, Helen Simbeard, and Helen Wilson were executed in Tranent on 5th May. Marion Lyne and Christian Cranstoun were put to death in Tranent on 14th May. Janet Man was burnt on the Castlehill on 11th May.]

1661-1688

Fountainhall's Historical Notices.

[Sir John Lauder of Fountainhall was a judge of the Court of Session, and as such is usually referred to by his judicial title of Lord Fountainhall. His country residence of Fountainhall near Pencaitland in East Lothian had formerly been known as Woodhead.

According to Chambers' *Traditions of Edinburgh* Sir John changed the name of his estate when he became a judge because he did not relish being known as "Lord Woodhead". Lauder was born in 1646, the son of an Edinburgh merchant. He was admitted as an advocate in 1668, knighted in 1681, and was elected member of parliament for the county of Haddington - East Lothian - in 1685. He continued to represent East Lothian in parliament until the Union of 1707, which he opposed. He was raised to the bench in 1689 with the title Lord Fountainhall, arid became a Lord of Justiciary in 1690. He declined the post of Lord Advocate in 1692 over the Massacre of Glencoe. He died in 1722. His voluminous *Historical Notices* were published in Edinburgh in 1848 by the Bannatyne Club.]

Volume 1, page 144.

It is not only the West which is fertile in witches, but Hadington in Eist Lothian also shelters such unhappy creatures. There was a certain Margaret Kirkwood in Haddington who hanged herself - although some say she was strangled by the Devil and other witches. This happened on a Sunday morning. A servant of hers called Elizabeth Moodie was in church, and created a noisy disturbance during the sermon, counting until she reached 59, which was her mistress's age. She then cried out, "The turn is done!" It turned out that this was at the very instant that her mistress was making away with herself.

At this she was arrested and questioned, but denied everything until she was searched and pricked. Then when the alleged marks were found on her, she confessed that she was a witch, and the particular circumstances involved. I myself heard her acknowledge this. She was burnt for it at the beginning of June 1677.

Margaret Kirkwood who hanged herself was wealthy, and there were several people who put in claims to inherit her forfeited estate. Amongst them was the town of Haddington, on the grounds that the town itself had the powers and duties of the office of sheriff. All the same, I do not think this gives them the right to the confiscated estates of those within their bounds who lay violent hands on themselves. If this were so, the town of Edinburgh would have this right, since ancient privilege and a clause in its charter gave the town rights to the confiscated estates of all who committed murder in the burgh. However they were forced to relinquish this right in their charter of 1636. Since the town of Hadington has a particular clause in its foundation charter excluding it from the sheriff's jurisdiction, at present their burgesses are outside the sheriff's jurisdiction... [A discussion follows of the legal ins and outs of this.]

That miserable creature Lissie Mudie who confessed that she was a witch also denounced five other women in the town of Haddington, two of them midwives, and a man, saying they were guilty of the same villainies. When she was confronted with them, she consistently stood by her accusations - although some said she was not in her right mind - and backed them up with particular indications and circumstances. However, they denied everything. I witnessed the examining and pricking of the man's body. He was pricked in two separate places - at his ribs, and on his shoulder. He seemed to feel pain, but no blood flowed. The pins were as long as your finger, and one of them was pushed in up to the head. The marks were a bluish colour, very small and did not protrude above the skin.

[Here I insert a paragraph where Fountainhall discusses witch-marks in a footnote.] The pricker said there were three kinds of marks; the "horn mark" which is very hard, the "breast mark" which is small, and the "feeling mark" which is sensible to pain. See *McKenzie's Criminals*, page 91. Also in another manuscript, page 21 onwards about witches put on trial then, and the pricker put in prison.

I was left very unsure and dissatisfied with this method of examination, as it seemed most unreliable, and the fellow could give me no account of the principles governing his art, but seemed to be a drunken foolish rogue ... There is no doubt that their methods of keeping suspects from sleeping, and pricking them, are a torture in themselves which no judge has the right to inflict except the Privy Council and the lords of the Criminal Court ... [Fountainhall then goes on to discuss "Martinus" on witch-marks.]

... Most of the poor creatures who are thus deluded by the grand imposter and enemy of mankind are of the meanest rank, and are either seduced by malice, poverty, ignorance, or covetousness. It is our good God's inexpressible mercy that the poor Devil does not have money at his command - even though many say that he is the master of all the mines and hidden treasures of the earth - otherwise he would debauch the greater part of the world.

[See *Trial by Commission* and *Satan's Invisible World* for a brief mention of this Haddington case.]

2nd May 1678.

Two witches had confessed at Salt Preston, and after receiving an application, the Privy Council granted an application to Prestongrange, St Germains, and Colstoun - for the Duke of Lauderdale excluded Mr John Preston as one inclined to burn too many witches. They were to try and judge those witches who had confessed, but not those whom they accused and whose characters they blackened. The two of them were burnt on the evidence of their confession, which had in no way been extorted.

[There are, however, good grounds to suspect much in the way of ill treatment and intimidation. See the petitions from victims of Prestongrange's baron bailie in *Justiciary Court Records* and *Trial by Commission*.]

9th, 10th, and 11th September 1678.

On those days eight or ten witches all, except one or two, poor miserable-looking women, were put on trial. Some of them were brought from the lands of Robert Hepburn of Keith, and others from the parishes of Ormiston, Crighton, and Pencaitland. The first of them had been accused by the two who were burnt in Salt Preston last May, and they revealed and named the rest; also denouncing seven in the Loanhead of Leswaid. If they had been permitted, they were ready to condemn by their accusations several gentlewomen and others of fashion. However, the judges forbade it, thinking it was either the product of malice or depression, or deception by the Devil, to claim that such people had been present at their meetings when in fact they were not there. And yet there was an outcry over this, as preventing them from revealing these enemies of mankind. However, they were permitted to name Mr Gideon Penman, who had been minister at Crighton, and who had been dismissed for various sexual indiscretions and other crimes. Two or three of the witches insisted that he was present at their meetings with the Devil, and that when the Devil called for him he asked, "Where is Mr Gideon my chaplain?" Usually Mr Gideon came behind in ail their dances, and drove on those who were slow. He denied everything and was freed on bail.

They declared in their confessions that the first thing the Devil made them do was to renounce their baptism. By laying one hand on the top of their head, and the other on the sole of heir foot, they gave up everything between the two to his service. At the time, one of them was pregnant with a child conceived in fornication, and in giving herself over to the Devil she excepted the child, at which the Devil was very angry.

He frequently had sex with them and kissed them, but his breath was like damp air. When they did the evil he demanded of them he beat them cruelly, for, they said, he was a most wicked and barbarous master. He dared to give them the Holy Sacrament, or Communion. The bread was like wafers, and the drink was sometimes blood, and sometimes black peat-bog water. He preached to them, and mocked them most blasphemously if they spoke of trusting in God, saying that God had left them miserable in the world, and neither he nor his son Jesus Christ ever appeared to them when called upon. The Devil did so, and would not cheat them.

They said that sometimes he transformed them into bees, ravens, or crows, and they would fly to certain remote places. However, it is impossible for the Devil to do this, to reduce their bodies to such a small amount of matter. It was thought by some that the Devil might take away their spirit, and convey it to these places leaving their bodies behind, but this would give him the power of resurrecting the dead, for death is nothing but the removal of the soul from the body. If this is done it is not in his power to reunite them. Thus he is only deluding them by depicting certain ideas, shapes, and objects to their fancies and imaginations when they are asleep, and in our sleep we can have very realistic experiences. However, in these diabolic trances their sleep is so deep that it is scarcely possible to waken them by pinching.

These confessions made many intelligent sober people very uneasy about how much trust could be put in them ...

There were one or two of them who denied everything and so were set at liberty. Nine of them, who seemed very rational and penitent, were sentenced upon their own confession to be strangled and then burnt. This was shortly afterwards carried out on five of them between Leith and Edinburgh, and the other four were burnt at Painston Muir [*Sic* See below.] within their own parish where they lived. The Privy Council gave a commission to Sir John Nicolson, John Clerk of Penicuick, John Johnston of Polton, and Mr John Preston, advocate, to judge the seven who were denounced as witches in Loanhead, with whom I spoke.

[The Bannatyne Club prints "were burnt at Painston neir within their own parish". However, as can be seen in the chapters *Trial by Commission* and *Justiciary Court Cases*, there is absolutely no doubt that these women were burnt at Peaston. I would guess that the Bannatyne Club's editor has misread Fountainhall's notes and transcribed "Paiston Mur" as "Painston neir". As previously remarked, this was the last authenticated witch burning in East Lothian.]

10th September 1678.

A certain Catherine Liddel lodged a complaint with the Privy Council against [blank] Rutherford, baron baillie to Morison of Prestongrange, and against David Cowan in Tranent, because they had seized her, an innocent woman, defamed her as a witch, and detained her under restraint as a prisoner. Cowan had pricked her with long pins in various places in her body, making her bleed, and torturing her most cruelly. Their defence was that she had been denounced by other witches, had a bad reputation, and was therefore arrested. However, she was treated so kindly that she was not bundled into any kind of public prison, but kept in a private house. She and her son in law had agreed to her being searched, consenting to it without expectation of injury or pain, in order to vindicate her and prove her innocence.

As for the pricker, he served his apprenticeship and learned his trade from Kincade, a famous pricker. Secondly, he never came without being sent for, because he was either sent for by sheriffs, magistrates of burghs, ministers, or by the baiilies of baronies. Thus what he did had official sanction, and he was committing no offence in obeying the orders of the Lord and the judiciary. Thirdly, the trade was not invalid or condemned by any of our laws. If it was not prohibited it must be permissible. Fourthly, all clergymen and lawyers who have written on witchcraft, such as Perkins, Del-rio etc, acknowledge that there are such marks, which they call *stigmata fagarum*. Why then may there not be an art whereby they may be recognised and distinguished from other marks on the body? Fifthly, on the grounds that if he law is at fault, then society is to blame, the Council may ban this method of investigation in future, but must pardon what was done in the past.

It was answered to this, firstly that there had been no consent, and that secondly, no-one can validly consent to his own torture, for no-one is ultimately the lord of the parts of his body [*i.e.* presumably, a person's body belongs not to him but to God]. As for the pricker, he was a cheat who abused the people for gain. The Chancellor recalled that he'd had Kincaid the pricker imprisoned in Kinross for abusing the people in that area.

The Lords of the Privy Council first declared the woman innocent, restored her good name and reputation, and ordered this to be publicly intimated in her parish church the following Sunday. They then censured Rutherford the baillie for being over hasty, and forbade him to proceed in such a way in future. It was decided that no inferior judge, much less a baron baillie, had the power to arrest, imprison, or detain any of the King's subjects under the claim that they had been denounced as being witches, or were suspected of being such. Either the Privy Council or the Lords of Justiciary must be immediately informed right at the outset, and a warrant obtained for their arrest, it was also decided that they must not make use of torture by pricking, depriving them of sleep, etc. All that was reserved to the Council and the Justiciary, and those who acted under commission from them. As a mark of their displeasure against the pricker, they ordered him to be imprisoned, to be detained at their pleasure.

Volume 2, page 872.

26th June 1688: An old woman Mattorgett [*i.e.* Catherine McTarget from Dunbar] was condemned on charges of witchcraft by a commission from the Privy Council to Mr Robert Lauder and some other gentlemen at Dumbar. She was brought before the Council and questioned. They were inclined to find her not guilty, and sent her back to prison. The main thing proven was her menacing and threatening those who refused to give her what she wanted, and some unfortunate accidents befalling them afterwards - that sort of thing. However, on 12th July she was brought before them again, and sent back to Dumbar to be burnt there if her judges pleased, because she had made a confession at some time, although she later retracted it. After they had read the evidence it was only carried by two votes that she was guilty.

[As previously remarked, there seems to be no actual record of Catherine McTarget's execution, but it is perhaps expecting too much that the commissioners in Dunbar would be lenient. If she was strangled and burnt, she would almost certainly be the last in East Lothian.]

1674

The Laws and Customs of Scotland in Matters Criminal: Sir George Mackenzie of Rosehaugh.

[Mackenzie was the son of the Earl of Seaforth's brother Simon Mackenzie of Lochslin. He was born in 1636, studied at St Andrews, Aberdeen, and Bourges in France. He qualified as an advocate in Edinburgh in 1656, entered Parliament for Ross-shire in 1669, and was appointed Lord Advocate in 1677. As Lord Advocate in the reigns of Charles II and James VII he prosecuted the rebellious Covenanters with rigour, thus earning his nickname of "Bluidy Mackenzie". He was dismissed from the post of Lord Advocate by the king in 1686 for opposing the king's plans to ease restrictions on Catholics. The "Glorious Revolution" of 1688 put paid to any hopes of reviving his political career. He died in 1691.

Mackenzie was the author of several works on Scots Law, politics, and history. He also ventured into poetry and fiction, and has been described as the first Scotsman to write pure classical English. He founded the Advocates' Library, the forerunner of the National Library of Scotland.

In the summer of 1661 Mackenzie was appointed along with two others to go to Musselburgh to judge several witchcraft cases there. These are the cases he refers to in paragraph 5 of his discussion of witchcraft quoted here. His experiences seem to have made him cautious and sceptical in his thinking regarding witchcraft, although he still upholds the orthodox view that it exists and deserves the death penalty, *The Laws and Customs of Scotland in Matters Criminal*, which contains Mackenzie's comments on witchcraft, was first published in 1674. My text has actually been taken from the second edition of 1699.

I summarise Mackenzie's introductory discussion of witchcraft, and give his ensuing remarks in full from paragraph 2 onwards. Mackenzie's prose is written in a standard English almost devoid of Scotticisms. I have, however, simplified it here and there for the sake of clarity.]

There can be no doubt that witches and witchcraft exist, and that witches ought to be punished with death. However, not only witches should be condemned, but judges who are over-eager to condemn and burn thousands of those they believe to be guilty of witchcraft. The following points should be made: -

1. Would anybody knowing of God's kindness and the Devil's malice, the rewards of Heaven and the torments of Hell, really enter voluntarily into the service of the Devil?

2. These poor persons who are ordinarily accused of this crime are poor ignorant creatures, often women who do not understand the nature of what they are accused of. Many of them mistake their own fears and apprehensions for witchcraft, and I shall give you two instances of this - one of a poor weaver who after he had confessed witchcraft, being asked how he saw the Devil, answered, "Like flies dancing about the candle." Another was a woman who asked seriously when she was accused, if a woman might be a witch and not know it. It is dangerous when those who are of all people the most simple, should be tried for a crime which is of all others the most mysterious.

3. These poor creatures when they are defamed become so confused with fear and the close confinement in which they are kept, and so starved for want of food and sleep - either of which is enough to distract the strongest reason - that even wiser or more serious people would hardly escape mental disorder. When people are confused by fear and apprehension, they will imagine very absurd and ridiculous things. Since no-one could escape profound depression ["melancholy"] on such an occasion and after such treatment, I must put it to physicians to consider what might be the effects of this depression, which has often made men who otherwise appeared stable enough, imagine they were horses or had lost their noses etc. Since it may make men err in things which are obvious to their senses, what is to be expected of things which transcend the wisest men's reason.

4. Most of these poor creatures are tortured by their keepers, who, being persuaded that they are serving God well, think it is their duty to vex and torment their poor prisoners. I know from my most certain knowledge, that most of all those who were ever arrested were tormented after this manner, and that this treatment was the foundation of all their confession. Even though the poor miscreants cannot prove this

treatment, since those doing it were the only witnesses, the judge should still be wary of it, suspecting that this is what first elicited the confession, and that they dare not retract it for fear of the same treatment.

5. When I was a Justice Depute I went to examine some women who had confessed judicially, and one of them, who was a poor silly creature, told me under secrecy that she had not confessed because she was guilty, but being a poor creature who had to work for a living, and having been defamed as a witch, she knew she would starve; for after that, no-one would give her food or lodging. All men would beat her and set dogs on her, and she therefore desired to be out of the world. On her knees she called God to witness what she said. Another told me that she was afraid that the Devil would lay claim to her after she was said to be his servant, and would haunt her, just as the minister said when he was desiring her to confess; and so she wished to die.

Really, ministers are often indiscreet in their zeal to have poor creatures confess to this, and I recommend to judges that the wisest ministers should be sent to them, and those who are sent should proceed cautiously.

6. Many of them confess things which all divines consider impossible, such as transforming their bodies into beasts and money into stones, going through walls and locked doors, and a thousand other ridiculous things which have no truth or existence but in their fancy.

7. The accusers are their masters or their neighbours whose children have died, and who are moved by grief to suspect the poor creatures. I also know of one who was burnt because the lady was jealous of her relationship with her husband. The crime of witchcraft is so odious that they are never assisted or defended by their relations.

8. The witnesses and jurors are afraid that if the suspects escape, they will die for it, and so they take an unwarrantably lax attitude. I have observed that hardly anyone ever escapes who is accused before a country jury of her neighbours.

9. Commissions are usually granted to gentlemen and others in the countryside whose judgment is suspect on this account, and who are not exactly enough acquainted with the nature of this crime, which is debateable enough even amongst the most learned. Nor do the persons accused have anyone to plead for them and to take notice of who are being led as witnesses. Thus many are admitted as witnesses who are unsuitable and suspect. Even if their confessions are sent to the Privy Council for scrutiny before such commissions are granted, the Council cannot know how these commissions came to be given, nor all the necessary circumstances, which cannot be obvious from a distance. Very many of these poor silly women repudiate at the stake the confessions they made in court, and yet have died very penitent. It might be presumed that few people would accuse themselves or confess when their own lives are threatened, and yet very many confess to this crime.

On what grounds may witches be apprehended?

I know that it is usual in Scotland not only for magistrates to apprehend witches on almost any accusation, but even gentlemen and landowners similarly make them prisoners and keep them so until they transfer them at their leisure to Justices of the Peace, magistrates, or to some public prison. However, all these procedures are most unwarrantable, for gentlemen and those invested with no official authority should on no account - without a special warrant - arrest anyone on suspicion of being a witch. To make an arrest is an Act of Jurisdiction, and I therefore think that no prison should accept anyone suspected of witchcraft, until they know that the person offered to them has been apprehended by lawful authority ...

... No one should be arrested except when it is obvious after investigation that she lies under many or significant suspicions ... or that the usual accoutrements of charming have been found in her house.

[Mackenzie goes on to explain that because witchcraft was an offence under Canon Law, kirk sessions had inherited the task of looking into "scandals" connected with witchcraft - alleged slanders and direct accusations. In pursuing their investigations sessions also took statements from witnesses and confessions from suspects. Mackenzie says that sessions ought to proceed with great caution, since so much importance is placed on these documents.

Mackenzie says that by the Act of Parliament of the reign of Queen Mary, lords of regalities and their deputes, and all other judges, are empowered and ordained to proceed against witchcraft. He interprets this as meaning that these persons may arrest and imprison suspects, but are not all competent to try such cases, which are reserved to the Court of Justiciary. Mackenzie knows of no cases where inferior courts have tried witchcraft cases. He grants that the Privy Council has often given commissions to laymen outwith Edinburgh to try witchcraft cases, but states that in his opinion this is "dangerous", and wonders why this procedure is followed in cases of witchcraft but not in murder cases.

Finally, Mackenzie summarises English Law as regards witchcraft. Death is the punishment for invoking or conjuring evil spirits; consulting, consorting with, or employing evil spirits; taking corpses or any part of them from graves to be used for witchcraft or charming; and using witchcraft by which anyone is "killed, destroyed, wasted, consumed, pined, or harmed in body or any part thereof". For using witchcraft to find hidden treasure or lost or stolen goods, to hurt or destroy anyone, the punishment is a year's imprisonment with six hours' exposure in the pillory once a quarter.

1685

Satan's Invisible World Discovered: George Sinclair.

[*Satan's Invisible World Discovered* was first published in Edinburgh in 1685. Its full title is *Satan's Invisible World Discovered; or, a choice Collection of modern Relations, proving evidently against the Saducees and Atheists of the present Age, that there are Devils, Spirits, Witches, and Apparitions, from authentick Records, Attestations of famous Witnesses, and undoubted Verity.* Its author, George Sinclair, "was probably the first person to study physics in its modern sense in Scotland, was the author of *Hydrostatics*, and in turn professor of philosophy and mathematics at Glasgow University" [James Sharp, in Goodare ed, 2002]. He was involved in schemes to improve Edinburgh's water supply, to drain the Earl of Winton's East Lothian coal mines, and in an attempt to salvage treasure using a primitive diving bell.

Sinclair's brother John was minister of Ormiston, and it was in his parish that East Lothian's last authenticated witch-burning took place. It is perhaps debatable whether George Sinclair's intention was in fact, as James Sharp claims, "to provide a defence of the reality of the spirit world as a bulwark against atheism", or whether he simply hoped that a potentially popular book of macabre tales might be a "nice little earner".

As might be expected with Sinclair's East Lothian connections, several of the tales in *Satan's Invisible World* are from the County. Sinclair's language and style are much more accessible to the modern reader that many of my sources. Nevertheless, I have simplified the language and punctuation here and there to ease the reader's progress. *Satan's Invisible World* is dedicated fulsomely to George Seton, Earl of Winton, who possessed extensive estates in East

Lothian, and whose coal pits in the Tranent area made him Scotland's greatest coal owner.

Sinclair's "Relation III" concerns Agnes Sampson, but since the North Berwick witches have already been dealt with thoroughly here and rehashed *ad nauseam* elsewhere, I have given her a miss. Sinclair has nothing new to say about her in any case.]

Relation XVII
Anent Hatteraik an old Warlock.

This man's name was Sandie Hunter, who called himself Sandie Hamilton, and it seems was called Hatteraick by the Devil, and this was taken up by others as a nickname. To begin with he was a cattle herd to a gentleman in East Lothian. He was much given to charming, and curing men and beasts by words and divining. His charms sometimes succeded, sometimes not. One day when he was herding his cattle on a hillside, the Devil came to him in the form of a physician, and said, "Sandie, you have followed my trade for too long, and never acknowledged me as your master. You must now contract with me to be my servant, and I will make you more perfect in your calling." At this, the man gave himself to the Devil, and received his mark with a new name. After this he became very well known throughout the area for his charming and curing diseases in men and beasts. He became a vagrant, like a Gypsy, getting meal, meat, and money by his charms through the ignorance of so many people at that time. Whenever he came to a house, no-one dared to refuse alms to Hatteraick.

One day he came to the gate of Samuelston, when a group of friends were setting off on horseback after dinner. A young gentleman, the Lady's brother, saw him, and switched him about the ears, saying, "What are you doing here, you old warlock?" Hatteraick went away grumbling and was heard to say, "You shall buy this dearly before too long." These were fateful words. The young gentleman escorted his friends for a good distance, then came back again for supper. After supper he took his horse, and crossing Tine-water to go home, he rode through a shadowy piece of river meadow commonly called the Allers. The evening was rather dark, and he met with a group of people there who disturbed him greatly - but most of this he would never reveal. Evil was to follow. The next day he became insane and had to be tied up for several days. When his sister Lady Samuelston heard of this she was heard to say, "Surely that knave Hatteraik is the cause of this truoble. Send for him immediately." When he came to her she said, "Sandie, what is this you have done to my brother William?" He replied, "I told him I would make him repent for striking me at the gate recently." She spoke to the rogue soothingly, and promised to fill his bag full of meal, with beef and cheese, and persuaded the fellow to cure him. He agreed to undertake the business, but said that first he must have one of his shirts. This was soon procured, and what tricks he played with it no-one knows, but within a short time the gentleman recovered his health. When Hatteraik came to receive his wages he told the lady, "Your brother William will leave the country very soon, but he will never return." Knowing the fellow's prophecies to be reliable, she caused her brother to will all his estate to her, to the defrauding of his younger brother George.

After this warlock had abused the people of the countryside for a long time he was finally arrested at Dunbar and burnt on the Castle Hill. This story was well known at that time throughout the area I got the information from the gentleman's own brother, and I have included it, not because there is anything of importance in it, but to give me an excuse to speak a little of charms ...

[He goes on to discuss charming in general

terms. Sinclair is confused about Hatteraik's identity. Alexander Hamilton and Alexander Hunter alias Sinclair were two different people. Indeed, an entry in the records of the Presbytery of Haddington for 12th November 1628 seems to indicate that Hatteraik was neither Hamilton nor Hunter/Sinclair, but another warlock named William Davidson - see *Other Church Records*. These three men were all contemporaries. However, the bewitching of Lady Samuelston's brother does not appear in the trial records of either Hamilton, Hunter/Sinclair, or Davidson - see "Burgh Records" and "Justiciary Court Records".]

Relation XXI Touching Isabel Heriot.

This woman was born in Peaston in the parish of Ormiston, and was for several years a useful servant to the minister there for all kinds of outdoor work. She was of low stature, small and slender, and dark-complexioned. Her head was set a little awry on her neck. She had a droll mocking sense of humour, and would speak to persons of a higher social class with great confidence.

After several years in his service the minister began to dislike her, particularly because she did not show any signs of improving her religious knowledge, although she had so much opportunity to know and learn. Because of this he dismissed her, and she went off to work elsewhere for a long time. After that she returned to Ormistoun village and hung around the minister's house from time to time, but without his knowledge. She fell ill about the beginning of the winter of 1680, and about the time of her death her face became extremely black. Three or four nights after she was buried, Isobel Murray, the widow of William Craig the church officer, saw her apparition about twelve o' clock at night, wearing her white robes just as she was put into her coffin, walking from the chapel towards the minister's "louping on stone" [mounting block], where she stopped briefly with her elbow leaning on it, as had been her custom when she was alive. After that she was observed to walk in at the minister's back gate towards the stable. We have only the bare testimony of this one woman for this.

A few nights after that some stones were thrown at the minister's house, and some thrown at the hall door and windows. The stones were found in the courtyard the next morning. When they landed they mostly fell softly. The minister - against whom the Devil's malice was chiefly directed - came in one night at the back door and was shutting it behind him when a large stone was thrown at him which hit the door very smartly, and left a mark and an impression there. She - or rather the Devil - did this in imitation of a prank she had played while alive. The minister had caused the servants to throw her out at the same door, and she threw a large stone at it violently, out of wrath and anger. The previously mentioned Isabel Murray, either coming into or going out of the minister's house one night was hit very sharply on her back with a stone. The servant who looked after the horses was going to bed in the stable after saying his prayers, when to his great amazement, something gripped him by the heel. He let out a loud cry and the mistress of the family and others came into the stable and found the lad in a state of great fear. The same night, several clods and stones were thrown, but no-one was touched. One remarkable thing was that an old horse-comb which had been missing for several years was thrown at the boy. It hit his bedstead with great violence, but injured nobody. The horses were found next morning standing and lying ail over the place, some of them in a great sweat. The same servant had several stones thrown at him when he was working in the garden. He was never touched by any of them except one, which hit him very accurately.

Sometimes the house was troubled indoors

by brief outbursts of noise and din. One time there was a burning coal thrown under one of the beds. One night one of the family had his nightcap taken off when he was in bed, and in the morning it was found in the fireplace full of cinders and ashes. If the Devil could have done more, he surely would have done it. This accounts for most of the trouble which bothered the family. It continued for eight or nine weeks, not every night, but now and then. During that time the members of the family sent up frequent and fervent prayers to God.

There was a great deal of talk about this ghost. Some things were spoken rashly, and some people invented lies and untruths out of malice. Somebody said mockingly, "Now let the minister and his brethren drive away the Devil with all their prayers!" Remarkably, the family had no more trouble after that.

For what follows we have only the word of Isabel Murray. She was coming home from church between sermons to Ormiston village, to check her house and garden in case wandering cows had come over the wall. Going down to her garden, she saw in the minister's garden next door, the apparition of Isabel Heriot in the very same clothes she was wearing when she was laid in her coffin. There was never one egg more like another than this apparition was to her - her face, stature, movements, speech and behaviour. The woman said her face was black "like the mouten sort" [?] - one of her own expressions - the very colour her face had been when she died. She saw her walking under the fruit trees, and over the beds where the seeds had been sown, bending down as if she was looking for something on the ground, and saying, "A stane, a stane," as she pronounced the word. She had gathered a considerable number of stones in her lap, which the woman saw thrown down at the roots of a bush near the bottom of the garden. Some might take these to be the stones which she frequently threw at night. When the woman saw her, she said with great confidence, "Wow, what are you doing here Isabel Heriot? I charge you to tell me, by the law you live by." She replied, or rather the Foul Fiend in her likeness replied, "I have come again bcause I wronged my master while I was his servant, for it was here that I stole his shekel." This was a Jewish shekel of gold which had been stolen from him several years before, with some other things. "I hid it under the hearth-stone in the kitchen, and when I left I took it to the Canongate and offered to sell it to a French woman who was lodging where I was in service. She asked me where I got it, and I told her I found it between Leith and Edinburgh. One night," she went on, "I was riding home late from the Town, and near the head of Fauside Brae the horse stumbled. I said, 'The Devil raise thee!' and at that the Foul Thief immediately appeared to me. He threatened that if I would not agree to destroy my master the minister he would throw me into a deep hole, which I suppose is still there. If I could not get power over my master, I should strive to destroy the schoolmaster."

Remarkably, one of the minister's servant women had given the schoolmaster's servant woman some linen to wash. Amongst it was a "cross-cloth" of strong linen, which could never be found again, although a careful search was made for it. Then one morning when the master awoke, he found it tied round his nightcap, to the great astonishment of himself and his wife. However, the Devil and the witches were able to do him no more harm. How this was done, or why, is a mystery; but it seems probable that they planned to strangle and destroy him during the night, which is their usual time for working and doing mischief. This I presume happened about the time when the Devil had ordered Isabel Heriot to destroy this honest man. Within two days a young child of his, a year old, fell sick and was quickly carried off by death, and no-one could tell the cause or the nature of the disease.

However, to proceed: she also confessed that the Devil met her a second time at Elfiston Mill, a quarter of a mile from Ormiston, and told what the Devil did to her. She also said, "I was coming home one night from Haddington market with corn for horse fodder, and met the Devil at Knock Hills. He told me to destroy Thomas Anderson who was riding with me. Because I refused he threw the corn off the horse." This Thomas Anderson was a man of strong Christian beliefs. It is well remembered even yet that she went away early the next morning and brought home her oats which had lain there all night. "Not only that," she said, "I cheated my master when I went to the market to buy oats, for I led him to believe that I gave more for the boll than I did. And do you not remember, Isabel Murray, that one night you came out of the minister's house and got a sore knock on the back with a stone? That was me, but it was not because of you, but because of your husband Willy Craig who threw me one day into the drain and gave me verbal abuse." She also told this woman that she would have liked to have spoken a word to her master, but after this conversation the woman began to be afraid and came running home in haste.

During all this time, such was the Lord's kindness to them, that no-one in the family met with any injury or harm, or saw anything. A certain witch, Isabel Elliot, confessed to the minister that his house and garden had been beseiged by witches on many occasions at night. This woman once asked the Devil why they were unable to get revenge on him, and he told her he was "locked up".

Isabel Heriot was never reputed to be a witch, or denounced for witchcraft by anyone, although some people mockingly called her so. She was certainly ignorant of religion in spite of the excellent opportunities se had for gaining knowledge. Her riding and travelling far and wide by night and day, coming home without fear, and her foul ill-nature, bred suspicion, if she had confessed a compact with the Devil before her death, it might have been good grounds for suspicion, but it was the trouble experienced by the family immediately after her death, and her apparition being seen, which caused everyone to say she had been a witch. However, these things are not infallible conclusive evidence.

What could her apparition have been? It must either have been her actual body animated and inhabited by the Devil - for her soul could not be brought back - or more probably the Devil taking on her shape or form, and acting and imitating her to the life.

I have ventured to publish this without the minister's knowledge, presuming to do so because of his goodness and love of truth, for the useful instruction of the world. Though it may be displeasing to his inclinations, it may upon reflection satisfy his more noble aspirations, for no aspect of the matter could reflect dishonourably upon him. The best of men and families have suffered from the Devil in extraordinary ways, and it is to their glory that they have overcome him by their faith, courage, and confidence in the arm of God. If I am mistaken in any way I should be excused, since I was not an eyewitness. What I have written about the apparition was for the most part from the woman's own mouth.

[There is no mention in "Relation XXI" of the Peaston witch burnings which took place in 1678, only seven years before the publication of Sinclair's book. Sinclair's brother John, as minister of Ormiston, was closely involved in the tracking down and interrogation of these women. I cannot help feeling that the ongoings described by Sinclair must in some way have been bound up with the Peaston witches, yet only one of them, Isabel Elliot, is mentioned, and then only briefly. Since the whole story of Isabel Heriot's apparition proceeds from a single eyewitness, Isabel Murray, it is tempting to speculate whether Murray had an ulterior motive in laying the blame for the strange occurrences in and around the minister's house on someone who was already dead.]

Relation XXIV Anent an apparition seen in Gladsmuir, with some other gleanings.

[Actually, nothing to do with witchcraft, but it does deal with the "supernatural", and it did happen in East Lothian.]

Among some of my notes written in the year 1666, I find reference to Richard Chaplain and and his brother George. They were both merchants in Haddington and were coming home late from Edinburgh on a Saturday night, the night of 4th November 1666. They were riding off the moor at a place called the Two Mile Cross, within two miles of their own home, when they saw four men in grey clothes and blue bonnets standing round a dead body wrapped in a winding sheet. Their dog was so terrified that it did not dare go forward, but came running back among their horses' feet. One of the brothers is still living, a sober and Christian man who can bear witness to this, if I have varied from this account it is only in minor details which do not alter the thing itself. It is all the more remarkable because it was about twenty days before the battle of Rullion Green.

Relation XXXIV [This tale concerns Helen Elliot in Culross, but Sinclair finishes with the passage below.]

... Which puts me in mind of a terrible gale in the Firth of Forth the day when Bessie Fouler was burnt at Musselburgh in May 1661. It seems the Devil had promised her that she would not die at that time, and so, looking out of the prison window, she spoke very confidently to the people below, saying, "You think to see me burnt today, but you will all be deceived." The hurricane predominated to such an extent that everybody suspected that indeed she would not die that day. The morning and the forenoon had been very calm.

Relation XXXV
[I include this brief reference from the end of Relation XXXV, suspecting that the minister concerned may have been a colleague of Sinclair's brother John, that the "Devil's piper" may have been John Douglas from Tranent, and that the song mentioned may have been "Hooly, the bed will fa". See *Justiciary Court Records*.]

... A reverend minister told me that a man who was the Devil's piper and a wizard, confessed to him that at a ball for dancing the Foul Spirit taught him a bawdy song to sing and play one night, and before two days had gone by all the young lads and girls of the town were singing it through the streets. It would be an abomination to quote it.

Relation XXXVI   Anent one Elizabeth Muidy at Haddington.

This woman was servant to Margaret Kirkwood in Haddington, a woman who had been of good reputation but became disturbed in mind before her death - but for what reason I have been unable to determine. It would appear she gave some of her friends to understand that she was inclined to do away with herself. She was therefore supervised with close attention, but was allowed the freedom to retire for private prayer, which she did frequently. One Sunday morning when everybody was at church and she was at home with only a servant maid, she went into some upstairs room as if she was going to her devotions. Before the maid knew what was happening, she had hanged herself. At that very moment her former servant Lissie Muidy who was in church, was observed to count on her fingers to 50 or 51. When she reached that number she cried out in a loud voice in front of everyone, "Now the turn is done!" She was taken out as being not in her right mind. When news came to the church that her former mistress had hanged herself she was taken away to prison. However, it is not clear what she confessed to. There are many other things reported of which I am unable to give an account. This tragedy took place just a few years ago at Haddington. [See *Trial by Commission* 1677.]

c. 1700

John Bell's "Tryal of Witchcraft"

John Bell, the son of a Glasgow merchant, became minister of Gladsmuir in East Lothian in 1701, having previously been minister of Broughton. He died in 1707 at the early age of 30, leaving a large family, several of whom distinguished themselves in various walks of life, including John Joseph Bell, professor of Scots Law at Edinburgh University, and Sir Charles Bell FRS, a "distinguished anatomist" in London. John Bell published a pamphlet entitled *The Tryal of Witchcraft: or witchcraft arraigned and condemned*. Martine's *Reminiscences* dates this as appearing in 1705, but the National Library of Scotland dates it as "1700?", giving the place of publication as "Glasgow?". The National Library shelfmark is 2.325[12], and BH043[06] on microfilm.

There has been occasional speculation that Bell drew on actual witchcraft cases in East Lothian for his pamphlet, but anyone hoping to find anything of the sort in *The Tryal of Witchcraft* will be disappointed. There is little to be gained from quoting Bell in full, so what follows is a summary.

Bell begins with a "Letter from a Friend" where an interested acquaintance is made to ask how you can tell whether a disease is caused by witchcraft, how can victims of such bewitchment be helped, and how can you prove that someone is a witch. Bell then sets out answers to the queries. He says that disease can indeed be caused by witchcraft. This is likely if the victim's condition baffles "wise and skillful physicians", if he vomits strange objects, if he displays inexplicable knowledge of past or future events during fits, or if he acquires superhuman strength. Various traditional remedies are not only unreliable, but may make things worse. The best remedy for disease caused by witchcraft is fasting and prayer.

As for what can prove that a person is a witch, Bell treads very cautiously. If harm follows cursing, that does not necessarily mean that the person doing the cursing caused the harm, even if she appears to delight in the victim's misfortune. If a victim names someone as the cause of his illness this may only be because his mind is disturbed.

Bell goes on to describe how the Devil draws prospective witches into entering his service. He discusses the witch-mark, "Sometimes like a blew spot, or a little tale, or reid spots like flea-biting, sometimes also the flesh is sunk in and hollow, and this is put in secret places, as among the hair of the head or eyebrows, within the lips, under the arm pits, and even in the most secret parts of the body." [This is quoted in Martine's *Reminiscences*.] Bell then discusses familiar spirits.

Next Bell tackles the problematic question of how we can be sure that someone has made a covenant with the Devil. Firstly, there will be a witch-mark which will be insensible and will not bleed when pricked. Also, suspects will foretell what turns out to be true, and speak of being transported to "forraign" places. They may secretly feed animals which they may send on errands; they will make images, give concoctions to people which cause pain or death, or work spells on items of clothing which have ill effects on those who subsequently wear them. Also, other confessing witches will have seen the suspect at their meetings. Those who claim to know how to counteract or heal witchcraft will be witches themselves, and in league with the Devil. Finally, a confession from the suspect will clinch the matter.

Bell has nothing new, or even particularly interesting to say about witchcraft. He quotes several learned authors, and gives various examples of bewitching to illustrate his points. However, none of the examples he gives are from East Lothian or even Scotland, and would all seem to be from England. Although Bell adheres to orthodox Church of Scotland belief about witchcraft, he does emphasise the extreme difficulty of proving that what seems to be witchcraft is in fact the genuine article, and the difficulty of proving that suspected witches are actually what their accusers claim them to be.

In short, Bell really has nothing to add to a study of East Lothian witchcraft, and is of passing interest only because he lived briefly in the county.

Reference is occasionally made to a manuscript of Bell's, supposedly *A Discourse of Witchcraft by Mr John Bell, Minister of the Gospel at Gladsmuir* dated 1705. This is mentioned for example in C. K. Sharp's *Historical Account of the Belief in Witchcraft in Scotland*, Glasgow, 1884. I have failed to trace this manuscript of Bell's. It is not in the National Library of Scotland, the Mitchell Library in Glasgow, nor in the libraries of Aberdeen or Edinburgh or St Andrews Universities. Inquiries to Glasgow University elicited no reply. It is not in the British Library in London, and the Curator of the Department of Manuscripts there "failed to locate a likely source on the National Record of Archives". I suspect that this manuscript no longer exists - if it ever did. In fact I would not be surprised if *A Discovery of Witchcraft* was simply the manuscript of the tract published as *The Tryal of Witchcraft*.

1722

The Laird of Coul's Ghost.

The tale of how the minister of Innerwick in East Lothian met the Laird of Coul's ghost is fairly well known. Or rather, it is fairly well known that there is a tale of how the minister of Innerwick met the Laird of Coul's ghost. The details of the story, how he met the ghost, and what passed between them are no longer common knowledge. It is therefore possible that the student of East Lothian witchcraft might think it worth while seeking out the story in case there should be some element of witchcraft in it. There is not. To save interested parties wasting time researching the tale, I give a summary of it below.

The biographical details of the Rev William Ogilvy are from *The Laird of Coul's Ghost: a Galloway Chapbook* by Frank Miller, reprinted from the Transactions of the Dumfriesshire and Galloway Natural History and Antiquarian Society, 21st October 1927.

William Ogilvy was apparently the younger son of a minor Dumfriesshire laird. He was born in 1689, graduated from Edinburgh University in 1706, and ordained chaplain to Ker's Regiment of Dragoons in 1712. He served with the army in Flanders, and was admitted minister of Innerwick in 1715, where he died in January 1729. The ghost, Thomas Maxwell of Coul in the parish of Buittle, was the cousin of Ogilvy's wife. Maxwell had been a businessman with an unsavoury reputation, and after his death on 18th January 1722 had supposedly appeared to a young man who had been an employee of his, and requested a further meeting. This young man was advised by his minister not to keep the appointment The minister's son, The Rev Robert Paton, was minister of the 2nd Charge in Haddington, and apparently discussed the matter with colleagues in East Lothian. Ogilvy, the minister of Innerwick, said that he would have advised the youth to keep the appointment, and would have gone along with him.

The manuscript of *The Laird of Coul's Ghost* was found among Ogilvy's papers after his death. His wife seems to have lent a copy of the original to an Edinburgh printer. After this man's death the copy fell into the hands of another printer who published it as a chapbook around 1750. Many subsequent reprints and editions followed. The National Library has several copies. The summary below is based on "Chapbooks Printed at Glasgow", shelfmark [AO].8/3.2

According to Ogilvy's account, he was returning from Thurston on the evening of 3rd February 1722 when he was overtaken by a figure on horseback who claimed to be the laird of Coul. After a vain attempt to strike the ghost with his cane, the minister entered into conversation with him, and found that the ghost was aware that Ogilvy had said that he would have gone with the young man to confront Coul. Realising that the minister was in a state of some consternation, the ghost said that he would speak to him again when he was in a calmer frame of mind, and galloped off through Innerwick churchyard.

On 5th March, Ogilvy was returning from baptising a shepherd's child at Harehead, when he was again overtaken by Coul on horseback. The minister was curious to know about the "other world", and engaged Coul in a lengthy conversation about it.

On 5th April, Ogilvy encountered Coul's ghost again as he was returning to Innerwick from Oldhamstocks. This time Coul gave Ogilvy an account of various frauds, forgeries, and dishonest dealings that he had perpetrated, and asked Ogilvy to go to his wife and request her to compensate the victims. Ogilvy asked for time to consider this mission. He was approached again by the ghost on 10th April, returning from Old Cambus "at the head of the heath called the Pees." He told Coul that he could not take on the commission, as it would be thought either that he was insane or that he had been deluded by the Devil.

Usually *The Laird of Coul's Ghost* is alluded to as a simple ghost story where a restless spirit tries to enlist the aid of a sympathetic mortal to undo the wrongs he had done on earth. However, the bulk of the narrative is taken up by Gout's descriptions of the spirit world, and it would seem sensible, therefore, to assume that this was the real point of Ogilvy's exercise. *The Laird of Coul's Ghost* is most likely a work of fiction, a parable used as a vehicle for Ogilvy's own speculations on the afterlife, the spirit world, and divine judgment. Much of it would not have accorded well with orthodox Presbyterian theology, and so it is not surprising that Ogilvy made no attempt to publish it, although he may have hoped to do so one day if the time ever seemed ripe. Possibly, however, *The Laird of Coul's Ghost* was simply a private means of self expression, a way of ordering his potentially controversial speculations on a topic which had gripped his interest.

Basically, the information imparted by Coul's ghost states that there is no heaven or hell for the dead until after Judgment Day. Until then their circumstances in the Other World are as varied as they were on earth. In any case, punishment for earthly sins must take account of how far the sinner was influenced by matters beyond his control.

Much space is given to the topic of guardian angels. Coul stated that not many individual humans have guardian angels, but families and communities do. Not only that, but Satan similarly sends out evil spirits to work on his behalf. The spirits of the dead are recruited both by God and Satan to assist in this work, and both sorts have regular meetings to discuss their progress. There are parallels here of course with the belief that witches met regularly with the Devil to give an account of their deeds, but as previously stated, witchcraft is not mentioned in *The Laird of Coul's Ghost*.

8. What was really going on?

What was most certainly going on as regards witchcraft in East Lothian in the late 16th and 17th centuries was the legally sanctioned slaughter of a great many women and more than a mere handful of men. We must be careful, however, to distinguish between what did in fact happen, and what popular perception imagines to have happened.

It is commonly imagined that witches in Scotland were burnt alive. In fact this was almost never the case. Condemned witches were strangled and their corpses were burnt. In the period under consideration (c. 1590 -1700) only one convicted witch was sentenced to be burnt alive in Scotland (Euphane MacCalyean), and there is some evidence to show that the sentence was not in fact carried out. (CSP Vol X, p. 508. Calderwood Vol V, p. 128.) An oft-quoted reference to witches being burnt alive at Brechin (RFC Vol 14, p. 605) is hearsay with no supporting evidence, and even if true would have been not only unusual but illegal. There is no record of any witch ever being burnt alive in East Lothian during the period covered by this discussion. Some commentators like to hint or even insist that some witches would be consigned to the flames merely unconscious or even half-conscious, but this is really only an attempt to talk up the horror of witchcraft executions. Would any self-respecting lokman make a public show of his lack of expertise by failing to dispatch his victims with professional efficiency? This after all was his living. No doubt it occasionally happened, but I would guess not often.

We also read of the ducking or floating of witches, the idea being that a guilty suspect would float and an innocent suspect would sink. In fact this could never have been part of the legal process in 17th century Scotland, and there is no record of any such thing ever happening in East Lothian.

The Church of Scotland has been cast in the role of chief persecutor, prosecutor, and executioner of witches, and it is frequently assumed that witches were tried and condemned by the Church. In fact, although church courts were empowered to deal with the relatively minor offence of charming, witchcraft could only be tried by the High Court of Justiciary, or by special local courts set up under "commissions" issued by the Privy Council or by Parliament. A kirk session finding itself dealing with what appeared to be witchcraft would have to refer the case to the "civil magistrate". In the countryside this would be the local landowner or his baron baillie, and the baillies of the town council in the case of burghs. The magistrate would have the suspect imprisoned and interrogated, and if enough evidence was gathered the suspect would either be sent for trial in the High Court in Edinburgh, or application would be made for a commission to try the suspect locally.

As has previously been observed, there seems often to have been a reluctance on the part of ministers and kirk sessions to recognise individual cases in their own parishes as witchcraft, and an attitude of leniency can sometimes be seen at a local level which is not usually present in the higher courts of the Church at the level of Presbytery and Synod. We can perhaps put down strictness at Presbytery and Synod to peer pressure. People in a group will do what individuals will not, since it is natural human behaviour to want to be "one of the boys" and subscribe to the ethos of the group. Individual ministers in their own parishes are more likely to have been swayed by doubts or feelings of sympathy. Also, if I may trail some anecdotal evidence: during a career in education I found that very few head teachers would ever admit to having discipline problems in their schools, even when the problems were common knowledge. I have a suspicion that 17th century ministers may have been inclined to turn a similarly blind eye to the problem of witchcraft. "What, witchcraft? No, a bit of charming maybe, but no witchcraft in my parish. They wouldn't dare!" To admit that the Devil's work was busily going ahead on your own particular patch would be to admit to weakness and lack of control on your part, so it would not be surprising if the usual reaction was to play it down and smooth it over at all costs, unless the problem was so blatant as to demand action.

Ministers and elders, then, were often involved in preliminary investigations before steps were taken to imprison the suspect, and they were also more often than not involved in the subsequent interrogations and taking of statements, along with local gentry, schoolmasters, and other dignitaries. Of course, kirk elders and local gentry were often the same people, and schoolmasters were often session clerks and clerks to baron courts, and so the Kirk did have a *de facto* role in processing witches. What the Church was absolutely not able to do was put witches on trial and pass sentence on them. This is made quite clear as early as 1608 in the case of Geillis Johnston in Musselburgh, who complained that Dalkeith Presbytery was pestering her with citations and summonses for witchcraft. The Privy Council summoned the ministers concerned and told them in no uncertain terms to back off. The Church could only act in an information gathering capacity.

What did often happen was that the interrogation process was so effective that the trial was a mere formality. If the minister and his elders brought the suspect to a confession in prison, and the suspect did not subsequently retract the confession, the trial was little more than a prelude to execution. That the accused was not expected to be acquitted is obvious from the fact that several condemned witches in East Lothian were executed on the same day as the trial, even though the arrangements for the execution, particularly the large amounts of fuel needed for the cremation of the body, must have had to be prepared in advance. During the witchcraft panic of 1649-50 the Church of Scotland was in a particularly strong position politically, and Haddington Presbytery had taken on the role of certifying evidence in witchcraft cases as being sufficient to apply for a commission. The Presbytery thus sent droves of suspects to almost inevitable death. Even so, however, it was the secular justice system which tried them, condemned them, and killed them.

If a suspect was tried by commission, the commissioners - usually such local figures of authority as lairds, or provosts and baillies of burgh councils - were empowered to set up the court, appoint its various officials, and choose a jury. The commissioners, or two or three of their number, would be appointed as judges for the occasion. The suspect was thus tried by her neighbours and acquaintances. If she had an unblemished reputation this would be to her advantage. Unfortunately this was hardly ever the case, and she was more likely to be processed by those who already "knew" her to be a witch. In the case of a High Court trial the judges were trained and qualified professionals, and the jury mostly Edinburgh tradesmen and merchants.

Not surprisingly, it is usually reckoned that the chances of acquittal were higher in High Court trials. It is sometimes said that the option of having a defence lawyer was only available in High Court trials. However, the records of some trials by commission in Haddington in the 1630s show that the accused was asked if she had anyone to speak on her behalf.

It is not easy to arrive at a precise total of the numbers of East Lothian people executed for witchcraft. In the case of witches tried and condemned by the High Court of Justiciary there are almost always records of the trial and the sentence passed. In the case of the Peaston witches in 1678 there are even signed statements from eyewitnesses of the executions, and a record of the expenses incurred. As far as commissions are concerned, we are operating on more uncertain ground. We might presume that if a commission was issued by the Privy Council, Parliament, or the Committee of Estates, a trial and execution would inevitably follow, but this, although highly likely, obviously would not necessarily be the case. The trial might be postponed and the charges eventually dropped, especially if it had been found impossible to bring the suspect to a confession. Then again, the trial might take place and result in acquittal. However unlikely that outcome might seem, it was always a possibility. Some suspects were indeed acquitted, and in the absence of records for the vast majority of trials by commission, we simply do not know how many more acquittals there were. Just as the records of some trials by commission in Haddington were kept with the records of the burgh council, it may be that others were kept with the baron court records or family papers of the landed proprietor who was the senior commissioner. Some of these may still survive, but their whereabouts is anybody's guess.

Similarly, just because Haddington Presbytery certified a vast number of cases in 1649-50 as being "sufficient to apply for a commission", it does not necessarily mean that a commission was in fact applied for, far less that a trial and subsequent execution took place. It is easy to produce a horrifyingly long list of those who were probably executed for witchcraft, but we should perhaps exercise some caution in making statements about the actual number of deaths.

The following is a list of residents of East Lothian "probably" executed for witchcraft.

1. In connection with the "North Berwick" plot: 1690/91

Agnes Sampson, John Cunningham (Fian), Geillis Duncan, Bessie Thomson. [Justiciary Court Records]

John Gordon (Greymeill), Margaret Dunn, Christian Tod, "Ersch Marioun", Gilbert McGill, John McGill, Catherine Grey. [Executions mentioned in a letter of the English Ambassador, and the trial of Beigis Tod. Janet Stratton and Donald Robertson may have survived. Robert Grierson died in custody.]

DEFINITE EXECUTIONS: 11

2. Death sentence passed.

1602 James Reid - Justiciary Court death sentence passed.

1607 Issobell Grierson - Justiciary Court death sentence passed.

1608 Beigis Tod - Justiciary Court death sentence passed.

1628 William Davidson - Commission. Death sentence passed.

1629 John Carfrae, Thomas Carfrae, Alison Borthwick, Alexander Sinclair, Besse Mak, Sara Keith. - Trials by commission. Death sentences passed.

1629 Issobell Young - Justiciary Court death sentence passed

1630 Alexander Hamilton - Justiciary Court

death sentence passed.

1631 Christian Paterson - Trial by commission. Death sentence passed.

1639 Anna Tait - Trial by commission. Death sentence passed.

1649 Jeanie Hunter, Marjorie Nisbet, Margaret Paterson, Jeamet Burgane, Margaret Bartillman, Agnes Broun, Margaret Robertson, Barbara Purdie, Helen Fairlie, John Weir, Heltein Lawson, Margaret Dickson, Isobel Murray, Agnes Hunter, Marione Richesone, John Dickson. - Trials by commission. Death sentences passed.

DEATH SENTENCES PASSED 30

3. Judged by Haddington Presbytery as giving "sufficient grounds for seeking a commission".

1649 Margaret Vaitch, Manie Haliburton, Agnes Clarkson, Patrick Watson, Marion Meik, Bessie Hodge, Isabel [?] , Margaret Dickson, [Long Blank, Haddington parish], [Blank, Dirleton parish], Sybella Wyllie, Elizabeth Hamiltoune, Margaret Hamilton, Margaret Fulleis, Marion Forrester, Helen Fairlie, Barbara Purdie, Helen Lawson, Marion Goodfellow, Margaret Robertson, Margaret Bartilman, Janet Burg, Margaret Paterson, Jean Hunter, George Ker, James Reid, Adam Moffat, Margaret Brotherstone, Jean Ker, Agnes Wilsone, Agnes Broun, [Long Blank, Pencaitland parish], Richard Umpherstone, Christina Leitch, Euphaim Wallace, Janet Smith, Margaret Fortune, Helen Umpherstone, Janet Thomson, [Blank], James Paterson, Bessie Johnstone, Adame Johnston, Margaret Murray, Marion Lawrie, Janet Carncrosse, Agnes Johnstone, Janet Cockbarne, Marione Hay, Christiana Forrest, James [Blank], Margaret Richesone, Isabel Boyd, Agnes Broun, Janet Wilson, Jennet Bard, Margaret Fodringhame, Catherine Whilley.

[Allowing one name for a blank in the records, and two for a long blank - at least 60.]

4. Commissions granted by the Privy Council 1600-1631.

1612 Christian Grinton, Janet Litster, Catherine Vertue, Euphane Young, Alesoun Denis, Alesoun Angus, Janet Harlaw, Jonet Henrie.

1622 Jonet Maglene, Helen Mine.

1624 Margaret Mewros, Jonet Acheson.

1628 Margaret Young, Agnes Rankin, Janet Reid, Margaret Ridpath, Bessie Roddell, Agnes Dempster, Agnes Liddell, Margaret Oliver, Barbara Maine, Janet Strauchane, Beatrix Cuthbertson, Janet Darby, Janet Boyd, Elspeth Hislop, Isobel Miller, Bessie Littil, Margaret Bain, William Davidson, Alesoun Tailyour, Alexander Hamilton, Margaret Baxter, Marion Bathcat.

1 629 Isobel Young, Sara Keith, Besse Make, Alexander Hunter, Beigis Wallace, Margaret Matheson, Marion Porteous.

[Commissions to detain and question several people were also issued. These suspects were referred to the Presbytery of Haddington for questioning four months later. No trials seem to have resulted.]

1630 Patrick Murray

1631 Cristian Paterson

TOTAL COMMISSIONS GRANTED BY THE PRIVY COUNCIL 1600-1631: 44

[Out of those persons named above 1600-1631, the following are known for certain to have been sentenced to death: William Davidson, Alexander Hunter/Sinclair, Isobel Young, Besse Mak, Sara Keith, Bessie Littil, Alexander Hamilton, Beigis Wallace, Margaret Matheson, Christian Paterson.

Total 10]

5. Commissions granted by the Committee of Estates 1649:-

Jean Craig, Agnes Affleck, Catherine Craig, Margaret Strachan, Margaret Gibson, Margaret Allane, Patrick Anderson, Margaret Pringle, Janet Cairnecross, Janet Paterson, Bessie Johnston, Andrew Johnston, Margaret Murray, Marioun Lawrie, James Dalgliesh, Geilles Wood, Rachael Horseburgh, Marion Broun, Elizabet Wilson, [Blank], Marion Broune, Isobell Keith, John Forrester, Elspet Douglas, Rachael Forrester, Janet Nicolson, Jonet Speid, Agnes Johnstoun, Janet Cockburne, Marjorie Hog, Margaret Temple, Margaret Hamilton, Christian Forrest, Agnes Cairns, Agnes Gourly, Agnes Gray, Janet Sympson, Marion Halyburton, Janet Paton, Margaret Oliver, John Steel, Marion Dobie, Marion Honeyman, Beatrix Dobson, Elspet Skuggal, Janet Baird, Margaret Fothringham, Catherine Veitch.

TOTAL OF COMMITTEE OF ESTATES COMMISSIONS 1649 : 48

6. Commissions granted by Parliament. 1649

Agnes Hunter, Margaret Dickson, Isobel Murray; ["Some Persons", Dirleton parish]; ["Certain Persons", North Berwick and Haddington]; ["Certain Persons", Humbie and Keith Marischal]; ["Certain Persons", Tranent]; ["Certain Persons, Haddington and Dirleton]; ["Certain Persons", Ormiston].

"Some Persons" and "Certain Persons" might be taken to indicate at least three people, giving an approximate total of 21

Thus, during the North Berwick affair there were 11 recorded executions of East Lothian people. Between 1591 and 1649, 30 people are known to have been sentenced to death.

Thus the number of known death sentences passed on East Lothian residents from 1590 up to 1649 is 41

During the same period the Privy Council granted commissions against 44 people. I have only counted commissions which were, or appear to have been, issued for arrest, examination, and trial. I have not included commissions for detention and questioning only, since there is not the same degree of probability that these would result in death for the suspect. In any case, many of these were followed by a separate commission for trial - which I have included in the count. The number of commissions issued for trial, therefore, was 44. Of these, 10 people are known to be included in the total of 41 definite death sentences. This leaves 34 others who are highly likely to have been executed, although there are no actual records of their deaths. Thus, there were 41 known executions, plus 34 likely executions, giving a total of 75 East Lothian people who were probably executed for witchcraft between 1590 and 1649.

TOTAL NUMBER OF EXECUTIONS BETWEEN 1590 AND 1649   75

The holocaust of 1649 presents some rather more difficult problems. During that year the Presbytery of Haddington certified that evidence against approximately sixty people was sufficient to seek commissions against them. However, there are no records for the Presbytery of Dunbar which may well have been doing the same. The parishes of Inveresk and Ormiston were included in the Presbytery of Dalkeith at that time, and the presbytery minutes for 1649 record evidence against five people from Ormiston as being sufficient to seek a commission. I have discounted here a note that eleven people "confessed witchcraft" because the records do not actually say that there was an intention to seek commissions against them. Thus, the records show that evidence against 65 people was deemed sufficient to seek a commission. To that must be added an unknown number from Dunbar.

In 1649, commissions for trial granted by

the Committee of Estates amounted to forty eight granted against East Lothian residents. Parliament granted commissions against three named persons, and five commissions against "some persons" or "several persons". As previously stated, we might give a conservative estimate here of commissions issued by Parliament against at least twenty one persons.

Thus we have a total of 65 commissions probably applied for (not including Dunbar Presbytery), and a minimum of 48 plus 21 commissions actually issued, in other words 69. Since it is unlikely that only four applications were made from Dunbar Presbytery, this would suggest that not all certified suspects actually had applications lodged against them, or that not all applications for commissions were granted. Probably both of these possibilities are in fact the case.

Records survive of twelve condemned witches being sentenced to death in Haddington in 1649, and one in Tranent. However, it would probably be unwise to suppose that they were the only ones executed. Records of the proceedings of vast majority of trials by commission do not exist, but that does not mean the trials did not take place. It is more likely, as previously suggested, that the records found their way into baron court or family papers, and are lost, destroyed, or lying unnoticed in some obscure archive.

If commissions were granted against a minimum of sixty nine people, it is tempting to believe that they would all have been tried and executed. This may not have been the case however. Some might never have come to trial. Some might have been condemned but not actually executed. An entry in the "Acts of the Parliaments of Scotland" for 7th August 1649 notes that it was decided that the "Committees of War" in each district were to investigate whether torture had been used on witchcraft suspects, and to report back before they were executed. Witchcraft suspects still in prison are believed to have been freed by the English army after the invasion and victory of 1650 (Larner 2000: p. 75). All of these factors might well bring the total of executed witches down below 69.

On the other hand, there were four persons executed in Haddington who do not seem to be named in commissions [John Dickson, Jeannie Hunter, Marjorie Nisbet, John Weir]. We might assume that they are included in Parliamentary commissions against "some persons" or "certain persons", but we cannot take this for granted. They might be additional suspects thrown up in the investigations into others. And if Haddington could throw up four "extra" executions, how many more might the rural commissions throw up?

Thus, although there are factors which might lower the total of deaths from 69, there is also the possibility that these "extra" executions might bring the total back up to, or beyond, 69. Let us then stick with this figure as the best we can do under the circumstances. In addition, one of the definite executions in 1649 was Jean Craig from Tranent, who was tried not by a commission but by a special sitting of the High Court of Justiciary in Tranent This requires us to round up the approximate number of likely East Lothian witchcraft executions in 1649 to 70.

The year 1650 also presents problems. Up to July of that year the Presbytery of Haddington was still certifying evidence against witchcraft suspects as "sufficient grounds for seeking a commission", and forty one people are named in the Presbytery minutes. However, there are no records of the Committee of Estates granting any commissions in 1650, and the Privy Council was not meeting at that time. After July 17th 1650 the Presbytery did not meet again until 13th August 1651, due to the invasion by Cromwell's army. It is tempting to believe that because there are no records of commissions being issued, that none were in fact issued. This of course may not be the case. It is obvious from presbytery and kirk session records that a number of witchcraft suspects were being held in Haddington in the first half of 1650. It would be nice to think that they were all released after the English invasion and victory, but how many had been executed prior to that? Perhaps none, but we do not know. In the absence of any records to the contrary, I will take the optimistic position that forty one people were suspected, a few were held in prison, but none were actually executed.

PROBABLE TOTAL OF EXECUTIONS 1649-50: 70

It is often thought that the English-dominated justice system during the Commonwealth period was more lenient as far as witchcraft was concerned. In fact there were several executions of East Lothian people.

1657 Janet Bruce. Tried by local J.P.s. Death sentence passed.

1658 Margaret Anderson. Justiciary Court death sentence passed.

1659 Helen Simberd, Marion Lynne, Marion Logan, Janet Crooks, John Douglas, Barbara Cochrane, Christian Cranstone, Jonet Man, Bessie Lacost, Jean Sydserf, Aleissone Fermer, Hellin Heriot, Marion Angus, Jonet Wood. All tried by the Justiciary Court. Death sentences passed.

TOTAL EXECUTED UNDER THE COMMONWEALTH 16

The Restoration of 1660 heralded another witchcraft panic in East Lothian, possibly sparked off by the Earl of Haddington's petition to Parliament of 3rd April 1661, where he famously claimed that things were so bad that his tenants were threatening to leave his land unless something was done. His claim that the laws were "silent" on witchcraft was a little odd, considering the fourteen witches executed in East Lothian only two years previously. The ensuing wave of persecution may well reflect the determination of the new order in church and state to show that they had no intention of remaining "silent" in the face of a challenge.

1661 Agnes Loch, Margaret Ramage, Jonet Lyte, Jonet Dale. [Tried and executed in Musselburgh but resident elsewhere.]
Justiciary Court trials.
Death sentences passed: 4
David Johnston:
Justiciary Court death sentence passed: 1

The year 1661 presents some of the same problems as 1649. Parliament issued large numbers of commissions in 1661. Some of these were for detention and questioning only, and some were for interrogation and trial. In some cases, further commissions were issued for the trial of those mentioned in commissions for questioning. Can we assume that all those not so named were freed? Can we assume that all those mentioned in commissions for trial were sentenced to death? Can we assume indeed that they even stood trial? The few surviving "Porteous Rolls" - lists of criminal cases in each sheriffdom - make it obvious that it was not uncommon for witchcraft suspects to flee from justice.

The Earl of Haddington's petition to Parliament lists Elspet Tailyeour, Margaret Bartilman, Marioun Quheit and Jonet Carfrae as having confessed. Agnes Williamson and Christiane Deanes had been named by these others; witchmarks had been found on them and they had confessed. The following people had been named but had not yet been arrested: Helen Deanes, George Milnetoune, Patrick Cathie, Anna Pilmore, Elizabeth Sinclair, Margaret Baptie, Jonet Maissone, Margaret Argyill, Elspet Crawford. The requested commission was granted immediately. I assume that those who had confessed would be tried and executed, as would Christian Deanes. Agnes Williamson was tried and acquitted.

This leaves five probable executions: 5

As for those named and not yet arrested commissions were subsequently granted for the trial of Maisson and Crawford, and one for Margaret "Barclay", who is in fact likely to be "Baptie": 3

The records of the Privy Council [2nd Ser. Vol viii, p.198] contain a renewed application for a commission against various suspects. In it Helen Deanes, Anna Pilmore, Elspeth Baillie, Isobel Richardson, and Elizabeth Lawson are described as having confessed. This is likely to have been enough to seal their fates. 5

During May and June of 1661 Parliamentary Commissions were also issued against Robert Crawffurd, Helen Cass[?], Bessie Doughty [Fisherrow]; Nicoll Steille, Isobel Steille, Isobel Cairns [as well as Baillie, Richardson and Lawson above-named];Bessie ffouler, Agnes Paterson, Katherine Cruikshank, Jonet Douglas [Musselburgh];

Catherine Coupland, Christine Watherstoun, Janet Wilson, Margaret Bannatyne [and Elspeth Crawford above-named]; Anna Kemp, Issobel Smith [i], Issobel Smith [ii], Margaret Ker, [Bolton area]; Bessie Knox [West Fenton] and Issobel Johnston [Gullane]; Jonat Wast, Issobel Cathie, Isobell Thomson, Christine Blak, Jonet Kemp [all Samuelston] and Barbara Scott [Rottenraw]; Jonet Hog [Prestonhaugh]; Merron Ingrahame, Euphane Bartleman, Christine Umpherston [Yester parish].

Named in Parliamentary Commissions 30

Thus it is possible that around 43 East Lothian people were tried and executed in 1661. Unfortunately there would seem to be no record of any of the trials. George Sinclair mentions the execution of Bessie Fouler in *Satan's Invisible World*, and Agnes Williamson's trial documents mention Margaret Bannatyne and Elizabeth/Elspeth Baillie as having been burnt for witchcraft, but these appear to be the only confirmations of execution.

LIKELY EXECUTIONS IN 1661: 43

1677 Elizabeth Moody [Haddington]. Privy Council Commission. Execution confirmed by Fountainhall and Sinclair.

1678 Agnes Kellie, Margaret Anderson [Prestonpans]. Privy Council commission. These are "the two who were burnt" [Fountainhall].

Helen Laing, Margaret Dodds, Marion Veitch, Isobel Eliot, [Peaston/Keith area]. Justiciary Court trial. Executions witnessed.

1688 Catherine McTarget [Dunbar]. Trial By Commission. Found guilty. The Privy Council was unhappy with the verdict and called her in for further questioning, but eventually sent her back to Dunbar "to be burnt there if her judges pleased" [Fountainhall].

EXECUTIONS AFTER 1661   8

Summary

Probable executions 1590 - 1649	75
Probable executions in 1649/50	70
Executions under the Commonwealth	16
Probable executions in 1661:	
Justiciary Court cases:	5
Trials by commission	30
Executions after 1661	8
Total	204

TOTAL OF LIKELY EAST LOTHIAN EXECUTIONS FOR WITCHCRAFT 1590 – 1700:   204

Thus, it is likely that somewhere in the region of 204 people were strangled and burnt in East

Lothian for witchcraft. However, I must again emphasise that although I think it likely that those who had commissions for trial granted against them would be executed, in the majority of cases we just do not know if that was in fact what happened. The actual total of deaths may therefore be lower than 204.

Compared with the figures given above, the numbers of those who stood trial and are known to have escaped with their lives, are small indeed.

1691   Barbara Napier. A high-profile "North Berwick" suspect, but not resident in East Lothian. Condemned to death but claimed pregnancy. Subsequently bailed.
1659   Janet Thomson, Marion Guild [Tranent]. Justiciary Court trials. Acquitted. Helen Cumine [Stenton]. Justiciary Court trial. Acquitted. Possibly insane.
1662   Agnes Williamson [Samuelston]. Justiciary Court trial. Acquitted.
James Welsh [Samuelston?] Commissioners refused to try him as he was a minor. Sent on to the Justiciary Court.   Sentenced to a year and a day in the "Correction House".

Other narrow escapes were John Hog and his wife in 1629 who were rigorously investigated but freed on bail, and Margaret Allan in 1661 whose accuser the Laird of Newhall dropped the charges at the last moment on the actual day of the trial.

It will be obvious that if there were indeed such things as "witch-hunts" and "witchcraft panics", then 1649 was the biggest panic of all. The main reason driving the 1649 "witch-hunt" was undoubtedly the fact that hard-line Calvinist Presbyterianism had finally gained the upper hand in Scotland, and it was possible to believe that church and state were becoming one, and that a physical manifestation of God's kingdom on earth (or at least on a tiny patch of the planet) was about to become reality. As Stuart Macdonald remarks in *The Witches of Fife*, "The times also encouraged the seeking out of all enemies of God, including witches, as the church sought to finally achieve its goal of building a godly society." [Macdonald 2002, p. 108]. There is an interesting contrast here with the Netherlands, also Calvinist and Presbyterian, where "from the beginning of the 17th century Dutch magistrates ceased completely to impose the death penalty for witchcraft or maleficent sorcery." [Ankarloo 2002, p. 80]. In the Netherlands however, "the clergy of the reformed church was not allowed to exert any considerable influences on legal practices and other secular matters, as they did for instance in Geneva and Scotland." [Ankarloo 2002, p. 81]. In Scotland in 1649, although government was in the hands of the Presbyterian party, there was much underlying instability. Not only was civil war about to erupt again after the execution of Charles I and the crowning of his son in Scotland as Charles II, but there was much "scarcity" [Larner 2000, Appendix 1], confirmed by Haddington Presbytery's reference of 31st October 1649 to "apprehension of great dearth and famine by reason of the unseasonableness of the weather." Given such daunting conditions, it might be thought all the more likely that the party in power would seek to curry divine favour by enthusiastic rooting out of "enemies of God".

The "panic" of 1661 is perhaps more difficult to explain. The restoration of the Stuart monarchy in 1660 ushered in an Episcopal religious and political establishment and there has always been a tendency to believe that Episcopacy is more tolerant and easy-going than Presbyterianism, which has acquired a reputation of being judgmental and intolerant. However, the Episcopal establishment post-1660 did not hesitate to treat dissident "Covenanters" with merciless harshness, and we might speculate whether witches were seen as a parallel threat to public order. Perhaps it was likelier that the "new brooms" of the Restoration took advantage of an easy target in order to be seen to be working wonders for the public good, while at the same time upholding the rule of law and common decency, and stamping governmental authority on the country at large. The Earl of Haddington's petition to Parliament making mention of his tenants' discontent would seem to indicate a grassroots feeling that witchcraft had been allowed to become an increasing problem under the Commonwealth and had reached the stage where "something must be done". Even the politicians of our more enlightened times are not above stage-managing minor problems so that their proactive and can-do initiatives will win kudos with the public and throw up a smokescreen to conceal their disinclination to tackle more difficult challenges.

The North Berwick trials smell strongly of a rather similarly sexed-up public relations exercise. The train of events in the North Berwick "panic" may have gone something like this: King James VI was a young man of little reputation and less charisma. His efforts to bring home a bride had become farcical, and cannot have done much either for his own image or that of the Scottish fleet. Hearing that Danish witches had been arrested for conjuring up the storms which had disrupted his wedding plans, James perhaps wonders if there has been a similar conspiracy at home. In East Lothian there is already some local agitation over witchcraft, possibly exacerbated by a feud between two minor lairds. Agnes Sampson, a "wise wife" of considerable reputation in the area, has been under investigation for witchcraft, and there is mention that she has been raising storms – supposedly a perennial activity of witches – and that there has been a meeting of witches at North Berwick where the King has been spoken of in disrespectful terms. Other suspicious characters are quickly pulled in, and willing hands set to work to provide the King with the answers he would appear to expect. More willing hands begin to orchestrate events to influence the King for reasons of their own. James, although genuinely intrigued by witchcraft, quickly sees an opportunity to stamp his authority on the country. The Church backs him up, seeing an opportunity to strengthen its case for a more authoritative national role. Various ambitious courtiers and politicians join in the game, seeing that backing the king enthusiastically may be an advantageous career move.

Suspicions about a local wise wife, coupled with a possible get-together of lesser lights with similar interests, where perhaps derogatory mention was made of the King by their master of ceremonies, quickly became a diabolical treason conspiracy, authenticated by confessions extracted by judicial and extra-judicial torture. Royal machismo and effectiveness were successfully demonstrated to the King's subjects, and as an added bonus James was able to rid himself of the menacing figure of his cousin the Earl of Bothwell.

It has already been hinted in Chapter 1 that there may well be more to David Seton's part in all this than meets the eye. Indeed, it might be even more interesting to speculate over the possible involvement behind the scenes of his master Robert, Lord Seton, head of one of Scotland's wealthiest, most ancient, and most influential aristocratic families – a family passionately devoted to the House of Stewart.

It is inconceivable that David Seton, a mere baron baillie, could have proceeded so prominently in all this without his master's full knowledge and approval. One might ask, "What was in it for Lord Seton?" A possible answer might be that although he was impeccably loyal to the King and on personally friendly terms with him, Lord Seton was a Catholic, and therefore always likely to be an object of suspicion in the eyes of Scotland's Protestant political establishment, particularly in the light of Catholic plotting and rebellion earlier in James's reign.

It would certainly do Lord Seton no harm to allow his "front man", the baron baillie of Tranent, to spark off the exposure of a diabolical plot against the King. The Kirk and the politicos could do little else but join in with enthusiasm. Just as the "North Berwick" show trials allowed the King to consolidate his power in Scotland, they may also have served to keep potential enemies of the House of Seton at bay.

How grateful would the King be for a friend's subtle but effective efforts on his behalf? In 1600 James created Lord Seton "Earl of Winton", ostensibly in recognition of Seton's father's loyal service to James's mother Queen Mary. But could it have also been a belated thankyou for services rendered a decade earlier?

Even the most cursory reading of the dittays makes it perfectly clear that there was little resemblance between what Agnes Sampson was charged with at the beginning of the affair, and the later accusations against Barbara Napier and Euphane MacCalyean. In short, the North Berwick affair was a series of show trials orchestrated to strengthen royal authority, and exploited by the Church and various individuals for reasons of their own. I do not see what other interpretation can be put on the North Berwick and Acheson's Haven saga, unless there is as yet undiscovered evidence which might shed further light on it.

"North Berwick" has had an undue influence on the way we perceive Scottish witchcraft. It should be remembered that its centring round a treason conspiracy, and the direct royal involvement in the interrogation of the suspects, make it utterly atypical of Scottish witchcraft cases.

The attempt to gain a clear perception of "What was really going on" in the field of Scottish witchcraft is not helped by historic attitudes to the subject. Hard on the heels of a hundred years of witch hunting came the Union with Engand in 1707. For many people, all that was English became all that was superior. England had traditionally taken a more lenient attitude towards witchcraft, and so the 17th century Scottish obsession with witches quickly came to be perceived by upwardly mobile Scots as shameful or laughable provincialism. The 18th century Scottish Enlightenment branded witchcraft beliefs as foolish and ignorant superstition, an attitude firmly backed by the Victorian philosophy of unstoppable human progress.

Throughout, "tolerant" English Episcopalians had shaken their heads in weary bemusement at the "fanatical" Presbyterian persecution of witches. This attitude hardened considerably with the advent of Socialism, which became a powerful influence in 20th century Scotland. The intellectual elite of Scottish socialism often had a particularly strong anticlerical bias, or at least an anti-Kirk bias. John Knox came to be reviled almost as the author of all Scotland's ills, and the Church of Scotland was given the lion's share of the blame for a holocaust of death and destruction perpetrated against innocent and defenceless old women.

All these factors contribute to a situation where for many people the question "What was really going on?" is meaningless, because they had been conditioned to believe that as far as witchcraft was concerned nothing can have been going on, since witchcraft and magic are impossible, and "real" witches are as much figments of the imagination as the fairies at the bottom of the garden.

Fortunately, in recent years there have been efforts made to get away from continually viewing witchcraft from the superior standpoint of lofty modernity, and attempts made to try to see it through the eyes of those who lived with it, feared it, used it, believed in it, and above all were familiar with it as one of the undeniable facts of life.

It is likely that there had always been a place for the "Wise Wife" in East Lothian peasant society. Illness, accident, disaster and death could strike at any time. Often enough the reasons for misfortune were obvious, but when they were not, the suspicion was that the victim was the target of malevolent magic, or "malefice" as it was defined in Scots law. The Wise Wife could diagnose malefice, and tell you how to counteract it. The Wise Wife could predict whether you would recover or die from sickness, and had a range of cures at her disposal. The Wise Wife could tell you the whereabouts of lost or stolen goods, help with love affairs, marriage and childbirth, and could foresee good or ill fortune. In an era devoid of anything resembling modern medicine, not to mention psychiatrists, social workers, and police, the Wise Wife was an important part of peasant society. In East Lothian, Agnes Sampson, the Wise Wife of Keith, is a prime example of the profession, consulted not only by the poor and ignorant but by the gentry as well. It is not altogether clear how the Wise Wife's customers perceived her powers - whether they were believed to be innate or learned, supernatural or practical.

A witch, in popular imagination, was a malevolent creature with power to do evil through sorcery. It is undeniable that there were "wise wives" in whom people could turn in time of need, and it is not improbable that there were others who would undertake to give you revenge on enemies, blight rivals' prospects, see off objectionable spouses, or dispose of unwanted pregnancies. Such people had no compunction about boosting their reputations by exploiting unease and inspiring terror. Catherine McTarget and Isobel Young seem to have acquired this sort of reputation.

Is addition, there were "charmers", people who specialised in finding stolen goods, or diagnosing and curing illness in livestock, or even in people.

It must be remembered too that ordinary people would have a range of cures and charms at their disposal, where folk medicine, magic, and religion mingled and merged. It was when their own best efforts in this field failed that they turned to the practitioners described above.

In the eyes of the Law and the Church in 17th century Scotland there was no debate about the origin of the powers of the wise wife, the witch, and the charmer. Any power they had came from the Devil. There was no inherent difference between the wise wife and the witch because both derived their power from the Devil and were thus servants of the Devil. It was held that such people had engaged in a formal pact with the Devil to renounce Christianity and enter Satan's service. Charmers were lesser offenders because they served the Devil through ignorant superstition and had not made a formal pact with him. Obviously charmers ran the risk of being arrested as witches, and it is surprising that some seemed to practise with impunity. John Lyndsay in Dirleton is a good example of a charmer who seems to have led a "charmed" life.

The belief that the witch's power came from the Devil was almost certainly not originally shared by the bulk of the population in Scotland. However, since this was the view of the elite of the country, in whom power resided, it was the rationale which counted, and was the belief which shaped official attitudes to witchcraft and governed the process by which society dealt with and disposed of witches.

Modern scholars agree that the notion that all magic and witchcraft was diabolically inspired gained ground first among the intellectuals and upper strata of continental European society. "Beginning in the early fifteenth century, many of the different kinds of offences that had earlier constituted the separate offences of magic, sorcery, divination, necromancy, and even learned natural magic, began to be considered in some places by some theologians and magistrates, both ecclesiastical and civil, as a single type of crime whose essence was defined as a conspiratorial alliance with the devil, whose purpose was to ruin human society, At its most comprehensive (and not all demonologists included all of the features that collectively came to distinguish it) individuals were believed to have made a pact with the devil, signed it with their blood, rendered homage and entered into sexual relations with him, travelled by flight to assemblies at which they participated in blasphemous rites, and carried with them, usually on their bodies, a mark or sign of their membership in the diabolical conspiracy of witches, and were sometimes accompanied by a familiar demon, often in the shape of an animal." [K. Jolly in Jolly et al., 2002, p.231].

This conception of magic and witchcraft was defined by Heinrich Krämer, a former inquisitor in Innsbruck, in his notorious book "Malleus Malificarum". The enthusiastic reception of Krämer's theories can be judged by the fact that thirteen editions of the "Malleus" appeared between 1487 and 1520, and sixteen more between 1574 and 1669 [Jolly 2002, p.231]. "Some of the omissions in the Malleus were compensated for in other works of demonology, so that by 1500 a reading of the 'Malleus' and a few other works provided a virtual encyclopedia for the investigation of diabolic sorcery and witchcraft" [Jolly 2002, p.240]. King James VI's *Daemonologie* was an unoriginal and derivative work, firmly grounded on this material. It did however provide clear guidelines for the investigation of witchcraft in 17th century Scotland, thus ensuring that the diabolic would be uppermost in the minds of the investigators. All the same, that was not always what concerned those at the "grassroots" who complained against witches in East Lothian.

What most worried the bulk of the population in East Lothian as far as witchcraft was concerned was not whether the local witch had done a deal with the Devil. What concerned them was "malefice" - the deliberate causing of misfortune, destruction, sickness, and death. As far as mere misfortune goes, the records contain an impressive list of mayhem allegedly caused by East Lothian witches.

Malefice [Misfortune].

1591 Agnes Sampson
Sinking ships. Raising a storm to stop the Queen coming to Scotland.
The ruination meant for David Seton landed on the possessions of a ploughman.
1591 John Cunningham
"Destroyed men at sea and on land, with corn cattle and goods."
1591 Euphane Macalyean
Tried to attract the laird of Pumpherston, and subsequently tried to impede his marriage with charms. Conjuring cats to raise storms.
1602 James Reid
Got a woman to lay raw meat under the doors of David Libberton's mill and stable to destroy his horses and cattle. Scattered enchanted stones to destroy Libberton's corn.
1607 Issobel Grierson
Spoiled Robert Peden's ale.
1608 Beigis Tod
Supposedly caused William Patterson's ale to fail [acquitted].
1611 Bessie Thomson
Alison Howison's cow stopped giving milk after Bessie fetched fire out of her house. [K.S. minutes.]
1612 Janet Lytster
Patrick Neilson bought a cow from Janet's husband. Janet was angry. The cow would not give milk for three days. When the cow started giving milk Patrick's wife sweated copiously and lost her appetite.

1628 William Davidson
Consulted with the Devil about laying on and taking off sickness, and undoing and destroying others.

1629 John and Thomas Carfrae, Alison Borthwick
John killed his neighbour's horses because he wouldn't lend him one. Alison took blood from her brother in law George Carfrae, and ever since his wealth declined. She killed Patrick Watherston's cow by witchcraft, and the meat was found to be like chicken, without blood.

1629 Issobell Young
Knocked George Sandie into the hopper of his mill, breaking the machinery. When the mill was repaired it wouldn't work for eleven days. She 'moved' the Laird of Broxmouth to put George out of the mill. She pulled her kerchief off in William Meslett's barn, and sixteen oxen and eight horses dropped dead soon after. She pulled her kerchief off as William Kellie came into her house. His house and barnyard caught fire. She prevented Jonet Hodge's butter from forming. She reduced Thomas Home and his widow to beggary. She caused the pigeons to leave Thomas Home's doocot She burned his widow Lilias Knowles's steading. She rode John Bryson's horses at night in the stable. His mare aborted her foal, and his horse wasted away and died. She quarrelled with Cuthbert Symson over a bolt of unsatisfactory cloth. His horse died and his worldly wealth vanished. Andrew Mertoun's cattle died and his worldly wealth vanished.

1629 John Hog and Margaret Nicolson
Patrick Carkettle claimed that John Hog boasts that whoever angers him or his family, he will destroy and overthrow them. James Sandie's horses went mad and one came to Markle where Hog lived. Hog was suspected to have caused this.

1630 Alexander Hamilton
Requested power to harm the Laird of Colstoun, but the Devil said he'd already granted that to somebody else.

1631 Cristiane Paterson
Caused the death, decay, and wasting away of Elizabeth Anderson's goods and livestock. She bewitched the corn and possessions of James Wadie in Saltoun and ruined him because he'd underpaid her for harvest work.

1634 Bitriche Milton
After Bitriche had supposedly caused Alexander Cugilton's daughter to become ill, Alexander's cow aborted her calf, the girl recovered, and the cow came into heat next morning. Crows were heard crying round the house. [K.S. minutes]

1643 Margaret Dickson
James Mill told her daughter off for pulling some of his wheat. Margaret predicted that he'd soon lose more than that. His livestock took "a kind of trembling disease" and some died. [Presb. minutes]

1649 Elspeth Dobbie
She came into a candlemaker's house when he was making candles. The white tallow turned bloody, and the white candles he was dipping were all red. [K.S. minutes].

1649 Margaret Vaitch
She took the milk from a cow which had knocked her over. She caused another cow to give blood instead of milk. She caused two pregnant cows never to give birth - their pregnancies dwindled away. [K.S. minutes].

1649 Jean Craig
Accused of causing "sickness in beasts and people, madness, and death." She bewitched the cattle of James Smith in Little Fawside - the cows gave blood instead of milk, and the oxen ran mad. She also bewitched James Smith's horses. Three died soon afterwards and three later.

1649 Jeannet Burgane
She, the Devil, and three others tied the tails of Patrick Cowden's oxen together, took hold of

the tails, and drew them backwards. As soon as she got home Patrick sent for her husband to come and bleed two of the oxen. The third died the next night.

1652 John Wilson

The application for a commission says he was guilty of malefice against the daughter of the Laird of Innerwick, and the widow of the Innerwick minister. No details given.

1657 Jonet Bruce

Her dog made to bite James Melvill. He threatened to throw it in the fire, and she threatened to do him a bad turn. That night his salt pan was overturned by an evil blast of wind and the contents spoiled. The house she was imprisoned in caught fire when a rat seized a lighted candle and ran into the thatch.

1658 Margaret Anderson

After a man shaved his head, she consulted with a charmer and prevented the hair growing back.

1659 Bessie Lacost, Jean Sydserff, Alleisson Fermer, Hellin Herriot, Marion Angus.

Their dittays say they caused misfortune, but no details are given.

1660 Jonet Spavine

She lent money to a man in Penston and he never prospered after that. [K.S. minutes].

1661 Margaret Allane

After a legal dispute between her son and James Hog, four horses in James's care died. One ran up and down the field for three hours then collapsed. The other three died within six months of the same disease. Back in 1650 she threatened William Tait for poinding her husband's goods for debt. William's horses and oxen began dying. This had continued ever since, bringing him to ruin.

1662 Agnes Williamson

George Cauldcleuch's horse had a piece of flesh cut out of its lip and died. Agnes was also accused of taking the strength and substance from George's meal. When James Carfra was wading over the Tyne he was knocked into the water by a whirlwind, and carried down to the East mill and over the dam. Thomas Crombie's malt kiln caught fire after Agnes predicted he would lose money. Several confessing witches blamed Agnes for this. Thomas Steel's house caught fire after he refused to lend her £10. [Acquitted].

1662 James Welsh

He claimed that the witches went one night to "cut" Patrick Baillie's mare, but Patrick sat up in the stable and prevented them. At Thrieplaw they planned to knock down the mill at Penston, but couldn't manage it because there was a man in the mill.

1678 Sara Cranston

According to her servant she "burst and rode to death" a horse belonging to her son.

1678 Helen Laing

Denied doing wrong to her husband or anyone else. Denied knowing that any other person did wrong to man woman or beast.

1678 Margaret Dodds

Denied ever doing harm to man, woman, beast or goods.

1678 Margaret Russell

Denied ever doing wrong to man or beast.

1678 Marion Veitch

The Devil required her to serve him by destroying her neighbours and blaspheming God's name; however God did not permit her to do these things.

1678 Marion Campbell

Absolutely denied ever doing harm to man, woman, or beast. When some people fell out with her she intended to do them harm, but could never have managed it

1672 Adam Gilles, Christian Watson

Helen Frater said that Christian used to come to her master asking for yeast on the Sabbath, and afterwards neither the yeast nor ale was any good. [K.S. minutes.]

1685 John Calder

Jean Finlison claimed John said he would "staint their ground". Two or three days later two of their cows died. [K.S. minutes.]

1688 Catherine McTarget

A woman in Spott refused to give Catherine milk, and her cow subsequently gave blood instead of milk, then died. John Milne's horse came into her garden and trampled her plants. She predicted the horse would break its neck and it did. She predicted John would never thrive, and he descended into extreme poverty. She dipped her fingers in George Colme's water pail then touched the sole of her foot - three of his cows and two bullocks subsequently died. She held dung to a bullock's mouth, and a cow in a barn nearby began to decline and never thrived afterwards. She threw her head-cloths at Janet Symentone and Janet's malt went bad. She sat on the stair opposite James Congaltone's house all night and he never thrived after that.

1703 Marion Lillie

William Colme blamed her for the loss of his livestock. Her son hanged a mad dog over Janet Logan's cow's fodder, which adversely affected the cow's supply of milk and butter. [K.S. minutes.]

While most of the "malefice" shown above is likely to be mere coincidence, it is not beyond the bounds of possibility that some "witches" were not above exploiting it to enhance their reputations. Also, although livestock were always vulnerable to disease, it is not impossible that on occasion they were physically interfered with. For example, a horse fed with ragwort might well "run mad", and a smart kick to the udder might cause a cow to give bloody milk.

Causing Illness.

An unhealthy man could not earn a living, and an unhealthy woman could not run a household. Sickness, therefore, could be even more devastating than mere misfortune.

1588 John McGill

A woman in Traprain was ill with an unspecified sickness, supposedly caused by McGill. Her family was advised to bring him into the house and she would recover as soon as she saw him.

1591 Agnes Sampson

She made a wax image of "Archie" for Barbara Napier which would cause him to pine away when melted by the fire. She met with others to plot the ruination of David Seton. They laid enchanted chords on the moor, but the malefice landed instead on a ploughman's daughter, who was plagued with hallucinations and possessed by an evil spirit. When the Gudewife of Galashiels omitted to pay Agnes for services rendered, Agnes caused her to be seized by a fit of madness, and her tongue swelled up.

1591 John Cunningham

Caused a man to be possessed by an evil spirit.

1591 Euphane MacCalyean

Bewitched her husband and her servant.

1602 James Reid

Roasted a wax image of David Libberton - result not known.

1607 Issobell Griersonne

She caused William Burnet to waste away and die in great pain. She laid a serious illness on Robert Peden and his wife.

1608 Beigis Tod

She caused Alexander Fairlie's son to fall ill, sweating and hallucinating. She was acquitted of casting a sickness on Robert Woid.

1611 Bessie Thomson

After a minor quarrel she promised a woman a bad turn and held her in sickness for a year. Another woman cut corn on Bessie's balk. Bessie was angry and the woman fell down sick on the rig she was cutting. [K.S. minutes.]

1628 William Davidson

He took a sickness off Agnes Sinclair and laid it on William Finlason.

1629 John Carfrae, Thomas Carfrae, Alison Borthwick

They consulted a witch, Margaret Hamilton, about killing the baron baillie of Yester's wife. Margaret bewitched her by sitting down to drink with her, and laid a "heavy sickness" on her.

1629 Alexander Sinclair

Isobel Turnbul in Longniddry collapsed after offering him grey bread instead of white.

1629 Besse Mak

Janet Broune fell ill after her husband doused Besse's fire. Bewitched James Robertson in Winton at Sara Keith's request. Besse spared his life because he was a crony of her son's.

1629 Issobell Young

She paralysed Thomas Kers for putting a summons in her lock. After her husband collapsed in the fields she laid his sickness at the threshold of their barn.

Her husband's nephew was first to come into the barn, and went mad. She caused a skin disease to break out on William Symson's wife's face. She paralysed Patrick Bryson down one side for cutting her pig's tether.

1631 Christiane Paterson

She laid a sickness on Janet Forrester and a serious illness on Elizabeth Anderson. She laid madness on her servant because she refused to sleep with the witch Margaret Muirhead.

1634 Bitriche Milton

Alexander Cugilton said he sent her a piece of pork with his daughter, and his other daughter became ill. When their cow aborted its calf the girl became well again. [K.S. minutes]

1642 Isobell Wood

She gripped John Howden by the arms after a quarrel. Shortly afterwards he lost the power of his arms and took a pain in his heels. His sister fell ill and was now bedridden. [Presb. minutes.]

1649 Jean Craig

She took Agnes Steille's milk away. She paralysed Thomas Crawfurd's son's legs, and caused James Cowan to tear continually at the skin of his face and to hide under beds and in roof cavities. She drove Beatrix Sandilands mad by blowing in her face.

1649 Helen Fairlie

Drove Jeanot Carfrae insane.

1657 Jonet Bruce

Robert Sandilands let her house to someone else. She came and urinated on his threshold and one of his children subsequently lost the power of his legs.

1659 Bessie Lacost, Jean Sydserff, Alleissonne Fermer, Hellin Heriot, Marion Angus

Their dittays say they all caused sickness and death but no details are given.

1661 Margaret Allane

Her fellow servant at Newhall was seized with fits of trembling. The same happened to Gilbert Lamb. She drove Thomas Hay insane. Any time the Laird of Newhall or his servants offended her they would be seized by fits of sweating and trembling.

1672 Adam Gilles, Christian Watson

Christian took a piece of turf off John Sandie's roof, and after that his wife was never well. [K.S. minutes.]

1688 Catherine McTarget

James Lauder's wife refused to give her ale, and subsequently took a violent pain in her hand; her baby fell ill and died within a month. Jean Johnston bought a sheep's head which Catherine had wanted, and subsequently became extremely ill. Catherine was refused drink by a servant in Cockburnspath post-house; the servant fell down as if dead and became delirious. Two girls found Catherine lying in the road. She suddenly jumped up and chased them. Both fell sick and the younger girl was struck dumb.

1703 Marion Lillie

Janet Logan blamed Marion for her child's sickness, and claimed she'd made her other son blind and dumb.

Death, of course, was the ultimate in mischief making.

Causing Death.

1591 John Cunningham
Helped to sink a ship.

1591 Euphane MacCalyean
Killed her nephew by witchcraft. Killed Eupham Pumphry. Killed two of the Laird of Pumpherston's children by witchcraft. Killed a six year old child by rubbing his face with a napkin. Helped to sink a ship.

1607 Issobell Griersonne
Caused William Burnet to waste away and die in great pain.

1608 Beigis Tod
Caused the death of the infant John Fairlie. [Charge dropped.]

1628 William Davidson
He bewitched and killed Eupham Cathie, and poisoned Isobel Wilson.

1629 John Carfrae, Thomas Carfrae, Alison Borthwick
They got the witch Margaret Hamilton to kill the wife of the baron baillie of Yester. Margaret then killed the baillie himself by rubbing a piece of enchanted gold on her hand. Thomas murdered his wife after consulting Margaret Hamilton. Alison was found guilty of murdering her child who had been fostered in Fala.

1629 Alexander Sinclair
He put on one of Lady Samuelston's husband's shirts and went away with it. The owner of the shirt died.

1629 Besse Mak
She killed Cuthbert Henderson's wife when she'd been asked to cure her.
She caused George Young to waste away and die, and killed Cuthbert Henderson when he was ill. She caused Janet Johnstoun to hang herself. She was art and part in the death of Lady Woodhead.

1629 Sara Keith
She gave her baby son to the Devil, who carried him out of the window in a whirlwind, leaving a lean deformed creature in the cradle, which cried for three days until it died.

1629 Issobell Young
When her son was fighting with another boy, the boy's sister nipped Issobell's son's leg. Issobell laid a sickness on her from which she died. She also laid a sickness on Thomas Home from which he died. She laid Alison Patterson's sickness on James Liddell and he died.

1629 John Hog, Margaret Nicolson
John Hog was very ill and expected to die. Euphane Yorstoun's baby died and Hog recovered. Patrick Carkettle claimed that Hog caused the death of the previous farmer of Markle, his wife, and two or three of their children.

1630 Alexander Hamilton
Lady Ormiston and her daughter refused to give him alms. He laid a ball of blue thread at lady Ormiston's gate, and she and her daughter fell ill and died.

1631 Christiane Paterson
She murdered John Keith in Hirdmestoun by laying a wasting disease on him.

1635 Anna Tait
She consulted with the Devil to murder her first husband in order to marry her present husband. She murdered her daughter and her daughter's unborn child with a mutchkin of white wine mixed with salt, in consultation with the Devil.

1649 Elspeth Dobbie
A child took a sore lip in her presence and subsequently died. She touched a woman's breast when she was feeding her baby, and the child never sucked again till it died. [K.S. minutes]

1649 Jean Craig
She rubbed her sister in law's baby with three enchanted stones, and the child died.

1657 Jonet Bruce
Margaret Strathearn's husband let Jonet's house to someone else. She threatened to make him shit his breeches for it. He had violent

diarrhoea for a year and a half and then died.

1659 Bessie Lacost, Jean Sydserff, Alleissonne Fermer, Hellin Heriot, Marion Angus

Their dittays say they all caused sickness and death, but no details are given.

1661 Margaret Allane

Lady Newhall was seized by fits of sweating and trembling after quarrelling with Margaret, and died blaming Margaret for her death.

1662 Agnes Williamson

John Veitch and his wife were in bed and woke to find Agnes and some other women sitting by the fire. He chased them out, and next morning their child was found dead in their bed. When Agnes was pregnant seven years before her trial, the child was "abstracted".

1678 Sara Cranston

Isobel Elliot claimed Sara was present at the contriving of the death of Kathrin Haliday's daughter.

1678 Jennet Burtoun

She claimed that Marion Keith gifted her year-old daughter to the Devil, and the child died within eight days.

1678 Helen Laing

Marion Veitch said Helen Laing killed her husband on his death bed, and pulled out his heart.

1678 Marion Veitch

Marion was present at, and an accessory to the killing of Helen Laing's husband. Also an accessory to the killing of William Thomson's daughter at Templehall.

1678 Marion Campbell

Marion Veitch said Marion Campbell was present when Helen Laing killed her husband, and also present when William Thomson's daughter was killed at Templehall.

1678 Isobel Elliot

Isobel named two women in Loanhead who killed a child of the Lasswade minister's.

1688 Catherine McTarget

Killed James Lauder's wife's baby. Patrick Ferguson refused Catherine's offer of bread and cheese, and his wife fell ill and died. A carter struck her for stealing coal from his cart, and he subsequently fell ill and died.

1697 Helen Hoge

She visited John Ochterlony when he was ill and was put out of the house. She prayed God's curse on him, that he would pine till he died. The night he died, John cried out that he could see Helen Hog.

Marion Lillie

Marion gripped Catherine Deans's belly, and she gave birth to a dead child six weeks later. Janet Haleburton miscarried after Marion gripped her belly.

This, then, was the kind of witchcraft activity which perturbed the general population in East Lothian. It should be obvious, however, that with this sort of thing it was very difficult to prove that the misfortune, injury, or death was actually caused by witchcraft. When the notorious witch Jean Craig blew in Beatrix Sandilands' face and Beatrix subsequently went mad, one might strongly suspect that Jean had caused her insanity, but proving it was a different matter. A fairly-conducted court - even a court by Commission - could seldom bring itself to convict solely on the evidence of malifice accusations.

Thus, in order to secure convictions, the pre-trial confession became of the utmost importance, and since the "guidelines" set out that a witch would have attended meetings, given herself to the Devil, and allowed herself to be marked, this was what the investigators strove to bring the suspect to confess. East Lothian witches, therefore, were not necessarily convicted because a farrago of magical or malicious activities had been proved against them. Many, perhaps most, died because they had confessed to the diabolic pact and to attending witches' meetings. When such a confession was obtained, and sustained in court, the subsequent trial was usually a mere formality, and some give the impression of being cursory in the extreme. That the suspects were not likely to be acquitted is indicated by the fact that some commissions for trial are marked "commission for burning" the accused. Also, as previously remarked, when accused persons were tried and executed the same day, it would seem likely that the preparations for execution were made before the trial. Considering the expenses involved in execution and cremation, these would not be incurred lightly.

Notwithstanding the fact that confessing the diabolic pact meant almost certain death, large numbers of witches in East Lothian made just such a confession. This is all the more puzzling since, as previously mentioned, the idea that magic was diabolic in origin was an alien notion imported from learned and academic circles in continental Europe. To the vast majority of modern minds the whole business is not only impossible, but laughable, that a woman could not only meet, converse with, and promise to serve the Devil himself, but also have sexual intercourse with him. Just as improbable is the idea that His Satanic Majesty should bother to turn up to preside over a meeting of a handful of illiterate peasant women of indeterminate age, jigging around in a damp hollow at the back of beyond in East Lothian.

Nevertheless, I have traced 77 cases where people resident in East Lothian were apparently recruited into witchcraft and underwent some form of initiation, sometimes receiving a new name, presumably as a parody of Christian baptism.

There follows a list of the circumstances of their recruitment, and the process used to initiate them.

1591 Agnes Sampson

After her husband's death the Devil in the likeness of a man promised to make her rich. She promised to serve him and was marked on the right knee. [However, she claimed to have learned her skill from her father. This would seem to suggest a less than complete identification of her "skill" with her service of the Devil.]

1591 John Cunningham

The Devil appeared to him dressed in white when he was lying in bed in Thomas Trumbil's house. The Devil marked him with a rod. Cunningham was known as "Fian", which has been taken to be a witch-name. Celtic mysticism buffs have pointed to the similarity between this name and that of the mythical Gaelic hero Fionn. If there is anything in the resemblance it might be worth pointing out that one of Fian's associates, Ersch Marion, was obviously a Gaelic speaker.

1598 Jonet Steill

When she was seriously ill thirteen years previously, a poor man who said he used to go around with the Jews washed her in south-running water and cured her.

1602 James Reid

He learned the trade of charming and curing from the Devil in Bynnie Craigs and Corstorphine Craigs.

1628 Wiliam Davidson

He renounced God and his baptism at Hirdmeston Mill at midnight, and became the Devil's servant. He was instructed in charming at the age of 32 by Bessie Gray. [Davidson may have been the notorious warlock known as "Hatteraik"].

1629 John Carfrae, Thomas
Carefrae, Alison Borthwick

According to Alexander Hamilton they swore on their knees to serve the Devil, possibly at a witch meeting on Coldingham Law.

1629 Alexander Sinclair alias Hunter

He renounced his baptism, and reputedly renewed his compact with the Devil annually at Norham.

1629 Sara Keith

George Harlaw refused to pay her a large

sum of money which he had owed to her late father. In despair she exclaimed, "May God or the Devil grant me revenge on this man!" The Devil appeared and promised her amends. She renounced God and her baptism. Her witch name was "Mistress Keith".

1629 Issobell Young

Her dittay says she renounced God and engaged in the service of Satan, but gives no further details.

1630 Alexander Hamilton

Coming from Nunland to Haddington, he met the Devil on Hugston Hills in the shape of a black man dressed all in black with a wand in his hand. Alexander agreed to be the Devil's servant. At a second encounter he renewed his promise to serve and renounced his baptism. The Devil gave him four shillings in English money.

1644 Andro Kerr

He learned charming and the words he used from his mother.

1646 George Beir

Knowing that George was a seventh son, the minister of Kelso told him to lay his hand on the sore part of a patient's body and say, "I touch thee, Lord cure thee," three times.

1649 Margaret Vaitch

Before the previous Easter the Devil appeared in the likeness of a gentleman and wanted to have sex with her. She refused and the Devil arranged to meet her in fourteen days' time. At the second encounter she had sex with the Devil, renounced her baptism, went down on her knees, and became the Devil's servant.

1649 Manie Haliburton

When her daughter was ill the Devil came to her house in the guise of a physician and sold her some ointment. He came back a week later and stayed all night. They had sex in the morning when her husband went out. The Devil came into her bed, they had sex, and he asked her to renounce Christ and her baptism, which she did.

1649 Agnes Clarkson

The piper's mother from Longniddry stayed the night with her and tried to persuade her to become the Devil's servant. The next morning the Devil burst into the house in the shape of a dog, turned into a black man, and had sex with her. He asked her to renounce God, Christ, and her baptism. She didn't actually do so in words, but felt that she had done so in effect by having sex with the Devil. Her witch name was "Nan Clark" or "Nan Clatt".

1649 Jeannie Hunter

Her sister got her out of bed and took her in behind the gardens where the Devil was waiting, telling the Devil that she'd brought someone who would be pleased to be his servant. The Devil embraced Jeannie and kissed her. Somebody came by, saying "God speed!", and everyone went away.

1649 Marjorie Nisbet

She saw a black man behind Patrick Hog's garden, who asked her to be his servant. The Devil asked her to leave the service of God and Christ, and forsake God and her baptism. She knelt down and threw a stone over her left shoulder. Her witch name was "Mugilie".

1649 Jean Craig

She saw the Devil in her own house in the likeness of a man. She renounced her baptism and became the Devil's servant.

1649 Margaret Paterson

Helen Gylour came to her house and asked her to come out and speak to a gentleman. She went with her to the east of the Three Mile House, where she found the Devil with three others. The Devil embraced her and kissed her. He asked her to become his servant and made her kneel, renounce her baptism and interest in Jesus Christ and become his servant. Her witch name was "Magdaline".

1649 Jeannet Burgane

Helen Gylour asked her to come to Patrick Hog's garden to have a word with a gentleman.

The Devil came to her, kissed her, and asked her to become his servant. She asked for a gift, and he agreed. He made her kneel, renounce her baptism and interest in Jesus Christ, and become his servant. [Jeannet seems to have done this again at a at a third encounter with the Devil.] Her witch name was "Jeanis".

1649 Margaret Bartillman

She met the Devil to the east of Penston with two others. The Devil ordered her to renounce God, Jesus Christ, and her baptism, and to become his servant. She knelt down and cast a clod of earth over her left shoulder. Her witch name was "Margaret Shortill".

1649 Agnes Broun

When she was living in Nisbet, Margaret Dickson came to her in the Devil's company with a pint of ale. She went with the Devil to the top end of Nisbet. He made her kneel and renounce God and her baptism. Her witch name was "Meg".

1649 Margaret Robison

She met the Devil while she was going looking for seed at four or five in the morning. The Devil took her by the shoulder and asked her to kneel and renounce her baptism. The Devil threw a cloak [or possibly a clod] over her shoulder. Her witch name was "Margaret Beals".

1649 Barbara Purdie

She was taken to a meeting by Isobel Murray in Pension. The Devil took her by the shoulder, asked her to forsake Christ and become his servant. He said she would never want. She knelt down, forsook Christ, and promised to serve the Devil.

1649 Helen Fairlie

She conceived a hatred of James Wilson after her mother's death. [Her mother seems to have been executed for witchcraft.] The Devil came to her in her father's house in the likeness of a man, promising to grant her revenge if she would forsake Christ and become his servant. This she did.

1649 John Weir

He was roused from his bed by his wife and another woman, and taken to Richard Broun's garden. His wife asked him to engage with the Devil. He knelt down, renounced God and Jesus Christ, believed in the Devil, and became his servant He asked for and was promised money.

1649 Hellein Watson

Isobel Murray asked her to come to Richard Broun's garden to have a word with someone. She saw a black man who asked her to be his servant She knelt down, renounced her baptism, and became his servant.

1649 Margaret Dickson

Her daughter was recovering from an illness. Margaret asked her to go and do some harvest work and she refused. Margaret said, "Since you are a burden to me, may either God or the Devil part me and you!" The Devil came to Margaret's bed that night and with "plausible conversation" persuaded her to become his servant and to have sex with him. He witch name was "Marrit".

1649 Isobell Murray

She was in bed when "the Spirit" took her out of bed. She walked round the garden, then knelt down, renounced her baptism, and became the Devil's servant. He made her throw a stone over her left shoulder. Her witch name was "Lisbie".

1649 Agnes Hunter

In her garden she met the Devil in the shape of a man in green clothes. He asked her to become his servant and she knelt down and renounced her baptism and Christ.

1649 John Dickson

Margaret Dickson asked him to come and see a man. When he came out she told him it was Lucifer. He renounced Christ and his baptism, and promised to become the Devil's servant. His witch name was "Grote Bage".

1652 John Wilson

There was a Baron Court case over a ball of yarn. On his way home from it he met Agnes

Henderson and her two daughters with the Devil in the hollow of Bilsdean. They had the yarn with them. The Devil told him to keep the piece of yarn he had, and not show it to anyone, and then he would always have enough work and money. At a second meeting in Bilsdean he renounced his baptism, got a new name, and had "carnal copulation" with the Devil. [This was most unusual for a man. However, he also said that the Devil met him sometimes in the shape of a man, and sometimes in the shape of a woman.] His witch name was "Saunders".

1657 Jonet Bruce

Her dittay says she made a covenant with the Devil, renounced her baptism, and received the mark, but gives no details.

1658 Margaret Anderson

She met the Devil in James Moneypenny's house in the Channonry of Ross. Possessed by vile and unclean thoughts, she entered into a pact with the Devil, had sex with him, and became his servant.

1659 Helen Wilsone

She was first taken to meetings by Agnes Thomson, and first met the Devil in her own house three years ago. She renounced her baptism, and the Devil nipped her shoulder.

1659 Helen Simberd

First met the Devil a year and a half previously. She renounced her baptism, received the Devil's mark, and the Devil kissed her.

1659 Marion Lynne

She attended a meeting at the Windmill near Prestonpans. She became the Devil's servant and renounced her baptism. The Devil kissed her and danced with her.

1659 Marion Logan

Shortly after she first saw the Devil, her servant Jean Craig [herself burnt for witchcraft in 1649] said she would get a gentleman to pay Marion's wages. The Devil appeared and told her not to worry about her wages, as he would pay them. He put a coin in her hand as a hiring penny, and had sex with her. He threw dirty water in her face and called her "Tapok" in the name of Beezebub *(sic)*.

1659 Janet Crooks

She was in the garden of Elphinstone [Tower?] with Anne Nesmeth when the Devil appeared. Anne introduced him to Janet. She renounced her baptism and became the Devil's servant.

1659 John Douglas

The Devil appeared in his house at night and asked if he would be piper to his servants. The Devil said he would want for nothing and nipped his neck.

1659 Barbara Cochrane

She first met the Devil at Meg Maitland's "feasts". [Meg had since been burnt as a witch.] She saw the Devil at Meg Maitland's. He kissed her and had sex with her.

1659 Elspeth Fowlar

The Devil appeared in her house and said she would lack none of life's necessities if she would become his servant. She became the Devil's servant, renounced her baptism, received her own name back again, and had sex with the Devil on the floor.

1659 Christian Cranstone

She learned curing from Jock Cranstoun in Humbie, and from Isobel Hepburn, a vagrant woman. Christian specifically denied renouncing her baptism.

1659 Janet Thomson

Janet Douglas, a witch, took her to the Shirrie Well in the Heugh at Tranent. The Devil appeared and Janet Douglas urged him to "devour" Janet Thomson. The Devil had sex with her and marked her. He asked her to renounce her baptism and become his servant. She had "no power" to refuse. They were then joined by ten or eleven masked witches and they danced.

1659 Mareon Guild/Yool

She attended a meeting three months previously at the Brae Green with the Devil and some witches, and engaged in the Devil's service. The next day the Devil appeared to her between the Black Gutter and Olivestob, gripped her left shoulder, and gave her his mark.

1659 Helen Cumine

She had two brief encounters with the Devil. Then Alison Fermor woke her at night and took her to the Gallow Hope. Alison was going so fast that Helen turned back. The Devil shouted, "Wait Janet!" He threw her down, made her renounce her baptism, and called her Janet.

1659 Jonet Man

One day when she was begging Alison Fermor said that there was an easier way to get assistance than that, and took her into her house where the Devil was sitting. The Devil had sex with her and asked her to renounce her baptism. She renounced Christ and all she had received from Christ, and became the Devil's servant. He touched her on the arm, leaving a pain. She promised to be ready to do whatever service he called her to. Then the Devil kissed her and went away. Witch name "Bessie".

1659 Bessie Lacost

Her dittay says she renounced her baptism. No other details given.

1659 Jean Sydserff

The Devil came to her bedside and asked her to be his servant and renounce her baptism. She refused at first, but he insisted and persuaded her. Witch name "Jonett".

1659 Alleissonne Fermer

She met the Devil in her garden. He asked her to be his servant but she refused. He asked her why not, when others were? He promised to give her revenge on anyone who wronged her. She consented to be his servant. He put one hand on her head and the other on her foot, and she said, "Now I renounce my baptism to thee. I renounce my baptism from Christ and give it to thee." Witch name "Jonnet".

1659 Hellin Heriot

The Devil appeared to her eight years previously when she was sitting by the fire in Bessie Lacost's house. He asked her to be his servant, and she agreed and renounced her baptism. Witch name "Bessie".

1659 Marion Angus

She was asked by Bessie Lacost and Alison Fermer to go to the Horn with them. They met several people, the Devil among them. The Devil told her to renounce her baptism, which she did saying, "I take my baptism from Christ and give it to you."

1661 Margaret Allane

Fourteen years previously Dina Kemp took her to Hodindean, where they saw witches dancing. The Devil left the dancers, took her by the hand, kissed her, asked her to be his servant, and said she would never want. She agreed to serve the Devil, and renounced her baptism by putting one hand on the crown of her head, the other on the sole of her foot, and giving him everything in between. Witch name "Jenni".

1661 [The following four women were tried in Musselburgh, but were not resident in the burgh, and therefore are probably not actual "East Lothian" witches.]

Agnes Loch

She met the Devil at the Sheriffhall Burn when she was returning from Dalkeith. She agreed to serve the Devil, and he promised her money. At a second encounter she had sex with the Devil and renounced her baptism.

Margaret Ramage

She met the Devil in Elspet Haliburton's house and renounced her baptism at a second encounter with him.

Jonet Lyle

She met the Devil at the back of Edmiston House. He asked her to be his housekeeper because his wife was dead. At a second encounter with the Devil she renounced her baptism and agreed to be his servant.

Jonet Dale

She met the Devil fourteen years previously,

with two other women. At a second encounter with him she renounced her baptism, and entered the Devil's service. Witch name "Jonet Cleirkeyes".

1661 David Johnston

The Devil appeared to him thirteen years previously at the Borough Muir when he was going to Edinburgh with a load of coal. The Devil said that if he served him he would never want, so he agreed. The Devil marked him at Wolmet Bank with his finger, and made him renounce his baptism. Witch name "William".

1661 Anna Kemp

She was enticed to the Back Burn by Margaret Ker. The Devil welcomed her, took her by the hand, and asked her to renounce her baptism, which she did, laying one hand on her head and the other on her feet, and gave soul and body to him. Witch name "Janet".

1661 Issobel Smyth [1]

Eight years previously Elizabeth Lawson asked her to come to her house to meet a gentleman. The Devil welcomed her, kissed her, and asked her to renounce her baptism and give soul and body to him, which she did, laying one hand on her head and the other on her feet.

1661 Issobel Smyth [2]

Margaret Ker and Anna Kemp asked her to join them, and she would never want. They took her to the Back Burn where she saw the Devil. The Devil asked her to be his servant, to renounce her baptism and Christ, and be his. He told her to lay one hand on her head and the other on her feet, and give herself to him, which she did. He said she would never lack the necessities of life. Witch name "Magie".

1661 Margaret Ker

A dog came into her house and pulled off her bedclothes. She got up and went to Bolton Muir. The Devil appeared as a man and asked her to be his servant. She agreed and the Devil asked her to renounce God and her baptism. She did so, laying one hand on her head and the other on her feet, and gave soul and body to him. Witch name "Elizabeth".

1661 Janet Baigbie

Bessie Todrig came to her window three nights running. She came out the third night and found the Devil at her door with Bessie. The Devil took her hand, laid a hand on her shoulder, and asked her to be his servant. She agreed. He asked her to renounce God and her baptism. She did so laying one hand on her head and the other on her feet, and gave soul and body to him. Witch name "Magie".

1661 Bessie Dawson [Lawson?]

She was gathering barley at Kirklandburn when the Devil appeared. She consented to be the Devil's servant, and renounced God and her baptism. She laid one hand on her head and the other on her feet, and gave herself to him. Witch name "Katherein".

1661 Bessie Todrig

The Devil came to her in her own house, stood at the end of the bed, laid his hand on her shoulder, and said she was his own. The Devil told her to renounce her baptism. She laid one hand on her head and one on her feet, and gave soul and body to him. The Devil told her to be a good servant to him, and to come when she was called.

1662 Agnes Williamson

She quarrelled with her husband about a sack. He went away with some meal, and the Devil came to her, had sex with her, marked her, and gave her a new name. Witch name "Maisie Luckifoot".

1662 James Welsh

He was at home alone and went out to the end of the barn to relieve himself. A girl appeared who wanted to have sex with him, but he refused. Then a man appeared and asked him what he did. James replied that he begged. The man asked him to become his servant, and he would never want He agreed to be the Devil's servant, and the Devil gave him two silver coins which James later found to be two pieces of slate. Witch name "James Scot".

1678 Jennet Burtoun

Two years previously her mistress got her out of bed saying that she must come and speak to a gentleman. She brought Jennet to the hall where she met a grim black man who took her in his arms and kissed her. The next night the Devil came again, had sex with her, and told her she must become his servant and come when he called her. She agreed. A fortnight later her mistress took her to a meeting where the Devil made her renounce her baptism. He made her put one hand on the crown of her head and the other under the sole of her foot, and deliver to the Devil all between her hands. He then gave her a new name. Witch name "Sara's Drudge".

1678 Elspeth Knox

When she was coming from Ormiston to Keith she lay down to sleep. Marion Veitch wakened her and brought the Devil to her. Jennet Burtoun was also there. Marion and Jennet left with the Devil. Eight weeks later she met the Devil at the Waird Haugh. She renounced her baptism, put one hand over the crown of her head and one under the sole of her foot, and gave over to the Devil all between her hands. The Devil gave her a new name. Witch name "Lady Know".

1678 Helen Laing

The Devil appeared to her seven years previously in her garden at Peaston. A year later she met the Devil at the Waird Burn and renounced her baptism. She denied receiving a new name.

1678 Agnes Dalgliesh

She was in Sara Cranstoun's house. A black man appeared, and Sara put her hand in his. At the second encounter Sara wakened her at midnight and took her to her front door where the Devil was waiting. The Devil kissed her and had sex with her, and at the Devil's request she renounced her baptism. The Devil made her put one hand on the crown of her head, and one on the sole of her foot, and give over to him all between her two hands. He gave her a new name. Witch name "Eppie".

1678 Margaret Dodds

The Devil appeared to her three years previously when she was in bed. She renounced her baptism at the Devil's request. He made her put one hand over the crown of her head and the other to her knee [because she was not able to put her hand on the sole of her foot], and give over to the Devil everything between her two hands. She denied getting a new name. According to Marion Campbell, however, Margaret's witch name was "Drodlin".

1678 Margaret Russell

Four and a half years previously she was coming from Seton to Winton. The Devil appeared and kissed Marion, who told Margaret that this was the Devil. At the Devil's request she renounced her baptism, putting one hand on the crown of her head and the other on the sole of her foot. She denied getting another name. However, according to Marion Campbell the Devil called Margaret "His Own Post Horse".

1678 Marion Veitch

The late Barbara Veitch took her to the Rid Ford where the Devil appeared to her. The Devil had sex with her, made her renounce her baptism, and gave her a new name. He made her put one hand on the crown of her head and the other at the sole of her foot, and deliver up to the Devil all between her two hands. Witch name "Broadback".

1678 Marion Campbell

Four and a half years previously she was coming from Seton to Winton with Margaret Russell when the Devil appeared. He kissed Marion and said she was his servant. She asked Margaret who he was, and she said she would find out later. A few days later she met the Devil in Ormiston Wood and he had sex with her. She met the Devil eight days later at Cousland

Dean. They had sex again, and the Devil made her renounce her baptism and become his servant, laying one hand on the crown of her head and the other on the sole of her foot, and giving him everything between her two hands. The Devil gave her a new name. Witch name Tousle[?].

1678 Isobel Elliot

Her mistress Helen Laing kept her home from church one Sunday because a friend was coming. Isobel came in from the well and found Helen Laing and Marion Campbell sitting with the Devil between them. The women went into the parlour, and the Devil came and kissed Isobel and suggested sex. She refused as she was pregnant, and the Devil said he would leave it until after her child had been delivered. She renounced her baptism in Helen Laing's house at the Devil's request. He baptised her on the face with a wave of his hand like a sprinkling of dew, and called her "Jean".

1688 Catherine McTarget

She said she was taught by a Highland woman, Margaret McLain. She told the Dunbar minister that she had renounced her baptism, but no details are given.

In many cases the exact circumstances of the first encounter with the Devil are either not clear or not mentioned. However, where the circumstances are clear, out of the 77 witchcraft cases given above 24 people claimed to have been introduced to the Devil by someone else, 18 claimed to have received a personal visit from the Devil, and 14 seem to have first met the Devil in a chance encounter.

The initiation ritual of putting one hand on the head, the other on the feet, and giving the Devil everything in between, seems to be a late introduction. It is mentioned in 16 cases - 7 in 1678, 8 in 1661, and 1 in 1659. In 1649 three people mention throwing a clod or stone over their shoulder on entering the Devil's service.

Thirty eight people seem to have been given a new name - forty if we count "Fian" and "Hatteraick", but only a couple of cases of mock baptism are recorded. The one thing which is common to almost all cases is the renunciation of baptism.

Modern readers trying to picture the Devil to themselves will probably imagine a naked but rough and hairy creature with human torso and head, but with horns, animal hindquarters and legs, and a tail - perhaps with the tip in the shape of an arrowhead. This unlikely looking apparition may also be coloured red and carry a trident. Seventeenth century East Lothian peasants tended to meet him in more prosaic guise. There follows a list of descriptions of the Devil's appearance given by 62 East Lothian witnesses.

1591 Geillis Duncan

A black man.

1591 Agnes Sampson

In the likeness of a man at the first encounter. Subsequently like a dog, like a pile of hay, like a foal or young horse. At North Berwick like a big black man in a hat and gown.

1591 John Cunningham

Dressed in white at the first encounter. Like a black man at North Berwick. According to *Newes from Scotland* he appeared all in black with a wand in his hand when Cunningham was in prison.

1591 Jannet Stratton

Like a black priest with black clothes. Like a hair mantle. Like a truss of hay.

1591 Barbara Napier

At North Berwick like a great black man, with a black beard like a goat and a high ridged nose like a hawk's beak. He wore a ragged black gown and a skull cap, and had a black book in his hand.

1602 James Reid

Sometimes in the likeness of a man,

sometimes like a horse.

1607 Issobel Grierson
Like a black man. Like a naked infant with an enchanted image in its hand. He appeared to William Burnet in Issobel's image.

1628 William Davidson
A tall black man. A great black dog which changed into a man.

1629 Besse Mak
A fine gentleman. A black dog.

1629 Sara Keith
A handsome boy. In the likeness of a man. Riding a fine spirited horse. In the likeness of a fine gentleman.

1629 John Hog, Margaret Nicolson
According to Alexander Hamilton, like a grim black man; a grim black man with a hat. Robert Quhyte claimed to have seen a big black man in Hog's house.

1630 Alexander Hamilton
A black man dressed all in black with a wand in his hand. Riding a black horse. A man dressed in grey in Saltoun Wood. When Alexander raised the Devil with his stick, he would appear like a crow, cat, or dog.

1635 Anna Tait
In the likeness of a man. A black man. In the likeness of a wind.

1649 Margaret Vaitch
In the likeness of a gentleman.

1649 Manie Haliburton
In the likeness of a man, calling himself a physician.

1649 Agnes Clarkson
A black dusky-coloured dog, then a black man. A black man with a staff in his hand.

1649 Jeannie Hunter
A man with grey-coloured clothes. He left her third meeting in the likeness of a black man.

1649 Marjorie Nisbet
Like a black man. Like a man, but with an unpleasant face, and black hair and black teeth.

1649 Jean Craig
Like a cat. In the likeness of a man.

1649 Margaret Paterson
Like a black man.

1649 Jeannet Burgane
A gentleman dressed in black, rough and hairy.

1649 Margaret Bartillman
He went away in the likeness of a dog.

1649 Agnes Broun
A man wearing black clothes.

1649 Barbara Purdie
In the likeness of a gentleman.

1649 Helen Fairlie
In the likeness of a man.

1649 John Weir
In the likeness of a gentleman.

1649 Helllein Lawsone
A black man. In the likeness of a man.

1649 Margaret Dicksone
A gentleman in green clothes.

1649 Isobell Murray
A great black dog. A rough man all black.

1649 Agnes Hunter
In the likeness of a gentleman, changing to a greyhound. Like a man in green clothes. Like a black man.

1649 MarionRicheson
Like a black shaggy foal. A man in dark-coloured clothes.

1649 John Dickson
Like a man. A black man. He left a meeting at Gladsmuir like a foal.

1652 John Wilson
Sometimes in the shape of a man, sometimes a woman

1659 Helen Wilsone
Like a big black man.

1659 Marion Logan
A gentleman. A black dog.

1659 Janet Crooks
In green clothes.

1659 John Douglas
Dressed in green. In the likeness of a big

black man.

1659 Barbara Cochrane
In green clothes. Dressed in green.

1659 Elspeth Foular
A great black man.

1659 Christian Cranstone
In green clothes. As he was going away he appeared bigger and uglier.

1659 Janet Thomson
A black cow, changing to a man in green clothes.

1659 Marion Guild
A black man. All in black with a side-cloak.

1659 Helline Cummine
Riding a horse which came plunging into the water at the Carfrae Burn.

1659 Jonet Man
A man in grey-coloured clothes with a hat on his head like a gentleman.

1659 Jean Sydserff
A man in grey clothes with a round bonnet on his head.

1659 Hellin Heriot
In grey clothes with a grey cap on his head. [At Ruchlaw he called himself "Simone".]

1659 Margaret Allane
In black clothes and a bonnet on his head. A black man.

1661 Agnes Loch *et al.*
A man dressed in green. In the likeness of a black man.

1661 David Johnston
A man in black clothes. A big grim-looking man in black clothes. In a black cloak with a hat on his head.

1661 Anna Kemp
A greyhound, changing to a man in black clothes.

1661 Issobell Smyth [1]
A gentleman.

1661 Issobell Smyth [2]
A black man in green clothes.

1661 Margaret Ker
First a dog, then a man.

1661 Janet Begbie
A man in black clothes - his hand was cold. In the likeness of a man.

1661 Bessie Dawson
A man in dark clothes.

1661 Bessie Todrig
A man in brown clothes with a different coloured cloak.

1662 James Welsh
A gentleman. Wearing dark clothes. Riding a horse with a gentlewoman behind him.

1662 John Kincaid
Witches had told him that they had an unpleasant smell after the Devil had sex with them, because he was inhabiting a corpse at the time.

1678 Helen Laing
A black man. A black man in black clothes.

1678 Agnes Dalgliesh
A black man in black clothes.

1678 Margaret Russell
A grim black man.

1678 Marion Campbell
A man in green clothes who had no breath.

It will be seen that although the Devil sometimes appeared as a beast, it was never as anything very exciting - not even as a lion or a bear, far less a dragon or the human/animal hybrid of modern myth. He often appears as a gentleman (a sight to inspire respect rather than terror), and often as a black man. Some writers have chosen to think that a "black man" indicates a man with dark hair, as it would in the Gaelic tradition, but here there is really no need to believe that a "black man" is anything other than what the words obviously mean. It is surprising, however, how often the Devil is neither black, nor of gentlemanly appearance, but simply "a man". Neither is his dress outlandish or startling. Green clothing (in eight cases) is as exotic as it gets. We should remember however that green was the colour traditionally associated with the fairies.

For women, the implication of giving themselves body and soul to the Devil was that he would take sexual advantage of his servants, usually around the time of their initiation, and often subsequently if the fancy took him. One would think that if Satan had wished to ensure his servants' future devotion, he would have made this experience rather special for them. However, it does not seem to have been much fun, as the following descriptions show. Throughout, as explained earlier, I have taken "cold nature" to mean a cold penis.

1591 Geillis Duncan
Cold penis.
1591 Agnes Sampson
Cold penis.
1629 Besse Mak
The Devil struggled with her and made her nose bleed.
1629 Sara Keith
The Devil had sex with her a year after her marriage when she was weeding flax in her garden.
1629 Margaret Nicolson
According to Alexander Hamilton the Devil rode Margaret like a beast.
1629 Alexander Hamilton
He describes a meeting in Duns where the Devil had sex with all the women present.
1629 Anna Tait
Had sex with him in her own bed.
1629 Agnes Murray
She saw the Devil lying in bed with Grissel Anderson.
1649 Margaret Vaitch
Cold penis.
1649 Manie Haliburton
Cold penis.
1649 Agnes Clarkson
Cold penis.
1649 Marjorie Nisbet
She thought him cold.
1649 Margaret Paterson
His penis was as cold as a clod of earth.
1649 Jeannet Burgane
Cold penis.
1649 Margaret Bartillman
Penis cold, like a lump of iron.
1649 Barbara Purdie
Penis cold and thin.
1649 Margaret Dickson
When she refused sex on one occasion the Devil flew at her like a wild animal and beat her. At her first encounter with the Devil she was sitting in Agnes Broun's house when the Devil came in and said he didn't know which of them to turn to. Agnes said, "Whichever of us you like." He turned to Margaret who winked at Agnes and told her to leave. However, the Devil pulled her back, joined their hands, and told them to be good servants.
1649 Isobel Murray
When the Devil had sex with her he was "like a rough man, all black".
1649 Agnes Hunter
Cold penis.
1649 Marione Richesone
She had sex with the Devil on the lid of a chest in Agnes Hunter's bedroom.
1659 Helen Wilson
The Devil had sex with her at night when she was sleeping, and he was very heavy on her.
1659 Elspeth Fowlar
She had sex "in the middle of the floor" immediately after renouncing her baptism.
1659 Christian Cranstone
The Devil's face was cold like lead. On another occasion he came to her when she was in bed, laid his face against her brow, and lay on her above the bedclothes.
1659 Jonnett Man
He had a cold penis and a strong smell of

earth.

1659 Marion Angus
His body was hard and cold.
1661 Anna Kemp
Cold penis.
1661 Issobell Smyth [1]
Cold penis.
1661 Issobell Smyth [2]
Cold penis.
1661 Margaret Ker
His penis was cold, which made her suspect something was wrong. His breath was unpleasant when he kissed her.
1662 John Kincaid
He said witches had told him they had an unpleasant smell after the Devil had sex with them, as he inhabited a corpse in order to do so.
1678 Elspeth Knox
He was as heavy as a horse and his penis was cold.
1678 Margaret Dodds
Cold penis and no breath.
1678 Agnes Dalgliesh
His mouth was as cold as lead and he had no breath. He was monstrously heavy on her and exceedingly cold.
1678 Marion Campbell
Cold penis.
1678 Isobel Eliot
She refused sex at first as she was pregnant. The Devil said he'd wait until after the birth of the child. He had the weight of four men and was very cold.

It was part of the academic perception of witchcraft that the Devil would mark his servants in some way. These witchmarks were supposed to be devoid of feeling and would not bleed if punctured. In England and elsewhere marks in the form of growths or tags of skin were often thought to be teats with which the witch would suckle familiar spirits in the form of imps or animals. This was almost never the case in Scotland and I came across no example of this belief in East Lothian. Interrogators did have East Lothian suspects searched systematically for witchmarks however, and almost always found them. Several people seem to have worked as professional prickers, including the infamous John Kincaid from Tranent. One might assume that pricking would cease after Kincaid was banned from practising in 1662. Certainly the upper echelons of society and the legal establishment seem to have lost faith in it, but there is evidence that suspects in East Lothian were still being pricked as late as 1688.

1591 Agnes Sampson
Marked on the right knee, according to her dittay. She thought at first she had been injured by one of her children lying in bed with her. The wound didn't heal for half a year. *Newes from Scotland* says she was marked in her "privities", but "Newes" is the 16th century equivalent of a tabloid scandal sheet.
1591 Geillis Duncan
Marked on her throat, according to *Newes from Scotland*.
1591 John Cunningham
The Devil marked him with a rod. No other details.
1629 Sara Keith
Marked on her right arm. The devil gripped her right arm and it was very painful when he marked her.
1629 Isobell Young
Marked under her right breast Issobell claimed this was the scar from a healed ulcer.
1632 James Balfore
It came to the attention of the Privy Council that James Balfore in Corsehouse near Tranent had been pricking witches. He was summoned for questioning and said that the first time he did this was when the Tranent minister ordered him to search a gardener's wife in Tranent. He found a mark under her arm, and she confirmed

that it was a witchmark. Since then he had exposed several people publicly in the church and in the tollbooth. His knowledge was found to be "only conjectural" and he was forbidden to practise again.

1635 Anna Tait
Marked on the cheek. She was nipped on the cheek by the Devil in the likeness of a wind.

1649 Manie Haliburton
Marked on the left side of the neck above the left shoulder. She voluntarily requested to be pricked by Kincaid. When he pricked her there was no feeling and no blood.

1649 Agnes Clarkson
Marked on the back of the left arm above the elbow.

1649 Marjorie Nisbet
Marked on the back of the left shoulder. The Devil nipped her.

1649 Jean Craig
Marked, according to her dittay - no details.

1649 John Weir
Nipped on the [illegible] bone. This nip was very painful for a long time afterwards.

1649 Margaret Dicksone
Marked by a nip under the right arm.

1649 Isobell Murray
The Devil in the shape of a black dog nipped her shoulder. This nip was very painful.

1649 Agnes Hunter
Marked when the Devil laid his hand on her shoulder.

1649 John Dickson
Marked when the Devil laid his hand on his left shoulder.

1657 Jonet Bruce
Pricked by Kincaid. She had four marks but no details are given. A rough diagram in the records shows the length of the pin Kincaid used to prick her.

1659 Helen Wilson
Marked when the Devil nipped her shoulder.

1659 Helen Simberd
Marked on her shoulder, over her heart, and a little above her left armpit.

1659 Janet Crooks
The records say she "admits she has the marks", but no details given.

1659 John Douglas
Marked on the roof of his mouth, and on the outside of his left leg - in spite of the fact that he said the Devil nipped his neck.

1659 Barbara Cochrane
She said she would be happy to admit she was the Devil's servant if any mark was found on her apart from "the normal marks women have". She was pricked by Kincaid and a mark was found on the back of her neck towards the left shoulder. Immediately she cried out in the magistrate's presence, "Foul thief, you have deceived me now! You have deceived me!" She then admitted that she was a witch.

1659 Christian Cranstone
Marked under the right armpit and on her leg. Kincaid put "a great long pin" into the mark under her armpit. Both marks were insensible to pain and there was no blood.

1659 Janet Thomson
Marked "on each side of her ears". Pricked by Kincaid. She said that after having sex with her the Devil put his hands round her neck. She supposed that was how she got the marks, but wasn't aware she had them. The minister said it was thought strange that the marks were in such sensitive places. She was acquitted of witchcraft.

1659 Mareon Guild
She was pricked by Kincaid. A mark was found beneath her left armpit with "a dug or teat of insensible flesh". The Devil gave her his mark by gripping her left shoulder. She was acquitted of witchcraft.

1659 Jonnett Mann
Marked on her right arm above the elbow. The Devil touched her right hand and arm,

which left a pain in her arm above the elbow.

1659 Alleissonne Fermer

Marked on the right shoulder. The Devil put his hand on her right shoulder, leaving it very painful. The pain lasted until the Devil came back and put his hand on it, and the pain disappeared.

1661 Margaret Allane

Marked on the shoulder and thigh.

1661 Agnes Loch

Marked on the shoulder and upper thigh.

1661 Margaret Ramage

Marked on the shoulder.

1661 David Johnston

The Devil marked him on the leg with his finger at Wolmet Bank.

1661 Issobell Smyth

The Devil put his hand on her neck at the Back Burn.

1662 Agnes Williamson

Marked on the shoulder. After she had quarreled with her husband the Devil came to her bed, had sex with her, marked her, and gave her a new name. Acquitted of witchcraft.

1662 James Welsh

Had several marks. He was marked between his thighs and his body, and was sore for forty eight hours.

1662 John Kincaid

Kincaid was questioned, and the records of this are among the Justiciary Court Processes. He said he had acquired his knowledge only by sight and by doing what witches told him to do. He seems to have used several ritualistic practices. He placed witches an ell from the wall and would not let them cross the threshold. Witches had told him to take them into the house backwards, and to keep them away from the wall and from water. He searched hands and arms first. He could tell witches by their unpleasant smell. Witches had told him the Devil left this smell on them after sex because he inhabited a corpse.

James Welsh claimed to have seen the Devil sitting with Kincaid at a meeting at Tranent Moor and it may be that official interest in Kincaid was sparked off as much by a suspicion that his "skills" were diabolic in origin, as by outrage at the cruelty of his procedures. However, the Records of the Privy Council for 31st March 1662 state, "Information has been received that great abuses have been committed by John Kincaid who takes upon himself the pricking and investigating of witches, through which in all probability many innocent people have suffered." Kincaid was imprisoned in the tollbooth of Edinburgh and only released after promising never to practise his profession again.

1677 Lissie Mudie

Fountainhall mentions Lissie Mudie in Haddington who denounced five women and a man. He writes, "I witnessed the examining and pricking of the man's body. He was pricked in two separate places - at his ribs and on his shoulder. He seemed to feel pain but no blood flowed. The pins were as long as your finger, and one of them was pushed in up to the head. The marks were of a bluish colour, very small, and did not protrude above the skin." Fountainhall discusses witchmarks in a footnote thus, "The pricker said there were three kinds of marks; the 'horn mark' which is very hard, the 'breast mark' which is small, and the 'feeling mark' which is sensible to pain...

... I was left very unsure and dissatisfied with this method of examination, as it seemed most unreliable, and the fellow could give me no account of tire principles governing his art, but seemed to be a drunken foolish rogue." [Fountainhall 1848: p144]. This drunken foolish rogue is quite likely to have been David Cowan, another Tranent man, on whom Kincaid's mantle seems to have fallen.

1678 John Rutherford, David Cowan

The baron baillie in Prestonpans, John

Rutherford, arrested and imprisoned Katherine Liddel there and had her pricked "to the great effusion of her blood". Her wounds seem to have become infected, since her complaint to the Privy Council claims that the skin was raised, her body highly swollen, and that her life was in danger. Rutherford was forbidden by the Privy Council to arrest anyone for witchcraft without a Privy Council warrant [RPC 13th Sept 1678], and David Cowan, who had done the actual pricking, was imprisoned. On 27th February 1679, Cowan, who seems to have been in prison since the previous September, pledged himself not to prick without a Privy Council warrant. Presumably he would then be released. In the same year, 1679, an attempt was made to prosecute Rutherford and Cowan for arresting Elspeth Chouslie in Prestonpans in June or July 1677. It was claimed Rutherford "brought a pricker in and stripped off her clothes in a most disrespectful and shameful manner." The eventual outcome of this case is not quite clear.

Although no mention is made in the records of the Peaston/Keith witches being pricked, if Lizzie Moodie and Elspeth Chouslie were pricked in 1677, and Katherine Liddel in 1678, it would not be surprising if the suspects from Keith and Peaston were treated similarly.

1688 Catherine McTarget

There is no mention of any official pricking, but while Catherine was standing in a crowd on Dunbar shore, a dumb man apparently stuck a pin into her shoulder, which she did not feel, and the significance was not lost on the bystanders.

What are we to make of the business of witchmarks? As previously observed, the idea that Satan would mark his servants originates in an academic perception of witchcraft, and before the North Berwick affair it seems unlikely that the general public believed their "wise wives" were so marked. However, once it became established in the minds of ministers, baron baillies, and their assistants that witchmarks were sure sign of guilt, such marks would be duly found and suspicions confirmed. Few people, especially after middle age, have bodies free from growths, tags, moles, scars, or other blemishes. When the marks were pricked they were supposed to be devoid of feeling and they were not supposed to bleed. One can only speculate about the methods of the prickers, but just as a modern-day injection from a skillful nurse or doctor does not usually result in shrieks of pain and fountains of blood, it would not seem beyond the bounds of possibility that a well-practised operator like Kincaid could slip a pin in almost unnoticed.

Then again, if we discount the notion that his servants were personally marked by the Devil himself, that does not mean that witches [or some witches] might not have been marked by someone, nor that such a mark might not have been the badge of some sort of association, or the sign of a chosen trade or lifestyle. For although some suspects seem to be surprised when their marks were discovered, and others give suspiciously imaginative accounts of how they were marked, many others give brief prosaic statements that they were "nipped" or "gripped".

The other aspect which was part and parcel of the "satanic" view of witchcraft, was that witches should meet regularly in groups with their master the Devil. In what we might call the "classical diabolism" of European witchcraft, witches were supposed to be organised into "covens" which would meet regularly to worship Satan. These meetings might also include dancing, feasting, and revelry, with blasphemous rituals, sacrifices, cannibalism, orgiastic or perverted sex, and [as Burns said] "mair o' horrible and awfu'". Almost all East Lothian witches admitted attending meetings with other witches, usually with the Devil present. The word "coven" is almost never used, and the numbers vary from two or three to over a hundred. It would be superfluous to provide a list of all the meetings attended by all East Lothian's witches. However, I found 74 individuals who either confessed to attending meetings, or were claimed by others to have done so. In passing, it is perhaps worth saying that it is sometimes difficult to distinguish in the records between a "meeting" with the Devil which was a mere encounter, and a "meeting" in the modern sense where several people were present. In the majority of cases there would appear to have been under ten people present, although numbers are often indeterminate, and expressed in terms of "divers other witches", "other notorious witches", "many people", and similar vague phrases. Large numbers were not usual. However, in the case of North Berwick in 1591 we find "over a hundred" [Agnes Sampson], "around sixty" [Geillis Duncan], and "seven score" [Barbara Napier]. At the Gallow Hope, Stenton, in 1659 we find "about forty" [Helline Cumine], At the Cow Park Burn and Mains Park Burn in the Keith/Peaston area in 1678 there were "about a hundred at both" [Agnes Dalgleish]. We might well be suspicious of these. None of the others in the Keith/Peaston cases mentioned gatherings of a hundred. Helen Cumming of Stenton was acquitted, and the records hint that she was insane. As for the North Berwick affair, it consisted largely of show trials with Government setting the agenda, and it would be rash to accept much of the evidence at face value.

The vast majority of meetings took place in secluded or out-of-the-way places - in woods, on moors, beside burns. The famous North Berwick case was exceptional in that the meeting took place in a church, but there seem to have been occasional meetings in yards and gardens, and even houses; for example: -

1629 The Carfraes
William Dennam's house in Haddington.

1629 John Hog and Margaret Nicolson
John Hog's house at Markle.
1649 Agnes Clarkson
On the green at Dirleton.
1649 The penston Witches
Various houses and gardens in Penston and Longniddry.
1659 The Stenton Witches
The courtyard at Ruchlaw.
1661 Issobell Smyth
Elizabeth Lawson's house. The great yard at Blance.
1661 James Welsh
A house in the West Port of Edinburgh.
1678 Marion Veitch
She said she and her associates "met also in houses for malifice".

Out of the 74 cases where meetings of some kind are mentioned, 33 specifically mention dancing. In most cases no detail is given, but three mention dancing for "about an hour". Four cases specifically mention dancing in a ring: -

1649 MarionRicheson
"The Devil had three others dancing round him in Alexander Maline's garden".
1659 Jonett Mann
"The Devil and Bessie Lacost led the ring."
1659 Alleissonne Fermer
"They were dancing in a ring at the Gallowhope when she fell and hurt her knee."
1659 Hellin Heriot
"At the Gallowhope they took hands and danced in a ring round the Broad Stone."

If there was dancing, we would expect music to dance to. However, this is not often mentioned. *Newes from Scotland* claims that Geillis Duncan played the "trump" at North Berwick. Other musical accompaniments mentioned are: -

1649 Hellen Fairlie

The Devil "played" at Butterdean and Three Mile House. [She does not mention what he played.]

1659 Helen Wilson

At the Windmill she heard a noise like the sound of "ane trump".

1659 John Douglas

He played his pipes at the Heuch and the Brae Green.

1659 Marion Guild

At the Brae Green Janet Watson played to them on "two stones".

1659 Jonnet Mann

At the Gallow Hope the Devil whistled.

1661 David Johnston

There was piping at the Grain Law.

1661 Issobell Smyth

There was a piper at the Back Burn.

1661 James Welsh

At all the meetings Patrick Cathie played his pipes.

1678 Margaret Dodds

There was a piper at Murraisburn.

In the Tranent/Prestonpans cases of 1659 it was mentioned that at the Heuch and the Brae Green where John Douglas played his pipes, they danced to the tune "Hulie, the bed will fall". According to Marion Logan, at the meeting at the windmill at Preston Links they danced a spring called "Kilt thy coat Maggie, and go thy ways with me".

Singing at meetings is mentioned only four times: -

1649 Marjorie Nisbet

Margaret Patterson said Marjorie Nisbet sang at the Three Mile House.

1649 John Weir

It was claimed that at one meeting his wife Margaret Dickson was "singing to you and holding you by the hand".

1649 Margaret Dickson

John Dickson also said that Margaret sang at a meeting.

1659 Helen Heriot

Helen said that they sang to each other as they danced at the Gallow Hope, and she also sang at Sandie's Hill.

The Devil was normally present at meetings. His physical appearance has already been investigated. Most witches had sex with the Devil at one of their early encounters with him. However, this does not often seem to have been at meetings where others were present. As previously mentioned, it is often difficult to distinguish in the records between a meeting and a one-to-one encounter, but occasionally some witches do seem to have had sex with the Devil at meetings in the presence of others - Alison Fermer and Marion Angus at the Gallow Hope in 1659 for instance. At Butterdean in 1649 the Devil had sex with Marion Fairlie "and all the rest", and Alexander Hamilton claimed in 1630 that the Devil had sex with all the women present at a meeting in Duns. Hamilton also claimed that at the same meeting a certain John Smith also had sex with all the women, and "usit them all behind and raid them like beastes". However, such debauchery seems to have been exceptionally rare. John Weir in 1649 said that the Devil kissed and embraced all the women but only shook him by the hand. John Wilson from Dunglass admitted in 1652 to "carnal copulation" with the Devil, but also said that the Devil appeared to him sometimes as a man and sometimes as a woman. Out of all the East Lothian cases Wilson is the only man mentioned as having sex with the Devil. It may be significant that while trawling the records for witchcraft cases I came across numerous cases of bestiality, but virtually no cases of homosexuality. In the context of 17th century East Lothian, "gay sex" was presumably too far beyond the pale even for Satan!

Thus, although sex with the Devil was almost

obligatory for witches, it seems to have usually taken place in private, and orgiastic or perverted sex is almost unheard of.

There are occasional mentions of witches asking the Devil for power at meetings, but a surprisingly small number. According to Alexander Hamilton in 1630, the Carfraes consulted with the Devil on how to lay on and take off sickness, and how to ruin people and take their lives. Also according to Hamilton, Margaret Nicolson asked for power to harm James Sandie, the miller at Linton Brig. Another of Hamilton's claims was that those who met the Devil at Duns asked leave to harm those that they had grudges against. In 1652 John Wilson said that at one meeting with the Devil Margaret Henrie asked the Devil for revenge on her master, and John himself asked for help to get money that was owed to him. Alison Fermer claimed in 1659 that Jonet Wood asked the Devil for revenge on James Crumbie. Jonet herself admitted asking the Devil for revenge on Crumbie for owing her money and for not marrying her. Helen Heriot, one of the same group of Stenton witches, asked for revenge on a English army supplier who had been quartered in her house.

Occasionally the Devil would ask what his servants had done since the last meeting. When Agnes Sampson and her associates met the Devil at a bridge near Foulstruther, he asked them if they had been good servants. Margaret Bartillman [1649] said the Devil asked her what service she had done. When she replied, "None," he told her she was a bad servant. He told those present that they should use every opportunity to draw others to his service. Helen Lawson [1649] said the Devil asked her how she was, and what she'd done since the last meeting. John Dickson [1649] said that at the third meeting he attended, the Devil asked what service they had done. James Welsh [1661] mentioned that David Shanks reported to Agnes Williamson that he had made two parcels and laid them at Patrick Baillie's door.

It would seem then that although it is popularly supposed that witches gathered to report on evil deeds performed and to ask their master for power to work mischief, and although these are important parts of the academic view of classical European witchcraft, they are mentioned in only a tiny number of East Lothian cases. That is not to say that such things did not occur more often, but if they did, why were they not deemed important enough to mention?

One of the most important activities of the "coven", according to academic European opinion, was the worship of their master the Devil, accompanied by blasphemous rites and perversions of the Mass. Part of the worship of the Devil consisted in kissing his backside. However, the worship of the Devil as some sort of deity is almost completely absent from the East Lothian cases. Certainly, the Devil appeared in the pulpit at North Berwick Church, and according to some accounts was dressed like a minister and preached a sermon, but this is hardly the same as being worshipped. His servants were then reported to have kissed his "erse", but this is the only time in the whole annals of East Lothian witchcraft that this practice is mentioned. In fact mention of any sort of ritual behaviour at meetings is extremely rare. The North Berwick trials mention the baptising and sacrificing of cats, and the passing of a wax image from hand to hand at Acheson's Haven. Beigis Tod's trial [1608] mentions baptising a cat and sacrificing it to the Devil. John Douglas, the Tranent piper [1659] said that the Devil kissed them all and said, "Goodnight my servants all," when he left. Elspeth Fowlar [1659] from the same Tranent group, mentioned that the Devil kissed each of them. Jonnet Mann [1659] from Stenton said that when the Devil took his leave, he said they were all his good and faithful servants, and they all answered, "My Lord, I am thy servant". Isobel Smyth [1661] describes herself and her company going from the Cadger Well towards Saltoun with lighted candles. James Welsh [1661] describes what could have been some sort of ritual at Samuelston Haugh where two people struck him with whip handles as the rest passed by. Finally, Issobell Elliot [1678] said that at meetings at Crichton, Midlothian, the Devil "gave them a kind of sacrament, preached to them, and blasphemed God." The Devil is often portrayed as appearing rather superior to his servants. Sara Keith [1629] describes him as riding a fine spirited horse, and James Welsh [1661] mentions the Devil appearing at one meeting on horseback with a gentlewoman behind him. And then, of course, the Devil is frequently described as appearing in the likeness of a gentleman.

Thus, religious ritual appears not to have been a normal feature of witchcraft meetings in East Lothian. It certainly appears to an extent at North Berwick and Acheson's Haven, but I have laboured the point before that the legal proceedings dealing with the North Berwick and Acheson's Haven events consisted of show trials with Government setting the agenda, and the evidence should be considered as highly suspect to say the least. As regards Issobell Elliot, none of the other Keith/Peaston suspects mention blasphemous eucharists, although such ongoings were a possibility, given that Gideon Penman, the disgraced minister of Crichton was denounced for his involvement with local witches. And as for the Devil appearing as a gentleman, this is hardly the same as appearing as a god!

Witch meetings sometimes involved eating and drinking. Alexander Hamilton [1630] talks of returning to the Hogs' house after meeting the Devil, and drinking and making merry till dawn. Agnes Broun [1649] said that Meg Dickson came with the Devil and a pint of ale. Helen Fairlie [1649] said that her group of witches had a "feast" in Thomas Dickson's house. According to Agnes Hunter, one of the same group, they had food and a quart of wine at Longniddry. John Wilson [1652] said that he and his companions drank, and ate a goose at the "Rutch House". Jean Sydserff [1659], one of the Stenton witches, told how Alison Fermer got ale for them at "Mr Robert's and Ruchlaw". Alison agreed that she had fetched ale at Robert Davidson's, and helped to drink wine at Ruchlaw. Helen Heriot confirmed that Alison got wine for them at Ruchlaw, and added that they had eaten some beef before they danced at the Gallow Hope. Jonet Wood also mentioned the wine from Ruchlaw, and said they finished off a whole barrel of Robert Davidson's ale. Jeannet Burgane [1649] was accused of being at a meeting near the Three Mile House at Gladsmuir where Marjorie Nisbet was sent to the Three Mile House for a quart of ale. The quart of ale is also mentioned in Marjorie's accusation. It will be seen that these occasional bouts of pleasant indulgence are a far cry from the drinking of blood, cannibalism, and the ingestion of foul concoctions which featured in the academic view of European witchcraft.

Another claim of the academic experts of early modern times was that witches would travel to their meetings by miraculous means. There is scant mention of this in my 74 major witchcraft cases. "Newes from Scotland" claimed that the North Berwick witches sailed in sieves and riddles, and this accusation actually appeared in Effie MacCalyean's dittay. John Cunningham [Fian] was accused of being carried through the air to North Berwick church. Interestingly, Agnes Sampson went there much more prosaically - on horseback, escorted by her son in law. Although the Devil himself sometimes "vanished away" from meetings, and occasionally arrived or departed in the shape of an animal, the only other mention of miraculous travel for his servants after the North Berwick affair was in the Keith/Peaston trials of 1678. Marion Campbell claimed that when she and the others went to meetings they sometimes went in their own shape, and sometimes as crows or magpies. Her associate Isobel Elliot declared that she and Marion Veatch attended a meeting where a child was poisoned, in the shape of bumble bees. Isobel further claimed to have gone to Loanhead in the shape of a crow while her body sat in Pencaitland Kirk. Obviously, then, between 1591 and 1678, miraculous travel to meetings was not a feature of the East Lothian witchcraft scene.

To recapitulate on East Lothian witchcraft meetings: We cannot help being struck by the extreme ordinariness of these get-togethers. Witches normally met in small groups of around ten or a dozen and often danced, sometimes to a piper. Occasionally there would be some eating and drinking. New recruits were sometimes initiated at meetings by formally renouncing Christianity, promising to serve the Devil, and on some occasions laying a hand on the head, a hand on the feet, and giving the Devil everything in between. More often than not, however, initiation seems to have occurred in private. The meetings were presided over by "the Devil", who was often a black man, sometimes a gentleman, but never, except in the later North Berwick trials, anything resembling a monster. He was sometimes heavy, sometimes hairy, and almost always endowed with a cold penis. It was usual for him to have sexual intercourse with new recruits, and he also favoured them with his attentions on subsequent occasions if it took his fancy. This was usually in private, or if it happened at meetings there is no indication that it was done before an audience [apart from some statements by the rather imaginative and unreliable Alexander Hamilton], and it may be assumed that the lucky lady concerned was usually discreetly taken aside. Although it is clear that the Devil and the witches were in a master-servant relationship, it is also quite clear that any sort of ritual or worship at meetings, apart from initiation, was virtually unknown. Not only that, but the Devil, apart from being sometimes black, sometimes hairy, and the owner of chilly genitalia, is often a singularly unimpressive figure. Indeed, when a meeting of the Pension witches in 1649 was disturbed by someone coming past, they all - including the Devil - scattered. This does not sound much like His Satanic Majesty. Nor is there any mention of cloven hooves, horns, tails, or any of the attributes of our modern image of the Devil. Our East Lothian Devil is a far cry from Lucifer, Son of the Morning.

There are two intertwined strands in East Lothian witchcraft. The one is the diabolic strand, deriving from an elite academic view of witchcraft activity, and as I have laboured to show above, it is almost always a very low-key diabolism indeed. The other strand is of native folk magic, which we can now proceed to examine more closely.

It is often supposed that the wise wife and the witch derived much of their skill from a knowledge of herbal medicine. This may well be true, but there is little evidence of it from the records. After trawling through every mention of witchcraft in East Lothian from all the records from kirk session minutes to Justiciary Court papers I have only managed to come up with the following rather sparse list of the use of herbs by witchcraft suspects.

1591 Agnes Sampson
She healed the lady of Kilbaberton with iris

steeped in wine and advised John Duncan's wife to take an egg steeped in vinegar for her disease.

1591 Geillis Duncan

A potion of flowers and herbs is mentioned, possibly to induce an abortion. Geillis was sent on one occasion to gather a broad-leaved grass.

1597 Jonet Stiell

She washed a patient with water from the Well of Saint Ann, mixed with watercress.

1612 Christian Grinton

Christian gave Catherine Gray a piece of rowan to keep in her purse and another to keep in her chest.

1628 William Davidson

He used a drink made from foxglove leaves to cure a man blasted with an evil spirit. When Agnes Sinclair was bewitched he cured her immediately with a salve made from foxglove leaves and fresh butter.

1629 Alexander Fortune [from Duns]

When Issobell Young had a greatly swollen belly he gave her a potion to drink made from oil, vinegar, onions, and mallows, and applied a waterproof cloth with wax and resin to her belly. When Issobell had an ulcer under one of her breasts he applied an ointment three times to the wound, made from "kemp leaves, bawort roots, curldodies, waybraid leaves". The wound remained unhealed. Kemps are the flower spikes of ribwort plantain, curldodies are ribwort plantain, and waybraid is plantain. I have been unable to find the meaning of bawort.

1629 Alexander Fairbairn [from Duns]

He cured Issobell Young's ulcer by making her swallow a handful of small stones and drinking two quarts of a drink made with bark.

1630 Alexander Hamilton

The Devil advised Alexander to cure Thomas Home by rubbing him with a woolen cloth dipped in a mixture of oil of animal fat, camomile oil, and heart fat.

1634 Marion Laing

Someone had advised Marion that foxglove leaves would either "end or mend" her sick child. She got Jeremie Fergison to gather foxglove leaves for her. The child died. [KS minutes].

1641 Agnes Broun

She told Margaret Wert to cut a piece of rowan tree "between the two Beltanes" and put it above the lintel to protect her child from witches and witchcraft. [KS minutes].

1649 Jean Craig

When her sister in law's child fell ill Jean promised to get south-running water and foxglove leaves for it but didn't do so.

1659 Christian Cranstone

She used to go to Humbie Wood to collect foxglove leaves, saying, "These I seek for God's sake." When she brought them back to the patient she would say, "This I give for God's sake, and may God give a blessing to it."

1678 Adam Gillies, Catherine Watson

When Adam feared his cow was bewitched Thomas Bookless advised him to tie grains of wheat with the same number of grains of salt to the cow's horn, and also said that rowan tree was good to keep on man and beast.

1688 Catherine McTarget

She cured Jean Johnston with broth made from five onions and sheep's entrails.

1688 John Watson

He gave Agnes Bartleman herbs to destroy the child she had conceived. He got them from the gardener of Wallyford. [KS minutes].

Of course the wheat and rowan mentioned above are being used as charms rather than medicine. Foxglove leaves seem to have been the wise wife's catch-all cure. Perhaps the two Alexanders from Duns had some genuine knowledge of the curative properties of wild plants, and possibly Agnes Sampson, but the others show few signs of having any such skill.

Whatever the means used, the records show that people regularly resorted to wise wives and witches for curing disease.

1591 Geillis Duncan
According to *Newes from Scotland* her skill in curing was one of the factors leading to her arrest.

1591 Agnes Sampson
Failed to cure John Thomson in Dirleton, who remained crippled. Caused John Peiry in Preston to recover when very ill. Brought Bessie Aikinhead in Haddington back to health.
Healed John Ker in Alexander Fairlie's house in Longniddry when he was expected to die. Healed John Duncan in Musselburgh.
Cured the Gudewife of Cameron who was walking with crutches. Healed the son of the laird of Reidhallis when the surgeons had given up on him. Cured Robert Dickson in Bolton who was wearing a bewitched doublet. Cured the wife of the sheriff of Haddington who was bewitched. Cured Alison Ker who had been bewitched for three years. Cured Robert Bailye's son in the Pans, who was seriously ill. Healed Lady Kilbabertoun when she was seriously ill. Cured Robert Kerse in Dalkeith who was bewitched.

1591 Euphane MacCalyean
Got Agnes Sampson to ease her labour pains.

1598 Jonet Steill
When she was seriously ill thirteen years ago with swollen hands and feet, she was washed in south-running water and healed by a poor man who said he used to go about with the Jews. [Presb. mins.]

1602 James Reid
Cured Sara Borthwick with south-running water, and salt and wheat scattered round her bed.
Tied three silk laces round John Crystie's waist to cure "swelling".

1608 Beigis Tod
Came to Alexander Fairlie with her two sons, and gave him "certain instructions" on how to treat himself.

1612 Christian Grinton
When it was suspected that Janet Lytster had bewitched Patrick Neilson's wife, Christian gave Patrick two fish and two for his wife. Patrick's wife stopped sweating after that and recovered her health.

1628 William Davidson
He told Andro Wilkiesone that he had been blasted by an evil spirit. He gave him a drink made from foxglove leaves and laid the sickness on Andro's nephew.
Cured Agnes Stanehouse with south-running water.
Cured John Hall with salted hake and raw flesh.
Cured James Halyday of madness with south-running water.

1629 Alexander Sinclair
Isobel Turnbul collapsed after offering him inferior bread. Alexander laid the sickness on a greyhound which fell down dead.

1629 Besse Mak
Besse was suspected of bewitching Janet Broun. She gave Janet a piece of meat. Janet roasted and ate it, and was cured.

1629 Sara Keith
She cured Agnes Litster with south-running water when she was expected to die. Cured the Stenhouse boys of blindness.

1629 Issobell Young
When Issobell's husband collapsed in the fields, she and Christian Grinton took the sickness off him, and laid it at the threshold of the barn. Alexander Fortoune of Duns cured her of a swollen belly with a potion and plaster. He treated an ulcer under one of her breasts with ointment but failed to heal it.

1630 Alexander Hamilton
When Thomas Home in Clerkington was bewitched, Hamilton rubbed him with a woolen cloth dipped in a mixture of oils and fat.

1631 Christiane Paterson

She laid madness on her servant Katherine Allan, then cured her.

1642 Isobel Wood

John Howden lost the power of his arms and believed Isobel had bewitched him. He sought his health from her and gradually recovered afterwards. Isobel said to him, "Goodman, if ever I did you any harm more than an unborn child could do, may the Lord make me like a crow to fly about the world, and may the same happen to you if it be otherwise." [Presb. mins.]

1643 Margaret Dickson

James Mill said Margaret offered to cure him by putting him through a hank of green yarn. Margaret denied this, and said she had told him to wind it round the affected part.

She advised John Sharp on the ritual that would cure his daughter if evil spirits had caused her illness.

She washed Isobel Johnston's child in south-running water twice. Isobel wouldn't let her do it a third time. She advised Isobel that the child was a changeling. [Presb. mins.]

1646 George Beir

He professed skill in curing "cruells" - "the king's seekness" [scrofula]. He had cured several people in Lothian and the Borders. He also had cured himself of the disease. [Presb. mins.]

1649 Margaret Dickson

Issobel Johnston asked Margaret to fetch south-running water to wash her sick child as others had advised. The Devil advised Margaret to do so but to let the mother wash the child herself. [This is presumably the 1643 case being dragged up again during the witchcraft panic of 1649.]

1649 Marion Richeson

When her child was ill she went to Agnes Hunter who said the child was bewitched. Agnes told her to go to a well below the Boggs before sunrise, and bring back a pint of water with which Agnes would wash the child.

1657 Jonet Bruce

She put a waterproof cloth on Alexander Johnston's child and rubbed him with oil when he was paralysed below the loins. He recovered in five days.

She smeared William Bryson with oils.

She agreed to cure John Phinnie's wife for £14, then asked for the gift of a child.

She claimed to a woman in Oxton that she could cure any disease.

She told Catherine Niblo that if she would become her servant for seven years, she would make her as expert in curing as herself.

Jonet was obviously in the habit of travelling the countryside and charging for her services.

1659 Christian Cranston

She learned how to cure from Jock Cranston in Humbie Wood, and from a vagrant woman called Isobel Hepburn.

She cured Patrick Cowan's son with south-running water. She seems to have been in the habit of using south-running water and foxglove leaves.

We see from this that much faith seems to have been placed in south-running water and foxglove leaves. Rubbing with oil also figures, as do enchanted threads. However, there is little here that could have had a directly beneficial medicinal effect, and we would appear to be in the realms of "faith healing".

Diagnosis sometimes also appears as part of the healer's art.

1591 Agnes Sampson

William Blackie sent his son's shirt to her. She said his sickness was caused by an elf-shot.

She said that the wife of the shepherd at Bearford would never be well living on the ground where she was, and that she should be transferred off that ground.

She said that that Isobel Hamilton was bewitched and that this had been done six or seven years previously.

According to the English ambassador, Agnes "knew when someone was bewitched by the smell of their linen clothes, or the sweat in them, and by looking at them".

When Agnes repeated her prayer, if it stopped once that meant the patient was bewitched. If the prayer stopped twice it meant the patient would die.

1657 Jonet Bruce

Jonet said that a sow of Margaret Stratheam's had had a wrong done to it which was meant for another, and that it would die.

1703 Marion Lillie

During the investigations into Marion Lillie, it was related that John Home in the Barns pricked William Colme's sick ewe with a penknife from front to back. He said it had lost the power of its hindquarters and was a hopeless case. [KS mins.]

There was a great demand for detectors of lost and stolen goods. This, although condemned by the Church, was viewed as charming rather than witchcraft, and treated much more leniently. Dumb persons seem to have been credited with special skills in this field.

1598 Jonet Steil

When inquiries were being made into Hary Broun's wife consulting Jonet about Mary's illness it was revealed that they had also consulted a dumb boy about missing articles. He was reputed to be a diviner and a soothsayer, and was supposedly possessed by an evil spirit.

1629 Alexander Sinclair

He knew Bessie Littil had a 5 merk piece in a cloth in her chest. He knew John Heres had gold that his wife didn't know about.

1629 Issobell Young

She knew that Janet Hoge had churned nine pounds of butter.

1629 John Hog, Margaret Nicolson

James Sandie's horses went mad. One of them came to Markle. It was suspected that this demonstrated that Hog was the perpetrator of the malefice.

1632 James Balfore

Balfore had been operating as a witch-pricker. He said that the first time he had done it he had been ordered to do so by the minister of Tranent. Since then he had publicly pricked several people in Tranent. His knowledge was found to be "only conjectural" and he was forbidden to practise.

1651 Robert Cockburn

Robert was a dumb boy, and people in Ormiston had been consulting him about stolen articles, asking him to "give some sign" indicating what had become of the missing articles or money. [Presb. mins].

1651 Dumb woman

People in Salt Preston had been consulting a dumb woman about stolen articles. [Presb mins].

1651 John Watherston

John Watherston in Yester was summoned for consulting with the parents of "the dumb boy in Peaston" about stolen money. [KS mins].

1651 Margaret Sivis

Margaret Sivis in the Nungate was summoned for consulting with the dumb boy in Peaston. [KS mins].

1653 Robert Paiston

Robert Paiston and his wife in Inveresk parish went to a dumb man to inquire about stolen cloth. Also, Helinor Stevenson went to a dumb man to inquire about stolen money. John Ker "turned the key" to find money stolen from a woman who consulted him. [KS mins.].

1662 John Kincaid

A notorious witch-pricker. When he was investigated and questioned he said that he acquired his knowledge only "by sight", and by doing what witches had told him to do. He said he could tell witches by their unpleasant smell. He was forbidden to practise.

1669 James Hog

He went to an Englishman named Seal in Newbattle to ask who had stolen corn and clothes from his house. Seal had promised the Presbytery not to meddle in such things, and directed James to David Ewart in Edinburgh, giving him a letter for Ewart. James sent his servant to Ewart with the letter and some money. Ewart sent back a letter describing the thief. [KS mins.].

1671 Robert White

Robert consulted a "wizard" in the Canongate about some stolen cloth. [KS mins.].

1672 Jean Pearson

Jean consulted "that person in the Cannogat" about the loss of the Countess of Tweedale's curtains for which she had been blamed. [KS mins.].

1673 David Blake

David was summoned for consulting a person in Edinburgh who claimed skill in discovering stolen goods, about clothes stolen in Yester a few months previously. [KS mins].

1678 David Cowan

Cowan was imprisoned in the tollbooth of Edinburgh for pricking Catherine Liddell in Prestonpans. Imprisoned in September 1678, in February 1679 he pledged himself not to prick in future without a warrant from the Privy Council.

1692 Agnes Lock

Agnes Lock in Prestongrange was advised by Doctor Mackie to go to Edinburgh to consult James Cathcart, an astrologer, about money stolen from her. Robert Irvine, overseer to the laird of Prestongrange, had written some figures and put them in water to inquire about her money. [KS mins].

1698 Dumb woman

Several people in Winton "came in to see the dumb woman", and several gave her a plack. Margaret Painstone and Jennet Mill were summoned for going to a dumb woman to enquire for something that was missing. They were sharply rebuked. [KS mins].

The official attitude of the Church and the Law was that victims of witchcraft should not take matters into their own hands. Prayer was the only approved remedy, along with reporting the suspected perpetrator to the requisite authorities. The trouble with such a law-abiding response was that it was usually rather difficult to produce credible evidence to those authorities. As even the most cursory glance at the East Lothian kirk session minutes will show, denouncing your neighbour to the kirk session for witchcraft was more likely to lead to your own humiliation as a slanderer, rather than to the trial and condemnation of the witch. Thus, it is not surprising that victims sometimes preferred their own methods to counteract witchcraft.

1590 John McGill

He was assaulted and dragged in to see Elspet Hepburn in Traprain, by members of her family. Agnes Sampson had advised that Elspeth would recover from her illness when she saw him. The implication is that they suspected McGill had bewitched her.

1591 Agnes Sampson

When Robert Kerse in Dalkeith was bewitched by a "westland warlock", Agnes took the sickness upon herself, kept it overnight with much groaning and obvious pain, then cast it into the close so that a dog or cat might get it. [It landed on Alexander Douglas, who died.]

1607 Issobell Griersonne

Robert Peden asked her thrice for his health for God's sake and recovered within 24 hours.

1608 Beigis Tod

She was suspected of bewitching Alexander Fairlie's son, and was asked to come and see him. She came with her two sons and gave him "certain instructions" on how to treat himself.

1612 Christian Grinton
She gave Catherine Gray a piece of rowan to keep in her purse and another to keep in her chest.

1612 Janet Litster
Patrick Nielson woke to find Janet Litster and others standing over him. He cried, "Lord be in this place!" and Janet gave a leap and "went away in an instant".

1629 Besse Mack
Janet Brown's husband carried her to Besse's house and asked her health three times for God's sake.

1629 Issobell Young
On the advice of a Highlandman. George Sandie asked Issobell for his luck three times for God's sake, and had a huge haul of herring after previously catching nothing. William Symson's wife asked Issobell for her health three times for God's sake, and was healed of her skin disease.

1632 Elspeth Meik
Robert Douglas believed Elspeth had taken his health from him, and knelt before her, asking his health from her three times for God's sake.

1641 Agnes Broun
Agnes told Margaret Weit to cut a piece of rowan tree "between the two Beltanes" and put it above the lintel to protect her child from witches and witchcraft.

1642 Isobel Wood
John Howden lost the power in his arms and took a pain in his heels after falling out with Isobel. He was advised to go to her and ask his health from her three times for God's sake.

1651 Bessie Heriot
It was reported to Yester kirk session that blood had been drawn from Bessie, baked on a girdle and eaten. No reason was given, and the matter was referred to the civil magistrate.

1669 William Weit
Bessie Clark thought that William had bewitched her child. She was advised by Lady Biel to blood him above the breath. She drew blood from around his nose several times with a needle, then fell on her knees three times asking for her child's health.

1688 Catherine McTarget
Two girls found Catherine lying in the road. She shot out her head and feet, terrifying them, and then chased them. Both fell sick, and the younger girl was struck dumb. Their father threatened Catherine with a knife and threatened to kill her if his daughter didn't speak again. She recovered her speech immediately.

1697 Helen Wyte
It was reported to Haddington kirk session that Margaret Thomson had taken blood from above Helen's brows.

1703 Marion Lillie
James Wood blooded her in the face.

William Colme was advised to take blood from her. He blamed her for his loss of livestock after he had forbidden her to keep a tethered ewe.

When Janet Logan's son fell ill she suspected Marion. She confronted her and threatened to tear her to pieces if anything happened to her son. He got better after that.

It will be seen, then, that rowan was thought to have protective powers, but if you had actually been bewitched the most popular remedy was to ask the witch for your health three times for God's sake. Another method was to draw blood from the perpetrator of the malifice from "above the breath". Bolder spirits might simply threaten to kill the witch.

It is a common belief nowadays that witches were in the habit of cursing those who offended them. It is certainly true that misfortune often followed causing such offence, but there are surprisingly few instances of outright cursing. Usually the offended witch would instead predict misfortune, sometimes specifically, sometimes in vague and enigmatic terms. It is often difficult to discern to what extent these predictions were considered simply as "unlawful" foreknowledge of an event, and to what extent they were believed to be the cause of the event. In some instances in the following list of predictions the witch is merely passing on knowledge of ill fortune in store, and in others would appear to be actively threatening.

1591 Agnes Sampson

Predicted that William Merkestoun was "bot ane deid man".

Predicted that if David Lyndsey lived past Wednesday he would not die. He recovered.

Predicted that no surgeon or medicine could help a man named Halyburton. He died.

She refused to go to Lady Rosline as she knew she wouldn't recover.

She predicted that Patrick Porteous would only live another eleven years.

She had foreknowledge of a storm the previous Michaelmas, and that it would cause much damage on land and sea.

Foretold that James Kirkaldy's wife would never recover.

Foretold Isobel Hamilton's death.

Predicted the death of James Libberton's wife.

Foretold the death of Patrick Hepburn's wife.

She had foreknowledge that the Queen would never reach Scotland unless the King fetched her.

According to *Newes from Scotland* she was able to tell the King what he had said to the Queen on their wedding night.

She used a prayer to predict whether a patient would recover or not. If the prayer stopped once the patient was bewitched. If it stopped twice the patient would die.

1591 John Cunningham

He had foreknowledge of a leak that sprang in the Queen's ship.

Predicted that Marion Weddel's son would die within fifteen days.

Predicted the death of Alexander Bowie's wife's son.

He claimed to be able to tell from people's date of birth, how long they would live and how they would die.

1608 Beigis Tod

Her daughter quarrelled with David Fairlie's wife over a comb. She said it would be the dearest comb David's wife had ever seen, and she would repent it from her heart. Since then David's wife's ale would never ferment. [Acquitted.]

1611 Bessie Thomson

After a minor quarrel Bessie promised a woman a bad turn, and held her in sickness for a year. [KS mins].

1628 John Carfrae,
Thomas Carfrae,
Alison Borthwick

Alison predicted misfortune to the beadle of Bothans Kirk. His cart wheel broke and his mare died.

1629 Alexander Sinclair

Predicted the death of John Heres. Foretold accurately that Isobel Turnbul would go to live in Ireland and then return.

1629 Besse Mack

Marion Allan refused to sell cloth to her. Besse said, "You will leave it to those who will give you less thanks for it." Marion fell ill and died.

1629 Issobell Young

Predicted that George Sandie's mill would lie idle when he least expected it, and when it was most needed.

She said that William Meslett and his wife would never again have as much money to lay out on land, and that they would have to sell and forfeit the land they had.

Predicted that two pet sheep of William Meslett's would break their necks. One of them did so.

1629 John Hog, Margaret Nicolson

It was claimed that when Hog was late in coming home, his wife put each of a horse's feet into a pan of water, and she would know he would come home safe.

1632 Alison Foular
Predicted that John Ewart would die in the same way as Alexander Jakson who was drowned in "the Creek". [KS mins].

1642 Isobel Wood
Isobel said to John Howden's sister, "Let God never allow your brother to prosper or thrive." John's sister fell ill and became bedridden. [Presb mins].

1643 Margaret Dickson
James Mill told Margaret's daughter off for pulling some ears of his wheat. Margaret said, "It won't be long until he loses a better quantity of goods." [Presb mins].

1662 Agnes Williamson
She said Thomas Steel would repent refusing to lend her £10. His house caught fire. She said Thomas Crumbie would lose 500 merks over and above what he lost at Whittinghame fair. His malt kiln caught fire.

1662 James Welsh
According to James, when the witches were sharing out peas from Samuelston Haugh, Janet Sympson wished that the owner would get no profit from them. The peas were all washed away in a flood.

1688 Catherine McTarget
A carter struck her for stealing coal. She said it would be dear coal to him, and he would never strike again. He fell ill and died.

She said that because Thomas Thomson's calf was calved at an ebb tide, it would roar until it died. It did.

She predicted that one of Thomas Ross's daughter's relatives would choke. Her father choked on a piece of beef and died.

John Milne's horse trampled plants in her garden. She predicted that the horse would break its neck and it did.

She predicted that John Milne would never thrive. He descended into extreme poverty. She predicted that the butcher James Reid would never draw blood from the cow he had bought from Catherine's husband. He fell ill and died.

She told the family at Knowes that they would get "barm enough" shortly, and their fermenting ale subsequently foamed out of the vessels up to the ceiling.

When she saw a sailor taking leave of his wife she observed, "It will be a long goodnight." He was lost in a shipwreck.

John White said he would rather see her hanged and burnt than give her any ale. Catherine wished that there would be a hanged man about his house before long. His next door neighbour subsequently hanged himself.

1697 Helen Whyte
Helen was heard to say that Alexander Brocky was sowing his corn but wouldn't see it cut down. She also said that witches would be the death of him. Alexander blamed her on his deathbed for his death. [KS mins].

1697 Helen Hoge
She came in to John Ouchterlony where he was lying seriously ill and accused him of raving about witches when none were there. She was put out of the house, but knelt down and prayed God's curse on him, that he should pine away till he declared her innocence. [KS mins].

1703 Marion Lillie
She prayed that the heavy curse of God might come on her slanderer Janet Logan and her supporters. She threatened to make William Combe repent not allowing her to keep a tethered ewe. Two of his mares "ramaged to death".

We have already mentioned the "elite" notion that witches travelled to meetings in miraculous ways, and found not much evidence for it in East Lothian. It was a common folk belief, however, that witches could change shape at will, and often did so on mischief-making expeditions. This is the belief, for example, behind the fisher superstition that hares were an unlucky sight. There seems also to have been a belief that witches were adept at entering houses when the doors and windows were locked and fastened.

1591 John Cunningham

He was stricken with trances and ecstasies, and his spirit carried to many mountains all over the world.

When chasing a cat in Tranent he was carried at great speed high above the ground and over high walls.

1607 Issobel Griersonne

She came into Adam Clark's house in the Pans in the shape of her own cat, accompanied by a great number of cats making a great noise and commotion.

1608 Beigis Tod

Appeared to Alexander Fairlie's son in the shape of a dog by day, and in her own shape by night.

1612 Janet Lytster

Patrick Neilson woke to find Janet standing over him, and three others with her. She tried to tear the child from his wife's arms. He cried, "Lord be in this house!" Janet gave a leap on the floor, and they all "went away in an instant".

1629 Sara Keith

Sara offered her baby son to the Devil, who took him out of the window in a whirlwind, leaving a lean deformed creature in the cradle which cried for three days till it died.

1629 Issobell Young

Christian Grinton was seen coming out of a hole in Issobell's roof in the shape of a cat.

Issobell was seen passing through William Sympson's courtyard in the shape of a hare.

She arrived in George Sandie's mill clean and dry on a night when the Brox Burn was in spate. She was accused of crossing the burn by "devlish and unlawful means of extraordinary transportation".

1630 Alexander Hamilton

He was carried to Coldingham Law by a spirit in the shape of a foal.

1649 Isobel Murray

She came home from her first encounter with the Devil in the shape of a cat.

1649 Jonet Bruce

She came into Robert Seatoun's house with two companions at midnight when the doors were shut, seized him, and pulled his nightshirt over his head.

1660 Jonet Spavine

Jonet and another four women came into Alison Murray's house at midnight when the doors were closed.

1661 Margaret Allane

Any time she was offended by her fellow servants in the household of the laird of Newhall, they were seized by sweating and trembling and Margaret was always found lying as if dead in a very deep sleep.

1678 Marion Veitch

She claimed to be present but invisible when Helen Laing and her servant killed Helen's husband and pulled out his heart.

1678 Marion Campbell

When she and the others went to meetings and returned they were sometimes in their own shape and sometimes in the shape of crows or magpies.

1678 Isobel Eliot

When Marion Veitch poisoned her grandchild, she and Isobel went to the house in the shape of bumble bees, and Marion carried the poison in her claws, wings, and mouth.

Isobel claimed to have left her body in Pencaitland Kirk, while she went to Loanhead in the shape of a crow to see a child she had nursed for someone there.

1697 Helen Hoge

Six hours before John Ouchterlony died he cried out, "There's Helen Hoge!" Those present saw nothing but a cat. When it was thrown out of the window, a woman's head appeared looking through the glass. [KS mins].

Whether a witch was curing or killing, healing or destroying, protecting or predicting, advising or detecting, her primary function was as a practitioner of popular folk magic, and she had a repertoire of charms, rituals, and "spells" to aid her in this. The records throw up an impressive list of such practices in East Lothian.

1591 Agnes Sampson

If she stopped once when reciting her prayer the patient was bewitched; if twice the patient would die. [See the section on the use of words.]

She was acquitted of going to Newton Church with other witches to dig up bodies and of taking joints from them to make enchanted powder.

She cured Robert Bailyie's son by probing his body with her hands and saying "some words of charming".

She took Robert Kerse's sickness on herself and kept it till morning with much groaning and obvious pain, then cast it out into the close so that a cat or a dog might get it.

The Devil appeared to her in the likeness of a dog, from whom she sought answers to her questions. She dismissed him by saying, "Depart by the law you live by." These words would conjure him away.

At Edmonstone, praying in the garden, she ordered the devil to come and speak to her, calling him "Elva" [More likely "Eloa" or "Hola".] The Devil came out of the well in the likeness of a dog, and came so near that Agnes was afraid and charged him to come no nearer. They discussed the Lady's health but there was no hope for her. The Devil said he intended to have one of the daughters. Agnes told him no, and he went away howling and remained in the well until after supper. When the ladies came into the garden the dog appeared out of the well, terrifying them. One of them was apparently drawn towards the well and had to be held back. She was carried to bed hysterical and was attended by Agnes and later by Agnes's son.

Agnes and others baptised a cat in a weaver's house, three of them putting their fingers in the chimney crook with their knuckles touching. They put the cat thrice through the links of the chain. After that they fastened four human joints to its feet at Beigis Tod's house. It was then taken to Leith and thrown in the sea. About eleven o'clock another group in Prestonpans had also thrown a cat in the sea. This caused a boat to sink between Leith and Kinghorn.

Agnes made a wax image to destroy Euphane MacCalyean's father in law, at Euphane's request. It was to be put under his bed.

She gave Euphane MacCalyean powder made from human joints and body parts, to be put under Euphane's bed before she gave birth.

She charmed cows and bullocks by going between them in pairs in the byre, striking their backs and repeating "Ave Maria" over and over again.

She and others pulled up the Devil on a rope at Ormiston Bridge as Agnes cried, "Haill, hola!" The Devil gave them pieces of glass braided in pieces of cord with other things. A thread was to be laid along the moor and the pieces of glass scattered, so that whoever passed first should die suddenly. This was meant for David Seton.

Agnes sent Anny Stratton and Bessie Thomson to Foulstruther House to ask for a handful of salt to be passed out to them from above the door. If they had succeeded in getting the salt ruination would have fallen on David Seton and his goods.

At North Berwick the men were turned anti-clockwise nine times, and the women six times. Graves were opened at the devil's command. The Devil enchanted "joints" from the corpses, and they were shared out. The Devil told them to keep the joints until they were dry, and make powder to do evil.

Agnes prepared a beautiful image of yellow wax for Barbara Napier, which she enchanted in the Devil's name under the name of "Archie".

She enchanted a ring with a stone in it for Barbara Napier, to influence Lady Angus to like and favour Barbara.

1590 John Cunningham

At North Berwick he and all the rest kissed Satan behind, some kissing his "erse".

Cunningham opened locks, especially in the house of David Seton junior in Tranent. He opened the gate guarding the front door while the key was lying on the table.

He opened the door in David Seton's mother's house by blowing in a woman's hand while he stood at the fireside.

At North Berwick graves were opened and women dismembered corpses with knives.

When he was riding to Tranent with a servant he made four candles appear on the horse's ears, and one on the staff the man was carrying.

He kept moles' feet in his purse, which had been given to him by the Devil so that he would never be short of money.

Newes from Scotland relates the long story of how he tried to obtain a girl's pubic hair so that she would be amenable to seduction. Hairs from a cow were substituted and the cow followed him around, presumably in the hope of mating with him.

Newes also says he had two pins inserted under his tongue to prevent him confessing.

According to Agnes Sampson, at North Berwick Cunningham "blew up the doors and blew in the lights".

1591 Geillis Duncan

Present when a cat was baptised and thrown in the sea. A toad and stale urine were laid in the king's way. An image in a cloth was passed from hand to hand at Acheson's haven.

1591 Janet Stratton

She described a toad being roasted and the drips from it being caught in a brass dish. They were mixed with stale urine, stirred in by Agnes Sampson with three fingers.

She also described the enchanting of a wax image where certain special persons stood in a ring and the image was passed round anti-clockwise. The image was yellow, less than half an ell long, and wrapped in cloth. As they handled it the name "James the Sixth" was spoken.

At the meeting where the image was handled, someone was instructed to procure an item of the King's linen.

1591 Barbara Napier

A toad was to be hung and roasted, and the drips mixed with stale urine, an adder skin, and the "thing" from the head of a new-born foal. This was to be laid in the King's way, or where it could drop on his head. The toad was set to drip for nine nights between three oyster shells and nine stones.

At North Berwick Fian blew up the church doors and blew in the lights. There were great black candles around the pulpit, and the women were turned around nine times anti-clockwise. Corpses were dug up and dismembered, and the nails and joints shared out to be dried and made into powder to do evil. Those present kissed the devil's arse. There was mention made at North Berwick of a wax image of the King.

1591 Euphane MacCalyean

She sent a wax image of her father in law to Agnes Sampson to be enchanted.

Agnes also enchanted a child's apron with something tied up in it. This was thrown in at John McGill's window. It contained clay images of McGill and his wife, sewn up in a shroud, and wrapped in an old black mutch with balls of different coloured wool.

Euphane was involved in conjuring cats to raise storms. A black dog was thrown in the sea which "skipped under the ship".

To ease her labour pains, Euphane got from Agnes Sampson a stone with a hole bored through it to be put under her pillow. Enchanted graveyard earth and powder were put in paper and rolled in her hair. He husband's shirt was folded up and put under the foot of her bed.

1598 Jonet Steill

She went on three different nights to the well of Saint Anne after sunset, and brought back water. She put the water in a tub and mixed it with watercress. She said the Creed and the Lord's Prayer in Latin as a man had taught her to do, stood Hary Broun in the tub, and she and his maidservant washed him. The water was then thrown out. [Presb mins].

1602 James Reid

He made use of south-running water on the Devil's instructions. He used south-running water from the well at Sheriff Braes to cure Sara Borthwick, and also scattered wheat and salt around her bed.

He took a piece of raw meat, made nine nicks in it, and got a woman to lay part of it under David Libberton's mill door, and part under his stable door to destroy his cattle and horses.

The Devil enchanted nine stones which Reid scattered on Libberton's land to destroy his corn.

Reid and two women roasted a wax image of Libberton.

Reid tied three silk laces round John Crystie's waist to cure "swelling". Crystie wore them for ten weeks and was cured.

1607 Issobell Griersone

She threw a piece of raw meat in at William Burnet's door.

She urinated on William Burnet's wife and in various parts of his house, and vanished when William named her. This was supposedly the Devil in Issobell's image.

Robert Peden asked her thrice for his health for God's sake and recovered within twenty four hours.

1608 Beigis Tod

She drew a cat nine times through her chimney crook. She drew a cat nine time through the iron gate of Seton, then christened it, calling it Margaret. When Beigis and her companions returned to the Dean Foot of Longniddry they cast the cat to the Devil.

1611 Bessie Manson

She put her child nine times into the hopper of a mill as it was grinding, and made the child drink from the horn of a living ox. Nine drinks from the horn of a living ox were supposed to effect the cure. The horn was obtained from Fisherrow, where an ox had broken its horn. [KS mins].

1612 Janet Lytster

Janet was believed to have bewitched Patrick Neilson's wife after Patrick bought her cow. Patrick's wife sweated copiously and lost her appetite, but recovered after the cow was burnt.

1628 William Davidson

He cured Agnes Stanehouse with south-running water from south-running wells. The water was fetched by her son, who had to leave a rag or two pins at the well. He was not to speak to anyone on the way. William washed her body, and her arms recovered their usual strength.

A witch in Hume gave Robert Spens's wife an enchanted shirt to put on Robert, and told her to get William to wash him in south-running water. The water was to be thrown away in an out-of-the-way place.

He cured John Hill by laying a piece of salted hake and a piece of raw flesh under his head.

He cured James Halyday of madness with a piece of salted hake and a piece of raw flesh.

1629 John Carfrae, Thomas Carfrae, Alison Borthwick

Alison took blood from her brother in law George Carfrae by biting his thumb. Ever since, his wealth declined.

They got the witch Margaret Hamilton to murder the wife of the baron baillie of Yester, which she achieved by rubbing a piece of enchanted gold.

1629 Alexander Sinclair

Lady Samuelston's husband died after Alexander put on one of his shirts and went away with it.

1629 Besse Mak

Janet Broun's husband carried her to Besse's house and asked her health three times for God's sake.

1629 Sara Keith

She used south-running water to cure Agnes Litster when she had a wasting disease.

She cured two of George Stanehouse's sons of blindness by anointing their eyes with south-running water.

1629 Issobell Young

She pulled the kerchief from her head and turned round three times anti-clockwise in William Meslett's barn.

She laid enchanted yarn at the door of Alison Patterson's house to take a sickness off Alison and lay it on another.

She took her kerchief off to Cuthbert Symson because of a disagreement over unsatisfactory cloth. His horse died and his worldly wealth vanished.

She was told by the Devil to cure livestock by digging a deep hole, and throwing in a live ox, a live cat, and some salt. The hole should face north between two lords' lands, or if not, should be in any inconspicuous place. The rest of the livestock should then be driven over it. Isobel's defence advocate said that in fact she had been advised to do this by their servant James Nisbet. When it didn't work Isobel's sons went to the Laird of Ley's house to borrow his curing stone. The Lady refused, but gave them some flagons of water the stone had been dipped in, which apparently did the trick.

On the advice of a Highlandman George Sandie asked Isobel for his luck three times for God's sake, and had a huge haul of herring after previouly catching nothing.

William Symson's wife asked Isobel for her health three times for God's sake, and her skin complaint cleared up.

1629 John Hog, Margaret Nicolson

When John was late home his wife would put each of the feet of a horse in the stable into a pan of water, and knew he would come home safe.

1630 Alexander Hamilton

Alexander would pay the Devil for services rendered with a loaf, a cat, a dog, or any beast he came by.

The Devil advised Alexander to harm the provost of Haddington by pulling three ears of corn out of each stack in the Provost's barnyard and burning them. The Provost's corn kiln caught fire and all the corn in it was burnt.

Thomas Hume had been bewitched by a woman who laid an enchanted blue thread in front of his door. To cure him, Alexander went to the Clerkington Burn and raised the Devil in the form of a crow, who told him to rub Hume with a woollen cloth dipped in a mixture of oil of animal fat, camomile oil, and heart fat. Alexander sacrificed a cat, and the Devil vanished with it.

At Saltoun Wood the Devil gave Alexander a ball of blue thread to lay at Lady Ormiston's gate at Woodhead. She and her daughter fell ill and died.

Hamilton said Home of Manderston's wife put a corpse's hand in a corner of his garden at Berwick to harm her husband.

The Devil told Hamilton that if he struck his stick three times on the ground saying, "Rise up Foul Thief," the Devil would appear.

1632 Elspeth Meik

Robert Douglas said that Elspeth had taken his health from him. He knelt before her and asked his health from her three times for God's sake. [KS mins].

1635 Anna Tait

On the Devil's advice she killed her daughter and the daughter's unborn child with a mutchkin of white wine mixed with salt.

1639 Bessie Hogg

Her sister Isobel asked her to ask David

Cowan's servant for ashes from "under the chimney" of Cowan's house. This was after Cowan's wife's delivery and before her being laid up in bed. [Presb mins].

1641 Agnes Broun

Agnes told Margaret Wait to put a piece of raw meat under her sick child's head, and he would recover. She was also to cut a piece of rowan "between the two Beltanes" and put it above the lintel to protect the child from witches and witchcraft. [KS mins].

1642 Isobel Wood

John Howden lost the power of his arms after quarrelling with her. He was advised to go to her and ask his health from her three times for God's sake. [Presb mins].

1643 Margaret Dickson

She advised John Sharp that if evil spirits were the cause of his daughter's illness, to take a peck of meal and bake it. He was then to take twelve empty eggshells and lay them and the bread in front of the fire, and his daughter behind the fire. About midnight he was to go round the house nine times, then come in again and say, "Rise up elf and go back where you should go in the Devil's name, and give me my daughter again." If the girl was to recover the bread and eggshells would be away; if not, they would still be there. Margaret admitted this, but said he was told to go round the house three times, not nine times.

Issobell Johnston said that Margaret washed her child and the child's shirt twice in south-running water, and put the shirt back on the child. Margaret wanted to wash the child a third time, but Issobell refused. The child was in a fever for thirteen weeks afterwards. Margaret advised her to put on a good fire and throw the child on it, for the child was not hers, but a hundred years old. She was to throw the child on to loose soil on the fire. Margaret was suspected of doing this to her own child, but denied it.

Margaret was suspected of offering to cure James Mill by putting him through a hank of green yarn. Margaret denied this, saying she had told him to wind the yarn round the affected part. [Presb mins].

1644 Tynninghame Parish

Public intimation was made by order of the Presbytery that nobody was to try to cure the "routing evil" by burying a live ox, as had been done recently in Whittinghame parish. [KS mins].

1644 Andro Kerr

He cured a bewitched ox by cutting its ear to bleed it, saying, "Three things are tain fra thee; the heart, the hand, and the eye maist. There is nane can remeid thee, bot the father, the sonne, and the haly ghaist." [Presb mins].

1646 George Beir

George professed skill in curing "cruells", the "king's seekness". He laid his hand on the affected part and said three times, "I touch thee; Lord cure thee." He then applied clean cloths [clothes?] to the patient and tied two black silk threads round the patient's neck. George claimed he was first instructed in curing by the Kelso minister, who realised he was a seventh son. George had also cured himself of the disease. [Presb mins].

1646 Andro Yool

He tied a live toad round a sheep's neck to cure a disease in the animal. He used no words or ritual. He had heard about this cure from George Brown of Dernidykes. Andro "thought it did them good." [Presb mins].

1646 Thomas Carfra, Jeane Deans

Thomas and Jean tied a live toad round a sheep's neck to cure "the kreakshaw", a disease of the leg joints. They said this was the cure used by Andro Yool. Thomas had been told about this by Jean Deans from Bolton parish. [Presb mins].

1647 Helen Bull

Helen was a midwife in the habit of laying a piece of bread in the bosom of children brought to be baptised. She said it was an old custom she had often seen followed. The Dirleton minister was to forbid this from the pulpit, since it was practised in Dirleton more than elsewhere. [Presb mins].

1648 Issabell Smith

Issabell turned a child twice round an oak tree on the advice of Agnes Anderson. She was also advised to cure the child by taking him between two barn doors and turning him three times head over heels. [KS mins].

1648 Agnes Anderson

Agnes advised Isobel Smith to take her child between two barn doors and turn it three times heels over head. Alternatively she should turn it three times round a post of oak saying words that Agnes would teach her. Isobel put the child twice round an oak tree but was afraid to do it a third time. The child recovered. This cure was for "maw turning" [nausea]. [Presb mins].

1648 Janet Symie

When it seemed that Janet Cosser's marriage to James Watson wouldn't come off, Agnes Anderson's daughter Janet Symie advised her to go in to James in the morning, look three times into his face, and three times at the ground. He would then either marry her or never do well. [Presb mins].

1649 Elspeth Dobbie

Elspeth touched the breast of a nursing mother. Her baby "never sucked again" and died. Elspeth was supposed to have taken the cloth off the child's head and put it in her pocket. She was also supposed to have taken the pin out of his clothes and put in an eyeless needle. [KS mins]

1649 Margaret Vaitch

A horse died in the street. When the flesh had been eaten off it, Margaret took the bones and boiled them, and used the grease to rub on her arm for gout. [KS mins].

1649 Agnes Gourley

When Anna Sympsone's milk did not have enough cream content, Agnes Gourley advised her to throw the milk into the drain. She said, "There are those under the earth who have as much need of it as those above ground." Agnes threw the milk into the drain herself. She also put salt and wheat bread into the cows' ears. She learned the charms from a "going man". [KS mins]

1649 Jean Craig

She rubbed her sister in law's baby with three enchanted stones. Later, when the child fell ill, she promised to get south-running water and foxglove leaves for it, but didn't do so. She blew in Beatrix Sandilands' face and Beatrix went mad. She threw down lumps of raw flesh in Beatrix Sandilands' house.

1649 Margaret Dicksone

Isobel Johnston asked Margaret to get south-running water for her sick child, as others had advised. The Devil advised Margaret to fetch the water, but to let the child's mother apply it.

1649 Marione Richesone

When her child was ill she went to Agnes hunter who told her to go to the well below the Boges before the sun rose, and to bring back a pint of water with which Agnes would wash the child, who was bewitched.

1651 Bessie Heriot

Blood was drawn from Bessie Heriot, baked on a girdle and eaten. No reason is recorded for this. The case was referred to the civil magistrate. [KS mins].

1651 Agnes Burnet

Agnes put a coffin nail between the corpse of a dead woman and the winding sheet. This was to stop her spirit coming back again. Agnes had heard of this from Bessie Crail in Saltoun. [KS mins].

1652 John Wilson

The Devil gave Margaret Henrie a wax image of Sir John Ruthven and told her to torment his body as she pleased.

The Devil gave John several silver coins which he was to stick in the walls of those who owed him money.

1652 Heilleine Baillie

Margaret Sinclair declared that Helleine Baillie was going up and down like a mad lion calling everybody witch and striving to blood them above the breath. [KS mins].

1653 Elspeth Wood

She got her son to steal a cow's tether, and after that the cow gave no milk but only blood. [KS mins].

1654 John Lyndsey

After John had been advising people about stolen property for many years, the Dirleton minister dealt privately with him as ordered by the Presbytery. John signed a confession acknowledging his guilt in that from time to time he had advised people regarding stolen goods "by that kind of divination called the turning of the key." He professed sorrow for all the trouble he had caused the Presbytery. [Presb mins].

1657 Jonet Bruce

Asked for items of John Phinnie's wife's clothing, probably headcloths.

Put a waterproof cloth on Alexander Johnston's child and rubbed the child with oil.

Smeared William Bryson with oils.

Urinated on the threshhold of Robert Sandelands' door when he let her house to another tenant.

She measured the length of Bessie Ronald's child with a length of velvet trimming. The child recovered from its sickness. When Bessie refused to give her more drink Jonet said, "You have the child, I have its measurements."

The flesh and bones of dead children were found in her plaid at Channelkirk.

1658 Margaret Anderson

When she was employed as a servant in Tarbet in Easter Ross a Gypsy woman came to the house claiming to have a knowledge of charming. Margaret took her into the great hall and asked her whether James Innes would marry her or not. The Gypsy asked her for a shilling and her linen apron, and told her to bring three straws from her bed. She told Margaret she was going to put them under the head of James's bed. The Gypsy then asked Margaret to turn her back, and when she turned round again the apron, straw, and shilling had disappeared. [With the Gypsy?]

1659 Christian Cranstone

Christian went to get south-running water. She took Patrick Cowan's son's mutch with her and left it beside the well. All the way to the well she repeated, "I seek it for God's cause." On the way back she would speak to no-one until she came to the patient, even though many people tried to speak to her.

When she went to Humbie Wood for foxglove leaves she used to say, "These I seek for God's cause." When she brought them back to the patient she used to say, "This I give for God's sake, and may God give a blessing to it."

When she went for south-running water she said, "I seek it for God's cause" all the way to the well, "muttering it in her mind". When she first came in to the patient she said, "God be here." [KS mins]

1661 Margaret Allan

She was seen going in among the horses which James Hog looked after, "saying certain words to herself", and four of the horses subsequently died.

1661 William Pettiloe

William had been going round the houses in East Barns looking for measuring vessels. He had been advised to do this to recover his health by an itinerant woman he met at Dryburn. [KS mins].

1662 Agnes Williamson

Agnes had been pregnant seven years previously, and when she was brought to bed the child was "substracted". Her husband buried some clothes in place of the "substracted" child.

Agnes was suspected of cutting off George Cauldcleuch's horse's lip.

According to James Welsh, Agnes and another woman "cut a horse lip of Patrick Baillie's".

James Welsh said David Shanks told Agnes Williamson that he had made two parcels and laid them at Patrick Baillie's door.

1662 John Kincaid

Kincaid would not let witches cross the threshold of the room where he searched them. [It's not quite clear what he means here. Does he mean that they were carried over the threshold?] They were placed an ell from the wall. He had been told by witches that he should always take them into the house backwards, and keep them away from the wall and from water. He always searched the hands and arms of suspects first.

1663 Adam Gilles,
Christian Watson

A witness saw one of their cows in the cattle fold had a cloth tied to one of its horns. When he opened it he found some grains of wheat and salt. Adam and Christian claimed they had been advised to do this by Thomas Bookless, a man of no fixed residence, after Adam had said he feared his cow was "forespoken". Thomas also said rowan was a good thing to keep on man or beast. Adam was adamant that he had done nothing wrong in this. Livestock was vulnerable to harm, and he would do all he could for their preservation. The Presbytery decided there was not enough evidence to prove that they were witches.

There was a long history of strife with their neighbours after this, and they were eventually referred to the sheriff in 1679 with a view to putting them out of the parish. [KS mins].

1669 Bessie Clark

Bessie thought William Weit had bewitched her child. She was advised by Lady Beil to blood him above the breath. She drew blood with a needle several times around his nose, then fell on her knees three times asking for her child's health. [KS mins].

1676 Margaret Shireff

A "testament" was given by North Berwick kirk session to Margaret and her children who were going to London to the King to be helped for "the creualls" [scrofula]. [KS mins].

1678 Jennet Burtoun

Jennet said that Marion Veitch gifted her year-old granddaughter to the Devil in the house of the girl's father at Templehall, in the presence of other witches. The child died within eight days.

1688 Catherine McTarget

She threw a horsehair tether down in John Lowrie's house. He fell ill and died.

She dipped her fingers in the water pail in George Colm's house, and touched her finger to the sole of her foot. Three of his cows and two of his bullocks ded.

She picked up a boy's bonnet and put it back on his head upside down. He developed a headache and died.

She picked up dung from the midden and held it to a bullock's mouth, muttering some words and charms. A cow in the barn nearby began to decline, and never thrived after that.

She took off her head-cloths and threw them at Janet Symontone. Janet's malt went bad.

She sat on the stair opposite James Cungiltone's house all night with her hair hanging over her eyes. He never thrived after that

She repeated three times, "If I break my nose I spoil my face, and when I spoil my face I break my fortune." Ever since, Patrick Mathie's daughter was in "a melancholy and troubled frame of mind".

1692 Agnes Lock

Robert Irvine, overseer to the Laird of Prestongrange wrote some figures and put them in water to enquire about Agnes's money. [KS mins].

1697 Helen Whyte

Somebody was supposed to have seen Helen turn three times anticlockwise. Margaret Thomson took blood from above Helen's brows. [KS mins].

1702 Marion Lillie

Her son Robert Kemp hanged a mad dog over Janet Logan's cow's fodder, which adversely affected the cow's milk and butter.

Marion threw down a pair of stockings in the road in front of Janet Logan's door.

James Wood blooded Marion in the face. William Colm was also advised to take blood from her. [KS mins].

Modern popular belief is that "magic spells" should normally be accompanied by "magic words". There are several interesting examples in the records of incantations and invocations. In view of the supposed diabolic origins of witchcraft, it is surprising how often these are thoroughly Christian. These forms of words are in fact "prayers", and were rightly so described by Agnes Sampson. Appeals to God, Christ, Mary, and the saints were in use well into the 19th century in the Catholic isles of Uist and Barra, as accompaniments to almost every aspect of daily life. Similar prayers and charms in East Lothian in the late 16th century, and in the 17th century, are without doubt a hangover from pre-Reformation days when the use of such forms of words would have been widespread.

1691 Agnes Sampson

Agnes used the following recitation to foretell whether a patient was bewitched or not, and whether he would five or die. If the prayer stopped once he was bewitched; if twice he would die. It is of course a vernacular version of the Creed. I give a modern translation of it in the chapter on "The North Berwick Witches".

I trow in Almychty God that wrocht
baith heavin and earth and all of nocht.
In his ain son Chryst Jesu,
in to that anaplie lord I trow;
was gotten of the haly ghaist,
borne of the Virgin Marie,
stoppit to heaven that all weill there
and sittis at his faderis rycht hand.
He bade us cum and there to dome
baith quick and deid as he thocht conuene.
I trow als in the Haly Ghaist,
in haly kirk my hoip is maist,
that halyschip quhar hallowars winnis
to ask forguenis of my sinnis,
and syne to ryis in flesch and bane,
the lyff that never mair is gane.
Thow sayis, Lord, lovit mocht ye be
that formed and made mankynd of me.
Thow coft me on the haly croce,
and lent me body, saul, and voce,
and ordanit me to heavinnis bliss,
wherefore I thank the Lord of this;
And all our hallowaris lovit be
to pray to them to pray to me
and keep me fra that fellon fea
and from the syn that saul wald slay.
Thow Lord, for thy bitter passioun in
to keip me frame syn and warldlie schame
and endless damnatioune.
Grant me the joy that never will be gane,
sweit Jesus Cristus. Amene.

Agnes also used the following "prayer and conjuration" as part of the ritual of healing, presumably only after she had determined whether the patient would live or die. As with her other incantation, this prayer is quite manifestly Christian, and far from invoking the Devil, quite specifically invokes Christ and God by name. The reference to the "virtues of the mass" would not recommend it to Agnes's interrogators, however.

All kindis of illis whatever may be,
in Crystis name I conjure ye.
I conjure ye baith mair and less
with all the vertewis of the mess.
And richt sa, be the naillis sa,

that naillit Jesus and na ma.
And richt sa be the samyn blude
that reikit owre the ruithfull ruid.
Furth of the flesch and of the bane,
and in the eird and in the stane
I conjure ye in Godis name.

Another obvious Catholic survival in Agnes's repertoire is her charming of cows and bullocks at Gosford and Herdmonstone by going between them in the byre, striking their backs, and repeating "Ave Maria".

When raising "the Devil" in the form of a dog, Agnes would call upon him by name, variously reported as "Elva", "Eloa", and "Hola". Did Agnes really think of this as the Devil? Or was "Hola" a familiar spirit on the English model? Or are we dealing with something much more primitive on the lines of a shamanic totem or spirit guide? Or is it more likely that we are dealing with a theatrical piece of hokum to impress the gullible? Bearing in mind the heavily religious content of Agnes's incantations it is tempting to make a connection with Christ's cry on the cross, "Eloi, Eloi, lama sabachthani?" [My God, my God, why hast thou forsaken me? - Mark Ch.16 v. 34.] Is Agnes really addressing a black dog as "My God"? Or again, is it just a fancy name to impress the gullible?

What a pity Agnes Sampson could not have been interviewed by a folklorist or ethnologist instead of the functionaries of the law!

1591 Jannet Stratton

As they were enchanting the wax image at Acheson's Haven, it was passed from hand to hand anti-clockwise, and "James the Sixth" was named as they handled it.

1598 Jonet Steill

When curing Hary Broun by washing him with water from St Anne's Well, she said the Creed and the Lord's Prayer in Latin as she had been taught to do by a "poor man who used to go about with the Jews".

1607 Issobell Griersonne

She said to Robert Peden's wife, "May the faggots of Hell land on you!" and "May you boil in Hell's cauldron!"

1612 Janet Lytster

When Patrick Neilson woke to find Janet and three other women standing over him he cried, "God be in this place!" and they all "went away in an instant".

1629 John Carfrae, Thomas Carfrae, Alison Borthwick

Alison was seen charming oxen. Some words were heard and her lips were seen moving. The witness coughed and interrupted her.

1630 Alexander Hamilton

When he wished to raise the Devil he said, "Rise up Foul Thief." He claimed that when they laid enchanted thread at Lady Ormiston's gate, the women were to "speak certain words". These words had been whispered to them by the Devil, but Hamilton hadn't heard them.

1643 Margaret Dickson

She advised John Sharp to lay oat bread and eggshells in front of the fire and his daughter behind the fire, and say, "Rise up elf, and go back where you should go in the Devil's name, and give me my daughter again." It was presumably suspected that the daughter was a changling. [Presb mins].

1644 Andro Kerr

Andro learned charming from his mother, who taught him to say when curing,

"Three things are tain fra thee; the heart, the hand, and the eye maist.

There is nane can remeid thee bot the Father, the Sonne, and the Haly Ghaist." [Presb mins].

1646 George Beir

When curing scrofula he had been told by the Kelso minster to say, "I touch thee; Lord cure thee." [Presb mins].

1649 Penston Witches

According to three of the accused, a witches' meeting was aborted when someone came by and said, "God speed". According to another the words were, "God be with you."

1657 Jonet Bruce

When Bessie Ronald refused to give her a drink after Jonet had cured her child, Jonet said, "You have the child. I have its measurements."

1659 Christian Cranstone

When she went to Humbie Wood for foxglove leaves she would say, "These I seek for God's cause." When she brought them back to the patient she would say, "This I give for God's sake, and may God give a blessing to it"

Going for south-running water she would "mutter in her mind" all the way to the well, "I seek it for God's cause." On coming back to the patient she would say "God be here" when she first came in.

1662 Agnes Williamson

Agnes's voice was heard crying, "Aha, aha!" outside George Cauldcleuch's house the right his horse had its lip cut off.

1688 Catherine McTarget

She said three times to Patrick Mathie's daughter, "If I break my nose I spoil my face, and when I spoil my face I break my fortune." The girl had been mentally disturbed ever since.

When she saw a sailor saying goodbye to his wife Catherine remarked, "It will be a long goodnight." He was subsequently lost at sea.

1703 Marion Lillie

Marion prayed that the heavy curse of God might come on Janet Logan and her supporters. [KS mins].

Parallels are often drawn between the "wise wife", and the shaman in more primitive communities. A common shamanic practice is consultation with, and reliance on, spirit guides which are often in animal form. Again, it was usual in some Native American societies for a young man to withdraw alone into some remote place to await the appearance of his totem.

There are traces in the records of witches summoning spirits or supernatural entities, often simply referred to as "the Devil". As P. G. Maxwell-Stuart remarks, "Such spirits are usually interpreted in the records to mean evil spirits or Satan himself, even though it is clear - and would have been clear to the original actors - that many of these spirits were sithean or spirit guides." [Maxwell-Stuart, 2001, p. 215]. However, there is very little in the East Lothian records in the way of evidence of spirit guides or spirit companions; nor do we see much of the imps or familiars which were such an important part of the English witchcraft scene.

The following are instances from the records of persons who apparently had the ability or means to summon the Devil or some other spirit or supernatural being.

1591 Agnes Sampson

Agnes could summon a spirit in the shape of a dog, variously called "Elva", "Eloa", or "Hola", and identified by her accusers as the Devil. She sought answers to her questions from him, and dismissed him by ordering him, "Depart, by the law you live by."

Janet Stratton claimed that Agnes had raised the Devil. Euphane MacCalyean consulted Agnes, who raised "the Spirit" as a voice.

1629 Alexander Sinclair /Hunter

Bessie Little said Alexander had a bee in a tin box, which he fed with drops of his blood. He went once a year to Norham to get a new bee.

1629 John Hog, Margaret Nicolson

There were rumours of strange rumbling noises in Hog's stable.

1629 Alexander Hamilton

The Devil told Alexander that he would appear to him if he struck the ground three times with his stick, saying, "Rise up Foul Thief."

Hamilton also describes being wakened by a spirit in the shape of a foal which carried him to a meeting.

1649 Jean Craig

It was claimed that she made ugly beasts like pups run round the knocking stone in Agnes Steill's house.

Jean also supposedly made ugly cats, "or rather devils in their likeness", leap and dance round the fire in John Parkie's house. One of them spoke. She caused James Cowan to be tormented by wicked spirits like ugly black dogs.

1657 Jonet Bruce

The house she was imprisoned in caught fire after a rat ran into the thatch with a lighted candle. When the house was burning a horse was seen on the roof. A raven flew over the burning house at the face of the woman into whose house Jonet had been transferred.

Some writers have made strenuous efforts to connect Scottish witchcraft to belief in fairies. Maxwell-Stuart, for example, seems to equate "sithean" [the Gaelic word for fairies] with spirit guides. [Maxwell-Stuart, 2001, p.215 - already quoted.] In their introduction to "Scottish Fairy Belief" the authors state, 'Witch trial testimonials are of crucial importance to this study." [Henderson & Cowan, 2001, p.3]. However, there is very little mention of fairies in the East Lothian records, nor much in the way of ghosts, poltergeists, and suchlike.

1591 Agnes Sampson

She had foreknowledge of events through "the spreit" - which Pitcairn equates with the Devil.

She had her questions answered by "Hola", a dog defined in her dittay as the Devil. She is described as raising "the spreit" to enchant an image of John Moscrop. She said William Black's son's sickness was caused by an elf shot.

1591 Euphane MacCalyean

Her dittay mentions Agnes Sampson raising the Spirit as a voice.

1629 Issobell Young

Witnesses' statements contain second-hand rumours that one of her oxen had been heard to speak.

1629 William Lermonth

Interviewed in the case of John Hog and his wife, William said several cats had come into his house and killed two of his cats. One of the invading cats spoke to him.

1630 Alexander Hamilton

He was wakened by a spirit in the shape of a foal, which carried him to a meeting at Coldingham Law.

1643 Margaret Dickson

Margaret told Issobel Johnston to put on a good fire and throw her child on it, as the child was not hers but a hundred years old. [The implication here is that the child is a changeling.]

1649 Jean Craig

Jean was blamed for ugly beasts like pups running round Agnes Steill's house; also for ugly cats, "or rather devils in their likeness", leaping round John Parkie's fire - one of which spoke to him. James Cowan was tormented by wicked spirits like ugly black dogs.

1649 Margaret Robison

Twenty or thirty years previously, when she was sleeping in James Fleming's barn, she was pulled up and down by the hair by some invisible creature, which also went to her mother's bed and said, "Old woman, you must shift."

1649 Agnes Gourley

When Anne Sympsone's milk was deficient in cream, Agnes advised her to throw the milk into the drain as "there are those under the earth who have as much need of it as those above ground."

1651 Agnes Burnet

Agnes put a coffin nail in a dead woman's shroud to stop her spirit coming back.

1657 Jonet Bruce

A rat carried off the candle and set fire to the house Jonet was being held in. A black horse appeared on the roof of the burning house. A raven flew over the burning house at the face of a woman who was watching.

1657 Dirleton Kirk Session

Marion Henderson was accused and found

guilty of calling Margaret Kemp "fairy lady, runt that the Devil rode upon".

1662 James Welsh

When he went out to the end of the barn to relieve himself, a "bonnie lass" appeared and wanted to lie with him.

When investigating the evidence for witchcraft in East Lothian we come across much that is fantastical, much that is unlikely, and much that is quite frankly impossible. Since the mid-eighteenth century, Enlightenment rationalism, Victorian practicality, and twentieth century materialism, have brought us to the point where until recently it was usual to dismiss everything in witchcraft confessions as nonsense. The almost compulsory standpoint was that witchcraft confessions were extorted by torture, or were the products of deluded minds. Christina Larner, the most respected authority on Scottish witchcraft, states baldly in *Enemies of God*, "Various methods were used to extract the confession. Officials used sleep deprivation, pricking for the witch's mark, threats of torture, and direct torture." [Larner 2000, p.107]. Sleep deprivation was certainly used. Sir George Mackenzie, the 17th Century legal luminary, wrote in his *Laws and Customs of Scotland* that witchcraft suspects were "starved for want of food and sleep". Larner says, "Known as 'waking' or 'watching' the witch, sleep deprivation was an almost routine method of extracting confession of the Demonic Pact." [Larner, 2000, p.107]. It is certainly not unlikely, judging by Mackenzie's comment, that lack of sleep was a factor in producing confessions. Also, Katherine Liddell, the Prestonpans witchcraft suspect, said "they kept her from sleep several nights and days with the intention of extorting any confession they pleased from her." However, there does not seem to be much evidence in the East Lothian records to support Larner's claim that this was "routine". Larner and others seem to have seized on the Scots word *waukin*, usually rendered in the records as "waking", which can indeed mean "waking" in the modern English sense, but also means "watching". As I have previously remarked, "waking" a witchcraft suspect means watching her, or guarding her, in the same sense as "waukin the fauld" means keeping an eye on your sheep. A "wake" is the overnight watching of a corpse, not an attempt to rouse it from its slumbers! A witchcraft suspect may have been kept awake by her guards, but there is no proof in the records that this was "routine".

For most of the period under discussion the use of torture was illegal without the express permission of the Privy Council. Having said that, it is perfectly obvious that there was much unofficial ill-treatment, which amounted to torture. Mackenzie in fact states, "Most of these poor creatures are tortured by their keepers."

Pricking for the witchmark does seem to have been almost routine, and is usually described as torture by modern writers, and certainly must often have been so. All the same, it ought to be remembered that one of the crucial points about the witchmark was that a witch would not feel pain if the mark was pricked. If a suspect confessed to save herself further pricking, that is one thing, but if she confessed after a "genuine" witchmark was found, surely the inference is that she would have felt no pain. And in fact the records in some cases at least say precisely that. It would not be surprising if pricking in many cases did indeed amount to torture, but it seems to me to be worth considering whether a skilled operator, like Kincaid perhaps, could perform the operation painlessly. After all, as I have previously remarked, injections in the doctor's surgery are not always accompanied by shrieks of agony and fountains of blood.

There follows a list of instances of obvious ill-treatment from the records, along with statements claiming the contrary. Evidence of pricking has already been dealt with in the section on witchmarks in this chapter.

1590 John McGill
Violently assaulted by his supposed victim's family.

1590 John Cunningham
According to *Newes from Scotland* he was severely tortured, first of all with the "bootes". After his escape and recapture he had needles forced under his fingernails, then had the nails torn out with pincers. The bones of his legs were then smashed in the "bootes".

1591 Agnes Sampson
According to "Newes" she had her head "thrawn" with a rope.

1591 Geillis Duncan
According to "Newes" she was tortured with the thumbscrews and had her head thrawn with a rope.

1591 Janet Stratton
Her final statement mentions "fear for her life", "fear of torture", and "compulsion".

1591 Euphane MacCalyean
There was certainly severe psychological pressure. She was sentenced to be burned alive, and in an attempt to encourage a confession, the King's instructions were to "show her the stake".

1629 Margaret Jo
Margaret was arrested and imprisoned by the Musselburgh baillies. They refused to put her on trial. The Privy Council ordered them either to free her or put her on trial within fifteen days. The baillies ignored the order and kept her fettered in irons. The baillies were summoned before the Council and ordered to free her from the irons and stocks in which she had been "miserably detained for twelve weeks". They had threatened to put her on trial at an hour's notice without allowing her to read her dittay. The Privy Council ordered that she should be put on trial by 25th November, and that her indictment should be produced by 20th November so that it could be passed to her advocate.

1629 John Carfrae, Thomas Carfrae, Alison Borthwick
Witnesses for the prosecution seem to have served on the jury.

1629 Janet Hardie, Janet Barclay
The Privy Council records for June 9th note that they had been arrested the previous March and imprisoned in Musselburgh tollbooth "in the stocks and in irons", and the baillies were refusing to put them on trial. The Privy Council remitted the case to the lord of the Regality.

1652 John Wilson
He had been arrested, escaped, and now seemingly had returned to Dunglass and turned himself in. The records say he confessed "freely of his own accord".

1659 Helen Simberd
Witnesses said she confessed voluntarily. She later denied everything.

1659 Janet Crooks
James Cowan and the rest of the witnesses testify that she confessed everything voluntarily without torture. She later denied everything.

1659 John Douglas
He said he was very much afraid to confess to begin with. They had threatened to put him in the [illegible] and the stocks. However, witnesses testified that no threats were made.

1659 Barbara Cochrane
Witnesses testified that she confessed voluntarily.

1659 Elspeth Foular
Elspeth died in prison of "ane flux".

1659 Janet Thomson
Janet claimed to have been threatened, and confessed out of fear of torture and "the gown". Her trial acquitted her.

1661 Agnes Lochand others.
George Mackenzie and two others were

appointed as judges to try their cases in Dalkeith and Musselburgh. Mackenzie later wrote in "The Laws and Customs of Scotland in Matters Criminal", published in 1674, that close confinement and deprivation of food and sleep confuses the suspects. He states, "Most of these poor creatures are tortured by their keepers, thinking they are serving God by so doing," and he says he "knows this to his certain knowledge." He says that judges should suspect that this torture is "the origin of the confession", and that fear of it "prevents retraction."

1661 David Johnston

[One of the Musselburgh witches above.] Johnstone said that when he was arrested he was put in "ane hair cloath". He said he was forced to say he had renounced his baptism. He retracted his confession, but said when questioned further that he would not deny what he had already confessed, whether it was true or not.

1661 Margaret Kerr

Confessed "without using any manner of violence or compulsion".

1661 Janet Bagbie

Confessed "without using any manner of violence or compulsion".

1661 Bessie Dawsone

Confessed "without using any manner of violence or compulsion".

1661 Bessie Todrig

Confessed "without using any manner of violence or compulsion, and without searching her". [Does this imply that her fellow suspects were searched?]

1661 Inveresk Kirk Session

It was intimated from the pulpit that anyone verbally abusing someone whose mother or other relative has been burnt for witchcraft would be liable to church censure and a civil penalty from the magistrate.

1662 Agnes Williamson

Agnes's lawyer claimed that her confession was illegal, and the result of torture. Some witnesses said she had confessed before she was put in the stocks. Thomas Steill said she was free when she confessed, but had been in he stocks before that, for her restraint, not to torture her. William Carrail said she was in the stocks before her confession.

1662 James Welsh

The Haddington magistrate says he was brought to a confession "after being laboured with".

1677 Elizabeth Moodie

The commission from the Privy Council against her specifically states, "... if she is found guilty after making a voluntary confession without any sort of torture of direct means being used against her to bring her to a confession".

1678 Agnes Kelly, Marjorie Anderson

The same conditions were stipulated in their Privy Council commission as in Elizabeth Moodie's. Fountainhall remarks that their confessions were "in no way extorted". [But see Elspeth Chouslie below.]

1678 Jennet Burtoun

Jennet gave a "free and voluntary confession".

1678 Elspeth Knox

On being questioned she confessed immediately "freely and voluntarily".

1678 Helen Laing

She gave a "free and voluntary confession made without any torture or threatening".

1678 Margaret Dodds

She gave a "free and voluntary confession made without any torture or threatening".

1678 Agnes Dalgleish

She confessed "freely and voluntarily without subjection to any threatening or torture".

1678 Margaret Russel

There was a "free and voluntary confession given without torture or threatening".

1678 Margaret Veitch

She confessed "without any compulsion or threatening".

1678 Marion Campbell

Marion "freely and voluntarily confessed without any threatening or torture whatever".

1678 Isobel Eliot

She gave a "free and voluntary confession".

1678/9 Elspeth Chouslie

She was denounced by Agnes Kellie, Marjorie Anderson, and Christian Lockart, confessing witches. The Prestonpans baron baillie and his officer arrested her, stripped her, and had her pricked by David Cowan from Tranent. She was kept in prison until she gave her bond to enter her person when required for trial. Later, the baron baillie attacked her house with soldiers, breaking down the door and smashing her windows. On another occasion he turned up at night armed with a sword and pistol, and threatened her. Elspeth claimed that Kellie, Anderson, and Lockart had been tortured, and denounced her, but had later retracted the accusation at the stake.

1678 Katherine Liddell

The Prestonpans baron baillie John Rutherford, and others, seized her and imprisoned her in the tdlbooth, and pricked her "to the great effusion of her blood". Her skin was raised, her body highly swollen, and her life was in danger. Also they "kept her from sleep several nights and days with the intention of extorting any confessions they pleased from her." Rutherford was forbidden to arrest or torture anyone without a warrant from the Privy Council. The pricker Cowan was imprisoned in Edinburgh in September 1678 and released on 27th February 1679 after pledging never to prick again without a Privy Council warrant.

It is obvious from the records that officially sanctioned torture does not appear to have been used in any of the East Lothian cases after the North Berwick affair, and in fact there was sometimes considerable effort made on the part of the interrogators to show that confessions were "free and voluntary". P. G. Maxwell-Stuart remarks cautiously, "... it is probably fair to say that the common assumption by nineteenth and early twentieth century writers on Scottish witchcraft that torture was routinely used against the panel [*i.e.* the accused] in such cases is likely to be exaggerated and to rest upon shaky foundations, especially since there are no means of telling whether a confession which appears in the records was or was not voluntary." [Maxwell-Stuart, 2001, p. 74-5].

It would be naive, however, to assume just because there was no official torture, that there was no ill-treatment. The cases of Elspeth Chouslie and Katherine Liddell make it clear that the baron baillie of Prestonpans made use of gross intimidation, sleep deprivation, and painful pricking. Since the Peaston/Keith witches were part of the same panic at the same time, one cannot help wondering if the interrogators there who claimed "free and voluntary confessions" were being absolutely truthful.

Then again, in the cases of Janet Thomson and David Johnston we read of "the gown", and a "hair cloth". Although other writers have mentioned suspects being kept in rough garments soaked in cold water or vinegar, we have no means of knowing precisely why "the gown" and the "hair cloth" inspired terror in Thomson and Johnston. We may bet, however, that these garments were not being used to keep the prisoners warm and dry!

There are several mentions of the stocks. It is easy to claim that prisoners were being confined in the stocks simply to prevent their escape, but of course if a suspect was kept sitting in her own urine and excrement, in the same position for days or weeks at a time in a cold damp cell, there is no real difference between close confinement and torture.

Mackenzie in his *Laws and Customs* states quite plainly, "Most of these poor creatures are tortured by their keepers, who being persuaded that they are serving God well, think it is their duty to vex and torment their poor prisoners." There is little reason to doubt him. One might consider recent cases of humiliation and abuse of Iraqi prisoners by low-ranking American military personel. There are also the famous psychological experiments where students were divided into "guards" and "prisoners", and the "guards" soon began to exhibit deliberately inhuman attitudes. There are the equally notorious "electric shock" experiments where perfectly normal human beings were more than willing to administer what they believed to be potentially fatal electric shocks to other participants [Haney, Banks & Zimbardo, Stanford University 1973; Stanley Milgram, Yale University,1974]. All these would suggest that many ordinary people given unlimited authority over prisoners, will take the opportunity to "play" with their charges.

On the other hand, we might perhaps question Mackenzie's motives. At the time of writing he was obviously having grave doubts about the validity of witchcraft confessions. Yet as a younger man he had been sent to Musselburgh and Dalkeith to judge several cases of witchcraft and had condemned [or was complicit in condemning] the "guilty" parties to death. When writing his *Laws and Customs* some seventeen years later, did he perhaps have an uneasy conscience about his part in this, and was he seeking to pass the buck by playing up the role of those who had extracted the confessions in the first place? Then again, what are we to make of the Haddington baillies drinking with witchcraft suspects in the tollbooth, and hobnobbing with them to the extent that the Synod of Lothian and Tweedale felt it necessary to advise Haddington to treat its witchcraft suspects more harshly? [See Kirk Session and Synod records.] Also, we find some suspects who categorically denied everything and refused to confess. Given that everybody is supposed to have a breaking point, does this not suggest that in some cases at least the treatment cannot have been unbearable?

A fair conclusion might be that actual torture was unusual, but that ill-treatment was widespread. Many confessions, therefore, were probably made out of a despairing and possibly misguided apprehension that a confession was the only way to end the misery.

This does not mean however that everything confessed by witchcraft suspects is necessarily false. Let us consider those who appear to have engaged in "wise wife" activities - curing, diagnosing, detecting, predicting, and counteracting witchcraft. Agnes Sampson is of course the most obvious example, but a glance at the relevant sections of this chapter will show that not only did many others engage in the same work, particularly healing, and not only were they frequently specifically sought out by their "patients", but both healer and patient often seem to have been satisfied that the cures had worked. It should not really be a matter for contention that such folk-healers existed. They have existed, and still exist, all over the world. Thus, when a "wise wife" confesses to washing someone's sick child in south-running water, what reason have we to doubt that she did in fact do so? When we read that Agnes Sampson healed John Ker in Alexander Fairlie's house in Longniddry when he had been expected to die we may be rather more sceptical. After all, most of the "cures" described - south-running water, foxglove leaves, enchanted threads, salt and wheat, live toads, drinking from the broken horn of a live ox, raw meat, charms and incantations - few if any can possibly have had any effective medicinal value.

However, modern science has demonstrated the power of the "placebo" effect whereby a patient will benefit from a pill or potion he believes to be effective, even when it is medicinally valueless. Neither should we ignore the psychological effect on well-being which stems from simply being listened to, treated with sympathy, and having an optimistic outcome predicted. Perhaps above all we should remember the quite amazing ability of the human metabolism to heal itself, sometimes in the most adverse circumstances. We should not forget that not only was the 16th/17th century "wise wife" operating in these areas, but so too is the modern medical practitioner, more often than he might readily admit; and this is without venturing into the realms of faith healing, homeopathy, acupuncture, and the whole gamut of "alternative" and "new age" treatments, all of which will happily produce their own evidence for successful healing and curing.

In short, I would contend that where a suspect confesses to activities connected with healing and curing disease in human beings and animals, there is little reason to doubt her. Modern scholarship tends to create a division between the activities of "cunning men" and "wise wives" on the one hand, and "witchcraft" on the other. I am not sure that this is entirely justified. The law of course made no distinction in most cases, but there is ample evidence from the East Lothian records that many of those engaging in "wise wife" activities were popularly considered to be "witches" by the ordinary folk they lived among. For example, when a little girl somewhere in Midlothian was made to sleep with Agnes Sampson, she was "frightened out of her wits" [Dalkeith Presb mins], presumably because of Agnes's reputation. William Davidson and Jonet Bruce were also obviously considered to be witches, although their activities revolved mainly around curing.

Thus, in as much as "wise wives" who practised healing and curing, detecting and diagnosing, preventing and counteracting witchcraft, were considered by the law of Scotland to be witches for so doing, and in as much as their neighbours also at least sometimes viewed them as such, we may say that witches did in fact exist in sixteenth and seventeenth century East Lothian.

The waters are perhaps more muddied when we come to examine the question of "malefice". If the main concern of the Kirk and the Law was that witches had entered into a covenant with Satan, the main concern of the population at large seems rather to have been the ability of witches to perpetrate "malefice", that is to cause sickness, ruin, misfortune or death. It will be seen from the relevant sections of this chapter that such accusations were legion. They were however very difficult to prove, which is why someone like Agnes Williamson, who seems to have had a formidable reputation as a witch, could nevertheless be acquitted in court. Others were not quite so fortunate. Jonet Bruce of Tranent was acquitted of almost all of the charges against her, but condemned to death as guilty of one [or perhaps two] of them. Isobel Young of East Barns was acquitted of half of the 24 charges against her but still could not escape the stake. Be that as it may, it was the difficulty of proving malefice which led to the crucial importance of obtaining confessions of the diabolic pact.

Many of the accusations of malefice must have been false, based on mere coincidence. If misfortune followed threats from a witch, or a quarrel with a witch, the cause was obvious to the victim and his family. Perhaps the witch would not even need to express hostility. Bearing in mind the Highland tradition of the "evil eye", and the East Lothian fisher superstition that certain individuals were unlucky to meet or even to mention, it would not be surprising if there was a feeling that even a perfectly ordinary encounter with a witch might have unfortunate results. Apart from that, there was the strong belief that sickness could be laid on as well as taken off. Contemporary logic decreed that if a witch took a sickness off someone, it could not simply disappear. The sickness had to go somewhere, perhaps to an animal, or possibly to some unsuspecting passer by - or even to a particular named victim.

Further, it is not implausible to suggest that if you could apply to a practitioner of folk magic to have an illness healed, you would be likely to believe that the same person had the ability to cause sickness. By extension, if it was possible to cause sickness, is it not logical to believe that other misfortunes could be similarly brought about? The opportunity or the means to take direct vengeance on an enemy or persecutor was not always available, but you could always pay a witch to take the wind from your enemy's sails for you. Thus it would not seem preposterous to suggest that "wise wives" could be employed from time to time by their customers to deliberately cause harm; that they took on the healing of patients fully aware that the cure might involve harming another; that they were perfectly prepared to set out to cause harm on occasion to avenge slights, insults, and bad turns for others. It is also more than likely that they were prepared to wreak vengeance for bad turns done to themselves, or cause misfortune simply to boost their own reputations. The records are full of accusations of such activities, and it is stretching credulity to suggest that they could all be nothing but imagination.

At a conference on witchcraft held at Edinburgh University on 25th January 2003, someone asked the speakers during the plenary session if in their opinion witches actually had the power to do what they were supposed to do. One speaker gave a very interesting reply to the effect that no-one with an academic reputation to defend could possibly admit to believing any such thing, but if you live in a society where everyone believes in witchcraft, then witchcraft works. There really ought to be nothing controversial in this statement. The power of suggestion can hardly be disputed. If a stage hypnotist can make a volunteer believe that the onion he is eating is an apple, or cause every muscle in the volunteer's body to go absolutely rigid, we should not be surprised if genuine physical symptoms followed a witch's threat to "see a black sight of you". If a hypnotherapist can regress a patient to childhood or into "past lives", what fevered imaginings could not be induced by a witch with a fearsome reputation over several parishes? Advertising, fashion, peer pressure, education, all influence modern thinking, behaviour, and perception of reality to an almost unlimited extent. The American psychologist Charles Tart has gone so far as to float the idea that these pressures and suggestions are so strong that the "normal" state of consciousness in a culture or society is in fact a sort of state of trance which he calls "consensus trance". Whether or not this is taking things to extremes, it cannot be denied that most human beings are very much open to suggestion - pathologically so, it might be argued, in view of the many "good things of life" which are in fact very mixed blessings.

The power of suggestion can be greatly enhanced by a little theatricality, an air of mystery, or just the feeling of the participant that he is involved in "something special". John Atkinson, the Victorian vicar of Danby in Yorkshire, described a visit by one of his informants to John Wrightson, "the Wise Man of Stokesley", early in the 19th century. His informant lived as a young man with a gamekeeper uncle who grazed some cattle on his master's ground. One bullock was afflicted by a mysterious illness which no-one could identify, far less cure. The gamekeeper sent his nephew to Wrightson, who received him in a robe and "strange-looking" headgear, sitting at a table set out with a globe, a skull, dried herbs, and other objects. Wrightson addressed him by name, told him why he had come, and seeing his astonishment, commented that there would be little use in coming to him for help if he wasn't able to tell why the visitor had come. He was also able to tell the youth the last thing his uncle had said before he left for Stokesley. Not only that, but he knew the symptoms of the sick bullock, and the very position it occupied in the byre. He said the beast was beyond help, but if they cut it open when it died they would find the growth which had caused the problem - a diagnosis which proved to be correct. [Atkinson, ed. O' Leary, 1983, p.56.]

Modern readers will find Wrightson's appearance as a comic-book wizard more amusing than awe-inspiring, but it certainly seems to have served its purpose in early 19th century Yorkshire, for he had an impressive reputation. We can detect hints of such theatricality in the records of East Lothian witchcraft. Quite apart from her confidence-inspiring "grave and matron-like" demeanour, it sounds rather as if Agnes Sampson's raising a spirit from the well at Edmiston in the shape of a black dog, was an elaborate piece of trickery designed to impress. If so, it certainly seems to have succeeded, terrifying the daughters of the house out of their wits. We also find Agnes taking Thomas Kerse's sickness upon herself, and keeping it all night with much groaning and apparent pain, before throwing it out for a dog or a cat to catch. On another occasion she raised a spirit as a voice only for Effie MacCalyean. Considering the "prayers" reproduced in Agnes's dittay, one used to predict whether the patient would live or die and the other used for curing - there is no mention of how Agnes repeated these prayers. We are conditioned to think of witches "mumbling" magic spells, but the repetition of such prayers could well have been performances stunning in their intensity.

There are other rituals mentioned in the records which seem deliberately intended to frighten or overawe. There is Isobel Young removing her kerchief and turning three times withershins when she wished a bad turn on those who displeased her. There is Jonet Bruce urinating at the threshold of her landlord's door; Jean Craig blowing in her victim's face and wishing a black sight of her; and perhaps most quietly menacing of all, Catherine McTarget sitting on the stair opposite James Cungilton's house all night with her hair hanging over her eyes. In a society where belief in the power of the witch to cause harm was almost universal, such actions would not only boost the witch's reputation, but must also often have had the desired effect on the victim. Alexander Sinclair/Hunter's reputation as a man of mystery can only have been enhanced by the bee he kept in a tin box, fed on drops of his own blood, and renewed annualy in Norham. When begging at the door, Alexander was able to tell one housewife where her money was hidden, and how much her nest-egg consisted of. Speaking of John Wrightson's ability to tell his clients what was seemingly impossible for him to know, Rev. Atkinson comments, "He must have known the district as if it were a map, and the people in it as the master knows his scholars. He must have had channels of information such that he could depend upon what they supplied him with, and yet such as not to be known or even suspected." [Atkinson, ed. O'Leary, 1983, p.56].

When James VI called Agnes Sampson's professional abilities into question, she could not resist proving herself by telling the King the first words he spoke to his young bride on his wedding night [according to *Newes from Scotland* anyway - there is no mention of this feat in Agnes's dittay.] We may be sure that like John Wrightson, Agnes had her "channels of information". We might, for example, consider the likelihood of the presence of the Queen's ladies and attendants in or near the bridal chamber, or ponder the possibility of confidences passed from the Queen to one or more of them. Since the Earl Marischal of Scotland had been responsible for all the wedding arrangements, we might speculate further on contact between this nobleman or his servants and attendants, and the Queen's ladies or their servants. And where was the Earl Marischal's Scottish home? Why, at Keith, a stone's throw from Agnes Sampson's own house! Need we doubt that Agnes would be on familiar terms with the Earl's servants? Thus, it is not hard to see how words whispered in secret in Scandinavia could "magically" wing their way to Nether Keith in East Lothian, especially if they were salacious or amusing. The fact that James and his bride apparently communicated in French makes little difference - all we need is one bilingual person somewhere in the chain of whispers.

If a "wise wife" could convince a king, and a highly educated, literate, and intelligent king at that, we should not be surprised if illiterate and superstitious peasants duly fell ill or went insane if their local witch wished a black sight of them.

To recapitulate, although many 18th, 19th, and 20th century writers have dismissed witchcraft confessions as nonsensical, there is no reason to doubt that in 16th and 17th century East Lothian there were those who made a living, full-time or part-time by curing disease in man and beast, counteracting witchcraft, and practising various odds and ends of folk magic. Nor need we doubt that on occasion at least some of these practitioners would deliberately set out to cause misfortune, illness, or even death. Part and parcel of such a career would be the acquisition of a professional reputation. The practitioner would be likely to take every opportunity to convey the impression of power and mystery, and to attain these ends might not be above intimidating or even terrifying. Deception and illusion would be part of the everyday stock-in-trade. No "wise wife" or witch could have managed a career spanning several decades [and some did] unless she was seen to be successful. We do not have to believe in "magic" to believe that there were successful witches. The powers of suggestion, the placebo effect, the workings of the subconscious, and human gullibility are quite enough to give us "magical" outcomes. So in answer to that mischievous question, "Could witches really do what they were supposed to do?" the simple answer is, 'Yes. A lot of the time anyway".

However, we now come up against the diabolic side of witchcraft. Very few modern readers are likely to believe in the existence of such a being as "the Devil", far less that he made regular appearances in out-of-the-way corners of East Lothian for open air dancing, and erotic adventures which seem to have been more frosty than steamy. Again, the stock response of many writers has been that this is all nonsense, the product of addled brains or of torture. It must be admitted that they may well be right. No-one who has read *The Gulag Archipelago*, for example, can be in any doubt that almost anybody can be made to confess to almost anything - a truth of which several British police forces seem to have been well aware over the past few decades. We must remember too that witchcraft confessions are more likely to have been cobbled together from a string of leading questions, than to have been spontaneous outpourings. The interrogators knew what they were looking for, and one suspects that the first question is more likely to have been, "When did you first meet the Devil?" than "Did you ever meet the Devil?"

We might imagine a scene something like the following: -

INTERROGATOR: *When did you first meet the Devil?*

SUSPECT: *I never met the Devil in my life.*

INT: *Come on, you must have met him. When was it?*

SUS: *I swear I never...*

[Baron baillie's "officer" advances menacingly.]

INT: *When was it? [Bellowing.]*

SUS: *Twenty years ago.*

INT: *Where was this?*

SUS: *I can't remember.*

[Wallop.]

531

INT: *Where was it? [Bellowing.]*
SUS: *At the Back Burn.*
INT: *Did he look like a black man?*
SUS: *A black man?*
INT: *A black man! Are you deaf?*
[Wallop!]
SUS: *Yes.*
INT: *Did you renounce your baptism?*
SUS: *No. Please don't... Yes.*
INT: *You renounced your baptism?*
SUS: *Yes.*
INT: *And you had sex with the Devil.*
SUS: *What? No, I never... No, please...*
[Wallop.]
INT: *Well?*
SUS: *Yes. Yes.*
INT: *Was his penis cold?*
SUS: *Cold? I can't remember... Aagh! No, please don't... Yes. Yes.*

Etc. etc. [Continued until the interrogator reaches the end of his mental list of "Things Witches Do".]

This is later cooked up into, "I first met the Devil twenty years ago at the Back Burn. He was in the shape of a black man. I renounced my baptism and the Devil had sex with me. His penis was cold..." The demoralised suspect would then acknowledge the confession, knowing all was now lost, perhaps also confirming that it was given voluntarily, without torture being used - after all, who could call a couple of dunts in the ribs "torture"? She would append her duly witnessed mark to the confession, and her fate was then pretty much sealed.

Then again, there would be the simple soul who remembered an erotic dream many years previously, and had it reinterpreted for her by her interrogators. There would be the poor creature so terrified out of her wits that she would blurt out anything to please her interrogators, just in the hope of being left alone. There may also have been those so socially conditioned as to dutifully do whatever their betters required of them, "even unto death". There must also have been the insane and the senile, whose wandering minds and alarming hallucinations could be trimmed and knocked into convincing shape by the interrogation team. There can be no doubt that many many times, suspects went to their deaths as a result of extorted confessions with hardly a grain of truth in them. This is particularly likely in the event of large-scale witchcraft panics, such as that of 1649.

Bearing in mind that many confessions can only have been false, is it possible that there could be any truth at all in any of them, as regards the diabolic aspects of witchcraft? Margaret Murray's book *The Witch Cult in Western Europe*, first published in 1921, became very influential during the course of the Twentieth Century. Basically, her theory was that what was popularly designated witchcraft was in fact a survival of pre-Christian pagan religion, whose devotees formed a network of organised groups meeting regularly for ritual worship. This was eagerly seized upon by a legion of other writers. Thus F. Marion McNeill in "The Silver Bough" –

"The organisation of the witch cult has been aptly described as a sort of Congregationalism. There was a 'minister' - the 'devil' or his substitute, the 'officer', and a body of 'elders' - the coven.

The coven consisted of twelve 'witches' (chiefly women), and the 'Devil' or 'officer' who managed the local affairs of the cult. Each coven had is Ring Leader (leader of the ring dance), its Piper, and its Maiden, the last two being peculiar to Scotland...

All the covens in the district were under the authority of a Grand-master or King Deil, the Horned God incarnate. (The witches had come to adopt the phraseology of the Christians.)" [McNeill, 1957, p.133.]

"Four times a year the witches held a festival known as a Sabbath... The main feature of the festival was a religious or magical ceremony in which the leading figure was the 'Devil', or

'King Deil' of the district in the disguise of a horned animal.

The proceedings opened with an act of homage to the 'Devil' ... Reports of magic accomplished either by individuals or by covens were then made and recorded in a book ... Then followed the religious service which in Catholic countries was comparable with Mass, but which in Scotland, as in Sweden, followed the rites of the Reformed Church ... The religious service was followed by the obscene fertility rites ... The dancing and feasting that ended the proceedings lasted until dawn, the crowing of the cock being the signal for dispersal." [McNeill, 1957, p.141-142.]

This "Pagan Survival" theory is still the explanation for witchcraft most likely to be found in modern newspaper or magazine articles. One suspects that is also the source from which much of modern "Wicca" has sprung, for although the New Age practitioners of Wicca like to persuade themselves that they are the bearers of a tradition going far back into the mists of time, much of what they purport to believe has "Margaret Murray" stamped all over it.

It will be recognised that the tightly organised meetings and practices described in "The Silver Bough" bear little resemblance to what appears in the records of East Lothian witchcraft. In fact few if any serious scholars have given any credence to the Pagan Survival theory since Norman Cohn showed conclusively in 1975 that Murray had been so selective with her supporting evidence as to render her conclusions quite unjustifiable. In other words, she simply ignored the vast body of evidence pointing in other directions. Christina Larner, the founder of serious witchcraft scholarship in Scotland, was able to write in *Enemies of God* that Cohn had "finally dispatched" Murray's witch cult theories. [Larner, 2000, p. 19].

On the basis of the evidence of the East Lothian records, is it at all likely that any aspect of diabolic witchcraft can have had any foundation in reality? Can any of it actually have happened? Most modern witchcraft scholars seem to take the view that the mediaeval and early modern learnèd view of witchcraft as something essentially evil and entirely diabolic in origin, is quite irreconcilable with the popular folk-magic "witchcraft" practised by the "wise wife". The usual conclusion to be drawn is that "wise wife" witchcraft existed, but diabolic witchcraft did not. Perhaps this may be too simplistic, however. Writing on witch trials in Denmark, Bengt Ankarloo remarks, "Nevertheless, just as in Sweden, traces of a popular concept of demonological witchcraft, although in a less developed form, are to be found in the trial records." [Ankarloo *et al*, 2002, Vol 4, p.83]. Would it be all that surprising if in Scotland too, something of the elite view of witchcraft had not rubbed off on the population at large? We might compare this with the activities at "Highland Games" where the costumes and events are mostly inventions of the 19th century literati and aristocracy, and bear little resemblance to the original dress, sports, and amusements of native Gaelic communities. Nevertheless, Highland Games are now patronised by crowds of locals, many of whom actually believe that they are participating in a genuine aspect of their Highland heritage.

It does not seem unreasonable to suggest that a diabolic strand spun by their "betters" might have become entwined in the more traditional witchcraft practices of the "lower orders". How seriously this was taken by the participants is another matter. When we read in David Calderwood's *History of the Kirk of Scotland* of Greymeal hiding behind the door at North Berwick to avoid kissing the Devil's backside "yet it behoved him also to kiss at last", it reads more like a glorious farce than an obscene act of blasphemous worship. We can almost hear the same howls of glee as when the class buffoon is pinioned and has his head rammed yet again down the toilet!

In considering diabolic witchcraft, let us begin with witch meetings. The word "coven" is never used. Ritual is almost entirely absent. There are religious overtones only at North Berwick, and according to a single witness, at Crichton in Midlothian in 1678. These meetings are not the hellish orgies, vile feasts, and blasphemous rituals of classical European witchcraft. They are usually relatively small get-togethers, often with dancing, sometimes with food and drink, sometimes with sex, occasionally with some reporting or requesting of favours. In fact, many of these East Lothian meetings bear more resemblance to nocturnal picnics than witches' sabbaths!

There is nothing out of the ordinary in people with shared interests meeting together from time to time. Rotary Clubs, Gardening Clubs, Flower Arrangers, Literary Associations do it all the time; it is part and parcel of human interaction. Would it be surprising if professional practitioners of folk magic met from time to time to discuss common interests? Would it be surprising if there was also a "fun" aspect to these meetings? Of course not - don't Rotarians meet to dine? Doesn't almost every organisation under the sun have its dinner dance, its Christmas night out? Would it be surprising if the "members" sometimes brought friends along? Would it be surprising if those practising a profession officially frowned upon, met to give each other material support and encouragement? Of course not - do trade unions and political parties not have their origins in just such gatherings? Would it be surprising if those practising a profession which had attracted much persecution preferred to meet in secret in out of the way places?

On the other hand, if for some reason you were organising some sort of Extraordinary General Meeting in an area where persecution had not yet got under way, with delegates arriving from a wide area, would you not arrange it for a venue which even total strangers could not miss? There is much that is dubious in the North Berwick evidence, and much that I suspect was concocted by the investigating authorities, but the very fact that the meeting was held at North Berwick is enough to suggest that some such meeting actually took place; for the hill Berwick Law is a prominent landmark visible from almost everywhere in East Lothian, unmistakable from Edinburgh, and clearly discernible from much of Midlothian.

In short, it might be thought that it is not only highly likely that practitioners of folk magic in any given area (and their admirers and hangers-on) would meet from time to time, but that it would be strange if they did not. Let us concede that if we are merely talking about a bit of discussion, some dancing and a bit of fun, and possibly a couple of pints and a bit of hanky-panky at the back of a dyke, witch meetings in East Lothian are perfectly possible. The sheer ordinariness of what was supposedly going on at most of them is perhaps the most compelling evidence.

If we can accept the possibility that there might have been occasional or even frequent get-togethers of witches for a bit of serious business and a bit of fun and frolic, we might perhaps take the further step of imagining loosely organised groups which like most gangs, clubs, or organisations, marked their exclusivity by having an initiation ceremony and a badge. After all, even Boy Scouts have an initiation ceremony and a badge. There would be nothing out of the ordinary in new recruits swearing to serve some mythical founder figure, guiding principle, or presiding spirit, with some degree of ritual attached, like for example, offering up in service all between the crown of the head and the sole of the foot. Ritual scarring or tattooing is a widespread phenomenon found in many societies, so the painful nip described by several witches, is a perfectly feasible way of giving the new recruit a permanent membership "badge". Receiving a new name too is not impossible. Does not Mary Brown become "Sister Concepta" on becoming a nun? Bear in mind that the suggestion is not that such things are probable, but that they are possible.

If meetings did indeed take place, we need not believe that everyone who attended or went through some form of initiation was a serious and assiduous practitioner of witchcraft. There are many members of Labour Clubs, British Legions, and Masonic Lodges who care little for the guiding principles of the organisation, but turn up regularly for the company and the cheap drink. In other words, many witch meetings could have been mainly or even entirely social in nature. This might seem all the more likely if we consider what alternative forms of entertainment were available for women in 17th century Scotland. The range of choice would not be wide! Thus, many women who were rounded up in witch hunts may only have gone along to meetings "for a laugh", and would know as much about witchcraft as about quantum theory. We might imagine, then, a very loose network of "witch clubs" which were taken seriously by a few stalwarts, but were used by the majority of participants entirely for social reasons.

The objection might be made that since witchcraft was a capital crime, no-one in her senses would take such risks simply "for a laugh". However, for much of the period under discussion, bestiality was also a capital crime punishable by strangulation at the stake and burning, just as witchcraft was. One might ask, who would risk such a fate just to have sex with a horse? And yet a search through any of the Justiciary Court boxes will show that bestiality was widespread. In modern times no effort has been spared to make people aware of the dangers of alcohol, smoking, taking drugs, and having unprotected sex. In spite of that, all of these remain very popular pastimes, with not a few hardy souls indulging in all of them. Knowledge of the dangers involved is not always an effective deterrent.

So far, so plausible. However, there are problems. We cannot but be struck by the overwhelmingly Christian content of the charms and prayers used by East Lothian witches. Karen Jolly remarks in *Witchcraft and Magic in Europe* (Vol. 3), "What is more surprising than the survival of these so-called 'pagan' remedies is to recognise the thoroughly Christian character of the bulk of charm formulas and their closeness to liturgical prayers, even in the early Middle Ages soon after conversion." (Jolly *et al.* 2002, Vol 3, p. 36.) It is difficult to believe that practitioners of folk magic which was essentially Christian in nature (albeit condemned by official Christianity) would renounce the God they obviously believed to be the source of their power. Although perusal of the 17th century Justiciary Court records shows the there were a few atheists around in those days, it is quite clear that for the overwhelming majority of the population, belief in the Christian God was taken for granted. It is difficult, therefore, to come to terms with the large number of witches who confessed to renouncing their baptism. What possible advantage could there have been to anyone in such an act, when it was implicitly believed by all that it would result in eternal damnation? Joining a group and attending meetings, either out of serious interest or "for a laugh", promising to serve some sort of guiding principle, receiving a mark - all this is feasible enough, but renouncing baptism does not make sense. Of course it might be argued that according to the Calvinist doctrine of Predestination, most people were bound for eternal damnation anyway. But how many ordinary folk in the rank and file of the Church of Scotland's congregations actually believed in this pessimistic view of the love of God?

Finally, of course, we come up against the figure of "the Devil". It beggars belief that droves of ordinary people from a thoroughly Christian society were blithely promising to devote themselves body and soul to the service of the personification of absolute evil. Throughout history, human beings have committed deeds of the most horrific and foulest wickedness, but usually in the pursuit of some higher cause - "the Flag", "the Empire", "Our Way of Life", "God", "Freedom", to name just a few. The evil is done under the illusion that the perpetrators are in some way doing good. Could anyone really thus delude herself if she was making a solemn vow to serve Satan?

This is where the apparent rationality of Margaret Murray's theories supply a handy escape route. The "Devil", in her view, is not "Satan", but the "Horned God", a pre-Christian personification of the forces of nature, represented at the "covens" by a man in disguise. His worshippers were in no danger of eternal damnation, because they did not believe in any such thing, nor in Satan, nor in the Christian God. They were pagans. This is a neat solution to the problem, but there is little hard evidence for it, and as previously mentioned, it has been abandoned by serious witchcraft scholars. Karen Jolly again: "By the mediaeval period the church may not have obliterated all signs of pre-Christian beliefs and practices in England, but it had effectively suppressed all vestiges of paganism as a religion and as a mode of worship." (Jolly *et al*, 2002, Vol 3, p.185.) There is no obvious reason why the situation in East Lothian in the Anglian south-east of Scotland should be any different.

If we consider the Devil as he is described in the records relating to his visits to East Lothian, it becomes clear that this is not the terrifying monster of mediaeval imagination, nor the pantomime demon of today. Nor is he the haughty fallen angel Lucifer, nor the majestic Prince of Darkness. Neither, however, does he bear any resemblance to the pagan Horned God.

The East Lothian Devil is astonishing only in his mundane ordinariness. Occasionally, granted, he may appear as a dog, a horse, or a puff of wind, but in the vast majority of cases he appears as "a man", "a gentleman", or "a black man". Nor, apart from occasional irritability, sporadic mild violence, a penchant for fornication, and a tendency to "vanish away", does he exhibit much in the way of satanic behaviour. He appears, in fact, most of the time to be thoroughly human, and apart from searching out new recruits and presiding at meetings, appears neither to have had much to do, nor to have commanded much respect. What are we to make of little incidents such as Margaret Paterson getting permission from the Devil to leave a meeting and go home because her children were crying? What do we make of a good-natured Devil who courteously greets the women with a kiss and an embrace, and the men with a handshake, then wishes his servants good night at the end of meetings? Can there be anything more down to earth than the scene where Margaret Dickson was sitting with Agnes Broun in Agnes's house, and the Devil comes in, remarking flirtatiously that he hardly knows which of them to turn to. Agnes says, 'Whichever of us you like," and the Devil turns to her. At this, Agnes winks at Margaret and asks her to leave. This is not Satanism, but good-natured rural banter! Not only that, but it has the ring of truth about it.

Just because suspects were mainly illiterate 17th century peasants does not mean that they were devoid of imagination. Scottish folk tales and ballads are full of wonder and magic. If suspects were making up their confessions, why was the Devil not a winged and shining warrior who carries his lovers off to marble palaces to feast from golden platters and fornicate on beds of silk? Why is he just an ordinary joe, so familiar and unthreatening that you wink to your friend behind his back?

One possibility, of course, is that this is precisely what he was (although here we come perilously close to Margaret Murrayism) - an ordinary man with the twin duties of recruiting and presiding over meetings. We need not believe in such a scenario that any of the group took his position as "the Devil" seriously. After all, farm workers recruited into the Horsemen's Society in 19th century Aberdeenshire had to "shake hands with the Devil" while blindfolded. It is unlikely that any of them thought of this as anything more than a bit of harmless hokum.

We might well suspect that the appearance of the Devil at witch meetings was a similar piece of nonsense, or perhaps something akin to the presence of the Abbot of Unreason or Lord of Misrule at pre-Reformation Christmas festivities.

There is of course the question of the Devil's sexual duties. Should we be surprised if a group of unconventional and mainly middle-aged women took advantage of an opportunity to spice up mundane or non-existent sex-lives? Would it be surprising if, as several writers have suggested, the poor Devil had to use an artificial [and therefore cold] penis to fulfill his obligations? Certainly, few of his partners are likely to have been particularly stimulating.

It is obvious then that the whole business of witch meetings and involvement with the Devil can be made to sound very plausible. There are sticking points, however - I have already mentioned the improbability of wholesale renunciations of baptism. Surely, though, the greatest difficulty of all is this: if the Devil was a real human being, engaged in recruitment, presiding at meetings, and providing sexual services, why is there not a single incidence of his identity being revealed? If witches could easily be made to supply long lists of their associates, if their interrogators could make them confess to pretty much anything, is it conceivable that no-one would ever reveal the identity of their local "devil"? The Devil is often in the shape of a man, a black man, or a fine gentleman, but he is never in the shape of Tommy Thomson from Tranent or Jockie Dickson from Dunbar. It would surely be quite impossible for local men to be "devils" without being betrayed on at least a few occasions. The way round this of course is to suggest that they could not be betrayed because their identities were kept secret. These "fine gentlemen" or "black men" were in disguise - and indeed "blacking up" is one of the most basic disguises there is. Perhaps the occasional genuine "fine gentleman" would not be averse to sowing some wild oats at the odd witch meeting "for a laugh", in a parish where he was not known. As for "black men", there must have been black servants in some 17th century lairds' homes. (Sooner or later someone will float the possibility of a connection between voodoo and Scottish witchcraft *via* African servants.) Much more readily available would be Gypsies, who in the early years after their arrival in Scotland were described in ballads as "black". Most were soon absorbed in the droves of native vagabonds and travelling folk, but in the beginning must have been as dark skinned as the Roma of eastern Europe still are. Gypsies would also have the advantage of being here today and gone tomorrow. Here, of course, we are in the realms of speculation, if not of fantasy. Interestingly, however, apparently "Earl of Hell" was "a favourite Gypsy title" in the south of Scotland (Gordon, 1980, p.124).

As a final summing up, then, is it possible to discern "What was really going on?" There need be no doubt that there were professional practitioners of folk magic - wise wives and vagabond tricksters, and all the indications are that they were colloquially known as witches and warlocks. There need be no doubt that some of these at least had reputations as effective performers. It seems likely also that sometimes there were those among them who were not above deliberately setting out to cause misfortune, illness, and even death. It is also likely that their "magic" worked often enough to preserve their reputations.

It is not impossible that some witches and their associates met together from time to time, possibly for business purposes, but more likely for social reasons. It is not altogether out of the question that on at least some occasions meetings might have been presided over by a "devil" and that sexual activities might have taken place. Nor is it beyond the bounds of possibility that admission to these groups might have involved an initiation ritual of some sort. On the other hand, since the interrogators of witchcraft suspects had preconceived ideas of witchcraft activities, it may well be that all the diabolic aspects of East Lothian witchcraft in the records are complete fabrications extorted by threats or ill-treatment.

We must avoid the "all or nothing" attitude, where either everything is true or everything is a farrago of ludicrous nonsense. We can accept what is probable, dismiss what is clearly impossible, but we should keep an open mind on the admittedly vast area in between. Sadly, until the day when a researcher turns up the diary of some "Samuel Pepys" or "Highland Lady" of East Lothian witchcraft, much of "what was really going on" must remain one of the many grey areas of 17th century history.

Bibliography.

Primary Sources.

Kirk Session Minutes: filed under CH2 in the National Archives of Scotland.
Records of the Presbytery of Haddington: CH2/185 in the National Archives of Scotland.
Presbytery of Dunbar : CH2/99
Presbytery of Dalkeith : CH2/242
Records of the Synod of Lothian and Tweedale: CH2/252
Dunbar Burgh records : B18/13
Haddington Burgh Records: GD1/413
[Transcriptions of Haddington Court and Council records.]
North Berwick Court Book: B56/6/1 In the National Archives of Scotland.
Register of the Privy Council, ed. John Hill Burton, Edinburgh, 1877.
Calendar of State Papers Relating to Scotland, Edinburgh, 1936.
Calender of Border Papers, ed. J. Bain, Edinburgh, 1894-6.
The Acts of the Parliaments of Scotland, ed. T. Thomson and C. Innes, Edinburgh, 1814-1875.
Records of the Committeee of Estates: PA11/8 and PA11/9 in the National Archives of Scotland.
Justiciary Court Records.
Boxes of *Court Processes*: JC26 in the National Archives of Scotland.
High Court Minute Books:JC6
*Books of Adjouma*l:JC2
Beigis Tod's dittay:JC40/3
Justiciary Cases 1624-1650: Vol 1, Ed. Stair A. Gillon, Stair Society, Edinburgh 1953.
ibid Vol. 3, Ed. J. Irvine Smith, Stair Society, Edinburgh, 1974.
Witchcraft in Early Modern Scotland: L Normand and G. Roberts, Exeter, 2000.
[Invaluable as a primary source because it contains the full texts of James VI's " Daemonologie" and the "North Berwick" pamphlet *Newes from Scotland,* and also previously unpublished Justiciary Court papers, the reference numbers of which I give in Chapter 1 of "Goodnight, My Servants All".]

Secondary Sources.

Allanson, John C. - *Countryman on the Moors* [Ed. John G. O' Leary], Oxford University Press, 1983.
Ankarloo], Bengt et al. - *Witchcraft and Magic in Europe Vol. 4 - the Period of the Witch Trials*, Athlone Press, London, 2002.
Bannatyne Club - *History and Life of James the Sext*, Anon., Edinburgh 1825.
Bannatyne Club - *Nicol's Diary*, Edinburgh, 1825.
Bell, John - *Tryal of Witchcraft,* Glasgow, c. 1700.
Black, G. T. - *Calendar of Cases of Witchcraft in Scotland 1510-1727*, New York, 1938.
Buchan, David [ed.] - *Folk Tradition and Folk Medicine in Scotland - The Writings of David Rorie.* Canongate, Edinburgh, 1994.
Calderwood, David - *History of the Kirk of Scotland*, Edinburgh, 1849.

Carmichael, Alexander - *Carmina Gadelica*, Floris Books, Edinburgh, 1992.

Davies, Owen - *Cunning Folk - Popular Magic in English History*, Hambledon and London, London, 2003.

Goodare, Julian [ed] - *The Scottish Witch-Hunt in Context*, Manchester University Press, Manchester, 2002.

Gordon, Anne - *Hearts on the Highway: Gypsies in South East Scotland*, Galashiels, 1980.

Henderson, Lizanne and Edward G. Cowan - *Scottish Fairy Belief*, Tuckwell Press, East Linton, 2001.

Larner, Christina - *Enemies of God*, John Donald, Edinburgh, 2001

Larner, C with C.H. Lee, H. McLachlan - *A Source Book of Scottish Witchcraft*, Glasgow, 1977, reprinted The Grimsay Press 2005.

Levack, Brian P. - *The Witch Hunt in Early Modern Europe*, 2nd edition, Longman, London and New York, 1995.

Lauder, John [Lord Fountainhall] - *Historical Notices*, Bannatyne Club, Edinburgh, 1848.

Macdonald, Stuart - *The Witches of Fife*, Tuckwell Press, East Linton, 2002.

McIntosh, Alastair – *Soil and Soul*, Aurum Press, London, 2004.

Mackenzie, George - *The Laws and Customs of Scotland in Matters Criminal*, Edinburgh, 1678.

Maclagan, R. C. - *Evil Eye in the Western Highlands*, 1st ed. London 1902, reprinted E.P. Publishing Ltd, 1972.

McNeill, F. Marion - *The Silver Bough, Vol 1 Scottish Folk Lore and Folk Belief*, William McLennan, Glasgow, 1957.

Martine, John – *Reminiscences and Notices of the Parishes of the County of Haddington*, East Lothian Council Library Services, 1999. (First published 1890 and 1894.)

Maxwell-Stuart, P.G. - *Satan's Conspiracy*, Tuckwell Press, East Linton, 2001.

Miller, Frank - *The Laird of Coul's Ghost: a Galloway Chap-Book*, Transactions of the Dumfriesshire and Galloway Natural History and Antiquarian Society, 1927.

Murray, Margaret - *The Witch Cult in Western Europe*, Oxford, 1921. Reprinted 1962.

Normand, L and G. Roberts - *Witchcraft in Early Modern Scotland*, Exeter, 2000.

Ogilvy, W. - *The Laird of Coul's Ghost*, Contained in "Chapbooks Printed at Glasgow", National Library of Scotland shelfmark [AO].8/3.2 .

Pettit, Edward [ed] - *Anglo Saxon Remedies Charms and Prayers from British Library MS Harley 585 The Lacunga"*, Edwin Mellen Press, Lampeter, 2001.

Pitcairn, Robert - *Criminal Trials in Scotland 1488-1624*, Edinburgh, 1833.

Pugh, Roy M. - *The Diet's Ain*, Harlaw Heritage, Balerno, 2001.

Sinclair, George - *Satan's Invisible World Discovered*, Edinburgh, 1685.

Spence, Lewis - *The Magic Arts in Celtic Britain*, Constable, London, 1995. (First published 1945).

Solzhenitsyn, Alexander, - *The Gulag Archipelago*, Colins/Fontana, 1974.

Spottiswood, Archbishop - *History of the Church of Scotland*, Edinburgh 1851, (First published 1655).

Index of People and Places

Spelling of names was inconsistent. Similar-sounding variants of the same name have been indexed together., e.g. see Acheson, below.

A

Abbay 183
Abbot 389, 537
Abercrombie 242
Aberdou[e]r 76, 234
Aberladie, Aberlady, Aberledie 67, 71, 154, 155, 163, 167, 228
Abernathie, Abernethie, Abernethy[e] 167, 179, 180, 184, 219, 220, 230, 231, 233
Acheson, Achesone, Achesoun, Achieson[e], Achiesoun, Aichiesoun 31, 35-37, 39, 40, 42, 45, 52, 55, 63, 77, 79, 211, 217, 222, 228, 280, 287, 292, 297-9, 303, 305, 307, 308, 310, 313, 318, 323, 376, 424, 466, 473, 499, 500, 512, 520 *and see Aitcheson, Atcheson*
Acheson's Haven 31, 35, 36, 37, 39, 42, 52, 55, 63, 376, 473, 499, 500, 520
Achinteck 395
Adam 29, 57, 83, 87-9, 96, 108-13, 115, 133, 136, 143, 163, 170, 172, 173, 222, 237, 242, 275, 276, 304, 335-8, 340, 341, 346, 396, 401, 402, 405, 407, 434, 466, 502, 510, 518
Adamson[e] 56, 79, 168, 205, 225, 283, 427, 428, 434
Adare 105
Aderstone, Adiestone, Adinstone, Adirstone, Adisone, Adniston 74, 75, 185, 201, 217, 230, 236
Adie 232
Affleck 230, 254, 258, 262, 269, 327, 364, 366, 467
Aikenhead, Aikenheid, Aikinhead 21, 360, 503
Aikwood 422
Aird 237
Airther 377
Aistbarnes, see East Barns
Aitcheso[u]n, Aitchieso[u]n, Aitchison 27, 44, 51, 97, 107, 291, 439 *and see Acheson, Atcheson*
Aitken 254, 266

Aiton, Aitun 229, 233
Aitun 233
Alan[e], Allain 72, 79, 116, 355, 374
Alderslie 198
Aldersto[u]n, Aldinstoun, Aldistone 74, 184, 189, 191, 220, 243
Aldhame 141
Alexander 18, 21-3, 27, 42, 45, 54, 56, 57, 68-71, 74, 76-9, 83, 84, 87, 91, 92, 99, 103, 107, 114-7, 119, 132-140, 146, 152, 153, 157, 168, 182, 184-6, 189-2, 195, 196, 201, 204, 211, 216-24, 227, 228, 230-3, 235-8, 242-5, 248, 252-4, 260-2, 269, 270, 277, 278, 281, 300, 303, 306, 307, 309, 310, 313, 318-25, 327-36, 340-3, 345-53, 356-62, 368, 371, 374-7, 379-85, 392, 393, 398, 400, 402-7, 409-11, 418, 420, 422-4, 428, 429, 434-6, 455, 465, 466, 476, 478, 479, 482, 483, 490, 492, 497-504, 506, 508-10, 513, 514, 517, 521, 527, 530, 540
Aliesone, Alisoun 291, 304, 307, 326, 356
Allan[e], Allene 68, 72, 79, 80, 88, 92, 115, 133, 188, 197, 216, 223, 230, 231, 238, 239, 334, 341, 356, 358-60, 364, 411, 413, 431, 467, 471, 504, 508, 517
Allat, Allot 191, 200
Allers 454
Allerstoun 232
Almonsson 39
Ambrois 216
Anderson[e] 73-6, 81, 105, 109, 110, 112, 131, 139, 145, 158, 160, 168, 172, 197, 200-2, 204-6, 210, 223, 225-7, 230, 232, 248, 251, 274, 305, 312, 327, 387, 388, 430, 431, 433, 435, 440, 457, 467, 469, 470, 476, 477, 479, 492, 516, 526
Angus 7, 18, 20, 28, 39, 42, 43, 47, 58, 60, 62, 140, 164, 217, 340, 343, 389-933, 446, 466, 469, 498, 512
Anislie 383
Antcaill 77

Ardbuckes 435
Argy[i]ll 87, 88, 235, 469
Arm[e]strang 133, 134, 362
Arnot 188, 217, 219, 222, 309, 316, 326, 347, 353
Arther 143, 144
Atcheson[e], Atchi[e]son 165, 166, 248, 254, 263, 284, 375 *and see Acheson, Aitcheson*
Athelstaneford 69, 424
Athin 423
Atholl 60
Atkinson 529, 530
Attkine 431
Auchemitie, Auchinmoutie 236, 398
Auchterlony 117
Aulderstoun 220
Auldham 141
Auldhamsto[c]k[i]s 312, 321, 337, 377
Ayrshire 247
Aytkine 98
Ayton[e], Aytoun[e] 75, 79, 80-2, 165-8, 200, 204, 208, 217, 220, 227

B

Bacbie 239
Back Burn[e] 239-41, 424, 487, 495, 498, 532
Ba[i]gbie 21, 94, 239, 240, 241, 242, 525
Bailhauches 423
Bail[l]ie 6, 71, 77-9, 82-4, 92, 97, 124, 126-8, 178, 179, 196, 211, 217, 219, 223, 225, 227, 237, 238, 240, 242, 368, 371, 374, 388, 407, 422, 423, 470, 477, 499, 517, 518
Bailyie, Bailzie 23, 28, 210, 280, 374, 511
Bain[n][e] 89, 205, 219, 278, 279, 466, 539
Bair[d] 96, 159, 232, 252, 260, 467
Bairfute 21, 341
Bairn[e]sfather 254, 263
Baize 205
Baker 57, 105
Balantine 432
Balcanquall, Balcanquell, Balcanquhall, Balcanquill 160, 161 190, 196, 223, 366, 371, 372
Bald 99, 237
Balenden 433, 434
Balentine 432
Balfore, Balfour[e] 86, 152, 223, 397, 407, 438, 493, 505

Ballenden 19
Ballenie 168
Balnetyne 360
Bamburgh 353
Banantyne 431
Bane[s] 190, 356
Bangley 23
Banklie 434
Bankreiff 154
Bannantyne 431
Banna[n]tyne, Banontyne 55, 56, 237, 280, 324, 360, 361, 413, 414, 418, 419, 422, 424, 428, 431, 446, 447, 449, 470, 539, 540
Baptie 98, 167, 235, 378, 380, 383, 384, 397, 418, 419, 422, 425, 469, 470
Bara 12, 19, 69, 71
Barber, Barbour 231
Barclay 220, 236, 435, 470
Bard 165, 466
Bardie 380, 384
Barker 145
Barlae Court 126
Barnes, Barnis, Barns 21, 55, 126, 191, 220, 237, 242, 243, 253, 262, 280, 282, 283, 288-93, 296, 298, 299, 303, 304, 306-8, 310, 311, 314-22, 324-6, 378, 505, 517, 528
Ba[r]ro, Barra 32, 232, 236, 237, 238, 242, 519
Barowmure 409
Bartelman, Bartieman, Bartil[l]man, Bartleman, 86, 93, 94, 98, 114, 163, 208, 210, 211, 227, 235, 238, 356, 407, 413, 422, 423, 466, 469, 470, 499, 502
Bartie 354
Bartram, Bartrem, Bartrim, Bartrome 21, 83, 179, 189, 191, 196
Bas[s] 61, 223, 387
Bas[s]inden, Bassenden 136
Bathan[e]s, Bathenes 41, 169, 238, 413
Bathcat[t] 185, 187, 219, 242, 280, 307, 466
Baxter 68, 155, 156, 219, 280, 307, 435, 466
Baylie[s] 239, 249, 414, 423, 424, 426
Beal[l]s 208, 484
Bearford 91, 504
Bee 140
Begbie 94, 145
Begto[u]n[e] 25, 30, 31, 35, 40,
Beil 304, 518

Beil[l] 110, 304, 326, 518
Beinsto[u]n 229, 231, 237, 238, 242, 336
Beir[e] 158, 159
Beirford 91
Belh[e]aven, Belhevin[e] 243, 253, 261, 326, 375
Bell 42, 56, 115, 119, 134, 168, 252, 328, 329, 343-6, 381, 385, 407, 408, 424, 433, 459, 460, 539
Belljebub 397
Bellne 311
Belpotis, Belpotts 138, 139
Belshes 249, 426
Belto[u]n 71, 126, 237, 253, 261
Bene, Benn 78, 135
Bennet 107, 112, 336, 409
Benstoun Milne 231
Berne 132
Berrie 101, 132
Berui[c]k, Berwick 1, 5, 7, 10, 14, 15, 17-21, 24, 27, 29-32, 36-8, 40-3, 45, 47-9, 51, 52, 55, 57, 59, 61, 63, 65, 99, 105, 106, 115, 150, 157, 158, 162, 165-70, 173, 211, 223, 274, 277, 280, 287, 314, 327, 351, 353, 356, 358, 362, 443, 445, 454, 465, 467, 471-3, 489, 496, 497, 499-501, 511, 512, 514, 518, 519, 526, 533, 534, 539
Berwickshire 57, 58, 324, 352
Bewar 241
Bichel 237
Bichet, Bichit 95
Biel 110, 507
Big[g]ar, Bigger 236, 237, 243
Biggin[s] 114
Bilsdene 376
Binnie 423
Birch Valley 186
Birnie 407, 416, 417
Bishop 166, 167, 196, 220, 221, 222, 309, 329, 335, 336, 340, 342, 344, 346, 347, 358, 360
Bisset 57
Bizet 117, 118, 119
Black 89, 97, 158, 179, 402, 422, 423, 424, 434, 486, 522, 539 *and see Blak*
Blackbarronie 77
Blackburn[e] 168, 196
Blackhall 216
Blackie 108, 504
Blacksheillis 179
Blaie 233

Blaikbie 182
Blaikie 68, 236
Blain 435
Blair 108, 230, 231, 232, 233, 243, 309, 353, 361
Blairquhan 61
Blak 87, 88, 89, 238, 356, 423, 470 *and see Black*
Blake 506
Blakeis 21
Blakestoun 243
Blake Gutter 398
Blance 208, 219, 220, 497
Blandilands 7
Blans[e] 179, 180, 184, 191, 241, 422, 423
Blause *see Blanse*
Blek 242
Blindschellis 21
Blowhen 61
Blunthorn 117
Blynschellis 16
Blythe 423
Blythswood 361
Bogle 68, 104, 408
Bogtoun 45
Boig 254, 264
Boigis 424
Bois 298
Boiswell 215
Bolto[u]n[e] 21, 69, 183, 237, 239, 240, 241, 360, 375, 424, 470, 487, 503, 515
Bookie 86
Bookles 108
Borroustounes 234
Borrowmore, Borrowmu[i]r[e] 409, 410
Borthui[c]k[e], Borthwick 172, 191, 192, 194, 195, 216, 220, 224, 227, 228, 230-3, 237, 238, 242, 244, 249, 274, 383, 426, 436, 465, 476, 503, 513
Bothans 101, 144, 193, 508
Bothuel[l], Bothwell 19, 35-41, 44, 47, 50, 54, 57-63, 472
Botton 145
Bouar[s] 120, 121
Bouden 125, 127
Bouglosse 168
Bouis 18
Bourhill 28
Bourhouse[s], Bourhousis, Bourhouss[es] 151, 217, 244, 256, 260, 263

543

Bourne Held 354
Bouston 68
Bower 88, 90, 239
Bowes 10, 23, 31, 36, 37, 40, 46, 47, 52, 53, 58
Bowie 508
Bown 208
Bowtoune 22
Boyd 70, 165, 218, 466
Bradie 364, 365
Braegrein, Brae Greane, Brae Green, Bragreen, Bragrein 397, 399, 402, 404, 405, 485, 498 *and see Braygrein*
Braidie 370
Braidwodsyde, Braidwoodsyd[e] 21, 195, 239, 242
Brandis Mylne, Brandsmyln 281, 293, 304
Braygrein, Bray Grein, Bra Green 396, 397, 398, 399, 404, 407 *and see Braegrein*
Breade 162
Breadwoodsyd 164
Brechenrig 105
Bre[i]chin 53, 54, 463
Breddin 146
Brig 42, 43, 44, 46, 283, 499
Brigend 408
Brigge Hallis 7
Brigishauch, Brigis Hauch 186, 187
Brig of Die 44, 46
Briswell 215
Broad Stonn 390
Brock, Brockie, Brocky 99, 131, 509
Broken Caisay of Nydrie 357
Broken Causway 350
Brok[i]sburne 304, 424
Broomhill 57
Brothersta[i]nes, Brotherstone[s], Brotherstones 87, 88, 89, 96, 163, 381, 382, 385, 386, 466
Broughton 459
Broun[e] 21, 28, 45, 71-4, 76-8, 80, 82-4, 91, 92, 98, 117, 121, 122, 150, 151, 152, 154, 163, 165, 168, 173, 178, 179, 187, 193, 200, 202, 204-6, 208, 210, 211, 226, 231, 236, 237, 242, 247, 248, 252-4, 260, 261, 262, 264, 270, 313, 314, 325, 328, 347, 350, 354, 360, 375, 377, 387, 422, 435, 466, 467, 479, 484, 492, 500, 503, 505, 513, 514, 520, 536 *and see Brown*
Brounfield Brownfield 164, 165 Brounhill 45
Broustene 364

Brown 47, 70, 91, 103, 104, 116, 146, 159, 178, 184, 189, 193, 195, 196, 208, 231, 232, 247, 253-5, 347, 435, 507, 515, 535 *and see Broun[e]*
Broxburne, Brox Burn 253, 261, 281, 326, 510
Broxmouth 281, 294, 476
Bruce 48, 244, 247, 378, 379, 380, 381, 382, 383, 385, 387, 446, 469, 477, 528, 530
Brumhoillis 17
Brunstoun Milne 407
Brunt 253
Bruntoun 433
Bruntylland 361
Brus 172
Bryanes 309
Bryesoun, Brys[s]on[n][e] 73, 104, 168, 253, 254, 257, 261, 265, 285, 287, 288, 290, 299-301, 306, 308, 310, 313, 314, 315, 316, 318, 321, 323, 325, 381, 385, 476, 479, 504, 517
Bucan 136
Buchquhannane, Buquhannane 28, 45
Buckon 93
Buikless 106
Buittle 460
Bull 159, 275, 277, 515
Burehousses 252
Burg 163, 466
Burgane, Burgone 208-11, 466, 476, 500
Burghley 10, 15, 31, 47, 59
Burn-syde 27
Burne 180, 233, 239, 349, 355, 362, 429, 435, 436
Burnehead, Burneheid 220, 221, 326
Burnet 91, 113, 114, 126, 168, 275, 277, 348, 351, 361, 478, 480, 490, 513, 516, 522
Burnhill 28
Burnmoore 73
Burnouses 243
Burntisland 8, 11
Burrowmuir 408
Burto[u]n 119, 214, 430, 431, 433, 488, 539
Butler 179, 184, 191, 208, 219, 220, 231, 235, 236-8, 240-2, 340
Butter 180, 227
Butterdain[e], Butterdeane 205, 236, 237
Bynnie Craigs 274, 482
Byres, Byris 21, 211, 231, 235, 409
Byrilaw 229

C

Cadger Well 241, 500
Cairintoune 434
Cairn[e]croce, Cairnecross 230, 399, 467 *and see Carncross*
Cairnehaugh 238
Cairn[e]s 56, 57, 230-2, 236-8, 240-2, 270, 418, 467, 470
Caldcl[e]uch 197, 223, 418
Calder 62, 143
Calderwood 53, 61, 62, 114, 154, 155, 157, 170, 218-20, 231, 249, 408, 426, 428-30, 432-4, 463, 533, 539
Caldro 75
Caldtoun 439
Caldwell 77
Callander 243, 244
Cameron 20, 21, 22, 503
Cam[p]bel[l] 12, 16, 19, 25, 26, 45, 49, 51, 427, 428, 431-5, 481, 488, 489, 501
Camroune-brig-end 28
Can[n]onga[i]t[e] 42, 50, 101, 147, 170, 418, 435, 456, 506, 539
Cant 244
Cantlie 240
Cap[h]ie 163, 164, 424
Carbarrie, Carbarry, Carberrie, Carberry 12, 19, 22, 27. 32, 58, 236, 237
Carbreath 98
Carein 166
Carentoune 427
Carey 59
Carfra[e] 21, 87, 115, 145, 153, 159, 191-5, 205, 220, 235, 364, 374, 392, 407, 409, 414, 418, 419, 421, 465, 469, 476, 477, 479, 482, 491, 513, 515
Carfraeburn[e] 395, 399
Cargill 110, 111
Caringtoun[e] 22, 27, 433
Carins 230
Carkettil, Carkettle 83, 93, 476, 480
Carlaverock 243
Carmicha[e]l[l] 6, 39, 57, 60, 71, 82, 161, 196, 197, 223, 540
Carncorse, Carncrosse, Carncroce 163, 230, 466 *and see Cairncroce*
Carnegy 217
Carn[e]s 270
Carrai[l]l 83-5, 94, 335, 338, 419, 525
Carram 91
Carrein 166
Carrick, Carrik 153, 220, 221, 356
Carriden, Carridine 145, 418
Carrie 19
Carrile 360
Carruthers 50
Cars[c]hoggill 41, 42
Carselwood 147
Carter 107, 375
Cass 236, 407, 470
Cassil[l][i]s, Cassleis 89, 340, 400
Castel[l]hill , Castell-hill, Castel Hill, Castlehill, Castle Hill 10, 30, 37, 43, 52, 56, 62, 115, 275, 277, 278, 309, 388, 399, 446, 454
Castleto[u]n, Castletowne 157, 158, 160
Catcune 171, 172
Cathcart 116, 197, 317, 506
Cathie 98, 167, 183, 184, 235, 238, 240, 242, 421, 422, 423, 469, 470, 480, 498
Cathil 392
Cathkit 77
Cathnes 244
Cauldcleuch 94, 414, 477, 518, 521
Cauldcoit Mure, Cauldcot Moor 350, 358
Caulder 124, 126, 128
Cawdewell 61
Chaimers, Chalmer[s] 117, 251, 370, 427, 431-4
Chambers 42, 59, 109, 447
Chancellor 38, 39, 43, 60, 160, 183, 216, 217, 243, 439, 446, 450
Chanceter 216
Channelkirk 154, 386, 387, 517
Chanonry of Ross 388
Chansler[e] 102
Chaplain 158, 458
Chapland 388
Charles 35, 113, 213, 214, 323, 326, 332, 333, 335, 336, 339-41, 346, 450, 459, 471, 529
Charteris 171, 418
Chengenkirk 154
Chesome 377
Chesterhall 253
Chirnside 59, 60
Chisholm[e] 254, 298, 376, 377

545

Chooshead 120
Chousley, Chouslie 439, 440, 496, 525, 526
Christie 115
Chrystiso[u]n[e] 67, 144, 158, 228
Cinglekirk 158
Cinquerrour 359
Claddo 171
Clark[e] 17, 110, 154, 224, 275, 276, 422, 483, 507, 510, 518
Clarkingtoun Mylne 355
Clarkson[e] 224, 228, 466
Clatt 224, 483
Clawie 42
Clegorne 99
Cleirkeyes 408, 487
Clerk[e] 38, 39, 43, 57, 66, 96, 106, 115, 136, 144, 155, 169, 170, 178, 215, 220, 222, 236, 251, 352, 358, 361, 381, 382, 404, 407, 438, 449
Clerk[e]son[e] 287, 292, 299, 308, 310
Clerkingto[u]n 11, 77, 222, 235, 236, 349, 355, 503, 514
Clifftonhall 48, 53
Clift 376, 377
Cluk 106
Clunie 132, 134, 135
Coalsto[u]n[e] 114, 200
Cochran[e] 356, 357, 395, 396, 397, 399, 402, 404, 405, 407, 418, 446, 469
Cock 409, 411
Cockbarne 164, 466
Cockbrandspethe 313 *and see Cockburnspath*
Cockburn[e] 37, 38, 74, 79-81, 83, 85, 97, 154, 163, 169, 171, 179, 184, 189, 191, 196, 198, 204, 208, 216, 219, 227, 231-3, 235-7, 242, 249, 253, 261, 349, 352, 354, 371, 426-34, 467 *and see Cokburn*
Cockburn[e]spath, Cockburn[e]speth, Cockburnes Peth 8, 217, 253, 254, 258, 261, 266, 267, 479 *and see Cockbrandspethe*
Cockenzie 135, 218
Cocklaw 253
Cocklemill 154
Cockpen 173
Coilstoun-mylne 21
Cokburn[e] 49, 50, 196, 226, 374 *and see Cockburn*
Cokeny 398
Colberspeath 219

Colbrand[i]speth 217, 326, 378
Coldenknowis 217
Coldingham 192, 353, 354, 356, 482, 510, 522
Coldingham Law 192, 353, 354, 356, 482, 510, 522
Colkiny 424
Colm 128, 254, 518, 519
Colm[b]e 124, 126, 127, 128, 256, 261, 264, 327, 331, 335, 336, 342, 343, 344, 346, 347, 352, 353, 358, 360, 361, 478, 505, 507
Colsto[u]n[e] 61, 135, 165, 236, 237, 242, 247, 248, 328, 350, 356, 448, 476
Colt 172, 236, 237
Coltheard 199, 200
Colvill[e] 243, 293, 340, 348, 362, 405, 409
Comb[e] 142, 509
Combulton 61
Coming 335, 336, 337, 338, 340, 346, 418, 483
Concker 105
Congalton Congilto[u]n[e] Congl[e]toun 28, 45, 61, 150, 238, 254, 258, 269, 364, 372
Conker, Conquer 105, 114
Constable 253, 540
Cook 54, 106, 170, 236, 244
Cootes 167
Cor[s]ehous[e] 167, 217, 223, 493
Corser 71, 238
Corstorphine 222, 482
Corstorphin Craigs 274
Cosser 160, 239, 516
Costertone 101
Cotthird 376
Couane 370, 403, 404, 406, 409
Coudin 92
Couk 279
Coul 440, 460, 461, 462, 540
Couper 14, 27, 74, 237, 362, 435
Coupland, 236, 237, 470
Courtney 157, 159, 164, 165
Cousing 116, 117
Cousland 12, 27, 32, 244, 431
Cousland Dean 431, 488
Couthard 377
Couts 166
Cove 259, 270
Cowan[e] 45, 83, 104, 132, 134, 153, 188, 211, 212, 244, 248, 249, 252, 364, 366, 367, 369,

371, 374, 383, 395, 396-8, 400, 402-6, 409, 428, 440, 449, 479, 495, 496, 504, 506, 515, 517, 522, 524, 526, 540
Cowburne, Cow Burne 429, 431, 432, 436
Cowdan[e] 78, 209
Cowie 31, 141, 248
Cowin 404, 405
Cowper 242, 429
Cowpland 239, 241
Cow Park Burn 497
Cra[f]f[o]ord 79, 80, 81, 83, 236, 237, 370
Crahill 261
Craig[e] 16, 60, 160-2, 211, 221, 229, 230, 253, 261, 317, 326, 334, 353, 362-72, 374, 397, 455, 457, 467, 468, 476, 481, 485, 530
Craighall 22, 222, 293, 324, 329, 351, 357, 361
Craigmillar 20, 21, 28
Craik 424
Crail[l] 114, 337, 516
Crailing 61
Cralo 418
Crambie 253, 261
Cranborn 244
Cranston Riddel, Cranstoun Ryddill 16, 42
Cransto[u]n[e] 16, 42, 49, 115, 191, 192, 195, 216, 220, 395, 396, 397, 399, 402-5, 407, 428, 429, 430, 431, 432, 433, 434, 436, 438, 446, 469, 485, 488, 504
Craprene 22
Crauford, Craufurd 365-7, 369
Crauswindhead 257
Craw 143, 300, 313
Crawfo[o]rd, Crawf[f]urd, 38, 166, 168, 235, 364, 366, 369, 370, 371, 374, 418, 469, 470, 479
Crawhill 253, 326
Creichto[u]n Creighton Crichto[u]n 57, 60, 101, 172, 214-6, 249, 360, 401, 426, 435, 436, 448, 500, 534
Crek 69
Criminal Trials 1, 5, 16, 21, 23, 42, 49, 274, 309, 540
Crombie 253, 254, 260, 261, 262, 414, 418, 477
Crook[e]s 132, 133, 395, 397, 399, 403, 405, 406, 407, 446, 469
Crose 424
Crosshill 430
Crosshouse 406

Cruiknowis 377
Cruiks 402
Cruikshank 237, 470
Crumb[i]e, Crumble 93, 242, 262, 389, 390, 419, 499, 509
Crummy 27
Crystie 274, 357, 503, 513
Crysti[e]son[e] 139, 274
Crystiesounis Mylne 274
Cubie 115
Cudbertsone 86
Cugilt[o][u]n 138, 139, 476, 479
Cuike 279
Culdcleuch 413, 414
Cullane 298
Cum[m]ine Cum[m]ing[e] 170, 173, 333, 338, 391-3, 395, 399, 423, 471, 479, 497
Cungilto[u]n[e] 423, 518, 530
Cun[n]i[n]gham[e] Cun[n]yngham[e 16, 17, 18, 34, 42, 61, 63, 78, 168, 243, 249, 375, 425, 426, 446, 465, 482, 489, 500, 512
Curr 108
Currie 214, 215
Cuthbertson[e] 42, 116-8, 119, 236, 253, 439, 466

D

Dailies 409, 410
Dale 407, 408, 469
Dalgl[i][e][i]sh 231, 408, 429, 431, 435, 467, 497, 525
Dalgownie 80
Dalkeith Dalkeyth 18, 20, 21, 23, 28, 30, 37, 61, 101, 152, 169, 171, 173, 192, 195, 214-6, 231, 232, 243, 387, 408-11, 464, 467, 486, 503, 506, 525, 527, 528, 539
Da[l]lliel, Dalyel, Dalziel[l] 134, 160, 161, 224, 228
Dame Bet 287
Danby 529
Danderhall, 25
Darby 466
Darg[u][e] 69, 70
Darleith 243, 244
Darlene 109
Darling 157, 218, 354
Darra 269
Darumpill 84
Daso[u]n[e] 92, 239, 326

Daurcin 242
Dausone 227, 253
Davidson[e] 117, 152, 170, 179, 182-4, 186-90, 219, 357, 375, 389, 412, 455, 465, 466, 476, 482, 500, 528
Davie 169, 279, 334, 341
Dawso[u]n[e] 118, 239, 240, 241, 525
Dayidson 390
Deall 409
Dean[e][s] 42, 91, 92, 94, 98, 125, 127-9, 145, 159, 235, 240, 242, 277, 278, 350, 413, 418, 421, 422, 431, 469, 470, 481, 489, 513, 515
Dells 409
Dempster 217, 466
Den[n]am 103, 192, 497
Denholm[e] 73, 103, 266, 326, 354
Denis 217, 466
Denmark 5, 6, 8, 15, 17, 30, 31, 44, 58, 59, 533
Dernidykes 159, 515
Dewar 91, 429
Dick Dik 71, 134, 135, 151, 162, 375, 403-6
Dickso[u]n[e] Dikso[u]n[e] 11, 21, 22, 26, 72, 83, 84, 85, 97, 101, 104, 145, 154, 155, 156, 157, 162, 166, 168, 200-2, 204-6, 208, 225-7, 229, 233, 304, 326, 356, 357, 368, 374, 410-2, 423, 424, 466, 467, 468, 476, 484, 498, 499, 500, 503, 536, 537
Dien-fute 277
Din 16
Dirilto[u]n Dirl[e]to[u]n[e] Dirletown[e] 21, 69, 105, 154, 155, 159-65, 170, 224, 228, 234, 237, 242, 466, 467, 474, 497, 503, 516, 517, 522
Dixon 143, 435
Dob[b]ie 74, 76, 77, 232, 236, 237, 467, 476, 480, 516
Dobson 422, 467
Dod[d][e]s 249, 426-8, 430-4, 438, 470
Dolsoun 232
Donal[d]so[u]n[e] 16, 68, 84, 276, 398
Donald the Man 62
Dornoch 122
Dougal[l] 236, 237, 238, 242
Doughty 236, 470
Douglas[s][e] 3, 19, 23, 41-3, 49-51, 56-8, 61, 76, 78, 98, 107, 142, 143, 160, 165, 169, 187, 216, 217, 219, 231, 236, 237, 243, 244, 253, 321, 322, 352, 370, 397, 403-7, 426, 446, 458, 467, 469, 470, 485, 498, 499, 506, 507, 514 *and see* Dowglas
Doune Hill 299, 308
Dounhill of Spott 310
Dounie 94
Dowcat Know 311
Dowglas[s] 67, 76, 217, 395, 399, 406, 426 *and see* Douglas
Downandson 313
Downie 11, 97
Drem 87, 228, 237, 254
Drew 89
Drum[m]ond 20, 26, 50, 51, 61, 80, 117, 119, 236
Drupes 172
Dryburghfurd 378
Dryburn 104, 517
Dryden Dein, Dene 185, 186
Drylawes Drylawis 304, 326
Drysdaill 214, 215
Duddingstone 49, 243
Duddo 357
Dudgeo[i]n 253, 260, 261, 332, 336
Duffus 244
Dumbar 108, 139, 141, 159-61, 174, 214, 216, 219, 232, 243, 244, 252-7, 259-66, 269, 270, 280, 282, 283, 285, 287, 291, 298, 299, 300, 302, 304, 305, 307, 310-2, 316, 317, 319, 323, 326, 327, 388, 389, 393, 418, 424, 450 *and see* Dunbar
Dumblane 220-2, 309, 327, 329-31, 335, 336, 342-4, 346, 358 *and see* Dunblane
Dumb Woman 505, 506
Dumfries 23, 30, 34, 37, 42, 57
Dumfriesshire 460, 540
Dun 30, 34, 37, 253, 326
Dunbar iv, 65, 70, 82, 104, 136, 159, 168, 171, 174, 177, 178, 216, 217, 253, 254, 256-9, 270, 293, 304, 305, 313, 316, 321, 337, 375, 402, 426, 439, 441, 446, 450, 454, 467, 468, 470, 489, 496, 537, 539 *and see* Dumbar
Dunblane 331, 335, 340, 342, 347, 358, 360 *and see* Dumblane
Duncan[e] 7, 8, 10, 11, 14-6, 18, 19, 22, 25, 27, 28, 30, 35-8, 40, 41, 44-6, 56-8, 61, 63, 69, 70, 152, 153, 160, 161, 179, 215, 216, 218-21, 232, 359, 360, 465, 497, 502, 503
Duncanlaw 166-8

Dunce 307, 310, 351, 352, 361, 362
Dune 69, 70
Dunfermline Dunfermling 216, 220
Dunglas[s][e] 254, 260, 267, 326, 375-8, 498, 524
Dunkanlaw 165
Dunlop 40
Dunn 465
Duns[e] 306, 317, 318, 324, 325, 352, 354, 356, 357, 358, 360, 492, 498, 499, 502, 503
Dunse 325, 349, 352, 353
Dwne 277
Dyit 79, 80
Dyn 25

E

Eastbarn[e]s East Barn[e]s 104, 220, 253, 254, 261, 262, 313, 322-5, 378, 517, 528 *and see* Eistbarns
Easter Broomhous 254
Eastie 165
Eastone 225
East Craig 334
East Hoipes 180
East Linton 46, 115, 327, 540
East Mill 414
Eccles 159
Eckfurd 365
Edgar, Edger 76, 329, 331, 356, 357
Edgcarnie 242
Edinburgh[e] Edenbroughe 6, 7, 10, 11, 16, 18, 21, 22, 25, 29-32, 37-44, 46, 49, 52-4, 56-63, 66, 68, 94, 99, 101, 115, 116, 147, 171, 173, 178, 213-5, 218-22, 231-3, 235, 243-5, 249, 251, 252, 260, 271, 274, 275, 277-80, 285, 293, 309, 316, 324-7, 329-32, 335, 336, 341-3, 346, 348, 351, 353, 355-62, 370, 377, 383, 388, 391, 393, 395, 39-403, 405, 409, 410, 412, 413, 418, 420-2, 425-7, 434, 435, 438, 439, 446, 447, 449, 450, 453, 456, 458-61, 463, 464, 487, 495, 497, 506, 526, 529, 534, 539, 540
Edington 357
Edmestoune Edmi[s]to[u]n[e] Edmonsto[u]n[e]11, 19, 25, 91, 434 486, 511, 530
Edyearis 53
Egliscarnie Egliscarno 237, 240, 241
Eidington 73
Eison 119
Eistbarn[e]s Estbarnes Est Barnes 219, 243, 244, 255, 280, 282, 283, 285, 287-93, 296, 303, 304, 306-8, 311-7, 319-21, 323, 324, 424 *and see* Eastbarns
Ekfurd 364
Elder 183, 188
Elfiston 457
Elgear 120
El[l]iot Elleat Elleot 178, 237, 243, 249, 426, 427, 428, 431, 432, 433, 434, 435, 436, 438, 457, 458, 470, 481, 493, 500, 501, 510, 526
Eliscamie 238
Eloa 12, 25, 27, 511, 520, 521
Elot 242, 436
Elphin[g]sto[u]n[e]s 38, 67, 217, 218, 230, 233, 361, 364, 370, 382, 397, 406 485
Elva 25, 511, 520, 521
Elvingsto[u]n 204, 208, 232, 233
England 5, 10, 17, 31, 34, 41, 47, 58, 60, 77, 168, 190, 199, 214, 220, 352, 356, 357, 393, 460, 473, 493, 536
Enterkine 426
Erdingtoune 21
Erske[i]n[e] 381, 385
Esk 19
Eskfoord 370
Estfeild 106
Eterkine 249
Ethie 330
Ewane 68
Ewart 85, 101, 102, 136, 137, 138, 506, 509
Ewingsto[u]n 230, 231, 233, 240, 242
Eyemouth 352, 358

F

Fa[a] 136, 288, 314, 315, 318, 379
Faicer 404
Fairbairn ffairbairn[e] 76, 310, 502
Fairlie, Fairly 15, 16, 19, 22, 36, 42, 162, 204, 206, 208-10, 218, 277-9, 317, 325, 466, 478, 480, 498, 500, 503, 506, 508, 510, 527
Fala, ffala, Fallay, ffallaw, Fall, Falle 56, 154, 188, 194, 195, 249, 310, 355, 384, 427-9, 436, 438, 480
Falconer 168, 424, 438
Falkland 59, 244

549

Farmer 392
Farstoun 244
Fauside Brae 456
Fean[n][e] 16, 18, 25, 27, 31, 34, 61, 446 *and see* Fian
Feinla 285
Fender 103, 316, 324
Fento[u]n 106, 153, 211, 224, 228, 470
Fentounbarnes ffentounbarnes 237, 242
Fentountoure 230
Fergis[t]on 138, 502
Fe[r]gus[s]on[e] Fegusson ffergison[e] ffergusone 82, 138, 168, 169, 224, 228, 237, 242, 254-6, 261, 263, 264, 284, 362, 411, 315, 481
Fermer, Fermo[u]r 389, 390, 391, 392, 393, 395, 399, 446, 469, 479, 481. 486, 498, 499, 500
Fernie 360
Feudar 277
ffairnie 135
ffalsyde ffawside 236, 237
ffife 417
ffin 440
ffine 379
ffuird 238
Fian, Fien[e] 6, 8, 10, 14, 15, 16, 20, 25, 28, 30, 37, 44, 45, 53, 63, 465, 482, 489, 500, 512 *and see* Fean
Fiery Hills 39, 40
Finie 379
Finlaso[u]n[e] Finlison Findleyson, 104, 120, 143, 182, 196, 218, 422, 423, 436, 478
Fintry 36
Firth of Forth 6, 458
Fis[c]herraw ffis[c]herraw Fisherrow 104, 106, 220, 236, 237, 407, 423, 470, 513
Fisher 57, 83, 434
Fleck ffleck 100, 103, 374, 405
Fleming, ffleming Flemyng 81, 164, 166, 208, 340, 522
Flemyng 340
Fleschear Flesher 173, 293
Fletcher 408
Flocker 356
Florence 61
Fockart Fokkart 404 424
Focker 401, 424
Fodringhame 165, 466

Fo[i]rman fforman 211, 228, 232
Foirtoun 303, 307, 318, 327
Fo[o]rd fford 115, 133, 134, 199, 242, 322, 429, 432, 488
For[r]est, fforest 72, 75, 83, 84, 92, 118, 120, 164, 204, 231, 245, 252, 260, 326, 419, 439, 466, 467
For[r]ester 57, 100, 121, 162, 196, 222, 223, 227, 231, 245, 254, 255, 263, 383, 396, 403, 404, 405, 406, 407, 426, 466, 467, 479
Forster 34, 139, 263
Forsyth 100
Forto[u]ne Fortun[e] 77, 163, 188, 324, 466, 502, 503
Fortonmoore 162
Foster, ffoster, 88, 89, 111, 164, 424
Fothringham[e], ffothringhame 232, 467
Foul[l]ar, Foul[l]er, ffoular ffou[l]ler, ffowler Fowl[l]ar Fowler 77, 78, 136, 137, 237, 395, 396, 402-5, 407, 431, 434, 458, 470, 499
Foulestruther 32
Foul[l]is 225, 277
Foulisch Strype 376
Foulordleyes 378
Foulster 14
Foulstruther, Fowlstruther 14, 15, 20, 27, 31, 35, 38, 42, 43, 499, 511
Fountainhall 186, 270, 438, 446-9, 470, 495, 525, 540
Fowles 114
foxglove 138, 182, 183, 199, 365, 370, 396, 402, 403, 502-4, 516, 517, 521, 527
Fran[c]k ffrank 71, 382, 386, 460, 540
Fraser 351, 362
Freirland[is] 217
Friskin 338
Frissell 68
Frud 312
Fru[i]d[e] 285, 287, 298, 304, 308, 312, 315-7, 323, 328, 346
Fuchcart Fukcart, 395, 400
Fulleis 466
Fuller 403-5
Furbos 61
Furde 219, 326
Fyen 45
Fy[f]fe ffyfe, 132, 416, 417, 419
Fysherraw Fysher Raw 106 *and see Fisherraw*

G

Ga 29, 174
Gaidhealtachd 56
Ga[i]rneto[u]n[e] Garnetoun Hill[i]s 74, 349, 350, 353, 354, 356, 357
Gaitgude 135
Galbraith 42
Gall 45
Galloway 278, 460, 540
Gallowhauch 399
Gallowhop[e] Gallow Hope 388-92, 395, 486, 497, 498, 500
Gallowlie 438
Gallowschelis 25
Games 231, 533
Gard[i]ner 55, 56, 118
Garvald 27, 35, 69, 71, 149, 184, 424
Garvatt Garvet[t] Garvit 27, 32, 142, 149
Gaw 25, 27
Gaylour 157
Gedde[s] Geddie[s] 19, 45, 376, 377
Geigging[?] Hillis 353
Getgood 244
Gewine 409
Gib[e]son[e] 84, 114, 230, 236, 467
Gifford 144, 411
Gilchrist 114
Gill[i][e]s 108-13, 170, 502
Gillohaslip, Gilwhaslip 397, 406
Gilmertoun 219, 238
Gilmoir 350
Gilmur, 134
Gimmersmilnes 88
Ginglekirk 382, 386
Gives 169
Gla[d]d[i]sm[o]or[e], Glad[i]smuir[e] 71, 72, 78, 185, 200, 202, 226, 245, 402, 403, 423, 424, 458, 459, 460, 490, 500
Gladsta[i]nes 98, 99
Glasgow 57, 62, 172, 446, 453, 459-61, 539, 540
Glass 68, 116
Glenca[i]rn[e] 71, 236, 244
Glorrat 237
Glover 418, 439, 440
Godscroft 43, 289, 301, 320
Godspeid 240
Goodacre 46
Goodaill 76
Goodear Goodeir 386, 395, 399
Goodfellow 163, 425, 466
Goodman 41, 152, 154, 504
Goold 72
Gordo[u]n[e] 33, 34, 45, 61, 168, 375, 465, 537, 540
Gorebridge 171
Gosford 26, 68, 245, 520
Gottray 240
Goudy 431
Gourdie 414
Gourla[y]bank 231, 232, 238
Gourlaw 154
Gourl[e]y, Gourlie 314, 436, 438, 467, 516, 522
Graham[e] 16, 24, 35, 36, 42, 44, 45, 47, 52, 58, 61, 62, 95, 409, 410
Grange 116, 119
Gray[e] 12, 14, 17, 22, 24, 26, 27, 34, 36, 45, 61, 71, 76, 82, 95, 102, 103, 114, 115, 149, 168, 180, 227, 232, 237, 252, 277, 287, 288, 291, 299, 310, 313, 314, 323, 328, 345, 357, 375, 387, 403, 404, 405, 434, 467, 482, 502, 507 *and see Grey*
Grayame 446
Graymeale, Graymeill, Greyme, Greymeal, Greymeill, Grey Meal 14, 15 10, 11, 14, 15, 25, 27, 28, 33, 34, 59, 60, 61, 277, 278, 465, 533
Greenlaw, Greinla[w] Grienlawis 88, 89, 407, 409, 410
Grege 118
Grein 98, 396, 397, 398, 408
Greive, Gri[e]ve 71, 84, 128, 431, 433
Grey 11, 14, 15, 27, 28, 102, 326, 465 *and see Gray*
Greyfriars Churchyard 243
Grierso[u]n[e] 7, 14, 15, 17, 25, 27, 35, 37, 38, 39, 40, 41, 44, 45, 46, 51, 63, 115, 245, 249, 275, 277, 427, 465, 475, 513
Grinlay 418
Grinto[u]n 102, 216, 284, 297, 308, 311, 312, 313, 315, 317, 323, 466, 502, 503, 507, 510
Grundisone 414
Grynto[u]n 291, 315
Guidfellow 326
Guild 107, 168, 395, 398, 399-402, 404, 407, 471
Guilly 122, 124, 128
Gulit 423

Gu[l]lan[e] Guillan Gulene Gylloun 28, 45, 67, 149, 238, 242, 304, 326, 424, 470
Guthrie 418
Guyler, Gylar, Gyler 154, 165, 166, 211, 212
Gy[l]lour[e] 75, 27, 205, 208, 209, 210, 483

H

Had[d]in[g]to[u]n[e] 6, 7, 21, 22, 29, 30, 34, 36, 37, 46, 49, 53, 58, 63, 65, 71-3, 75, 79, 87, 94, 101, 110, 115, 130, 141, 149-54, 158-60, 162, 163, 165-71, 173-5, 178-80, 189-92, 196-8, 200, 204, 208, 211-3, 219-29, 231-42, 244, 247, 248, 251, 252, 273, 282, 287, 291, 311, 313, 323, 332, 336, 341, 343, 348, 349, 351-4, 356-8, 360-2, 369, 370, 372, 375, 387, 412, 413, 420, 421, 423, 425, 439, 447, 448, 455, 457-60, 464-72, 483, 495, 497, 503, 507, 514, 525, 527, 539, 540
Haddo 171
Hadtheraike 152
Hafflandbarne 343
Hagstoun 196
Hailes Hail[l]is 57, 58, 140, 150, 231
Hair 434
Hairt 214, 275, 277
Haistie 87, 92, 168, 376, 377
Haitsyd 326
Hakit 16
Halcartoun 244
Hal[l]eburton Ha[l]li[e]burto[u]n[e] Hal[l]yburtoune Hailyburton Helebourtone 21, 129, 130, 224, 228, 232, 235-8, 240-2, 408-10, 466, 467, 481, 486, 508
Half Land Barne 340
Hall 78, 147, 210, 221, 236, 260, 319, 428, 503
Hal[l]hill 41, 253, 260
Hal[l]iday, Halyday Helliday 84, 144, 183, 427, 43-4, 481, 503, 513
Halyeort 16
Hamelto[u]n 330, 332, 335, 356, 357, 358, 361
Ham[m]ilt[t]o[u]n[n][e] Hammyltoun 18, 22, 23, 71, 78, 79, 83, 115, 116, 152, 153, 162, 182, 185, 186, 191-5, 204-6, 214, 216, 217, 219-23, 227, 231, 236, 237, 252, 254, 260, 277, 304, 305, 307, 315, 319, 322, 323, 327, 329-32, 335, 336, 339-43, 346--62, 377, 382, 386, 400, 420, 435, 454, 455, 465-7, 476, 479, 480, 482, 483, 490,
492, 498-504, 508, 510, 513, 514, 520-2
Hannin 108
Hansey 228
Haprig 205
Hardie 220, 524
Hare[s] 191, 431
Harehead 461
Harlaw, Harlow 106, 145, 184, 216, 217, 242, 244, 335, 337, 338, 355, 466, 482, 540
Harmestoun Harmistoun 232, 235, 242
Harpardane 238
Harper 42, 115, 405
Harriot 326
Harvie 411
Hastie 82, 87, 166, 167, 168
Hastings 67
Hatterai[c]k[e] 152, 454, 455, 482, 489
Hawch of Laide 312
Hawhill 326
Hawick 178
Hawie 244
Hawthorne 393
Hay[e] 79, 80, 81, 114, 115, 117, 164, 191, 192, 193, 195, 216, 220, 232, 235, 236, 237, 238, 242, 251, 391, 424, 466, 479
Haymouth 234
Headone 120
Heamone 77
Heidrik 283
Heislip 215
Helden 326
Hempseid 434
Henderso[u]n[n][e] 69, 70, 85, 109, 133, 142, 143, 144, 187, 236, 237, 243, 259, 269, 277, 376, 480, 485, 522, 540
Hendrie, Hendry 83, 87, 102, 243, 313, 314, 402, 404 *and see Henry*
Henillis 28
Henrie, Henry 34, 49, 68, 119, 151, 157, 170, 183, 186, 216, 217, 253, 376, 377, 435, 466, 499, 516 *and see Hendry*
Henryso[u]n[e] 57, 377
Henson 434
Hepburn[e][s] 23, 29, 57, 58, 88, 89, 91, 100, 118, 150, 162, 163, 174, 184, 189, 191, 204, 208, 216, 217, 219-21, 229, 231, 232, 236-8, 242, 243, 247, 249, 337, 356, 360, 387, 396, 398,

402, 413, 426-30, 432-4, 438, 448, 485, 504, 506, 508
Hercus 108
Herd 422
Herdma[n]ston, Her[d]misto[u]n[e], Herdmonstone 26, 61, 76, 88, 159, 179, 231, 421, 520 *and see Hirdmanston*
Herdrid 323
Her[i]es 190, 298, 505, 508
Her[r]i[o]t[t] Herote Heryott 146, 193, 356, 364, 376, 377, 382, 386, 389-93, 446, 455-7, 469, 499, 500, 516
Hermitage 57
Herring 77
Herrone 376
Heuch 157, 158, 205, 405, 406, 498
Heugh 396, 403, 485
Heugh of Tranent 396, 397
Hewat, Hewit 376, 377
Hewit 377
Hiefield 237, 242
Hielie 430, 431
Hieslop 133
Hill 10, 37, 43, 52, 56, 58, 62, 68, 107, 115, 183, 192, 200, 214, 275, 287, 299, 308, 309, 351, 387, 388, 389, 390, 391, 407, 423, 498, 513, 539
Hiltoun 187
Hinklie 357
Hirdman[e]sto[u]n Hirdmestoun Hirdmestown Hirdmisto[u]n Hirmestoun[e] 26, 179, 180, 182-4, 186, 189, 196, 197, 219, 223, 480 *and see Herdmanston*
Hislop 104, 133, 218, 466
Hismestoune 26
Hodge[s] 106, 162, 245, 247, 289, 300, 318, 378, 379, 380-2, 396, 399, 402, 403, 405, 406, 409, 423, 466, 476
Hodindean 412, 486
Hog[e] Hogg[e] 88, 89, 101, 108, 109, 115, 116-9, 134, 153, 204, 209, 210, 221, 224, 227, 231, 238, 253, 254, 261, 267, 304, 315, 326-47, 351, 352, 358, 362, 376, 377, 407, 410-2, 434, 467, 470, 471, 476, 477, 480, 481, 483, 490, 497, 505, 508, 510, 517, 521, 522
Hog[g]ard Hoggart 72, 83
Hogis 329
Hola 12, 14, 27, 511, 520, 521, 522

Holieday 168
Holyrood 44
Holyroodhouse 39, 59
Home Hoom[e] 43, 51, 52, 68, 107, 146, 158, 169, 179, 182, 216, 217, 219, 222, 223, 236-8, 242-4, 253, 254, 262, 266, 267, 283, 287, 289, 290, 292, 294, 296, 298, 300, 301, 304-6, 308, 311-3, 318, 322, 326, 327, 347, 349, 351-3, 355-8, 362, 376, 388, 389, 405, 422, 476, 480, 502, 503, 505, 514
Home of Godscroft 43, 289, 300
Honeyman 232, 467
Hope, Hoip[is] 21, 222, 293, 309, 324, 329, 331, 335, 340, 344, 346-8, 351, 356-8, 361, 486, 497, 498, 500
Hopper 217, 243, 291
Hoppringell 326
Hoprig 78
Hordweill 321
Horn 389, 486
Horseburgh 231, 467
Horsemen's Society 537
Houm[e] 126, 421
Housto[u]n 307, 325, 331
How 119, 154, 170, 224, 259, 266, 316, 322, 323, 335, 338, 354, 445, 456, 473, 533
Howat 170, 376
Howda[i]ne, Howden, Howdine, Howdone 120, 151, 153, 154, 183, 393, 430, 479, 504, 507, 509, 515
Howie 275
How[i][e]son[e] 107, 173, 182, 383, 435, 475
Howlatsone 82
Howname Hownome 197, 198, 199
Hucheson[e] 85
Hucksto[u]n[e] 382, 386
Hugsto[u]n Hills 348, 353, 354, 483
Huiesoune 402
Hukstoun 352
Hum 320
Humbie Humby 6, 99, 114, 154, 158, 163, 164, 230, 234, 249, 353, 355, 396, 402, 426, 428-30, 432, 433, 467, 485, 502, 504, 517, 521
Humbiemylne 431
Hume 60, 95, 212, 261, 319, 320, 391, 435, 436, 513, 514
Huntar, Hunter 71, 72, 77, 78, 88, 89, 97, 98, 133, 136, 137, 140, 145, 152, 153, 163, 165, 168-70,

183, 185, 189, 190, 191, 200-2, 204, 208-11,
   219, 220, 225-7, 231-3, 244, 362, 372, 411, 422,
   423, 425, 430, 433, 439, 454, 455, 466-8, 492,
   500, 504, 521, 530
Huntington 348
Hutso[u]n[e] 17, 94, 242

I

Incarne 21
Inchcairn[e] Inchcarne 235-7
Inglis 24, 90, 204, 208, 232, 233, 243, 244, 270,
   378
Ingrahame 238, 470
Innerkeithing 234
Innerleithen 244
I[n]nerw[e]i[c]k 102, 216, 217, 244, 253, 261, 280,
   289, 315, 317, 324, 326, 377, 460, 461, 477
Innes 214, 233, 253, 254, 260, 388, 517, 539
Inveresk 21, 104, 171, 172, 216, 232, 407, 467,
   505, 525
Inverkeithing 234
Ireland 190, 191, 323, 352, 362, 393, 508
Irvine 116, 362, 364, 506, 518, 539

J

Jackson[e] 98, 254, 264
Jaimesone 139
Jakson[e] 85, 136, 137, 264, 509
James 5-8, 11, 16, 19, 21-3, 26-8, 30, 34, 35, 40-3,
   47, 52, 53, 57, 58, 63, 68, 73-87, 89-94, 96, 99,
   100-4, 106, 108, 114-21, 124, 126-8, 130, 132,
   133, 136, 139, 141, 143, 144, 149, 151, 152,
   154-6, 158, 160, 161, 163-7, 169-71, 173, 178,
   179, 182-4, 186, 188, 189, 191, 192, 194-200,
   204, 205, 208, 211, 214-8, 220, 221, 223, 224,
   227, 228, 230-3, 235-8, 240, 242, 243, 245, 248,
   249, 252-5, 257, 258, 260-3, 266, 267, 269, 270,
   274, 275, 277-80, 291, 293, 302, 304, 305, 307,
   317-9, 325-7, 329-37, 339, 341, 342, 345, 346,
   349, 352-60, 362-4, 366-72, 374-7, 378, 381-8,
   395-8, 400, 402-7, 409, 410, 412-4, 418-23,
   425-435, 439, 440, 443-6, 450, 453, 465, 466,
   467, 471-3, 475, 476, 477-81, 484, 485, 487,
   488, 493, 495, 499, 500, 503-9, 512-20, 522,
   524, 530, 531, 539
James VI 5, 30, 34, 41, 58, 63, 443, 472, 475, 530

Jamieson 117
Jedburghe 316
Johns[t]o[u]n[e] 68, 72, 73, 77, 86, 88, 112, 113,
   118, 119, 142, 156, 163, 164, 167, 168, 187,
   197-200, 202, 215, 217, 226, 230-3, 237, 238,
   242-5, 254, 261, 269, 328, 367, 371, 380-2, 384,
   396, 402, 407-10, 424, 435, 449, 464, 466, 467,
   469, 470, 479, 480, 487, 495, 498, 502, 504,
   515-7, 522, 525, 526
Johnsto[u]nburn[e] 230-3, 237, 242, 244, 249, 426
Jollie 237
Jossie 236, 237
Justice 38, 42, 43, 48, 57, 215, 216, 221, 229, 244,
   245, 252, 275-7, 293, 309, 327, 329, 331, 336,
   342, 346, 353, 356, 358-61, 369, 376, 377, 393,
   400, 401, 407, 416, 418, 420, 421, 425, 427,
   438, 452

K

Kamaway 432
Kathie 167
Keddie, Keddy 248, 439
Keir 329, 333, 335, 336, 340, 341
Keith. Keyt[h] 5, 6, 26, 27, 29, 30, 62, 63, 99, 100,
   150, 153, 173, 179, 182, 184-9, 197, 219, 220,
   230-4, 237, 247, 249, 426-36, 438, 446, 448,
   465-7, 470, 474, 479-81, 483, 488, 496, 497,
   500, 501, 526, 531
Keithbank Folds 430
Keithmarshall Keith Marishall, Keith Marschell
   Keith Marshall, 231, 232, 233, 237
Keiver 390
Kellie, Kelly 11, 77, 116, 247, 253, 254, 261, 270,
   284, 288, 298, 300, 306, 308, 310, 314, 318,
   327, 440, 470, 476, 525, 526
Kelso 60, 158, 483, 515, 520
Kemp[e] 69, 70, 101, 122, 124, 125, 127, 146, 211,
   237, 238-42, 254, 264, 381, 385, 412, 422, 470,
   486, 487, 519, 523
Kennedie 80, 92, 145
Ker[r] 11, 22, 43, 49, 79, 80, 90, 104, 115, 116, 157,
   158, 160, 162, 163, 225, 229, 236, 237, 239-241,
   254, 267, 289, 300, 304, 320, 387, 388, 412, 420,
   421, 427, 434, 460, 466, 470, 487, 503, 505, 527
Kerd 387
Keresone 323
Keringtoun[e] 45, 150

Kers[e] 23, 282, 295, 296, 308, 317, 323, 479, 503, 506, 511, 530
Kilbaberto[u]n[e] 11, 23, 501
Kilgour 401
Killene Mure 349, 354
Kilspindie 219
Kincade, Kincaid Kinka[i]d[e] 77, 142, 164, 228, 243-5, 382, 383, 387, 396, 403, 405, 406, 410, 411, 413, 422, 425, 428, 449, 450, 493-6, 518, 523
King 5-8, 10-12, 15, 17-19, 22, 29, 31, 34-9, 41, 43-55, 57-63, 112, 113, 118, 158, 174, 178, 213, 214, 236, 260, 292, 305, 324, 361, 408-10, 443, 446, 450, 472, 473, 475, 508, 512, 518, 524, 530, 532, 533
Kinghorn 26, 511
Kingsburn 40
Kinloch 238
Kirkaldy Kirkadye Kirkaldie 22, 87, 402, 508
Kirkcudbright 57
Kirkland 139-41, 169, 235-42
Kirklandburn 487
Kirklandis of Bolton 183
Kirktoun 153, 220, 221, 360
Kirkwood 74, 87, 88, 141, 164, 165, 252, 253, 260, 261, 263, 326, 447, 458
Kirk of Garvett 27
Kirk Session 29, 65-7, 69, 71, 72, 99, 100, 113, 118, 120-22, 131, 140, 142, 144, 147, 149, 168, 240, 421, 527, 539
Kniblo 379, 382, 383
Knocks 142
Knock Hills 457
Knoll[i]s Knowllis 118, 318, 319, 321-3
Knous Know Knowes Knowis 143, 254, 257, 265, 266, 289, 290, 300, 301, 306, 311, 430, 488, 509
Knox[e] 70, 135, 143, 158, 237, 244, 429, 430, 431, 435, 470, 473
Krige 132
Kummin[e] 108, 109
Kyle, Kyll 21, 80, 184, 236
Kyllismure 216, 217

L

Lacost 388-93, 395, 423, 446, 469, 486, 497
Lady Well 292
Laidlaw 178
Laing[e] 115, 138, 249, 427, 428, 431-4, 438, 470, 481, 489, 510
Lairhill 228
Lairmoth 78
Laistoun 231
Laiswaid 433
Lamb[e] 77, 97, 98, 158, 211, 239, 254, 267, 269, 398, 412, 424, 479
Lambe Burn 158
Lam[m]ingto[u]n[e] 78, 90, 233, 249, 368, 372, 374, 426
Lammerlaw 96
Lanark 57
Lanarkshire 78
Landels 95
Lang-Nydrie
Langnid[d]r[i]e, Langnuddr[i]e, Langnuderie, Langnudr[i]e, Langnudrye, Langnydrie, Lang Nydrie 22, 190, 201, 204, 218, 219, 225, 277-9, 364
Lanson 135
Larner 1, 216, 252, 273, 443, 468, 471, 523, 533, 540
Lason[e] 90, 237
Lauch 423
Lauder 28, 45, 79, 81, 107, 152, 180, 221, 228, 243, 244, 252, 254, 257, 260, 266, 326, 360, 375, 438, 446, 447, 450, 479, 481, 540
Lauderda[i]l[l][e] 56, 151, 154, 217, 240, 382, 386, 407, 408, 448
Laurie, Laury, Lawrie 103, 163, 230, 254, 256, 263, 264, 295, 466, 467
Lauson[e], Lawson[e] 162, 204-6, 208, 227, 238, 239, 241, 242, 253, 261, 350, 404, 435, 466, 470, 487, 497, 499
Lauthian 180
Lawder 79, 80, 81, 211, 220, 221
Lawfield 216
Layeshope 423
Laying 223, 249, 426, 434
Learmonth Learmouth Learmuith Leirmont Leirmont[h] Leirmouth Leirmuith Lermonth[e] Lermott Lermouth[e] 57, 86, 98, 179, 184, 189, 298, 304, 326, 328, 329, 331-5, 337, 338, 341, 346, 347, 375, 522
Lefinstown 173
Leitch 163, 466

Leith 6-8, 11, 15-7, 19, 25, 26, 34, 35, 51, 280, 438, 449, 456, 511
Lenchop 25
Lennox 38, 39
Leslie 108, 110, 111, 407
Les[s]wa[i]d[e] 428, 433, 435, 448
Letham[e] 178, 235, 237
Lethington 340
Levingstoun, Levi[n]ston, Levin[g]to[u]n[e] 60, 163, 163, 180, 196, 224, 228, 237
Libberto[u]n[e] 23, 274, 475, 478, 508, 513
Liddail[l], Lid[d][l]el[l] 121, 217, 248, 257, 291, 302, 307, 318, 382, 386, 424, 434, 449, 466, 480, 496, 506, 523, 526
Liddesdale 57
Lie 302
Likkit 45
Lillie 121, 122, 124-31, 376, 505
Lindores 73
Lind[e]say, Lindsey, Linsay[e] Linsey 48, 92-4, 155, 160-3, 165, 166, 169, 170, 211, 212, 323, 423
Linkhops 26
Links 211, 259, 261, 269, 289, 300, 315, 350, 357, 398, 424, 498
Linkup 17, 19
Linn 119
Lintoun 174, 253
Lint Hauch 431
Lister 183
Lithgow 166
Litill Newton 184
Lit[t]le Fawsyd[e] 363, 367, 369, 371, 374, 476
Litster 186, 197, 216, 217, 376, 377, 466, 503, 507, 514
Littel[l] 84, 111, 367
Littil 189, 219, 367, 466, 505
Little 77, 126, 191, 369, 371, 433, 476, 521
Littledean 12
Livingto[u]n[e] 92, 93, 242
Livy 294
Loanhead 433, 435, 448, 449, 481, 501, 510
Loch 20, 36, 82, 83, 210, 227, 407, 408, 469, 486, 491, 495, 524
Lochard 127
Loche 352
Lochend 217, 252, 260

Lochhall 205
Lochhouses 131
Lochland 122, 124
Lock 116, 506, 518
Lockart 440, 526
Locke 116
Lockhed 439
Logan[e] 45, 122, 124-30, 154, 172, 253, 262, 397-9, 404, 435, 446, 469, 478, 479, 498, 507, 509, 519, 521
Logie 425
Lolluller 356
Lonesay 169
Long 114, 466
Longniddry, Longnidrie 16, 113, 218, 224, 230, 278, 372, 479, 483, 497, 500, 503, 513, 527
Lorimer Lorimo[o]re Lorimour[e] 78, 79, 87, 88, 418
Lo[u]thian[e] Lowthian v, 1-3, 5, 6, 21, 23, 29, 35, 42, 43, 47-50, 56-8, 66, 67, 93, 104, 121, 147, 171-5, 177, 180, 213, 232, 238, 249, 252, 273, 274, 280, 293, 324, 352, 357, 376-8, 387, 389, 391, 393, 395, 396, 402, 403, 407, 408, 425, 426, 435, 436, 438, 439, 441, 443, 446, 447, 449, 450, 453, 454, 458-60, 463-5, 467-72, 474, 475, 481, 482, 486, 489, 493, 496-501, 504, 506, 509, 511, 519, 521-3, 526-8, 530, 531, 533-6, 538-40
Lougan 255
Lough Hall 78
Low 118, 329, 426
Lowrie 282, 296, 297, 327, 404, 424, 518
Lucifer. 200, 484
Luckifoot, 416
Luffness 439
Lukit 27
Lumhnay Mains 439
Lum[m]isden, Lumsdean 218, 259, 287, 298, 304, 307, 308, 318
Lyddell 164, 171, 427, 428
Lyl[l]e 74, 82, 131, 157, 158, 267, 407, 408, 424
Lyn 325, 395
Lynd[e]say, Lynds[e]y 21, 154, 155, 161, 162, 164, 165, 174, 283, 291, 296, 311, 341, 343, 344, 474, 508, 517
Lyn[n]e 398, 399, 446, 469
Lyntone Mill 339

Lynton Brigges 311
Lynto[u]n 174, 283, 304, 311, 326, 330, 331, 335-8, 341-3, 346, 354
Lyo[u]n[n] 20, 28, 39, 42, 215
Lystoun 230
Lyte 469
Lytster 102, 103, 475, 503, 510, 513, 520

Mc

McAirtour, McCairtour 309, 350
Macall, Maccail, McCaill, McColl 74, 75, 79, 81, 128
MacCalyean MaccAlzean Mackallean Mackalzon Mak[c]alzean[e] Makkaillen McCalyan[e] McCalyanis McCalyean McCalyeane McCalyeanne 7, 19, 20, 26, 35-40, 44-6, 47-9, 51-7, 60-3, 299, 463, 473, 475, 480, 500, 503, 511, 512, 521, 522, 524, 530
McCrie 146
Maccullo, McCulloch McKullo 257, 266, 418
Macelat, Macelet 325
McG[h]ie 162, 228
Macgill McGill 16, 22, 26, 28-30, 36, 42, 45, 49, 50, 51, 59, 149, 150, 219, 293, 435, 465, 478, 506, 512, 524
Mack 507, 508
Mackae 197
Mackanquell 368
Mackendly 132, 133
Mackenell 60
Mackenzie McKenz[i]e 99, 162, 243, 387, 388, 447, 450, 451, 453, 523-7, 540
Mackgie 159, 160-4
Mackgill 30, 34
McKie 257, 387
Mackie 506
McKinnel 146
McLachlan xv, 1, 540
McLain McLane McClain 259, 260, 270, 489
Macklennen 111
Macklurge McLurge 107, 435
McMath 428, 433
Macnab McNab 87, 88, 98
Macktargatt Mactaggart Mactargatt Mactarget[t] Mattorgett McTargaret McTarget[t] 177, 178, 213, 252-5, 260, 262, 263, 270, 426, 439, 450, 470, 474, 478, 530

M

Madeis Loup 308
Maen 423
Mag[h]ie 162, 165-7, 169, 239, 241, 487
Magkie 159
Maglene 217, 466
Mahoun 40
Maiday's Lowpe Maiddeyis Loupe 287, 310
Main[e] 80, 81, 98, 466
Mains Park Burn[e] 429, 497
Mair 436
Mairsone 120
Mairtoun 292, 319
Maislet 240
Mais[s]on[e] 79, 86, 223, 235, 236, 343, 469, 470
Maitland 52, 60, 397, 405, 430, 431, 446, 485
Mak 182, 184, 185, 186, 189, 465, 466
Makcoull 240
Make 220, 466
Makg[h]ie 160, 163, 170, 224, 225, 228, 372
Makgil[l] 149, 185, 186
Makie 116, 195
Makmirrie 92
Maldsly 171
malefice 65, 145, 374, 400, 413, 416, 474, 475, 477, 478, 505, 528
Mallire 201
Man 62, 132, 391-3, 395, 399, 446, 469, 529
Manderson[ne] Mandersto[u]n[e] 98, 130, 131, 222, 223, 326, 347, 348, 351-3, 357, 358, 361, 362, 390, 391, 514
Mann 499
Manners 132, 424
Mansoun 105, 106
Mar 53, 54, 217
Marchbanks 245, 247
Marioun[e] 25, 27, 28, 30, 34, 37, 45, 68-70, 82, 107, 114, 158, 165, 182, 183, 188, 191, 201, 202, 204, 205, 225, 230, 232, 235, 277, 299, 300, 307, 310, 328, 329, 423, 465, 467, 469
Maristoun 240
Marjoribanks 49, 378-81, 402, 403, 405, 406
Markesto[u]n 21, 61
Markil[l] Markal Markle 160, 161, 221, 231, 279, 316, 328-46, 351, 362, 476, 480, 497, 505
Marr 133

Marrit 202, 484
Mart[e]in[e] 76, 94, 95, 132-4, 137, 168, 422-4, 427, 459, 540
Maselate 321
Mas[s]on[e] 72, 88, 342, 197, 344
Math[i]eson[e] 145, 221, 363, 368, 369, 372, 466
Mathie 217, 240, 254, 256, 264, 265, 518, 521
Maxwell 38, 46, 48, 56, 237, 242, 460, 521, 522, 526, 540
Maxwell-Stuart 38, 46, 48, 56, 521, 522, 526, 540
Mayne 362
Mayston 171
Mayten 171
Mearnes, Mearnis 376, 377
Measlit 165
Medles 425
Meik[ke], Miek 67, 422, 466, 507, 514
Meik[k]ie 73, 86, 242
Meik[k]le 408, 422, 424
Meikle pinkerton Mekill Pinkertoun 283, 311
Meirton 292
Melro[i]s[e] Mewros 217, 280, 284, 287, 291, 292, 297-9, 303-5, 307, 308, 310, 311, 317, 318, 323, 466
Melvill[e] 41, 378, 383, 384, 386, 477
Melvine 80
Menteith 326, 435
Menzies 96
Merkestoun 508
Merkhous[s] 145
Merkill 328, 332, 333, 336, 337, 362
Merss 357
Merstone, Merstoun 254, 262
Mertoun[e] 302, 307, 318, 319, 374, 476
Meslet[t] Meslit 283, 284, 287, 296, 297, 308, 311-7, 476, 508, 514
Mesone 398
Middlemast Middlemost 96
Midlothian 57, 104, 171, 172, 244, 249, 387, 426, 436, 500, 528, 534
Mill 25, 30, 37, 40, 42, 44, 76, 88, 107, 114, 154, 155, 156, 159, 313, 321, 339, 342, 376, 414, 421, 422, 424, 457, 476, 482, 504, 506, 509, 515
Millar, Miller 99, 106, 218, 231, 232, 238, 253, 261, 314, 460, 466, 540
Millen, Milne 86, 231, 254, 258, 262, 269, 403, 407, 478, 509

Milnetoun[e] Milnetowne 231, 235, 469
Milto[u]n[e] 16, 101, 138, 139, 242, 476
Mindrum 199
Mine 466
Miraklis 201
Mirrielawis Mirrilies 22, 423
Mirst 138
Mitchell 72, 105, 109, 157, 169, 197, 220, 221, 360, 375, 398, 460
Mitchelso[u]n[e] 214, 215
Moffat 103, 163, 243, 429, 466
Moirtoun 307
Moitis 44
Moniepenny 388
Monkrig[e] 179, 184, 189, 192, 196, 204, 237, 350, 356
Montgumbrie 121
Montrose 60
Moodie Moody Moddy 247, 249, 428, 447, 470, 496, 525
Moor[e] 79, 100, 142, 226, 247, 249, 358, 422, 427, 438, 495 *and see Muir, Mure*
More House 397
More Shote 202
Morgone 375
Morham[e] 105, 231, 241
Mori[e]son[e] 135, 248, 449
Morrison's Haven 35, 39, 42, 116
Morto[u]n 38, 131, 217, 244, 292, 303, 325
Morvindean 121
Moscrop 20, 26, 42, 48, 49, 50, 51, 522
Mosley 395, 399
Mott 14, 20, 35, 37, 40
Mowat 353, 357, 358, 360
Mowbray 42
Muddy, Mudie, Mu[i]dy 383, 428, 436, 447, 458, 495
Muet 128
Muffet 103
Muir 116, 121, 128, 133, 134, 160, 249, 408, 449, 487 *and see Moor, Mure*
Muirhead, Muirheid 152, 180, 196, 197, 479
Munkrig 229
Mure 32, 72, 217, 239, 240, 241, 252, 260, 304, 308, 326, 349, 350, 354 *and see Muir, Moor*
Murebrow 364
Murraisburn[e] 428, 498

Murray[s] Murrey 27, 45, 72, 75, 79, 86, 89, 90, 120, 133, 134, 163, 168, 200-2, 204-6, 208, 210, 222, 226, 227, 230, 233, 236, 237, 242-4, 252, 253, 259-61, 322, 434, 455-8, 466, 467, 484, 510, 532, 533, 536, 540
Musselburgh Mussilbrugh Mussil[l]burgh Mussulburgh 22, 44, 65, 104, 106, 167, 171, 173, 211, 214-6, 218-20, 231, 232, 236, 237, 243, 244, 274, 407-10, 423, 451, 458, 464, 469, 470, 486, 503, 524, 525, 527
Mutis 25
Myl[e]s Myllis 17, 396, 402
Myller 275, 276
Mylne 98, 191, 274, 293, 304, 309, 355
Mylnehill 430
Mynram 199
Myreside 291, 302, 318

N

Naipare Naiper Naper Napier 7, 19, 20, 28, 31, 35-43, 46, 48, 49, 52, 53, 56, 57, 60-3, 364, 369, 370, 471, 473, 478, 497, 511, 512
Na[i]smith Nesmith 217, 397, 406
Nalsone 403
Nather Howdene 151
Natoun, Neato[u]n[e] 22, 26, 243
Neill 222, 223, 348, 351, 353, 356-8, 361, 362
Neilson[e] 89, 102, 139, 253, 329, 337, 340, 341, 424, 475, 503, 510, 513, 520
Neitherdein Netherdeane Netterdene 220 230, 233
Nelans Burne 180
Ne[a]lson 199, 407
Nemoe 398
Nerkeith 233
Nesbit[t] Neisbeit 180, 182, 202, 205, 208, 209, 386
Netherbow 434
Netherkeith Nether Keith 99, 230, 430, 436, 531
Netherton 233
Netterdaill Netterstaill 179, 180, 184
Nevin 37
Newbane 423
Newbattle Newbotle Newbottall Newbottle 101, 216, 243, 357, 506
Newbyth 252, 260
Newcastell 349, 353, 354

Newes from Scotland 2, 5, 6, 8, 10, 15, 18, 19, 30, 31, 56, 493, 500, 512, 524, 530
Newhall 146, 238, 412, 413, 471, 479, 481, 510
Newhaven 116
Newmiln[e][s] Newmyln Newmyln[e] 73, 92, 160, 232, 304, 326, 423
Newto[u]n 11, 16, 22, 145, 184, 195, 214, 215, 232, 236-8, 244, 411, 511
Newtonlies 254, 263
Niblo 504
Nicholl 57
Nicol[l]son[n][e] Nicelsone Niclsone Nicolsoun[e] Nycolsone 21, 28, 45, 69, 70, 93, 107, 133, 136, 140, 221, 224, 231, 304, 326, 327, 329, 330, 332-9, 341-7, 364, 369, 370, 377, 378, 380, 400, 401, 404, 423-5, 449, 467, 476, 480, 490, 492, 497, 499, 505, 508, 514, 521
Nid[d]rie, Nydrie 277, 350, 357, 385
Nielso[u]n[e] 105, 110, 111
Nimil 18, 19
Nisbet, Nisbit[t], Nisbot Nysbett 39, 49, 88, 96, 139, 155, 157, 180, 186, 202, 208-11, 226, 243, 253, 290, 301, 302, 304, 306, 318, 325-7, 375, 381, 391, 421, 422, 424, 466, 468, 484, 498, 500, 514
Norham[e] 190, 306, 482, 521, 530
Norime 323
Normand 5, 6, 10-12, 15, 18-20, 26, 27, 35, 36, 38, 39, 41, 46-9, 54-6, 443, 445, 539, 540
Norram 314
Northrig 54
Northumberland 347, 435
North Belton 253
North Berwick Northberuik Northberwick 1, 5, 7, 10, 14, 15, 17-21, 24, 27, 29-32, 36-8, 40-3, 45, 48, 49, 51, 52, 55, 57, 59, 61, 63, 65, 99, 105, 106, 115, 150, 157, 158, 160, 162, 165-70, 173, 211, 223, 228, 234, 274, 277, 280, 287, 314, 327, 375, 443, 445, 446, 454, 465, 467, 471-3, 489, 496, 497, 499, 500, 501, 511, 512, 518, 519, 526, 533, 534, 539
Norvie 438
Nungate 82, 89, 92, 169, 505
Nunland 220, 221, 236-8, 348, 353, 483
Nuntands 357
Nymbill 216
Nymmo 423

O

Oarther 168
Ogil[e], Ogill Ogle 283, 288, 296, 297, 304, 306, 311-8
Ogilvie, Ogilbie, Ogilby Ogilvy 49, 55-7, 85, 86, 146, 409, 460, 461, 540
Oldhamstocks 113, 461
Old Cambus 461
Old Craighall 22
Olestop 428
Oliphant 348, 351, 361
Oliver 168, 172, 217, 229, 232, 236, 237, 378, 408, 418, 466, 467
Olivestob 398, 399, 486
Orm 265, 266
Orm[e] 254, 257, 258, 265, 266
Ormesto[u]n[e] Ormisto[u]n 14, 35, 38, 113, 165, 168, 169, 171-3, 184, 191, 201, 216, 219, 230, 232, 234, 243, 244, 249, 350, 353, 355, 356, 360, 400, 410, 411, 426, 427, 429-36, 448, 453, 455-7, 467, 480, 488, 505, 511, 514, 520
Oslo 6, 7
Oswald 160, 163, 236, 350
Oswell 167
Ouchterlony 118, 119, 509, 510
Overhaills 238
Overke[i]th, Overkeyt[h] 101, 150, 151, 232, 233, 434, 435
Overthornton 103
Over Boltoun 239, 240, 241
Over Boltoun More 239
Over Haillis 150
Over Keith, Over Keyt 100, 153, 230, 231, 430
Over Libbertoune 23
Ovir Saltoun 182, 183
Oxton 382, 504

P

Painestoun, Painistoune, Painkertoun, Painson, Painsto[u]n[e], Paisto[u]n[e] Panestoune, Panisto[u]n[e] Pannistoune Paysto[u]n, 12, 69, 75-7, 81, 83, 86, 88, 90, 91, 104, 114, 145, 189, 200-2, 204-6, 208, 209, 225-7, 230-3, 249, 369, 374, 377, 411, 419, 423, 433, 435, 438, 449, 505, 506
Palmer 188
Pankaitland 167
Pannes, Pannis, Pans Pannis 17, 23, 25, 34, 40, 41, 236, 237, 275, 276, 277, 289, 300, 319, 320, 350, 357, 365, 372, 374, 378, 379, 382, 398, 503, 510.
Pannistoune Heuch 205
Pap 55
Papill 232
Pargill 61
Park[i][e] 11, 168, 193, 195, 363, 365, 366, 368-70, 374, 375, 429, 497, 522
Part 193, 329, 374, 388, 393, 499, 531
Pat[t]erso[u]n[e] Patisone 27, 45, 86, 87, 89, 93, 107, 114, 120, 163, 171, 196, 197, 205, 208-11, 217, 223, 229, 230, 237, 254, 258, 266, 267, 279, 280, 291, 302, 307, 318, 326, 413, 422, 426, 434, 435, 466, 467, 470, 475, 476, 480, 498, 514, 536
Paton 172, 232, 460, 467
Pearson 147
Peasto[u]n[e] 82, 134, 249, 251, 426-8, 430, 434-6, 438, 441, 449, 455, 457, 465, 470, 488, 496, 497, 500, 501, 505, 526
Peasto[u]n Moore 249, 427
Pedane Peddane Peden 275-7, 475, 478, 506, 513, 520
Peebles 167
Peeres, Peires 375, 376
Peiry 21, 503
Penca[i]tland Pencatlane 61, 91, 113, 154-7, 163, 164, 168, 171, 182, 183, 186, 219, 230-2, 249, 424, 427-30, 433, 435, 446, 448, 466, 501, 510
Pencraik Penkraik 192, 354
Penman 172, 173, 215, 216, 249, 426, 448, 500
Pennicook 244
Penny 145
Pensto[u]n[e] 71, 72, 78, 84, 86, 89-91, 157, 162, 363, 368, 369, 371, 372, 374, 477, 484, 497, 520
Pepper 353, 423
Peppercraig Pepper Craig 353, 354
Peris 21
Pestoun 427-9, 431, 432, 434
Peter 56, 78, 93, 138, 187, 245, 364, 372
Pethhead Pethheid 304, 326
Pettigrew 326
Pettiloe 104, 517
Phinnie 384, 386, 387, 504, 517

Pickiltillane Pickletillane Pikkiltillim 220, 221, 354
Pilmoir Pilmoore Pilmore Pilmure 85, 236-42, 414, 422, 469, 470
Pincarto[u]n[e] Pinkerto[u]n 216, 217, 253, 261, 283, 287, 292, 304, 310-2, 326
Piper's Mother 224
Pirie 119
Pitcairn 1, 5, 16, 18, 21-6, 28, 34, 42, 43, 49, 52, 56, 59, 274-8, 522, 540
Plaine 114
Playfair 221
Pleasants 253
Plewlandhill 179, 230, 231-3
Poerk 80
Pogie 18
Pollock 434
Polton 449
Polwart 11
Pople 142
Poppilhall 304, 308, 326
Porteous 12, 22, 27, 133, 150, 151, 221, 439, 440, 466, 469, 508
Post House 267, 269
Potterawe 435
Potts 404
Praintatoun 151
Pressmenen Pressmennan 126, 260
Presto[u]n 16, 21, 44, 60, 91, 111, 119, 169, 170, 214, 216, 217, 221, 231, 236, 237, 243, 247, 248, 275, 289, 292, 300, 303, 307, 318-20, 325, 331, 332, 338, 350, 357, 363, 364, 365, 368, 371, 378, 379, 382, 383, 398, 400, 402, 407, 439, 448, 449, 498, 503, 505
Presto[u]ngrange 116, 119, 177, 248, 440, 448, 449, 506, 518
Prestonhaugh 115, 238, 470
Prestonkirk 115, 140, 141
Prestonpanns Prestonpan[e]s Prestoune Pann[e]s Prestounpannis Prestounpan[n][e]s 8, 10, 16, 17, 20, 25, 26, 31, 35, 39-41, 44, 63, 115, 117, 118, 177, 217, 218, 221, 247, 248, 275, 277, 289, 347, 365, 367, 370, 374, 382, 383, 384, 395, 398, 439, 440, 470, 485, 495, 496, 498, 506, 511, 523, 526
Primrois, Prymrois 197, 219, 293, 294, 326
Pringall[e] Pringel[l] Pringle 165, 166, 172, 230, 231, 249, 254, 258, 265, 266, 391, 427, 430, 433, 434, 438, 467
Provan[e] 60, 68, 240, 241
Pumfrastoune Pumphers[t]on 20, 49-51, 475, 480
Pumphray 50
Purdie 78, 162, 204, 205, 206, 208, 227, 466
Purves, Purvis 117, 178, 252, 253, 260-7, 269, 270, 287, 288, 297, 298, 305, 306, 314, 316-9, 364, 383, 395, 400, 401, 404-6
Putonmilne 325

Q

Qilmour 364
Quarioir 376
Queensfer[r]ie 234, 244
Quhitelaw Quhytlaw 27, 45
Quhitlie 193, 195
Quhittinghame 199, 217
Quhyt[e] Quheit, Quyte 21, 26, 45, 210, 235, 304, 327, 329, 334, 336, 340, 343-6, 351, 362, 469, 490
Quhyt[e]kirk 304, 326

R

Ra[e], Ray 68, 77, 95, 120, 135-9, 251, 252, 436
Raeburn[e] 332, 423
Raff 71
Ramage 236, 237, 408, 469
Ramanoe Ram[m]anous 165, 167
Ramma[d]ge 133, 407, 408
Ramsay, Ramsey 27, 29, 42, 45, 116, 173, 216, 230, 243, 245, 364, 369, 372, 410, 411, 428, 429, 435
Randerstoun 249
Rankin[e] Ranking 37, 84, 217, 466
Raschaw 151
Ratchiman 231
Reck 139
Redhall Redhaule Reidhallis 11, 22, 61, 503
Reedhouse Reidhouse 68, 332
Reid, Read, Reed, Rid 68, 71, 72, 86, 88, 89, 112, 115-7, 149, 163, 217, 236, 242, 255, 262, 274, 275, 356, 357, 362-4, 368, 369, 372, 374, 400, 407, 429, 432, 465, 466, 488, 509, 513
Reidpeth Ridpath Ridpeth 84, 85, 217, 377, 378, 466,

Rento[u]n[e] 78, 82, 83, 91, 120, 368
Resto[u]n[e] 22, 254, 262, 270
Reyming 362
Rhine 409
Richeso[u]n[e] Rich[i]eson[e] Ritchardsone Ritchesone Ritchison Rychesoun 21, 27, 45, 86, 163, 164, 200-2, 204, 205, 215, 225-7, 236-8, 240, 242, 256, 263, 390, 440, 466, 470, 492, 516
Riddel[l] 16, 75, 217
Rig 236, 237
Rigwoodie Rigwoody Witch 121, 122
Rind 244
Ritchie 36, 52, 58, 362
Robert 1, 5, 6, 7, 10, 14-7, 21-3, 25, 27, 28, 31, 35, 37, 38, 40, 42, 44-6, 48, 49, 51, 54-8, 63, 67, 71, 72, 74, 75, 79, 80, 82, 85, 90-4, 100, 104, 107, 109-9, 122, 124-7, 131-4, 136-8, 141-3, 147, 150, 151, 154, 157, 160-3, 165-9, 172, 174, 179, 182-4, 189, 190, 191, 195, 196, 198, 211, 216-21, 223, 225, 229-32, 236, 237, 240, 241, 243-5, 247, 249, 252-4, 260, 261, 274-9, 304, 308, 326, 327, 329, 334, 335, 337, 340, 343-8, 351, 361, 362, 364, 366, 371, 375-83, 385, 387-91, 395, 396, 398-404, 407, 408, 414, 418, 420, 422-30, 432-5, 438, 448, 450, 460, 465, 470, 472, 475, 478, 479, 490, 500, 503, 505-7, 510, 511, 513, 514, 517-20, 540
Robertoun 236, 293, 348, 362
Robertso[u]n[e] v, 3, 35, 74, 115, 119, 163, 173, 210, 211, 229, 236, 237, 248, 331, 385, 404, 407, 408, 434, 439, 465, 466, 479
Robeso[u]n[e] Robesounis Rob[i][e]son[e] 21, 24, 25, 31, 35-8, 40, 41, 44-6, 54-6, 78, 86, 92, 116, 188, 208, 253, 260, 261, 422
Robswalls 423
Roddell 466
Roger 151
Roman[o]es Rom[m]an[n]os Romannus 81, 95, 97
Ronald, Ronold, 381, 385, 517, 521
Ronderstoun 426
Roslen, Rosline 21, 61, 508
Ros[s] 254, 255, 262, 388, 298, 407, 450, 485, 509, 517
Rothes 243, 244
Rotsone 330
Rottenraw Rottinraw Rottonraw 75, 238, 349, 355, 470
Rowting Stair 428
Roxburgh 243, 244
Rucheid 353
Ruchlaus Close Ruchlawes Closse 256, 263
Ruchlaw 217, 232, 389, 390, 491, 497, 500
Ruscastle 98
Russel[l] 42, 49, 59, 62, 116, 133, 201, 205, 225, 424, 427, 428, 430-4, 435, 488, 525
Rutherfo[o]rd[e] 236-8, 252, 316, 439, 440, 449, 450, 496, 526
Ruthven 376, 377, 516

S

Saidler 81
Saltcoatts Saltcottis Saltcotts 106, 224, 228, 242
Salto[u]n[e] 21, 37, 40, 44, 87, 114, 120, 122, 152, 154, 163-5, 168, 169, 179, 180, 182-8, 197, 219, 220, 223, 241, 350, 355, 358, 359, 360, 422, 423, 430, 476, 490, 500, 514, 516
Saltounmylne Saltoun Mill 37, 44, 423
Saltpanhall 254, 267
Saltpans 8
Saltpresto[u]n[e] Salt Presto[u]n[e] 61, 169, 170, 236, 237, 248, 357, 398, 402, 403, 448, 505
Sam[m]elsto[u]n[e] Sam[m]ilsto[u]n[e]e 23, 77, 83, 85, 86, 87, 88, 89, 92, 93, 94, 179, 183, 238, 240, 356, 421, 423
Sampso[u]n[e] 7, 8, 10, 11, 15-7, 19, 21, 25, 29-32, 34-45, 47, 48, 50, 51, 58, 60-3, 99, 132, 133, 150, 172-5, 274, 280, 440, 446, 454, 465, 472-4, 497, 499, 500, 502, 503, 506, 512, 519, 520, 522, 527, 528, 530, 531
Samuelsto[u]n[e] Samwelstoun 71, 72, 86, 87, 89, 91, 158, 187, 189, 191, 197, 222, 223, 235, 237, 238, 347, 351, 413, 414, 418, 422, 424, 454, 455, 470, 471, 480, 500, 509, 513
Sanct Androis 307
Sanders 355
Sandersdale 439
Sanderson[e] 83, 86, 94, 168, 355, 422
Sand[i]e 75, 110, 111, 157, 281, 282, 293, 294, 295, 304, 309, 317, 323, 327, 328, 330, 332, 333, 334, 335, 336, 339, 341, 342, 345, 346, 358, 362, 389, 390, 424, 454, 476, 479, 498, 499, 505, 507, 508, 510, 514
Sand[i]elan[d][i]s 42, 53, 110, 254, 266, 363, 365,

366, 368, 369, 370, 371, 372, 374, 378, 381, 385, 479, 481, 516, 517
Sand[i]s Sandes 84, 119, 184, 196, 197, 204, 208, 211, 227, 329
Sat[h]an 8, 17, 18, 23, 46, 152, 172, 191, 240, 283, 292, 303, 329, 348-50, 353, 355, 360, 376, 383, 388, 406, 410, 444, 446, 448, 453, 461, 470, 474, 483, 492, 496, 498, 512, 521, 528, 536, 540
Saunders 377, 485
Saundersdean 439
Scaitraw 216, 217
Schaipland 387
Schakes 423
Schankes 426
Scharp[e] 242, 393
Schaw 45, 57
Scheil 28
Scheilfield 186
Schoirswoid Schoreswood Schor[i]swood[e] Schorswood 187, 357, 422
Schyreff Braes 274
Scot[t] 86, 133, 134, 145, 159, 193, 195, 218, 222, 231, 232, 238, 383, 396, 398, 400-6, 410, 411, 422, 470, 488
Scottistarvet Scot[t]istarvit 358
Scoug[h]al[l] 11, 111
Scugail Scug[g]all Scuggil[l] 71, 77-81, 136
Seal 31, 101, 506
Seatain Seato[u]n[n][e] Seitoun Seto[u]n[e] Seyto[u]n[e] 6, 7, 14, 16, 17, 25, 27, 31, 32, 34, 35, 38, 42, 43, 45, 48, 49, 54-6, 61, 77, 83, 97, 115, 116, 119, 132, 133, 190, 211, 216-9, 230, 236, 237, 242, 248, 277-9, 364, 374, 380, 381, 385, 396-8, 402, 404, 405, 407, 427, 431, 453, 472, 473, 475, 478, 488, 510-3
Selby 31, 34, 47
Selkirk 57, 434, 435
Sendert 326
Seutie 396
Shanks Shenkis 94, 139, 143, 144, 168, 499, 518
Shannoch 98
Sharp[e] 88, 155, 156, 206, 354, 453, 460, 504, 515, 520
Shaw 57, 362
Sheal[l] Sheill, Shiel[l] 70, 71, 88, 90, 411, 429, 431, 432
Sheriffhall 22, 408, 486

Sheriff Braes 513
Shi[r]reff[e] Shirrif[f] 112, 253, 254, 257, 258, 265, 518
Shirrie Well 406, 485
Shor[e]swood 78, 96, 421
Shortill 208, 484
Shortus 135, 141
Sibbet 61, 337
Sigis 329
Sim[b][e][a]rd 395, 398, 399, 446, 469
Simnel[l] 389, 391, 393
Sim[p]son[e] 72, 74, 78, 79, 83, 133, 145, 205, 253, 254, 267, 321, 433, 439 *and see Sympson*
Sincla[i]r[e] Sincler 61, 72, 75, 82-4, 92, 114, 115, 132, 152, 154, 168, 169, 172, 179, 180, 182, 184, 189-91, 195, 197, 200, 219-21, 231, 232, 235, 242, 249, 252, 260, 282, 354, 355, 360, 400, 407, 413, 423, 426, 427, 429, 432, 434, 453-5, 457, 458, 465, 466, 469, 470, 478, 502, 517, 530, 540
Sives Sivis 82, 91, 505
Skaitbush Skedsbush 191 230
Skaitraw Skateraw 102, 216
Sked[d] 146, 158, 253, 261, 326
Skene Skin 49, 143
Skirvin[e] Skirv[e]ing 144, 179, 230, 231-3, 436
Sk[o]ug[g]all Skug[a]il 11, 136, 141, 166, 168, 232, 237, 467
Sleich[e] 79, 80, 82, 198, 208, 232, 354, 360
Sligh 165
Sluit 352
Smail, Sm[e][a]ll 254, 269, 335, 426
Smart 108, 112, 113, 218, 277
Sme[i]to[u]n[e] Smertoun Smeytoun 217, 229, 231, 236-8, 280, 362
Smith Smyt[h][e] 16, 73-75, 82, 83, 85, 87-9, 98, 99, 102, 115, 119, 142, 151, 153, 160, 163, 165, 167, 182, 188, 195, 211, 216, 223, 232, 236, 237, 239-41, 252-4, 260, 261, 264, 265, 270, 280, 282-5, 288, 289, 292, 293, 295, 297, 302, 304, 308, 310-21, 324, 325, 352, 360, 362-4, 367, 369, 371, 372, 374, 380, 382, 385, 386, 412, 422, 430, 466, 470, 476, 498, 500, 516, 539
Smithsone 371, 374
Smout 118
Somervail[l] Somervale Somerval[l] 98, 245, 436, 438

Sonnes, Sonus 436, 438
south-running water 150, 151, 156, 182, 183, 186, 202, 226, 274, 365, 370, 396, 482, 502-4, 513-7, 521, 527
Southesk 244
Spans 422
Sparrow 25, 40
Spavine 89, 90, 432, 477, 510
Speid 231, 467
Speir[e][s] 92, 93, 228
Spence, Spens[e] 17, 21, 26, 75, 151, 182, 364, 374, 395, 400, 401, 404, 406, 431, 513, 540
Spilmersford Spilmourfu[i]rd Spinnelfoord 14, 25, 27, 30, 35, 422
Spot[t][e] 121, 122, 126, 127, 130, 131, 216, 217, 243, 244, 252, 254, 255, 256, 260, 263, 264, 287, 291, 299, 302, 308, 310, 326, 478
Spot[t][i]swood 30, 62, 93, 249, 540
Staig[e] 201, 225
Stainehill, Staniehill 236 236, 237
Stalker 228
Standarts 253
Stanehous 182, 186
Steal, Steel[l][e] Steil[l][e] 12, 26, 48, 119, 139, 150, 151, 172, 232, 237, 362, 363, 365-71, 374, 397, 414, 418, 419, 467, 470, 477, 479, 505, 509, 521, 522, 525
Steine 82, 92
Steinson Steinstone 96, 418
Stenhouse 21, 503
Stento[u]n[e] 131, 164, 238, 253, 375, 388-93, 395, 399, 423, 446, 471, 497, 499, 500
Stevens[t]on[e] Stevinson[e] 104, 132, 168, 245, 248, 252, 254, 256, 263, 422, 505
Steward, Stewart 40, 58, 86, 87, 140, 141, 162, 163, 233, 472
Stillcart 26
Stillie 77, 86, 88, 89, 94, 242, 422
Stirling 44, 60, 228, 229
Stobart 159
Stob[b]eis 16, 19, 26
Stob[be]stane, Stob Stane 220, 221, 350, 356
Stobe 326
Stoddart, Stoddirt 77, 78, 105
Stokesley 529
Stone Well 396
Storie 150, 209

Stow ot Weddell 151
Strachan Straquhan Strauchan[e] Strayn[e] 73, 93, 218, 230-32, 236, 237, 243, 409, 466, 467
Straitton[e] 27, 44, 46
Strathear[e]n, Stratherne 16, 21, 132, 133, 379, 384, 480
Stra[y]to[u]n[e], Stratton 12, 14, 27, 31, 35-41, 45, 54-6, 465, 511, 521
Strong 93, 94, 136, 137
Struethers, Strutheris, Struthers 329, 330, 335
Stuart 38, 46, 48, 56-8, 107, 471, 521, 522, 526, 540
St Androis 217, 340
St Germa[i]ns 230, 248, 448
Summer 91
Summervaile 95
Su[n]niesyd 407, 408
Svingstone 208
Swanstoun 182
Sweden 356, 357, 360, 533
Swintoun 236, 237, 238
Sydserf[e], Sydserff[e] 107, 217, 232, 389-93, 446, 469,500
Symie 160, 516
Symontone, Symontoun 254, 258, 269, 518
Symson[e] 100, 197, 232, 281, 285, 291, 297, 298, 301, 302, 306, 308, 315-8, 375, 376, 378, 424, 428, 434, 467, 476, 479, 507, 509, 510, 514, 516, 522 *and see Simpson*
Sytoun 211

T

Taes 83, 92
Tail 85
Tailer, Tailloure, Tailly[e]or, Tailly[o]ur, Taily[e]our Tailyour, Tailzeour, Taylor 27, 68, 92, 116, 182, 186, 219, 235, 419, 422, 423, 466, 469
Tait[t], Tate 77, 197-200, 243, 326, 377, 378, 412, 435, 466, 477
Tantallon 107, 111, 340
Tarbat 387, 388
Temple 224, 231, 253, 428, 467
Templefield 196, 223, 237
Templehall 114, 428, 431-6, 481, 518
Terman 228
Thin 83
Thomason[e], Thomeson[e], Thomesoun

Thompson[e] Thomsome Thomson[e]
Thomsoun[e] Tomson 7, 10, 14, 15, 21, 25, 27,
35, 37, 40, 41, 44-6, 56, 57, 63, 71, 75, 76, 81,
89, 91-3, 99, 106, 109, 119, 121, 134, 145, 155,
156, 163, 168, 186, 196, 214, 218, 231-3, 238,
254, 259, 261, 269, 313, 317, 328, 329, 339, 346,
350, 357, 360, 375, 380, 385, 395, 396, 398-402,
404, 406, 407, 422-4, 426, 429, 430-3, 435, 439,
440, 465, 466, 470, 471, 475, 481, 485, 503,
507, 509, 511, 519, 526, 537, 539
Thomtonloch 139, 377
Thraitonley 376
Three Mile House, Thrie Mile House, Thrie Myll
  Hous 78, 185, 186, 205, 209, 210, 483, 498, 500
Threiplaw, Thrieplaw 423, 477
Thrieburnfurde 187
Thursetun 253
Thurston 103, 313, 461
Tinble 372
Tine-water 454
Tod 16, 277, 278, 279, 280, 353, 356, 360, 465,
  475, 499, 511, 539
Toddis 26
Todrig 96, 238, 239, 240, 241, 423, 487
Tofts 158
Tollbooth 43, 179, 180, 184, 186, 187, 196, 198,
  211, 252, 260, 393
Torsenze 25
Tosh 424
Trabroun 185
Traill 173
Tranent 3, 6, 14, 16, 17, 21, 31, 34, 38, 48, 49, 54-
  7, 63, 67, 71, 81, 82, 92, 132-4, 140-2, 158, 160,
  161, 164, 167, 174, 189-91, 217-9, 221, 223,
  228-30, 234, 243, 245, 247, 248, 252, 277, 278,
  362-6, 368-72, 374, 378, 380-5, 395-407, 410,
  411, 422, 424, 425, 439, 446, 449, 454, 458,
  467, 468, 471, 473, 485, 493, 495, 498, 499,
  505, 510, 512, 526, 528, 537
Traprain, Trapren[e] 22, 29, 150, 326, 478, 506
Trent 75, 85, 163, 167, 226, 227, 240, 241, 387,
  388
Triplaw 103
Trisk 16
Trotter 208
Trumbil[l], Trumble 16, 364, 402, 482
Tuedale 71

Tulleis 162
Turnbul[l] 89, 130, 133, 190, 191, 218, 219, 244,
  400-2, 479, 503, 508
Turner, Turnour 115, 145, 216, 230
Turnour 216
Turuett 169
  357
Tweed 47, 357
Tweedale, Tweeddall, 29, 147, 172, 173, 244, 506,
  527, 539
Tweedmouth, Tueidmouth, Twedismouth,
  Tweidmouth, 222, 223, 348, 351, 356, 357, 361
Tweedside 357
Two Mile Cross 458
Tyne 14, 84, 136, 185, 414, 418, 477
Tyne Water 14, 185
Tyn[n]inghame, Tynyngham 11, 75, 135, 142, 211,
  253

U

Ugston 357
Uist 519
Umferstoun, Umphersto[u]n[e],,
  Umphrasto[u]n[e] 163, 238, 239, 289, 300, 315,
  318, 466, 470
Umphrais 17
Utterston[e] 135, 138
Uttersyde 114

V

Vaitch 74, 75, 85, 89, 94, 229, 249, 427, 429, 433,
  466, 476
Vaith 229
Vans 21
Vause 252
Vea[t]ch 75, 414, 419, 435, 436, 438, 501
Vei[t]ch[e] 75, 167, 168, 233, 249, 356, 414, 419,
  426, 428-36, 438, 467, 470, 481, 488, 510, 518
Vernor 91, 232
Vert Vertie Vertue 68, 216, 217, 254, 261, 466
Vint 116, 119

W

Waddel[l] 119, 364
Wa[d]dersto[u]n 179, 186, 195, 236
Wade 223

Wadell 71, 374
Wadie 197, 476
Wairdhaugh 433
Waird Burn 488
Waird Hauch 429, 430, 431
Wait 72, 73, 112, 392, 486, 515
Waker 86, 87, 429
Wakraft 315
Wakterstoun 195
Walderstoun 182, 192, 194
Waldie 68
Walker 91, 103, 153, 218, 254, 257, 262, 269, 424, 429, 435
Walkerland 220, 221, 360
Wallace 25, 35, 40, 45, 61, 163, 178, 208, 211, 216, 217, 221, 254, 262, 295, 362, 363, 365, 367, 370, 436, 438, 466
Wallacemill 104
Walliford 114
Walter 42, 55, 88, 108, 113, 146, 218, 219, 224, 228, 383, 400, 401, 402, 407, 409, 423, 431
Wamphray 439
Wands 253
Ward Burn 434, 436, 438
Warrock 435
Wast 238, 240, 288, 308, 314, 361, 422, 470
Wat[e] 72, 306, 317, 318, 321, 391, 395
Wathersto[u]n[e], Wathirstone 74, 75, 77-9, 83, 85, 86, 145, 146, 169, 237, 470, 476, 505
Watso[u]n[e] 21, 35, 85, 108, 111, 114, 118, 134, 160, 162, 167, 224, 228, 243, 402, 404, 466, 498, 516
Watt 7, 103, 290, 314, 321, 322
Waugh 134, 435
Waughtoun 216
Wed[d]el[l], Wed[d]le 18, 56, 151, 218, 219, 381, 382, 385, 386, 508
Wedderburn[e] 115, 216, 217, 245
Weir[e] 56, 78, 83, 132, 202, 204, 205, 206, 208, 210, 226, 418, 419, 425, 426, 466, 468, 498
Weit 110, 112, 507, 518
Weitscha 106
Weitschot 158
Well Myrs 126
Well of Saynt An 151
Welsh 94, 238, 420-2, 471, 495, 499, 500, 518
West 42, 48, 50, 153, 224, 228, 231, 239, 242, 243, 253, 259, 261, 269, 288, 318, 326, 405, 421-3, 447, 470, 497
Westbank 254
Westbyres 232
Wester Broomhou[i]s[e] 253, 260
Wester Gladsmore 403
Wester Monkrig[e] 179, 184, 189, 196, 204
Westfenton West Fentoun 224, 238
Westhall 326
Westoun 158
Westpans 236, 237
West Barnes, Wastbarnes, Westbarnes 244, 261, 262, 314, 243, 253, 314, 318, 326
West Field 239
West Lothian 48, 50
Weymes Weymis 243, 317, 318, 352
Wheatlie 145
Wheit 107
Whilley Whylae 82, 466
Whinton 116
Whitburgh 233
Whit[e] 112, 147, 205, 509
Whitekirk 135, 142
Whithouse 436
Whitlae Whitl[e]y Whitlaw 163, 164, 165
Whittinghame 139, 142, 143, 232, 253, 509, 515
Whittle 161
Whyt[e] 99, 125-128, 131, 161, 168, 170, 229, 231, 259, 270, 326, 419, 433, 509, 519
Whyteburgh 231, 233
Whytfurd 105
Whytlaw 143, 144, 232
Whytloch 389
Whytt 439
Whyttinghame 414
Wickedshaw 104
Wife of Noram 313
Wightman 79, 81, 82, 84, 126, 127, 253, 261, 418, 439
Wilkie 42, 77, 96, 179, 184, 189, 191, 196, 198, 208
Wilkiesone 182, 503
Wil[l]iamson[e] 85-7, 91, 115, 168, 235, 242, 244, 352, 399, 413, 414, 419-24, 439, 469-71, 499, 518, 528
Wilso[u]n[e] 81, 85, 92, 93, 96, 105, 109, 110, 116, 132, 133, 140, 163-5, 182-4, 194, 204, 215, 231,

236, 237, 279, 344, 350, 352, 356, 360, 362, 364, 370, 375-8, 381, 385, 387, 395, 398, 399, 418, 423, 429, 435, 446, 466, 467, 470, 477, 480, 484, 498, 499, 500
Windegoul 17
Windymain[e]s 427, 434
Winla[e], Winlay 77, 78, 368, 371, 374
Winto[u]n[e] 38, 77, 91, 182, 184, 188, 218, 219, 231, 364, 374, 424, 427, 431, 434, 435, 453, 473, 479, 488, 506
Woddrington 34
Wolf[e] 287, 288, 299, 310, 313, 314, 318
Wolfstar 14
Wollmet Bank 409
Wolmet 232, 408, 409, 410, 487, 495
Wo[o]d, Woid 18, 30, 53, 79, 83, 84, 97, 98, 101, 126, 139, 142, 146, 153, 154, 172, 182, 186, 194, 216, 231, 232, 236, 238, 240, 242, 243, 253, 254, 258-61, 269, 270, 278, 279, 289, 300, 304, 320, 326, 350, 355, 357, 364, 374, 388-90, 392, 396, 402, 422-4, 430-3, 435, 467, 469, 478, 488, 490, 499, 500, 502, 504, 507, 514, 517, 519, 521
Woodfoote 238
Woodhall 231
Wo[o]dhead, Wod[e]heid, Woidheid, Woodheid 38, 185-7, 197, 249, 350, 352, 359, 360, 412, 427-31, 433, 438, 446, 447, 480, 514
Wood and Hannay 30, 53
Woolans 143
Woolmet 231
Wright's Houses 62
Wrightson 529, 530
Wrycht 27, 45
Wyl[l]ie 364, 372
Wyllie 162, 196, 364, 372, 466
Wyntoun 220
Wyte 99, 507

Y

Yarrow 143
Yeaman[e] Yeoman 46, 97, 107, 222, 347, 351
Yellowstanes 341
Ye[a]ster 101, 144, 145, 146, 147, 169, 171, 191, 192, 193, 194, 195, 243, 411, 470, 479, 480, 505, 506, 507, 513
Yeul, Yool[e], Yooll, Youl[e], Yule, Yull 102, 108, 112, 159, 195, 239, 389, 400, 401, 407, 428, 429, 431-3, 485, 515
Yewart 253
Yong 242, 311-7, 327
Yorkshire 529, 530
Yorkstane 96
Yo[u]rsto[u]n[e] 140, 142, 331-42, 345, 346, 429, 480
Young[e] 21, 74, 75, 79, 80, 83, 85, 87, 91, 98, 118, 122, 124, 126-8, 132, 182, 186, 188, 200, 217, 220, 226, 227, 229, 233, 235-8, 253, 280-2, 287, 289, 291-3, 300, 306-10, 312-7, 319-27, 377, 418, 465, 466, 474, 476, 480, 502, 528, 530

www.ingramcontent.com/pod-product-compliance
Lightning Source LLC
Chambersburg PA
CBHW080719300426
44114CB00019B/2425